THE PRINCETON REVIEW

STUDENT ADVANTAGE
GUIDE TO
THE BEST 310
COLLEGES

1997 EDITION

Books in The Princeton Review Series

Cracking the ACT
Cracking the ACT with Sample Tests on CD-ROM
Cracking the CLEP (College-Level Examination Program)
Cracking the GED
Cracking the GMAT
Cracking the GMAT with Sample Tests on Computer Disk
Cracking the GRE
Cracking the GRE with Sample Tests on Computer Disk
Cracking the GRE Biology Subject Test
Cracking the GRE Literature in English Subject Test
Cracking the GRE Psychology Subject Test
Cracking the LSAT
Cracking the LSAT with Sample Tests on Computer Disk
Cracking the LSAT with Sample Tests on CD-ROM
Cracking the MAT (Miller Analogies Test)
Cracking the SAT and PSAT
Cracking the SAT and PSAT with Sample Tests on Computer Disk
Cracking the SAT and PSAT with Sample Tests on CD-ROM
Cracking the SAT II: Biology Subject Test
Cracking the SAT II: Chemistry Subject Test
Cracking the SAT II: English Subject Tests
Cracking the SAT II: French Subject Test
Cracking the SAT II: History Subject Tests
Cracking the SAT II: Math Subject Tests
Cracking the SAT II: Physics Subject Test
Cracking the SAT II: Spanish Subject Test
Cracking the TOEFL with Audiocassette
Flowers & Silver MCAT
Flowers Annotated MCAT
Flowers Annotated MCATs with Sample Tests on Computer Disk
Flowers Annotated MCATs with Sample Tests on CD-ROM

Culturescope Grade School Edition
Culturescope High School Edition
Culturescope College Edition

SAT Math Workout
SAT Verbal Workout

All U Can Eat
Don't Be a Chump!
How to Survive Without Your Parents' Money
Speak Now!
Trashproof Resumes

Biology Smart
Grammar Smart
Math Smart
Reading Smart
Study Smart
Word Smart: Building an Educated Vocabulary
Word Smart II: How to Build a More Educated Vocabulary
Word Smart Executive
Word Smart Genius
Writing Smart

Grammar Smart Junior
Math Smart Junior
Word Smart Junior
Writing Smart Junior

Business School Companion
College Companion
Law School Companion
Medical School Companion

Student Access Guide to College Admissions
Student Advantage Guide to the Best 310 Colleges
Student Advantage Guide to America's Top Internships
Student Advantage Guide to Business Schools
Student Advantage Guide to Law Schools
Student Advantage Guide to Medical Schools
Student Advantage Guide to Paying for College
Student Advantage Guide to Summer
Student Advantage Guide to Visiting College Campuses
Student Advantage Guide: Help Yourself
Student Advantage Guide: The Complete Book of Colleges
Student Advantage Guide: The Internship Bible
Hillel Guide to Jewish Life on Campus
International Students' Guide to the United States
The Princeton Review Guide to Your Career

Also available on cassette from Living Language

Grammar Smart
Word Smart
Word Smart II

THE PRINCETON REVIEW

STUDENT ADVANTAGE
GUIDE TO
THE BEST 310
COLLEGES

1997 EDITION

**By Edward T. Custard
John Katzman,
Tom Meltzer,
and Zachary Knower,**

Random House, Inc.
New York 1996
http://www.randomhouse.com

Princeton Review Publishing, L.L.C.
2315 Broadway, 3rd Floor
New York, NY 10024
E-mail: info@review.com

ISBN 0-679-77122-0
ISSN 1008-8454

9 8 7 6 5 4 3 2 1

1997 Edition

FOREWORD

Every year, over two million high school graduates go to college. To make sure they end up at the *right* school, they spend several hundred million dollars on the admissions process. This money pays for countless admissions officers and counselors, a bunch of standardized tests (and preparation for them), and many books like—but not as good as—this one.

It's so expensive because most admissions professionals have a thing about being in control. As a group, colleges resist almost every attempt to standardize or otherwise simplify the process. Admissions officers want you to believe that every admissions decision that they render occurs within systems of weights, measures, and deliberations that are far too complex for you to comprehend. They shudder at the notion of having to respond to students and their parents in down-to-earth language that might reveal the arbitrary nature of a huge percentage of the admissions and denials that they issue during each cycle. That would be admitting that good luck and circumstance play a major part in many successful applications. So, in flight from public accountability, they make the process a lot more mysterious than it needs to be.

Even the most straightforward colleges hide the information you would want to know about the way they'll evaluate your application: What grades and SATs are they looking for? Do their reported SAT averages include minority students, athletes, and legacies (kids whose parents went to their school)? Exactly how much do extracurricular activities count? What percentage of the aid that they give out is loans and what percentage is in grants?

We couldn't get answers to these questions from many colleges. In fact, we couldn't get answers to *any* questions from some schools. Others who supplied this information to us for earlier editions of this guide have since decided that they never should have in the first place. After all, knowledge is power.

Colleges seem to have the time and money to create beautiful brochures (which generally show that all college classes are held under a tree on a beautiful day); why not just tell you what sort of students they're looking for, and what factors they'll use to consider your application?

Until the schools demystify the admissions process, this book is your best bet. It's not a phone book containing every fact about every college in the country. And it's not a memoir written by a few graduates in which they describe their favorite dining halls or professors. We've given you the facts you'll need to apply to the few hundred best schools in the country. And enough information about them—which we gathered from hundreds of counselors and admissions officers and tens of thousands of students—to let you make a smart decision about going there.

One note: we don't talk a lot about majors. This is because most high school students really don't know what they want to major in—and the ones who do almost always change their minds by the beginning of junior year. Choosing a school by the reputation of a single department is often a terrible idea.

As complicated and difficult as the admissions process is, we think you'll love college itself—especially at the schools listed in this book.

Good luck in your search.

—John Katzman
June 1996

ACKNOWLEDGMENTS

Ed owes an enormous debt to Edward T. Custard Sr., his father, an auto worker whose understanding of the importance of a college education is the main reason that his son is an author today. And special thanks to Jeanne Krier, whose public relations efforts on behalf of *Best Colleges* have helped it to become the best-seller of its kind.

Chris Kensler and Eric Owens wrote, edited, and managed the immensity of much of this year's edition. Along with Christine Chung, whose diligence and management skills proved invaluable, they contributed substantial segments of their lives to it in the process. Here's hoping they can now find a hobby. Thanks also to the lovely PJ Waters, the lively Bruno Blumenfeld, the savvy Kristin Fayne-Mulroy, and the talented Meredith McGowan for their writing and editing assistance.

Special thanks to Richard Infield and the best programmer alive today, Irina Tabachnik. Their technical expertise and cheerful disposition made this book possible. And without Jefferson "Jake" Nichols none of the information on these pages would have made it out of our database and into this book.

We owe enormous gratitude to not one but *two* David Kims, Jason Park, Seung Lee, Kathy Tatochenko, Joseph Hassett, Cindy Severino, Jason Behan, Daniel Bae, and Young Lee, all of whom processed the endless torrent of surveys and helped out in countless other ways.

During the editorial crunch, Louisa Harding Gilman reviewed and refined all 310 entries like the true professional she is. A lifetime achievement award goes to Lee Elliott, who served as principal editor on earlier editions of this book in the face of technical and emotional challenges. Kudos also to Dan "Padre" Saraceno for his unique ability to fill in *any* gap, and to Scott White for his assistance with the Counselor-O-Matic. Many thanks as well to Jane Lacher, Jeannie Yoon, and Evan R. Schnittman, three people who really know how to get things done.

Credit for redesigning the book belongs to Julian Ham and the omnipotent pagemaking genius of Meher Khambata, who took a good thing and made it better. Thanks also to Meher's staff: John Bergdahl, Adam Hurwitz, Peter Jung, Sara Kane, Illeny Maaza, Russell Murray, Glen Pannell, Dinica Quesada, Lisa Ruyter, and Chris Thomas, whose superior and efficent desktop publishing work was invaluable.

Some of the quantitative data in this book were compiled and supplied by Wintergreen/Orchard House, Inc. of New Orleans, Louisiana—a major college research and database publishing organization. We thank Don Beatty and Andrea Krasker at Wintergreen/Orchard House for their technical assistance and patience. For further information about Wintergreen/Orchard House's extensive college, financial aid, and vo-tech school databases, call 1-800-321-9479.

Contents

PART 1

INTRODUCTION

How to Use
This Book

There was a void in the college guide market and we have filled it. No other book provides in-depth descriptions of schools *and* in-depth statistics about admissions, financial aid, and student body demographics. And, more important, no other college guide is based on the input of so many students.

More than 56,000 students at the 310 colleges included in this guide participated in the survey. Except at some extremely small schools (undergraduate enrollment below 1,000), we heard from at least 100 students on every one of the campuses described between these covers.

On our survey, we asked students to answer seventy multiple-choice questions on subjects ranging from the school's administration to their social lives and from the quality of food to the quality of teaching. We asked them to tell us what other schools they had applied to. Finally, we asked students for their comments.

The combination of the ratings and comments form the substance of our articles about the schools. We wanted you to hear from as many of your (potential) future classmates as possible, to get a real sense of how happy they are when they're in their classrooms and in their campus organizations; at their fraternity parties and at their student rallies; on their way to get extra help from a professor or on their way into town to blow off some steam; getting food from their meal plans; and getting the financial aid packages that determine whether they'll return for the following semester. The idea is, if you know about their responses in advance, you can figure out if you'd be happy at a school before you go there.

We also received completed surveys from over fifty independent college counselors. We asked them to recommend schools in their regions for inclusion in *Best Colleges*, and we used their recommendations to help formulate our list of the nation's best schools. We also asked for comments on these schools' academic departments, admissions and financial aid policies, and hospitality toward groups that fall into the "high risk" category regarding marginalization—that is, minorities and those with physical and learning disabilities. The counselors' comments on these subjects are incorporated into the text. Fresh counselor feedback is solicited annually.

How did we get it done? The Princeton Review has offices in over fifty American cities. Every year over 60,000 students enroll in our SAT and graduate test preparation courses; those students are either on their way to college or have just graduated. Some of our teachers attend the featured schools; others have recently graduated and still live in the area; we even teach our courses on some of these campuses. Because of this, we already had in place the kind of army necessary to get a project this massive accomplished: All we had to do was mobilize it. Although some colleges didn't exactly welcome us with open arms, the students themselves were great, even at those schools where we showed up during finals week. Their insightful comments are what's most valuable about *Best Colleges*.

This book also contains several indexes. One is a compilation of entertaining quotations from students across the country that we just couldn't resist including. Another lists the top and bottom schools in various categories, based on the results of our student surveys. **When you look at the bottom schools in a category, please remember that *every* school in this book is an excellent institution—that's why it's in a guide to the best colleges.** A third index lists the names and business addresses of the independent college counselors who contributed to the creation of this book.

Finally, there is an Index of Programs for Students with Learning Disabilities that includes brief descriptions of the programs schools offer and the phone numbers of the offices to contact for information. If you are interested in programs for learning disabled students, we suggest you call the numbers provided because these programs vary widely from school to school.

HOW THIS BOOK IS ORGANIZED

Each of the colleges and universities listed in this book has its own two-page spread. To make it easier to find information about the schools of your choice, we've used the same format for every school. Look at the sample pages below:

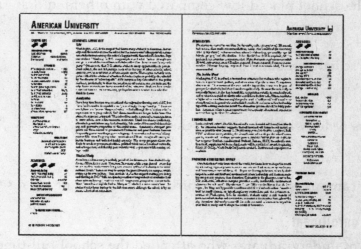

Each spread has nine major components. First, at the very top of the spread you will see the school's address, telephone and fax numbers for the admissions office, the telephone number for the financial aid office, and the school's web site and/or e-mail address. Second, there are two "sidebars" (the narrow columns on the outside of each page, which consist mainly of statistics) divided into the categories of Life, Academics, Admissions, and Financial Facts. Third, there are four headings in the main body text or "write-up" called Students Speak Out, Admissions, Financial Aid, and From the Admissions Office. Here's what each part contains:

The Sidebars

The sidebars contain various statistics culled either from our own surveys, from questionnaires sent to the schools, or from Wintergreen/Orchard House, Inc., a major college research and database publishing organization. Keep in mind that not every category will appear for every school, since in some cases the information is not reported or not applicable.

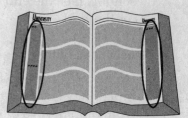

Here is what each heading tells you:

Quality of Life Rating

How happy students are with their lives outside the classroom. This rating is given on a scale of one to four arrows. One arrow is the equivalent of a grade of

60 to 69; two are equivalent to a grade of 70 to 79; three are equivalent to a grade of 80 to 89; and four are equivalent to a grade of 90 to 100. The ratings were determined using the results from our surveys. We weighed several factors, including students' overall happiness, the beauty, safety, and location of the campus, comfort of dorms, food quality, and ease in dealing with the administration. Note that even if a school's rating is in the low 60s, it does not mean that the quality of life is horrible—there are no "failing" schools. A low ranking just means that the school placed low compared with others in *Best 310 Colleges*.

Type of school

Whether the school is public or private.

Affiliation

Any religious order with which the school is affiliated.

Environment

Whether the campus is located in an urban, suburban, or rural setting.

FT undergrad enrollment

The number of undergraduates who attended the school full-time.

% male/% female *through* # countries represented

The demographic breakdown of the full-time undergraduate student body and what percent of the student body live on campus, belong to Greek organizations, spend their weekends on campus, and, finally, the number of countries represented by the student body.

What's Hot/What's Not

Summarizes the results of our survey. These lists show what the students we surveyed felt unusually strongly about, both positively and negatively, at their schools (see the end of the introduction for a more detailed explanation of items on the list).

Academic Rating

On a scale of one to four arrows, how hard students work at the school and how much they get back for their efforts. The ratings are determined based on results from our surveys of students and administrators. Factors weighed included how many hours students studied, how vigorously they did assigned readings and attended all classes, and the quality of students the school attracts; we also considered the student/teacher ratio, the students' assessments of their professors' abilities and helpfulness, and the students' assessment of the school's administration (in those areas where administrators directly affect the quality of education).

Calendar

The school's schedule of academic terms. A "semester" schedule has two long terms, usually starting in September and January. A "trimester" schedule has three terms, one usually before Christmas and two after. A "quarterly" schedule has four terms, which go by very quickly: the entire term, including exams, usually lasts only nine or ten weeks. A "4-1-4" schedule is like a semester schedule, but with a month-long term in between the fall and spring semesters. When a school's academic calendar doesn't match any of these traditional schedules we note that by saying "other." For schools that have "other" as their calendar it is best to call the admissions office for details.

Student/teacher ratio

The ratio of full-time faculty members to undergraduates.

% profs PhD/tenured

Percentage of professors who have a doctorate in their primary field of instruction and the percentage of professors who have been tenured at the institution.

Profs interesting

The average of the answers given in our survey in response to the question, "In general, how good are your instructors as teachers?"

Profs accessible

The average of the answers given in our survey in response to the question, "In general, how accessible are your instructors outside the classroom?"

Hours of study per day

The average number of hours studied per day outside of class as reported by students in our survey.

Most popular majors

The three most popular majors at the school.

% grads who pursue

The percentage of graduates who continue their education in law, business, medicine, or other graduate studies within a year of receiving their bachelor's degrees.

Admissions Rating

How competitive admission is at the school, on a scale of one to four arrows. This rating is determined by several factors, including the class rank of entering freshmen, test scores, and percentage of applicants accepted. By incorporating all these factors, our competitiveness rating adjusts for "self-selecting" applicant pools. Swarthmore, for example, has a very high competitiveness rating, even though it admits a surprisingly large proportion of its applicants. Swarthmore's applicant pool is "self-selecting"; that is, nearly all the school's applicants are exceptional students.

% of applicants accepted

The percentage of applicants to which the school offered admission.

% acceptees attending

The percentage of those who were accepted who eventually enrolled.

Average verbal SAT, Average math SAT, Average ACT

The average test scores for entering freshmen. *SAT scores in this book are all "recentered" scores.* When specific averages were not available, we approximated scores using ranges provided by the school. Please note that these numbers are *averages*; so about half of the students accepted at the school scored *below* the number in each category. Don't be discouraged from applying to the school of your choice even if your combined SAT scores are 80 or even 120 points below that average, because you may still have a chance of getting in. Remember that many schools emphasize other aspects of your application (e.g., your grades, how good a match you make with the school) more heavily than test scores.

Average TOEFL

The minimum test score necessary for entering freshmen who are required to take the TOEFL (Test of English as a Foreign Language). Most schools will require all international or non-US citizens to take the TOEFL in order to be considered for admission, but there are a few schools that do not.

Average HS GPA or avg.

We report this on a scale of 1–4. This is one of the key factors in college admissions, if not the biggest factor. But keep in mind, again, that half of the GPAs at any given school fall below the school's average; don't be discouraged if yours does too. Most importantly, be sure to keep your GPA as high as possible straight through until graduation from high school.

Graduated top 20%, top 40%, top 60% of class

Of those students for whom class rank was reported, the percentage of entering freshman who ranked in the top twenty, forty, and sixty percent of their high school classes.

Early decision deadline

The deadline for submission of application materials under the early decision or early action plan. Early decision is generally for students for whom the school is a first choice. The applicant commits to attending the school if admitted; in return, the school renders an early decision, usually in December or January. If accepted, the applicant doesn't have to spend the time and money to apply to other schools. In most cases, students may apply for early decision to only one school. Early action is similar to early decision, but less binding; applicants need not commit to attending the school and in some cases may apply early action to more than one school. The school, in turn, may not render a decision, choosing to defer the applicant to the regular admissions pool. Each school's guidelines are a little different; it's a good idea to call and get full details if you plan to pursue one of these options.

Regular admission deadline

The date by which all materials must be postmarked (we'd suggest, "received in the office") to be considered for regular admission for the fall term.

Regular admission notification

The date by which you can expect a decision on your application under the regular admission plan.

Non-fall registration

Some schools will allow applicants or transfers to matriculate at times other than the fall term—the traditional beginning of the academic calendar year. Other schools will only allow you to register for classes if you can begin in the fall term. A simple "yes" or "no" in this category indicates the school's policy on non-fall registration.

Applicants also look at

These lists were formulated with data from our on-campus surveys and information solicited directly from the colleges. We asked students to list all the schools to which they applied and those at which they were accepted. Schools they named most often appear in these three lists. When students consistently rejected a school in favor of the featured school, that school appears under "and rarely prefer"; schools that split applicants on a relatively even basis with the featured school appear under "and sometimes prefer"; and schools that students usually chose over the featured school appear under "and often prefer." For example, students in our survey who are accepted at both Princeton and the University of Pennsylvania generally choose Princeton. Therefore, on Princeton's feature page, U Penn appears in the "and rarely prefer" category (because students rarely preferred U Penn to Princeton), and on U Penn's feature page, Princeton appears in the "and often prefer" category (because students often prefer Princeton to U Penn). Admissions officers are given the opportunity to annually review and suggest alterations to these lists for their schools.

Student rating of FA

Based on their survey responses, students' satisfaction with the financial aid they receive. Again, this is on a scale of one to four arrows.

In-state tuition

The tuition at the school for a resident of the school's state. Usually much lower than out-of-state tuition for state-supported public schools.

Out-of-state tuition

The tuition at the school for a nonresident of the school's state. This entry appears only for public colleges, since tuition at private colleges is generally the same regardless of state of residence.

Room & board

Estimated room and board costs.

Est. book expense

Estimated annual cost of necessary textbooks.

% frosh receiving aid

According to the school's financial aid department, the percentage of freshmen financial aid applicants who received some form of aid.

% undergrads receiving aid

According to the school's financial aid department, the percentage of all undergrads who receive some form of financial aid.

% aid is need-based

According to the school's financial aid department, the percentage of all financial aid awarded that is based strictly on demonstrated financial need.

% frosh rec. grant (avg)

The percentage of full-time freshmen who applied for/received grants or scholarships, and the average grant or scholarship value.

% frosh rec. loan (avg)

The percentage of full-time freshmen who applied for/received loans, and the average amount of loan.

% UGs w/ job

The percentage of undergrads employed part-time on campus and their average annual earnings.

Off-campus job outlook

According to school sources, the chances of finding off-campus part time employment: *excellent*, *good*, *fair*, or *poor*.

THE WRITE-UP

Students Speak Out

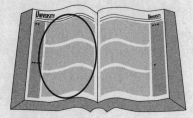

This section summarizes the results of the surveys we distributed to students at the school. It also includes information from the surveys completed by independent college counselors and incorporates statistics provided by the schools themselves and Orchard House. It is divided into three subheadings: Life, Academics, and Student Body. The Life section describes life outside the classroom and addresses questions ranging from "How nice is the campus?" and "How comfortable are the dorms?" to "How popular are fraternities and sororities?" and "How easily and frequently do students of different ethnic origins interact?" The Academics section reports how hard students work and how satisfied they are with the education they are getting and also tells you which academic departments our respondents rated favorably. The Student Body section tells you about what type of student the school traditionally attracts and how the students view the level of interaction between different groups.

All quotes in these sections are from students' essay responses to our surveys except, where noted, when we cite an area college counselor. **We choose quotes based on the accuracy with which they reflect our survey results;** those students who wrote entertaining but nonrepresentative essays will find excerpts of their work in part three of the book, a section titled "My Roommate's Feet Really Stink."

Admissions

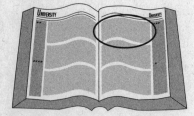

This section tells you what aspects of your application are most important to the school's admissions officers. It also lists the high school curricular prerequisites for applicants, which standardized tests (if any) are required, and special information about the school's admissions process (e.g., Do minority students and legacies, for example, receive special consideration? Are there any unusual application requirements for applicants to special programs?).

The Inside Word

Pay attention here: This section contains our own insights into each school's admissions process. Our source for this section is an educational consultant and former college admissions director who has been in college counseling for almost twenty years and who knows personally many of the admissions officers about whom he writes.

Financial Aid

This section summarizes the financial aid process at the school: what forms you need and what types of merit-based aid and loans are available. Information about need-based aid is contained in the financial aid sidebar. Because schools are now required to accept the FAFSA (Free Application for Federal Student Aid), many schools are requiring a different combination of need-analysis forms than they did in the past. For schools from which we did not receive current information, you will see the phrase "The school has traditionally required...," followed by the need-analysis forms the school required last time we heard from them. While this section includes specific deadline dates for submission of materials as reported by the colleges, we strongly encourage students seeking financial aid to file all forms—federal, state, and institutional—as soon as they become available. In the world of financial aid, the early birds almost always get the best worms. (Provided, of course, that they're eligible for a meal!)

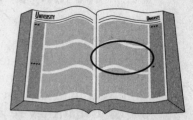

From the Admissions Office

This section contains text supplied by the colleges in response to our invitation that they use this space to "speak directly to the readers of our guide." For schools that did not respond, we excerpted an appropriate passage from the school's catalog or admissions literature.

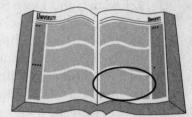

What Did We Learn from the Survey?

As well as providing us with invaluable information about specific undergraduate programs, our questionnaires, when viewed collectively, also provided some interesting information about the nation's elite college population. While it is impossible to say anything universally true about all 56,000 of our respondents (except that they're all college students), the following generalizations accurately represent what the vast majority of them told us. We hope that what you read on these next few pages will challenge some of your preconceptions about what college life is like and thereby help you more wisely select the undergraduate program that will make you happiest.

Life

When it comes to location, respondents to our survey overwhelmingly prefer cities to suburbs, towns, and rural sites. All but two of the schools that ranked in the top twenty for student satisfaction with location are in major cities (except University of Colorado–Boulder, which, according to students, is practically a ski resort, and Deep Springs College—deep as in "deep in the desert," where the desire for isolation can't help but be a factor in student decisions to enroll). Five are in New York City, giving the "Big Apple" the unofficial title of best college town. Boston, a former coholder of the crown, is home to three of the schools. Atlanta and Washington, D.C., both placed more than one school in the top twenty. On the bottom of the pile are decaying industrial cities (Bethlehem, PA; Worcester, MA) and quiet towns well removed from major metropolitan areas (Middletown, CT; Crawfordsville, IN; Annandale, NY). In addition, most of the low-ranking school locations are cursed with bad weather for much of the year. The importance of a school's location is often undervalued by those shopping for colleges; while it shouldn't be your prime concern, remember that you will be living in the city/town you choose for the next four years. College can be a very stressful experience, and other factors that can increase or relieve that stress—such as location and how well you fit in with your fellow students—should not be dismissed.

Another thing we learned: small schools inhibit what is generally considered a "normal" social scene. At schools with fewer than 1,500 students, we were told, students rarely date in the traditional sense; they either "settle down" with someone for four years, or they "hook up" once and then spend the next few weeks trying to avoid the person they hooked up with. Or, they have no love lives at all. The reason is that at these schools the community is small: everybody knows about and is involved in everyone else's business, making it hard to go out on a casual date without becoming the talk of the campus. Schools of this size are often those at which the Greeks dominate social life, although the Greeks can be dominant at larger schools as well. Keep your eyes open for such schools: There is a definite type of person who fits into a Greek-dominated scene, and a type who does not. Those who fit in tend to be from white upper-middle-class backgrounds and hold conventionally conservative political and social attitudes. Those who don't fit this mold often find life at Greek-dominated schools depressingly stifling. If you're unsure how you'll fit in at such a school, go visit one for a few days.

And now, an editorial message from the Princeton Review (Are you listening, URI?*): campus-wide drinking prohibitions don't work! Such regulations douse school spirit (few students are interested in any campus-sponsored activity if they know security guards will be actively enforcing no-drinking rules), provoke the students (who resent what they consider the school's intrusion into their personal lives), and encourage drinking and driving. "Dry campus" policies simply don't prevent students from drinking: In some cases, students actually reported that such policies encouraged their drinking because it provided both the challenge and the enjoyment inherent in disobeying a dumb rule. At a few "dry" schools we found that, ironically, the policy had served to increase the popularity of illegal narcotics (which are easier to conceal). On most campuses, by the way, drinking remains much more popular than drug use. Drugs are not entirely ubiquitous, but except at a few women's schools and at Brigham Young, drinking is a substantial fact of life on every college campus in the country. If you're looking to avoid a drinking- and drug-based social scene in college, your best bet is probably at a large school, where the sheer number of students allows social communities of all types to flourish. Don't get us wrong: there's plenty of drinking going on at big schools, but there are also more alternatives.

*After appearing as the number one party school in *Best Colleges* for three consecutive years, the University of Rhode Island began the 1995-96 school year by instituting a ban on alcohol. Students report that prior to this publicity, the university showed little or no concern regarding alcohol consumption on the part of its students. Can you say "knee-jerk?" We knew that you could.

Academics

By far the most important factor influencing students' satisfaction with their academic programs is the quality of their professors. By quality we mean not only academic qualifications (degrees earned, major articles published, major awards won) but also the professors' abilities to serve as teachers. Year after year, students at the nation's most famous research-oriented universities learn that academic prestige and the ability/desire to teach undergraduates do not go hand in hand. At such schools, professors are often preoccupied with their graduate students (those studying for master's and doctoral degrees) or their own research. Some will have to cancel classes so they can appear on CNN, others will disappear midsemester to attend an international symposium, leaving you and your classmates in the hands of a teaching assistant (often a brilliant, incomprehensible graduate student with an attitude). Remember that most of what you learn in college, while difficult, is pretty basic material to scholars. You do not need the world's foremost expert on particle physics to teach you any college physics course; what you need is someone who knows how to make that material intelligible to undergraduates. Those students most satisfied with their academic programs are generally those at small, undergraduate-oriented schools where professors' attentions are turned entirely to teaching and helping students. This can't be stressed enough: If you go to Harvard or Caltech expecting to be showered with your professors' attention and interest, you are almost certainly in for a big letdown.

Students

It has come to be an accepted truism that college students get more conservative with each passing year. This may in fact be true, but we were surprised to find that the national student population is not as conservative as we had been led to believe. Our survey showed us that American college students as a whole still fall slightly to the left of "middle-of-the-road," or centrist, politics. As a rule, the farther a student body leans to the left, the more pervasive the influence of political correctness. The farther a student body leans to the right, the more likely it is that alternative lifestyles and ideologies, such as homosexuality or feminism, will meet with overt hostility.

Minority representation at many top schools remains distressingly low. The most prestigious, high-profile schools (the Ivies, for example) have little trouble attracting qualified minority students. The next tier of schools, however—those that are excellent but are less well known or are located in more remote areas—lack either the ability or desire to attract minority students of similar quality. To make matters worse, the few minority students who attend such schools are often made uncomfortable by the lack of a substantial peer group. The inability of these schools to help their few minority students fit in dissuades other minorities from attending these schools, thereby perpetuating the problem. While ethnically oriented and single-sex schools offer an excellent alternative for those uncomfortable at predominantly white, upper-class schools, they don't address the larger problem of how to create an undergraduate atmosphere in which students of all backgrounds can study together and reap the benefits of their diversity of experiences. We offer no solutions—we'll leave that debate to the nation's educators, sociologists, and politicians—but as you read this guide, look at the descriptions of the student body and the student body demographic breakdowns, and think about how comfortable you'll be among your peers at the schools described.

The most important thing we learned from our survey is that there is a tremendous diversity of educational opportunities available in the United States. Look through *Best 310 Colleges*, and you will surely find at least one school that is just right for you (whether you get accepted there is another question). We also found that motivated, thoughtful, and intelligent people—56,000 of whom took the time to fill out our survey—are out there taking advantage of those opportunities. Good luck to you in your quest to join them.

COLLEGE ADMISSION GOES ELECTRONIC

College admission is finally moving onto the "information superhighway." Here are a couple of ways to use your computer to best effect.

Looking For Colleges Online

First off, *we've* provided a lot of information about colleges and college admissions through our online services on the Internet, America Online, and the Microsoft Network.

The Internet is the most interesting of all online information services, because the colleges themselves have posted information there. You can connect to the 'net through an *Internet service provider* or through America Online, CompuServe, the Microsoft Network, or Prodigy. (If you've never played with the Internet, you'll find these last four companies the easiest way to get started.) Once you're on the Internet, you can reach colleges directly (we've listed each college's address at the top right of its entry) or through our own World Wide Web (also known as the Web, the graphical interface to the Internet) page.

The Internet changes every day—content is added or deleted, and sites change their look and feel regularly. Addresses (known as URLs) change; some sites disappear completely. All of the URLs that we have provided in our guides were accurate and functioning at the time of publication. The simplest way to get at all this college information is to go directly to our server on the Web. We've set up a search engine and posted some of the information in this book, so you can access virtually every college and university Internet site by just clicking. We've also established message threads for admissions and testing questions, and posted useful (we hope) career and internship advice, info about all of our books and software, an extensive phone list of useful numbers, and hotlinks to our favorite educational sites on the Internet.

Our boards on America Online and the Microsoft Network offer more information and a very different look and feel. One of the most popular features of these boards is our Student Message areas, where you can create your own topic folders and post questions for other students and for our own online admissions and testing experts. We also feature regularly scheduled live online forums where you can get answers in real time to your questions about admission, testing, and just about anything else to do with college or grad school directly from our experts and special guests.

To reach the Princeton Review at any of these sites, or to e-mail us, use the following addresses:

- e-mail: info@review.com
- World Wide Web: http://www.review.com
- America Online: keyword "princeton review"
- Microsoft Network: go to: "princeton review"

Applying To College Via Electronic Application

Once you've gathered all the information that you need about colleges and universities and have decided where to apply, you may not need to leave your computer keyboard. Just a handful of years ago electronic applications were *never* going to happen. Today, colleges are scrambling to make electronic versions of their applications available.

The colleges and universities that currently accept electronic applications are identified in our write-ups by the icon you see at right. You can get many of them directly from the colleges through the mail or by downloading them off the school's Internet site.

One especially good package is called Apply!, and is available for both Macintosh and Windows platforms. Through Apply! you have access to electronic applications from hundreds of colleges and universities. The software produces an exact duplicate of each college's application, complete with logos and graphics. Once you've received your Apply! software, you simply fill out the application(s) onscreen, print, and submit directly to the college or university admissions office(s). Apply! software is available on CD-ROM only, and is free of charge. To order Apply! call 1-800-WE-APPLY, e-mail them at apply@aol.com, or write them at Apply Technology, Inc., 50 Mall Road, Suite 210, Burlington, Massachusetts 01803.

Another package is the Common Application, an electronic version of the notorious paper forms that purport to be a quick and easy way to apply to several colleges with one application. We aren't big fans of the paper version and can't endorse the electronic one either—unlike Apply!, the application is generic, and stands out like a sore thumb in a stack of the college's own forms. If colleges really wanted you to use the common application, they wouldn't bother printing their own. (A few, including Harvard, don't use any other app.) Unless it is the college's primary application, the message you send when you use the common app. is that this school is not your first choice; this is all the reason that we need to advise against using it when the college prints its own app.

None of the few other electronic application packages that are currently available excite us either. College Link is a package that has gotten some attention, but it includes one major flaw—you've got to send your completed disk back to the source, where the applications are then printed and returned to you to sign and then send on to the admissions office. This is a needless step that delays the submission of your application. Some colleges have already put their application forms online, allowing you to fill them out and submit them via the Internet, but this is probably two or three years off for most admissions offices.

A final note of advice: No matter which form of electronic application you choose, if you go the electronic route you must still contact the admissions office for an application packet. You're taking a risk if you don't. This is the *only* way that you can be sure to have all the information and materials that you need to put together the strongest candidacy possible. Despite the increasing online presence of colleges and the convenience of the electronic medium, "snail mail" remains an integral part of the process.

Touring Colleges Via Videotape

A critical part of choosing the right college to attend is visiting the campuses of those that you're considering. It's most likely that you'll apply to several colleges, which can send travel expenses soaring if you attempt to visit every one. And videos from the admissions office are far from the next best thing to being there—some of them are scripted and staged almost as elaborately as a Hollywood production! We've found an alternative.

The Klass Report College Video Tours can help to ease the hit on your parents' wallet and give you the chance to get a closer, objective look at the colleges you're considering. Their videos are full-length, unaffiliated, unbiased tours of major colleges and universities. Each tour includes the entire campus: academic and athletic buildings, housing, frats and sororities, the surrounding area, transportation, shopping and entertainment options, and student hangouts are all visited via the video lens. Candid interviews with students are also included to help clue you in on campus life. Once you've viewed Klass Report videos, you'll be better able to decide which campuses to put on your travel schedule.

We've identified schools for which the Klass Report has video tours by placing a video cassette icon in the upper right corner of the college's entry.

The Klass Report College Video Tours cost $19.95 per school; if you order three or more you'll receive one free. To order, or to get more information, call 1-800-638-1330, write The Klass Report, 317 Madison Avenue, Suite 206, New York, NY 10017, or visit their web site at http://www.klassreport.com/videos.

What's Hot/What's Not

Our What's Hot/What's Not lists, located in the Campus Life sidebar on each school's two-page spread, are based entirely on the results of our on-campus surveys. In other words, the appearance on these lists of such categories as "financial aid," "ethnic diversity," and "library" are based on the opinions of the students we surveyed at those schools (NOT on any numerical analysis of library size, endowment, etc.). "Hot" items are defined as those that are unusually popular on a campus; "not," those that are unpopular. Some of the terms that appear in these lists are not entirely self-explanatory; these terms are defined below:

different students interact: We asked students whether students from different class and ethnic backgrounds interacted frequently and easily. This heading shows up on "Not" lists as "student body is cliquish."

Greeks: Fraternities and sororities are "Greek" organizations. They often host parties and provide meals and housing for some members. At schools with few or no official Greek organizations, this heading appears on the "Not" list.

honesty *or* cheating: We asked students how prevalent cheating is at their school. If students reported cheating to be rare, "honesty" shows up in the "Hot" list, and if students reported cheating to be reportedly prevalent, "cheating" is listed.

students are happy: This category reflects student responses to the question "Overall, how happy are you with your school?" This heading shows up on "Not" lists as "students are unhappy."

profs teach upper courses *or* TAs teach upper courses: At some large universities, you'll continue to be taught by teaching assistants even in your upper-level courses. It is safe to assume that when "TAs teach upper courses" appears on a "Not" list, TAs also teach a disproportionate number of intro courses as well.

religion: We asked students how religious they are. Their responses are reflected by this category.

diverse student body: We asked students whether their student body is made up of diverse social and ethnic groups. This category reflects their answers to this question. Note that this category is not limited to *ethnic diversity* (which you can figure out by looking at the student body demographics). This heading shows up as "lack of diversity on campus" on "Not" lists.

town-gown relations: We asked students whether they got along with local residents; their answers are reflected by this category.

If you have any questions, comments, or suggestions, please e-mail your insights to us over the Internet at Books@review.com. We appreciate your input and want to make our books as useful to you as they can be.

GLOSSARY

ACT: The American College Test. Like the SAT but less tricky. Many schools accept either SAT or ACT scores; if you consistently get blown away by the SAT, you might want to consider taking the ACT instead.

college prep curriculum: 16 to 18 academic credits (each credit equals a full year of a high school course), usually including: 4 years of English, 3 to 4 years of social studies, and at least 2 years each of science, mathematics, and foreign language.

core curriculum: Students at schools with core curricula must take a number of required courses, usually in such subjects as world history, western civilization, writing skills, and fundamental math and science.

CSS Profile: The College Scholarship Service Profile has replaced the Financial Aid Form (FAF). An optional financial aid form required by some colleges in addition to the FAFSA.

distribution requirements: Students at schools with distribution requirements must take a number of courses in various subject areas, such as foreign language, humanities, natural science, and social science. Distribution requirements do not specify which courses you must take, only which types of courses.

FAFSA: The Free Application for Federal Student Aid. Schools are required by law to accept the FAFSA; some require that applicants complete at least one other form to be considered for financial aid.

4-1-4: A type of academic schedule. It's like a semester schedule, but with a short semester (usually one month long) between the two semesters. Most schools offer internship programs or nontraditional studies during the short semester.

GDI: "God-damned independents," a term frequently used by students in fraternities and sororities to describe those not in fraternities and sororities.

Greek system, Greeks: Fraternities and sororities.

humanities: These include such disciplines as art history, drama, English, foreign languages, music, philosophy, and religion.

merit-based grant: A scholarship (not necessarily full) given to students because of some special talent or attribute. Artists, athletes, community leaders, and geniuses are typical recipients.

natural sciences: These include such disciplines as astronomy, biology, chemistry, genetics, geology, mathematics, physics, and zoology.

need-based grant: A scholarship (not necessarily full) given to students because they would otherwise be unable to afford college. Student need is determined on the basis of the FAFSA. Some schools also require the CSS Profile and/or institutional applications.

p.c.: Politically correct—a genuine buzzword on campuses today. It signifies either (1) an enlightened awareness of how society rewards certain members and punishes others solely on the basis of class, ethnicity, and gender; or (2) an unrelenting, humorless hypersensitivity on all issues even remotely related to class, ethnicity, and gender.

priority deadline: Some schools will list a deadline for admission and/or financial aid as a "priority deadline," meaning that while they will accept applications after that date, all applications received prior to the deadline are assured of getting the most thorough, in some instances potentially more generous, appraisal possible.

RA: Residence assistant (or residential adviser). Someone, usually an upperclassman or graduate student, who supervises a floor or section of a dorm, usually in return for free room and board. RAs are responsible for enforcing the drinking and noise rules.

SAT: Scholastic Assessment Test. A college entrance exam required by many schools; some schools will accept either the ACT or the SAT.

SAT II Subject Tests: Subject-specific exams administered by the Educational Testing Service (the SAT people). These tests are required by some, but not all, admissions offices. English Writing and Math Level I or IIc are the tests most frequently required.

social sciences: These include such disciplines as anthropology, economics, geography, history, international studies, political science, psychology, and sociology.

TA: Teaching assistant. Most often a graduate student, a TA will often teach discussion sections of large lectures. At some schools, TAs and graduate students teach a large number of introductory-level and even some upper-level courses. At smaller schools professors generally do all the teaching.

work-study: A government-funded financial aid program that provides assistance to financial aid recipients in return for work in the school's library, labs, etc.

Schools
Ranked by
Category

One of the great things about a multiple-choice survey is that the results give you lots of numbers. We wanted to present those numbers to you in a fun and informative way; hence, the following rankings of schools in sixty-one categories. In the following lists, the top twenty schools in each category are listed *in descending order.* Remember, of course, that our survey included only students at the most competitive colleges, and that all schools appearing on negative lists have many assets that counterbalance their various deficiencies.

Although these lists are presented mostly for fun, they can be used to help you clarify some of the choices you have to make in picking the right college. As you read through them, focus on those categories that are important to you: Do you want to go to a school where discussion takes up most of the class time? Would you prefer only to be lectured to? Do you care? Do you want to go to a school where students party nonstop? Or would you rather go somewhere with a subdued social scene? By looking through these lists, you should be able to get a good idea of what are and are not important considerations to you.

We've broken the rankings down into nine categories: Academics; Administration; Quality of Life; Politics; Demographics; Social Life; Extracurriculars; Parties; and Schools by Type. Under each list heading, we tell you the survey question or assessment that we used to tabulate the list. For the Schools by Type rankings, we combined student responses to several questions to determine whether a school was a "jock" school, a "party" school, and so on. These lists have changed considerably since the first edition of this book, as we have had time to rethink what truly defines a school's character. For instance, we now factor students' answers to the questions "How happy are you at school?" and "How many hours a day do you study?" into our party school calibrations. After all, as some of our readers have pointed out, at some schools students drink and do drugs to relieve the stress of their demanding curricula. We are proud to report that, thanks to such readers' diligence and our recalibrations, no such student bodies taint our list.

Be aware that all of these lists are based on our survey results. Therefore, they do not reflect our opinions, nor do they perfectly reflect reality; that is to say, we can't tell you at which schools registration is actually the biggest hassle. What we can tell you is at which school students are most pissed off about registration hassles. Our feeling is that students' self-perceptions are quite valuable. After all, when you get down to it, what better way is there to judge a school than by how its students feel about it?

ACADEMICS

Best overall academic experience for undergrads
Based on The Princeton Review Academic Rating

Princeton University
Williams College
Deep Springs College
Washington and Lee University
Swarthmore College
Dartmouth College
Pomona College
Haverford College
Davidson College
Wesleyan University
Bryn Mawr College
California Institute of Technology
Amherst College
Harvey Mudd College
Harvard and Radcliffe Colleges
University of Chicago
Rice University
Wellesley College
Carleton College
Reed College

The toughest to get into
Based on The Princeton Review Admissions Rating

Harvard and Radcliffe Colleges
Juilliard School
Cooper Union
U.S. Military Academy
Deep Springs College
Princeton University
U.S. Naval Academy
Rice University
Stanford University
Yale University
Massachusetts Institute of Technology
Brown University
Dartmouth College
California Institute of Technology
Williams College
Amherst College
Columbia University
Georgetown University
Duke University
Cornell University

Their students never stop studying

How many out-of-class hours do you spend studying each day (exclude class time)?

Deep Springs College
California Institute of Technology
Harvey Mudd College
San Francisco Conservatory of Music
Rhode Island School of Design
Massachusetts Institute of Technology
Swarthmore College
U.S. Naval Academy
Reed College
Smith College
Carleton College
Maryland Institute, College of Art
Wabash College
Eastman School of Music
College of the Holy Cross
Mount Holyoke College
Parsons School of Design
Bryn Mawr College
Rose-Hulman Institute of Technology
Cooper Union

Their students (almost) never study

How many out-of-class hours do you spend studying each day (exclude class time)?

Emerson College
University of Missouri-Columbia
Louisiana State University-Baton Rouge
Stephens College
Seton Hall University
Bellarmine College
State University of New York at Albany
Auburn University
University of Kansas
University of Tennessee-Knoxville
City University of New York-Queens College
George Mason University
Warren Wilson College
University of California-Irvine
University of Wisconsin-Madison
Trenton State College
Providence College
University of Miami
Bentley College
Pepperdine University

Professors bring material to life

Are your instructors good teachers?

Deep Springs College
Randolph-Macon Woman's College
St. John's College (New Mexico)
College of the Atlantic
Sarah Lawrence College

Carleton College
Agnes Scott College
Washington and Lee University
Mount Holyoke College
St. John's College (MD)
Hollins College
Sweet Briar College
Davidson College
Rhodes College
Wabash College
Marlboro College
University of the South
Austin College
Reed College
Simon's Rock College of Bard

Professors suck all life from materials

Are your instructors good teachers?

University of Missouri-Columbia
City University of New York-Hunter College
University of Toronto
State University of New York at Stony Brook
Hampton University
Temple University
Georgia Institute of Technology
City University of New York-Queens College
State University of New York at Albany
Michigan State University
University of California-Los Angeles
Florida A&M University
Marquette University
Rensselaer Polytechnic Institute
University of Arizona
University of Maine
New York University
Rutgers University-Rutgers College
West Virginia University
California Institute of Technology

Professors make themselves accessible

Are your instructors accessible outside the classroom?

Deep Springs College
U.S. Military Academy
Randolph-Macon Woman's College
Agnes Scott College
St. John's College (MD)
Harvey Mudd College
Carleton College
Davidson College
St. John's College (New Mexico)
College of the Atlantic
Sweet Briar College
Washington and Lee University
Hollins College
U.S. Naval Academy
Wabash College

Mount Holyoke College
University of the South
Whitman College
Claremont McKenna College
Dartmouth College

Professors make themselves scarce
Are your instructors accessible outside the classroom?

University of Missouri-Columbia
City University of New York-Hunter College
Pennsylvania State University-University Park
Parsons School of Design
Temple University
University of Toronto
City University of New York-Queens College
New Jersey Institute of Technology
University of California-Los Angeles
University of Minnesota-Twin Cities
University of Arizona
Georgia Institute of Technology
School of the Art Institute of Chicago
Johns Hopkins University
State University of New York at Stony Brook
University of California-Irvine
West Virginia University
University of Oklahoma
State University of New York at Buffalo
Marquette University

Class discussions encouraged
How much of your overall course time is devoted to discussion (as opposed to lectures)?

St. John's College (New Mexico)
St. John's College (MD)
Eugene Lang College
Deep Springs College
Goddard College
Sarah Lawrence College
Simon's Rock College of Bard
State University of New York at Buffalo
Virginia Tech
Marlboro College
University of California-Santa Barbara
University of Vermont
Clarkson University
St. Mary's College (CA)
Reed College
Harvard and Radcliffe Colleges
New York University
Hampshire College
St. Louis University
University of Massachusetts-Amherst

Class discussions rare
How much of your overall course time is devoted to discussion (as opposed to lectures)?

McGill University
Montana Tech of the University of Montana
Pennsylvania State University-University Park
Georgia Institute of Technology
University of Toronto
Texas A&M University-College Station
New Mexico Institute of Mining & Technology
University of California-Davis
Grove City College
Calvin College
University of Missouri-Rolla
University of Delaware
University of Wisconsin-Madison
Michigan Technological University
Rice University
Case Western Reserve University
Loyola Marymount University
California Institute of Technology
University of Oregon
Louisiana State University-Baton Rouge

TAs teach too many upper-level courses
How many upper-level classes are taught by teaching assistants?

University of Alabama
Eastman School of Music
University of Missouri-Columbia
University of California-Los Angeles
Marquette University
West Virginia University
University of Illinois—Urbana-Champaign
Duquesne University
Auburn University
University of Kansas
University of Michigan-Ann Arbor
University of Iowa
Temple University
University of North Carolina-Chapel Hill
Drexel University
Purdue University-West Lafayette
Indiana University-Bloomington
University of California-Berkeley
City University of New York-Hunter College
State University of New York at Stony Brook

ADMINISTRATION

Great libraries
Based on students' assessments of library facilities

Eastman School of Music
Mount Holyoke College
Princeton University
Smith College
Dartmouth College
U.S. Naval Academy
Cornell University
University of Chicago
Wake Forest University
Auburn University
University of Washington
Bucknell University
Washington and Lee University
University of Rochester
Grinnell College
St. Olaf College
Texas Christian University
University of Southern California
Claremont McKenna College
Lehigh University

This is a library?
Based on students' assessments of library facilities

Tuskegee University
University of Dallas
Hiram College
Deep Springs College
Catholic University of America
Hampton University
Spelman College
Whittier College
Illinois Wesleyan University
Wesleyan College
Lewis & Clark College
Tufts University
San Francisco Conservatory of Music
Boston Conservatory
Stevens Institute of Technology
Valparaiso University
Georgia Institute of Technology
Fisk University
Siena College
Hanover College

Students happy with financial aid
Based on students' assessments of their individual financial aid packages

Deep Springs College
U.S. Military Academy
U.S. Naval Academy
Wabash College

Lake Forest College
Hollins College
Lehigh University
California Institute of Technology
Claremont McKenna College
Pomona College
Pitzer College
College of Wooster
Cooper Union
Washington and Lee University
Lafayette College
Sweet Briar College
University of the South
Knox College
Wellesley College
Smith College

Students dissatisfied with financial aid
Based on students' assessments of their individual financial aid packages

Howard University
University of Massachusetts-Amherst
College of the Holy Cross
Loyola Marymount University
Hampton University
University of Vermont
New York University
University of California-Santa Barbara
American University
Loyola University of Chicago
Tuskegee University
University of Pittsburgh
Virginia Tech
Rhode Island School of Design
Spelman College
Temple University
University of Minnesota-Twin Cities
City University of New York-Hunter College
Yale University
Florida A&M University

School runs like butter
Overall, how smoothly is your school run?

U.S. Military Academy
Claremont McKenna College
Washington and Lee University
Randolph-Macon Woman's College
Williams College
Harvey Mudd College
St. John's College (New Mexico)
Pomona College
Hollins College
Princeton University
Davidson College
Wabash College
Bucknell University

Calvin College
Whitman College
Rose-Hulman Institute of Technology
University of Puget Sound
Swarthmore College
Sweet Briar College
U.S. Naval Academy

Long lines and red tape
Overall, how smoothly is your school run?

Hampton University
Tuskegee University
University of Massachusetts-Amherst
Columbia University
University of Vermont
State University of New York at Stony Brook
Bennington College
Howard University
Florida A&M University
Southwestern University
Boston Conservatory
Morehouse College
University of Arizona
University of Minnesota-Twin Cities
Bard College
Boston University
City University of New York-Hunter College
State University of New York at Buffalo
Temple University
Emerson College

QUALITY OF LIFE

Happy students
Overall, how happy are you?

Washington and Lee University
College of the Atlantic
Deep Springs College
Dartmouth College
Hollins College
Sweet Briar College
Mount Holyoke College
Randolph-Macon Woman's College
Colby College
Wofford College
College of the Holy Cross
St. Lawrence University
University of the South
Colgate University
St. Mary's College (CA)
Amherst College
Carleton College
Williams College
Brown University
Kenyon College

Unhappy students
Overall, how happy are you?

University of Missouri-Columbia
Hampton University
New Jersey Institute of Technology
State University of New York at Stony Brook
Tuskegee University
Stevens Institute of Technology
Illinois Institute of Technology
City University of New York-Queens College
University of Arizona
Marquette University
Hofstra University
Rensselaer Polytechnic Institute
University of Maryland-College Park
University of Toronto
Seton Hall University
U.S. Naval Academy
City University of New York-Hunter College
Georgia Institute of Technology
Johns Hopkins University
Temple University

Beautiful campus
Based on students' ratings of campus beauty

Mount Holyoke College
Washington and Lee University
College of the Atlantic
Sweet Briar College
Colgate University
Furman University
University of the South
Colby College
Dartmouth College
Hollins College
Wellesley College
Hanover College
Rhodes College
St. Mary's College (CA)
Swarthmore College
University of California-Santa Cruz
Agnes Scott College
Vassar College
Warren Wilson College
Williams College

Campus is tiny, unsightly or both
Based on students' ratings of campus beauty

Illinois Institute of Technology
Berklee College of Music
New Jersey Institute of Technology
Boston Conservatory
Cooper Union
New York University
University of Dallas

Parsons School of Design
Massachusetts Institute of Technology
Boston University
Golden Gate University
State University of New York at Albany
State University of New York at Stony Brook
City University of New York-Hunter College
Eastman School of Music
Drexel University
School of the Art Institute of Chicago
Case Western Reserve University
Georgia Institute of Technology
Temple University

Great food
Based on students' ratings of campus food

Deep Springs College
Bowdoin College
Sweet Briar College
College of the Atlantic
Randolph-Macon Woman's College
Cornell University
Dartmouth College
Colby College
Dickinson College
James Madison University
Miami University
Gettysburg College
Bryn Mawr College
University of Richmond
Smith College
San Francisco Art Institute
Hollins College
Trinity University
Davidson College
Bennington College

Is it food?
Based on students' ratings of campus food

New College of the University of South Florida
St. John's College (MD)
Fisk University
New Mexico Institute of Mining & Technology
Hampton University
State University of New York at Albany
Tuskegee University
Worcester Polytechnic Institute
St. Mary's College of Maryland
Catawba College
Berklee College of Music
Carnegie Mellon University
Golden Gate University
St. Bonaventure University
San Francisco Conservatory of Music
Stevens Institute of Technology
Earlham College

Oglethorpe University
Westminster College (PA)
Emerson College

Dorms like palaces
Based on students' ratings of dorm comfort

Agnes Scott College
Trinity University
Hollins College
Smith College
Mount Holyoke College
Loyola College (MD)
Randolph-Macon Woman's College
Sweet Briar College
Bryn Mawr College
College of the Atlantic
Williams College
George Washington University
Bowdoin College
New College of the University of South Florida
Skidmore College
Dartmouth College
Bates College
Scripps College
Wellesley College
Claremont McKenna College

Dorms like dungeons
Based on students' ratings of dorm comfort

Hampton University
Tuskegee University
City University of New York-Hunter College
Florida State University
University of Oregon
Emerson College
State University of New York at Stony Brook
U.S. Military Academy
Florida A&M University
Southwestern University
Morehouse College
University of Arizona
Howard University
Baylor University
Fisk University
Michigan Technological University
University of California-Riverside
University of Idaho
University of Massachusetts-Amherst
Berklee College of Music

The best quality of life
Based on The Princeton Review Quality of Life Rating

College of the Atlantic
Deep Springs College
Dartmouth College
Hollins College

Sweet Briar College
Mount Holyoke College
Randolph-Macon Woman's College
University of Richmond
Davidson College
Skidmore College
Harvard and Radcliffe Colleges
Brigham Young University
Agnes Scott College
Smith College
Washington and Lee University
Marlboro College
Colby College
Bowdoin College
Rhodes College
University of California-Santa Cruz

POLITICS

Students most nostalgic for Reagan
Based on students' assessment of their personal political views

Brigham Young University
Grove City College
Hampden-Sydney College
Samford University
U.S. Military Academy
Baylor University
Louisiana State University-Baton Rouge
Rose-Hulman Institute of Technology
U.S. Naval Academy
Calvin College
Furman University
Texas A&M University-College Station
Washington and Lee University
Creighton University
University of Kansas
Wofford College
Randolph-Macon College
University of Dallas
Millsaps College
Ohio Northern University

Students most nostalgic for George McGovern
Based on students' assessment of their personal political views

Reed College
Hampshire College
Goddard College
Eugene Lang College
College of the Atlantic
The Evergreen State College
Bard College
Sarah Lawrence College

New College of the University of South Florida
University of California-Santa Cruz
Deep Springs College
Oberlin College
San Francisco Art Institute
Bennington College
Macalester College
Grinnell College
Carleton College
Earlham College
Pitzer College
Simon's Rock College of Bard

Most politically active
How popular are political/activist groups?

The Evergreen State College
Swarthmore College
Earlham College
Grinnell College
Goddard College
College of the Atlantic
Oberlin College
Agnes Scott College
New College of the University of South Florida
Smith College
Georgetown University
George Washington University
Brown University
Claremont McKenna College
Eugene Lang College
Mount Holyoke College
University of California-Santa Cruz
Sarah Lawrence College
Bryn Mawr College
Guilford College

Election? What election?
How popular are political/activist groups?

San Francisco Conservatory of Music
California Institute of Technology
Berklee College of Music
U.S. Military Academy
New Mexico Institute of Mining & Technology
Eastman School of Music
Illinois Institute of Technology
Harvey Mudd College
Montana Tech of the University of Montana
Parsons School of Design
Stephens College
Juilliard School
Stevens Institute of Technology
Worcester Polytechnic Institute
Boston Conservatory
Rochester Institute of Technology
Babson College

Pennsylvania State University-University Park
Golden Gate University
Rhode Island School of Design

DEMOGRAPHICS

Diverse student population
Is your student body made up of diverse social and ethnic types?

Harvard and Radcliffe Colleges
George Mason University
University of Miami
Massachusetts Institute of Technology
Berklee College of Music
Boston University
Juilliard School
Columbia University
Mount Holyoke College
Occidental College
Rutgers University-Rutgers College
State University of New York at Buffalo
Temple University
Wellesley College
Brown University
Cooper Union
Clark University
George Washington University
Manhattanville College
New York University

Homogeneous student population
Is your student body made up of diverse social and ethnic types?

Washington and Lee University
Hampden-Sydney College
Grove City College
Reed College
Miami University
Bucknell University
Villanova University
Deep Springs College
Gettysburg College
St. Lawrence University
Morehouse College
University of Richmond
University of Vermont
University of the South
College of the Atlantic
Dickinson College
Colby College
College of the Holy Cross
Providence College
University of New Hampshire

Students from different backgrounds interact
Do different types of students (black/white, rich/poor) interact frequently and easily?

U.S. Military Academy
U.S. Naval Academy
Cooper Union
North Carolina School of the Arts
Eastman School of Music
St. John's College (MD)
Bennington College
California Institute of Technology
Boston Conservatory
Harvey Mudd College
Marlboro College
Juilliard School
San Francisco Conservatory of Music
Mount Holyoke College
Whittier College
Simon's Rock College of Bard
Berklee College of Music
Bryn Mawr College
New College of the University of South Florida
Parsons School of Design

Race/class relations strained
Do different types of students (black/white, rich/poor) interact frequently and easily?

Miami University
Vanderbilt University
Villanova University
Hampden-Sydney College
Washington and Lee University
St. Lawrence University
Cornell University
University of California-Santa Barbara
Emory University
University of Vermont
Duke University
Syracuse University
University of Notre Dame
Baylor University
University of Richmond
Fairfield University
Gettysburg College
Providence College
Boston College
Northwestern University

Gay community accepted
Is there very little discrimination against homosexuals?

Deep Springs College
Bennington College
North Carolina School of the Arts
College of the Atlantic
Sarah Lawrence College

Marlboro College
Hampshire College
Bryn Mawr College
Simon's Rock College of Bard
Smith College
San Francisco Conservatory of Music
Reed College
Boston Conservatory
Warren Wilson College
Bard College
St. John's College (New Mexico)
New College of the University of South Florida
Eugene Lang College
Oberlin College
Juilliard School

Alternative lifestyles not an alternative
Is there very little discrimination against homosexuals?

U.S. Military Academy*
U.S. Naval Academy*
Washington and Lee University
Hampden-Sydney College
University of Alabama
Morehouse College
Grove City College
College of the Holy Cross
Clarkson University
University of Notre Dame
Howard University
Baylor University
Lafayette College
Texas Christian University
Brigham Young University
Samford University
Colorado School of Mines
Ripon College
Texas A&M University-College Station
St. Lawrence University
* Didn't ask, didn't tell.

Students pray on a regular basis
Are students very religious?

Brigham Young University
Grove City College
Furman University
Loyola Marymount University
Samford University
College of the Holy Cross
University of Dallas
University of Notre Dame
Baylor University
Calvin College
U.S. Military Academy
Valparaiso University
Brandeis University
Fisk University

Creighton University
St. Olaf College
U.S. Naval Academy
Pepperdine University
Morehouse College
The College of William and Mary

Students ignore God on a regular basis
Are students very religious?

Reed College
Bennington College
Bard College
College of the Atlantic
San Francisco Art Institute
Eugene Lang College
Sarah Lawrence College
Deep Springs College
Hampshire College
New College of the University of South Florida
California Institute of the Arts
Grinnell College
Marlboro College
Macalester College
Goddard College
Lewis & Clark College
Vassar College
Beloit College
Emerson College
School of the Art Institute of Chicago

SOCIAL LIFE

Great college towns
Based on students' ratings of the surrounding town or city

Deep Springs College
Columbia University
Oglethorpe University
McGill University
American University
Eugene Lang College
Georgetown University
Juilliard School
Emerson College
Harvard and Radcliffe Colleges
George Washington University
Southern Methodist University
Emory University
San Francisco Art Institute
Macalester College
Agnes Scott College
Boston University
Parsons School of Design
University of Colorado, Boulder
Barnard College

More to do on-campus
Based on students' ratings of the surrounding town or city

U.S. Military Academy
Union College (NY)
Bennington College
Vassar College
Tuskegee University
New Jersey Institute of Technology
Earlham College
Rensselaer Polytechnic Institute
Rose-Hulman Institute of Technology
University of the Pacific
Yale University
Beloit College
Clark University
Wesleyan University
Lafayette College
Bard College
Wheaton College (MA)
Eastman School of Music
University of Notre Dame
Connecticut College

Town-gown relations are good
Do students get along well with members of the local community?

Deep Springs College
U.S. Naval Academy
Brigham Young University
Calvin College
Furman University
Samford University
Grove City College
Randolph-Macon Woman's College
Davidson College
St. Olaf College
Guilford College
Wofford College
Texas Christian University
U.S. Military Academy
Hollins College
Texas A&M University-College Station
Agnes Scott College
San Francisco Conservatory of Music
Creighton University
Montana Tech of the University of Montana

Town-gown relations are strained
Do students get along well with members of the local community?

Bennington College
Sarah Lawrence College
Vassar College
Lehigh University
California Institute of the Arts

Earlham College
Union College (NY)
Tuskegee University
Bates College
Morehouse College
Lafayette College
University of Virginia
Bard College
Yale University
College of Wooster
Illinois Institute of Technology
Howard University
Hobart and William Smith Colleges
Fordham University
Gettysburg College

Students pair off on "old-fashioned" dates
Do students date frequently?

Florida A&M University
Southwestern University
Morehouse College
Stephens College
University of Alabama
Howard University
Louisiana State University-Baton Rouge
Agnes Scott College
Hampton University
Brigham Young University
Florida State University
Loyola Marymount University
Texas A&M University-College Station
Randolph-Macon Woman's College
Spelman College
Fisk University
Sweet Briar College
Tuskegee University
University of Kentucky
University of Tennessee-Knoxville

Students socialize in a more casual fashion
Do students date frequently?

Deep Springs College
College of the Holy Cross
California Institute of Technology
Stanford University
Williams College
Bowdoin College
Trinity University
Amherst College
Vassar College
Duke University
Wake Forest University
Haverford College
Bryn Mawr College
Princeton University
Georgetown University

University of Chicago
Rice University
Brown University
Cooper Union
Carleton College

EXTRACURRICULARS

Students pack the stadiums
How popular are intercollegiate sports?

University of Notre Dame
Duke University
University of North Carolina-Chapel Hill
University of Southern California
Williams College
University of Michigan-Ann Arbor
Syracuse University
U.S. Military Academy
U.S. Naval Academy
Florida State University
Auburn University
University of Kansas
Wake Forest University
University of Miami
Wabash College
University of Kentucky
Indiana University-Bloomington
Pennsylvania State University-University Park
University of Alabama
Texas A&M University-College Station

Intercollegiate sports unpopular or nonexistent
How popular are intercollegiate sports?

Deep Springs College
Eugene Lang College
Goddard College
San Francisco Conservatory of Music
School of the Art Institute of Chicago
College of the Atlantic
Juilliard School
Maryland Institute, College of Art
New College of the University of South Florida
Boston Conservatory
Eastman School of Music
Bennington College
North Carolina School of the Arts
California Institute of the Arts
San Francisco Art Institute
Parsons School of Design
Reed College
Rhode Island School of Design
Berklee College of Music
Sarah Lawrence College

Everyone plays intramural sports
How popular are intramural sports?

U.S. Naval Academy
U.S. Military Academy
Wabash College
University of Notre Dame
Trinity University
Loyola Marymount University
Colgate University
Carleton College
St. John's College (MD)
Rice University
Massachusetts Institute of Technology
Williams College
Furman University
Siena College
University of Richmond
Whitman College
College of the Holy Cross
Rose-Hulman Institute of Technology
Santa Clara University
University of Miami

Nobody plays intramural sports
How popular are intramural sports?

Eugene Lang College
San Francisco Conservatory of Music
School of the Art Institute of Chicago
Juilliard School
Goddard College
Boston Conservatory
Maryland Institute, College of Art
San Francisco Art Institute
California Institute of the Arts
Parsons School of Design
Eastman School of Music
North Carolina School of the Arts
Golden Gate University
Bennington College
Rhode Island School of Design
Berklee College of Music
Sarah Lawrence College
College of the Atlantic
Simmons College
Deep Springs College

Great college radio station
How popular is the radio station?

Emerson College
Goddard College
Loyola Marymount University
Brown University
The Evergreen State College
Guilford College

DePauw University
Union College (NY)
Whitman College
Denison University
Bates College
Syracuse University
St. Bonaventure University
Wittenberg University
Grinnell College
Illinois Wesleyan University
Knox College
Oberlin College
Franklin & Marshall College
Skidmore College

College newspaper gets read
How popular is the newspaper?

Loyola Marymount University
Howard University
Syracuse University
University of North Carolina-Chapel Hill
Union College (NY)
Louisiana State University-Baton Rouge
Mount Holyoke College
University of Virginia
Tufts University
Pennsylvania State University-University Park
Washington and Lee University
University of Georgia
University of Kansas
University of Florida
Georgetown University
DePauw University
Emerson College
Northwestern University
Texas Christian University
Brandeis University

College theater is big
How popular are theater groups?

Boston Conservatory
Sarah Lawrence College
Emerson College
North Carolina School of the Arts
Juilliard School
Vassar College
California Institute of the Arts
Oberlin College
Skidmore College
Marlboro College
University of Pennsylvania
Brandeis University
Drew University
Carleton College
Simon's Rock College of Bard

Yale University
Wesleyan University
University of Dallas
St. Olaf College
Brigham Young University

<hr>

PARTIES

Lots of beer
How widely used is beer?

University of the South
Washington and Lee University
DePauw University
Siena College
Lafayette College
Lehigh University
Randolph-Macon College
Rollins College
University of Wisconsin-Madison
Union College (NY)
Fairfield University
University of North Carolina-Chapel Hill
Austin College
Loyola University New Orleans
Pennsylvania State University-University Park
University of Delaware
University of Kansas
Catholic University of America
Dartmouth College
Dickinson College

Lots of hard liquor
How widely used is hard liquor?

Washington and Lee University
Tulane University
DePauw University
University of the South
Syracuse University
University of Wisconsin-Madison
Siena College
Centenary College of Louisiana
Bennington College
Lafayette College
Randolph-Macon College
Louisiana State University-Baton Rouge
University of Vermont
Emory University
Loyola University New Orleans
University of Florida
Hampden-Sydney College
Loyola College (MD)
Union College (NY)
Rollins College

Scotch and soda, hold the scotch
How widely used is hard liquor?

Brigham Young University
Deep Springs College
Golden Gate University
U.S. Military Academy
Harvard and Radcliffe Colleges
College of the Holy Cross
Grove City College
Agnes Scott College
Clarkson University
Morehouse College
Cooper Union
Samford University
City University of New York-Queens College
U.S. Naval Academy
Haverford College
Spelman College
Wellesley College
Calvin College
St. Louis University
Bryn Mawr College

Reefer madness
How widely used is marijuana?

Bennington College
University of California-Santa Barbara
Sarah Lawrence College
University of California-Santa Cruz
Trinity College (CT)
California Institute of the Arts
Emerson College
Bard College
School of the Art Institute of Chicago
Vassar College
New College of the University of South Florida
The Evergreen State College
"University of Colorado, Boulder"
Reed College
University of Vermont
Syracuse University
Rhode Island School of Design
St. Lawrence University
Eugene Lang College
University of Wisconsin-Madison

Don't inhale
How widely used is marijuana?

U.S. Military Academy
U.S. Naval Academy
Deep Springs College
Brigham Young University
Golden Gate University
Agnes Scott College
Rose-Hulman Institute of Technology
Wesleyan College

Grove City College
Cooper Union
Stevens Institute of Technology
San Francisco Conservatory of Music
Samford University
Randolph-Macon Woman's College
University of Notre Dame
Calvin College
Wellesley College
Bryn Mawr College
College of the Holy Cross
Furman University

Major frat and sorority scene
How popular are fraternities/sororities?

Washington and Lee University
Wabash College
Lehigh University
Randolph-Macon College
Union College (NY)
Lafayette College
DePauw University
Southern Methodist University
Wofford College
Birmingham-Southern College
St. Lawrence University
Hanover College
Dartmouth College
Westminster College (PA)
Gettysburg College
University of Illinois-Urbana-Champaign
Millsaps College
Texas Christian University
Bucknell University
Ursinus College

SCHOOL BY TYPE

Party schools
Based on a combination of survey questions concerning the use of alcohol and drugs, hours of study each day, and the popularity of the Greek system

Florida State University
George Washington University
University of Florida
University of California-Santa Barbara
Emerson College
University of Wisconsin-Madison
St. Mary's College of Maryland
SUNY Albany
Colgate University
University of Vermont
Syracuse University
St. Lawrence University
University of Dayton

Sarah Lawrence College
Millsaps College
Louisiana State University-Baton Rouge
Lafayette College
University of South Carolina
Hobart/William Smith Colleges
University of Iowa

Stone-cold sober schools
Based on a combination of survey questions concerning the use of alcohol and drugs, hours of study each day, and the popularity of the Greek system

Deep Springs College
Brigham Young University
U.S. Military Academy
U.S. Naval Academy
Golden Gate University
Grove City College
Samford University
Wesleyan College
Spelman College
Calvin College
Wellesley College
Cooper Union
Bryn Mawr College
Furman University
Mount Holyoke College
California Institute of Technology
Stevens Institute of Technology
San Francisco Conservatory of Music
Agnes Scott College
Smith College

Jock schools
Based on a combination of survey questions concerning the popularity of the Greek system, intercollegiate and intramural sports, theater, and cigarettes

Dartmouth College
Wabash College
Colgate University
Duke University
Bowdoin College
Baylor University
Florida A&M University
Southwestern University
Rose-Hulman Institute of Technology
Wake Forest University
University of Missouri-Columbia
Texas Christian University
University of Florida
Hampden-Sydney College
University of Illinois—Urbana-Champaign
Bucknell University
Georgia Institute of Technology
Texas A&M University-College Station

Florida State University
University of Virginia

Aesthete schools
Based on a combination of survey questions concerning the popularity of the Greek system, intercollegiate and intramural sports, theater, and cigarettes

North Carolina School of the Arts
Juilliard School
Eugene Lang College
Sarah Lawrence College
California Institute of the Arts
Goddard College
Boston Conservatory
San Francisco Conservatory of Music
School of the Art Institute of Chicago
Reed College
Simon's Rock College of Bard
College of the Atlantic
Marlboro College
St. John's College (New Mexico)
Maryland Institute, College of Art
New College of the University of South Florida
Rhode Island School of Design
Oberlin College
Hampshire College
Vassar College

Birkenstock-wearing, tree-hugging, clove-smoking vegetarians
Based on a combination of survey questions concerning political persuasion, the use of alcohol, marijuana and hallucinogens, the prevalence of religion, and the popularity of student government

Bard College
Hampshire College
Reed College
The Evergreen State College
California Institute of the Arts
New College of the University of South Florida
Sarah Lawrence College
Vassar College
San Francisco Art Institute
Macalester College
Eugene Lang College
University of California-Santa Cruz
Maryland Institute, College of Art
Goddard College
Oberlin College
School of the Art Institute of Chicago
Rhode Island School of Design
Bates College
Beloit College
University of Wisconsin-Madison

Future Rotarians and Daughters of the American Revolution

Based on a combination of survey questions concerning political persuasion, the use of alcohol, marijuana and hallucinogens, the prevalence of religion, and the popularity of student government

Brigham Young University
Grove City College
U.S. Naval Academy
Samford University
U.S. Military Academy
Furman University
Baylor University
Wesleyan College
Calvin College
Randolph-Macon Woman's College
Deep Springs College
Pepperdine University
Villanova University
Creighton University
Hollins College
Sweet Briar College
St. Olaf College
Valparaiso University
Loyola College (MD)
University of Notre Dame

PART 2

THE BEST COLLEGES

AGNES SCOTT COLLEGE

141 EAST COLLEGE AVENUE, DECATUR, GA 30030   ADMISSIONS: 404-638-6285   FAX: 404-638-6414

CAMPUS LIFE

Quality of Life Rating   92
Type of school   private
Affiliation   Presbyterian Church USA
Environment   metropolis

STUDENTS
FT undergrad enrollment   514
% male/female   0/100
% from out of state   50
% live on campus   86
% spend weekend on campus   75
% transfers   8
% from public high school   81
% African-American   14
% Asian   3
% Caucasian   77
% Hispanic   3
% international   3
# of countries represented   12

WHAT'S HOT
campus easy to get around
off-campus food
dorms
student government
old-fashioned dating

WHAT'S NOT
college radio
drugs
hard liquor
health facilities
intramural sports

ACADEMICS

Academic Rating   93
Profs Interesting Rating   98
Profs Accessible Rating   98
Calendar   semester
Student/teacher ratio   8:1
% profs PhD/tenured   99/99
Hours of study per day   3.63

MOST POPULAR MAJORS
psychology
international relations
political science

STUDENTS SPEAK OUT

Life

Agnes Scott, a small women's school in Atlanta, is surrounded by so many large coed schools that its single-sex status does not hurt its social life. Although one student reports that "developing a romantic relationship can prove difficult if you do not have the time or motivation to get involved with the Georgia Tech or Emory frat scene," most student responses emphasize students' access to "the opportunities of a big city with many area colleges: social events (frat parties), sporting events (football, basketball, baseball), and friendships." Explains another student: "Being in Atlanta is wonderful. We have the advantage of a small, beautiful campus in the midst of a metropolitan area—definitely the best of both worlds." On-campus life centers on study, clubs ("We have many great leadership opportunities on campus," reported one student), and two "major formals, one each semester."

Academics

Most small schools are hamstrung in their efforts to offer students a full range of studies. Tiny Agnes Scott, however, allows students to cross-register at 18 other area colleges and universities. The result is that Scott students get "the best of both worlds: the friendly comforts of a small college and the opportunities of a larger school." Most students take almost all their classes at Scott, where they enjoy a capable, energetic faculty. Explains one student, "The faculty is the highlight of the school. They are very interested in our education and enjoy building relationships with the students." Students here work hard and told us that "the classwork isn't out of reach but it is very demanding." Warns one, "Scott is the paper-writing capital of the South. When you get here, be prepared to write." Despite the intense (and sometimes stressful) academic atmosphere, "competition among students is minimal. Instead, you are constantly pushed to improve your own performance regardless of your ranking in the class." Curricular highlights include the Global Awareness Program, which sends undergraduates overseas for the "pleasantly unsettling experience" of discovering "that [their] view of the world is not universally shared." Students live under an honor code that allows them to leave dorm doors unlocked and take tests unproctored. Sums up one student: "As a senior I can honestly say that I have learned far more about myself as an individual than I would have at a large coeducational institution. This school is dedicated to getting rid of the girl and educating women."

Student Body

In their descriptions of each other, Scott students mention the strong sense of community that is felt on campus. Writes one, "Agnes Scott is great if you want to graduate having made a lot of friends that seem almost like family; the bonds formed here are unique." Black students (who are moderately well represented in the student body) tell us that "It's difficult being black on this campus. All activities are either geared toward the majority (white heterosexuals) or call for a lot of interaction with Emory or Tech." In general, the student body is liberal.

AGNES SCOTT COLLEGE

ADMISSIONS

The admissions committee considers (in descending order of importance): HS record, class rank, test scores, recommendations, essay. *Also considered (in descending order of importance):* extracurriculars, personality, special talents. Either the SAT or ACT is required. An interview is recommended. Admissions process is need-blind. *High school units required/recommended:* 16 total units are recommended; 4 English recommended, 3 math recommended, 1 science recommended, 2 foreign language recommended, 1 social studies recommended. Rank in top third of secondary school class recommended. TOEFL is required of all international students.

The Inside Word

Women's colleges are enjoying a renaissance of late and to top it off, Agnes Scott has always been a great choice for strong students. Don't be deceived by the college's generous admit rate—we're talking about a small applicant pool of well-qualified candidates, and one of the best small liberal arts colleges to be found anywhere. Look for greater selectivity as the college recruits students from further afield and application totals continue to increase at top women's colleges. The admissions process can't get any more personalized than it is at Agnes Scott—every candidate is assigned her own specific admission advisor, who works with the student throughout the process.

FINANCIAL AID

Students should submit: FAFSA, a copy of parents' most recent income tax filing. The Princeton Review suggests that all financial aid forms be submitted as soon as possible after January 1. *The following grants/scholarships are offered:* Pell, SEOG, academic merit, the school's own scholarships, the school's own grants, state scholarships, state grants, private scholarships, foreign aid. *Students borrow from the following loan programs:* Stafford, unsubsidized Stafford, PLUS, the school's own loan fund, private loans. College Work-Study Program is available. Institutional employment is available.

FROM THE ADMISSIONS OFFICE

"Agnes Scott's size offers many advantages. Students can look forward to individual attention from professors and much stimulating classroom discussion with women who were among the top students in their secondary schools. They also have the opportunity to make friends with women from more than 33 states and 12 foreign countries. "Agnes Scott offers students the chance to study off-campus through cross-registration with 18 colleges in the Atlanta area. The Global Awareness Program enables students to travel and study abroad. "Students are encouraged to preview Agnes Scott through the College's interactive multimedia presentation available on Macintosh and IBM-compatible CD-ROM. Using the latest multimedia technology, this hands-on presentation includes a look at our campus; summary of academic programs; video footage and conversations with students, faculty and alumnae; and a glimpse of Atlanta."

ADMISSIONS

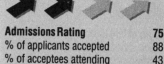

Admissions Rating	75
% of applicants accepted	88
% of acceptees attending	43

FRESHMAN PROFILE

Average verbal SAT	600
Average math SAT	560
Average ACT	NR
Average TOEFL	NR
Graduated top 20% of class	63
Graduated top 40% of class	94
Graduated top 60% of class	NR
Average HS GPA or Avg.	3.4

DEADLINES

Early decision	3/1
Regular admission	NR
Regular notification	rolling
Non-fall registration	yes

APPLICANTS ALSO LOOK AT

AND OFTEN PREFER

U. Georgia
Emory

AND SOMETIMES PREFER

Randolph-Macon Woman's
Smith
Rhodes
Hollins
Sweet Briar

AND RARELY PREFER

UNC-Chapel Hill

FINANCIAL FACTS

Financial Aid Rating	94
Tuition	$13,800
Room & board	$5,800
Estimated book expense	$450
% frosh receiving aid	97
% undergrads receiving aid	93
% aid is need-based	60
% frosh w/ grant (avg)	93 ($9,668)
% frosh w/ loan (avg)	65 ($2,625)
% UGs w/ job (avg)	58 ($1,300)
Off-campus job outlook	good

UNIVERSITY OF ALABAMA

Box 870132, Tuscaloosa, AL 35487-0132 ADMISSIONS: 800-933-2262 Fax: 205-348-6010

CAMPUS LIFE

Quality of Life Rating 75
Type of school public
Affiliation none
Environment city

STUDENTS
FT undergrad enrollment 13,167
% male/female 49/51
% from out of state 32
% live on campus 41
% spend weekend on campus 50
% transfers 33
% from public high school 85
% in (# of) fraternities 16 (27)
% in (# of) sororities 24 (17)
% African-American 12
% Asian 1
% Caucasian 84
% Hispanic 0
% international 3
# of countries represented 102

WHAT'S HOT
old-fashioned dating
health facilities
intercollegiate sports
intramural sports
college radio

WHAT'S NOT
support groups
campus difficult to get around
theater
students are unhappy
religion

ACADEMICS

Academic Rating 68
Profs Interesting Rating 72
Profs Accessible Rating 63
Calendar semester
Student/teacher ratio 17:1
% profs tenured 97
Hours of study per day 2.97

MOST POPULAR MAJORS
marketing
accounting
psychology

STUDENTS SPEAK OUT

Life

The majority of "'Bama bound" students are Alabama natives who come for the strong traditions, such as tappings on Honors Day, Westminster chimes that ring on the quarter hour, and the student ambassador corps. There are over 200 clubs and organizations on campus, and one-fifth of the undergraduate population pledges a fraternity or sorority ("People are very concerned with acceptance, appearances, and Greek life"). Outside of organized channels, many students create their own entertainment: "we go to parties, hang out with friends and go on trips to beaches, camping, etc.," writes one student. Religious activity at this Southern school can enrich one's social life: "I have had the same room and roommate for two years and we would still be roommates next year if I was not getting married to someone who found me in our YA Christian Fellowship group." And as for near-religious experience: "Aerobics are big."

Academics

The most sensible way for the University of Alabama to educate 15,500 undergraduates is to divide 'em up, so students choose their home from nine divisions: arts and sciences, commerce and business administration, communication, education, engineering, human environmental sciences, nursing, social work, and New College, a special program that emphasizes independent study. To further personalize attention to their future alumni, 'Bama provides extensive academic support and tutoring. The excellent honors programs also offer smaller, research-oriented courses of study. With all of these self-contained options, students we hear from affirm that this large institution succeeds, for the most part, in its mission to create a cozy universe of study. The for-the-most-part "highly accessible" professors also contribute to the perception that individual attention is attainable here despite the school's size. One student beams that "My advisor is very comforting in that she believes in me and that I can do whatever I put my mind to...My teachers and advisor stop me to talk when I see them anywhere." Overall, most we hear from are more than satisfied with their school: "The University of Alabama is one of the best universities in the country...I wouldn't want to go anywhere else."

Student Body

Surprisingly for a school with so many students milling around campus, prospective students need not fear they will become free-floating loners in an anonymous crowd. Alabama respondents describe an ultra-friendly atmosphere: "Even people that you don't know will give you a friendly smile as they pass. It is easy to make friends because of the diversity on campus. It is easy to find a group to fit into." Things are not all peaches and cream, however; race relations can be strained, and one student reports that "Racism is a hot issue on campus." Indeed, most people report that minority students experience negative attitudes here and that the university needs to buttress the support groups to make positive changes in this crucial area of college life.

ADMISSIONS

The admissions committee considers (in descending order of importance): HS record, test scores, recommendations, class rank. *Also considered (in descending order of importance):* special talents. Either the SAT or ACT is required. An interview is required of some applicants. Admissions process is need-blind. *High school units required/recommended:* 20 total units are required; 4 English required, 3 math required, 3 science required, 1 foreign language required, 3 social studies required, 1 history required. Minimum composite ACT score of 22 (combined SAT I score of 1030) and minimum 2.0 GPA in core courses required. *Special Requirements:* A portfolio is required for art program applicants. An audition is required for music program applicants. TOEFL is required of all international students.

The Inside Word

There's no mystery in Alabama's formula-driven approach to admission; any solid "B" student is likely to meet with success. What selectivity there is in the process exists mainly due to the volume of applications, not high academic expectations on the part of the university. Recommendations are not likely to play a significant role in the admission of applicants unless they are borderline candidates.

FINANCIAL AID

Students should submit: FAFSA, the school's own financial aid form. The Princeton Review suggests that all financial aid forms be submitted as soon as possible after January 1. *The following grants/scholarships are offered:* Pell, SEOG, academic merit, athletic, the school's own scholarships, the school's own grants, state scholarships, state grants, private scholarships, private grants, federal nursing scholarship, ROTC, foreign aid. *Students borrow from the following loan programs:* Stafford, unsubsidized Stafford, Perkins, PLUS, the school's own loan fund, supplemental loans, private loans. Applicants will be notified of awards beginning April 1. College Work-Study Program is available. Institutional employment is available.

FROM THE ADMISSIONS OFFICE

Since its founding in 1831 as the first public university in the state, The University of Alabama has been committed to providing the best, most complete education possible for its students. Our commitment to that goal means that as times change, we sharpen our focus and methods to keep our graduates competitive in their fields. By offering outstanding teaching in a solid core curriculum enhanced by multimedia classrooms and campus-wide computer labs, The University of Alabama keeps its focus on the future while maintaining a traditional college atmosphere. Extensive international study opportunities, internship programs, and co-operative education placements help our students prepare for successful futures. Consisting of 14 colleges and schools offering 275 degrees in over 150 fields of study, the University gives its students a wide range of choices and offers courses of study at the bachelor's, master's, specialist, and doctoral levels.

ADMISSIONS

Admissions Rating	77
% of applicants accepted	77
% of acceptees attending	48

FRESHMAN PROFILE

Average verbal SAT	NR
Average math SAT	NR
Average ACT	23
Average TOEFL	500
Graduated top 20% of class	61
Graduated top 40% of class	92
Graduated top 60% of class	99
Average HS GPA or Avg.	3.2

DEADLINES

Early decision	3/1
Regular admission	8/1
Regular notification	rolling
Non-fall registration	yes

APPLICANTS ALSO LOOK AT

AND OFTEN PREFER

Oglethorpe U.
Loyola U. New Orleans
Birmingham-Southern Coll.
Samford U.
Rhodes Coll.

AND SOMETIMES PREFER

Michigan State U.
Auburn U.
U. Georgia
Florida State U.
Vanderbilt U.

FINANCIAL FACTS

Financial Aid Rating	80
In-state tuition	$2,374
Out-of-state tuition	$5,924
Room & board	$3,285
Estimated book expense	$610
% frosh receiving aid	50
% undergrads receiving aid	50
% aid is need-based	64
% frosh w/ grant (avg)	47 ($3,034)
% frosh w/ loan (avg)	37 ($3,607)
% UGs w/ job (avg)	19 ($2,042)
Off-campus job outlook	fair

ALFRED UNIVERSITY

SAXON DRIVE, ALFRED, NY 14802   ADMISSIONS: 800-541-9229   FAX: 607-871-2198

CAMPUS LIFE

Quality of Life Rating **76**
Type of school   private
Affiliation   none
Environment   town

STUDENTS

FT undergrad enrollment	1,911
% male/female	53/47
% from out of state	30
% live on campus	65
% spend weekend on campus	90
% transfers	10
% from public high school	83
% in (# of) fraternities	23 (7)
% in (# of) sororities	16 (5)
% African-American	5
% Asian	2
% Caucasian	88
% Hispanic	3
% international	NR
# of countries represented	5

WHAT'S HOT
college radio
Greeks
old-fashioned dating
drugs
beer

WHAT'S NOT
off-campus food
political activism
health facilities
Alfred, NY
religion

ACADEMICS

Academic Rating	**82**
Profs Interesting Rating	85
Profs Accessible Rating	86
Calendar	semester
Student/teacher ratio	12:1
% profs PhD/tenured	88/87
Hours of study per day	3.18

MOST POPULAR MAJORS
ceramic engineering science
business administration
psychology

STUDENTS SPEAK OUT

Life
One AU student describes his predicament as being "stranded in the middle of nowhere." AU students definitely wish the school were somewhere else. It's a testimony to the school's other fine qualities that its students scored well in our overall happiness category despite giving the surrounding area very low grades. Alfred and the nearby mountains are great for those who love outdoor activities, but with Rochester and Buffalo each almost two hours away (and with roadways icy much of the school year), social distractions are hard to come by. Reports one student, "Alfred is a great small university. But if you want to have a wild time while in school, this is not the place." Students get bored in their spare time, as evidenced by the high popularity levels of alcohol and drugs. Bring your Scrabble board.

Academics
Alfred University is famous for its studies in ceramics and glassworks. How many schools offer even one major in these fields? AU offers three: ceramic art and design, engineering, and science. Furthermore, the ceramics program is publicly funded, and its students pay about one-third the tuition that those enrolled in the school's private divisions pay. More than one-tenth of the students major in the visual and performing arts, but AU is not simply an art school. In fact, almost a quarter of the students are engineers, and there are large business and pre-med populations. Says one student, "It's amazing that such a fantastic education can be found in Grizzly Adams country." A demanding core curriculum requires that all students pursue a liberal arts program in addition to the rigors of their majors. Students report that classes are small, the administration is helpful, and the professors are both accessible and talented teachers. Reports one student (clearly destined for a career in public relations), "Take big-school education and mix it comfortably with small-school personal attention. Throw in a little small-town security and you have the recipe for Alfred University. If you miss a lot of classes, you can expect to be contacted by your professor to find out why."

Student Body
Remote Alfred attracts few minority students: the solid majority of students are white. The male/female ratio favors the women, and guys who don't find girlfriends at Alfred will be hard pressed to find them anywhere else in the area. Students reported that there is a noticeable gay community but that it is not well integrated into the mainstream of the Alfred student body. In fact, some argued that there is no mainstream of the student body: Reported one student, "Due to the small size of the university, there are many tight cliques and sometimes discriminatory groups. Students here are not altogether independent." Not everyone agreed, however, and quite a few respondents voiced more encouraging opinions. One such student wrote that "everyone is friendly and very accepting of the diverse group of people who are here."

ALFRED UNIVERSITY

ADMISSIONS

The admissions committee considers (in descending order of importance): HS record, class rank, test scores, recommendations, essay. *Also considered (in descending order of importance):* extracurriculars, alumni relationship, geographical distribution, special talents, personality. Either the SAT or ACT is required. An interview is recommended. Admissions process is need-blind. *High school units required/recommended:* 16 total units are required; 4 English required, 3 math required, 1 science required, 3 science recommended, 2 foreign language recommended, 3 social studies required, 4 social studies recommended. Two or three units of mathematics and two or three units of social studies required. *Special Requirements:* A portfolio is required for art program applicants. TOEFL is required of all international students. *The admissions office says:* "Each applicant's folder is read by the counselor who travels and recruits in the applicant's geographic area. The counselor is then familiar with the strengths and characteristics of the applicant's high school and can be better prepared to evaluate the compatibility between the applicant and the institution."

The Inside Word

There's no questioning the high quality of academics at Alfred, especially in their internationally known ceramics program. Still, the university's general lack of name recognition and relatively isolated campus directly affect both the applicant pool and the number of admitted students who enroll, and thus keeps selectivity relatively low for a school of its caliber. (The exception is clearly in ceramic arts, where candidates will face a very rigorous review.) If you're a back-to-nature type looking for a challenging academic environment, Alfred could be just what the doctor ordered. And if you're a standout academically, you may find that they're generous with financial aid, too—they are serious about competing for good students.

FINANCIAL AID

Students should submit: FAFSA, the school's own financial aid form (due: rolling), state aid form, a copy of parents' most recent income tax filing. The Princeton Review suggests that all financial aid forms be submitted as soon as possible after January 1. *The following grants/scholarships are offered:* Pell, SEOG, academic merit, the school's own scholarships, the school's own grants, state scholarships, state grants, private scholarships, private grants, ROTC, foreign aid. *Students borrow from the following loan programs:* Stafford, unsubsidized Stafford, Perkins, PLUS, the school's own loan fund. Applicants will be notified of awards beginning: rolling. College Work-Study Program is available. Institutional employment is available.

FROM THE ADMISSIONS OFFICE

"The admissions process at Alfred University is the foundation for the personal attention that a student can expect from this institution. Each applicant is evaluated individually and can expect genuine, personal attention at Alfred University."

ADMISSIONS

Admissions Rating	73
% of applicants accepted	85
% of acceptees attending	35

FRESHMAN PROFILE

Average verbal SAT	640
Average math SAT	570
Average ACT	26
Average TOEFL	550
Graduated top 20% of class	40
Graduated top 40% of class	70
Graduated top 60% of class	90
Average HS GPA or Avg.	NR

DEADLINES

Early decision	12/1
Regular admission	2/1
Regular notification	mid-March
Non-fall registration	yes

APPLICANTS ALSO LOOK AT

AND OFTEN PREFER
SUNY Geneseo

AND SOMETIMES PREFER
SUNY Buffalo
SUNY Albany
U. Rochester
Syracuse

AND RARELY PREFER
Clarkson U.
RIT
U. Mass., Amherst

FINANCIAL FACTS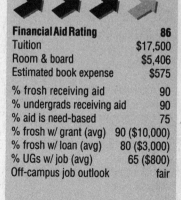

Financial Aid Rating	86
Tuition	$17,500
Room & board	$5,406
Estimated book expense	$575
% frosh receiving aid	90
% undergrads receiving aid	90
% aid is need-based	75
% frosh w/ grant (avg)	90 ($10,000)
% frosh w/ loan (avg)	80 ($3,000)
% UGs w/ job (avg)	65 ($800)
Off-campus job outlook	fair

AMERICAN UNIVERSITY

4400 MASSACHUSETTS AVENUE, NW, WASHINGTON, DC 20016-8001   ADMISSIONS: 202-885-6000   FAX: 202-885-6014

CAMPUS LIFE

Quality of Life Rating   **77**
Type of school	private
Affiliation	Methodist Church
Environment	metropolis

STUDENTS

FT undergrad enrollment	4,982
% male/female	41/59
% from out of state	90
% live on campus	65
% spend weekend on campus	13
% transfers	26
% from public high school	60
% in (# of) fraternities	20 (7)
% in (# of) sororities	25 (8)
% African-American	7
% Asian	5
% Caucasian	69
% Hispanic	5
% international	14
# of countries represented	130

WHAT'S HOT
political activism
Washington
ethnic diversity on campus
drugs
old-fashioned dating

WHAT'S NOT
inefficient administration
unattractive campus
intercollegiate sports
beer
students are unhappy

ACADEMICS

Academic Rating	**80**
Profs Interesting Rating	77
Profs Accessible Rating	80
Calendar	semester
Student/teacher ratio	14:1
% profs PhD/tenured	92/68
Hours of study per day	3.21

MOST POPULAR MAJORS
communication
international studies
political science

% GRADS WHO PURSUE...
Law 28

STUDENTS SPEAK OUT

Life

Washington, D.C., is the magnet that draws many students to American University, and those who choose the school for this reason aren't disappointed: American students are among the *Best 310's* happiest with their school's location. Says one student, "Washington, D.C., is a great place with a lot of action. At night you can go to one of dozens of bars and clubs rather than to some mandatory rush party." Others note that D.C. affords students many opportunities in government-related jobs and internships. As is often the case at urban schools, school spirit is low, as is interest in intercollegiate sports. Washington certainly competes with AU for students' attention. But school spirit is probably also affected by the absence of "school spirits": AU's campus is dry. One effect of this policy has been, predictably, to drive the social scene off campus and into frats and the city. Some students are fairly resentful of the situation. Students here smoke more pot than students elsewhere, perhaps because it's easier to smoke than to drink in dorms.

Academics

For a long time location was considered the only major drawing card of AU, but the school's academic reputation and, accordingly, its applicant pool, have recently been on the rise. Many students note that although the school once had a reputation as a party school, that characterization no longer holds true. One student's response is typical: "This school has made a successful transition from a 'party school' into a fine academic institution. I find the classes challenging, stimulating, and interesting. Unfortunately, this trade-off has resulted in a striking and pervasive stagnation of the social scene." American's strongest programs are those related to government: Professors and guest lecturers here are frequently government bigwigs or ex-bigwigs. Also notable is American's Cooperative Education Program, which serves about 500 students (in all majors, not just in business and technical fields) annually. The co-op program allows students to work at government offices, political think-tanks, broadcast networks, and arts agencies, and thereby gain valuable work experience while earning college credit.

Student Body

American students are particularly proud of the diversity of their student body. As one AU student puts it, "American University is like a trip abroad—every day we are in close contact with foreigners, especially those of us living in the international dorm. There's no way to escape the great diversity on campus, which makes up its own culture." Says another, "AU is the original melting pot, living and thriving in D.C." Still, a surprising number of respondents characterize their classmates as having the attitude of a homogeneous group of rich white folks. More than a few complain that snobbery and ostentation are common here. The student body leans farther to the left than most, although the school is by no means a hotbed of radicalism.

FINANCIAL AID: 202-885-6100

WEB SITE: HTTP://WWW.AMERICAN.EDU/

ADMISSIONS

The admissions committee considers (in descending order of importance): HS record, test scores, class rank, recommendations, essay. *Also considered (in descending order of importance):* extracurriculars, alumni relationship, personality, special talents, geographical distribution. Either the SAT or ACT is required; SAT is preferred. An interview is recommended. *High school units required/recommended:* 15 total units are required; 4 English required, 3 math required, 3 science recommended, 2 foreign language required, 2 social studies recommended, 2 history recommended.

The Inside Word

Washington, D.C. is indeed a tremendous attraction for students who aspire to careers in government, politics, and other areas of public service. Georgetown skims most of the cream of the crop off the top of this considerable pool of prospective students, but American does quite nicely. Because the university is nationally known it also has formidable competition outside its own backyard, and as a result its yield of admits who enroll is on the low side. This necessitates a higher admit rate than one might expect at a school with considerable academic strength and an impressively credentialed faculty. If you're an active leadership type with a strong academic record the admissions process should be fairly painless—American offers a great opportunity for a quality educational experience without having to plead for admission.

FINANCIAL AID

Students should submit: FAFSA, the school's own financial aid form (due March 1). The Princeton Review suggests that all financial aid forms be submitted as soon as possible after January 1. *The following grants/scholarships are offered:* Pell, SEOG, academic merit, athletic, the school's own scholarships, the school's own grants, private scholarships, private grants. *Students borrow from the following loan programs:* Stafford, unsubsidized Stafford, Perkins, PLUS, the school's own loan fund, supplemental loans. Applicants will be notified of awards beginning March 15. College Work-Study Program is available. Institutional employment is available.

FROM THE ADMISSIONS OFFICE

"Our students not only learn about the world, but learn how to shape the world by interacting regularly with decision makers and leaders in every profession and from every corner of the world. If you are looking to be academically challenged in a rich multicultural environment where leadership and decision making are put into practice, then American University is the place you want to be. Our residential, suburban campus provides a safe, comfortable environment where students from all fifty states and over 130 countries live and work. Our expert, teaching faculty provide a well-rounded liberal arts education characterized by small classes, an interdisciplinary curriculum, and the extensive resources of Washington, D.C. In addition, students enjoy a rich variety of professional internship and cooperative education opportunities throughout the city. American University offers all the tools you need to become an expert in your field of study and to shape the world of tomorrow."

ADMISSIONS

Admissions Rating	77
% of applicants accepted	78
% of acceptees attending	29

FRESHMAN PROFILE

Average verbal SAT	610
Average math SAT	590
Average ACT	26
Average TOEFL	550
Graduated top 20% of class	58
Graduated top 40% of class	87
Graduated top 60% of class	98
Average HS GPA or Avg.	3.2

DEADLINES

Early decision	11/15
Regular admission	2/1
Regular notification	4/1
Non-fall registration	yes

APPLICANTS ALSO LOOK AT

AND OFTEN PREFER

Georgetown U.
UNC-Chapel Hill
Northwestern U.
Emory
Boston U.

AND SOMETIMES PREFER

Catholic U.
Dickinson
Boston Coll.
George Washington
U. Maryland, Coll. Park

AND RARELY PREFER

U. Delaware
Loyola Marymount

FINANCIAL FACTS

Financial Aid Rating	68
Tuition	$17,515
Room & board	$7,004
Estimated book expense	$450
% frosh receiving aid	60
% undergrads receiving aid	70
% aid is need-based	35
% frosh w/ grant (avg)	NR
% frosh w/ loan (avg)	NR%
UGs w/ job (avg)	NR ($1,500)
Off-campus job outlook	excellent

AMHERST COLLEGE

Amherst, MA 01002

ADMISSIONS: 413-542-2328   FAX: 413-542-2040

CAMPUS LIFE

Quality of Life Rating	89
Type of school	private
Affiliation	none
Environment	suburban

STUDENTS

FT undergrad enrollment	1,600
% male/female	56/44
% from out of state	85
% live on campus	98
% spend weekend on campus	95
% transfers	3
% from public high school	54
% African-American	8
% Asian	12
% Caucasian	68
% Hispanic	9
% international	2
# of countries represented	25

WHAT'S HOT
political activism
campus easy to get around
registration is a breeze
students are happy
dorms

WHAT'S NOT
infrequent dating
hard liquor
religion
drugs
beer

ACADEMICS

Academic Rating	95
Profs Interesting Rating	96
Profs Accessible Rating	92
Calendar	other
Student/teacher ratio	9:1
% profs PhD/tenured	91/91
Hours of study per day	3.46

MOST POPULAR MAJORS
English
political science
economics

STUDENTS SPEAK OUT

Life
Several years ago, fraternities and sororities were abolished at Amherst College. This move by the administration has had a deadening effect on campus social life; one student describes the current social scene as "nonexistent." The last few years have been trying ones, as "socially, Amherst is still struggling to find its niche. Students turn to small private parties to make up for the lack of campus events." Weekend "tap" parties (usually beer-oriented and held in upperclass dorms) are "still well-attended (especially by Five College women)." Despite the voids in their social world, students are still committed to the Amherst tradition of playing hard, and report overall that they are extremely happy. With their own lovely campus, the small town of Amherst, and the four other colleges at their doorstep, students at Amherst find plenty of diversions.

Academics
The professors are the heart and soul of the solid liberal arts education available at Amherst, one of the country's most highly regarded four-year colleges. Amherst profs garner rave reviews from students, who describe them as "outstanding," "concerned," and "friendly." Small classes, mostly taught by the professors themselves, maximize the learning experience and ensure the faculty's accessibility. Enthuses one sophomore, "I spend about two hours a week talking with a chemistry professor whom I consider a very good friend. I don't think that happens very often at big schools." Students here work hard, but don't feel they are competing for grades; most truly consider learning to be its own reward. (Writes one student, "There is pressure here but it comes from yourself. Students are stressed out, but it's because most are incredibly active.") "Incredibly active" indeed: Amherst students enjoy the many opportunities to get involved that the small school affords them. Remarks one, "Amherst allows me to do so many things I could never do on a large campus: play two sports, or be student treasurer and editor of a magazine and also row crew." When students tire of their own college community, it is easy to take a class or audition for a play at one of the other four schools in the Five College Consortium (UMass - Amherst, Smith, Hampshire, and Mount Holyoke); the Five College system, according to students, "gives you all the opportunities of a large university, without any of the drawbacks."

Student Body
Amherst is definitely a cultural mix, boasting a minority population that constitutes over a quarter of the student body. Although most are proud of this surprisingly diverse group, there are scattered complaints that most students are still from the upper- or upper-middle classes. ("Ethnic and social diversity are different. Amherst is ethnically diverse, but most come from the same socioeconomic levels," explains one student.) There is some truth to the reputation of Amherst students looking like "J. Clones," but the efforts of the administration in this area are admirable compared to those of some other colleges we have seen.

FINANCIAL AID: 413-542-2296

ADMISSIONS

The admissions committee considers (in descending order of importance): HS record, test scores, class rank, recommendations, essay. *Also considered (in descending order of importance):* extracurriculars, personality, special talents, alumni relationship, geographical distribution. Either the SAT or ACT is required. Admissions process is need-blind. *High school units required/recommended:* 19 total units are recommended; 4 English recommended, 4 math recommended, 3 science recommended, 4 foreign language recommended, 2 social studies recommended, 2 history recommended. Rank in top tenth of secondary school class recommended. *Special Requirements:* TOEFL is required of all international students. Resumes recommended; slides and specific audiotapes accepted.

The Inside Word

With the surge in applications to the most highly selective colleges, it's only going to get tougher to gain admission here. At Amherst, you've got to make a strong match all around, and given their swelling applicant pool it's very important that you make your case in as direct a fashion as possible. If you're a special interest candidate such as a legacy or recruited athlete you may get a bit of a break from the admissions committee, but you'll still need to show sound academic capabilities and potential. Those without such links have a tougher task. On top of taking the toughest courses available to them and performing at the highest of their abilities, they must be strong writers who use their skill with a pen to show that they are intellectually curious self-starters who will contribute to the community and profit from the experience. In other words, you've got to have a strong profile and a very convincing application in order to get admitted.

FINANCIAL AID

Students should submit: FAFSA (due May 1), CSS Profile (due February 15), the school's own financial aid form (due February 15), state aid form (due May 1), Divorced Parents form (due February 15), a copy of parents' most recent income tax filing. The Princeton Review suggests that all financial aid forms be submitted as soon as possible after January 1. *The following grants/scholarships are offered:* Pell, SEOG, the school's own grants, state scholarships, state grants, private scholarships, foreign aid. *Students borrow from the following loan programs:* unsubsidized Stafford, Perkins, PLUS, the school's own loan fund, supplemental loans, private loans. Applicants will be notified of awards beginning in April. College Work-Study Program is available. Institutional employment is available.

FROM THE ADMISSIONS OFFICE

"Amherst College looks, above all, for men and women of intellectual promise who have demonstrated qualities of mind and character that will enable them to take full advantage of the college's curriculum...Admission decisions aim to select from among the many qualified applicants those possessing the intellectual talent, mental discipline, and imagination that will allow them most fully to benefit from the curriculum and contribute to the life of the college and of society. Whatever the form of academic experience—lecture course, seminar, conference, studio, laboratory, independent study at various levels—intellectual competence and awareness of problems and methods are the goals of the Amherst program, rather than the direct preparation for a profession."

ADMISSIONS

Admissions Rating	97
% of applicants accepted	19
% of acceptees attending	45

FRESHMAN PROFILE

Average verbal SAT	690
Average math SAT	670
Average ACT	29
Average TOEFL	600
Graduated top 20% of class	90
Graduated top 40% of class	NR
Graduated top 60% of class	NR
Average HS GPA or Avg.	NR

DEADLINES

Early decision	NR
Regular admission	12/31
Regular notification	4/10
Non-fall registration	no

APPLICANTS ALSO LOOK AT

AND OFTEN PREFER
Harvard/Radcliffe
Princeton
Yale

AND SOMETIMES PREFER
Brown
Williams
Stanford
Dartmouth

AND RARELY PREFER
U. Virginia
Vassar
Tufts

FINANCIAL FACTS

Financial Aid Rating	90
Tuition	$20,710
Room & board	$560
Estimated book expense	$660
% frosh receiving aid	55
% undergrads receiving aid	55
% aid is need-based	NR
% frosh w/ grant (avg)	45 ($15,146)
% frosh w/ loan (avg)	52 ($2,447)
% UGs w/ job (avg)	66 ($1,375)
Off-campus job outlook	fair

Arizona State University

Tempe, AZ 85287-1203   Admissions: 602-965-7788   Fax: 602-965-3610

CAMPUS LIFE

Quality of Life Rating	**78**
Type of school	public
Affiliation	none
Environment	metropolis

STUDENTS

FT undergrad enrollment	23,637
% male/female	51/49
% from out of state	29
% live on campus	25
% spend weekend on campus	NR
% transfers	50
% from public high school	NR
% in (# of) fraternities	12 (26)
% in (# of) sororities	10 (14)
% African-American	3
% Asian	4
% Caucasian	75
% Hispanic	9
% international	1
# of countries represented	32

WHAT'S HOT
old-fashioned dating
Tempe
health facilities
campus food
computer facilities

WHAT'S NOT
student government
dorms
campus difficult to get around
theater
beer

ACADEMICS

Academic Rating	**66**
Profs Interesting Rating	65
Profs Accessible Rating	64
Calendar	semester
Student/teacher ratio	20:1
% profs PhD/tenured	86/92
Hours of study per day	3.15

MOST POPULAR MAJORS
management
marketing
psychology

STUDENTS SPEAK OUT

Life

Commenting on the quality of life at Arizona State University, one student tells us, "ASU is a country club; who wouldn't want to come here?" The school has excellent sports and recreation facilities, a "beautiful, nondepressing campus," and weather that is "warm and sunny 340 days of the year." No wonder most students tell us that they're having a great time. Fraternities and sororities are active participants in the school's social life, but they are by no means the only game in town. Many students live off campus (there's limited availability of dorm rooms), and parties in their apartment complexes are plentiful; the city of Tempe also offers a wide choice of night-spots. Most students come here knowing that ASU is a party school, and, while they don't ignore their studies, they certainly find time to party and date.

Academics

One student sums up the ASU experience this way: "There is an education for you here. The teaching is excellent and the facilities superior. Nothing, however, is handed to you; you must want an education and seek it out. With 45,000 students (undergrad and grad), the majority of the student body is focused on socializing rather than learning." That's ASU in a nutshell: a fine school with plenty of opportunities for a great education and even more opportunities to have a good time. One quarter of the students pursue business-related degrees in an excellent program ("the school basically caters to business majors," complains an elementary education student). The engineering college, attended by six percent of undergrads, is also nationally renowned. For an institution with a "party school" reputation, students work pretty hard: They average over three hours of study a day, and indicate that they take class attendance and course reading seriously. Their complaints focus on the sometimes difficult-to-negotiate bureaucracy (writes one respondent, "The red tape gets pretty tangled...[and] causes a lot of stress—but, you'll get through"). As is often the case at large public universities, space in required courses is too frequently limited, causing a lot of frustration for upperclassmen. Says one, "It is much easier to get the schedule you want when you're a freshman or sophomore. In my case, the registrar incorrectly processed my preregistration, but I'm still the one who has to fight for my classes." However, going to a large school also has its benefits, as one undergrad explains: "It's a pleasure to attend a school that offers so many services, such as Mac and IBM computers, the finest rec center in the country, a fantastic campus paper, and literally hundreds of clubs to be involved with."

Student Body

With over 20,000 undergraduates, ASU has a student body that's not easy to categorize. Most of the students are Arizona natives and, like most Arizona residents, they are politically conservative. Among minority students here, Latinos are by far the best represented. The stereotypical Sun Devil is relatively well-off and involved in the Greek system.

FINANCIAL AID: 602-965-4045

WEB SITE: HTTP://INFO.ASU.EDU/

ADMISSIONS

The admissions committee considers (in descending order of importance): HS record, class rank, test scores, recommendations. *Also considered (in descending order of importance):* special talents. Either the SAT or ACT is required. *High school units required/recommended:* 11 total units are required; 4 English required, 3 math required, 2 science required, 1 social studies required, 1 history required. Minimum combined SAT I score of 930 (composite ACT score of 22), rank in top quarter of secondary school class, or minimum 3.0 GPA recommended of in-state applicants; minimum combined SAT I score of 1010 (composite ACT score of 24), rank in top quarter of secondary school class, or minimum 3.0 GPA recommended of out-of state applicants. *Special Requirements:* An audition is required for music program applicants. TOEFL is required of all international students.

The Inside Word

A college preparatory curriculum and solid grades should lead to hassle-free admission. Another formula and cutoff admission process. Candidates who don't fill the bill through the formula can appeal their denial and submit additional information for consideration.

FINANCIAL AID

Students should submit: FAFSA, a copy of parents' most recent income tax filing. The Princeton Review suggests that all financial aid forms be submitted as soon as possible after January 1. *The following grants/scholarships are offered:* Pell, SEOG, academic merit, athletic, the school's own scholarships, the school's own grants, state scholarships, private scholarships, private grants, ROTC. *Students borrow from the following loan programs:* Stafford, Perkins, PLUS, the school's own loan fund, private loans. Applicants will be notified of awards beginning April 1. College Work-Study Program is available. Institutional employment is available.

FROM THE ADMISSIONS OFFICE

"ASU is a place where students from all fifty states and abroad come together to live and study in one of the nation's premier collegiate environments. Situated in Tempe, ASU boasts a physical setting and climate second to none. ASU offers more than 150 academic programs of study leading to the BS and BA in eight undergraduate colleges and one school. Many of these programs have received national recognition for their quality of teaching, innovative curricula, and outstanding facilities. ASU's Honors College, the only Honors College in the Southwest that spans all academic disciplines, provides unique and challenging experiences for its students and was recently named one of eight 'best buys' in honors education by Money magazine."

ADMISSIONS

Admissions Rating	69
% of applicants accepted	80
% of acceptees attending	38

FRESHMAN PROFILE

Average verbal SAT	540
Average math SAT	540
Average ACT	23
Average TOEFL	500
Graduated top 20% of class	40
Graduated top 40% of class	69
Graduated top 60% of class	91
Average HS GPA or Avg.	3.2

DEADLINES

Early decision	4/15
Regular admission	8/10
Regular notification	rolling
Non-fall registration	yes

APPLICANTS ALSO LOOK AT

AND OFTEN PREFER
UCLA
U. Colorado, Boulder

AND SOMETIMES PREFER
USC
Brigham Young
UC-Irvine
U. Arizona

AND RARELY PREFER
San Diego St.
Northern Arizona

FINANCIAL FACTS

Financial Aid Rating	77
In-state tuition	$1,884
Out-of-state tuition	$7,912
Room & board	$4,690
Estimated book expense	$700
% frosh receiving aid	42
% undergrads receiving aid	58
% aid is need-based	86
% frosh w/ grant (avg)	30 ($1,960)
% frosh w/ loan (avg)	25 ($2,400)
% UGs w/ job (avg)	17 ($1,900)
Off-campus job outlook	excellent

UNIVERSITY OF ARIZONA

TUCSON, AZ 85721-0007   ADMISSIONS: 520-621-3237   FAX: 520-621-3237

CAMPUS LIFE

Quality of Life Rating   **70**
Type of school   private
Affiliation   none
Environment   metropolis

STUDENTS
FT undergrad enrollment   21,511
% male/female   49/51
% from out of state   28
% live on campus   18
% spend weekend on campus   90
% transfers   34
% from public high school   90
% in (# of) fraternities   15 (25)
% in (# of) sororities   15 (20)
% African-American   3
% Asian   5
% Caucasian   71
% Hispanic   14
% international   3
# of countries represented   117

WHAT'S HOT
drugs
old-fashioned dating
intercollegiate sports
hard liquor
student publications

WHAT'S NOT
students are unhappy
dorms
campus difficult to get around
inefficient administration
support groups

ACADEMICS

Academic Rating   **69**
Profs Interesting Rating   62
Profs Accessible Rating   61
Calendar   semester
Student/teacher ratio   20:1
% profs PhD/tenured   93/97
Hours of study per day   2.83

MOST POPULAR MAJORS
psychology
political science
accounting

STUDENTS SPEAK OUT

Life

As one student writes, "On campus there is ALWAYS something to do." Outdoor activities abound in this resort-like environment. With approximately 300 days of sunshine per year, parties and concerts are held outside in all seasons. Social life is continuous and lively and the university's reputation for partying is well deserved. One student offers a simple view of the partying lifestyle: "Life is pleasant as long as you're not getting arrested." Fraternities and sororities are popular, but certainly not the only options. Some students live on campus, but dorm rooms are small and hard to get. Most upperclassmen move to nearby apartments. Sports are very big at the U of A, "particularly men's basketball and football," according to student fans. Most agree that a car is necessary for getting around, and for making road trips (skiing, surfing, and drinking for those under twenty-one are all available only a few hours away in various directions). The city of Tucson does not receive positive reviews, ("Tucson is...too dangerous to be out without a car very late."), but that may be the only aspect of life that students do not enjoy. As one student puts it, "The Gulf of California is so near that I can bask in the sun and scuba dive often. There's also a ski area nearby (one hour away) and Sabino Canyon to hike in. Do I REALLY have to leave in May?"

Academics

Although the University of Arizona has a long-standing reputation as a party school, students here can obtain an excellent undergraduate education if they know where to look. The U of A boasts several outstanding offerings, including a demanding engineering program, and strong departments in astronomy, cell biology, chemistry, English, nursing, and most of the social sciences. The liberal arts tend to suffer from underfunding while athletics tend to get good funding. A junior writes that she "wonder[ed] sometimes why they cancel classes like drawing when everyone wants in. Oops, I forgot. It's because football is more important than art." One student writes "The U of A is a good school for students who know exactly what they want to major in, don't need career guidance, and are personally motivated." Self-discipline is the key. If you want to blow off work, no one will stop you. Overall, students give professors average marks for those at a public university. Many agree that if students take the initiative, faculty members are willing to help.

Student Body

Most students here are from Arizona, but the out-of-state contingent is growing. U of A boasts a significant minority population, about half of which is made up of Latino students. Just about the only group of students who seem to not mix well are the Greek students: fraternities, that is. One sophomore writes that "The student body gets along pretty well. There is a division between those in fraternities and sororities and people who aren't in them." Another adds that "The Greeks isolate themselves from the rest of the community." A transfer student from Michigan, however, notes that U of A wasn't just like any other state school: "I feel the people out here are very friendly. I attended the University of Michigan last year and the difference is like night and day."

FINANCIAL AID: 520-621-1858

ADMISSIONS

The admissions committee considers (in descending order of importance): HS record, class rank, test scores, recommendations, essay. *Also considered (in descending order of importance):* extracurriculars, special talents, alumni relationship, geographical distribution, personality. Either the SAT or ACT is required. Admissions process is need-blind. *High school units required/recommended:* 11 total units are required; 4 English required, 3 math required, 4 math recommended, 2 science required, 2 foreign language recommended, 1 social studies required, 1 history required. Eighteen units recommended. Minimum combined SAT I score of 1040 (composite ACT score of 22), rank in top half of secondary school class, or minimum 2.5 GPA required of in-state applicants; minimum combined SAT I score of 1110 (composite ACT score of 24), rank in top quarter of secondary school class, or minimum 3.0 GPA required of out-of-state applicants. *Special Requirements:* TOEFL is required of all international students. Additional requirements for architecture, education, engineering, music, theatre, and pharmacy program applicants. *The admissions office says:* "Also, all applicants are considered based on student goals and past experiences, so appropriate additional information is considered."

The Inside Word

Universities like Arizona who use formulas and cutoffs in the admissions process rarely do more than glance at anything else that candidates submit with their applications. High-volume processing means that very little time is spent on individual applicants—you either have what is required or you don't.

FINANCIAL AID

Students should submit: FAFSA, the school's own financial aid form. The Princeton Review suggests that all financial aid forms be submitted as soon as possible after January 1. *The following grants/scholarships are offered:* Pell, SEOG, academic merit, athletic, the school's own scholarships, the school's own grants, state scholarships, state grants, private scholarships, private grants, federal nursing scholarship, ROTC, foreign aid. *Students borrow from the following loan programs:* Stafford, unsubsidized Stafford, Perkins, PLUS, the school's own loan fund, state loans, federal nursing loans, private loans. College Work-Study Program is available. Institutional employment is available.

FROM THE ADMISSIONS OFFICE

"Surrounded by mountains and the dramatic beauty of the Sonoran desert, the University of Arizona offers a top-drawer education in a resort-like setting. Some of the nation's highest ranked departments make their homes at this oasis of learning in the desert. In addition to producing cloudless sunshine 350 days per year, the clear Arizona skies provide an ideal setting for one of the country's best astronomy programs. Other nationally rated programs include nursing, sociology, management information systems, anthropology, creative writing, and computer and aerospace engineering. The university balances a strong research component with an emphasis on teaching—faculty rolls include Nobel and Pulitzer prizewinners. Famous Chinese astrophysicist and political dissident Fang Lizhi continues his landmark studies here; he teaches physics to undergraduates. The wealth of academic choices—the university offers 125 majors—is supplemented by an active, progressive campus atmosphere, conference-winning basketball and football teams, and myriad recreational opportunities."

ADMISSIONS

Admissions Rating	70
% of applicants accepted	83
% of acceptees attending	34

FRESHMAN PROFILE

Average verbal SAT	620
Average math SAT	560
Average ACT	23
Average TOEFL	500
Graduated top 20% of class	50
Graduated top 40% of class	78
Graduated top 60% of class	93
Average HS GPA or Avg.	3.3

DEADLINES

Early decision	11/1
Regular admission	4/1
Regular notification	rolling
Non-fall registration	yes

APPLICANTS ALSO LOOK AT

AND OFTEN PREFER

UC-Irvine
U. Washington

AND SOMETIMES PREFER

U. Colorado, Boulder
UCLA
UC-Santa Barbara
U. Wisconsin, Madison
Ohio U.

AND RARELY PREFER

Baylor
Arizona St.
Northern Arizona

FINANCIAL FACTS

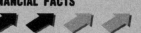

Financial Aid Rating		73
Tuition		$1,884
Room & board		$4,190
Estimated book expense		$620
% frosh receiving aid		59
% undergrads receiving aid		65
% aid is need-based		NR
% frosh w/ grant (avg)	54	($2,248)
% frosh w/ loan (avg)	24	($5,347)
% UGs w/ job (avg)	23	($1,973)
Off-campus job outlook		good

COLLEGE OF THE ATLANTIC

105 Eden Street, Bar Harbor, ME 04609   Admissions: 800-528-0025   Fax: 207-288-2328

CAMPUS LIFE

Quality of Life Rating	**98**
Type of school	private
Affiliation	none
Environment	town

STUDENTS

FT undergrad enrollment	217
% male/female	39/61
% from out of state	79
% live on campus	50
% spend weekend on campus	90
% transfers	21
% from public high school	62
% African-American	1
% Asian	1
% Caucasian	95
% Hispanic	2
% international	5
# of countries represented	9

WHAT'S HOT
students are happy
campus is beautiful
campus food
campus feels safe
leftist politics

WHAT'S NOT
religion
intercollegiate sports
Greeks
health facilities
lack of diversity on campus

ACADEMICS

Academic Rating	**90**
Profs Interesting Rating	98
Profs Accessible Rating	97
Calendar	trimester
Student/teacher ratio	8:1
% profs PhD/tenured	80/85
Hours of study per day	3.23

% GRADS WHO PURSUE...
Law 5, Med 8, MBA 3, MA 22

STUDENTS SPEAK OUT

Life
Many students at College of the Atlantic, a tiny college nestled in Maine's rocky coastline (on Mount Desert Island), agree that their island is "the most beautiful place in the whole world." The excellent dining hall (which serves some of the best college food in the country, according to our surveys) offers a spectacular view of the island, attesting to the students' good taste in surroundings. Students here are in love with the outdoors and spend as much time as possible there. It's not uncommon to see people biking to school or walking down by the ocean in ten-degree weather, and new arrivals are urged to "bring all their camping, hiking, and canoeing equipment!" The closely knit "family atmosphere" of COA also allows students a "unique opportunity to explore democracy" through the college's "self-governance system, which is based on the New England town meeting." Only first-year students live in dorms, although more residential halls are under construction; most others live in nearby Bar Harbor. The social scene is soft-pedaled here, with a decided lack of mainstream college activities (no fraternities, sororities, beer bashes, etc.—although that ever-popular mainstay, pot-smoking, is alive and well). But the "self-starter" attitude carries over to social life, and people enjoy finding their own ways to have fun.

Academics
College of the Atlantic offers its 200-plus students degrees in a single major: Human Ecology. COA's alternative, interdisciplinary approach wins raves from most participants, who love the focus and "self-directed" nature of their education. Mainly, courses deal with the relationships of humans to marine and ecological issues; the handful of full-time professors are all experts in these and related topics. Because of its small size, COA boasts exceptional faculty-student relationships. Most students call instructors by their first names and feel like "equals in the classroom; we're not like sponges at the mercy of a professor." Within the broad range encompassed by Human Ecology, students design their own programs of concentration. Remarks one glowingly, "If you want control of your education (instead of enrolling with a ten-page book of requirements) and are motivated enough to do what it takes, you can really get a lot out of this place." Dedication is key; grades are given only at the student's request, so students must be self-motivated to keep up with the workload here. Warns one, "If you're not a self-starter, don't come here."

Student Body
Students at COA tend to be white, politically left-leaning, accepting of the visible and vocal gay population, and generally happy with their choice of college. Bar Harbor in winter is quite an isolated, sheltered place, however, and some worry about the future: "Due to COA's size and uniform student population, it is easy to universalize problems and think of cute, idealistic solutions. I wonder if I will be adequately prepared for the real world after graduation."

ADMISSIONS

The admissions committee considers (in descending order of importance): HS record, essay, recommendations, class rank, test scores. *Also considered (in descending order of importance):* personality, extracurriculars, alumni relationship, geographical distribution, special talents. An interview is recommended. Admissions process is need-blind. *High school units required/recommended:* 17 total units are recommended; 4 English recommended, 4 math recommended, 3 science recommended, 2 foreign language recommended, 1 social studies recommended, 2 history recommended. Rank in top half of secondary school class or minimum 3.0 GPA recommended. TOEFL is required of all international students. *The admissions office says:* "(The admissions process) is intentionally personal—we do not quantify our applicants in any way (and) we place a strong emphasis on writing throughout the admissions process."

The Inside Word

COA's singular academic emphasis results in a highly self-selected applicant pool. Fortunately for the college, its focus on human ecology strikes a chord that is timely in its appeal to students. Enrolling here is definitely opting to take an atypical path to higher education. Admissions evaluations emphasize what's on your mind over what's on your transcript, which makes thoughtful essays and an interview musts for serious candidates. It also makes the admissions process a refreshing experience in the relatively uniform world of college admission. The admissions committee includes a few current students, who have full voting rights as members.

FINANCIAL AID

Students should submit: FAFSA, the school's own financial aid form, Divorced Parents form, a copy of parents' most recent income tax filing. The Princeton Review suggests that all financial aid forms be submitted as soon as possible after January 1. *The following grants/scholarships are offered:* Pell, SEOG, academic merit, the school's own scholarships, the school's own grants, state scholarships, state grants, private scholarships, private grants, foreign aid. *Students borrow from the following loan programs:* Stafford, unsubsidized Stafford, Perkins, PLUS, the school's own loan fund, state loans, private loans. Applicants will be notified of awards beginning April 1. College Work-Study Program is available. Institutional employment is available.

FROM THE ADMISSIONS OFFICE

"College of the Atlantic was created two decades ago at a time when it was becoming evident that conventional education was inadequate for citizenship in our increasingly complex and technical society. The growing interdependence of environmental and social issues and the limitations of academic specialization demand a wider vision. COA's founders created a pioneering institution dedicated to the interdisciplinary study of human ecology, a college in which students overcome narrow points of view and integrate knowledge across traditional academic lines."

ADMISSIONS

Admissions Rating	80
% of applicants accepted	74
% of acceptees attending	37

FRESHMAN PROFILE

Average verbal SAT	640
Average math SAT	610
Average ACT	26
Average TOEFL	550
Graduated top 20% of class	60
Graduated top 40% of class	96
Graduated top 60% of class	100
Average HS GPA or Avg.	3.6

DEADLINES

Early decision	1/1
Regular admission	3/1
Regular notification	4/1
Non-fall registration	yes

APPLICANTS ALSO LOOK AT

AND OFTEN PREFER

Tufts
Bard

AND SOMETIMES PREFER

Evergreen St.
Marlboro
Hampshire
Eckerd

AND RARELY PREFER

U. New Hampshire
U. Maine, Orono
U. Rhode Island

FINANCIAL FACTS

Financial Aid Rating	90
Tuition	$16,170
Room & board	$4,850
Estimated book expense	$450
% frosh receiving aid	60
% undergrads receiving aid	59
% aid is need-based	90
% frosh w/ grant (avg)	58 ($6,705)
% frosh w/ loan (avg)	59 ($2,625)
% UGs w/ job (avg)	60
Off-campus job outlook	good

AUBURN UNIVERSITY

Auburn, AL 36849   Admissions: 334-844-4080   Fax: 334-844-6179

CAMPUS LIFE

Quality of Life Rating	**77**
Type of school	public
Affiliation	none
Environment	suburban

STUDENTS

FT undergrad enrollment	16,468
% male/female	53/47
% from out of state	37
% live on campus	17
% spend weekend on campus	75
% transfers	37
% from public high school	82
% in (# of) fraternities	20 (31)
% in (# of) sororities	28 (17)
% African-American	6
% Asian	1
% Caucasian	91
% Hispanic	1
% international	NR
# of countries represented	46

WHAT'S HOT

intercollegiate sports
library
student government
intramural sports
student publications

WHAT'S NOT

registration is a pain
students are cliquish
campus difficult to get around
theater
lack of diversity on campus

ACADEMICS

Academic Rating	**68**
Profs Interesting Rating	64
Profs Accessible Rating	65
Calendar	quarter
Student/teacher ratio	16:1
% profs tenured	90
Hours of study per day	2.54

MOST POPULAR MAJORS

psychology
marketing
mechanical engineering

% GRADS WHO PURSUE...

Law 3, Med 2, MBA 10, MA 6

STUDENTS SPEAK OUT

Life

Auburn University is a large community that provides its students a vast array of activities. Writes one student, "There are a lot of school-sponsored activities like movies, concerts, guest speakers and comedians that I enjoy seeing." Opportunities to participate in jazz and classical ensembles, theater and dance companies, and TV, radio, and newspaper production are available. The students' main rallying point, however, is the football team. The Tigers, who have produced many professional players, are immensely popular with the students; other sporting events (especially men's basketball) are also well attended. Auburn's twenty-eight fraternities and eighteen sororities figure prominently in the school's social scene and provide housing for the majority of students who do not live on campus. Students give the town of Auburn (pop. 30,000) below-average grades. Montgomery, a city of 200,000, is about an hour away by car. When students yearn for the "big city," they head for Atlanta, about ninety minutes away.

Academics

Located in the heart of Alabama, Auburn is very much a product of its region. Tradition, conservatism, school spirit, and an academic philosophy that strongly emphasizes the pragmatic are hallmarks of the university and of its students. Because it is a land-grant institution, Auburn excels in agricultural studies; agricultural engineering and veterinary medicine are also both exceptional. The schools of architecture, pharmacy, nursing, and engineering are highly regarded; the business school is considered "up and coming." A large university, Auburn is subdivided by field of specialization into eleven smaller schools; all students, however, must complete a core program of math, science, social science, fine arts, literature, and writing. Students complain that "The college is factionalized and different departments fight over everything. There is constant fighting with the board of trustees." Students also complain that teachers are both uninspiring in class and difficult to get extra help from outside of class. On the positive side, students note that the school is extremely affordable, especially for native Alabamans.

Student Body

For a public university, Auburn does a good job of drawing out-of-state students; about one third of Auburn's undergrads come from outside Alabama (mostly from neighboring states). Auburn does a less admirable job of attracting minority students, however; despite the fact that twenty-five percent of Alabama's residents are black, African Americans make up a very small percentage of the Auburn student body. Respondents report that on-campus race relations—what few opportunities exist for them—are troubled. Within their own groups, students are "very friendly." In the end, a disturbing number of students size up their student body as similar to (yet not as biting as) this respondent who writes that "students are either Southern rednecks or Greek freaks."

FINANCIAL AID: 334-844-4723

WEB SITE: HTTP://MALLARD.DUC.AUBURN.EDU/

ADMISSIONS

The admissions committee considers (in descending order of importance): test scores, HS record. *Also considered (in descending order of importance):* alumni relationship, geographical distribution, special talents. Either the SAT or ACT is required. Admissions process is need-blind. *High school units required/recommended:* 12 total units are required; 15 total units are recommended; 4 English required, 3 math required, 2 science required, 3 science recommended, 1 foreign language recommended, 3 social studies required, 4 social studies recommended. Minimum composite ACT score of 18 required of in-state applicants; minimum composite ACT score of 22 required of out-of-state applicants. Minimum 2.5 GPA required of all applicants. Slightly lower test scores may be offset by higher GPA and vice versa. *Special Requirements:* An audition is required for music program applicants. TOEFL is required of all international students. Portfolio may replace audition for theatre program applicants. Higher standards may be required of architecture and engineering program applicants.

The Inside Word

Auburn is another "follow the numbers" admission institution—if you have what they require, you're in with little sweat.

FINANCIAL AID

Students should submit: FAFSA, the school's own financial aid form. The Princeton Review suggests that all financial aid forms be submitted as soon as possible after January 1. *The following grants/scholarships are offered:* Pell, SEOG, academic merit, athletic, the school's own scholarships, state grants, private scholarships, ROTC. *Students borrow from the following loan programs:* Stafford, unsubsidized Stafford, Perkins, PLUS, the school's own loan fund, health professions loans, private loans. Applicants will be notified of awards beginning June 1. College Work-Study Program is available. Institutional employment is available.

FROM THE ADMISSIONS OFFICE

"Auburn University is a comprehensive land-grant university serving Alabama and the nation. The university is especially charged with the responsibility of enhancing the economic, social, and cultural development of the state through its instruction, research, and extension programs. In all of these programs the university is committed to the pursuit of excellence. The university assumes an obligation to provide an environment of learning in which the individual and society are enriched by the discovery, preservation, transmission, and application of knowledge; in which students grow intellectually as they study and do research under the guidance of competent faculty; and in which the faculty develop professionally and contribute fully to the intellectual life of the institution, community, and state. This obligation unites Auburn University's continuing commitment to its land-grant traditions and the institution's role as a dynamic and complex comprehensive university."

ADMISSIONS

Admissions Rating	72
% of applicants accepted	90
% of acceptees attending	44

FRESHMAN PROFILE

Average verbal SAT	580
Average math SAT	590
Average ACT	24
Average TOEFL	550
Graduated top 20% of class	49
Graduated top 40% of class	76
Graduated top 60% of class	92
Average HS GPA or Avg.	3.2

DEADLINES

Early decision	NR
Regular admission	9/1
Regular notification	rolling
Non-fall registration	yes

APPLICANTS ALSO LOOK AT

AND OFTEN PREFER

North Carolina St.
Clemson
Furman
Georgia Tech.
Vanderbilt

AND SOMETIMES PREFER

U. Tennessee, Knoxville
Florida St.

AND RARELY PREFER

U. Alabama

FINANCIAL FACTS

Financial Aid Rating	80
In-state tuition	$2,250
Out-of-state tuition	$6,750
Room & board	$4,098
Estimated book expense	$600
% frosh receiving aid	43
% undergrads receiving aid	34
% aid is need-based	NR
% frosh w/ grant (avg)	12 ($2,100)
% frosh w/ loan (avg)	20 ($3,214)
% UGs w/ job (avg)	15 ($1,800)
Off-campus job outlook	good

Austin College

900 North Grand Avenue, Sherman, TX 75090-4440 · Admissions: 903-813-3000 · Fax: 903-813-3199

CAMPUS LIFE

Quality of Life Rating	76
Type of school	private
Affiliation	Presbyterian Church USA
Environment	suburban

STUDENTS

FT undergrad enrollment	1,047
% male/female	46/54
% from out of state	8
% live on campus	76
% spend weekend on campus	60
% transfers	14
% from public high school	92
% in (# of) fraternities	26 (10)
% in (# of) sororities	24 (6)
% African-American	3
% Asian	7
% Caucasian	77
% Hispanic	10
% international	2
# of countries represented	16

WHAT'S HOT
beer
cigarettes
political activism
different students interact
campus feels safe

WHAT'S NOT
off-campus food
college radio
Sherman
student publications
town-gown relations

ACADEMICS

Academic Rating	90
Profs Interesting Rating	97
Profs Accessible Rating	95
Calendar	4-1-4
Student/teacher ratio	13:1
% profs tenured	98
Hours of study per day	3.77

MOST POPULAR MAJORS
psychology
biology
business administration

% GRADS WHO PURSUE...
Law 3, Med 7, MBA 4

STUDENTS SPEAK OUT

Life

"One thing is for certain," explains one student, "this is definitely NOT Austin, Texas." Most agree that "AC isn't in a great location," and consider Sherman too quiet (although a few look on the bright side—"Sherman is the ideal college town—no distractions!" writes one). The social scene is equally dead: Sums up one student, "Most of the students come here to get a good education, not to find a significant other." This emphasis on work before play leaves some students cold. One complains, "You have to wait four years for a date." Fraternity and sorority parties form the nucleus of AC's social world. Drinking, not surprisingly, is popular, and for some makes up for the "lack of an exciting social scene"; beer and hard liquor are more popular here than at most colleges, although the town's "dry" regulations sometimes put a damper on things alcoholic. Most students live on campus in "comfortable dorms." Prospective students must prepare themselves for AC's strong work ethic and occasionally partyless weekends, but most will find plenty to do.

Academics

Austin College (located in Sherman, a suburb north of Dallas, not in Austin) is a small liberal arts school "big enough to have facilities that larger schools have but small enough that you can really get to know the faculty and other students." Students here are "highly competitive" and "definitely have academics as their first priority"; over 40 percent proceed to graduate school when they leave AC. Excellent student-faculty relations and small classes are AC's greatest attributes; professors are "very personable" and receive high grades for teaching and accessibility. One student writes, "I am on a first-name basis with all of my teachers, and I feel that they are there for my benefit, not their own." The strongest departments at AC are reportedly political science/international relations, education, business and management. The three-course, interdisciplinary Heritage of Western Culture program is widely praised by students, one of whom describes it as "what makes this school worthwhile." On the downside, many students complain that the administration is not terribly responsive to students. As one student puts it, "It's very frustrating when the administration makes decisions that affect no one but the student body, and yet doesn't give us an appropriate vote on the issues." All in all, however, students are very satisfied with AC. Sums up one student: "Since the day I walked on this campus I've been bombarded with new ideas about politics, the traditional family, and religion. I've come to see the value of all three."

Student Body

Austin College is predominantly white, Texan, and conservative; some students "wish we had more diversity in the student body." There is no visible gay community on campus. For the motivated, pre-professional student who enjoys a close-knit, intense atmosphere, Austin College could be the perfect undergraduate destination.

FINANCIAL AID: 903-813-2900   E-MAIL: OPAGE@AUSTINC.EDU   WEB SITE: HTTP://WWW.AUSTINC.EDU/

ADMISSIONS

The admissions committee considers (in descending order of importance): HS record, class rank, test scores, recommendations, essay. *Also considered (in descending order of importance):* extracurriculars, personality, special talents, alumni relationship, geographical distribution. Either the SAT or ACT is required. An interview is recommended. Admissions process is need-blind. *High school units required/recommended:* 16 total units are recommended; 4 English recommended, 3 math recommended, 3 science recommended, 2 foreign language recommended, 1 social studies recommended, 2 history recommended. Additional units of mathematics and foreign language strongly recommended. TOEFL is required of all international students. *The admissions office says:* "Class rank is considered a more valuable tool in determining the competitive nature of the student. GPA is required, however the rank in class (not GPA) will be used to determine scholarship awards and, in some cases, actual admission or denial."

The Inside Word

Austin continues to be a prize find among lesser-known colleges. The college's emphasis on academic quality and its very sincere approach to recruitment of students has paid off handsomely. Efforts to increase minority representation on campus have been a big success—few small colleges have as impressive a level of diversity. Out-of-state students will continue to be quite appealing to the admissions committee, as their number is still rather low.

FINANCIAL AID

Students should submit: FAFSA, the school's own financial aid form. The Princeton Review suggests that all financial aid forms be submitted as soon as possible after January 1. *The following grants/scholarships are offered:* Pell, SEOG, academic merit, the school's own scholarships, the school's own grants, state grants, private scholarships, foreign aid. *Students borrow from the following loan programs:* Stafford, unsubsidized Stafford, Perkins, PLUS, the school's own loan fund, supplemental loans, state loans, private loans. College Work-Study Program is available. Institutional employment is available.

FROM THE ADMISSIONS OFFICE

"Austin College has more than a track record for excellent education. We have a tradition of consistently graduating students who go on to successful and fulfilling careers. Our formula for success is simple: we offer quality of education that provides breadth of understanding and depth of knowledge. You learn to think critically and develop problem-solving skills. We are a residential college that provides opportunity for involvement, participation and experience which lasts a lifetime. You will be taught by our faculty who are here to teach undergraduates, because that is Austin College's primary mission."

ADMISSIONS

Admissions Rating	76
% of applicants accepted	79
% of acceptees attending	32

FRESHMAN PROFILE

Average verbal SAT	660
Average math SAT	590
Average ACT	24
Average TOEFL	600
Graduated top 20% of class	67
Graduated top 40% of class	85
Graduated top 60% of class	93
Average HS GPA or Avg.	NR

DEADLINES

Early decision	12/1
Regular admission	2/1
Regular notification	rolling
Non-fall registration	yes

APPLICANTS ALSO LOOK AT

AND OFTEN PREFER
Rice
Trinity U.
U. Texas-Austin

AND SOMETIMES PREFER
Southwestern
Baylor
Texas A&M
SMU

FINANCIAL FACTS

Financial Aid Rating	89
Tuition	$11,280
Room & board	$4,342
Estimated book expense	$412
% frosh receiving aid	90
% undergrads receiving aid	89
% aid is need-based	49
% frosh w/ grant (avg)	87 ($6,416)
% frosh w/ loan (avg)	63 ($4,140)
% UGs w/ job (avg)	35 ($1,300)
Off-campus job outlook	good

BABSON COLLEGE

BABSON PARK, MA 02157-0310   ADMISSIONS: 800-488-3696   FAX: 617-239-4006

CAMPUS LIFE

Quality of Life Rating   **83**
Type of school   private
Affiliation   none
Environment   metropolis

STUDENTS
FT undergrad enrollment   1,725
% male/female   64/36
% from out of state   63
% live on campus   85
% spend weekend on campus   80
% transfers   17
% from public high school   49
% in (# of) fraternities   10 (5)
% in (# of) sororities   8 (2)
% African-American   3
% Asian   7
% Caucasian   61
% Hispanic   5
% international   21
# of countries represented   70

WHAT'S HOT
beer
campus food
health facilities
dorms
student government

WHAT'S NOT
music associations
college radio
theater
political activism
registration is a pain

ACADEMICS

Academic Rating   **84**
Profs Interesting Rating   84
Profs Accessible Rating   87
Calendar   semester
Student/teacher ratio   12:1
% profs PhD/tenured   90/72
Hours of study per day   3.26

MOST POPULAR MAJORS
marketing
economics
finance/investments

% GRADS WHO PURSUE...
Law 3

STUDENTS SPEAK OUT

Life
While students like the off-campus food, the comfortable dorms, and the level of both campus safety and campus beauty, they still complain about the quality of their social lives at Babson College. One student writes that Babson had "too much sexual tension because of the bad male/female ratio." Men outnumber women by a long shot, which means that many students take the short train to Boston (which receives extremely high ratings) for fun. For students who do stay on campus, options are available. One student notes that she "go[es] to student-group sponsored activities almost every weekend, bands, or DJs in the auditorium." Students tell us that frats play at best a nominal role on campus, despite the fact that many go Greek. Another student notes that social life at Babson is "tough if you're gay." Student evaluations support this statement.

Academics
"If you are not ready to put a picture of [Andrew or Dale] Carnegie on your wall, don't come here," writes one student in capital letters on the back of his survey. It's pretty accurate advice: After all, Babson College is the school where everybody majors in some business field. Marketing, entrepreneurial studies, accounting, economics, finance, banking—all are popular majors at this school for tomorrow's business leaders. Students give their professors, most of whom have extensive "real-world" experience in business, good marks. One student comments that students at Babson are more connected to the corporate networking that takes place in life-after-school because, "At a business school, its great to have access to teachers who were high in the business world." On a more personal note, another student notes the professors are "very dedicated," and care about the students. Babson also provides students with their first taste of corporate competitiveness. One student reports "Competition is fierce. I've often found myself lying to my classmates about how much time I spend studying for exams, hoping it will influence them not to study as seriously. We'll do anything to get ahead." Almost all our respondents express satisfaction with their academic programs, and frustration at the administration. A familiar comment is that Babson is "a school that teaches the best business practices and doesn't use them."

Student Body
It shouldn't come as a surprise that Babson's student body is among the most politically conservative in the country. After all, these aren't just college students—they're the future chairpersons of the Federal Reserve. The business structure of Babson makes it a competitive environment that doesn't exactly breed camaraderie. One student writes, "A lot of the boys are extremely cocky and immature—and they wonder why they're lonely." Perhaps the common background best explains the student environment: "Most students come from middle- to upper-class backgrounds. Many have family businesses or their own businesses. We are extremely driven and goal-oriented and we have high expectations of ourselves." Minority representation at Babson is low.

ADMISSIONS

The admissions committee considers (in descending order of importance): HS record, class rank, test scores, essay, recommendations. *Also considered (in descending order of importance):* extracurriculars, personality, special talents, alumni relationship, geographical distribution. Either the SAT or ACT is required. An interview is recommended. Admissions process is need-blind. *High school units required/recommended:* 16 total units are required; 4 English required, 4 math required, 1 science required, 2 foreign language recommended, 2 social studies required. TOEFL is required of all international students.

The Inside Word

All applications are read by two or three admissions officers. Minority representation, including that of women, remains low, which makes for a very advantageous situation for such candidates. Legacies are also well-accommodated by Babson's committee. In this age of corporate "downsizing" it has become much more commonplace for students to pursue college programs that lead directly to career paths, and Babson has benefited handsomely from this trend. When this trend and the College's fine reputation are combined, the result is a relatively challenging admissions process despite a relatively modest freshman academic profile. On top of this, the College is also recruiting further afield than in the past. Be wary of overconfidence when applying.

FINANCIAL AID

Students should submit: FAFSA (due February 1), CSS Profile (due February 1), state aid form (due February 1), a copy of parents' most recent income tax filing (due February 1). The Princeton Review suggests that all financial aid forms be submitted as soon as possible after January 1. *The following grants/scholarships are offered:* Pell, SEOG, academic merit, the school's own scholarships, the school's own grants, state scholarships, state grants. *Students borrow from the following loan programs:* Stafford, unsubsidized Stafford, Perkins, PLUS, state loans. Applicants will be notified of awards beginning April 1. College Work-Study Program is available. Institutional employment is available.

FROM THE ADMISSIONS OFFICE

"While many students think of a business school as demanding good quantitative skills, Babson College also places high value on communication skills, both oral and written. We carefully evaluate students' preparation in English and other courses that stress writing and speaking. Given that management is now a worldwide activity, we also encourage students to pursue foreign language study."

ADMISSIONS

Admissions Rating	85
% of applicants accepted	41
% of acceptees attending	35

FRESHMAN PROFILE

Average verbal SAT	560
Average math SAT	590
Average ACT	NR
Average TOEFL	610
Graduated top 20% of class	57
Graduated top 40% of class	84
Graduated top 60% of class	99
Average HS GPA or Avg.	NR

DEADLINES

Early decision	12/1
Regular admission	2/1
Regular notification	4/1
Non-fall registration	yes

APPLICANTS ALSO LOOK AT

AND OFTEN PREFER

Pennsylvania
Georgetown U.
New York U.
Tufts U.

AND SOMETIMES PREFER

George Washington U.
Bryant
Boston Coll.
Boston U.

AND RARELY PREFER

Bentley
Providence
U. New Hampshire
U. Connecticut
U. Mass., Amherst

FINANCIAL FACTS

Financial Aid Rating	78
Tuition	$18,185
Room & board	$7,530
Estimated book expense	$500
% frosh receiving aid	54
% undergrads receiving aid	49
% aid is need-based	96
% frosh w/ grant (avg)	45 ($9,800)
% frosh w/ loan (avg)	51 ($3,000)
% UGs w/ job (avg)	20 ($1,200)
Off-campus job outlook	fair

BARD COLLEGE

P.O. Box 5000, Annandale-on-Hudson, NY 12504-5000   Admissions: 914-758-7472   Fax: 914-758-5208

CAMPUS LIFE

Quality of Life Rating 77
Type of school private
Affiliation none
Environment town

STUDENTS
FT undergrad enrollment 1,072
% male/female 48/52
% from out of state 74
% live on campus 85
% spend weekend on campus 75
% transfers 13
% from public high school 60
% African-American 7
% Asian 3
% Caucasian 74
% Hispanic 5
% international 10
# of countries represented 48

WHAT'S HOT
sex
cigarettes
leftist politics
drugs
hard liquor

WHAT'S NOT
religion
computer facilities
town-gown relations
Annandale-on-Hudson
inefficient administration

ACADEMICS

Academic Rating 90
Profs Interesting Rating 91
Profs Accessible Rating 84
Calendar 4-1-4
Student/teacher ratio 10:1
% profs PhD/tenured 95/95
Hours of study per day 3.51

MOST POPULAR MAJORS
social sciences
literature
fine arts

% GRADS WHO PURSUE...
Law 5, Med 4, MBA 2, MA 40

STUDENTS SPEAK OUT

Life

Bard's lovely campus is located in the relatively isolated small town of Annandale-on-Hudson, New York. Students agree that not much is happening in Annandale or in nearby Red Hook ("it's a ghost town, but very pretty"), and those without cars can feel "stranded on campus." The seclusion of the college "bores many people into fleeing to New York City, but the others stay here and find interesting ways of entertaining themselves." Actually, the social life here can be lively; there are no fraternities or sororities ("not PC" says one student), but many think "some dorms have become like them." Theater is very popular on campus—not surprisingly, given the number of drama majors here. Living conditions overall are "not princely," although the nicest dorms are appealing. Some students gripe that "we have buildings from the time of Lincoln, and plumbing from the time of Plato."

Academics

Bard College offers its 1,000-plus students a "rich academic environment," "attentive and demanding" professors, and a "strong element of independence" in its curriculum. Described by its students as "sink-or-swim," Bard has many strengths, perhaps the most outstanding of which is the individual attention each student receives. Everyone is required to complete a Senior Project before graduation (a thesis-type paper or other original work), and many describe this experience as "absolutely the most valuable part of a Bard education." Another high-quality asset is the school's progressive Excellence and Equal Cost Program (EEC), which makes Bard available to top students at a state school price. One recipient gratefully acknowledges that "the EEC scholarship is the only way I could afford a private school"; another tells us that "the EEC program makes Bard a place to think." Students emphasize that an independent streak is essential for successful Bard students; writes one, "If you take the initiative and have interest, you get all the encouragement and opportunity you need." Students give high marks to their professors for both in-class and out-of-class performance. Visual and performing arts students make up nearly one-third of Bard's student body; liberal arts and social science majors are also popular and are reportedly excellent.

Student Body

Nearly one in ten Bard students is a foreign national, lending a real international flavor to the campus. The typical Bard student is extremely liberal politically, so much so that the school is described as a "left-wing free-for-all." Members of this politically correct vortex, according to one student, "work so hard to be nonconformist that everyone ends up with similar values, causing intolerance of differing (conservative) perspectives."

FINANCIAL AID: 914-758-7526

WEB SITE: HTTP://WWW.BARD.EDU

ADMISSIONS

The admissions committee considers (in descending order of importance): HS record, essay, recommendations, class rank. *Also considered (in descending order of importance):* extracurriculars, personality, special talents. An interview is recommended. Admissions process is need-blind. Bard's Immediate Decision Plan allow students to attend a seminar, interview with the admissions committee, and receive an admit/deny decision on the same day. *High school units required/ recommended:* 4 English recommended, 4 math recommended, 4 science recommended, 4 foreign language recommended, 4 social studies recommended, 4 history recommended. Rank in top two-fifths of secondary school class recommended. TOEFL is required of all international students.

The Inside Word

The Immediate Decision Plan, if nothing else, represents the ultimate acceleration of the admissions process. It is also tangible proof that Bard puts the needs of its applicants ahead of, or at least on a par with, the college's own interests (this is admirable and, unfortunately, uncommon). Applicants tend to be cerebral sorts, with and without solid grades from high school. Bard is highly selective, but it's the match that counts more than having the right numerical profile.

FINANCIAL AID

Students should submit: FAFSA (due March 1), CSS Profile (due March 1), state aid form (due March 1), a copy of parents' most recent income tax filing (due March 1). The Princeton Review suggests that all financial aid forms be submitted as soon as possible after January 1. *The following grants/scholarships are offered:* Pell, SEOG, academic merit, the school's own scholarships, the school's own grants, state scholarships, state grants, private scholarships, private grants, foreign aid. *Students borrow from the following loan programs:* Stafford, unsubsidized Stafford, Perkins, PLUS. Applicants will be notified of awards beginning April 1. College Work-Study Program is available. Institutional employment is available.

FROM THE ADMISSIONS OFFICE

"The awakening of thought. Everything seems quite ordinary, at first. You are sitting in a class, reading at home, practicing, working, or making something in a studio. Your mind connects with an ongoing tradition of inquiry and study. The world becomes more vivid and interesting after an authentic experience like that. The engagement required to follow through with your ideas becomes a priority, and the search for a college becomes, as it should be, the quest for a truly higher education. If you approach Bard in this spirit, you will find yourself in the company of young men and women who also are interested in college as a profound, life-changing experience. Like you, they have tasted the transformative power of great thoughts and ideals."

ADMISSIONS

Admissions Rating	90
% of applicants accepted	53
% of acceptees attending	29

FRESHMAN PROFILE

Average verbal SAT	670
Average math SAT	620
Average ACT	NR
Average TOEFL	550
Graduated top 20% of class	73
Graduated top 40% of class	93
Graduated top 60% of class	99
Average HS GPA or Avg.	NR

DEADLINES

Early decision	12/1
Regular admission	1/31
Regular notification	4/7
Non-fall registration	yes

APPLICANTS ALSO LOOK AT

AND OFTEN PREFER
Middlebury Coll.
Colby
Bowdoin
Brown

AND SOMETIMES PREFER
Sarah Lawrence
Vassar
Oberlin
NYU

AND RARELY PREFER
Hampshire
Antioch
Evergreen St.
Bennington

FINANCIAL FACTS

Financial Aid Rating	88
Tuition	$20,864
Room & board	$6,520
Estimated book expense	$750
% frosh receiving aid	68
% undergrads receiving aid	68
% aid is need-based	90
% frosh w/ grant (avg)	68 ($12,500)
% frosh w/ loan (avg)	62 ($2,500)
% UGs w/ job (avg)	42 ($1,000)
Off-campus job outlook	fair

BARNARD COLLEGE

3009 BROADWAY, NEW YORK, NY 10027-6598   ADMISSIONS: 212-854-2014   FAX: 212-854-6220

CAMPUS LIFE

Quality of Life Rating	90
Type of school	private
Affiliation	none
Environment	metropolis

STUDENTS

FT undergrad enrollment	2,276
% male/female	0/100
% from out of state	61
% live on campus	90
% spend weekend on campus	95
% transfers	16
% from public high school	61
% African-American	4
% Asian	25
% Caucasian	62
% Hispanic	5
% international	3
# of countries represented	36

WHAT'S HOT
health facilities
support groups
New York
ethnic diversity on campus
off-campus food

WHAT'S NOT
intramural sports
intercollegiate sports
beer
political activism
campus food

ACADEMICS

Academic Rating	90
Profs Interesting Rating	89
Profs Accessible Rating	87
Calendar	semester
Student/teacher ratio	12:1
% profs tenured	93
Hours of study per day	3.32

MOST POPULAR MAJORS
English
psychology
political science

% GRADS WHO PURSUE...
Law 7, Med 7, MA 15

STUDENTS SPEAK OUT

Life

Barnard College students describe themselves as "chic, sophisticated, and very New York." They prize the varied experiences they have daily as residents of the Big Apple. One woman writes, "It's great to learn about chemistry, other cultures, and religions in the classroom, and self-defense in the subway." The "small-town school setting" of the Barnard campus within the big-city setting of New York creates a supportive, safe home base for students and allows them to absorb urban culture at the same time. The social scene is tied into that of Columbia, although Barnard's own extracurricular activities have been beefed up lately in an effort to increase unity. Athletic teams draw members from both sides of the street, as do some dorms and cafeterias (the only kosher one is at Barnard). Most students live on campus, partly due to the outrageous rents in the area. The dating scene is plagued by the competition between Barnard and Columbia women; between the two undergraduate populations, women outnumber men three to one.

Academics

Women at Barnard are in the unique position of having several educational environments at their disposal. First there is Barnard, considered "extremely empowering" for women; then there is Columbia University, with its Ivy League academics; and finally, there's New York City, famous for just about everything. Classes at Barnard are small and taught by well-respected professors (never teaching assistants). Students gave high ratings to the faculty for being "accessible and willing to help" (one certain advantage Barnard has over Columbia University). English, foreign languages, political science, and the natural sciences are strong departments here; premedical studies are particularly competitive. Arts students can combine their talents with a liberal arts education in an interdisciplinary option unique to Barnard. Barnard students may take courses at Columbia U, and nearly all do. Women here love the fact that they "have access to all of Columbia, but do not have to deal with its bureaucracy." Columbia-Barnard relations aren't entirely amicable, however. Some students feel that Barnard is neglected by the university because it refused to merge with Columbia U, choosing instead to remain a single-sex institution. Students in our surveys praised their deans, and have a warm relationship with the Barnard administration as a whole.

Student Body

Barnard students have long been known as feminists. Intense, liberal political commitment is common. There is a visible and very well-accepted gay community here. A substantial minority population creates a diverse atmosphere: with the campus, Columbia, and New York City to choose from, students are hard-pressed to run out of social, cultural, and other options. For the "strong-minded, determined, intellectual woman," Barnard should not be overlooked.

ADMISSIONS

The admissions committee considers (in descending order of importance): HS record, test scores, recommendations, essay, class rank. *Also considered (in descending order of importance):* extracurriculars, alumni relationship, geographical distribution, personality, special talents. Either the SAT or ACT is required. An interview is recommended. Admissions process is need-blind. *High school units required/recommended:* 16 total units are recommended; 4 English recommended, 3 math recommended, 3 science recommended, 2 foreign language recommended, 1 social studies recommended, 1 history recommended. Rank in top tenth of secondary school class or minimum 3.5 GPA recommended. *Special Requirements:* TOEFL is required of all international students. Audition required of applicants to exchange program with the Juilliard School or Manhattan School of Music. *The admissions office says:* "Every application is read two times by admissions officers and all decisions are made by a committee. No formulas are used in the selection process. We attract women who are independent in spirit; who want to be in New York City for the richness and opportunities it provides and who describe themselves as 'serious'."

The Inside Word

The college's admissions staff is open and accessible, which is not always the case at highly selective colleges with as long and impressive a tradition of excellence. The admissions committee's expectations are high, but their attitude reflects a true interest in who you are and what's on your mind. Students have a much better experience throughout the admissions process when treated with sincerity and respect. Perhaps this is why Barnard continues to attract and enroll some of the best students in the country.

FINANCIAL AID

Students should submit: FAFSA (due February 1), CSS Profile (due February 1), the school's own financial aid form (due February 1), Divorced Parents form (due February 1), a copy of parents' most recent income tax filing (due February 1). The Princeton Review suggests that all financial aid forms be submitted as soon as possible after January 1. *The following grants/scholarships are offered:* Pell, SEOG, the school's own scholarships, the school's own grants, state scholarships, state grants, private scholarships, private grants. *Students borrow from the following loan programs:* Stafford, unsubsidized Stafford, Perkins, PLUS, the school's own loan fund, state loans, private loans. Applicants will be notified of awards beginning April 3. College Work-Study Program is available. Institutional employment is available.

FROM THE ADMISSIONS OFFICE

"Barnard College, a small distinguished liberal arts college for women, affiliated with Columbia University, is located in the heart of New York City. The College enrolls women from all over the United States, Puerto Rico, and the Caribbean. Sixty countries, including France, England, Hong Kong, and Greece are also represented in the student body. Students pursue their academic studies in over thirty-five majors, and are able to cross-register at Columbia University."

ADMISSIONS

Admissions Rating	92
% of applicants accepted	45
% of acceptees attending	40

FRESHMAN PROFILE

Average verbal SAT	670
Average math SAT	640
Average ACT	28
Average TOEFL	600
Graduated top 20% of class	89
Graduated top 40% of class	100
Graduated top 60% of class	100
Average HS GPA or Avg.	3.6

DEADLINES

Early decision	12/15
Regular admission	1/15
Regular notification	4/1
Non-fall registration	yes

APPLICANTS ALSO LOOK AT

AND OFTEN PREFER

Yale
Columbia U.
Brown
Stanford

AND SOMETIMES PREFER

Dartmouth
Pennsylvania
Georgetown U.
Brandeis U.
U. Michigan-Ann Arbor

AND RARELY PREFER

NYU
George Washington U.
Boston Coll.
Boston U.
SUNY Binghamton

FINANCIAL FACTS

Financial Aid Rating	80
Tuition	$19,576
Room & board	$8,374
Estimated book expense	$630
% frosh receiving aid	60
% undergrads receiving aid	55
% aid is need-based	100
% frosh w/ grant (avg)	53 ($16,300)
% frosh w/ loan (avg)	50 ($2,600)
% UGs w/ job (avg)	30 ($1,013)
Off-campus job outlook	excellent

BATES COLLEGE

23 CAMPUS AVENUE, LEWISTON, ME 04240   ADMISSIONS: 207-786-6000   FAX: 207-786-6025

CAMPUS LIFE

Quality of Life Rating	84
Type of school	private
Affiliation	none
Environment	city

STUDENTS

FT undergrad enrollment	1,636
% male/female	49/51
% from out of state	89
% live on campus	93
% spend weekend on campus	75
% transfers	5
% from public high school	65
% African-American	2
% Asian	4
% Caucasian	86
% Hispanic	2
% international	2
# of countries represented	26

WHAT'S HOT
college radio
support groups
dorms
health facilities
campus food

WHAT'S NOT
Greeks
town-gown relations
Lewiston
religion
off-campus food

ACADEMICS

Academic Rating	91
Profs Interesting Rating	93
Profs Accessible Rating	92
Calendar	4-4-1
Student/teacher ratio	11:1
% profs PhD/tenured	96/98
Hours of study per day	3.31

MOST POPULAR MAJORS
biology
psychology
English

STUDENTS SPEAK OUT

Life

Bates College has no fraternities or sororities, and most students are glad about it. Writes one student, "The lack of fraternities and sororities creates a very friendly atmosphere within the school by eliminating exclusion and hierarchy." There is an active social scene because, as one student explained, "we are a very strong community. Participation in sports, clubs, and especially student organizations is strongly encouraged within the school." As for parties, "During the week, the library is packed and students are hard at work. On the weekends, everyone unwinds and parties." Students drink a good deal to ward off the cold weather and the academic pressures. One frequently cited negative is that the small student body inhibits the dating scene. Students praise the food and the dormitories, and several mentioned that, for those who choose to live off campus, huge Victorian houses are nearby and affordable.

Academics

The Puritan work ethic is alive and well at Bates College. Not only do students at this fine liberal arts school work hard, but they do so knowing that the rewards of their labor will be less than they desire: Bates professors are notoriously difficult graders. Oddly, most students don't seem to mind. In fact, they seem to relish the challenge. It helps that students feel professors and administrators go out of their way to create an atmosphere conducive to learning. Professors teach all courses and provide "a lot of personal attention," particularly to students who fall behind in their classes. More than a few go beyond the call of duty, helping students with personal as well as academic problems. Students appreciate the administration's liberal governance of the school. As one puts it, "With few rules and regulations, students have to learn to be responsible for themselves, a skill they will need in the real world." Psychology, history, and biology are the most popular majors here, and the visual and performing arts programs are beginning to flourish.

Student Body

Bates draws students from all over New England: only slightly more than a tenth of the students are natives of Maine. The student body is predominantly white and preppy, with a very small minority population. Even though most students are happy here, there is a significant minority for whom the atmosphere is a touch limited. One such dissenter is fed up with the "many annoying, self-righteous preps, and the multitudes of wanna-be crunchies." Still, most describe their fellow students as "friendly, down-to-earth, and amiable." As a whole the students "are particularly interested in social and political issues, which makes class discussions energetic and interesting."

ADMISSIONS

The admissions committee considers (in descending order of importance): HS record, class rank, essay, recommendations. *Also considered (in descending order of importance):* extracurriculars, special talents, geographical distribution, alumni relationship, personality. An interview is recommended. Admissions process is need-blind. *High school units required/recommended:* 4 English recommended, 3 math recommended, 2 science recommended, 3 foreign language recommended. SAT I, ACT, and SAT II are optional. TOEFL is required of all international students.

The Inside Word

Whether or not it considers test scores, the admissions office here will weed out weak students showing little or no intellectual curiosity. Students with high SAT I scores should always submit them. If you are serious about Bates, it is important to have solid grades in challenging courses; without them, you are not a viable candidate for admission. Though competition for students between the college and its New England peers has intensified greatly over the past couple of years, Bates is holding its own. It remains a top choice among its applicants, and as a result selectivity is on the rise.

FINANCIAL AID

Students should submit: FAFSA (due February 10), CSS Profile (due February 10), Divorced Parents form (due February 10), a copy of parents' most recent income tax filing (due April 15). The Princeton Review suggests that all financial aid forms be submitted as soon as possible after January 1. *The following grants/scholarships are offered:* Pell, SEOG, the school's own scholarships, the school's own grants, state scholarships, state grants, private scholarships, private grants, foreign aid. *Students borrow from the following loan programs:* Stafford, unsubsidized Stafford, Perkins, PLUS, the school's own loan fund, state loans, private loans. Applicants will be notified of awards beginning April 3. College Work-Study Program is available. Institutional employment is available.

FROM THE ADMISSIONS OFFICE

"The people on the Bates admissions staff read your applications carefully, several times. We get to know you from that reading. Your high school record and the quality of your writing are particularly important. We strongly encourage a personal interview, either on campus or with an alumni representative."

ADMISSIONS

Admissions Rating	95
% of applicants accepted	36
% of acceptees attending	35

FRESHMAN PROFILE

Average verbal SAT	720
Average math SAT	650
Average ACT	NR
Average TOEFL	600
Graduated top 20% of class	85
Graduated top 40% of class	100
Graduated top 60% of class	100
Average HS GPA or Avg.	NR

DEADLINES

Early decision	NR
Regular admission	1/15
Regular notification	4/3
Non-fall registration	yes

APPLICANTS ALSO LOOK AT

AND OFTEN PREFER

Amherst
Wesleyan U.
Tufts
Williams
Bowdoin

AND SOMETIMES PREFER

Middlebury Coll.
U. Vermont
Colby
Colgate

FINANCIAL FACTS

Financial Aid Rating	79
Tuition	NR
Room & board	NR
Estimated book expense	$650
% frosh receiving aid	45
% undergrads receiving aid	49
% aid is need-based	100
% frosh w/ grant (avg)	41 ($12,078)
% frosh w/ loan (avg)	44 ($3,855)
% UGs w/ job (avg)	46 ($1,400)
Off-campus job outlook	good

BAYLOR UNIVERSITY

Waco, TX 76798

Admissions: 817-755-1811   Fax: 817-755-3843

CAMPUS LIFE

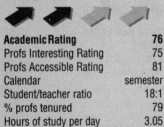

Quality of Life Rating	76
Type of school	private
Affiliation	Baptist Church
Environment	city

STUDENTS

FT undergrad enrollment	9,785
% male/female	44/56
% from out of state	23
% live on campus	26
% spend weekend on campus	NR
% transfers	17
% from public high school	NR
% in (# of) fraternities	20 (17)
% in (# of) sororities	25 (13)
% African-American	4
% Asian	6
% Caucasian	79
% Hispanic	8
% international	4
# of countries represented	68

WHAT'S HOT
religion
Greeks
intramural sports
intercollegiate sports
campus food

WHAT'S NOT
students are cliquish
dorms
sex
theater
Waco

ACADEMICS

Academic Rating	76
Profs Interesting Rating	75
Profs Accessible Rating	81
Calendar	semester
Student/teacher ratio	18:1
% profs tenured	79
Hours of study per day	3.05

MOST POPULAR MAJORS
biology
psychology
education

STUDENTS SPEAK OUT

Life

While acknowledging Baylor's pretty campus, most students bemoan the lack of things to do in Waco. Says a student about the lack of dating destinations, "Creative dating is fun for awhile but...after three trips to the Davidian compound, you'd rather save gas." Another way to alleviate Waco boredom is to join a frat or sorority, which students here do to such an extent that one student recommends, "if you think frats and sororities are rent-a-friend societies, go somewhere else." Chimes in another, "If you don't like conservative things or have a conservative ideology you may be ostracized." Other students suggest that if you have strong, conservative Christian values, Baptist-affiliated Baylor can be a fine choice whether you choose to go Greek or not. Drug and alcohol policies are quite strict at Baylor, and the use of any intoxicating substances besides beer and liquor is generally frowned upon by students. Even dancing was traditionally banned here as too risque until 1996, when Baylor held its first-ever dance (though pelvic gyrations were strictly monitored). Many students mention "the Baylor Bubble," a kind of netherworld where real-life problems and expectations magically disappear in a haze of smiling student sameness. Many are able to function quite well within this bubble, while others function just fine outside it. Just make sure you're not on the bubble about your lifestyle when considering this unique school.

Academics

"I feel that the academics are very challenging, yet very attainable because of the high-quality professors." Yes, Baylor undergrads are quite happy with their education. "Baylor has a really close personal interaction between students and professors," writes one. "This is the 'Ivy League-looking' and academically profound university in Texas." Cautions another respondent, however, "Professors and administrators tend to have a paternalistic attitude, though they are typically excellent." Getting your preferred classes as a freshman isn't as hard to do as at most other large institutions, and studying more than three hours a day is fairly rare. Don't forget, though, "Baylor is a school dedicated to Christian principles of education." The Baptist church exerts a strong influence on social and academic life. At least it's supposed to. Writes one disillusioned junior, "The only reason I went here was I thought it would be a good Christian atmosphere—NOT."

Student Body

A senior writes, "Our student body consists of three sections: 1) Baptists; 2) Greeks; 3) Other (this small number is rising however)." Shouts another, "Materialistic [students] need to get out of the 90210 lifestyle!" Coming from another angle, a satisfied student writes, "Many of the students at Baylor come from a similar background, so I find it easy to get along with them." Well, you get the picture. Predominantly white and often perceived as "shallow, rich, and snobby," the Baylor student body has an image problem. Even the religious segment of the population gets called on the mat. "Students here at Baylor are very religious," writes a junior, "but they are somewhat hypocritical and afraid to meet new people." But enough with the negativity! Even with the "strong trend toward conformity" at Baylor, or maybe because of it, an overwhelming majority of students are glad to be there. "They are so respectable and such a great group of people," writes a junior. However, there is widespread prejudice reported against minorities, women, and gays. Perhaps you can look at it philosophically, as this student does: "Some are mean, some treat you bad, but that's life."

FINANCIAL AID: 817-755-2611

WEB SITE: HTTP://WWW.BAYLOR.EDU/

ADMISSIONS

The admissions committee considers (in descending order of importance): class rank, test scores, HS record, recommendations, essay. Also considered (in descending order of importance): personality, alumni relationship, extracurriculars, geographical distribution, special talents. Either the SAT or ACT is required. An interview is recommended. Admissions process is need-blind. High school units required/recommended: 16 total units are required; 4 English required, 3 math required, 2 science required, 3 science recommended, 2 foreign language recommended, 1 social studies required, 1 history required. Minimum combined SAT I score of 1100 (composite ACT score of 24) and rank in top half of secondary school class recommended. Priority given to applicants ranking in top tenth of secondary school class. Special Requirements: A portfolio is required for art program applicants. An audition is required for music program applicants. TOEFL is required of all international students.

The Inside Word

A largely self-selected applicant pool and the need for a fairly large freshman class each year makes for a high admit rate. If your values reflect those of the community at Baylor, the chances are you will be offered admission.

FINANCIAL AID

Students should submit: FAFSA, the school's own financial aid form. The Princeton Review suggests that all financial aid forms be submitted as soon as possible after January 1. The following grants/scholarships are offered: Pell, SEOG, academic merit, athletic, the school's own scholarships, the school's own grants, state scholarships, state grants, private scholarships, private grants, ROTC, foreign aid. Students borrow from the following loan programs: Stafford, unsubsidized Stafford, Perkins, PLUS, the school's own loan fund, state loans, federal nursing loans, private loans. College Work-Study Program is available. Institutional employment is available.

FROM THE ADMISSIONS OFFICE

"Baylor University, chartered by the Republic of Texas in 1845, is one of the world's major academic church-related institutions providing liberal arts and professional education in a Christian environment. Baylor's student body comes from all 50 states and 60 foreign countries. The university's number of National Merit Scholars places it in the top 1 percent of all colleges nationwide...In addition, the Templeton Foundation has repeatedly named Baylor as one of America's top character-building colleges. Professors teach 96 percent of all courses; the student-faculty ratio is 18 to 1 and the typical class numbers 35. There are 140 bachelor's programs and 70 master's programs as well as numerous doctoral, professional, and specialist programs. More than 225 student organizations provide opportunities for social, intellectual, physical, spiritual, and professional development. One of the most inexpensive major private universities in the country, Baylor is consistently ranked by national organizations as one of the best buys in higher education. Take a closer look...There is a place for you at Baylor."

ADMISSIONS

Admissions Rating			75
% of applicants accepted			NR
% of acceptees attending			NR

FRESHMAN PROFILE

Average verbal SAT	570
Average math SAT	590
Average ACT	24
Average TOEFL	540
Graduated top 20% of class	63
Graduated top 40% of class	89
Graduated top 60% of class	NR
Average HS GPA or Avg.	NR

DEADLINES

Early decision	10/1
Regular admission	rolling
Regular notification	rolling
Non-fall registration	yes

APPLICANTS ALSO LOOK AT

AND OFTEN PREFER
SMU

AND SOMETIMES PREFER
U. Oklahoma
Tulane
TCU

AND RARELY PREFER
Texas A&M
Austin
Southwestern
U. Texas-Austin
Trinity U.

FINANCIAL FACTS

Financial Aid Rating	75
Tuition	$7,740
Room & board	$4,035
Estimated book expense	$634
% frosh receiving aid	70
% undergrads receiving aid	70
% aid is need-based	60
% frosh w/ grant (avg)	54 ($3,993)
% frosh w/ loan (avg)	52 ($3,534)
% UGs w/ job (avg)	14 ($1,113)
Off-campus job outlook	good

BELLARMINE COLLEGE

NEWBURG ROAD, LOUISVILLE, KY 40205   ADMISSIONS: 502-452-8131   FAX: 502-456-3331

CAMPUS LIFE

Quality of Life Rating	**81**
Type of school	private
Affiliation	Roman Catholic Church
Environment	metropolis

STUDENTS

FT undergrad enrollment	1,306
% male/female	41/59
% from out of state	20
% live on campus	33
% spend weekend on campus	80
% transfers	19
% from public high school	55
% in (# of) fraternities	1 (1)
% in (# of) sororities	(1)
% African-American	3
% Asian	1
% Caucasian	94
% Hispanic	1
% international	1
# of countries represented	14

WHAT'S HOT
town-gown relations
off-campus food
Louisville
old-fashioned dating
religion

WHAT'S NOT
library
health facilities
college radio
support groups
computer facilities

ACADEMICS

Academic Rating	**78**
Profs Interesting Rating	85
Profs Accessible Rating	84
Calendar	semester
Student/teacher ratio	13:1
% profs PhD/tenured	82/84
Hours of study per day	2.51

MOST POPULAR MAJORS
business administration
accounting
nursing

% GRADS WHO PURSUE...
Law 6, Med 7, MBA 9, MA 6

STUDENTS SPEAK OUT

Life

Many at Bellarmine College complain, "Students are apathetic about school events. We definitely need more school spirit." As a result, students write that much of their social life occurs off campus. "Partying off campus is very hot," wrote one, while several others praised the school's hometown of Louisville. "There's a great arts center downtown, with plays, musicals, and orchestra," explains one student. Adds another, "We have a Hillside concert which is popular. Also there's the Derby at the beginning of May, which is what makes Kentucky famous." Students also noted that "there are lots of other colleges in the area." As with many small schools, Bellarmine's size is both its chief asset and a drawback; the Bellarmine community is so small that it has trouble sustaining a vibrant social scene.

Academics

Bellarmine is a small Catholic liberal arts college in Kentucky that "is a great school for people who don't want to get lost in the shuffle of a large school. Professors know your name after the first week of class. You're not a Social Security number here." As another student noted, "Classes are small enough so that the student can have individual attention if needed. This is important to me." Students agree that a caring atmosphere is what sets Bellarmine apart. "Bellarmine is a very academic and challenging school. The professors are demanding but also understanding, very caring and very hard-working," wrote one student. Another added that "Most of the professors are very easy to talk to, glad to help if you need out-of-class time." All this attention pays off in heavy dividends for the dedicated student; about one-fifth of Bellarmine graduates go on to a graduate program. All this is more impressive given that, at two and a half hours per day, the average Bellarmine student studies considerably less than the average student elsewhere. Some complain that Bellarmine's size means "there are fields of study that are very limited because there are only one or two profs available for those areas." But mostly students express satisfaction with the amount of personal attention the school affords them. Wrote one student, "I like Bellarmine because the administration is nice and act like they want what the students want." The most popular majors are business, accounting, nursing and psychology.

Student Body

Wrote one student of his classmates, "Most students here are from about the same background: white, upper-middle-class, Catholic." Some respondents noted that a lot of students fit the description "religious right-winger," with others reporting that discrimination against gays is considered acceptable by some. Others countered that the students generally live in harmony among themselves. Minority representation is sparse; wrote one student, "There are very few minorities at Bellarmine. I have never in four years had a black student in a class, and only one black prof in all that time."

ADMISSIONS

The admissions committee considers (in descending order of importance): HS record, class rank, test scores, recommendations, essay. *Also considered (in descending order of importance):* extracurriculars, alumni relationship, geographical distribution, personality, special talents. Either the SAT or ACT is required. An interview is recommended. *High school units required/recommended:* 4 English required, 3 math required, 4 math recommended, 2 science required, 3 science recommended, 2 foreign language recommended, 2 social studies required. Minimum combined SAT I score of 1000 (composite ACT score of 21), rank in top half of secondary school class, and minimum 2.5 GPA recommended. *Special Requirements:* An audition is required for music program applicants. TOEFL is required of all international students.

The Inside Word

Bellarmine's admissions process follows the typical small liberal arts college approach fairly closely—solid grades, test scores, and course selection from high school combined with a broad complement of extracurriculars generally will add up to an admit. The applicant pool is very regional here; students who hail from outside the college's normal markets may benefit from the appeal that their relative scarcity brings to their candidacies.

FINANCIAL AID

Students should submit: FAFSA (due March 15). The Princeton Review suggests that all financial aid forms be submitted as soon as possible after January 1. *The following grants/scholarships are offered:* Pell, SEOG, academic merit, athletic, the school's own scholarships, the school's own grants, state scholarships, state grants, private scholarships, private grants, ROTC, foreign aid, United Negro College Fund. *Students borrow from the following loan programs:* Stafford, unsubsidized Stafford, Perkins, PLUS, the school's own loan fund, private loans. College Work-Study Program is available. Institutional employment is available.

FROM THE ADMISSIONS OFFICE

"A wealth of opportunity awaits you on our 120-acre campus nestled in one of Louisville's most desirable neighborhoods. Here you'll have the chance to learn from an outstanding faculty deeply committed to teaching. Our small class size makes getting to know your professors and classmates easy, while providing a stimulating learning environment. Many students also take advantage of international study in nearly forty countries through the college's foreign exchange program."

ADMISSIONS

Admissions Rating	68
% of applicants accepted	88
% of acceptees attending	48

FRESHMAN PROFILE

Average verbal SAT	550
Average math SAT	530
Average ACT	24
Average TOEFL	550
Graduated top 20% of class	66
Graduated top 40% of class	89
Graduated top 60% of class	97
Average HS GPA or Avg.	3.4

DEADLINES

Regular admission	rolling
Regular notification	rolling
Non-fall registration	yes

APPLICANTS ALSO LOOK AT

AND SOMETIMES PREFER

U. Louisville
Hanover
Transylvania
Miami U.

AND RARELY PREFER

Ohio U.
Ohio State U.-Columbus
U. Dayton
U. Kentucky
Indiana U.-Bloomington

FINANCIAL FACTS

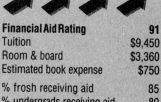

Financial Aid Rating	91
Tuition	$9,450
Room & board	$3,360
Estimated book expense	$750
% frosh receiving aid	85
% undergrads receiving aid	80
% aid is need-based	57
% frosh w/ grant (avg)	84 ($5,127)
% frosh w/ loan (avg)	54 ($2,739)
% UGs w/ job (avg)	15 ($2,250)
Off-campus job outlook	excellent

BELOIT COLLEGE

700 COLLEGE STREET, BELOIT, WI 53511

ADMISSIONS: 608-363-2500   FAX: 608-363-2075

STUDENTS SPEAK OUT

Life

The social scene at Beloit College is jumping. Practically all activity takes place on campus, where almost everyone resides: Even seniors, who are allowed to move off campus, usually stay in dorms in order to be near the fun. One student explains, "Off-campus, the only thing to do is drive to Madison or Chicago...Our campus is not inherently exciting like a city would be. We entertain ourselves by debating ideas with friends, drinking and smoking, listening to music. Fun is a state of mind at Beloit." Live music forms the center of one large social scene ("Live bands are an integral part of my entertainment—usually two per week."). Extracurriculars are many and varied (thanks in part to the "significant activity fee," which prompts some complaints). Especially popular are the radio station and intramural sports of all types. All this activity concentrated among such a small student body creates an intense but positive atmosphere; as a result, students report themselves happier with their overall college experience than most students elsewhere.

Academics

While many consider Beloit a "safety school," the college does an outstanding job of convincing its students that enrolling at Beloit is a great choice. Don't be fooled by the high admission rate: Beloit is an excellent liberal arts college, with stellar departments in anthropology, English, biochemistry, economics, and geology. In nearly all areas, academics are considered "very demanding," with an emphasis on student participation. Writes one student, "There is a strong emphasis on participation in field experiences and internships, which is also a tremendous asset." Students rate most aspects of their academic life highly, praising the small class size ("the low teacher-student ratio makes learning easier and more enjoyable") and the exceptional faculty accessibility ("My teachers are easy to get hold of and usually very flexible. Our unofficial motto here is: Everything is negotiable!"). Some students note that the school's size limits considerably the number of courses available, while others counter, "The size offers students opportunities other schools don't: Students have art shows, curate shows, intern at campus museums, design, direct, and star in plays."

Student Body

Regarded as more funky than its Midwestern neighbors, Beloit "is a comfortable place for liberals and individualists." Others qualify that "There are two groups here, jocks and hippies, and they rarely intermingle." Sums up one student, "The size of the college and student body, as it is quite small, fosters a very intimate community feeling, at times verging on incestuous. By the same token, it creates a very strong bond of intimacy."

FINANCIAL AID: 608-363-2663

WEB SITE: HTTP://WWW.BELOIT.EDU

ADMISSIONS

The admissions committee considers (in descending order of importance): HS record, test scores, recommendations, essay, class rank. *Also considered (in descending order of importance):* extracurriculars, personality, special talents, alumni relationship. Either the SAT or ACT is required. An interview is recommended. *High school units required/recommended:* 16 total units are required; 4 English recommended, 3 math recommended, 3 science recommended, 2 foreign language recommended, 3 social studies recommended. Rank in top half of secondary school class recommended. *The admissions office says:* "In application review, we are conscious that as much can be learned from failure as success, and that quantitative results are never adequate measures of human character. We believe each student is an individual; as such, each application is reviewed in a holistic manner—one at a time."

The Inside Word

Beloit expects to find evidence of sensitivity and thoughtfulness in successful candidates. There is tough competition for students among colleges in the Midwest, which gives those Beloit applicants who don't show consistent strength a bit of a break.

FINANCIAL AID

Students should submit: FAFSA (due April 1), the school's own financial aid form (due April 1), state aid form (due April 1). The Princeton Review suggests that all financial aid forms be submitted as soon as possible after January 1. *The following grants/scholarships are offered:* Pell, SEOG, academic merit, the school's own scholarships, the school's own grants, state scholarships, state grants, private scholarships, foreign aid. *Students borrow from the following loan programs:* Stafford, unsubsidized Stafford, Perkins, PLUS, the school's own loan fund. Applicants will be notified of awards beginning: rolling. College Work-Study Program is available. Institutional employment is available.

FROM THE ADMISSIONS OFFICE

"While Beloit students clearly understand the connection between college and career, they are more apt to value learning for its own sake than for the competitive advantage that it will afford them in the workplace. As a result, Beloit students adhere strongly to the concept than an educational institution, in order to be true to its own nature, must imply and provide a context in which a free exchange of ideas can take place. This precept is embodied in the mentoring relationship that takes place between professor and student and the dynamic, participatory nature of the classroom experience."

ADMISSIONS

Admissions Rating	75
% of applicants accepted	73
% of acceptees attending	29

FRESHMAN PROFILE

Average verbal SAT	630
Average math SAT	590
Average ACT	26
Average TOEFL	525
Graduated top 20% of class	48
Graduated top 40% of class	82
Graduated top 60% of class	95
Average HS GPA or Avg.	3.4

DEADLINES

Early decision	12/1
Regular admission	3/1
Regular notification	rolling
Non-fall registration	yes

APPLICANTS ALSO LOOK AT

AND OFTEN PREFER

Carleton
U. Wisconsin-Madison
Lawrence
Grinnell
Oberlin

AND SOMETIMES PREFER

Macalester
Colorado Coll.
Wooster
Kenyon
U. Illinois, Urbana-Champaign

AND RARELY PREFER

Knox
Ripon
Northwestern
Lewis & Clark
Gustavus Adophus

FINANCIAL FACTS

Financial Aid Rating	93
Tuition	$18,030
Room & board	$3,846
Estimated book expense	$350
% frosh receiving aid	86
% undergrads receiving aid	78
% aid is need-based	98
% frosh w/ grant (avg)	88 ($10,050)
% frosh w/ loan (avg)	78 ($4,224)
% UGs w/ job (avg)	83 ($1,280)
Off-campus job outlook	fair

BENNINGTON COLLEGE

BENNINGTON, VT 05201

ADMISSIONS: 800-833-6845   FAX: 802-442-5401

CAMPUS LIFE

Quality of Life Rating   84
Type of school   private
Affiliation   none
Environment   town

STUDENTS

FT undergrad enrollment   373
% male/female   37/63
% from out of state   94
% live on campus   98
% spend weekend on campus   95
% transfers   NR
% from public high school   91
% African-American   1
% Asian   1
% Caucasian   81
% Hispanic   4
% international   8
# of countries represented   17

WHAT'S HOT
drugs
different students interact
hard liquor
political activism
campus easy to get around

WHAT'S NOT
college radio
town-gown relations
religion
Bennington, VT
student publications

ACADEMICS

Academic Rating   84
Profs Interesting Rating   95
Profs Accessible Rating   95
Calendar   other
Student/teacher ratio   7:1
% profs tenured   59
Hours of study per day   3.42

MOST POPULAR MAJORS
literature
drama

STUDENTS SPEAK OUT

Life
Bennington College is a nontraditional school, and its nontraditional atmosphere extends to its social life. There are "no frats or football games here," and "the 'date' is an outmoded concept." Partly because of the small number of students and the isolation of the rural Vermont campus, life can get "claustrophobic" at times. One student comments that it "is not for the socially squeamish." Sports are becoming more popular here. The most widespread extracurricular activities, according to our surveys, are drinking and enjoying controlled substances (though there is little pressure to join in—people are "generally considerate toward those who choose not to"). Social freedoms are many; Bennington students may even select roommates of the opposite sex if they are so inclined. Artistic pursuits abound, and many believe the best thing about Bennington is that "all forms of expression are given space."

Academics
Bennington offers its students the rare chance to design their own academic programs of study, and then to follow through under close faculty supervision. The educational philosophy at this proudly different school is "centered around nurturing independence, creativity and self-determination." Grades are replaced by written evaluations, conventional classes by "seminars and tutorials," and exams by final papers and projects. Classes are small, facilities are excellent, and teachers are very accessible. The school is currently in the aftermath of a big shakeup in which all departments were dissolved and tenure was abolished. National attention and controversy were drawn to Bennington and its president, who dismissed a large portion of the faculty in order to institute this radical shift away from academic business-as-usual. Because of these dramatic changes, we advise a cautious look for those considering the college. As always, the strongest programs here are arts-related, and creativity of all kinds is emphasized; indeed, the idea behind the changes was that only professional "practitioners" should be teachers—working choreographers teach dance, fiction writers teach literature, etc. Interdisciplinary majors are now the norm: "I found my voice in oil paints, children's literature, and anthropological ethnographies," says one student. All in all, Bennington has a lot to offer the creative, especially those with "that one overriding passion." As one student warns, "There is a great deal of academic freedom here, and it requires a disciplined student to get the most out of Bennington."

Student Body
If you are looking for acceptance of alternative lifestyles or beliefs, Bennington may be the place for you. There are "so many nonconformists that it is actually the conservatives who don't conform." Many students are self-described "outcasts" or "misfits," perhaps because of their artistic leanings. Bennnington College is "not for everyone," cautions one student, but for those who like its emphasis on individual academic development, it offers a rigorous and potentially rewarding education.

ADMISSIONS

The admissions committee considers (in descending order of importance): essay, HS record, recommendations, class rank, test scores. *Also considered (in descending order of importance):* personality, special talents, extracurriculars. Either the SAT or ACT is required. An interview is required. Admissions process is need-blind. *High school units required/recommended:* 21 total units are recommended; 4 English recommended, 4 math recommended, 3 science recommended, 4 foreign language recommended, 3 social studies recommended, 3 history recommended. TOEFL is required of all international students. *The admissions office says:* "We do not evaluate the applications with a 'standard formula.' The Committee spends considerable time with the applicant by requiring interviews and giving close scrutiny to essays and recommendations. It is a process that resists formulas and subdivisions."

The Inside Word

Attending Bennington requires much soul-searching; for intellectually curious students it can be a godsend, but for those who lack self-motivation it can represent a sidetracking of progress toward their degree. Campus controversy regarding the refocusing of academic offerings and faculty retrenchment makes the decision even tougher. Selectivity has declined, but one shouldn't be overconfident about admission. Candidates will encounter a thorough review process that places great emphasis on matchmaking, which means that strong essays and solid interviews are a must. Intellectual types whose high school grades are inconsistent with their potential will find an opportunity for forgiveness here if they can write well and demonstrate self-awareness and a capacity to thrive in the college's self-driven environment. Minority students are rarities in the applicant pool, and thus enjoy "most-favored candidate" status—provided they fit Bennington's profile.

FINANCIAL AID

Students should submit: FAFSA (due March 1), the school's own financial aid form (due March 1), a copy of parents' most recent income tax filing. The Princeton Review suggests that all financial aid forms be submitted as soon as possible after January 1. *The following grants/scholarships are offered:* Pell, SEOG, academic merit, the school's own scholarships, the school's own grants, state scholarships, state grants, private scholarships, private grants, foreign aid. *Students borrow from the following loan programs:* Stafford, PLUS, the school's own loan fund. Applicants will be notified of awards beginning in mid-March. College Work-Study Program is available. Institutional employment is available.

FROM THE ADMISSIONS OFFICE

"Bennington is designed for students with the motivation and maturity to give shape to their own academic lives. It invites you not merely to study the subject you are learning but to put into practice, to act, to compose, to write, to do science: to make the choices through which you become an educated person. Faculty guide the process, but students make it their own at every stage, leaving Bennington prepared to think and create for themselves."

ADMISSIONS

Admissions Rating	80
% of applicants accepted	59
% of acceptees attending	35

FRESHMAN PROFILE

Average verbal SAT	650
Average math SAT	570
Average ACT	20
Average TOEFL	500
Graduated top 20% of class	12
Graduated top 40% of class	28
Graduated top 60% of class	48
Average HS GPA or Avg.	NR

DEADLINES

Early decision	12/1
Regular admission	2/1
Regular notification	3/31
Non-fall registration	yes

APPLICANTS ALSO LOOK AT

AND OFTEN PREFER

Vassar
Smith
Bard
Swarthmore

AND SOMETIMES PREFER

Boston Coll.
U. Vermont
Sarah Lawrence
Hampshire
NYU

AND RARELY PREFER

U. New Hampshire
U. Connecticut

FINANCIAL FACTS

Financial Aid Rating	85
Tuition	NR
Room & board	NR
Estimated book expense	$300
% frosh receiving aid	88
% undergrads receiving aid	82
% aid is need-based	93
% frosh w/ grant (avg)	80 ($17,400)
% frosh w/ loan (avg)	85 ($2,343)
% UGs w/ job (avg)	70 ($925)
Off-campus job outlook	fair

BENTLEY COLLEGE

175 FOREST STREET, WALTHAM, MA 02154-4705

ADMISSIONS: 617-891-2244   FAX: 617-891-3414

CAMPUS LIFE

Quality of Life Rating   **81**
Type of school   private
Affiliation   none
Environment   metropolis

STUDENTS
FT undergrad enrollment   3,168
% male/female   59/41
% from out of state   42
% live on campus   67
% spend weekend on campus   40
% transfers   22
% from public high school   58
% in (# of) fraternities   (8)
% in (# of) sororities   (6)
% African-American   3
% Asian   7
% Caucasian   68
% Hispanic   4
% international   11
# of countries represented   66

WHAT'S HOT
computer facilities
ethnic diversity on campus
health facilities
cigarettes
drugs

WHAT'S NOT
registration is a pain
theater
political activism
support groups

ACADEMICS

Academic Rating   **75**
Profs Interesting Rating   76
Profs Accessible Rating   80
Calendar   semester
Student/teacher ratio   16:1
% profs PhD/tenured   86/84
Hours of study per day   2.70

MOST POPULAR MAJORS
accountancy
marketing
finance

% GRADS WHO PURSUE...
Law 2, MBA 5

STUDENTS SPEAK OUT

Life

Bentley College is located in Waltham, a Boston suburb that is fifteen minutes from Harvard Square by shuttle bus. Says one student, "The location is amazing; secluded, safe, yet with easy access to Boston." Students here definitely find time to party: Weekends start on Thursday nights and run through Sunday, during which bar- and club-hopping are popular. When the weather allows, students spend nights hanging out around the beautiful campus or going to frat parties. Boston's proximity notwithstanding, frats and sororities play a big role in Bentley social life. "The Greeks add a huge number of activities to Bentley and the community," reports one student; says another, "Bentley College would be nothing without Greek life." School spirit is strong, although some students wish for a more serious athletic program. One student's remarks typify the prevalent attitude here: "Your college years are the best years of your life, and Bentley College allows you to enjoy them as well as get an excellent education that will provide the world with great business leaders in the very near future."

Academics

If you're interested in pursuing an undergraduate business degree, you really should check out Bentley. Practically every student here is studying accounting, business administration, or marketing (those few who don't pursue business programs have to write their own curricula), so BC students definitely hobnob with some of the business leaders of tomorrow. Core curriculum requirements demand that students receive a good grounding in basic business theory, ethics and computers regardless of major (liberal arts requirements are less demanding and less successful). Bentley is particularly strong in the study of international business; its Center for International Business Education and Research, run in conjunction with Tufts University, allows students opportunities to study, pursue research projects, and travel. Students are enthusiastic about their professors, whom they repeatedly describe as extra helpful outside of class. And even though students don't work too hard here—about two and two-thirds hours a night—most agree that they are getting a top-notch education in an extremely pleasant environment. It's also a school whose star is on the rise, as one student notes: "Bentley is a conservative business school that is moving in the direction of being more well rounded in academics, political views, and social aspects of what college is all about." Note: students must have their own personal computers (which can be bought or rented through the school and financed though a local bank at attractive rates).

Student Body

Students here are very conservative, although many just plain don't care about politics. "Preppy" is a word that classmates frequently use to describe each other. International students make up a good portion of the minority population here, and separate groups mostly stay separate.

FINANCIAL AID: 617-891-3441

WEB SITE: HTTP://WWW.BENTLEY.EDU/

ADMISSIONS

The admissions committee considers (in descending order of importance): class rank, HS record, test scores, essay, recommendations. *Also considered (in descending order of importance):* extracurriculars, geographical distribution, personality, special talents, alumni relationship. Either the SAT or ACT is required. An interview is recommended. *High school units required/recommended:* 16 total units are recommended; 4 English recommended, 4 math recommended, 1 science recommended, 2 foreign language recommended, 2 social studies recommended. Minimum 2.0 GPA required. TOEFL is required of all international students.

The Inside Word

If you're a solid "B" student there's little challenge to encounter in the admissions process here. The college's appealing greater Boston location and career-oriented academic strengths account for a sizable applicant pool, and the moderate selectivity that it enjoys.

FINANCIAL AID

Students should submit: FAFSA. The Princeton Review suggests that all financial aid forms be submitted as soon as possible after January 1. *The following grants/scholarships are offered:* Pell, SEOG, academic merit, athletic, the school's own scholarships, the school's own grants, state scholarships, state grants, private scholarships, private grants, ROTC. *Students borrow from the following loan programs:* Stafford, Perkins, PLUS, state loans. Applicants will be notified of awards beginning April 5. College Work-Study Program is available. Institutional employment is available.

FROM THE ADMISSIONS OFFICE

"If you are interested in studying business and want to be in the Boston area, you should consider Bentley College. Founded in 1917, Bentley is a four-year, accredited, coeducational institution recognized for excellence in accounting, business, and financial management education. Located in Waltham, Massachusetts, it is the eighth largest of eighty-seven independent institutions of higher education in the commonwealth. The 110-acre campus is located on the crest of Cedar Hill in Waltham; nine miles west of Boston. Most of the college's forty-four buildings were constructed after moving to this campus in 1968. Bentley offers eight bachelor of science degrees in business-related fields as well as a bachelor of arts program where a student may design his or her own field of concentration. The college also awards a master's degree in six business concentrations."

ADMISSIONS

Admissions Rating	75
% of applicants accepted	66
% of acceptees attending	32

FRESHMAN PROFILE

Average verbal SAT	560
Average math SAT	560
Average ACT	NR
Average TOEFL	550
Graduated top 20% of class	46
Graduated top 40% of class	82
Graduated top 60% of class	95
Average HS GPA or Avg.	NR

DEADLINES

Early decision	NR
Regular admission	2/15
Regular notification	4/1
Non-fall registration	yes

APPLICANTS ALSO LOOK AT

AND OFTEN PREFER
Babson
Boston Coll.
Boston U.

AND SOMETIMES PREFER
U. Connecticut
Northeastern
U. Mass., Amherst
U. New Hampshire
Fairfield

AND RARELY PREFER
Bryant

FINANCIAL FACTS

Financial Aid Rating	76
Tuition	$14,770
Room & board	$6,180
Estimated book expense	$630
% frosh receiving aid	68
% undergrads receiving aid	61
% aid is need-based	72
% frosh w/ grant (avg)	71 ($7,970)
% frosh w/ loan (avg)	60 ($4,770)
% UGs w/ job (avg)	26 ($2,000)
Off-campus job outlook	excellent

BERKLEE COLLEGE OF MUSIC

1140 BOYLSTON STREET, BOSTON, MA 02215-3693   ADMISSIONS: 800-421-0084   FAX: 617-536-2623

CAMPUS LIFE

Quality of Life Rating	74
Type of school	private
Affiliation	none
Environment	metropolis

STUDENTS

FT undergrad enrollment	2,700
% male/female	82/18
% from out of state	42
% live on campus	33
% spend weekend on campus	80
% transfers	43
% from public high school	NR
% African-American	6
% Asian	4
% Caucasian	84
% Hispanic	5
% international	39
# of countries represented	70

WHAT'S HOT
ethnic diversity on campus
music associations
different students interact
lab facilities
Boston

WHAT'S NOT
unattractive campus
student government
political activism
student publications
campus food

ACADEMICS

Academic Rating	82
Profs Interesting Rating	83
Profs Accessible Rating	70
Calendar	semester
Student/teacher ratio	8:1
% profs PhD	9
Hours of study per day	3.68

MOST POPULAR MAJORS
professional music
music production/engineering
performance

STUDENTS SPEAK OUT

Life
"Life at Berklee? Three words: music, twenty-four, seven." This attitude is reflected in one way or another by almost all Berklee undergrads. To live, breathe, eat, and sleep music twenty-four hours a day is why students come here: "Life is cool because we're here for music. That's all we think about." In those rare moments when students are not thinking about music, they find the city of Boston to be a great source of distraction: "There is a lot to do in Boston. Civilization is within reach. And it has the advantages of a big city without the major drawbacks," says one. Another student remarks: "It offers a great escape from possible music burnout." The recent establishment of a student newspaper and student government may help matters as well. Nearly all of the Berklee students surveyed, while thriving in this musically saturated environment, comment upon the huge amount of pressure they experience: "Berklee is even more difficult than a traditional college."

Academics
The Berklee administration receives favorable marks, but in the eyes of students they still have a long way to go before the school is run in a way that matches the first-rate musical education available here. One student gripes, "There are heaps of bureaucratic crap, no communication between upper-level management and students, and no student government. Our money seems to disappear." Others rail against the administration's insensitivity ("The administration is a stone-cold moneymaking machine"), and the dearth of scholarships ("You can only get scholarships if you play jazz. That sucks"). Teachers, however, do receive sensitivity points: "The teachers are just like us—they understand what we're going through because they've been through it." In fact, professors receive respectable marks all around; students cite their talent ("The professors are excellent—personable, bright individuals who are well-informed and professional"), accessibility ("My teachers are available for extra help if needed") and professionalism ("Your professors are people who are making a living at what they teach. It's what it's all about"). Berklee's facilities receive mostly average marks, but are not without their detractors. Complaints are aimed at the library facilities ("Why does the library close early on the weekends when most students want that time to study?"), practice space ("For drummers it sucks. Drum lockers are way too small, and practice room doors open inward. And the practice rooms are too small, too"), and the food served on campus ("I'm learning a lot here, but the line at the cafeteria for bad food is not fun"). Still, most students would agree with this sophomore's statement: "For music, there is no other place to be."

Student Body
The monumentally lopsided male/female ratio is a source of much dissatisfaction at Berklee. Most of the undergrads feel that the school "needs more women" or, perhaps more to the point, that "the lack of women here really sucks." There are, however, many international students, which is a big plus for most: "Everyone comes from everywhere here. It's a diverse makeup. You hang with people from all over the world." About his fellow students, another notes: "They are very diverse (from all over the world) which is quite nice, and we all have the same thing in common—we love music."

FINANCIAL AID: 617-266-1400

WEB SITE: HTTP://WWW.BERKLEE.EDU

ADMISSIONS

The admissions committee considers (in descending order of importance): HS record, recommendations, class rank, test scores. *Also considered (in descending order of importance):* extracurriculars, special talents, alumni relationship, personality. Either the SAT or ACT is required. An interview is recommended. *High school units required/recommended:* 16 total units are required; 4 English required, 1 math required, 1 science required, 2 social studies required. No more than 3 units of nonacademic electives are recommended. Minimum of 2 years of musical study and/or significant experience in some phase of music required of all applicants. *Special Requirements:* TOEFL is required of all international students. Special application and interview required of music production/engineering program applicants. *The admissions office says:* "Applicants are expected to be knowledgeable in written music theory fundamentals, including rhythmic notation, melodic notation, in treble and bass clefs, key signatures, major scales, intervals, and construction of triads and seventh chords."

The Inside Word

There is no question that getting in to Berklee is much easier than one would expect at a music school of such world renown. Unfortunately, this is not necessarily a favorable circumstance for applicants. Musicians at Berklee are strictly ranked by talent, and while many are admitted, only the best get to study privately with the top faculty members. Yet these big-name musicians are exactly those whom Berklee uses in advertising and admissions literature to tout its programs. Students need to seriously and objectively assess their musical talent before they enroll if they are banking on access to Berklee's best. Other faculty members are talented, but don't hold a candle to the top tier.

FINANCIAL AID

Students should submit: FAFSA (due March 31), the school's own financial aid form (due March 31), state aid form (due March 31), a copy of parents' most recent income tax filing (due March 31). The Princeton Review suggests that all financial aid forms be submitted as soon as possible after January 1. *The following grants/scholarships are offered:* Pell, SEOG, academic merit, the school's own scholarships, the school's own grants, state scholarships, state grants, private scholarships, foreign aid. *Students borrow from the following loan programs:* Perkins, PLUS, supplemental loans, state loans, private loans. Applicants will be notified of awards beginning rolling. College Work-Study Program is available. Institutional employment is available. Freshmen are discouraged from working.

FROM THE ADMISSIONS OFFICE

"Berklee College of Music is a selective college that believes deeply in sharing its musical and educational expertise with qualified applicants from a wide variety of musical backgrounds, interests, and career goals. With nearly half a century of institutional experience, Berklee has established its ability to identify the fundamental musical knowledge and staff skills necessary for entering students to function effectively and be placed in a comfortable peer-learning environment. Musical and educational success also depends on individual student motivation, maturity, and commitment to take advantage of Berklee's unique resources."

ADMISSIONS

Admissions Rating	75
% of applicants accepted	76
% of acceptees attending	47

FRESHMAN PROFILE

Average verbal SAT	NR
Average math SAT	NR
Average ACT	NR
Average TOEFL	500
Graduated top 20% of class	NR
Graduated top 40% of class	NR
Graduated top 60% of class	NR
Average HS GPA or Avg.	NR

DEADLINES

Regular admission	rolling
Regular notification	rolling
Non-fall registration	yes

APPLICANTS ALSO LOOK AT AND SOMETIMES PREFER

Boston Cons.
Oberlin
U. Miami

FINANCIAL FACTS

Financial Aid Rating	70
Tuition	$13,290
Room & board	$7,390
Estimated book expense	$400
% frosh receiving aid	48
% undergrads receiving aid	90
% aid is need-based	35
% frosh w/ grant (avg)	22 ($2,426)
% frosh w/ loan (avg)	56 ($8,466)
% UGs w/ job (avg)	26 ($2,500)
Off-campus job outlook	good

BIRMINGHAM-SOUTHERN COLLEGE

ARKADELPHIA ROAD, BIRMINGHAM, AL 35254   ADMISSIONS: 205-226-4686   FAX: 205-226-4627

CAMPUS LIFE

Quality of Life Rating   **86**
Type of school   private
Affiliation   United Methodist Church
Environment   city

STUDENTS
FT undergrad enrollment   1,333
% male/female   46/54
% from out of state   25
% live on campus   82
% spend weekend on campus   75
% transfers   18
% from public high school   71
% in (# of) fraternities   62 (6)
% in (# of) sororities   70 (7)
% African-American   14
% Asian   0
% Caucasian   82
% Hispanic   1
% international   NR
# of countries represented   7

WHAT'S HOT
Greeks
school runs like butter
campus feels safe
hard liquor
religion

WHAT'S NOT
college radio
sex
student publications
campus food
drugs

ACADEMICS

Academic Rating   **85**
Profs Interesting Rating   92
Profs Accessible Rating   90
Calendar   4-1-4
Student/teacher ratio   12:1
% profs PhD/tenured   76/88
Hours of study per day   3.17

MOST POPULAR MAJORS
business administration
biology
English

% GRADS WHO PURSUE...
Law 8, Med 8, MBA 6, MA 21

STUDENTS SPEAK OUT

Life

"Southern is like a small town overlooking a large city. Its strengths and weaknesses are the same—its size. Everyone here knows you, but everyone knows you, too." This sage opinion is shared by many BSC students. While the size of this close-knit school is generally seen as an advantage, it also makes some students feel as though they're living in a fishbowl. The city of Birmingham receives great marks for off-campus diversions—cultural events, restaurants, and other activities are available at all hours ("There are great bars in Birmingham where great bands play"; "Four a.m. trips to local twenty-four hour restaurants are very common"). Outdoor activities like hiking and camping in local state parks are also options. There's plenty to do on campus as well, especially around Frat Row. With nearly half of its population pledging fraternities and sororities, the BSC social scene revolves heavily around its Greek organizations. Non-Greek members, however, are generally encouraged to participate in Greek events and parties: "The Greek system is great and brings a lot of social opportunities to campus." Another elaborates, "The mixers are very popular, probably due to the themes such as Country Club, Road Warriors, and Dazed and Confused. Another on-campus draw is a coffee house called the Cellar ("Oftentimes there are poetry readings or bands that play there.") Still, with all these distractions, students spend a lot of time on their studies. "BSC tries to encourage a balance of both social and academic life. There are a lot of activities provided which are a lot of fun, but you are also expected to devote an equal amount of time to books."

Academics

BSC is a strong liberal arts college that is also well known for its business and management programs. Academics here can be pretty rigorous (according to one upperclassman, "once you become a senior, sleeping is a luxury"), but students here seem willing to accept that. Most of our respondents have nothing but good things to say about BSC's administration, faculty, and staff. Many report painless registration experiences with an administrative staff that took the time and effort to get to know each student. One student writes, "Here at BSC we are individuals, not just numbers." Another declares, "The administrators make an effort to know every student by name." Even the school's president is found to be friendly and interested in the affairs of each student: "Where else do you have a college president who knows not only your face and name, but what activities you're involved in and who you're dating?" The faculty scores high in the students' ratings for their accessibility and skills in teaching. "They are all extremely knowledgeable, yet maintain levels of teaching which are comfortable and informative for the students" is a very typical response. One sophomore notes that her "exceptional professors" are "very willing to meet with students outside of class—they are the best part of my academic experience here."

Student Body

BSC students seem to genuinely like and get along with their fellow students. "We are family oriented and collectively concerned for one another. When students pass on campus, an exchange is always made," is how one student puts it, a sentiment shared by a majority of BSC undergrads. Some students comment on the lack of diversity (over seventy percent of the BSC student population is white), and say that there is little interaction between ethnic groups. Still, one student notes that "although the school's student makeup is fairly limited to upper-middle-class whites, the tolerance level is higher than one would expect."

ADMISSIONS

The admissions committee considers (in descending order of importance): HS record, class rank, test scores, recommendations, essay. *Also considered (in descending order of importance):* personality, special talents, alumni relationship, extracurriculars, geographical distribution. Either the SAT or ACT is required. An interview is recommended. Admissions process is need-blind. *High school units required/recommended:* 12 total units are required; 4 English required, 3 math required, 3 science required, 2 foreign language recommended, 2 social studies required, 2 history required. Minimum composite ACT score of 21 (SAT I scores of 400 in both verbal and math) and minimum 2.0 GPA required. *Special Requirements:* A portfolio is required for art program applicants. An audition is required for music program applicants.

The Inside Word

Birmingham-Southern's lack of widespread national recognition by students and parents results in a small applicant pool, the majority of whom are admitted. Most of the admits are looking for a quality southern college, recognize a good situation here, and decide to enroll. Our impression is that few regret their decision. In a reflection of the entire administration, the admissions staff is truly personal and very helpful to prospective students.

FINANCIAL AID

Students should submit: FAFSA (due March 31), the school's own financial aid form (due March 31), state aid form (due March 31), a copy of parents' most recent income tax filing (due March 31). The Princeton Review suggests that all financial aid forms be submitted as soon as possible after January 1. *The following grants/scholarships are offered:* Pell, SEOG, academic merit, athletic, the school's own scholarships, the school's own grants, state scholarships, state grants, private scholarships, ROTC. *Students borrow from the following loan programs:* Stafford, Perkins, PLUS, the school's own loan fund, private loans. Applicants will be notified of awards beginning: rolling. College Work-Study Program is available. Institutional employment is available.

FROM THE ADMISSIONS OFFICE

"Respected publishers continue to recognize Birmingham-Southern College as one of the top-ranked liberal arts colleges in the nation. One guide highlights our small classes and the fact that we still assign each student a 'faculty-cum-mentor,' to assure individualized attention to our students. One notable aspect of our academic calendar is our January interim term, a four-week period in which students can participate in special projects in close collaboration with faculty members, either on- or off-campus. "One dimension of Birmingham-Southern's moral focus is the commitment to volunteerism. In fact, former President George Bush visited the campus to present our Conservancy group one of his 'Points of Light' volunteer service awards. "The Center for Leadership Studies assists students in realizing their leadership potential by combining the academic study of leadership with significant community service."

ADMISSIONS

Admissions Rating	79
% of applicants accepted	85
% of acceptees attending	43

FRESHMAN PROFILE

Average verbal SAT	670
Average math SAT	630
Average ACT	26
Average TOEFL	500
Graduated top 20% of class	68
Graduated top 40% of class	83
Graduated top 60% of class	92
Average HS GPA or Avg.	3.3

DEADLINES

Early decision	1/5
Regular admission	3/1
Regular notification	rolling
Non-fall registration	yes

APPLICANTS ALSO LOOK AT

AND OFTEN PREFER
Vanderbilt
Rhodes

AND SOMETIMES PREFER
Samford
U. Alabama
U. Auburn
U. of the South
Furman U.

AND RARELY PREFER
LSU.-Baton Rouge
Tulane U.

FINANCIAL FACTS

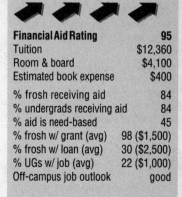

Financial Aid Rating	95
Tuition	$12,360
Room & board	$4,100
Estimated book expense	$400
% frosh receiving aid	84
% undergrads receiving aid	84
% aid is need-based	45
% frosh w/ grant (avg)	98 ($1,500)
% frosh w/ loan (avg)	30 ($2,500)
% UGs w/ job (avg)	22 ($1,000)
Off-campus job outlook	good

BOSTON COLLEGE

CHESTNUT HILL, MA 02167 ADMISSIONS: 617-552-3100 FAX: 617-552-0798

CAMPUS LIFE

Quality of Life Rating 78
Type of school private
Affiliation Roman Catholic Church
(Society of Jesus)
Environment metropolis

STUDENTS
FT undergrad enrollment 9,079
% male/female 47/53
% from out of state 70
% live on campus 71
% spend weekend on campus 75
% transfers 2
% from public high school 58
% African-American 3
% Asian 7
% Caucasian 78
% Hispanic 5
% international 3
# of countries represented 86

WHAT'S HOT
sex
off-campus food
student government
campus food
lab facilities

WHAT'S NOT
music associations
students are cliquish
computer facilities
theater
library

ACADEMICS

Academic Rating 80
Profs Interesting Rating 72
Profs Accessible Rating 71
Calendar semester
Student/teacher ratio 15:1
% profs tenured 95
Hours of study per day 3.47

MOST POPULAR MAJORS
English
finance
psychology

% GRADS WHO PURSUE...
Law 8, Med 3, MBA 5, MA 9

STUDENTS SPEAK OUT

Life

Boston College was at one time considered a party school, but times change, and the results of our survey indicate that BC has moved along. Students here report an average amount of beer and drug consumption: BC students aren't teetotalers, but neither are they the party animals they once were. The campus is officially dry, but students say that local bars that will serve them can be found ("A fake ID is key!" reports one student). BC has no fraternities or sororities, but the lack of a Greek system doesn't limit the number of parties, which are plentiful during weekends. Intercollegiate and intramural sports are popular on-campus activities, and many students become involved in community-service-oriented organizations. Downtown Boston, with its vital, college-oriented night life, is only twenty minutes away by car or public transportation.

Academics

To those unacquainted with the school, the name "Boston College" evokes the image of a tiny liberal arts school tucked away in Cambridge. This image couldn't be more inaccurate: Boston College, which is neither a college (it's a university) nor in Boston (it's in Chestnut Hill), is a large Jesuit school whose greatest strengths lie in its schools of business, nursing, and education. On the other hand, the liberal arts, while good, are "not as strong as they are reputed to be," according to one college counselor. In all academic areas, BC pursues the Jesuit ideals of developing the intellect and serving the community. The Jesuit spirit is particularly evident in the school's optional PULSE program, which allows students to combine courses in philosophy and ethics with community service in order to "address the relationship of self and society, the nature of community, the mystery of suffering, and the practical difficulties of developing a just society." Other optional course sequences, such as Perspectives on Western Culture and the Faith, Peace, and Justice Program, provide students with the opportunity to concentrate a sizable part of their undergraduate study on global social, philosophical, and theological questions. One drawback of BC is its size; students here complain that professors are often inaccessible and that administrative chores, such as registration, "suck."

Student Body

Despite a relatively large minority population, BC students consider themselves more alike than different. For example, one student inaccurately reports, "People here are all white Irish-Catholic beer-drinking clones and are damn proud of it, too." Agrees another, "People think BC is very homogeneous, but you come here because you want to be around people like yourself." Perhaps this misconception arises from the large Catholic population, the underrepresentation of black students, and the fact that "BC is a very cliquish place. As a result, you have to be extremely dynamic in order to make the most of it."

FINANCIAL AID: 617-552-3320

WEB SITE: HTTP://INFOEAGLE.BC.EDU/

ADMISSIONS

The admissions committee considers (in descending order of importance): HS record, test scores, class rank, essay, recommendations. *Also considered (in descending order of importance):* personality, special talents, alumni relationship, extracurriculars, geographical distribution. Either the SAT or ACT is required. An interview is recommended. *High school units required/recommended:* 20 total units are recommended; 4 English recommended, 4 math recommended, 3 science recommended, 4 foreign language recommended, 2 social studies recommended, 1 history recommended. *Special Requirements:* 2 units of lab science including chemistry required of nursing program applicants. 4 units of college-preparatory math strongly recommended of School of Management applicants. *The admissions office says:* "Boston College seeks a student body with a diversity of talents, attitudes, backgrounds, and interests to produce a vital community atmosphere. As a Jesuit institution, Boston College also chooses responsible and concerned students who are interested in the ideals of commitment and service to others."

The Inside Word

Applications have increased by more than a third over the past four years. BC is tough to get into; we more than recommend a strong college-preparatory curriculum in high school—it's a must in order to have a shot. With a large percentage of its students coming from parochial high schools such applicants are treated well, but there is little room for relaxation in the process. Applicants need to show strong SAT I and SAT II scores, but keep the tests in perspective— BC is interested in the whole package.

FINANCIAL AID

Students should submit: FAFSA, the school's own financial aid form, a copy of parents' most recent income tax filing. The Princeton Review suggests that all financial aid forms be submitted as soon as possible after January 1. *The following grants/scholarships are offered:* Pell, SEOG, academic merit, athletic, the school's own scholarships, the school's own grants, state scholarships, state grants, private scholarships, private grants, federal nursing scholarship, ROTC. *Students borrow from the following loan programs:* Stafford, unsubsidized Stafford, Perkins, PLUS, state loans, federal nursing loans, private loans. Applicants will be notified of awards beginning April 1. College Work-Study Program is available. Institutional employment is available.

FROM THE ADMISSIONS OFFICE

"Boston College students enjoy the quiet, suburban atmosphere of Chestnut Hill, with easy access to the cultural and historical richness of Boston. Junior Year Abroad and Scholar of the College Program offer students flexibility within the curriculum. Facilities opened in the past ten years include: the O'Neill Library, Robsham Theater Arts Center, Conte Forum (sports), and a chemistry center. Ten Presidential Scholars enroll in each freshman class with a half-tuition scholarship irrespective of need, and funding is available to meet full demonstrated need. These students, selected from the top one percent of the Early Notification applicant pool, participate in the most rewarding intellectual experience offered at the university."

ADMISSIONS

Admissions Rating	92
% of applicants accepted	41
% of acceptees attending	35

FRESHMAN PROFILE

Average verbal SAT	630
Average math SAT	640
Average ACT	NR
Average TOEFL	NR
Graduated top 20% of class	NR
Graduated top 40% of class	NR
Graduated top 60% of class	NR
Average HS GPA or Avg.	NR

DEADLINES

Early decision	NR
Regular admission	NR
Regular notification	4/15
Non-fall registration	yes

APPLICANTS ALSO LOOK AT

AND OFTEN PREFER

Georgetown U.
Notre Dame

AND SOMETIMES PREFER

Villanova
Coll. of the Holy Cross
Boston U.
Syracuse
Fairfield

AND RARELY PREFER

U. Vermont
U. Connecticut
U. New Hampshire

FINANCIAL FACTS

Financial Aid Rating	77
Tuition	$17,890
Room & board	$7,270
Estimated book expense	$500
% frosh receiving aid	69
% undergrads receiving aid	66
% aid is need-based	89
% frosh w/ grant (avg)	74 ($8,839)
% frosh w/ loan (avg)	43 ($3,500)
% UGs w/ job (avg)	21 ($2,000)
Off-campus job outlook	good

BOSTON CONSERVATORY

8 THE FENWAY, BOSTON, MA 02215   ADMISSIONS: 617-536-6340   FAX: 617-536-3176

CAMPUS LIFE

Quality of Life Rating   **79**
Type of school   private
Affiliation   none
Environment   metropolis

STUDENTS
FT undergrad enrollment   326
% male/female   30/70
% from out of state   74
% live on campus   30
% spend weekend on campus   100
% transfers   33
% from public high school   NR
% African-American   4
% Asian   4
% Caucasian   65
% Hispanic   4
% international   23
# of countries represented   36

WHAT'S HOT
theater
music associations
different students interact
Boston
off-campus food

WHAT'S NOT
computer facilities
lab facilities
unattractive campus
intramural sports
intercollegiate sports

ACADEMICS

Academic Rating   **86**
Profs Interesting Rating   77
Profs Accessible Rating   71
Calendar   semester
Student/teacher ratio   5:1
% profs PhD   5
Hours of study per day   3.72

MOST POPULAR MAJORS
music
musical theatre
dance

STUDENTS SPEAK OUT

Life

The Boston Conservatory is located in the city's Back Bay area, convenient to both Cambridge and downtown Boston. The student body is small, which might be blamed for the lack of an active social scene among students, if everybody wasn't so busy. "Not much time for friends unless you're really organized," one student wrote. Living in a major cultural center, undergrads are not deprived of entertainment or good food. While the former is provided on campus as well as off ("We put on great shows!" one student exclaimed), the latter is not. More than one respondent to our survey sees fit to report that, on campus, "the food sucks." Still, most students report being either very happy or happy at college, and maybe part of the reason is that some students find time to kick back and let off steam. Women outnumber men by more than two to 1, but still, a music major tells us there is "lots of drugs and alcohol, lots of sex. By senior year, you've learned your lesson." It is clear that students are happy here largely because they are doing what they want to do: as one student puts it, "entertainment and practicing our instruments are not separate entities."

Academics

The Conservatory offers study in Music Composition, Performance, and Education, and in Dance and Musical Theater. Professors get generally high marks from the undergrads we surveyed, who find them both able and accessible. "You get lots of individual attention because of the small student body," one student writes. The administration doesn't fare as well. While the majority of students agree that their school's staff operates fairly well, some survey respondents saw fit to criticize it. "Administration needs improving," is the kindest comment we received. As in the past, students also blame the school's "minuscule" endowment for the lack of timely investment in the repair of stages and studios. "Acoustically, the theater is the Black Hole of Calcutta," one student complains. Another writes, "It's just too bad about the school's facilities; we spend enough." Still, students at the Boston Conservatory are certainly dedicated to their art: more than half of those surveyed claim to do four or more hours of work a day outside of class. The curriculum is intense; students are required to complete a heavy course load in theory and history in addition to giving regular performances. Professors who teach these non-performance-oriented courses are not as highly praised among those surveyed as professors in the dance and musical theater departments. One student writes: "I would only recommend this school for certain programs."

Student Body

Students hold in high regard one another's talents and dedication. "The Boston Conservatory's strongest attribute is its motivated student body," one writes. Others are quick to mention the lack of competition and the generally supportive attitude students here share. Still, the heavy schedules and smallness of the school population contribute, for some, to a feeling of dislocation. One respondent claims that, "Students tend to socialize within their own department." "There is not a great deal of association among ourselves," a music major wrote, "other than that we all share the same ambitions and goals and follow the same struggle to attain them." The Boston Conservatory attracts a large number of foreign students, which many of the American students acknowledge as a big part of the school's appeal. Most also agree that there is little discrimination of any kind here.

FINANCIAL AID: 617-536-6340

ADMISSIONS

The admissions committee considers (in descending order of importance): HS record, test scores, essay, recommendations. *Also considered (in descending order of importance):* extracurriculars, special talents, alumni relationship, personality. Admissions process is need-blind. *High school units required/recommended:* 19 total units are recommended; 4 English recommended, 2 math recommended, 2 science recommended, 3 foreign language recommended, 4 social studies recommended. Minimum combined SAT I score of 950 (composite ACT score of 23) and minimum 2.7 GPA required. *Special Requirements:* An audition is required for music program applicants. TOEFL is required of all international students. Audition required of all applicants. *The admissions office says:* "Each student [is] evaluated on [an] individual basis for proper 'fit' to our school and its programs. Applicants with a significantly weaker academic performance will be recommended for admission into the Conservatory Diploma Program for one year, following which admission to the bachelor's degree program may be requested."

The Inside Word

Students applying to Boston Conservatory should put the overwhelming amount of effort they spend on their applications on preparing for the audition. Everything else will get a look, but admissions decisions have little do with your grades or anything else besides your performance background and potential. The Conservatory is a good option for musicians who are not ready for places like Juilliard, Manhattan, or Eastman.

FINANCIAL AID

Students should submit: FAFSA (due March 1), the school's own financial aid form (due March 1). The Princeton Review suggests that all financial aid forms be submitted as soon as possible after January 1. *The following grants/scholarships are offered:* Pell, SEOG, the school's own scholarships, private scholarships. *Students borrow from the following loan programs:* Stafford, unsubsidized Stafford, PLUS, the school's own loan fund. Applicants will be notified of awards beginning April 1. College Work-Study Program is available. Institutional employment is available.

FROM THE ADMISSIONS OFFICE

"Any student who is serious about training for a professional performing arts career should apply and audition. Each applicant is evaluated based on talent and ability in his or her chosen field. The Conservatory offers a challenging environment where each student receives individual attention. With our small student body everyone is a known quantity and receives support and encouragement to achieve his or her best."

ADMISSIONS

Admissions Rating	77
% of applicants accepted	50
% of acceptees attending	50

FRESHMAN PROFILE

Average verbal SAT	540
Average math SAT	510
Average ACT	NR
Average TOEFL	550
Graduated top 20% of class	NR
Graduated top 40% of class	NR
Graduated top 60% of class	NR
Average HS GPA or Avg.	2.6

DEADLINES

Regular admission	3/1
Regular notification	4/1
Non-fall registration	no

APPLICANTS ALSO LOOK AT

AND OFTEN PREFER
Juilliard

AND SOMETIMES PREFER
New England Music
SUNY Purchase
U. Cincinnati
U. the Arts
Eastman School of Music

FINANCIAL FACTS

Financial Aid Rating	78
Tuition	$14,300
Room & board	$6,075
Estimated book expense	$500
% frosh receiving aid	90
% undergrads receiving aid	75
% aid is need-based	52
% frosh w/ grant (avg)	79 ($4,684)
% frosh w/ loan (avg)	47 ($3,293)
% UGs w/ job (avg)	25 ($450)
Off-campus job outlook	excellent

BOSTON UNIVERSITY

121 BAY STATE ROAD, BOSTON, MA 02215   ADMISSIONS: 617-353-2300   FAX: 617-353-9695

CAMPUS LIFE

Quality of Life Rating   **81**
Type of school   private
Affiliation   none
Environment   metropolis

STUDENTS
FT undergrad enrollment	14,598
% male/female	44/56
% from out of state	73
% live on campus	60
% spend weekend on campus	80
% transfers	9
% from public high school	71
% in (# of) fraternities	5 (5)
% in (# of) sororities	7 (9)
% African-American	4
% Asian	15
% Caucasian	71
% Hispanic	6
% international	12
# of countries represented	90

WHAT'S HOT
ethnic diversity on campus
Boston
political activism
cigarettes
student publications

WHAT'S NOT
computer facilities
unattractive campus
inefficient administration
student government
dorms

ACADEMICS

Academic Rating	**77**
Profs Interesting Rating	66
Profs Accessible Rating	68
Calendar	semester
Student/teacher ratio	13:1
% profs PhD/tenured	82/81
Hours of study per day	2.91

MOST POPULAR MAJORS
management
communications
engineering

STUDENTS SPEAK OUT

Life

Says one BU student, "Boston University is located in one of the best cities in which to receive an education. There are at least 100,000 other students in the metropolitan area during the school year." Another insists that "if you are a BU student you have to take advantage of the city. There is so much to do and so many things to see." Students here enjoy the Boston club scene as well as easy access to Fenway Park, home of the Red Sox. BU's campus itself, however, is not much to brag about: it's big, spread out, and has a major roadway running through the middle of it. Students tell us that "at BU people love to hook up," perhaps compensating for the lack of campus unity in other social venues.

Academics

Even though BU is a private institution, the school has a lot in common with many major public institutions. For one thing, BU is a pretty big school. The diversity of programs available here is amazing (the school offers majors in over eighty categories). The bureaucracy is also amazing—amazingly scary, if anything goes wrong. And it's easy to get overlooked here. Says one student, "One must be aggressive and independent; you can get lost in the crowd if you don't participate in school activities." Says another, "BU is supposedly dedicated to celebrating the individual, but at a school of 14,000 this is an oxymoron." Some believe, though, that a good academic program is always within your grasp. Brags one undergrad, "BU is an incredible university, and its resources are extraordinary (and they'd better be because of the price one pays to go here)." Engineering and General Studies both received praise for the individual attention their students get. The College of Arts and Sciences, on the other hand, while good, is seen as "too large and impersonal" by many of its students. Still, if students don't aggressively pursue quality, they can easily find themselves mired in mediocrity. Most of their classmates are lax about studying (fewer than two and three quarters hours a day), and one complains that "the school offers too many 'high school level' classes for kids who aren't as talented academically, but the kids' parents are rich enough to send their children to a 'respectable' university, when in fact they are paying $23,000 to go to high school all over again."

Student Body

BU students' biggest gripe has to do with the level of seriousness with which some of their classmates attack their work. Says one, "A lot of people here don't take the education seriously. Some are only here to find a spouse who will make them financially secure. It's sad because they bring down BU's reputation and potential to be an extraordinary college." Students here feel strongly that they are part of a diverse and harmonious community, although the school does not have an exceptionally large minority population. A noticeable portion of the student body comes from ritzy Boston suburbs, but there are a lot of ritzy international suburbs represented as well.

ADMISSIONS

The admissions committee considers (in descending order of importance): HS record, test scores, class rank, essay, recommendations. *Also considered (in descending order of importance):* special talents, alumni relationship, extracurriculars, personality. Either the SAT or ACT is required. An interview is required of some applicants. Admissions process is need-blind. *High school units required/recommended:* 21 total units are required; 26 total units are recommended; 4 English required, 4 math required, 4 science required, 2 foreign language required, 3 foreign language recommended, 4 social studies required, 3 history recommended. Specific admissions requirements vary by college. SAT II chemistry, math level I or IIc, and writing required of applicants to accelerated medical/dental programs; foreign language recommended. SAT II English, foreign language, and math level I or IIc required of applicants to University Professors Program. SAT II writing recommended of applicants to College of Communication. *Special Requirements:* A portfolio is required for art program applicants. An audition is required for music program applicants. TOEFL is required of all international students. Interview required of finalists to accelerated medical and dental programs. Interview and portfolio required of applicants to some theatre programs (management, stage design, and technical). Portfolio and/or audition required of applicants to School of Arts. *The admissions office says:* "BU does recommend a college preparatory curriculum, including a full complement of math, science, and foreign language courses."

The Inside Word

Boston is one of the nation's most popular college towns, and BU benefits tremendously. A high volume of applications does more toward making BU selective than anything else. Those who aren't up to traditional standards can even "back door" through the less-selective College of General Studies, which allows students to transfer to other divisions of the University once they prove themselves academically.

FINANCIAL AID

Students should submit: FAFSA (due February 15), CSS Profile (due February 15), state aid form (due February 15), a copy of parents' most recent income tax filing. The Princeton Review suggests that all financial aid forms be submitted as soon as possible after January 1. *The following grants/scholarships are offered:* Pell, SEOG, academic merit, athletic, the school's own scholarships, the school's own grants, state scholarships, state grants, private scholarships, private grants, ROTC. *Students borrow from the following loan programs:* Perkins, PLUS, supplemental loans, state loans, private loans. Applicants will be notified of awards beginning mid-March. College Work-Study Program is available. Institutional employment is available.

FROM THE ADMISSIONS OFFICE

"The spirit of Boston University is in the possibilities. With more than 250 major and minor concentrations led by a faculty dedicated to the art of teaching, the University's academic opportunities are nearly unrivaled among American institutions of higher learning. Beyond the classroom, Boston University students—who come from all 50 states and more than 130 foreign countries—may choose to participate in any of the more than 300 student organizations, from environmental groups to intramural ice broomball teams. Students find abundant opportunities for growth and enjoyment not only in the city of Boston but in cities throughout the world where Boston University students study and work."

ADMISSIONS

Admissions Rating	81
% of applicants accepted	63
% of acceptees attending	29

FRESHMAN PROFILE

Average verbal SAT	680
Average math SAT	620
Average ACT	26
Average TOEFL	550
Graduated top 20% of class	71
Graduated top 40% of class	94
Graduated top 60% of class	99
Average HS GPA or Avg.	3.3

DEADLINES

Early decision	11/1
Regular admission	1/15
Regular notification	4/15
Non-fall registration	yes

APPLICANTS ALSO LOOK AT

AND OFTEN PREFER

Harvard/Radcliffe
Pennsylvania
Cornell U.
Boston Coll.
Georgetown U.

AND SOMETIMES PREFER

NYU
Syracuse
RIT
Notre Dame

AND RARELY PREFER

U. New Hampshire
Rutgers U.-Rutgers Coll.

FINANCIAL FACTS

Financial Aid Rating	72
Tuition	$20,570
Room & board	$7,050
Estimated book expense	$475

% frosh receiving aid	65
% undergrads receiving aid	59
% aid is need-based	77
% frosh w/ grant (avg)	65 ($12,795)
% frosh w/ loan (avg)	58 ($3,852)
% UGs w/ job (avg)	25 ($1,500)
Off-campus job outlook	excellent

BOWDOIN COLLEGE

BRUNSWICK, ME 04011   ADMISSIONS: 207-725-3100   FAX: 207-725-3101

CAMPUS LIFE

Quality of Life Rating	**91**
Type of school	private
Affiliation	none
Environment	town

STUDENTS

FT undergrad enrollment	1,521
% male/female	49/51
% from out of state	86
% live on campus	80
% spend weekend on campus	95
% transfers	2
% from public high school	57
% in (# of) fraternities	37 (8)
% African-American	2
% Asian	8
% Caucasian	81
% Hispanic	3
% international	3
# of countries represented	27

WHAT'S HOT
campus food
dorms
campus easy to get around
campus feels safe
beer

WHAT'S NOT
infrequent dating
cigarettes
lack of diversity on campus
religion
sex

ACADEMICS

Academic Rating	**91**
Profs Interesting Rating	92
Profs Accessible Rating	94
Calendar	semester
Student/teacher ratio	11:1
% profs PhD/tenured	94/67
Hours of study per day	3.73

MOST POPULAR MAJORS
government/legal studies
biology
history

% GRADS WHO PURSUE...
Law 9, Med 12, MBA 37, MA 17

STUDENTS SPEAK OUT

Life

Bowdoin College is located in picturesque Brunswick, Maine, a small town just minutes from the ocean. Portland is 25 miles away, and bus service to Boston (120 miles away) is right on campus. Brunswick itself may not be a hub of cultural opportunities, but Bowdoin's outdoorsy students never want for things to do:" You are easily within one hour of great rock climbing, rafting, kayaking, hiking, or any outdoor activity you could possibly want." Skiing is an hour away and is another popular weekend diversion. Claims one booster, "Bowdoin is a college for those who enjoy the outdoors, parties, and a good education." On campus, the small-college atmosphere strikes some as warmly intimate, others as claustrophobic: explains one student, Bowdoin is "a wonderful place to grow intellectually, but the social sphere is very stifling and 'elite,' with little to do during the limited time students have to take breaks (especially if they have no cars)." The huge and gleaming new Smith Union, however, seems to have added a jolt of energy to campus life. Students rarely "date"; they either settle into long relationships or...well, as one student puts it, "As for dating, Bowdoin is the world's most expensive contraceptive." In any case, most students feel that the "strong friendships" they form here compensate. Both intercollegiate and intramural sports are popular, and the fraternities have survived after becoming coed. A final note: Bowdoin's cafeterias serve up some of the nation's best food!

Academics

Recent years have seen something of a transformation at Bowdoin, almost all of which seem to have been for the better of the 200-year-old liberal arts college. No Puritans, the administration at Bowdoin—Nathaniel Hawthorne's alma mater— struck a progressive chord with its mandate that fraternities go coed, and while some initially saw the move as strong-arming, it seems to have been a success. Other big changes include the establishment of a Coastal Studies Center right on the ocean, which will house the College's strong programs in biology, geology, and environmental studies. Students here are given lots of academic independence, with the result that "Independent study is huge"—well over half the students complete year-long research projects under close faculty guidance. Study abroad is also popular, especially since financial aid is guaranteed for these costs as well. But despite the intellectual independence Bowdoin offers, students tell of a homey atmosphere and personal attention. Reports one student: "The second night I was here, I was invited to a professor's house for tea and a chance to play with his new kittens." Students respond to this balance by studying hard and succeeding after graduation: nearly three-fourths proceed to graduate school, with a surprising number going on to medical school.

Student Body

The students at Bowdoin agree that theirs is "not a diverse community," but are quick to add that "the students want it to be diverse and the administration is 'seeking diversity,'" including outreach programs to students from poor areas of Maine. In general, Bowdoin students are more left-leaning than most, though conservative voices are heard, and the large and vocal liberal faction has its detractors: writes one student, "Most students are liberal until they graduate, then they become investment bankers." Wealthy New Englanders are well represented here, but as one student explains, "Despite what was said in one college guidebook I had, Bowdoin students do not all look alike."

FINANCIAL AID: 207-725-3273

ADMISSIONS

The admissions committee considers (in descending order of importance): HS record, class rank, recommendations, essay, test scores. *Also considered (in descending order of importance):* extracurriculars, personality, special talents, alumni relationship, geographical distribution. An interview is recommended. *High school units required/recommended:* 4 English recommended, 4 math recommended, 3 science recommended, 4 foreign language recommended, 4 social studies recommended. SAT I or ACT scores required at matriculation; may be submitted with application if applicant wishes them to be considered. Rank in top tenth of secondary school class and minimum 3.5 GPA recommended. *Special Requirements:* TOEFL is required of all international students. Portfolio recommended of art program applicants. Sample or tape recommended of music program applicants. *The admissions office says:* "The admissions committee focuses a great deal of its attention on each candidate's academic record, intellectual interests, and overall ability to thrive in a challenging academic environment. To enhance the educational scope and stimulation of the Bowdoin community, special consideration is given to applicants who represent a culture, region, or background that will contribute to the diversity of the college. Added consideration is also given to candidates who have demonstrated talents in leadership, communication, social service, and other fields that will contribute to campus life."

The Inside Word

This is one of the twenty or so most selective colleges in the country. Virtually everyone who applies is well-qualified academically, which means criteria besides grades and test scores become critically important in candidate review. Who you are, what you think, where you are from, and why you are interested in Bowdoin are the sorts of things that will determine whether you get in or not-provided you meet their high academic standards.

FINANCIAL AID

Students should submit: FAFSA (due March 1), the school's own financial aid form (due March 1), a copy of parents' most recent income tax filing. The Princeton Review suggests that all financial aid forms be submitted as soon as possible after January 1. *The following grants/scholarships are offered:* Pell, SEOG, the school's own scholarships, the school's own grants, state scholarships, state grants, private scholarships, private grants, foreign aid. *Students borrow from the following loan programs:* Stafford, Perkins, PLUS, the school's own loan fund, state loans, private loans. Applicants will be notified of awards beginning April 5. College Work-Study Program is available. Institutional employment is available. Freshmen are discouraged from working.

FROM THE ADMISSIONS OFFICE

"This is an exciting time in the 202-year history of Bowdoin College. A new $4.8 million campus center has just opened, construction is about to begin on a $14 million science center, and a new residence hall is in the final design stages. The College has also announced that it will build a new Coastal Studies Center on 118 acres of nearby seacoast property that is already being utilized by students doing field and marine research. The Bowdoin College Library, containing over 825,000 volumes, is one of the largest and most renowned undergraduate college libraries in the U.S. Recently the library has been enriched by a new array of computerized services providing access to a wealth of information resources on campus, and in libraries and electronic information networks around the world."

ADMISSIONS

Admissions Rating	92
% of applicants accepted	30
% of acceptees attending	36

FRESHMAN PROFILE

Average verbal SAT	610
Average math SAT	680
Average ACT	NR
Average TOEFL	600
Graduated top 20% of class	91
Graduated top 40% of class	99
Graduated top 60% of class	100
Average HS GPA or Avg.	NR

DEADLINES

Early decision	1/1
Regular admission	1/1
Regular notification	early April
Non-fall registration	yes

APPLICANTS ALSO LOOK AT

AND OFTEN PREFER

Brown
Dartmouth
Harvard/Radcliffe
Williams
Middlebury Coll.

AND SOMETIMES PREFER

Princeton
Cornell U.
Bates
Colby
Wesleyan U.

FINANCIAL FACTS

Financial Aid Rating	76
Tuition	$21,410
Room & board	$6,030
Estimated book expense	$650
% frosh receiving aid	46
% undergrads receiving aid	46
% aid is need-based	100
% frosh w/ grant (avg)	42 ($13,940)
% frosh w/ loan (avg)	44 ($3,000)
% UGs w/ job (avg)	40 ($600)
Off-campus job outlook	fair

BRANDEIS UNIVERSITY

415 SOUTH STREET, P.O. BOX 9110, WALTHAM, MA 02254-9110   ADMISSIONS: 617-736-3500   FAX: 617-736-3536

CAMPUS LIFE

Quality of Life Rating	81
Type of school	private
Affiliation	none
Environment	suburban

STUDENTS

FT undergrad enrollment	2,929
% male/female	45/55
% from out of state	75
% live on campus	90
% spend weekend on campus	NR
% transfers	9
% from public high school	75
% African-American	3
% Asian	8
% Caucasian	78
% Hispanic	3
% international	5
# of countries represented	55

WHAT'S HOT
theater
religion
student publications
music associations
support groups

WHAT'S NOT
Waltham
beer
sex
students are cliquish
intercollegiate sports

ACADEMICS

Academic Rating	86
Profs Interesting Rating	89
Profs Accessible Rating	91
Calendar	semester
Student/teacher ratio	10:1
% profs PhD	87
Hours of study per day	3.07

MOST POPULAR MAJORS
psychology
sociology
economics

% GRADS WHO PURSUE...
Law 22, Med 16, MBA 2, MA 12

STUDENTS SPEAK OUT

Life

Most Brandeis University students admit that the social life at their school is slow, but social and cultural activities do exist for those willing to make an effort. In the words of one student, "There is an opportunity to meet wonderful people here and have a good time, but don't come if you're looking for a party school." Another asserts that the school is "great socially, but only if you get involved (clubs, etc.). You've got to find your social life, because it won't find you." Brandeis has an underground Greek scene, but there is an "open animosity" toward the Greeks among administrators and many students. The new athletic center "provides a great outlet for non-academic activity"; students who don't feel like working out often go there to watch the Boston Celtics practice. Of Brandeis's home city, one student writes: "Waltham is a blue-collar area, but it does have a lot of good stores. It's easy to get to downtown Boston, but it's still forty-five minutes away." There is a weekend shuttle van that takes students to Cambridge and Boston. Students note that junkets to Boston are invariably expensive but also necessary to maintain your sanity on this academically intense campus.

Academics

Brandeis University is one of the rare schools that manages to function well both as a research center and as an undergraduate institution. The school's research orientation attracts some of the nation's top scholars; the school's dedication to undergraduate education guarantees that those scholars teach college students. Of the stellar faculty, students report that "there are some AMAZING professors, and a few (but very few) turkeys." More surprising, given the emphasis on research, is that "the professors are wonderful; brilliant, accessible and extremely interested in their students." Brandeis produces a large number of pre-professionals—one in six students goes on to law school, one in eleven to medical school—without skimping on traditional liberal arts and science studies. Some students find Brandeis's core curriculum (math, science, humanities, and foreign language) excessive: They take at least two semesters to complete. Overall, however, students appreciate the school's academic philosophy. Writes one student, "The liberal principles on which this university was founded provide an atmosphere conducive for the interrelation of different ideas, values, cultures, and lifestyles. Anyone with an open mind will love this place, anyone with a closed mind will hate it." Economics, English, Life Sciences, Theater Arts, and Near Eastern and Jewish studies are among the many excellent majors here.

Student Body

"Informed," "open-minded," "liberal," and "socially committed" are terms that appear frequently in students' descriptions of each other; so, too, unfortunately, does "spoiled" (Brandeis is one of the country's most expensive schools). Students are liberal socially and politically, and, by their own account, very accepting of diversity and alternative lifestyles. Nearly two thirds of Brandeis's undergraduates are Jewish. Comments one student, "At other schools, everyone may look different, but they often think exactly the same. Some of us might look the same, but since heritage is the draw, the political and social ideas are vastly different."

FINANCIAL AID: 617-736-3700   WEB SITE: HTTP://WWW.BRANDEIS.EDU/

ADMISSIONS

The admissions committee considers (in descending order of importance): HS record, class rank, recommendations, test scores, essay. *Also considered (in descending order of importance):* extracurriculars, personality, special talents, alumni relationship. Either the SAT or ACT is required; SAT is preferred. An interview is recommended. *High school units required/recommended:* 12 total units are recommended; 4 English recommended, 3 math recommended, 1 science recommended, 3 foreign language recommended, 1 history recommended. *Special Requirements:* TOEFL is required of all international students. Essay required of all applicants. Foreign language recommended in 12th year. One unit of advanced mathematics recommended of prospective science majors. Science unit(s) must be chosen from chemistry, physics, and biology.

The Inside Word

While the university has a reputation for quality, the low yield of admits who actually choose to attend Brandeis results in a higher acceptance rate than one might expect. Weak students will still find it difficult to gain admission. The option of submitting ACT scores instead of SAT and SAT II Subject Test scores should be the hands down choice of any candidate who doesn't have to take SAT IIs for any other reason.

FINANCIAL AID

Students should submit: FAFSA, CSS Profile, the school's own financial aid form (due February 15), state aid form. The Princeton Review suggests that all financial aid forms be submitted as soon as possible after January 1. *The following grants/scholarships are offered:* Pell, SEOG, academic merit, the school's own scholarships, the school's own grants, state scholarships, state grants, private scholarships, private grants, foreign aid. *Students borrow from the following loan programs:* Stafford, unsubsidized Stafford, Perkins, PLUS, the school's own loan fund. Applicants will be notified of awards beginning April 1. College Work-Study Program is available. Institutional employment is available.

FROM THE ADMISSIONS OFFICE

"Featuring an innovative core curriculum as the centerpiece of its flexible interactive academic structure, Brandeis provides its graduates with the intellectual skills and versatility necessary to assure them success as graduate or professional students, workers, and citizens. The entire academic experience at Brandeis is characterized by unequaled access to faculty, an approach to learning that stresses the interconnectedness of knowledge, and the opportunity to choose courses that best fit one's interests and academic goals."

ADMISSIONS

Admissions Rating	85
% of applicants accepted	66
% of acceptees attending	29

FRESHMAN PROFILE

Average verbal SAT	720
Average math SAT	640
Average ACT	NR
Average TOEFL	630
Graduated top 20% of class	78
Graduated top 40% of class	100
Graduated top 60% of class	100
Average HS GPA or Avg.	NR

DEADLINES

Early decision	NR
Regular admission	2/1
Regular notification	4/1
Non-fall registration	yes

APPLICANTS ALSO LOOK AT

AND OFTEN PREFER

Cornell U.
Columbia
Colgate
Brown
Amherst

AND SOMETIMES PREFER

Union Coll. (NY)
Tufts
Pennsylvania

AND RARELY PREFER

Binghamton U.
Boston U.
Clark

FINANCIAL FACTS

Financial Aid Rating	80
Tuition	$20,470
Room & board	$6,950
Estimated book expense	$410
% frosh receiving aid	59
% undergrads receiving aid	59
% aid is need-based	85
% frosh w/ grant (avg)	NR ($13,621)
% frosh w/ loan (avg)	53 ($3,493)
% UGs w/ job (avg)	45 ($1,385)
Off-campus job outlook	good

BRIGHAM YOUNG UNIVERSITY

Provo, UT 84602   Admissions: 801-378-2500   Fax: 801-378-4264

STUDENTS SPEAK OUT

Life

It's not the case that all Brigham Young University students are Mormon, but it is true that those who aren't sometimes have trouble fitting in. "This is a very homogeneous school in that practically everyone is LDS [Latter-day Saint], white, and intolerant of different views than those of the Mormon church," writes one student. Provo is not a hugely eventful town, according to the students we surveyed, but that isn't much of a problem for most. There are movies and dances on campus, and when students aren't studying they're reportedly thinking, "When will I find my eternal mate?" "Life at BYU outside class is all about getting married." The student who wrote that was exaggerating slightly. Sometimes it's also about hiking, mountain biking, rock climbing, going to basketball and football games, or skiing at one of the five resorts that are within forty-five minutes of campus. Every student must live according to an honor code, which prohibits the use of drugs, including alcohol, tobacco, and caffeine. A couple of students claim that the code is occasionally violated by people they know, but most feel that the restrictions are a definite plus. One comments that "the best thing about BYU activities is not worrying about fights, who has to stay sober to drive home, etcetera." "People (here) know how to have fun without getting wasted," another writes. "They're creative!"

Academics

By most accounts, the course load at BYU is demanding. In addition to concentrating on a traditional major (business and management, communication, and engineering are among the most popular here) each student must pass seven religion courses by graduation. "All I have time for is work and study," one respondent to our survey remarks. "No life, no fun, no nothing." Others find time for the leisure activities mentioned in the section above; most find time for regular church attendance (it is required for LDS students), and many also fit into their hectic schedules the volunteer and missionary work that is expected in the LDS community. Several respondents comment on the competitiveness of their fellow students. "The student body is extremely serious about their studies and intent on overachieving," one puts it. Others are concerned by the hold that the Church-controlled administration has on community discourse. "It seems to be very easy for professors to get in trouble with the administration," a student writes, "so they seem nervous about discussing controversial issues, particularly ethics and politics." Our survey respondents are divided on the basic quality of the faculty, some praising their professors' "caring" and "inspiring" natures, others lodging complaints similar to those made by students at any large university. Some students feel that their professors' preoccupation with research and funding interferes with their commitment to their students, while a couple echo this remark: "I think some of my professors need to make learning more exciting!! They're boring!!"

Student Body

"Conformity is king," writes one student of the environment at BYU. But even those who expressed concern about the homogeneity and conservatism of their classmates also mentioned the exceptional courtesy and friendliness that characterize the typical BYU student. It is a very social campus, where, everyone seems to agree, dating is extremely popular. The positive attitude here is a boon to most students ("It's almost impossible to not get along with your classmates."), and mildly bizarre to a few ("The student body here is too happy sometimes."). Regardless, students clearly have a great deal of respect for their peers. "I really enjoy how fast people become friends here," one student writes.

ADMISSIONS

The admissions committee considers (in descending order of importance): HS record, test scores, essay, recommendations, class rank. *Also considered (in descending order of importance):* personality, extracurriculars, special talents. ACT is preferred. An interview is recommended. *High school units required/recommended:* 18 total units are recommended; 4 English recommended, 3 math recommended, 2 science recommended, 2 foreign language recommended, 2 history recommended. Minimum ACT score in mid-20s and minimum 3.0 GPA recommended. TOEFL is required of all international students. *The admissions office says:* "Applicants must meet published application deadlines to be considered. Our applicants have agreed to abide by the University 'Code of Honor' and 'Dress and Grooming' guidelines prior to enrolling."

The Inside Word

Despite the high acceptance rate, this is a rigorous application process which will quickly and efficiently eliminate candidates who make a poor match. Most eliminate themselves by not applying to begin with, as the matchmaking places the greatest weight on the ideological fit.

FINANCIAL AID

Students should submit: FAFSA (due April 15), the school's own financial aid form (due April 15), state aid form (due April 15), a copy of parents' most recent income tax filing (due April 15). The Princeton Review suggests that all financial aid forms be submitted as soon as possible after January 1. *The following grants/ scholarships are offered:* Pell, academic merit, athletic, the school's own scholarships, the school's own grants, private scholarships, ROTC. *Students borrow from the following loan programs:* Stafford, PLUS, the school's own loan fund. Applicants will be notified of awards beginning: rolling. Institutional employment is available.

FROM THE ADMISSIONS OFFICE

"The mission of Brigham Young University—founded, supported, and guided by the Church of Jesus Christ of Latter-day Saints—is to assist individuals in their quest for perfection and eternal life. That assistance should provide a period of intensive learning in a stimulating setting where a commitment to excellence is expected and the full realization of human potential is pursued. All instruction, programs, and services at BYU, including a wide variety of extracurricular experiences, should make their own contribution toward the balanced development of the total person. Such a broadly prepared individual will not only be capable of meeting personal challenge and change but will also bring strength to others in the tasks of home and family life, social relationships, civic duty, and service to mankind."

ADMISSIONS

Admissions Rating	81
% of applicants accepted	76
% of acceptees attending	83

FRESHMAN PROFILE

Average verbal SAT	NR
Average math SAT	NR
Average ACT	27
Average TOEFL	500
Graduated top 20% of class	55
Graduated top 40% of class	98
Graduated top 60% of class	NR
Average HS GPA or Avg.	3.7

DEADLINES

Early decision	NR
Regular admission	2/15
Regular notification	rolling
Non-fall registration	yes

APPLICANTS ALSO LOOK AT

AND OFTEN PREFER
U. Utah
Utah St.

AND RARELY PREFER
Boston U.
U. Texas-Austin
UC-Berkeley
U. Michigan, Ann Arbor
U. Washington

FINANCIAL FACTS

Financial Aid Rating	88
Tuition	NR
Room & board	$3,740
Estimated book expense	$900
% frosh receiving aid	NR
% undergrads receiving aid	74
% aid is need-based	NR
% frosh w/ grant (avg)	54
% frosh w/ loan (avg)	14
% UGs w/ job (avg)	30 ($3,328)
Off-campus job outlook	good

BROWN UNIVERSITY

45 PROSPECT STREET, BOX 1876, PROVIDENCE, RI 02912   ADMISSIONS: 401-863-2378   FAX: 401-863-9300

CAMPUS LIFE

Quality of Life Rating	**87**
Type of school	private
Affiliation	none
Environment	city

STUDENTS

FT undergrad enrollment	5,730
% male/female	48/52
% from out of state	97
% live on campus	89
% spend weekend on campus	90
% transfers	3
% from public high school	80
% in (# of) fraternities	12 (11)
% in (# of) sororities	2 (2)
% African-American	6
% Asian	15
% Caucasian	67
% Hispanic	5
% international	7
# of countries represented	63

WHAT'S HOT
college radio
ethnic diversity on campus
students are happy
support groups
theater

WHAT'S NOT
infrequent dating
religion
student government
intramural sports
library

ACADEMICS

Academic Rating	**91**
Profs Interesting Rating	82
Profs Accessible Rating	80
Calendar	semester
Student/teacher ratio	8:1
% profs PhD/tenured	98/99
Hours of study per day	3.58

MOST POPULAR MAJORS
biological/medical sciences
history
English/American literature

% GRADS WHO PURSUE...
Law 8, Med 9, MBA 1, MA 8

STUDENTS SPEAK OUT

Life

Brown University students see each other as intelligent, talented, and less competitive than students at other top-tier schools. "It's the laid-back Ivy League," as one puts it. With no core requirements, students seem happy about the freedom they are trusted with and often blur the boundary between their academic and social lives. Students reportedly socialize a great deal, meeting to discuss philosophy and politics in small groups. Dating, however, is not a frequent phenomenon, according to many of the students. One student claims, "Social life's great except that dating is nonexistent. If you wanna be celibate for four years, come to Brown!" While the sleepy character of Providence drives students looking for urban excitement to travel to Boston, or even New York, many undergrads maintain that it's not really necessary to leave campus for entertainment's sake. "The great thing about Brown is the constant bombardment of notices and announcements you get regarding the myriad activities going on," one writes. "On any given weekend night, I could go hear a cappella, go to a `Euro' party, attend some intellectual forum, go to the Grad Center Bar and play pool, go to an artsy movie, hear a campus band at our pub, the Underground, or just hang around with friends."

Academics

Brown University's unusual curriculum and grading policies are generally appreciated by its students. While advisors tend to steer students toward well-rounded elective choices, freedom from curriculum requirements is very liberating and, respondents tell us, motivating. Students are given even more freedom when it comes to grades, with two low-key options to choose from. Courses can be taken either ABC/No Credit, wherein any grade below a C does not appear on the student's transcript, or Satisfactory/No Credit, a pleasant version of Pass/Fail that leaves out the failing part. (One pays for such policies, apparently. Fewer than half of Brown's students receive financial aid and the admissions process is not need-blind.) Professors are praised highly for their intelligence and accessibility. "My psychology professor practically begs us to e-mail him and stop by his office! The professors really make an effort to help students learn." Advisors are quite accessible as well: "It actually shocks me how easy it is to meet with a dean. But then Brown has so many." Students like to point out how motivated and happy they are, a condition some attribute to a lack of undue stress. "We're a $6.00 train ride from Harvard, so we can always get a bunch of students to go there on weekends to laugh at how miserable the students look. But, of course, half of us will end up there for grad school anyway."

Student Body

"The student body is amazingly diverse, but groups with different backgrounds tend to remain segregated from each other." This is the consensus among respondents to our survey. While Brown students are widely noted for their respect and tolerance, disparate groups apparently don't mix here any more easily than on many campuses that are less acclaimed for such virtues. Brown also has a fairly wealthy student body, which can cause some rancor as well. "I think classism is a big issue, because of non-need-blind admissions," one student wrote. Still, the vast majority of our respondents expressed deep admiration for their classmates and satisfaction with their social lives. "I've never felt more comfortable with my peers than at Brown."

FINANCIAL AID: 401-863-2721

WEB SITE: HTTP://WWW.BROWN.EDU/

ADMISSIONS

The admissions committee considers (in descending order of importance): HS record, recommendations, class rank, essay, test scores. *Also considered (in descending order of importance):* personality, extracurriculars, special talents, alumni relationship, geographical distribution. Either the SAT or ACT is required; SAT is preferred. Admissions process is not need-blind. *High school units required/recommended:* 16 total units are required; 4 English required, 3 math required, 3 science required, 3 foreign language required, 2 history required. Electives should be from computer science, foreign language, history, math, or science. Different distributions of units required of S.B. program applicants and eight-year liberal arts/medical education program applicants. TOEFL is required of all international students.

The Inside Word

The cream of just about every crop applies to Brown. Gaining admission requires more than just a superior academic profile from high school. Some candidates, such as the sons and daughters of Brown graduates (who are admitted at virtually double the usual acceptance rate) have a better chance for admission than most others. Minority students benefit from extravagant courtship, particularly once admitted. Ivies like to share the wealth, and distribute offers of admission across a wide range of constituencies. Candidates from states that are overrepresented in the applicant pool, such as New York, have got to be particularly distinguished in order to have the best chance at admission. So do those who attend high schools with many seniors applying to Brown, as it is rare for more than 2 or 3 students from any one school to be offered admission.

FINANCIAL AID

Students should submit: FAFSA (due February 1), the school's own financial aid form (due January 1), state aid form (due February 1), a copy of parents' most recent income tax filing (due April 15). The Princeton Review suggests that all financial aid forms be submitted as soon as possible after January 1. *The following grants/scholarships are offered:* Pell, SEOG, the school's own scholarships, the school's own grants, state scholarships, state grants, private scholarships, private grants, foreign aid. *Students borrow from the following loan programs:* Stafford, Perkins, PLUS, the school's own loan fund. Applicants will be notified of awards beginning April 2. College Work-Study Program is available. Institutional employment is available.

FROM THE ADMISSIONS OFFICE

"It is our pleasure to introduce you to a unique and wonderful learning place: Brown University. Brown was founded in 1764 and is a private, co-educational, Ivy League university in which the intellectual development of undergraduate students is fostered by a dedicated faculty on a traditional New England campus."

ADMISSIONS

Admissions Rating	99
% of applicants accepted	22
% of acceptees attending	49

FRESHMAN PROFILE

Average verbal SAT	680
Average math SAT	670
Average ACT	31
Average TOEFL	600
Graduated top 20% of class	93
Graduated top 40% of class	99
Graduated top 60% of class	NR
Average HS GPA or Avg.	NR

DEADLINES

Early decision	NR
Regular admission	1/1
Regular notification	4/1
Non-fall registration	yes

APPLICANTS ALSO LOOK AT

AND OFTEN PREFER

Harvard/Radcliffe
Princeton
Yale
Stanford

AND SOMETIMES PREFER

Swarthmore
Amherst
Williams
Smith

AND RARELY PREFER

Tufts
Georgetown U.
Bowdoin
Oberlin

FINANCIAL FACTS

Financial Aid Rating	82
Tuition	$20,608
Room & board	$5,926
Estimated book expense	$720

% frosh receiving aid	35
% undergrads receiving aid	35
% aid is need-based	100
% frosh w/ grant (avg)	28 ($10,313)
% frosh w/ loan (avg)	29 ($3,200)
% UGs w/ job (avg)	55 ($1,600)
Off-campus job outlook	good

BRYN MAWR COLLEGE

101 NORTH MERION AVENUE, BRYN MAWR, PA 19010-2899   ADMISSIONS: 610-526-5152   FAX: 610-526-7471

STUDENTS SPEAK OUT

Life

Bryn Mawr students are divided on the subject of the social life on campus: some are grateful for the lack of a tumultuous "scene," and others are moved to complain about it. Philadelphia is close by, as are coed colleges Swarthmore and Haverford, so those who need a diversion unavailable on campus can find it without too much trouble. Most agreed, however, that time for seeking diversions is decidedly scant. "The schoolwork is always at the center of our lives. This makes having fun somewhat difficult because you're always thinking about it. There aren't many big parties...People usually hang out in small groups on campus." Students here frequently attend cultural events, and many are politically active, as well. "There is always a crusade, whether it is to save the whales, protect victims of sexual abuse, or to free somebody or other. The funny thing is, everybody genuinely cares." Many respondents to our survey remark on their happiness and level of comfort. "Bryn Mawr is like no other campus I've visited--it is almost as if Bryn Mawr is isolated from society's discriminations." One diversion that is unavailable to "Mawrters" is interaction with male students. "My advice," one wrote, "is to go to Philly, go to the different campuses (Haverford and Swarthmore), and if faced with a choice between a `ford and a Swattie, pick the Swattie."

Academics

"No matter how much they complain about it, the people here like to work hard. That's part of the reason they're here and not at Smith," says one Bryn Mawr student. Everyone agrees about the demanding nature of the workload and the expectations of the faculty. "Bryn Mawr College is clearly committed to my education, some days more than I am. Profs know you by name within the first month, even in the larger intro classes!" Unlike at most colleges, the administration gets high marks, but the professors receive the most praise of all. One student refers to them as "goddesses," and many remark on their dedication. "Profs are involved and interested, from academic problems to the occasional middle-of-a-lab-exam nervous breakdown." While the workload is not generally considered unreasonable ("People work hard here but they don't get stressed—they're interested in the work."), it takes getting used to for some: "The feeling of my heart pounding (from caffeine and lack of sleep) in my chest and the sight of my fingernails gnawed to the cuticle—this is what I will most distinctly remember about my academic experience at Bryn Mawr." Still, the honor code allows students to schedule their own exams, and they can also take courses at fellow consortium-member campuses Haverford and Swarthmore.

Student Body

Bryn Mawr has a small student body with a strong sense of community. Most undergrads expressed the utmost regard for their classmates' personalities and abilities. "There is a very high level of respect for one another's ideas, beliefs, and personal dignity." Many are struck by being in a place with so many people as serious as themselves. "We are a very particular group of women—ambitious, unrelenting—and we drive ourselves very hard." Of course, for some, the atmosphere, populated by high-powered academic achievers, can be a bit much sometimes: Bryn Mawr has a "diverse but single-minded group of women who need to relax," one student writes. The political scene is not as fraught with controversy as at some schools, but not everybody sees this as a positive thing. One respondent feels that, "A real problem here is the general assumption that everyone will automatically espouse a particular political agenda. I don't think we think through our political responses here, and we don't like to hear opposing views."

FINANCIAL AID: 610-526-5245　　E-MAIL: MPMCP@BRYNMAWR.EDU　　WEB SITE: HTTP://WWW.BRYNMAWR.EDU/COLLEGE

ADMISSIONS

The admissions committee considers (in descending order of importance): HS record, recommendations, test scores, class rank, essay. *Also considered (in descending order of importance):* personality, special talents, alumni relationship, extracurriculars, geographical distribution. Either the SAT or ACT is required; SAT is preferred. An interview is recommended. Admissions process is need-blind. *High school units required/recommended:* 16 total units are required; 4 English required, 3 math required, 1 science required, 4 foreign language required, 1 history required. TOEFL is required of all international students.

The Inside Word

Do not be deceived by Bryn Mawr's admit rate; its student body is among the best in the nation academically. Outstanding preparation for graduate study draws an applicant pool which is well-prepared and intellectually curious. The admissions committee includes eight faculty members and four seniors. Each applicant is reviewed by four readers, including at least one faculty member and one student.

FINANCIAL AID

Students should submit: FAFSA (due January 15), CSS Profile (due January 15), the school's own financial aid form (due January 15), state aid form (due January 15), Divorced Parents form (due January 15), a copy of parents' most recent income tax filing (due January 15). The Princeton Review suggests that all financial aid forms be submitted as soon as possible after January 1. *The following grants/scholarships are offered:* Pell, SEOG, the school's own scholarships, the school's own grants, state scholarships, state grants, private scholarships, private grants, ROTC, foreign aid. *Students borrow from the following loan programs:* Stafford, Perkins, PLUS, the school's own loan fund, state loans, private loans. Applicants will be notified of awards beginning April 15. College Work-Study Program is available. Institutional employment is available.

FROM THE ADMISSIONS OFFICE

"Prepare to be surprised. One wouldn't ordinarily assume that a small institution could offer as diverse a range of opportunities as many large universities, or that some of the residence halls at a women's college would be coeducational, or that a campus looking like the English countryside could exist within twenty minutes of downtown Philadelphia. But Bryn Mawr is not an ordinary institution. Bryn Mawr was founded in 1885 to extend to women the opportunity for rigorous academic training, including the study of Greek, mathematics, and philosophy, that was then available only to men. Being small, it could offer a kind of attention to the needs and concerns of its students that large universities could not. Being new and somewhat arrogant, it could challenge educational convention whenever that seemed important. Those traditions continue, and Bryn Mawr is today very much a demanding and caring place where both ideas and individuals matter very much."

ADMISSIONS

Admissions Rating	89
% of applicants accepted	58
% of acceptees attending	35

FRESHMAN PROFILE

Average verbal SAT	670
Average math SAT	640
Average ACT	NR
Average TOEFL	650
Graduated top 20% of class	87
Graduated top 40% of class	99
Graduated top 60% of class	100
Average HS GPA or Avg.	NR

DEADLINES

Early decision	NR
Regular admission	1/15
Regular notification	4/15
Non-fall registration	no

APPLICANTS ALSO LOOK AT
AND OFTEN PREFER

Brown
Yale
Princeton

AND SOMETIMES PREFER

Wellesley
Swarthmore
Smith
Mount Holyoke
Vassar

AND RARELY PREFER

Haverford
Skidmore

FINANCIAL FACTS

Financial Aid Rating	82
Tuition	$20,210
Room & board	$7,870
Estimated book expense	$600
% frosh receiving aid	53
% undergrads receiving aid	52
% aid is need-based	100
% frosh w/ grant (avg)	53 ($13,582)
% frosh w/ loan (avg)	53 ($3,000)
% UGs w/ job (avg)	50 ($1,382)
Off-campus job outlook	good

BUCKNELL UNIVERSITY

LEWISBURG, PA 17837

ADMISSIONS: 717-524-1101   FAX: 717-524-3760

CAMPUS LIFE

Quality of Life Rating	**86**
Type of school	private
Affiliation	none
Environment	town

STUDENTS

FT undergrad enrollment	3,342
% male/female	51/49
% from out of state	68
% live on campus	85
% spend weekend on campus	85
% transfers	4
% from public high school	74
% in (# of) fraternities	47 (12)
% in (# of) sororities	52 (8)
% African-American	3
% Asian	3
% Caucasian	91
% Hispanic	2
% international	1
# of countries represented	30

WHAT'S HOT
lab facilities
library
school runs like butter
registration is a breeze
Greeks

WHAT'S NOT
lack of diversity on campus
cigarettes
students are cliquish
off-campus food
drugs

ACADEMICS

Academic Rating	**90**
Profs Interesting Rating	90
Profs Accessible Rating	91
Calendar	semester
Student/teacher ratio	13:1
% profs PhD/tenured	94/95
Hours of study per day	3.60

MOST POPULAR MAJORS
economics
biology
English

% GRADS WHO PURSUE...
Law 5, Med 4, MBA 2, MA 13

STUDENTS SPEAK OUT

Life

Bucknell University makes up for its remote locale with its many clubs and campus-sponsored activities and its "country club setting" (writes one student, "This is definitely the prettiest college campus in the United States. We have our own 18-hole golf course and plans for a boathouse on the river in addition to a new athletic complex.") One student explains, "The activities and clubs at Bucknell offer something for everyone! There's always an activity going on. Sometimes it's hard to decide what to do!" Sports of all kinds are extraordinarily popular here; students rate their intercollegiate sports teams (especially basketball) as "great" and both intramurals and outdoor activities attract lots of fanatic participation. Still, many students complain that "It gets really boring. Lewisburg is small: we're stranded amidst lots of dairy farms. The only things to do here are drink and go to frat parties, go to the bar (there are only two in town), and see a movie. No wonder we drink a lot."

Academics

Affectionately known as "the Bubble" for its idyllic, secluded atmosphere, Bucknell commands respect in many areas. "The workload is tough," writes one engineer, a sentiment echoed by science, economics, and business majors. Competition for grades is stiff ("We're in the cutthroat zone-be careful!"), perhaps because success here pays off: many of Bucknell's graduates proceed on to some graduate program. Students here love their professors ("I have been consistently impressed with the dedication, competence, availability, and approachability of my Bucknell professors.)" Writes one student, "There is a strong sense of community that exists because of size and location, even though the school is fairly large. There is a real nice small-school feeling to it. Professors can be e-mailed and called at home and are very willing to meet one-on-one." Bucknell students also dole out high marks to their deans, bursar, and registrar. This is one of the few schools where the students actually like the administration.

Student Body

Bucknell is "very homogeneous" with a small percentage of minorities. Writes one of the few, "Life as a minority can be difficult at times, yet the minority community has worked to make first-years feel at home. Bucknell has much to work on as far as its conservative views, but, from the little I've seen, they are making progress."

FINANCIAL AID: 717-524-1331

ADMISSIONS

The admissions committee considers (in descending order of importance): HS record, class rank, test scores, recommendations, essay. *Also considered (in descending order of importance):* alumni relationship, extracurriculars, personality, special talents, geographical distribution. Either the SAT or ACT is required; SAT is preferred. An interview is recommended. Admissions process is not need-blind. *High school units required/recommended:* 16 total units are required; 4 English required, 3 math required, 2 science required, 2 foreign language required, 2 social studies required, 2 history required. *Special Requirements:* An audition is required for music program applicants. TOEFL is required of all international students. *The admissions office says:* "At Bucknell, each applicant has every piece of his or her credentials read and evaluated by professional staff. It is a personal, hands-on process, one that is not driven by a formula or indices, but one that attempts to assess an individual's capability for becoming a productive and contributing member of the Bucknell community."

The Inside Word

Each application is read by two admissions officers. If you are serious about attending Bucknell and have strong grades and test scores, there is little to get in your way. Still, overconfidence or a so-so match can throw a wrench in the plans of some—the university increased its wait list by nearly 25 percent last year, and has decreased acceptances for the past two years.

FINANCIAL AID

Students should submit: FAFSA (due February 1), CSS Profile (due February 1), state aid form, a copy of parents' most recent income tax filing (due February 1). The Princeton Review suggests that all financial aid forms be submitted as soon as possible after January 1. *The following grants/scholarships are offered:* Pell, SEOG, the school's own scholarships, state scholarships, state grants, private scholarships, ROTC. *Students borrow from the following loan programs:* Stafford, unsubsidized Stafford, Perkins, PLUS. Applicants will be notified of awards beginning March 25. College Work-Study Program is available. Institutional employment is available.

FROM THE ADMISSIONS OFFICE

"Bucknell offers a unique learning environment and is one of a few primarily undergraduate colleges which offers the opportunity to investigate both the human and technical aspects of life in the twenty-first century. A major curricular revision was implemented by the faculty in 1993. All students enrolling in the College of Arts and Sciences will complete: a first year foundation seminar; distributional requirements which include four humanities courses, two social science courses, and three courses in natural science and mathematics; broadened perspectives for the twenty-first century consisting of one course each in natural and fabricated worlds and on human diversity; departmental, college, or interdepartmental majors; and a capstone seminar or experience during the senior year. Bucknell also requires a minimum writing competency for graduation."

ADMISSIONS

Admissions Rating	88
% of applicants accepted	55
% of acceptees attending	25

FRESHMAN PROFILE

Average verbal SAT	620
Average math SAT	640
Average ACT	NR
Average TOEFL	550
Graduated top 20% of class	78
Graduated top 40% of class	96
Graduated top 60% of class	100
Average HS GPA or Avg.	3.4

DEADLINES

Early decision	NR
Regular admission	1/1
Regular notification	4/1
Non-fall registration	no

APPLICANTS ALSO LOOK AT

AND OFTEN PREFER

Cornell U.
Middlebury Coll.
Duke
Northwestern U.

AND SOMETIMES PREFER

Boston U.
Colgate
Villanova
Penn State U.
Lehigh

AND RARELY PREFER

Lafayette

FINANCIAL FACTS

Financial Aid Rating	80
Tuition	$20,230
Room & board	$5,075
Estimated book expense	$600
% frosh receiving aid	48
% undergrads receiving aid	60
% aid is need-based	100
% frosh w/ grant (avg)	39 ($11,079)
% frosh w/ loan (avg)	60 ($3,400)
% UGs w/ job (avg)	43 ($1,500)
Off-campus job outlook	poor

CALIFORNIA INSTITUTE OF THE ARTS

24700 McBean Parkway, Valencia, CA 91355   Admissions: 805-545-2787   Fax: 805-254-8352

CAMPUS LIFE

Quality of Life Rating   **68**
Type of school   private
Affiliation   none
Environment   suburban

STUDENTS
FT undergrad enrollment	674
% male/female	64/36
% from out of state	60
% live on campus	50
% spend weekend on campus	60
% transfers	16
% from public high school	NR
% African-American	7
% Asian	7
% Caucasian	68
% Hispanic	8
% international	11
# of countries represented	30

WHAT'S HOT
drugs
theater
music associations
different students interact
leftist politics

WHAT'S NOT
town-gown relations
intramural sports
religion
intercollegiate sports
off-campus food

ACADEMICS

Academic Rating	**92**
Profs Interesting Rating	85
Profs Accessible Rating	72
Calendar	semester
Student/teacher ratio	7:1
Hours of study per day	3.43

STUDENTS SPEAK OUT

Life

It's a good thing that the students at Cal Arts are creative, because they are generally forced to entertain themselves. The campus is located in Valencia, a hard town to get around in without a car, and not much of a draw with one. Still, people are able to find diversions. "Always there is someone showing work, "explains one undergrad. "Parties here are fun," another writes, but the frequency of his classmates' festivities has an effect on this student's sleeping habits: "(For fun) I like to hang out of my door at 3 a.m. and yell at everyone to shut up because I'm trying to sleep." While that may make the campus sound like some huge, unremitting party scene, the focus of most people's leisure time here is taking in their classmates' presentations. "There is no lack of artistic inspiration, product, or shows at this school," a student writes. "There is always something exciting happening here." Musical organizations, theater productions, and the radio station are popular among students at Cal Arts; the student government, newspaper, and activist organizations are somewhat less so. The administration's drug and alcohol policy is comparatively lenient, a fact not under-appreciated by the student body. One member of it writes, "Even though there are many drugs at this school the school is very safe. I think people are adult enough to know what they're doing and that's cool."

Academics

Cal Arts students describe themselves as "fiercely creative" and praise the school for its small size ("I get all the individual help that I want.") and its freedom ("This is a great place to come and do your own thing and be as creative as you can be. You make your own program, practically."). Cal Arts offers courses in six divisions: the schools of Art, Dance, Music, Theater, Critical Studies, and Film and Video; the film department's most prestigious major is Animation. As with most BFA programs, humanities fall by the wayside, something to consider if you're expecting a varied, liberal arts-type education in addition to the courses in your major. "The undergraduate experience here is not very well-rounded," one student writes, "I think Cal Arts has more to offer the graduate student." One film major sees fit to point out that "Technologically, the school is a little behind the times when it comes to digital media, but there's still plenty to take advantage of." Much of the faculty is made up of adjunct professors—active in the fields in which they teach—and students praise them for their egalitarian approach: "The professors here are very relaxed and friendly. Since there are few students in each area its easy to befriend professors and administrators. It's a very equal to equal relationship." In most cases, students come here just to learn how to practice their art, and appreciate the single-minded concentration: "It's a great place to study if you are focused and motivated, and not just simply talented and rich."

Student Body

"My fellow students are totally cool—everyone is pretty open to new things. They're kind of wild, too...People stay out of each other's business here." Several Cal Arts students mention their classmates' "open-mindedness," while others advise prospective applicants to "come with an open mind." However, most of those who describe their classmates as "flaky" describe nothing more specifically unusual than a preponderance of green hair. The majority seems to feel as this student does: "It is exciting to be with so many talented people in one place."

ADMISSIONS

Special Requirements: A portfolio is required for art program applicants. An audition is required for music program applicants. TOEFL is required of all international students. Portfolio required of visual arts and music composition program applicants. Audition required of performing arts program applicants. *The admissions office says:* "Admissions is based entirely on audition or portfolio."

The Inside Word

Cal Arts fits into a great niche. It's very small and focused on the arts alone. It's more contemporary in its orientation and direction than the majority of other music schools with national reputations. It eclipses the scope and quality of virtually all the for-profit contemporary music and art schools which are often found in ads in magazines aimed at teens. There are few better overall choices for students seeking practical career training in the arts and a bachelor's degree. Getting in isn't easy, and neither is graduating. But those who make it through have one of the most practical arts degrees to be found. As is usually the case at such schools, your audition or portfolio counts far more than any other application materials.

FINANCIAL AID

Students should submit: FAFSA (due March 2), the school's own financial aid form (due March 2), state aid form (due March 2), a copy of parents' most recent income tax filing. The Princeton Review suggests that all financial aid forms be submitted as soon as possible after January 1. *The following grants/scholarships are offered:* Pell, SEOG, the school's own scholarships, the school's own grants, state scholarships, state grants, private scholarships, private grants. *Students borrow from the following loan programs:* Stafford, unsubsidized Stafford, Perkins, PLUS, the school's own loan fund, supplemental loans. Applicants will be notified of awards beginning April 1. College Work-Study Program is available. Institutional employment is available. Freshmen are discouraged from working.

FROM THE ADMISSIONS OFFICE

"California Institute of the Arts is a single complex of five professional schools-Art, Dance, Film and Video, Music, and Theater-conceived as a community of artists. The institute is a training ground, a performance center, and a laboratory of the arts. Interaction among the arts is a fundamental premise of the Institute, and the several schools have developed numerous special programs, such as performance art, electronic art, video art, and world music, that cross traditional disciplinary lines. Whenever possible, the faculty resources of each school are available to all other schools. The faculty members are all working artists and eminent educators, and the standards of all five schools are professional. Students are accepted as artists on the assumption that they come to the institute to develop the talents they bring."

ADMISSIONS

Admissions Rating	83
% of applicants accepted	36
% of acceptees attending	66

FRESHMAN PROFILE

Average verbal SAT	NR
Average math SAT	NR
Average ACT	NR
Average TOEFL	550
Graduated top 20% of class	NR
Graduated top 40% of class	NR
Graduated top 60% of class	NR
Average HS GPA or Avg.	NR

DEADLINES

Early decision	NR
Regular admission	rolling
Regular notification	rolling
Non-fall registration	no

APPLICANTS ALSO LOOK AT

AND SOMETIMES PREFER
USC

AND RARELY PREFER
UCLA
NYU
Pratt Inst.
Loyola Marymount U.

FINANCIAL FACTS

Financial Aid Rating	74
Tuition	$16,350
Room & board	$5,520
Estimated book expense	$450
% frosh receiving aid	40
% undergrads receiving aid	69
% aid is need-based	89
% frosh w/ grant (avg)	85 ($5,122)
% frosh w/ loan (avg)	85 ($4,695)
% UGs w/ job (avg)	35
Off-campus job outlook	good

CALIFORNIA INSTITUTE OF TECHNOLOGY

1201 EAST CALIFORNIA BOULEVARD, PASADENA, CA 91125   ADMISSIONS: 818-395-6341   FAX: 818-683-3026

CAMPUS LIFE

Quality of Life Rating	74
Type of school	private
Affiliation	none
Environment	suburban

STUDENTS

FT undergrad enrollment	923
% male/female	75/25
% from out of state	60
% live on campus	90
% spend weekend on campus	90
% transfers	7
% from public high school	85
% African-American	1
% Asian	29
% Caucasian	56
% Hispanic	5
% international	9
# of countries represented	29

WHAT'S HOT
lab facilities
computer facilities
different students interact
honesty
dorms

WHAT'S NOT
cigarettes
infrequent dating
sex
beer
drugs

ACADEMICS

Academic Rating	95
Profs Interesting Rating	62
Profs Accessible Rating	68
Calendar	trimester
Student/teacher ratio	3:1
% profs PhD	100
Hours of study per day	4.43

MOST POPULAR MAJORS
engineering/applied science
physics
biology

% GRADS WHO PURSUE...
Law 2, Med 13, MA 85

STUDENTS SPEAK OUT

Life
Sums up one student, "Life here is work, work, work. The weekend is spent catching up on work. Often, I calculate how many hours are in the weekend and find that it is less than the number of hours it will take me to finish my work. On a good night I may get five or six hours of sleep, but usually on weekdays I get three or four." Stressful? You judge: One student reports that "I like to run up on the roof, scream 'I'm Fun Man,' and throw off parachute men." Others relieve stress by pulling pranks: Explains one student, "Pranks are a big source of fun and distraction. Converting a friend's room into a disco bar while he was gone was memorable." In their few seconds of spare time, students hang out on a beautiful campus ("a lovely location when you have the time to enjoy it") and participate in a fairly active intramural sports program ("The best thing about Caltech: sports. You don't have to be a potential big-leaguer to get lots of playing time"). A unique housing system "combines the features of dorms and the Greek system. After a 'shopping week,' students are matched with 'specialty houses,' each with a different personality: some emphasize sports, others different social activities and attitudes."

Academics
Caltech's attitude is a lot more relaxed than you'd think for one of America's top schools. Professors maintain an informal air ("I like the fact that during my entire academic career, I've only seen one of my professors in a tie") and assist students in the execution of their notorious pranks, and students take freshman classes pass/fail, mostly collaborate on class work, and take most exams at home—the hallmarks of a school that already knows its students are brilliant. Caltech students put in an average of four and a half hours of study per day, tops in the nation. Opportunities here "for undergraduates to do research are unbelievable. Everyone that I know that wanted a school-year or summer job got one. Furthermore, what the undergrads do is real research and not test-tube cleaning." Students also benefit from the most intimate technical undergraduate education available anywhere: Caltech's faculty-student ratio is a remarkable 1:3. "The accessibility of faculty is amazing...Nobel prizewinners are available to anyone." Adds another, "The workload is huge, but all efforts are made to help students learn to deal with it. It is amazing to see people who are the best in their fields taking an interest in freshmen." Students tell us that faculty are unusually accessible outside the classroom but give them very poor grades for their teaching skills.

Student Body
One-third of Caltech's students are minorities; well over half of the minority students are Asian. Students are "extremely intense. This place is not for the weak of heart. Death by science." One student describes his classmates as "a bunch of nerds and borderline psychotics," adding, "I guess I fit in." Faculty and student body are still predominantly male, and several women complained that sexism is a problem.

FINANCIAL AID: 818-683-3026

WEB SITE: HTTP://WWW.CALTECH.EDU/

ADMISSIONS

The admissions committee considers (in descending order of importance): HS record, test scores, recommendations, class rank, essay. *Also considered (in descending order of importance):* extracurriculars, personality, special talents. *High school units required/recommended:* 15 total units are required; 3 English required, 4 math required, 2 science required, 1 history required. Additional units of English or history, foreign language, geology, biology, or other lab sciences recommended. *The admissions office says:* "Because we are so small, our admissions process is very individualized—every application is reviewed three times and discussed in small committees, so we get to know every applicant very well."

The Inside Word

A mere glance at Cal Tech's freshman profile can discourage all but the most self-confident of high school seniors. It should. The impact of grades and test scores on the admissions process is minimized significantly when virtually every freshman was in the top fifth of his or her high school class and has a 1400 SAT. The admissions office isn't kidding when they emphasize the personal side of their criteria. Six students are on the admissions committee; every file is read at least twice. The process is all about matchmaking, and the Tech staff is very interested in getting to know you. Don't apply unless you have more than high numbers to offer.

FINANCIAL AID

Students should submit: FAFSA (due January 15), CSS Profile (due January 15), state aid form (due January 15), a copy of parents' most recent income tax filing (due January 15). The Princeton Review suggests that all financial aid forms be submitted as soon as possible after January 1. *The following grants/scholarships are offered:* Pell, SEOG, academic merit, the school's own scholarships, the school's own grants, state grants, private scholarships, ROTC, foreign aid. *Students borrow from the following loan programs:* Stafford, unsubsidized Stafford, Perkins, PLUS, the school's own loan fund. Applicants will be notified of awards beginning April 15. College Work-Study Program is available. Institutional employment is available. Freshmen are discouraged from working.

FROM THE ADMISSIONS OFFICE

"Admission to the freshman class is based on many factors—some quantifiable, some not. What you say in your application is important! And, because we don't interview students for admission, your letters of recommendation are weighed heavily. High school academic performance is very important, as is a demonstrated interest in math, science, and/or engineering. We are also interested in your character, maturity, and motivation. We are very proud of the process we use to select each freshman class. It's very human, it has great integrity, and we believe it serves all the students who apply, justly. If you have any questions about the process or about Cal Tech in general, write us a letter or give us a call. We'd like to hear from you!"

ADMISSIONS

Admissions Rating	99
% of applicants accepted	25
% of acceptees attending	46

FRESHMAN PROFILE

Average verbal SAT	700
Average math SAT	770
Average ACT	NR
Average TOEFL	NR
Graduated top 20% of class	100
Graduated top 40% of class	100
Graduated top 60% of class	100
Average HS GPA or Avg.	3.9

DEADLINES

Early decision	11/1
Regular admission	1/1
Regular notification	April
Non-fall registration	no

APPLICANTS ALSO LOOK AT

AND OFTEN PREFER
Stanford
Harvard/Radcliffe
Princeton

AND SOMETIMES PREFER
MIT
UC-Berkeley
Harvey Mudd
Georgia Tech.
RPI

AND RARELY PREFER
Virginia Poly. Inst.

FINANCIAL FACTS

Financial Aid Rating	94
Tuition	$18,000
Room & board	$5,478
Estimated book expense	$795
% frosh receiving aid	74
% undergrads receiving aid	69
% aid is need-based	98
% frosh w/ grant (avg)	62 ($13,000)
% frosh w/ loan (avg)	53 ($3,435)
% UGs w/ job (avg)	60 ($1,800)
Off-campus job outlook	good

CALIFORNIA POLYTECHNIC STATE UNIVERSITY

SAN LUIS OBISPO, CA 93407-0005   ADMISSIONS: 805-756-2311   FAX: 805-756-5400

CAMPUS LIFE

Quality of Life Rating	**86**
Type of school	private
Affiliation	none
Environment	suburban

STUDENTS

FT undergrad enrollment	13,623
% male/female	58/42
% from out of state	4
% live on campus	17
% spend weekend on campus	NR
% transfers	36
% from public high school	91
% in (# of) fraternities	8 (18)
% in (# of) sororities	5 (7)
% African-American	2
% Asian	13
% Caucasian	59
% Hispanic	15
% international	NR
# of countries represented	44

WHAT'S HOT
*San Luis Obispo
health facilities
off-campus food
students are happy
computer facilities*

WHAT'S NOT
*theater
music associations
students are cliquish
cigarettes
dorms*

ACADEMICS

Academic Rating	**72**
Profs Interesting Rating	69
Profs Accessible Rating	71
Calendar	quarter
Student/teacher ratio	20:1
% profs PhD	52
Hours of study per day	2.93

MOST POPULAR MAJORS
business administration
agricultural business
mechanical engineering

STUDENTS SPEAK OUT

Life

Students give San Luis Obispo surprisingly good grades for a tiny town. Writes one, "If there were more industry here in SLO, I would never leave! It is a beautiful town with friendly people"; another describes it as "a homey college town with quaint coffee shops and restaurants." Another student notes that the school is "located halfway between the Bay Area and Los Angeles, so it provides a meeting place for northern and southern California students. Also, it is located fifteen minutes from the beach and is surrounded by green hills with grazing cows." Social life is reportedly "laid-back" and "unexciting" despite an active Greek scene and the large amount of free time students enjoy (by technical school standards, the three hours a day students study here is very reasonable). Notably lacking from student surveys are any hair-pulling expressions of stress and frustration that we found at other tech schools. In fact, students report themselves to be among the nation's happiest, making them by far the most serene architecture and engineering students in the country.

Academics

California Polytechnic State University in San Luis Obispo stands out among the Cal State schools because it's hard to get in (the most competitive in the State system) and it's a hands-on school for scientific study. Cal Poly emphasizes a real-world approach to practical problem solving for all students ("The focus on campus is industry-related knowledge, not a research grant or thesis," reports one undergrad), including freshmen: In fact, applicants must declare a major and begin a course of study during their first semester. Architecture and engineering are the best-known majors here, although agribusiness/agricultural sciences are also supposed to be excellent. The business school, furthermore, is beginning to establish a good reputation. Liberal arts majors are also available: English and journalism students in our survey express satisfaction with their programs. Students report that, despite the large enrollment, "the academic standards are high, and the classes are small." Several also note that "the most attractive quality of Cal Poly is the professors' commitment to the undergraduate students and their learning." To others, however, Cal Poly's most attractive quality is its tuition, cheap for everyone but positively a steal for state residents. The mix of quality programs and affordability leads many students in our survey to comment that Cal Poly is "a great deal for students."

Student Body

Cal Poly draws its student body almost entirely from in-state. Despite a significant minority population, students report that the school is "not ethnically diverse"; another student went so far as to say that "everyone looks and acts the same." Hispanics and Asians both constitute substantial populations. Students are generally "quite conservative, mostly Republican," and very practical and goal-oriented. Men outnumber women substantially, but the split is not too lopsided for a tech school.

California Polytechnic State University-San Luis Obispo

FINANCIAL AID: 805-756-2927

WEB SITE: HTTP://WWW.CALPOLY.EDU/

ADMISSIONS

The admissions committee considers (in descending order of importance): HS record, test scores. *Also considered (in descending order of importance):* extracurriculars, geographical distribution. Either the SAT or ACT is required. *High school units required/recommended:* 15 total units are required; 4 English required, 3 math required, 1 science required, 2 foreign language required, 1 history required. Electives should include 1 unit of visual/performing arts. *Special Requirements:* A portfolio is required for art program applicants. An audition is required for music program applicants. TOEFL is required of all international students. *The admissions office says:* "California Polytech uses the following formula to determine whether a candidate is admitted: multiply your high school GPA (on a 0 to 4 scale, add one point to your grade in each honors-level course) by 800 plus your combined SAT score. If you took the ACT, multiply your GPA by 200 and add 10 times your ACT composite score. The cut-offs for California residents are 2800 (SAT) or 694 (ACT); for non-residents, the cutoffs are 3402 (SAT) or 842 (ACT). Required high school curriculum: English, 4 yrs; mathematics, 3 yrs. (including algebra I and II and geometry); foreign language, 2 yrs.; lab science, U.S. history, art, 1 yr. each; academic electives, 3 yrs. total."

The Inside Word

While it is tough to get admitted, Cal Poly doesn't spend much time on frills in the admissions process. Satisfy the formulas or else!

FINANCIAL AID

Students should submit: FAFSA (due May 1), the school's own financial aid form (due March 1), state aid form (due March 1), a copy of parents' most recent income tax filing (due March 1). The Princeton Review suggests that all financial aid forms be submitted as soon as possible after January 1. *The following grants/scholarships are offered:* Pell, SEOG, academic merit, athletic, the school's own scholarships, the school's own grants, state scholarships, state grants, private scholarships, ROTC. *Students borrow from the following loan programs:* Stafford, Perkins, PLUS, the school's own loan fund, state loans. Applicants will be notified of awards beginning in April. College Work-Study Program is available. Institutional employment is available.

FROM THE ADMISSIONS OFFICE

"From row crops to computers, Cal Poly believes the best way for someone to learn something is to do it. That's been the school's philosophy since it began. Learn by doing, the university calls it. Cal Poly students gain invaluable first-hand experience both on campus and off. On-campus opportunities such as the daily student-run newspaper and real-world agricultural enterprise projects make hands-on learning a daily reality, not just a catch phrase. Off-campus work with government agencies and major national corporations for both academic credit and a salary is available through various programs that include the largest Cooperative Education Program in the western United States. With its approach to education and success in applying it, Cal Poly has built a solid statewide and national reputation."

ADMISSIONS

Admissions Rating	80
% of applicants accepted	56
% of acceptees attending	41

FRESHMAN PROFILE

Average verbal SAT	620
Average math SAT	590
Average ACT	23
Average TOEFL	NR
Graduated top 20% of class	63
Graduated top 40% of class	87
Graduated top 60% of class	97
Average HS GPA or Avg.	3.5

DEADLINES

Early decision	NR
Regular admission	11/30
Regular notification	rolling
Non-fall registration	yes

APPLICANTS ALSO LOOK AT

AND SOMETIMES PREFER

UC-Berkeley
UC-Santa Cruz
UCLA
UC-Santa Barbara
UC-Davis

AND RARELY PREFER

U. Pacific

FINANCIAL FACTS

Financial Aid Rating	78
Tuition	$2,033
Room & board	$5,044
Estimated book expense	$648
% frosh receiving aid	50
% undergrads receiving aid	49
% aid is need-based	85
% frosh w/ grant (avg)	34 ($2,939)
% frosh w/ loan (avg)	40 ($3,311)
% UGs w/ job (avg)	12 ($1,500)
Off-campus job outlook	good

THE BEST COLLEGES ■ 105

UNIVERSITY OF CALIFORNIA-BERKELEY

BERKELEY, CA 94720   ADMISSIONS: 510-642-3175   FAX: 510-643-8245

CAMPUS LIFE

Quality of Life Rating   **75**
Type of school   public
Affiliation   none
Environment   metropolis

STUDENTS
FT undergrad enrollment   21,138
% male/female   52/48
% from out of state   10
% live on campus   25
% spend weekend on campus   NR
% transfers   30
% from public high school   82
% in (# of) fraternities   14 (42)
% in (# of) sororities   13 (17)
% African-American   6
% Asian   39
% Caucasian   32
% Hispanic   14
% international   3
# of countries represented   100

WHAT'S HOT
health facilities
drugs
ethnic diversity on campus
leftist politics
library

WHAT'S NOT
support groups
campus difficult to get around
campus food
inefficient administration
students are unhappy

ACADEMICS

Academic Rating   **83**
Profs Interesting Rating   64
Profs Accessible Rating   62
Calendar   semester
Student/teacher ratio   17:1
% profs PhD   95
Hours of study per day   3.14

MOST POPULAR MAJORS
engineering
molecular/cell biology
English

STUDENTS SPEAK OUT

Life

Since the revolutionary days of the 1960s, "Cal" and the surrounding city of Berkeley have been hotbeds of political and social activism. "People take themselves too seriously. Everyone needs to seriously relax, especially about politics," one student notes. Adding to the intensity of emotion is the size of the student body, which alone would mean a diversity of opinions. The campus itself is idyllic, but the surrounding neighborhood is not. One student warns that "the homelessness and squalor...are difficult for some to get used to." On-campus housing is scarce, so many students live off campus. Some choose to live in the nine student-run co-ops near campus. Others go the way of the Greeks, who are not the center of campus life but an active part. Comments one student: "life at school is overwhelming; there's too much going on at any one time." For those who need to get away from campus, the city of Berkeley is lively, and a bit farther away, San Francisco is accessible.

Academics

No matter how you judge academic excellence, UC-Berkeley is the nation's finest public university. "UC-Berkeley offers what I think to be the most challenging and competitive classes in the nation," writes one student, and others agree. Many of its academic programs are exceptional—particularly noteworthy are the engineering program, all hard sciences, and the English and history departments—and the faculty is internationally recognized as stellar. An overwhelming majority of Berkeley students are bound for some graduate program almost immediately after graduation. The most common complaint is that undergrads are often shortchanged on professor interaction: "The professors are mostly writing books, which leaves the TAs with a lot more time to teach," is a familiar comment. Classes can have enrollment of 1,000 students or more. Berkeley's size (more than 21,000 full-time undergraduate, graduate and research students) can make the bureaucratic hassles a nightmare. One student identifies the typical administrative experience: "Here at UC-Berkeley you have the choice of getting help from every possible office or being ignored on a grand scale." Many students feel that the administration's attitude is one of "indifferent hostility." Berkeley life is big, busy, rigorous, and challenging but, at least for one student, "Words can not express how grateful I am for this experience."

Student Body

Ethnic diversity at Berkeley is "impressive," and includes large Asian and Hispanic populations. People note the large size of the student body encourages students to form small "cliques" based on ethnic groups or social interests, which tend to limit the exposure of each group to others. The gay community is large, visible, and well accepted. Do not let this plurality of students fool you into believing, though, that Berkeley is all about understanding and helping each other. Academically, the student body is very competitive, and self-described as "cutthroat."

FINANCIAL AID: 510-642-6442

WEB SITE: HTTP://WWW.BERKELEY.EDU/

ADMISSIONS

The admissions committee considers (in descending order of importance): HS record, test scores, essay, recommendations. *Also considered (in descending order of importance):* geographical distribution, extracurriculars, personality, special talents. Either the SAT or ACT is required. *High school units required/recommended:* 15 total units are required; 4 English required, 3 math required, 4 math recommended, 2 science required, 3 science recommended, 2 foreign language required, 3 foreign language recommended. Minimum 3.4 GPA required of out-of-state applicants. In-state applicants with minimum 3.3 GPA are eligible regardless of test scores. Applicants with minimum combined SAT I score of 1400 (composite ACT score of 31) and minimum combined SAT II scores of 1730 (in-state) or 1850 (out-of-state), with no score below 530 on any one test, are eligible on the basis of test scores alone. *Special Requirements:* An audition is required for music program applicants. TOEFL is required of all international students. *The admissions office says:* "Additional course work in all areas is recommended. Special: residents must have either a 3.3 GPA or do well on a standardized test to be considered for admission. Nonresidents must earn a 3.4 average (the eligibility index applies to residents only). Any student who fails to meet the academic requirements may gain admission on the basis of test scores alone if (1) his/her SAT I is 1300 or higher (ACT composite: 31 or higher), and (2) his/her combined SAT II Subject Test scores exceed a minimum score (1650 for residents, 1730 for non-residents), and none is lower than 500."

The Inside Word

The State of California's plan to discontinue affirmative action in the UC admission process has created much uncertainty regarding the future of candidate selection in the system. There is little room for deviation in any applicant's statistical profile, but out-of-state students will find the going even tougher, with available spaces few and far between. Initial candidate evaluation is in the form of computer screening for minimum admissibility standards. Berkeley is the most selective division of the university system.

FINANCIAL AID

Students should submit: FAFSA. The Princeton Review suggests that all financial aid forms be submitted as soon as possible after January 1. *The following grants/ scholarships are offered:* Pell, SEOG, academic merit, athletic, the school's own scholarships, the school's own grants, state scholarships, state grants, private scholarships, private grants, ROTC. *Students borrow from the following loan programs:* Stafford, Perkins, PLUS, the school's own loan fund, health professions loans, private loans. Applicants will be notified of awards beginning April 21. College Work-Study Program is available. Institutional employment is available.

FROM THE ADMISSIONS OFFICE

"One of the top public universities in the nation and the world, the University of California-Berkeley offers a vast range of courses and a full menu of extracurricular activities. Berkeley's academic programs are internationally recognized for their excellence. Undergraduates can choose one of 100 majors. Or, if they prefer, they can design their own. Many departments are first-rate, including sociology, mathematics, and physics, as are the poets, scholars, and award-winning researchers who comprise Berkeley's faculty. Access to one of the foremost university libraries enriches studies. There are 23 specialized libraries on campus and distinguished museums of anthropology, paleontology, and science."

ADMISSIONS

Admissions Rating	91
% of applicants accepted	40
% of acceptees attending	40

FRESHMAN PROFILE

Average verbal SAT	640
Average math SAT	650
Average ACT	NR
Average TOEFL	550
Graduated top 20% of class	NR
Graduated top 40% of class	NR
Graduated top 60% of class	NR
Average HS GPA or Avg.	3.8

DEADLINES

Early decision	11/30
Regular admission	NR
Regular notification	3/15
Non-fall registration	yes

APPLICANTS ALSO LOOK AT

AND OFTEN PREFER
Stanford

AND SOMETIMES PREFER
UCLA
UC-San Diego
UC-Santa Barbara
UC-Santa Cruz

AND RARELY PREFER
UC-Davis
Occidental

FINANCIAL FACTS

Financial Aid Rating	73
In-state tuition	$4,232
Out-of-state tuition	$7,699
Room & board	$6,466
Estimated book expense	$675
% frosh receiving aid	73
% undergrads receiving aid	61
% aid is need-based	97
% frosh w/ grant (avg)	52 ($5,529)
% frosh w/ loan (avg)	51 ($2,100)
% UGs w/ job (avg)	29 ($2,672)
Off-campus job outlook	excellent

UNIVERSITY OF CALIFORNIA-DAVIS

Davis, CA 95616-8678   Admissions: 916-752-8111   Fax: 916-752-6363

CAMPUS LIFE

Quality of Life Rating	**82**
Type of school	public
Affiliation	none
Environment	suburban

STUDENTS

FT undergrad enrollment	17,596
% male/female	48/52
% from out of state	2
% live on campus	21
% spend weekend on campus	NR
% transfers	35
% from public high school	85
% in (# of) fraternities	10 (29)
% in (# of) sororities	9 (19)
% African-American	3
% Asian	31
% Caucasian	47
% Hispanic	11
% international	1
# of countries represented	33

WHAT'S HOT
campus food
intramural sports
library
student publications
town-gown relations

WHAT'S NOT
cigarettes
student government
theater
registration is a pain
music associations

ACADEMICS

Academic Rating	**77**
Profs Interesting Rating	67
Profs Accessible Rating	71
Calendar	quarter
Student/teacher ratio	19:1
% profs tenured	98
Hours of study per day	2.88

MOST POPULAR MAJORS
psychology
biological sciences
agricultural/managerial econ.

% GRADS WHO PURSUE...
Law 4, Med 5, MBA 2, MA 16

STUDENTS SPEAK OUT

Life
"The size of Davis can be fairly intimidating [to entering students], but with time it seems to shrink and become more understandable." UC-Davis is big—a bicycle is a help—while the town of Davis is small. A "very relaxed atmosphere in a bike-friendly town," is the majority opinion with a student body that is generally very satisfied with its school. But there can be a dark side to Davis: "For fun I leave. Davis is a rural community in the middle of dullsville." If you like life fast and furious once in awhile, Sacramento is your nearest urban oasis, otherwise, get used to spending time on a campus judged beautiful and safe by its students. UC-Davis also sports comfortable dorms, good dorm food, and decent health facilities. Alcohol and drug policies are on the strict side, which might be a problem at times with drinking and pot rated as very popular. Frats are well attended. One reason may be that "there aren't many organizations or clubs to join." Let's hope this computer science major can't be trusted when he says, "When [we] are on the verge of insanity, we listen to 'Mr. Tambourine Man' by William Shatner." That would just not be a good sign.

Academics
"I like classes and think that they are generally taught well, "says one student, "but I believe the problem is with labs and discussion." While students are for the most part happy with their professors ("Excellent professors—very devoted to students") they do have consistent problems with the school's large discussion sections. TA's also teach a decent number of these classes, something that does not sit well with most UC-Davis undergrads. "Most of the time TAs don't know what they are talking about," says one disgruntled sophomore. Getting into the classes you want as a freshman is also often a problem, but as you progress, it gets easier. Dealing with the UC-Davis bureaucracy can be frustrating. Says a senior, "I stood in line for 3-4 hours for financial aid during the fall quarter the last two years only to be sent somewhere else. I hate the system." Indeed, as with most large universities, "help is there, but hard to find." The school's library and computer systems both received stellar marks from students. Adds one, "Davis is on the cutting edge of all technological advancements."

Student Body
"Since Davis is so big, any comment would be a huge generalization." This cogent comment by a senior sums up perfectly the varied responses students gave about themselves. Nobody agreed about anything (except one topic that we'll discuss later). Here are a few of the conflicting comments: "Students are friendly and nice—not uptight"; "Most are socially maladjusted dorks, lots of people who really know how to study"; "Most resort to heavy drinking on weekends"; "Students at UC-Davis are very motivated and very tenacious"; "Students are very down to earth and academic but also athletic." See! Davis is obviously big enough for a diversity of students and opinions. The only thing students seem to agree on is that there is an appalling lack of interaction among people with different skin colors. Observes a white female, "For a school that supports ethnic diversity I find it ironic that most races only interact with people of their own race." Actual discrimination on the basis of race, sex, or sexual preference is also a concern with some, but not most, UC-Davis undergrads. Most students are sexually active, few are religious. At Davis, there are plenty of niches to choose from; just don't look for the school to be one big happy family.

ADMISSIONS

The admissions committee considers (in descending order of importance): HS record, test scores, essay, recommendations. *Also considered (in descending order of importance):* special talents, extracurriculars, personality. Either the SAT or ACT is required. Admissions process is need-blind. *High school units required/recommended:* 15 total units are required; 4 English required, 3 math required, 2 science required, 2 foreign language required. Minimum 3.30 GPA required of in-state applicants; 2.82-3.29 GPA requires specific SAT I or ACT scores. Minimum 3.4 GPA required of out-of-state applicants. Applicants with minimum combined SAT I score of 1300 (composite ACT score of 31) and minimum combined SAT II scores of 1650 (in-state) or 1730 (out-of-state) with no score below 500 on any one test, are eligible on the basis of test scores alone. TOEFL is required of all international students. *The admissions office says:* "Residents must have either a 3.3 GPA or do well on a standardized test. Non-residents must earn a 3.4 average (the eligibility index applies to residents only). Any student who fails to meet the academic requirements may gain admission on the basis of test scores alone if (1) his/her SAT is 1300 or higher (ACT composite: 31 or higher), and (2) his/her combined SAT II Subject Test scores exceed a minimum score (1760 for residents, 1400 for non-residents), and none is lower than 530."

The Inside Word

The State of California's plan to discontinue affirmative action in the UC admission process has created much uncertainty regarding the future of candidate selection in the system. A higher percentage of students are admitted to Davis than to Berkeley or UCLA, but don't forget that the UC system in general is geared toward the best and brightest of California's high school students.

FINANCIAL AID

Students should submit: FAFSA, state aid form (due March 2). The Princeton Review suggests that all financial aid forms be submitted as soon as possible after January 1. *The following grants/scholarships are offered:* Pell, SEOG, academic merit, the school's own scholarships, the school's own grants, state grants, private scholarships, private grants, ROTC. *Students borrow from the following loan programs:* Stafford, Perkins, PLUS, the school's own loan fund, health professions loans. College Work-Study Program is available. Institutional employment is available. Freshmen are discouraged from working.

FROM THE ADMISSIONS OFFICE

"The quality of undergraduate instruction is a prime concern of the faculty, students, and administration at Davis. Creative teaching and academic innovation are encouraged by several programs, including the Distinguished Teaching Awards (for which students can nominate outstanding faculty members), and a $25,000 prize for undergraduate teaching and scholarly achievement (believed to be among the largest of its kind in the nation). Student Viewpoint, a student-written and published evaluation of classes and instructors, is compiled each year from course questionnaires completed by students."

ADMISSIONS

Admissions Rating	76
% of applicants accepted	71
% of acceptees attending	26

FRESHMAN PROFILE

Average verbal SAT	560
Average math SAT	590
Average ACT	24
Average TOEFL	500
Graduated top 20% of class	100
Graduated top 40% of class	NR
Graduated top 60% of class	NR
Average HS GPA or Avg.	3.7

DEADLINES

Early decision	11/30
Regular admission	NR
Regular notification	3/15
Non-fall registration	yes

APPLICANTS ALSO LOOK AT

AND OFTEN PREFER

UC-Berkeley
UCLA

AND SOMETIMES PREFER

UC-Santa Barbara
UC-Santa Cruz
U. Washington

AND RARELY PREFER

UC-San Diego
UC-Irvine
UC-Riverside

FINANCIAL FACTS

Financial Aid Rating	75
In-state tuition	$4,332
Out-of-state tuition	$7,698
Room & board	$5,520
Estimated book expense	$858
% frosh receiving aid	NR
% undergrads receiving aid	52
% aid is need-based	80
% frosh w/ grant (avg)	NR
% frosh w/ loan (avg)	NR
% UGs w/ job (avg)	NR
Off-campus job outlook	good

UNIVERSITY OF CALIFORNIA-IRVINE

IRVINE, CA 92717

ADMISSIONS: 714-824-6703

CAMPUS LIFE

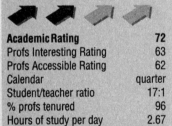

Quality of Life Rating	77
Type of school	public
Affiliation	none
Environment	suburban

STUDENTS

FT undergrad enrollment	13,541
% male/female	47/53
% from out of state	4
% live on campus	29
% spend weekend on campus	NR
% transfers	30
% from public high school	87
% in (# of) fraternities	(17)
% in (# of) sororities	(12)
% African-American	2
% Asian	46
% Caucasian	32
% Hispanic	12
% international	NR
# of countries represented	NR

WHAT'S HOT
religion
campus food
ethnic diversity on campus
Greeks
political activism

WHAT'S NOT
hard liquor
beer
intercollegiate sports
Irvine
inefficient administration

ACADEMICS

Academic Rating	72
Profs Interesting Rating	63
Profs Accessible Rating	62
Calendar	quarter
Student/teacher ratio	17:1
% profs tenured	96
Hours of study per day	2.67

MOST POPULAR MAJORS
biological sciences
economics

STUDENTS SPEAK OUT

Life

Because well over half of UC-Irvine students commute, social life here sucks. "To meet people one must take an active role, joining a club or going Greek," says one student. Says another, "There is little school spirit or unity unless you're in a frat or sorority." About fifteen percent of UCI students go Greek, but frats and sororities don't have their own houses, so even this "essential" part of UCI social life is limited in what it can contribute. "School functions are numerous," reports one student, but few respondents voice an enthusiasm for them. If suburban diversions excite you, there's Irvine ("clean, safe, and not too exciting"). The beach is only five miles from campus, a fact that lead one student to assert that UCI is "a great school if you want to ride some tasty waves and catch a hair-raising buzz." Nighttime parties by the ocean are not uncommon. Excellent skiing is within an hour's drive, as is the sprawling city of Los Angeles.

Academics

The social scene here is so dead that even when students are discussing academics, they feel compelled to mention it: "excellent education, terrible social life" is a comment UCI undergrads echo over and over again. The school is best known for its biology department—"very competitive and challenging, but the rewards are great if you're a survivor," says one bio major. The results are impressive: the school sends an astonishing seventeen percent of its graduates on to medical school. The ecological sciences department is also popular; science students in general note excellent facilities and numerous opportunities to participate in research among UCI's chief advantages. Outside the sciences, academics are less challenging: students here study an average of two hours, forty minutes a day, which is pretty low. Students also complain about inaccessible profs—a common complaint at research-oriented universities like UCI—and large classes. Of those departments outside the sciences, economics, English, and political science are the strongest. All UCI students must complete "breadth requirements," meaning that they must take three courses each in the natural sciences, social sciences, and humanities to graduate. Honors programs are available in most areas of study (although, curiously, not in the natural sciences).

Student Body

Nearly half of UCI's students are Asian, and about a third are white, providing for a uniquely diverse student body. Unfortunately, since there's little in the way of a social scene, interaction is minimal. Still, people do get along here. Ethnic animosity is reportedly "not a problem". Irvine students are pretty conservative, but mostly apathetic; they don't care about politics. The vast majority of students are from California, with many coming from ritzy Orange County.

FINANCIAL AID: 714-824-6261

WEB SITE: HTTP://PEG.CWIS.UCI.EDU/

ADMISSIONS

The admissions committee considers (in descending order of importance): HS record, test scores, essay, class rank, recommendations. *Also considered (in descending order of importance):* extracurriculars, special talents. Either the SAT or ACT is required. *High school units required/recommended:* 16 total units are required; 4 English required, 3 math required, 1 science required, 3 science recommended, 2 foreign language required, 3 foreign language recommended, 2 history required. Applicants with minimum 3.3 GPA are eligible regardless of test scores. Applicants with GPA below 3.3 but above 2.81 may be considered if they achieve composite or combined test score specified on the Eligibility Index. *Special Requirements:* TOEFL is required of all international students. Civil engineering, economics, electrical engineering, mechanical engineering, and psychology program applicants must meet higher standards. *The admissions office says:* "Some majors have limited enrollments and place prerequisites on admission. Also, be aware of the filing periods for applications: Nov. 1-30, fall quarter; July 1-31, winter quarter; Oct. 1-31, spring quarter."

The Inside Word

The State of California's plan to discontinue affirmative action in the UC admission process has created much uncertainty regarding the future of candidate selection in the system. Few out-of-state students consider Irvine, which lessens the competition among those applicants who are well-qualified.

FINANCIAL AID

Students should submit: FAFSA, a copy of parents' most recent income tax filing. The Princeton Review suggests that all financial aid forms be submitted as soon as possible after January 1. *The following grants/scholarships are offered:* Pell, SEOG, academic merit, athletic, the school's own scholarships, the school's own grants, state scholarships, state grants, private scholarships, ROTC, foreign aid. *Students borrow from the following loan programs:* Stafford, unsubsidized Stafford, Perkins, PLUS, the school's own loan fund, health professions loans. College Work-Study Program is available. Institutional employment is available.

FROM THE ADMISSIONS OFFICE

"UCI offers programs designed to provide students with a foundation on which to continue developing their intellectual, aesthetic, and moral capacity. The programs and curricula are based on the belief that a student's collective university experience should provide understanding and insight, which are the bases for an intellectual identity and lifelong learning. An important aspect of the educational approach at UCI is the emphasis placed on student involvement in independent study, research, and the creative process as a complement to classroom study. Independent research in laboratories, field study, involvement in writing workshops, and participation in fine arts productions are normal elements of the UCI experience."

ADMISSIONS

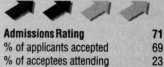

Admissions Rating	71
% of applicants accepted	69
% of acceptees attending	23

FRESHMAN PROFILE

Average verbal SAT	530
Average math SAT	580
Average ACT	NR
Average TOEFL	550
Graduated top 20% of class	NR
Graduated top 40% of class	NR
Graduated top 60% of class	NR
Average HS GPA or Avg.	NR

DEADLINES

Early decision	11/1
Regular admission	11/30
Regular notification	3/15
Non-fall registration	yes

APPLICANTS ALSO LOOK AT

AND OFTEN PREFER

UC-Berkeley
UC-Davis
UCLA
UC-Riverside
Stanford

AND SOMETIMES PREFER

USC
UC-San Diego
UC-Santa Cruz
UC-Santa Barbara

FINANCIAL FACTS

Financial Aid Rating	78
In-state tuition	$4,300
Out-of-state tuition	$7,699
Room & board	$5,824
Estimated book expense	$600

% frosh receiving aid	NR
% undergrads receiving aid	49
% aid is need-based	84
% frosh w/ grant (avg)	NR
% frosh w/ loan (avg)	NR
% UGs w/ job (avg)	10 ($5,500)
Off-campus job outlook	excellent

UNIVERSITY OF CALIFORNIA-LOS ANGELES

405 HILGARD AVENUE, LOS ANGELES, CA 90024   ADMISSIONS: 310-825-3101   FAX: 310-206-1206

CAMPUS LIFE

Quality of Life Rating	**78**
Type of school	public
Affiliation	none
Environment	metropolis

STUDENTS

FT undergrad enrollment	23,619
% male/female	50/50
% from out of state	3
% live on campus	24
% spend weekend on campus	NR
% transfers	35
% from public high school	85
% in (# of) fraternities	13 (34)
% in (# of) sororities	12 (19)
% African-American	6
% Asian	30
% Caucasian	42
% Hispanic	14
% international	NR
# of countries represented	65

WHAT'S HOT
political activism
religion
campus food
town-gown relations
music associations

WHAT'S NOT
beer
campus difficult to get around
hard liquor
cigarettes
sex

ACADEMICS

Academic Rating	**82**
Profs Interesting Rating	61
Profs Accessible Rating	60
Calendar	quarter
Student/teacher ratio	17:1
% profs tenured	100
Hours of study per day	2.88

MOST POPULAR MAJORS
psychology
economics
biology

% GRADS WHO PURSUE...
Law 11, Med 6, MBA 4, MA 16

STUDENTS SPEAK OUT

Life

"Talk about diversity—Los Angeles is the epitome of a diverse culture," writes one student. All that diversity is there for the taking by UCLA students, provided they have cars: public transportation, says one succinct student, "sucks." L.A. is a major city with much in the way of night life and "wonderful weather," and not surprisingly, students give their location a big thumbs-up. Those who stay on campus find it "a great place to get involved. Because of its size, almost anyone can find a particular niche to fit into." Agrees another, "UCLA's size helps it offer a huge variety of extracurricular activities. There's always something to do here." There is an active Greek scene and it's pretty easy to find parties any night of the week, but, given the enormity of the school, it's also easy to avoid them if you want. Students can choose from hundreds of clubs and community service organizations. Intercollegiate sports, especially football and basketball, are huge; "I bleed blue and gold," writes one student, expressing a popular sentiment.

Academics

Like most large universities, UCLA offers a lot to those who are "capable of taking advantage of things. Opportunities to learn, do research, and have fun are present in great quantity." Students agree that UCLA is best for the go-getter: Writes one, "To gain the most from this place, one must take advantage of the plethora of activities (internships, research with professors, sororities and fraternities, community service programs...)." If you fit the bill, however, UCLA offers a veritable universe of quality programs at cut-rate prices. Popular and reportedly excellent departments include economics, psychology, sociology, and political science/government. Premed-related hard sciences, liberal arts, and performing and creative arts (the film/television programs are among the nation's best) are also substantial. Classes can be large, but complaints about classrooms the size of shopping malls and inaccessible profs are rare for a school of this size: More characteristic is the comment, "Occasionally classes are hard to get into, but the professors get the information across and classes aren't inhibited by their large sizes." Complaints about bureaucratic red tape are more common. Says one student, "I feel like a hapless microbe swimming through a quagmire of numbers, unknown faces, and bureaucracy." The situation is exacerbated by the fact that "like all universities, UCLA is experiencing financially difficult times."

Student Body

As one student explains, "UCLA is the great melting pot of the West!" Less than half of UCLA's student body is white. About a third are Asian; Hispanics make up the next largest minority group, and black students number more than 1,500. Students report a moderately well-blended and copacetic community, although several complained that self-imposed racial segregation is too common. The political mainstream is left-of-center, but with 24,000-plus students, every political view is well represented. More than nine tenths of the students are from California.

ADMISSIONS

The admissions committee considers (in descending order of importance): HS record, test scores, essay, recommendations. *Also considered (in descending order of importance):* geographical distribution, special talents, extracurriculars. Either the SAT or ACT is required. *High school units required/recommended:* 15 total units are required; 4 English required, 3 math required, 4 math recommended, 2 science required, 3 science recommended, 2 foreign language required, 3 foreign language recommended. Minimum 2.82 GPA required of in-state applicants; minimum 3.4 GPA required of out-of-state applicants. In-state applicants with minimum 3.3 GPA are eligible regardless of test scores; in-state applicants with minimum combined SAT I score of 1100 (composite ACT score of 27) and minimum combined SAT II score of 1650 (with minimum score of 500 on any one test) are eligible on the basis of test scores alone. *Special Requirements:* A portfolio is required for art program applicants. An audition is required for music program applicants. Additional requirements for applicants to School of the Arts and School of Theatre, Film, and Television. *The admissions office says:* "Residents must either have a 3.3 GPA or do well on a standardized test. Non-residents must have taken the same courses but must earn a 3.4 average (the eligibility index applies to residents only). Any student who fails to meet the academic requirements may gain admission on the basis of test scores alone if (1) his/her combined SAT is 1300 or higher (ACT composite: 31 or higher), and (2) his/her combined SAT II scores exceed a minimum score (1650 for residents, 1730 for nonresidents), and none is lower than 500."

The Inside Word

The State of California's plan to discontinue affirmative action in the UC admission process has created much uncertainty regarding the future of candidate selection in the system. UCLA is the second most selective university in the UC system. Out-of-state applicants are subject to the same requirements as at Berkeley, but will find their prospects a little better because UCLA accepts a larger freshman class.

FINANCIAL AID

Students should submit: FAFSA. The Princeton Review suggests that all financial aid forms be submitted as soon as possible after January 1. *The following grants/ scholarships are offered:* Pell, SEOG, academic merit, athletic, the school's own scholarships, the school's own grants, state scholarships, state grants, private scholarships, private grants, federal nursing scholarship, ROTC. *Students borrow from the following loan programs:* Stafford, unsubsidized Stafford, Perkins, PLUS, the school's own loan fund, state loans, federal nursing loans, health professions loans, private loans. Applicants will be notified of awards beginning April 1. College Work-Study Program is available. Institutional employment is available.

FROM THE ADMISSIONS OFFICE

"UCLA has earned a worldwide reputation for the excellence of its academic programs, the achievements of its students and faculty, and the beauty of its campus. Acclaimed both as a major public university and a major research university, UCLA is at once distinguished and dynamic, academically rigorous and responsive. UCLA is generally considered among the nation's top half-dozen universities and one of the two leading public university campuses. With some 35,000 students and more than 18,000 faculty and staff, UCLA has no equal in the ethnic and cultural diversity of its student body, its faculty and staff, and its curricular and extracurricular offerings."

ADMISSIONS

Admissions Rating	89
% of applicants accepted	50
% of acceptees attending	35

FRESHMAN PROFILE

Average verbal SAT	590
Average math SAT	610
Average ACT	NR
Average TOEFL	NR
Graduated top 20% of class	100
Graduated top 40% of class	100
Graduated top 60% of class	100
Average HS GPA or Avg.	3.9

DEADLINES

Early decision	11/30
Regular admission	NR
Regular notification	3/15
Non-fall registration	no

APPLICANTS ALSO LOOK AT

AND OFTEN PREFER
UC-Berkeley

AND SOMETIMES PREFER
UC-San Diego

AND RARELY PREFER
UC-Santa Barbara
UC-Irvine
UC-Davis
UC-Riverside
UC-Santa Cruz

FINANCIAL FACTS

Financial Aid Rating	73
In-state tuition	$3,893
Out-of-state tuition	$7,699
Room & board	$5,859
Estimated book expense	$874
% frosh receiving aid	70
% undergrads receiving aid	84
% aid is need-based	75
% frosh w/ grant (avg)	40 ($5,000)
% frosh w/ loan (avg)	72 ($4,000)
% UGs w/ job (avg)	75 ($5,500)
Off-campus job outlook	good

UNIVERSITY OF CALIFORNIA-RIVERSIDE

900 UNIVERSITY AVENUE, RIVERSIDE, CA 92521   ADMISSIONS: 909-787-3411   FAX: 909-787-7368

CAMPUS LIFE

Quality of Life Rating	**69**
Type of school	public
Affiliation	none
Environment	city

STUDENTS

FT undergrad enrollment	7,103
% male/female	47/53
% from out of state	1
% live on campus	31
% spend weekend on campus	NR
% transfers	33
% from public high school	90
% in (# of) fraternities	12 (14)
% in (# of) sororities	13 (12)
% African-American	5
% Asian	39
% Caucasian	36
% Hispanic	19
% international	4
# of countries represented	51

WHAT'S HOT
old-fashioned dating
health facilities
religion
ethnic diversity on campus
library

WHAT'S NOT
dorms
hard liquor
student government
beer

ACADEMICS

Academic Rating	**74**
Profs Interesting Rating	63
Profs Accessible Rating	64
Calendar	quarter
Student/teacher ratio	16:1
% profs PhD/tenured	95/98
Hours of study per day	2.97

MOST POPULAR MAJORS
business administration
biology
psychology

STUDENTS SPEAK OUT

Life

There's not a whole lot to do in Riverside, but students at UC-Riverside say the revitalization of the area that is underway has spruced up the downtown area considerably. On campus, the "musical scene is hot," and the student program board regularly draws big-name bands. In addition, "Comedy shows and the Coffee House series are becoming trendy." Of course, Riverside students can always climb in their cars and drive the hour or so it takes to get to Los Angeles and the beaches to the west, or the mountains to the east. Dormitory and frat parties are common (about fifteen percent of the students go Greek), and UCR students seem to enjoy themselves without getting loaded: alcohol consumption here is very low, particularly for a secular school. Dorm space accommodates only about one-third of Riverside's undergrads, but dorm life is "absolutely a plus" for the campus. Cheap off-campus housing is reportedly easy to come by, and undergrads with families find the subsidized housing "fantastic." The sports program has some standout teams; most noteworthy are the men's and women's karate teams, which have won six national championships, and the nationally ranked men's baseball team.

Academics

Probably because of its location, UC-Riverside is often a second choice for students who wish to attend a University of California campus. Many students cite the fact that they did not get into UCLA as their reason for attending UCR. Still, Riverside has a lot to offer, and in certain respects, even surpasses its more famous sister campuses. It is the smallest of the UC campuses—much smaller than all others except Santa Cruz. Yet it is large enough to offer a broad range of course choices and several highly regarded departments, especially in the sciences. The prestigious biomedical program puts selected students on track for a degree from UCLA medical school (in one year less than it would take otherwise). Liberal arts programs have a solid reputation, as does business/management. Like most UC schools, Riverside is a research center, but since Riverside's student body is relatively small, its undergraduates often have the chance to participate in their professors' research projects. Says one Riverside undergrad, "Our school doesn't have the resources of UCLA, its size, or prestige. But you learn well here." Professors are well-liked. One creative writing major extols the "Pulitzer Prize-nominated faculty" who are "charismatic, insightful, and approachable."

Student Body

The average Riverside student is truly the average college student: of the sixty-seven questions we ask every student we survey, UCR students' responses are close to the Best 310's average on sixty-one of them. Yet the UCR campus is by no means homogeneous. One student calls campus diversity "average for SoCal," which means that there's a pretty diverse student body, including sizable Asian and Hispanic populations. "As a Latino, I have had incredible opportunities to excel and learn in an environment rich with different perspectives," one senior tells us.

University of California-Riverside

ADMISSIONS

The admissions committee considers (in descending order of importance): HS record, test scores, class rank, essay, recommendations. *Also considered (in descending order of importance):* extracurriculars, special talents, geographical distribution. Either the SAT or ACT is required. Admissions process is need-blind. *High school units required/recommended:* 15 total units are required; 4 English required, 3 math required, 2 science required, 2 foreign language required, 2 history required. Minimum 3.4 GPA required of out-of-state applicants. In-state applicants with minimum 3.3 GPA are eligible regardless of test scores. Applicants with minimum combined SAT I score of 1300 (composite ACT score of 31) and minimum combined SAT II scores of 1650 (in-state) or 1730 (out-of-state), with no score below 500 on any one test, are eligible on the basis of test scores alone. TOEFL is required of all international students. *The admissions office says:* "Supplemental criteria for evaluation include (1) talents and experiences; (2) hardship circumstances; (3) cultural, ethnic, & geographic factors to ensure diversity."

The Inside Word

The State of California's plan to discontinue affirmative action in the UC admission process has created much uncertainty regarding the future of candidate selection in the system. Despite this, Riverside's admit rate is sufficiently high enough to mean smooth sailing for those who suit the formulas well.

FINANCIAL AID

Students should submit: FAFSA. The Princeton Review suggests that all financial aid forms be submitted as soon as possible after January 1. *The following grants/scholarships are offered:* Pell, SEOG, academic merit, athletic, the school's own scholarships, the school's own grants, state scholarships, state grants, private scholarships, private grants, ROTC. *Students borrow from the following loan programs:* Stafford, Perkins, PLUS, the school's own loan fund, private loans. Applicants will be notified of awards beginning May 1. College Work-Study Program is available. Institutional employment is available. Freshmen are discouraged from working.

FROM THE ADMISSIONS OFFICE

"The University of California-Riverside offers the quality, rigor, and facilities of a major research institution, while still assuring its undergraduates personal attention and a sense of community. Academic programs, teaching, advising, and student services all reflect the supportive attitude that characterizes the campus. Among the exceptional opportunities are the accelerated biomedical sciences program, unique in the UC system, in which students can earn both the BS and MD degrees in seven years instead of eight; the University Honors Program; a BS degree in business administration; and the only bachelor's degree in creative writing in the UC system. The College of Engineering offers degrees in chemical, electrical, and environmental engineering, and computer science."

ADMISSIONS

Admissions Rating	73
% of applicants accepted	78
% of acceptees attending	21

FRESHMAN PROFILE

Average verbal SAT	530
Average math SAT	560
Average ACT	22
Average TOEFL	550
Graduated top 20% of class	95
Graduated top 40% of class	100
Graduated top 60% of class	100
Average HS GPA or Avg.	3.6

DEADLINES

Early decision	11/30
Regular admission	NR
Regular notification	3/31
Non-fall registration	yes

APPLICANTS ALSO LOOK AT

AND OFTEN PREFER

UC-Berkeley
UCLA
UC-Davis

AND SOMETIMES PREFER

UC-Irvine
California Poly. St.
Claremont Coll.-Pomona
UC-Santa Barbara
UC-Santa Cruz

AND RARELY PREFER

U. San Diego
USC

FINANCIAL FACTS

Financial Aid Rating	74
In-state tuition	$4,092
Out-of-state tuition	$8,394
Room & board	$5,705
Estimated book expense	$880
% frosh receiving aid	60
% undergrads receiving aid	60
% aid is need-based	NR
% frosh w/ grant (avg)	NR ($5,000)
% frosh w/ loan (avg)	50 ($2,625)
% UGs w/ job (avg)	20
Off-campus job outlook	good

UNIVERSITY OF CALIFORNIA-SAN DIEGO

9500 GILMAN DRIVE, LA JOLLA, CA 92093   ADMISSIONS: 619-534-4831   FAX: 619-534-5723

CAMPUS LIFE

Quality of Life Rating	**83**
Type of school	public
Affiliation	none
Environment	metropolis

STUDENTS

FT undergrad enrollment	11,248
% male/female	38/62
% from out of state	3
% live on campus	29
% spend weekend on campus	NR
% transfers	25
% from public high school	NR
% in (# of) fraternities	12 (14)
% in (# of) sororities	12 (8)
% African-American	3
% Asian	28
% Caucasian	47
% Hispanic	12
% international	1
# of countries represented	70

WHAT'S HOT
intramural sports
health facilities
dorms
campus food
off-campus food

WHAT'S NOT
sex
theater
cigarettes
student government
campus difficult to get around

ACADEMICS

Academic Rating	**80**
Profs Interesting Rating	65
Profs Accessible Rating	65
Calendar	quarter
Student/teacher ratio	19:1
% profs PhD/tenured	94/97
Hours of study per day	3.01

MOST POPULAR MAJORS
general biology
psychology
biochemistry/cell biology

% GRADS WHO PURSUE...
Law 5, Med 6, MBA 2, MA 9

STUDENTS SPEAK OUT

Life

There is no agreement among students on the quality of social life at UC-San Diego. On the one hand are students like the one who tells us that "there are many social opportunities for the outgoing student." On the other hand are those who tell us, "Don't go to UCSD if you're looking for a good time. It's Nerdville!" Most would agree with the student who reports, "Here, academics are emphasized more than anything else, although extracurricular activities are a must for anyone who does not want to be classified as a deadbeat or a study bum. Overall, the location is beautiful and the weather is a great addition to our learning environment." The Greek system is "growing rapidly" and is hoping to provide housing in the near future. On-campus social life is slow, partly because the school's "dry campus" policy is aggressively enforced by campus security, but intramural sports are very popular. While few would agree with the enthusiastic sophomore who writes "San Diego is by far the greatest city in the U.S.," the area is safe, the campus is great (and near the beach), and the weather is amazing.

Academics

Because the huge University of California-San Diego is divided into five smaller colleges (all five offer a range of liberal arts and science courses; they differ mostly in terms of requirements), students here feel they get the benefits of attending both a small college and a large university. Says one, "Because of the separate colleges, one is able to be in small surroundings and also, when desired, a larger university setting. It's easy to meet people in one's smaller college, and it's also a lot more fun in the midst of the larger college atmosphere." Warns another student, "Make sure that you attend the college that best fits your career goals, otherwise you'll have to stick around trying to finish requirements you don't need for your major." UCSD is a world-class research center with all the benefits and drawbacks that implies. On the upside, academics are tough but thorough, and professors are often hard at work on some major medical, science, or engineering project. The downside is that some of these professors are reportedly lousy teachers, while others' interests lie in advanced research, not in basic undergraduate subject matter. Hard sciences, math, and engineering dominate the academic scene, but there are also plenty of social science and art students. Reports one undergrad, "It's a school for the more serious-minded student who has long-term goals in mind."

Student Body

UCSD has a large minority population made up mostly of Asian and Latino students. Students here are serious; says one, "I was surprised how studious the school environment is. In general I would say it is very mellow, low-key, and casual with a 'whatever' attitude. People need to loosen up and have more fun." Another tells us that "if you are really into computers, you'll fit in." Commenting on the looks of UCSD women, one man reports, "There's a saying I've heard around: Nine out of ten girls in California look good—the tenth goes to UCSD." A female student counters: "Although you've probably seen the baseball and water polo teams in YM magazine, not one quarter of the guys come close to that level of desirability."

FINANCIAL AID: 619-534-4480   WEB SITE: HTTP://WWW.UCSD.EDU/

ADMISSIONS

The admissions committee considers (in descending order of importance): HS record, test scores, essay, class rank, recommendations. *Also considered (in descending order of importance):* extracurriculars, special talents. Either the SAT or ACT is required. *High school units required/recommended:* 15 total units are required; 4 English required, 3 math required, 4 math recommended, 2 science required, 2 foreign language required, 3 foreign language recommended, 2 history required. Minimum 3.4 GPA required of out-of-state applicants. In-state applicants with minimum 3.3 GPA are eligible regardless of test scores. Applicants with minimum combined SAT I score of 1100 (composite ACT score of 27) and minimum combined SAT II scores of 1650 (in-state) or 1730 (out-of-state), with no score below 500 on any one test, are eligible on the basis of test scores alone. TOEFL is required of all international students. *The admissions office says:* "Residents must either have a 3.3 GPA or do well on a standardized test. Non-residents must have taken the same courses but must earn a 3.4 average (the eligibility index applies to residents only). Any student who fails to meet the academic requirements may gain admission on the basis of test scores alone if (1) his/her combined SAT I is 1300 or higher (ACT composite: 31 or higher), and (2) his/her combined SAT II scores exceed a minimum score (1650 for residents, 1730 for non-residents), and none is lower than 500."

The Inside Word

The State of California's plan to discontinue affirmative action in the UC admission process has created much uncertainty regarding the future of candidate selection in the system. Increased national awareness and its reputation for excellence in the marine sciences is making UCSD more and more popular among high school seniors. Even greater selectivity cannot be far behind.

FINANCIAL AID

Students should submit: FAFSA, state aid form. The Princeton Review suggests that all financial aid forms be submitted as soon as possible after January 1. *The following grants/scholarships are offered:* Pell, SEOG, academic merit, the school's own scholarships, the school's own grants, state scholarships, state grants, private scholarships. *Students borrow from the following loan programs:* Stafford, unsubsidized Stafford, Perkins, PLUS, the school's own loan fund. Applicants will be notified of awards beginning in March. College Work-Study Program is available. Institutional employment is available.

FROM THE ADMISSIONS OFFICE

"UCSD is recognized for the exceptional quality of its academic programs. In 1986, the Ford Foundation cited UCSD as one of the six top public institutions in the country based upon the strength and balance of our academic programs, the proportions of undergraduates who go on to earn Ph.D.s, and the ethnic diversity of the student body. One feature that sets UCSD apart from most universities in the United States is that its family of five colleges—Revelle, Muir, Third, Warren, and Fifth—are modeled on the Cambridge and Oxford systems found in Great Britain. This arrangement allows our students to enjoy the benefits of a large university without the disadvantages of size found in many of today's mega-universities. Each college offers a distinctive curriculum that allows our students to choose an academic program that best suits their individual interests and educational plans. At UCSD, students have a choice about what they learn, and how they learn."

ADMISSIONS

Admissions Rating	83
% of applicants accepted	64
% of acceptees attending	22

FRESHMAN PROFILE

Average verbal SAT	590
Average math SAT	600
Average ACT	NR
Average TOEFL	550
Graduated top 20% of class	NR
Graduated top 40% of class	NR
Graduated top 60% of class	NR
Average HS GPA or Avg.	3.8

DEADLINES

Early decision	NR
Regular admission	11/30
Regular notification	3/15
Non-fall registration	no

APPLICANTS ALSO LOOK AT

AND OFTEN PREFER

Stanford
UC-Berkeley
UCLA

AND SOMETIMES PREFER

UC-Davis

AND RARELY PREFER

UC-Riverside
UC-Irvine
UC-Santa Barbara
UC-Santa Cruz

FINANCIAL FACTS

Financial Aid Rating	73
In-state tuition	$4,620
Out-of-state tuition	$13,081
Room & board	$6,557
Estimated book expense	$612
% frosh receiving aid	50
% undergrads receiving aid	46
% aid is need-based	NR
% frosh w/ grant (avg)	45 ($5,000)
% frosh w/ loan (avg)	35 ($2,000)
% UGs w/ job (avg)	25 ($3,000)
Off-campus job outlook	excellent

UNIVERSITY OF CALIFORNIA-SANTA BARBARA

SANTA BARBARA, CA 93106

ADMISSIONS: 805-893-2485   FAX: 805-893-8779

CAMPUS LIFE

Quality of Life Rating 87
Type of school public
Affiliation none
Environment city

STUDENTS
FT undergrad enrollment 15,525
% male/female 48/52
% from out of state 4
% live on campus 22
% spend weekend on campus NR
% transfers 29
% from public high school 82
% in (# of) fraternities 13 (21)
% in (# of) sororities 13 (18)
% African-American 3
% Asian 16
% Caucasian 66
% Hispanic 12
% international 1
# of countries represented 48

WHAT'S HOT
drugs
political activism
student publications
hard liquor
intramural sports

WHAT'S NOT
students are cliquish
inefficient administration
lack of diversity on campus
religion
town-gown relations

ACADEMICS

Academic Rating 74
Profs Interesting Rating 63
Profs Accessible Rating 66
Calendar quarter
Student/teacher ratio 18:1
% profs PhD/tenured 100/100
Hours of study per day 2.85

MOST POPULAR MAJORS
business economics
sociology
English

% GRADS WHO PURSUE...
Law 15, Med 7, MBA 6, MA 17

STUDENTS SPEAK OUT
Life
The verdict is in: UCSB is a party school! Students here report that they drink more, do more drugs, and lust after each other more than students anywhere else. "It's easy to have too much fun and not enough school," says one student, although another reports that "UCSB offers a quiet atmosphere during the week when I need to study, but it turns into a raging party on the weekends when I need to let loose." It takes a good deal of self-restraint for a student to get through UCSB in four years. Not only are there parties, but also the beach—which is on campus—and the perennially amazing weather. Many students live off campus in notorious Isla Vista, accommodating to party animals but off-putting to those squeamish about nonstop partying (says one resident, it "gets really loud and old after about a month"). A typical student attitude: "UCSB would be a great place if you didn't have to study."

Academics
UC-Santa Barbara's academic reputation is not as well developed as its social reputation. As one student puts it, "Because of the amount of partying going on, the university's image is sometimes tarnished regarding the quality of education. Personally, I think this school balances academics and social life really well." Most students agree, although few who come here aren't previously aware of the school's reputation. UCSB is a large university that provides students the chance to pursue almost anything. Economics is the most popular choice, and the school "has many state-of-the-art facilities for science majors, especially physics, marine biology, engineering, and geology," reports one undergrad. Complaints focused on the quality of instruction—"UC schools are top-notch in research, but I must say the undergrad curriculum can be rather dry, due to the system's goal of research over teaching"—and the quarterly schedule of classes—"quarters go by way too fast for effectively studying the liberal arts," says one English major. As at many large universities, it can sometimes be a chore to get courses you need to graduate and to cut through bureaucratic red tape when you have to deal with administrators.

Student Body
"Warning: Everyone here is blonde," is how a UCSB student characterizes his classmates. Says another, students here are "not as stuffy as at UC-Davis nor is it as bizarre as at UC-Santa Cruz." Like most large schools, there are lots of subcommunities here, and the trick is finding the folks you fit in with. Despite the sizable minority population, groups of different ethnicity do not mix particularly well. "Outside of a pretty campus and an education, the community of Santa Barbara has nothing to offer African-Americans," complains one black student. Adds an Asian student, "This school is not ethnically diverse at all, but I'm getting used to it."

FINANCIAL AID: 805-893-2432   WEB SITE: HTTP://WWW.UCSB.EDU/

ADMISSIONS

The admissions committee considers (in descending order of importance): HS record, test scores, essay. *Also considered (in descending order of importance):* extracurriculars, special talents. Either the SAT or ACT is required. *High school units required/recommended:* 15 total units are required; 4 English required, 3 math required, 2 science required, 2 foreign language required, 1 social studies required, 1 history required. Electives should include 1 unit of visual/performing arts. Minimum 2.82 GPA required of in-state applicants; those with minimum combined SAT I score of 1300 (composite ACT score of 31) and combined SAT II score of 1650 (with minimum score of 500 on any one SAT II) are eligible on the basis of test score alone. Minimum 3.4 GPA required of out-of-state applicants; those with combined SAT I score of 1300 (composite ACT score of 31) and combined SAT II score of 1730 (with minimum score of 500 on any one SAT II) are eligible on the basis of test score alone. *Special Requirements:* A portfolio is required for art program applicants. An audition is required for music program applicants. TOEFL is required of all international students. Audition required of performing arts program applicants.

The Inside Word

The State of California's plan to discontinue affirmative action in the UC admission process has created much uncertainty regarding the future of candidate selection in the system. There should ultimately be little effect for most candidates at Santa Barbara—plug into the UC admissions formula and grab your board!

FINANCIAL AID

Students should submit: FAFSA (due March 2). The Princeton Review suggests that all financial aid forms be submitted as soon as possible after January 1. *The following grants/scholarships are offered:* Pell, SEOG, academic merit, athletic, the school's own scholarships, the school's own grants, state scholarships, state grants, private scholarships, private grants, ROTC, foreign aid. *Students borrow from the following loan programs:* Stafford, Perkins, PLUS, the school's own loan fund. Applicants will be notified of awards beginning May 15. College Work-Study Program is available. Institutional employment is available.

FROM THE ADMISSIONS OFFICE

"The University of California-Santa Barbara is a major research institution offering undergraduate and graduate education in the arts, humanities, sciences and technology, and social sciences. Large enough to have excellent facilities for study, research, and other creative activities, the campus is also small enough to foster close relationships among faculty and students. The faculty numbers more than 900. A member of the most distinguished system of public higher education in the nation, UC-Santa Barbara is committed equally to excellence in scholarship and instruction. Through the general education program, students acquire good grounding in the skills, perceptions, and methods of a variety of disciplines. In addition, because they study with a research faculty, they not only acquire basic skills and broad knowledge but also are exposed to the imagination, inventiveness, and intense concentration that scholars bring to their work."

ADMISSIONS

Admissions Rating	73
% of applicants accepted	83
% of acceptees attending	20

FRESHMAN PROFILE

Average verbal SAT	530
Average math SAT	560
Average ACT	NR
Average TOEFL	500
Graduated top 20% of class	100
Graduated top 40% of class	100
Graduated top 60% of class	100
Average HS GPA or Avg.	3.5

DEADLINES

Early decision	NR
Regular admission	11/30
Regular notification	3/15
Non-fall registration	yes

APPLICANTS ALSO LOOK AT

AND OFTEN PREFER

UC-Berkeley
UCLA

AND SOMETIMES PREFER

UC-Riverside
UC-Davis
UC-Santa Cruz
Pomona
Loyola Marymount

AND RARELY PREFER

U. Pacific

FINANCIAL FACTS

Financial Aid Rating	68
In-state tuition	$4,098
Out-of-state tuition	$7,699
Room & board	$5,900
Estimated book expense	$630
% frosh receiving aid	NR
% undergrads receiving aid	49
% aid is need-based	NR
% frosh w/ grant (avg)	NR
% frosh w/ loan (avg)	NR
% UGs w/ job (avg)	NR
Off-campus job outlook	fair

University of California-Santa Cruz

Santa Cruz, CA 95064   Admissions: 408-459-4008   Fax: 408-459-4163

CAMPUS LIFE

Quality of Life Rating   **91**
Type of school   public
Affiliation   none
Environment   suburban

STUDENTS
FT undergrad enrollment   8,876
% male/female   40/60
% from out of state   8
% live on campus   48
% spend weekend on campus   NR
% transfers   32
% from public high school   75
% African-American   4
% Asian   10
% Caucasian   58
% Hispanic   18
% international   1
# of countries represented   49

WHAT'S HOT
drugs
leftist politics
campus is beautiful
off-campus food
college radio

WHAT'S NOT
religion
intercollegiate sports
student government
intramural sports
Greeks

ACADEMICS

Academic Rating   **81**
Profs Interesting Rating   77
Profs Accessible Rating   79
Calendar   trimester
Student/teacher ratio   19:1
% profs PhD   99
Hours of study per day   3.07

MOST POPULAR MAJORS
psychology
biology
literature

% GRADS WHO PURSUE...
Law 4, Med 1, MBA 3, MA 12

STUDENTS SPEAK OUT

Life

"This school is beautiful—a haven for open-minded people, tucked away in the woods." And so agree many of the students who answered our survey. One student writes, "A midday stroll through the redwoods, watching the sun set over Monterey Bay from the Great Meadow—how can you say enough about the campus?" There is certainly a throwback quality of life at Santa Cruz with many of the students enjoying nature ("I count the stars on clear nights."), non-organized athletics, and free-living. One student lists his favorites activities as "rock-climbing, surfing, concerts, and LSD." Another student tries to capture the positive outlook of life at UCSC: "This campus is generally into mind expansion. Whether through hallucinogens or philosophy classes, people here are trying to figure out what's up. Personally, I've never been more in touch with nature, or my place in it." It's not difficult to imagine that Political Correctness is a big issue with many of the students. A veggie undergrad says, "Santa Cruz is super tolerant. It's okay to not eat meat!" And a third-year biology student asks, "Where else are there rubberwear parties put on by the HIV prevention education program?" The party scene is controlled, with many students explaining that life is not at all about big frat parties with a hundred kegs. "The best parties are small and private. For many of us the life is off campus in Santa Cruz and San Francisco."

Academics

This "little big school" has a large number of professors ("progressive thinkers who encourage critical discussion") that are leaders in their fields. A literature student writes, "The teachers that I have are so energetic that it is contagious. I get so excited to learn every day." This fact, along with UCSC's optional grading system, leave the students with a "very encouraging environment for undergraduates." One student explains, "Since Santa Cruz has a `no grades' policy, it's very challenging to make the best of my education and to not slack off." Another student adds, "The narrative evaluation system destroys competitiveness and leads to a perfect cooperative learning experience." Challenging classes are a big part of the Santa Cruz experience. As this undergrad colorfully points out, "The engineering programs are as tough and grueling as any debate with a fundamentalist on crack." Registration gets mixed reviews, although that could be explained by the fairly large campus and typical state school bureaucracy. One student offers, "The registration system (called Teleslug) is very organized." A smooth registration at a pretty big school is obviously important to students for a couple of reasons, as this student writes, "UCSC has such a large variety of classes that you can easily fulfill your graduation requirements with classes that are interesting and relevant to your interests." Other aspects of the administration, such as "excellent advising facilities" and "high tech library and computer facilities" are worth mentioning as well.

Student Body

Included among its many strengths, UCSC is culturally diverse. However, time and again respondents mentioned a lack of ethnic influence. "White middle-class liberals with a PC twist," writes a junior sociology major. A great number of student are not "typical" in that many live off-campus and are not fresh out of high school. One student declares, "I'm a single mom of three, live in family housing, and just love Santa Cruz!" Of course politically the campus swings way to the left, but the students only rank themselves average in their commitment.

FINANCIAL AID: 408-459-2963

ADMISSIONS

The admissions committee considers (in descending order of importance): HS record, test scores, essay, recommendations, class rank. *Also considered (in descending order of importance):* extracurriculars, special talents, geographical distribution, personality. Either the SAT or ACT is required. *High school units required/recommended:* 15 total units are required; 4 English required, 3 math required, 4 math recommended, 2 science required, 3 science recommended, 2 foreign language required, 1 social studies required, 1 history required. Minimum 3.4 GPA required of out-of-state applicants. In-state applicants with minimum 3.3 GPA are eligible regardless of test scores. Applicants with minimum combined SAT I score of 1300 (composite ACT score of 27) and minimum combined SAT II scores of 1650 (in-state) or 1730 (out-of-state), with no score below 500 on any one test, are eligible on the basis of test scores alone. *Special Requirements:* An audition is required for music program applicants. TOEFL is required of all international students. *The admissions office says:* "Residents must either have a 3.30 GPA or higher. A lower GPA (min. 2.82) can be offset by a corresponding test score. Non-residents must have taken the same courses but must earn a 3.4 average (the eligibility index applies to residents only). Any student who fails to meet the academic requirements may gain admission on the basis of test scores alone if (1) his/her combined SAT is 1300 or higher (ACT composite: 31 or higher), and (2) his/her combined SAT II scores exceed a minimum score (1650 for residents, 1730 for non-residents), and none is lower than 500."

The Inside Word

The State of California's plan to discontinue affirmative action in the UC admission process has created much uncertainty regarding the future of candidate selection in the system. Don't be deceived by the high acceptance rate at Santa Cruz—there are lots of engaging, intellectually-motivated students here, and only active learners should apply. The University has been especially welcoming to minority students of late, admitting more students from all four of the tracked ethnic minority groups last year.

FINANCIAL AID

Students should submit: FAFSA (due May 2), state aid form (due March 2), a copy of parents' most recent income tax filing. The Princeton Review suggests that all financial aid forms be submitted as soon as possible after January 1. *The following grants/scholarships are offered:* Pell, SEOG, academic merit, the school's own grants, state grants, private scholarships, private grants. *Students borrow from the following loan programs:* Stafford, Perkins, PLUS, the school's own loan fund, private loans. Applicants will be notified of awards beginning April 1. College Work-Study Program is available. Institutional employment is available.

FROM THE ADMISSIONS OFFICE

"UC-Santa Cruz's dual commitment to rigorous undergraduate education and research is affirmed by its outstanding libraries, computer facilities, and studios for the creative and performing arts, and a new natural sciences building that expands state-of-the-art biology, biochemistry, and biophysics labs. UCSC's rich curriculum leaves its graduates with the impression of a strong liberal arts education-an understanding of the many social, historical, and scientific developments that shape the world."

ADMISSIONS

Admissions Rating	78
% of applicants accepted	83
% of acceptees attending	19

FRESHMAN PROFILE

Average verbal SAT	570
Average math SAT	560
Average ACT	NR
Average TOEFL	NR
Graduated top 20% of class	NR
Graduated top 40% of class	NR
Graduated top 60% of class	NR
Average HS GPA or Avg.	3.4

DEADLINES

Early decision	NR
Regular admission	11/30
Regular notification	3/15
Non-fall registration	yes

APPLICANTS ALSO LOOK AT

AND OFTEN PREFER

Stanford
UCLA
UC-Berkeley

AND SOMETIMES PREFER

UC-Davis
UC-Riverside
UC-Santa Barbara

AND RARELY PREFER

Santa Clara
Scripps
U. Colorado, Boulder

FINANCIAL FACTS

Financial Aid Rating	84
In-state tuition	$4,109
Out-of-state tuition	$11,808
Room & board	$6,081
Estimated book expense	$633
% frosh receiving aid	43
% undergrads receiving aid	50
% aid is need-based	95
% frosh w/ grant (avg)	76 ($4,239)
% frosh w/ loan (avg)	45 ($2,804)
% UGs w/ job (avg)	3 ($1,500)
Off-campus job outlook	good

CALVIN COLLEGE

3201 Burton Street, SE, Grand Rapids, MI 49546 · Admissions: 800-688-0122 · Fax: 616-957-8551

CAMPUS LIFE

Quality of Life Rating 90
Type of school private
Affiliation Christian Reformed Church
Environment city

STUDENTS
FT undergrad enrollment 3,699
% male/female 45/55
% from out of state 45
% live on campus 57
% spend weekend on campus 80
% transfers 11
% from public high school 42
% African-American 1
% Asian 3
% Caucasian 94
% Hispanic 1
% international 8
# of countries represented 28

WHAT'S HOT
town-gown relations
religion
school runs like butter
music associations
students are happy

WHAT'S NOT
sex
drugs
beer
hard liquor
lack of diversity on campus

ACADEMICS

Academic Rating 84
Profs Interesting Rating 93
Profs Accessible Rating 90
Calendar 4-1-4
Student/teacher ratio 17:1
% profs PhD/tenured 77/82
Hours of study per day 3.52

MOST POPULAR MAJORS
business
English
engineering

% GRADS WHO PURSUE...
Law 1, Med 5, MBA 4, MA 8

STUDENTS SPEAK OUT

Life
Life at Calvin College is "absolutely blissful" for many of the students. One happy student writes, "I am so thankful that I am at Calvin college. There is so much to do here, and I am truly blessed." Calvin is affiliated with the Christian Reform Church and, as one student points out, "It is not only religiously affiliated, it is also religious." Some students insist that they are party animals, but overall, shotgunning beers and dropping acid are not among the more popular activities at Calvin. One student explains, "Most of the time we sit around and discuss issues of theology." The campus provides a great deal of entertainment, including dances, talent shows, and theater productions. "Concerts and dramas are abundant. I often don't have to go off campus to have fun," writes an English major. The city of Grand Rapids and the surrounding countryside are given good marks. One student says, "There are woods here. They are beautiful and fun to play in. The squirrels are nice and friendly." Some students complain of the "closed mindedness," but for the majority of them, Calvin is "a beautiful campus that is filled with positive energy." One student sums it up: "Life here at Calvin is challenging. We are challenged to grow in our faith and to think and form our opinions on life issues."

Academics
An intensive core curriculum (thirteen courses that require students to demonstrate competence in the liberal arts, sciences, and math, as well as spoken rhetoric, writing, a foreign language, and physical education) has helped Calvin build a solid academic reputation. One student writes, "Calvin College is an incredibly challenging learning environment. We students are pushed to examine our beliefs in class and in our life." The professors in particular are given exceptionally high marks ("They lead without getting in the way. They live what they teach"), particularly as far as their accessibility is concerned: "Professors at Calvin are like ice cream—here when you need 'em, easy to take, and good for the soul." All right then. The administration also seems attentive to the students' needs, as this respondent mentions: "The administration regularly meets with students and has our interests in mind." Education is the school's strongest department, with other pre-professional tracks such as law, nursing, and accounting being popular as well. An honors program, which offers special "honors only" classes, extra sections for already available courses, and the opportunity to test out of core requirements demonstrates the flexibility of Calvin College. Students praise the small class size and the amount of class discussion. However, one common complaint from the students is that the computer and library facilities have limited hours.

Student Body
"The general attitude of most students is summed up by the phrase, `If you ain't Dutch, you ain't much,'" explains one Calvin student. "I wish variety was more encouraged and widespread," writes another. The student body ratio of whites to minorities is over 9:1, which constitutes a problem as far as diversity goes ("My fellow students are a bunch of ethnocentric, shallow, spoiled white kids who are in for a big shock when they enter the real world"), but as one student points out, "About 60 percent of the students are Christian Reformed. There is a very strong sense of community." Not surprisingly, Calvin College students are extremely conservative politically and formal dating is popular. In part due to its religious affiliation, some bias is expressed toward homosexuals.

CALVIN COLLEGE

ADMISSIONS

The admissions committee considers (in descending order of importance): HS record, class rank, test scores, recommendations, essay. *Also considered (in descending order of importance):* personality, alumni relationship, extracurriculars, special talents. Either the SAT or ACT is required; ACT is preferred. An interview is recommended. Admissions process is need-blind. *High school units required/recommended:* 16 total units are required; 3 English required, 4 English recommended, 2 math required, 3 math recommended, 2 science required, 3 science recommended, 2 foreign language recommended, 3 social studies required. Required social studies units should include history. Required math units must include algebra and geometry. Minimum composite ACT score of 20 (combined SAT I score of 810) and minimum 2.5 GPA required. *The admissions office says:* "One essay question asks applicants to interact with the faith-perspective that lies at the heart of Calvin's curriculum."

The Inside Word

Calvin's applicant pool is highly self-selected and small. Nearly all candidates get in, and over half choose to enroll. The freshman academic profile is fairly solid, but making a good match with the college philosophically is much more important for gaining admission than anything else.

FINANCIAL AID

Students should submit: FAFSA, the school's own financial aid form. The Princeton Review suggests that all financial aid forms be submitted as soon as possible after January 1. *The following grants/scholarships are offered:* Pell, SEOG, academic merit, the school's own scholarships, the school's own grants, state scholarships, state grants, private scholarships, private grants, foreign aid. *Students borrow from the following loan programs:* Stafford, unsubsidized Stafford, Perkins, PLUS, the school's own loan fund, supplemental loans, state loans, private loans. Applicants will be notified of awards beginning March 15. College Work-Study Program is available. Institutional employment is available.

FROM THE ADMISSIONS OFFICE

"Calvin is one of North America's largest and oldest Christian colleges. Our graduates have an outstanding record for career placement, and an impressive number of students pursue graduate studies. We encourage students to question, to examine, and to make their own decisions. Our 4-1-4 calendar, with its one-month Interim Term, offers opportunities for intensive studies here and abroad. Fully ninety-five percent of our professors hold the highest degree in their field, and our student-professor ratio is 16:1. We seek to live by the foundational principles of our faith heritage: the sovereignty of God, the Lordship of Jesus Christ, the goal of individual service, and the wonder of God's grace."

ADMISSIONS

Admissions Rating	73
% of applicants accepted	89
% of acceptees attending	55

FRESHMAN PROFILE

Average verbal SAT	600
Average math SAT	590
Average ACT	25
Average TOEFL	550
Graduated top 20% of class	50
Graduated top 40% of class	74
Graduated top 60% of class	88
Average HS GPA or Avg.	3.4

DEADLINES

Early decision	3/1
Regular admission	8/1
Regular notification	rolling
Non-fall registration	yes

APPLICANTS ALSO LOOK AT

AND OFTEN PREFER
Hope

AND SOMETIMES PREFER
U. Michigan, Ann Arbor
Wheaton Coll. (IL)
Grand Valley St.

AND RARELY PREFER
Michigan Tech.
Michigan St.

FINANCIAL FACTS

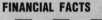

Financial Aid Rating	89
Tuition	$10,995
Room & board	$3,895
Estimated book expense	$410
% frosh receiving aid	90
% undergrads receiving aid	90
% aid is need-based	80
% frosh w/ grant (avg)	80 ($4,250)
% frosh w/ loan (avg)	60 ($3,700)
% UGs w/ job (avg)	35 ($1,200)
Off-campus job outlook	excellent

CARLETON COLLEGE

ONE NORTH COLLEGE STREET, NORTHFIELD, MN 55057　　　ADMISSIONS: 800-995-2275　　FAX: 507-663-4526

CAMPUS LIFE

Quality of Life Rating	88
Type of school	private
Affiliation	none
Environment	town

STUDENTS

FT undergrad enrollment	1,752
% male/female	50/50
% from out of state	77
% live on campus	92
% spend weekend on campus	95
% transfers	3
% from public high school	76
% African-American	3
% Asian	9
% Caucasian	83
% Hispanic	4
% international	1
# of countries represented	15

WHAT'S HOT
intramural sports
theater
lab facilities
leftist politics
students are happy

WHAT'S NOT
Greeks
infrequent dating
religion
campus food
off-campus food

ACADEMICS

Academic Rating	95
Profs Interesting Rating	98
Profs Accessible Rating	97
Calendar	trimester
Student/teacher ratio	11:1
% profs PhD/tenured	83/74
Hours of study per day	4.07

MOST POPULAR MAJORS
biology
English
history

% GRADS WHO PURSUE...
Law 8, Med 9, MBA 10, MA 40

STUDENTS SPEAK OUT

Life

Carleton College is located in Northfield, in the middle of rural Minnesota. "Just survive the winters, and you'll love this place," insists one student. Students must entertain themselves ("Northfield is not a metropolis, so you've got to be creative"), even though the college makes every effort to sponsor events like movies, concerts, plays, and dances. This student explains one particularly popular pastime: "Traying is a winter tradition—sliding down snow-covered hills on cafeteria trays." And the students seem resigned to make the best of the art of conversation: "Other nights it's watching the fish swim in your room and hanging out with friends." Athletics are important at Carleton, whether it's organized meets or pick-up games of basketball. As this student writes, "Sports, either intercollegiate or intramural, give people a break from the everyday academic life and serve as an outlet for built-up energy." Many of the students mentioned dorm parties ("I love dorm life—minus the food") as a highlight, and the college has a very lenient policy with regard to alcohol. But it seems as if the students respect the responsibility given them and don't take advantage of this freedom. One student says, "Students who prefer to have fun without alcohol are accepted just as well as they would be if they were drinkers." The students at Carleton take academics very seriously, but there appears to be a good blend. As this senior majoring in history writes, "Light-hearted as well as serious pursuits engage most students."

Academics

"Academics are the central pillar of most students' lives here, and rightly so." Carleton College is a truly excellent liberal arts school. "This is the result of the highly qualified people that attend this institution," writes one student. Indeed, its student body is one of the most academically accomplished in the country, but the faculty can also take some credit for making Carleton special. One student explains, "Even in the intro classes the professors try to convey the liberal arts experience—how different disciplines fit together and what makes their own scholarly activities important to them." The professors are "engaging," "accessible," and "caring," going out of their way to make the student comfortable by hosting potluck dinners and handing out their home phone numbers. An English student says simply, "Professors here are teachers, not writers." The administration gets high marks from the students in terms of ease of registration and campus policy. "The administration treats us like adults," writes one student. Carleton's only problem might be with its reputation, or lack thereof, outside of its region. But this is bound to change, as its virtues continue to draw the driven-to-learn student. This junior is full of praise: "Carleton has the integrity, drive, and pride of any great eastern school mixed with the charming, casual, friendly atmosphere of the small-town midwest."

Student Body

Despite being a geographically diverse bunch, "the students resist cliques" according to many Carleton students. Three-quarters of the student body are white (and many of these from middle-upper class backgrounds), but acceptance is a way of life at Carleton ("We are, in a word, 'respectful.'"). The wealthy students have a tendency to "act poor." As this student comments, "The rich students dress the 'poorest' but the Birkenstocks give them away." Politically the campus is liberal although the level of commitment is negligible: "Political activism is virtually nonexistent."

FINANCIAL AID: 507-663-4190

ADMISSIONS

The admissions committee considers (in descending order of importance): HS record, recommendations, class rank, test scores, essay. *Also considered (in descending order of importance):* extracurriculars, personality, special talents, alumni relationship, geographical distribution. Either the SAT or ACT is required. An interview is recommended. Admissions process is not need-blind. *High school units required/recommended:* 4 English recommended, 4 math recommended, 3 science recommended, 3 foreign language recommended, 2 social studies recommended. *The admissions office says:* "Of importance [in the admissions process] are superior academic achievement; personal qualities and interests; participation in extracurricular activities; and potential for development as a student and a graduate of the college."

The Inside Word

Admission to Carleton would be even more difficult if the College had more name recognition. Current applicants should be grateful for this, because standards are already rigorous as they stand. Only severe competition with the best liberal arts colleges in the country prevents an even lower admit rate.

FINANCIAL AID

Students should submit: FAFSA (due February 15), CSS Profile (due February 15), state aid form (due February 15), Divorced Parents form (due February 15), a copy of parents' most recent income tax filing (due February 15). The Princeton Review suggests that all financial aid forms be submitted as soon as possible after January 1. *The following grants/scholarships are offered:* Pell, SEOG, academic merit, the school's own scholarships, the school's own grants, state scholarships, state grants, foreign aid. *Students borrow from the following loan programs:* Stafford, unsubsidized Stafford, Perkins, PLUS, the school's own loan fund, state loans. College Work-Study Program is available. Institutional employment is available.

FROM THE ADMISSIONS OFFICE

"Carleton, a residential, coeducational liberal arts college, is located about thirty-five miles south of Minneapolis-St. Paul. More than eighty percent of those entering as freshmen graduate within four years, nearly ninety percent in five years. About seventy-five percent enter graduate or professional school within five years of graduation. Carleton ranks first of all liberal arts colleges in the number of its graduates who earned Ph.D.s in the laboratory sciences in the years 1979-1988, and sixth in the number who earned Ph.D.s in all fields."

ADMISSIONS

Admissions Rating	93
% of applicants accepted	48
% of acceptees attending	32

FRESHMAN PROFILE

Average verbal SAT	630
Average math SAT	660
Average ACT	30
Average TOEFL	NR
Graduated top 20% of class	90
Graduated top 40% of class	95
Graduated top 60% of class	100
Average HS GPA or Avg.	NR

DEADLINES

Early decision	1/15
Regular admission	1/15
Regular notification	4/15
Non-fall registration	no

APPLICANTS ALSO LOOK AT

AND OFTEN PREFER

Amherst
Williams
Swarthmore
Stanford
Pennsylvania

AND SOMETIMES PREFER

Wesleyan U.
Haverford
Vassar
St. Olaf
Macalester

AND RARELY PREFER

Reed
U. Minnesota, Twin Cities
Oberlin

FINANCIAL FACTS

Financial Aid Rating	89
Tuition	$20,171
Room & board	$4,125
Estimated book expense	$550
% frosh receiving aid	77
% undergrads receiving aid	83
% aid is need-based	94
% frosh w/ grant (avg)	57 ($9,302)
% frosh w/ loan (avg)	54 ($2,878)
% UGs w/ job (avg)	80 ($1,800)
Off-campus job outlook	fair

CARNEGIE MELLON UNIVERSITY

5000 FORBES AVENUE, PITTSBURGH, PA 15213   ADMISSIONS: 412-268-2082   FAX: 412-268-7838

STUDENTS SPEAK OUT

Life

"All I do is work," says one exhausted Carnegie Mellon undergrad, and he is not alone in this opinion. Work is a large part of the CMU experience. "Class is your life...People have very little time for things other than classes." Yet a few other options do exist, and students mention parties as the stress-relief of choice, with the occasional foray into the Pittsburgh club scene as a second option. Some male students feel a bit hampered by the male-female ratio—"It really sucks that there are so few women here"—but few mention it as reducing the enjoyment of the CMU experience. One possible explanation for this might be the students' marks on Pittsburgh—which varied from the horrible—"I'm just trying to get a job and get out of Pittsburgh"—to the surprised and positive—"Pittsburgh has a lot of attractive women, strangely enough." Complaints of student spirit/apathy and lack of interest in their Division III athletic program leads some students to "get away from [CMU] for fun," but the majority of students seem to enjoy the hard work, the camaraderie and the educational experience Carnegie Mellon provides.

Academics

Carnegie Mellon's two major areas of study are very different—engineering and the fine arts. Drama, architecture, and the hard sciences are also quite popular and top notch. CMU students learn to be aggressive very quickly. One freshman writes, "We are taught 'you've got to survive, whatever it takes.'" CMU is best suited to the ambitious student already focused on his or her career choice. One student remarks, "Carnegie Mellon is the place to go if you know what you want to study, if you are an overachiever, and if you like to work a lot." Students work a whopping four hours a day outside of class. "The professors are excellent, but the workload is unbearable," is a groan commonly voiced by students. Classes are relatively small and professors are rated above average, but students still get the feeling that "they all do research as their number-one priority." One student embraces both sides of the CMU culture as he writes, "Carnegie Mellon is an excellent school with excellent faculty. If you come here, though, you'll learn to live on pizza and no sleep!"

Student Body

Because the school attracts both hard-core scientists and hard-core artists, the student body has "a strange mix of nerds and posing art majors on campus." Most, however, are very positive about the other students in their own discipline. The school has a large minority population, much of which is Asian. The diversity of the student body, unsurprisingly, lends itself to a variety of opinions on political, religious, and social issues. One student, who identified himself as left-wing, writes that students "are either politically radical or politically reactionary. There is very little in between." One other important tidbit—one student, surprised at the enthusiasm of others, writes that "the manner in which many students openly express their sexuality also takes a while to get used to."

FINANCIAL AID: 412-268-2068   WEB SITE: HTTP://WWW.CMU.EDU/

ADMISSIONS

The admissions committee considers (in descending order of importance): HS record, class rank, test scores, recommendations, essay. *Also considered (in descending order of importance):* personality, special talents, alumni relationship, extracurriculars, geographical distribution. Either the SAT or ACT is required. An interview is recommended. Admissions process is need-blind. *High school units required/recommended:* 16 total units are required; 4 English required. Specific requirements vary as follows: 4 English, 4 math, 1 chemistry, 1 physics, and 6 electives for Carnegie Institutes of Technology (CIT); 4 English, 4 math, 1 chemistry, and 6 electives for Mellon College of Science; 4 English, 3 math, 1 science, and 8 electives for College of Humanities and Social Sciences (H&SS) and School of Industrial Management (IM); 4 English, 4 math, 1 physics, and 7 electives (2 foreign languages recommended) for College of Fine Arts (CFA) Department of Architecture; 4 English and 12 electives (2 foreign languages recommended) for CFA Department of Art, Drama, and Music; 4 English, 2 math, 1 science, and 9 electives for CFA Department of Design. *Special Requirements:* A portfolio is required for art program applicants. An audition is required for music program applicants. Audition required of drama program applicants (acting and music theatre options). Portfolio required of drama program applicants (production option). Design projects required of design program applicants.

The Inside Word

The admissions office reports that it uses "no cutoffs, no formulas" in assessing its applicant pool. Don't get too excited. It doesn't necessarily mean that applicants are looked at in a more personal fashion. Carnegie Mellon requires candidates to submit even more standardized test scores than do many universities that are more selective and use sliding scales. Copious test scores are hard for admissions officers to ignore, especially if they have asked for them in the first place, and the process can't help but become less personal. A very low yield of admits who enroll keeps selectivity moderate, but you must have strong numbers to gain admission.

FINANCIAL AID

Students should submit: FAFSA (due February 15), the school's own financial aid form (due February 15), state aid form (due May 1), a copy of parents' most recent income tax filing (due March 15). The Princeton Review suggests that all financial aid forms be submitted as soon as possible after January 1. *The following grants/scholarships are offered:* Pell, SEOG, academic merit, the school's own scholarships, the school's own grants, state scholarships, state grants, private scholarships, private grants, ROTC. *Students borrow from the following loan programs:* Stafford, Perkins, PLUS, state loans, private loans. College Work-Study Program is available. Institutional employment is available.

FROM THE ADMISSIONS OFFICE

"Carnegie Mellon is a private, coeducational university with approximately 4,300 undergraduates, 2,500 graduate students, and 425 full-time faculty members. The university's 103-acre campus is located in the Oakland area of Pittsburgh, five miles from downtown. The university is composed of seven colleges: the Carnegie Institute of Technology (engineering); the College of Fine Arts; the College of Humanities and Social Sciences (combining liberal arts education with professional specializations); the Graduate School of Industrial Administration (undergraduate business is industrial management); the Mellon College of Science; the School of Computer Science; and the School of Urban and Public Affairs.

ADMISSIONS

Admissions Rating	88
% of applicants accepted	54
% of acceptees attending	22

FRESHMAN PROFILE

Average verbal SAT	630
Average math SAT	730
Average ACT	NR
Average TOEFL	600
Graduated top 20% of class	78
Graduated top 40% of class	95
Graduated top 60% of class	100
Average HS GPA or Avg.	3.4

DEADLINES

Early decision	NR
Regular admission	2/1
Regular notification	4/15
Non-fall registration	no

APPLICANTS ALSO LOOK AT

AND OFTEN PREFER
Cornell U.
Tufts
Pennsylvania

AND SOMETIMES PREFER
Case Western Reserve
Washington U.

AND RARELY PREFER
U. Pittsburgh
Boston U.
Syracuse
Penn State U.

FINANCIAL FACTS

Financial Aid Rating	79
Tuition	$18,600
Room & board	$5,850
Estimated book expense	$450
% frosh receiving aid	74
% undergrads receiving aid	71
% aid is need-based	75
% frosh w/ grant (avg)	93 ($11,759)
% frosh w/ loan (avg)	65 ($3,892)
% UGs w/ job (avg)	44 ($1,450)
Off-campus job outlook	good

CASE WESTERN RESERVE UNIVERSITY

10900 EUCLID AVENUE, CLEVELAND, OH 44106   ADMISSIONS: 216-368-4450   FAX: 216-368-5111

CAMPUS LIFE

Quality of Life Rating	**68**
Type of school	private
Affiliation	none
Environment	metropolis

STUDENTS

FT undergrad enrollment	3,079
% male/female	57/43
% from out of state	39
% live on campus	75
% spend weekend on campus	85
% transfers	14
% from public high school	70
% in (# of) fraternities	33 (17)
% in (# of) sororities	15 (5)
% African-American	7
% Asian	12
% Caucasian	68
% Hispanic	2
% international	6
# of countries represented	40

WHAT'S HOT
ethnic diversity on campus
different students interact
Greeks
Cleveland
college radio

WHAT'S NOT
campus difficult to get around
unattractive campus
political activism
intercollegiate sports
dorms

ACACEMICS

Academic Rating	**80**
Profs Interesting Rating	65
Profs Accessible Rating	69
Calendar	semester
Student/teacher ratio	8:1
% profs PhD/tenured	95/37
Hours of study per day	3.35

MOST POPULAR MAJORS
mechanical engineering
psychology
biology

% GRADS WHO PURSUE...
Law 3, Med 8, MBA 2, MA 22

STUDENTS SPEAK OUT

Life

Encompassing two distinct programs, liberal arts and engineering, Case Western is like two separate schools on a single campus. This division, according to some students, affects the social scene because engineering students have much less time to let it hang. One engineering student offers, "Social life? My best friend in my spare time is my pillow." But there are favorite activities among the student body. One student writes, "Fraternity parties and the movies are very popular. And if you have a car and are over twenty-one, there's always the Flats." On this note, many of the students warn that "you really need a car" in order to appreciate all that Cleveland has to offer. As this student says, "There's not much to do on campus, but off campus is surrounded by clubs, museums, parks, and malls." Finding a date at Case "is about like finding decent food on campus." (On-campus fare receives low marks.) But from the point of view of this junior studying biology, "The recent influx of women nursing students has changed the dating scene for the better." In the end, Case is a lot like any college. It is up to the student to be creative and take the initiative. "Some people like to say, 'Case is full of geeks!' But school and life are what you make of it, and there are plenty of us that go out, party, and have fun."

Academics

In many ways Case could be labeled a "sleeper," since it offers so many strong departments for undergraduate study. The university was formed by the union of Western Reserve University (a traditional liberal arts college) and the Case Institute of Technology (an engineering and physical sciences college). While engineers make up the largest student group, undergrads report that "many different groups exist here." One engineering student advises, "expect to work like a dog and learn a lot on your own." Indeed, the workload is intense. Some undergrads mention that much of the work is left up to the student ("A lot of professors are here for research and not for teaching.") while others report that the professors do a fantastic job. As this student writes, "in terms of ability, availability, and general helpfulness, CWRU professors are brilliant." Case undergrads love the small class size and the fact that many classes are taught by professors and not TAs. With respect to the administration, however, the student are less supportive: "The administration (president included) has forgotten that we, the students, should be the main concern, not the other way around." Another writes, "The education is excellent, but this school does not run efficiently." The health facilities, computers, and library receive less-than-spectacular marks from Case students.

Student Body

Nearly one-third of Case's undergrads are minorities (of these, the Asian population is by far the biggest) and the school is proud of its large international population. One student mentions how inspiring diversity can be: "The student body is very diverse. There are many minority/cultural groups that hold events sponsoring their groups. Many students who are not in the group attend these events." One student classifies CWRU students as "very studious, serious, diverse, and conservative." Perhaps all the hard work takes its toll on the students at Case; their commitment to politics is strikingly low: "We all seem to get along fairly well, but the student body leans toward apathy."

FINANCIAL AID: 216-368-4530   E-MAIL: XX329@PO.CWRU.EDU   WEB SITE: HTTP://WWW.CWRU.EDU/

ADMISSIONS

The admissions committee considers (in descending order of importance): HS record, class rank, test scores, recommendations, essay. Also considered (in descending order of importance): special talents, extracurriculars, alumni relationship, geographical distribution, personality. Either the SAT or ACT is required. An interview is recommended. Admissions process is need-blind. High school units required/recommended: 16 total units are required; 4 English required, 3 math required, 1 science required, 3 foreign language recommended, 4 social studies recommended. Special Requirements: A portfolio is required for art program applicants. An audition is required for music program applicants. TOEFL is required of all international students. 4 units of math and 2 units of lab science, including chemistry, required of math and science program applicants. 4 units of math, 1 unit of chemistry, and 1 unit of physics required of engineering program applicants. 2 units of lab science, including chemistry, required of premedical studies program applicants. Portfolio required of art education program applicants. Audition required of music education program applicants. SAT II (math I or II and chemistry and/or physics) recommended of engineering, math, and science program applicants. The admissions office says: "Rather than require students to apply to a specific school, CWRU admits its students to the university without regard to intended major (with the exception of the nursing program, which limits undergraduate enrollment). A student can keep options open during the admissions process and, if admitted based on overall academic performance and promise, choose to begin study in any area."

The Inside Word

Case Western faces tough competition, and they handle it very well. The university received a record number of applications last year, and as a result it's quite a bit tougher to get admitted. Even if you solidly meet the academic profile, don't be complacent—Case's freshman profile reflects well on the academic preparedness of its candidates, and due to their good fortune they've got an opportunity to be significantly more choosy about who gets an offer.

FINANCIAL AID

Students should submit: FAFSA (due February 1), CSS Profile (due February 1), state aid form (due February 1). The Princeton Review suggests that all financial aid forms be submitted as soon as possible after January 1. The following grants/scholarships are offered: Pell, SEOG, academic merit, the school's own scholarships, the school's own grants, state scholarships, state grants, private scholarships, ROTC. Students borrow from the following loan programs: Stafford, Perkins, PLUS, the school's own loan fund. Applicants will be notified of awards beginning early April. College Work-Study Program is available. Institutional employment is available.

FROM THE ADMISSIONS OFFICE

"CWRU's note to you is not self-promoting. We would rather use this space to send a simple message: To thine own self be true. Filter the word-of-mouth, the slick guidebook ratings, and flattering college-generated literature through your own sense of what will work for you. Read no further in this guidebook if you haven't already taken thoughtful stock of your own needs. If you know yourself well, then have the confidence to look beyond the surface impressions and discover how less glamorous or well-known colleges may very well meet your individual needs."

ADMISSIONS

Admissions Rating	83
% of applicants accepted	77
% of acceptees attending	22

FRESHMAN PROFILE

Average verbal SAT	NR
Average math SAT	NR
Average ACT	NR
Average TOEFL	550
Graduated top 20% of class	92
Graduated top 40% of class	99
Graduated top 60% of class	100
Average HS GPA or Avg.	NR

DEADLINES

Early decision	January
Regular admission	2/1
Regular notification	4/1
Non-fall registration	yes

APPLICANTS ALSO LOOK AT

AND OFTEN PREFER
Northwestern U.
Carnegie Mellon
U. Michigan, Ann Arbor

AND SOMETIMES PREFER
Marquette
Boston U.

AND RARELY PREFER
Ohio State U.-Columbus
Purdue U.-West Lafayette
Penn State U.

FINANCIAL FACTS

Financial Aid Rating	87
Tuition	$17,100
Room & board	$4,860
Estimated book expense	$585
% frosh receiving aid	94
% undergrads receiving aid	84
% aid is need-based	64
% frosh w/ grant (avg)	93 ($11,550)
% frosh w/ loan (avg)	67 ($4,819)
% UGs w/ job (avg)	80 ($1,200)
Off-campus job outlook	good

CATAWBA COLLEGE

2300 West Innes Street, Salisbury, NC 28144   Admissions: 800-228-2922   Fax: 704-637-4444

CAMPUS LIFE

Quality of Life Rating   **74**
Type of school   private
Affiliation   United Church of Christ
Environment   suburban

STUDENTS
FT undergrad enrollment   969
% male/female   49/51
% from out of state   50
% live on campus   66
% spend weekend on campus   NR
% transfers   18
% from public high school   NR
% African-American   7
% Asian   1
% Caucasian   89
% Hispanic   1
% international   1
# of countries represented   9

WHAT'S HOT
old-fashioned dating
different students interact
town-gown relations
theater
intercollegiate sports

WHAT'S NOT
campus food
student publications
college radio
political activism

ACADEMICS

Academic Rating   **75**
Profs Interesting Rating   81
Profs Accessible Rating   81
Calendar   semester
Student/teacher ratio   14:1
% profs PhD/tenured   71/83
Hours of study per day   2.91

MOST POPULAR MAJORS
business
communication arts
elementary education

% GRADS WHO PURSUE...
Law 1, Med 1, MBA 5, MA 3

STUDENTS SPEAK OUT

Life

Students complain that the Catawba College community, while exciting academically, is a bore socially. "There is not a whole lot for students to do for fun on weekends on campus. There are no fraternities and no radio station," writes one student. One student more optimistically assesses that "The only real problem is that the town closes down early and the student body sometimes lacks school spirit." Still, students agree that Catawba has a "very beautiful campus," and many enjoy participating in sports activities, to the point of excluding nearly everything else. Rules governing on-campus behavior are widely perceived as overly strict, but, as one upright student notes, "Students believe the rules here are strict and say so, but they don't acknowledge that none of the rules go beyond the laws of the state and city. They should realize when they are caught by the school that they are lucky that the school simply punishes them and doesn't turn them over to the authorities."

Academics

Catawba students gush shamelessly about the academic experience their school offers. "If you like personal attention, easily available professors, a close, family-like student body, then Catawba is your kind of place! I couldn't ask for a better place," writes one satisfied student. Adds another, "Catawba is an exceptional college, deserving only of those who want to learn and are excited about learning. This place gives you a wonderful experience that combines spirituality and academics." Students report that "Catawba's teaching staff is beyond excellent; the professors earnestly show concern for the subjects they teach and for the students as well, while at the same time inspiring students to learn and encouraging interest." Another student explains, "There is extremely good interaction between faculty and students, and the faculty bend over backwards to help students who need it." Students single out for praise the school's arts programs ("excellent and accessible to all, regardless of major") and the freshman orientation program: "Our freshman program is excellent in helping freshmen make the adjustment from high school to college, which keeps many students from dropping out after first year." Pre-professional programs—business, education, and communications—are most popular among students.

Student Body

Catawba students report that "lots of Southern hospitality" permeates their community. Students deeply committed to their religion are not uncommon, but do not dominate the student body. One student explains that even though there aren't any frats, people do coalesce into cliques: "Groups are very segregated through sports (soccer players, football players stick together)." A few students tell us that even though they get along with their friendly peers, they are saddened that "many are homophobic and closed-minded." Half the student body is drawn from outside North Carolina, many from states to the South. Blacks make up the majority of the school's small minority population.

FINANCIAL AID: 704-637-4416

ADMISSIONS

The admissions committee considers (in descending order of importance): HS record, test scores, class rank, recommendations, essay. *Also considered (in descending order of importance):* special talents, alumni relationship, extracurriculars, personality. Either the SAT or ACT is required; SAT is preferred. An interview is recommended. Admissions process is need-blind. *High school units required/recommended:* 16 total units are required; 4 English required, 2 math required, 2 science required, 2 foreign language recommended, 2 social studies required. *Special Requirements:* An audition is required for music program applicants. TOEFL is required of all international students. Minimum 2.5 GPA required of applicants to sports medicine and teacher education programs.

The Inside Word

Catawba's applicant pool is mainly from the Southeast, which tends to give candidates from far afield some extra appeal. There is serious competition for students among similar colleges in this neck of the woods, and the admissions staff here has to work hard to bring in the freshman class each year. They succeed because they are truly friendly and personal in their dealings with students and their families, and the college seems to have carved a worthwhile niche for itself amid the myriad choices available in the area.

FINANCIAL AID

Students should submit: FAFSA (due March 1), the school's own financial aid form (due March 1), state aid form (due March 1). The Princeton Review suggests that all financial aid forms be submitted as soon as possible after January 1. *The following grants/scholarships are offered:* Pell, SEOG, academic merit, athletic, the school's own scholarships, the school's own grants, state scholarships, state grants, private scholarships, private grants. *Students borrow from the following loan programs:* Stafford, unsubsidized Stafford, Perkins, PLUS, the school's own loan fund, private loans. College Work-Study Program is available. Institutional employment is available.

FROM THE ADMISSIONS OFFICE

Perhaps one of Catawba's greatest assets is location, location, location. The town of Salisbury (http://www.ol.salisbury.no.us/) is a small city of 26,000 people, a leader in the historic preservation movement, and a place with a rare wealth of opportunities in the arts. The town embraces the college, and vice-versa. Catawba College has just significantly upgraded the computer technology made available to students. A fiber-optic loop has been completed, and our three computer labs are equipped with 486 and Pentium chip computers, many of which have sound cards and ten watt speakers. The library has also been electronically upgraded with the addition of the same on-line system used by the Museum of Natural History.

ADMISSIONS

Admissions Rating	65
% of applicants accepted	82
% of acceptees attending	33

FRESHMAN PROFILE

Average verbal SAT	500
Average math SAT	510
Average ACT	NR
Average TOEFL	500
Graduated top 20% of class	28
Graduated top 40% of class	53
Graduated top 60% of class	71
Average HS GPA or Avg.	2.8

DEADLINES

Early decision	NR
Regular admission	NR
Regular notification	rolling
Non-fall registration	yes

APPLICANTS ALSO LOOK AT

AND SOMETIMES PREFER

UNC-Chapel Hill
UNC-Charlotte

AND RARELY PREFER

UNC, Wilmington
UNC, Greensboro
North Carolina St.
Elon
Appalachian St.

FINANCIAL FACTS

Financial Aid Rating	95
Tuition	$9,972
Room & board	$4,200
Estimated book expense	$600
% frosh receiving aid	89
% undergrads receiving aid	87
% aid is need-based	39
% frosh w/ grant (avg)	87 ($5,450)
% frosh w/ loan (avg)	50 ($3,646)
% UGs w/ job (avg)	33 ($883)
Off-campus job outlook	fair

CATHOLIC UNIVERSITY OF AMERICA

620 MICHIGAN AVENUE, WASHINGTON, DC 20064 | ADMISSIONS: 202-319-5305 | FAX: 202-319-6533

CAMPUS LIFE

Quality of Life Rating	**83**
Type of school	private
Affiliation	Roman Catholic Church
Environment	metropolis

STUDENTS

FT undergrad enrollment	2,182
% male/female	45/55
% from out of state	95
% live on campus	57
% spend weekend on campus	75
% transfers	27
% from public high school	41
% in (# of) fraternities	1 (1)
% in (# of) sororities	1 (1)
% African-American	5
% Asian	4
% Caucasian	76
% Hispanic	5
% international	11
# of countries represented	103

WHAT'S HOT
beer
theater
student government
religion
cigarettes

WHAT'S NOT
library
town-gown relations
computer facilities
lab facilities
health facilities

ACADEMICS

Academic Rating	**80**
Profs Interesting Rating	74
Profs Accessible Rating	81
Calendar	semester
Student/teacher ratio	10:1
% profs tenured	95
Hours of study per day	3.42

MOST POPULAR MAJORS
nursing
politics
architecture

% GRADS WHO PURSUE...
Law 17, Med 8, MBA 6, MA 54

STUDENTS SPEAK OUT

Life

Catholic University is located in Washington, D.C., which provides both its so-cial upside and social downside. Washington is a great college town, home not only to CUA but also to American, Georgetown, George Washington, Howard, and the President of the United States. CUA's neighborhood, however, is less appealing. "Dangerous" and "feels a bit unsafe due to the crime level" came to our attention as comments students made regarding the northeast D.C. area sur-rounding campus. Washington is still the CUA students favorite stamping ground; college bars abound, and "the people at Catholic love to drink." All activities on campus are dry, however. Fraternities and sororities are practically nonexistent. The school also rates above the national average on responses to questions involving student flings. As one devout CUA student writes, "for fun, I go into church and pray for my fellow students."

Academics

Although it's the official university of the Roman Catholic Church in America, Catholic U. has a lot more than religious study to offer. One student writes, "For the Catholic University of America, my classes have a distinctly secular, non-preachy bent." Strong programs include drama, music, architecture, nursing, and preprofessional studies. Students enjoy a close-knit academic community united by religion and by a demanding core curriculum. A great help in over-coming the difficulty of the academic environment is the approachability of the teachers: "CUA boasts a 10 to 1 student-teacher ratio. It is easy to get to know and be friends with teachers." Even the personal attention shown by the admin-istration is praised by the students: "When I was in high school I visited CUA two times, once the spring of my junior year and again in the fall of my senior year. When I returned that fall I walked into the Admissions office, unan-nounced, and the Dean of Admissions remembered my name." CUA requires its liberal arts and sciences students (who make up the majority of the undergradu-ates) to complete an extensive core curriculum; these requirements chew up approximately half the credits necessary for graduation, leaving students with few opportunities to take elective courses. Students rate their library among the lowest in the country—fortunately, D.C. is home to the Library of Congress, which is excellent.

Student Body

The Catholic University student body is fairly homogenous; nearly four-fifths of the students are Catholic, and close to the same percentage is white. "Everyone here (almost) is white, Republican, and straight," comments one student. An-other adds that there is a "definite clash between drinkers/partiers and nerds." But the students do seem to get along. One student mentions that "the thing that attracted me to the school [was] its personality. Everyone still says, 'Hello!' "An overall warning from one student might be appropriate: "Catholic University. Don't let the name fool you! The students are great and generally easy to get along with, but don't underestimate how much fun Catholics have or what they do to have it."

ADMISSIONS

The admissions committee considers (in descending order of importance): HS record, class rank, recommendations, essay, test scores. *Also considered (in descending order of importance):* extracurriculars, personality, special talents, alumni relationship, geographical distribution. Either the SAT or ACT is required. *High school units required/recommended:* 17 total units are required; 21 total units are recommended; 4 English required, 3 math required, 4 math recommended, 3 science required, 4 science recommended, 2 foreign language required, 4 foreign language recommended, 4 social studies required. *Special Requirements:* An audition is required for music program applicants. TOEFL is required of all international students. Biology, chemistry, language, math, and social science required of nursing program applicants. *The admissions office says:* "We are looking for a well-rounded student [who demonstrates a] balance of academics, activities, and community service." CUA also notes that "students are evaluated on the basis of the whole application package."

The Inside Word

This is not the place to try radical approaches to completing your admissions application. Smooth sailing for solid students and even friendlier for candidates from the top parochial schools in their applicant pool.

FINANCIAL AID

Students should submit: FAFSA (due January 15), CSS Profile (due January 15), the school's own financial aid form (due January 15), state aid form (due January 15), a copy of parents' most recent income tax filing (due January 15). The Princeton Review suggests that all financial aid forms be submitted as soon as possible after January 1. *The following grants/scholarships are offered:* Pell, SEOG, academic merit, the school's own scholarships, the school's own grants, state scholarships, state grants, private scholarships, private grants, ROTC. *Students borrow from the following loan programs:* Stafford, unsubsidized Stafford, Perkins, PLUS, the school's own loan fund, federal nursing loans, private loans. Applicants will be notified of awards beginning April 1. College Work-Study Program is available. Institutional employment is available.

FROM THE ADMISSIONS OFFICE

"The Catholic University of America's friendly atmosphere, rigorous academic programs, and emphasis on time-honored values attract students from most states and more than 100 foreign countries. Its 154-acre, tree-lined campus is ten minutes from the nation's capital. Distinguished as the national university of the Catholic Church in the United States, CUA is the only institution of higher education established by the U.S. Catholic bishops. Students from all religious traditions are welcome. CUA offers undergraduate degrees in more than 50 major areas. With Capitol Hill and The Smithsonian Institution minutes away via the Metrorail rapid transit system, students enjoy a residential campus in an exciting city of historical monuments, theaters, ethnic restaurants, and parks."

ADMISSIONS

Admissions Rating	82
% of applicants accepted	75
% of acceptees attending	32

FRESHMAN PROFILE

Average verbal SAT	600
Average math SAT	570
Average ACT	25
Average TOEFL	500
Graduated top 20% of class	41
Graduated top 40% of class	68
Graduated top 60% of class	84
Average HS GPA or Avg.	3.1

DEADLINES

Early decision	11/15
Regular admission	2/15
Regular notification	4/1
Non-fall registration	yes

APPLICANTS ALSO LOOK AT

AND OFTEN PREFER

Notre Dame
U. Virginia
Boston Coll.
Georgetown U.

AND SOMETIMES PREFER

Coll. of the Holy Cross
William and Mary
Villanova
Loyola Coll. (MD)
U. Scranton

AND RARELY PREFER

American
Fordham U.
LaSalle U.
George Washington U.

FINANCIAL FACTS

Financial Aid Rating	86
Tuition	$15,561
Room & board	$6,846
Estimated book expense	$480
% frosh receiving aid	79
% undergrads receiving aid	72
% aid is need-based	60
% frosh w/ grant (avg)	74 ($7,818)
% frosh w/ loan (avg)	75 ($2,625)
% UGs w/ job (avg)	35 ($1,000)
Off-campus job outlook	excellent

CENTENARY COLLEGE OF LOUISIANA

2911 CENTENARY BOULEVARD, SHREVEPORT, LA 71104   ADMISSIONS: 318-869-5131   FAX: 318-869-5026

CAMPUS LIFE

Quality of Life Rating	**74**
Type of school	private
Affiliation	United Methodist Church
Environment	city

STUDENTS

FT undergrad enrollment	753
% male/female	43/57
% from out of state	46
% live on campus	56
% spend weekend on campus	70
% transfers	15
% from public high school	80
% in (# of) fraternities	25 (4)
% in (# of) sororities	20 (2)
% African-American	6
% Asian	2
% Caucasian	87
% Hispanic	1
% international	2
# of countries represented	12

WHAT'S HOT
hard liquor
cigarettes
beer
music associations
theater

WHAT'S NOT
health facilities
support groups
registration is a pain
library
dorms

ACADEMICS

Academic Rating	**82**
Profs Interesting Rating	89
Profs Accessible Rating	90
Calendar	4-4-1
Student/teacher ratio	11:1
% profs PhD/tenured	94/64
Hours of study per day	2.92

MOST POPULAR MAJORS
business
education

% GRADS WHO PURSUE...
Law 4, Med 4, MBA 10, MA 10

STUDENTS SPEAK OUT

Life

Centenary College is described by a number of dejected students as having "no school spirit." A sophomore notes that "Students go to games, but they don't cheer or shout. Students miss a lot of good opportunities and free events." The administration takes a protective attitude toward students, requiring that all but married students live on campus and participate in the meal plan. One student comments that this enforced living inspires "a true feeling of community. Almost everyone knows everyone else, so you don't go unnoticed." As for social events, one student notes that "Centenary is a five-day-a-week campus. The Greek system provides for much of the entertainment on the weekends." Partying (drinking beer, in particular) rocks at Centenary. "It's scary—it's a blast. It goes way too fast," rhymes one student. Students like Shreveport—primarily for its legal drinking age of 18. Other than the drinking age, Centenary students give Shreveport only average marks, but this doesn't keep them from having a good time. One student writes: "Here people think about drinking, smoking, sex, and school in that order. At any given moment, you can find a bar that will let anyone eighteen and older in." Centenary students are above the national average in their love of beer.

Academics

Students at Centenary, a Methodist school in Shreveport, Louisiana, agree that the faculty is the best thing about the college. The faculty is well respected and well liked. One student notes that "my professors are also my friends." This seems to make the students work harder. Another student comments that "It's kind of like a big family. You want to make them proud of you." Centenary has an 11 to 1 student/teacher ratio, which translates into small classes and close attention. With a student body under a thousand, students and teachers understand and know each other. Centenary's no-nonsense approach to a "classic" college education includes a number of distribution requirements in the humanities and sciences, an Honor Code, and a Cultural Perspectives program that requires students to attend cultural events. Among the preprofessional fields, business and management and education are the most popular. While the faculty is appreciated, the administration receives low marks. One student notes "[the administration] never asks our opinion."

Student Body

Centenary students agree that the school's student body is "very homogeneous." The school's ten percent minority population translates, in real numbers, to about seventy students. Because Centenary is so small, there is a "strong gossip 'grapevine.' Even if you don't know a student personally, you know something about them." But this small student body also fosters a sense of friendship, noted by many Centenary students. Centenary is a conservative environment in which "students are in general fairly well-informed and willing to jump into an argument and defend themselves and their beliefs." The male/female ratio at the school prompts one woman to write that "we could use more men—it's unbalanced as is."

ADMISSIONS

The admissions committee considers (in descending order of importance): HS record, test scores, essay, recommendations, class rank. *Also considered (in descending order of importance):* personality, extracurriculars, special talents, alumni relationship. Either the SAT or ACT is required. An interview is required. Admissions process is need-blind. *High school units required/recommended:* 4 English required, 3 math required, 3 science required, 2 foreign language required, 3 social studies required. Minimum composite ACT score of 21 (combined SAT I score of 970) and minimum 2.5 GPA in core classes recommended. *Special Requirements:* An audition is required for music program applicants. TOEFL is required of all international students.

The Inside Word

Centenary has a very small applicant pool, and thus has to admit the vast majority in order to meet its freshman enrollment goals. Its reputation, though regional, is quite solid, and the college does a good job of enrolling its admits. A very friendly and efficient admissions office no doubt contributes to such success.

FINANCIAL AID

Students should submit: FAFSA (due April 15), the school's own financial aid form (due April 15), state aid form (due April 15), a copy of parents' most recent income tax filing (due April 15). The Princeton Review suggests that all financial aid forms be submitted as soon as possible after January 1. *The following grants/scholarships are offered:* Pell, SEOG, academic merit, athletic, the school's own scholarships, the school's own grants, state scholarships, state grants, private scholarships, private grants, ROTC. *Students borrow from the following loan programs:* Stafford, Perkins, PLUS, state loans, private loans. Applicants will be notified of awards beginning April 15. College Work-Study Program is available. Institutional employment is available.

FROM THE ADMISSIONS OFFICE

"Centenary students work closely with a gifted faculty and inquisitive peers. Small classes and interactive learning keep our students coming back after class to ask that extra question...or working a little longer to produce their very best. Our students were the leaders of their schools and communities. We know college should not be an end to their activities, but a furthering of their experiences. Centenary College provides ample and varied opportunities to further leadership experiences in an atmosphere of integrity and honesty encouraged by the Honor Code. Our students come for experiential learning through our service-learning program. They participate in a global classroom through our intercultural and study-abroad programs. They develop their career paths with the help of dedicated faculty, staff, and internship mentors. Come visit Centenary College, get the facts, and find out if we are best for you."

ADMISSIONS

Admissions Rating	71
% of applicants accepted	83
% of acceptees attending	46

FRESHMAN PROFILE

Average verbal SAT	570
Average math SAT	570
Average ACT	25
Average TOEFL	550
Graduated top 20% of class	60
Graduated top 40% of class	79
Graduated top 60% of class	90
Average HS GPA or Avg.	3.5

DEADLINES

Early decision	NR
Regular admission	5/1
Regular notification	rolling
Non-fall registration	yes

APPLICANTS ALSO LOOK AT

AND OFTEN PREFER

Tulane
Trinity U.

AND SOMETIMES PREFER

Louisiana State U.-Baton Rouge
U. New Orleans
U. Southwestern Louisiana
Millsaps
Austin

AND RARELY PREFER

TCU
SMU

FINANCIAL FACTS

Financial Aid Rating	97
Tuition	$10,400
Room & board	$3,800
Estimated book expense	$650
% frosh receiving aid	91
% undergrads receiving aid	90
% aid is need-based	33
% frosh w/ grant (avg)	90 ($6,282)
% frosh w/ loan (avg)	59 ($2,874)
% UGs w/ job (avg)	30 ($1,200)
Off-campus job outlook	good

School of the Art Institute of Chicago

37 South Wabash Avenue, Chicago, IL 60603

Admissions: 800-232-7242   Fax: 312-899-1840

CAMPUS LIFE

Quality of Life Rating **73**

Type of school	private
Affiliation	none
Environment	metropolis

STUDENTS

FT undergrad enrollment	1,237
% male/female	46/54
% from out of state	72
% live on campus	15
% spend weekend on campus	NR
% transfers	48
% from public high school	NR
% African-American	4
% Asian	7
% Caucasian	75
% Hispanic	7
% international	6
# of countries represented	23

WHAT'S HOT
cigarettes
drugs
leftist politics
Chicago
sex

WHAT'S NOT
intramural sports
intercollegiate sports
support groups

ACADEMICS

Academic Rating	**80**
Profs Interesting Rating	64
Profs Accessible Rating	62
Calendar	semester
Student/teacher ratio	13:1
% profs PhD/tenured	80/87
Hours of study per day	3.54

% GRADS WHO PURSUE...
MA 65

STUDENTS SPEAK OUT

Life

The School of the Art Institute of Chicago is located in downtown Chicago, near many established art galleries (art openings, frequently featuring free food, are a favorite pastime of Art Institute undergrads). The majority of the students live off campus, and depend on Chicago for their entertainment. The city offers a thriving art community which nicely compliments the school, as well as countless other draws. "The city provides exposure to a large amount of activities and people. I've become more open-minded than I've ever been in my life!" says one student. Schoolwork takes up the bulk of time, with nearly half of the students spending at least four hours a day working outside of class. A student reports that "School is like a job. I commute from my apartment, put 8-12 hours in, and then go home. I enjoy people in my classes, but this isn't exactly a campus-y type of school." Some students complain about the lack of community between the students, but for the most part students seem to like each other and are happy. "There is a community feeling here," said one student, "but it's a lot different from a normal university's atmosphere. People are accepting and friendly." Drinking and drug use are accepted as the norm, and parties are popular.

Academics

There are no specific majors at the Art Institute, but instead concentrations of study, which allow students the freedom to explore a wide range of classes in more than one area. "The school overall can be an excellent experience if you are a very motivated student," writes one student. Popular areas of interest include graphic arts, filmmaking, fashion, architecture, and art education. Students are also required to take academic classes outside of the arts. For the most part, undergrads tend to like their professors ("My teachers are excellent and my classes are open and interesting"), though one dissenter refers to the instructors as "high paid baby-sitters." Nearly all of the students surveyed unanimously condemn the administration (one student simply writes "great instructors, administration sucks"), specifically in terms of financial aid. "If the bottom line is economics it's no wonder I'm paying so much to receive so little," complains one student, while another opines, "The administration is unorganized to the point where you would think they were corrupt." Still, the facilities at the School of the Art Institute of Chicago are one of the best aspects of the college, receiving high marks from undergrads. Most agree that students at The School of the Art Institute of Chicago work very hard. "At this art school, you bust your ass or get out—it's not for the weak of mind." However, one person calls the student body "a bunch of slackers." Most classes are relatively small.

Student Body

The Art Institute's student body leans to the left politically. Students seem to be open to diversity, even if they are not actually diverse themselves, with the majority of students being white. "Everyone really gets along and I like them, but everyone seems to be an upper-middle-class white." "It's the only place I know where dyed hair, body piercings, and tattoos are normal," offers another, while another cheers "we're all terrible weirdos—Hurrah!" A less enthusiastic student remarks "We're always trying to be individuals in one way or another, and that can be a problem."

FINANCIAL AID: 312-899-5106

ADMISSIONS

The admissions committee considers (in descending order of importance): HS record, test scores, recommendations, essay, class rank. *Also considered (in descending order of importance):* special talents, alumni relationship, extracurriculars, geographical distribution, personality. Either the SAT or ACT is required. An interview is recommended. Admissions process is need-blind. Minimum SAT I score of 420 verbal (ACT English score of 18) required. Applicants should have as much art experience as possible. *Special Requirements:* A portfolio is required for art program applicants. TOEFL is required of all international students. *The admissions office says:* "Immediate Decision Option allows prospective students to visit the school for a day, interview, have their portfolios reviewed, and receive an admissions decision."

The Inside Word

It is hard to imagine a more stimulating setting than the Art Institute of Chicago in which to pursue an arts education. Admission is highly competitive; in addition to strong artistic talents, candidates should demonstrate serious dedication to an arts career. When applying here and at other highly selective arts institutions, it is especially important to be meticulous in following all instructions in completing the application and submitting an appropriate portfolio. The Art Institute is small, very prestigious, and extremely particular about who is offered a spot in the entering class.

FINANCIAL AID

Students should submit: FAFSA (due April 1), the school's own financial aid form (due April 1), state aid form (due April 1). The Princeton Review suggests that all financial aid forms be submitted as soon as possible after January 1. *The following grants/scholarships are offered:* Pell, SEOG, academic merit, the school's own scholarships, the school's own grants, state scholarships, state grants, private scholarships, private grants. *Students borrow from the following loan programs:* Stafford, unsubsidized Stafford, Perkins, PLUS. College Work-Study Program is available. Institutional employment is available.

FROM THE ADMISSIONS OFFICE

Recognized as an innovator in the arts since its inception more than 100 years ago, and internationally esteemed as a school of art and design, the School of the Art Institute of Chicago offers a comprehensive college education centered in the visual and related arts. The School of the Art Institute of Chicago's primary purpose is to foster the conceptual and technical education of the artist in a highly professional and studio-oriented environment. Believing that the artist's success is dependent on both creative vision and technical expertise, the School encourages excellence, critical inquiry, and experimentation. The teaching of studio art, the complementary programs in art history, theory, and criticism and liberal arts, the visiting artists, and the collections and exhibitions of one of the world's finest museums all contribute to the variety, the challenge, and the resonance of the educational experience. An education of this sort is rare and, for the artist, irreplaceable.

ADMISSIONS

Admissions Rating	78
% of applicants accepted	71
% of acceptees attending	35

FRESHMAN PROFILE

Average verbal SAT	530
Average math SAT	570
Average ACT	NR
Average TOEFL	525
Graduated top 20% of class	35
Graduated top 40% of class	NR
Graduated top 60% of class	NR
Average HS GPA or Avg.	NR

DEADLINES

Early decision	3/15
Regular admission	8/15
Regular notification	rolling
Non-fall registration	yes

APPLICANTS ALSO LOOK AT

AND OFTEN PREFER
RISD
North Carolina School of the Arts

AND SOMETIMES PREFER
Maryland Inst., Coll. of Art
San Francisco Art Inst.

AND RARELY PREFER
Parsons

FINANCIAL FACTS

Financial Aid Rating	82
Tuition	$16,320
Room & board	$6,980
Estimated book expense	$1,980
% frosh receiving aid	74
% undergrads receiving aid	69
% aid is need-based	90
% frosh w/ grant (avg)	74 ($6,900)
% frosh w/ loan (avg)	70 ($3,455)
% UGs w/ job (avg)	32 ($1,284)
Off-campus job outlook	excellent

UNIVERSITY OF CHICAGO

1116 EAST 59TH STREET, CHICAGO, IL 60637   ADMISSIONS: 312-702-8650   FAX: 312-702-4199

CAMPUS LIFE

Quality of Life Rating	**71**
Type of school	private
Affiliation	none
Environment	metropolis

STUDENTS

FT undergrad enrollment	3,431
% male/female	54/46
% from out of state	70
% live on campus	64
% spend weekend on campus	94
% transfers	3
% from public high school	70
% in (# of) fraternities	14 (9)
% in (# of) sororities	5 (2)
% African-American	4
% Asian	27
% Caucasian	60
% Hispanic	5
% international	3
# of countries represented	43

WHAT'S HOT

library
lab facilities
political activism
computer facilities
dorms

WHAT'S NOT

student government
infrequent dating
sex
intercollegiate sports
town-gown relations

ACADEMICS

Academic Rating	**95**
Profs Interesting Rating	78
Profs Accessible Rating	81
Calendar	quarter
Student/teacher ratio	6:1
% profs PhD	100
Hours of study per day	3.72

MOST POPULAR MAJORS

economics
biological sciences
English

% GRADS WHO PURSUE...

Law 18, Med 12, MBA 7, MA 54

STUDENTS SPEAK OUT

Life

Chicago is a wonderful city, but Hyde Park, where the University of Chicago is located, is not one of its most hopping spots. Nor is it one of the city's safest, but given its reputation, student complaints about the neighborhood are surprisingly few. Because students here are extremely studious and competitive, social life is a drag. One undergrad sums up life at UC this way: "A small school surrounded by poor ghettos on Chicago's South Side with few women in the student body or the faculty hardly makes for an enjoyable social situation. When you consider also the stoic design of the buildings and the Chicago weather, you'll see that there is very little reason for being here unless the academic situation wasn't nearly perfect (and it is nearly perfect—at least in the physics department)." Sums up one student, "I chose this school for its excellent academic reputation, and any other criteria are ridiculous."

Academics

If you're serious about getting a great undergraduate education and can tolerate a slow social scene in a dreary neighborhood, you can't do much better than the UC. The school puts students through their paces with a demanding core curriculum that makes up half the credits necessary for an undergraduate degree. These mandatory courses in humanities, mathematics, science, and foreign languages, when coupled with major requirements, leave little room in the undergrad schedule for electives. When students do take electives, however, it's usually in graduate-level courses (grads make up more of the university's population than do the undergrads): "thus," concludes one undergrad, "an academically motivated undergraduate can receive a very stimulating education." Students here recognize that few other schools extend this much respect to their undergrads. Says one, "This school treats its undergrads like grad students. If a student is ready and willing to put the kind of intensity into his/her schoolwork that's required here, then it can be very rewarding." Be aware that expectations are also very high. The school is on a quarterly schedule, which tends to make courses go by quickly, and also more easily facilitates semesters off for work and travel.

Student Body

Chicago students have a well-known "geek" reputation. Says one gleefully, "The U of Chicago is the place where even a geek/loser/nerd can fit in." A classmate disagrees: "The people here, although widely described as geeks, are down-to-earth and tend to get to know each other as people rather than judging by appearances. People here talk about real things." The traditional student social interaction is available, but "you have to work really hard at this school—really hard!" Chicago students are very intense, and perhaps a little unkempt—"It's not so much that students are unattractive here as that they care less about appearances," says one student. Yet one student counters that image: "I'm sick of hearing people complain about the women here being ugly—they're not; in fact, some people prefer the way women look when they don't make a three-foot hole in the ozone layer every morning preparing their hair so they can look like Barbie dolls." So there! To sum it all up: "A small college, full of brilliant neurotics, in the midst of a great city."

ADMISSIONS

The admissions committee considers (in descending order of importance): HS record, class rank, essay, recommendations, test scores. *Also considered (in descending order of importance):* extracurriculars, personality, special talents. Either the SAT or ACT is required. An interview is recommended. Admissions process is need-blind. *High school units required/recommended:* 19 total units are recommended; 4 English recommended, 4 math recommended, 4 science recommended, 3 foreign language recommended, 2 social studies recommended, 2 history recommended. Rank in top fifth of secondary school class recommended. TOEFL is required of all international students.

The Inside Word

While excellent grades in tough courses and high test scores are the norm for applicants to the university, what really counts is what's on your mind. This is a cerebral institution, and thinkers stand out in the admissions process. Think about yourself, think about what you'd like to know more about, think about why you want to attend the university. Once you have some answers, begin writing your essays. And remember that universities that are this selective and recommend interviews should always be taken up on their recommendation.

FINANCIAL AID

Students should submit: FAFSA, the school's own financial aid form, a copy of parents' most recent income tax filing. The Princeton Review suggests that all financial aid forms be submitted as soon as possible after January 1. *The following grants/scholarships are offered:* Pell, SEOG, academic merit, the school's own scholarships, the school's own grants, state scholarships, state grants, private scholarships, private grants, ROTC, foreign aid. *Students borrow from the following loan programs:* Stafford, Perkins, PLUS, private loans. Applicants will be notified of awards beginning April 1. College Work-Study Program is available. Institutional employment is available.

FROM THE ADMISSIONS OFFICE

"Chicago is a place where talented young intellectuals, writers, mathematicians, and scientists come to learn in a setting that rewards hard work and prizes initiative and creativity. It is also a place where collegiate life is urban, yet friendly and open, and free of empty traditionalism and snobbishness. Chicago is the right choice for students who know that they would thrive in an intimate classroom setting. Classes at Chicago are small, emphasizing discussion with faculty members whose research is always testing the limits of their chosen fields. Our students: they take chances; they delight us when they pursue a topic on their own for the fun of it; they display an articulate voice in papers and in discussion; they do not accept our word for everything but respect good argument; they are fanciful or solid at the right time. Most often they are students who choose the best courses available, who take a heavier load than necessary because they are curious and not worried about the consequences, who let curiosity and energy spill over into activities and sports, who are befriended by the best and toughest teachers, and who finish what they set out to do."

ADMISSIONS

Admissions Rating	92
% of applicants accepted	54
% of acceptees attending	31

FRESHMAN PROFILE

Average verbal SAT	680
Average math SAT	660
Average ACT	29
Average TOEFL	600
Graduated top 20% of class	89
Graduated top 40% of class	100
Graduated top 60% of class	NR
Average HS GPA or Avg.	NR

DEADLINES

Early decision	NR
Regular admission	1/15
Regular notification	4/1
Non-fall registration	no

APPLICANTS ALSO LOOK AT

AND OFTEN PREFER
Harvard/Radcliffe
Yale
Princeton
Columbia U.
Swarthmore

AND SOMETIMES PREFER
Northwestern U.
Johns Hopkins

AND RARELY PREFER
Loyola U. Chicago
U. Illinois, Urbana-Champaign
U. Rochester

FINANCIAL FACTS

Financial Aid Rating	80
Tuition	$19,875
Room & board	$7,258
Estimated book expense	$1,000
% frosh receiving aid	75
% undergrads receiving aid	69
% aid is need-based	95
% frosh w/ grant (avg)	66 ($13,995)
% frosh w/ loan (avg)	56 ($2,450)
% UGs w/ job (avg)	80 ($1,900)
Off-campus job outlook	excellent

CUNY-HUNTER COLLEGE

695 PARK AVENUE, NEW YORK, NY 10021 · ADMISSIONS: 212-772-4490 · FAX: 212-772-4554

CAMPUS LIFE

Quality of Life Rating **69**

Type of school	public
Affiliation	none
Environment	metropolis

STUDENTS

FT undergrad enrollment	8,897
% male/female	27/73
% from out of state	2
% live on campus	1
% spend weekend on campus	1
% transfers	39
% from public high school	70
% in (# of) fraternities	2 (2)
% in (# of) sororities	1 (2)
% African-American	22
% Asian	15
% Caucasian	41
% Hispanic	22
% international	NR
# of countries represented	21

WHAT'S HOT

ethnic diversity on campus
different students interact
leftist politics
New York
political activism

WHAT'S NOT

registration is a pain
dorms
lab facilities
beer
unattractive campus

ACADEMICS

Academic Rating **66**

Profs Interesting Rating	60
Profs Accessible Rating	60
Calendar	semester
Student/teacher ratio	18:1
% profs tenured	85
Hours of study per day	2.96

MOST POPULAR MAJORS

psychology
English
sociology

STUDENTS SPEAK OUT

Life

Hunter College is a commuter school that sports a lone residence hall. Most Hunter students live with their parents or on their own in New York City. Says one, "Everyone has their own lives outside of school as there isn't a dorm/campus atmosphere here." Yes, Hunter, which has "a certain rawness," is about as urban as you can get, with campuses uptown and downtown in the Big Apple. This lack of a traditional campus can make forging friendships tough. Explains one freshman, "I like the students but it can be difficult to establish friendships, as it is a commuter school." A really diverse commuter school, mind you, a quality that students are very happy about. This mixed metaphor sums it up quite well: "At Hunter it is one big melting pot with a hell of a backbone as support for all ethnic groups." Students love studying in New York ("This is NY! Anything goes!") although it is quite expensive to eat, not to mention live, both on and off campus (those who are in the dorms give them low marks). Unlike most colleges, frats and beer do not rule Hunter. Instead, for diversion, many students turn to cigarettes, by far their drug of choice, and "clubbing" at New York's many hot nightspots.

Academics

"You can thank Governor George Pataki and his outrageous budget cuts for many of the problems [at Hunter]," rages one Hunter College junior. Statewide cuts have had a bad effect on Hunter, sparking student protest, and limiting access to the library, computers, and other college facilities. Still, most Hunter undergrads are satisfied with the level of instruction. Says one, breezily, "I have had some excellent professors, many of whom I'd love to spend some time with outside class, throwing back some beers and ranting about popular culture." Another is not quite as complimentary, "So far my professors seem to be competent in their fields, but competency and mastery are two different ballparks, and the professors at Hunter don't seem to participate in that sport." With fine programs in English, urban planning, pre-med sciences, nursing, and education, to name a few, Hunter has a lot to offer for a very affordable (in-state) tuition. However, students must jump through hoops to get that education. They rate registration procedures as incredibly tough, and the bursar and library fared only slightly better in our surveys. Says one, "You have to scream at [the administration] to get them to do what they're supposed to do." In these trying budgetary times, those screams might just keep getting louder.

Student Body

Hunter undergrads are a friendly group of independent students who have their own thing going on and are at school for one reason: to get an education. "I really enjoy the diversity of students and faculty and I feel it greatly contributes to my overall education," beams a satisfied philosophy major. With similar African-American, Asian, Caucasian, and Hispanic populations, Hunter is truly colorful, and lacks many problems associated with discrimination that more homogeneous student bodies must contend with. Another adds, "Fortunately, there is little of the judgment and social hierarchy going on that exists in high school." While women still outnumber men (Hunter was women-only for most of its existence), the gap is closing, though not fast enough for some: "We need men!" Dating and sexual activity are both popular, but not to the extent they are at most traditional campuses. Says one, "Students at Hunter pair off with their friends for study reasons." Hunter also sponsors an array of clubs and associations for students who want further contact with their classmates outside of class.

ADMISSIONS

The admissions committee considers (in descending order of importance): HS record, test scores, class rank. Admissions process is need-blind. *High school units required/recommended:* 16 total units are recommended; 4 English recommended, 3 math recommended, 2 science recommended, 2 foreign language recommended, 4 social studies recommended. Minimum combined SAT I score of 900, rank in top third of secondary school class, or minimum grade average of 80 required. *Special Requirements:* A portfolio is required for art program applicants. An audition is required for music program applicants. An RN is required for nursing program applicants. TOEFL is required of all international students. Auditions required of dance, music, and theatre program applicants. R.N. required of applicants to R.N. pathway nursing program.

The Inside Word

Nothing personal here; applications are processed through CUNY's enormous central processing center. Follow the numbers—and be sure to have followed the new high school curriculum requirements—and gain admission.

FINANCIAL AID

Students should submit: FAFSA (due May 1). The Princeton Review suggests that all financial aid forms be submitted as soon as possible after January 1. *The following grants/scholarships are offered:* Pell, SEOG, academic merit, the school's own scholarships, the school's own grants, state scholarships, state grants, private scholarships, foreign aid. *Students borrow from the following loan programs:* Perkins, PLUS, the school's own loan fund, supplemental loans. College Work-Study Program is available. Institutional employment is available.

FROM THE ADMISSIONS OFFICE

Hunter College, the second oldest college in the City University of New York, is a coeducational, fully accredited college, with a large and diverse faculty in the liberal arts and sciences and in several professional schools. In most of its programs the college offers both undergraduate and graduate degrees. Hunter's total enrollment is over 18,400. Of these students, about 8,200 are full-time undergraduates. An additional 6,100 part-time students are divided between degree and nondegree programs. Over 4,000 graduate students are studying in the arts and sciences and teacher education programs and at the schools of Social Work, Health Sciences, and Nursing. The Thomas Hunter Honors program offers students special academic challenge in a small-group setting. The Freshman Block program keeps classmates together in the same courses as they pursue pre-health science, pre-nursing, pre-med or honors programs. The unique Public Service Scholars program, which offers internships in New York City government; the Minority Access to Research Careers (MARC); and Minority Biomedical Research Support (MBRS) programs, to name just a few, permit students to earn academic credit while participating in scientific research and/or gaining valuable career experience. Undergraduates interested in social work careers may enter a five-year program leading to a master's degree from the Hunter College School of Social Work, rated among the top ten in the nation.

ADMISSIONS

Admissions Rating	72
% of applicants accepted	49
% of acceptees attending	51

FRESHMAN PROFILE

Average verbal SAT	470
Average math SAT	480
Average ACT	NR
Average TOEFL	500
Graduated top 20% of class	42
Graduated top 40% of class	81
Graduated top 60% of class	93
Average HS GPA or Avg.	83.0

DEADLINES

Early decision	NR
Regular admission	1/15
Regular notification	rolling
Non-fall registration	yes

APPLICANTS ALSO LOOK AT

AND OFTEN PREFER

CUNY Queens
NYU

AND SOMETIMES PREFER

Fordham
Iona
SUNY Stony Brook

FINANCIAL FACTS

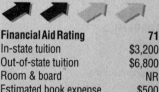

Financial Aid Rating	71
In-state tuition	$3,200
Out-of-state tuition	$6,800
Room & board	NR
Estimated book expense	$500
% frosh receiving aid	NR
% undergrads receiving aid	74
% aid is need-based	NR
% frosh w/ grant (avg)	NR
% frosh w/ loan (avg)	NR
% UGs w/ job (avg)	NR
Off-campus job outlook	good

CUNY-QUEENS COLLEGE

65-30 KISSENA BOULEVARD, FLUSHING, NY 11367   ADMISSIONS: 718-997-5600   FAX: 718-997-5617

CAMPUS LIFE

Quality of Life Rating   **68**
Type of school	public
Affiliation	none
Environment	metropolis

STUDENTS
FT undergrad enrollment	8,999
% male/female	41/59
% from out of state	1
% live on campus	NR
% spend weekend on campus	NR
% transfers	42
% from public high school	55
% African-American	9
% Asian	16
% Caucasian	61
% Hispanic	14
% international	1
# of countries represented	32

WHAT'S HOT
ethnic diversity on campus
leftist politics
religion
library
different students interact

WHAT'S NOT
beer
students are unhappy
hard liquor
political activism
support groups

ACADEMICS

Academic Rating   **65**
Profs Interesting Rating	61
Profs Accessible Rating	60
Calendar	semester
Student/teacher ratio	18:1
% profs tenured	87
Hours of study per day	2.65

MOST POPULAR MAJORS
accounting
communication arts/sciences
elementary education

% GRADS WHO PURSUE...
Law 9, Med 4, MBA 5, MA 80

STUDENTS SPEAK OUT

Life

Queens College, like others in the CUNY system, is solely a commuter school. There are no dorms at all, so most students live at home, although many find housing nearby, perhaps in order to avoid parking hassles. Most students here work at some type of job outside of school. Perhaps this necessity contributes to the lack of a typical collegiate party atmosphere. The social scene is "quiet," and mostly focused on "hanging out in the student union or cafeteria." Recently, however, social activities have been promoted; concerts, parties, and other student government-sponsored events are on the rise. Dating in the traditional sense is very popular as well, as life at this commuter college does not completely end after class. Sports are also now receiving more attention at Queens; the college boasts over twenty NCAA Division II teams, including a strong men's tennis team. The campus is "very safe and pretty clean," quite a compliment for an urban New York school. In general, many extracurricular and social options exist here for students who have the desire to go after them, but most still opt for weekends at home.

Academics

Many people consider Queens College the finest school in the CUNY system. Students rate their courses overall as "excellent." Particularly sharp departments are English, music, accounting, computer science, biology, and chemistry. The constantly improving facilities also earn praise, especially the first-rate library building. Areas of complaint mostly have to do with the faculty and administration: Students give their professors low marks for teaching ability and accessibility, and slam the administration for inefficiency (registration is a red-tape nightmare, many classes are overcrowded, "not enough advising" is available, and too often the course catalog does not accurately reflect the course offerings). Budget problems in the CUNY system, New York City, and New York State have caused service to diminish while tuition charges rise, causing predictable dissatisfaction among students. However, students still consider their school a bargain, given the overall value of their curriculum and facilities.

Student Body

One of the greatest attributes of Queens College is its diversity. All types of students come here. Minority students make up almost half the school's population. There is also a "high foreign student population," and the school's affordability, as well as its considerable merit-based scholarship offerings, allows students of all income levels to enroll. The political climate reflects the cultural mix of the students: neither liberal nor conservative, but accepting of different points of view. Queens College students can leave after four years with a solid education behind them, as well as the invaluable experience of interaction with virtually all kinds of people.

ADMISSIONS

The admissions committee considers (in descending order of importance): HS record, class rank, test scores, recommendations, essay. *Also considered (in descending order of importance):* extracurriculars, special talents. SAT is preferred. Admissions process is need-blind. *High school units required/recommended:* 17 total units are recommended; 4 English recommended, 3 math recommended, 3 science recommended, 3 foreign language recommended, 4 social studies recommended. Minimum combined SAT I score of 1020, rank in top third of secondary school class, or minimum 3.0 GPA or grade average of 80 required. SAT II recommended of scholarship applicants. TOEFL is required of all international students. *The admissions office says:* "Queens College seeks to admit freshmen who have completed a strong academic program in high school with a B+ average. Admission is based on a variety of factors, including grade point average, the academic program, and test scores. Those applying to the SEEK (Search for Education, Elevation, and Knowledge) program need not meet those requirements. SEEK "helps economically and educationally disadvantaged students" and provides those students with "intensive academic services (possibly including a stipend for educational expenses). Apply by January 15."

The Inside Word

Applicants to Queens follow the usual CUNY application procedures, which have gotten tougher with the implementation of new high school curriculum requirements. Candidates for the Aaron Copeland School of Music must also successfully pass through a rigorous audition process.

FINANCIAL AID

Students should submit: FAFSA, the school's own financial aid form (due August 1). The Princeton Review suggests that all financial aid forms be submitted as soon as possible after January 1. *The following grants/scholarships are offered:* Pell, SEOG, the school's own scholarships, state grants, private scholarships. *Students borrow from the following loan programs:* Stafford, unsubsidized Stafford, Perkins, PLUS. College Work-Study Program is available. Institutional employment is available. Freshmen are discouraged from working.

FROM THE ADMISSIONS OFFICE

"Queens College is dedicated to the idea that a great education should be accessible to talented young people of all backgrounds—ethnic and financial. It is a global gathering place for ideas. The college's colorful kaleidoscope of tongues, talents, and cultures—sixty-six different native languages are spoken here—provides an extraordinary educational environment. A strong liberal arts curriculum ensures students an education for a full career and a full life. Opportunities abound with special programs developed for honors students; students in prelaw, pre-med, and business; adults; 'fresh start' students; foreign language speakers. In all their diversity, students come first."

ADMISSIONS

Admissions Rating	66
% of applicants accepted	81
% of acceptees attending	49

FRESHMAN PROFILE

Average verbal SAT	500
Average math SAT	520
Average ACT	NR
Average TOEFL	500
Graduated top 20% of class	34
Graduated top 40% of class	70
Graduated top 60% of class	87
Average HS GPA or Avg.	82.0

DEADLINES

Early decision	1/15
Regular admission	NR
Regular notification	rolling
Non-fall registration	yes

APPLICANTS ALSO LOOK AT

AND OFTEN PREFER
CUNY Hunter
St. John's U. (NY)
Hofstra

AND SOMETIMES PREFER
Fordham
SUNY Albany
SUNY Binghamton
SUNY Buffalo
SUNY Stony Brook

FINANCIAL FACTS

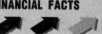

Financial Aid Rating	74
In-state tuition	$3,200
Out-of-state tuition	$6,800
Room & board	NR
Estimated book expense	$600
% frosh receiving aid	50
% undergrads receiving aid	50
% aid is need-based	100
% frosh w/ grant (avg)	60 ($3,000)
% frosh w/ loan (avg)	5 ($2,000)
% UGs w/ job (avg)	5 ($700)
Off-campus job outlook	good

CLAREMONT MCKENNA COLLEGE

890 COLUMBIA AVENUE, CLAREMONT, CA 91711   ADMISSIONS: 909-621-8088   FAX: 909-6218516

STUDENTS SPEAK OUT

Life

Note: The Claremont Colleges are five small undergraduate schools (Claremont McKenna, Harvey Mudd, Pitzer, Pomona, and Scripps) and one graduate school sharing a central location and facilities. Each school serves a distinct purpose and maintains its own faculty and campus. Cross-registration is encouraged. Life at Claremont McKenna College is a good mix of academics, athletics, cultural get-togethers, and parties. One student writes, "The best thing about CMC is the five-college community and the Athenaeum (interesting speakers on everything from politics to music and great gourmet food)." Many of the parties at the five colleges occur at CMC or Harvey Mudd, since the other campuses have stricter alcohol policies. And beer gets a mention in many of the students responses. As this student point out, "Maybe we don't drink as hard as some colleges, but we sure drink a lot more often." There are lots of on-campus planned activities (Homecoming, Wild Video Dance Party, the Night in Vienna Dinner, and Monte Carlo Night, for example) along with fun rooms for pool and foosball. For those interested in a change of nightlife, L.A. is a half-hour drive, and San Diego is within easy reach. The town of Claremont gets disparaging comments from many of the students. As this one explains, "Claremont is entirely useless as a college town—all boutiques and pricey restaurants. I suppose it's good for the occasional cup of coffee." Student government is "huge" here and given a good amount of freedom by the administration to voice the students' concerns.

Academics

"If I had a personal talk with God about creating a great school, He would create CMC," wrote one student. Another admirer adds, "CMC is what east coast Ivy League schools used to be—a tight-knit community of intellectuals, a faculty with commitment to both students and the school, and a financial aid office that rocks the world." Indeed, if your goals include a successful professional career or graduate school (particularly law school), then you should definitely consider Claremont McKenna. As one student reports, "The school emphasizes competition and encourages financial success." Students definitely benefit from the five-college flexibility and CMC offers "research opportunities with profs" who are "both plentiful and enjoyable." And working with these "brilliant" professors seems to be just fine with CMC undergrads. The glowing comments include this little note, "One professor took us all out for dinner and then to hear Danny Glover read poetry by Langston Hughes." In general, the "professors are accessible and willing to work with you." And this accessibility is the rule for both freshman and seniors alike: "My first English teacher was #1 in his class at Harvard and he teaches freshman lit. He's awesome!" The bursar's office and deans both receive high marks. One student says, "CMC is a great place to be if you don't want to be a number." Students lauded the "seamless registration" as well as the library and computer facilities on campus.

Student Body

Over one-third of CMC's ambitious students are minorities, but this doesn't necessarily ensure diversity: "My fellow students are pampered, prep-school brats who have little respect for others." And as one student proclaims, "Minorities are accepted as long as they act white." Still, discrimination does not seem to be a problem. "As a minority, I personally have never experienced discrimination," says one. The student body is very career-oriented and politically conservative: "CMC is a campus with little appreciation for the protest. We prefer intellectual discussion over a brute show of political force."

FINANCIAL AID: 909-621-8356

WEB SITE: HTTP://WWW.MCKENNA.EDU

ADMISSIONS

The admissions committee considers (in descending order of importance): HS record, test scores, recommendations, essay, class rank. *Also considered (in descending order of importance):* extracurriculars, personality, special talents, alumni relationship. Either the SAT or ACT is required. An interview is recommended. Admissions process is need-blind. *High school units required/recommended:* 12 total units are required; 20 total units are recommended; 4 English required, 3 math required, 4 math recommended, 2 science required, 3 science recommended, 2 foreign language required, 2 social studies recommended, 1 history required. Electives from listed areas recommended. Full program of challenging work is more important than specific number or distribution of units. TOEFL is required of all international students. *The admissions office says:* "Because of the nature of CMC, we place extra emphasis on leadership ability/potential and extracurricular involvement. Our students typically have strong interpersonal skills. They also rate high in self-confidence, assertiveness, and motivation."

The Inside Word

Although applicants have to possess solid academic qualifications in order to gain admission to Claremont McKenna, the importance of making a good match should not be underestimated. Colleges of such small size and selectivity devote much more energy to determining whether the candidate as an individual fits than they do to whether a candidate has the appropriate test scores.

FINANCIAL AID

Students should submit: FAFSA, state aid form (due February 1), a copy of parents' most recent income tax filing (due May 1). The Princeton Review suggests that all financial aid forms be submitted as soon as possible after January 1. *The following grants/scholarships are offered:* Pell, SEOG, academic merit, the school's own scholarships, the school's own grants, state scholarships, state grants, private scholarships, ROTC. *Students borrow from the following loan programs:* Stafford, unsubsidized Stafford, Perkins, PLUS, the school's own loan fund. Applicants will be notified of awards beginning April 1. College Work-Study Program is available. Institutional employment is available.

FROM THE ADMISSIONS OFFICE

"CMC's mission is clear: to educate students for meaningful lives and responsible leadership in business, government, and the professions. While many other colleges champion either a traditional liberal arts education with emphasis on intellectual breadth, or training that stresses acquisition of technical skills, CMC offers a clear alternative. Instead of dividing the liberal arts and working world into separate realms, education at CMC is rooted in the interplay between the world of ideas and the world of events. By combining the intellectual breadth of liberal arts with the more pragmatic concerns of public affairs, CMC students gain the vision, skills, and values necessary for leadership in all sectors of society."

ADMISSIONS

Admissions Rating	93
% of applicants accepted	41
% of acceptees attending	31

FRESHMAN PROFILE

Average verbal SAT	680
Average math SAT	680
Average ACT	30
Average TOEFL	600
Graduated top 20% of class	93
Graduated top 40% of class	100
Graduated top 60% of class	NR
Average HS GPA or Avg.	3.8

DEADLINES

Early decision	11/15
Regular admission	1/15
Regular notification	4/1
Non-fall registration	no

APPLICANTS ALSO LOOK AT

AND OFTEN PREFER

Stanford
Georgetown U.

AND SOMETIMES PREFER

Pomona
UC-Berkeley
UCLA

AND RARELY PREFER

UC-San Diego
UC-Davis
UC-Irvine

FINANCIAL FACTS

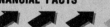

Financial Aid Rating	89
Tuition	$18,320
Room & board	$6,010
Estimated book expense	$1,500
% frosh receiving aid	60
% undergrads receiving aid	72
% aid is need-based	76
% frosh w/ grant (avg)	60 ($9,790)
% frosh w/ loan (avg)	65 ($3,000)
% UGs w/ job (avg)	55 ($900)
Off-campus job outlook	fair

CLARK UNIVERSITY

950 MAIN STREET, WORCESTER, MA 01610-1477   ADMISSIONS: 508-793-7431   FAX: 508-793-8821

CAMPUS LIFE

Quality of Life Rating   **72**
Type of school   private
Affiliation   none
Environment   city

STUDENTS
FT undergrad enrollment	1,850
% male/female	41/59
% from out of state	63
% live on campus	70
% spend weekend on campus	70
% transfers	14
% from public high school	73
% African-American	3
% Asian	4
% Caucasian	61
% Hispanic	3
% international	17
# of countries represented	63

WHAT'S HOT
ethnic diversity on campus
cigarettes
drugs
leftist politics
different students interact

WHAT'S NOT
Worcester
town-gown relations
unattractive campus
campus food
intramural sports

ACADEMICS

Academic Rating	**81**
Profs Interesting Rating	79
Profs Accessible Rating	78
Calendar	semester
Student/teacher ratio	11:1
% profs PhD/tenured	98/99
Hours of study per day	3.37

MOST POPULAR MAJORS
psychology
government/international relations
biology

% GRADS WHO PURSUE...
Law 4, MBA 6, MA 9

STUDENTS SPEAK OUT

Life
Life at Clark University means dealing with life in Worcester (pronounced "Woostah," as if you're in a Pepperidge Farm ad), where, evidently, never is heard an encouraging word. "There is a lot of frustration about location," one student comments. Students do like the campus, however, rating it safe, comfortable, and convenient. There are no fraternities or sororities here. This, combined with the apparent unfriendliness of Worcester, leads to a pretty dull social life. "If you don't drink or do drugs, that cuts out about eighty-five percent of your fun," says one student. While this is certainly an exaggeration, drinking does seem to be a prevalent pastime. The consensus: "Worcester is no cultural Nirvana, but the school is cool." Fortunately, Boston is only forty miles away and is easily accessible by bus.

Academics
"Individualism" is the buzzword at Clark. Students frequently cite their autonomy in their comments to us. Clark is "a good choice, unless you're the kind of person who must fit into a particular crowd or have constant supervision," says one student. "Clark's the kind of place individuals come to contribute themselves to education and college life." Another praises the university as "allowing the perfect opportunity to find one's self." Psychology and geography are the two most famous departments here, although economics and political science are quite popular. Social science and natural science departments are generally considered stronger than the liberal arts here (except for the English department, which is good). Although a research university, Clark has many more undergraduate students than graduate students, allowing undergraduates to participate to an unusually large degree as research assistants. An added plus is that classes are small, so it's easier to get individual attention. Says one business management major, "In my freshman year, all of my classes had fewer than twenty students. I love Clark!" Clark is a member of the Worcester Consortium, which allows undergraduates to take courses at any of nine other schools in the area.

Student Body
As one student puts it, "Clark boasts about having one of the most diverse student populations around; this, however, is an understatement." Most of the diversity is provided by foreign nationals. Hanging out with so many international students "really opens your eyes to different cultures." Still, students complain that their classmates are cliquish—an almost inevitable result of the fractured social life here (see "Life," above). Clark students are famous for their apathy, and some seem strangely proud of this. Says one, "I get really sick of that infamous Clark apathy, but hey, what can you do?"

FINANCIAL AID: 508-793-7478

WEB SITE: HTTP://WWW.CLARKU.EDU/

ADMISSIONS

The admissions committee considers (in descending order of importance): HS record, class rank, test scores, recommendations, essay. *Also considered (in descending order of importance):* extracurriculars, personality, special talents, alumni relationship, geographical distribution. Either the SAT or ACT is required. An interview is recommended. *High school units required/recommended:* 16 total units are recommended; 4 English recommended, 3 math recommended, 3 science recommended, 2 foreign language recommended, 2 social studies recommended. TOEFL is required of all international students. *The admissions office says:* "If a student plans to major in math or science, three or more years of math and science courses are strongly recommended."

The Inside Word

Clark is surrounded by formidable competitors, and its selectivity suffers because of it. Most "B" students will encounter little difficulty gaining admission. Given the University's solid academic environment and access to other member colleges in the Worcester Consortium, it can be a terrific choice for students who are not up to the ultra-competitive admission expectations of "top tier" universities.

FINANCIAL AID

Students should submit: FAFSA (due February 1), CSS Profile (due February 1), state aid form (due February 1), Divorced Parents form (due February 1), a copy of parents' most recent income tax filing (due February 1). The Princeton Review suggests that all financial aid forms be submitted as soon as possible after January 1. *The following grants/scholarships are offered:* Pell, SEOG, academic merit, the school's own scholarships, the school's own grants, state scholarships, state grants, private scholarships, private grants, ROTC, foreign aid. *Students borrow from the following loan programs:* Stafford, unsubsidized Stafford, Perkins, PLUS, the school's own loan fund, state loans, private loans. Applicants will be notified of awards beginning April 1. College Work-Study Program is available. Institutional employment is available.

FROM THE ADMISSIONS OFFICE

"Founded in 1887 as the nation's first all-graduate university, Clark is an independent, residential college. Joining Harvard and Yale as New England's charter members in the Association of American Universities, Clark has an international reputation for quality instruction and advanced research. More than 800 courses per semester are offered in the humanities, sciences, social sciences, education, and visual and performing arts."

ADMISSIONS

Admissions Rating	76
% of applicants accepted	78
% of acceptees attending	26

FRESHMAN PROFILE

Average verbal SAT	600
Average math SAT	570
Average ACT	NR
Average TOEFL	600
Graduated top 20% of class	53
Graduated top 40% of class	84
Graduated top 60% of class	96
Average HS GPA or Avg.	3.1

DEADLINES

Early decision	January
Regular admission	2/1
Regular notification	4/1
Non-fall registration	yes

APPLICANTS ALSO LOOK AT

AND OFTEN PREFER

Tufts
Boston Coll.
Brandeis
Vassar

AND SOMETIMES PREFER

Connecticut Coll.
Syracuse
U. New Hampshire
Skidmore Coll.
U. Mass., Amherst

AND RARELY PREFER

Wheaton Coll. (MA)

FINANCIAL FACTS

Financial Aid Rating	80
Tuition	$19,600
Room & board	$4,250
Estimated book expense	$500
% frosh receiving aid	72
% undergrads receiving aid	71
% aid is need-based	98
% frosh w/ grant (avg)	74 ($10,595)
% frosh w/ loan (avg)	60 ($2,979)
% UGs w/ job (avg)	32 ($1,300)
Off-campus job outlook	good

CLARKSON UNIVERSITY

Box 5605, POTSDAM, NY 13699   ADMISSIONS: 315-268-6479   FAX: 315-268-7647

CAMPUS LIFE

Quality of Life Rating **74**
Type of school   private
Affiliation   none
Environment   town

STUDENTS
FT undergrad enrollment   2,212
% male/female   76/24
% from out of state   28
% live on campus   86
% spend weekend on campus   95
% transfers   18
% from public high school   88
% in (# of) fraternities   25 (16)
% in (# of) sororities   20 (3)
% African-American   1
% Asian   2
% Caucasian   89
% Hispanic   1
% international   3
# of countries represented   23

WHAT'S HOT
intercollegiate sports
Greeks
campus feels safe
registration is a breeze
different students interact

WHAT'S NOT
hard liquor
student publications
campus difficult to get around
unattractive campus
drugs

ACADEMICS

Academic Rating   **77**
Profs Interesting Rating   66
Profs Accessible Rating   76
Calendar   semester
Student/teacher ratio   15:1
% profs PhD   90
Hours of study per day   2.95

MOST POPULAR MAJORS
civil engineering
mechanical engineering
engineering/management

% GRADS WHO PURSUE...
Law 2, Med 2, MBA 1, MA 8

STUDENTS SPEAK OUT
Life
Isolated Clarkson University is located in Potsdam, a remote town near the Canadian border. Winters are long and cold, and the bleakness can be discouraging for newcomers. One senior tells us "almost everyone I've talked to says that during the first year he wanted to transfer out, but by the time he graduated he thought Clarkson was the best and was happy he stayed. Clarkson and even Potsdam grow on you. Men outnumber women three to one. Downtown [Potsdam] is key! It gives you a chance to meet new people and interact with SUNY-Potsdam students. Fraternity life and the bars are the things to do!" Clarkson boasts a student-run television station, which, according to one student is "one of the best in the country (WCKN-TV 31). It's entirely owned and operated by the students with very little faculty involvement, yet we rival 'professional' stations." The hockey team is excellent, and other winter sports are understandably popular.

Academics
For northeasterners looking for a solid engineering education who would rather do without the intense competition at MIT and RPI, Clarkson may be the place. Explains one CU undergrad, "The level of competitiveness here is very low. Students are willing to help you at all times—it's not a fight to see who is the best, it's more of a 'let's all get through this together' kind of thing." Others agree that "there's no cutthroat atmosphere, which makes life easier." Two thirds of Clarkson's students are engineers; practically all the rest study business and management (the notable exception is a small group of premeds). Professors are helpful and accessible, particularly for those at an engineering-intensive school. Says one student, "The professors here are very interested in the successful progress of their students. Professors will work with students in a way that is unique, from what I've been told about major universities." Academics are challenging but not unreasonably demanding. Students put in about three hours of study a day outside the classroom. Required courses, which include liberal arts courses as well as basic math and computer sciences, are considered difficult. Administrators receive good grades across the board.

Student Body
Clarkson's student body is overwhelmingly white. With around 200 minority classmates, minority students can feel a little out of place. One student complains that many of his classmates "have small-town, upstate New York mentalities. There are lots of 'brains' but very few intellectuals." All the same, students are generally friendly and easygoing: Says one student, "People here don't think they're above anyone else—that's what's so great about them."

FINANCIAL AID: 315-268-6471   E-MAIL: DBROWN@DARIUS.CLARKSON.EDU   WEB SITE: HTTP://FIRE.CLARKSON.EDU/

ADMISSIONS

The admissions committee considers (in descending order of importance): HS record, class rank, test scores, recommendations, essay. *Also considered (in descending order of importance):* personality, alumni relationship, extracurriculars, geographical distribution, special talents. Either the SAT or ACT is required. An interview is recommended. *High school units required/recommended:* 16 total units are required; 4 English required, 3 math required, 2 science required, 3 science recommended. Rank in top quarter of secondary school class recommended. TOEFL is required of all international students. *The admissions office says:* "We do not use cutoffs, but rather evaluate the overall match between student and Clarkson. Throughout the process, we are accessible to the students, their family, and their guidance counselor."

The Inside Word

Clarkson's acceptance rate is too high for solid applicants to lose much sleep about gaining admission. Serious candidates should interview anyway. If you are particularly solid and really want to come here, it could help you get some scholarship money. Women and minorities will encounter an especially friendly admissions committee.

FINANCIAL AID

Students should submit: FAFSA (due February 15), the school's own financial aid form (due February 15), a copy of parents' most recent income tax filing (due February 15). The Princeton Review suggests that all financial aid forms be submitted as soon as possible after January 1. *The following grants/scholarships are offered:* Pell, SEOG, academic merit, athletic, the school's own scholarships, the school's own grants, state scholarships, state grants, private scholarships, private grants, ROTC. *Students borrow from the following loan programs:* Stafford, Perkins, PLUS. Applicants will be notified of awards beginning April 15. College Work-Study Program is available. Institutional employment is available. Freshmen are discouraged from working.

FROM THE ADMISSIONS OFFICE

"Clarkson is a blend of vivid contrasts. High-powered academics in a cooperative, friendly community; technically oriented students who enjoy people; a unique location that serves as gateway to all kinds of outdoor recreation and to social and cultural activities of four colleges within a ten-mile radius. Our students are described as smart, hard-working, outgoing, energized, fun-loving, and team players. Our academic programs: rigorous, relevant, flexible and nationally respected. Our teachers: demanding, approachable, concerned, accomplished and inspiring. Clarkson alumni, students, and faculty share an exceptionally solid bond and the lifetime benefits that come from an active, global network of personal and professional ties."

ADMISSIONS

Admissions Rating	74
% of applicants accepted	84
% of acceptees attending	31

FRESHMAN PROFILE

Average verbal SAT	600
Average math SAT	620
Average ACT	NR
Average TOEFL	550
Graduated top 20% of class	66
Graduated top 40% of class	90
Graduated top 60% of class	98
Average HS GPA or Avg.	3.0

DEADLINES

Early decision	NR
Regular admission	NR
Regular notification	rolling
Non-fall registration	yes

APPLICANTS ALSO LOOK AT

AND OFTEN PREFER

RIT
SUNY at Buffalo
RPI
U. Vermont
Penn State U.

AND SOMETIMES PREFER

Worcester Poly.
U. Connecticut
U. Rochester
Alfred
Lehigh

AND RARELY PREFER

Syracuse

FINANCIAL FACTS

Financial Aid Rating	82
Tuition	$16,770
Room & board	$5,830
Estimated book expense	$500
% frosh receiving aid	90
% undergrads receiving aid	85
% aid is need-based	75
% frosh w/ grant (avg)	75 ($6,300)
% frosh w/ loan (avg)	90 ($4,000)
% UGs w/ job (avg)	40 ($800)
Off-campus job outlook	good

CLEMSON UNIVERSITY

105 SIKES HALL, CLEMSON, SC 29634-5124   ADMISSIONS: 803-656-2287   FAX: 803-656-2464

CAMPUS LIFE

Quality of Life Rating	**81**
Type of school	public
Affiliation	none
Environment	town

STUDENTS

FT undergrad enrollment	11,695
% male/female	55/45
% from out of state	28
% live on campus	52
% spend weekend on campus	NR
% transfers	23
% from public high school	80
% in (# of) fraternities	15 (25)
% in (# of) sororities	25 (15)
% African-American	9
% Asian	2
% Caucasian	89
% Hispanic	0
% international	NR
# of countries represented	37

WHAT'S HOT
old-fashioned dating
intercollegiate sports
town-gown relations
Greeks
intramural sports

WHAT'S NOT
dorms
theater
campus difficult to get around
student publications
support groups

ACADEMICS

Academic Rating	**72**
Profs Interesting Rating	66
Profs Accessible Rating	64
Calendar	semester
Student/teacher ratio	18:1
% profs PhD/tenured	75/86
Hours of study per day	2.89

MOST POPULAR MAJORS
management
civil engineering
marketing

STUDENTS SPEAK OUT

Life

You'd have a hard time finding a group of people anywhere who care more about football than do Clemson University students. Many students write "GO TIGERS!" across the bottom of their surveys, and it's this undying devotion to the pigskin that fuels students' ardent school spirit. Beyond football games, social options are limited. Even the school's loudest boosters admit the lack of variety. Writes one, "In the fall after football games there is a lot to do, but in the spring it gets pretty dull." Parties are relatively easy to come by, however. As one student writes, "There are not a whole lot of enriching cultural events, but the people are friendly and there's something going on every night of the week." Area bars, frats, and dorms are popular sites for getting together and drinking, although lately the school has begun to enforce drinking age laws pretty vigorously. One student complains, "By trying to eliminate alcohol on campus, the administration is cutting its own throat. People come here for the academics and because it's a party school, but the level of fun has definitely dropped." Visitation restrictions in single-sex dorms are also strictly enforced. But students are happy that Clemson's location provides excellent outdoor recreation opportunities. Reports one student, "Good weekend getaways are just an hour away. We've got the mountains for skiing close by."

Academics

Clemson is the school for South Carolinians who want to put their careers on track while also enjoying beautiful mountain scenery, easygoing classmates, and top-notch college football. More than one-quarter of the students pursue business and management majors; pre-medicine and engineering are also popular, as is education. Considering the school's size, access to professors is good. Explains one student, "For a big university the classes are very small, similar to high school classes, except biology and chemistry, which can reach about 150 students." However, as one student warns, "Lately classes are getting larger due to budget cuts, and tuition is definitely on the rise!" Professors receive below-average marks, especially from premeds and engineers, "mostly because so many don't speak English very well," according to one student. Students definitely take a laid-back approach to study—their two and a half hours a day of studying ranked among the bottom five percent—but the school is nonetheless "great for people who want to get away from the fast-paced urban life while still getting a good education." Cost is a major drawing card: even for those from out of state, this public university charges an extremely affordable tuition.

Student Body

Over two-thirds of Clemson students are native South Carolinians. Nearly ninety percent are white, but almost all the rest are black, so there is a sizable African-American population here. Students are very conservative politically—they ranked fourteenth most conservative in the country. They are also quite religious and tend toward conformity. "Variety is hidden or ousted," complains one student. Within those parameters, the student body is laid-back and friendly in the Southern tradition.

FINANCIAL AID: 864-656-2280   WEB SITE: HTTP://WWW.CLEMSON.EDU/

ADMISSIONS

The admissions committee considers (in descending order of importance): class rank, HS record, test scores, recommendations, essay. *Also considered (in descending order of importance):* alumni relationship, geographical distribution, personality. Either the SAT or ACT is required; SAT is preferred. An interview is required of some applicants. Admissions process is need-blind. *High school units required/recommended:* 14 total units are required; 4 English required, 3 math required, 2 science required, 2 foreign language required, 3 social studies required. Minimum combined SAT I score of 1050, rank in top quarter of secondary school class, and minimum 2.5 GPA recommended. *Special Requirements:* A portfolio is required for art program applicants. TOEFL is required of all international students. Interview required of architecture program applicants. Choice of major is considered due to enrollment capacities in certain areas. *The admissions office says:* "Candidates for the College of Architecture should present a portfolio for review by the faculty early in the candidate's senior year."

The Inside Word

Admission by formula. Out-of-state students are in abundance; such applicants will find little difference in admissions standards from those for state residents.

FINANCIAL AID

Students should submit: FAFSA (due April 1), the school's own financial aid form (due April 1). The Princeton Review suggests that all financial aid forms be submitted as soon as possible after January 1. *The following grants/scholarships are offered:* Pell, SEOG, academic merit, athletic, the school's own scholarships, the school's own grants, state grants, private scholarships, private grants, ROTC. *Students borrow from the following loan programs:* Stafford, unsubsidized Stafford, Perkins, PLUS, private loans. Applicants will be notified of awards beginning May 1. College Work-Study Program is available. Institutional employment is available.

FROM THE ADMISSIONS OFFICE

"Clemson University is a comprehensive land-grant university with approximately 16,000 students. Noted for its academic excellence, Clemson offers over 70 undergraduate degree programs in five academic colleges. Programs such as Calhoun College, the Honors Program, and study abroad are available to outstanding students. The campus is situated in the foothills of the Blue Ridge Mountains, with numerous outdoor opportunities available for students. Clemson has over 250 clubs and organizations, and the spirit that our students show for the university is unparalleled."

ADMISSIONS

Admissions Rating	74
% of applicants accepted	80
% of acceptees attending	41

FRESHMAN PROFILE

Average verbal SAT	560
Average math SAT	570
Average ACT	24
Average TOEFL	550
Graduated top 20% of class	53
Graduated top 40% of class	85
Graduated top 60% of class	96
Average HS GPA or Avg.	3.2

DEADLINES

Early decision	NR
Regular admission	5/1
Regular notification	rolling
Non-fall registration	yes

APPLICANTS ALSO LOOK AT

AND OFTEN PREFER
UNC-Chapel Hill
Duke
U. Georgia

AND SOMETIMES PREFER
Furman
James Madison
U. South Carolina, Columbia
Wake Forest
Vanderbilt

AND RARELY PREFER
U. Florida
Auburn U.

FINANCIAL FACTS

Financial Aid Rating	79
In-state tuition	$2,922
Out-of-state tuition	$8,126
Room & board	$3,770
Estimated book expense	$600
% frosh receiving aid	59
% undergrads receiving aid	55
% aid is need-based	51
% frosh w/ grant (avg)	58 ($3,300)
% frosh w/ loan (avg)	40 ($1,750)
% UGs w/ job (avg)	25 ($1,100)
Off-campus job outlook	good

COLBY COLLEGE

MAYFLOWER HILL, WATERVILLE, ME 04901   ADMISSIONS: 800-723-3032   FAX: 207-872-3474

CAMPUS LIFE

Quality of Life Rating	**91**
Type of school	private
Affiliation	none
Environment	town

STUDENTS

FT undergrad enrollment	1,785
% male/female	45/55
% from out of state	89
% live on campus	89
% spend weekend on campus	99
% transfers	4
% from public high school	62
% African-American	2
% Asian	5
% Caucasian	91
% Hispanic	2
% international	5
# of countries represented	45

WHAT'S HOT
campus food
campus is beautiful
students are happy
campus feels safe
beer

WHAT'S NOT
lack of diversity on campus
religion
Greeks
cigarettes
students are cliquish

ACADEMICS

Academic Rating	**92**
Profs Interesting Rating	94
Profs Accessible Rating	96
Calendar	4-1-4
Student/teacher ratio	10:1
% profs PhD/tenured	97/55
Hours of study per day	3.47

MOST POPULAR MAJORS
English
biology
economics

% GRADS WHO PURSUE...
Law 12, Med 10, MBA 10, MA 35

STUDENTS SPEAK OUT

Life

Colby College students report that they enjoy their lives at school immensely. They love their beautiful, secluded campus; they love outdoor sports even during the "frozen tundra" winter months in Maine; and they love their classes. All in all, they consider Colby "a really groovy place" to spend four years. Even the food here gets respect. Writes one student, the dining halls "are always thinking of new ways to feed the herds. 'Tuesday wok night' is a favorite." A slight glitch in this collegiate utopia may be the pervasiveness of mind-altering substances in Colby's social life ("if you don't drink or smoke drugs, Colby will not be a very fun place"). However, the administration has recently taken steps to educate the community about alcohol use, and more and more students are opting to live in "chem-free" dorms. If you're up for the lifestyle described as typical here, Colby might be the place for you. As one student sums up, "We work intensely, party with determination, work out religiously, and spend what leisure time is left recuperating."

Academics

"The best things about Colby College," wrote one student, "are the excellence and approachability of the professors." This respect for the faculty prevails throughout the student body. Professors are warmly described over and over as "committed," "outstanding," "always available," and so on. Particularly impressive are the fields of "government and economics; students would be hard-pressed to find better departments in comparable colleges." English and other humanities majors are also popular, and the school has a small but dedicated contingent of visual and performing arts students. Colby, a small college nestled in quaint Waterville, Maine, has often received praise for its dedicated faculty and "surprisingly intellectual" student body. Its history has been dotted with various pioneering moves such as the admission of women in 1871 (making it the first coed institution in the Northeast), and the establishment of an enrichment program for its students called "Jan Plan." This program allows students to study nontraditional subjects or intern during the month of January (and year-round for top seniors), and the experience generates rave reviews.

Student Body

"Okay, so we're not too diverse," one student wryly admits; the few minority students who attend Colby tend to "segregate themselves" from the white mainstream. "A minority student at Colby," notes one student, "is someone who does not drive a Volvo with Connecticut plates with a golden retriever in the back." The Colby administration is striving for a more heterogeneous student body.

FINANCIAL AID: 207-872-3379   E-MAIL: WRCOTTER@COLBY.EDU   WEB SITE: HTTP://WWW.COLBY.EDU/

ADMISSIONS

The admissions committee considers (in descending order of importance): HS record, recommendations, class rank, test scores, essay. *Also considered (in descending order of importance):* extracurriculars, personality, special talents, alumni relationship, geographical distribution. Either the SAT or ACT is required. An interview is recommended. Admissions process is not need-blind. *High school units required/recommended:* 16 total units are recommended; 4 English recommended, 3 math recommended, 2 science recommended, 3 foreign language recommended, 2 social studies recommended. TOEFL is required of all international students.

The Inside Word

Colby's admissions office has in the past expressed an unwillingness to work with independent educational consultants. Candidates who have contracted with such individuals should keep their relationship personal when dealing with the college. This is a very conservative campus, and admission is best approached in the same fashion. Colby continues to be both very selective and successful in converting admits to enrollees, which makes for a perpetually challenging admissions process.

FINANCIAL AID

Students should submit: FAFSA (due February 1), the school's own financial aid form (due February 1). The Princeton Review suggests that all financial aid forms be submitted as soon as possible after January 1. *The following grants/scholarships are offered:* Pell, SEOG, the school's own grants, state scholarships, state grants, private scholarships, private grants, foreign aid. *Students borrow from the following loan programs:* Stafford, unsubsidized Stafford, Perkins, PLUS, the school's own loan fund, state loans. Applicants will be notified of awards beginning April 1. College Work-Study Program is available. Institutional employment is available.

FROM THE ADMISSIONS OFFICE

"As the twelfth oldest independent college of liberal arts in the nation, Colby values the tradition of liberal learning and has maintained and enriched its core curriculum. The Colby Plan, adopted in 1989, embraces a series of ten educational precepts reflecting the faculty's sense of the principal elements of a liberal education. They are intended as a guide for course choices and as a framework for education beyond college. Recent program changes include a renewed emphasis in the natural sciences and enhanced opportunities for study abroad. Students praise the faculty for their strong commitment to teaching and to close interaction beyond the classroom. Colby replaced its fraternity system—abolished in 1984—with a system of four residential commons, which has increased opportunity for leadership and participation in campus governance for both men and women. Colby's campus, in central Maine, is generally regarded as one of the most handsome in the nation."

ADMISSIONS

Admissions Rating	92
% of applicants accepted	38
% of acceptees attending	35

FRESHMAN PROFILE

Average verbal SAT	650
Average math SAT	640
Average ACT	27
Average TOEFL	620
Graduated top 20% of class	92
Graduated top 40% of class	99
Graduated top 60% of class	100
Average HS GPA or Avg.	NR

DEADLINES

Early decision	1/1
Regular admission	1/15
Regular notification	4/1
Non-fall registration	yes

APPLICANTS ALSO LOOK AT

AND OFTEN PREFER
Bowdoin
Dartmouth
Williams
Brown
Middlebury Coll.

AND SOMETIMES PREFER
Colgate
Boston Coll.
Bates
Holy Cross

AND RARELY PREFER
Trinity
U. New Hampshire
Hamilton
U. Vermont

FINANCIAL FACTS

Financial Aid Rating	84
Tuition	$20,070
Room & board	$5,650
Estimated book expense	$500
% frosh receiving aid	49
% undergrads receiving aid	41
% aid is need-based	100
% frosh w/ grant (avg)	43 ($13,223)
% frosh w/ loan (avg)	47 ($2,950)
% UGs w/ job (avg)	65 ($1,450)
Off-campus job outlook	fair

COLGATE UNIVERSITY

13 OAK DRIVE, HAMILTON, NY 13346   ADMISSIONS: 315-824-7401   FAX: 315-824-7544

STUDENTS SPEAK OUT

Life

Colgate University, a small, upstate New York liberal arts school, has a reputation both for the strength of its academics and the wildness of its social scene. "I don't leave Colgate on the weekends for fear of missing something," informs one typical Colgate University respondent. Students write that they "work hard and party hard" so many times that it could be the unofficial school motto. Fraternities and sororities play an important role, one that the administration is trying to curtail through stricter enforcement of drinking policies and frat regulations. "No matter how hard the administration tries," one student responds, "they're not going to get us to stop partying." Be assured, though, that beyond partying, there is no shortage of extracurricular activities at Colgate. Says one undergrad, "This is a place where almost anyone can make a difference, whether they wish to excel in music, art, theater, or sports." A community service group, "Volunteer Colgate," is run by students and offers a wide range of volunteer options—from literacy programs to a project aimed at building houses for the homeless. The campus is in a remote area, but many students regard this as an asset. Writes one, "We're located in the middle of a beautiful farm area. A trek on cross-country skis brings one to overgrown apple orchards, crumbling stone walls, and glades with bubbling springs where deer prints dot the snow."

Academics

One Colgate student describes the student body as "characterized by highly intelligent underachievers who enjoy an active social life." Administrators have recently beefed up academic and admissions requirements, thereby improving the school's programs and student profile. Political science, the most popular major, is reportedly the least demanding; among the other popular majors, English, economics, and psychology, students reported the most demanding curricula. One student notes that "the outdoor education program is great. We take first-year students out during the year for activities such as hiking, rock climbing, winter camping, and ice climbing. Minimal impact camping and survival are offered for credit." All students must take general education courses, which cover introductory material in the liberal arts and sciences. All professors, regardless of their field of expertise, teach all "gen ed" courses, leading one student to complain that "the interdisciplinary approach to 'gen ed' results in biology professors teaching *The Odyssey*. They end up teaching things that they remember from high school."

Student Body

Most students feel that there's a certain similarity about their classmates. Writes one, "Everyone here was captain of their football, lacrosse, or field hockey team in high school, or was student government president or yearbook editor." The atmosphere is congenial. Says one student, "The other students are really friendly and easy to get along with. Unfortunately, this can be chalked up to the homogeneity of the campus." The minority population is composed mostly of blacks and Asians. Blacks and whites agree that black students remain alienated from the social mainstream.

FINANCIAL AID: 315-824-7431

ADMISSIONS

The admissions committee considers (in descending order of importance): HS record, recommendations, class rank, test scores, essay. *Also considered (in descending order of importance):* extracurriculars, special talents, alumni relationship, geographical distribution, personality. Either the SAT or ACT is required. An interview is recommended. *High school units required/recommended:* 16 total units are recommended; 4 English recommended, 4 math recommended, 3 science recommended, 3 foreign language recommended, 2 social studies recommended. TOEFL is required of all international students.

The Inside Word

Like many colleges, Colgate caters to some well-developed special interests. Athletes, minorities, and legacies (the children of alumni) are among the most special of interests and benefit from more favorable consideration than applicants without particular distinction. Students without a solid, consistent academic record, beware—the university wait-listed 1000 students last year. Heightened visibility from its basketball team's conference championship and NCAA tournament appearance could give apps a boost and further increase selectivity.

FINANCIAL AID

Students should submit: FAFSA, the school's own financial aid form, a copy of parents' most recent income tax filing. The Princeton Review suggests that all financial aid forms be submitted as soon as possible after January 1. *The following grants/scholarships are offered:* Pell, SEOG, the school's own scholarships, the school's own grants, state scholarships, state grants, private scholarships, private grants. *Students borrow from the following loan programs:* Stafford, unsubsidized Stafford, Perkins, PLUS, the school's own loan fund, state loans, private loans. Applicants will be notified of awards beginning April 1. College Work-Study Program is available. Institutional employment is available.

FROM THE ADMISSIONS OFFICE

"When the Roper Organization asked graduates from 1980-92 'What most influenced your decision to attend Colgate,' the key factor—cited on ninety percent of their responses—was academic reputation. Asked 'how well Colgate measured up to your expectations academically,' ninety-seven percent of those same graduates responded positively. Students and faculty alike are drawn to Colgate by the quality of its academic programs. Faculty initiative has given the college a rich mix of learning opportunities that includes general education, 45 academic concentrations, and a wealth of off-campus study groups in the United States and abroad. But there is more to Colgate than academic life, including nearly eighty student organizations, athletics and recreation at all levels, and a full complement of living options set within a campus described as one of the most beautiful in the country. For students in search of a busy and varied campus life, Colgate is a place to learn and grow."

ADMISSIONS

Admissions Rating	90
% of applicants accepted	36
% of acceptees attending	30

FRESHMAN PROFILE

Average verbal SAT	651
Average math SAT	645
Average ACT	28
Average TOEFL	640
Graduated top 20% of class	84
Graduated top 40% of class	89
Graduated top 60% of class	100
Average HS GPA or Avg.	NR

DEADLINES

Early decision	11/15
Regular admission	1/15
Regular notification	4/1
Non-fall registration	yes

APPLICANTS ALSO LOOK AT

AND OFTEN PREFER

Williams
Dartmouth
Cornell U.
Duke
Middlebury Coll.

AND SOMETIMES PREFER

Boston U.
Boston Coll.
Colby
Tufts

AND RARELY PREFER

Hamilton
Lehigh
Lafayette
Bucknell

FINANCIAL FACTS

Financial Aid Rating	78
Tuition	$21,525
Room & board	$5,935
Estimated book expense	$500
% frosh receiving aid	42
% undergrads receiving aid	44
% aid is need-based	100
% frosh w/ grant (avg)	40 ($15,861)
% frosh w/ loan (avg)	33 ($2,478)
% UGs w/ job (avg)	50
Off-campus job outlook	poor

COLORADO COLLEGE

14 EAST CACHE LA POUDRE ST., COLORADO SPRINGS, CO 80903   ADMISSIONS: 719-389-6344   FAX: 719-389-6816

STUDENTS SPEAK OUT

Life

Situated among the scenic Rocky Mountains, Colorado College has a movie-like setting that promotes inner peace. "When I am stressed about a test, I just look at the mountains and feel one hundred percent better." Colorado's beautiful wilderness leads the students to do outdoor activities for fun: "Most people use the outdoors (i.e., camping, hiking, cycling, skiing, etc.) for enjoyment." For some, coming to CC is like traveling through time: "At CC, the general trend is 'the 1960s are back.' "Beer and pot are very popular with students. Students are active in intramural sports and extracurricular organizations, which are reportedly numerous. The Greek system is active, but not oppressive in the social life of CC. One student sums up the CC experience best by writing us that "It's a never-ending summer camp with winter sports and excellent classes—Camp Colorado College."

Academics

CC takes a unique approach to the academic calendar. Rather than have students take multiple courses simultaneously, CC breaks each semester into three-and-a-half-week blocks ("the block plan") during which students take one course intensively. At the end of each block, students get a four-day "block break" to cleanse their minds before starting in on their next course. "There are only two types of students who graduate from here," reports one undergrad, "those who love the block plan and those who are neutral about it. Those who hate it, leave." Students report that the block plan is excellent for humanities and the social sciences, but "the block plan is difficult for subjects like chemistry." Students just love the fact that they are taught only by professors—CC has no TAs. "CC is an incredible environment. I don't know any other school where the teachers are so involved with their students, so accessible, and understanding," notes one student. Another student commented that "my professors are closer to being friends [than merely teachers]."

Student Body

The student body of CC is almost hippie-level liberal and environmentally aware. "Students at CC are not caught up in make-up, hairspray, or trying to impress," writes one student. As a result, many find the student body "nurturing," and "more concerned with helping each other than cutting each others' throats." Some Easterners feel right at home out here. Some don't: "Get out your carabiners and rock climbing shoes, guys," writes one female eastern transplant, "all the boys here climb...Not a lot of fashion lovers or urbanites." Though the block program leads to intensive study, the students don't lose their perspective on life: "We don't take much too seriously." Past initiatives of the student government include a failed quest to change the mascot from a tiger to a trout.

ADMISSIONS

The admissions committee considers (in descending order of importance): HS record, class rank, test scores, essay, recommendations. *Also considered (in descending order of importance):* extracurriculars, special talents, personality, alumni relationship, geographical distribution. Either the SAT or ACT is required. Admissions process is need-blind. *High school units required/recommended:* 16 total units are required; 18 total units are recommended. TOEFL is required of all international students. *The admissions office says:* "CC seeks students who demonstrate academic excellence, uncommon talents and interests, and a commitment to the idea of a liberal arts education. Economic and geographic diversity and the potential for making significant contributions to the college community are also factors considered for admission."

The Inside Word

Colorado is seeking thinkers with personality. This makes for an admissions process that gives more credit to the match a candidate makes than simply to good numbers. Tough high school courses are nonetheless a strong factor in admission. The college is a rarity—an institution that admits that geography plays a part in admissions. Minority recruitment is improving, but needs to play an even bigger part. Students who view Colorado College as a safety beware—the admissions committee employs a policy of denying candidates who, though strong academically, demonstrate little real interest in attending.

FINANCIAL AID

Students should submit: FAFSA (due February 15), CSS Profile (due January 15), Divorced Parents form (due March 1), a copy of parents' most recent income tax filing. The Princeton Review suggests that all financial aid forms be submitted as soon as possible after January 1. *The following grants/scholarships are offered:* Pell, SEOG, academic merit, athletic, the school's own scholarships, the school's own grants, state scholarships, state grants, private scholarships, private grants, ROTC, foreign aid. *Students borrow from the following loan programs:* Stafford, Perkins, PLUS. Applicants will be notified of awards beginning April 1. College Work-Study Program is available. Institutional employment is available.

FROM THE ADMISSIONS OFFICE

"Students enter Colorado College for intense academic challenges and an empowering community. The Block Plan breaks the mold of the 'common classroom,' enabling students to become scholars who apply textbook knowledge in practical ways. Independent and creative, CC students push the boundaries of discovery. The college encourages students, with advice and special funds, to pursue serious research, preparing them for graduate level work and the job market. Colorado College also takes advantage of its location. CC's off-campus programs—including the distinguished Southwest Studies program—are centered at the 'Baca' campus, a college-operated conference retreat in Colorado's San Luis Valley. Classes ranging from medieval history to ecology to landscape drawing use this site. And more than half the student body contributes to the community service program, which sponsors eighteen volunteer groups that work in Colorado Springs and the surrounding rural areas."

ADMISSIONS

Admissions Rating	87
% of applicants accepted	60
% of acceptees attending	30

FRESHMAN PROFILE

Average verbal SAT	640
Average math SAT	620
Average ACT	28
Average TOEFL	NR
Graduated top 20% of class	74
Graduated top 40% of class	95
Graduated top 60% of class	100
Average HS GPA or Avg.	NR

DEADLINES

Early decision	11/15
Regular admission	1/15
Regular notification	April
Non-fall registration	yes

APPLICANTS ALSO LOOK AT

AND OFTEN PREFER

Stanford
Dartmouth
Carleton
Middlebury Coll.

AND SOMETIMES PREFER

Macalester
Reed
Occidental
U. Colorado-Boulder

AND RARELY PREFER

U. Vermont
Kenyon
Lewis and Clark Coll.

FINANCIAL FACTS

Financial Aid Rating	85
Tuition	$19,026
Room & board	$4,824
Estimated book expense	$525
% frosh receiving aid	54
% undergrads receiving aid	55
% aid is need-based	90
% frosh w/ grant (avg)	49 ($10,300)
% frosh w/ loan (avg)	39 ($2,780)
% UGs w/ job (avg)	42 ($1,200)
Off-campus job outlook	good

COLORADO SCHOOL OF MINES

1500 ILLINOIS STREET, GOLDEN, CO 80401-9952   ADMISSIONS: 303-273-3220   FAX: 303-273-3165

CAMPUS LIFE

Quality of Life Rating	76
Type of school	public
Affiliation	none
Environment	metropolis

STUDENTS

FT undergrad enrollment	2,194
% male/female	76/24
% from out of state	31
% live on campus	23
% spend weekend on campus	65
% transfers	23
% from public high school	90
% in (# of) fraternities	20 (6)
% in (# of) sororities	20 (2)
% African-American	2
% Asian	5
% Caucasian	78
% Hispanic	6
% international	9
# of countries represented	67

WHAT'S HOT
health facilities
town-gown relations
different students interact
religion
campus feels safe

WHAT'S NOT
sex
cigarettes
theater
college radio
drugs

ACADEMICS

Academic Rating	82
Profs Interesting Rating	77
Profs Accessible Rating	77
Calendar	semester
Student/teacher ratio	14:1
% profs PhD	95
Hours of study per day	3.25

MOST POPULAR MAJORS
engineering
chemical engineering
mathematics

% GRADS WHO PURSUE...
Law 1, Med 1, MBA 2

STUDENTS SPEAK OUT

Life
Some students go to college to party, party, party. Some don't. Most of students' time at Colorado School of Mines is spent in classrooms, libraries, and labs, rather than bars or frat parties. After classes are over, students here study, on average, almost four hours a day. Many students combine social life and study by forming "study and support groups." One student describes leisure time this way: "We do chemical experiments on the cafeteria food. We have excellent fireworks on E-Days. We think about graduation." Others "meet and drink a beer, comment about sports or a good play, movie, or scientific program on TV. Plus, we hike every chance we get." When the pressure gets to be too much, students can travel to Denver (fifteen miles away) or Boulder. Says one student, "If you are looking for a party, CU in Boulder is only twenty minutes away; but one cannot party too much or he'll wind up at CU permanently."

Academics
For Coloradans seeking a career in engineering, math, or science, CSM is a natural first choice. A state school, CSM provides state residents (who make up two-thirds of the student body) with a first-rate education at cut-rate prices. CSM offers so much in the way of quality programs and career placement services, however, that even a Tennessee native writes that CSM "is really one of the last great deals in America." According to CSM, close to ninety percent of its graduates are placed in jobs or graduate programs by graduation day, and the school projected ninety-five percent placement within six months. Students concur: "CSM is a lot of work, but the job placement rate makes it worth it." Another student elaborates, "The best thing about the school is the cooperation with industry. The career placement center has a very high placement rate. With their help, I was able to get a summer job at a precious metals refinery in South Africa." Course work at CSM is both tough and time-consuming. Writes one student, "This school is hard. You can't comprehend, out there, what that really means. They test you two levels of comprehension above what they teach you, but if you can do it, the education you get is unbelievable." Particularly demanding is the Engineering Practices Introductory Course Sequence (EPICS), an engineering core curriculum that drives away a good number of freshmen every year. Profs here get mixed reviews: "Some teachers make class very exciting and others make their classes nap sessions. The classes I fall asleep in are the ones I skip. I don't learn anything anyway; I'd rather sleep in bed."

Student Body
Writes one student, "Everyone is here for one purpose: to learn and get a degree in math and the sciences. The majority of students are conservative and consequently everyone gets along pretty good." Some students report that "people here are generally geeky." Minority representation is sparse.

FINANCIAL AID: 303-273-3301   E-MAIL: ADMIT@MINES.COLORADO.EDU   WEB SITE: HTTP://GN.MINES.COLORADO.EDU/:80/

ADMISSIONS

The admissions committee considers (in descending order of importance): HS record, class rank, test scores, recommendations, essay. *Also considered (in descending order of importance):* alumni relationship, extracurriculars, geographical distribution. Either the SAT or ACT is required. An interview is recommended. Admissions process is need-blind. *High school units required/recommended:* 16 total units are required; 4 English required, 4 math required, 3 science required, 2 social studies required. Rank in top third of secondary school class recommended. TOEFL is required of all international students. *The admissions office says:* "While we are selective, we also try to be low-key, personable, and straightforward about the business of college admissions. We also are willing to take a chance with the unusual student (the one that doesn't fit the standard mold). The typical CSM student is directed, motivated, hardworking, and decent. They care about and take pride in themselves and the school."

The Inside Word

Although the admissions process is rigorous and straightforward in its focus on the academic, the admissions staff is more personable than at most technically oriented schools. Minorities and women are in demand.

FINANCIAL AID

Students should submit: FAFSA (due March 1), the school's own financial aid form (due March 1), a copy of parents' most recent income tax filing. The Princeton Review suggests that all financial aid forms be submitted as soon as possible after January 1. *The following grants/scholarships are offered:* Pell, SEOG, academic merit, athletic, the school's own scholarships, the school's own grants, state scholarships, state grants, private scholarships, ROTC. *Students borrow from the following loan programs:* Stafford, unsubsidized Stafford, Perkins, PLUS, the school's own loan fund, state loans, private loans. Applicants will be notified of awards beginning April 1. College Work-Study Program is available. Institutional employment is available.

FROM THE ADMISSIONS OFFICE

"CSM is a uniquely western school, not a typical college or university located in the west. The social environment is informal and friendly, and the academic environment is competitive but not cutthroat. Founded as a school of mining and geology, today we do much more. Nearly forty percent of our students major in our broad-based, interdisciplinary, nontraditional engineering program which offers course concentrations in civil, electrical, and mechanical engineering. Another twenty percent are studying chemical engineering. Our fastest-growing new area is environmental sciences and engineering. We're not the right school for everyone. But if the fit is there, CSM is a good place to spend your college years."

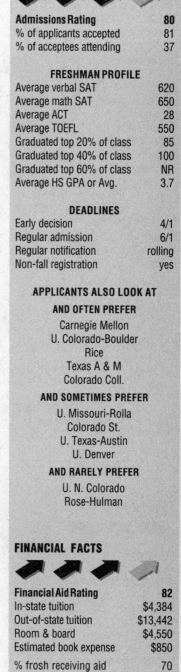

ADMISSIONS

Admissions Rating	80
% of applicants accepted	81
% of acceptees attending	37

FRESHMAN PROFILE

Average verbal SAT	620
Average math SAT	650
Average ACT	28
Average TOEFL	550
Graduated top 20% of class	85
Graduated top 40% of class	100
Graduated top 60% of class	NR
Average HS GPA or Avg.	3.7

DEADLINES

Early decision	4/1
Regular admission	6/1
Regular notification	rolling
Non-fall registration	yes

APPLICANTS ALSO LOOK AT

AND OFTEN PREFER

Carnegie Mellon
U. Colorado-Boulder
Rice
Texas A & M
Colorado Coll.

AND SOMETIMES PREFER

U. Missouri-Rolla
Colorado St.
U. Texas-Austin
U. Denver

AND RARELY PREFER

U. N. Colorado
Rose-Hulman

FINANCIAL FACTS

Financial Aid Rating	82
In-state tuition	$4,384
Out-of-state tuition	$13,442
Room & board	$4,550
Estimated book expense	$850

% frosh receiving aid	70
% undergrads receiving aid	70
% aid is need-based	70
% frosh w/ grant (avg)	65 ($4,000)
% frosh w/ loan (avg)	45 ($4,700)
% UGs w/ job (avg)	30 ($800)
Off-campus job outlook	fair

UNIVERSITY OF COLORADO, BOULDER

Campus Box 30, Boulder, CO 80309   Admissions: 303-492-6301   Fax: 303-492-7115

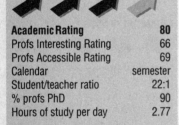
STUDENTS SPEAK OUT

Life

Located shoulder-to-shoulder with the Rockies, skiing, hiking, biking, and climbing are all accessible to the student body, which seems to take full advantage of these opportunities. Boulder itself is part of campus life: "It's not just 'CU life'—it's 'Boulder life.' People are very active and enjoy fitness activities. It is generally a very healthy town. But there's also a big drinking/party scene." Students rate the school above the national average in terms of beer, alcohol, and substances. Denver is only a thirty-minute drive away, so the students get the best of both worlds—the rural feel of the picturesque mountains and the urban accessibility of a suburban community. Partying and dating are attended almost as much as classes, and some students note a trend of the campus turning into a more "mellow, caring place," sometimes referred to ironically as "The People's Republic of Boulder."

Academics

The attitude of plenty of students attending University of Colorado-Boulder can be summed up by the one who writes "I chose this school because I love to ski." And while UC-Boulder is located in one of the most desirable (and beautiful) locations in the nation, undergrads warn that the "classes are definitely challenging." Business and management majors are very popular and reputedly excellent; the engineering school also garners praise for its program, although some students believe the professors "substitute math for thinking," removing the creative element from the engineering program. The school is large enough and good enough to provide solid offerings in most traditional college majors—political science, psychology, premedical sciences, and biology are all noted in our survey. Where the educational experience is appreciated, the administration is noted by students as a major pain. "The administration is defined by red tape. No one in the administration has a clue what anyone else is doing," notes one student. Changing a course of study was also mentioned as difficult: "When I need help, like switching my major, people send me around in circles." These disappointments, however, are showing signs of relief for the students. "In general, CU is an excellent school and there's a real sense that it's evolving in the right direction."

Student Body

Minority representation is low at UC-Boulder. One student writes that "it is the least diverse campus in the U.S." But other comments indicate that "CU is so damn big that everyone has to get along with someone! It's just a matter of finding them." Many students, while praising their immediate group of friends, describe other students as "rich kids with nothing to do." The typical CU-Boulder student is described as having "lots of glitter in the eyes and flowers in the hair," but in a good way. The community spirit and overall respect of the students for each other makes the student body a positive, productive group which supports each other as much as it can in such a large institution.

FINANCIAL AID: 303-492-5091   WEB SITE: HTTP://WWW.COLORADO.EDU/

ADMISSIONS

The admissions committee considers (in descending order of importance): HS record, class rank, test scores, recommendations, essay. *Also considered (in descending order of importance):* alumni relationship, geographical distribution, extracurriculars, personality, special talents. Either the SAT or ACT is required. Admissions process is need-blind. *High school units required/recommended:* 18 total units are required; 4 English required, 4 math required, 3 science required, 3 foreign language required, 3 social studies required. *Special Requirements:* An audition is required for music program applicants. 4 units of math required of business/administration and engineering/applied science program applicants. Chemistry and physics required of engineering/applied science program applicants. 3 units of foreign language and 3 units of social studies required of arts/sciences and business/administration program applicants. *The admissions office says:* "Students [are strongly encouraged] to include courses or activities in the fine and performing arts, and the visual arts. In-state applicants and children/relatives of alumni receive extra consideration."

The Inside Word

Much controversy erupted in Colorado a few years ago when university figures indicated that more out-of-state students had been admitted than resident students. In response, the out-of-state population has already been reduced slightly. Non-Coloradans will definitely find the going a bit tougher because of these circumstances.

FINANCIAL AID

Students should submit: FAFSA (due April 1). The Princeton Review suggests that all financial aid forms be submitted as soon as possible after January 1. *The following grants/scholarships are offered:* Pell, SEOG, academic merit, athletic, the school's own scholarships, the school's own grants, state scholarships, state grants, private scholarships, private grants, ROTC. *Students borrow from the following loan programs:* Stafford, unsubsidized Stafford, Perkins, PLUS, the school's own loan fund, state loans. Applicants will be notified of awards beginning rolling. College Work-Study Program is available. Institutional employment is available.

FROM THE ADMISSIONS OFFICE

Share in the excitement of a major research and teaching university located in one of the most spectacular environments in the country. The University of Colorado at Boulder is one of thirty public institutions belonging to the prestigious Association of American Universities (AAU). The Boulder Campus is the only member in the Rocky Mountain Region. Ranking tenth among all public universities in federally funded research, the university offers tremendous academic, cultural, ethnic, and geographic diversity. The Boulder campus, the largest in the CU system, offers more than 2,500 courses each semester and over 150 areas of study. Over the past year two major actions were implemented that affect the accessibility of alcohol on the University of Colorado at Boulder campus. A two year moratorium on the sale of alcohol at Folsom Stadium was enacted, to be effective fall 1997. And sororities and fraternities implemented a ban on the serving of alcohol at all sorority and fraternity gatherings.

ADMISSIONS

Admissions Rating	75
% of applicants accepted	76
% of acceptees attending	34

FRESHMAN PROFILE

Average verbal SAT	580
Average math SAT	590
Average ACT	25
Average TOEFL	500
Graduated top 20% of class	54
Graduated top 40% of class	87
Graduated top 60% of class	98
Average HS GPA or Avg.	3.5

DEADLINES

Early decision	NR
Regular admission	2/15
Regular notification	rolling
Non-fall registration	yes

APPLICANTS ALSO LOOK AT

AND OFTEN PREFER
UC-Berkeley
Stanford
UC-Santa Cruz

AND SOMETIMES PREFER
Northwestern U.
Colorado St.
Arizona St.
U. Arizona
Oregon St.

AND RARELY PREFER
U. Oregon
U. Vermont

FINANCIAL FACTS

Financial Aid Rating	80
In-state tuition	$2,602
Out-of-state tuition	$13,320
Room & board	$4,162
Estimated book expense	$540
% frosh receiving aid	54
% undergrads receiving aid	45
% aid is need-based	NR
% frosh w/ grant (avg)	NR ($3,000)
% frosh w/ loan (avg)	41 ($7,600)
% UGs w/ job (avg)	70 ($1,500)
Off-campus job outlook	excellent

COLUMBIA UNIVERSITY

212 HAMILTON HALL, NEW YORK, NY 10027   ADMISSIONS: 212-854-2521   FAX: 212-854-1209

STUDENTS SPEAK OUT

Life

Ask Columbia University students what they love most about their school and almost all will say New York City. A whopping eighty-four percent rated New York a great place to go to school—that from a notoriously iconoclastic student body. "No other city gives students the street-smarts, awareness, and overall life experience," gushes one student. As another points out, "Where else can you eat Ethiopian food one night, see The Will Rogers Follies the next, catch a Lizzie Borden film the next..." Because the city offers many opportunities for extracurricular activity and entertainment, school organizations and frats play a relatively small role at Columbia. One student complains that there is "very little campus life and school spirit," and several athletes groan that student support of teams is poor. "If you're looking for the typical all-American college scene," says one, "this is not the place for you."

Academics

Coursework at Columbia is challenging, most notably in a number of required courses. These courses, known as the core curriculum, demand that students spend a good deal of time mastering western classics. One student notes: "Columbia promised the core would change my life. It did; now I have no life." High-quality instruction in just about any field is available to students, and world-renowned scholars can be found in nearly every department. However, don't expect individual attention. "You can enrich your mind here, but good luck finding an advisor who knows your name," complains one student. Several students grouse about professors who are more interested in their graduate students and their own research than in their undergrad courses. Overall, however, students report their professors were good teachers; class size also got high marks. The administration receives poor grades. "Aside from the core curriculum, Columbia has one more requirement: Bureaucracy I, a four-year course in surviving the trials of mountains of red tape," says one student. "Be prepared for many frustrating episodes with the registrar, bursar, and library if you go here." Almost half of Columbia's graduates move on to professional schools within a year; one in four undergrads is a future lawyer! The engineering school is also world-class.

Student Body

The Columbia student body is still among the more left-leaning in the nation, although many students tell us that this isn't as true as it once was. Students give themselves high marks in ethnic diversity/interaction, and openness/acceptance of alternative lifestyles, all hallmarks of a liberal student body. A growing conservative population finds its liberal classmates self-righteous. "Too many 'I'm gonna change the world' people," says one such student. Minorities make up about a quarter of Columbia's student body, with Asians by far the largest minority group.

FINANCIAL AID: 212-854-3711

ADMISSIONS

The admissions committee considers (in descending order of importance): HS record, class rank, essay, recommendations, test scores. *Also considered (in descending order of importance):* extracurriculars, personality, special talents, alumni relationship, geographical distribution. Either the SAT or ACT is required. An interview is recommended. Admissions process is need-blind. *High school units required/recommended:* 16 total units are recommended; 4 English recommended, 3 math recommended, 3 science recommended, 3 foreign language recommended, 3 social studies recommended. Written evaluation/recommendation from school official and two recommendations from teachers of academic classroom subjects required; midyear report of first term of 12th year recommended. TOEFL is required of all international students. *The admissions office says:* "Columbia seeks to attract candidates from a variety of backgrounds. It is misleading, therefore, to take a list or ranking of admissions criteria as definitive; it is safe to say, however, that a student's academic record (rigor of program and grades received) is the single most important factor in the admissions decision..."

The Inside Word

The Ivies are getting even tougher, and Columbia is no exception. It is less selective than most of its compatriots, but offers the advantage of being a bit more open and frank in discussing the admissions process with students, parents, and counselors—refreshing amid the typical shrouds of Ivy mystique.

FINANCIAL AID

Students should submit: FAFSA (due January 1), the school's own financial aid form (due January 1), a copy of parents' most recent income tax filing (due January 1). The Princeton Review suggests that all financial aid forms be submitted as soon as possible after January 1. *The following grants/scholarships are offered:* Pell, SEOG, the school's own scholarships, state scholarships, ROTC, foreign aid. *Students borrow from the following loan programs:* Stafford, Perkins, PLUS, the school's own loan fund. Applicants will be notified of awards beginning April 5. College Work-Study Program is available. Institutional employment is available.

FROM THE ADMISSIONS OFFICE

"Located in the world's most international city, Columbia University offers a diverse student body a solid and broad liberal arts curriculum foundation coupled with more advanced study in specific departments."

ADMISSIONS

Admissions Rating	97
% of applicants accepted	23
% of acceptees attending	43

FRESHMAN PROFILE

Average verbal SAT	680
Average math SAT	650
Average ACT	NR
Average TOEFL	600
Graduated top 20% of class	95
Graduated top 40% of class	100
Graduated top 60% of class	NR
Average HS GPA or Avg.	NR

DEADLINES

Early decision	NR
Regular admission	1/1
Regular notification	4/3
Non-fall registration	no

APPLICANTS ALSO LOOK AT

AND OFTEN PREFER
Harvard/Radcliffe
Yale
Princeton
Stanford
Duke

AND SOMETIMES PREFER
Brown
Pennsylvania
Dartmouth
Tufts

AND RARELY PREFER
Wesleyan U.
Binghamton U.
Vassar
Barnard

FINANCIAL FACTS

Financial Aid Rating	72
Tuition	$19,730
Room & board	$6,864
Estimated book expense	$800
% frosh receiving aid	56
% undergrads receiving aid	53
% aid is need-based	100
% frosh w/ grant (avg)	NR ($14,338)
% frosh w/ loan (avg)	NR
% UGs w/ job (avg)	NR
Off-campus job outlook	excellent

CONNECTICUT COLLEGE

270 MOHEGAN AVENUE, NEW LONDON, CT 06320-4196   ADMISSIONS: 203-439-2200   FAX: 203-439-4301

CAMPUS LIFE

Quality of Life Rating 80
Type of school   private
Affiliation   none
Environment   suburban

STUDENTS

FT undergrad enrollment	1,615
% male/female	44/56
% from out of state	81
% live on campus	97
% spend weekend on campus	NR
% transfers	7
% from public high school	52
% African-American	5
% Asian	3
% Caucasian	82
% Hispanic	3
% international	1
# of countries represented	51

WHAT'S HOT

sex
student government
leftist politics
lab facilities
college radio

WHAT'S NOT
New London
Greeks
student publications
campus food
religion

ACADEMICS

Academic Rating	87
Profs Interesting Rating	90
Profs Accessible Rating	91
Calendar	semester
Student/teacher ratio	11:1
% profs PhD/tenured	91/94
Hours of study per day	3.08

MOST POPULAR MAJORS
government
history
English

% GRADS WHO PURSUE...
Law 6, Med 4, MBA 2, MA 11

STUDENTS SPEAK OUT

Life

One student sums up the Connecticut College social scene this way: "There's a big emphasis on drinking, which I don't like. Every Thursday (when the weekend starts) there's a dance party and the drinking starts. It continues through Saturday night. Sometimes there's even a keg for Monday night football." Agrees another, "Academically, Connecticut College is close to perfect. But social life (basically drinking and/or dancing) gets a little monotonous." Recently, however, the drinking scene has taken less and less prominence, students report. The sameness of social life isn't helped by the town of New London ("It's dull!"). New York and Boston are each about two hours away by car, a little too far for regular visits but close enough for the occasional road trip. Students are active in intramural sports and provide a strong support base for their Division III teams. For the community-minded, "The school has some great volunteer programs."

Academics

Connecticut College's best feature, according to one student, is "the fact that such diverse departments are strong. Arts, drama, and dance attract a certain type of student, philosophy and psychology another, and a strong athletics department attracts yet another type." It is surprising that such a small school provides quality education in so many areas. Although the arts department is its best-known and best (its lack of film courses not withstanding), the school also features an excellent center for international studies as well as uniformly solid liberal arts and social sciences departments. A set of core requirements prevents students from escaping Connecticut College without some understanding of literature, history, and hard sciences. What students seem to appreciate most, however, is the homey atmosphere of the school. Writes one: "On the plus side, members of the faculty are readily accessible and one does not get lost in the crowd. Also, our campus has several small dining halls, providing a better environment for getting together with friends or profs. This does, of course, have its downside: There are few secrets on a campus of 1,600 people."

Student Body

Connecticut's small student body has a total minority population of a little over 200. Many of the white students seem to all be cut from the same mold. Writes one, "I wish there was more diversity. This is a white, rich kid school. It's changing, but slowly...not everyone is from the country club." Students are politically farther to the left than most, but not particularly active. Several students rag on their classmates for their complacency. Writes one, "Most of the people here are prep school kids who are smart but lazy or unmotivated. As a public school student I feel a bit out of place. If you plan to bring a car, it better be a Saab—the unofficial car of Connecticut College." The college itself reports that Fords, Chevys, Toyotas and Hondas are more popular than Saabs, which account for less than 4% of all registered student vehicles.

FINANCIAL AID: 860-439-2059   WEB SITE: HTTP://CAMEL.CONNCOLL.EDU/

ADMISSIONS

The admissions committee considers (in descending order of importance): HS record, class rank, recommendations, essay, test scores. *Also considered (in descending order of importance):* extracurriculars, personality, special talents, geographical distribution, alumni relationship. An interview is recommended. *High school units required/recommended:* 18 total units are required; 4 English required, 3 math required, 2 science required, 3 foreign language required, 2 social studies required. *Special Requirements:* TOEFL is required of all international students. Audition required of dance program applicants. *The admissions office says:* "We spend a lot of time looking at each applicant as an individual, evaluating qualities and accomplishments within the context of each one's academic and personal environment. We look for students whose achievements have been characterized by stretch-going beyond the minimums and demonstrating real enthusiasm for learning in all its forms. And we look for each applicant's potential for success in our environment, that of a creative and flexible liberal arts curriculum and a diverse and involved student body."

The Inside Word

Late in 1994, Connecticut became the most recent college to drop the SAT I as a requirement for admission, citing the overemphasis that the test receives from the media and, in turn, students. The college is judicious about keeping their acceptance rate as low as possible. Candidates undergo a rigorous review of their credentials, and should be strong students in order to be competitive. Still, the college's competition for students is formidable, and students who are wait-listed will usually find they have a reasonable chance to be admitted, especially if they plan to enroll if offered a place in the class.

FINANCIAL AID

Students should submit: FAFSA (due February 1), the school's own financial aid form (due February 1), Divorced Parents form (due February 1), a copy of parents' most recent income tax filing (due February 1). The Princeton Review suggests that all financial aid forms be submitted as soon as possible after January 1. *The following grants/scholarships are offered:* Pell, SEOG, the school's own grants, state scholarships, state grants. *Students borrow from the following loan programs:* Stafford, unsubsidized Stafford, Perkins, PLUS, the school's own loan fund. Applicants will be notified of awards beginning April 1. College Work-Study Program is available. Institutional employment is available.

FROM THE ADMISSIONS OFFICE

"Distinguishing characteristics of the diverse student body at this small, highly selective college are honor and tolerance. Student leadership is pronounced in all aspects of the college's administration from exclusive jurisdiction of the honor code and dorm life through active representation on the president's academic and administrative cabinets. Differences of opinion are respected and celebrated as legitimate avenues to new understanding. Students come to Connecticut College seeking opportunities for independence and initiative and find them in abundance."

ADMISSIONS

Admissions Rating	88
% of applicants accepted	50
% of acceptees attending	29

FRESHMAN PROFILE

Average verbal SAT	660
Average math SAT	620
Average ACT	25
Average TOEFL	600
Graduated top 20% of class	71
Graduated top 40% of class	95
Graduated top 60% of class	NR
Average HS GPA or Avg.	NR

DEADLINES

Early decision	NR
Regular admission	1/15
Regular notification	4/1
Non-fall registration	no

APPLICANTS ALSO LOOK AT

AND OFTEN PREFER
Wesleyan U.
Vassar
Bowdoin
Tufts

AND SOMETIMES PREFER
Trinity Coll. (CT)
Colgate
Bates
U. Vermont
Colby

AND RARELY PREFER
U. Connecticut
Dickinson

FINANCIAL FACTS

Financial Aid Rating	80
Tuition	$18,740
Room & board	$6,300
Estimated book expense	$500
% frosh receiving aid	50
% undergrads receiving aid	51
% aid is need-based	100
% frosh w/ grant (avg)	45 ($14,025)
% frosh w/ loan (avg)	50 ($426)
% UGs w/ job (avg)	70 ($1,050)
Off-campus job outlook	good

UNIVERSITY OF CONNECTICUT

STORRS, CT 06269   ADMISSIONS: 203-486-3137   FAX: 203-486-1476

CAMPUS LIFE

Quality of Life Rating	73
Type of school	public
Affiliation	none
Environment	town

STUDENTS

FT undergrad enrollment	11,958
% male/female	49/51
% from out of state	15
% live on campus	66
% spend weekend on campus	70
% transfers	30
% from public high school	NR
% in (# of) fraternities	10 (16)
% in (# of) sororities	10 (9)
% African-American	6
% Asian	4
% Caucasian	85
% Hispanic	3
% international	NR
# of countries represented	18

WHAT'S HOT
sex
intercollegiate sports
beer
student publications
hard liquor

WHAT'S NOT
campus difficult to get around
off-campus food
lab facilities
inefficient administration
political activism

ACADEMICS

Academic Rating	72
Profs Interesting Rating	67
Profs Accessible Rating	68
Calendar	semester
Student/teacher ratio	NR
% profs tenured	90
Hours of study per day	3.11

MOST POPULAR MAJORS
English
economics
psychology

STUDENTS SPEAK OUT

Life

Storrs, Connecticut is not Paris, London or even New Brunswick. Writes one student, "I'd really love Storrs if I were able to eat hay and lay eggs. As it is, the ducks seem to have the most fun here. You can tell by all the quacking every morning." Another called the town "a very poor location that does not offer any off-campus entertainment." While most students agree (they gave the town a grade of D+), many counter that the university itself offers "a diverse range of extracurricular activities and opportunities to enhance the students' college career." Writes another, "You have to get involved! Join cheerleading, take advantage of the extensive study-abroad program, go scuba diving, or become an athlete. Do anything but sit on your butt and complain. And then you'll enjoy UConn." Students are ardent sports fans, and although "basketball is clearly the most important sport," many will tell you that "UConn sports is more than just men's basketball. Our soccer, hockey, and women's basketball teams are all well-followed." In fact, the women hoopsters were 1995 NCAA champs! Drinking is a very popular way to pass the time, but one student warns that "there are only three bars anywhere near campus: I call it the 'three-bar rotation.'" When students get tired of hanging around Storrs, "Hartford is only forty-five minutes away, and we are a short train ride from Boston or New York City."

Academics

Once known as an agricultural school, University of Connecticut is, in the words of one student, "More than the cow/agriculture school down the road; it is now an admired institute of learning in the arts and sciences." The school has enhanced its reputation by developing a strong engineering program (which attracts ten percent of the student body) and solid undergraduate business departments (sixteen percent of the students pursue business majors). In fact, the other popular majors, English and psychology, are about as far from the farm as one can get. As at most large universities, "The choices are unlimited and if you utilize your resources, you really can get the best of all worlds." Or, as another student puts it, "There is a lot here but nobody will hold your hand and show it to you." Student complaints center almost entirely on the effects of recent budget cuts, which "have been creating a lot of bureaucratic difficulties."

Student Body

Most UConn students are in-state students, and nearly nine-tenths are white. Minority students will find themselves part of a decent-sized community, especially important given that the school is out in the boondocks. Discussing student body demographics, a student who had transferred from an expensive private college writes, "My previous school had nothing but a bunch of rich yuppies who liked the Dead. I love UConn; it's much more like the real world."

FINANCIAL AID: 203-486-2819

WEB SITE: HTTP://WWW.UCONN.EDU/

ADMISSIONS

The admissions committee considers (in descending order of importance): HS record, class rank, test scores, recommendations, essay. *Also considered (in descending order of importance):* special talents, alumni relationship, extracurriculars, geographical distribution, personality. Either the SAT or ACT is required; SAT is preferred. Admissions process is need-blind. *High school units required/recommended:* 16 total units are required; 4 English required, 3 math required, 2 science required, 2 foreign language required, 2 social studies required. Minimum combined SAT I score of 900 and rank in top third of secondary school class recommended of in-state applicants; minimum combined SAT I score of 1000 and rank in top quarter of secondary school class recommended of out-of-state applicants. *Special Requirements:* An audition is required for music program applicants. TOEFL is required of all international students. Audition required of drama program applicants. *The admissions office says:* "No formulas or cutoffs are used. Every application is read by at least one person."

The Inside Word

While no formulas or cutoffs may be used at UConn in the admissions process, getting in is still simply a matter of decent courses, grades, and tests. The recent high national profiles of the UConn men's and women's basketball teams will undoubtedly result in an increase in applications, and in turn a slight increase in selectivity.

FINANCIAL AID

Students should submit: FAFSA (due February 15), the school's own financial aid form (due February 15). The Princeton Review suggests that all financial aid forms be submitted as soon as possible after January 1. *The following grants/scholarships are offered:* Pell, SEOG, academic merit, athletic, the school's own scholarships, the school's own grants, state scholarships, state grants, private scholarships. *Students borrow from the following loan programs:* Stafford, Perkins, PLUS. Applicants will be notified of awards beginning April 1. College Work-Study Program is available. Institutional employment is available.

FROM THE ADMISSIONS OFFICE

"Located in the wooded hills of northeastern Connecticut, the University of Connecticut offers tremendous educational opportunities to talented students. An education at the university is a study in contrasts: small school opportunities at a major university, an excellent liberal arts foundation with the opportunity to continue in professional, specialized fields, and the advantage of a major university in a rural setting. The university's location lends itself to many things—a collegiate setting, a comfortable existence, academics, athletics and rural opportunities. Yet at the same time UConn is accessible to Hartford (one-half hour), Boston (one and one-half hours), or New York (two and one-half hours). The University of Connecticut is a blend of people, ideas, and opportunities."

ADMISSIONS

Admissions Rating	71
% of applicants accepted	69
% of acceptees attending	29

FRESHMAN PROFILE

Average verbal SAT	560
Average math SAT	560
Average ACT	NR
Average TOEFL	NR
Graduated top 20% of class	48
Graduated top 40% of class	90
Graduated top 60% of class	99
Average HS GPA or Avg.	NR

DEADLINES

Early decision	NR
Regular admission	4/1
Regular notification	rolling
Non-fall registration	yes

APPLICANTS ALSO LOOK AT

AND OFTEN PREFER
Tufts
Boston Coll.
Boston U.

AND SOMETIMES PREFER
Villanova
U. Mass.-Amherst
Providence
Fairfield
U. Rhode Island

AND RARELY PREFER
Central Connecticut St.
Siena
Bentley
Clarkson U.
U. Maine-Orono

FINANCIAL FACTS

Financial Aid Rating	69
In-state tuition	$3,900
Out-of-state tuition	$11,890
Room & board	$5,124
Estimated book expense	$700
% frosh receiving aid	35
% undergrads receiving aid	37
% aid is need-based	85
% frosh w/ grant (avg)	25 ($2,030)
% frosh w/ loan (avg)	36 ($1,800)
% UGs w/ job (avg)	20 ($1,500)
Off-campus job outlook	good

COOPER UNION

41 COOPER SQUARE, NEW YORK, NY 10003 · ADMISSIONS: 212-353-4120 · FAX: 212-353-4343

CAMPUS LIFE

Quality of Life Rating 75
Type of school private
Affiliation none
Environment metropolis

STUDENTS
FT undergrad enrollment 933
% male/female 65/35
% from out of state 41
% live on campus 19
% spend weekend on campus 60
% transfers 18
% from public high school 65
% in (# of) fraternities 20 (2)
% in (# of) sororities 10 (2)
% African-American 8
% Asian 26
% Caucasian 51
% Hispanic 8
% international 8
# of countries represented 33

WHAT'S HOT
different students interact
ethnic diversity on campus
off-campus food
New York
dorms

WHAT'S NOT
sex
unattractive campus
health facilities
college radio
drugs

ACADEMICS

Academic Rating 92
Profs Interesting Rating 77
Profs Accessible Rating 74
Calendar semester
Student/teacher ratio 7:1
% profs PhD/tenured 60/60
Hours of study per day 3.83

MOST POPULAR MAJORS
fine arts
electrical engineering
architecture

% GRADS WHO PURSUE...
Law 3, Med 3, MA 51

STUDENTS SPEAK OUT

Life
"The toughest thing about going out is never finding someplace to go, it's finding someone who'll stop working and go with you." Not too many people would be at a loss for a social life at Cooper Union in Greenwich Village of New York City. There's a ton of great restaurants, cafes, and clubs nearby. But budgeting your free time with an amazingly tough course load is not easy ("If you can work all day and be happy, Cooper is the place for you!"). And the pressure to excel is intense ("Work hard or get kicked out!"). For some students at Cooper, friendships develop easily in this environment ("It is amazing how you can learn to get along with some people when you end up spending 20 hours a week in class and then another 40 hours a week studying"). Others agree with this sophomore: "There is no time left for real friendship." Perhaps Cooper could heed this senior's advice: "This school needs a student union where students can go relax and unwind." Dating is almost nonexistent.

Academics
"I don't think that many people realize what a really great school this is." Without a doubt the students of Cooper Union enjoy the best deal in higher education; they are not charged any tuition and they only have to pay a few hundred dollars in fees. As this student points out, "For $400 a year, I couldn't even get a plane ticket to go to a comparable school." The catch is that Cooper only offers studies in art, architecture, and engineering. But if you know that you will someday want a career in one of these fields, check this student's comment out: "I sincerely doubt that one could find a school anywhere in the universe that beats Cooper Union in the academics." Many of the classes are taught by professors with a lot of experience in the real world, and for the most part they received good marks: "The profs are top rate with a great deal of insight into their fields." Some students hint that the professors often dump huge loads of work on them ("Professors put your brain through spartan academic training").

Student Body
Over one-third of Cooper's students are minority students. Most of the students categorize each other as "friendly," "genuinely nice," and "polite." And, unlike some larger schools where academic competition gets in the way of friendships, at Cooper the students feel that they have to work together to get anything accomplished ("The work here REQUIRES group effort!") Other students do mention "clumping," primarily due to the different majors but also due to race. As with many commuter schools, the students have difficulties with hanging out off campus, leading to "two different sets of friends."

ADMISSIONS

The admissions committee considers (in descending order of importance): HS record, test scores, recommendations, class rank. *Also considered (in descending order of importance):* special talents, personality, extracurriculars. Admissions process is need-blind. *The admissions office says:* "We concentrate very heavily on the importance of an appropriate match-we are so focused, there must be a demonstrated passion for the profession-you can't simply change majors here."

The Inside Word

It is ultra-tough to gain admission to Cooper Union, and will only get tougher. Loads of people apply here, and national publicity and the addition of dorms have brought even more candidates to the pool. Not only do students need to have top academic accomplishments but they also need to be a good fit for Cooper's off-beat milieu.

FINANCIAL AID

Students should submit: FAFSA (due May 15), a copy of parents' most recent income tax filing (due May 15). The Princeton Review suggests that all financial aid forms be submitted as soon as possible after January 1. *The following grants/scholarships are offered:* Pell, SEOG, the school's own scholarships, the school's own grants, state scholarships, private scholarships, private grants. *Students borrow from the following loan programs:* Stafford, unsubsidized Stafford, Perkins, PLUS, the school's own loan fund, state loans. Applicants will be notified of awards beginning April 1. College Work-Study Program is available. Institutional employment is available. Freshmen are discouraged from working.

FROM THE ADMISSIONS OFFICE

"Each of the three schools, architecture, art, and engineering, adheres strongly to preparation for its profession and is committed to a problem-solving philosophy of education in a unique, scholarship environment. A rigorous curriculum and group projects reinforce this unique atmosphere in higher education and contribute to a strong sense of community and identity in each school. With McSorley's Ale House and the Joseph Papp Public Theater nearby, the Cooper Union remains at the heart of the city's tradition of free speech, enlightenment, and entertainment. Cooper's Great Hall has hosted national leaders, from Abraham Lincoln to Booker T. Washington, from Mark Twain to Samuel Gompers, from Susan B. Anthony to Betty Friedan and, more recently, President Bill Clinton. "

ADMISSIONS

Admissions Rating	99
% of applicants accepted	13
% of acceptees attending	65

FRESHMAN PROFILE

Average verbal SAT	670
Average math SAT	760
Average ACT	NR
Average TOEFL	550
Graduated top 20% of class	90
Graduated top 40% of class	100
Graduated top 60% of class	100
Average HS GPA or Avg.	3.3

DEADLINES

Early decision	NR
Regular admission	NR
Regular notification	4/1
Non-fall registration	no

APPLICANTS ALSO LOOK AT
AND OFTEN PREFER

Cornell U.
UC-Berkeley
NYU
Columbia U.
MIT

AND SOMETIMES PREFER

Harvey Mudd
Georgia Tech.
RIT

FINANCIAL FACTS

Financial Aid Rating	86
Tuition	$0
Room & board	$5,200
Estimated book expense	$1,200
% frosh receiving aid	51
% undergrads receiving aid	51
% aid is need-based	100
% frosh w/ grant (avg)	45 ($4,500)
% frosh w/ loan (avg)	47 ($2,000)
% UGs w/ job (avg)	35 ($3,000)
Off-campus job outlook	excellent

CORNELL UNIVERSITY

ITHACA, NY 14853   ADMISSIONS: 607-255-5241   FAX: 607-255-0659

CAMPUS LIFE

Quality of Life Rating   **81**
Type of school   private
Affiliation   none
Environment   suburban

STUDENTS
FT undergrad enrollment   13,262
% male/female   53/47
% from out of state   51
% live on campus   58
% spend weekend on campus   90
% transfers   14
% from public high school   79
% in (# of) fraternities   32 (45)
% in (# of) sororities   27 (19)
% African-American   4
% Asian   16
% Caucasian   58
% Hispanic   6
% international   5
# of countries represented   78

WHAT'S HOT
campus food
library
student publications
campus is beautiful
Greeks

WHAT'S NOT
students are cliquish
student government
campus difficult to get around
registration is a pain
town-gown relations

ACADEMICS

Academic Rating   **90**
Profs Interesting Rating   69
Profs Accessible Rating   64
Calendar   semester
Student/teacher ratio   8:1
% profs tenured   95
Hours of study per day   3.61

MOST POPULAR MAJORS
biological sciences
applied economics/business mgmt
mechanical engineering

% GRADS WHO PURSUE...
Law 6, Med 9, MBA 1, MA 13

STUDENTS SPEAK OUT

Life
The social life at Cornell University often gets crushed under the heavy workload students carry. Explains one student, "There is very little time to do anything except study. When there are a few free moments, most students pack in as much fun or sleep as they can stand because they don't know when they'll get the opportunity again!" Says another student, "the isolated setting makes it the most charming Ivy League school, but it also makes it more intense, since there's only the school here." The setting is beautiful, sort of like a state park with academic buildings. The most striking features are the gorges, legendary as the sites of stressed-out suicides. Students write that rumors of Cornell being the suicide capital of academia "are highly embellished." The weather is dreary. "Overcast, raining, sleeting, and generally ugly—we say 'it's Ithacating,'" writes one student. Because of its remote location and because students have "little interaction with the town 'down the hill,'" frats play an important role on the social scene. Drinking is popular but difficult. "The administration is really strict on underage drinking," explains one student. Among intercollegiate sports, "hockey, lacrosse, and wrestling are big-time"; participation in intramural sports is above average, and the area offers plenty of opportunities for lovers of the outdoors and winter sports.

Academics
As one student aptly puts it, "Cornell University is known as the easiest Ivy to get into and the most difficult to stay in." Our survey showed that no other Ivy League student body works harder, bearing out claims that "the profs expect blood from you, and mostly they get it." Cornell is also unique among the Ivies in that it is not an entirely private university. Three schools, agriculture and life sciences, human ecology, and industrial and labor relations, are publicly funded, and at these schools in-state tuition is about one-third that charged students in the Ivy schools. Industrial and labor relations and veterinary sciences are tops among the public divisions; among the private ones, engineering, hotel management, and the liberal arts departments are all first-rate. The premedical program is also highly regarded, but one student warns that, even by Cornell standards, "competition among premeds is cutthroat." Students must apply to one of the seven divisions of the school, but transferring among them is commonplace.

Student Body
Almost one-quarter of the Cornell student body is made up of minority students. About half of those are Asians, and the rest are evenly split between blacks and Latinos. Cornell's blend of Ivy League private divisions and state-funded public divisions creates a uniquely diverse student body. Writes one undergrad, "Cornell is the definition of diversity in its student body, faculty, and opportunities."

FINANCIAL AID: 607-255-5145   E-MAIL: ADMISSIONS-MAILBOX@CORNELL.EDU   WEB SITE: HTTP://WWW.CORNELL.EDU/

ADMISSIONS

The admissions committee considers (in descending order of importance): HS record, class rank, essay, recommendations, test scores. *Also considered (in descending order of importance):* extracurriculars, special talents, personality, alumni relationship, geographical distribution. Either the SAT or ACT is required. An interview is required of some applicants. Admissions process is need-blind. *High school units required/recommended:* 16 total units are required; 4 English required, 3 math required, 2 science recommended, 2 foreign language recommended, 2 social studies recommended. Other requirements vary significantly depending upon program. Applicants must have satisfactory knowledge of subjects required by individual colleges for admission to those colleges. *Special Requirements:* TOEFL is required of all international students. Interview and portfolio required of applicants to College of Architecture, Art, and Planning. Interview required of applicants to School of Hotel Administration and School of Industrial and Labor Relations.

The Inside Word

Cornell is the largest of the Ivies, and its admissions operation is a reflection of the fairly grand scale of the institution: complex and somewhat intimidating. Candidates should not expect contact with admissions to reveal much in the way of helpful insights on the admissions process, as the university seems to prefer to keep things close to the vest. Cornell is not the easiest Ivy to gain admission to, and only applicants with top accomplishments will be viable (though the admissions staff has used a limited number of 'wild cards' in the past to admit candidates they personally advocated for, but who faced an uphill climb with the committee). The university is a very positive place for minorities, and the public side is a value that's hard to beat.

FINANCIAL AID

Students should submit: FAFSA, the school's own financial aid form, a copy of parents' most recent income tax filing. The Princeton Review suggests that all financial aid forms be submitted as soon as possible after January 1. *The following grants/scholarships are offered:* Pell, SEOG, the school's own scholarships, the school's own grants, state scholarships, state grants, private scholarships, private grants, ROTC, foreign aid. *Students borrow from the following loan programs:* Stafford, Perkins, PLUS, the school's own loan fund. Applicants will be notified of awards beginning April 2. College Work-Study Program is available. Institutional employment is available.

FROM THE ADMISSIONS OFFICE

"A demanding course structure with an informal atmosphere stimulates extensive interaction between students and faculty. Cornell encourages students to develop communication and critical thinking skills and challenge themselves in a wide breadth of campus activities, clubs, organizations and intercollegiate sports."

ADMISSIONS

Admissions Rating	96
% of applicants accepted	33
% of acceptees attending	47

FRESHMAN PROFILE

Average verbal SAT	670
Average math SAT	670
Average ACT	NR
Average TOEFL	NR
Graduated top 20% of class	96
Graduated top 40% of class	100
Graduated top 60% of class	NR
Average HS GPA or Avg.	NR

DEADLINES

Early decision	NR
Regular admission	1/1
Regular notification	mid-April
Non-fall registration	yes

APPLICANTS ALSO LOOK AT

AND OFTEN PREFER
Harvard/Radcliffe
Yale
Princeton
Brown
Dartmouth

AND SOMETIMES PREFER
Pennsylvania
Wesleyan U.
Williams
Amherst

AND RARELY PREFER
U. Mass., Amherst
U. Rochester
Purdue U.-West Lafayette

FINANCIAL FACTS

Financial Aid Rating	72
Tuition	$20,000
Room & board	$6,238
Estimated book expense	$520
% frosh receiving aid	60
% undergrads receiving aid	70
% aid is need-based	100
% frosh w/ grant (avg)	75 ($10,630)
% frosh w/ loan (avg)	48 ($4,730)
% UGs w/ job (avg)	44 ($900)
Off-campus job outlook	good

CREIGHTON UNIVERSITY

2500 CALIFORNIA, OMAHA, NE 68178 | ADMISSIONS: 800-282-5835 | FAX: 402-280-2685

STUDENTS SPEAK OUT

Life

Creighton University students give Omaha average grades, an improvement since we first surveyed the school three years ago. Notes one student, "Life at school is pretty fun. The town helps. There are lots of things to do in Omaha, from the parties on the weekends to school functions such as sports events. We rarely run out of things to do." Students are religious; as at many Catholic schools, the level of participation in community service programs is high. Social life revolves around the Greek system and drinking. Writes one student, "Social activities are always associated with frats and sororities, so if one is not a member there is not a lot offered." Adds another, "There is a big tension between fraternity people and non-fraternity people." Men enjoy a favorable male/female ratio, and students report an active dating scene. The cost of living at Creighton is surprisingly high. Students report average weekly out-of-pocket expenses of sixty-five dollars (excluding rent and groceries). The reason: "Omaha has exceptional restaurants—people eat out a lot."

Academics

As one student explains, "Getting into Creighton University isn't as hard as getting into Harvard or Yale. But staying here takes a lot of work!" Undergrads study over three and a half hours a day here (well over the national average) and take class attendance very seriously. Over one-quarter of the students pursue degrees in pre-medical sciences (reportedly Creighton's toughest program) and another quarter study business and administration, with almost half those students proceeding to earn MBAs and MDs after graduation. Students must complete a set of liberal arts core requirements that account for over one-third of the courses they take here. Professors "are generally incredibly bright. They'll confuse you, stomp you, and rock your world. In the end, you come out a changed person." Another adds, "I feel real comfortable contributing to class discussion. The environment here is academically oriented. The faculty motivates the student body and promotes a positive attitude towards learning." An Honors Program rewards top students with smaller classes, courses that take a comprehensive approach to understanding the arts and sciences, and the opportunity to conduct an independent research project during senior year.

Student Body

Creighton draws students from a wide geographic radius. Fewer than half the students are from Nebraska. More than half the students are Catholic. Twelve percent of Creighton's undergrads are minority students. Asian students make up the single largest minority population; writes one black student, "Students are very supportive. However, as an African-American I can safely say that there is little knowledge and awareness of our cultural diversity." The student body is religious and generally very conservative politically and socially. Alternative lifestyles are predictably frowned upon here.

FINANCIAL AID: 402-280-2731

WEB SITE: HTTP://BLUEJAY.CREIGHTON.EDU/

ADMISSIONS

The admissions committee considers (in descending order of importance): HS record, class rank, test scores, recommendations, essay. *Also considered (in descending order of importance):* extracurriculars, personality, special talents. Either the SAT or ACT is required; ACT is preferred. An interview is recommended. Admissions process is need-blind. *High school units required/recommended:* 16 total units are required; 4 English required, 3 math required, 2 science required, 2 foreign language required, 2 social studies required. Minimum composite ACT score of 20, rank in top half of secondary school class, and minimum 2.5 GPA required. TOEFL is required of all international students.

The Inside Word

In this world of literal translation, even colleges and universities with admit rates that are higher than Creighton's refer to themselves as selective. While it should not be particularly difficult to get in, some don't. The fact that the university places little weight on essays or interviews and gives greater weight to letters of recommendation is a peculiar twist that denies applicants a real voice in the process.

FINANCIAL AID

Students should submit: FAFSA, the school's own financial aid form, state aid form, a copy of parents' most recent income tax filing. The Princeton Review suggests that all financial aid forms be submitted as soon as possible after January 1. *The following grants/scholarships are offered:* Pell, SEOG, academic merit, athletic, the school's own scholarships, the school's own grants, state scholarships, state grants, private scholarships, private grants, federal nursing scholarship, ROTC. *Students borrow from the following loan programs:* Stafford, unsubsidized Stafford, Perkins, PLUS, federal nursing loans, health professions loans, private loans. Applicants will be notified of awards beginning March 1. College Work-Study Program is available. Institutional employment is available.

FROM THE ADMISSIONS OFFICE

"An unusually high percentage (nearly one-third) of the freshmen class each year at Creighton considers itself pre-professional, hoping to eventually gain entry to the professional programs of medicine, dentistry, pharmacy, occupational therapy, physical therapy and law. The competitiveness of these programs, coupled with the substantial financial investment involved in choosing a quality, private undergraduate education might indicate that Creighton students are, indeed, motivated to succeed. Beyond academic excellence, we would say the single most identifiable characteristic of a Creighton education is the value-centered approach to study. No matter what the student's major, he or she will always feel the influence of the Jesuit tradition on campus, encouraging students to examine the moral, as well as the factual dimension of issues."

ADMISSIONS

Admissions Rating	70
% of applicants accepted	93
% of acceptees attending	33

FRESHMAN PROFILE

Average verbal SAT	NR
Average math SAT	NR
Average ACT	25
Average TOEFL	500
Graduated top 20% of class	49
Graduated top 40% of class	72
Graduated top 60% of class	87
Average HS GPA or Avg.	3.5

DEADLINES

Early decision	NR
Regular admission	8/1
Regular notification	rolling
Non-fall registration	yes

APPLICANTS ALSO LOOK AT

AND OFTEN PREFER

Iowa St.
Notre Dame
U. Colorado-Boulder

AND SOMETIMES PREFER

U. Iowa
Marquette
DePaul

AND RARELY PREFER

U. Wisconsin- Madison

FINANCIAL FACTS

Financial Aid Rating	88
Tuition	$11,160
Room & board	$4,548
Estimated book expense	$553
% frosh receiving aid	88
% undergrads receiving aid	68
% aid is need-based	53
% frosh w/ grant (avg)	57 ($3,316)
% frosh w/ loan (avg)	53 ($4,227)
% UGs w/ job (avg)	50 ($1,500)
Off-campus job outlook	excellent

UNIVERSITY OF DALLAS

1845 EAST NORTHGATE DRIVE, IRVING, TX 75062-4799 · ADMISSIONS: 214-721-5266 · FAX: 214-721-5417

STUDENTS SPEAK OUT

Life

University of Dallas is not a party school, as students keep reminding us. Says one, "If you like personal attention and don't want to feel like a number, this is the place for you. If you require a large social scene, sports, or fraternities/sororities (there are none at UD), go elsewhere." Although drinking is not unheard of here, many students' idea of a good time is staying up all night drinking coffee and discussing Plato and Nietzsche. "Life at this school is rigorous and not for the faint-hearted!" offers one student. One junior beams, "This is probably the last place where you can sit down at dinner and hear the majority of students talking about Dante and Milton." The campus is "really ugly, but this matters little in the big picture," says a typical student. Students are disappointed with the lack of adequate health services or counseling services. Students don't seem to date much here at UD.

Academics

"Traditional" is the word UD students use to describe their school's approach to academics. Students study a core curriculum (which includes literature, science and math) and work hard to receive a classical education: "UD is a place where one can almost forget that he is not in the 13th century studying in a medieval college." Almost all students spend their sophomore year at the school's Rome campus (an experience students uniformly praise). Then there are the professors here, whom UD students rank in the top ten percent in the nation. Says a typical student, "The professors are wonderful. We have no TAs or grad students teaching. They are also everywhere—on the mall, at lunch, etc. Discussions do not stop in class but move outside or to the Rat. By the same token, before you complain about a class or a professor, you have to look over your shoulder to make sure they're not eating at the next table." Explains another, "The professors are extremely enthusiastic about the subjects. They make it a joy to go to class." All departments are good, but many students singled out the English department and the history department for their excellence. About the only negative we heard was that the library is inadequate; many students prefer studying in local restaurants, and they use SMU's library for research.

Student Body

Only about three quarters of the students at UD are Catholic, but almost all are religious and conservative. "The student body is composed of all sorts, but those seeking a strong religious community can easily find it," says one student. "There is a fairly strong conflict between the very Catholic right-wing students and the rest of the student body," offers another. Students are outspoken about their beliefs, and this sometimes leads to "extreme" arguments. Still, there is an atmosphere of discussion and mutual respect which marks the student body. Students here are self-confident. Several students agree with the one who called her classmates "some of the smartest, wittiest, and overall entertaining people you'll ever meet." Liberals have a tough go of it here. "I'm pro-choice and people here wear me out about it," says one student.

ADMISSIONS

The admissions committee considers (in descending order of importance): HS record, class rank, test scores, essay, recommendations. *Also considered (in descending order of importance):* personality, alumni relationship, extracurriculars, special talents. Either the SAT or ACT is required. An interview is recommended. Admissions process is need-blind. *High school units required/recommended:* 14 total units are required; 18 total units are recommended; 4 English required, 3 math required, 4 math recommended, 3 science required, 4 science recommended, 2 foreign language required, 3 foreign language recommended, 2 social studies required, 3 social studies recommended. TOEFL is required of all international students. *The admissions office says:* "[We pay] attention to the individual record. The review process takes the total student record into consideration, not just standardized test scores. Our typical student is distinguished by a serious nature, and a time commitment to learning, a real desire to read the great books in their entirety and spend time discussing them."

The Inside Word

The university's conservative nature places significant emphasis on "fit" in the admissions process. Having a solid academic background counts, but what kind of match a candidate makes with Dallas can be even more important.

FINANCIAL AID

Students should submit: FAFSA, the school's own financial aid form. The Princeton Review suggests that all financial aid forms be submitted as soon as possible after January 1. *The following grants/scholarships are offered:* Pell, SEOG, academic merit, the school's own scholarships, the school's own grants, state scholarships, state grants, private scholarships, private grants, ROTC. *Students borrow from the following loan programs:* Stafford, unsubsidized Stafford, Perkins, PLUS, state loans. Applicants will be notified of awards beginning March 30. College Work-Study Program is available. Institutional employment is available.

FROM THE ADMISSIONS OFFICE

"Quite unabashedly, the curriculum at the University of Dallas is based on the supposition that truth and virtue exist and are the proper objects of search in an education. The curriculum further supposes that this search is best pursued through an acquisition of philosophical and theological principles on the part of a student and has for its analogical field a vast body of great literature—perhaps more extensive than is likely to be encountered elsewhere—supplemented by a survey of the sweep of history and an introduction to the political and economic principles of society. An understanding of these subjects, along with an introduction to the quantitative and scientific worldview and a mastery of a language, is expected to form a comprehensive and coherent experience, which, in effect, governs the intellect of a student in a manner that develops independence of thought in its most effective mode."

ADMISSIONS

Admissions Rating	76
% of applicants accepted	91
% of acceptees attending	38

FRESHMAN PROFILE

Average verbal SAT	630
Average math SAT	590
Average ACT	26
Average TOEFL	550
Graduated top 20% of class	62
Graduated top 40% of class	87
Graduated top 60% of class	96
Average HS GPA or Avg.	NR

DEADLINES

Early decision	12/1
Regular admission	3/1
Regular notification	rolling
Non-fall registration	yes

APPLICANTS ALSO LOOK AT

AND OFTEN PREFER

U. Texas, Austin
U. Texas, Dallas
Trinity U.

AND SOMETIMES PREFER

Baylor
St. Louis
U. Denver
U. Texas, Arlington
SMU

FINANCIAL FACTS

Financial Aid Rating	95
Tuition	$11,380
Room & board	$4,830
Estimated book expense	$250
% frosh receiving aid	95
% undergrads receiving aid	89
% aid is need-based	64
% frosh w/ grant (avg)	94 ($6,933)
% frosh w/ loan (avg)	83 ($3,665)
% UGs w/ job (avg)	47
Off-campus job outlook	good

DARTMOUTH COLLEGE

HANOVER, NH 03755   ADMISSIONS: 603-646-2875   FAX: 603-646-1216

CAMPUS LIFE

Quality of Life Rating	**95**
Type of school	private
Affiliation	none
Environment	town

STUDENTS

FT undergrad enrollment	4,286
% male/female	54/46
% from out of state	91
% live on campus	92
% spend weekend on campus	90
% transfers	NR
% from public high school	65
% in (# of) fraternities	41 (17)
% in (# of) sororities	28 (7)
% African-American	7
% Asian	10
% Caucasian	57
% Hispanic	5
% international	5
# of countries represented	54

WHAT'S HOT

computer facilities
students are happy
library
campus feels safe
campus food

WHAT'S NOT

cigarettes
infrequent dating
religion
student government
drugs

ACADEMICS

Academic Rating	**97**
Profs Interesting Rating	93
Profs Accessible Rating	96
Calendar	other
Student/teacher ratio	11:1
% profs tenured	94
Hours of study per day	3.38

MOST POPULAR MAJORS

government
history
biological sciences

STUDENTS SPEAK OUT

Life

"Football games, fraternity parties, ice sculptures—Dartmouth's all-around atmosphere and 'study hard, party hard' philosophy cannot be beat!" sums up one student. Fraternity parties are the center of social life here, and while administrators have tried to curtail the Greeks' influence, they have had little success. A new campus alcohol policy prohibits kegs at parties at dorms and at school-recognized fraternities, and while our survey results indicate that students still drink regularly, the policy has some students up in arms. Complains one frat member, "The fraternities have taken the brunt of the administration's assault on drinking. The system is fighting back, but I do not see change in the near future." The social scene is "very male-oriented. If you're looking for male bonding, strong athletics, hard drinking, and lots of studying, Dartmouth is the place." Beyond the campus confines, "There is not much to do, but Hanover is a quaint, charming town. The countryside is beautiful and there are tons of outdoor activities. We own our own ski mountain twenty minutes from campus." The campus is gorgeous, and the food ranks among the best in the country.

Academics

It's no breeze getting through Dartmouth, and those who succeed here do it the old-fashioned way—hard work. Still, among all the Ivy League student bodies we surveyed, Dartmouth students wrote the least about their academic programs; they also wrote the most about social conditions on campus. Don't conclude that these students blow off their studies. It's just that they perceive schoolwork as a chore to be completed, and completed well, so they can get on with their social lives. This practically anti-intellectual attitude might well be summed up by the student who writes, "The faculty here really seems to care...about what I have no idea." The challenging academic program features distribution requirements that oblige students to take four courses each in the natural sciences, social sciences, and humanities. Students must also demonstrate writing and foreign language proficiency. Political science, economics, and English are among the most popular of the fine departments here. Students also offered praise to the foreign language departments, computer science, and engineering. Students gave their professors excellent marks (best in the Ivy League).

Student Body

While hardly the most conservative students in the nation, Dartmouth students do fall to the right of center. Although one student notes that "our conservative reputation is overrated—all political, ethical, and moral groups are represented," much more common were comments such as "don't come here if you are liberal, artsy, or antisocial; you won't enjoy yourself." Complains one detractor, "I've had a difficult time here because of my reluctance to adopt a pretentious, pseudo-friendly, beer-loving exterior. Those who stray from the prototype are seen as flaunting their uniqueness. There is no in-between." Nearly one-fourth of the students are minorities, with Asians and African-Americans making up a large portion of the minority population.

ADMISSIONS

The admissions committee considers (in descending order of importance): HS record, class rank, essay, recommendations, test scores. *Also considered (in descending order of importance):* extracurriculars, personality, special talents, alumni relationship, geographical distribution. Either the SAT or ACT is required; SAT is preferred. An interview is recommended. *High school units required/recommended:* 17 total units are recommended; 4 English recommended, 4 math recommended, 3 science recommended, 3 foreign language recommended, 3 social studies recommended. TOEFL is required of all international students. *The admissions office says:* "Admissions to Dartmouth is highly selective. The competition for admission is a function of both the number of applicants as well as their outstanding credentials. A large and well-qualified applicant pool offers Dartmouth the opportunity to enroll a freshman class that is not only very capable but also broad in the variety of backgrounds, talents, and interests represented."

The Inside Word

As is the case with those who apply to any of the Ivies or other highly selective colleges, candidates to Dartmouth are up against, or benefit from, many institutional interests that go unmentioned in discussions of appropriate qualifications for admission. This makes an already stressful process even more so for most candidates.

FINANCIAL AID

Students should submit: FAFSA, the school's own financial aid form (due February 1), a copy of parents' most recent income tax filing (due February 1). The Princeton Review suggests that all financial aid forms be submitted as soon as possible after January 1. *The following grants/scholarships are offered:* Pell, SEOG, the school's own scholarships, the school's own grants, state scholarships, state grants, ROTC, foreign aid. *Students borrow from the following loan programs:* Stafford, Perkins, PLUS, the school's own loan fund, state loans. Applicants will be notified of awards beginning in April. College Work-Study Program is available. Institutional employment is available.

FROM THE ADMISSIONS OFFICE

"Today Dartmouth's mission is to endow its students with the knowledge and wisdom needed to make creative and positive contributions to society. The college brings together a breadth of cultures, traditions, and ideas to create a campus that is alive with ongoing debate and exploration. The educational value of such discourse cannot be underestimated. From student-initiated roundtable discussions that attempt to make sense of world events, to the late-night philosophizing in a dormitory lounge, Dartmouth students take advantage of their opportunities to learn from each other. The unique benefits of sharing in this interchange are accompanied by a great sense of responsibility. Each individual's commitment to the Principles of Community ensures the vitality of this learning environment."

ADMISSIONS

Admissions Rating	99
% of applicants accepted	23
% of acceptees attending	48

FRESHMAN PROFILE

Average verbal SAT	690
Average math SAT	680
Average ACT	NR
Average TOEFL	NR
Graduated top 20% of class	97
Graduated top 40% of class	100
Graduated top 60% of class	100
Average HS GPA or Avg.	NR

DEADLINES

Early decision	NR
Regular admission	January
Regular notification	4/15
Non-fall registration	no

APPLICANTS ALSO LOOK AT

AND OFTEN PREFER
Harvard/Radcliffe
Princeton
Yale
Stanford

AND SOMETIMES PREFER
Amherst
Williams
Wesleyan U.
Columbia U.
Duke

AND RARELY PREFER
Cornell U.
Northwestern U.
Middlebury Coll.

FINANCIAL FACTS

Financial Aid Rating	79
Tuition	$20,805
Room & board	$5,865
Estimated book expense	NR
% frosh receiving aid	49
% undergrads receiving aid	40
% aid is need-based	100
% frosh w/ grant (avg)	42 ($14,660)
% frosh w/ loan (avg)	44 ($2,900)
% UGs w/ job (avg)	55 ($1,500)
Off-campus job outlook	good

DAVIDSON COLLEGE

P.O. BOX 1737, DAVIDSON, NC 28036   ADMISSIONS: 800-768-0380   FAX: 704-892-2016

CAMPUS LIFE

Quality of Life Rating **93**
Type of school   private
Affiliation   Presbyterian Church USA
Environment   metropolis

STUDENTS
FT undergrad enrollment   1,614
% male/female   52/48
% from out of state   79
% live on campus   93
% spend weekend on campus   NR
% transfers   1
% from public high school   60
% in (# of) fraternities   65 (6)
% in (# of) sororities   71
% African-American   4
% Asian   3
% Caucasian   87
% Hispanic   2
% international   3
# of countries represented   32

WHAT'S HOT
campus easy to get around
town-gown relations
school runs like butter
campus food
honesty

WHAT'S NOT
drugs
infrequent dating
lack of diversity on campus
college radio
cigarettes

ACADEMICS

Academic Rating **96**
Profs Interesting Rating   97
Profs Accessible Rating   97
Calendar   semester
Student/teacher ratio   12:1
% profs PhD/tenured   94/98
Hours of study per day   3.80

MOST POPULAR MAJORS
biology
English
psychology

% GRADS WHO PURSUE...
Law 13, Med 12, MBA 7, MA 36

STUDENTS SPEAK OUT

Life
Students at Davidson College work hard and play hard, enjoying the challenge of balancing the two: "We spend a lot of time studying, but our extracurricular activities keep us sane." Extracurricular activities, particularly athletics "are very popular—a high percentage of students are involved in some way." Another way in which Davidson depressurizes the highly charged academic environment is by employing the honor system rather than rigidly proctoring every exam, test and quiz. Does it work? One student responds, "There is absolutely no cheating here. There is no stealing here. I leave my door and window open all the time." Davidson's Greek system carries much of the burden of social activities, but on the whole, "Greek life isn't the center of campus." Charlotte is a hop, skip and a jump away—but only gets average marks. Some students complain that "dating is nearly nonexistent," but others state that socially, because of the small size, you can "create your own atmosphere."

Academics
Davidson students love the quality and caring nature of their professors. "Davidson's focus is on the students," writes one undergraduate. The faculty is referred to as "excellent," and it is particularly noted that "professors are always there for you." The students respond well to this specific and unique attention: "Davidson is a truly 'personal' school. I have not felt so welcomed, challenged, encouraged or supported at any other place." Students study, on average, close to four hours a day (not including classes). Very few student bodies work any harder. Davidson offers preprofessional course sequences for those interested in law, medicine, business, and engineering. Engineers may also participate in a 3-2 B.A./B.S. program. Davidson's Dean Rusk Program in International Studies sponsors speakers, conferences and provides grant support for students pursuing careers with an international focus. Other notable features of a Davidson education are the core curriculum (which heavily emphasizes the social and natural sciences), and the option to pursue a two-year, five-course interdisciplinary Humanities program.

Student Body
Davidson's small size and remote location make for a tight-knit college community. "There is a wonderful feeling of community at Davidson," remarks one student. Yet this concentration of size and space also gets on some people's nerves: "there is no anonymity, so you have to like an environment where you're going to know by name two-thirds of the people you pass on the way to class—and probably the name of the person they hooked up with last weekend as well." Students feel very positive about the student body as a whole, but some students noted the "precious little diversity" that marked the student body. "Everyone looks like they walked out of the J. Crew Catalog," notes one student, "white, preppy, [and] Southern." One student sums up the Davidson experience this way: "If you are looking for a politically inactive, conservative campus and the best possible liberal arts education in the world, then Davidson is the place for you."

ADMISSIONS

The admissions committee considers (in descending order of importance): HS record, class rank, recommendations, essay, test scores. *Also considered (in descending order of importance):* personality, special talents, alumni relationship, extracurriculars, geographical distribution. Either the SAT or ACT is required. An interview is recommended. *High school units required/recommended:* 17 total units are required; 4 English required, 3 math required, 4 math recommended, 3 science required, 4 science recommended, 2 foreign language required, 4 foreign language recommended, 1 history required, 2 history recommended. TOEFL is required of all international students. *The admissions office says:* "These are minimum requirements. Additional course work is recommended. Candidates must take a minimum of 4 academic courses each year in secondary school with 5 per year as 'standard'."

The Inside Word

Even though Davidson is little known outside of the South, harbor no illusions regarding ease of admission. Getting in is every bit as tough as staying in, because an amazingly high percentage of those who are admitted choose to attend. Look for admission to become even more difficult as the college's name recognition increases.

FINANCIAL AID

Students should submit: FAFSA (due February 1), the school's own financial aid form (due February 1), state aid form (due June 1), Divorced Parents form (due February 1), a copy of parents' most recent income tax filing (due March 15). The Princeton Review suggests that all financial aid forms be submitted as soon as possible after January 1. *The following grants/scholarships are offered:* Pell, SEOG, academic merit, athletic, the school's own scholarships, the school's own grants, state scholarships, state grants, private scholarships, private grants, ROTC, foreign aid. *Students borrow from the following loan programs:* Stafford, unsubsidized Stafford, Perkins, PLUS, the school's own loan fund. Applicants will be notified of awards beginning April 1. College Work-Study Program is available. Institutional employment is available.

FROM THE ADMISSIONS OFFICE

"Davidson College is one of the nation's premier academic institutions, a college of the liberal arts and sciences respected for its intellectual vigor, the high quality of its faculty and students, and the achievements of its alumni. It is distinguished by its strong honor system, close interaction between professors and students, an environment that encourages both intellectual growth and community service, and a commitment to international education. Davidson places great value on student participation in extracurricular activities, intercollegiate athletics, and intramural sports. The college has a strong regional identity, which includes traditions of civility and mutual respect, and has historic ties to the Presbyterian Church."

ADMISSIONS

Admissions Rating	94
% of applicants accepted	37
% of acceptees attending	45

FRESHMAN PROFILE

Average verbal SAT	660
Average math SAT	650
Average ACT	29
Average TOEFL	600
Graduated top 20% of class	95
Graduated top 40% of class	100
Graduated top 60% of class	NR
Average HS GPA or Avg.	NR

DEADLINES

Early decision	NR
Regular admission	1/15
Regular notification	4/1
Non-fall registration	no

APPLICANTS ALSO LOOK AT

AND OFTEN PREFER

Dartmouth
Duke
UNC-Chapel Hill

AND SOMETIMES PREFER

Emory
William and Mary
Princeton
Virginia
U. of the South

AND RARELY PREFER

Rhodes
North Carolina St.
Wake Forest
Vanderbilt
Wofford

FINANCIAL FACTS

Financial Aid Rating	86
Tuition	$19,631
Room & board	$5,636
Estimated book expense	$650
% frosh receiving aid	56
% undergrads receiving aid	63
% aid is need-based	75
% frosh w/ grant (avg)	60 ($10,507)
% frosh w/ loan (avg)	30 ($3,125)
% UGs w/ job (avg)	40 ($1,200)
Off-campus job outlook	fair

UNIVERSITY OF DAYTON

300 COLLEGE PARK, DAYTON, OH 45469-1611   ADMISSIONS: 800-837-7433   FAX: 513-229-4545

STUDENTS SPEAK OUT

Life

The University of Dayton is an apparent oxymoron, a Catholic party school. Explains one student, "UD is like a very conservative parent with rebellious children." Although a few students report that the administration is beginning to crack down on drinking ("the school is shutting us down abruptly, not gradually," writes one very upset undergrad), the vast majority reports that the party rages on. One student jokes that UD is "a drinking institution with a learning problem"; writes another, "There is a tremendous amount of pressure here to drink beer excessively." Fraternities and sororities, surprisingly, are not the dominant presence they are on most "party" campuses. Students enjoy intramural and intercollegiate sports and participate actively in campus clubs and community-service organizations. The city of Dayton receives below-average marks from UD undergrads, but students do report that relations with locals are amiable. Commuters complain that "parking on campus is a constant battle between campus security; be prepared to spend money."

Academics

Students at the University of Dayton repeatedly emphasize two aspects of the UD experience. One is the party scene described above. The other is the sense of community they enjoy. Writes one, "The best thing about UD is how much the faculty, staff, and administration are dedicated to academics. Professors are very willing to see students individually. The faculty even voted to lower their raises for next year in order to put more money into financial aid." Students agree that UD is a school for the preprofessional student; liberal arts take a backseat here to business and management, engineering, communications, and education. Like most Catholic schools, UD has a broad set of general education requirements. Students report that they study an average of two and three-quarters hours a day, which places them among the bottom twenty-five percent of students we surveyed. For those looking for a greater challenge, UD offers both a University Scholars Program, which offers enrollees special classes, seminars, and symposiums (about twenty percent of UD undergraduates participate in the program), and an even more rigorous Honors Program. Honors students, who make up only three percent of the undergraduate population, follow a prescribed four-year, interdisciplinary curriculum that culminates in a senior thesis.

Student Body

About three quarters of UD's students are Roman Catholic. Just over half are from Ohio. Minority enrollment is extremely small. The student body is among the most politically conservative of any school of all the colleges we surveyed. One student describes it as "politically conservative but socially liberal—what a mix!"

ADMISSIONS

The admissions committee considers (in descending order of importance): HS record, test scores, class rank, recommendations, essay. *Also considered (in descending order of importance):* extracurriculars, special talents. Either the SAT or ACT is required. An interview is recommended. Admissions process is need-blind. *High school units required/ recommended:* 18 total units are recommended; 4 English recommended, 3 math recommended, 3 science recommended, 2 foreign language recommended, 2 social studies recommended. Rank in top two-thirds of secondary school class recommended; minimum test scores and GPA vary depending on program. *Special Requirements:* An audition is required for music program applicants. TOEFL is required of all international students. Completion of math courses through algebra II and trigonometry recommended of business administration, computer science, engineering, mathematics, and natural sciences program applicants. *The admissions office says:* "All 6,000+ applications are reviewed individually with attention given to ALL areas-grades, rank, scores, curriculum, activities, recommendations, and counselor feedback. All visitors are given the opportunities for an individual admission interview as well as financial aid."

The Inside Word

While Dayton may review all applicants individually, with such a high admit rate it is rather unlikely that many get much scrutiny. Keep in mind that the admissions office didn't even mention the required essay in discussing its review process.

FINANCIAL AID

Students should submit: FAFSA, the school's own financial aid form, state aid form, a copy of parents' most recent income tax filing. The Princeton Review suggests that all financial aid forms be submitted as soon as possible after January 1. *The following grants/scholarships are offered:* Pell, SEOG, academic merit, athletic, the school's own scholarships, the school's own grants, state grants, private scholarships, private grants, ROTC, foreign aid. *Students borrow from the following loan programs:* Stafford, unsubsidized Stafford, Perkins, PLUS, the school's own loan fund, state loans, private loans. Applicants will be notified of awards beginning March 15.

FROM THE ADMISSIONS OFFICE

"The University of Dayton is a medium-sized, residential institution, and is respected as one of the nation's leading Catholic universities. We offer the resources and diversity of a comprehensive university and the attention and accessibility of a small college. Our respected programs of study, impressive 110-acre campus, advanced research facilities, NCAA Division I intercollegiate athletics, international alumni network, and access to the Dayton metropolitan community are big-school advantages. Small class sizes, undergraduate emphasis, student-centered faculty and staff, residential campus, and friendliness are all attractive small-school qualities. The University of Dayton is committed to student success. Our educational mission is to recognize the talents you bring as an individual and help you reach your potential."

ADMISSIONS

Admissions Rating	71
% of applicants accepted	89
% of acceptees attending	34

FRESHMAN PROFILE

Average verbal SAT	590
Average math SAT	600
Average ACT	25
Average TOEFL	500
Graduated top 20% of class	45
Graduated top 40% of class	71
Graduated top 60% of class	89
Average HS GPA or Avg.	3.2

DEADLINES

Early decision	NR
Regular admission	rolling
Regular notification	rolling
Non-fall registration	yes

APPLICANTS ALSO LOOK AT

AND OFTEN PREFER
Miami U.
Notre Dame

AND SOMETIMES PREFER
Ohio U.
Ohio State U.-Columbus
Purdue U.-West Lafayette
Indiana U.-Bloomington

AND RARELY PREFER
U. Illinois, Urbana-Champaign
Marquette

FINANCIAL FACTS

Financial Aid Rating	83
Tuition	$13,170
Room & board	$4,430
Estimated book expense	$500
% frosh receiving aid	90
% undergrads receiving aid	84
% aid is need-based	63
% frosh w/ grant (avg)	98 ($4,700)
% frosh w/ loan (avg)	75 ($2,170)
% UGs w/ job (avg)	82 ($5,200)

Deep Springs College

HC72 Box 45001, Dyer, NV 89010   Admissions: 619-872-2000   Fax: 619-872-4466

CAMPUS LIFE

Quality of Life Rating   **96**

Type of school	private
Affiliation	none
Environment	rural

STUDENTS

FT undergrad enrollment	25
% male/female	100/0
% from out of state	88
% live on campus	100
% spend weekend on campus	NR
% transfers	NR
% from public high school	NR
% African-American	0
% Asian	12
% Caucasian	88
% Hispanic	0
% international	16
# of countries represented	NR

WHAT'S HOT

campus food
Dyer
honesty
political activism
registration is a breeze

WHAT'S NOT

beer
infrequent dating
intercollegiate sports
off-campus food
hard liquor

ACADEMICS

Academic Rating   **98**

Profs Interesting Rating	99
Profs Accessible Rating	99
Calendar	semester
Student/teacher ratio	4:1
% profs PhD	80
Hours of study per day	4.67

STUDENTS SPEAK OUT

Life

As one Deep Springs College student puts it, "We give up beer and women for sixty miles of sand." (Actually, according to several students, while "it is against rules to drink alcohol during the school term, on our breaks drinking is common.") Television, drugs, and contact with anyone but the Deep Springs community are other things students here forsake. Leaving campus, except for urgent family matters and ranch business, is prohibited, although the rigorous physical activity has been known to leave students too tired to even want to leave. One student clarified the sentiment: "Dairy barn at 5:00 a.m. = Bedtime at 10:00 p.m." Explains one student, "Students have a love/hate relationship with the school. The absence of women is frustrating, socially, morally, and intellectually. Drugs and alcohol have no place in a schedule jammed with academics, labor, and student government. Coffee and cigarettes are good." It's fair to say that student life at Deep Springs is unique: "This is the only place I can imagine where the students would organize a Derrida reading group that meets every Sunday at midnight in the dairy barn. This place rocks!" The surrounding area, while devoid of civilization and its diversions, is breathtakingly beautiful and accommodating to skiers and hikers.

Academics

Men looking for the unconventional undergraduate experience, look no farther: Deep Springs College provides that in spades to its few students. This two-year college (enrollment: twenty-six) furnishes students with an intense workload that includes not only academics but ranch work as well. Deep Springs is located on a remote desert ranch on which labor is mandatory. Here's how it works: Students attend small, discussion-oriented classes in the morning, then spend the afternoons working their jobs, during which the classroom discussions are often continued. Jobs include such unglamorous titles as ditch digger and general laborer. One lucky guy gets to be a cowboy. According to the school, "The labor program is not a way for students to pay for their time [here]...nor is its purpose to teach skills. The labor program exists to help students develop self-discipline, self-reliance, and an awareness of their responsibilities to the...community." Students play a role in every aspect of the school's governance, from assigning work to recommending courses to reviewing and deciding upon admissions applications. For those suited to this type of life, Deep Springs "helps students gain a perspective on and understanding of the way things work in any community" and "forces you to succeed, to fail, and to evaluate yourself. It is a place where you can realize your full potential." Sums up one student: "Higher education was born of a need for something beyond manual labor, but that intermediary step was lost in intervening years. Deep Springs was born of the need to re-establish the complete progression." After two years, students transfer to more conventional four-year colleges, which often include the nation's top schools.

Student Body

Deep Springs provides full scholarships for all students, so economic background is no barrier to acceptance here. The student body is largely white (there are Asians, but no black or Hispanic students), liberal, and extremely bright. One student reports, "Most years there is one gay student on campus. Homophobia doesn't exist here."

ADMISSIONS

The admissions office says: "Our admissions process is the most intense in the country. Finalists write seven essays and undergo a two-hour-long intensive interview. All applicants accepted for the second stage must travel to Deep Springs for a three-day visit. The deadline for the first stage [of the application process] is November 15, so don't be caught off-guard."

The Inside Word

There is no admissions staff at Deep Springs. Along with faculty, students make up the admissions committee. There is likely to be no more rigorous, personal, or refreshing an admissions process to be found in U.S. higher education. This place requires serious commitment, and only the strong survive. Thorough self-assessment is a must before applying.

FROM THE ADMISSIONS OFFICE

"Founded in 1912, Deep Springs College lies isolated in a high desert valley of California, 30 miles from the nearest town. Its enrollment is limited to 26 students, each of whom receives a full scholarship valued at over $20,000 covering tuition, room, and board. The students engage in a rigorous academic program, govern themselves, and participate in the operation of the cattle and alfalfa ranch, which is owned by the school. After two or three years, they transfer to other schools to complete their studies. Students regularly transfer to Berkeley, Cornell, Harvard, and Yale. Students make up eight of the ten members of the Applications Committee."

ADMISSIONS

Admissions Rating	99
% of applicants accepted	7
% of acceptees attending	86

FRESHMAN PROFILE

Average verbal SAT	740
Average math SAT	750
Average ACT	NR
Average TOEFL	NR
Graduated top 20% of class	100
Graduated top 40% of class	100
Graduated top 60% of class	100
Average HS GPA or Avg.	NR

DEADLINES

Early decision	NR
Regular admission	11/15
Regular notification	4/5
Non-fall registration	no

APPLICANTS ALSO LOOK AT
AND SOMETIMES PREFER

Harvard/Radcliffe
Yale
U. Chicago
UC-Berkeley
Swarthmore

FINANCIAL FACTS

Financial Aid Rating	99
Tuition	$0
Room & board	$0
Estimated book expense	$500
% frosh receiving aid	100
% undergrads receiving aid	100
% aid is need-based	NR
% frosh w/ grant (avg)	NR
% frosh w/ loan (avg)	NR
% UGs w/ job (avg)	100

UNIVERSITY OF DELAWARE

Newark, DE 19716

Admissions: 302-831-8123   Fax: 302-831-6905

CAMPUS LIFE

Quality of Life Rating **83**
Type of school   public
Affiliation   none
Environment   town

STUDENTS
FT undergrad enrollment   13,290
% male/female   43/57
% from out of state   58
% live on campus   53
% spend weekend on campus   75
% transfers   17
% from public high school   76
% in (# of) fraternities   18 (25)
% in (# of) sororities   18 (15)
% African-American   5
% Asian   3
% Caucasian   89
% Hispanic   2
% international   2
# of countries represented   77

WHAT'S HOT
beer
hard liquor
computer facilities
student publications
library

WHAT'S NOT
student government
political activism
music associations
students are cliquish
campus difficult to get around

ACADEMICS

Academic Rating **80**
Profs Interesting Rating   69
Profs Accessible Rating   75
Calendar   4-1-4
Student/teacher ratio   15:1
% profs PhD/tenured   87/68
Hours of study per day   2.95

MOST POPULAR MAJORS
psychology
biological sciences
engineering

% GRADS WHO PURSUE...
Law 4, Med 1, MBA 3

STUDENTS SPEAK OUT

Life

We find few student complaints about social life at U of D. As one student puts it, "There are so many social opportunities at Delaware, it is possible to go out every night of the week." Beer and hard liquor are the social lubricants of choice, and "parties are common--but you can have a life if you don't get plastered every weekend." Another comments that "It's not possible to party 24 hours a day, 7 days a week and still do well, but I have a pretty active weekend social life and a 3.5 cum." Intercollegiate sports, particularly football and basketball (the men's basketball team made it to the NCAA tournament in 1992 and 1993), are popular. Campus-wide events include Homecoming and Greek-related parties and contests. Other bonuses: the campus is "gorgeous" and "the town of Newark is the perfect college town. It's on Main Street, which is composed of all kinds of shops and places to eat. Plus, there is a good nightclub and a good bar where a lot of students hang out."

Academics

The University of Delaware is a popular choice among area students: Marylanders, Pennsylvanians, and New Jersey natives, as well as home staters, are among those attracted by U of D's reasonable price tag and great reputation. Psychology, business/accounting/economics, education, nursing, and engineering (the last bolstered by its proximity to and close relationship with Du Pont) are most popular and are considered the best that U of D offers. Students report that "most teachers are pretty cool and are willing to help students when needed." As at many large schools, students sometimes complain of large classes and an administration that "can be a little out of touch." But actions speak louder than words; our surveys show that most students feel Delaware is smoothly run. The University's new student services center centralizes administrative functions, and is winning national regard as a model to be imitated. Together with an award-winning campus-wide computer networking system, the center is a strong sign of administrative commitment. U of D has a noteworthy Honors Program, ideal for budget-conscious achievers who seek a challenging, intimate college experience.

Student Body

Delaware's student body is mainly Caucasian, leading one student to observe, "This feels like an all-white university." Adds another student, "The U of D has a very diverse campus with many people of different social backgrounds; however, the diverse groups rarely interact. Also, I hardly ever see any black students." One student tells us that "although some homophobia exists...the school is generally welcoming to diversity." On the whole, U of D students are politically apathetic, but one student mentions that "the people who do choose to be involved are very committed and active."

ADMISSIONS

The admissions committee considers (in descending order of importance): HS record, test scores, class rank, recommendations, essay. *Also considered (in descending order of importance):* alumni relationship, geographical distribution, special talents. Either the SAT or ACT is required; SAT is preferred. Admissions process is need-blind. *High school units required/recommended:* 16 total units are required; 19 total units are recommended; 4 English required, 4 English recommended, 2 math required, 4 math recommended, 2 science required, 3 science recommended, 2 foreign language required, 4 foreign language recommended, 1 social studies required, 2 social studies recommended, 2 history required, 2 history recommended. TOEFL is required of all international students. *The admissions office says:* "[In our admissions process] the academic record is weighted more than SATs. A minimum SAT score is not used. Students can be admitted directly to most majors. Engineering, business, and science majors are more competitive."

The Inside Word

Most students applying to Delaware face a moderately selective admissions process focused mainly on grades and tests. Those who seek to enter the university's honors program need to be far more thorough in completing their applications and much better prepared academically in order to gain admission. The honors program has high expectations; from what we know, it appears to be well worth it.

FINANCIAL AID

Students should submit: FAFSA (due March 15). The Princeton Review suggests that all financial aid forms be submitted as soon as possible after January 1. *The following grants/scholarships are offered:* Pell, SEOG, academic merit, athletic, the school's own scholarships, the school's own grants, state scholarships, state grants, private scholarships, private grants, ROTC. *Students borrow from the following loan programs:* Stafford, unsubsidized Stafford, Perkins, PLUS, supplemental loans, federal nursing loans, private loans. Applicants will be notified of awards beginning April 1. College Work-Study Program is available. Institutional employment is available.

FROM THE ADMISSIONS OFFICE

"The University of Delaware is, by design, one of the smallest major research universities in the nation, with a long-standing commitment to teaching and servicing undergraduates. It is one of only a few in the country designated as a land-grant, sea-grant, and space-grant institution. The university received the 1994 CAUSE Award for Excellence in Campus Networking for its use of a campus-wide network to enhance teaching, learning, research, administration, and community service. The University of Delaware offers the wide range of majors and course offerings expected of a university, but in spirit remains a small place, where you can interact with your professors and feel at home. The most experienced and knowledgeable faculty teach introductory courses and they welcome students who seek their advice and counsel. Faculty invite students to participate in their research and scholarship and are especially encouraging to those who want to engage in learning beyond the classroom."

ADMISSIONS

Admissions Rating	76
% of applicants accepted	71
% of acceptees attending	32

FRESHMAN PROFILE

Average verbal SAT	580
Average math SAT	570
Average ACT	NR
Average TOEFL	550
Graduated top 20% of class	49
Graduated top 40% of class	84
Graduated top 60% of class	99
Average HS GPA or Avg.	3.2

DEADLINES

Early decision	11/15
Regular admission	1/1
Regular notification	rolling
Non-fall registration	yes

APPLICANTS ALSO LOOK AT

AND OFTEN PREFER
James Madison

AND SOMETIMES PREFER
Trenton St.
Widener
Rutgers U.-Rutgers Coll.
Penn State U.
U. Rhode Island

AND RARELY PREFER
Dickinson
Providence

FINANCIAL FACTS

Financial Aid Rating	83
In-state tuition	$3,860
Out-of-state tuition	$10,730
Room & board	$4,420
Estimated book expense	$530
% frosh receiving aid	76
% undergrads receiving aid	58
% aid is need-based	NR
% frosh w/ grant (avg)	60 ($4,000)
% frosh w/ loan (avg)	60 ($2,625)
% UGs w/ job (avg)	15 ($1,000)
Off-campus job outlook	good

DENISON UNIVERSITY

Box H, Granville, OH 43023   Admissions: 800-282-4766   Fax: 614-587-6417

STUDENTS SPEAK OUT

Life

The Greeks play a huge role in the Denison social universe—the school ranked twelfth among all schools in this book in terms of the importance of frats and sororities to campus life. Says one student, "If you aren't in a fraternity or sorority, your social life is nonexistent." Without the Greeks, most students fear, DU would have no social life. One student explains, "There is a lack of social alternatives here at Denison. It's not necessarily the fault of the administration, but rather it's because the school is located in a small-town in central Ohio." Accordingly, moves by the university to rein in Greek excesses have scared all students. Says one, "A lot of pressure has been put on the Greeks to make reforms. However, since Greek life is the ONLY social scene within a ten-mile radius, Greeks have really come together in a joint effort to remain an active part of Denison." University efforts notwithstanding, DU remains a party school, although students agree that the partying gets less intense each year. "If you come looking for a constant party scene, you'll be about five years too late," says one student. There are plenty of opportunities for students to participate in clubs and organizations: intramural sports, the school paper, and especially the radio station are very popular. Says one student, "Denison is the perfect size for getting involved in different activities and feeling a real part of the campus community. It is also big enough to offer a wide variety of classes and activities, and wonderful opportunities."

Academics

Until recently, Denison had a reputation as a party school, and it was common knowledge that students could breeze through many of their courses. This is no longer true: writes one student, "Academics are becoming increasingly more stringent; our goal of becoming 'little Dartmouth' is coming together well." The faculty are highly regarded by many students, the administration by few. Many mention sentiments to the effect that "students are not given an equal voice, and things are often done behind our backs." Denison is a university in name, but in fact it's a small liberal arts college. Small classes, caring, personable professors, and rigorous academics take precedence over prestige-garnering research and publication. Psychology, English, and economics are among the most popular of the many strong departments here; the school also has its fair share of pre-meds. Over the past year, Denison has opened a new science hall, including a planetarium, and begun construction on a biological field station. Majors have been added in environmental studies, biochemistry, and music, technology, and the arts.

Student Body

Denison students are pretty cynical about the makeup of their student body. Says one, "Denison does not allow for great diversity of social background. If you come here, prepare to conform to the image of upper class, wealthy, and well bred." Another writes: "Denison is still a haven for rich, underachieving prep schoolers, but the student body is changing. Recent additions include: students who like to study, those against the Greek system, and those whose names aren't Skip or Bailey." The vast majority of the students are white.

ADMISSIONS

The admissions committee considers (in descending order of importance): HS record, test scores, class rank, recommendations, essay. *Also considered (in descending order of importance):* personality, special talents, alumni relationship, extracurriculars, geographical distribution. Either the SAT or ACT is required. An interview is required of some applicants. Admissions process is need-blind. *High school units required/recommended:* 16 total units are required; 4 English recommended, 3 math recommended, 3 science recommended, 3 foreign language recommended, 2 social studies recommended, 1 history recommended. Recruitment, enrollment, and financial support of minority applicants. *The admissions office says:* "The quality of your academic performance and your GPA in your junior and senior years are the most important factors. Important also is the quality, rather than the quantity, of your extracurricular accomplishments."

The Inside Word

Applicants who statistically are below Denison's freshman profile should proceed with caution. One of the simplest ways for a university to promote a reputation as an increasingly selective institution is to begin to cut off the bottom of the admit pool. Only lack of success against heavy competition for students prevents Denison from being more aggressive in this regard.

FINANCIAL AID

Students should submit: FAFSA, the school's own financial aid form, a copy of parents' most recent income tax filing. The Princeton Review suggests that all financial aid forms be submitted as soon as possible after January 1. *The following grants/scholarships are offered:* Pell, SEOG, academic merit, the school's own scholarships, the school's own grants, state scholarships, state grants, private scholarships, private grants, foreign aid. *Students borrow from the following loan programs:* Stafford, unsubsidized Stafford, Perkins, PLUS, the school's own loan fund, private loans. Applicants will be notified of awards beginning April 1. College Work-Study Program is available. Institutional employment is available.

FROM THE ADMISSIONS OFFICE

"Denison University's concern for the success of each student is reflected in its innovative and extensive First Year Program, including June Orientation, Freshman Studies, excellent academic support services, and a First Year Center, which get first-year students off to a strong start. In small classes—many of them seminar size—active learning is the norm. Faculty are committed to sharing their own high academic standards and to helping students attain them through a strong faculty-based advising system. Unique opportunities to do original research and publishing with faculty members, and state-of-the-art equipment in the sciences, set Denison apart from other undergraduate schools. Writing and discourse are integral components of most courses. Outside the classroom, more than 90 student-run organizations offer students many options for developing leadership skills. The uncommon beauty of the campus and its meticulously maintained facilities make Denison a beautiful place to learn."

ADMISSIONS

Admissions Rating	72
% of applicants accepted	84
% of acceptees attending	32

FRESHMAN PROFILE

Average verbal SAT	600
Average math SAT	600
Average ACT	25
Average TOEFL	550
Graduated top 20% of class	56
Graduated top 40% of class	79
Graduated top 60% of class	93
Average HS GPA or Avg.	3.3

DEADLINES

Early decision	January
Regular admission	2/1
Regular notification	4/1
Non-fall registration	yes

APPLICANTS ALSO LOOK AT

AND OFTEN PREFER

Northwestern U.
Miami U.
Kenyon
DePauw

AND SOMETIMES PREFER

Wittenberg
Ohio State U.-Columbus
Ohio Wesleyan
Dickinson
Vanderbilt

AND RARELY PREFER

Skidmore
Hobart & William Smith

FINANCIAL FACTS

Financial Aid Rating	86
Tuition	$17,770
Room & board	$4,720
Estimated book expense	$600
% frosh receiving aid	97
% undergrads receiving aid	86
% aid is need-based	77
% frosh w/ grant (avg)	98 ($11,368)
% frosh w/ loan (avg)	61 ($2,331)
% UGs w/ job (avg)	51 ($1,700)
Off-campus job outlook	fair

UNIVERSITY OF DENVER

UNIVERSITY PARK, DENVER, CO 80208

ADMISSIONS: 800-525-9495   FAX: 303-871-3301

CAMPUS LIFE

Quality of Life Rating	**82**
Type of school	private
Affiliation	none
Environment	suburban

STUDENTS

FT undergrad enrollment	2,779
% male/female	47/53
% from out of state	58
% live on campus	48
% spend weekend on campus	NR
% transfers	8
% from public high school	NR
% in (# of) fraternities	(9)
% in (# of) sororities	(4)
% African-American	3
% Asian	6
% Caucasian	85
% Hispanic	6
% international	11
# of countries represented	56

WHAT'S HOT
Greeks
registration is a breeze
Denver
drugs
off-campus food

WHAT'S NOT
student publications
theater
college radio
lab facilities
religion

ACADEMICS

Academic Rating	**78**
Profs Interesting Rating	80
Profs Accessible Rating	81
Calendar	quarter
Student/teacher ratio	13:1
% profs PhD/tenured	87/90
Hours of study per day	3.00

MOST POPULAR MAJORS
biology
business
communication

% GRADS WHO PURSUE...
Law 5, Med 2, MBA 4, MA 11

STUDENTS SPEAK OUT

Life

Many University of Denver students are skiing fanatics, and more than a few choose the school for its location. "You don't need to know how to ski when you come here," writes one student, "but you better be ready to learn." Explains another, "Skiing and partying are big. If you have time, you go to class." The social scene centers on fraternity parties, which pleases many but not all undergrads. Although students at similarly-sized schools often complain that their surroundings become claustrophobic at times, DU students have no such complaints, probably because they are located on the outskirts of a major city. In fact, students report that they enjoy the small student body ("Everywhere you go on campus, including parties, social functions, the cafeteria, etc., you see someone you know," explains one student. "That is very comforting.") Students also note that the small student body allows for "Great opportunity for student action and involvement." Sums up one respondent: "If you enjoy outdoor activities and a small campus, then DU is great. Most freshmen have a more active social life than an academic one, but then, not all of them come back."

Academics

University of Denver is a place where business and pleasure successfully mix. The school's business and management programs, which claim over half the student body, are excellent. And while the proximity of the nation's best ski resorts presents a major distraction, most students seem to find the time to get their work done before hitting the slopes—the average student puts in over three hours of study a day and takes class attendance and assignments fairly seriously. Music, communications, international studies, and hotel, tourism, and restaurant management are among the other recommended departments here, and one sophomore brags that "this is probably one of the few universities in the nation where undergraduates work directly with doctors involved in such things as ozone depletion and global warming." All students must complete a set of core requirements covering basic humanities, social science, and natural science materials. Students report that "The classes are small and the teachers are extremely helpful." Students also give the core curriculum ("a good, broad introduction to a variety of areas") a thumbs-up. Note: DU runs on a quarterly schedule, so terms go by very quickly.

Student Body

The student body of DU is pretty homogeneous: Asians, blacks, and Hispanics combined make up about 15 percent of the population. Writes one African-American student, "DU offers little or no attraction for minority students. It seems that the school makes little effort to attract minority students from the local urban community," though the school claims they are concerned and making strides in this area. Otherwise, students are happy about the makeup of their classes. One student reports that "A lot of people are environmentally conscious. Students are friendly and caring, and show many similar interests. We are a tight-knit group."

Financial Aid: 303-871-2681 E-mail: Admission@du.edu Web Site: http://www.du.edu/

ADMISSIONS

The admissions committee considers (in descending order of importance): HS record, test scores, class rank, recommendations, essay. *Also considered (in descending order of importance):* extracurriculars, personality, special talents. Either the SAT or ACT is required. An interview is recommended. *High school units required/recommended:* 4 English recommended, 3 math recommended, 3 science recommended, 2 foreign language recommended. Minimum combined SAT I score of 850 (composite ACT score of 18), rank in top quarter of secondary school class, and minimum 2.8 GPA recommended. *Special Requirements:* An audition is required for music program applicants. TOEFL is required of all international students. Essay required of all applicants. Portfolio recommended of art program applicants. *The admissions office says:* "The committee on admissions selects students whose backgrounds show that enrollment at the University of Denver will be mutually rewarding. In selecting the freshman class, the committee on admissions considers all available information, including evidence of academic maturity and independence, general contributions to the school and the community, extracurricular activities, and leadership."

The Inside Word

Any good student will find getting admitted to Denver to be a fairly straightforward process.

FINANCIAL AID

Students should submit: FAFSA, a copy of parents' most recent income tax filing. The Princeton Review suggests that all financial aid forms be submitted as soon as possible after January 1. *The following grants/scholarships are offered:* Pell, SEOG, academic merit, athletic, the school's own scholarships, the school's own grants, state scholarships, state grants, private scholarships, private grants, ROTC, foreign aid. *Students borrow from the following loan programs:* Stafford, unsubsidized Stafford, Perkins, PLUS, private loans. Applicants will be notified of awards beginning April 1. College Work-Study Program is available. Institutional employment is available.

FROM THE ADMISSIONS OFFICE

The University of Denver is the oldest independent university in the Rocky Mountain region, founded in 1864 before Colorado became a state. The 125-acre University Park campus is located in a residential neighborhood eight miles southeast of downtown Denver. Reflecting the school mascot, our students tend to be pioneers—congenial, determined, daring individualists with a passion for living and learning. Like the old West pioneers, our students journey from all 50 states and more than 92 countries. That pioneering spirit extends to our academic programs, which begin with a core curriculum recognized for its excellence by the National Endowment for the Humanities. And our students benefit from a new Partners in Scholarship program that offers research grants to undergraduates. The living community includes special residence hall floors focusing on wellness, leadership, honors, and international interests. Denver is a great place to study and launch a career. Denver's robust economy—diversified by tourism, high technology, telecommunications, and government—continues to defy national trends. That's good news for University alumni, half of whom stay in the region to live and work after graduation.

ADMISSIONS

Admissions Rating	72
% of applicants accepted	69
% of acceptees attending	29

FRESHMAN PROFILE
Average verbal SAT	560
Average math SAT	560
Average ACT	24
Average TOEFL	580
Graduated top 20% of class	51
Graduated top 40% of class	82
Graduated top 60% of class	95
Average HS GPA or Avg.	3.2

DEADLINES
Early decision	NR
Regular admission	2/15
Regular notification	rolling
Non-fall registration	yes

APPLICANTS ALSO LOOK AT
AND OFTEN PREFER
U. Colorado-Boulder
AND SOMETIMES PREFER
U. Puget Sound
U. Vermont

FINANCIAL FACTS

Financial Aid Rating	88
Tuition	$16,740
Room & board	$5,538
Estimated book expense	$555
% frosh receiving aid	58
% undergrads receiving aid	60
% aid is need-based	65
% frosh w/ grant (avg)	NR ($8,609)
% frosh w/ loan (avg)	46 ($3,041)
% UGs w/ job (avg)	25 ($1,400)
Off-campus job outlook	excellent

DePAUL UNIVERSITY

1 EAST JACKSON BOULEVARD, CHICAGO, IL 60604-2287   ADMISSIONS: 800-433-7285   FAX: 312-362-5749

CAMPUS LIFE

Quality of Life Rating   80
Type of school   private
Affiliation   Roman Catholic Church
                  (Vincentian Fathers)
Environment   metropolis

STUDENTS
FT undergrad enrollment	6,137
% male/female	43/57
% from out of state	25
% live on campus	25
% spend weekend on campus	60
% transfers	48
% from public high school	64
% in (# of) fraternities	3 (3)
% in (# of) sororities	2 (2)
% African-American	10
% Asian	7
% Caucasian	69
% Hispanic	13
% international	2
# of countries represented	60

WHAT'S HOT
Chicago
off-campus food
registration is a breeze
different students interact
leftist politics

WHAT'S NOT
student publications
health facilities
lab facilities
unattractive campus
support groups

ACADEMICS

Academic Rating	**75**
Profs Interesting Rating	69
Profs Accessible Rating	70
Calendar	trimester
Student/teacher ratio	13:1
% profs tenured	88
Hours of study per day	2.80

MOST POPULAR MAJORS
accountancy
finance
marketing

STUDENTS SPEAK OUT
Life
Due to a substantial commuter population, DePaul University "lacks a typical college atmosphere." Clubs and the Greeks fill the social void for many who live on campus. Says one student, "There is a club here for everyone. The DePaul Community Service Association is very popular, as is the Residence Hall Council. There's a walking club and even an Elvis Lives Club." Those who live at DePaul are housed at the Lincoln Park campus. The neighborhood around it is not unlike Washington, D.C.'s Georgetown; although it's a little preppy for some tastes, it offers a lot in the way of clubs, record stores, and inexpensive dining. Beyond Lincoln Park is the rest of Chicago, "a terrific city with a lot of culture and history; it's also Partytown USA." Chicago also provides preprofessional students plenty of internship opportunities, opportunities arranged by the university. The campuses themselves are unspectacular. Reports one student, "We need more grass (lawn, that is)." It's obvious the administration listened to this student, as a huge new grass-filled quad has been constructed.

Academics
DePaul is a Catholic school with a preprofessional emphasis. Business administration, accounting, management, and marketing are popular majors here, as are computer science and political science (a popular choice with pre-law students). DePaul also boasts a nationally renowned drama department. Says one drama major, "We have one of the finest theater schools anywhere, which means there is plenty of talent abounding here." The campus is home to the Reskin Theater, which allows DePaul theatre students ample opportunities to perform. Although a medium-sized school, DPU offers several of the benefits of a small college. Classes are usually small, and professors take genuine interest in their students' progress. Says one student, "The best thing about DePaul is the student/teacher ratio. You really get to know your professors." Reports another, "The instructors set high standards, and encourage us to do the same and not do things by way of the status quo." The quarterly academic schedule draws some complaints ("it does not allow students the time for play"), as did the number and difficulty level of required liberal arts courses. The school is divided into two campuses: downtown (at the Loop), where most of the preprofessional studies take place, and uptown (Lincoln Park) for liberal arts, science, music, and theatre students.

Student Body
About half of DePaul's students are Catholic. Many of the students are from Chicago's less-wealthy suburbs and were "not really aware of the city" before attending DePaul. One Hispanic woman explains that "although DePaul is located in the city, it caters to the suburbs. I would say that in all my classes I have been the only Latina and the only person born and raised in the city." For the most part, however, students have praise for their classmates, characterizing them as "helpful" and "sociable." Students here are liberal and particularly open-minded for those attending religious schools.

FINANCIAL AID: 312-362-8526

WEB SITE: HTTP://WWW.DEPAUL.EDU/

ADMISSIONS

The admissions committee considers (in descending order of importance): HS record, class rank, test scores, recommendations, essay. *Also considered (in descending order of importance):* extracurriculars, personality, alumni relationship, special talents. Either the SAT or ACT is required. An interview is recommended. Admissions process is need-blind. *High school units required/recommended:* 16 total units are required; 4 English required, 2 math required, 2 science required, 2 social studies required, 2 history required. Additional units of math and science recommended. *Special Requirements:* An audition is required for music program applicants. An RN is required for nursing program applicants. TOEFL is required of all international students. Audition required of theater program applicants. *The admissions office says:* "No cutoffs or formulas are used in considering applicants. A student's total academic record and extracurricular or co-curricular activities are considered."

The Inside Word

Applicants to DePaul will find the admissions staff is genuinely committed to helping students. Candidates whose academic qualifications fall below normally acceptable levels are reviewed for other evidence of potential for success. The Latino student presence on campus has begun to increase significantly, due in large part to the university's major commitment to active involvement in the National Hispanic Institute, an organization that works with top Hispanic students from junior high through college.

FINANCIAL AID

Students should submit: FAFSA. The Princeton Review suggests that all financial aid forms be submitted as soon as possible after January 1. *The following grants/scholarships are offered:* Pell, SEOG, academic merit, athletic, the school's own scholarships, the school's own grants, state scholarships, state grants, private scholarships, private grants, ROTC. *Students borrow from the following loan programs:* Stafford, Perkins, PLUS, state loans, private loans. College Work-Study Program is available. Institutional employment is available.

FROM THE ADMISSIONS OFFICE

"Founded by the Vincentian Order in 1898, DePaul is the second largest Catholic university in the country, including two main campuses: The Lincoln Park campus, located amidst one of Chicago's most exciting neighborhoods—filled with century-old brownstone homes, theaters, cafes, clubs, and shops—is home to DePaul's College of Liberal Arts & Sciences, the School of Education, the Theatre School, and the School of Music, as well as residence halls and academic and recreational facilities. The focal point of this campus is a new library with its soaring three-story reading room that overlooks a landscaped quad. The Loop Campus, located in Chicago's downtown—a world-class center for business, government, law, and culture—is home to DePaul's College of Commerce, the Law School, and the School of Computer Science and Information Systems."

ADMISSIONS

Admissions Rating	**71**
% of applicants accepted	72
% of acceptees attending	33

FRESHMAN PROFILE

Average verbal SAT	570
Average math SAT	560
Average ACT	25
Average TOEFL	550
Graduated top 20% of class	62
Graduated top 40% of class	90
Graduated top 60% of class	NR
Average HS GPA or Avg.	3.4

DEADLINES

Early decision	11/15
Regular admission	8/15
Regular notification	rolling
Non-fall registration	yes

APPLICANTS ALSO LOOK AT

AND OFTEN PREFER
Northwestern U.
U. Chicago
Illinois Tech.
Northeastern
Notre Dame

AND SOMETIMES PREFER
U. Illinois, Urbana-Champaign
Loyola U. Chicago
Boston U.
Indiana U.-Bloomington

AND RARELY PREFER
Purdue U.-West Lafayette

FINANCIAL FACTS

Financial Aid Rating	**78**
Tuition	$11,856
Room & board	$3,000
Estimated book expense	$600
% frosh receiving aid	NR
% undergrads receiving aid	65
% aid is need-based	NR
% frosh w/ grant (avg)	68 ($2,800)
% frosh w/ loan (avg)	55 ($2,460)
% UGs w/ job (avg)	28 ($2,000)
Off-campus job outlook	excellent

DePauw University

313 South Locust Street, Greencastle, IN 46135

ADMISSIONS: 800-447-2495   FAX: 317-658-4007

CAMPUS LIFE

Quality of Life Rating	75
Type of school	private
Affiliation	United Methodist Church
Environment	town

STUDENTS

FT undergrad enrollment	2,090
% male/female	45/55
% from out of state	58
% live on campus	95
% spend weekend on campus	90
% transfers	2
% from public high school	85
% in (# of) fraternities	78 (15)
% in (# of) sororities	72 (11)
% African-American	7
% Asian	2
% Caucasian	85
% Hispanic	4
% international	2
# of countries represented	15

WHAT'S HOT
beer
hard liquor
college radio
Greeks
cigarettes

WHAT'S NOT
off-campus food
Greencastle
students are cliquish
political activism
town-gown relations

ACADEMICS

Academic Rating	89
Profs Interesting Rating	87
Profs Accessible Rating	85
Calendar	4-1-4
Student/teacher ratio	12:1
% profs PhD/tenured	79/70
Hours of study per day	3.71

MOST POPULAR MAJORS
communication arts/sciences
political science
English writing

% GRADS WHO PURSUE...
Law 10, Med 5, MBA 15, MA 20

STUDENTS SPEAK OUT

Life

Despite the school's many good qualities, DePauw University students ranked only in the middle of the national pack in terms of overall satisfaction with their school. A major source of unhappiness is the limit of social options. There is essentially one: the Greek system. Nearly everybody goes Greek, and while this arrangement is satisfactory to many, it isn't satisfactory to everyone. Writes one student, "The campus is extremely Greek and the social system is hardly navigable without the correct Greek letters on your chest." Writes another, "If there was another school just like DePauw, but without the Greek system, I'd be much happier there." The town of Greencastle is "much too rural" and "offers little in terms of entertainment." Positive aspects of life at DePauw include a popular intramural sports program ("intramurals are more popular spectator sports than the college-affiliated programs"), an excellent college radio station, and the food. Of the last, one student writes, "With apologies to Mom, the food here is better than what I get at home. After all, it's tough to beat a Belgian waffle maker, self-serve ice cream, salad bar, and all around first-class 'grub' with all the fixings."

Academics

Several features set DePauw University apart from the "small liberal arts school" pack. One is the winter semester, a month-long term in which students pursue "many outstanding opportunities to do things you can't do in the classroom." Writes one student, "During the winter term I've had friends who interned at hospitals, law firms, and went on mission trips. I stayed on campus to learn production and news aspects of the college radio station." Another unique aspect of campus life is the strong student participation in community service. According to one student, "The level of volunteer involvement with the community is amazing." Students get involved "through their church or through the campus ministries center." In most other ways a conventional liberal arts school, DePauw offers excellent, challenging programs in letters and social sciences (several respondents note that the new media-studies center is very good). Students enjoy a great deal of contact with professors: wrote one, "The teachers could not be more accessible. The caring academic environment makes it impossible for someone to slip through the cracks unless he or she wants to." DePauw students are encouraged to participate in the overseas studies program, which sends students practically everywhere in the world.

Student Body

Several students tell us that DePauw has recently stepped up efforts to attract minority students. One student reports, "I have close friends from Argentina, South Africa, and Hawaii. It's a much healthier environment this way." Still, the predominant tone of the student body remains wealthy and WASPy. Writes one black student, "DePauw is a good school, but academics are only a part of education. DePauw students are rich and often ignorant of other racial and ethnic backgrounds, which makes it a chore for other groups to interact. We constantly have to tolerate their ignorance!" Another student writes that "the student body is divided by fraternity, sorority, race, and politics. The place is socially fragmented."

FINANCIAL AID: 317-658-4030

ADMISSIONS

The admissions committee considers (in descending order of importance): HS record, class rank, test scores, essay, recommendations. *Also considered (in descending order of importance):* extracurriculars, personality, special talents, alumni relationship, geographical distribution. Either the SAT or ACT is required. An interview is recommended. Admissions process is need-blind. *High school units required/recommended:* 15 total units are required; 4 English required, 3 math required, 3 science required, 4 science recommended, 2 foreign language required, 4 foreign language recommended, 1 social studies required, 2 social studies recommended, 2 history required. *Special Requirements:* An audition is required for music program applicants. Separate applications required of Honor Scholars, Management Fellows, Media Fellows, and Science Research Fellows program applicants. *The admissions office says:* "We set no arbitrary limits on class rank, GPA, or results of SAT I/ACT test results. Our committee on admissions reviews each application carefully. Our students typically are involved in many activities and compete for leadership positions. There is a strong commitment to and participation in community service, both in the U.S. and Third World countries.""

The Inside Word

Students considering DePauw should not be deceived by the university's high acceptance rate. The impressive freshman profile indicates a high level of self-selection in the applicant pool.

FINANCIAL AID

Students should submit: FAFSA (due February 15), CSS Profile (due February 15), the school's own financial aid form (due February 15), state aid form (due March 1), a copy of parents' most recent income tax filing. The Princeton Review suggests that all financial aid forms be submitted as soon as possible after January 1. *The following grants/scholarships are offered:* Pell, SEOG, academic merit, the school's own scholarships, the school's own grants, state scholarships, state grants, private scholarships, private grants, ROTC. *Students borrow from the following loan programs:* Stafford, unsubsidized Stafford, Perkins, PLUS, the school's own loan fund, federal nursing loans. College Work-Study Program is available. Institutional employment is available.

FROM THE ADMISSIONS OFFICE

"A love for learning; a willingness to serve others; the reason and judgment to lead; an interest in engaging worlds you don't know; the courage to question your assumptions; and a strong commitment to community—in sum, these describe DePauw University students. Preprofessional and career exploration opportunities coexist with the liberal arts and are encouraged through Winter Term in which 700 students regularly participate in off-campus internships. This represents more students in experiential learning opportunities than at any other liberal arts college in the nation. Other innovative programs include the Honor Scholar Program as well as the Management Fellows Program, Media Fellows Program, and Science Research Fellows Program, which all include a semester-long internship in the junior year."

ADMISSIONS

Admissions Rating	**79**
% of applicants accepted	81
% of acceptees attending	33

FRESHMAN PROFILE

Average verbal SAT	620
Average math SAT	620
Average ACT	25
Average TOEFL	500
Graduated top 20% of class	71
Graduated top 40% of class	96
Graduated top 60% of class	99
Average HS GPA or Avg.	NR

DEADLINES

Early decision	NR
Regular admission	2/15
Regular notification	4/1
Non-fall registration	yes

APPLICANTS ALSO LOOK AT

AND OFTEN PREFER

Denison
Indiana U.-Bloomington
Miami U.
Purdue
Butler

AND SOMETIMES PREFER

Hanover
Rhodes
Vanderbilt
Wittenberg
Northwestern

AND RARELY PREFER

Ohio Wesleyan
Ball State
Lake Forest
Coll. of Wooster

FINANCIAL FACTS

Financial Aid Rating	**85**
Tuition	$15,175
Room & board	$5,245
Estimated book expense	$550
% frosh receiving aid	89
% undergrads receiving aid	82
% aid is need-based	69
% frosh w/ grant (avg)	87 ($10,393)
% frosh w/ loan (avg)	54 ($2,630)
% UGs w/ job (avg)	35 ($700)
Off-campus job outlook	fair

DICKINSON COLLEGE

P.O. Box 1773, Carlisle, PA 17013-2896 ADMISSIONS: 717-245-1231 Fax: 717-245-1442

CAMPUS LIFE

Quality of Life Rating	82
Type of school	private
Affiliation	none
Environment	town

STUDENTS

FT undergrad enrollment	1,789
% male/female	44/56
% from out of state	58
% live on campus	90
% spend weekend on campus	85
% transfers	1
% from public high school	62
% in (# of) fraternities	35 (9)
% in (# of) sororities	35 (5)
% African-American	1
% Asian	3
% Caucasian	94
% Hispanic	2
% international	3
# of countries represented	31

WHAT'S HOT

campus food
beer
dorms
sex
hard liquor

WHAT'S NOT

lack of diversity on campus
town-gown relations
students are cliquish
library
Carlisle

ACADEMICS

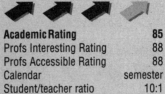

Academic Rating	85
Profs Interesting Rating	88
Profs Accessible Rating	88
Calendar	semester
Student/teacher ratio	10:1
% profs PhD/tenured	98/99
Hours of study per day	3.22

MOST POPULAR MAJORS

political science
English
history

% GRADS WHO PURSUE...

Law 13, Med 5, MBA 11, MA 30

STUDENTS SPEAK OUT

Life

As one Dickinson College undergrad puts it, "You need to make sure a small school is what you're looking for before you come here. You really have to plunge yourself into activities and get to know the people here if you want to be happy. There may not be much to do on weekends, but you can always find something to do if you're involved." Dickinson offers students tons of clubs, lectures, and arts outlets. Most students find the Greek houses the single most attractive diversion; almost half the students pledge, and many others go to their frequent parties. Warns one student, "The school's social structure is harsh. If you aren't Greek, you aren't the social norm, and as a result you are shut out of campus social life." Currently "there is a lot of drinking on campus," although "It feels as though the administration is attempting to destroy all partying on this campus, with or without alcohol. To many students, it is the prime means of socialization and stress release." Students recommend Dickinson's location; wrote one, "This area is always beautiful and alive. I can't think of another place I'd rather be." Another added, "Carlisle is a very picturesque town with the bare essentials close by."

Academics

Dickinson is a small liberal arts college known for its gorgeous location, an excellent overseas education program, and the loving attention it lavishes on its undergraduates. Students here enjoy a capable, accessible faculty who motivate and push students to achieve their best, with the result that over half of all graduates pursue advanced academic degrees. Dickinson students take their studies seriously, but unlike their counterparts at Pennsylvania rival Franklin and Marshall, do not report feeling overwhelmed by them. Reports one student, "Dickinson students are extremely active academically, but they are socially and co-curricularly active as well. If you're not the type to get involved, don't bother coming." Students also brag that "The administration here works for the students, not vice versa." Students here praise their professors.

Student Body

Dickinson's student body is predominantly white and middle- to upper-middle class. Writes one student, "There is a very strong sense of community, like living in an incredibly small town." Students consider themselves generally left of center politically, but report that their tolerance of gay and alternative lifestyles is being tested by the "in-your-face" style of on-campus activists. One student reports, "The gay rights/equal rights issue is beginning to gather steam and will eventually explode, perhaps soon." Complains another, "In general, there is an open attitude toward homosexuality on campus. However, the gay community stays in the focus because of their constant demands for equality. It's almost always in our faces; that's what causes the hostility."

FINANCIAL AID: 717-245-1308   E-MAIL: ADMIT@DICKINSON.EDU   WEB SITE: HTTP://WWW.DICKINSON.EDU/

ADMISSIONS

The admissions committee considers (in descending order of importance): HS record, recommendations, essay, class rank. *Also considered (in descending order of importance):* personality, extracurriculars, alumni relationship, geographical distribution, special talents. An interview is recommended. Admissions process is need-blind. *High school units required/recommended:* 16 total units are required; 4 English required, 3 math required, 3 science required, 2 foreign language required, 3 foreign language recommended, 2 social studies required. TOEFL is required of all international students.

The Inside Word

Dickinson's admissions process is typical of most small, conservative liberal arts colleges. The best candidates for such a place are those with solid grades and broad extracurricular involvement—the stereotypical "well-rounded student." Those who dance to the beat of a different drummer aren't likely to fit well here. Admissions selectivity is kept in check by a strong group of competitor colleges that fight tooth and nail for their cross-applicants.

FINANCIAL AID

Students should submit: FAFSA, CSS Profile, state aid form, Divorced Parents form, a copy of parents' most recent income tax filing. The Princeton Review suggests that all financial aid forms be submitted as soon as possible after January 1. *The following grants/scholarships are offered:* Pell, SEOG, academic merit, the school's own scholarships, the school's own grants, state scholarships, state grants, private scholarships, private grants, ROTC, foreign aid. *Students borrow from the following loan programs:* Stafford, Perkins, PLUS, the school's own loan fund, state loans, private loans. Applicants will be notified of awards beginning March 30. College Work-Study Program is available. Institutional employment is available.

FROM THE ADMISSIONS OFFICE

"Dickinson's curriculum may be classified as traditional liberal arts characterized by considerable flexibility and diversity. There is a pattern of distribution to courses (not a core curriculum) which offers a great deal of choice. One of the special features is the Freshman Seminar Program, a distinctive vehicle of transition. There are over 35 seminars from which to choose; seminar participants are often housed together; in most cases, seminar instructors are also faculty advisers to the students; and the seminar is the first class, starting during orientation. Also, some introductory science and math courses are taught by the innovative workshop method, eliminating lecture and traditional labs in favor of a hands-on computer format. Dickinson has 10 centers in nine countries, and 40% of the students will participate in these or other programs abroad at some point in their college careers."

ADMISSIONS

Admissions Rating	74
% of applicants accepted	84
% of acceptees attending	22

FRESHMAN PROFILE

Average verbal SAT	600
Average math SAT	590
Average ACT	NR
Average TOEFL	550
Graduated top 20% of class	39
Graduated top 40% of class	59
Graduated top 60% of class	67
Average HS GPA or Avg.	NR

DEADLINES

Early decision	NR
Regular admission	2/15
Regular notification	3/30
Non-fall registration	yes

APPLICANTS ALSO LOOK AT

AND OFTEN PREFER
Cornell U.
Georgetown U.
James Madison
Swarthmore
Middlebury Coll.

AND SOMETIMES PREFER
Bucknell
Franklin & Marshall
Gettysburg
Lafayette
Connecticut Coll.

AND RARELY PREFER
Fairfield
Rutgers U.-Rutgers Coll.

FINANCIAL FACTS

Financial Aid Rating	81
Tuition	$19,600
Room & board	$5,270
Estimated book expense	$600
% frosh receiving aid	67
% undergrads receiving aid	70
% aid is need-based	100
% frosh w/ grant (avg)	61 ($12,102)
% frosh w/ loan (avg)	62 ($3,263)
% UGs w/ job (avg)	60 ($816)
Off-campus job outlook	good

DREW UNIVERSITY

MADISON AVENUE, MADISON, NJ 07940 — ADMISSIONS: 201-408-3739 — FAX: 201-408-3068

CAMPUS LIFE

Quality of Life Rating	**86**
Type of school	private
Affiliation	United Methodist Church
Environment	metropolis

STUDENTS

FT undergrad enrollment	1,348
% male/female	40/60
% from out of state	43
% live on campus	87
% spend weekend on campus	70
% transfers	10
% from public high school	66
% African-American	4
% Asian	8
% Caucasian	65
% Hispanic	5
% international	1
# of countries represented	15

WHAT'S HOT
computer facilities
theater
college radio
campus is beautiful
student government

WHAT'S NOT
Greeks
health facilities
campus food
lack of diversity on campus
dorms

ACADEMICS

Academic Rating	**86**
Profs Interesting Rating	93
Profs Accessible Rating	93
Calendar	semester
Student/teacher ratio	12:1
% profs tenured	93
Hours of study per day	3.03

MOST POPULAR MAJORS
political science
English
psychology

% GRADS WHO PURSUE...
Law 4, Med 3, MA 15

STUDENTS SPEAK OUT

Life

One student seems to say it best when he describes Drew University as "calm, yet good fun." To judge by the students' responses, social life at Drew is what you make of it. One bored student says simply, "The social life is lame." But many others gave the school huge marks for effort: "The student activities office at Drew is incredible. They work hard to provide a lot of fun activities on campus." And many other students have a different idea of a good time: "For fun for me, there is the beautiful surrounding area and writing." Students at Drew report that they don't pressure one another into doing things they don't want to do. A sophomore student majoring in English says, "Drew gives you the opportunity to do a lot of things. No one thing is `the thing to do' and no one is pushed to do anything they don't want to do." And another sophomore adds, "There is no peer pressure here. I am not a drinker and at parties I've never had a problem." Madison, the school's hometown, is apparently fun to look at, but not good for much else: "Madison is a beautiful town, but the people are condescending and snobby." "Not a problem," says one, "there's always New York City!" NYC's accessibility offers many of the more "bored" students a chance to get off campus and see some action.

Academics

Drew is a small liberal arts school that is nearly unknown outside its region. A senior majoring in biology says, "You really don't appreciate how valuable a school like Drew is until you take a class at Huge State U." In general, the students have almost nothing but praise for the level of Drew's academics and, in particular, the effort of its professors. One student says, "Academics are very challenging. I will definitely be proud of a degree received from Drew." Another adds, "The professors are extremely accessible, and the classes are taught by true scholars [all classes at Drew are taught by professors], not teaching assistants." High-profile innovations here include the Computer Initiative and Knowledge Initiative programs (almost half of the students graded the computer facilities as "excellent"), which together provide every student with a computer ("I'm leaving here with my own laptop!" Perhaps the only area that could be noted as a weakness is the bursar's office, which receives only passing marks from the students. For the most part, the administration, including the president, makes every attempt to get to know each student personally. "The women's rugby team is only a club sport, yet President Kean makes the effort to come to our games and even our practices to support us." Perhaps this first-year student says it best: "This place is cool."

Student Body

For a few years now, Drew has tried to recruit minority students and students outside its immediate area. One student is beginning to see a change: "There are students from all over here, which erases problems between students regardless of race or anything." Another student is more cautious: "I feel very comfortable here and I have made a lot of great friends. Diversity is emphasized, but I think we could use more interaction." Politically, students rank themselves left of center, but generally they think of themselves as merely average when it comes to political involvement. However, as this student states, "I think the student body is very concerned about not getting screwed. We come together on issues that concern us."

ADMISSIONS

The admissions committee considers (in descending order of importance): class rank, HS record, test scores, essay, recommendations. *Also considered (in descending order of importance):* special talents, extracurriculars, personality. Either the SAT or ACT is required; SAT is preferred. An interview is recommended. *High school units required/recommended:* 16 total units are recommended; 4 English recommended, 3 math recommended, 2 science recommended, 2 foreign language recommended, 2 social studies recommended. TOEFL is required of all international students. *The admissions office says:* "The university is interested in the student as an individual—the special strengths, talents, and extracurricular activities of each applicant are considered. Rank in the highest quarter of the secondary school class is desirable."

The Inside Word

Drew suffers greatly from the annual mass exodus of New Jersey's college-age residents and a lack of recognition by others. Application totals have increased slightly, but the university must begin to enroll more of its admitted students before any significant change in selectivity will occur. This makes Drew a great choice for solid students, and easier to get into than it should be given its quality.

FINANCIAL AID

Students should submit: FAFSA. The Princeton Review suggests that all financial aid forms be submitted as soon as possible after January 1. *The following grants/scholarships are offered:* Pell, SEOG, academic merit, the school's own scholarships, the school's own grants, state scholarships, state grants, ROTC. *Students borrow from the following loan programs:* Stafford, Perkins, PLUS, state loans, private loans. College Work-Study Program is available. Institutional employment is available.

FROM THE ADMISSIONS OFFICE

"'Drew University commits itself to being an intimate and significant community,' said a 1980 mission description by the university's Long-Range Planning Committee. Its three schools, each with separate missions, share a common purpose: to increase and transmit knowledge of all aspects of human life. The university distinguishes itself by its high academic standards, by the strength of its commitment to ethical values, by its global awareness, and by its assumption that all knowledge is interrelated. Drew strives to give concise expression to these commitments in its curriculum, in the quality of its teaching, in the extra-classroom student life, and in the encouragement of its lifelong learning. Because each generation recreates the nation, Drew's objective is education for responsible citizenship and leadership."

ADMISSIONS

Admissions Rating			80
% of applicants accepted			81
% of acceptees attending			21

FRESHMAN PROFILE

Average verbal SAT	620
Average math SAT	600
Average ACT	26
Average TOEFL	550
Graduated top 20% of class	69
Graduated top 40% of class	89
Graduated top 60% of class	97
Average HS GPA or Avg.	3.3

DEADLINES

Early decision	NR
Regular admission	2/15
Regular notification	3/15
Non-fall registration	yes

APPLICANTS ALSO LOOK AT

AND SOMETIMES PREFER

George Washington
Penn State U.
Fairfield
U. Rochester
Franklin & Marshall

AND RARELY PREFER

Rutgers U.-Rutgers Coll.
Hofstra
SUNY Purchase
U. Minnesota, Twin Cities

FINANCIAL FACTS

Financial Aid Rating	85
Tuition	$19,132
Room & board	$5,834
Estimated book expense	$920
% frosh receiving aid	89
% undergrads receiving aid	80
% aid is need-based	55
% frosh w/ grant (avg)	95 ($9,066)
% frosh w/ loan (avg)	75 ($3,224)
% UGs w/ job (avg)	65 ($825)
Off-campus job outlook	good

DREXEL UNIVERSITY

32ND AND CHESTNUT STREETS, PHILADELPHIA, PA 19104 ADMISSIONS: 215-895-2400 FAX: 215-895-6679

STUDENTS SPEAK OUT

Life

Located in the heart of Philadelphia, not far from the University of Pennsylvania, Drexel offers the community feel of a campus and the diverse options of a major city. Drexel's neighborhood, however, is dullsville: "The neighborhood leaves much to be desired." While the neighborhood is unexciting, it is by no means considered dangerous. No students complained about local crime, and some even praised the university efforts to keep Drexel a safe and livable place—"the campus has good security; I always feel safe." The lack of local options, however, means that students often leave the campus for fun, which has an effect on school support. Put bluntly by one student, "DU lack[s] school spirit." Several explanations emerge for this void: "The lack of popular athletics and the city environment" are blamed. Another student suggests the rigors of the quarterly schedule were the sticking point. The on-campus social scene is slow, partly due to a lousy male-to-female ratio, and partly due to a large commuter population. Perhaps the best recommendation for the growing social life of Drexel within Philadelphia comes from the following anecdote: "Recently, guys in bars have incorporated into their pickup lines the fact that they are students at Drexel, but more than half of them aren't. At least it's comforting to know that some people feel the 'Drexel Experience' is respectable, even if they are losers who can't get dates."

Academics

Drexel University, like Bentley and Northeastern, provides its largely preprofessional undergraduate students with a "co-op" program, which extends the undergraduate program to five years, but finds employment for those students in the field of their concentration for over half their stay at Drexel. Comments on the "co-op" program are unilaterally positive: "It's absolutely the best thing a college education can offer: experience. It lets you know what you are spending your 60K for." A huge percentage of Drexel students go immediately to graduate school following graduation. Students also like the fact that, upon arrival, they immediately began to study in the field of their choosing. One student comments that "you are thrown into the thick of your major right from the beginning; you don't have to wait until junior year to realize if you like it or not." The school is on a quarterly schedule, which means "terms are tough because they're only 10 weeks."

Student Body

Drexel attracts a diverse student body; more than one in ten students is black, and there is also a sizable Asian population. Aside from sharing a lack of school spirit, the student body seems to have another trait in common: "my fellow students are very competitive." Most liberal arts majors feel out of place here. As one student explains, "Drexel prepares you for the cutthroat corporate world of 'all for me, nothing for you' competition and the 'every man for himself attitude of the nineties.'" But high marks on dating proves the student body isn't all about work and professionalism. In fact, the student body provides a diversity and mutual support comparable to other urban preprofessional colleges. As one student puts it, "The fellow students are very nice around here except when someone tries to sing in a cowboy shirt and beat-up old hat."

ADMISSIONS

The admissions committee considers (in descending order of importance): HS record, test scores, essay, recommendations, class rank. Also considered (in descending order of importance): extracurriculars, personality, special talents, alumni relationship. Either the SAT or ACT is required. An interview is recommended. Admissions process is need-blind. High school units required/recommended: 16 total units are recommended; 4 English recommended, 3 math recommended, 1 science recommended, 1 social studies recommended. Elective units must be in English, history, math, science, social science, foreign language, or mechanical drawing. Special Requirements: TOEFL is required of all international students. One additional unit in both math and science required of applicants to College of Engineering, College of Science, and to commerce/engineering program offered by College of Business and Administration. The admissions office says: "Drexel students are very motivated and desire knowledge with a real-world application. Drexel's education is fast-paced and requires students to stay on top of their work."

The Inside Word

Drexel's distinct nature creates a high level of self-selection in the applicant pool, and most decent students are admitted.

FINANCIAL AID

Students should submit: state aid form (due May 1). The Princeton Review suggests that all financial aid forms be submitted as soon as possible after January 1. The following grants/scholarships are offered: Pell, SEOG, academic merit, athletic, the school's own scholarships, the school's own grants, state scholarships, state grants, private scholarships, private grants, ROTC. Students borrow from the following loan programs: Stafford, Perkins, PLUS, the school's own loan fund, state loans, private loans. College Work-Study Program is available. Freshmen are discouraged from working.

FROM THE ADMISSIONS OFFICE

"The goal of every Drexel major is to prepare you for success in the professional world or in graduate school. For this reason, the Drexel education goes beyond solid course work. It places a high priority on firsthand experience, on completing your own design projects, research, or original creative work. And it stresses technology, understanding the innovations that are reshaping the world, even in areas that haven't traditionally been seen as high-tech. Along the way, it provides plenty of personal help to make sure you succeed. The cooperative education, or co-op, is the added dimension that really sets Drexel apart. Through co-op, you switch between periods of full-time studies on campus and periods of full-time professional employment. What also sets Drexel apart is the use of computers. Each student has personal access to a Macintosh. In virtually every career area, from chemistry to corporate communication, one of the most important tools professionals use to do their jobs is the computer. Drexel students use the Macintosh extensively, preparing for a lifetime of working with computers after they graduate."

ADMISSIONS

Admissions Rating		69
% of applicants accepted		85
% of acceptees attending		38

FRESHMAN PROFILE

Average verbal SAT	550
Average math SAT	560
Average ACT	NR
Average TOEFL	510
Graduated top 20% of class	42
Graduated top 40% of class	71
Graduated top 60% of class	89
Average HS GPA or Avg.	3.1

DEADLINES

Early decision	1/1
Regular admission	5/1
Regular notification	rolling
Non-fall registration	yes

APPLICANTS ALSO LOOK AT

AND OFTEN PREFER
American
Boston U.
U. Delaware

AND SOMETIMES PREFER
U. Maryland, Coll. Park
Temple
Lehigh
Penn State U.
Villanova

AND RARELY PREFER
LaSalle
Northeastern

FINANCIAL FACTS

Financial Aid Rating	66
Tuition	$13,080
Room & board	$4,980
Estimated book expense	$500
% frosh receiving aid	60
% undergrads receiving aid	NR
% aid is need-based	98
% frosh w/ grant (avg)	NR ($3,367)
% frosh w/ loan (avg)	NR ($3,242)
% UGs w/ job (avg)	NR
Off-campus job outlook	excellent

DUKE UNIVERSITY

2138 CAMPUS DRIVE, BOX 90586, DURHAM, NC 27708   ADMISSIONS: 919-684-3214   FAX: 919-684-8941

CAMPUS LIFE

Quality of Life Rating **81**
Type of school   private
Affiliation   United Methodist Church
Environment   city

STUDENTS
FT undergrad enrollment   6,380
% male/female   54/46
% from out of state   87
% live on campus   88
% spend weekend on campus   NR
% transfers   3
% from public high school   66
% in (# of) fraternities   42 (23)
% in (# of) sororities   42 (12)
% African-American   8
% Asian   12
% Caucasian   72
% Hispanic   5
% international   .6
# of countries represented   43

WHAT'S HOT
intercollegiate sports
campus food
intramural sports
student publications
registration is a breeze

WHAT'S NOT
infrequent dating
students are cliquish
town-gown relations
Durham
cigarettes

ACADEMICS

Academic Rating   **92**
Profs Interesting Rating   71
Profs Accessible Rating   72
Calendar   semester
Student/teacher ratio   9:1
% profs tenured   97
Hours of study per day   3.11

MOST POPULAR MAJORS
biology
history
psychology

% GRADS WHO PURSUE...
Law 11, Med 12, MBA 1

STUDENTS SPEAK OUT

Life
Duke University is divided into two beautiful campuses separated by a mile of woodland: a shuttle bus carries students from one to the other. The campus boasts Gothic architecture, sprawling lawns, and a real Arthurian forest. According to several students "Durham NC is not a college town at all, so unless you have a car to go to nearby UNC Chapel Hill, you must be prepared to seek out things to do on campus." There are many, as long as you don't need alcohol to enhance them. "The scene has completely changed as a result of the new alcohol policy. There are still parties...but things are much more closed and drinking has been forced behind closed doors." Fraternities and sororities still dominate social life, but many remark that life has become appreciably more dull since the administration instituted the stricter policies. Duke students continue to find release via their first love, sports, especially Blue Devils basketball. One woman told us, "Basketball is life. I'm camping out all week for the Carolina game."

Academics
Duke students love their school. Where else would a student complain that "the administration is trying to turn this place into Harvard, which it should not be, because as we are now, this is a better place to go to college"? Duke students have good reasons to be proud: they attend one of the nation's most competitive universities and enjoy incredible resources, a beautiful campus, and an academic program that is thorough but not backbreaking: in fact, the number of hours the average Duke student puts in each day—about three hours and ten minutes—is nothing compared to other highly competitive institutions. The undergraduate division of the school is divided, with a School for Engineering for engineers and the Trinity College of Arts and Sciences for everyone else. Political science, economics, history, and engineering are the favorite majors of this largely preprofessional student body, although departments are uniformly excellent. About 40% of the students go on to grad school. Most of the graduate programs here are world class, yet students did not report that they felt abandoned by their professors. They do feel alienated from the administration, however: "The administration at Duke is tyrannically limiting social options of students." Luckily, "Students and professors salvage an academic experience which administration does its best to ruin."

Student Body
The student body is "intellectual, yet cool, fun, and relaxed," according to one sophomore. The typical student is conservative, well-off, and white, and although minority representation has increased, groups coalesce and rarely intermingle. As one senior remarks, "I think, in general, we're a pretty snazzy bunch of kids, but we could stand to interact across 'groups' (whether ethnic, frat, whatever) a little more." Other students agree, and add that more recruitment and support would be helpful: "I feel that the student body is too homogeneous—racially, socio-economically, politically, ideologically. Things must change and catch up to the real world."

FINANCIAL AID: 919-684-6225

WEB SITE: HTTP://WWW.DUKE.EDU/

ADMISSIONS

The admissions committee considers (in descending order of importance): HS record, recommendations, class rank, test scores, essay. *Also considered (in descending order of importance):* extracurriculars, personality, special talents, alumni relationship, geographical distribution. Either the SAT or ACT is required. An interview is recommended. *High school units required/recommended:* 15 total units are recommended; 4 English required, 3 math recommended, 3 science recommended, 3 foreign language recommended, 2 social studies recommended. *Special Requirements:* TOEFL is required of all international students. 4 units of math and 1 unit of physics or chemistry required of engineering program applicants. *The admissions office says:* "Every application is reviewed by two or more readers before the candidate is presented to the full admissions committee. Candidates are rated on a one-to-five scale (with five as the highest rating) on six different categories: quality of the academic program, performance in secondary school course work, recommendations, personal qualities, performance on standardized tests, and quality of the essays. While applicants are reviewed by the admissions committee by school and by region, there are no school or regional quotas."

The Inside Word

The way in which Duke discusses its candidate-review process should be a basic model for all schools to use in their literature. Just about all highly selective admissions committees use rating systems similar to the one described above, but few are willing to publicly discuss them.

FINANCIAL AID

Students should submit: FAFSA (due February 1), CSS Profile, a copy of parents' most recent income tax filing. The Princeton Review suggests that all financial aid forms be submitted as soon as possible after January 1. *The following grants/scholarships are offered:* Pell, SEOG, academic merit, athletic, the school's own scholarships, the school's own grants, state scholarships, state grants, private scholarships, private grants, ROTC. *Students borrow from the following loan programs:* Stafford, Perkins, PLUS, the school's own loan fund, state loans, health professions loans. College Work-Study Program is available. Institutional employment is available.

FROM THE ADMISSIONS OFFICE

"The Duke University motto, Erudito et Religio, reflects a fundamental faith in the union of knowledge and religion, the advancement of learning, the defense of scholarship, the love of freedom and truth, a spirit of tolerance, and a rendering of the greatest service to the individual, the state, the nation, and the church. Through changing generations of students, the objective has been to encourage individuals to achieve, the extent of their capacities, an understanding and appreciation of the world in which they live, their relationship in it, their opportunities, and their responsibilities."

ADMISSIONS

Admissions Rating	97
% of applicants accepted	28
% of acceptees attending	40

FRESHMAN PROFILE

Average verbal SAT	690
Average math SAT	700
Average ACT	30
Average TOEFL	NR
Graduated top 20% of class	94
Graduated top 40% of class	99
Graduated top 60% of class	100
Average HS GPA or Avg.	NR

DEADLINES

Early decision	12/1
Regular admission	1/2
Regular notification	4/5
Non-fall registration	yes

APPLICANTS ALSO LOOK AT

AND OFTEN PREFER
Brown

AND SOMETIMES PREFER
Dartmouth
Davidson
Emory

AND RARELY PREFER
Wake Forest
Vanderbilt
William and Mary
Georgia Tech.

FINANCIAL FACTS

Financial Aid Rating	78
Tuition	$20,520
Room & board	$6,605
Estimated book expense	$686
% frosh receiving aid	43
% undergrads receiving aid	38
% aid is need-based	90
% frosh w/ grant (avg)	39 ($11,162)
% frosh w/ loan (avg)	26 ($2,800)
% UGs w/ job (avg)	28 ($1,400)
Off-campus job outlook	good

600 FORBES AVENUE, PITTSBURGH, PA 15282   ADMISSIONS: 800-456-0590   FAX: 412-642-9055

CAMPUS LIFE

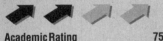

Quality of Life Rating   **75**
Type of school	private
Affiliation	Roman Catholic Church
	(Spiritan Congregation)
Environment	metropolis

STUDENTS
FT undergrad enrollment	4,736
% male/female	43/57
% from out of state	20
% live on campus	49
% spend weekend on campus	65
% transfers	13
% from public high school	65
% in (# of) fraternities	14 (3)
% in (# of) sororities	14 (2)
% African-American	5
% Asian	2
% Caucasian	86
% Hispanic	1
% international	3
# of countries represented	83

WHAT'S HOT
religion
drugs
Pittsburgh
old-fashioned dating
hard liquor

WHAT'S NOT
political activism
support groups
library
students are unhappy
computer facilities

ACADEMICS

Academic Rating   **75**
Profs Interesting Rating	67
Profs Accessible Rating	65
Calendar	semester
Student/teacher ratio	16:1
% profs PhD/tenured	94/94
Hours of study per day	2.98

MOST POPULAR MAJORS
pharmacy
nursing
physical therapy

% GRADS WHO PURSUE...
Law 9, Med 2, MBA 13, MA 29

STUDENTS SPEAK OUT

Life

Duquesne University has made major alterations to the campus in recent years, and students are split on the issue of their campus's appearance: one writes that it was "beautiful, and getting more so every year," while another (who feel money to upgrade campus beauty could be better spent on the library and science labs) says the changes made the school "look like an amusement park." Commuters, of whom there are many, gripe that the parking situation is "terrible." The large commuter population contributes to Duquesne's dead social scene. One student refers to DU as "the social black hole of Pittsburgh," and others voice such opinions as "if you're not planning on going home every weekend, don't come here. There is no weekend life." Residents must deal with restrictive dorm policies ("you can't even sneeze in the dorms without getting in trouble") and a mentality that "treats all sex-related subjects as taboo, even though the students desperately need information." Still, the school is located "in the coolest part of the city (Pittsburgh). We are right downtown and have access to everything." Don't be confused about what city you're in, though. Another student notes that "Pittsburgh is a lot different from Philly," and many students seemed to find Pittsburgh not the most vibrant of cities. Fraternities and sororities are popular, and students participate actively in intramural sports.

Academics

Duquesne is a Roman Catholic school serving a serious-minded, career-oriented student body. Almost a third of the students here study business and management. Students in the pharmacy department claim it's the university's best, while psychology, occupational therapy, and physical therapy also receive raves. DU's professors receive good grades, and many respondents note how helpful instructors were outside the classroom. Strong academics and supportive professors help the school overcome several shortcomings. The biggest problem is the library, described as "confusing, outdated, worthless, and poorly lit" by one student. Says another, "As for the library, plan on spending a lot of time at the University of Pittsburgh." Students also complain that, despite the school's moderate size, it's easy to get lost in the crowd: writes one, "Duquesne is a good school if you know what you want to major in and what kind of classes you need to take. If you don't know exactly what you need, don't expect to get any help from an adviser." Registration, financial aid, and bill-paying all rate low on the national scale. Finally, students dislike the fact that there are "hidden" charges, such as student activities fees: writes one undergrad, "Everything here is à la carte—be prepared to spend a lot to get the whole deal."

Student Body

Over half of Duquesne's students are Catholic. Minority populations are small. Although foreign nationals make up only four percent of the student body, they are clearly a noticeable presence, because many students complain of the preferential treatment they felt internationals receive.

ADMISSIONS

The admissions committee considers (in descending order of importance): HS record, class rank, test scores, recommendations, essay. *Also considered (in descending order of importance):* special talents, extracurriculars, personality, alumni relationship, geographical distribution. Either the SAT or ACT is required; SAT is preferred. An interview is recommended. *High school units required/recommended:* 16 total units are recommended; 4 English recommended, 2 math recommended, 2 science recommended, 2 foreign language recommended, 2 social studies recommended. Minimum combined SAT I score of 1000, rank in top three-fifths of secondary school class, and minimum 2.5 GPA recommended. *Special Requirements:* An audition is required for music program applicants. *The admissions office says:* "[We have] rolling admissions. We have a strong bond with many high schools and take the counselors' recommendation very seriously."

The Inside Word

With such a high admit rate, the admissions process should create little anxiety in all but the weakest candidates.

FINANCIAL AID

Students should submit: FAFSA, the school's own financial aid form (due May 1). The Princeton Review suggests that all financial aid forms be submitted as soon as possible after January 1. *The following grants/scholarships are offered:* Pell, SEOG, academic merit, athletic, the school's own scholarships, the school's own grants, state scholarships, state grants, private scholarships, private grants, ROTC, foreign aid. *Students borrow from the following loan programs:* Stafford, unsubsidized Stafford, Perkins, PLUS, the school's own loan fund, federal nursing loans, health professions loans. College Work-Study Program is available. Institutional employment is available.

FROM THE ADMISSIONS OFFICE

"Duquesne University was founded in 1878 by the Holy Ghost Fathers. Although it is a private, Roman Catholic institution, Duquesne is proud of its ecumenical reputation, and almost half of the student body is non-Catholic. The total university enrollment is 8,569. Duquesne University's attractive and secluded campus is set on a 40-acre hilltop ('the bluff') overlooking the large corporate metropolis of Pittsburgh's Golden Triangle. It offers a wide variety of educational opportunities, from the liberal arts to modern professional training. Duquesne is a medium-sized university striving to offer personal attention to its students while having the versatility and opportunities of a true university. A deep sense of tradition is combined with innovation and flexibility to make the Duquesne experience both challenging and rewarding. The Palumbo Convocation/Recreation Complex features a 6,300-seat arena, home court to the University's Division I basketball teams; racquetball and handball courts; weight rooms and saunas. Extracurricular activities are recognized as an essential part of college life, complementing academics in the process of total student development. Students are involved in nearly 100 university-sponsored activities, and Duquesne's location gives students the opportunity to enjoy sports and cultural events both on campus and citywide. There are four residence halls with the capacity to house 2,750 students."

ADMISSIONS

Admissions Rating	72
% of applicants accepted	82
% of acceptees attending	42

FRESHMAN PROFILE

Average verbal SAT	570
Average math SAT	540
Average ACT	24
Average TOEFL	500
Graduated top 20% of class	NR
Graduated top 40% of class	88
Graduated top 60% of class	NR
Average HS GPA or Avg.	3.5

DEADLINES

Early decision	12/1
Regular admission	7/1
Regular notification	rolling
Non-fall registration	yes

APPLICANTS ALSO LOOK AT

AND OFTEN PREFER
West Virginia
Penn State U.

AND SOMETIMES PREFER
Ohio State U.-Columbus
Marquette

AND RARELY PREFER
U. Pittsburgh

FINANCIAL FACTS

Financial Aid Rating	78
Tuition	$11,662
Room & board	$5,580
Estimated book expense	$550
% frosh receiving aid	94
% undergrads receiving aid	85
% aid is need-based	61
% frosh w/ grant (avg)	87 ($6,823)
% frosh w/ loan (avg)	72 ($3,469)
% UGs w/ job (avg)	17 ($1,980)
Off-campus job outlook	good

EARLHAM COLLEGE

NATIONAL ROAD WEST, RICHMOND, IN 47374 ADMISSIONS: 800-327-5426 FAX: 317-983-1560

STUDENTS SPEAK OUT

Life

Students report that "Life becomes very self-contained here at Earlham. It's easy to lose touch with outside events. You hang out with friends a lot talking, watching videos, cooking dinner, drinking beer, or stepping out to catch a movie. There's a chance you may go on a date, but not a big chance." Ironically, Earlham students maintain more contact with "outside events" than do most other students; their Quaker backgrounds and deep commitment to political activity keep them connected. As one student tells us, "Most people are involved in causes. I, for instance, work on campus as a rape crisis interventionist. Most activities are centered around such causes; this is a very political school." Social life on campus is cozy and casual: "Earlham students can easily entertain themselves. Large parties are unnecessary because students are confident enough in themselves to not have to party." Of their home town, students write that "Richmond is not a college town, and therefore there's a lack of things to do off campus. You need a car to get to stuff in town, and road trips to Oxford and Dayton are necessary. When we get a three-day weekend, everyone makes big plans. I went on a bus trip to the Grand Canyon for Spring Break."

Academics

Earlham undergraduates report that the intimate and dynamic classroom experience is what appeals to them most about their school. Wrote one, "The professors are excellent. The Quaker zeitgeist attracts teachers who are very willing to help and create a comfortable atmosphere. This place is very conducive to learning." Added another, "From what I've seen so far, there is much more of a focus on thinking and integrating themes and ideas here at Earlham than on learning for the sake of memorization or just having the knowledge." Professors are "caring, brilliant, and very demanding. They are genuinely interested in who I am as a person and are pleased by questions. I especially appreciate the emphasis on discussion. It's by talking through my ideas and others' that I really learn. Help is given whenever it is needed." Summed up one student, "Earlham is exactly what I wanted my college to be: very challenging academically, with a caring community of professors and students, and still enough time to goof off and relax if I feel the need. I made the right choice."

Student Body

The diversity of Earlham's student body is created mostly by the number of out-of-state students. Minorities make up a significant but still small proportion of the student body. Students pride themselves on being open-minded ("Most students are very accepting and understanding of different lifestyles and background than their own") and politically off to the left: "Students here are very politically active. The overall political affiliation is way to the left. Right wingers, beware! Your views are not considered acceptable here." Summed up one student: "It's the people at EC and the academic community who keep life colorful and unpredictable."

ADMISSIONS

The admissions committee considers (in descending order of importance): HS record, class rank, essay, test scores, recommendations. *Also considered (in descending order of importance):* personality, extracurriculars, special talents, alumni relationship, geographical distribution. Either the SAT or ACT is required; SAT is preferred. An interview is recommended. Admissions process is need-blind. *High school units required/recommended:* 15 total units are required; 4 English required, 3 math required, 2 science required, 3 science recommended, 2 foreign language required, 4 foreign language recommended, 2 social studies required. Additional units of mathematics and social studies/history recommended. Minimum SAT I scores of 500 in both verbal and math and minimum 2.8 GPA recommended. TOEFL is required of all international students.

The Inside Word

Like most colleges with a Friends affiliation, Earlham has a sincere interest in the person it admits. Essays and interviews carry virtually as much weight as the numbers. Quakers, minorities, legacies, and state residents receive special consideration in the admissions process, but special consideration is what this place is really all about. Earlham deserves a much higher national public awareness level than it has. Hopefully, this entry will help.

FINANCIAL AID

Students should submit: FAFSA (due March 1), the school's own financial aid form (due March 1), state aid form (due March 1), a copy of parents' most recent income tax filing. The Princeton Review suggests that all financial aid forms be submitted as soon as possible after January 1. *The following grants/scholarships are offered:* Pell, SEOG, academic merit, the school's own scholarships, the school's own grants, state scholarships, state grants, private scholarships, private grants, foreign aid. *Students borrow from the following loan programs:* Stafford, unsubsidized Stafford, Perkins, PLUS, the school's own loan fund, private loans. College Work-Study Program is available. Institutional employment is available.

FROM THE ADMISSIONS OFFICE

"The world is full of people with good intentions. What it needs is people with the intellect, the vision, the skills, and the energy to back up their good intentions. It needs people who are able to make a difference. Although only a few students identify themselves as Quakers, Earlham retains those humanistic values of its tradition that have relevance to students of all backgrounds."

ADMISSIONS

Admissions Rating	75
% of applicants accepted	77
% of acceptees attending	30

FRESHMAN PROFILE

Average verbal SAT	620
Average math SAT	560
Average ACT	26
Average TOEFL	580
Graduated top 20% of class	47
Graduated top 40% of class	76
Graduated top 60% of class	92
Average HS GPA or Avg.	3.3

DEADLINES

Early decision	12/1
Regular admission	2/15
Regular notification	4/1
Non-fall registration	yes

APPLICANTS ALSO LOOK AT

AND OFTEN PREFER

Macalester
Kenyon

AND SOMETIMES PREFER

Oberlin
Vassar
Guilford
Carleton

AND RARELY PREFER

Antioch

FINANCIAL FACTS

Financial Aid Rating	94
Tuition	$17,312
Room & board	$4,412
Estimated book expense	$550
% frosh receiving aid	71
% undergrads receiving aid	62
% aid is need-based	95
% frosh w/ grant (avg)	68 ($9,595)
% frosh w/ loan (avg)	50 ($2,975)
% UGs w/ job (avg)	42 ($1,275)
Off-campus job outlook	poor

EASTMAN SCHOOL OF MUSIC

26 GIBBS STREET, ROCHESTER, NY 14604-2599   ADMISSIONS: 800-388-9695   FAX: 716-274-1088

CAMPUS LIFE

Quality of Life Rating **75**
Type of school   private
Affiliation   none
Environment   city

STUDENTS

FT undergrad enrollment	483
% male/female	47/53
% from out of state	83
% live on campus	75
% spend weekend on campus	100
% transfers	8
% from public high school	NR
% in (# of) fraternities	18 (14)
% in (# of) sororities	13 (9)
% African-American	6
% Asian	9
% Caucasian	70
% Hispanic	1
% international	14
# of countries represented	25

WHAT'S HOT
library
music associations
different students interact
ethnic diversity on campus
dorms

WHAT'S NOT
intercollegiate sports
intramural sports
student publications
unattractive campus
Rochester

ACADEMICS

Academic Rating	**90**
Profs Interesting Rating	76
Profs Accessible Rating	71
Calendar	semester
Student/teacher ratio	7:1
% profs PhD/tenured	84/90
Hours of study per day	4.00

MOST POPULAR MAJORS
music

% GRADS WHO PURSUE...
MA 65

STUDENTS SPEAK OUT

Life

Life at the Eastman School of Music "is fantastic: very busy, full, harried, and difficult, but fantastic." Another student elaborates: "Life at school is generally fun. Being a music school, there's a good chance of burnout from lack of variety. To get out, people try to go to another school or to parties in town. There aren't many of those, though." Students give Rochester ("unsafe and unattractive") a big thumbs-down; notes one respondent, "There is not a lot to do in Rochester. Everything in town is closed at 5 p.m. and places to eat are too far to walk to. Most activities are in the dorms and the River Campus."

Academics

While other top schools flourish in major media centers, Eastman is hidden away in Rochester, New York. For the dedicated classical musician interested in piling a well-rounded liberal arts education on top of four hours of practice a day, Eastman is a first-rate choice. Explains one student, "Among conservatories and other schools of specialization, Eastman offers the least narrow scope of education, and the University of Rochester (at which Eastman students can take classes) can be a valuable complement to the intensive music program." Students describe the atmosphere as high pressure—one wrote that "at least twenty percent of each class drops out during sophomore year. Why? Because the pressure here can sometimes strangle you. It seems painful at times, but when you are away from here, you realize that your intense training is starting to pay off." Facilities are excellent ("the library is totally burnin'!" writes one student), professors are "top-notch, cream of the crop," TAs "teach a lot of the classes, but many of them have been here for years, longer than some professors, so they are usually good teachers," and administrators keep the school running (mostly) smoothly. In short: "Eastman is a place for serious musicians who are crazy enough to care more about music than making a living."

Student Body

Eastman has a very small minority population, and, of course, all the students are serious, classical-and-jazz trained musicians, but within those parameters there is some diversity among this small student body. There is a substantial gay community and there is a group of conservative, religious students. There are string musicians, horn players, and even some vocalists! All right, so there isn't that much diversity here. Many students note that their classmates are particularly caring and supportive. One relates this story: "Recently my main professor died. It was an incredible blow to myself and to others in his studio. Even though this tragedy occurred at the beginning of the year, the care and support I received was awesome. People here are intensely focused in their individual instrument/major, but people think about each other a lot too."

FINANCIAL AID: 716-275-3226

ADMISSIONS

The admissions committee considers (in descending order of importance): HS record, recommendations, class rank, test scores, essay. *Also considered (in descending order of importance):* extracurriculars, personality, alumni relationship, geographical distribution, special talents. Either the SAT or ACT is required. An interview is recommended. Admissions process is need-blind. *High school units required/recommended:* 15 total units are recommended; 4 English recommended, 3 math recommended, 2 science recommended, 2 foreign language recommended, 4 social studies recommended. *Special Requirements:* Physics required of physics and physics/astronomy program applicants; recommended of engineering program applicants. Chemistry strongly recommended of biology, chemical engineering, chemistry, and nursing program applicants. Audition required of B.Mus. program applicants; recommended of B.A. music program applicants. *The admissions office says:* "Achievement in the major area of musical interest [is] most important. Personal attention is given to each applicant, not only by admissions office staff but by faculty and students."

The Inside Word

Eastman is not only a major challenge once a student is enrolled—it's super tough to get admitted in the first place. Students who are considering the school need to be well versed in classical repertoire and have a solid foundation in music theory. Besides the audition itself, these considerations are much more important than anything else. If you are not solid enough to be competitive at Juilliard, you're probably not Eastman material either.

FINANCIAL AID

Students should submit: FAFSA, CSS Profile, the school's own financial aid form (due January 15), state aid form, a copy of parents' most recent income tax filing (due May 31). The Princeton Review suggests that all financial aid forms be submitted as soon as possible after January 1. *The following grants/scholarships are offered:* Pell, SEOG, academic merit, the school's own scholarships, the school's own grants, state scholarships, state grants, private scholarships, private grants, ROTC, foreign aid. *Students borrow from the following loan programs:* Stafford, unsubsidized Stafford, Perkins, PLUS, the school's own loan fund, federal nursing loans, private loans. Applicants will be notified of awards beginning March 15. College Work-Study Program is available. Institutional employment is available.

FROM THE ADMISSIONS OFFICE

"When industrialist and philanthropist George Eastman founded the School in 1921, he stressed the importance of providing a broad foundation in the liberal arts for all musicians. The School's strong humanities department allows Eastman students to refine their language and writing skills and to explore a variety of intellectual interests. George Eastman established the School as the first professional school of the University of Rochester. This further expands the opportunities open to Eastman students, allowing them to take advantage of a wide variety of course offerings in other colleges of the University. The outstanding resources of the School's downtown campus contribute to a stimulating educational experience. Superb performance halls, the nation's largest and most complete academic music library, and the modern Student Living Center distinguish the campus."

ADMISSIONS

Admissions Rating	93
% of applicants accepted	37
% of acceptees attending	52

FRESHMAN PROFILE

Average verbal SAT	600
Average math SAT	650
Average ACT	NR
Average TOEFL	550
Graduated top 20% of class	70
Graduated top 40% of class	92
Graduated top 60% of class	NR
Average HS GPA or Avg.	NR

DEADLINES

Early decision	NR
Regular admission	1/15
Regular notification	4/15
Non-fall registration	yes

APPLICANTS ALSO LOOK AT

AND OFTEN PREFER

Juilliard
Oberlin Conservatory

AND SOMETIMES PREFER

SUNY Purchase
Manhattan School of Music
Berklee
New England Conservatory
Peabody Conservatory

AND RARELY PREFER

Mannes Coll. of Music
Skidmore

FINANCIAL FACTS

Financial Aid Rating	87
Tuition	$17,850
Room & board	$6,930
Estimated book expense	$650
% frosh receiving aid	87
% undergrads receiving aid	85
% aid is need-based	85
% frosh w/ grant (avg)	89 ($8,000)
% frosh w/ loan (avg)	77 ($2,625)
% UGs w/ job (avg)	40 ($2,800)
Off-campus job outlook	good

ECKERD COLLEGE

4200 54TH AVENUE SOUTH, ST. PETERSBURG, FL 33711   ADMISSIONS: 800-456-9009   FAX: 813-866-2304

CAMPUS LIFE

Quality of Life Rating **84**
Type of school   private
Affiliation   Presbyterian Church USA
Environment   metropolis

STUDENTS
FT undergrad enrollment   1,330
% male/female   48/52
% from out of state   70
% live on campus   78
% spend weekend on campus   75
% transfers   20
% from public high school   80
% African-American   3
% Asian   2
% Caucasian   79
% Hispanic   4
% international   12
# of countries represented   57

WHAT'S HOT
town-gown relations
sex
different students interact
students are happy
hard liquor

WHAT'S NOT
library
campus food
health facilities
Greeks
unattractive campus

ACADEMICS

Academic Rating   **84**
Profs Interesting Rating   88
Profs Accessible Rating   86
Calendar   4-1-4
Student/teacher ratio   13:1
% profs PhD/tenured   84/65
Hours of study per day   3.43

MOST POPULAR MAJORS
international business
marine science
management

% GRADS WHO PURSUE...
Law 8, Med 6, MBA 13, MA 25

STUDENTS SPEAK OUT

Life

"Life? Life's a beach!" An overwhelming majority of the students respond with the big thumbs up on the beach and waterfront program at Eckerd College. One student explains, "I love this school because of the waterfront program. We can go sailing, canoeing, or swimming whenever we want for free." The beach certainly contributes to the "laid back and informal attitude" on campus. However, the result of this casual attitude can be negative. As this student responds, "Students are typically detached from reality. They live in their own country-club style. We rarely have student rallies in reaction to current events." Along with the waterfront program the university apparently makes other attempts to keep the students happy on campus. "Most activities are held on campus making Eckerd a tightly knit community." Another student is more specific: "Theme dances, comedians, singers, and bands happen all the time on campus" All of these on-campus choices are good, because as this junior said, "St. Pete blows!" There are those that feel like beer plays too big a role at Eckerd: "This school would be super boring if we weren't wasted all the time." The campus itself is officially dry, but one student explains that "there isn't really any control over alcohol and drug use."

Academics

Eckerd is a good liberal arts school with dedicated and helpful professors. "Students come first and foremost," applauds one student. Another says, "Professors are very accessible and truly want to help us learn." The level of attention and the quality of instruction at Eckerd have a positive effect on the students. A junior studying biology writes, "Academics are taken very seriously by almost the entire student body." Despite the truly rigorous core requirements ("Freshmen, beware of Western Heritage!") Eckerd lets the student take control of their own education. Check out what this student has to say: "The opportunities for student research are phenomenal for an undergraduate institution." And this student: "Overall, a great place for student leadership possibilities." The glowing reports for the academics at Eckerd do not carry over to evaluation of the administration. This student jokes (we hope?), "The administration don't have their heads on so good." But the students' concern is no laughing matter. Most echo this response from a senior in English: "Our administration is more worried about filling their own pockets than caring about what the students need." The president was mentioned in many of the harshest responses, and he seems to be the scapegoat for problems other than financial concerns from this liberal student body's point of view: "The president refuses to let the health center offer condoms and it's against the rules for any student group to pass them out." The community-oriented campus seems to stick together through good or bad. Pre-professional studies and the marine sciences are both strong.

Student Body

As you can imagine, Eckerd students generally hang together, with little or no involvement in the community of St. Petersburg. The student body is generally white and upper-middle class with serious goals for their professional future. This is a popular sentiment: "The students are, or can be, wonderfully supportive and willing to help other out, but they can be awfully cliquey." There is, however, a strong number of international students, and Eckerd's PEL program is growing, so people of various walks of life are joining the college community. Glows one undergrad, "It's easy to be yourself."

FINANCIAL AID: 813-864-8334

ADMISSIONS

The admissions committee considers (in descending order of importance): HS record, test scores, essay, class rank, recommendations. *Also considered (in descending order of importance):* personality, special talents, extracurriculars. Either the SAT or ACT is required. An interview is recommended. Admissions process is need-blind. *High school units required/recommended:* 18 total units are required; 22 total units are recommended; 4 English required, 3 math required, 4 math recommended, 3 science required, 4 science recommended, 2 foreign language required, 3 foreign language recommended, 2 social studies required, 2 history required. Minimum combined SAT I score of 1000 (composite ACT score of 22) and minimum 2.5 GPA recommended. TOEFL is required of all international students. *The admissions office says:* "We do everything we can to personalize the admissions process, to be helping professionals, and to assess the personal qualities of our applicants. Eckerd students tend to have a strong inclination toward community volunteer service, and a strong commitment to improve environmental quality..."

The Inside Word

Budding marine biologists are by far the strongest students at Eckerd. They make up a significant percentage of the college's total applicant pool and do much to provide for a more impressive freshman profile. Applications totals remain steady.

FINANCIAL AID

Students should submit: FAFSA (due March1), the school's own financial aid form (due March 1). The Princeton Review suggests that all financial aid forms be submitted as soon as possible after January 1. *The following grants/scholarships are offered:* Pell, SEOG, academic merit, athletic, the school's own scholarships, the school's own grants, state scholarships, state grants, private scholarships, private grants, ROTC, foreign aid. *Students borrow from the following loan programs:* Stafford, unsubsidized Stafford, Perkins, PLUS, the school's own loan fund. Applicants will be notified of awards beginning March 1. College Work-Study Program is available. Institutional employment is available.

FROM THE ADMISSIONS OFFICE

"Eckerd College students come from 49 states and 55 countries. They are attracted to this international environment and participate extensively in our study abroad programs. International business, international relations and, international studies majors are popular here. We characterize Eckerd students as competent givers. The Academy of Senior Professionals draws to campus distinguished persons who have retired from fields our students aspire to enter. Academy members, such as novelist James Michener, enrich classes and offer valuable counsel for career planning."

ADMISSIONS

Admissions Rating	74
% of applicants accepted	76
% of acceptees attending	29

FRESHMAN PROFILE

Average verbal SAT	600
Average math SAT	580
Average ACT	26
Average TOEFL	550
Graduated top 20% of class	39
Graduated top 40% of class	58
Graduated top 60% of class	68
Average HS GPA or Avg.	3.3

DEADLINES

Early decision	1/15
Regular admission	NR
Regular notification	rolling
Non-fall registration	yes

APPLICANTS ALSO LOOK AT

AND OFTEN PREFER

Rollins
U. Florida
U. South Florida

AND SOMETIMES PREFER

Stetson
U. Miami
Florida St.

FINANCIAL FACTS

Financial Aid Rating	94
Tuition	$16,450
Room & board	$4,450
Estimated book expense	$600
% frosh receiving aid	82
% undergrads receiving aid	82
% aid is need-based	75
% frosh w/ grant (avg)	77 ($9,000)
% frosh w/ loan (avg)	60 ($3,000)
% UGs w/ job (avg)	43 ($1,000)
Off-campus job outlook	excellent

EMERSON COLLEGE

100 BEACON STREET, BOSTON, MA 02116   ADMISSIONS: 617-578-8600   FAX: 617-578-8609

STUDENTS SPEAK OUT

Life
One of Emerson College's attractions is the city of Boston, which students rave about. Explains one student, "Within walking distance is Fenway Park, the Theater District, Copley Square (noted for its many shops), and several dance clubs. There's even a paintball range and an indoor mini-golf club up the street." Time outside the classroom is often spent working in the school's radio and television stations and theaters, although students also find the time to hit the town. There is, surprisingly, a Greek scene here. Drugs are popular, not surprising among a student body that prides itself on its lack of conventionalism ("For fun, people go to the parks and take a lot of drugs, mostly, shrooms and marijuana. Everyone has colored hair, body piercing, tattoos, drug paraphernalia, sex paraphernalia, etc. I love this school, America the beautiful!").

Academics
Emerson College is named after nineteenth-century scholar Charles Wesley Emerson, but, considering the school's emphasis on communication, it could just as easily be named after the company that dominated radio manufacturing during that medium's Golden Age. Although 14 percent of the students major in liberal arts, communications and performing arts are Emerson's specialty. According to many of the students, Emerson is "the best hands-on school in America for students of television, film, theater, writing, and radio." Accordingly, students devote relatively little time to conventional college study (e.g., reading, writing papers, etc.). That doesn't mean they're not devoted to their schoolwork, though. "We compete like hell," writes one student. "Emerson is the Ivy League for misfits." Students are extremely satisfied with class sizes ("more than ideal") and the quality of their instructors. On the negative side, students have a contentious relationship with the school's administration ("The administration is very secretive about their decisions, and do not always consider the best interests of the students. Plus, they're very disorganized."). Also, many students note that "There's not a lot of communication between departments: there is absolutely no networking among different majors, which is unfortunate for a communication school!"

Student Body
Emerson students perceive themselves as outsiders. Says one, "Emerson is a school for people who didn't fit in in high school. We're all misfits and freaks." A few dissenters accuse their fellow students of being posers. Says one, "Too many people trying to be weird for attention without anything to say." Most students concede that the student body is homogeneous; explains one, "This is primarily a white upper-middle-class school with alternative students. It would be nice to see more diversity." Gay students will find a welcome atmosphere here ("When it comes to being gay, Emerson couldn't be a better place to spend your college career").

ADMISSIONS

The admissions committee considers (in descending order of importance): HS record, class rank, test scores, recommendations, essay. *Also considered (in descending order of importance):* extracurriculars, special talents, alumni relationship, personality. Either the SAT or ACT is required. Admissions process is need-blind. *High school units required/recommended:* 20 total units are required; 4 English required, 2 math required, 3 math recommended, 2 science required, 2 foreign language recommended, 2 social studies required. *Special Requirements:* TOEFL is required of all international students. Audition required of acting and musical theatre program applicants. *The admissions office says:* "Applicants may apply under Early Action (November 15 deadline) or under Regular Admission (February 1 deadline). Applicants are encouraged to submit their materials as early in the senior year as possible. Priority is given to applications received by February 1."

The Inside Word

Being in Boston does more for Emerson's selectivity than do rigorous admissions standards.

FINANCIAL AID

Students should submit: FAFSA, the school's own financial aid form, a copy of parents' most recent income tax filing. The Princeton Review suggests that all financial aid forms be submitted as soon as possible after January 1. *The following grants/scholarships are offered:* Pell, SEOG, academic merit, the school's own scholarships, the school's own grants, state scholarships, state grants, private scholarships, private grants. *Students borrow from the following loan programs:* Stafford, unsubsidized Stafford, Perkins, PLUS, state loans, private loans. Applicants will be notified of awards beginning March 15. College Work-Study Program is available. Institutional employment is available.

FROM THE ADMISSIONS OFFICE

"Founded in 1880 by Charles Wesley Emerson, noted preacher, orator, and teacher, Emerson has grown into a college offering its more than 2,600 students comprehensive undergraduate and graduate curricula in the communication arts and sciences and the performing arts. From the original concentration on oratory, have evolved specialization in such fields as mass communication (radio and television broadcasting, film, and journalism), theater arts, communication studies, communication disorders, writing, literature, and publishing. As the issues facing business, industry, and government grow larger and more complex, effective communication will grow more important, even crucial. Emerson has been selected as one of the 52 schools in the world as a new Media Center site by a consortium of hardware and software companies like Apple Computer, SuperMatch technology, Eastman Kodak and Adobe System. Emerson students and faculty will gain extraordinary access to advanced new technologies, technologies that will enable us to continue to explore the high tech frontiers of our fields. Emerson today, is preparing to educate those men and women who will bear the burden of that communication in the next century. Emerson College is accredited by New England Association of Schools and Colleges, Inc., and is a member of the Council of Graduate Schools."

ADMISSIONS

Admissions Rating	74
% of applicants accepted	70
% of acceptees attending	40

FRESHMAN PROFILE

Average verbal SAT	600
Average math SAT	530
Average ACT	NR
Average TOEFL	550
Graduated top 20% of class	43
Graduated top 40% of class	86
Graduated top 60% of class	94
Average HS GPA or Avg.	3.0

DEADLINES

Early decision	11/15
Regular admission	2/1
Regular notification	4/10
Non-fall registration	yes

APPLICANTS ALSO LOOK AT

AND OFTEN PREFER

Boston U.
NYU
Syracuse

AND SOMETIMES PREFER

U. Mass., Amherst
Ithaca

FINANCIAL FACTS

Financial Aid Rating	80
Tuition	$15,936
Room & board	$7,850
Estimated book expense	$500
% frosh receiving aid	79
% undergrads receiving aid	73
% aid is need-based	90
% frosh w/ grant (avg)	89 ($8,076)
% frosh w/ loan (avg)	72 ($3,323)
% UGs w/ job (avg)	33 ($1,500)
Off-campus job outlook	good

EMORY UNIVERSITY

200 BOIFFEVILLET JONES CENTER, ATLANTA, GA 30322 · ADMISSIONS: 800-727-6036

STUDENTS SPEAK OUT

Life

Emory University provides its students with both an expansive wooded campus and convenient access to Atlanta. One student writes us that "Atlanta is very accessible to Emory students and those that aren't interested in the Greek system on the weekend will find plenty to do in the city. There are also many non-Greek private Emory parties." Social life, however, stays mainly on campus, where the Greek system rules. Some students note that "A lot revolves around the Greek system. For many, they see it as their only outlet." Social life isn't lacking, and with the 1996 Olympics in town, Emory is going to be an exciting campus to attend. One student writes to us that "Life at school is quite busy. With all the lectures, organizations, intramural sports, club meetings held, and hanging out with friends, it's difficult to remember sometimes you're here for an education."

Academics

Emory, long touted as the South's "up and coming" contender for Ivy League students, is tired of that label. One student notices that "It is already one of the nation's truly great undergraduate programs." And that statement holds a lot of weight. Two-thirds of Emory students go on to graduate school within five years of graduation, many to medical school. "Pre-med is by far the most popular path for students, making this a very cutthroat university," writes one student. Also impressive are the university's expanding facilities, particularly in the physical and life sciences. Psychology, political science, and business degrees are popular, and the faculty in those departments are reportedly excellent. The professors, in general, receive high marks. One political science junior notes that "The professors are generally interested in the students and enjoy talking outside of class." The administration seems less helpful, and minority students seem to have more gripes about the administration than white students. Writes one African-American student, "The administration generally appears to be friendly but when black people need help...You have to fight for everything." One frequent knock on the university is that it's a pre-professional factory.

Student Body

Emory students have two views of themselves. The first is the unflattering one. One junior writes that "Emory does not attract people from diverse backgrounds by any means. With few exceptions, the people are 'middle-class, parochial minded, apathetic, and career oriented.'" The other view is the flattering one. A sophomore describes the student body: "I think there is a group of friends for everyone who comes to Emory. No matter who you are, you can find a way to fit in. Some social groups are more prominent than others, for example, the Greek system, but there are plenty of other kinds of people. You just have to look." Students from 80 foreign countries and many geographically diverse regions populate the student body. Minority students are well represented, but don't necessarily feel tremendously accepted. There is a large and active gay community that, while not having conquered homophobia, is progressive and visible.

ADMISSIONS

The admissions committee considers (in descending order of importance): HS record, test scores, recommendations, essay, class rank. *Also considered (in descending order of importance):* alumni relationship, extracurriculars, geographical distribution, special talents, personality. Either the SAT or ACT is required. *High school units required/recommended:* 16 total units are required; 4 English required, 3 math required, 2 science required, 2 foreign language required, 2 social studies required. Minimum 3.0/3.5 GPA required. *Special Requirements:* An audition is required for music program applicants. *The admissions office says:* "Primarily school achievement record, with careful examination of program content. Diversity of interests, background, and special talents sought."

The Inside Word

Only the fact that Emory competes with some of the best universities in the country prevents its admissions process from being even more competitive. As the South continues to increase its population and presence on the national scene, Emory will continue to increase its selectivity and prestige.

FINANCIAL AID

Students should submit: FAFSA (due April 1), state aid form, a copy of parents' most recent income tax filing (due May 1). The Princeton Review suggests that all financial aid forms be submitted as soon as possible after January 1. *The following grants/scholarships are offered:* Pell, SEOG, academic merit, the school's own scholarships, the school's own grants, state scholarships, state grants, private scholarships, federal nursing scholarship. *Students borrow from the following loan programs:* Stafford, Perkins, PLUS, the school's own loan fund, state loans, federal nursing loans, health professions loans, private loans. Applicants will be notified of awards beginning April 15. College Work-Study Program is available. Institutional employment is available.

FROM THE ADMISSIONS OFFICE

"The combination Emory offers you is really a rarity in today's college marketplace. As an Emory student, you can still have the benefits of a small liberal arts college, while enjoying the wider opportunities found in a major university. Emory College is the four-year undergraduate division of the university and provides a broad, rigorous liberal arts curriculum. At the same time, Emory University, with its nine major divisions, numerous centers for advanced study, and a host of prestigious affiliated institutions, provides the larger context, thus enriching your total college experience."

ADMISSIONS

Admissions Rating	89
% of applicants accepted	49
% of acceptees attending	25

FRESHMAN PROFILE

Average verbal SAT	650
Average math SAT	650
Average ACT	29
Average TOEFL	600
Graduated top 20% of class	NR
Graduated top 40% of class	NR
Graduated top 60% of class	NR
Average HS GPA or Avg.	3.7

DEADLINES

Early decision	NR
Regular admission	1/15
Regular notification	4/1
Non-fall registration	no

APPLICANTS ALSO LOOK AT

AND OFTEN PREFER

Brown
Northwestern U.
Duke

AND SOMETIMES PREFER

Wake Forest
Washington U.
Pennsylvania

AND RARELY PREFER

Rhodes
SMU
Tulane

FINANCIAL FACTS

Financial Aid Rating	82
Tuition	$18,770
Room & board	$6,220
Estimated book expense	$600
% frosh receiving aid	54
% undergrads receiving aid	62
% aid is need-based	79
% frosh w/ grant (avg)	54 ($10,037)
% frosh w/ loan (avg)	44 ($3,632)
% UGs w/ job (avg)	44 ($1,800)
Off-campus job outlook	good

EUGENE LANG COLLEGE

65 WEST 11TH STREET, NEW YORK, NY 10011   ADMISSIONS: 212-229-5665   FAX: 212-229-5355

CAMPUS LIFE

Quality of Life Rating	85
Type of school	private
Affiliation	none
Environment	metropolis

STUDENTS

FT undergrad enrollment	374
% male/female	29/71
% from out of state	40
% live on campus	40
% spend weekend on campus	NR
% transfers	50
% from public high school	55
% African-American	7
% Asian	3
% Caucasian	46
% Hispanic	10
% international	7
# of countries represented	12

WHAT'S HOT
off-campus food
leftist politics
New York
drugs
cigarettes

WHAT'S NOT
Greeks
intramural sports
lab facilities
intercollegiate sports
college radio

ACADEMICS

Academic Rating	85
Profs Interesting Rating	92
Profs Accessible Rating	89
Calendar	semester
Student/teacher ratio	9:1
% profs PhD	95
Hours of study per day	2.94

MOST POPULAR MAJORS
writing/literature
art/culture/society
social science/urban studies

STUDENTS SPEAK OUT

Life

With not much of a traditional campus, many Eugene Lang undergrads refer in their comments to the city of New York. One student writes, "Eugene Lang is unlike any other school in the respect that we're in the cultural mecca of the world, learning in small discussion classes—we can sample tastes of life right outside the door." The university does make an attempt to provide the students with activities "like parties and events," but "not many students show. Usually we go to private parties or to the clubs in Greenwich Village." It's true that the Village might be the ideal location for the student who appreciates life in a teeming metropolis where museums, art galleries, restaurants, and coffee bars abound. But "don't leave home without it," because life ain't cheap in NYC: "New York and Eugene Lang are conspiring to leave me in poverty forever." The students mention that the workload is manageable ("There is a lot of work here, but I have found I have time to do what I want") and that constructive pursuits "like internships and volunteering" are popular. This student characterizes his peers and the college they attend: "Lang attracts a certain kind of student: politically correct, liberal-minded, creative, and of superior intelligence, mostly of Ivy-League caliber, but who seek something 'different' in a college experience."

Academics

Lang, the undergraduate division of the New School for Social Research, is best suited to the needs of the independent undergrad who is interested in the humanities and social sciences. There are no required courses except a first-year writing requirement, all classes are taught in a seminar format and limited to sixteen students, and the college provides an incredible amount of personal attention, bestowing upon the student almost complete autonomy. There is a huge range of disciplines (political science, history, political anthropology, hard science, English and psychology) for the student to concentrate on, so this student's advice seems sound: "Eugene Lang is a school you attend if you already have a pretty clear idea of what you want to do. There is not much support for students in the 'undecided' category." Many students thrive under the self-imposed pressure to succeed. As this student remarks, "The students here learn not because we have to, but because we want to." The professors receive very high marks from the students for both the quality of instruction ("profs are great—super intelligent") and accessibility. There is "little to no bureaucratic feeling," and Lang has an administration that "really tries to get on a first-name basis with every student." One student writes, "The deans are always there when you need to work out a problem." The library and health facilities receive low marks, which is a sore spot for some of the students. "We pay almost as much in tuition as NYU students, but don't equal them in facilities," although a new multi-million dollar computer building may change that perception. In any case, one student responds well to that argument: "I think it's fair to say that we are paying all this money for the quality of classes and profs."

Student Body

Ethnic diversity is clearly a strong-suit of Eugene Lang with almost half the student population representing minorities, and the different types of students interact frequently and easily. One student says, "From the purple-haired, nose-ringed extremist to the prep—everyone's cool." Many of the students live off campus, but some pointed out that in order to make friends at the college it's important to live in the dorms for your freshman year. Not surprisingly, the political affiliation of the students leans way to the left with a better-than-average commitment. Traditional dating is not very popular.

FINANCIAL AID: 212-229-8930   E-MAIL: LANG@NEWSCHOOL.EDU   WEB SITE: HTTP://WWW.LANG.NEWSCHOOL.EDU/

ADMISSIONS

The admissions committee considers (in descending order of importance): HS record, recommendations, test scores, essay, class rank. *Also considered (in descending order of importance):* extracurriculars, personality, special talents. Either the SAT or ACT is required. An interview is required. Admissions process is need-blind. *High school units required/recommended:* 16 total units are required; 4 English recommended, 3 math recommended, 2 science recommended, 2 foreign language recommended, 1 social studies recommended, 2 history recommended. *Special Requirements:* A portfolio is required for art program applicants. An audition is required for music program applicants. Portfolio and home exam required of B.A./B.F.A. program applicants. *The admissions office says:* "We seek to gain a complete picture of the applicant's ability to succeed in a rigorous and nontraditional liberal arts program by reviewing grade/subject patterns in the transcript; ability to write and communicate evidence of self-directedness, maturity and enthusiasm for learning."

The Inside Word

An extremely small applicant pool prevents the admissions committee from being picky, though to be fair the college draws a very self-selected and intellectually curious pool, and applications are up. Those who demonstrate little self-motivation will find themselves denied.

FINANCIAL AID

Students should submit: FAFSA, the school's own financial aid form, state aid form, a copy of parents' most recent income tax filing. The Princeton Review suggests that all financial aid forms be submitted as soon as possible after January 1. *The following grants/scholarships are offered:* Pell, SEOG, the school's own scholarships, the school's own grants, state scholarships, state grants, private scholarships, private grants, foreign aid. *Students borrow from the following loan programs:* Stafford, unsubsidized Stafford, Perkins, PLUS, the school's own loan fund, state loans, private loans. Applicants will be notified of awards beginning April 1. College Work-Study Program is available. Institutional employment is available.

FROM THE ADMISSIONS OFFICE

"Eugene Lang College offers students of diverse backgrounds an innovative and creative approach to a liberal arts education, combining stimulating classroom activity of a small, intimate college with rich resources of a dynamic, urban university-the New School for Social Research. The curriculum at Lang College is challenging and flexible. Class size, limited to 15 students, promotes energetic and thoughtful discussions and writing is an essential component of all classes. Students design their own program of study within one of five interdisciplinary concentrations in the Social Sciences and Humanities. They also have the opportunity to pursue a five-year B.A./B.F.A., B.A./M.A., or B.A./M.S.T. at one of the university's five other divisions. Our Greenwich Village location means all the cultural treasures of the city-museums, libraries, music, theater-are literally at your doorstep."

ADMISSIONS

Admissions Rating		73
% of applicants accepted		77
% of acceptees attending		38

FRESHMAN PROFILE

Average verbal SAT	610
Average math SAT	540
Average ACT	28
Average TOEFL	600
Graduated top 20% of class	51
Graduated top 40% of class	NR
Graduated top 60% of class	NR
Average HS GPA or Avg.	NR

DEADLINES

Early decision	11/15
Regular admission	2/1
Regular notification	4/1
Non-fall registration	yes

APPLICANTS ALSO LOOK AT

AND OFTEN PREFER
NYU
Bard

AND SOMETIMES PREFER
Hampshire
Sarah Lawrence

AND RARELY PREFER
Reed
Bennington

FINANCIAL FACTS

Financial Aid Rating	81
Tuition	$15,650
Room & board	$8,132
Estimated book expense	$800
% frosh receiving aid	67
% undergrads receiving aid	69
% aid is need-based	85
% frosh w/ grant (avg)	64 ($7,301)
% frosh w/ loan (avg)	70 ($3,200)
% UGs w/ job (avg)	30 ($2,000)
Off-campus job outlook	good

THE EVERGREEN STATE COLLEGE

OLYMPIA, WA 98505   ADMISSIONS: 206-866-6000   FAX: 206-866-6823

CAMPUS LIFE

Quality of Life Rating   **82**
Type of school   public
Affiliation   none
Environment   suburban

STUDENTS

FT undergrad enrollment	3,410
% male/female	43/57
% from out of state	25
% live on campus	33
% spend weekend on campus	30
% transfers	56
% from public high school	95
% African-American	3
% Asian	5
% Caucasian	85
% Hispanic	3
% international	NR
# of countries represented	16

WHAT'S HOT
college radio
leftist politics
drugs
support groups
political activism

WHAT'S NOT
student government
religion
intercollegiate sports
intramural sports
music associations

ACADEMICS

Academic Rating	**82**
Profs Interesting Rating	94
Profs Accessible Rating	88
Calendar	quarter
Student/teacher ratio	22:1
% profs PhD/tenured	74/76
Hours of study per day	3.35

MOST POPULAR MAJORS
education
environmental studies

% GRADS WHO PURSUE...
Law 1, Med 3, MBA 6, MA 4

STUDENTS SPEAK OUT

Life

Life on the beautiful campus of The Evergreen State College reflects the environment. One student writes, "Life here is centered around nature and the discovery of self. It's not unusual to find someone meditating or frequently walking to the beach." Popular activities include hiking ("Evergreen's campus is 1000 acres of forest"), biking, swimming, camping, movies (the city of Olympia hosts a gay and lesbian film festival), and "group activities like the Frisbee team are cool." One undergrad mentions an interesting part of campus life: "There is a vegetarian cafe that is a student-run collective on campus." Since the school is located in the state capital of Olympia, it is easy to see many of the students focus their life on politics. As this student writes, "I love it. Evergreen rocks. We think about politics, activism, and subverting the dominant paradigm." Some students react negatively to all the talk of politics ("PC is way out of control"), but as a student body, "political/activist groups are extremely vocal."

Academics

The Evergreen State College offers the best of both worlds to the incoming student: the price of a public university combined with the student body, class size, instructor accessibility, and educational philosophy of a private school. Even some private schools could learn from TESC. Instead of enrolling in individual courses, the students study in one comprehensive program designed to examine a major academic topic—often a philosophical question, such as the nature of democracy—from several different academic viewpoints. They take team-taught classes from professors in various disciplines and meet in small groups to discuss potential areas of overlap and definition. Some of these "courses" last one quarter, while others last a full year. The students receive written evaluations but no grades are given. In this way, the self-motivated student is driven by an inner desire to learn, not the external rewards system of passing grades. The students laud the accessibility ("Intimidation is zero!") and the intensity of the teaching method: "The professors are excellent. They know how to keep you awake and motivated." And at least one ecology major knows the reason: "The absence of graduate students and the publish-or-perish policies for the professors lets them concentrate wholly on the students." Administration receives passing marks, but more than one student suggests that you make a copy of all your paperwork before turning it in to the financial aid office. The computer, library, and lab facilities are all good, according to the students.

Student Body

Evergreen might the last bastion of hippiedom. Many undergrads see the student body as "Hippies and Hipsters trying to figure it out." But other students dislike such categorization. As this student writes, "There is more to Evergreen than just hippies." Right, there are Hipsters too. Ethnic diversity is somewhat lacking with the ratio of white students to minority students at about 4:1. Perhaps as far as diversity goes, this student is right: "It's amazing the diversity there can be in a bunch of liberal white kids." At Evergreen, traditional dating is not as popular as politics.

FINANCIAL AID: 206-866-6000

ADMISSIONS

The admissions committee considers (in descending order of importance): HS record, test scores. Either the SAT or ACT is required. Admissions process is need-blind. *High school units required/recommended:* 16 total units are required; 4 English required, 3 math required, 2 science required, 2 foreign language required, 3 social studies required. Minimum 2.0 GPA required. TOEFL is required of all international students. *The admissions office says:* "[Our students] are seriously involved with their education; [each] designs [his or her] own major; making a difference is a widely held objective. [Our students] are interested in the process of learning...as opposed to studying for a grade."

The Inside Word

Evergreen is one of the rare breed of "alternative" colleges—places where intellectual curiosity and a high level of self-motivation are much more important than grades and test scores in the admissions process. Students with inconsistencies in their academic background will find an admissions committee that is quite reasonable and willing to hear what you have to say for yourself in the way of explanation. A visit is a good idea for all candidates.

FINANCIAL AID

Students should submit: FAFSA. The Princeton Review suggests that all financial aid forms be submitted as soon as possible after January 1. *The following grants/scholarships are offered:* Pell, SEOG, academic merit, athletic, the school's own scholarships, the school's own grants, state scholarships, state grants, private scholarships. *Students borrow from the following loan programs:* Stafford, unsubsidized Stafford, Perkins, PLUS, private loans. Applicants will be notified of awards beginning April 15. College Work-Study Program is available. Institutional employment is available.

FROM THE ADMISSIONS OFFICE

"Evergreen is a liberal arts and sciences college with some very special features. Studies at Evergreen are interdisciplinary. Students study major fields by drawing knowledge from several different academic disciplines to develop an understanding of the relationships between the arts, humanities, and natural and social sciences. An education at Evergreen emphasizes cooperative learning in place of competition and relies heavily on small discussion groups involving faculty members and students."

ADMISSIONS

Admissions Rating	71
% of applicants accepted	82
% of acceptees attending	45

FRESHMAN PROFILE

Average verbal SAT	580
Average math SAT	540
Average ACT	24
Average TOEFL	525
Graduated top 20% of class	40
Graduated top 40% of class	75
Graduated top 60% of class	90
Average HS GPA or Avg.	3.2

DEADLINES

Early decision	NR
Regular admission	3/1
Regular notification	4/1
Non-fall registration	no

APPLICANTS ALSO LOOK AT

AND OFTEN PREFER
U. Washington
UC-Santa Cruz

AND SOMETIMES PREFER
Western Washington
U. Puget Sound

AND RARELY PREFER
U. Oregon

FINANCIAL FACTS

Financial Aid Rating	74
In-state tuition	$2,439
Out-of-state tuition	$8,625
Room & board	$5,000
Estimated book expense	$500
% frosh receiving aid	50
% undergrads receiving aid	47
% aid is need-based	77
% frosh w/ grant (avg)	NR ($4,072)
% frosh w/ loan (avg)	44 ($4,392)
% UGs w/ job (avg)	38
Off-campus job outlook	good

FAIRFIELD UNIVERSITY

North Benson Road, Fairfield, CT 06430-7524   Admissions: 203-254-4100   Fax: 203-254-4199

STUDENTS SPEAK OUT

Life

"Just try finding a sober Jesuit on a Friday night." According to its undergrads, Fairfield University students—and faculty—place a huge emphasis on alcohol in their social life. Well over three-quarters of the students have something to say, good or bad, about beer. Most responses were along this line: "If there is no beer, there is no fun!" Many also mention famed beach parties on Long Island Sound as the height of students' debauchery. Other students sound frustrated with the lack of imagination in this social scene: "It is a difficult school if you don't like to socialize or drink at parties." There are a few students who note a change in the works at Fairfield. One student says, "There has definitely been a greater effort to provide non-alcoholic activities since I started at Fairfield." For off-campus activities that offer some variety and a breather from the hectic college schedule, there's always New Haven and NYC close by. Perhaps the fairest assessment comes from this level-headed student: "Fairfield offers the perfect balance between working hard and playing hard." Finally, for those students who choose to use their free time helping others rather than getting blasted, check out this comment: "Fairfield's community service opportunities are unparalleled. If you want to help, Fairfield's the place for you."

Academics

"My bio professor and my dad are the only people who still call me Suzy!" Comments like these are fairly common at Fairfield University, as student after student praises the professors' friendliness, teaching skills, and knowledge. One student gushes, "Most professors possess Socratic wisdom in their realm of expertise." Another student offers, "The professors are clear, articulate, and extremely knowledgeable about their fields." Accessibility was also mentioned by many of the students. This is important, one points out, "because when you go from high school to college, some people need to feel like they're not getting left behind." In general, the administration received high marks. One student writes, "Administration really cares about school and students, especially the Jesuits-in-residence." There are a couple of negatives at Fairfield, however. For instance, the library could use a lift: "The library is awful. It is small and too hot, and the 70s orange carpet's got to go. I get nauseated when I'm in there." Another area for improvement could be how the college handles money. Consider this statement from a biology student: "The bursar's office and financial aid office do not communicate." As if that weren't bad enough, one student added, "They're not totally inefficient, just very unfriendly."

Student Body

One Fairfield student puts it succinctly: "My fellow students are rich and Catholic." It's true that the university is homogenous; over eighty percent of the students are white and upper class. But the prevailing sentiment here seems to be, "Even though we all look alike, we're good kids." Concerning the issue of diversity, some students feel like they're moving in the right direction: "Issues dealing with race and sexuality are being addressed proactively by students and faculty alike. We are working towards a more diverse campus, which is for the benefit of all." Some students complain about "all the cliques," "the spoiled rich kids," and "the snobs" at Fairfield, but others feel the university's reputation is not deserved.

ADMISSIONS

The admissions committee considers (in descending order of importance): HS record, class rank, test scores, recommendations. *Also considered (in descending order of importance):* personality, alumni relationship, extracurriculars, special talents. Either the SAT or ACT is required; SAT is preferred. An interview is recommended. *High school units required/recommended:* 17 total units are required; 3 English required, 4 English recommended, 3 math required, 2 science required, 2 foreign language required, 3 social studies required, 1 history required. Rank in top two-fifths of secondary school class recommended. TOEFL is required of all international students. *The admissions office says:* "Students at Fairfield University learn that academic achievement should be coupled with social concerns so that 20% of them are involved in serving at area kitchens and shelters for the homeless, working with children whose parents have AIDS, tutoring inner city children and volunteering to assist the needy in Appalachia, Ecuador, Haiti, and Mexico."

The Inside Word

The lack of essays or an interview in the admissions process goes a long way toward stocking the applicant pool, as does solid support from parochial high schools.

FINANCIAL AID

Students should submit: FAFSA (due February 15), a copy of parents' most recent income tax filing (due May 1). The Princeton Review suggests that all financial aid forms be submitted as soon as possible after January 1. *The following grants/scholarships are offered:* Pell, SEOG, academic merit, athletic, the school's own scholarships, the school's own grants, state scholarships, state grants, private scholarships, private grants. *Students borrow from the following loan programs:* Stafford, unsubsidized Stafford, Perkins, PLUS, state loans, federal nursing loans, private loans. Applicants will be notified of awards beginning April 1. College Work-Study Program is available. Institutional employment is available.

FROM THE ADMISSIONS OFFICE

"Fairfield University's primary objectives are to develop the creative intellectual potential of its students and to foster in them ethical and religious values and a sense of social responsibility. Fairfield recognizes that learning is a lifelong process and sees the education which it provides as a foundation upon which its students may continue to build within their chosen areas of scholarly study or professional development. It also seeks to foster in its students a continuing intellectual curiosity and to develop leaders. As the key to the lifelong process of learning, Fairfield has developed a core curriculum (60 credits), to introduce all students to the broad range of liberal learning. The core helps some students discover where their interests truly lie and conveys a broad understanding that makes them more flexible even in their areas of specialty."

ADMISSIONS

Admissions Rating	72
% of applicants accepted	71
% of acceptees attending	23

FRESHMAN PROFILE

Average verbal SAT	580
Average math SAT	580
Average ACT	25
Average TOEFL	500
Graduated top 20% of class	36
Graduated top 40% of class	60
Graduated top 60% of class	65
Average HS GPA or Avg.	2.7

DEADLINES

Early decision	NR
Regular admission	3/1
Regular notification	4/1
Non-fall registration	no

APPLICANTS ALSO LOOK AT

AND OFTEN PREFER

Georgetown U.
Coll. of the Holy Cross
Trinity Coll. (CT)
Boston Coll.
Villanova

AND SOMETIMES PREFER

Fordham
U. Mass., Amherst
U. Connecticut
Siena

AND RARELY PREFER

Syracuse

FINANCIAL FACTS

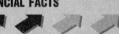

Financial Aid Rating	76
Tuition	$16,000
Room & board	$6,600
Estimated book expense	$500
% frosh receiving aid	76
% undergrads receiving aid	66
% aid is need-based	88
% frosh w/ grant (avg)	73 ($6,132)
% frosh w/ loan (avg)	52 ($4,500)
% UGs w/ job (avg)	11 ($1,200)
Off-campus job outlook	good

FISK UNIVERSITY

1000 17TH AVENUE NORTH, NASHVILLE, TN 37208   ADMISSIONS: 615-329-8665   FAX: 615-329-8715

STUDENTS SPEAK OUT

Life

The most attractive aspect of life at Fisk is the strong sense of community fostered by its size. "Fisk has a family-type atmosphere. Students here interact well with each other, as well as with members of the community," is how one student puts it. The campus is currently undergoing necessary renovations: both the dorms and campus received low marks from students. Also, the food here gets poor ratings from students. One student informs us that "it's hard to do anything outdoors because we are located in a bad area, but we still have fun in the dorms."

Academics

Although it may not be as well known as Howard or Tuskegee universities, Fisk boasts a record its main competitors for black students can't touch: over half of Fisk's graduates go on to graduate school within a year of graduation. It is much smaller than either of those other two schools, and admissions accordingly are more competitive. Despite its small size, an excellent, well-rounded education is readily available at Fisk, as Fiskites constantly reminded us. "Educationally, Fisk is an excellent school," reported one undergrad. "The professors really care about us as students and as people. The personal attention we receive from our instructors is great. Fisk provides me with the small classroom atmosphere and the role models I need to succeed." Black perspectives are emphasized in all classes; one student told us that "Fisk University teaches young black Americans not only how to survive in the future but also how our ancestors survived the past." The liberal arts are popular here, as are business administration and pre-law programs. Most complaints we heard concerned administrators ("very uncooperative," said one student) and the fact that "a lack of resources restricts complete educational enrichment." Also, it can be difficult to study at the library, which serves as a campus social center. Still, few schools are attended by such adamant boosters (see "Student Body," below).

Student Body

Although the administration, social life, and living conditions could be better, Fisk students almost unanimously sing the praise of their university: "Fisk...forever!" is their rallying cry. Comments such as "I'll send my children to Fisk and their children, too, if it is left up to me" are the rule rather than the exception. Students feel that, when all is said and done, they are getting an excellent education in an African-American setting, and that the importance of that cannot be overemphasized. The typical Fiskite is politically liberal, socially conservative, religious, serious about study, and holds his fellow students in high regard. As one student sums it up, "Fisk University, like many others, has its problems. On the whole, though, it is excellent, and I can honestly say that the best and the brightest of the black community are being educated here."

FISK UNIVERSITY

FINANCIAL AID: 615-329-8735

WEB SITE: HTTP://WWW.FISK.EDU/

ADMISSIONS

The admissions committee considers (in descending order of importance): HS record, class rank, test scores, recommendations, essay. *Also considered (in descending order of importance):* personality, alumni relationship, extracurriculars, special talents. Either the SAT or ACT is required. *High school units required/recommended:* 15 total units are recommended; 4 English recommended, 2 math recommended, 1 science recommended, 1 foreign language recommended, 1 history recommended. Electives should include units relating to intended major. Math units must include algebra and plane geometry. SAT II is considered. *Special Requirements:* TOEFL is required of all international students. Several years of applied music (preferably piano) and participation (as performer and listener) in various musical activities required of music program applicants. *The admissions office says:* "Fisk University seeks to enroll men and women who will benefit from a liberal arts experience, designed to equip them for intellectual and social leadership. It is the policy of Fisk University to grant admission to applicants showing evidence of adequate preparation and the ability to successfully pursue college studies at Fisk."

The Inside Word

While a solid academic record is central to getting in, applicants to Fisk should not underestimate the personal side of admissions criteria. A high level of motivation and involvement in your school, church, and/or community goes a long way toward a successful candidacy here.

FINANCIAL AID

Students should submit: FAFSA (due April 20). The Princeton Review suggests that all financial aid forms be submitted as soon as possible after January 1. *The following grants/scholarships are offered:* Pell, SEOG, academic merit, the school's own scholarships, the school's own grants, state grants, United Negro College Fund. *Students borrow from the following loan programs:* Stafford, Perkins, PLUS. College Work-Study Program is available.

FROM THE ADMISSIONS OFFICE

"Founded in 1866, the University is coeducational, private, and one of America's premier historically black universities. The first black college to be granted a chapter of Phi Beta Kappa Honor Society, Fisk serves a national student body, with an enrollment of 900 students. There are residence halls for men and women. The focal point of the 40-acre campus and architectural symbol of the University is Jubilee Hall, the first permanent building for the education for blacks in the South, and named for the internationally renowned Fisk Jubilee Singers, who continue their tradition of singing the Negro spiritual. From its earliest days, Fisk has played a leadership role in the education of African-Americans. Faculty and alumni have been among America's intellectual leaders. Among them include Fisk graduates Nikki Giovanni, poet/writer; John Hope Franklin, historian/scholar; David Lewis, professor/recipient of the prestigious Pulitzer Prize; Hazel O'Leary, U.S. Secretary of Energy; John Lewis, U.S. Representative-GA; W.E.B. DuBois, the great social critic and co-founder of the NAACP. Former Fisk students, whose distinguished careers bring color to American culture include Judith Jamison, director of the Alvin Ailey Dance Company and Johnetta B. Cole, president of Spelman College. In proportion to its size, Fisk continues to contribute more alumni to the ranks of scholars pursuing doctoral degrees than any other institution in the United States."

ADMISSIONS

Admissions Rating	68
% of applicants accepted	80
% of acceptees attending	25

FRESHMAN PROFILE

Average verbal SAT	500
Average math SAT	530
Average ACT	NR
Average TOEFL	550
Graduated top 20% of class	27
Graduated top 40% of class	47
Graduated top 60% of class	70
Average HS GPA or Avg.	3.1

DEADLINES

Early decision	NR
Regular admission	6/15
Regular notification	rolling
Non-fall registration	yes

APPLICANTS ALSO LOOK AT

AND OFTEN PREFER
Howard
Morehouse
Spelman

AND SOMETIMES PREFER
Vanderbilt
Penn State U.

AND RARELY PREFER
Clark Atlanta

FINANCIAL FACTS

Financial Aid Rating	74
Tuition	$7,212
Room & board	$4,224
Estimated book expense	$600
% frosh receiving aid	80
% undergrads receiving aid	82
% aid is need-based	95
% frosh w/ grant (avg)	16 ($2,000)
% frosh w/ loan (avg)	80 ($4,000)
% UGs w/ job (avg)	NR
Off-campus job outlook	good

FLORIDA A&M UNIVERSITY

TALLAHASSEE, FL 32307 ADMISSIONS: 904-599-3796 FAX: 904-561-2428

CAMPUS LIFE

Quality of Life Rating 70
Type of school public
Affiliation none
Environment city

STUDENTS
FT undergrad enrollment 8,074
% male/female 43/57
% from out of state 28
% live on campus 28
% spend weekend on campus NR
% transfers 46
% from public high school 85
% in (# of) fraternities (4)
% in (# of) sororities (4)
% African-American 89
% Asian 1
% Caucasian 7
% Hispanic 1
% international 1
# of countries represented 84

WHAT'S HOT
old-fashioned dating
sex
student government
leftist politics
college radio

WHAT'S NOT
cigarettes
registration is a pain
dorms
inefficient administration
lab facilities

ACADEMICS

Academic Rating 70
Profs Interesting Rating 61
Profs Accessible Rating 63
Calendar semester
Student/teacher ratio 13:1
% profs PhD 51
Hours of study per day 2.92

MOST POPULAR MAJORS
business administration
health professions
liberal arts

STUDENTS SPEAK OUT

Life
Explains one student, "Social life is dictated by the sororities and frats," and by all indication, the Greek system is the king of student social life. Students seem happier on campus than off—Tallahassee earns only average support, while on-campus life receives some raves. One student notes, "There are parties galore. We have our own rendition of the Apollo, the 'Stoop,' for fun. Many organizations accessible on campus make up for the dead life of Tallahassee." Most social events take place on the weekends, and on campus. Some popular student events are Greek Week, Homecoming and Harambee. Religious and community service events draw large turnouts. FAMU athletic life is also healthy; over fifty percent of the student body participates in some intramural sport. A sophomore comments, "I love FAMU; I would suggest it to anyone. It's a great learning experience filled with ups and downs."

Academics
The teachers at Florida Agricultural & Mechanical University (FAMU) receive heaps of praise from the students. One student writes, "I've found my professors to be helpful, concerned, and creative to make the environment conducive to learning." These statements are heartening for a school that is approaching its centennial (1997), and especially heartening for a school with such a business focus. Only twenty-five percent of the student body goes on to graduate study within five years, compared to thirty-five percent who get jobs in business and remain in that same profession. The most popular majors are, indeed, business and the health professions, but students enjoyably report a lack of cutthroat behavior among the student body. FAMU offers over thirty-five undergraduate degrees, and the liberal arts major is popular. The hard sciences (chemistry, physics, and animal sciences) have the fewest declared undergraduate majors. FAMU offers internships in Washington D.C. and study abroad in Italy and England. The administration receives lower marks than the faculty. One student comments, "I often wonder what it is they do." Many students offered negative comments about the bureaucracy in the administration and financial aid offices. FAMU has one of the most comprehensive Learning Disabilities aids in the country. The Learning Development & Evaluation Center offers special accommodations and considerations to students who require them—included are taped lectures, alternative (non-essay) tests, and note-takers.

Student Body
A mainly in-state institution, FAMU is proud of its home-grown student body. One student notes that "There is much diversity as well as unity on campus. In general, students tend to be friends. The organizations (frats and sororities) work together...Regardless of differences, people tend to interact well with each other. The black community here has proved to be united and strong when a worthy cause comes along." FAMU's homogeneity provided a feeling of comfort and care, "like family."

FINANCIAL AID: 904-599-3730

ADMISSIONS

The admissions committee considers (in descending order of importance): HS record, test scores, recommendations, class rank, essay. *Also considered (in descending order of importance):* personality, alumni relationship. Either the SAT or ACT is required. *High school units required/recommended:* 19 total units are required; 4 English required, 3 math required, 3 science required, 2 foreign language required, 3 social studies required. Minimum combined SAT I score of 900 (composite ACT score of 21) and minimum 2.5 GPA required. TOEFL is required of all international students.

The Inside Word

FAMU's admissions staff does a terrific job. Collectively, they are warm, compassionate, and skilled counselors. This goes a long way towards explaining why the university has enrolled the highest number of National Achievement Scholars of any school in the country. There's a lot to like about the way these guys do business—they never lose sight of the notion that they are educators first and marketers second. Other colleges would do well to study FAMU's approach.

FINANCIAL AID

Students should submit: FAFSA. The Princeton Review suggests that all financial aid forms be submitted as soon as possible after January 1. *The following grants/scholarships are offered:* Pell, SEOG, academic merit, athletic, the school's own scholarships, the school's own grants, state scholarships, state grants, private scholarships, private grants, ROTC. *Students borrow from the following loan programs:* Stafford, Perkins, PLUS, the school's own loan fund, state loans, private loans. Applicants will be notified of awards beginning in May. College Work-Study Program is available.

FROM THE ADMISSIONS OFFICE

"FAMU encourages applications for admission from qualified applicants regardless of sex, culture, race, religion, ethnic background, age or disability. We are committed to enrolling the best possible students and we are interested in applicants who have demonstrated superior academic ability and outstanding personal qualities. For more than a century, the primary goals of FAMU have been to promote academic excellence and to improve the quality of life for those individuals it serves and their society. FAMU is located in the capital city of Florida (Tallahassee) and is a four-year public, general purpose, land-grant institution. It offers undergraduate and graduate programs designed to meet the needs of a diverse student population."

ADMISSIONS

Admissions Rating	73
% of applicants accepted	62
% of acceptees attending	54

FRESHMAN PROFILE

Average verbal SAT	490
Average math SAT	480
Average ACT	21
Average TOEFL	500
Graduated top 20% of class	NR
Graduated top 40% of class	NR
Graduated top 60% of class	NR
Average HS GPA or Avg.	3.1

DEADLINES

Early decision	2/1
Regular admission	5/1
Regular notification	rolling
Non-fall registration	yes

APPLICANTS ALSO LOOK AT

AND SOMETIMES PREFER

Tuskegee
Spelman
Morehouse
Florida St.
Howard

AND RARELY PREFER

U. South Florida
U. Florida
Hampton

FINANCIAL FACTS

Financial Aid Rating	75
In-state tuition	$1,908
Out-of-state tuition	$7,200
Room & board	$2,884
Estimated book expense	$250
% frosh receiving aid	52
% undergrads receiving aid	72
% aid is need-based	60
% frosh w/ grant (avg)	81 ($969)
% frosh w/ loan (avg)	20 ($1,000)
% UGs w/ job (avg)	10 ($1,360)
Off-campus job outlook	good

FLORIDA STATE UNIVERSITY

2249 UNIVERSITY CENTER, TALLAHASSEE, FL 32306-1009   ADMISSIONS: 904-644-6200   FAX: 904-644-0197

CAMPUS LIFE

Quality of Life Rating   **86**

Type of school	public
Affiliation	none
Environment	city

STUDENTS

FT undergrad enrollment	19,880
% male/female	45/55
% from out of state	16
% live on campus	18
% spend weekend on campus	NR
% transfers	44
% from public high school	67
% in (# of) fraternities	20 (26)
% in (# of) sororities	20 (20)
% African-American	8
% Asian	2
% Caucasian	77
% Hispanic	3
% international	1
# of countries represented	68

WHAT'S HOT

intercollegiate sports
old-fashioned dating
town-gown relations
health facilities
sex

WHAT'S NOT

dorms
cigarettes
registration is a pain
campus difficult to get around
inefficient administration

ACADEMICS

Academic Rating   **76**

Profs Interesting Rating	74
Profs Accessible Rating	72
Calendar	semester
Student/teacher ratio	NR
% profs tenured	87
Hours of study per day	2.73

MOST POPULAR MAJORS

criminology
communication
psychology

STUDENTS SPEAK OUT

Life

Sports and parties form the center of FSU social life. "Sports are almost a religion here, especially football," writes one student, whose attitude was seconded by the number of students complaining about the way in which football tickets are distributed. One student sums up life at FSU this way: "People drink for fun. A lot of people do silly frat and sorority functions. The Student Union is always showing movies and providing concerts and comedians for students here, which is especially good for students who don't have cars to go off campus." FSU also boasts a "great gym, recreational facilities, and campus food services." Students give Tallahassee ugly marks, although they note that "Tallahassee has great access to outdoor fun: camping, running, biking, etc. The weather is also suited for such activities, most of the time. Most people who mainly use drinking and socializing for fun get sick of Tallahassee quickly, because it's somewhat limited in new places to go."

Academics

Florida State University is a school better known for its party atmosphere than for its academics. Even its most vocal supporters, of which there are many, rarely mention the quality of the academics without also mentioning the quality of their leisure time. "Classes are great, but this school is so much fun it's sometimes hard to get motivated," explains one student. Serious students here must contend with the temptation to join their classmates, who tend to take it easy academically, and the hospitable climate and surroundings. For the strong-willed, however, an excellent education is available at a bargain-basement price. FSU's strengths are definitely in preprofessional and career-oriented programs; business, education, engineering, nursing, and hotel management are among the strongest departments. Performing arts are also excellent, particularly music and theater. Students give their professors subpar grades but note that the quality of instruction varies widely from department to department. One political science major notes that "professors are kind and considerate and care about students." The FSU experience, in a nutshell: "One can easily feel overwhelmed at a school this size, but only if they allow themselves. It's a friendly place, not to mention fun, plus there are excellent professors."

Student Body

Over three-quarters of FSU students are native Floridians. Minorities make up fifteen percent of the student body. Blacks make up half the minority population. Because FSU is particularly lenient in accepting transfer credit from junior and community colleges, many students arrive here as sophomores and juniors; transfers make up twelve percent of the student body. Several students note that "The one thing you notice here is how friendly people are—students, staff, everybody. People go out of their way to make a difference here, at the school, in town, and for the future."

FINANCIAL AID: 904-644-0539   E-MAIL: GOPHER@FSU.EDU   WEB SITE: HTTP://WWW.FSU.EDU/

ADMISSIONS

The admissions committee considers (in descending order of importance): HS record, test scores, class rank, recommendations, essay. *Also considered (in descending order of importance):* special talents, alumni relationship, extracurriculars, geographical distribution, personality. Either the SAT or ACT is required. Admissions process is need-blind. *High school units required/recommended:* 19 total units are required; 4 English required, 3 math required, 3 science required, 2 foreign language required, 3 social studies required. Minimum composite ACT score of 24 (combined SAT I score of 1000). *Special Requirements:* A portfolio is required for art program applicants. An audition is required for music program applicants. TOEFL is required of all international students. Audition required of B.F.A. theatre program applicants. Departmental application required of motion picture, television, and recording arts program applicants. *The admissions office says:* "One of the most unique qualities of Florida State University is that there isn't a typical student. There are as many perspectives as there are FSU students. An ideal of individualism permeates every facet of student life at FSU—academically, culturally, politically, and socially."

The Inside Word

The high volume of applicants has everything to do with Florida State's selectivity, which continues to increase as budgets hold enrollment fairly level. Non-Floridians will find FSU's selection process to be a bit more welcoming than UF's, but just as impersonal. Performing arts auditions are quite competitive.

FINANCIAL AID

Students should submit: FAFSA, the school's own financial aid form, state aid form, a copy of parents' most recent income tax filing. The Princeton Review suggests that all financial aid forms be submitted as soon as possible after January 1. *The following grants/scholarships are offered:* Pell, SEOG, academic merit, athletic, the school's own scholarships, the school's own grants, state scholarships, state grants, private scholarships, private grants. *Students borrow from the following loan programs:* Stafford, unsubsidized Stafford, Perkins, PLUS, the school's own loan fund, state loans. Applicants will be notified of awards beginning in April. College Work-Study Program is available. Institutional employment is available.

FROM THE ADMISSIONS OFFICE

"Florida State University encourages applications for admission from qualified students regardless of sex, culture, race, religion, ethnic background, age or disability. Most Florida students accepted to the university have at least a 'B' average in all academic subjects (grades 9-12) and test scores of at least 24 (composite) on the Enhanced ACT or 1000 (verbal plus math) on the SAT. Non-Florida applicants will ordinarily be held to higher standards. In the case of applicants who do not meet these qualifications, a variety of additional factors are considered. These include the pattern and quality of courses and curriculum, grade trends, class rank, educational objectives, record of extracurricular activities, leadership, and school recommendations. Applicants who bring to the university community other important attributes may receive additional consideration. These include talented writers and performing artists, applicants having special ties to the university, students with significant life and career experiences, skilled athletes, and members of minority groups under-represented in our student body."

ADMISSIONS

Admissions Rating	77
% of applicants accepted	73
% of acceptees attending	33

FRESHMAN PROFILE

Average verbal SAT	580
Average math SAT	590
Average ACT	25
Average TOEFL	550
Graduated top 20% of class	67
Graduated top 40% of class	95
Graduated top 60% of class	99
Average HS GPA or Avg.	NR

DEADLINES

Early decision	December
Regular admission	3/1
Regular notification	rolling
Non-fall registration	yes

APPLICANTS ALSO LOOK AT

AND SOMETIMES PREFER

Georgia Tech.
Wake Forest
Florida A & M
Rollins
U. Florida

AND RARELY PREFER

Wesleyan Coll.
Stetson
U. Colorado, Boulder

FINANCIAL FACTS

Financial Aid Rating	81
In-state tuition	$1,780
Out-of-state tuition	$6,700
Room & board	$4,285
Estimated book expense	$600
% frosh receiving aid	50
% undergrads receiving aid	48
% aid is need-based	59
% frosh w/ grant (avg)	31 ($2,325)
% frosh w/ loan (avg)	54 ($3,819)
% UGs w/ job (avg)	10 ($3,354)
Off-campus job outlook	good

UNIVERSITY OF FLORIDA

UNDERGRADUATE ADMISSIONS, 226 TIGERT HALL, GAINESVILLE, FL 32611   ADMISSIONS: 904-392-1365   FAX: 904-392-3987

CAMPUS LIFE

Quality of Life Rating	83
Type of school	public
Affiliation	none
Environment	city

STUDENTS

FT undergrad enrollment	26,553
% male/female	52/48
% from out of state	8
% live on campus	21
% spend weekend on campus	95
% transfers	6
% from public high school	NR
% in (# of) fraternities	15 (28)
% in (# of) sororities	15 (18)
% African-American	6
% Asian	6
% Caucasian	75
% Hispanic	10
% international	1
# of countries represented	114

WHAT'S HOT
health facilities
student publications
hard liquor
intercollegiate sports
old-fashioned dating

WHAT'S NOT
registration is a pain
dorms
campus difficult to get around
theater
music associations

ACADEMICS

Academic Rating	80
Profs Interesting Rating	67
Profs Accessible Rating	69
Calendar	semester
Student/teacher ratio	17:1
% profs PhD/tenured	97/89
Hours of study per day	2.76

MOST POPULAR MAJORS
psychology
finance
English

STUDENTS SPEAK OUT

Life
Even though almost half of the University of Florida students polled rank fraternities "extremely popular," not one went into detail on the influence of the Greeks at the school. The crackdown by school officials on free-for-all beer orgies seems to have worked. One student explains, "I'm glad I didn't join a frat even though a lot of my friends did. Now I can do whatever I want!" And contrary to one student's response ("The town provides little recreation option besides bars"), there seems to be a great deal to do in Gainesville and on the beautiful campus. There is an art museum, a professional theater, a well-respected student newspaper, and even a television station to go along with the bars, restaurants, and coffee shops around town. Of course the highlighted activity takes place at The Swamp, UF's stadium. One student says, "Gator football is the Alpha and the Omega at the University of Florida." If you don't particularly care for pigskins, the gridiron, or the SEC, you'd better be careful. As this student mentions, "People here eat, breathe, and sleep 'Gator,' whether you are into football or not, denying your orange and blue affiliation is sacrilegious." Some students mention their "laid-back" attitude, but others describe the pressure to conform. One student offers her outlook: "Everything is a fad, whether it be clothes, or a drug, or music."

Academics
The Sunshine State has affordable, quality schools, and the University of Florida might be the best of the bunch. UF offers excellent programs in career-track majors (a few of the more popular majors are business, journalism, engineering, and premeds). As with any large university, however, there is going to be some slipping through the cracks. The majority of Florida undergrads have serious complaints. "Administration is a pain in my ass," says one outspoken junior majoring in biology. And certainly a scary thought is entertained by this student: "Considering you never see the school's administration or professors, it's hard to comment on them." One student, however, offers a little hope: "It is very frustrating, but if you can get through the red tape, you can find a great education." Without a doubt school authorities have a tough task when laying down the law for so many students ("A sardine has more opportunities to express his personality and I had more freedom as a ten-year-old."), but as one student points out, "Individuality almost has to be compromised for general consensus." Underclassmen generally find themselves in huge classes, often taught by TAs, but most students feel like the quality of instruction is high: "Academically, UF is a great school." More than one mentions that "UF provides very unique ways of learning." The school's computer, health, and library facilities received extremely high marks.

Student Body
UF's affordability for in-state students ensures a healthy number of Floridians within the student body. However, many of the students mention diversity and interaction ("good chemistry!") as a strong suit. As this junior in biology insists, "The student body here is great!! Diversity is a wonderful part of this institution." And for those potential students worried about the size of the university, check out this student's comment: "You always have a group of friends no matter how large your school is." The formal dating scene receives high marks and praise from the respondents, although apparently not all see it that way, "Serious relationships are rare. Just hang out and hook up!"

ADMISSIONS

The admissions committee considers (in descending order of importance): HS record, test scores, recommendations. *Also considered (in descending order of importance):* extracurriculars, geographical distribution, personality, special talents. Either the SAT or ACT is required; SAT is preferred. Admissions process is need-blind. *High school units required/recommended:* 19 total units are required; 4 English required, 3 math required, 3 science required, 2 foreign language required, 3 social studies required. Minimum combined SAT I score of 970 (composite ACT score of 20) and minimum 2.0 GPA required. *Special Requirements:* A portfolio is required for art program applicants. An audition is required for music program applicants. TOEFL is required of all international students. Audition required of theatre and music program applicants.

The Inside Word

Practically every other high school graduate in the state applies to UF, which gives the admissions staff a huge pool of candidates to choose from. The selection process is driven by numbers, with little personal attention afforded anyone but athletes, legacies, minorities, and National Merit Scholars. Out-of-state students will find that getting into this "party school" isn't too easy. With budget cuts further restricting enrollment levels, it won't be long before admission to Florida is as difficult for out-of-staters as it is at such top public universities as North Carolina and Virginia.

FINANCIAL AID

Students should submit: FAFSA, the school's own financial aid form. The Princeton Review suggests that all financial aid forms be submitted as soon as possible after January 1. *The following grants/scholarships are offered:* Pell, SEOG, academic merit, athletic, the school's own scholarships, the school's own grants, state scholarships, state grants, private scholarships, private grants, ROTC. *Students borrow from the following loan programs:* Stafford, unsubsidized Stafford, Perkins, PLUS, the school's own loan fund, state loans, health professions loans, private loans. College Work-Study Program is available. Institutional employment is available. Freshmen are discouraged from working.

FROM THE ADMISSIONS OFFICE

University of Florida students come from more than 100 countries, all 50 states, and every one of the 67 counties in Florida. Nineteen percent of the student body is comprised of graduate students. Approximately 2,300 black students, 3,300 Hispanic students, and 2,200 Asian-American students attend UF. Ninety percent of the entering freshmen rank above the national mean of scores on standard entrance exams. UF consistently ranks near the top among public universities in the number of new National Merit and Achievement scholars in attendance.

ADMISSIONS

Admissions Rating	84
% of applicants accepted	67
% of acceptees attending	44

FRESHMAN PROFILE

Average verbal SAT	620
Average math SAT	640
Average ACT	27
Average TOEFL	550
Graduated top 20% of class	83
Graduated top 40% of class	83
Graduated top 60% of class	83
Average HS GPA or Avg.	3.4

DEADLINES

Early decision	11/1
Regular admission	2/1
Regular notification	3/24
Non-fall registration	yes

APPLICANTS ALSO LOOK AT

AND OFTEN PREFER

Georgia Tech.
Tulane
Florida St.

AND SOMETIMES PREFER

Clemson
West Virginia
U. South Florida
Florida A & M

AND RARELY PREFER

U. Miami
Howard

FINANCIAL FACTS

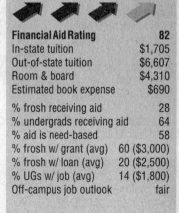

Financial Aid Rating	82
In-state tuition	$1,705
Out-of-state tuition	$6,607
Room & board	$4,310
Estimated book expense	$690
% frosh receiving aid	28
% undergrads receiving aid	64
% aid is need-based	58
% frosh w/ grant (avg)	60 ($3,000)
% frosh w/ loan (avg)	20 ($2,500)
% UGs w/ job (avg)	14 ($1,800)
Off-campus job outlook	fair

FORDHAM UNIVERSITY

113 WEST 60TH STREET, NEW YORK, NY 10023   ADMISSIONS: 800-367-3426   FAX: 718-367-9404

STUDENTS SPEAK OUT

Life
Fordham's main campus is in the Bronx, and the good side and the bad side of this location was the subject of many students' essays. While most students agree that the campus itself was safe and self-contained, many feel that some of the immediately surrounding neighborhoods are dangerous. The biggest problems occur at night: students enjoy the area bars and are not always cautious enough when returning home. Says one student, "You have to be smart about where you go at night." Still, there is a Little Italy nearby that is safe and chock-full of excellent restaurants. The Botanical Gardens and the Bronx Zoo, both of which are spectacular, are very close by. And, of course, there's Manhattan, accessible by subway or by the school-run shuttle bus. The Bronx campus is "absolutely beautiful—trees, old buildings...It's hard to believe it's in the middle of the Bronx!" Students who wish to stay on campus will find "enough activities, clubs, and organizations to suit anyone's needs." Many students get involved in neighborhood affairs by joining community service groups. Sports are popular, and the school's baseball team is top-notch.

Academics
One independent college counselor accurately characterizes Fordham as "an all-purpose Catholic university." Students pursue a wide range of studies: business, hard sciences, and the liberal arts all attract their fair share. A core curriculum provides, according to one biology major, "a solid liberal arts core, backed by one of the best science departments in the state." Students give Fordham good grades for class size. Although they give their professors only average grades, many students comment that profs are helpful and friendly. FU maintains two campuses: one is large, beautiful, and in the Bronx; the other is small, but gradually expanding, and near New York City's Lincoln Center. Explains one student, "One of the best things about Fordham is that there are two campuses. It is very easy to take advantage of opportunities on both campuses, as there is an intercampus transportation system." For pre-professionals, New York City provides plenty of internship opportunities.

Student Body
The typical Fordham student is bright, conservative, and Catholic. There is some friction between residents and commuters: residents tend to view commuters as "working class," and commuters see residents as stuck-up parochial school graduates. The real problem is that these two populations rarely get the chance to interact, so each group's preconceived notion of the other is almost never challenged. The conservatism of students and administrators can, at times, get oppressive: explains one student, "Since this is a Jesuit institution, not all viewpoints get expressed, particularly liberal ones about gays and premarital sex." The latter seems to bother students more than the former. One student sums up his experience saying, "Fordham—where you can drink like fish but you can't have sex."

ADMISSIONS

The admissions committee considers (in descending order of importance): HS record, class rank, test scores, recommendations, essay. *Also considered (in descending order of importance):* alumni relationship, extracurriculars, geographical distribution, personality, special talents. Either the SAT or ACT is required. An interview is recommended. Admissions process is need-blind. *High school units required/recommended:* 18 total units are required; 22 total units are recommended; 4 English required, 3 math required, 4 math recommended, 1 science required, 2 science recommended, 2 foreign language required, 2 social studies required, 4 social studies recommended. *Special Requirements:* TOEFL is required of all international students. 4 units of math and 1 unit each of chemistry and physics required of science program applicants. Stronger math background required of applicants to College of Business. *The admissions office says:* ""Interviews and tours are recommended for all applicants." The school catalog states that the admissions committee looks for "personal characteristics such as strength of character, intellectual and extracurricular interests, special talents, and potential for growing and developing within the environment and academic programs offered.""

The Inside Word

Candidates are reviewed by a committee made up of admissions officers, faculty, administrators, and deans. Admission to Fordham isn't nearly as competitive as it once was, but a solid flow of applicants from metropolitan area parochial schools keeps their student profile sound.

FINANCIAL AID

Students should submit: FAFSA, the school's own financial aid form. The Princeton Review suggests that all financial aid forms be submitted as soon as possible after January 1. *The following grants/scholarships are offered:* Pell, SEOG, academic merit, athletic, the school's own scholarships, the school's own grants, state scholarships, state grants, private scholarships, private grants, ROTC. *Students borrow from the following loan programs:* Stafford, Perkins, PLUS, the school's own loan fund, state loans, private loans. Applicants will be notified of awards beginning April 1. College Work-Study Program is available.

FROM THE ADMISSIONS OFFICE

"Fordham, an independent institution offering an education based on the Jesuit tradition, has two major campuses in New York City. The Rose Hill campus is an 85-acre traditional campus located next to the New York Botanical Garden and the Bronx Zoo. The Rose Hill campus is the largest 'green' campus in New York. The Lincoln Center campus, with a new 20-story residence hall, is located in the middle of Manhattan across from one of the world's greatest cultural centers, Lincoln Center for the Performing Arts. Fordham offers its students a variety of majors, concentrations and programs that can be combined with an extensive internship program. Fordham works with more than 2,000 organizations in the New York metropolitan area to arrange internships for students in fields such as business, communications, medicine, law and education."

ADMISSIONS

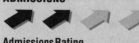

Admissions Rating	74
% of applicants accepted	68
% of acceptees attending	36

FRESHMAN PROFILE

Average verbal SAT	600
Average math SAT	560
Average ACT	NR
Average TOEFL	550
Graduated top 20% of class	54
Graduated top 40% of class	81
Graduated top 60% of class	94
Average HS GPA or Avg.	3.2

DEADLINES

Early decision	NR
Regular admission	2/1
Regular notification	3/1
Non-fall registration	yes

APPLICANTS ALSO LOOK AT

AND OFTEN PREFER

NYU
Binghamton U.
Columbia U.
Boston U.
Villanova

AND SOMETIMES PREFER

SUNY Albany
SUNY Stony Brook
George Washington
Boston Coll.
Siena

AND RARELY PREFER

St. John's U. (NY)
Iona
Hofstra

FINANCIAL FACTS

Financial Aid Rating	82
Tuition	$14,900
Room & board	$7,063
Estimated book expense	$500
% frosh receiving aid	85
% undergrads receiving aid	80
% aid is need-based	90
% frosh w/ grant (avg)	80 ($6,800)
% frosh w/ loan (avg)	76 ($2,200)
% UGs w/ job (avg)	40 ($1,600)
Off-campus job outlook	excellent

FRANKLIN & MARSHALL COLLEGE

UNDERGRADUATE ADMISSIONS, P.O. BOX 3003, LANCASTER, PA 17604-3003   ADMISSIONS: 717-291-3951   FAX: 717-291-4389

CAMPUS LIFE

Quality of Life Rating	**81**
Type of school	private
Affiliation	none
Environment	suburban

STUDENTS

FT undergrad enrollment	1,794
% male/female	53/47
% from out of state	65
% live on campus	74
% spend weekend on campus	80
% transfers	1
% from public high school	61
% in (# of) fraternities	45 (9)
% in (# of) sororities	30 (3)
% African-American	3
% Asian	11
% Caucasian	81
% Hispanic	4
% international	5
# of countries represented	50

WHAT'S HOT
college radio
library
Greeks
computer facilities
campus easy to get around

WHAT'S NOT
infrequent dating
town-gown relations
students are cliquish
intramural sports
Lancaster

ACADEMICS

Academic Rating	**90**
Profs Interesting Rating	91
Profs Accessible Rating	95
Calendar	semester
Student/teacher ratio	11:1
% profs tenured	98
Hours of study per day	3.74

MOST POPULAR MAJORS
government
English
business administration

% GRADS WHO PURSUE...
Law 10, Med 9, MBA 3, MA 9

STUDENTS SPEAK OUT

Life
Greek life is the center of student life at Franklin & Marshall, even though the administration has withdrawn official recognition. Many respondents praise the social scene, while others are less positive. A senior student majoring in psychology admits, "One of the big problems is frat life. It totally consumes the school. Those interested in doing something else will have to search to find it. This is not necessarily bad, just limiting." Another student takes a stronger view: "Life here without fraternities would suck unless you like chilling with the Amish." Still, at least some find other things to do at F & M: "There are the frats, but activist groups (gay rights, human rights, etc.) are gaining in prominence." A junior geology major agrees, "There are so many campus clubs that I wish I had more time to do everything I am interested in." Lancaster receives only passing marks as a college town, but many students pick out the restaurants as a particular bonus: "Lancaster has an excellent variety of restaurants."

Academics
Academics at Franklin & Marshall are no joke. One student sighs, "Rigorous, man, rigorous." While many students respond with comments about the demanding workload, most of them in the same breath are praising the efforts of the professors, deans, and the administration for providing them with a cool environment. As one student puts it, "I have had a rich academic experience, and I don't think F & M gets a good enough reputation for the demanding work load of the courses." Another student offers, "My professors are very knowledgeable. They really know what they are talking about—more importantly, they are my friends." A good number of students share anecdotes about professors waking up in the middle of the night to answer a question, hosting laid-back potluck dinners, or attending intramural sporting events. At F & M the majority of the students also feel good about the administration. One student insists, "This is the real reason to come to Franklin & Marshall: the approachability of administration." Another agrees, "The deans and administration are awesome!" So it's not too hard to see why so many students put up with the demands at Franklin & Marshall; most of them feel like they've got a good support group behind them. And with F & M's solid reputation, many students feel like they are bound to succeed after graduation. As one student points out, "Not a liberal arts college, really, but a pre-professional school."

Student Body
Over three-quarters of the students are white, with Asian students being the largest percentage of the minority population. A number of happy students had lots of glowing comments: "supportive," "caring," "friendly." There were some students who remarked about the diversity of the campus ("students from over forty countries!"), but many more criticize the "cloning" at Franklin & Marshall. One student jokes, "The J. Crew catalog basically sums up the students at F & M." Politically, the school is conservative. According to one student, "The school finds new ways to display its conservatism every day. They all need to lighten up and get the sticks out of their 'beep.'"

FINANCIAL AID: 717-291-3991

ADMISSIONS

The admissions committee considers (in descending order of importance): HS record, class rank, recommendations, test scores, essay. *Also considered (in descending order of importance):* extracurriculars, personality, special talents, alumni relationship, geographical distribution. Either the SAT or ACT is required. An interview is recommended. *High school units required/recommended:* 17 total units are recommended; 4 English recommended, 4 math recommended, 3 science recommended, 3 foreign language recommended, 3 social studies recommended. *Special Requirements:* TOEFL is required of all international students. Portfolio, audition, and interview recommended for demonstration of special skills or talent. *The admissions office says:* "Graded writing samples are accepted in place of standardized tests from students in the top ten percent of their high school classes."

The Inside Word

Admissions committees who are as particular as F & M's is about secondary school course selection quite often impose severe consequences on candidates who come up short. Applicants who are serious about attending the college should definitely interview; it will also help to make it known if F & M is one of your top choices. The college loses a lot of its admits to competitor colleges, and will take notice of a candidate who is likely to enroll.

FINANCIAL AID

Students should submit: FAFSA, state aid form, a copy of parents' most recent income tax filing. The Princeton Review suggests that all financial aid forms be submitted as soon as possible after January 1. *The following grants/scholarships are offered:* Pell, SEOG, academic merit, the school's own scholarships, the school's own grants, state scholarships, state grants, private scholarships, private grants, ROTC, foreign aid. *Students borrow from the following loan programs:* Stafford, unsubsidized Stafford, Perkins, PLUS, the school's own loan fund, state loans, private loans. Applicants will be notified of awards beginning March 24. College Work-Study Program is available. Institutional employment is available.

FROM THE ADMISSIONS OFFICE

"Franklin and Marshall students choose from a variety of fields of study, traditional and interdisciplinary, that typify liberal learning. Professors in all of these fields are committed to a common purpose, which is to teach students to think, speak and write with clarity and confidence. Whether the course is in theatre or in physics, the class will be small, engagement will be high, and discussion will dominate over lecture. Thus throughout his or her four years, beginning with the First Year Seminar, a student at Franklin and Marshall is repeatedly invited to active participation in intellectual play at a high level. Our graduates consistently testify to the high quality of an F & M education as a mental preparation for life."

ADMISSIONS

Admissions Rating	84
% of applicants accepted	66
% of acceptees attending	23

FRESHMAN PROFILE

Average verbal SAT	630
Average math SAT	620
Average ACT	26
Average TOEFL	600
Graduated top 20% of class	75
Graduated top 40% of class	97
Graduated top 60% of class	100
Average HS GPA or Avg.	NR

DEADLINES

Early decision	NR
Regular admission	2/1
Regular notification	4/1
Non-fall registration	yes

APPLICANTS ALSO LOOK AT

AND OFTEN PREFER

Pennsylvania
Hamilton
Cornell U.
Haverford
Lafayette

AND SOMETIMES PREFER

Lehigh
Bucknell
Dickinson
Colgate
Skidmore

AND RARELY PREFER

Gettysburg
Boston U.
Tufts

FINANCIAL FACTS

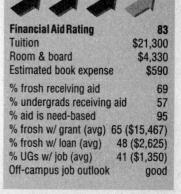

Financial Aid Rating	83
Tuition	$21,300
Room & board	$4,330
Estimated book expense	$590

% frosh receiving aid	69
% undergrads receiving aid	57
% aid is need-based	95
% frosh w/ grant (avg)	65 ($15,467)
% frosh w/ loan (avg)	48 ($2,625)
% UGs w/ job (avg)	41 ($1,350)
Off-campus job outlook	good

FURMAN UNIVERSITY

3300 POINSETT HIGHWAY, GREENVILLE, SC 29613 | ADMISSIONS: 864-294-2034 | FAX: 864-294-3127

CAMPUS LIFE

Quality of Life Rating   **85**
Type of school	private
Affiliation	none
Environment	metropolis

STUDENTS
FT undergrad enrollment	2,256
% male/female	45/55
% from out of state	70
% live on campus	60
% spend weekend on campus	75
% transfers	1
% from public high school	75
% in (# of) fraternities	35 (9)
% in (# of) sororities	35 (8)
% African-American	4
% Asian	2
% Caucasian	93
% Hispanic	1
% international	2
# of countries represented	17

WHAT'S HOT
religion
campus is beautiful
town-gown relations
intramural sports
music associations

WHAT'S NOT
sex
drugs
lack of diversity on campus
library
beer

ACADEMICS

Academic Rating   **86**
Profs Interesting Rating	92
Profs Accessible Rating	93
Calendar	trimester
Student/teacher ratio	12:1
% profs PhD/tenured	90/86
Hours of study per day	3.38

MOST POPULAR MAJORS
political science
health/exercise science
business administration

% GRADS WHO PURSUE...
Law 3, Med 4, MBA 1, MA 24

STUDENTS SPEAK OUT

Life

Students refer to Furman University as "the Country Club of the South" because of its large, well-manicured campus and sports facilities (tennis courts, softball fields, and an eighteen-hole golf course). Not surprisingly, students here are very athletic, and sports, both intramural and intercollegiate, are very popular. School-sponsored activities, while numerous, are less popular because the campus is dry. (Writes one student, "The school needs to open up a bit and get rid of this dry campus, but other than that everyone is really friendly.") Other on-campus regulations include an unpopular dorm visitation schedule (though visitation hours were recently extended). Social life centers on the fraternities and sororities located off campus, whose parties provide a haven for drinkers. Extracurricular clubs and community service groups located on campus also serve as gathering spots and are strongly supported by students. As one mentions, "Furman's got so much community you'd think you were in Mr. Rogers' neighborhood." All in all, Furman is "a very close-knit community," but only for those who can live within the administration's precepts; as one student who couldn't cope put it, "For the typical Furman student, the big issues are whether condoms should be on campus and how many Baptist teachers there are. It's prison."

Academics

Furman is a small school best known for its lush campus. But Furman is also a solid academic institution, especially for the pre-professional-minded student: over forty percent of the school's undergraduates proceed from here to graduate programs within a year of graduation. Political science, biology, health and exercise science are the most popular majors, but premedical majors, the visual and performing arts, and English are all considered strong by undergraduates. All students must complete a range of distribution requirements, which include both a religion course and an African or Asian studies course. Students report that "academically, Furman is rather strenuous; however, the professors are extremely helpful and accessible." Extra praise is heaped on the "new president, who has brought in a new, young perspective to the administration."

Student Body

Furman's religious orientation and small minority population are contributing factors toward what most students would admit is a "pretty homogeneous student body." One student characterizes her classmates this way: "The majority of students are very religious, study all the time, and are conscientious about finding a lifetime partner." Most students are "narrowly focused on doing well and preparing their futures for success," which leads one to report, "Students are academically and socially successful, though, as a whole, somewhat lacking in depth." Furman students are among the most conservative and most religious student bodies we surveyed, and, unsurprisingly, "the gay lifestyle at Furman is met with hostility and extreme moral disapproval."

FINANCIAL AID: 864-294-2204   E-MAIL: SHI_DAVID/FURMAN@FURMAN.EDU   WEB SITE: HTTP://WWW.FURMAN.EDU/

ADMISSIONS

The admissions committee considers (in descending order of importance): HS record, test scores, essay, class rank. *Also considered (in descending order of importance):* extracurriculars, personality, alumni relationship, special talents. Either the SAT or ACT is required. Admissions process is need-blind. *High school units required/recommended:* 4 English recommended, 4 math recommended, 3 science recommended, 3 foreign language recommended, 3 social studies recommended. Minimum 3.0 GPA in college prep courses recommended. *Special Requirements:* An audition is required for music program applicants. TOEFL is required of all international students. *The admissions office says:* "While our Early Decision process is not binding by application, it does require a response date of February 1."

The Inside Word

While Furman is selective academically, a high level of self-selection on the part of its applicants makes for a high acceptance rate. Good students who truly want to be here will encounter little resistance from the admissions committee.

FINANCIAL AID

Students should submit: FAFSA (due February 1), CSS Profile (due February 1), the school's own financial aid form (due February 1), state aid form (due June 30), Divorced Parents form (due February 1). The Princeton Review suggests that all financial aid forms be submitted as soon as possible after January 1. *The following grants/scholarships are offered:* Pell, SEOG, academic merit, athletic, the school's own scholarships, the school's own grants, state scholarships, state grants, private scholarships, private grants, ROTC, foreign aid. *Students borrow from the following loan programs:* Stafford, unsubsidized Stafford, Perkins, PLUS, the school's own loan fund, state loans, private loans. Applicants will be notified of awards beginning March 15. College Work-Study Program is available. Institutional employment is available.

FROM THE ADMISSIONS OFFICE

"Furman University offers an excellent liberal arts education and quality of life. Outside the classroom, the university places a high value on community service. Furman is regularly recognized as one of the nation's top educational bargains."

ADMISSIONS

Admissions Rating	78
% of applicants accepted	80
% of acceptees attending	30

FRESHMAN PROFILE

Average verbal SAT	610
Average math SAT	610
Average ACT	26
Average TOEFL	600
Graduated top 20% of class	77
Graduated top 40% of class	96
Graduated top 60% of class	100
Average HS GPA or Avg.	3.6

DEADLINES

Early decision	12/1
Regular admission	2/1
Regular notification	3/15
Non-fall registration	no

APPLICANTS ALSO LOOK AT

AND OFTEN PREFER

Wake Forest
Duke
UNC-Chapel Hill
Washington and Lee
Vanderbilt

AND SOMETIMES PREFER

Emory
Davidson
U. South Carolina, Columbia
Georgia Tech.
Wofford

AND RARELY PREFER

Clemson
Auburn U.

FINANCIAL FACTS

Financial Aid Rating	81
Tuition	$15,360
Room & board	$4,304
Estimated book expense	$600
% frosh receiving aid	63
% undergrads receiving aid	69
% aid is need-based	60
% frosh w/ grant (avg)	47 ($8,500)
% frosh w/ loan (avg)	63 ($2,600)
% UGs w/ job (avg)	27 ($1,200)
Off-campus job outlook	good

GEORGE MASON UNIVERSITY

4400 UNIVERSITY DRIVE, FAIRFAX, VA 22030   ADMISSIONS: 703-993-2400   FAX: 703-993-8707

CAMPUS LIFE

Quality of Life Rating   **77**
Type of school   public
Affiliation   none
Environment   suburban

STUDENTS

FT undergrad enrollment	9,508
% male/female	45/55
% from out of state	10
% live on campus	12
% spend weekend on campus	NR
% transfers	51
% from public high school	93
% in (# of) fraternities	10 (20)
% in (# of) sororities	8 (10)
% African-American	7
% Asian	14
% Caucasian	69
% Hispanic	5
% international	3
# of countries represented	83

WHAT'S HOT

ethnic diversity on campus
town-gown relations
old-fashioned dating
political activism
religion

WHAT'S NOT

campus difficult to get around
students are unhappy
intramural sports
hard liquor
unattractive campus

ACADEMICS

Academic Rating	**74**
Profs Interesting Rating	68
Profs Accessible Rating	66
Calendar	semester
Student/teacher ratio	17:1
% profs tenured	95
Hours of study per day	2.65

MOST POPULAR MAJORS

business administration
psychology
English

STUDENTS SPEAK OUT

Life

George Mason is "basically a commuter school, but if you never live on or near campus you really miss out." The administration is aiming to increase the number of campus dwellers by building new dorms, but for the time being most people still drive to school and scramble for parking spaces. Greek organizations dominate the social scene on campus ("Greek life or no life"), and off-campus partying mostly takes place in private houses and apartments, with lots of drinking the main attraction. Some just don't have time to party ("working and living off campus take up a lot of the time that could be spent socializing"), and those that do wish the parties were better and more numerous. Luckily, D.C. is close (about half an hour away) and accessible without a car, so "most people go into the city for fun." Many students think campus life would improve if GMU had a football team.

Academics

George Mason, a Virginia state school located southwest of Washington, D.C., has been building its reputation as an up-and-coming powerhouse for quite a while. The consensus among students is that "Mason is getting better and better every year." Students describe its strong and improving faculty as "generally extremely good." Competitive programs in economics, business, and communications help further the perception of this school as a major new force in higher education. However, Mason has been growing unevenly and not all departments are standouts. New facilities support the school's image of progress, but unfortunately other important resources, most notably the library, are still substandard. The administration has trouble keeping up with the school's growth, creating a public relations problem with the students, who largely perceive administrators as excessively concerned with the school's reputation at the expense of their welfare. The biggest problem here is that class offerings are limited and classes fill too quickly. Several students note that "If it was not for the beer and alcohol, I feel that no one could bear the whole 6 years it takes to graduate." Despite these quirks, however, Mason has demonstrated a tremendous surge in quality over the past few years, and should not be overlooked.

Student Body

George Mason boasts a student body that is "incredibly diverse." It is a source of pride here that "the people tend to be more open-minded and there is a better opportunity to expand your horizons." The student body contains enough international students for it to be "easy to walk across campus and not hear a single conversation in English." Undergraduates frequently find continuing education students in their classes, particularly those taught in the evening; writes one undergraduate, "Many students are older and married with children. Many viewpoints are expressed in class discussions."

ADMISSIONS

The admissions committee considers (in descending order of importance): HS record, essay, recommendations, test scores, class rank. *Also considered (in descending order of importance):* alumni relationship, extracurriculars, personality, special talents. Either the SAT or ACT is required. An interview is required. Admissions process is need-blind. *High school units required/recommended:* 16 total units are required; 22 total units are recommended; 4 English required, 3 math required, 4 math recommended, 1 science required, 3 science recommended, 2 foreign language required, 3 foreign language recommended, 3 social studies required, 4 social studies recommended. *Special Requirements:* A portfolio is required for art program applicants. An audition is required for music program applicants. TOEFL is required of all international students. *The admissions office says:* "Those denied admission are encouraged to contact an admissions officer to discuss plans for future enrollment possibilities at GMU."

The Inside Word

George Mason is a popular destination for college for two key reasons: its proximity to Washington, D.C. and the fact that it is not nearly as difficult to gain admission at GMU as it is at UVA or William and Mary, the two flagships of the Virginia state system. The university's quality faculty and impressive facilities make it worth taking a look if low-cost, solid programs in the D.C. area are high on your list.

FINANCIAL AID

Students should submit: FAFSA. The Princeton Review suggests that all financial aid forms be submitted as soon as possible after January 1. *The following grants/scholarships are offered:* Pell, SEOG, academic merit, athletic, the school's own scholarships, the school's own grants, state scholarships, state grants, private scholarships, private grants, federal nursing scholarship, ROTC. *Students borrow from the following loan programs:* Stafford, unsubsidized Stafford, Perkins, PLUS, the school's own loan fund, state loans, private loans. College Work-Study Program is available. Institutional employment is available.

FROM THE ADMISSIONS OFFICE

"George Mason University president, George Johnson, is fond of saying, 'To build a great university, get good people first; the bricks and mortar will follow.' Over the past decade, the university has acquired one of the finest faculties in the nation. Roger Wilkins, who is a distinguished Clarence J. Robinson professor, a Pulitzer Prize-winning journalist, and former Assistant U.S. Attorney General, loves to say, 'At George Mason, you will never be told 'No, you can't do that here.' Instead, we say, 'Let's do it. Let's try it and see what happens.'"

ADMISSIONS

Admissions Rating	74
% of applicants accepted	79
% of acceptees attending	40

FRESHMAN PROFILE

Average verbal SAT	580
Average math SAT	570
Average ACT	NR
Average TOEFL	570
Graduated top 20% of class	NR
Graduated top 40% of class	NR
Graduated top 60% of class	NR
Average HS GPA or Avg.	3.0

DEADLINES

Early decision	12/1
Regular admission	2/1
Regular notification	4/1
Non-fall registration	yes

APPLICANTS ALSO LOOK AT

AND OFTEN PREFER

U. Virginia
Georgetown U.
William and Mary
James Madison
Virginia Tech.

AND SOMETIMES PREFER

George Washington

FINANCIAL FACTS

Financial Aid Rating	73
In-state tuition	$4,212
Out-of-state tuition	$11,604
Room & board	$4,930
Estimated book expense	$580
% frosh receiving aid	46
% undergrads receiving aid	39
% aid is need-based	76
% frosh w/ grant (avg)	34 ($3,132)
% frosh w/ loan (avg)	40 ($3,849)
% UGs w/ job (avg)	5 ($1,600)
Off-campus job outlook	good

GEORGE WASHINGTON UNIVERSITY

WASHINGTON, DC 20052 ADMISSIONS: 800-447-3765 FAX: 202-994-0458

CAMPUS LIFE

Quality of Life Rating **89**
Type of school private
Affiliation none
Environment metropolis

STUDENTS
FT undergrad enrollment	5,630
% male/female	48/52
% from out of state	87
% live on campus	54
% spend weekend on campus	90
% transfers	17
% from public high school	80
% in (# of) fraternities	16 (13)
% in (# of) sororities	12 (8)
% African-American	7
% Asian	11
% Caucasian	61
% Hispanic	4
% international	2
# of countries represented	93

WHAT'S HOT
Washington
dorms
ethnic diversity on campus
campus feels safe
health facilities

WHAT'S NOT
unattractive campus
beer
library
drugs
inefficient administration

ACADEMICS

Academic Rating **76**
Profs Interesting Rating 74
Profs Accessible Rating 77
Calendar semester
Student/teacher ratio 14:1
% profs tenured 93
Hours of study per day 2.96

MOST POPULAR MAJORS
international affairs
business administration
biology

% GRADS WHO PURSUE...
Law 5, Med 3, MBA 3, MA 11

STUDENTS SPEAK OUT

Life
As at most urban schools, the major influence on quality of life at George Washington University is the city itself. One student explains it: "D.C. provides a wealth of opportunities for work and entertainment." Like NYU, BU, and many other "downtown" schools, GW has no discernible campus. School spirit and a strong sense of community among students are, accordingly, low. "Much of the school is split up into cliques," explains one senior, "such as Deadheads, fraternities, ROTCs, internationals, African-Americans, and the leftover malcontents. And, sorry, I forgot the left- and right-wingers, the most tedious of all." "The majority of people here love to party," says another, "but they don't party together." Fortunately, the student body is diverse enough that, eventually, students find where they fit in. Warning to those who think all city dwellers are wild partiers: a relatively large proportion of students come here looking to get married. Dorms are reportedly comfortable and safe, which will definitely be news to alumni.

Academics
Politics is the hot ticket at GW. The school is located in downtown D.C., just a few blocks down the street from the White House, so both the faculty and guest-lecturer rosters are well populated with government bigwigs. "Where else can you attend lectures by political aides and notables, where else can you be taught by an aide to four presidents?" asks one undergrad. Not surprisingly, the international affairs and pre-law programs are strong, too: one in ten graduates goes on to law school within a year. Students report that they study only two hours a day, lowest in the country, reaffirming the school's reputation as a party school and raising the question of how demanding the course work is. The library gets low marks—"the minuscule amount of information available there is generally obsolete and extremely difficult to locate"—but students have access to the Library of Congress, America's library.

Student Body
"Many people describe GW as a segregated melting pot," reports one student. Indeed, GW has a pretty diverse student body, particularly loaded with international students. "We have everything from the NY/Long Island fraternity contingent to Arab/Middle East oil barons and diplomats," is the way one woman puts it. She doesn't mention African-American students, who make up a small percentage of the student body. The school has a large contingent of nineties-style pot-smoking hippies, Deadhead preppies, and lots of their detractors. A comment we commonly hear at other schools was "the students are so friendly here." Not at GW: what we most often hear here was that "students all have attitudes." Don't say you weren't warned.

FINANCIAL AID: 202-994-6620

ADMISSIONS

The admissions committee considers (in descending order of importance): HS record, class rank, test scores, recommendations, essay. *Also considered (in descending order of importance):* alumni relationship, extracurriculars, geographical distribution, personality, special talents. Either the SAT or ACT is required. An interview is recommended. Admissions process is need-blind. *High school units required/recommended:* 16 total units are required; 4 English required, 2 math required, 2 science required, 2 foreign language required, 1 social studies required, 1 history required. *Special Requirements:* An audition is required for music program applicants. TOEFL is required of all international students. 4 units of math (2 algebra, 1 plane geometry, 1/2 plane trigonometry, 1/2 precalculus), 1 unit of physics, and 1 unit of chemistry required of engineering program applicants.

The Inside Word

The low percentage of admitted students who enroll at GW works to keep the admit rate relatively high. For strong students, this is definitely a low-stress admissions process. The university's location and access to faculty with impressive credentials are the main reasons for GW's sound freshman profile.

FINANCIAL AID

Students should submit: FAFSA, CSS Profile, a copy of parents' most recent income tax filing. The Princeton Review suggests that all financial aid forms be submitted as soon as possible after January 1. *The following grants/scholarships are offered:* Pell, SEOG, academic merit, athletic, the school's own scholarships, the school's own grants, state scholarships, state grants, private scholarships, private grants, ROTC, foreign aid. *Students borrow from the following loan programs:* Stafford, unsubsidized Stafford, Perkins, PLUS. Applicants will be notified of awards beginning April 1. College Work-Study Program is available. Institutional employment is available.

FROM THE ADMISSIONS OFFICE

"At GW, we welcome students who show a measure of impatience with the limitations of traditional education. At many universities, the edge of campus is the real world, but not at GW, where our campus and Washington, D.C., are seamless. We look for bold, bright students who are ambitious, energetic, and self-motivated. Here, where we are so close to the centers of thought and action in every field we offer, we easily integrate our outstanding academic tradition and faculty connections with the best internship and job opportunities of Washington, D.C. A generous scholarship and financial assistance program attracts top students from all parts of the country and the world."

ADMISSIONS

Admissions Rating	86
% of applicants accepted	59
% of acceptees attending	27

FRESHMAN PROFILE

Average verbal SAT	630
Average math SAT	600
Average ACT	27
Average TOEFL	550
Graduated top 20% of class	67
Graduated top 40% of class	94
Graduated top 60% of class	99
Average HS GPA or Avg.	NR

DEADLINES

Early decision	NR
Regular admission	NR
Regular notification	rolling
Non-fall registration	yes

APPLICANTS ALSO LOOK AT

AND OFTEN PREFER

Georgetown U.
U. Virginia
Boston U.
Emory
NYU

AND SOMETIMES PREFER

Tufts
U. Vermont
U. Maryland, Coll. Park
American
Catholic

FINANCIAL FACTS

Financial Aid Rating	77
Tuition	$18,300
Room & board	$6,328
Estimated book expense	$700
% frosh receiving aid	78
% undergrads receiving aid	70
% aid is need-based	66
% frosh w/ grant (avg)	75 ($9,926)
% frosh w/ loan (avg)	51 ($5,499)
% UGs w/ job (avg)	NR ($2,450)
Off-campus job outlook	excellent

GEORGETOWN UNIVERSITY

37TH AND O STREETS, NW, WASHINGTON, DC 20057   ADMISSIONS: 202-687-3600   FAX: 202-687-5084

STUDENTS SPEAK OUT

Life

Time and again the students of Georgetown University praise the city of Washington, D.C. and the university for offering a ton of stuff to do. One student says, "Georgetown's social life is one of the best in the nation." Adds another, "GU is in a great city with tons of off campus cultural and social activities. It's never boring!" But bring your cash card, because the fun doesn't come cheap. One student responds, "Everything here costs something—the school will drain you for all you are worth." And keep in mind that some feel social skills here are limited. One frustrated student says, "My main problem here is the parties. For the people here a party is just getting drunk." Not every activity involves beer and money; campus clubs are very popular, as are intramural sports. And Georgetown is unique in another respect. One student brags, "Where else can you find a school like GU with a basketball ranking of number 2 in the country?" Even though the dating scene is a little frigid, you probably won't be lonely ("group activity is very common"). And the school's affiliation with the Catholic church is only apparent in its poor reproductive health services (counseling, availability of birth control/medical treatment). All in all, students dig life at Georgetown.

Academics

Georgetown divides the university into five self-contained schools: Arts and Sciences, Business Administration, Nursing, Foreign Service, and Language and Linguistics. A couple of students mention that this tends to split up the students, even though every student is required to take a certain number of core requirements, including courses in liberal arts and religious studies. But no matter which school you're in, get ready to hit the books ("We enjoy studying!"), because most of the students study 3 to 5 hours every day. The professors receive high grades from the students. One student says, "All my profs take a genuine interest in how I do." And another one adds, "It's nice to go to a school where professors are always being consulted by the media and politicians alike." However, she warns about the school's celebrity faculty, "It is a rare occurrence to actually get [those] professors for a class." Overall, both class registration and the bursar receive poor grades, and many students mention the huge amount of red tape and bureaucracy. A first-year chemistry student says, "Many of the procedures you have to go through are frustrating." A laid-back political science student agrees, "Administration is a bit distant." But some students point out other positive aspects of the administration. "The school's administration is good for me, because it is possible to see my dean whenever I am having troubles with any courses." Another advantage of GU's academics is that learning is not limited to class: "Georgetown has offered me a wide range of activities both inside and outside the classroom."

Student Body

"The people here are very smart, but they are not nerds," insists one freshman chemistry student. It's true, a lot Georgetown students are very serious about their academics ("most have a passion for academics"), though they are not particularly intellectual; they place a high priority on landing a job once they are finished with college. This can be good and bad, as one sophomore points out, "Students at Georgetown are extremely pre-professional. I find it difficult to get anyone to participate in something that isn't going to enhance a resume." As far as diversity goes, a good percentage of the students are foreign nationals, and minority groups have small but not invisible numbers. GU can be proud of this student's praise: "I am very happy to get along so well with students of different social, cultural, and ethnic groups."

ADMISSIONS

The admissions committee considers (in descending order of importance): HS record, test scores, class rank, recommendations, essay. *Also considered (in descending order of importance):* extracurriculars, alumni relationship, geographical distribution, personality, special talents. Either the SAT or ACT is required. An interview is required. *High school units required/recommended:* 4 English recommended, 3 math recommended, 2 science recommended, 2 foreign language recommended, 2 social studies recommended. *Special Requirements:* TOEFL is required of all international students. 4 units of math and 3 units of science required of math and science program applicants. Chemistry, biology, and physics required of nursing program applicants. Language background required of foreign service and language program applicants. *The admissions office says:* "Students who plan a program in mathematics or science should include four years of math and at least three years of science. Candidates for the nursing program (are recommended to include) one year of biology, one year of chemistry, and one year of physics."

The Inside Word

It was always tough to get admitted to Georgetown, but in the early 1980s Patrick Ewing and the Hoyas created a basketball sensation that catapulted the place into position as one of the most selective universities in the nation. There has been no turning back since. GU gets almost ten applications for every space in the entering class, and the academic strength of the pool is impressive. Virtually 50 percent of the entire student body took AP courses in high school. Candidates who are wait-listed here should hold little hope for an offer of admission; over the past several years Georgetown has taken very few off their lists.

FINANCIAL AID

Students should submit: FAFSA, a copy of parents' most recent income tax filing. The Princeton Review suggests that all financial aid forms be submitted as soon as possible after January 1. *The following grants/scholarships are offered:* Pell, SEOG, athletic, the school's own scholarships, the school's own grants, state scholarships, state grants, private scholarships, private grants, ROTC. *Students borrow from the following loan programs:* Stafford, unsubsidized Stafford, Perkins, PLUS, federal nursing loans, private loans. Applicants will be notified of awards beginning April 1. College Work-Study Program is available. Institutional employment is available.

FROM THE ADMISSIONS OFFICE

"Georgetown was founded in 1789 by John Carroll, who concurred with his contemporaries Benjamin Franklin and Thomas Jefferson in believing that the success of the young democracy depended upon an educated and virtuous citizenry. Carroll founded the school with the dynamic, Jesuit tradition of education, characterized by humanism and committed to the assumption of responsibility and action. Georgetown is a national and international university, enrolling students from all fifty states and over 100 foreign countries. Undergraduate students are enrolled in one of five undergraduate schools: the College of Arts and Sciences, School of Foreign Service, School of Languages and Linguistics, Georgetown School of Business, and the Georgetown School of Nursing. All students share a common liberal arts core and have access to the entire university curriculum."

ADMISSIONS

Admissions Rating	97
% of applicants accepted	24
% of acceptees attending	47

FRESHMAN PROFILE

Average verbal SAT	670
Average math SAT	650
Average ACT	29
Average TOEFL	550
Graduated top 20% of class	88
Graduated top 40% of class	98
Graduated top 60% of class	100
Average HS GPA or Avg.	NR

DEADLINES

Early decision	NR
Regular admission	1/10
Regular notification	4/1
Non-fall registration	no

APPLICANTS ALSO LOOK AT

AND OFTEN PREFER
Duke
Harvard/Radcliffe
U. Virginia
Yale
Stanford

AND SOMETIMES PREFER
Pennsylvania
U. Chicago
Cornell U.
Boston Coll.

AND RARELY PREFER
Syracuse
Tulane
Emory

FINANCIAL FACTS

Financial Aid Rating	86
Tuition	$19,230
Room & board	$7,131
Estimated book expense	NR
% frosh receiving aid	54
% undergrads receiving aid	52
% aid is need-based	65
% frosh w/ grant (avg)	51 ($11,051)
% frosh w/ loan (avg)	39 ($2,661)
% UGs w/ job (avg)	48 ($2,500)
Off-campus job outlook	excellent

GEORGIA INSTITUTE OF TECHNOLOGY

225 NORTH AVENUE, NW, ATLANTA, GA 30332 ‖ ADMISSIONS: 404-894-4154 ‖ FAX: 404-853-9163

CAMPUS LIFE

Quality of Life Rating **70**
Type of school | public
Affiliation | none
Environment | metropolis

STUDENTS

FT undergrad enrollment	8,821
% male/female	73/27
% from out of state	37
% live on campus	62
% spend weekend on campus	82
% transfers	15
% from public high school	85
% in (# of) fraternities	30 (31)
% in (# of) sororities	27 (8)
% African-American	10
% Asian	11
% Caucasian	75
% Hispanic	4
% international	21
# of countries represented	71

WHAT'S HOT
intercollegiate sports
Atlanta
off-campus food
intramural sports
ethnic diversity on campus

WHAT'S NOT
library
unattractive campus
campus difficult to get around
students are unhappy
support groups

ACADEMICS

Academic Rating	**76**
Profs Interesting Rating	60
Profs Accessible Rating	61
Calendar	quarter
Student/teacher ratio	20:1
% profs PhD/tenured	91/58
Hours of study per day	3.13

MOST POPULAR MAJORS
mechanical engineering
electrical engineering
industrial engineering

STUDENTS SPEAK OUT

Life
Some students at the Georgia Institute of Technology report that after hitting the books, there is very little time for social activities. This student declares, "I came here to learn, not to enrich my social life." Of course, some students disagree and do find the time to unwind. And apparently they get pretty creative: "Soapy, sudsing fountains manage to mysteriously pop up on campus during the weekends." Attending athletic events (especially against the University of Georgia and ACC rivals Duke and Florida State) and working out at the student athletic complex are two popular things to do. And there's always Atlanta, with excellent restaurants (food off campus is given very high marks), bars, and concerts. With almost a third of students pledging, Greek life is a big part of the culture at Tech. According to one student, "Social life revolves around the Greeks," although there are plenty of other campus clubs and organizations. Students rank alcohol (especially beer) as very popular, and most of them point to the level of day-to-day stress as the reason for this ("Tech is a pressure cooker"). But drinking is not the only outlet for Tech students. The university sponsors over 170 organizations including a model UN team and an improvisational comedy troupe. For this senior in physics, "The student organizations at Tech are what makes this school so great." In the end, Georgia Tech students know how to have a good time. "If we didn't," says one, "we'd probably die."

Academics
"Dedication to your college career is required to survive at Tech." Time and again the students mention that study time is crucial to success. Some students choose to think of life at Tech as an investment. As this student writes, "The most important thing at Tech is to remember you only get out what you put in." Many students mention the academic competition as a drag ("too many competing egos"), but others find this to be a positive motivating force: "It's like the students and professors are all urging you along to graduate." The professors are given average marks, but most students find them "accessible" and "helpful." Some students feel like the professors concentrate too much on research, and that they make tests too difficult: "Georgia Tech is often harder than it should be." TAs staff labs and recitations, which can be frustrating: one student grumbles that "the first two years are usually spent listening to TAs correcting themselves." Some tell us that "administration is a major headache," and wish for more support in their times of stress.

Student Body
Georgia Tech can brag about its racial diversity, with almost one-third of the student body population representing minorities. And the students appreciate this: "It's great to have such diversity." Geographical diversity is not as strong due to cheap in-state tuition for Georgia natives. Interaction is also not always the best, with one undergrad reporting "no mingling between the 'niches' and 'cliques'." Still, overall, the sentiment that "Tech is a fairly open, friendly community" rules. And as this senior civil engineering student writes, "Tech graduates are known to be able to go out into the real world and be very successful. We are an extremely independent breed." Politically, the students are pretty middle-of-the-road with a better-than-average level of commitment.

FINANCIAL AID: 404-894-4160

ADMISSIONS

The admissions committee considers (in descending order of importance): HS record, test scores. Also considered (in descending order of importance): alumni relationship, special talents. Either the SAT or ACT is required; SAT is preferred. High school units required/recommended: 16 total units are required; 4 English required, 4 math required, 3 science required, 2 foreign language required, 1 social studies required, 2 history required. Chemistry required of engineering and science program applicants. TOEFL is required of all international students. The admissions office says: "We have an Apply By Computer program which provides on-line access and we waive the application fee for students who use the ABC program. Georgia residents and children/relatives of alumni receive extra consideration."

The Inside Word

Tech follows strict formulas in the admissions process; candidates must have solid grades and test scores in order to be competitive. It may be easier to gain admission for some quarters rather than others; fall is likely to be the most selective because the fall applicant pool is by far the year's largest.

FINANCIAL AID

Students should submit: FAFSA (due March 1), the school's own financial aid form (due March 1). The Princeton Review suggests that all financial aid forms be submitted as soon as possible after January 1. The following grants/scholarships are offered: Pell, SEOG, academic merit, athletic, the school's own scholarships, the school's own grants, state scholarships, state grants, private scholarships, private grants, ROTC. Students borrow from the following loan programs: Stafford, unsubsidized Stafford, Perkins, PLUS, the school's own loan fund, state loans, private loans. Applicants will be notified of awards beginning April 15. College Work-Study Program is available. Institutional employment is available.

FROM THE ADMISSIONS OFFICE

Georgia Tech is ranked third among engineering schools and 25th among business schools, and is called a great buy among science/technology schools by national publications. Tech consistently ranks in the top three among public colleges in the percentage of National Merit and National Achievement Scholars and has the largest voluntary cooperative education program in America. Tech's low cost, focus on experiential education, and reputation with employers and graduate schools insures students receive the greatest return on their educational investment. However, the only way you can know if Georgia Tech is the right place for you is to visit the campus. Seeing is believing and we strongly encourage you to come to Atlanta, take one of our student-guided walking tours, and speak with current students and faculty. It is the only way you can be sure you are making the best decision for you.

ADMISSIONS

Admissions Rating	86
% of applicants accepted	62
% of acceptees attending	40

FRESHMAN PROFILE

Average verbal SAT	630
Average math SAT	660
Average ACT	NR
Average TOEFL	620
Graduated top 20% of class	90
Graduated top 40% of class	99
Graduated top 60% of class	100
Average HS GPA or Avg.	3.6

DEADLINES

Early decision	NR
Regular admission	2/1
Regular notification	3/15
Non-fall registration	yes

APPLICANTS ALSO LOOK AT

AND OFTEN PREFER

UC-Berkeley
Duke
Mass. Tech.
UNC-Chapel Hill

AND SOMETIMES PREFER

Florida St.
U. Florida
U. Georgia
Clemson

AND RARELY PREFER

Carnegie Mellon
Auburn U.
Emory
Virginia Tech.

FINANCIAL FACTS

Financial Aid Rating	76
In-state tuition	$2,685
Out-of-state tuition	$8,946
Room & board	$5,700
Estimated book expense	$900
% frosh receiving aid	60
% undergrads receiving aid	68
% aid is need-based	56
% frosh w/ grant (avg)	56 ($2,700)
% frosh w/ loan (avg)	40 ($2,625)
% UGs w/ job (avg)	NR
Off-campus job outlook	excellent

UNIVERSITY OF GEORGIA

ATHENS, GA 30602   ADMISSIONS: 706-542-2112   FAX: 706-542-1466

CAMPUS LIFE

Quality of Life Rating	87
Type of school	public
Affiliation	none
Environment	suburban

STUDENTS

FT undergrad enrollment	22,000
% male/female	45/55
% from out of state	20
% live on campus	35
% spend weekend on campus	70
% transfers	34
% from public high school	87
% in (# of) fraternities	16 (26)
% in (# of) sororities	21 (22)
% African-American	6
% Asian	2
% Caucasian	90
% Hispanic	1
% international	2
# of countries represented	127

WHAT'S HOT

health facilities
student publications
campus food
cigarettes
off-campus food

WHAT'S NOT

student government
theater
registration is a pain
dorms
lab facilities

ACADEMICS

Academic Rating	73
Profs Interesting Rating	66
Profs Accessible Rating	68
Calendar	quarter
Student/teacher ratio	14:1
% profs PhD/tenured	75/65
Hours of study per day	2.73

MOST POPULAR MAJORS

general business
pre-medicine
pre-journalism

STUDENTS SPEAK OUT

Life

Like Boulder and a relative handful of other college towns, Athens is a magnet that has prompted many a high school grad to head to University of Georgia. Some feel "Athens is the reason to go to this school." According to one student, "The best part of Georgia is the social and cultural aspect...[Athens] is a college town with lots of arts, entertainment, outdoor activities, bars, and clubs. There is never a lack of something to do." There may not be a college town that has had more of an impact on youth culture over the past ten years than Athens, a wellspring of musical talent that spawned the "alternative rock" of REM and the B-52s, among others. Campus life is also thriving—although only a third of all students live there, the University reports that over two-thirds are on campus on weekends. A total of 48 frats and sororities no doubt do their share to keep things lively, as do sports—especially the football team. The annual clash between the Bulldogs and the Florida Gators is one of the biggest rivalries in college football. For those less enamored of a social life centered on partying, 300 campus organizations provide plenty of alternatives.

Academics

"My overall academic experience at the University of Georgia has been a positive one. Honors classes, ease of registration, diversity on campus and most of all the high caliber of professors have enhanced my college experience." Such comments typify those we received from the majority of students surveyed at UGA. Few universities of its size have earned as much overall praise from their students. Many of the students we polled here didn't apply anywhere else. UGA's hometown, Athens, and the faculty are the focus of much student commentary. "[T]he professors I have had are exceptionally great. UGA is a very competitive school academically, and the standards are high." "Professors are very approachable, and downright cool." According to one senior who returned after a hiatus, the magnetism of the faculty is apparently quite strong: "I go to this university because I like the professors in anthropology...I had to jump off the Dead tour to come back...I'm really into anthropology." The most impressive thing about this is that these sentiments come from students in virtually every college and school UGA has. One reason may be Georgia's surprisingly small student to faculty ratio, unusual for a school of its grand scale. Not that academic life is perfect on campus; as at most schools of its size, lecture classes are quite large, with limited class discussion, and there is little hand-holding by faculty and administrators. Enrollment is greatest in programs within the disciplines of business, social sciences, education, and natural sciences.

Student Body

The Georgia student body is overwhelmingly white. Because we're talking about a huge undergraduate population, the small percentage of minority students translates into sizable numbers on campus. The mix is further enhanced by students from 125 foreign countries. Even so, the student body at Georgia is no melting pot. One student mentions that "most of the students are very conservative. Although the student body is socially and ethnically diverse, they usually prefer to interact with their own kind more than...with other racial, sexual, religious, social, or political groups." Despite such segmenting, it is apparent from our surveys that students here don't feel much friction between their fellow classmates: "The people I've met so far have had open minds and the ability to accept people for who they are." A senior points out that Georgia students are "either geeks, freaks, or Greeks—UGA has something for everyone."

FINANCIAL AID: 706-542-6147

ADMISSIONS

The admissions committee considers (in descending order of importance): HS record, test scores, recommendations, essay. *Also considered (in descending order of importance):* special talents. Either the SAT or ACT is required; SAT is preferred. Admissions process is need-blind. *High school units required/recommended:* 15 total units are required; 4 English required, 3 math required, 3 science required, 2 foreign language required, 3 social studies required. Minimum combined SAT I score of 900 (or equivalent ACT score) and minimum 3.0 GPA recommended. *Special Requirements:* An audition is required for music program applicants. TOEFL is required of all international students. SAT II in foreign language required of applicants planning to continue study of that language. Plane geometry, trigonometry, chemistry, and physics recommended of B.S. program applicants. Combined SAT I score of 1000 recommended of business administration program applicants.

The Inside Word

UGA is one of the more popular choices among Southern college-bound students. The admissions process is very straightforward, but few large universities have as much success as Georgia in converting admits to enrollees, which makes candidate evaluation fairly selective. Since student satisfaction and interest in the university shows no sign of a decline to come any time soon, look for circumstances to remain the same for the foreseeable future.

FINANCIAL AID

Students should submit: the school's own financial aid form, a copy of parents' most recent income tax filing. The Princeton Review suggests that all financial aid forms be submitted as soon as possible after January 1. *The following grants/scholarships are offered:* Pell, SEOG, academic merit, athletic, the school's own scholarships, the school's own grants, state scholarships, state grants, private scholarships, private grants, ROTC. *Students borrow from the following loan programs:* Stafford, Perkins, PLUS, the school's own loan fund, state loans, health professions loans, private loans. Applicants will be notified of awards beginning May 1. College Work-Study Program is available. Institutional employment is available.

FROM THE ADMISSIONS OFFICE

The University of Georgia mission statement: "The University of Georgia, a land-grant and sea-grant university, is the state's oldest, most comprehensive, and most diversified institution of higher education. Its constituents are numerous, and the scope of its programs in graduate, professional, and undergraduate education is the most extensive in the state. As Georgia's leading institution of higher learning, the University has the following major purpose: to disseminate knowledge through teaching in the academic disciplines and fields of professional study that make universities distinctive; related to this purpose are programs and other opportunities for students' intellectual, professional, and personal development; to advance knowledge through research, scholarly inquiry, and the creative arts; related to both teaching and research is the conservation and enhancement of the state's and the nation's intellectual, cultural, and environmental heritage; to provide service to the public through consultation, technical assistance, short-term instruction, training, and other opportunities for continued learning, growth, and development. Since the quest for knowledge is universal, a global perspective is necessary to provide students with educational opportunities consistent with the international dimensions of their future careers and personal lives."

ADMISSIONS

Admissions Rating	80
% of applicants accepted	60
% of acceptees attending	47

FRESHMAN PROFILE

Average verbal SAT	590
Average math SAT	580
Average ACT	NR
Average TOEFL	NR
Graduated top 20% of class	85
Graduated top 40% of class	99
Graduated top 60% of class	NR
Average HS GPA or Avg.	3.3

DEADLINES

Early decision	NR
Regular admission	2/1
Regular notification	3/30
Non-fall registration	yes

APPLICANTS ALSO LOOK AT

AND OFTEN PREFER

Duke
UNC-Chapel Hill
Georgia Tech.

AND SOMETIMES PREFER

Emory
Florida State
U. South Carolina-Columbia
U. Tennessee-Knoxville
Furman

AND RARELY PREFER

Clemson
Georgia State
U. Florida

FINANCIAL FACTS

Financial Aid Rating	90
In-state tuition	$2,542
Out-of-state tuition	$6,829
Room & board	$3,820
Estimated book expense	$555
% frosh receiving aid	95
% undergrads receiving aid	60
% aid is need-based	NR
% frosh w/ grant (avg)	NR ($1,200)
% frosh w/ loan (avg)	NR ($2,625)
% UGs w/ job (avg)	25 ($2,500)
Off-campus job outlook	good

GETTYSBURG COLLEGE

GETTYSBURG, PA 17325-1484   ADMISSIONS: 800-431-0803   FAX: 717-337-6008, 717-337-6145

CAMPUS LIFE

Quality of Life Rating   **85**
Type of school   private
Affiliation   Lutheran Church
Environment   town

STUDENTS
FT undergrad enrollment   1,983
% male/female   49/51
% from out of state   75
% live on campus   85
% spend weekend on campus   90
% transfers   5
% from public high school   77
% in (# of) fraternities   55 (11)
% in (# of) sororities   45 (5)
% African-American   3
% Asian   4
% Caucasian   90
% Hispanic   2
% international   4
# of countries represented   35

WHAT'S HOT
campus food
Greeks
beer
sex
hard liquor

WHAT'S NOT
lack of diversity on campus
students are cliquish
town-gown relations
infrequent dating
religion

ACADEMICS

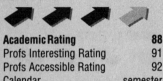

Academic Rating   **88**
Profs Interesting Rating   91
Profs Accessible Rating   92
Calendar   semester
Student/teacher ratio   11:1
% profs tenured   95
Hours of study per day   3.48

MOST POPULAR MAJORS
business administration/management
political science
psychology

% GRADS WHO PURSUE...
Law 7, Med 6, MBA 5, MA 17

STUDENTS SPEAK OUT

Life
Gettysburg is, of course, the home of a famous Civil War battle and Lincoln's famous speech. As a result, students encounter a lot of tourists, especially during the early part of the fall term and the end of spring. Area bars welcome students, but most extracurricular activities seem to take place on campus. Students report high participation in sports, clubs, and organizations. "Greek life dominates socially" and beer consumption is heavy. As one student notes, "If they offered a major in Alcohol, Gettysburg would have many Rhodes Scholars." For students not so into the Greek scene, and these number quite a few of our respondents, the "Student Senate did instate a coffee house which has become very popular with non-Greeks." And "The Lincoln Diner is an excellent hang-out spot within walking distance of the college." Because of the small, affluent student body, some feel Gettysburg is "basically a glorified version of a rich-kid suburban high school, complete with all of the gossip you could ever wish for."

Academics
Gettysburg College was created in 1832 as a Lutheran school. Although no longer attended solely by Lutherans (the church affiliation is mostly nominal), leftovers of the school's religious origins remain. The school has an honor code, for one thing; it also has a policy making class attendance mandatory ("If you're not at class the professor knows where you live and will send for you!"); and Gettysburg has a "strong commitment to the liberal arts and the moral dimension of learning." Gettysburg believes all undergraduates should receive a varied academic program, and, accordingly, students here spend nearly three semesters completing a range of distribution requirements. The school's chief asset is its dedicated faculty, which, coupled with a favorable student/teacher ratio, provides students with lots of personal attention. Writes one student, "Professors will commonly invite students to their home for picnics, get togethers, etc. "Academics are of high quality but not overly demanding, despite the administration's recent efforts to toughen up performance requirements. Some complain that "there are two kinds of administrative practices at Gettysburg College: one for students and one for fraternity houses." Business and management are favorite fields; English, premedical sciences, and psychology are also popular.

Student Body
Gettysburg's student body is overwhelmingly white, wealthy, and conservative. One student observes, "Students here are wealthy, very alike, very athletically inclined, and fun loving. Diversity at the school is not an applicable word in the sense of racial, ethnic, or cultural 'diversity.' Diversity at Gettysburg is 'plaid or stripes?' or more so, 'J.Crew or Polo?'" And another writes, "If they were casting a live-action Barbie movie, they could definitely find a number of Kens and Barbies here." Despite the reportedly friendly atmosphere, some say there are too many "rich alcoholic snobs."

ADMISSIONS

The admissions committee considers (in descending order of importance): HS record, class rank, test scores, recommendations, essay. *Also considered (in descending order of importance):* personality, special talents, alumni relationship, extracurriculars, geographical distribution. Either the SAT or ACT is required. An interview is recommended. Admissions process is need-blind. *High school units required/recommended:* 16 total units are recommended; 4 English recommended, 3 math recommended, 3 science recommended, 3 foreign language recommended, 3 social studies recommended. Participation in accelerated, enriched, and advanced courses recommended. *Special Requirements:* A portfolio is required for art program applicants. An audition is required for music program applicants. TOEFL is required of all international students. Audition and interview required of art and music program applicants. *The admissions office says:* "The admissions office reports that students can expect "a careful, individual review of their applications. We particularly value: (1) high school achievement, including the choice of challenging courses; (2) personal qualities and talents which will contribute to the community. Evidence of leadership, creativity, integrity, commitment, and service to community are welcomed."

The Inside Word

Gettysburg's small size definitely allows for a more personal approach to admission. The low yield of admitted students who enroll serves to temper the college's selectivity, even though the committee puts much energy into matchmaking. It's just that most Gettysburg types are good students and also match up well with competitor colleges, often choosing to attend elsewhere.

FINANCIAL AID

Students should submit: FAFSA (due February 15), CSS Profile (due March 15), state aid form, Divorced Parents form (due March 15). The Princeton Review suggests that all financial aid forms be submitted as soon as possible after January 1. *The following grants/scholarships are offered:* Pell, SEOG, academic merit, the school's own scholarships, the school's own grants, state scholarships, state grants, private scholarships, private grants, foreign aid. *Students borrow from the following loan programs:* Stafford, Perkins, PLUS, the school's own loan fund, state loans, private loans. Applicants will be notified of awards beginning April 1. College Work-Study Program is available. Institutional employment is available.

FROM THE ADMISSIONS OFFICE

"Four major goals of Gettysburg College, to best prepare students to enter the twenty-first century, include: first, to accelerate the intellectual development of our first-year students by integrating them more quickly into the intellectual life of the campus; second, to use interdisciplinary courses combining the intellectual approaches of various fields; third, to encourage students to develop an international perspective through course work, study abroad, association with international faculty, and a variety of extracurricular activities; and fourth, to encourage students to develop (1) a capacity for independent study by ensuring that all students work closely with individual faculty members on an extensive project during their undergraduate years and (2) the ability to work with their peers by making the small group a central feature in college life."

ADMISSIONS

Admissions Rating	82
% of applicants accepted	68
% of acceptees attending	24

FRESHMAN PROFILE

Average verbal SAT	610
Average math SAT	600
Average ACT	26
Average TOEFL	550
Graduated top 20% of class	70
Graduated top 40% of class	95
Graduated top 60% of class	100
Average HS GPA or Avg.	3.5

DEADLINES

Early decision	Fall
Regular admission	2/15
Regular notification	4/1
Non-fall registration	yes

APPLICANTS ALSO LOOK AT

AND OFTEN PREFER

William and Mary
James Madison
Lafayette
Lehigh
Bucknell

AND SOMETIMES PREFER

Dickinson
Franklin and Marshall Coll.
U. Delaware
Hobart & William Smith

AND RARELY PREFER

Penn State U.
Muhlenberg

FINANCIAL FACTS

Financial Aid Rating	89
Tuition	$20,744
Room & board	$4,522
Estimated book expense	$500
% frosh receiving aid	53
% undergrads receiving aid	52
% aid is need-based	95
% frosh w/ grant (avg)	53 ($12,875)
% frosh w/ loan (avg)	45 ($3,010)
% UGs w/ job (avg)	35 ($1,310)
Off-campus job outlook	good

GODDARD COLLEGE

PLAINFIELD, VT 05667   ADMISSIONS: 800-468-4888   FAX: 802-454-8017

CAMPUS LIFE

Quality of Life Rating **90**
Type of school   private
Affiliation   none
Environment   rural

STUDENTS
FT undergrad enrollment   246
% male/female   41/59
% from out of state   82
% live on campus   90
% spend weekend on campus   90
% transfers   45
% from public high school   95
% African-American   3
% Asian   1
% Caucasian   89
% Hispanic   0
% international   2
# of countries represented   4

WHAT'S HOT
college radio
leftist politics
honesty
different students interact
town-gown relations

WHAT'S NOT
lab facilities
intercollegiate sports
intramural sports
religion
health facilities

ACADEMICS

Academic Rating   **86**
Profs Interesting Rating   95
Profs Accessible Rating   92
Calendar   semester
Student/teacher ratio   7:1
% profs PhD/tenured   52/71
Hours of study per day   3.41

STUDENTS SPEAK OUT
Life
Goddard College stresses the ideal of "rounded education and rounded lives." Community action is promoted here, and everyone must work for the college in some constructive way several hours per week. Because of Goddard's tiny size, each individual has a "tremendous opportunity" to get involved in various activities, including the popular school newspaper, radio station, and Woman's Center. Social life is mostly centered in the dorms, and can get pretty laid back: "there's no frats, no sports, no crap—everyone just chills." Religious activity is not popular, although many students cite "spiritual and/or pagan clubs" as well attended. The campus itself is quite beautiful and secluded. Skiing trails are nearby, and there are plenty of places to hike. Students rate themselves as very happy overall ("Life at Goddard is a beautiful thing"). Even the cafeteria food is considered high quality (which may be one reason the college president frequently lunches with students there). Connoisseurs of rural life especially love Goddard's quiet atmosphere.

Academics
Goddard College, a self-proclaimed alternative school, is definitely not "typical, traditional, or boring." Classes are "small discussion groups in which everyone participates. There are no grades or exams, which alleviates any pressure that interferes with the business of learning." Students enjoy exceptionally close relationships with their professors, whom they respect and rate very highly as teachers. All students attend "community-based meetings with students/faculty/staff. We are a part of the decision making and governance here." Written evaluations substitute for grades, and most students value the individual attention they receive. But, as one student aptly writes, "Beware, ye pre-professionals!" Goddard students learn how "not to become a piece of the capitalist/corporate powers which control our lives and thought!" The emphasis here is on more holistic values like "re-learning to be sensitive, integrated human beings who love life on this planet too much to abandon themselves to the materialism of the modern world." Many feel that students must be "independent, self-directed, and focused to attend—there's no hand-holding here." If prospective students are searching for the "balance between idealism, reality, the individual and the community," Goddard may prove to be just the place for them.

Student Body
It is safe to say that this school "would be an uncomfortable place for a person with a conservative background." Despite the cultural homogeneity of the population (a black student comments, "I am the diverse ethnic type"), there are alternative lifestyles aplenty. One student queries, "Where else could I run around naked with a bunch of queer activists without raising the eyebrows of students, faculty, staff, and administration alike." Goddard prides itself on it opposition to "isms: sexism is challenged openly and daily, as are racism and classism."

FINANCIAL AID: 802-454-8311   E-MAIL: PRES@EARTH.GODDARD.EDU   WEB SITE: HTTP://WWW.SUN.GODDARD.EDU

ADMISSIONS

The admissions committee considers (in descending order of importance): essay, recommendations, HS record, test scores. *Also considered (in descending order of importance):* extracurriculars, personality, special talents. An interview is required. Admissions process is need-blind. TOEFL is required of all international students. *The admissions office says:* "Goddard aims to bring students into the college, not keep them out. Admissions criteria have to do with an applicant's interest in attending Goddard, readiness to do so, and willingness to embrace the evolving Goddard educational program fully. Underlying these must be a thorough understanding of what Goddard is and is not, what the curriculum and programs can and cannot offer."

The Inside Word

A small applicant pool, the need to have an entering class each year, and a high level of self-selection among candidates makes for Goddard's high acceptance rate. Even though students are not banging down the doors to get into the college, applicants should prepare themselves for a fairly demanding experience. The committee here wants to know a lot about the people who apply, none of which can be supplied in the clean and neat form of transcripts or score reports. This place is not for everyone, and careful self-assessment is the toughest part of the admissions process.

FINANCIAL AID

Students should submit: FAFSA. The Princeton Review suggests that all financial aid forms be submitted as soon as possible after January 1. *The following grants/scholarships are offered:* Pell, SEOG, the school's own grants, state scholarships, state grants, private scholarships. *Students borrow from the following loan programs:* Stafford, Perkins, PLUS, the school's own loan fund, private loans. College Work-Study Program is available.

FROM THE ADMISSIONS OFFICE

"Goddard is a small, coeducational liberal arts college that has an international reputation for appealing to the creative, independent student. Its commitment is to adventurous, capable persons who want to make their own educational decisions and work closely with the faculty. Individually designed programs can be pursued on or off campus."

ADMISSIONS

Admissions Rating	72
% of applicants accepted	72
% of acceptees attending	39

FRESHMAN PROFILE

Average verbal SAT	590
Average math SAT	520
Average ACT	NR
Average TOEFL	550
Graduated top 20% of class	NR
Graduated top 40% of class	NR
Graduated top 60% of class	NR
Average HS GPA or Avg.	NR

DEADLINES

Early decision	NR
Regular admission	NR
Regular notification	rolling
Non-fall registration	yes

APPLICANTS ALSO LOOK AT

AND OFTEN PREFER

New College
Reed
Oberlin
Hampshire
Bennington

AND SOMETIMES PREFER

Antioch
Marlboro
Coll. of the Atlantic

FINANCIAL FACTS

Financial Aid Rating	88
Tuition	$15,246
Room & board	$4,749
Estimated book expense	NR
% frosh receiving aid	85
% undergrads receiving aid	72
% aid is need-based	100
% frosh w/ grant (avg)	80
% frosh w/ loan (avg)	NR
% UGs w/ job (avg)	NR
Off-campus job outlook	good

GOLDEN GATE UNIVERSITY

536 MISSION STREET, SAN FRANCISCO, CA 94105   ADMISSIONS: 415-442-7800   FAX: 415-495-2671

CAMPUS LIFE

Quality of Life Rating   **73**
Type of school   private
Affiliation   none
Environment   metropolis

STUDENTS
FT undergrad enrollment   454
% male/female   45/55
% from out of state   20
% live on campus   NR
% spend weekend on campus   NR
% transfers   NR
% from public high school   NR
% African-American   10
% Asian   17
% Caucasian   60
% Hispanic   9
% international   63
# of countries represented   66

WHAT'S HOT
different students interact
ethnic diversity on campus
San Francisco
registration is a breeze
town-gown relations

WHAT'S NOT
theater
beer
hard liquor
drugs
health facilities

ACADEMICS

Academic Rating   **76**
Profs Interesting Rating   67
Profs Accessible Rating   66
Calendar   trimester
Student/teacher ratio   16:1
% profs PhD   49
Hours of study per day   3.12

MOST POPULAR MAJORS
management
information systems
institutional/hotel/restaurant

STUDENTS SPEAK OUT
Life
As one Golden Gate student puts it, "Don't come here for the football team, because we don't have one. We don't even have a cheerleader squad. We come here to learn and eventually to become prominent figures in our society." Students certainly don't come here for the social life, because there is none. Most of the mainstays of typical college life—dormitories, parties, drinking, sports, clubs—simply don't exist here. However, "The Plaza Cafe, a new addition to our campus, has successfully increased student life on campus—more people meet each other." Fortunately the school is in downtown San Francisco, a city with a very active social scene of its own. Off-campus housing is available but distressingly expensive, as is almost everything else: students report that cost-of-living expenses here are extremely high. As one student sums it up, "GGU caters to mostly career-oriented people and the classes are mostly at night, so there isn't much interaction after school. It's not boring, but can be."

Academics
In nearly every aspect, Golden Gate University is atypical of the schools included in this book. Most of its undergraduates study part time, and many were out of high school for several years before returning to college; it has no campus or campus life to speak of; and, with a large number of its students in graduate programs, its orientation is decidedly toward graduate, not undergraduate study. Golden Gate has several excellent qualities to recommend it, however. For one, the school is located in downtown San Francisco, certainly an exceptional place to spend four years. Second, it attracts a bright, motivated, and unusually diverse student body. Finally, and most importantly, Golden Gate offers fine undergraduate business programs. Golden Gate's Cooperative Education and Internship Program allow students to study and work concurrently in the San Francisco business community. The only complaint we hear from students is that "this school's reputation isn't nearly as good as it should be, given the quality of instruction I receive." Students praise "the small classes and the opportunity to be taught by business professionals rather than professional teachers" whose "frequent use of case studies...will be very useful when we graduate and start our careers," and the fact that "the school allows the motivated student to get a good degree quickly."

Student Body
The Golden Gate student body boasts a minority population verging on the 50 percent mark as well as a large number of international students. Students report that interaction among undergrads of different ethnicities and backgrounds is frequent, despite the rarity of school-supported venues in which undergrads can congregate. To no one's surprise, the student body at this business-oriented school is politically somewhat conservative, although decidedly less so than at other similar schools. Students admire one another for their tenacity: "My fellow students are good people, hard working and ambitious," says one.

FINANCIAL AID: 415-442-7270

ADMISSIONS

The admissions committee considers (in descending order of importance): HS record, test scores, essay, recommendations. *Also considered (in descending order of importance):* extracurriculars, personality, special talents. *High school units required/recommended:* 16 total units are required; 3 English recommended, 2 math recommended, 1 science recommended, 1 foreign language recommended, 1 social studies recommended. Minimum 3.0 GPA required. SAT I or ACT required of applicants lacking specified units or minimum GPA. TOEFL is required of all international students.

The Inside Word

Golden Gate's focus is unique, and requires a high level of independence, self-discipline, and motivation. Grades may be the most important factor in admission, but candidates who are lacking in the aforementioned personal qualities stand the greatest likelihood of denial.

FINANCIAL AID

Students should submit: FAFSA, the school's own financial aid form, state aid form (due March 2), a copy of parents' most recent income tax filing. The Princeton Review suggests that all financial aid forms be submitted as soon as possible after January 1. *The following grants/scholarships are offered:* Pell, SEOG, academic merit, the school's own scholarships, the school's own grants, state scholarships, state grants, private scholarships. *Students borrow from the following loan programs:* Stafford, unsubsidized Stafford, Perkins, PLUS, the school's own loan fund, private loans. College Work-Study Program is available. Institutional employment is available.

FROM THE ADMISSIONS OFFICE

"Golden Gate University is an ideal choice for men and women who are serious about their careers. Here, students work together with faculty who are leaders in their fields to build foundations for achievement in the world today and in the years ahead. Convenience, practical education and personalized attention are the norm. Classes are small to encourage interaction between students and instructors. A full range of graduate and undergraduate courses are offered during the day, evenings, or on weekends to accommodate the needs of working adults as well as full-time students. Located in the financial district of San Francisco, Golden Gate's largest campus is convenient to business and social opportunities and has just completed a major renovation of classrooms and library. The university also has campuses and programs throughout California. Golden Gate remains one of the most affordable private universities in northern California. A full range of financial aid and scholarships, including full-tuition scholarships for transfer students and under-represented minorities, are available for those who need financial assistance to pursue their studies. Golden Gate is a multi-cultural institution. The university celebrates its diverse student body and seeks staff and faculty members reflective of the community."

ADMISSIONS

Admissions Rating	74
% of applicants accepted	76
% of acceptees attending	51

FRESHMAN PROFILE

Average verbal SAT	NR
Average math SAT	NR
Average ACT	NR
Average TOEFL	525
Graduated top 20% of class	NR
Graduated top 40% of class	NR
Graduated top 60% of class	NR
Average HS GPA or Avg.	NR

DEADLINES

Early decision	NR
Regular admission	NR
Regular notification	rolling
Non-fall registration	yes

APPLICANTS ALSO LOOK AT
AND SOMETIMES PREFER
San Francisco St.

FINANCIAL FACTS

Financial Aid Rating	76
Tuition	$8,190
Room & board	NR
Estimated book expense	$600
% frosh receiving aid	50
% undergrads receiving aid	30
% aid is need-based	55
% frosh w/ grant (avg)	31 ($2,754)
% frosh w/ loan (avg)	40 ($7,133)
% UGs w/ job (avg)	10 ($2,000)
Off-campus job outlook	good

GONZAGA UNIVERSITY

EAST 502 BOONE AVENUE, SPOKANE, WA 99258-0001   ADMISSIONS: 800-572-9658   FAX: 509-484-2818

CAMPUS LIFE

Quality of Life Rating	**83**
Type of school	private
Affiliation	Roman Catholic Church
	(Society of Jesus)
Environment	city

STUDENTS

FT undergrad enrollment	2,707
% male/female	47/53
% from out of state	49
% live on campus	47
% spend weekend on campus	40
% transfers	26
% from public high school	68
% African-American	1
% Asian	4
% Caucasian	73
% Hispanic	3
% international	10
# of countries represented	46

WHAT'S HOT
religion
town-gown relations
library
school runs like butter
computer facilities

WHAT'S NOT
sex
lack of diversity on campus
drugs
Greeks
cigarettes

ACADEMICS

Academic Rating	**84**
Profs Interesting Rating	92
Profs Accessible Rating	90
Calendar	semester
Student/teacher ratio	16:1
% profs PhD/tenured	76/88
Hours of study per day	3.52

MOST POPULAR MAJORS
management

STUDENTS SPEAK OUT

Life

Students describe campus life at Gonzaga University as mixed: "There are two sets of people—the religious people and the partiers. The partiers party all the time, the religious ones party sometimes." Despite the heavy drinking, people here are very health- and exercise-oriented. A typical student describes his activities: "I party, ski, rock-climb, mountain bike and play intramurals for fun." And for those who don't drink, "There's always something going on: plays, movies, free skiing. The school offers a lot of activities on weekends for people who don't want to go to parties." Also, the campus ministry "is terrific for providing opportunities to meet students and faculty through retreats." Basketball games "are widely attended, a real morale booster," as are Gonzaga's major annual events—Charity Ball, Spring Formal, Octoberfest, and Aprilfest. Students have mixed feelings about Spokane. Writes one, "Spokane definitely is not the place to go for exciting nightlife or safe drivers, but it's a fun town, easy to get around."

Academics

Students describe Jesuit-run Gonzaga as though it were a small liberal arts college. Writes one typical respondent, "I appreciate Gonzaga's commitment to personalization. For the first time in my life, I feel like I'm learning because I want to." Gonzaga offers many of the features of an intimate college, including a small student body (says one undergrad, "I think the size is ideal—we are a real community. I know all of my professors and 90 percent of my classmates"), a dedicated, caring faculty ("The priority of the professors is the students and teaching, not doing research and writing articles. Because I'm a student and not a magazine, I think that's pretty damn important"), and a core curriculum rich in liberal arts requirements. But since Gonzaga is a university, it is also dedicated to encouraging research opportunities and developing cutting-edge facilities. The finest of these is the Center for Information and Technology, a $20 million multimedia center providing students with access to numerous computer databases and satellite communications. Students do have some gripes: they complain that class availability is often limited, that the "financial aid office needs to be more cooperative and less condescending," and that "math teaching lags." The most popular majors—business, engineering, communication, and education—receive a solid thumbs-up from students.

Student Body

Writes one student: "I get along fine with all the students. Most are a lot like me (white, conservative, Catholic) so it is easy to interact with them." Nearly every respondent describes the atmosphere as extremely friendly, as long as it remains homogeneous: "People should be recruited because of what they have to offer, not because of their race or sex." International students, GU's most prominent non-white group, "stay pretty much to themselves." Students note that "because this is a Catholic school, there is discrimination in religious matters, i.e., homosexuality."

FINANCIAL AID: 509-328-4220   E-MAIL: CONNAL@GU.GONZAGA.EDU   WEB SITE: HTTP://WWW.GONZAGA.EDU/

ADMISSIONS

The admissions committee considers (in descending order of importance): HS record, test scores, recommendations, essay, class rank. *Also considered (in descending order of importance):* personality, alumni relationship, extracurriculars, special talents. Either the SAT or ACT is required. An interview is recommended. Admissions process is need-blind. *High school units required/recommended:* 17 total units are required; 4 English required, 3 math required, 1 science required, 2 foreign language required, 1 history required. Minimum SAT I scores of 450 in both verbal and math and minimum 2.8 GPA required. *Special Requirements:* A portfolio is required for art program applicants. An audition is required for music program applicants. TOEFL is required of all international students. R.N., A.D.N., or L.P.N. required of nursing program applicants. *The admissions office says:* "We are real people with whom applicants can talk. We want to 'meet' them by phone if not in person. It helps us if they take the time to become 'real' to us."

The Inside Word

As with many religiously affiliated universities, getting in to Gonzaga is much more a matter of making a good match philosophically than having high grades and test scores. An above average academic record should be more than adequate to gain admission.

FINANCIAL AID

Students should submit: FAFSA, the school's own financial aid form (due February 1). The Princeton Review suggests that all financial aid forms be submitted as soon as possible after January 1. *The following grants/scholarships are offered:* Pell, SEOG, academic merit, athletic, the school's own scholarships, the school's own grants, state scholarships, state grants, private scholarships, private grants, federal nursing scholarship, ROTC. *Students borrow from the following loan programs:* Stafford, unsubsidized Stafford, Perkins, PLUS, the school's own loan fund, federal nursing loans, private loans. Applicants will be notified of awards beginning April 1. College Work-Study Program is available. Institutional employment is available.

FROM THE ADMISSIONS OFFICE

"We at Gonzaga wish you the very best as you enter your college years. Take your applications and admissions process with a grain of salt. Humor is of the essence. Remember, the application isn't you, and colleges' decisions, positive or negative, do not really touch you—it only feels that way. If they are interested, let the college folks get to know you a bit. Let them see you in a way not afforded by their applications. Finally, don't be a wallflower. Ask questions—you might get answers! Good luck!"

ADMISSIONS

Admissions Rating	72
% of applicants accepted	81
% of acceptees attending	41

FRESHMAN PROFILE

Average verbal SAT	590
Average math SAT	580
Average ACT	25
Average TOEFL	520
Graduated top 20% of class	61
Graduated top 40% of class	89
Graduated top 60% of class	96
Average HS GPA or Avg.	3.6

DEADLINES

Early decision	3/1
Regular admission	4/1
Regular notification	rolling
Non-fall registration	yes

APPLICANTS ALSO LOOK AT

AND OFTEN PREFER
Notre Dame
U. San Diego
Marquette

AND SOMETIMES PREFER
Santa Clara
U. Puget Sound
U. Washington
Lewis and Clark Coll.
Washington St.

AND RARELY PREFER
Loyola Marymount
Central Washington

FINANCIAL FACTS

Financial Aid Rating	88
Tuition	$14,900
Room & board	$4,670
Estimated book expense	$650
% frosh receiving aid	88
% undergrads receiving aid	87
% aid is need-based	65
% frosh w/ grant (avg)	86 ($6,549)
% frosh w/ loan (avg)	64 ($4,252)
% UGs w/ job (avg)	31 ($2,000)
Off-campus job outlook	excellent

GOUCHER COLLEGE

1021 DULANEY VALLEY ROAD, BALTIMORE, MD 21204   ADMISSIONS: 800-638-4278   FAX: 410-337-6123

STUDENTS SPEAK OUT

Life

Students describe the atmosphere at Goucher as "intimate." Explains one, "Building friendships and getting to know people is extremely easy"; says another, "Because the school is so small, the rumor mill is always buzzing. You've got to watch what you do and who you do it with. But tight friendships and honest relationships are the advantage." While many complain that "social life is limited because of the school's size and the male/female ratio," there are, according to one student, "plenty of opportunities for involvement in organizations. We have everything from a gay/lesbian organization to a math and computer science club." Other students are less enthusiastic: "There are two things to do at Goucher for fun: 1) drink or 2) die of boredom." The truth seems to lie somewhere in-between. The Goucher administration is currently working to build a competitive intercollegiate athletic program. The campus is located in Towson, an upscale suburb north of Baltimore, and students agreed that it provides an excellent setting for studies. Writes one, "On campus it's like you're in the country, but outside the gates is a great city."

Academics

As one student at the formerly all-women Goucher College explains, "We're still struggling to get an identity because we only went coed in 1987." Certain components of the school's new identity are already in place, chief among which are a commitment to a broad-ranging liberal arts core curriculum, excellent premedical science departments, and an "amazing, very friendly, and extremely accessible" faculty. All students must complete distribution requirements covering eight academic disciplines. One student notes that the core places "a strong emphasis on liberal arts and writing proficiency." Several students describe the premed program as "fantastic." Dance, English, communications, and women's studies also drew students' praise. The students save their kindest words for the faculty. Writes a typical respondent, "The best thing about Goucher is the professors. They treat us with respect. We have their home phone numbers and call them by their first names." Students rank the professors here among the top five percent in the nation for out-of-class accessibility. With a 10 to 1 student/faculty ratio, classes are "generally small" and in-class discussions are a major part of most courses. On the other end of the spectrum is the food at Goucher, which receives uniformly negative (if not angry) reviews.

Student Body

Goucher is a predominantly white school. One student characterizes her classmates as "mostly liberal and open-minded." One of her conservative classmates agrees, writing, "If you are a right-winger and want to know what it feels like to be in the minority, come here; it's like sleeping in the enemy's camp. Not a day will go by that your ideals are not challenged. After you leave here, you'll be able to argue anything with anyone."

FINANCIAL AID: 410-337-6141

ADMISSIONS

The admissions committee considers (in descending order of importance): HS record, essay, recommendations, class rank, test scores. *Also considered (in descending order of importance):* extracurriculars, alumni relationship, personality, special talents. Either the SAT or ACT is required, SAT II required. An interview is recommended. Admissions process is need-blind. *High school units required/recommended:* 15 total units are required; 4 English required, 3 math required, 2 science required, 2 foreign language required, 2 social studies required. *The admissions office says:* "We [try to make the admissions process] as personal as possible, meeting students' individual needs. We accomplish this through individually tailored visits to campus, personalized mailings, and consistent follow-through by staff. Our application reading and decision making are very humane; we keep in mind that each file represents a person."

The Inside Word

Requiring SAT IIs is excessive for a college with Goucher's high admit rate. Applicants must comply nevertheless, but shouldn't be too concerned about getting in if their grades are solid.

FINANCIAL AID

Students should submit: FAFSA, the school's own financial aid form, state aid form (due March 1), a copy of parents' most recent income tax filing. The Princeton Review suggests that all financial aid forms be submitted as soon as possible after January 1. *The following grants/scholarships are offered:* Pell, SEOG, academic merit, the school's own scholarships, the school's own grants, state scholarships, state grants, private scholarships. *Students borrow from the following loan programs:* Stafford, Perkins, PLUS, the school's own loan fund, state loans, private loans. Applicants will be notified of awards beginning April 1. College Work-Study Program is available. Institutional employment is available.

FROM THE ADMISSIONS OFFICE

"While maintaining a strong commitment to liberal arts education, Goucher has expanded that concept to include an internationalized curriculum and a greater focus on interdisciplinary study. At the heart of the recently revised core curriculum is the common intellectual experience, a one-year course required of all freshmen. Taught in small sections, it was designed by students and faculty. There is also an honors program, and all students must choose an internship, study abroad, or independent study to broaden their classroom experience. The college boasts impressive facilities in technology, science, arts, and athletics. A strong merit-awards program offers scholarships ranging from partial tuition to full tuition and room and board."

ADMISSIONS

Admissions Rating	77
% of applicants accepted	70
% of acceptees attending	31

FRESHMAN PROFILE

Average verbal SAT	610
Average math SAT	580
Average ACT	NR
Average TOEFL	550
Graduated top 20% of class	47
Graduated top 40% of class	74
Graduated top 60% of class	84
Average HS GPA or Avg.	3.3

DEADLINES

Early decision	NR
Regular admission	2/1
Regular notification	4/1
Non-fall registration	yes

APPLICANTS ALSO LOOK AT

AND OFTEN PREFER

UNC-Chapel Hill
Connecticut Coll.
Syracuse

AND SOMETIMES PREFER

Agnes Scott
Hobart & William Smith
Allegheny
Muhlenberg
Gettysburg

AND RARELY PREFER

Adelphi

FINANCIAL FACTS

Financial Aid Rating	87
Tuition	$16,530
Room & board	$6,260
Estimated book expense	$500
% frosh receiving aid	70
% undergrads receiving aid	65
% aid is need-based	58
% frosh w/ grant (avg)	87 ($13,000)
% frosh w/ loan (avg)	NR ($2,700)
% UGs w/ job (avg)	45 ($1,200)
Off-campus job outlook	good

GRINNELL COLLEGE

GRINNELL, IA 50112

ADMISSIONS: 515-269-3600   FAX: 515-269-4800

CAMPUS LIFE

Quality of Life Rating   **84**
Type of school   private
Affiliation   none
Environment   town

STUDENTS
FT undergrad enrollment   1,295
% male/female   45/55
% from out of state   86
% live on campus   85
% spend weekend on campus   96
% transfers   8
% from public high school   79
% African-American   4
% Asian   4
% Caucasian   77
% Hispanic   3
% international   10
# of countries represented   42

WHAT'S HOT
computer facilities
college radio
library
leftist politics
sex

WHAT'S NOT
off-campus food
Greeks
religion
intramural sports
intercollegiate sports

ACADEMICS

Academic Rating   **93**
Profs Interesting Rating   92
Profs Accessible Rating   93
Calendar   semester
Student/teacher ratio   10:1
% profs tenured   96
Hours of study per day   3.71

MOST POPULAR MAJORS
economics
English
history

STUDENTS SPEAK OUT

Life

Although Grinnell College is a "very intellectual" school, life here doesn't begin and end in the classroom. Explains one student, "There is not a lot to do in the town of Grinnell during the weekends, yet we never get bored. Campus dances and concerts attract a lot of people every Friday and Saturday nights. Further, all movies, plays, sports, or any other activities are free of charge, which we definitely cannot complain about. We have a lot of work during the week, but we know how to have a great time on weekends." However, another warns, "The college provides a lot of extracurricular activities but it cannot escape the fact that it lies in the middle of Iowa, an area that can be quite suffocating for those accustomed to the fast pace of urban life." Grinnell has no Greek system, and the whole idea of frats and sororities is generally loathed by the student body."

Academics

Iowa is, by midwestern standards, a hot spot of liberalism, and nowhere in the state is this more apparent than at Grinnell. As one out-of-state student puts it, "I wanted a school with lots of non-mainstream thought and action. Believe it or not, I found it in the middle of Iowa." An unconventional approach to undergraduate education is evidenced by the school's lack of a core curriculum (one student writes approvingly, "Having no core curriculum allows students to expand their knowledge in fields of interest outside of their majors") and the large degree of autonomy allowed students in both academic and social pursuits. As at many small liberal arts schools, students here enjoy small classes and enthusiastic, dedicated professors. One student characterizes Grinnell this way: "Academics are extremely rigorous and challenging. You have to like to think to be happy here. Stress is moderate to high. There's always more to do, but classes are informal and teachers are easy to find, great to talk to." Students also give high marks to the administration; one student writes, "Advisors try to help as much as possible without getting on your case." Best of all, despite the school's excellent academic reputation, many students report, "This is a very laid-back school without competition among students. This creates an atmosphere most conducive to learning."

Student Body

Writes one Grinnell College student, "Grinnell seems to be a haven for students who were unique in some way in high school. This makes for a very diverse, very interesting campus." Adds another, "The student body is comprised of individuals who aren't afraid to be themselves. This is one of the friendliest places on Earth." Tolerance of alternative lifestyles, unsurprisingly, is high; one student tells us, "A great sense of community and sensitivity exists on campus. Many groups on campus actively work to create feminist, ethnic, and GLB (gay-lesbian-bisexual) dialogue and activities." The only negative: "Students get along well, but they have an exaggerated notion of self-importance which often makes them insufferable."

FINANCIAL AID: 515-269-3250

ADMISSIONS

The admissions committee considers (in descending order of importance): HS record, class rank, test scores, recommendations, essay. *Also considered (in descending order of importance):* extracurriculars, personality, special talents, alumni relationship, geographical distribution. Either the SAT or ACT is required. An interview is recommended. Admissions process is not need-blind. *High school units required/recommended:* 16 total units are required; 4 English required, 3 math required, 3 science recommended, 3 foreign language recommended, 3 social studies recommended. TOEFL is required of all international students. *The admissions office says:* "Intellectual curiosity, motivation, and depth and breadth of out-of-class involvement are stressed."

The Inside Word

Grinnell has plenty of academically talented applicants. This enables the admissions committee to put a lot of energy into matchmaking, and gives candidates who have devoted time and energy to thought about themselves, their future, and Grinnell the opportunity to rise to the top. All applicants should consider interviewing; you're likely to leave with a positive impression.

FINANCIAL AID

Students should submit: FAFSA, the school's own financial aid form, a copy of parents' most recent income tax filing. The Princeton Review suggests that all financial aid forms be submitted as soon as possible after January 1. *The following grants/scholarships are offered:* Pell, SEOG, academic merit, the school's own scholarships, the school's own grants, state scholarships, state grants, foreign aid. *Students borrow from the following loan programs:* Stafford, Perkins, PLUS, the school's own loan fund. Applicants will be notified of awards beginning April 1. College Work-Study Program is available. Institutional employment is available.

FROM THE ADMISSIONS OFFICE

"Grinnell students are involved and committed to academic work and involved in community and volunteer service. Students are independent and can exercise that independence in Grinnell's open-style curriculum. Grinnell hopes to produce individualism, social commitment, and intellectual self-awareness in its graduates."

ADMISSIONS

Admissions Rating	88
% of applicants accepted	64
% of acceptees attending	28

FRESHMAN PROFILE

Average verbal SAT	670
Average math SAT	650
Average ACT	29
Average TOEFL	550
Graduated top 20% of class	87
Graduated top 40% of class	98
Graduated top 60% of class	100
Average HS GPA or Avg.	NR

DEADLINES

Early decision	2/1
Regular admission	NR
Regular notification	4/1
Non-fall registration	no

APPLICANTS ALSO LOOK AT

AND SOMETIMES PREFER

Carleton
U. Iowa
Washington U.
Oberlin
Macalester

AND RARELY PREFER

Kenyon
U. Minnesota
Denison

FINANCIAL FACTS

Financial Aid Rating	93
Tuition	$16,236
Room & board	$4,782
Estimated book expense	$400
% frosh receiving aid	88
% undergrads receiving aid	83
% aid is need-based	85
% frosh w/ grant (avg)	86 ($9,876)
% frosh w/ loan (avg)	43 ($3,480)
% UGs w/ job (avg)	56 ($1,000)
Off-campus job outlook	fair

GROVE CITY COLLEGE

100 CAMPUS ROAD, GROVE CITY, PA 16127-2104   ADMISSIONS: 412-458-2100   FAX: 412-458-3395

STUDENTS SPEAK OUT

Life

"We have good clean fun the way people should. This kind of fun promotes true social interaction and promotes lasting friendships." No, Grove City College is not a party school by any means! Predictably, at this Christian college strongly affiliated with the Presbyterian church, social life is tame and restricted. Explains one student, "Parties are off campus, so they're avoidable if you like, and available if you like." Another describes typical on-campus social activities: "We watch the campus movie, bowl, do aerobics, and participate in multiple activities." The town leaves much to be desired: "There is very little to do in the community, so the school creates a lot of activities." These activities include prayer groups and intramural athletics, both of which are quite popular. On-campus dorms, where most students live, are rated quite high by students, though the food fares poorly. Drug and alcohol use at Grove City is among the lowest in the country. As for reproductive health services, they're not available at GCC: "The school refuses to believe that sex is going on and therefore won't offer any reproductive health service."

Academics

Grove City is a conservative school dedicated to combining liberal arts and religious instruction into a cohesive academic program. Class and chapel attendance are compulsory. The courseload is fairly rigorous. Says one student, "The classes are challenging and the professors demanding." Students study over three hours a day on average. Profs at GCC are generally respected, though some wish they would take their language down a notch: "Our profs are very intelligent, almost too much at times. I wish they would teach to our level." While profs may reach too high sometimes, much of class time is spent in discussion, instead of lecture, which students appreciate. Another adds of the profs, "They are usually men and women of God and are not ashamed of their beliefs." The administration doesn't fare as well, partly due to its strict adherence to rules some feel are outdated. "Due to the extreme care taken in maintaining the high reputation of the school, academic innovation through the classroom, and especially the newspaper, is stifled." Indeed, the school paper does not allow student opinion that dissents from that of the administration. Another rails against a perceived double standard, "The administration discriminates against women by having curfew and sign-in at night [for first-semester women]. Men aren't required!" While such concerns aren't uncommon, most students are very satisfied with their education at GCC. "I can put my overall academic experience in one sentence: This is the BEST school on earth!"

Student Body

"Grove City is very strict, political, and right wing." It's also very white, and over half the students come from Pennsylvania. Discrimination on the basis of race and sex is a concern for undergrads. Explains one, "For the most part everyone gets along but the stupid cliques (like in high school) still exist: sororities, fraternities, and housing groups." Greek life is quite popular on campus, as is, of course, religion. "Grove City is made up of mostly religious students. About 1/3 of the students are highly religious to the point of looking down on others. 2/3 or so have religious values or maybe just a little religious background." Most students report that they date frequently, while few report being very sexually active. Says one, "Grove City College is a friendly place. People respect each other, are helpful and cooperative, and are just plain nice."

FINANCIAL AID: 412-458-2163

ADMISSIONS

The admissions committee considers (in descending order of importance): class rank, HS record, test scores, essay, recommendations. Also considered (in descending order of importance): personality, extracurriculars, special talents, alumni relationship, geographical distribution. Either the SAT or ACT is required. An interview is recommended. Admissions process is need-blind. High school units required/recommended: 16 total units are required; 4 English required, 3 math required, 2 science required, 3 foreign language required, 2 social studies required, 1 history required. Special Requirements: An audition is required for music program applicants. TOEFL is required of all international students. 4 units of math (including trigonometry) and 3 units of lab science required of engineering, math, and sciences program applicants.

The Inside Word

If you're looking for a northeastern college with a Christian orientation, Grove City is a pretty good choice, but it's getting tougher to get in as we speak. Applications and standards are on the rise, and the college is fast becoming the newest addition to the lofty realm of the highly selective. Minorities are in short supply, and will encounter a somewhat friendlier admissions process. All students should definitely follow the college's recommendation and interview.

FINANCIAL AID

Students should submit: FAFSA (due April 15), the school's own financial aid form (due April 15). The Princeton Review suggests that all financial aid forms be submitted as soon as possible after January 1. The following grants/scholarships are offered: academic merit, the school's own scholarships, the school's own grants, state scholarships, state grants, private scholarships, private grants, foreign aid. Students borrow from the following loan programs: Stafford, unsubsidized Stafford, PLUS, the school's own loan fund, state loans, private loans. Applicants will be notified of awards beginning June 1. Institutional employment is available.

FROM THE ADMISSIONS OFFICE

"A good college education doesn't have to cost a fortune. For decades, Grove City College has offered a quality education at costs among the lowest nationally. The 1990s have brought increased national academic acclaim to Grove City College. In the 1995 issue of Money Guide, 'Best College Buys Now' ranked GCC fourth in the mid-Atlantic region and eleventh in their top one hundred honor roll of public and private four-year colleges across the country. Grove City College is a place where professors teach. You will not see graduate assistants or teacher's aides in the classroom. Our professors are also active in the total life of the campus. More than one hundred student organizations on campus afford opportunity for a wide variety of co-curricular activities. Outstanding scholars and leaders in education, science, and international affairs visit the campus each year. The environment at GGC is friendly, secure, and dedicated to high standards. Character building is emphasized and traditional Christian values are supported."

ADMISSIONS

Admissions Rating	87
% of applicants accepted	48
% of acceptees attending	51

FRESHMAN PROFILE

Average verbal SAT	620
Average math SAT	620
Average ACT	26
Average TOEFL	550
Graduated top 20% of class	82
Graduated top 40% of class	96
Graduated top 60% of class	99
Average HS GPA or Avg.	3.7

DEADLINES

Early decision	11/15
Regular admission	2/15
Regular notification	3/15
Non-fall registration	yes

APPLICANTS ALSO LOOK AT

AND SOMETIMES PREFER

Pennsylvania State U.
Allegheny
Wheaton (IL)
Westminster (PA)
Hillsdale

AND RARELY PREFER

Slippery Rock
Indiana U. (PA)

FINANCIAL FACTS

Financial Aid Rating	84
Tuition	$6,478
Room & board	$3,652
Estimated book expense	$650
% frosh receiving aid	58
% undergrads receiving aid	53
% aid is need-based	60
% frosh w/ grant (avg)	49 ($2,540)
% frosh w/ loan (avg)	41 ($3,919)
% UGs w/ job (avg)	37 ($604)
Off-campus job outlook	good

GUILFORD COLLEGE

5800 WEST FRIENDLY AVENUE, GREENSBORO, NC 27410　　ADMISSIONS: 910-316-2100　　FAX: 910-316-2954

CAMPUS LIFE

Quality of Life Rating 85
Type of school　　　　　private
Affiliation　　　Society of Friends
Environment　　　　　suburban

STUDENTS
FT undergrad enrollment　　1,093
% male/female　　　　　48/52
% from out of state　　　　67
% live on campus　　　　　83
% spend weekend on campus　95
% transfers　　　　　　　13
% from public high school　62
% African-American　　　　7
% Asian　　　　　　　　　1
% Caucasian　　　　　　　86
% Hispanic　　　　　　　2
% international　　　　　　3
# of countries represented　25

WHAT'S HOT
　college radio
　town-gown relations
　political activism
　support groups
　student government

　　　　　WHAT'S NOT
　　　　　campus food
　　　　　　　Greeks
　　　　music associations
　　　　　lab facilities
　　　registration is a pain

ACADEMICS

Academic Rating 83
Profs Interesting Rating　　92
Profs Accessible Rating　　91
Calendar　　　　　semester
Student/teacher ratio　　14:1
% profs PhD/tenured　　89/70
Hours of study per day　3.28

MOST POPULAR MAJORS
management
psychology
justice/policy studies

% GRADS WHO PURSUE...
Law 3, Med 3, MBA 3, MA 12

STUDENTS SPEAK OUT

Life

The Quaker tradition at Guilford College gives students "a distinctive amount of influence" on campus. Explains one student, "Community decision making, an integral part of the Quaker tradition, is taken seriously and the student government has authentic responsibility and power." The downside of this is that "the Quaker process means no decisions are made without a ton of bureaucracy. All decisions are made by committee, and those committees are run by consensus. Everyone has a voice, but it's so slow!" GC's 300 acre campus is Georgian and "as postcard-beautiful as it is in the brochure." Campus life is quiet, although "there's always something like a lecture, poetry reading, or a film available. Also, there are always panel discussions happening on campus, on topics from homosexuality to Buddhism. Students are encouraged to think and question, not just absorb like a sponge." The lack of fraternities, combined with the unappealing nature of their hometown ("Guilford is not a city, nor is it a beautiful country town. It is a horrible, mediocre, froufrou mixture of the two") leads some students to complain of boredom. Writes one, "Guilford is a great school for people who don't want to have fun."

Academics

Guilford, a small, Quaker-run liberal arts school, is notable for the combination of attention and autonomy it provides its undergraduates. A student notes that "We receive lots of personal attention. If you show up for class without having done the reading, it's painfully obvious." Another reports: "The Quaker philosophy is important in the supportive, free thinking, inquisitive nature of Guilford's academic environment." Notes one, "We call our professors by their first names because of the Quaker idea that teachers are peers, not authority figures." Guilford's curriculum contains few distribution requirements, and even these can by bypassed with good scores on AP exams. Students are not entirely on their own-they must work closely with a faculty adviser in fashioning their program-but a Guilford education allows students an unusual amount of freedom in pursuing their studies. Also notable is the school's excellent study-abroad program, which more than thirty percent of the students enjoy for at least one semester. One student sums up Guilford this way: "A small liberal arts college with fine science, education, and social science departments. An oasis of progressive thinking and quality traditional academics."

Student Body

The general atmosphere at Guilford is one of acceptance. Writes one student, "Gay couples are seen holding hands on campus, interracial couples are accepted, athletes and 'alternative' people are seen hanging out together. There's a very safe feeling." Students, who describe themselves as "hippies with an attitude," are "highly concerned about political issues." They are also highly concerned about academic achievement. One student remarks, "People here are very work-oriented. The atmosphere is not exactly competitive, but it is very stressful."

FINANCIAL AID: 910-316-2354

WEB SITE: HTTP://WWW.GUILFORD.EDU/

ADMISSIONS

The admissions committee considers (in descending order of importance): HS record, class rank, test scores, essay, recommendations. *Also considered (in descending order of importance):* extracurriculars, geographical distribution, personality, special talents, alumni relationship. Either the SAT or ACT is required. An interview is recommended. Admissions process is need-blind. *High school units required/recommended:* 18 total units are required; 21 total units are recommended; 4 English required, 3 math required, 4 math recommended, 2 science required, 2 foreign language required, 3 foreign language recommended, 2 social studies required, 3 social studies recommended, 1 history required. TOEFL is required of all international students.

The Inside Word

Guilford is indeed a sleeper, and is likely to become more selective as it becomes better known. Its current acceptance rate is high mainly because the competition includes many of the best colleges and universities east of the Mississippi.

FINANCIAL AID

Students should submit: FAFSA (due March 1), the school's own financial aid form (due March 1), a copy of parents' most recent income tax filing. The Princeton Review suggests that all financial aid forms be submitted as soon as possible after January 1. *The following grants/scholarships are offered:* Pell, SEOG, academic merit, the school's own scholarships, the school's own grants, state scholarships, state grants, private scholarships, private grants, ROTC. *Students borrow from the following loan programs:* Stafford, unsubsidized Stafford, Perkins, PLUS, the school's own loan fund, state loans, private loans. College Work-Study Program is available. Institutional employment is available.

FROM THE ADMISSIONS OFFICE

"At Guilford we take pride in the fact that we strive to empower our enrolled students to exercise some influence in what happens on campus day to day. We encourage prospective students to do no less. Show some active interest in your application for admission and make sure that we know the unique ways you will contribute to Guilford. Although academic achievement and preparation are extremely important as we review applicants' files, we truly want to look beyond those factors to find men and women with broad perspectives, social concerns, untapped potential, and a love for learning."

ADMISSIONS

Admissions Rating	70
% of applicants accepted	82
% of acceptees attending	30

FRESHMAN PROFILE

Average verbal SAT	590
Average math SAT	560
Average ACT	24
Average TOEFL	550
Graduated top 20% of class	27
Graduated top 40% of class	46
Graduated top 60% of class	54
Average HS GPA or Avg.	3.2

DEADLINES

Early decision	12/1
Regular admission	2/1
Regular notification	4/1
Non-fall registration	yes

APPLICANTS ALSO LOOK AT

AND OFTEN PREFER

UNC-Chapel Hill
Davidson
Oberlin
Duke
U. Virginia

AND SOMETIMES PREFER

Earlham
UNC, Greensboro
Swarthmore
Wake Forest
Warren Wilson

AND RARELY PREFER

U. Richmond
Elon
Randolph-Macon

FINANCIAL FACTS

Financial Aid Rating	95
Tuition	$14,180
Room & board	$5,270
Estimated book expense	$550
% frosh receiving aid	92
% undergrads receiving aid	79
% aid is need-based	81
% frosh w/ grant (avg)	52 ($8,795)
% frosh w/ loan (avg)	59 ($3,350)
% UGs w/ job (avg)	31 ($1,250)
Off-campus job outlook	good

Gustavus Adolphus College

800 West College Avenue, St. Peter, MN 56082-1498   Admissions: 507-933-7676   Fax: 507-933-6270

CAMPUS LIFE

Quality of Life Rating   **81**
Type of school   private
Affiliation   none
Environment   town

STUDENTS

FT undergrad enrollment	2,361
% male/female	46/54
% from out of state	31
% live on campus	90
% spend weekend on campus	85
% transfers	7
% from public high school	92
% in (# of) fraternities	22 (6)
% in (# of) sororities	20 (6)
% African-American	2
% Asian	3
% Caucasian	92
% Hispanic	1
% international	1
# of countries represented	22

WHAT'S HOT

intramural sports
music associations
computer facilities
school runs like butter
students are happy

WHAT'S NOT

infrequent dating
off-campus food
lack of diversity on campus
St. Peter
drugs

ACADEMICS

Academic Rating   **85**
Profs Interesting Rating	86
Profs Accessible Rating	87
Calendar	4-1-4
Student/teacher ratio	13:1
% profs tenured	84
Hours of study per day	3.28

MOST POPULAR MAJORS

biology
psychology
English

% GRADS WHO PURSUE...

Law 5, Med 5, MBA 8, MA 15

STUDENTS SPEAK OUT

Life

Gustavus students enjoy an exceptionally strong sense of on-campus fellowship. Writes one, "Gustavus is a community. Sometimes there are little family squabbles, sometimes a little stress-but those are the things that keep Gustavus the friendly, supportive community it continues to be." Students participate in over 100 student organizations ranging from literary clubs to faith-centered groups. Most popular is the intramural sports program, which involves over eighty percent of the students. Gustavus's Division III sports teams are also popular, especially football and women's tennis and gymnastics. Greek fraternities and sororities have been recognized since 1993, with one in three students participating." Of the town of Saint Peter, one student warns, "There is very little to do in town, so most people drink every weekend and that's all." Road trips lead either to Minneapolis-St. Paul or Mankato.

Academics

Like many other colleges, Gustavus Adolphus requires students to complete a core curriculum. But unlike other schools, Gustavus offers its students a choice of two cores. Curriculum I resembles distribution requirements; students in this program must spend about one-third of their time taking courses in different liberal arts areas. Curriculum II, open to only sixty freshmen a year, offers fewer courses but presents material in a sequence designed to help students better "develop a comprehensive understanding of global society." Neither curriculum interferes with a student's ability to study abroad (more than 40 percent of the students study overseas for at least one month). Although Gustavus leans heavily on the liberal arts, the school also seems to understand the career orientation of its students; the school sponsors semester-long and summer internship programs. Internships are also available during the short January term (which some students use to study abroad). Students particularly praise the nursing school, and students in all departments appreciate "the friendly atmosphere and cooperative nature of the college." Typical of this cooperative nature is the adopt-a-prof program, "where each floor/section adopts a prof. When the floor/section does an activity, the prof is involved whenever possible."

Student Body

The Gustavus student body is predominantly white, Nordic, Lutheran, and from Minnesota. Students express the desire for more diversity on campus, but the lack of diversity doesn't lead to tension for minorities. Students "are very friendly. Everyone says 'hi' to each other."

FINANCIAL AID: 507-933-7527   E-MAIL: ADMISSION@GAC.EDU   WEB SITE: HTTP://WWW.GAC.EDU/

ADMISSIONS

The admissions committee considers (in descending order of importance): HS record, essay, test scores, class rank, recommendations. *Also considered (in descending order of importance):* personality, special talents, alumni relationship, extracurriculars, geographical distribution. Either the SAT or ACT is required. An interview is recommended. Admissions process is need-blind. *High school units required/recommended:* 17 total units are required; 4 English required, 3 math required, 4 math recommended, 2 science required, 3 science recommended, 2 foreign language required, 2 social studies required, 2 history required. Rank in top third of secondary school class recommended. TOEFL is required of all international students. *The admissions office says:* "We encourage all students to visit the campus, and will meet students flying into the Minneapolis-St. Paul airport and transport them to and from the campus. Many applicants have self-selected Gustavus with twenty percent not applying to another college. We are interested in recruiting more students from the West and the South. Relatives/children of alumni receive extra consideration, and are 'especially encouraged' to apply. Minorities also receive extra consideration."

The Inside Word

While the college refers to itself as a national liberal arts college, the applicant pool is decidedly regional and mostly from Minnesota. The pool is also small and highly self-selected, which explains the high acceptance rate and solid freshman profile. Minorities and those who hail from far afield will find their applications met with enthusiasm by the admissions committee.

FINANCIAL AID

Students should submit: FAFSA (due June 1), the school's own financial aid form (due June 1). The Princeton Review suggests that all financial aid forms be submitted as soon as possible after January 1. *The following grants/scholarships are offered:* Pell, SEOG, academic merit, the school's own scholarships, state scholarships, state grants, private scholarships, private grants, federal nursing scholarship, ROTC, foreign aid. *Students borrow from the following loan programs:* Stafford, unsubsidized Stafford, Perkins, PLUS, the school's own loan fund, supplemental loans, state loans, federal nursing loans, private loans. College Work-Study Program is available. Institutional employment is available.

FROM THE ADMISSIONS OFFICE

"Gustavus Adolphus, a national liberal arts college with a strong tradition of quality teaching, is committed to the liberal arts and sciences, to its Lutheran history, to innovation as evidenced by the 4-1-4 calendar, Curriculums I and II, and the writing program, and to affordable costs with its unique Guaranteed Cost Plan, Partners in Scholarship Program and first-year participation in the new government direct loan program. Excellent facilities with most recent buildings being Olin Hall for physics and mathematics, Confer Hall for the Humanities, and Lund Center for physical education, athletics, and health."

ADMISSIONS

Admissions Rating	77
% of applicants accepted	82
% of acceptees attending	43

FRESHMAN PROFILE

Average verbal SAT	670
Average math SAT	600
Average ACT	25
Average TOEFL	550
Graduated top 20% of class	59
Graduated top 40% of class	88
Graduated top 60% of class	99
Average HS GPA or Avg.	NR

DEADLINES

Early decision	2/15
Regular admission	4/15
Regular notification	rolling
Non-fall registration	yes

APPLICANTS ALSO LOOK AT
AND SOMETIMES PREFER

Carleton
St. Olaf
U. Minnesota
U. Wisconsin, Madison
Macalester

FINANCIAL FACTS

Financial Aid Rating	92
Tuition	$14,760
Room & board	$3,600
Estimated book expense	$400
% frosh receiving aid	77
% undergrads receiving aid	73
% aid is need-based	95
% frosh w/ grant (avg)	84 ($8,087)
% frosh w/ loan (avg)	87 ($3,780)
% UGs w/ job (avg)	60 ($1,400)
Off-campus job outlook	fair

HAMILTON COLLEGE

CLINTON, NY 13323   ADMISSIONS: 315-859-4421   FAX: 315-859-4457

STUDENTS SPEAK OUT

Life

Hamilton is a small school in a small town (Clinton, New York). The closest city is Utica, but most of Hamilton's social life happens on its two gorgeous campuses. Explains one student, "There's always something to do, from schoolwork to partying (on weeknights, too) to participating in clubs and intramurals, and finally, to attending guest lectures and plays." For many, the setting is perfect (writes one student, "There is plenty of time during graduate school to enjoy a big university in a city. Come to Hamilton to experience the small college community life"), but it's certainly not for hard-core urbanites. These days, students feel there are big changes in the air at Hamilton, "but it's nothing that doesn't reflect society's changes in general: concern with alcohol and drugs, how people socialize, diversity, etc." Says one student, "We used to rage 24-7, now it's a lot calmer," particularly due to the recent residential life decision to close frat houses. The comfortable and attractive dorms at Hamilton receive high marks.

Academics

Hamilton College may not have the big-name scholars nearby Ivy League institutions have, but the typical Hamilton student gets something Ivy students don't: an exceptional amount of personal attention from "first-rate" professors. "I believe I have gotten more out of small classes and personal interactions with professors than my friends who have been taught by TAs at Harvard and Princeton," writes one Hamiltonian. Reports another, "The accessibility of professors is fantastic. Some will invite you over to their homes for dinner and offer you a beer. That's the great thing about being at a small school." Students here pursue popular liberal arts and social science majors: political science, English, and economics have the highest enrollment. Demanding core requirements in a broad range of subjects eat up over one quarter of the credits necessary for an undergraduate degree.

Student Body

Hamilton students, as one puts it, "do tend to be homogeneous—mostly white with money, from prep schools." Another describes what he called "the Hamilton uniform: Dockers, Champion turtlenecks, L.L Bean or Colombia Siri jackets, knit sweaters, something from Lands' End, and a New England haircut." Adds a black student (one of about fifty), "if you're not Caucasian, the adjustment here is tremendous. The school has a great deal to offer to many different people, but it needs more diversity. Also, more attention needs to be paid to women's issues here." About ninety international students "help create a more diverse student body. It's a wonderful situation for both local and international students." There appears to be considerable division over political issues: the student body is by and large conservative, but there are enough left-leaning students and faculty to draw majority complaints about political correctness, multiculturalism, and the existence of a women's studies center.

ADMISSIONS

The admissions committee considers (in descending order of importance): HS record, class rank, recommendations, test scores, essay. Also considered (in descending order of importance): alumni relationship, personality, extracurriculars, special talents, geographical distribution. Either the SAT or ACT is required. An interview is recommended. Admissions process is need-blind. High school units required/recommended: 16 total units are recommended; 4 English recommended, 3 math recommended, 2 science recommended, 3 foreign language recommended, 3 social studies recommended. Only academic subjects may be counted. TOEFL is required of all international students. The admissions office says: "We place most of our emphasis on the high school record when judging academic potential."

The Inside Word

Gaining admission to Hamilton is difficult, and would be more so if the college didn't lose many of its shared applicants to competitor schools. The college's position as a popular safety for the top tier of northeastern colleges has always benefited the quality of its applicant pool, but it translates into a tough fight when it comes to getting admits to enroll. Although selectivity has risen slightly, Hamilton remains in the position of losing many of its best candidates to other more prestigious schools. Students who view Hamilton as their first-choice college should definitely make it plain to the admissions committee—such news can often be influential, especially under circumstances like those mentioned here.

FINANCIAL AID

Students should submit: FAFSA (due February 1), CSS Profile (due February 1). The Princeton Review suggests that all financial aid forms be submitted as soon as possible after January 1. The following grants/scholarships are offered: Pell, SEOG, the school's own scholarships, the school's own grants, state scholarships, state grants, private scholarships, private grants, foreign aid, United Negro College Fund. Students borrow from the following loan programs: Stafford, unsubsidized Stafford, PLUS, the school's own loan fund, private loans. Applicants will be notified of awards beginning April 1. College Work-Study Program is available. Institutional employment is available.

FROM THE ADMISSIONS OFFICE

"One of Hamilton's most important characteristics is the exceptional interaction that takes place between students and faculty members. Whether in class or out, they work together, challenging one another to excel. Academic life at Hamilton is rigorous, and emerging from that rigor is a community spirit based on common commitment. It binds together student and teacher, and stimulates self-motivation, thus making the learning process not only more productive but also more enjoyable and satisfying." Hamilton's Bristol Scholars program is merit-based, offering six to eight awards of up to $10,000 for each of the student's four years at Hamilton. Both the Bristol and the need-based Schambach Scholars program also offer special research opportunities with faculty on campus.

ADMISSIONS

Admissions Rating	83
% of applicants accepted	48
% of acceptees attending	28

FRESHMAN PROFILE

Average verbal SAT	610
Average math SAT	600
Average ACT	NR
Average TOEFL	600
Graduated top 20% of class	68
Graduated top 40% of class	94
Graduated top 60% of class	100
Average HS GPA or Avg.	NR

DEADLINES

Early decision	NR
Regular admission	1/15
Regular notification	4/1
Non-fall registration	no

APPLICANTS ALSO LOOK AT

AND OFTEN PREFER

Dartmouth
Bowdoin
Cornell U.
Middlebury Coll.
Williams

AND SOMETIMES PREFER

Trinity Coll. (CT)
Colby
Bucknell
Colgate
Bates

AND RARELY PREFER

Hobart & William Smith
Skidmore

FINANCIAL FACTS

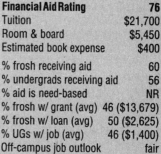

Financial Aid Rating	76
Tuition	$21,700
Room & board	$5,450
Estimated book expense	$400
% frosh receiving aid	60
% undergrads receiving aid	56
% aid is need-based	NR
% frosh w/ grant (avg)	46 ($13,679)
% frosh w/ loan (avg)	50 ($2,625)
% UGs w/ job (avg)	46 ($1,400)
Off-campus job outlook	fair

HAMPDEN-SYDNEY COLLEGE

HAMPDEN-SYDNEY, VA 23943

ADMISSIONS: 800-755-0733   FAX: 804-223-6350

CAMPUS LIFE

Quality of Life Rating   **83**
Type of school	private
Affiliation	Presbyterian Church
	(Synod of the Virginias)
Environment	town

STUDENTS
FT undergrad enrollment	971
% male/female	100/0
% from out of state	46
% live on campus	97
% spend weekend on campus	75
% transfers	7
% from public high school	57
% in (# of) fraternities	37 (11)
% African-American	3
% Asian	2
% Caucasian	93
% Hispanic	1
% international	NR
# of countries represented	4

WHAT'S HOT
health facilities
hard liquor
political activism
honesty
town-gown relations

WHAT'S NOT
lack of diversity on campus
students are cliquish
music associations
theater
off-campus food

ACADEMICS

Academic Rating   **84**
Profs Interesting Rating	95
Profs Accessible Rating	94
Calendar	semester
Student/teacher ratio	13:1
% profs PhD/tenured	79/79
Hours of study per day	3.24

MOST POPULAR MAJORS
economics
history
political science

% GRADS WHO PURSUE...
Law 5, Med 4, MBA 5, MA 11

STUDENTS SPEAK OUT

Life

The all-male Hampden-Sydney campus isn't as all-male as you might think. Says one, "With so many girls visiting on the weekend, Thursday night is like Christmas Eve." (Don't forget to leave out milk and cookies, guys!) The dominant Greek culture does throw numerous parties that attract female undergrads from schools in the surrounding area. "Fraternities provide the perfect environment for a coed setting." And what a campus the women are coming to. A country-club atmosphere pervades HSC, from its well-manicured lawns to its livable dorms to its nice off-campus frats. Outside of fraternity and academic life, many students here are community-minded. Says one, "I'm involved in the student-run fire department and also in the local rescue squad." While almost all HSC students are happy with their situation, one notes, "It's high school all over again."

Academics

"HSC is an institution where we enter as boys so that we may be able to leave as men. The Honor Code is one of our strongest and most-revered traditions." Tradition, honor, and character are all traits that HSC undergrads aspire to and defend. Predominantly southern, many following in the footsteps of fathers and brothers, students at HSC are serious about their school and education. Well, most of them are: "If you kiss ass like me, then you'll get an A" says one. States another, "Classes are very rigorous, and the professors expect work to be done outside of class." Imagine that. About three hours a day of out-of-class studying is the average for HSC students. Teachers' involvement with their students is high: "Professors are great and work extremely hard to make sure you do your best. If you're not in class some professors will hunt you down and find out exactly why." Odds are all your professors will know you by name: the lectures are tiny, with much class time taken up by discussion, discussion that sometimes takes on a certain tone: "At HSC, not only do you have quality faculty, but an all-men classroom atmosphere that permits 'politically-not-so-correct' discussions." All students must complete a rigorous set of required courses that take up close to half the credits needed for graduation. Says one, "The school may be easy to get into, but it's very, very difficult academically and hard to stay in." Another adds, "The teachers and the competitive level push you to be the best." Academic facilities (labs, the library, computers) all receive very high marks, as do the health services, registration, and the overall administration of the school.

Student Body

"It's a conservative's seventh heaven," explains one member of the ultra-conservative student body at Hampden-Sydney College. This student adds, "Most of our students are conservative, white, upper-middle-class males. These shared qualities are not apt to create conflict. Most of our arguments are over which fraternity threw the best party over the weekend." Says another, more soberly, "We all care deeply for our school. There is a lot of tradition in being an all-male campus. The student body recognizes this tradition and maintains it well." Diversity is not even an issue at this school because it almost doesn't exist, although one student would like us to understand, "Simply because we all wear J. Crew doesn't mean that we are all alike." One minority student adds, "Being one of the few international students on campus, I've realized that although the student body is for the most part ethnically homogenous, I haven't run into the difficulties one would expect from in a school that would be labeled as underrepresenting minorities." One other thing—if you are gay, this place is probably not for you. There is active discrimination against gays from the students at HSC.

ADMISSIONS

The admissions committee considers (in descending order of importance): HS record, class rank, recommendations, test scores, essay. *Also considered (in descending order of importance):* alumni relationship, extracurriculars, personality, special talents, geographical distribution. Either the SAT or ACT is required. An interview is recommended. Admissions process is need-blind. *High school units required/recommended:* 16 total units are required; 4 English required, 3 math required, 2 science required, 2 foreign language required, 1 social studies required. Minimum combined SAT I score of 1020-1250, rank in top two-fifths of secondary school class. TOEFL is required of all international students. *The admissions office says:* "We are in written contact with our prospects throughout the latter part of their junior year and senior year. We strongly encourage campus visits, personal interviews, conferences with professors and coaches, and overnight stays when possible."

The Inside Word

Hampden-Sydney is one of the last of its kind. Understandably, the applicant pool is heavily self-selected, and a fairly significant percentage of those who are admitted choose to enroll. This enables the admissions committee to be more selective, which in turn requires candidates to take the process more seriously than might otherwise be necessary. Students with consistently sound academic records should have little to worry about nonetheless.

FINANCIAL AID

Students should submit: FAFSA (due March 1), CSS Profile (due March 1), state aid form (due July 31). The Princeton Review suggests that all financial aid forms be submitted as soon as possible after January 1. *The following grants/scholarships are offered:* Pell, SEOG, academic merit, the school's own scholarships, the school's own grants, state grants, private scholarships, private grants, ROTC. *Students borrow from the following loan programs:* Stafford, unsubsidized Stafford, Perkins, PLUS, the school's own loan fund, private loans. Applicants will be notified of awards beginning March 15. College Work-Study Program is available. Institutional employment is available.

FROM THE ADMISSIONS OFFICE

"The spirit of Hampden-Sydney is its sense of community. As one of only 950 students, you will be in small classes and find it easy to get extra help or inspiration from professors when you want it. Many of our professors live on campus and enjoy being with students in the snack bar, as well as in the classroom. They give you the best, most personal education as possible. A big bonus of small-college life is that everybody is invited to go out for everything, and you can be as much of a leader as you want to be. From athletics, to debating, to publications, to fraternity life, this is part of the process that produces a well-rounded Hampden-Sydney graduate."

ADMISSIONS

Admissions Rating	71
% of applicants accepted	83
% of acceptees attending	42

FRESHMAN PROFILE

Average verbal SAT	590
Average math SAT	560
Average ACT	24
Average TOEFL	570
Graduated top 20% of class	25
Graduated top 40% of class	50
Graduated top 60% of class	68
Average HS GPA or Avg.	3.0

DEADLINES

Early decision	Fall
Regular admission	3/1
Regular notification	4/15
Non-fall registration	yes

APPLICANTS ALSO LOOK AT

AND OFTEN PREFER

William and Mary
U. Virginia

AND SOMETIMES PREFER

Washington and Lee
James Madison
Vanderbilt
UNC-Chapel Hill

AND RARELY PREFER

Randolph-Macon

FINANCIAL FACTS

Financial Aid Rating	95
Tuition	$13,878
Room & board	$4,707
Estimated book expense	$700
% frosh receiving aid	82
% undergrads receiving aid	79
% aid is need-based	80
% frosh w/ grant (avg)	75 ($5,300)
% frosh w/ loan (avg)	66 ($6,100)
% UGs w/ job (avg)	19 ($850)
Off-campus job outlook	fair

HAMPSHIRE COLLEGE

ADMISSIONS OFFICE, 893 WEST STREET, AMHERST, MA 01002   ADMISSIONS: 413-582-5471   FAX: 413-582-5631

CAMPUS LIFE

Quality of Life Rating	**85**
Type of school	private
Affiliation	none
Environment	town

STUDENTS

FT undergrad enrollment	1,073
% male/female	42/58
% from out of state	81
% live on campus	95
% spend weekend on campus	NR
% transfers	11
% from public high school	72
% African-American	4
% Asian	3
% Caucasian	80
% Hispanic	3
% international	3
# of countries represented	24

WHAT'S HOT
leftist politics
honesty
campus feels safe
theater

WHAT'S NOT
student government
religion
student publications
beer
intercollegiate sports

ACADEMICS

Academic Rating	**84**
Profs Interesting Rating	91
Profs Accessible Rating	80
Calendar	4-1-4
Student/teacher ratio	12:1
% profs PhD	82
Hours of study per day	3.30

MOST POPULAR MAJORS
creative writing
film/photography
art

STUDENTS SPEAK OUT

Life

Just about anything goes at Hampshire College, but "peer pressure is low. There are plenty of virgin teetotalers who are accepted here." Some are disappointed with the somewhat smothering social life, but most admit to having fun. One wryly remarks, "Hampster relationships are never a problem, if you're one of the dozen or so people who are still whimsical enough to date anyone." Antonio's Pizza is a local favorite for those late-night munchies. Anyone seeking escape can easily slip out to another college (Hampshire is part of the Five College Consortium, which includes Amherst, Smith, Mount Holyoke, and UMass-Amherst).

Academics

Students at Hampshire College, a small school known for its philosophy of alternative, self-directed education, responded to our questions with a flood of well-written essays. The unusually high number of thoughtful responses from Hampshire is telling. Students here are used to creative thinking and fluent writing, because those skills are expected of them daily. Hampsters "have no tests, grades, credits, or majors. Instead, we have course papers, self- and teacher evaluations, the divisional system, and concentrations." This unusual academic structure is hailed by many as progressive and challenging. Since students design their own programs, there are "no cheesy English 101 requirements." Rather than "teaching countless empty facts, the system teaches students to think independently and to write well." Warns one student, "Don't think this place is a breeze just because we don't believe in grades. Written evaluations can be harsh, and you'll never write—and revise—as many papers anywhere as you will here." All agreed that if prospective students are not "extremely motivated," they should not come to Hampshire. Many artistic types can be found here. Witness the excellent film and photography departments, which are so popular that they "close out students who aren't majors." Most students believe Hampshire's system really works; but one complaint is that the school is "so alternative that after two years you are trapped in a nontransferable system." A few gripe about the administration, calling it "tyrannical and impossible to interact with," but overall student opinion of Hampshire is very high. It is "Okay to draw outside the lines here," and most appreciate the opportunity to do just that.

Student Body

Hampsters are a very tolerant and accepting group. One says that "gays, lesbians, and bisexuals are active and accepted here, but not in a way that limits heterosexuals, many of whom attend LGBA-sponsored dances." Retro clothing and purple, blue, green, orange, or nonexistent hair are more common here than are different shades of skin color, but Hampshire is diverse in its own way.

ADMISSIONS

The admissions committee considers (in descending order of importance): HS record, essay, recommendations, class rank. *Also considered (in descending order of importance):* extracurriculars, personality, special talents. An interview is recommended. Admissions process is need-blind. *High school units required/recommended:* 20 total units are recommended. TOEFL is required of all international students. *The admissions office says:* "We require every applicant to submit an analytic writing sample in addition to the personal statement."

The Inside Word

Don Quixote would be a fairly solid candidate for admission to Hampshire. The admissions committee (and it really is one, unlike at many colleges) looks to identify thinkers, dreamers, and the generally intellectually curious. It is important to have a solid record from high school, but high grades only go so far toward impressing the committee. Those who are denied usually lack self-awareness and are fairly poor communicators as well. Candidates should expect their essays to come under close scrutiny.

FINANCIAL AID

Students should submit: FAFSA, CSS Profile, the school's own financial aid form (due February 15), state aid form, Divorced Parents form. The Princeton Review suggests that all financial aid forms be submitted as soon as possible after January 1. *The following grants/scholarships are offered:* Pell, SEOG, academic merit, the school's own scholarships, the school's own grants, state scholarships, state grants, private scholarships, private grants, foreign aid. *Students borrow from the following loan programs:* unsubsidized Stafford, Perkins, PLUS, state loans, private loans. Applicants will be notified of awards beginning April 1. College Work-Study Program is available. Institutional employment is available.

FROM THE ADMISSIONS OFFICE

"Students tell us they like our application. It is less directive and more open-ended than most. Rather than assigning an essay topic, we ask to learn more about you as an individual and invite your ideas. Instead of asking for a list of activities, we ask you to describe your involvement in a dozen different kinds of personal, artistic, social, and intellectual activities. This approach parallels the work you will do at Hampshire, defining the questions you will ask, and the courses and experiences that will help you to answer them."

ADMISSIONS

Admissions Rating	76
% of applicants accepted	68
% of acceptees attending	28

FRESHMAN PROFILE

Average verbal SAT	640
Average math SAT	580
Average ACT	NR
Average TOEFL	610
Graduated top 20% of class	46
Graduated top 40% of class	80
Graduated top 60% of class	93
Average HS GPA or Avg.	3.1

DEADLINES

Early decision	11/15
Regular admission	2/1
Regular notification	4/1
Non-fall registration	yes

APPLICANTS ALSO LOOK AT
AND OFTEN PREFER

Bates
Vassar
Smith
New College
Oberlin

AND SOMETIMES PREFER

Reed
Sarah Lawrence
Bennington
Antioch
NYU

AND RARELY PREFER

Bard
Goddard

FINANCIAL FACTS

Financial Aid Rating	77
Tuition	$22,600
Room & board	$5,990
Estimated book expense	$400
% frosh receiving aid	55
% undergrads receiving aid	62
% aid is need-based	99
% frosh w/ grant (avg)	55 ($13,000)
% frosh w/ loan (avg)	53 ($2,625)
% UGs w/ job (avg)	50
Off-campus job outlook	fair

HAMPTON UNIVERSITY

HAMPTON, VA 23368

ADMISSIONS: 804-727-5328   FAX: 804-727-5084

CAMPUS LIFE

Quality of Life Rating 65
Type of school private
Affiliation none
Environment city

STUDENTS
FT undergrad enrollment	4,556
% male/female	40/60
% from out of state	82
% live on campus	50
% spend weekend on campus	NR
% transfers	NR
% from public high school	NR
% in (# of) fraternities	(5)
% in (# of) sororities	(3)
% African-American	90
% Asian	0
% Caucasian	9
% Hispanic	0
% international	NR
# of countries represented	NR

WHAT'S HOT
sex
old-fashioned dating
college radio
leftist politics
hard liquor

WHAT'S NOT
inefficient administration
dorms
registration is a pain
students are unhappy
campus food

ACADEMICS

Academic Rating 70
Profs Interesting Rating 60
Profs Accessible Rating 62
Calendar semester
Student/teacher ratio 18:1
% profs PhD 60
Hours of study per day 2.92

MOST POPULAR MAJORS
accounting
biology
psychology

% GRADS WHO PURSUE...
Law 3, Med 1, MBA 4, MA 17

STUDENTS SPEAK OUT

Life

Hampton students are serious, and as a result, they don't seem to need much of a social life. Some comments we received include: "Hampton isn't a big city so there is not a lot to do in terms of entertainment," "There are few social activities on campus," and "There's relatively little to do at Hampton. People are too absorbed in themselves to notice what is going on around them." Part of this may be due to the dry nature of Hampton, the city. Located between Virginia Beach and colonial Williamsburg, Hampton has a 204-acre waterfront campus and offers much by its location. Popular student events are the Virginia Beach Party, Greek cabarets, and traveling to other Virginia schools to party. This adds to the appeal of off-campus life. As one student notes, "Off-campus housing is cheap and luxurious. We live better than most college students. A car helps a lot down here. After freshman year you kind of need a car and most people have one." Put more bluntly, "Hampton University is very dry and boring unless you have access to a car, and the on-campus activities are few and far between. But what can you expect, because Hampton is a dry city?" HU students are very proud of its CIAA teams, particularly its tennis team, which has won the CIAA twenty times out of the past twenty-one years.

Academics

Let's not beat around the bush: Hampton students work hard and get results. Over 40 percent of Hampton students go on to graduate school within five years. A whopping 60 percent of students enter the profession of their choice immediately following graduation. There is a waiting list each year for corporations who wish to recruit students from Hampton. Hampton is a coeducational, nonsectarian, historically black university that "remains faithful to its traditional commitment of coping with the problems of educating students whose academic and personal growth, potential and promise may have been inhibited by a lack of economic, social, and educational opportunity." Hampton offers forty-seven different undergraduate majors, of which business, arts and letters, and pure and applied sciences are the most popular. Hampton students give their professors mixed to positive reviews and give the administration comparatively negative comments. Students write that the professors "are highly accessible and very concerned with each interested student. If you care, they care." One student notes about the administration that "seriously, they don't care if you live or die as long as tuition is paid." Students also have negative comments about the new grading policy which they believe will "cause GPAs to drop and long lines with the administration and professors." The Hampton Museum is internationally known for its collection of Oceanic Asian and American Indian artifacts, as well as American and African contemporary works.

Student Body

One student writes that "this school is a historically black university and therefore made of a pretty homogeneous group. Many different groups in the African-American community are represented, yet we all seem to mesh well (especially against the administration)." Hampton students do seem to get around the "cutthroat" behavior of most pre-business schools and find a sense of community.

FINANCIAL AID: 800-624-3341

WEB SITE: HTTP://WWW.CS.HAMPTONU.EDU/

ADMISSIONS

The admissions committee considers (in descending order of importance): HS record, test scores, essay, recommendations, class rank. *Also considered (in descending order of importance):* alumni relationship, extracurriculars, geographical distribution, personality, special talents. Either the SAT or ACT is required. *High school units required/recommended:* 17 total units are required; 4 English required, 3 math required, 2 science required, 2 history required. Minimum combined SAT I score of 800, rank in top half of secondary school class, and minimum 2.0 GPA required. TOEFL is required of all international students.

The Inside Word

Hampton has less general visibility than such better-known historically black colleges as Morehouse, Spelman, and Howard, but it has just as much of a tradition of academic quality. In recent years the university's profile has been boosted by hosting national workshops on counseling minority students in the college admissions process. Candidates can expect a personal and caring experience in the admissions process.

FINANCIAL AID

Students should submit: FAFSA, the school's own financial aid form, state aid form. The Princeton Review suggests that all financial aid forms be submitted as soon as possible after January 1. *The following grants/scholarships are offered:* Pell, SEOG, academic merit, athletic, the school's own scholarships, the school's own grants, state grants, private scholarships, private grants, ROTC, foreign aid. *Students borrow from the following loan programs:* Stafford, Perkins, PLUS, state loans, federal nursing loans, private loans. College Work-Study Program is available.

FROM THE ADMISSIONS OFFICE

"Hampton attempts to provide the environment and structures most conducive to the intellectual, emotional, and aesthetic enlargement of the lives of its members. The University gives priority to effective teaching and scholarly research while placing the student at the center of its planning. Hampton will ask you to look inwardly at your own history and culture and examine your relationship to the aspirations and development of the world."

ADMISSIONS

Admissions Rating	72
% of applicants accepted	52
% of acceptees attending	38

FRESHMAN PROFILE

Average verbal SAT	NR
Average math SAT	NR
Average ACT	NR
Average TOEFL	600
Graduated top 20% of class	NR
Graduated top 40% of class	NR
Graduated top 60% of class	NR
Average HS GPA or Avg.	NR

DEADLINES

Early decision	NR
Regular admission	3/15
Regular notification	rolling
Non-fall registration	yes

APPLICANTS ALSO LOOK AT

AND OFTEN PREFER

Florida A & M
Tuskegee
Spelman

AND SOMETIMES PREFER

U. Maryland, Coll. Park
Howard
Virginia Tech.

FINANCIAL FACTS

Financial Aid Rating	62
Tuition	$7,662
Room & board	$3,468
Estimated book expense	$600
% frosh receiving aid	NR
% undergrads receiving aid	60
% aid is need-based	NR
% frosh w/ grant (avg)	NR
% frosh w/ loan (avg)	NR
% UGs w/ job (avg)	NR
Off-campus job outlook	good

HANOVER COLLEGE

P.O. BOX 108, HANOVER, IN 47243

ADMISSIONS: 812-866-7021   FAX: 812-866-7172

CAMPUS LIFE

Quality of Life Rating	**77**
Type of school	private
Affiliation	Presbyterian Church
Environment	rural

STUDENTS

FT undergrad enrollment	1,075
% male/female	48/52
% from out of state	40
% live on campus	98
% spend weekend on campus	60
% transfers	1
% from public high school	80
% in (# of) fraternities	44 (5)
% in (# of) sororities	45 (4)
% African-American	0
% Asian	0
% Caucasian	96
% Hispanic	0
% international	2
# of countries represented	19

WHAT'S HOT
Greeks
campus is beautiful
intramural sports
campus easy to get around
campus feels safe

WHAT'S NOT
student publications
library
lack of diversity on campus
off-campus food
Hanover

ACADEMICS

Academic Rating	**87**
Profs Interesting Rating	87
Profs Accessible Rating	92
Calendar	4-4-1
Student/teacher ratio	11:1
% profs tenured	82
Hours of study per day	3.52

MOST POPULAR MAJORS
business administration
English
psychology

% GRADS WHO PURSUE...
Law 4, Med 8, MBA 15, MA 8

STUDENTS SPEAK OUT

Life

"Most of the fun at Hanover involves the Greek life," explains one Hanover College student, "but the school also provides entertaining activities each weekend such as musical groups, speakers, and theater productions." Greek life is indeed huge at Hanover. More than half the students join fraternities and sororities, and most Greek parties are open to Greeks and independents alike. Apart from such activities, Hanover has little to offer for some. "We live in a cornfield," explains one, "all people do is drink." Yes they do; beer is huge at Hanover, a dry campus that tends to get soaked on weekends. But others feel differently about their town: "Because of its relative isolation (Kentuckiana), I was at first worried that I would be bored at Hanover. But I have discovered that there is a ton of stuff to do here, if a person is willing to participate." Another adds, "The Student Planning Board has been working hard to bring more activities to the campus. I've seen a lot of improvement." Still, one sad student adds "Things have been more boring since they discontinued Thursday afternoon pony rides. The pony's very ill. They think it's terminal, I'm afraid." Very funny.

Academics

Professors at Hanover are adored by their students. "Basically, the professors here are more concerned with your grades than those of their own children," explains one. Interaction between student and profs is so prevalent that dining with profs is common: "I have eaten at three different faculty homes," says one sophomore. Tiny classes and the amount of class time spent in discussion does a lot to foster close relationships. So does required classroom attendance! Says another of his academic experience, "I literally had to ask friends at a big school what a TA was. I didn't know!" While the administration receives passing marks for facilities and services (except registration, which is a real bear for freshmen), its paternalistic attitude is often remarked upon: "The administration is at least as authoritarian as the former Soviet Union," rails one, "A student placed a Jamaican flag in his window and was forced to remove it because it 'detracted from the building's appearance.' Right." These problems with the administration do little to dampen students' enthusiasm for their school, however. Beams one, "I love this place! I attended a much larger state school last year and I can't believe how much better this school is." Indeed, with its huge endowment and impressive student/teacher ratio, Hanover is a school with the means to provide a great, personalized education.

Student Body

Hanover College does not have a diverse student body. Almost everyone is white, and with such a small student population, minority populations can be prohibitively small. "We are too much of an archetype of the average American Midwest kid," explains such a student. Another concurs, "Our student body is homogenous—too many upper middle class white Midwesterners. We need diversity just to keep from being boring!" Interaction between races is fairly rare, but open discrimination is not a problem (though it is for homosexuals). Greek life also tends to segregate the campus, "After fall term of the freshman year, noticeable differences in social structure appear between the Greek house and independents."

FINANCIAL AID: 812-866-7030

WEB SITE: HTTP://WWW.HANOVER.EDU/

ADMISSIONS

The admissions committee considers (in descending order of importance): HS record, class rank, test scores, recommendations, essay. *Also considered (in descending order of importance):* personality, extracurriculars, alumni relationship, geographical distribution, special talents. Either the SAT or ACT is required. An interview is recommended. Admissions process is need-blind. *High school units required/recommended:* 18 total units are required; 4 English required, 3 math required, 4 math recommended, 2 science required, 3 science recommended, 2 foreign language required, 3 foreign language recommended, 2 social studies required, 3 social studies recommended, 2 history required, 3 history recommended. Minimum combined SAT I score of 900 and rank in top half of secondary school class recommended. TOEFL is required of all international students. *The admissions office says:* "Alumni children receive some special consideration."

The Inside Word

Despite significant national publicity in recent years, Hanover still has a relatively small applicant pool. There is no doubt that these candidates are capable academically-few schools have as impressive a graduation rate or percentage of its alums going on to grad school. It pays to put some energy into the completion of the application process, especially given the sizable percentage of students awarded academic scholarships.

FINANCIAL AID

Students should submit: FAFSA (due March 1), CSS Profile (due March 1), a copy of parents' most recent income tax filing (due March 1). The Princeton Review suggests that all financial aid forms be submitted as soon as possible after January 1. *The following grants/scholarships are offered:* Pell, academic merit, the school's own scholarships, the school's own grants, state scholarships, state grants, private scholarships, private grants, foreign aid. *Students borrow from the following loan programs:* Stafford, unsubsidized Stafford, PLUS. Institutional employment is available.

FROM THE ADMISSIONS OFFICE

"Hanover College offers a unique community to all who live here. With ninety-five percent of our students and seventy-five percent of our faculty and staff residing on campus, the pursuit of academic excellence extends well beyond the confines of the classroom. This is enhanced by a caring faculty, ninety-five percent of whom hold earned doctoral degrees. The desire to meet academic challenges and the strong sense of community may be the two greatest contributors to the ninety-two percent retention rate of which Hanover is quite proud. These contributions are also apparent in that over the past five years more than sixty-five percent of our graduates have advanced their educational degrees. Hanover's total cost qualifies the college as one of the best values in the nation; and, its sizable endowment, on a dollar per student ratio, places it in the top ten percent nationally."

ADMISSIONS

Admissions Rating	76
% of applicants accepted	78
% of acceptees attending	39

FRESHMAN PROFILE

Average verbal SAT	650
Average math SAT	590
Average ACT	25
Average TOEFL	550
Graduated top 20% of class	63
Graduated top 40% of class	91
Graduated top 60% of class	99
Average HS GPA or Avg.	3.3

DEADLINES

Early decision	3/1
Regular admission	NR
Regular notification	4/1
Non-fall registration	yes

APPLICANTS ALSO LOOK AT

AND SOMETIMES PREFER
Indiana U.-Bloomington
DePauw
Centre
Butler
Franklin Coll.

AND RARELY PREFER
Ball St.
Purdue U.-West Lafayette
Wittenberg
Indiana St.

FINANCIAL FACTS

Financial Aid Rating	83
Tuition	$8,800
Room & board	$3,485
Estimated book expense	$700
% frosh receiving aid	70
% undergrads receiving aid	83
% aid is need-based	80
% frosh w/ grant (avg)	62 ($4,000)
% frosh w/ loan (avg)	42 ($1,000)
% UGs w/ job (avg)	33 ($900)
Off-campus job outlook	fair

HARVARD AND RADCLIFFE COLLEGES

BYERLY HALL, 8 GARDEN STREET, CAMBRIDGE, MA 02138   ADMISSIONS: 617-495-1551   FAX: 617-495-0500

CAMPUS LIFE

Quality of Life Rating   **93**
Type of school   private
Affiliation   none
Environment   metropolis

STUDENTS
FT undergrad enrollment   7,098
% male/female   56/44
% from out of state   84
% live on campus   96
% spend weekend on campus   NR
% transfers   6
% from public high school   68
% African-American   8
% Asian   19
% Caucasian   45
% Hispanic   7
% international   6
# of countries represented   88

WHAT'S HOT
ethnic diversity on campus
Cambridge
political activism
students are happy
different students interact

WHAT'S NOT
hard liquor
drugs
beer
infrequent dating
college radio

ACADEMICS

Academic Rating   **95**
Profs Interesting Rating   76
Profs Accessible Rating   70
Calendar   semester
Student/teacher ratio   8:1
% profs tenured   97
Hours of study per day   3.61

MOST POPULAR MAJORS
government
economics
biology

% GRADS WHO PURSUE...
Law 19, Med 17, MBA 12, MA 18

STUDENTS SPEAK OUT

Life
One thing that clearly sets Harvard apart from Yale is its safe and attractive location. Yale is located in dingy, unfriendly downtown New Haven, while Harvard is located in very student-friendly Cambridge, minutes away from Boston. Another difference between the two is quality of dorms. You guessed it: Harvard's are great, Yale's are gross. Partly because of the workload, the staples of social life at most other schools—partying and dating—are relatively uncommon here. Another impediment to social life, according to one student, is that "Harvard makes students work very hard—they have no time to socialize and interact with others—so when placed into social situations, they don't know how to act." There is no Greek system here, but there are several exclusive, upper-crust social clubs (membership by invitation only). Biggest negative of life here: the weather stinks.

Academics
Harvard is one of the best academic universities in the country, period. If you attend school here, you will learn from world-famous scholars in small classes, do research in excellent facilities, and probably feel privileged to be at the nation's most famous institution. Not surprisingly, Harvard students love everything about their school (although, oddly, they are not among the ten happiest student bodies in the nation). The school is a hub of intellectual activity in America, home to a distinguished faculty, and often host to visiting politicians and scholars. Says one student, "There is always so much going on—lectures, visiting speakers, events—it's just a matter of going out and finding what you want!" Students give their profs average marks, as students often do at schools with considerable graduate populations. Even those who disliked their instructors, though, were happy with Harvard. Says one, "The resources available for learning (libraries, labs, friends) are the redeeming qualities that make it worthwhile coming here." Says another, "Harvard has all the resources: career services advisors, great people academically and administratively at many different levels. But students must go out and tap these resources themselves—there's not much hand-holding here." Students give the administration a big thumbs-up. Once discrete all-male and all-female colleges, Harvard and Radcliffe are now separate entities in name only.

Student Body
The students have a reputation for arrogance. Of course, Harvard students feel they're entitled to be arrogant. "Lots of huge egos, but, unfortunately, many are well deserved," reports one student. "Brilliant" is the word most often used by Harvard students to describe each other; "preppy" is the second most common description. Still, many students indicated surprise at how heterogeneous the student body here is. A gay student tells us that while "there is a rather large proportion of preppie snobs, it's easy to avoid them if you want. Everyone and anyone can find his/her niche among the incredibly diverse students." Says one freshman, "I wholeheartedly recommend applying to all you dweebs out there."

ADMISSIONS

The admissions committee considers (in descending order of importance): class rank, essay, HS record, recommendations, test scores. *Also considered (in descending order of importance):* extracurriculars, personality, alumni relationship, geographical distribution, special talents. Either the SAT or ACT is required. An interview is recommended. Admissions process is need-blind. *High school units required/recommended:* 19 total units are recommended; 4 English recommended, 4 math recommended, 4 science recommended, 4 foreign language recommended, 3 history recommended. Applicants are urged to pursue the most rigorous four-year programs in English, math, foreign language, and sciences. TOEFL is required of all international students.

The Inside Word

It just doesn't get any tougher than this. Candidates to Harvard face dual obstacles—an awe-inspiring applicant pool and, as a result, admissions standards that defy explanation in quantifiable terms. Harvard denies admission to the vast majority, and virtually all of them are top students. This boils down committee decisions to splitting hairs, which is quite hard to explain and even harder for candidates to understand. Rather than being as detailed and direct as possible about the selection process and criteria, Harvard keeps things close to the vest—before, during, and after. These guys even refuse to admit that being from South Dakota is an advantage. Thus the admissions process does more to intimidate candidates than to empower them. Moving to the Common Application seemed to be a small step in the right direction, but with the current explosion of applicants and a super-high yield of enrollees, things are not likely to change dramatically.

FINANCIAL AID

Students should submit: FAFSA, the school's own financial aid form, Divorced Parents form, a copy of parents' most recent income tax filing. The Princeton Review suggests that all financial aid forms be submitted as soon as possible after January 1. *The following grants/scholarships are offered:* Pell, SEOG, the school's own scholarships, state scholarships, state grants, private scholarships, private grants, ROTC, foreign aid. *Students borrow from the following loan programs:* Stafford, unsubsidized Stafford, Perkins, PLUS, the school's own loan fund, state loans. Applicants will be notified of awards beginning April 1. College Work-Study Program is available. Institutional employment is available.

FROM THE ADMISSIONS OFFICE

"The admissions committee looks for energy, ambition, and the capacity to make the most of opportunities. Academic ability and preparation are important, and so is intellectual curiosity-but many of the strongest applicants have significant nonacademic interests and accomplishments as well. There is no formula for admission and applicants are considered carefully, with attention to future promise."

ADMISSIONS

Admissions Rating	99
% of applicants accepted	12
% of acceptees attending	75

FRESHMAN PROFILE

Average verbal SAT	740
Average math SAT	720
Average ACT	NR
Average TOEFL	600
Graduated top 20% of class	NR
Graduated top 40% of class	NR
Graduated top 60% of class	NR
Average HS GPA or Avg.	NR

DEADLINES

Early decision	12/15
Regular admission	1/1
Regular notification	4/3
Non-fall registration	no

APPLICANTS ALSO LOOK AT

AND SOMETIMES PREFER

Princeton
Stanford
Yale
Swarthmore

AND RARELY PREFER

Northwestern U.
Georgetown U.
Amherst
Williams
Pennsylvania

FINANCIAL FACTS

Financial Aid Rating	81
Tuition	$18,838
Room & board	$6,710
Estimated book expense	NR
% frosh receiving aid	78
% undergrads receiving aid	67
% aid is need-based	100
% frosh w/ grant (avg)	46 ($12,478)
% frosh w/ loan (avg)	58 ($3,200)
% UGs w/ job (avg)	75 ($2,250)
Off-campus job outlook	excellent

HARVEY MUDD COLLEGE

301 EAST 12TH STREET, CLAREMONT, CA 91711-5990　　　ADMISSIONS: 909-621-8011　　FAX: 909-621-8360

CAMPUS LIFE

Quality of Life Rating 79
Type of school | private
Affiliation | none
Environment | suburban

STUDENTS

FT undergrad enrollment	628
% male/female	75/25
% from out of state	57
% live on campus	97
% spend weekend on campus	90
% transfers	1
% from public high school	80
% African-American	1
% Asian	24
% Caucasian	68
% Hispanic	5
% international	10
# of countries represented	10

WHAT'S HOT
computer facilities
lab facilities
school runs like butter
different students interact
honesty

WHAT'S NOT
cigarettes
student publications
sex
religion
intercollegiate sports

ACADEMICS

Academic Rating	**95**
Profs Interesting Rating	94
Profs Accessible Rating	97
Calendar	semester
Student/teacher ratio	8:1
% profs PhD	100
Hours of study per day	4.41

MOST POPULAR MAJORS
engineering
physics

STUDENTS SPEAK OUT

Life

"Where do you go to breakfast after being awake for fifty hours and discuss quantum physics, chemistry, and sex at the same time?" Maybe the same place where "lunchtime conversation ranges from UNIX to poetry"? Both colleges are one and the same: they are Mudd, a school where students revel in their brainy, cluttered academic lives: "For fun, we fantasize about having free time," explains one preoccupied undergrad. Everyone lives on-campus at Mudd, which isn't a problem for most: "This campus is safe and small, everything is within walking distance." Indeed, the town of Claremont received high marks for accessibility and overall beauty. Dorm food at Mudd sucks, however. Intramural sports are big. Greek life is nonexistent, but we're told that "unicycling and juggling are both moderately popular." Many drink beer, few smoke cigarettes or pot. See, "Everybody does homework. After that, they all relax...in their own ways." Vive la difference, Mudders!

Academics

Note: The Claremont Colleges are five small undergraduate schools (Claremont McKenna, Harvey Mudd, Pitzer, Pomona, and Scripps) and one graduate school sharing a central location and facilities. Each school serves a distinct purpose and maintains its own faculty and campus. Cross-registration is encouraged. Harvey Mudd College offers programs in engineering, biology, chemistry, physics, mathematics, and computer science. The first year of each program is basically laid out for incoming freshman, and that first year (as well as subsequent years) is tough. The average student studies over four hours a day! Says one, "Grades, social life, sleep: pick any two of three." No one seems to mind the long hours, partly due to the universal respect they have for their profs and administation. "The faculty's primary concern is not with grad students, not with research, not with publishing, but with the success and well-being of the students." Another adds "There is much more emphasis placed on understanding the material than on grades." Yes, "professors are pretty damn helpful." And about the administration, "The fact that I don't notice the administration leads me to believe that it runs well." Facilities, especially labs and computers, are ranked extremely high by students. Classes are small, and TAs rarely teach. One students sums up the serious academic experience at Mudd quite well: "Classes at Mudd are like hard liquor. They're hard to swallow, but the result is all good."

Student Body

"Students are...eccentric.," says one student. "Yeah, we like each other. When the heat is on and the books are three feet deep, not killing the guy next to you is liking each other," explains another Mudder. Both tell the truth. Undergrads at Mudd are a fairly homogenous group (mostly whites and Asians) who get along well with one another. Discrimination on any basis is not reported as a problem: "There are no well-defined cliques or outcasts." Not only that, Mudders help each other out with homework, go to cheap campus movies en masse (few date due to the man-heavy student ratio), and bond over their intense workloads. "Everyone's willing to help everyone else both on school and personal levels."

FINANCIAL AID: 909-621-8055

ADMISSIONS

The admissions committee considers (in descending order of importance): HS record, class rank, test scores, recommendations, essay. *Also considered (in descending order of importance):* extracurriculars, personality, special talents, alumni relationship. SAT is preferred. An interview is recommended. *High school units required/recommended:* 4 English required, 4 math required, 3 science required, 2 foreign language required, 2 social studies required. Minimum SAT I scores of 580 verbal and 660 math and rank in top tenth of secondary school class recommended. TOEFL is required of all international students. *The admissions office says:* "HMC students are focused on math/science/technology, yet are not ready to pursue a narrow specialty in those fields. Students coming to HMC are also joining the Claremont College culture. They will be taking classes on the other Claremont campuses and are likely to be involved in college activities such as sports programs, performing arts, journalism, etc."

The Inside Word

Harvey Mudd is a place for serious students, and its admissions process is designed to screen out all but the best. Not to say that they don't have a sense of humor out there in Claremont. The college attracted national attention in the past by mailing recruitment literature that poked fun at the overly serious world of college admissions while at the same time showcasing the school's academic quality. Any admissions staff that contributes to the lessening of student stress in the college search and admissions process is to be commended.

FINANCIAL AID

Students should submit: FAFSA, CSS Profile, the school's own financial aid form (due February 1), state aid form. The Princeton Review suggests that all financial aid forms be submitted as soon as possible after January 1. *The following grants/scholarships are offered:* Pell, SEOG, the school's own scholarships, the school's own grants, state scholarships, state grants, private scholarships, private grants, ROTC. *Students borrow from the following loan programs:* Stafford, unsubsidized Stafford, Perkins, PLUS, the school's own loan fund. Applicants will be notified of awards beginning April 1. College Work-Study Program is available. Institutional employment is available. Freshmen are discouraged from working.

FROM THE ADMISSIONS OFFICE

"Students interested in HMC must have a talent and passion for science and mathematics. The college offers majors in mathematics, physics, engineering, chemistry, biology and computer science. 'Mudders' have very diverse interests. Because nearly one-third of the course work at HMC is in the humanities and social sciences, HMC students also enjoy studying economics, psychology, philosophy, history, the fine arts and literature."

ADMISSIONS

Admissions Rating	95
% of applicants accepted	41
% of acceptees attending	31

FRESHMAN PROFILE

Average verbal SAT	710
Average math SAT	740
Average ACT	NR
Average TOEFL	600
Graduated top 20% of class	NR
Graduated top 40% of class	NR
Graduated top 60% of class	NR
Average HS GPA or Avg.	NR

DEADLINES

Early decision	NR
Regular admission	1/15
Regular notification	4/1
Non-fall registration	no

APPLICANTS ALSO LOOK AT

AND OFTEN PREFER
Stanford
MIT

AND SOMETIMES PREFER
Cornell U.
Rice

AND RARELY PREFER
Worcester Poly.
Virginia Tech.

FINANCIAL FACTS

Financial Aid Rating	85
Tuition	$18,100
Room & board	$6,920
Estimated book expense	$700
% frosh receiving aid	83
% undergrads receiving aid	75
% aid is need-based	100
% frosh w/ grant (avg)	81 ($9,927)
% frosh w/ loan (avg)	84 ($1,851)
% UGs w/ job (avg)	57 ($1,374)
Off-campus job outlook	good

HAVERFORD COLLEGE

370 LANCASTER AVENUE, HAVERFORD, PA 19041-1392   ADMISSIONS: 610-896-1350   FAX: 610-896-1338

CAMPUS LIFE

Quality of Life Rating	**87**
Type of school	private
Affiliation	none
Environment	metropolis

STUDENTS

FT undergrad enrollment	1,115
% male/female	50/50
% from out of state	82
% live on campus	96
% spend weekend on campus	85
% transfers	2
% from public high school	61
% African-American	4
% Asian	8
% Caucasian	83
% Hispanic	5
% international	5
# of countries represented	27

WHAT'S HOT
campus easy to get around
registration is a breeze
political activism
honesty
dorms

WHAT'S NOT
Greeks
infrequent dating
hard liquor
religion
beer

ACADEMICS

Academic Rating	**97**
Profs Interesting Rating	95
Profs Accessible Rating	96
Calendar	semester
Student/teacher ratio	10:1
% profs PhD/tenured	94/55
Hours of study per day	3.67

MOST POPULAR MAJORS
English
history
biology

% GRADS WHO PURSUE...
Law 5, Med 7, MBA 1, MA 9

STUDENTS SPEAK OUT

Life

If you go here, you'll find that Haverford is a great place to study. Just ask any undergrad about social life and you'll be told: "Haverford is a great place to study." Social life definitely runs a distant second to academics here. Writes one typical respondent, "It's not a big party school, but you can find good pals to drink with regardless." There is a smaller partying contingent—one member writes, "One third of us go out drinking on weekends and try to do enough to make up for the other two thirds"—but quiet weekends seem more the rule than the exception. Haverford has no Greek system. For off-campus activity, Philadelphia is only twenty minutes away by train. Many student activities are run jointly with the school down the road. Reports one student, "Haverford is pretty hard to evaluate without taking Bryn Mawr into account. Virtually everything is bi-college." There is a closeness at Haverford that comes from having a small student body (fewer than 1,200). Sometimes that closeness is overwhelming. Writes one student, "This place can seem a little too small, especially when I realize that I know everyone here by face."

Academics

Haverford College has a reputation as one of the finest small colleges in the country. Students here give high marks to most of the academic environment, citing their easy interaction with professors, relatively painless dealings with campus bureaucrats, and satisfaction with the school's Honor Code. One student tells us that "the Honor Code is probably the most unique thing about Haverford. Students take the Code very seriously and on the whole it provides an atmosphere of trust. Many exams are self-scheduled, which makes exam period more relaxed." Students stress the ease of cross-registration at nearby Bryn Mawr; says one, "The two schools function together as one academic entity." Premedical studies are popular here—one in ten students goes on to medical school—as are English, history, and philosophy. Students carry a heavy workload (about three and three quarters hours of studying a day), but most seem comfortable with it and would agree that "Haverford is a wonderful place for the mind to germinate."

Student Body

Haverford has a seventeen percent minority population, nearly half of which is made up of Asians. African-Americans and Hispanics make up the other large minority groups here. Haverford has an equal number of men and women, but Haverford/ Bryn Mawr combine for a 3 to 1 female/male ratio. The student body leans to the left, but with its right foot on the ground. One black student calls Haverford "a small liberal arts school with a semi-liberal attitude." The Honor Code affects student relations as well as academics. One student sums it up this way: "Some say the code restricts people in the minority view because they don't want to offend the majority. I think it's just the opposite, the code creates an atmosphere where people are more likely to listen to and respect views that are different from theirs."

FINANCIAL AID: 610-896-1350

WEB SITE: HTTP://WWW.HAVERFORD.EDU/

ADMISSIONS

The admissions committee considers (in descending order of importance): HS record, class rank, recommendations, test scores, essay. *Also considered (in descending order of importance):* extracurriculars, personality, alumni relationship, geographical distribution, special talents. Either the SAT or ACT is required. An interview is recommended. Admissions process is need-blind. *High school units required/recommended:* 12 total units are required; 4 English required, 3 math required, 1 science required, 3 foreign language required, 1 social studies required. TOEFL is required of all international students.

The Inside Word

Candidate evaluation at Haverford is quite thorough, and the applicant pool is sizable and strong. Applicants who are successful through the initial academic review are then carefully considered for the match they make with the college. This part of the process is especially important at small schools like Haverford, and students should definitely spend some time assessing the reasons for their interest in attending before responding to essays and interviewing. Interviewing is a must.

FINANCIAL AID

Students should submit: FAFSA (due January 31), CSS Profile (due January 31), the school's own financial aid form (due January 31), state aid form, Divorced Parents form (due January 31), a copy of parents' most recent income tax filing. The Princeton Review suggests that all financial aid forms be submitted as soon as possible after January 1. *The following grants/scholarships are offered:* Pell, SEOG, the school's own grants, state grants, foreign aid. *Students borrow from the following loan programs:* Stafford, unsubsidized Stafford, Perkins, PLUS, the school's own loan fund. Applicants will be notified of awards beginning April 15. College Work-Study Program is available. Institutional employment is available.

FROM THE ADMISSIONS OFFICE

"Haverford strives to be a college in which integrity, honesty, and concern for others are dominant forces. The college does not have many formal rules; rather, it offers an opportunity for students to govern their affairs and conduct themselves with respect and concern for others. Each student is expected to adhere to the Honor Code as it is adopted each year by the Students' Association. Haverford's Quaker roots show most clearly in the relationship of faculty and students, in the emphasis on integrity, in the interaction of the individual and the community, and through the college's concern for the uses to which its students put their expanding knowledge. Haverford's 1,100 students represent a wide diversity of interests, backgrounds, and talents. They come from public, parochial and independent schools across the United States, Puerto Rico, and 27 foreign countries. Students of color are an important part of the Haverford community. The Minority Coalition, which includes Asian, black, and Hispanic students' associations, works with faculty and administration on matters directly concerned with the quality of life at the college."

ADMISSIONS

Admissions Rating	95
% of applicants accepted	37
% of acceptees attending	31

FRESHMAN PROFILE

Average verbal SAT	690
Average math SAT	680
Average ACT	NR
Average TOEFL	600
Graduated top 20% of class	92
Graduated top 40% of class	99
Graduated top 60% of class	100
Average HS GPA or Avg.	NR

DEADLINES

Early decision	11/15
Regular admission	1/15
Regular notification	4/15
Non-fall registration	no

APPLICANTS ALSO LOOK AT

AND OFTEN PREFER

Princeton
Harvard/Radcliffe
Yale
Brown
Wellesley

AND SOMETIMES PREFER

Amherst
Swarthmore
Williams
Pennsylvania
Bryn Mawr

AND RARELY PREFER

Vassar
Middlebury Coll.
Earlham

FINANCIAL FACTS

Financial Aid Rating	89
Tuition	$20,692
Room & board	$6,810
Estimated book expense	$750
% frosh receiving aid	45
% undergrads receiving aid	45
% aid is need-based	100
% frosh w/ grant (avg)	33 ($13,266)
% frosh w/ loan (avg)	NR ($2,176)
% UGs w/ job (avg)	NR
Off-campus job outlook	good

HENDRIX COLLEGE

1601 HARKRIDER STREET, CONWAY, AR 72032-3080   ADMISSIONS: 501-450-1362   FAX: 501-450-1200

CAMPUS LIFE

Quality of Life Rating	**81**
Type of school	private
Affiliation	United Methodist Church
Environment	suburban

STUDENTS

FT undergrad enrollment	953
% male/female	45/55
% from out of state	23
% live on campus	78
% spend weekend on campus	75
% transfers	3
% from public high school	87
% African-American	5
% Asian	2
% Caucasian	89
% Hispanic	0
% international	1
# of countries represented	7

WHAT'S HOT
campus easy to get around
college radio
student government
different students interact
campus is beautiful

WHAT'S NOT
health facilities
Greeks
support groups
Conway
off-campus food

ACADEMICS

Academic Rating	**87**
Profs Interesting Rating	95
Profs Accessible Rating	95
Calendar	trimester
Student/teacher ratio	12:1
% profs PhD/tenured	87/100
Hours of study per day	3.46

MOST POPULAR MAJORS
biology
psychology
economics/business

% GRADS WHO PURSUE...
Law 7, Med 9, MBA 1, MA 20

STUDENTS SPEAK OUT

Life
Hendrix College is the typical small school. With nearly 1,000 students and located in a town that doesn't offer much, students must rely heavily on one another for entertainment. Says one, "People generally just hang out together and enjoy the scenery of Arkansas. We go camping, to concerts, or do homework!!!" Reports another, "The students are so stressed out by week's end that often drinking begins as soon as classes end. Hendrix drunks tend to be philosophical drunks. Drunk = friendly and philosophical." The campus is beautiful and the school energetically supports extracurricular activities, intramural sports, and clubs; notes one student, "Hendrix's small size gives everyone a chance to participate in the life of the college to the degree they wish." There is no Greek life here, and students generally want to keep it that way; the Student Senate recently organized a mock-Olympics celebrating fifty years of a Greek-free campus.

Academics
Hendrix students give their school a thumbs-up in almost every academic category. The profs are great teachers and are very accessible outside the classroom ("The professors are the number one reason to come to this school"); the student-teacher ratio is good, and most classes are small; most important, students ranked high in our "overall happiness" category. Over one-third of Hendrix graduates go on to grad school, including a considerable number who proceed to medical school. "Science classes are openly competitive and premed oriented," explains one premed. Economics, political science, and humanities programs are also popular here. Hendrix's general education requirements are flexible but demanding: While students are offered a number of choices in fulfilling these, all mean a great deal of work in the fields of Western civilization, humanities, social sciences, natural sciences, and a foreign language. Of the school's academic schedule, students report that "we are on a trimester system, which is extremely rigorous, but I like the pace—no time to get bored." A final note: Hendrix offers several attractive study-abroad options, including the Hendrix-in-Oxford plan, which allows students to spend their junior year at Oxford University in England.

Student Body
For a southern school, Hendrix is liberal. Students seriously value diversity and tolerance, and they definitely stand out among the other residents of Conway. As one student puts it, "It's not for every student, but only those willing to be open-minded and experience new ideas, lifestyles, and religious beliefs that often challenge the more conservative, Bible Belt tradition of this area." Minorities are sparsely represented; reports one, "Being a black student here is hard because most things done here are done the way white students want it. Most times black students get together and do things on their own." There is a visible hippie contingent; also accounted for are "redneck reactionaries, metal fans, and poseurs."

FINANCIAL AID: 501-450-1368

ADMISSIONS

The admissions committee considers (in descending order of importance): HS record, test scores, recommendations, essay. *Also considered (in descending order of importance):* extracurriculars, geographical distribution, personality, special talents. An interview is recommended. Admissions process is need-blind. *High school units required/recommended:* 13 total units are recommended; 4 English recommended, 3 math recommended, 2 science recommended, 1 foreign language recommended, 3 social studies recommended. TOEFL is required of all international students.

The Inside Word

Hendrix has a small but well-qualified applicant pool. The college is a sleeper, and is an especially good bet for students with strong grades who lack the test scores usually necessary for admission to colleges on a higher level of selectivity. Look for Hendrix to get tougher as they continue to garner attention from national publications. This place has been making the lists, and it is solid.

FINANCIAL AID

Students should submit: FAFSA, the school's own financial aid form. The Princeton Review suggests that all financial aid forms be submitted as soon as possible after January 1. *The following grants/scholarships are offered:* Pell, SEOG, academic merit, the school's own scholarships, the school's own grants, state scholarships, state grants, private scholarships, private grants, ROTC, foreign aid. *Students borrow from the following loan programs:* Stafford, Perkins, PLUS, private loans. College Work-Study Program is available. Institutional employment is available.

FROM THE ADMISSIONS OFFICE

"Students who choose Hendrix are bright, eager learners. They have high aspirations; many go on to pursue advanced degrees in graduate and professional schools. Each year the average ACT and College Board scores of the incoming class are in the eighty-fifth to ninetieth percentile range nationally. But Hendrix students expect more from the school than academic challenge. For most, there is a desire to balance their schedules with other kinds of activity—from ensemble practice to a game of intramural racquetball. Everyone fits in; the small campus engenders a sense of openness and belonging. Among the recent graduating class, two hundred seniors are recipients of offers to study biochemistry at Yale, English at the University of Virginia, electrical engineering at Duke, business administration at Harvard, medicine at Johns Hopkins, theology at Claremont, and law at Georgetown."

ADMISSIONS

Admissions Rating	78
% of applicants accepted	90
% of acceptees attending	43

FRESHMAN PROFILE

Average verbal SAT	610
Average math SAT	580
Average ACT	26
Average TOEFL	600
Graduated top 20% of class	40
Graduated top 40% of class	70
Graduated top 60% of class	85
Average HS GPA or Avg.	3.5

DEADLINES

Early decision	4/1
Regular admission	NR
Regular notification	rolling
Non-fall registration	yes

APPLICANTS ALSO LOOK AT

AND OFTEN PREFER
Tulane
Vanderbilt
Millsaps
Oglethorpe

AND SOMETIMES PREFER
U. of the South
Rhodes
U. Arkansas
Southern Methodist U.

FINANCIAL FACTS

Financial Aid Rating	81
Tuition	$9,325
Room & board	$3,195
Estimated book expense	$500
% frosh receiving aid	86
% undergrads receiving aid	81
% aid is need-based	61
% frosh w/ grant (avg)	84 ($4,883)
% frosh w/ loan (avg)	49 ($2,976)
% UGs w/ job (avg)	39 ($1,381)
Off-campus job outlook	good

Hiram College

Hiram, OH 44234   Admissions: 800-362-5280   Fax: 216-569-5494

CAMPUS LIFE

Quality of Life Rating   **73**
Type of school   private
Affiliation Christian Church (Disciples of Christ)
Environment   rural

STUDENTS
FT undergrad enrollment   847
% male/female   47/53
% from out of state   20
% live on campus   93
% spend weekend on campus   70
% transfers   12
% from public high school   90
% African-American   6
% Asian   1
% Caucasian   92
% Hispanic   1
% international   2
# of countries represented   8

WHAT'S HOT
sex
campus feels safe
campus easy to get around
theater
beer

WHAT'S NOT
library
off-campus food
campus food
student publications
Hiram

ACADEMICS

Academic Rating   **84**
Profs Interesting Rating   91
Profs Accessible Rating   93
Calendar   semester
Student/teacher ratio   10:1
% profs PhD/tenured   86/93
Hours of study per day   3.11

MOST POPULAR MAJORS
biology
management
psychology

STUDENTS SPEAK OUT

Life

Students give their hometown of Hiram the big thumbs-down; reports one student, "The two famous things to do here are playing at the Crestwood Elementary playground and singing in the Bell Tower." Writes another, "The Hiram area is very beautiful, but one must seek out fun and entertainment. We go to movies, bike, play cards, go to town, read, play football with fellow students: not a real team, although the college's is not any better." Life does feature "an incredible number of student-run activities"; still, most students that we surveyed agree that "social life leaves much to be desired." Adding to the situation is the fact that Hiram "has a weekend migration problem." Hiram has no Greek system, but it does have "social clubs," which are fairly popular and which serve the same function as the Greeks do elsewhere. Cleveland and Akron are less than an hour away by car. Writes one student, "Cleveland is cool and it's really close by. There are a lot of dance clubs and fun things to do there."

Academics

An excellent biology department—"one of the best in the nation," according to more than one student—sets Hiram apart from the nation's other fine small liberal arts schools. About one seventh of the students here pursue bio degrees, taking advantage of the dedicated faculty and top notch facilities (including "superior" laboratories and an off campus field station/greenhouse/nature reserve). Pre-business and liberal arts majors are also strong and popular, although the "arts" reportedly suffer from a lack of support from the school ("Hiram College, while very strong in the sciences, is in danger of losing the 'arts' in liberal arts," complains one biology student). Students give the faculty high grades, reporting that "the faculty is very accommodating. If motivated, a student will find endless opportunities and plenty of inventive people with whom to collaborate." Students are less happy with the administration, however, complaining that "most of the time, one gets the feeling that, to the administration, the students' needs and input don't count." The Hiram Plan divides each semester into two sessions, twelve and three weeks respectively. The three week sessions will be devoted to experiential learning through study abroad, research, internships, and field trips.

Student Body

Hiram's predominantly white, middle-class student body go about their studies with a workmanlike attitude. Hiram attracts intellectually curious students. Students are generally "friendly and very accepting," although they also report that a contingent of fundamentalist students openly disapprove of the gay community. Also be aware that "the Hiram student body is so small that eventually everyone knows everyone else, which can be a problem."

ADMISSIONS

The admissions committee considers (in descending order of importance): HS record, test scores, recommendations, essay, class rank. *Also considered (in descending order of importance):* extracurriculars, personality, special talents, alumni relationship, geographical distribution. Either the SAT or ACT is required. An interview is required of some applicants. Admissions process is need-blind. *High school units required/recommended:* 16 total units are required; 4 English required, 3 math required, 3 science required, 2 foreign language recommended, 1 social studies required, 2 history required. TOEFL is required of all international students. *The admissions office says:* "Minority students and alumni relations receive special consideration."

The Inside Word

Students with consistent academic records will find little difficulty in gaining admission. The applicant pool is decidedly local; out-of-state candidates benefit from their scarcity.

FINANCIAL AID

Students should submit: FAFSA, the school's own financial aid form, state aid form (due October 1), a copy of parents' most recent income tax filing. The Princeton Review suggests that all financial aid forms be submitted as soon as possible after January 1. *The following grants/scholarships are offered:* Pell, SEOG, academic merit, the school's own scholarships, the school's own grants, state scholarships, state grants, private scholarships, private grants. *Students borrow from the following loan programs:* Stafford, unsubsidized Stafford, Perkins, PLUS, the school's own loan fund, private loans. College Work-Study Program is available. Institutional employment is available.

FROM THE ADMISSIONS OFFICE

"Every student can expect a sense of belonging—a sense of community. Hiram's location and setting fosters a very tight-knit community. There are no in-groups and out-groups; no cliques. It is a very friendly community. Politics vary from left to right; student clothing comes in all styles; there is no Hiram type. All this makes for a pretty tolerant and independent-minded student body—a community in the best sense of the word. Our Extramural Studies program is unusual. Unlike most schools, these are our programs. Hiram students take Hiram courses abroad, taught by Hiram faculty. The college travels all over the world. Nearly forty percent of our students take advantage of the EMS program, despite the fact that they are not required to do so. Our two field stations are distinctive. The James H. Barrow Field Station is one of only a handful of such facilities in the country. It offers science students—generally biology majors—opportunities to do significant undergraduate research. The second station—Northwoods Station in the Upper Peninsula of Michigan—is a Hiram microcosm: the huge lodge and five or six sleeping cabins were built entirely by Hiram faculty and students. They maintain the station together. The station is the only development on Little Lost Lake. Hiram is also an affiliate of Shoals Marine Laboratory."

ADMISSIONS

Admissions Rating	75
% of applicants accepted	88
% of acceptees attending	41

FRESHMAN PROFILE

Average verbal SAT	600
Average math SAT	570
Average ACT	24
Average TOEFL	550
Graduated top 20% of class	58
Graduated top 40% of class	83
Graduated top 60% of class	95
Average HS GPA or Avg.	3.4

DEADLINES

Early decision	2/1
Regular admission	3/15
Regular notification	rolling
Non-fall registration	yes

APPLICANTS ALSO LOOK AT

AND OFTEN PREFER
Miami U.
Kenyon
Wooster

AND SOMETIMES PREFER
Wittenberg
Ohio Wesleyan

AND RARELY PREFER
Ohio State U.-Columbus
Mount Union
Kent State

FINANCIAL FACTS

Financial Aid Rating	90
Tuition	$15,000
Room & board	$4,720
Estimated book expense	$500
% frosh receiving aid	88
% undergrads receiving aid	93
% aid is need-based	60
% frosh w/ grant (avg)	96 ($9,573)
% frosh w/ loan (avg)	71 ($2,554)
% UGs w/ job (avg)	81 ($1,500)
Off-campus job outlook	fair

Hobart and William Smith Colleges

Geneva, NY 14456   Admissions: 800-245-0100   Fax: 315-781-3560

CAMPUS LIFE

Quality of Life Rating	81
Type of school	private
Affiliation	none
Environment	town

STUDENTS

FT undergrad enrollment	1,764
% male/female	49/51
% from out of state	51
% live on campus	82
% spend weekend on campus	90
% transfers	7
% from public high school	63
% in (# of) fraternities	30 (7)
% African-American	5
% Asian	1
% Caucasian	89
% Hispanic	4
% international	2
# of countries represented	19

WHAT'S HOT
campus food
lab facilities
drugs
intercollegiate sports
student government

WHAT'S NOT
town-gown relations
Geneva
religion
students are cliquish
music associations

ACADEMICS

Academic Rating	84
Profs Interesting Rating	88
Profs Accessible Rating	88
Calendar	trimester
Student/teacher ratio	13:1
% profs PhD/tenured	97/98
Hours of study per day	3.36

MOST POPULAR MAJORS
English
psychology
individual majors

% GRADS WHO PURSUE...
Law 7, Med 5, MBA 6, MA 30

STUDENTS SPEAK OUT

Life

Once upon a time, Hobart and William Smith Colleges were widely regarded as a haven for "those who followed the Grateful Dead and played lacrosse." In the past decade, though, the school has come a long way in its struggle to remake its image. Deadheads and bong-toting lacrosse players still maintain a visible campus presence but, with Jerry Garcia now playing that great arena in the sky, the times at HWS are a-changin'. "The college is slowly moving away from the total party school toward an atmosphere of intellectual stimulation," relates a senior. While many students welcome the new emphasis on academics, others hanker for the good old days. "No kegs on the quad is a depressing change," for instance. "Some people still go to parties, get drunk, and hook up, but now more and more people are studying on Saturday nights. What is the world coming to?" laments a disgruntled senior. However, counters a junior, "those students who become involved with campus programs and issues are most happy; those who do not complain too much." Most students live on campus and some gripe that the "segregated nature of the dormitory setup (i.e. single-sex dorms)" adversely affects socializing. "The only way to really get to know guys is at frat parties and the bars," explains one woman. The surrounding town of Geneva "does not have much to offer in terms of entertainment." However, its choice location "on the banks of historic Seneca Lake in the beautiful Finger Lakes region of New York State" provides HWS students with opportunities for many "outdoorsy" activities.

Academics

The separate but intertwined Hobart and William Smith Colleges offer students an unusual mix of both coeducational and single-sex environments. Under the "coordinate system," the two colleges share the same campus and classes, yet operate under the guidance of "very different" administrations. The female students of William Smith especially appreciate the emphasis on gender issues and "the excellent support for women" provided by their college within the larger coed framework. The widely praised trimester calendar at HWS "allows students to concentrate on only three classes at a time." Students applaud the quality of course offerings and the "amazing" professors who "show a great willingness to work with students." A biology major reports that "the department prepares each student individually for medical school by putting together applications, and giving mock interviews." HWS students are given ample freedom to design their own programs of study, and "taking full advantage of the benefits of a liberal arts college is big here," declares a geoscience major with a dance minor. However, the abundance of academic freedom leaves some students scholastically unfocused. "It is possible to make the most out of your education or to slide by with little work and still maintain a 2.0 GPA," asserts a sophomore. Most students agree that HWS has a "great administration." They also single out the housing office and the computer and lab facilities as more than satisfactory.

Student Body

The typical HWS student grew up in the Northeast, is white, "fairly liberal," politically apathetic, and not poor. "I own a Pontiac Sunbird and I feel totally out of place because everyone else owns a Saab," explains a student with a mild case of Swede envy. Overall, the student population is "homogenous but most people are very friendly and outgoing" and there is a "a strong sense of unity among the students." The campus may be diversifying in at least one aspect, however—age: as of Spring 1995, Hobart and William Smith Colleges are inviting alumni who graduated at least five years ago to take tuition-free classes for as many semesters as they want, provided there's room among undergraduates.

HOBART AND WILLIAM SMITH COLLEGES

ADMISSIONS

The admissions committee considers (in descending order of importance): HS record, test scores, recommendations, class rank, essay. *Also considered (in descending order of importance):* extracurriculars, personality, special talents, alumni relationship, geographical distribution. Either the SAT or ACT is required; SAT is preferred. An interview is recommended. Admissions process is need-blind. *High school units required/recommended:* 18 total units are required; 4 English required, 3 math required, 2 science required, 2 foreign language required, 2 history required. TOEFL is required of all international students. *The admissions office says:* "The admissions process tends to be highly individualized, even more so than at other small (warm, fuzzy) liberal arts colleges, we've been told by prospective students. We encourage students to spend at least a day on campus with a student host in order to observe the colleges in action. This is a place where students do a lot of exploring and experience a number of interesting intellectual collisions with other students and faculty. Our students tend to be pretty daring and adventurous, whether it's a matter of swimming in the lake in March, arguing politics with a dean, or taking a non-traditional course."

The Inside Word

The college's out-of-the-way location unfortunately turns off many admits: Hobart and William Smith lose a lot of students to their competitors, who are many and strong. This helps open up the gates a bit for more candidates.

FINANCIAL AID

Students should submit: FAFSA, CSS Profile, state aid form, Divorced Parents form, a copy of parents' most recent income tax filing. The Princeton Review suggests that all financial aid forms be submitted as soon as possible after January 1. *The following grants/scholarships are offered:* Pell, SEOG, academic merit, the school's own scholarships, the school's own grants, state scholarships, state grants, private scholarships, private grants, foreign aid. *Students borrow from the following loan programs:* Stafford, unsubsidized Stafford, Perkins, PLUS. Applicants will be notified of awards beginning April 1. College Work-Study Program is available. Institutional employment is available.

FROM THE ADMISSIONS OFFICE

"Hobart and William Smith Colleges seek students with a sense of adventure and a commitment to the life of the mind. Inside the classroom, students find the academic climate to be rigorous, with a faculty that is deeply involved in teaching and working with them. Outside, they discover a supportive community that helps to cultivate a balance and hopes to foster an integration among academics, extracurricular activities, and social life. Hobart and William Smith, as coordinate colleges, have an awareness of gender differences and equality and are committed to respect and a celebration of diversity."

ADMISSIONS

Admissions Rating	76
% of applicants accepted	76
% of acceptees attending	22

FRESHMAN PROFILE

Average verbal SAT	600
Average math SAT	590
Average ACT	26
Average TOEFL	NR
Graduated top 20% of class	51
Graduated top 40% of class	82
Graduated top 60% of class	95
Average HS GPA or Avg.	3.3

DEADLINES

Early decision	NR
Regular admission	2/1
Regular notification	4/1
Non-fall registration	no

APPLICANTS ALSO LOOK AT

AND OFTEN PREFER

Colgate
Trinity Coll. (CT)
Connecticut Coll.
Hamilton
Union Coll. (NY)

AND SOMETIMES PREFER

Skidmore
Kenyon
Gettysburg
St. Lawrence
Dickinson

FINANCIAL FACTS

Financial Aid Rating	82
Tuition	$19,962
Room & board	$6,075
Estimated book expense	$600
% frosh receiving aid	69
% undergrads receiving aid	68
% aid is need-based	99
% frosh w/ grant (avg)	66 ($12,000)
% frosh w/ loan (avg)	59 ($2,625)
% UGs w/ job (avg)	40 ($1,000)
Off-campus job outlook	fair

HOFSTRA UNIVERSITY

HEMPSTEAD, NY 11550 ADMISSIONS: 516-463-6700 FAX: 516-564-4296

CAMPUS LIFE

Quality of Life Rating **71**
Type of school private
Affiliation none
Environment suburban

STUDENTS
FT undergrad enrollment 6,589
% male/female 47/53
% from out of state 17
% live on campus 50
% spend weekend on campus 90
% transfers 34
% from public high school 70
% in (# of) fraternities 16 (19)
% in (# of) sororities 16 (13)
% African-American 5
% Asian 5
% Caucasian 80
% Hispanic 5
% international 4
# of countries represented 67

WHAT'S HOT
drugs
health facilities
library
college radio
old-fashioned dating

WHAT'S NOT
students are unhappy
support groups
off-campus food
campus difficult to get around
beer

ACADEMICS

Academic Rating **72**
Profs Interesting Rating 67
Profs Accessible Rating 71
Calendar semester
Student/teacher ratio 15:1
% profs PhD/tenured 90/69
Hours of study per day 2.74

MOST POPULAR MAJORS
psychology
accounting
marketing

% GRADS WHO PURSUE...
Law 5, Med 2, MBA 11, MA 15

STUDENTS SPEAK OUT

Life

The Hofstra campus is beautiful, maybe a little too beautiful. One student jokes, "Hofstra needs to stop spending millions of dollars on those tulips that we get fined $100 if we touch!" Indeed, great time and expense is spent keeping Hofstra picture-perfect. Once a commuter school, Hofstra now houses over half its students on its pretty campus in dorms that receive decent marks. "Except for the food, life on campus is great," explains one undergrad. Adds another, "If you make an effort to get involved, you'll get involved, but it's far easier if you live on campus." The town of Hempstead doesn't fare well in students' eyes. "There's only once place to go, McHebe's. Everyone is there, every night." Luckily, neighboring towns make up for some of Hempstead's inadequacies, and New York City is a 45-minute train ride away. Frats and sororities are pretty popular for on-campus diversion, as are beer and pot. "Campus life is fun when it comes to parties. People know how to have a good time, sometimes too much."

Academics

"All I can say is that a teacher's popularity is directly related to whether their classes begin before 1:00 P.M. or not." Well, class schedule notwithstanding, Hofstra profs receive good grades from their students, being judged both competent and accessible. Says a sophomore studying accounting, "Professors are interesting. They bring a lot to the classroom and students leave classes with much to look forward to next session." The lectures and discussions are invariably quite small at Hofstra, so student-teacher interaction is high. Hofstra is definitely a career-oriented school. Business and management, marketing, engineering, and computer science are among its popular majors. Its career-oriented students take their classes seriously, but studying averages out at fewer than 3 hours per day. Of note at Hofstra are its annual Presidential Conferences, which draw scholars and administration officials to discuss a different presidency each year, and its annual Shakespeare Festival, run through the drama department. Lab facilities, computer facilities, and the library at Hofstra all receive very high marks from students, and the school is run fairly well as far as undergrads are concerned.

Student Body

"The students here are like animals in the sense that they're all sprouting antlers, if you know what I mean." If this undergrad means that students are competitive with one another, we understand. He's not the only one who thinks so. "There is constant competition and...nasty attitudes among students," adds one. Another comments, somewhat mysteriously, "The students are generally nice. Still, I don't trust them." Hofstra boasts a fairly homogenous population that is around three-quarters New Yorkers and almost half Long Island commuters (think big hair and gold chains). Says one, "The ethnic makeup is poor. It is not a diverse school." Indeed, discrimination on the basis of race, sex, and sexual preference is a concern among students, though not a pervasive problem. "Black and white students should interact more," offers one.

FINANCIAL AID: 516-463-6680   E-MAIL: HOFSTRA@HOFSTRA.EDU   WEB SITE: HTTP://WWW.HOFSTRA.EDU/

ADMISSIONS

The admissions committee considers (in descending order of importance): HS record, class rank, test scores, recommendations, essay. *Also considered (in descending order of importance):* extracurriculars, personality. Either the SAT or ACT is required. An interview is recommended. Admissions process is need-blind. *High school units required/recommended:* 17 total units are required; 4 English required, 2 math required, 3 math recommended, 2 science required, 3 science recommended, 2 foreign language required, 3 social studies required. Minimum combined SAT I score of 1000 and rank in top third of secondary school class recommended. *Special Requirements:* A portfolio is required for art program applicants. An audition is required for music program applicants. TOEFL is required of all international students. *The admissions office says:* "Applicants who do not meet high school curricular standards will be given careful consideration by the admissions committee to determine from achievements and from assessment of abilities and maturity the probability of [their] success..."

The Inside Word

Hofstra wants to be national and has positioned itself very well with impressive facilities, appealing program offerings, and an effective national ad campaign. However, the current student profile just isn't strong enough academically to draw top students on a national level: too many of Hofstra's best applicants choose to attend elsewhere. This makes the university a good choice for students who would not be strong candidates at some of its competitors.

FINANCIAL AID

Students should submit: FAFSA (due March 1), the school's own financial aid form (due March 1), a copy of parents' most recent income tax filing. The Princeton Review suggests that all financial aid forms be submitted as soon as possible after January 1. *The following grants/scholarships are offered:* Pell, SEOG, academic merit, athletic, the school's own scholarships, the school's own grants, state grants, private scholarships, ROTC. *Students borrow from the following loan programs:* Stafford, unsubsidized Stafford, Perkins, PLUS, the school's own loan fund. College Work-Study Program is available. Institutional employment is available.

FROM THE ADMISSIONS OFFICE

Founded in 1935, Hofstra University has grown to be recognized both nationally and internationally for its resources, academic offerings, accreditations, conferences, and cultural events. Academically Hofstra is comprised of six schools: College of Liberal Arts and Sciences, School of Education, Frank G. Zarb School of Business, School of Communication, New College and Hofstra Law School. Focused on undergraduate education, Hofstra places great emphasis on the role of the student in the life of the University. Students come from 45 states and 72 countries. Hofstra also offers graduate programs in business, education, liberal arts and law. Students have easy access to the theater and cultural life of New York City, yet have a learning environment on Long Island on a 238-acre campus that is also a registered arboretum and accredited museum. Admission information sessions are offered daily at 10:15 a.m. and 2 p.m. Please call the Admissions Center for an appointment at 1-800-HOFSTRA.

ADMISSIONS

Admissions Rating	70
% of applicants accepted	82
% of acceptees attending	25

FRESHMAN PROFILE

Average verbal SAT	540
Average math SAT	550
Average ACT	23
Average TOEFL	NR
Graduated top 20% of class	50
Graduated top 40% of class	84
Graduated top 60% of class	98
Average HS GPA or Avg.	3.0

DEADLINES

Early decision	NR
Regular admission	2/15
Regular notification	rolling
Non-fall registration	yes

APPLICANTS ALSO LOOK AT

AND OFTEN PREFER

NYU
Cornell U.
Binghamton U.
Syracuse
Boston U.

AND SOMETIMES PREFER

Fordham
Rutgers U.
SUNY Stony Brook
SUNY at Albany
Siena

FINANCIAL FACTS

Financial Aid Rating	70
Tuition	$11,670
Room & board	$6,180
Estimated book expense	NR
% frosh receiving aid	78
% undergrads receiving aid	72
% aid is need-based	74
% frosh w/ grant (avg)	74 ($3,825)
% frosh w/ loan (avg)	62 ($2,625)
% UGs w/ job (avg)	25
Off-campus job outlook	excellent

HOLLINS COLLEGE

P.O. BOX 9707, ROANOKE, VA 24020   ADMISSIONS: 800-456-9595   FAX: 703-362-6642

CAMPUS LIFE

Quality of Life Rating	95
Type of school	private
Affiliation	none
Environment	city

STUDENTS

FT undergrad enrollment	816
% male/female	0/100
% from out of state	69
% live on campus	95
% spend weekend on campus	60
% transfers	12
% from public high school	65
% African-American	4
% Asian	2
% Caucasian	88
% Hispanic	2
% international	2
# of countries represented	17

WHAT'S HOT
student government
support groups
dorms
students are happy
campus is beautiful

WHAT'S NOT
drugs
college radio
library
intramural sports
beer

ACADEMICS

Academic Rating	89
Profs Interesting Rating	98
Profs Accessible Rating	97
Calendar	4-1-4
Student/teacher ratio	9:1
% profs tenured	95
Hours of study per day	3.34

MOST POPULAR MAJORS
English
psychology
history

% GRADS WHO PURSUE...
Law 2, Med 2, MBA 3, MA 20

STUDENTS SPEAK OUT

Life
"Going to an all-women's school at first was hard to get used to. Now I am genuinely happy with my decision. It has made me a stronger, more independent, and much more confident person." Once known as a finishing school for young Southern women, Hollins College is now a fine liberal arts institution with a satisfied student body. Still, being at Hollins means men are two hours away, which leads some to "suitcase" it to coed colleges for any sort of social life. Says one undergrad, "If there was a better social life this school would be perfect." The campus itself, at the foot of the Blue Ridge mountains, is as close to perfect as you get, and the dorms, where almost everyone lives, are big, comfortable, and serve excellent food. There is no Greek system on campus, so students have to make their own fun when they do stay on campus. "The activities at Hollins are amazingly impressive," praises one, while another adds "For fun we have 'Til Tuesdays, where a band comes and plays the latest music." For some, the fun never stops: "I love Hollins so much I stayed here over the summer, and we don't offer summer school!"

Academics
"The professors here are wonderful and always willing to meet with students. In fact, I'm late for a meeting with my history teacher right now." We hope she made it on time. Yes, Hollins undergrads are quite happy with their academic experience. "You can walk up to the Dean's office without an appointment and pretty much be guaranteed to see him within a few minutes—I even go chat with professors I don't know for advice about majors," beams one. Indeed, the accessibility of profs and the administration received incredibly high marks. Some concern is raised about the difficulty of classes (or rather, the lack thereof): "Professors are nice, almost too nice. Classes could be more academically challenging." Adds another, "Hollins is the type of school where you set your own level of challenge." Liberal arts and the social sciences are the school's specialties, with especially good programs in psychology and creative writing: "Our creative writing program is amazing." States another of Hollins' improved recruiting, "This year's freshman class is very strong academically." Another unique aspect of Hollins is its honor code, which allows exams to be scheduled by the student and taken without a teacher present. Sighs one student in relief, "The independent exam system saves my butt every summer." Lab facilities, the computer system, and health services all received high marks, with only the library being found somewhat lacking.

Student Body
"Hollins seems to be in a transitional period. The Southern traditional student is still prominent [but there are] more alternative and diverse students." We're not sure what an "alternative student" is, but you get the picture. There is still a contingent of "BMW-driving pearl and T-shirt girls," whom the local community calls "bowheads" because "they tie their hair in ponytails with unattractive gold and green bows." But Hollins is attracting more minority students, most of whom enjoy their experience at Hollins, but feel somewhat separated from the mainstream. Says one, "As a minority student, I feel accepted but not as though I belong." Offers another, "I realize I have to be a 'trailblazer' for others and educate my peers." Still, discrimination on the basis of race is not seen as a problem by most, and discrimination on the basis of sex is, you guessed it, nil! Dating is very popular with Hollins undergrads, and most describe themselves as sexually active. Sums up one, "For the most part students at Hollins are a typical college community. You have snobs, nerds, religious fanatics, partiers, and those that keep to themselves."

FINANCIAL AID: 540-362-6332   E-MAIL: MOBRIEN@MATTY.HOLLINS.EDU   WEB SITE: HTTP://WWW.HOLLINS.EDU/

ADMISSIONS

The admissions committee considers (in descending order of importance): HS record, class rank, test scores, recommendations, essay. *Also considered (in descending order of importance):* extracurriculars, special talents, personality, alumni relationship, geographical distribution. Either the SAT or ACT is required. An interview is recommended. Admissions process is need-blind. *High school units required/recommended:* 16 total units are recommended; 4 English recommended, 3 math recommended, 3 science recommended, 3 foreign language recommended, 3 social studies recommended. Minimum combined SAT I score of 900, rank in top two-fifths of secondary school class, and minimum 3.0 GPA recommended. *Special Requirements:* Letter of recommendation required. *The admissions office says:* "Alumnae relations are taken into consideration. Applicants may request that the admissions office disregard SAT results if GPA and other academic credentials indicate that test scores are not a good indicator of academic ability."

The Inside Word

Only candidates who overtly display their lack of compatibility with the Hollins milieu are likely to encounter difficulty in gaining admission. A high level of self-selection and its weak, but improving, freshman profile allow most candidates to relax.

FINANCIAL AID

Students should submit: FAFSA, a copy of parents' most recent income tax filing. The Princeton Review suggests that all financial aid forms be submitted as soon as possible after January 1. *The following grants/scholarships are offered:* Pell, SEOG, academic merit, the school's own scholarships, the school's own grants, state grants, private scholarships, private grants, foreign aid. *Students borrow from the following loan programs:* Stafford, unsubsidized Stafford, Perkins, PLUS, private loans. College Work-Study Program is available. Institutional employment is available.

FROM THE ADMISSIONS OFFICE

"As a liberal arts college dedicated to high achievement for women, Hollins celebrates and encourages the success—whether in the classroom, in the laboratory, on stage, or on the athletic field—of each student. A spirit of independent inquiry, the free exchange of ideas, and a love for learning characterize life on campus. At Hollins, creativity and imaginative thinking are applauded with the same vigor that rewards academic achievement."

ADMISSIONS

Admissions Rating	72
% of applicants accepted	81
% of acceptees attending	40

FRESHMAN PROFILE

Average verbal SAT	600
Average math SAT	540
Average ACT	24
Average TOEFL	550
Graduated top 20% of class	53
Graduated top 40% of class	84
Graduated top 60% of class	94
Average HS GPA or Avg.	3.2

DEADLINES

Early decision	NR
Regular admission	2/15
Regular notification	rolling
Non-fall registration	yes

APPLICANTS ALSO LOOK AT

AND OFTEN PREFER
U. Virginia
William and Mary
James Madison
Smith
Vanderbilt

AND SOMETIMES PREFER
UNC-Chapel Hill
Randolph-Macon Woman's Coll.
Sweet Briar
Mount Holyoke

FINANCIAL FACTS

Financial Aid Rating	96
Tuition	$14,000
Room & board	$5,745
Estimated book expense	$500
% frosh receiving aid	79
% undergrads receiving aid	77
% aid is need-based	56
% frosh w/ grant (avg)	52 ($9,446)
% frosh w/ loan (avg)	40 ($4,000)
% UGs w/ job (avg)	52 ($1,700)
Off-campus job outlook	good

COLLEGE OF THE HOLY CROSS

COLLEGE STREET, WORCESTER, MA 01610-2395   ADMISSIONS: 508-793-2443   FAX: 508-793-3888

CAMPUS LIFE

Quality of Life Rating	86
Type of school	private
Affiliation	Roman Catholic Church
	(Society of Jesus)
Environment	city

STUDENTS

FT undergrad enrollment	2,738
% male/female	47/53
% from out of state	60
% live on campus	86
% spend weekend on campus	95
% transfers	2
% from public high school	45
% African-American	2
% Asian	3
% Caucasian	91
% Hispanic	2
% international	NR
# of countries represented	13

WHAT'S HOT
religion
students are happy
political activism
intramural sports
campus is beautiful

WHAT'S NOT
infrequent dating
hard liquor
lack of diversity on campus
drugs
Worcester

ACADEMICS

Academic Rating	92
Profs Interesting Rating	93
Profs Accessible Rating	91
Calendar	semester
Student/teacher ratio	13:1
% profs tenured	94
Hours of study per day	3.98

MOST POPULAR MAJORS
English
economics
history

% GRADS WHO PURSUE...
Law 7, Med 3, MBA 1, MA 7

STUDENTS SPEAK OUT

Life

As one Holy Cross student explains, "Students here tend to complain about a lot of things, but really, it's all a facade. No one would want to be anywhere else." Indeed, Holy Cross students rank among the top ten percent of all student bodies surveyed in terms of overall satisfaction. But they do complain. Topping the list of annoyances is the city of Worcester, the non-existent dating scene, the food, and the lack of diversity among the student body (see "Students," below). Students have positive things to say about the campus, which, reports one, "is so beautiful and secure, you almost forget you're in the city of Worcester." They also report favorably on the quality and safety of the dorms. Sports, both intramural and intercollegiate, are very popular. Drug use is minimal, but drinking is not: "This school is fifty percent hard work, fifty percent hangover," writes one student. Says another, "I have yet to find a student in any department who does not work hard at course work and still does not have an excellent time on weekends." There are no fraternities and sororities.

Academics

Holy Cross students give their school high grades in practically every one of our academic categories. Professors teach all courses and receive praise both for their skills as instructors and for their accessibility outside the classroom. Writes one student, "The faculty are totally accessible and unbelievably talented." Academics are challenging—students put in nearly four hours of work a day beyond class attendance—yet none complain that the work is excessive or superfluous. Administrators receive high marks, too, and one student tells us it is because "they genuinely care about all of us." Concludes one Indiana native, "I can honestly say that Holy Cross is the Notre Dame of New England, with a few differences: HC is half the size, the campus is prettier, [nearby Boston] is more exciting, and we don't have parietals [restricted dorm visitation rights] here. It's a highly competitive, Irish Catholic institution with an excellent football team." Students major in the traditional variety of humanities and social sciences subjects, and about one-fourth proceed to graduate school within a year of graduation. Holy Cross is a member of the Worcester Consortium, which allows students to take classes at any of ten area schools.

Student Body

Over ninety percent of Holy Cross students are white, and the minority population is pretty evenly divided among Asians, Hispanics, and African-Americans, so each individual minority population is small. One student reports that "the administration seems to be concerned with making the school more diverse; more minority-focused scholarships and recruiting plans have surfaced." So far, however, these efforts have had little effect on student body demographics. Most students are Catholic, and there is a visible preppy population. Writes one student, "If you wonder where the Gap and J. Crew families reside, they're here at Holy Cross." If there are any gay students here, their presence is unacknowledged and considered unwelcome by fellow students. The college has, however, recognized Allies, a gay organization.

ADMISSIONS

The admissions committee considers (in descending order of importance): HS record, class rank, test scores, recommendations, essay. *Also considered (in descending order of importance):* personality, special talents, alumni relationship, extracurriculars, geographical distribution. Either the SAT or ACT is required; SAT is preferred. An interview is recommended. Admissions process is need-blind. *High school units required/recommended:* 22 total units are recommended; 4 English recommended, 4 math recommended, 4 science recommended, 4 foreign language recommended, 3 social studies recommended, 3 history recommended. TOEFL is required of all international students. *The admissions office says:* "The Holy Cross admissions process is distinguished by the presence of two Early Decision options; the ability to admit the class without regard to family finances; recognition of the applicants' energy and time commitment beyond the classroom."

The Inside Word

The applicant pool at Holy Cross is strong; students are well advised to take the most challenging courses available to them in secondary school. Everyone faces fairly close scrutiny here, but, as is the case virtually everywhere, the college does have its particular interests. The admissions committee takes good care of candidates from the many parochial schools that are the source of dozens of solid applicants each year.

FINANCIAL AID

Students should submit: FAFSA (due February 1), CSS Profile (due February 1), state aid form, Divorced Parents form (due February 1), a copy of parents' most recent income tax filing. The Princeton Review suggests that all financial aid forms be submitted as soon as possible after January 1. *The following grants/scholarships are offered:* Pell, SEOG, the school's own scholarships, state scholarships, ROTC. *Students borrow from the following loan programs:* Stafford, unsubsidized Stafford, Perkins, PLUS, private loans. Applicants will be notified of awards beginning April 1. College Work-Study Program is available. Institutional employment is available.

FROM THE ADMISSIONS OFFICE

"When applying to Holy Cross, two areas deserve particular attention. First, the essay should be developed thoughtfully, with correct language and syntax in mind. That essay reflects for the Board of Admissions how you think and how you can express yourself. Second, activity beyond the classroom should be clearly defined. Since Holy Cross is 2,700 students, the chance for involvement/participation is exceptional. The Board reviews many applications for academically qualified students. A key difference in being accepted is the extent to which a candidate participates in-depth beyond the classroom—don't be modest, define who you are."

ADMISSIONS

Admissions Rating	87
% of applicants accepted	50
% of acceptees attending	40

FRESHMAN PROFILE

Average verbal SAT	630
Average math SAT	610
Average ACT	NR
Average TOEFL	550
Graduated top 20% of class	84
Graduated top 40% of class	98
Graduated top 60% of class	100
Average HS GPA or Avg.	NR

DEADLINES

Early decision	12/15
Regular admission	1/15
Regular notification	4/1
Non-fall registration	yes

APPLICANTS ALSO LOOK AT

AND OFTEN PREFER

Dartmouth
Georgetown U.
Notre Dame
Boston Coll.
Tufts

AND SOMETIMES PREFER

Bowdoin
Colgate
Villanova
Providence
U. Mass., Amherst

AND RARELY PREFER

Fairfield

FINANCIAL FACTS

Financial Aid Rating	65
Tuition	$18,900
Room & board	$6,500
Estimated book expense	$400
% frosh receiving aid	66
% undergrads receiving aid	64
% aid is need-based	99
% frosh w/ grant (avg)	52 ($10,621)
% frosh w/ loan (avg)	57 ($3,694)
% UGs w/ job (avg)	46 ($1,200)
Off-campus job outlook	fair

HOWARD UNIVERSITY

2400 SIXTH STREET, NW, WASHINGTON, DC 20059   ADMISSIONS: 800-822-6363   FAX: 202-806-5934

STUDENTS SPEAK OUT

Life

Howard students gave their hometown lower grades than did other D.C. undergrads, partly because their neighborhood is not entirely safe, and partly because Howard students are more involved with their college experiences than with the city. Says one undergrad, "One of the things I like most about Howard that you don't find at other schools is the school spirit. You don't find as many people at other schools as you do here that are truly happy and excited to attend their school." Dating is the key to social life here, and fraternities and sororities are also very popular. Sitting around and drinking beer, one of the staples of the white college experience, is not popular. Also, Howard continues to have a major housing problem: the school currently guarantees housing for freshman only and can accommodate fewer than half the other students.

Academics

Among the great universities geared predominantly toward serving African-Americans, Howard remains the most famous and arguably the best (see also Fisk, Morehouse, Spelman, and Tuskegee). Instruction here naturally reflects black perspectives (just as, at most universities, instruction reflects white attitudes, albeit without acknowledgment). Says one African-American student, "I'm glad I chose Howard because it taught me a lot about my race." Practical concerns seem to be the main motivating factor when students choose their courses of study: one in five pursues a degree in business administration. Also, because it is attached to an excellent medical school, Howard offers a full complement of premed science courses. Its liberal arts departments, however, are also strong. Students have kind words for their professors— "Professors are excellent because they truly care about their students' succeeding in school; there are no office hours when it comes to a student needing additional help," says one. Unfortunately, the administration must learn from the ways of the faculty members before students bestow such approval upon them.

Student Body

Because Howard is such a prominent black institution, some students here feel pressure to present themselves as exemplary students. Explains one: "The things that go on here are the same as what goes on at other schools; just because we are the Mecca doesn't mean we should be put on some kind of pedestal. But when something goes wrong with a Howard student, it's like we just robbed a bank or something. Remember, we are human, too." Politically, the student body leans farther to the left than most, and they are a relatively religious group. They are also happy to be at Howard: in terms of happiness, students here ranked in the top third of the schools we surveyed. Men have a decided advantage in the dating game. Says one man, "Howard is the gateway to meeting the best-looking women in the country."

FINANCIAL AID: 202-806-2800   WEB SITE: HTTP://WWW.HOWARD.EDU/

ADMISSIONS

The admissions committee considers (in descending order of importance): class rank, HS record, test scores, recommendations. *Also considered (in descending order of importance):* alumni relationship, extracurriculars, special talents. Either the SAT or ACT is required. *High school units required/recommended:* 16 total units are required; 4 English required, 2 math required, 2 science required, 2 foreign language required. *Special Requirements:* TOEFL is required of all international students. Audition, tape, or portfolio required of College of Fine Arts program applicants. *The admissions office says:* "For admission to most majors, a student should have a combined SAT I score of 800 or above or ACT composite of 20, rank in the top half of his/her graduation class, or have a C+ average."

The Inside Word

A large applicant pool and solid yield of acceptees who enroll is a combination that adds up to selectivity for Howard. Pay strict attention to the formula.

FINANCIAL AID

Students should submit: FAFSA. The Princeton Review suggests that all financial aid forms be submitted as soon as possible after January 1. *The following grants/scholarships are offered:* Pell, SEOG, academic merit, athletic, the school's own scholarships, the school's own grants, state scholarships, state grants, private scholarships, private grants, federal nursing scholarship, ROTC, foreign aid. *Students borrow from the following loan programs:* Stafford, Perkins, PLUS, health professions loans. Applicants will be notified of awards beginning May 1. College Work-Study Program is available. Institutional employment is available. Freshmen are discouraged from working.

FROM THE ADMISSIONS OFFICE

"Since its founding, Howard has stood among the few institutions of higher learning where African-Americans and other minorities have participated freely in a truly comprehensive university experience. Thus, Howard has assumed a special responsibility to prepare its students to exercise leadership wherever their interest and commitments take them. Howard has issued approximately 67,000 degrees, diplomas, and certificates to men and women in the professions, the arts and sciences, and the humanities. The university has produced and continues to produce a high percentage of the nation's African-American professionals in the fields of medicine, dentistry, pharmacy, engineering, nursing, architecture, religion, law, music, social work, education, and business. There are more than 12,000 students from across the nation and approximately 109 countries and territories attending the university. Their varied customs, cultures, ideas, and interests contribute to the university's international character and vitality. Approximately 2,000 faculty members represent the largest concentration of African-American scholars in any single institution of higher education."

ADMISSIONS

Admissions Rating	75
% of applicants accepted	58
% of acceptees attending	33

FRESHMAN PROFILE

Average verbal SAT	510
Average math SAT	480
Average ACT	20
Average TOEFL	NR
Graduated top 20% of class	NR
Graduated top 40% of class	NR
Graduated top 60% of class	NR
Average HS GPA or Avg.	NR

DEADLINES

Early decision	11/1
Regular admission	4/15
Regular notification	rolling
Non-fall registration	yes

APPLICANTS ALSO LOOK AT

AND OFTEN PREFER

Morehouse
Spelman
Hampton

AND SOMETIMES PREFER

George Washington
U. Maryland, Coll. Park
Florida A&M

AND RARELY PREFER

Morgan St.

FINANCIAL FACTS

Financial Aid Rating	65
Tuition	$8,105
Room & board	$4,755
Estimated book expense	$620
% frosh receiving aid	NR
% undergrads receiving aid	63
% aid is need-based	NR
% frosh w/ grant (avg)	NR
% frosh w/ loan (avg)	NR
% UGs w/ job (avg)	6 ($200)
Off-campus job outlook	good

UNIVERSITY OF IDAHO

MOSCOW, ID 83844-3133 · ADMISSIONS: 208-885-6326 · FAX: 208-885-9061

CAMPUS LIFE

Quality of Life Rating	**83**
Type of school	public
Affiliation	none
Environment	town

STUDENTS

FT undergrad enrollment	7,398
% male/female	57/43
% from out of state	29
% live on campus	65
% spend weekend on campus	60
% transfers	27
% from public high school	96
% in (# of) fraternities	26 (28)
% in (# of) sororities	19 (8)
% African-American	1
% Asian	2
% Caucasian	88
% Hispanic	2
% international	2
# of countries represented	78

WHAT'S HOT
health facilities
music associations
town-gown relations
intercollegiate sports
old-fashioned dating

WHAT'S NOT
dorms
cigarettes
campus difficult to get around
lab facilities
library

ACADEMICS

Academic Rating	**69**
Profs Interesting Rating	66
Profs Accessible Rating	69
Calendar	semester
Student/teacher ratio	17:1
% profs PhD	84
Hours of study per day	3.14

MOST POPULAR MAJORS
mechanical engineering
elementary education
electrical engineering

STUDENTS SPEAK OUT

Life
Students describe life in and around Moscow, Idaho, as quiet and sedate. "Life here in Moscow is boring if you're under twenty-one. Most people go out to bars, or else they leave town to go skiing, to the lake, whatever," writes one student. Writes another, "Life in Moscow is cool. It's big enough that we have movies and a mall, but small enough that if I go for a run or ride my bike, I can be out in the middle of a rolling wheat field in three minutes to enjoy the peace and quiet." Agrees a third, "The town is nice. People are pleasant, and I feel safe here. The environment is clean and, while it's quiet, there's enough activity to keep you entertained." Entertainment is low key, often comprised of "dancing, visiting friends, working out to keep stress down, studying." Like most college students, Idaho undergrads drink; explains one, "Life at this school is controlled by the weather. The colder it gets, the drunker we get." In most ways, in fact, Idaho is like a scaled-down version of larger state universities; as one student explains, "The U of I has a great deal of activities available for nearly all interests: sports, frats/sororities, outdoor activities, etc." A large number of men, almost one-third of them, pledge a fraternity. Also popular are "lots of out-of-door activities. Idaho is a virtual playground for the camper, climber, mountain biker, etc."

Academics
Students at the University of Idaho describe their academic experiences as a mixed bag. Depending on their majors, students either rave about instructors ("Professors in the College of Education are cool"; "The architecture professors can relate to us on a personal level. Overall, my academic experience has been a good one"), or rage against them ("Most labs are taught by TAs and some cannot speak English very well. Most of the time is spent trying to figure out what they said instead of doing the lab"; "There is much variation in the teaching staff. I have had teachers that were excellent and others that had no business teaching"). The University of Idaho is strongest in its popular engineering, business, education, forestry, and agriculture departments. The administration, students report, "is like most—full of red tape and rules that don't bend."

Student Body
A student boasts that "the U of I has the most unpretentious student body of all the schools I've attended." Others point out that it's "an extremely liberal campus, in contrast with the prevailing view of north Idaho," although students are generally more politically conservative than students nationwide. U of I attracts a relatively large proportion of its students—almost one quarter—from out of state. U of I has a small student body for a state school, but the student body still divides itself along the lines of major—and fraternity—affiliation; "People tend to hang out with those from their own college or major," notes one student.

FINANCIAL AID: 208-885-6312

WEB SITE: HTTP://WWW.UIDAHO.EDU/UIDAHO-HOME.HTML

ADMISSIONS

The admissions committee considers (in descending order of importance): HS record, test scores, class rank. Either the SAT or ACT is required. *High school units required/recommended:* 4 English required, 3 math required, 3 science required, 1 foreign language recommended, 3 social studies required. Applicants evaluated on a sliding scale based on secondary school GPA and ACT or SAT I scores. TOEFL is required of all international students.

The Inside Word

Idaho's admissions process is typical of large universities, and easy to deal with—it doesn't get any more straightforward than this. A small number of college-age students in Idaho means out-of-staters face little in the way of any constraints above and beyond in-state standards.

FINANCIAL AID

Students should submit: FAFSA, the school's own financial aid form. The Princeton Review suggests that all financial aid forms be submitted as soon as possible after January 1. *The following grants/scholarships are offered:* Pell, SEOG, academic merit, athletic, the school's own scholarships, the school's own grants, state scholarships, state grants, private scholarships, ROTC. *Students borrow from the following loan programs:* Perkins, the school's own loan fund, supplemental loans, private loans. College Work-Study Program is available. Institutional employment is available.

FROM THE ADMISSIONS OFFICE

"The University of Idaho combines the best of both worlds. We are the major research university in the state of Idaho, the state's land grant university, and a safe, residential environment. Moscow's small size and the supportive surrounding community provide the ideal atmosphere for a total learning experience."

ADMISSIONS

Admissions Rating	67
% of applicants accepted	85
% of acceptees attending	47

FRESHMAN PROFILE

Average verbal SAT	540
Average math SAT	550
Average ACT	23
Average TOEFL	550
Graduated top 20% of class	42
Graduated top 40% of class	82
Graduated top 60% of class	97
Average HS GPA or Avg.	3.4

DEADLINES

Early decision	NR
Regular admission	8/1
Regular notification	rolling
Non-fall registration	yes

APPLICANTS ALSO LOOK AT
AND SOMETIMES PREFER

Boise St.
Washington St.

FINANCIAL FACTS

Financial Aid Rating	79
In-state tuition	$1,620
Out-of-state tuition	$7,000
Room & board	$3,600
Estimated book expense	$866
% frosh receiving aid	65
% undergrads receiving aid	60
% aid is need-based	60
% frosh w/ grant (avg)	35 ($1,000)
% frosh w/ loan (avg)	60 ($2,600)
% UGs w/ job (avg)	45 ($2,000)
Off-campus job outlook	good

ILLINOIS INSTITUTE OF TECHNOLOGY

3300 SOUTH FEDERAL STREET, CHICAGO, IL 60616   ADMISSIONS: 800-448-2329   FAX: 312-567-3004

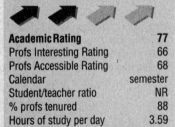
STUDENTS SPEAK OUT

Life

IIT students are uniformly negative about life outside their classrooms and labs. Chief among their complaints is the area surrounding the school: IIT, like the University of Chicago, is located on the South Side of Chicago, a notoriously rundown neighborhood, and IIT students are certainly thinking of relations with their immediate neighbors when they rank "town-gown relations" the fourth worst in the country. Positive notes: The school is just across the expressway from Comiskey Park (good news for White Sox fans), and is also near the Lincoln Park Zoo and Grant Park; all forms of public transportation make stops right on campus. Students also rank their campus among the nation's ugliest: clearly, they were unimpressed that the boxy, urban campus was largely designed by famous architect (and former director of the College of Architecture) Ludwig Mies van der Rohe. Students also report that they have neither the time nor the opportunities for a "normal" social life—intense academic pressure. Because half the students commute, many others go home every weekend, and the male/female ratio is so skewed, very little dating or partying happens (what little drinking there is, could be categorized as the "stress relief"—as opposed to "social"—variety). Finally, do not forget those Chicago winters, during which the temperature frequently drops near zero degrees...Kelvin!

Academics

IIT has redefined its undergraduate program and changed its curriculum. The undergraduate program now focuses on three areas, engineering, architecture, and a new pre-professional track. Eighty percent of the undergraduates are engineers. Like most engineering students, the undergraduates of IIT work hard (nearly four hours a day) and must endure an extremely stressful academic environment. Besides engineering, architecture and computer science are also reputedly excellent; liberal arts departments, on the other hand, exist almost solely to teach courses required by the core curriculum. That core, which applies to students in all divisions, mandates twelve hours of humanities and twelve hours of social sciences, as well as twelve hours of natural science/engineering and eight hours of math (the engineering core demands more hours of science and math). All divisions offer an honors program, and all but design offer five-year graduate/undergraduate degree programs. Cooperative programs are available in most fields, allowing students the opportunity to put their educations to use in the business and research worlds. Research opportunities on campus are also reportedly numerous.

Student Body

IIT draws a good mix of students from different ethnic and social backgrounds. Because the students essentially share the same general academic interests, and because the student body is predominantly male, IIT students can seem a little similar, but, by tech school standards, IIT has a well-balanced student body. Nearly half the students are from out of state.

ADMISSIONS

The admissions committee considers (in descending order of importance): HS record, class rank, test scores, recommendations, essay. *Also considered (in descending order of importance):* extracurriculars, personality. Either the SAT or ACT is required. An interview is recommended. Admissions process is need-blind. *High school units required/recommended:* 11 total units are required; 4 English required, 3 math required, 2 science required, 1 social studies required, 1 history required. Minimum combined SAT I score of 1150 (composite ACT score of 25) required. TOEFL is required of all international students. *The admissions office says:* "The admissions office considers each application on its individual merits, always looking for superior ability as determined through previous academic records, recommendations, statements by the student, leadership experiences, aptitudes, and goals. The student's record of achievement in high school, however, most often provides the best prediction of success at IIT."

The Inside Word

IIT's applicant pool is small and includes a strong element of self-selection. This means the majority get in, but not without solid academic preparation. While the committee evaluates other criteria, the bottom line is that candidates need fairly solid grades and better than average test scores in order to get admitted.

FINANCIAL AID

Students should submit: FAFSA, the school's own financial aid form. The Princeton Review suggests that all financial aid forms be submitted as soon as possible after January 1. *The following grants/scholarships are offered:* Pell, SEOG, academic merit, athletic, the school's own scholarships, the school's own grants, state scholarships, state grants, private scholarships, private grants, ROTC, foreign aid. *Students borrow from the following loan programs:* Stafford, unsubsidized Stafford, Perkins, PLUS, the school's own loan fund, state loans, private loans. College Work-Study Program is available. Institutional employment is available.

FROM THE ADMISSIONS OFFICE

"IIT is committed to providing undergraduate education of the highest quality. We believe that every one of our students has the ability to make significant contributions to society. Our goal is to help you attain the knowledge, skills, ethical perspective, and motivation you will need to realize that potential. Our university is especially well suited to prepare you to seize the opportunities and address the real problems of a rapidly changing, increasingly complex world. The IIT scholars with whom you will study contribute to the nation's intellectual wealth in areas ranging from ethics and management to design processes, mathematical problems, and theoretical physics. Our multicultural student body and our location in the heart of one of America's most ethnically diverse cities make the undergraduate experience an ideal way to prepare for tomorrow's global society."

ADMISSIONS

Admissions Rating	80
% of applicants accepted	64
% of acceptees attending	25

FRESHMAN PROFILE

Average verbal SAT	600
Average math SAT	650
Average ACT	26
Average TOEFL	550
Graduated top 20% of class	70
Graduated top 40% of class	94
Graduated top 60% of class	99
Average HS GPA or Avg.	NR

DEADLINES

Early decision	NR
Regular admission	NR
Regular notification	rolling
Non-fall registration	yes

APPLICANTS ALSO LOOK AT

AND OFTEN PREFER

UC-Berkeley
U. Illinois, Urbana-Champ.
Northwestern U.
Abilene Christian

AND SOMETIMES PREFER

Purdue U.-West Lafayette
Case Western Reserve
Southern Illinois U.
Marquette

FINANCIAL FACTS

Financial Aid Rating	75
Tuition	$15,280
Room & board	$4,795
Estimated book expense	$800
% frosh receiving aid	89
% undergrads receiving aid	85
% aid is need-based	84
% frosh w/ grant (avg)	87 ($8,764)
% frosh w/ loan (avg)	31 ($5,919)
% UGs w/ job (avg)	NR
Off-campus job outlook	fair

ILLINOIS WESLEYAN UNIVERSITY

Box 2900, Bloomington, IL 61702-2900　　　ADMISSIONS: 309-556-3031　　FAX: 309-556-3411

CAMPUS LIFE

Quality of Life Rating 74
Type of school　　　private
Affiliation　　　　　none
Environment　　　　suburban

STUDENTS
FT undergrad enrollment　　1,829
% male/female　　　　　　48/52
% from out of state　　　　14
% live on campus　　　　　86
% spend weekend on campus　90
% transfers　　　　　　　　3
% from public high school　83
% in (# of) fraternities　24 (6)
% in (# of) sororities　　24 (6)
% African-American　　　　3
% Asian　　　　　　　　　4
% Caucasian　　　　　　　86
% Hispanic　　　　　　　　1
% international　　　　　　3
# of countries represented　24

WHAT'S HOT
college radio
music associations
theater
town-gown relations
Greeks

WHAT'S NOT
library
political activism
support groups
students are cliquish
students are unhappy

ACADEMICS

Academic Rating 88
Profs Interesting Rating　　77
Profs Accessible Rating　　82
Calendar　　　　　　　　4-4-1
Student/teacher ratio　　　13:1
% profs PhD/tenured　　　92/59
Hours of study per day　　3.53

MOST POPULAR MAJORS
business administration
biology
English

% GRADS WHO PURSUE...
Law 6, Med 5, MBA 1, MA 17

STUDENTS SPEAK OUT

Life
Many students at Illinois Wesleyan mention the high level of participation in extracurricular clubs here. Writes one, "People are encouraged to get involved in a wide range of activities, from frats to the scuba club." Students get pretty excited about their Division III sports teams, but intramural sports are not among the many popular extracurriculars. Nor is partying. Writes one student, "This is not a party school. Alcohol rules are strict, and controlled substances are rare." Because the school is so small, it's hard to maintain any degree of anonymity. Writes one student, "Some students aren't comfortable with the small-school, 'everyone knows everyone' scene, because one mistake and you can't recover. There's no new social group to go to who doesn't know you or the reputation you just earned." Students give Bloomington below-average grades. Explains one, "Usually I enjoy the small-town feel at this school, but weekends can get pretty boring."

Academics
You'd think students would take pride in IWU's recognition as the best regional university in the Midwest, right? Wrong! Most of our respondents used the school's ranking as a jumping-off point for their own gripes. Many start their responses in this manner: "It's supposed to be the best in the area, but..." The old cliché is true: It is lonely at the top. Compared with other schools in its class, IWU has very competitive admissions. It's also very versatile, strong in the fine arts (particularly drama and music) and able to send twenty percent of its students on to professional programs (one in ten goes on to pursue an MBA). Classes are small, and, for a private school, tuition is pretty reasonable. So what's the problem? Mostly it's the perception that the administration, in its eagerness to maintain the school's new-found prominence, is "thoroughly disorganized" and ignoring the needs of the students. Music students complain that distribution requirements take too much time away from their music studies, and fear that when they graduate they won't be able to compete with conservatory students in the job market. Others complain that important facilities, such as the library, are outdated (a new library is planned, and a new science center opened this year), and still others that financial aid packages are meager. Still, one student points out, "There's $15 million being invested in a new athletic center—why?" And, while several students positively note the small class size and instructor accessibility, our survey showed overall student dissatisfaction in these categories. Mel Brooks once said, "It's good to be the king!" Well, maybe not.

Student Body
IWU students characterized all their classmates as "overwhelmingly conservative," but those who filled out our survey fell to the left-of-center on the political spectrum. Did we hit the small mother lode of liberals here? More likely, the student body isn't quite as homogeneously white, rich, and Republican as students think. Over three-quarters of the students are from in-state, many from the Chicago area. Writes one out-of-state student, "I'm from Minnesota and I feel like a foreign student."

ADMISSIONS

The admissions committee considers (in descending order of importance): HS record, class rank, test scores, essay, recommendations. *Also considered (in descending order of importance):* special talents, extracurriculars, alumni relationship, geographical distribution, personality. Either the SAT or ACT is required. An interview is recommended. Admissions process is need-blind. *High school units required/recommended:* 15 total units are required; 4 English required, 4 math required, 3 science required, 2 foreign language required, 2 social studies required. Minimum combined SAT I score of 1000 (composite ACT score of 24), rank in top third of secondary school class, and minimum 3.0 GPA recommended. *Special Requirements:* A portfolio is required for art program applicants. TOEFL is required of all international students. Audition required of music and drama program applicants. Biology, chemistry, algebra, and geometry required of nursing program applicants. Additional math and science required of pre-engineering and science program applicants.

The Inside Word

Illinois Wesleyan is selective enough that serious candidates should exceed the suggested curriculum requirements in order to better their chances for admission.

FINANCIAL AID

Students should submit: FAFSA (due March 1), CSS Profile (due March 1), state aid form. The Princeton Review suggests that all financial aid forms be submitted as soon as possible after January 1. *The following grants/scholarships are offered:* Pell, SEOG, academic merit, the school's own scholarships, the school's own grants, state scholarships, state grants, private scholarships, private grants, ROTC, foreign aid. *Students borrow from the following loan programs:* Stafford, unsubsidized Stafford, Perkins, PLUS, the school's own loan fund, federal nursing loans, private loans. College Work-Study Program is available. Institutional employment is available.

FROM THE ADMISSIONS OFFICE

"Illinois Wesleyan University strives to provide a liberal education of high quality for all of our students. An Illinois Wesleyan education is distinctive in giving a liberal arts direction to the curricula of the professional schools and programs and in allowing liberal arts majors access to a wide variety of professional courses as electives. We believe that our most important educational goal is liberation from ignorance and complacency. Because we assume that the mind is the key to the educated person, we hope to foster during the college years the knowledge, values, and skills that will sustain all of us over a lifetime of learning. We intend, moreover, to prepare our students for responsible citizenship and leadership in a democratic society and global community. We want Illinois Wesleyan to reflect the ethnic, racial, and cultural diversity of the world. Above all, whatever their course of studies, we wish to enable Wesleyan graduates to lead useful, creative, fully realized lives."

ADMISSIONS

Admissions Rating	86
% of applicants accepted	54
% of acceptees attending	33

FRESHMAN PROFILE

Average verbal SAT	620
Average math SAT	610
Average ACT	27
Average TOEFL	550
Graduated top 20% of class	73
Graduated top 40% of class	96
Graduated top 60% of class	100
Average HS GPA or Avg.	3.4

DEADLINES

Early decision	NR
Regular admission	NR
Regular notification	rolling
Non-fall registration	yes

APPLICANTS ALSO LOOK AT

AND OFTEN PREFER

U. Illinois, Urbana-Champ.
Northwestern U.
U. Chicago
Notre Dame
Indiana U.-Bloomington

AND SOMETIMES PREFER

DePauw
Northern Illinois
Southern Illinois-Edwardsville
Illinois State

AND RARELY PREFER

Eastern Illinois
Bradley

FINANCIAL FACTS

Financial Aid Rating	75
Tuition	$15,410
Room & board	$4,290
Estimated book expense	$400
% frosh receiving aid	86
% undergrads receiving aid	85
% aid is need-based	86
% frosh w/ grant (avg)	82 ($7,836)
% frosh w/ loan (avg)	55 ($2,923)
% UGs w/ job (avg)	55 ($1,400)
Off-campus job outlook	excellent

University of Illinois—Urbana-Champaign

506 South Wright Street, Urbana, IL 61801 ADMISSIONS: 217-333-0302 FAX: 217-333-9758

STUDENTS SPEAK OUT
Life
Says one student of the social scene, "It's about as good as you can have in an area that's completely surrounded by farms." Writes another, "Socially, the university offers an extremely wide variety of...bars." Still, it's not as if University of Illinois students are completely cut off from civilization. Explains one, "Both cities, Champaign and Urbana, are accessible with mass transit and offer decent shopping and dining." An "excellent transportation system" makes cars unnecessary for traveling off campus. Of course, at a school of this size, one rarely needs to leave campus for entertainment. Parties at dorms and off-campus housing are frequent, and fraternities and sororities play a dominant role in the lives of those who go Greek. Students ardently follow their intercollegiate sports teams, the Fighting Illini, particularly in football and basketball. One of the few controversies at the school centers on the team mascot, a Native American chief whom some perceive as an offensive racial stereotype.

Academics
The University of Illinois attracts an almost entirely in-state student body, but, as one student explains, "that can only be attributed to the cheap price for in-state students. It sure isn't because of the quality of the school." This huge university's greatest assets are its competitive engineering and business programs, but because of its size the school supports many other less-touted but fine programs (mostly career-track majors). Although the University of Illinois is very big, a good education is easily within reach for the student who doesn't need to be led by the hand to find it. True, lecture classes can reach four-digit enrollments, but discussion sections are much smaller. True, students never meet some of their professors, but they do have access to an unbelievable variety of "lectures, seminars, plays, performances, speakers, sports, and other presentations that are readily available for anyone interested." And, the school boasts some of the most studious public school students in the country, in part because one-fifth of the student body is made up of engineers. As one student explains, "I came from a small town and was worried about this school's size, but I wouldn't be happier anywhere else. The possibilities are endless." Still, students voice some of the complaints common at many large schools: those most often mentioned concerned TAs ("you're lucky if your TA speaks English," writes a finance major) and the time-consuming registration process. The University reports that on-line registration is now in operation, and can be completed in ten minutes.

Student Body
Practically every student here is from the state of Illinois. One student reports that, despite the low tuition rates, "for a public school, Illinois students are pretty affluent. Most are seeking a good job and family—the things they were given in their home life." Writes another, "Because this is a large college, you will find a group to associate with, but you will also have the opportunity to meet people from very diverse backgrounds." Asians make up the largest minority population, blacks the second largest. Both black and white students reported that race relations are acrimonious. One African American student writes that U of I is "a great school, but the student body and faculty need to be better educated about minorities and their cultures."

ADMISSIONS

The admissions committee considers (in descending order of importance): HS record, class rank, test scores, recommendations, essay. *Also considered (in descending order of importance):* geographical distribution, special talents. Either the SAT or ACT is required. Admissions process is need-blind. *High school units required/recommended:* 15 total units are required; 4 English required, 3 math required, 4 math recommended, 2 science required, 2 foreign language required, 4 foreign language recommended, 2 social studies required. *Special Requirements:* An audition is required for music program applicants. Professional interest statement recommended for some programs.

The Inside Word

Few candidates are deceived by Illinois' relatively high acceptance rate; the university has a well-deserved reputation for expecting applicants to be strong students, and those who aren't usually don't bother to apply. Despite a jumbo applicant pool, the admissions office reports that every candidate is individually reviewed, which deserves mention as rare in universities of this size.

FINANCIAL AID

Students should submit: FAFSA. The Princeton Review suggests that all financial aid forms be submitted as soon as possible after January 1. *The following grants/scholarships are offered:* Pell, SEOG, academic merit, athletic, the school's own scholarships, the school's own grants, state scholarships, state grants, private scholarships, private grants, ROTC. *Students borrow from the following loan programs:* Stafford, Perkins, PLUS, the school's own loan fund, health professions loans, private loans. Applicants will be notified of awards beginning May 15. College Work-Study Program is available. Institutional employment is available.

FROM THE ADMISSIONS OFFICE

"The campus has been aptly described as a collection of neighborhoods constituting a diverse and vibrant city. The neighborhoods are of many types: students and faculty within a department; people sharing a room or house; the members of a professional organization, a service club, or an intramural team; or simply people who, starting out as strangers sharing a class or a study lounge or a fondness for a weekly film series, have become friends. And the city of this description is the university itself—a rich cosmopolitan environment constructed by students and faculty to meet their educational and personal goals. The quality of intellectual life parallels that of other great universities, and many faculty and students who have their choice of top institutions select Illinois over its peers. While such choices are based often on the quality of individual programs of study, another crucial factor is the 'tone' of the campus life that is linked with the virtues of midwestern culture. There is an informality and a near-absence of pretension which, coupled with a tradition of commitment to excellence, creates an atmosphere that is unique among the finest institutions."

ADMISSIONS

Admissions Rating	82
% of applicants accepted	72
% of acceptees attending	50

FRESHMAN PROFILE

Average verbal SAT	NR
Average math SAT	NR
Average ACT	27
Average TOEFL	NR
Graduated top 20% of class	77
Graduated top 40% of class	95
Graduated top 60% of class	99
Average HS GPA or Avg.	NR

DEADLINES

Early decision	11/15
Regular admission	1/1
Regular notification	rolling
Non-fall registration	yes

APPLICANTS ALSO LOOK AT

AND OFTEN PREFER

Northwestern U.
Purdue
U. Wisconsin-Madison
Indiana U.
Washington U.

AND SOMETIMES PREFER

U. Michigan-Ann Arbor
Northern Illinois
Miami U.

AND RARELY PREFER

U. Kentucky
Loyola U. Chicago
Illinois State
Southern Illinois-Edwardsville

FINANCIAL FACTS

Financial Aid Rating	73
In-state tuition	$3,150
Out-of-state tuition	$8,174
Room & board	$4,560
Estimated book expense	$500
% frosh receiving aid	76
% undergrads receiving aid	82
% aid is need-based	60
% frosh w/ grant (avg)	48 ($1,830)
% frosh w/ loan (avg)	58 ($2,500)
% UGs w/ job (avg)	45 ($1,250)
Off-campus job outlook	good

INDIANA UNIVERSITY-BLOOMINGTON

300 NORTH JORDAN AVENUE, BLOOMINGTON, IN 47405 | ADMISSIONS: 812-855-0661 | FAX: 812-855-5102

CAMPUS LIFE

Quality of Life Rating	85
Type of school	public
Affiliation	none
Environment	suburban

STUDENTS

FT undergrad enrollment	26,152
% male/female	46/54
% from out of state	36
% live on campus	50
% spend weekend on campus	80
% transfers	NR
% from public high school	NR
% in (# of) fraternities	12 (34)
% in (# of) sororities	11 (24)
% African-American	4
% Asian	3
% Caucasian	88
% Hispanic	2
% international	2
# of countries represented	135

WHAT'S HOT
intercollegiate sports
library
intramural sports
Greeks
campus is beautiful

WHAT'S NOT
registration is a pain
students are cliquish
campus difficult to get around
student government
dorms

ACADEMICS

Academic Rating	73
Profs Interesting Rating	65
Profs Accessible Rating	71
Calendar	semester
Student/teacher ratio	19:1
% profs tenured	84
Hours of study per day	3.03

MOST POPULAR MAJORS
biology
psychology
criminal justice

STUDENTS SPEAK OUT

Life

Bloomington, home of Indiana University, is "the perfect college town, not a big city but always open to students," according to our respondents. The campus itself, according to one junior, is "one of the most beautiful places I've ever seen," where, as another mentions, "there are a million and one things to do..., which was nice before I turned twenty-one." But now, "I love hangin' out at Sports—the bar scene is a pretty good one around here and it's made my senior year a great one." Athletics, as the bar's name suggests, are a very important part of nonacademic life. Intercollegiate sports are universally popular—men's basketball, however, is the big draw—and intramural programs are also well attended. Day-to-day social life basically revolves around fraternities and sororities, acceptance to which can be brutally competitive. Students also "go camping, we go to musicals, free jazz at the Encore Cafe, [and] hang out on this awesome campus." Our survey shows that IU has earned its reputation as a party school: alcohol and drugs (particularly hallucinogens) are on-campus favorites.

Academics

Indiana University's national reputation may rest on its killer athletic teams, but Indiana residents and students know, and others are beginning to learn, that IU is a fine academic university. Students particularly praise the top-notch business and journalism schools, the excellent psychology departments, and the competitive School of Music. A journalism student characterizes his department as "not excessively competitive, while still maintaining academic excellence." In all departments, students agree that "the opportunities are there, but size is a big deterrent." Indeed, as at most state schools, classes can be less than intimate. Most agree that professors must be sought for help but are excellent teachers. One student notes, "My professors are witty, memorable, and accurate." New registration procedures seem to have sped up the process considerably, putting to rest an age-old gripe of IU students. But as always, assertiveness is the key to success at IU; as one student sums up, "IU is big only if you make it that way! Administrators and professors are more than willing to help if you take the initiative. Success is yours if you seek it." Once you learn the ropes, you can find "the big school opportunities with the experience of a small campus."

Student Body

Around three-fifths of IU students are from in-state, which translates to a relatively high percentage of out-of-staters for a state school. The percentage of minorities in the student body is low, but since the school is large, the minority population is as well. Some undergrads find the students to be an interesting mix: "This campus is incredibly diverse. You have your beer-drinking crazy partiers and your snobby (not so snobby) intellectuals, your realists, your idealists, and some people who just don't know who they are." But most report that "there is not an honest outreach to unite different types of students," particularly along racial lines, in this conservative school. Although people get along superficially, "everyone knows their boundaries," because, as one student reports, "racial hate still resides on our campus." Racial tension became more publicly painful to African-American students during and after the O.J. Simpson trial.

INDIANA UNIVERSITY-BLOOMINGTON

FINANCIAL AID: 812-855-3278

WEB SITE: HTTP://WWW.INDIANA.EDU/

ADMISSIONS

The admissions committee considers (in descending order of importance): HS record, class rank, recommendations, test scores. *Also considered (in descending order of importance):* alumni relationship, extracurriculars, personality, special talents. Either the SAT or ACT is required. An interview is recommended. Admissions process is need-blind. *High school units required/recommended:* 14 total units are required; 19 total units are recommended; 4 English required, 3 math required, 1 science required, 2 social studies required. Rank in top third of secondary school class and completion of nineteen year-long academic courses recommended. Primary attention given to the number of strong college-preparatory courses taken, their level of difficulty, student's willingness to accept challenge, and grade trends. Students with modest class rank but rising grades in challenging academic programs are encouraged to apply. *Special Requirements:* An audition is required for music program applicants. *The admissions office says:* "University-bound students should establish a solid foundation at the high school level in English (the school requires four years), laboratory sciences (one year), and social sciences (two years) if they intend to compete in any academic program offered by Indiana University. Society's increasing demands for mathematical analysis and computing make a broad background in mathematics, including algebra and trigonometry (three years total required), essential for many fields of study. The study of a foreign language is desirable but not required for admission."

The Inside Word

A high volume of applicants makes Indiana's formula-driven admissions process relatively selective for a university of its size. Candidates to the School of Music face a highly selective audition process.

FINANCIAL AID

Students should submit: FAFSA, the school's own financial aid form, a copy of parents' most recent income tax filing. The Princeton Review suggests that all financial aid forms be submitted as soon as possible after January 1. *The following grants/scholarships are offered:* Pell, SEOG, academic merit, athletic, the school's own scholarships, the school's own grants, state scholarships, state grants, private scholarships, private grants, federal nursing scholarship, ROTC. *Students borrow from the following loan programs:* Stafford, Perkins, PLUS, the school's own loan fund, state loans, federal nursing loans, health professions loans, private loans. Applicants will be notified of awards beginning March 15. College Work-Study Program is available. Institutional employment is available.

FROM THE ADMISSIONS OFFICE

"Indiana University is a traditional university located in Bloomington, Indiana. The campus is known for its spacious, wooded beauty, classic limestone buildings, and wide variety of trees and flowers. Bloomington is a wonderful college town. The liberal arts curriculum offers students a wide range of academic options combined with built-in flexibility."

ADMISSIONS

Admissions Rating	70
% of applicants accepted	82
% of acceptees attending	44

FRESHMAN PROFILE

Average verbal SAT	550
Average math SAT	550
Average ACT	24
Average TOEFL	NR
Graduated top 20% of class	47
Graduated top 40% of class	86
Graduated top 60% of class	NR
Average HS GPA or Avg.	NR

DEADLINES

Early decision	2/15
Regular admission	NR
Regular notification	rolling
Non-fall registration	yes

APPLICANTS ALSO LOOK AT

AND OFTEN PREFER
Notre Dame
U. Illinois, Urbana-Champ.

AND SOMETIMES PREFER
U. Wisconsin-Madison
U. Iowa
Ohio State-Columbus
Purdue U.-West Lafayette

AND RARELY PREFER
Wabash
Bellarmine
SUNY Buffalo

FINANCIAL FACTS

Financial Aid Rating	78
In-state tuition	$3,570
Out-of-state tuition	$10,700
Room & board	$3,863
Estimated book expense	$625
% frosh receiving aid	57
% undergrads receiving aid	68
% aid is need-based	90
% frosh w/ grant (avg)	60 ($1,100)
% frosh w/ loan (avg)	30 ($2,253)
% UGs w/ job (avg)	NR
Off-campus job outlook	excellent

IOWA STATE UNIVERSITY

314 ALUMNI HALL, AMES, IA 50011-2010 ADMISSIONS: 800-262-3810 FAX: 515-294-2592

CAMPUS LIFE

Quality of Life Rating	**81**
Type of school	public
Affiliation	none
Environment	suburban

STUDENTS

FT undergrad enrollment	20,208
% male/female	57/43
% from out of state	23
% live on campus	42
% spend weekend on campus	NR
% transfers	33
% from public high school	92
% in (# of) fraternities	14 (35)
% in (# of) sororities	14 (20)
% African-American	3
% Asian	2
% Caucasian	87
% Hispanic	2
% international	6
# of countries represented	116

WHAT'S HOT
old-fashioned dating
library
intramural sports
college radio
Greeks

WHAT'S NOT
political activism
cigarettes
students are cliquish
support groups
campus difficult to get around

ACADEMICS

Academic Rating	**67**
Profs Interesting Rating	64
Profs Accessible Rating	63
Calendar	semester
Student/teacher ratio	18:1
% profs PhD/tenured	87/83
Hours of study per day	3.00

MOST POPULAR MAJORS
finance
mechanical engineering
elementary education

% GRADS WHO PURSUE...
Law 1, Med 1, MA 15

STUDENTS SPEAK OUT

Life

Ames, Iowa, is a small city of 50,000 whose slow pace is just fine for many of Iowa State's undergraduates. One reports, "Ames is a college town, not a huge metropolis. The people are easy to know and friendly. ISU is the best decision I ever made." Still, if you're looking for big-city action, ISU probably won't suit your needs. One undergrad complains that "Iowa State University is a well-thought-out campus without an active campus town surrounding it." Des Moines is a half hour away, but most students' social lives begin and end on campus. The campus is beautiful and easy to get around. One student writes that "from one corner to another is a thirteen-minute walk." Another reports, "The campus is absolutely beautiful. There is always something to do—whether you choose a school-related activity or a party." Fraternities and sororities play a major role here: They are more popular at only thirteen other schools included in this book. ISU students aren't sports nuts, unlike students at most large universities, but they do take an active interest in their teams and cherish their rivalry with the University of Iowa. Says one, "There is a big intrastate rivalry between the University of Iowa and Iowa State University, and finally after years of lopsidedness, ISU is taking over. It's about time, ISU!"

Academics

Iowa State University has earned its reputation as one of the country's leading agricultural schools. But engineering and agricultural sciences aren't the only things taught at this land-grant institution: career-oriented programs of all types attract the school's 25,000 students to Ames. A little over one-tenth of the students study agriculture, but a much larger proportion, about one-third, study Arts and Sciences; another one-fifth pursue engineering degrees, and one in ten studies education. Business and management studies are also popular, as are other career-oriented majors. Our respondents are happy with programs as varied as landscape architecture, speech communication, and graphic design. Students tell us that the school was unusually well run for a large university: they give good grades in most administrative categories. Says one, "I think the academic advising here is exceptional. Advisors want to know what you want from your education and really help you achieve it." Although professors receive only average grades, several students mention how helpful instructors are. "The profs really care about teaching you and also care whether you excel," reports one accounting major. As at most state universities, students complain that classes of all difficulty levels are too often taught by graduate students, and class sizes are predictably too large.

Student Body

ISU students are extremely happy with their choice, particularly for students at a large university. It's probably because of "the school's most unique quality: the friendliness of the students." They must be particularly well adjusted, because they reported an active dating scene despite a somewhat lopsided male/female ratio. Students are generally conservative and serious, and the minority population is relatively small.

FINANCIAL AID: 515-294-2223   E-MAIL: INFO@IASTATE.EDU   WEB SITE: HTTP://WWW.IASTATE.EDU/

ADMISSIONS

The admissions committee considers (in descending order of importance): class rank, HS record, test scores, recommendations. *Also considered (in descending order of importance):* special talents. Either the SAT or ACT is required; ACT is preferred. Admissions process is need-blind. *High school units required/recommended:* 12 total units are required; 4 English required, 3 math required, 3 science required, 2 social studies required. Rank in top half of secondary school class required. *Special Requirements:* TOEFL is required of all international students. 1 additional unit of social studies and 2 units of a single foreign language required of applicants to College of Liberal Arts and Sciences. *The admissions office says:* "Students applying to the College of Liberal Arts and Sciences are required to have completed an additional year of social studies and two years of a single foreign language."

The Inside Word

With a decided lack of mystery in the admissions process and a super-high acceptance rate, Iowa State still attracts a solid student body. What we have here is living proof of the value of a good reputation and a little national press.

FINANCIAL AID

Students should submit: FAFSA. The Princeton Review suggests that all financial aid forms be submitted as soon as possible after January 1. *The following grants/ scholarships are offered:* Pell, SEOG, academic merit, athletic, the school's own scholarships, the school's own grants, state scholarships, state grants, private scholarships, private grants, ROTC, foreign aid. *Students borrow from the following loan programs:* unsubsidized Stafford, Perkins, PLUS, the school's own loan fund, supplemental loans, health professions loans, private loans. Applicants will be notified of awards beginning April 1. College Work-Study Program is available. Institutional employment is available.

FROM THE ADMISSIONS OFFICE

"Iowa State University offers all the advantages of a major university along with the friendliness and warmth of a residential campus. There are more than 100 undergraduate programs of study in the Colleges of Agriculture, Business, Design, Education, Engineering, Family and Consumer Sciences, Liberal Arts and Sciences, and Veterinary Medicine. Our 1,700 faculty members include Rhodes Scholars, Fulbright Scholars, and National Academy of Sciences and National Academy of Engineering members. Recognized for its high quality of life, Iowa State has taken practical steps to make the university a place where students feel like they belong. Iowa State has been recognized for the high quality of campus life and the exemplary out-of-class experiences offered to its students. Along with a strong academic experience, students also have opportunities for further developing their leadership skills and interpersonal relationships through any of the more than 500 student organizations, 60 intramural sports, and a multitude of arts and recreational activities."

ADMISSIONS

Admissions Rating	**69**
% of applicants accepted	87
% of acceptees attending	47

FRESHMAN PROFILE

Average verbal SAT	NR
Average math SAT	NR
Average ACT	NR
Average TOEFL	500
Graduated top 20% of class	49
Graduated top 40% of class	80
Graduated top 60% of class	96
Average HS GPA or Avg.	3.3

DEADLINES

Early decision	NR
Regular admission	NR
Regular notification	rolling
Non-fall registration	yes

APPLICANTS ALSO LOOK AT

AND OFTEN PREFER

U. Iowa
U. Kansas
U. Northern Iowa

AND SOMETIMES PREFER

U. Wisconsin-Madison
U. Michigan-Ann Arbor
Purdue U.-West Lafayette
U. Minnesota

AND RARELY PREFER

Kansas State
Illinois State
Creighton

FINANCIAL FACTS

Financial Aid Rating	**84**
In-state tuition	$2,470
Out-of-state tuition	$8,284
Room & board	$3,508
Estimated book expense	$664
% frosh receiving aid	75
% undergrads receiving aid	48
% aid is need-based	61
% frosh w/ grant (avg)	68 ($1,720)
% frosh w/ loan (avg)	NR ($2,407)
% UGs w/ job (avg)	15 ($1,835)
Off-campus job outlook	excellent

UNIVERSITY OF IOWA

107 CALVIN HALL, IOWA CITY, IA 52242-1396   ADMISSIONS: 800-553-4692   FAX: 319-335-1535

CAMPUS LIFE

Quality of Life Rating   **88**
Type of school   public
Affiliation   none
Environment   suburban

STUDENTS
FT undergrad enrollment   16,048
% male/female   47/53
% from out of state   31
% live on campus   30
% spend weekend on campus   NR
% transfers   26
% from public high school   88
% in (# of) fraternities   14 (25)
% in (# of) sororities   15 (19)
% African-American   3
% Asian   4
% Caucasian   89
% Hispanic   2
% international   3
# of countries represented   89

WHAT'S HOT
town-gown relations
intercollegiate sports
Iowa City
off-campus food
student publications

WHAT'S NOT
student government
campus difficult to get around
lab facilities
inefficient administration
health facilities

ACADEMICS

Academic Rating   **70**
Profs Interesting Rating   65
Profs Accessible Rating   70
Calendar   semester
Student/teacher ratio   15:1
% profs tenured   99
Hours of study per day   3.16

MOST POPULAR MAJORS
business administration
engineering
communication studies

STUDENTS SPEAK OUT

Life
Iowa City is small, but students seen to actually like its size. Writes one, "Iowa City is the greatest college town in the nation...I feel sorry for anyone who's never been here for a visit." Because the university is the city's chief industry, Iowa City is more accommodating to students than are most small cities. Local bars and clubs provide fun diversions for students, who report that drinking is both popular and easy to do, even for those under twenty-one. Intercollegiate sports provide another rallying point for students. Football, wrestling, and basketball are most popular. The Greeks are active but not dominant. The school is so large and so diverse that no one organization or activity could overwhelm social life here. For road trips, Chicago is less than four hours away by car, "which in the Midwest is just a hop, skip, and a jump," reports one student.

Academics
Peppered among the many large midwestern public universities that serve the preprofessional crowd are a few institutions that also do a little more. University of Iowa is one that does an excellent job producing the lawyers, doctors, businessmen, engineers, and teachers of tomorrow while also providing one of the region's intellectual centers—"the Athens of the Midwest," as several students describe it. Writes one economics major, "Almost every academic discipline and combination thereof can be found here. Best of all, the students here live and work in a friendly environment where learning is more than just rote memorization—it's learning who you are and how you can best use the skills you gain during your years in Iowa City." Among the university's nationally renowned departments are journalism, English (especially the creative writing program), film theory and production, and molecular biology. Humanities and social science departments are, in general, stronger here than at most schools. Students in the liberal arts college must complete a massive battery of distribution requirements; students in the other schools are allowed to focus more specifically on one area of study. Regardless, the school is tough. Writes one student, "Graduate in four years? Yeah, right!" As at most large schools, classes are often huge, professors inaccessible, and the bureaucracy running the institution a complete pain. Students report that the generally friendly atmosphere on campus makes some of the school's drawbacks a little easier to bear.

Student Body
"The UI is very, very white!" writes one student, and to a certain extent, they are right; UI's minority population is small. Still, students report that theirs is a diverse student body. "UI is a diverse place in every respect," says one student. "Students here come from a wide variety of social and economic backgrounds, and there are many foreign students, which adds a unique international dimension to the school." Liberal politics is the rule rather than the exception here, although, with over 15,000 undergraduates, all perspectives are represented.

ADMISSIONS

The admissions committee considers (in descending order of importance): class rank, HS record, test scores, recommendations. *Also considered (in descending order of importance):* special talents, alumni relationship, extracurriculars, personality. Either the SAT or ACT is required. An interview is recommended. Admissions process is need-blind. *High school units required/recommended:* 15 total units are required; 4 English required, 3 math required, 3 science required, 2 foreign language required, 3 social studies required. Rank in top half of secondary school class required of in-state applicants; rank in top 30% of secondary school class required of out-of-state applicants; admissions index based on class rank and ACT or SAT I scores used for all applicants who do not meet these requirements. *Special Requirements:* A portfolio is required for art program applicants. An audition is required for music program applicants. TOEFL is required of all international students. Specific requirements vary by college.

The Inside Word

Iowa's admissions process is none too personal, but on the other hand, candidates know exactly what is necessary to get admitted. The majority of applicants are fairly good students, most get in, and a lot choose to attend. That helps make Iowa the solid academic community it is.

FINANCIAL AID

Students should submit: FAFSA, the school's own financial aid form, a copy of parents' most recent income tax filing. The Princeton Review suggests that all financial aid forms be submitted as soon as possible after January 1. *The following grants/scholarships are offered:* Pell, SEOG, academic merit, athletic, the school's own scholarships, the school's own grants, state scholarships, state grants, private scholarships, private grants, federal nursing scholarship, ROTC. *Students borrow from the following loan programs:* Stafford, unsubsidized Stafford, Perkins, PLUS, the school's own loan fund, federal nursing loans, health professions loans, private loans. Applicants will be notified of awards beginning rolling. College Work-Study Program is available. Institutional employment is available.

FROM THE ADMISSIONS OFFICE

"The University of Iowa has strong programs in the creative arts, being the home of the first Writers Workshop and now housing the world-renowned International Writing Program. It also has strong programs in communication studies, journalism, political science, English, and psychology, and was the birthplace of the discipline of speech pathology and audiology. It offers excellent programs in the basic health sciences and health care programs, led by the top-ranked College of Medicine and the closely associated University Hospitals and Clinics."

ADMISSIONS

Admissions Rating	72
% of applicants accepted	86
% of acceptees attending	41

FRESHMAN PROFILE

Average verbal SAT	570
Average math SAT	580
Average ACT	25
Average TOEFL	530
Graduated top 20% of class	44
Graduated top 40% of class	76
Graduated top 60% of class	96
Average HS GPA or Avg.	3.4

DEADLINES

Early decision	NR
Regular admission	NR
Regular notification	rolling
Non-fall registration	yes

APPLICANTS ALSO LOOK AT

AND OFTEN PREFER
Northwestern U.
U. Illinois, Urbana-Champ.

AND SOMETIMES PREFER
Iowa State
U. Northern Iowa
Indiana U.-Bloomington
Drake
Grinnell

AND RARELY PREFER
Illinois State
U. Wisconsin-Madison
Cornell Coll.
U. Missouri-Rolla

FINANCIAL FACTS

Financial Aid Rating	73
In-state tuition	$2,470
Out-of-state tuition	$9,068
Room & board	$3,890
Estimated book expense	$694
% frosh receiving aid	65
% undergrads receiving aid	65
% aid is need-based	65
% frosh w/ grant (avg)	30 ($1,450)
% frosh w/ loan (avg)	33 ($1,823)
% UGs w/ job (avg)	55 ($2,048)
Off-campus job outlook	excellent

JAMES MADISON UNIVERSITY

UNDERGRADUATE ADMISSIONS, HARRISONBURG, VA 22807   ADMISSIONS: 540-568-6147   FAX: 540-568-3332

STUDENTS SPEAK OUT

Life
Harrisonburg may not be the nation's entertainment capital, but some JMU students find enough to keep them busy on campus, with activities that range from "philosophical conversation at the on campus coffee house" to "going to a play at the experimental theater on campus." They can also "work out, join an outdoors club, play tennis or soccer, hear a band, see a movie for $1.50, or go hiking." Outdoor activities rank high, probably because the campus is so beautiful, and there aren't enough campus-based activities to occupy everyone. One happy student explains, "People either play sports or alter their minds to have fun, unless they are out bickering about something." Alcohol dominates social life, but according to this student it is easier for some than others to partake: "For fun we throw parties and if you're non-black they don't get broken up by police." Fraternities play a central but not overwhelming role in social circles and when students get tired of the "cow pasture community," they usually head off to Richmond or Washington, D.C., both within driving distance.

Academics
James Madison University is a true bargain. Reasonably priced for both in-state and out-of-state students, JMU provides many strong programs in comfortable surroundings to a diverse and friendly student body. Students told us that business and music are the school's standouts. Other departments receiving thumbs-up were English, political science, psychology, history, and the international relations department. Students report that, while classes at the introductory levels tend to be somewhat big, "The professors seem almost hurt if you don't call them at home." Instructors overall receive enthusiastic praise from many students. Others, however, fear that academic standards might be suffering, noting that "the school's population is growing without a proportional increase in teachers and staff." And some distrust the administration and worry that institutional politics adversely affect the quality of their education: "The administration is extremely conservative. The professors are extremely liberal...The constant fighting between the administration and the professors stagnates our education." Students also complain that "Although the phone registration process is easy, getting the classes you want as an underclassman is next to impossible" and "the library is deficient."

Student Body
JMU is nearly nine-tenths white, the rest African-American, and primarily from Virginia. According to one student, "JMU students are active, intelligent, and highly motivated." Most people use the word "friendly" to describe their peers: "The typical JMU student is friendly, hard-working, and beer-loving." However, that warmth doesn't flow in all directions. One black woman used to a more integrated social scene in high school wishes "there were more racial interaction. Like at parties and social events...It's completely segregated here." Students describe stratification of other variations: "There are many socially isolated cliques of social/career/religion origin."

FINANCIAL AID: 540-568-6644   WEB SITE: HTTP://WWW.JMU.EDU/

ADMISSIONS

The admissions committee considers (in descending order of importance): HS record, class rank, test scores, essay, recommendations. *Also considered (in descending order of importance):* extracurriculars, personality, special talents, alumni relationship, geographical distribution. Either the SAT or ACT is required; SAT is preferred. An interview is required of some applicants. Admissions process is need-blind. *High school units required/recommended:* 22 total units are recommended; 4 English recommended, 4 math recommended, 4 science recommended, 4 foreign language recommended, 1 social studies recommended, 2 history recommended. Minimum combined SAT I score of 800 required of all applicants; rank in top half of secondary school class recommended of in-state applicants and rank in top third of secondary school class recommended of out-of-state applicants. *Special Requirements:* A portfolio is required for art program applicants. An audition is required for music program applicants. TOEFL is required of all international students. Supplemental application and interview required of nursing program applicants.

The Inside Word

James Madison has prospered from the applications of students faced with severe competition for admission to UVA and William and Mary. Third place on the Virginia public university totem pole is not a bad spot to be, as JMU's admissions committee will attest. Pay attention when they stress that your high school schedule should be chock-full of challenging academic courses.

FINANCIAL AID

Students should submit: FAFSA (due February 15). The Princeton Review suggests that all financial aid forms be submitted as soon as possible after January 1. *The following grants/scholarships are offered:* Pell, SEOG, athletic, the school's own scholarships, the school's own grants, state scholarships, state grants, private scholarships, private grants, federal nursing scholarship, ROTC. *Students borrow from the following loan programs:* Stafford, unsubsidized Stafford, Perkins, PLUS, state loans, federal nursing loans, private loans. Applicants will be notified of awards beginning April 15. College Work-Study Program is available. Institutional employment is available.

FROM THE ADMISSIONS OFFICE

"James Madison University has been described as the 'Ultimate University.' It is a close-knit community that possesses a unique atmosphere for living and learning. The special kind of spirit on campus emphasizes excellence in all aspects of a student's life. Students are challenged both inside and outside the classroom by talented and caring faculty and staff and by other JMU students who are friendly, diverse, and actively involved in their own educations. The individuals who comprise the JMU student body make the most of their college experiences by creating and participating in a rich variety of educational, social, and extracurricular programs. Looking toward the twenty-first century, the university is committed to preparing students for the complex challenges of a rapidly changing, global society. The College of Integrated Science and Technology, the Classroom of the twenty-first century, and a growing number of study abroad opportunities are only a few examples of this commitment. JMU students truly love and appreciate the beautiful campus, supportive collegiate environment and challenging academic programs at what they feel is the 'Ultimate University.'"

ADMISSIONS

Admissions Rating	80
% of applicants accepted	53
% of acceptees attending	37

FRESHMAN PROFILE
Average verbal SAT	600
Average math SAT	600
Average ACT	NR
Average TOEFL	570
Graduated top 20% of class	NR
Graduated top 40% of class	NR
Graduated top 60% of class	NR
Average HS GPA or Avg.	NR

DEADLINES
Early decision	12/1
Regular admission	1/15
Regular notification	4/1
Non-fall registration	no

APPLICANTS ALSO LOOK AT
AND OFTEN PREFER
Virginia
William and Mary
U. North Carolina
Duke

AND SOMETIMES PREFER
Virginia Tech
George Mason
American
Mary Washington

AND RARELY PREFER
West Virginia U.
Clemson
Hampden-Sydney
Dickinson

FINANCIAL FACTS

Financial Aid Rating	78
In-state tuition	$4,104
Out-of-state tuition	$8,580
Room & board	$5,088
Estimated book expense	$500
% frosh receiving aid	59
% undergrads receiving aid	59
% aid is need-based	NR
% frosh w/ grant (avg)	35 ($2,535)
% frosh w/ loan (avg)	52 ($2,400)
% UGs w/ job (avg)	30 ($1,200)
Off-campus job outlook	good

JOHNS HOPKINS UNIVERSITY

3400 NORTH CHARLES STREET, BALTIMORE, MD 21218   ADMISSIONS: 410-516-8171   FAX: 410-516-6025

CAMPUS LIFE

Quality of Life Rating	67
Type of school	private
Affiliation	none
Environment	metropolis

STUDENTS

FT undergrad enrollment	3,427
% male/female	62/38
% from out of state	86
% live on campus	65
% spend weekend on campus	100
% transfers	4
% from public high school	59
% in (# of) fraternities	30 (13)
% in (# of) sororities	25 (5)
% African-American	5
% Asian	21
% Caucasian	67
% Hispanic	2
% international	5
# of countries represented	36

WHAT'S HOT
ethnic diversity on campus
leftist politics
lab facilities
dorms
library

WHAT'S NOT
students are unhappy
sex
campus food
off-campus food
infrequent dating

ACADEMICS

Academic Rating	88
Profs Interesting Rating	62
Profs Accessible Rating	62
Calendar	4-1-4
Student/teacher ratio	10:1
% profs PhD/tenured	99/99
Hours of study per day	3.46

MOST POPULAR MAJORS
biology
international studies
biomedical engineering

% GRADS WHO PURSUE...
Law 7, Med 25, MBA 5, MA 33

STUDENTS SPEAK OUT

Life
Johns Hopkins University's undergraduate campus is located in Baltimore's Homewood section, a residential area that provides very few social opportunities. On-campus social life is slow too; explains one RA, "It is very hard to get people to participate in fun activities because of the extremely heavy workload. For many activities I arrange for my dorm (like movie night), nobody shows up because, even though it is pass/fail for first semester freshmen, they still say they have too much work to have fun." School spirit is low; writes one respondent, "Complaining about Hopkins is Hopkins students' favorite activity. Everyone is proud of Hopkins only because he or she has gotten through it." On a positive note, students report that "the campus is very serene—you wouldn't know you were in a city," and that "Baltimore is a lot better than people think. There are great restaurants, the Inner Harbor, and we're close to D.C. and Philly. There are on-campus activities every weekend."

Academics
Although Johns Hopkins houses a prestigious undergraduate institution, the school's primary focus is on its graduate departments. Those who choose JHU must be prepared for a tremendous workload and advanced coursework. Hopkins demands that its students be prepared to think and work independently. For those up to the challenge, the rewards are gratifying; writes one student, "Departments are graduate-oriented. Because of this, I have brought the level of my studies up to the graduate level (by the end of my sophomore year). I feel that I am lucky to have graduate students among the people I consider my peers." For those expecting a more traditional liberal-arts-college education—the kind typified by a caring faculty and an attentive administration—the experience can be disheartening. Reports one student, "The administration seems inaccessible. There are times at JHU when it seems that undergraduate classes are seen as annoying appendages that limp behind the rest of the department. Many profs don't take undergraduates seriously." Premed is the marquee major here. As one student explains, "I'm premed and there's no place I would rather be. The academics are a killer, no joke, but for those few who survive, the world is their oyster." The English, writing, history, political science and engineering departments are all among the best around.

Student Body
With three-quarters of its students going on to some kind of graduate school, Hopkins' student body is an ambitious, hardworking lot. Says one undergrad, "Students here tend to be more self-sufficient, mature, and work-oriented. Professional school plans come easy to a JHU graduate." Many respondents say their classmates are overly competitive, although several countered that "Grades are on a curve, so competition is high. However, I have never encountered the cutthroat attitude Hopkins is famous for. Students are friendly, if somewhat preoccupied with studies."

ADMISSIONS

The admissions committee considers (in descending order of importance): HS record, test scores, class rank, recommendations, essay. *Also considered (in descending order of importance):* extracurriculars, personality, alumni relationship, geographical distribution, special talents. Either the SAT or ACT is required; SAT is preferred. An interview is recommended. Admissions process is not need-blind. *High school units required/recommended:* 20 total units are recommended; 4 English recommended, 4 math recommended, 3 science recommended, 3 foreign language recommended, 3 social studies recommended, 3 history recommended. TOEFL is required of all international students.

The Inside Word

The admissions process at Hopkins demands to be taken seriously. Competition with the best colleges and universities in the country keeps the acceptance rate artificially high. Make certain that your personal credentials-essays, recommendations, and extracurricular activities-are impressive.

FINANCIAL AID

Students should submit: FAFSA, the school's own financial aid form (due January 15), a copy of parents' most recent income tax filing (due January 15). The Princeton Review suggests that all financial aid forms be submitted as soon as possible after January 1. *The following grants/scholarships are offered:* Pell, SEOG, academic merit, athletic, the school's own scholarships, the school's own grants, state scholarships, state grants, private scholarships, private grants, ROTC. *Students borrow from the following loan programs:* Stafford, Perkins, PLUS, the school's own loan fund, supplemental loans. Applicants will be notified of awards beginning April 1. College Work-Study Program is available. Institutional employment is available.

FROM THE ADMISSIONS OFFICE

"The admissions process at Johns Hopkins is a highly competitive one, but also a highly personal process. Our staff gets to know you through your application essays and extracurricular activities. We would also like to know you personally through one of a variety of campus programs we offer, including individual interviews, overnight visits with current students and open houses. We are not a huge university and we seek to build a true 'community' of scholars; as we get to know each other we hope you will sense this and seek to be a part of it."

ADMISSIONS

Admissions Rating	**94**
% of applicants accepted	42
% of acceptees attending	26

FRESHMAN PROFILE

Average verbal SAT	730
Average math SAT	680
Average ACT	31
Average TOEFL	600
Graduated top 20% of class	93
Graduated top 40% of class	99
Graduated top 60% of class	NR
Average HS GPA or Avg.	3.8

DEADLINES

Early decision	NR
Regular admission	1/1
Regular notification	4/1
Non-fall registration	no

APPLICANTS ALSO LOOK AT

AND OFTEN PREFER
Harvard/Radcliffe
Stanford
MIT
Virginia
Princeton

AND SOMETIMES PREFER
Yale
Brown
Duke
Columbia

AND RARELY PREFER
Cornell U.
Georgetown U.
UC-Berkeley
U. Maryland-Coll. Park

FINANCIAL FACTS

Financial Aid Rating	**75**
Tuition	$19,750
Room & board	$6,955
Estimated book expense	$500
% frosh receiving aid	54
% undergrads receiving aid	58
% aid is need-based	95
% frosh w/ grant (avg)	40 ($13,749)
% frosh w/ loan (avg)	45 ($3,500)
% UGs w/ job (avg)	50 ($1,900)
Off-campus job outlook	good

Juilliard School

60 LINCOLN CENTER PLAZA, NEW YORK, NY 10023-6590　　ADMISSIONS: 212-799-5000　　FAX: 212-724-0263

CAMPUS LIFE

Quality of Life Rating	**82**
Type of school	private
Affiliation	none
Environment	metropolis

STUDENTS

FT undergrad enrollment	484
% male/female	46/54
% from out of state	79
% live on campus	48
% spend weekend on campus	90
% transfers	18
% from public high school	NR
% African-American	10
% Asian	30
% Caucasian	52
% Hispanic	5
% international	7
# of countries represented	50

WHAT'S HOT

music associations
off-campus food
ethnic diversity on campus
theater
New York

WHAT'S NOT

computer facilities
student government

ACADEMICS

Academic Rating	**93**
Profs Interesting Rating	80
Profs Accessible Rating	66
Calendar	semester
Student/teacher ratio	3:1
Hours of study per day	3.32

MOST POPULAR MAJORS

piano
dance
violin

STUDENTS SPEAK OUT

Life

"Life at school is engulfed by practice and study. What time there is left, New York has plenty of things to help fill." At one of the world's finest conservatories, what else would you expect? With no real campus (Juilliard is housed in Lincoln Center), what social life students have is based in the Big Apple. "Living in New York City, its easy to find something new to do. Our location in Lincoln Center and frequently donated tickets offers us a unique opportunity to see the finest artists of our time in concert." Explains another, "Juilliard is a place for people who know their goals and are determined to attain them. It's not a place for one who is unsure about his career and talent." Still, the competitive nature of the students and the crush of humanity that is New York can bring feelings of anxiety: "I feel like a tadpole." Juilliard has enacted measures to make the transition a bit easier, and to bring freshmen into contact with each other more often outside of class. Freshmen are required to live on-campus the first year. It makes it easier to meet and make friends." Freshman dorms receive so-so marks, though the food on campus is horrible. Luckily, about 20 billion restaurants are beckoning, another reason students love New York (which they also find surprisingly safe). Few forget why they are here, "You're at Lincoln Center and NYC—the crotch of the American artistic world."

Academics

"The Juilliard school has an incredible faculty that is devoted to producing professional artists in the 21st century." That remark sums up the reverence most students at Juilliard feel for their professors, many of whom are their private instructors in their chosen disciplines. Gushes another, "The teachers are, frankly, the best in the country and possibly the world." All together now: "The professors are gods." But good teaching can only get you so far at Juilliard. You know the motto, "Practice, practice, practice." Notes one undergrad, "Juilliard is different from other colleges in that it is a training ground/forum for professionals." Yes, this is an intense, focused group of pre-professional artists, and with private instruction, they each have tailored curricula to match their passions. General classes are small, and what services there are at Juilliard get decent marks from undergrads. Of the administration a student says, "Juilliard is like an arrangement between students and the administration. If you help in making the school run smoothly, you can usually get what you want." For the chance at an artistic career that is both personally fulfilling and envied by millions, jumping though a few administrative hoops is a small price to pay.

Student Body

"You will have lots of acquaintances but not that many close friends." That is the long and short of it at Juilliard, a campus-less school some students see as cutthroat and ultracompetitive. "Everybody fends for themselves," says one. Of her fellow students, this sophomore explains, "They are very closed. They are very talented. There is not much interaction." Another counters with this humble assessment: "We are creative people working to become true artists. We are all the best and most promising new talents and will be changing the face of the arts in this country over the next fifty years. We are all very supportive of each other regardless of the discipline." This drama student concurs: "Despite the rumors about Juilliard being full of competitive individuals, my experience here has been nothing but supportive." A diverse group that judges itself by talent, not skin color or sexual preference, the Juilliard student body is among the most accepting in the nation.

ADMISSIONS

The admissions committee considers (in descending order of importance): class rank, HS record, essay. *Also considered (in descending order of importance):* special talents, personality. Preparation in proposed major required. *Special Requirements:* An audition is required for music program applicants. TOEFL is required of all international students. Personal audition required of dance, drama, and music program applicants. *The admissions office says:* "The audition is of critical importance and is a one-shot deal. Also, we do have quotas in orchestral instruments, so what you play can have an impact on how easy or hard it is to get in. Applicants must have had extensive prior study in their major area of interest. It is to an applicant's advantage to apply early to the drama division [because auditions are first-come, first-served]. In dance and music it is to an applicant's advantage to audition in March."

The Inside Word

Self-confidence is a prerequisite for all students who apply to Juilliard. The talent in the applicant pool is phenomenal, and the unforgiving nature of auditions mandates months of preparation by most candidates. Not that it is any different in the real world; when it comes to the arts, this is it.

FINANCIAL AID

Students should submit: FAFSA, the school's own financial aid form, a copy of parents' most recent income tax filing. The Princeton Review suggests that all financial aid forms be submitted as soon as possible after January 1. *The following grants/scholarships are offered:* Pell, SEOG, academic merit, the school's own scholarships, the school's own grants, state scholarships, state grants, private scholarships, private grants, foreign aid. *Students borrow from the following loan programs:* Stafford, Perkins, PLUS, the school's own loan fund, private loans. College Work-Study Program is available. Institutional employment is available.

FROM THE ADMISSIONS OFFICE

"The Juilliard School, founded in 1905, is a private college of the performing arts. Degrees are offered through the divisions in Dance, Drama, and Music. Juilliard is located at Lincoln Center, the home of the New York Philharmonic, Metropolitan Opera, New York City Ballet, etc., and Juilliard students interact with these constituencies regularly. A regular series of Master Classes are taught regularly by visiting artists. The faculty consist of renowned teachers/artists. Prominent alumni include: Leontyne Price, opera singer; Itzhak Perlman, violinist; Wynton Marsalis, trumpet player; Kevin Kline, Kelly McGillis, Robin Williams, Christopher Reeve, and Patti LuPone, actors; and Paul Taylor, choreographer."

ADMISSIONS

Admissions Rating	99
% of applicants accepted	12
% of acceptees attending	79

FRESHMAN PROFILE

Average verbal SAT	NR
Average math SAT	NR
Average ACT	NR
Average TOEFL	NR
Graduated top 20% of class	NR
Graduated top 40% of class	NR
Graduated top 60% of class	NR
Average HS GPA or Avg.	NR

DEADLINES

Early decision	NR
Regular admission	NR
Regular notification	1 month after audition
Non-fall registration	no

APPLICANTS ALSO LOOK AT

AND SOMETIMES PREFER
Curtis Inst. of Music
Manhattan School of Music
NYU-Tisch Arts

AND RARELY PREFER
Eastman School
New England Conservatory
Oberlin

FINANCIAL FACTS

Financial Aid Rating	75
Tuition	$13,000
Room & board	$6,300
Estimated book expense	NR
% frosh receiving aid	100
% undergrads receiving aid	100
% aid is need-based	100
% frosh w/ grant (avg)	86% frosh w/
loan (avg)	44 ($3,000)
% UGs w/ job (avg)	65 ($1,500)
Off-campus job outlook	good

KALAMAZOO COLLEGE

1200 ACADEMY STREET, KALAMAZOO, MI 49006-3295   ADMISSIONS: 800-253-3602   FAX: 616-337-7390

STUDENTS SPEAK OUT

Life

Because of the unique K Plan (see below), students at Kalamazoo College have a hard time keeping track of their friends from quarter to quarter. Many students (especially juniors) disappear to all corners of the earth during their various global jaunts. Furthermore, Kalamazoo has an unusual housing policy that requires students to participate in a housing lottery every three months or so (one nomadic junior suggests the college "should offer a self-help cassette entitled 'Learning to Deal with Moving Anxiety'"). But many students view this campus-in-flux as a benefit, constantly stimulating new friendships and improving coping skills. Kalamazoo is "definitely not a party school (a [restrictive] alcohol policy keeps the kegs largely untapped)," although many claim to have figured out ways to drink despite the rules. Some simply wait until their trips abroad; one marvels, "You can have a brew in the Hofbrau Haus, slam some vodka in Red Square, and drink tequila south of the border—all while you study and explore foreign cultures." Most students we asked are glad that drinking and Greek life (there is no Greek system here) are not the focus of the campus social life. Life in Kalamazoo is slow; explains one student, "Public transportation stops at 6 P.M. and doesn't run on Sundays, so it's hard to go to dinner or the movies." Adds another, "You pray for a car or a friend with one."

Academics

Two Kalamazoo College students discussing their undergraduate experiences can describe two (or more) entirely different campuses (in different languages if you'd like). What most consider this school's greatest asset is an imaginative and "really well put together" program called the K Plan, which allows for an unparalleled amount of foreign travel and study by all students who are interested. Most are. More than eighty percent of students "go abroad at least once in their four years at Kalamazoo." The same tuition students pay in Michigan covers all foreign expenses, thanks to an endowment specifically for this purpose, so financial need does not preclude participation in the program. Not everything good about Kalamazoo is off campus. The college itself offers "fast-paced and challenging academics" in a "small, personalized atmosphere" (even smaller than one might think, given the fact that many students are away at any given time). Premed is popular and "incredibly competitive, but the strenuous curriculum genuinely prepares students for med school." Be forewarned that "The eleven-week academic quarter means classes get intense quickly."

Student Body

There is a t-shirt popular at Kalamazoo: "The World Is Our Campus." This applies not only to the K Plan, but also to the feeling of diversity on the campus itself. The college's heterogeneous atmosphere belies the low percentage of minority students and the high percentage of Michigan natives. As one student explains, "Students are from generally the same socioeconomic background, but they do represent a diverse spectrum of political, moral, and social views." Overall, students describe themselves as "very liberal, but with a good mix."

KALAMAZOO COLLEGE

FINANCIAL AID: 616-337-7192

WEB SITE: HTTP://WWW.KZOO.EDU/

ADMISSIONS

The admissions committee considers (in descending order of importance): HS record, class rank, test scores, essay, recommendations. *Also considered (in descending order of importance):* extracurriculars, geographical distribution, special talents, alumni relationship, personality. Either the SAT or ACT is required. An interview is recommended. Admissions process is need-blind. *High school units required/recommended:* 16 total units are recommended; 4 English recommended, 4 math recommended, 3 science recommended, 2 foreign language recommended, 1 social studies recommended, 2 history recommended. Minimum rank in top two-fifths of secondary school class and minimum 3.0 GPA recommended.

The Inside Word

K-Zoo's applicant pool is small and self-selected academically, which leads to the unusual combination of a very high acceptance rate and an impressive freshman profile. The admissions committee expects candidates to show evidence of serious academic intent, suitability for the college, and a willingness to contribute to the life of the college. Those who underestimate the evaluation process risk denial.

FINANCIAL AID

Students should submit: FAFSA, a copy of parents' most recent income tax filing. The Princeton Review suggests that all financial aid forms be submitted as soon as possible after January 1. *The following grants/scholarships are offered:* Pell, SEOG, academic merit, the school's own scholarships, the school's own grants, state scholarships, state grants, private scholarships, private grants, foreign aid. *Students borrow from the following loan programs:* Stafford, unsubsidized Stafford, Perkins, PLUS, state loans. College Work-Study Program is available. Institutional employment is available.

FROM THE ADMISSIONS OFFICE

"The educational program offered by Kalamazoo College combines traditional classroom instruction with experiential education. During their four years, students move freely from working and learning in groups to pursuing individual academic and artistic projects. The Kalamazoo Plan, or 'K' Plan, enables every student to participate in four different educational experiences: on-campus learning, a career development internship, overseas study, and a senior project. The Career Development internship is typically done during the sophomore year allowing students to 'try on' a career. Eighty-five percent of all Kalamazoo College students choose to participate in this valuable experience. The Senior Individualized Project (SIP) provides students with the opportunity to make use of all their experiences at the college. They may choose to do research, a thesis, creative or artistic work, or other work related to their major. All students complete a Senior Individualized Project prior to graduation."

ADMISSIONS

Admissions Rating	74
% of applicants accepted	89
% of acceptees attending	30

FRESHMAN PROFILE

Average verbal SAT	620
Average math SAT	610
Average ACT	27
Average TOEFL	590
Graduated top 20% of class	81
Graduated top 40% of class	96
Graduated top 60% of class	NR
Average HS GPA or Avg.	3.5

DEADLINES

Early decision	NR
Regular admission	2/15
Regular notification	rolling
Non-fall registration	yes

APPLICANTS ALSO LOOK AT

AND OFTEN PREFER

U. Michigan-Ann Arbor
Northwestern U.
Georgetown U.
Dartmouth

AND SOMETIMES PREFER

Notre Dame
Oberlin
Earlham
Macalester
Michigan State

AND RARELY PREFER

Albion
Alma
Hope
Wooster
DePauw

FINANCIAL FACTS

Financial Aid Rating	88
Tuition	$16,173
Room & board	$5,262
Estimated book expense	$525
% frosh receiving aid	90
% undergrads receiving aid	87
% aid is need-based	56
% frosh w/ grant (avg)	91 ($8,000)
% frosh w/ loan (avg)	55 ($3,550)
% UGs w/ job (avg)	39 ($875)
Off-campus job outlook	good

UNIVERSITY OF KANSAS

126 STRONG HALL, LAWRENCE, KS 66045 · · · · · ADMISSIONS: 913-864-3911 · · · FAX: 913-864-5221

CAMPUS LIFE

Quality of Life Rating **85**
Type of school · · · · · · · · · · public
Affiliation · · · · · · · · · · · none
Environment · · · · · · · · · suburban

STUDENTS
FT undergrad enrollment · · · · 18,087
% male/female · · · · · · · · · 49/51
% from out of state · · · · · · · · 30
% live on campus · · · · · · · · · 20
% spend weekend on campus · · · · NR
% transfers · · · · · · · · · · · 30
% from public high school · · · · · NR
% in (# of) fraternities · · · · · 21 (27)
% in (# of) sororities · · · · · · 23 (18)
% African-American · · · · · · · · · 3
% Asian · · · · · · · · · · · · · · 3
% Caucasian · · · · · · · · · · · · 77
% Hispanic · · · · · · · · · · · · · 3
% international · · · · · · · · · · · 7
# of countries represented · · · · 109

WHAT'S HOT
intercollegiate sports
student publications
beer
Lawrence
off-campus food

WHAT'S NOT
registration is a pain
lab facilities
student government
campus difficult to get around
inefficient administration

ACADEMICS

Academic Rating **68**
Profs Interesting Rating · · · · · · 63
Profs Accessible Rating · · · · · · 66
Calendar · · · · · · · · · · · semester
Student/teacher ratio · · · · · · 15:1
% profs tenured · · · · · · · · · · 96
Hours of study per day · · · · · · 2.59

MOST POPULAR MAJORS
journalism
psychology
business

STUDENTS SPEAK OUT

Life

"There is a unique quality to the town of Lawrence, and it is an easy place to call home." University of Kansas undergrads, for the most part, love their college town: "It's a beautiful campus and a fun place to live. There is a wide variety of affordable social activities." More specifically, adds this English major, "There is an amazing music scene here. All well-known bands and quality local/regional bands play here all the time." "Everyone always has an excuse to go out and get a beer," adds another satisfied Jayhawk. A philosophy major with a similar take on life seconds that emotion, "Lawrence in general consists in going out to drink or staying home to get high." That is, until basketball season starts! "In the winter/spring [life] centers around our basketball team," explains one of many Jayhawk fans. With low-rated dorms and on-campus food that is generally called inedible, most move off-campus or to the Greek system as soon as they can. Yet, "People on this campus seem to be very proud to attend this school."

Academics

KU has great preprofessional schools, which you must apply to separately, in architecture and engineering. It also has great schools in pharmacy, nursing, journalism, and education. Being an undergrad at Kansas is no academic walk in the park. "Classes are large and mostly TAs teach classes," explains a frustrated sophomore, echoing the two criticisms most often stated by students. "Classes are hard to get in as you move into your major," adds a communications major. Indeed, for the most part, it sounds like "a student here is simply a Social Security number," though the school's new president has been trying to change that perception. "Computer facilities are woefully inadequate for technical students," reports a technical student. Take heart though—new computer facilities are in the works, and meanwhile, the kids do love their library! Profs also receive fair marks, and their accessibility doesn't seem to be much of a problem for students seeking help outside of class. Offers one particularly upbeat undergrad, "The university is one of the most underrated, excellent, and well-rounded academic institutions in the country. It's a real sleeper!" Adds another, somewhat more soberly, "When compared to our peer schools, they seem much more organized than we are. However, this university is a great value." Another student concurs absolutely, "Even though I have had several problems enrolling and paying my fees, the positive academic experience I had outweighs them."

Student Body

Kansas students, the majority of whom are from in-state, are generally happy with the people they have chosen to spend four important years of their lives with. Says a senior studying biology, "I have made a lot of friends from all over the country." Adds another undergrad, "It is very easy to get to know students within your major." A bit of a wet blanket, this sociology major offers, "There does not appear to be a lot of cultural diversity (some, but not much)." Whatever the case, a diverse student body is what most undergrads perceive ("Everyone is very friendly and there is very little discrimination/prejudice"; "The diversity of students enables people from a more sheltered background to experience new views and ways of life"; "I think there is a lot of diversity here. Everyone can find their niche"). Even so, discrimination on the basis of skin color or sexual preference is indeed a concern of many Kansas undergrads, but hardly perceived as a problem. Maybe it's because undergrads are too busy dating and mating to worry about much else! Few describe themselves as religious, so they're certainly not spending their quality time praying.

FINANCIAL AID: 913-864-4700   E-MAIL: REH@CO.WPO.UKANS.EDU   WEB SITE: HTTP://KUFACTS.CC.UKANS.EDU

ADMISSIONS

The admissions committee considers (in descending order of importance): HS record, test scores, class rank, recommendations. *Also considered (in descending order of importance):* special talents. Either the SAT or ACT is required. An interview is recommended. Admissions process is need-blind. *High school units required/recommended:* 15 total units are recommended; 4 English recommended, 3 math recommended, 3 science recommended, 2 foreign language recommended, 3 social studies recommended. Open admissions policy for in-state applicants who are graduates of accredited secondary schools. Minimum composite ACT score of 24 (combined SAT I score of 1090) and minimum 2.0 GPA required of out-of-state applicants. *Special Requirements:* An audition is required for music program applicants. Portfolio may be requested of art or design program applicants. *The admissions office says:* "All graduates of accredited Kansas high schools are currently automatically offered admission, but new admissions standards will go into effect in 2001. All students are recommended to exceed the course distributional minimums, particularly in mathematics and English."

The Inside Word

A no-sweat approach to admissions. So who gets denied? Weak out-of-state candidates, who are apparently in large supply in the Kansas applicant pool. But in-state students too may have to face the music with new admissions standards starting in 2001.

FINANCIAL AID

Students should submit: FAFSA (due March 15), the school's own financial aid form (due March 15), state aid form. The Princeton Review suggests that all financial aid forms be submitted as soon as possible after January 1. *The following grants/scholarships are offered:* Pell, SEOG, academic merit, athletic, the school's own scholarships, state scholarships, private scholarships, private grants, ROTC. *Students borrow from the following loan programs:* Stafford, unsubsidized Stafford, Perkins, PLUS, health professions loans. Applicants will be notified of awards beginning May 1. College Work-Study Program is available. Institutional employment is available.

FROM THE ADMISSIONS OFFICE

"Many undergraduate students have achieved distinction at the University of Kansas. KU has been a leader among public universities in producing national fellowship winners. In recent years KU students have won top honors in national competitions in debate, theater, aerospace engineering, and international moot court, and have achieved national recognition in medical technology, design, music, journalism, and the sciences. More than seventy percent of KU's students are undergraduates. More than ninety percent of KU undergraduates pursue their studies on the Lawrence campus. Total fall enrollment in 1989 was 28,773. In 1989-1990, KU granted approximately 3,500 bachelor's degrees."

ADMISSIONS

Admissions Rating	73
% of applicants accepted	68
% of acceptees attending	64

FRESHMAN PROFILE

Average verbal SAT	NR
Average math SAT	NR
Average ACT	23
Average TOEFL	570
Graduated top 20% of class	55
Graduated top 40% of class	85
Graduated top 60% of class	98
Average HS GPA or Avg.	NR

DEADLINES

Early decision	2/1
Regular admission	4/1
Regular notification	rolling
Non-fall registration	yes

APPLICANTS ALSO LOOK AT

AND OFTEN PREFER
Kansas State

AND SOMETIMES PREFER
Purdue U.-West Lafayette
Indiana U.-Bloomington
Michigan State

FINANCIAL FACTS

Financial Aid Rating	76
In-state tuition	$1,766
Out-of-state tuition	$7,484
Room & board	$3,544
Estimated book expense	$700
% frosh receiving aid	34
% undergrads receiving aid	37
% aid is need-based	66
% frosh w/ grant (avg)	NR
% frosh w/ loan (avg)	NR ($5,028)
% UGs w/ job (avg)	13
Off-campus job outlook	good

UNIVERSITY OF KENTUCKY

100 W.D. FUNKHOUSER BUILDING, LEXINGTON, KY 40506   ADMISSIONS: 606-257-2000   FAX: 606-257-4000

CAMPUS LIFE

Quality of Life Rating 82
Type of school public
Affiliation none
Environment city

STUDENTS
FT undergrad enrollment 14,964
% male/female 51/49
% from out of state 20
% live on campus 25
% spend weekend on campus 60
% transfers 38
% from public high school NR
% in (# of) fraternities 16 (22)
% in (# of) sororities 16 (17)
% African-American 5
% Asian 1
% Caucasian 88
% Hispanic 0
% international 4
# of countries represented 113

WHAT'S HOT
intercollegiate sports
old-fashioned dating
health facilities
student publications
off-campus food

WHAT'S NOT
registration is a pain
campus difficult to get around
support groups
dorms
library

ACADEMICS

Academic Rating 73
Profs Interesting Rating 65
Profs Accessible Rating 73
Calendar semester
Student/teacher ratio 16:1
% profs PhD 95
Hours of study per day 2.89

MOST POPULAR MAJORS
accounting
psychology
finance

STUDENTS SPEAK OUT

Life

University of Kentucky's social calendar is dominated by sports, particularly men's football and basketball. One student's entire essay consists of the sentence "Rick Pitino rules my life!" No further explanation seems necessary to the writer, who assumes that everyone in the country knows UK's basketball coach. Students report that partying is popular, noting that UK's dry-campus policy is "a joke, since there are bars right across the street from the dorms," and that, within the popular Greek system "alcohol is a big deal." Students give the city of Lexington good grades ("Lexington is a great town for music. They have some great bands that come through"), and note that Louisville is within driving distance.

Academics

It's hard to tell whether University of Kentucky students take more pride in their school's academic programs or in its basketball teams. "While Kentucky may be known for its shoeless hillbillies," writes one student, "the University of Kentucky is a veritable educational stalwart. And, we have the most loyal basketball following on earth. In fact, a lot of students choose UK, believe it or not, because of the basketball!" Those who register at UK because of its basketball team receive, at no additional cost, the opportunity for an excellent education at bargain-basement prices. Students praise all business and management departments ("we have top-notch instructors," claims one management major), laying claim to "one of the best accounting programs in the nation." Other popular majors are in career-oriented fields such as communications, health sciences, education, and engineering; the last is perhaps UK's most underrated program. The school requires all students to complete general education requirements, meaning that everyone dabbles at least a little in the liberal arts. Top high school students can qualify for the honors program, which, according to one enrollee, "provides students with an exceptional opportunity to obtain an Ivy League education at a state school." Students give their professors good grades, especially for accessibility outside the classroom. Student complaints center on the availability of required classes, the registration-by-phone system, and the fact that "advisors are not well informed about requirements for specific majors."

Student Body

Most of UK's student body hails from the Bluegrass State. Over ninety percent of the students are white: approximately 1,000 black students make up the single largest minority population. Many students "just aren't very serious about their studies," and must be avoided if one is to escape the "party-'til-you-fail" trap. Also, "There seems to be a sizable amount of racial tension in all directions," although the responses of minority students were particularly discouraging. Students are generally conservative both politically and socially.

UNIVERSITY OF KENTUCKY

FINANCIAL AID: 606-257-3172

WEB SITE: HTTP://WWW.UKY.EDU/

ADMISSIONS

The admissions committee considers (in descending order of importance): HS record, test scores. *Also considered (in descending order of importance):* extracurriculars, geographical distribution, special talents. Either the SAT or ACT is required; ACT is preferred. *High school units required/recommended:* 12 total units are required; 4 English required, 3 math required, 2 science required, 2 foreign language recommended, 1 social studies required, 1 history required. Minimum composite ACT score of 19 and minimum 2.0 GPA required of in-state applicants; minimum composite ACT score of 20 and minimum 2.0 GPA required of out-of-state students. *Special Requirements:* An audition is required for music program applicants. TOEFL is required of all international students. Exam required of architecture program applicants. *The admissions office says:* "Apply early. "Admission to the University of Kentucky is offered on a competitive basis to students who can demonstrate the ability to succeed in an academically demanding environment. The admissions policy is based on an evaluation of a student's standardized test scores, high school grade point average, and completion of a minimum pre-college curriculum. Students whose scores and grades predict a high probability of achieving a C average or better the freshman year at UK will be accepted automatically."

The Inside Word

High volume of applications has more to do with Kentucky's selectivity than any other factor. Given the recent successes of the Wildcats in NCAA basketball, more apps are likely to be on the way.

FINANCIAL AID

Students should submit: FAFSA. The Princeton Review suggests that all financial aid forms be submitted as soon as possible after January 1. *The following grants/scholarships are offered:* Pell, SEOG, academic merit, athletic, the school's own scholarships, state grants, private scholarships, ROTC, United Negro College Fund. *Students borrow from the following loan programs:* Stafford, Perkins, PLUS, state loans, federal nursing loans, health professions loans. College Work-Study Program is available. Institutional employment is available.

FROM THE ADMISSIONS OFFICE

"The University of Kentucky offers you an outstanding learning environment and quality instruction through its excellent faculty. Of the 1,606 full-time faculty, ninety-eight percent hold the doctorate degree or the highest degree in their field of study. "Many are nationally and internationally known for their research, distinguished teaching, and scholarly service to Kentucky, the nation, and the world. Yet, with a student/teacher ratio of only 16 to 1, UK faculty are accessible and willing to answer your questions and discuss your interests."

ADMISSIONS

Admissions Rating	74
% of applicants accepted	72
% of acceptees attending	44

FRESHMAN PROFILE

Average verbal SAT	NR
Average math SAT	NR
Average ACT	25
Average TOEFL	527
Graduated top 20% of class	NR
Graduated top 40% of class	NR
Graduated top 60% of class	NR
Average HS GPA or Avg.	3.4

DEADLINES

Early decision	NR
Regular admission	6/1
Regular notification	rolling
Non-fall registration	yes

APPLICANTS ALSO LOOK AT

AND OFTEN PREFER

Vanderbilt
Miami U.
Indiana U.-Bloomington

AND SOMETIMES PREFER

U. Tennessee-Knoxville
Eastern Kentucky
Western Kentucky
Transylvania
Bellarmine

AND RARELY PREFER

U. Illinois, Urbana-Champ.
Purdue U.-West Lafayette
Ohio State-Columbus
Florida State

FINANCIAL FACTS

Financial Aid Rating	84
In-state tuition	$2,260
Out-of-state tuition	$6,780
Room & board	$3,078
Estimated book expense	$450
% frosh receiving aid	48
% undergrads receiving aid	52
% aid is need-based	NR
% frosh w/ grant (avg)	NR ($1,800)
% frosh w/ loan (avg)	NR ($2,625)
% UGs w/ job (avg)	72
Off-campus job outlook	excellent

KENYON COLLEGE

GAMBIER, OH 43022-9623

ADMISSIONS: 800-848-2468   FAX: 614-427-2634

CAMPUS LIFE

Quality of Life Rating **89**
Type of school   private
Affiliation   Episcopal Church
Environment   rural

STUDENTS
FT undergrad enrollment   1,516
% male/female   48/52
% from out of state   75
% live on campus   100
% spend weekend on campus   95
% transfers   4
% from public high school   68
% in (# of) fraternities   25 (8)
% in (# of) sororities   2 (2)
% African-American   4
% Asian   4
% Caucasian   88
% Hispanic   2
% international   2
# of countries represented   25

WHAT'S HOT
sex
support groups
students are happy
campus is beautiful
beer

WHAT'S NOT
off-campus food
religion
lack of diversity on campus
student publications
infrequent dating

ACADEMICS

Academic Rating **91**
Profs Interesting Rating   96
Profs Accessible Rating   96
Calendar   semester
Student/teacher ratio   10:1
% profs PhD/tenured   96/65
Hours of study per day   3.46

MOST POPULAR MAJORS
English
history
psychology

% GRADS WHO PURSUE...
Law 16, Med 8, MBA 16, MA 38

STUDENTS SPEAK OUT

Life

As one Kenyon College student puts it, "Community makes Kenyon. I feel that I know everyone, from the president to my professor's dog Barney." Kenyon is the embodiment of the small college, where the outside world rarely intrudes on campus life. For many, Kenyon's size is one of its great assets: as one student tells us, "After visiting many universities and large schools I've realized how highly I value Kenyon's close-knit community." Most students live on campus and rarely go home, so for some the community can get a little too close. One student puts it this way: "Kenyon is a small place, which leads, after a time, to intensive familiarity (not always a good thing). I went abroad junior year, which was wonderful, and it's really cool how Kenyon supports the Junior Year Abroad program. I think they realize four years here can be a bit much." The "isolated" town of Gambier "can become very dull very quickly," and a car for excursions to Columbus or to nearby ski areas is recommended. Only twelve percent of the students go Greek, and there are no Greek houses. Still, one student reports that weekends "are filled with frat parties. Either people do that, or they make their own parties or watch movies. There are also musical and theatrical productions, movies, concerts, lectures, and debate." The campus is "small, quiet, and beautiful, conducive to long walks with nothing but your thoughts. One can be alone here in the most noble sense."

Academics

Students at Kenyon College rank their profs in the top ten percent in this book for their teaching skills and among the twenty most accessible outside of class. Such are the benefits of attending a small liberal arts college where practically all the professors live near campus. Says one student, "I feel that it's important to stress the student/faculty relationships here. Almost all our faculty hold their Ph.D.s, but that doesn't deter them from interacting in all aspects of life at Kenyon." The English department is universally acclaimed and is so popular that it's difficult for those not majoring in English to get into English classes. Most departments are nearly as good. Students report that class sizes are excellent and give administrators very high marks. They also note that the school encourages students to focus intensively in specific areas of study and to pursue independent studies, both of which help to prepare students for graduate studies. This program suits the needs of Kenyon undergraduates perfectly, as over half go on to graduate school within a year of graduation. Preprofessional tracks are popular: a big sixteen percent of the students go on to study law and another ten percent pursue medicine.

Student Body

Kenyon students "are mostly white, middle-class, and interested in learning. They come from households where the parents are well-educated and affluent. They tend to be a little self-absorbed and not so interested in others of different backgrounds." Within the predominantly white and wealthy student body, however, there is some diversity; reported one student, "There is a very diverse set of people here: hippies, jocks, and preps, but we all get along." Students consider their classmates "very liberal!"

318 ■ THE BEST 310 COLLEGES

FINANCIAL AID: 614-427-5430   E-MAIL: ADMISSIONS@KENYON.EDU   WEB SITE: HTTP://WWW.KENYON.EDU/

ADMISSIONS

The admissions committee considers (in descending order of importance): HS record, class rank, test scores, recommendations, essay. *Also considered (in descending order of importance):* personality, special talents, alumni relationship, extracurriculars, geographical distribution. Either the SAT or ACT is required. An interview is recommended. Admissions process is need-blind. *High school units required/recommended:* 20 total units are required; 24 total units are recommended; 4 English required, 3 math required, 4 math recommended, 2 science required, 4 science recommended, 3 foreign language required, 4 foreign language recommended, 1 social studies required, 2 social studies recommended, 1 history required, 2 history recommended. Minimum combined SAT I score of 1150, rank in top quarter of secondary school class, and honors courses in secondary school recommended. TOEFL is required of all international students. *The admissions office says:* "We look for students who have taken AP or honors courses in two or more subjects. Students who have outstanding achievement in activities, e.g., athletics, drama, music, community service, leadership, and sound academic records, are given preference."

The Inside Word

Kenyon pays close attention to matchmaking in the course of candidate selection, and personal accomplishments are just as significant as academic ones. Applicants who rank the college high among their choices should definitely interview.

FINANCIAL AID

Students should submit: FAFSA (due February 15), the school's own financial aid form (due February 15), state aid form (due February 15). The Princeton Review suggests that all financial aid forms be submitted as soon as possible after January 1. *The following grants/scholarships are offered:* Pell, SEOG, academic merit, the school's own scholarships, the school's own grants, state scholarships, state grants, private scholarships, private grants. *Students borrow from the following loan programs:* Stafford, unsubsidized Stafford, Perkins, PLUS, the school's own loan fund, state loans, private loans. Applicants will be notified of awards beginning April 1. College Work-Study Program is available. Institutional employment is available.

FROM THE ADMISSIONS OFFICE

"We at Kenyon College seek through liberal education to enhance our understanding of humanity, society, art, and nature. We expect to develop our awareness of our private capacities and creative talents, even as we seek to improve our ability to formulate our ideas rigorously and communicate them effectively to others. And while we strive to further our intellectual independence so as to be free of dogmatic thinking, we seek to find a basis for moral judgments in a thorough understanding of both our environment and our cultural heritage."

ADMISSIONS

Admissions Rating	85
% of applicants accepted	65
% of acceptees attending	27

FRESHMAN PROFILE

Average verbal SAT	700
Average math SAT	620
Average ACT	28
Average TOEFL	550
Graduated top 20% of class	65
Graduated top 40% of class	93
Graduated top 60% of class	99
Average HS GPA or Avg.	3.5

DEADLINES

Early decision	NR
Regular admission	2/15
Regular notification	4/1
Non-fall registration	no

APPLICANTS ALSO LOOK AT

AND OFTEN PREFER

Miami U.
U. Michigan-Ann Arbor
Hamilton
Middlebury Coll.
Oberlin

AND SOMETIMES PREFER

Bowdoin
Bates
Carleton
Colgate
Denison

AND RARELY PREFER

Colby
Hobart & William Smith

FINANCIAL FACTS

Financial Aid Rating	87
Tuition	$21,370
Room & board	$3,820
Estimated book expense	$800

% frosh receiving aid	40
% undergrads receiving aid	41
% aid is need-based	82
% frosh w/ grant (avg)	60 ($11,936)
% frosh w/ loan (avg)	42 ($3,710)
% UGs w/ job (avg)	45 ($900)
Off-campus job outlook	poor

KNOX COLLEGE

GALESBURG, IL 61401

ADMISSIONS: 800-678-5669   FAX: 309-341-7070

CAMPUS LIFE

Quality of Life Rating	**80**
Type of school	private
Affiliation	none
Environment	suburban

STUDENTS

FT undergrad enrollment	1,094
% male/female	46/54
% from out of state	43
% live on campus	90
% spend weekend on campus	90
% transfers	12
% from public high school	85
% in (# of) fraternities	35 (5)
% in (# of) sororities	15 (2)
% African-American	5
% Asian	5
% Caucasian	79
% Hispanic	3
% international	7
# of countries represented	33

WHAT'S HOT

college radio
library
theater
ethnic diversity on campus
support groups

WHAT'S NOT

Galesburg
town-gown relations
student government
religion
off-campus food

ACADEMICS

Academic Rating	**91**
Profs Interesting Rating	94
Profs Accessible Rating	96
Calendar	3-3
Student/teacher ratio	12:1
% profs PhD/tenured	90/86
Hours of study per day	3.58

MOST POPULAR MAJORS

political science
sociology/anthropology
biology

% GRADS WHO PURSUE...

Law 2, Med 6, MBA 4, MA 20

STUDENTS SPEAK OUT

Life

Galesburg, Illinois, is a small town. As one student puts it, "If you're looking for excitement, don't go to college in the middle of a cornfield." The seclusion of the college creates an "intimate" sense of community on campus, however, which many students appreciate. Extracurricular activities are everywhere. Especially popular are theater groups and the student newspaper. Fraternities and sororities help liven up the social scene and fortunately engender little bad feeling. According to one student, "The boundary between the Greeks and the rest of the students virtually does not exist." Drinking can be major: a senior comments colorfully, "If someone actually remains sober for an extended period of time, their friends start to express concern for their welfare," though students also show respect for each others' choices. We receive numerous complaints about the dating scene on campus. The consensus was that "dating is nonexistent: either you're in a relationship, or you hang out with your buddies and bitch about it." Living conditions are first-rate. The large suites at Knox are among the most luxurious in the nation. Also noteworthy is the fact that a new food service provider has improved students' relationships with gastroenterologists in Galesburg.

Academics

With just over one thousand undergraduates, Knox College is a small liberal arts school, and as such its strengths lie in the personal attention and academic challenges it provides. Probably its greatest strength is its ability to "enliven and personalize academics." To achieve this goal, Knox allows, and in fact expects, students to participate in the school's governance: most faculty and administration boards have student members with voting powers. Students here bestow extremely high marks on their professors, both for excellent teaching and for their extraordinary level of accessibility. One student writes, "Knox is here to meet your needs. Professors are always available to speak with you." Another marvels that many students meet with instructors even after courses end. In general, all levels of the administration at Knox display an attitude of caring ("The faculty are extremely responsive to student needs"). The academic atmosphere is challenging, and requirements are strict ("medieval monks didn't write as much as we do here"): all students must complete an introductory course, Freshman Preceptorial, that focuses on communication and reasoning as well as a broad set of distribution requirements. These rigors pay off for many. One grateful senior writes, "If I didn't end up at Knox, there's no way I'd be going into a Ph.D. program next year. This school has a way of giving the right intellectual kicks in the butt at the right time." Forty percent of Knox graduates go on to graduate programs.

Student Body

Although most students at Knox are from the Midwest, many feel that "the diversity is unmatched." Approximately one-fifth of the students are minorities, with African-Americans and Asians making up most of that population. Political activism is not widespread, and disparate viewpoints are generally well accepted on campus.

FINANCIAL AID: 309-341-7149   E-MAIL: RNAHM@KNOX.EDU   WEB SITE: HTTP://WWW.KNOX.EDU/

ADMISSIONS

The admissions committee considers (in descending order of importance): HS record, class rank, recommendations, essay, test scores. *Also considered (in descending order of importance):* extracurriculars, personality, alumni relationship, geographical distribution, special talents. Either the SAT or ACT is required. An interview is recommended. Admissions process is need-blind. *High school units required/recommended:* 15 total units are required; 4 English recommended, 3 math recommended, 3 science recommended, 2 foreign language recommended, 3 social studies recommended. Rank in top half of secondary school class required. TOEFL is required of all international students. *The admissions office says:* "[Approximately two-thirds of our consideration] is placed upon the difficulty of the applicant's academic program combined with his/her performance. We review each application and accompanying documents thoroughly. The key to admissibility is for a student to have successfully completed his/her school's most challenging curriculum and demonstrate integrity, initiative, and leadership."

The Inside Word

A small applicant pool necessitates Knox's high acceptance rate. The student body is nonetheless well qualified, and candidates should show solid academic accomplishment.

FINANCIAL AID

Students should submit: FAFSA, the school's own financial aid form, state aid form. The Princeton Review suggests that all financial aid forms be submitted as soon as possible after January 1. *The following grants/scholarships are offered:* Pell, SEOG, academic merit, the school's own scholarships, the school's own grants, state scholarships, state grants, private scholarships, private grants, foreign aid. *Students borrow from the following loan programs:* Stafford, unsubsidized Stafford, Perkins, PLUS, the school's own loan fund, state loans. Applicants will be notified of awards beginning April 1. College Work-Study Program is available. Institutional employment is available.

FROM THE ADMISSIONS OFFICE

"Economists talk about the importance of finding your niche—knowing that one special thing you do better than anyone else. At Knox, we specialize in changing people's lives. Knox isn't an elitist school with mile-high hoops for applicants to jump through. We work hard at finding those students who will flourish here and giving them the freedom to do so. The result is a top-notch academic school with a remarkably unpretentious sense of itself."

ADMISSIONS

Admissions Rating	78
% of applicants accepted	81
% of acceptees attending	36

FRESHMAN PROFILE

Average verbal SAT	610
Average math SAT	600
Average ACT	27
Average TOEFL	620
Graduated top 20% of class	69
Graduated top 40% of class	98
Graduated top 60% of class	NR
Average HS GPA or Avg.	NR

DEADLINES

Early decision	12/1
Regular admission	2/15
Regular notification	3/31
Non-fall registration	yes

APPLICANTS ALSO LOOK AT
AND OFTEN PREFER
U. Kansas
Northwestern U.

AND SOMETIMES PREFER
Bradley
Grinnell
Beloit
U. Illinois, Urbana-Champ.

FINANCIAL FACTS

Financial Aid Rating	97
Tuition	$17,571
Room & board	$4,662
Estimated book expense	$400
% frosh receiving aid	90
% undergrads receiving aid	89
% aid is need-based	89
% frosh w/ grant (avg)	90 ($11,671)
% frosh w/ loan (avg)	66 ($3,065)
% UGs w/ job (avg)	66
Off-campus job outlook	good

LAFAYETTE COLLEGE

EASTON, PA 18042-1770   ADMISSIONS: 610-250-5100   FAX: 610-250-9850

CAMPUS LIFE

Quality of Life Rating   **78**
Type of school   private
Affiliation   United Presbyterian Church
Environment   suburban

STUDENTS
FT undergrad enrollment   2,009
% male/female   54/46
% from out of state   75
% live on campus   98
% spend weekend on campus   90
% transfers   1
% from public high school   68
% in (# of) fraternities   11 (11)
% in (# of) sororities   67 (6)
% African-American   3
% Asian   3
% Caucasian   88
% Hispanic   1
% international   5
# of countries represented   50

WHAT'S HOT
beer
Greeks
hard liquor
sex
campus easy to get around

WHAT'S NOT
town-gown relations
Easton
music associations
off-campus food
students are cliquish

ACADEMICS

Academic Rating   **84**
Profs Interesting Rating   86
Profs Accessible Rating   90
Calendar   4-1-4
Student/teacher ratio   11:1
% profs tenured   99
Hours of study per day   3.26

MOST POPULAR MAJORS
economics/business
government/law
biology

% GRADS WHO PURSUE...
Law 7, Med 6

STUDENTS SPEAK OUT

Life
Lafayette College has a party-school reputation, one that its students earn Thursday through Sunday nights every week. "I wish I could give beer a higher mark than an A!" one student comments on our grading system. Drinking laws, and the school's efforts to enforce them, seem to have had little impact on consumption. Fraternities and sororities rank fourth most popular in the country (one of the few schools that nosed Lafayette out of first place is arch-rival Lehigh): if you have any problems with the Greek system, be careful, as social life here revolves around it. Despite the fact that many students come here to enjoy frat life, the school maintains, at best, a polite relationship with the frats. This is one cause of animosity between students and administrators. Another is an enforced meal plan: students are required to prepay for $250 worth of food at the "food court" per semester. To add insult to injury, "The price of food is high and the quality is poor." For go-getters, there are plenty of campus groups and organizations to become involved with. The town of Easton "stinks," says one student. "The townies hate the students, but we're up on the hill pretty much segregated from them. The only time we go into town is for restaurants, movies, and bars." The campus is beautiful and easy to get around.

Academics
Lafayette is a liberal arts college that also boasts a nationally renowned engineering program. One-third of the students pursue engineering degrees: other popular majors include psychology, computer science, business, and liberal arts. All students here must complete a core curriculum that stresses a comprehensive approach to academic subjects. While students here are satisfied with their academic programs and work hard at them during the week, most also view them as a responsibility to be endured: their real enthusiasm is for social life, which almost all addressed in their comments to us.

Student Body
Lafayette has a homogeneous student population. "White, conservative, and preppy" describes most students pretty accurately. A small minority population exists on the fringes—"There isn't even a black frat or sorority"—complains one African-American student. If there is a gay population, it's invisible and, by students' accounts, unwelcome. For those who fit the mold, LC provides a very homey atmosphere. Many students voice the same sentiment as the one who reports, "There's something on this campus that you can't get a sense of when you read about it in a book. It's almost a feeling of family. When I return from visiting another school, I suddenly feel like I'm home." A skewed male-female ratio must make for a pheromone-laced atmosphere at parties.

ADMISSIONS

The admissions committee considers (in descending order of importance): HS record, class rank, essay, recommendations, test scores. *Also considered (in descending order of importance):* extracurriculars, personality, alumni relationship, geographical distribution, special talents. SAT is preferred. An interview is recommended. Admissions process is need-blind. *High school units required/ recommended:* 13 total units are required; 4 English required, 3 math required, 2 science required, 2 foreign language required. TOEFL is required of all international students. *The admissions office says:* "Lafayette looks for the student who tries to stretch in secondary school. Honors courses, advanced placement work, a range of serious electives, and evidence of willingness to take risks will always count for more than spectacular marks in 'soft' subjects."

The Inside Word

Applications are reviewed three to five times and evaluated by as many as nine different committee members. Engineering cāndidates face a significantly more rigorous evaluation process than applicants with other academic interests. In all cases, students who continually seek challenges and are willing to take risks academically win out over those who play it safe in order to maintain a high GPA.

FINANCIAL AID

Students should submit: FAFSA, the school's own financial aid form, state aid form, a copy of parents' most recent income tax filing. The Princeton Review suggests that all financial aid forms be submitted as soon as possible after January 1. *The following grants/scholarships are offered:* Pell, SEOG, academic merit, athletic, the school's own scholarships, the school's own grants, state scholarships, state grants, private scholarships, private grants, ROTC, foreign aid. *Students borrow from the following loan programs:* Stafford, Perkins, PLUS, the school's own loan fund, state loans, private loans. Applicants will be notified of awards beginning March 18. College Work-Study Program is available. Institutional employment is available.

FROM THE ADMISSIONS OFFICE

"We choose students individually, one by one, and we hope that the ones we choose will approach their education the same way, as a highly individual enterprise. Our first-year seminars have enrollments limited to fifteen or sixteen students each in order to introduce the concept of learning not as passive receipt of information but as an active, participatory process. Our low average class size and 11 to 1 student-teacher ratio reflect that same philosophy. We also devote substantial resources to our Marquis Scholars Program, to one-on-one faculty-student mentoring relationships, and to other programs in engineering within a liberal arts context, giving Lafayette its distinctive character, articulated in our second-year seminars exploring values in science and technology. Lafayette provides an environment in which its students can discover their own personal capacity for learning, for personal growth, and for leadership."

ADMISSIONS

Admissions Rating	82
% of applicants accepted	60
% of acceptees attending	22

FRESHMAN PROFILE

Average verbal SAT	660
Average math SAT	600
Average ACT	NR
Average TOEFL	550
Graduated top 20% of class	60
Graduated top 40% of class	93
Graduated top 60% of class	93
Average HS GPA or Avg.	NR

DEADLINES

Early decision	1/15
Regular admission	NR
Regular notification	4/1
Non-fall registration	no

APPLICANTS ALSO LOOK AT

AND OFTEN PREFER

Pennsylvania
Tufts
Boston Coll.
Cornell U.

AND SOMETIMES PREFER

Gettysburg
Bucknell
Lehigh
Colgate
Hamilton

AND RARELY PREFER

Dickinson
Franklin & Marshall
Penn State-U. Park

FINANCIAL FACTS

Financial Aid Rating	81
Tuition	$20,308
Room & board	$6,335
Estimated book expense	$600
% frosh receiving aid	50
% undergrads receiving aid	60
% aid is need-based	99
% frosh w/ grant (avg)	48 ($13,812)
% frosh w/ loan (avg)	41 ($3,220)
% UGs w/ job (avg)	50 ($839)
Off-campus job outlook	good

LAKE FOREST COLLEGE

555 NORTH SHERIDAN ROAD, LAKE FOREST, IL 60045   ADMISSIONS: 847-735-5000   FAX: 847-735-6291

STUDENTS SPEAK OUT

Life

Campus life at Lake Forest College means participating in a close-knit community. As one student puts it, "This school is so small that everyone knows your business before you do." In fact, "It's very easy to feel trapped on this campus, especially if you don't have a car." The small town location can indeed be frustrating: "Our town is not a college town and therefore it is difficult to find a restaurant/grocery store open late." Others enjoy the aesthetics: "It's a gorgeous campus where fraternity parties are the weekend highlights." Administration efforts to curtail the once-rampant partying seem to have worked, but sufficiently entertaining activities have not been created to fill the vacuum, so people tend to look elsewhere for weekend life. "To have fun without alcohol, you MUST leave campus and go to Chicago. You can only drink so much beer with drunken assholes before you either have to transfer or go to the city." As for the romantic scene, people tell us that "students 'hook-up' but rarely date other students."

Academics

LFC is a small school whose excellent and caring professors set it apart from the "small liberal arts college" pack. Students uniformly praise their teachers, for the most part declaring that, instruction-wise, this is the best school they could ever hope to attend. A tone of self-justification definitely permeates many comments, such as the following: "With class sizes of about 15 students who are being taught by a Ph.D, academics are incredible here. Students are strongly challenged, unlike many students at large Big Ten universities." It's to be expected that LFC students might feel slightly in the shadow of the large (national stature- and student body-wise) schools in nearby Chicago, but some are confident that national prominence is near at hand for the school they love: "Lake Forest College is one stop below the 'Ivy League' status that Princeton and Harvard receive and is striving to attain academic excellence." An excellent education is certainly available here, but how vigorously students pursue that education varies. The recently implemented General Education Curriculum requires two courses in each of the liberal arts areas (Natural and Mathematical Sciences, Humanities, Social Science) and two Cultural Diversity Courses.

Student Body

"The past description of this school being a getaway for snobby kids who went to boarding schools on the East Coast is fading quickly. This past freshman class is not only larger, but more diverse, than previous classes." Maybe so, but people still say things like, "overall, the students seem to be more concerned with clothing and wealth than learning and studying. It's kind of like high school with ashtrays and nicer cars." Superficially, things are okay for most: "People get along fine. If it weren't for sororities and fraternities they would probably get along better." But one student remarks, "we are a bit segregated when it comes to race and everyone is extremely homophobic—I think that is our greatest problem."

ADMISSIONS

The admissions committee considers (in descending order of importance): HS record, recommendations, essay, class rank, test scores. *Also considered (in descending order of importance):* extracurriculars, personality, alumni relationship, special talents. Either the SAT or ACT is required. An interview is recommended. Admissions process is need-blind. *High school units required/recommended:* 16 total units are recommended; 4 English recommended, 4 math recommended, 2 science recommended, 2 foreign language recommended, 2 social studies recommended, 2 history recommended. Accelerated courses recommended. TOEFL is required of all international students.

The Inside Word

Candidates with good grades will meet with little resistance on the road to acceptance. But remember that Lake Forest definitely has a prep-school-at-the-college-level feel. It pays to keep the admissions committee's eagerness to assess the whole person in mind when completing the application.

FINANCIAL AID

Students should submit: FAFSA, the school's own financial aid form. The Princeton Review suggests that all financial aid forms be submitted as soon as possible after January 1. *The following grants/scholarships are offered:* Pell, SEOG, academic merit, the school's own scholarships, the school's own grants, state scholarships, state grants, private scholarships, private grants, foreign aid. *Students borrow from the following loan programs:* Stafford, unsubsidized Stafford, Perkins, PLUS, the school's own loan fund. Applicants will be notified of awards beginning upon admission. College Work-Study Program is available. Institutional employment is available.

FROM THE ADMISSIONS OFFICE

"Students today must think in global terms. Lake Forest College provides a point of entry for students interested in our international world. The campus is located in the tranquil suburban community of Lake Forest, IL, population 18,000. A fifty-minute train ride takes you to the heart of Chicago, one of America's most exciting cities. It is a world-class center for business, the arts, science, industry, international culture and sports, and serves as a real life laboratory to supplement coursework and to enrich personal life. The 1,000 Lake Forest College students represent forty-eight states and thirty-four countries throughout the world. The are encouraged and supported by a nationally prominent faculty to raise their awareness and understanding of their individual roles and responsibilities. As liberally educated persons, they intend to be prepared for the demands of a constantly changing world. Each new class of entering students helps to define the educational process by dint of their breadth of individual background and accomplishment. The students of Lake Forest know that by putting forth a serious effort and by taking an active role in their education, they will be shaping a more confident and satisfying future. The saying, 'You'll go further than you ever thought you could' has long applied to students at Lake Forest College."

ADMISSIONS

Admissions Rating	77
% of applicants accepted	70
% of acceptees attending	36

FRESHMAN PROFILE

Average verbal SAT	580
Average math SAT	560
Average ACT	24
Average TOEFL	550
Graduated top 20% of class	53
Graduated top 40% of class	83
Graduated top 60% of class	94
Average HS GPA or Avg.	3.3

DEADLINES

Early decision	1/1
Regular admission	3/1
Regular notification	3/15
Non-fall registration	yes

APPLICANTS ALSO LOOK AT

AND OFTEN PREFER

Kenyon
Connecticut Coll.
DePauw

AND SOMETIMES PREFER

U. Illinois, Urbana-Champ.
Bradley
Valparaiso
Cornell Coll.
U. Iowa

AND RARELY PREFER

Hollins

FINANCIAL FACTS

Financial Aid Rating	97
Tuition	$18,750
Room & board	$4,400
Estimated book expense	$600
% frosh receiving aid	83
% undergrads receiving aid	76
% aid is need-based	90
% frosh w/ grant (avg)	83 ($13,049)
% frosh w/ loan (avg)	61 ($2,625)
% UGs w/ job (avg)	60 ($1,575)
Off-campus job outlook	good

LAWRENCE UNIVERSITY

APPLETON, WI 54912   ADMISSIONS: 800-227-0982   FAX: 414-832-6606

STUDENTS SPEAK OUT

Life
"Appleton can be boring," laments a Lawrence University freshman studying biology, but that doesn't mean that Lawrence undergrads are bored. "People go to campus events—there's usually sixty things going on at once," explains one freshman. The school's conservatory attracts many music-minded students, so the variety of music on campus is quite extraordinary. Adds an art history major, "I [am] surprised at the marijuana use!" Yes, Lawrence students tend to drink and smoke with the same vigor and singularness of purpose as their brethren across this great land of ours, but they go one step further: "A popular winter activity of students on-campus is to steal trays from the cafeteria and use them to sled down Memorial Hill." Now that's crazy. While Lawrence has five fraternities and three sororities, one student explains, "I am in a sorority and it saddens me that the Greek system is not more popular." "The town is smelly," winces one student, but it's cheap too. Students spend less than $20 a week on average. "The small college atmosphere takes away a lot of the stress," explains a senior, a good reason that students at Lawrence are generally satisfied with the quality and tenor of their daily lives.

Academics
"The professors are always easily accessible. I was impressed when a calculus professor walked across campus to discuss his class with me," beams a freshman biology major at Lawrence University. This comment is indicative of the respect verging on love that students feel for their highly accessible profs. Explains this English major, "I know all of my professors' office, as well as home, phone numbers. They want us to call them if we are having problems." The only fairly negative comment? It's hard for some students to stay awake. "Bring a BIG cup of coffee to some classes," advises one. It's a good thing the students like their profs so much, because Lawrence doesn't employ TAs to teach any classes (classes that are tiny, by the way). The conservatory at LU is excellent. If you do have trouble with any aspect of your Lawrence experience, "advisors here are totally helpful." Getting into the courses you need shouldn't be much of a problem, especially after your first year. Academic facilities (labs, library, computers) are top-notch, with the school's health facilities the only campus service that fares poorly.

Student Body
"The student body is like one gigantic family. I feel very close to my brothers and sisters, yet I don't know a lot of my distant relatives." Most Lawrence undergrads agree with this familial metaphor. "People at Lawrence aren't afraid to disagree with each other," explains one, while another adds, "The student body is one of the top reasons I chose Lawrence. It has a very friendly atmosphere." Some students, maybe the black sheep, don't subscribe to the happy family theory: "This is where the rich Ivy League rejects turn to ease their pain!" Malcontents are in the minority though. Discrimination is a concern, but not a pervasive problem. Diversity is expected by students at Lawrence. "We have students from all over, so we all accept each other. I have met so many people who are different than myself and learned a lot from these people," explains a chemistry major. A music major concurs, "The international student population is very important in making the campus more diverse." Maybe the biggest cultural difference one faces is the language barrier that must be confronted upon entering Appleton. "Everyone pronounces 'Wisconsin' with a 'g' instead of a 'c'." Can't we all just get along?

FINANCIAL AID: 414-832-6583

WEB SITE: HTTP://WWW.LAWRENCE.EDU/

ADMISSIONS

The admissions committee considers (in descending order of importance): HS record, class rank, essay, test scores, recommendations. *Also considered (in descending order of importance):* special talents, alumni relationship, personality, extracurriculars, geographical distribution. Either the SAT or ACT is required. An interview is recommended. Admissions process is need-blind. *High school units required/recommended:* 4 English recommended, 3 math recommended, 3 science recommended, 3 foreign language recommended, 2 social studies recommended, 2 history recommended. *Special Requirements:* An audition is required for music program applicants.

The Inside Word

Although the admit rate is fairly high, getting into Lawrence demands an above average academic record. Students who are serious about the university should stick with a very challenging high school course load straight through senior year, put significant energy into their application essays, and definitely interview.

FINANCIAL AID

Students should submit: FAFSA, the school's own financial aid form, a copy of parents' most recent income tax filing. The Princeton Review suggests that all financial aid forms be submitted as soon as possible after January 1. *The following grants/scholarships are offered:* Pell, SEOG, academic merit, the school's own scholarships, the school's own grants, state scholarships, state grants, private scholarships, private grants, foreign aid. *Students borrow from the following loan programs:* Stafford, unsubsidized Stafford, Perkins, PLUS, the school's own loan fund, private loans. College Work-Study Program is available. Institutional employment is available.

FROM THE ADMISSIONS OFFICE

"Lawrence students are characterized by their energy, commitment to community service respect for each other, and desire to achieve to their full potential. Campus activities are abundant, off-campus study programs are popular (more than half of the students take advantage of them), small classes are the norm (65% of the classes have 10 or fewer students in them), and, yes, winters are for the hardy! But the diversity of interests and experiences, the drive to excel, the wealth of cultural opportunities presented by the art, theatre, and music departments, the quality of research students undertake alongside Ph.D. faculty, and the general friendly attitude of everyone at the university contribute to an excitement that more than outweighs the challenge of winter."

ADMISSIONS

Admissions Rating	82
% of applicants accepted	68
% of acceptees attending	31

FRESHMAN PROFILE

Average verbal SAT	630
Average math SAT	620
Average ACT	27
Average TOEFL	620
Graduated top 20% of class	60
Graduated top 40% of class	89
Graduated top 60% of class	97
Average HS GPA or Avg.	3.5

DEADLINES

Early decision	1/1
Regular admission	2/1
Regular notification	4/1
Non-fall registration	no

APPLICANTS ALSO LOOK AT

AND OFTEN PREFER
Carleton

AND SOMETIMES PREFER
Earlham
Oberlin

AND RARELY PREFER
Augustana (IL)

FINANCIAL FACTS

Financial Aid Rating	91
Tuition	$18,744
Room & board	$4,309
Estimated book expense	$1,500
% frosh receiving aid	87
% undergrads receiving aid	86
% aid is need-based	90
% frosh w/ grant (avg)	86 ($11,227)
% frosh w/ loan (avg)	55 ($2,625)
% UGs w/ job (avg)	50 ($1,500)
Off-campus job outlook	good

LEHIGH UNIVERSITY

BETHLEHEM, PA 18015-3035

ADMISSIONS: 610-758-3100   FAX: 610-6758-4361

STUDENTS SPEAK OUT

Life

At most schools, one or two respondents write, "At our school, we work hard and party hard." At Lehigh, one out of every ten students wrote that on his survey. For Lehigh undergrads, "work hard, party hard" is not just a hackneyed cliché, it's a way of life. Social life here is dominated by the Greek system: students ranked the popularity of fraternities and sororities third in the country. Those who live for frat parties are never disappointed. Reports one student, "Once Thursday rolls around, the social atmosphere takes the place of academics. The strong Greek system results in free-flowing alcohol and everybody 'hooking up.'" Despite efforts by the state and the school to curb underage drinking, alcohol is still a mainstay of Lehigh life. The Greek houses and a beautiful campus keep most social life on campus, as does the lack of attractions in the town of Bethlehem, a town described as "boring" by the one respondent who mentioned it at all. When campus life gets oppressive, most students blow off steam by traveling to Philadelphia (an hour and a half away) or New York (two hours away).

Academics

Lehigh University maintains a prestigious engineering school, a College of Business and Economics, and a College of Arts and Sciences. By all accounts, the first two are excellent." One student expresses what is pretty much the consensus: "We have an incredibly demanding school for engineering and business. Lehigh has been trying to improve its Arts and Sciences, but it is not yet worth the money to come here if you are undecided as to what you're going to study. Computer engineering [this student's major] is really tough, but you'll be prepared socially and academically for your future." Engineering and business students agree that "the courses are quite hard and require many hours of preparation." Students here are extremely goal-oriented; many take advantage of the numerous accelerated undergraduate/graduate degree programs here, and double majors and demanding independent studies are also popular. Still, undergrads do not work so hard as to preclude an active social life. Students gave the administration and library high marks.

Student Body

Lehigh draws its students primarily from Pennsylvania and the rest of the Eastern Seaboard. The school has only a small minority population, made up mostly of Asian students. One Asian student writes to tell us that they maintain a tight-knit community, participating in activities and trips on an almost weekly basis. By both groups' accounts, interaction between the Asian and white communities is minimal. The predominant feel of the student body is white, conservative, jockish, and well-off. The male/female ratio here is around 2 to 1, even worse (for men) than at "party school" rival Lafayette.

FINANCIAL AID: 610-758-3181   E-MAIL: INADO@LEHIGH.EDU   WEB SITE: HTTP://WWW.LEHIGH.EDU/

ADMISSIONS

The admissions committee considers (in descending order of importance): HS record, class rank, test scores, recommendations, essay. *Also considered (in descending order of importance):* extracurriculars, personality, special talents, alumni relationship, geographical distribution. Either the SAT or ACT is required. An interview is recommended. Admissions process is not need-blind. *High school units required/recommended:* 16 total units are required; 4 English required, 3 math required, 2 science required, 2 foreign language required, 2 social studies required. *Special Requirements:* TOEFL is required of all international students. Chemistry and math through trigonometry required of engineering program applicants.

The Inside Word

Liberal arts candidates will find the admissions process to be much friendlier to them than it is to engineering and business applicants. Students without solidly impressive academic credentials will have a rough time getting in regardless of their choice of programs. So will unenthusiastic but academically strong candidates who have clearly chosen Lehigh as a safety.

FINANCIAL AID

Students should submit: FAFSA, CSS Profile, Divorced Parents form (due February 15), a copy of parents' most recent income tax filing. The Princeton Review suggests that all financial aid forms be submitted as soon as possible after January 1. *The following grants/scholarships are offered:* Pell, SEOG, academic merit, athletic, the school's own scholarships, the school's own grants, state scholarships, state grants, private scholarships, private grants, ROTC. *Students borrow from the following loan programs:* Stafford, unsubsidized Stafford, Perkins, PLUS, the school's own loan fund, state loans, private loans. Applicants will be notified of awards beginning April 1. College Work-Study Program is available. Institutional employment is available.

FROM THE ADMISSIONS OFFICE

"Lehigh is a comprehensive, national university located in Bethlehem, which is sixty miles north of Philadelphia and eighty miles southwest of Manhattan. It offers a wide range of degree programs (more than seventy majors) in arts and science, business and economics, and engineering and applied science. Lehigh has always prided itself on preparing students for a rewarding and useful life. Our philosophy has always been that the most effective way to learn is to do. We encourage you to pursue your college career to its fullest potential. The best way to find out if Lehigh is right for you is to come visit our campus and talk to some of our students and faculty."

ADMISSIONS

Admissions Rating	85
% of applicants accepted	60
% of acceptees attending	27

FRESHMAN PROFILE

Average verbal SAT	600
Average math SAT	620
Average ACT	NR
Average TOEFL	580
Graduated top 20% of class	75
Graduated top 40% of class	97
Graduated top 60% of class	99
Average HS GPA or Avg.	NR

DEADLINES

Early decision	1/1
Regular admission	2/15
Regular notification	4/1
Non-fall registration	yes

APPLICANTS ALSO LOOK AT

AND OFTEN PREFER

Pennsylvania
Cornell U.

AND SOMETIMES PREFER

Lafayette
Penn State-U. Park
Bucknell
Union (NY)
Colgate

AND RARELY PREFER

Boston U.
Boston Coll.
Villanova
Syracuse
Gettysburg

FINANCIAL FACTS

Financial Aid Rating	81
Tuition	$20,500
Room & board	$6,020
Estimated book expense	$850
% frosh receiving aid	56
% undergrads receiving aid	58
% aid is need-based	98
% frosh w/ grant (avg)	51 ($11,625)
% frosh w/ loan (avg)	48 ($3,100)
% UGs w/ job (avg)	NR
Off-campus job outlook	fair

LEWIS & CLARK COLLEGE

615 S.W. PALATINE HILL ROAD, PORTLAND, OR 97219-7899   ADMISSIONS: 800-444-4111   FAX: 503-768-7055

CAMPUS LIFE

Quality of Life Rating   **82**
Type of school   private
Affiliation   none
Environment   metropolis

STUDENTS
FT undergrad enrollment	1,837
% male/female	43/57
% from out of state	68
% live on campus	55
% spend weekend on campus	95
% transfers	20
% from public high school	73
% African-American	2
% Asian	10
% Caucasian	78
% Hispanic	3
% international	6
# of countries represented	37

WHAT'S HOT
Portland
college radio
theater
leftist politics
health facilities

WHAT'S NOT
library
religion
inefficient administration
hard liquor
beer

ACADEMICS

Academic Rating	**83**
Profs Interesting Rating	83
Profs Accessible Rating	87
Calendar	semester
Student/teacher ratio	13:1
% profs PhD/tenured	94/62
Hours of study per day	3.21

MOST POPULAR MAJORS
psychology
English

% GRADS WHO PURSUE...
Law 10, Med 1, MBA 1, MA 13

STUDENTS SPEAK OUT

Life

Lewis & Clark's campus "is gorgeous. You can just go out and wander around the woods, ravine, or rose garden. The grass is lush and relaxing. It's great fun!" To make matters even better, the school is located on the outskirts of Portland, so students enjoy both serene immediate surroundings and access to a thriving, moderately large city. Extracurricular clubs and organizations are popular. Reported one student, "This school allows for a lot of artistic and creative freedom. There are student-directed one-act plays, a student-run radio station, and newspaper." Another pointed out, "Many activities are free. Every Saturday there's a movie, and most Fridays there are halfway decent bands at the dorms. Outdoor trips on weekends are wonderful escapes from campus and can cost between ten and sixty-five dollars." On-campus partying has been somewhat cut down by the administration's decision to enforce more aggressively Oregon's drinking-age laws: "Because the alcohol policy here is so strict, most parties take place off campus."

Academics

Lewis and Clark College is a liberal arts school whose reputation rests on a variety of strong academic departments, a progressive General Education curriculum, a popular overseas studies program, and a dedicated faculty. For a small school, L&C offers a remarkable choice of quality programs. The international affairs department is its most famous, but the school's success in sending students to graduate and professional programs attests to the soundness of its other curricular offerings. Students also reported satisfaction with their English and foreign language courses. All students must complete a core curriculum that stresses "liberal" perspectives, critical thought, and understanding of non-Western culture. This progressive approach permeates all study here. Explained one student, "This is a great place to learn to synthesize material. I don't know where else I could study mitosis and, in another class, turn it into a mime piece for high school students." More than half the students take advantage of the overseas studies program, which sends students virtually everywhere in the world. Best of all, the school subsidizes the program so that all students can afford it. Students also praised their professors, saying that "they have an obvious love for the subjects they teach." The administration, on the other hand, "is awfully unpopular. They make a lot of unilateral policy changes the students don't support."

Student Body

"The school is making an honest effort to diversify the student body," wrote one student. "The changes are slow, but evident." Students are "very friendly and rather on the 'crunchy granola' side," and consider themselves very liberal politically. One student summed up the student body this way: "This place is a mixture of a ton of Frisbee players, a couple of athletes, and a handful of people who just don't know what they're doing."

FINANCIAL AID: 503-768-7090   E-MAIL: ADMISSIONS@LCLARK.EDU   WEB SITE: HTTP://WWW.LCLARK.EDU/

ADMISSIONS

The admissions committee considers (in descending order of importance): HS record, class rank, test scores, essay, recommendations. *Also considered (in descending order of importance):* alumni relationship, extracurriculars, geographical distribution, personality, special talents. Either the SAT or ACT is required. An interview is recommended. Admissions process is need-blind. *High school units required/recommended:* 18 total units are recommended; 4 English recommended, 3 math recommended, 3 science recommended, 2 foreign language recommended, 3 social studies recommended. Portfolio Path, in which applicants submit portfolio of materials demonstrating academic strengths, may be substituted for standardized test scores. Portfolio must include graded writing.

The Inside Word

The low percentage of accepts who choose to enroll significantly inhibits Lewis & Clark's ability to be very selective. Admissions evaluations are nonetheless thorough, and the Portfolio Path is an intriguing option that guarantees a purely personal evaluation. Few colleges of Lewis & Clark's quality are as accommodating to students.

FINANCIAL AID

Students should submit: FAFSA (due March 1), the school's own financial aid form (due March 1). The Princeton Review suggests that all financial aid forms be submitted as soon as possible after January 1. *The following grants/scholarships are offered:* Pell, SEOG, academic merit, the school's own scholarships, the school's own grants, state scholarships, state grants, private scholarships, private grants, foreign aid. *Students borrow from the following loan programs:* Stafford, unsubsidized Stafford, Perkins, PLUS, state loans, private loans. Applicants will be notified of awards beginning April 1. College Work-Study Program is available. Institutional employment is available.

FROM THE ADMISSIONS OFFICE

"Applicants cite a variety of reasons why they are drawn to Lewis & Clark. Many have to do with the multiple environments experienced by out students, including (1) a small arts and sciences college with a 13 to 1 student/faculty ratio; (2) a location only six miles from downtown Portland (metropolitan population 1.5 million); (3) being in the heart of the Pacific Northwest, which provides our College Outdoors Program nearly one hundred trips per year; and, (4) the rest of the world. "More than fifty percent of our graduates included an overseas program in their curriculum. Over the past thirty-four years, our students and faculty have studied in sixty-three countries or geographical areas. Our international curriculum had undergone a total review to better prepare graduates going into the twenty-first century."

ADMISSIONS

Admissions Rating	78
% of applicants accepted	77
% of acceptees attending	20

FRESHMAN PROFILE

Average verbal SAT	610
Average math SAT	600
Average ACT	26
Average TOEFL	550
Graduated top 20% of class	59
Graduated top 40% of class	85
Graduated top 60% of class	100
Average HS GPA or Avg.	NR

DEADLINES

Early decision	11/15
Regular admission	2/1
Regular notification	4/1
Non-fall registration	yes

APPLICANTS ALSO LOOK AT

AND OFTEN PREFER
Colorado Coll.

AND SOMETIMES PREFER
U. Puget Sound
Willamette
U. Oregon
UC-Santa Cruz
Reed

AND RARELY PREFER
UC-Santa Barbara

FINANCIAL FACTS

Financial Aid Rating	86
Tuition	$17,740
Room & board	$5,780
Estimated book expense	$1,500
% frosh receiving aid	65
% undergrads receiving aid	64
% aid is need-based	85
% frosh w/ grant (avg)	61 ($9,734)
% frosh w/ loan (avg)	59 ($3,625)
% UGs w/ job (avg)	49 ($1,200)
Off-campus job outlook	good

LOUISIANA STATE UNIVERSITY-BATON ROUGE

BATON ROUGE, LA 70803-2750 ADMISSIONS: 504-388-1175 FAX: 504-388-5991

CAMPUS LIFE

Quality of Life Rating | **87**
Type of school | public
Affiliation | none
Environment | city

STUDENTS
FT undergrad enrollment | 16,663
% male/female | 50/50
% from out of state | 12
% live on campus | 22
% spend weekend on campus | NR
% transfers | 22
% from public high school | NR
% in (# of) fraternities | 14 (20)
% in (# of) sororities | 15 (15)
% African-American | 9
% Asian | 4
% Caucasian | 80
% Hispanic | 2
% international | 3
# of countries represented | 101

WHAT'S HOT
student publications
old-fashioned dating
political activism
hard liquor
off-campus food

WHAT'S NOT
campus difficult to get around
lab facilities
inefficient administration
theater
dorms

ACADEMICS

Academic Rating | **72**
Profs Interesting Rating | 69
Profs Accessible Rating | 71
Calendar | semester
Student/teacher ratio | 18:1
% profs PhD/tenured | 78/86
Hours of study per day | 2.41

MOST POPULAR MAJORS
general studies
psychology
elementary education

STUDENTS SPEAK OUT

Life

Although Louisiana State University sponsors tons of extracurricular cultural and educational events on campus, the two centers of LSU social life remain partying and intercollegiate sports. Students find plenty of special occasions to party—Mardi Gras, St. Patrick's Day, Homecoming, a music festival called Groovin' on the Grounds, and the spring frat rush are the biggest—and plenty of mundane occasions as well. Of sports, writes another student, "They make our world go round. The football team was horrible this year and so, consequently, was the whole semester." The Greek system "is strong, but it has grown weaker recently as it has been under evaluation by the administration." The city of Baton Rouge hosts an active bar and live music scene; students complain, however, that the school is located in one of the city's less desirable neighborhoods. New Orleans is one and a half hours away by car; many students travel there for Mardi Gras.

Academics

Nearly one-fifth of LSU undergraduates pursue degrees in fields related to business and management, and it is about these departments that students here are most generous in their praise. Writes one marketing major, "LSU has a strong and successful business department. Many professors have had practical experience beforehand in their field, while many still consult part time on the side. Upper-level class size averages about 25." An accounting major adds, "All my accounting professors have been great." Students are less pleased with other aspects of their education; even when discussing LSU's relatively low tuition, most students voice concern over a continuing state budget crisis that has already resulted in many fee increases. Other complaints center on the college counseling staff ("College counselors don't always lead you in the right decision in meeting major requirements. They act as if they don't have time to discuss your situation," writes one student; several suggest consulting instead with the staff of your major department). Students in the sciences, engineering, and computer sciences programs complain that their professors are poor teachers: some, they feel, have little aptitude and less desire for instructing undergraduates, and many simply cannot speak English well. LSU has recently decided to demand more of undergraduates; about one-third of an undergraduate's credits will now go toward distribution requirements.

Student Body

More than ninety percent of LSU students are from in-state. The vast majority of students are white, conservative, Christian, and hold strong-mostly negative-views on multiculturalism and tolerance of gays. "Race discrimination is unfortunately very much alive at LSU and in the state of Louisiana in general," complains a typical minority student; writes another undergrad, "Rush Limbaugh is very popular here." Student life is marked by "strong social distinctions between blacks and whites, gays and straights, Greeks and GDIs"; about the only time all students rally together is during football games.

ADMISSIONS

The admissions committee considers (in descending order of importance): HS record, test scores. *Also considered (in descending order of importance):* extracurriculars, special talents. Either the SAT or ACT is required; ACT is preferred. Admissions process is need-blind. *High school units required/recommended:* 17 total units are required; 4 English required, 3 math required, 3 science required, 2 foreign language required, 3 social studies required. Minimum 2.3 GPA required. *Special Requirements:* A portfolio is required for art program applicants. An audition is required for music program applicants. TOEFL is required of all international students. *The admissions office says:* "Applicants not meeting course units and/or grades or test score minimums may be considered by the admissions committee."

The Inside Word

LSU's admissions process is a straight numbers game. The university is rare among formula-driven institutions in recognizing that some good students fall through the cracks in such systems. It is commendable that LSU's admissions committee is also willing to take a closer, more personal look if circumstances warrant.

FINANCIAL AID

Students should submit: FAFSA. The Princeton Review suggests that all financial aid forms be submitted as soon as possible after January 1. *The following grants/scholarships are offered:* Pell, SEOG, academic merit, athletic, the school's own scholarships, state scholarships, state grants, ROTC. *Students borrow from the following loan programs:* Stafford, unsubsidized Stafford, Perkins, PLUS, state loans. College Work-Study Program is available. Institutional employment is available.

FROM THE ADMISSIONS OFFICE

"Throughout its history, LSU has served the people of Louisiana, the region, the nation, and the world through extensive, multipurpose programs encompassing instruction, research, and public service."

ADMISSIONS

Admissions Rating	71
% of applicants accepted	80
% of acceptees attending	62

FRESHMAN PROFILE

Average verbal SAT	NR
Average math SAT	NR
Average ACT	23
Average TOEFL	500
Graduated top 20% of class	45
Graduated top 40% of class	71
Graduated top 60% of class	88
Average HS GPA or Avg.	3.1

DEADLINES

Early decision	NR
Regular admission	6/1
Regular notification	rolling
Non-fall registration	yes

APPLICANTS ALSO LOOK AT

AND SOMETIMES PREFER

Centenary
Florida State
U. Florida

AND RARELY PREFER

Southern Methodist
TCU
Spring Hill

FINANCIAL FACTS

Financial Aid Rating	88
In-state tuition	$2,663
Out-of-state tuition	$5,963
Room & board	$3,610
Estimated book expense	$634
% frosh receiving aid	71
% undergrads receiving aid	60
% aid is need-based	39
% frosh w/ grant (avg)	51 ($3,325)
% frosh w/ loan (avg)	33 ($4,275)
% UGs w/ job (avg)	28 ($1,580)
Off-campus job outlook	excellent

LOYOLA COLLEGE (MD)

4501 NORTH CHARLES STREET, BALTIMORE, MD 21210-2699 ADMISSIONS: 800-221-9107 FAX: 410-617-2768

CAMPUS LIFE

Quality of Life Rating **90**
Type of school private
Affiliation Roman Catholic Church
Environment suburban

STUDENTS

FT undergrad enrollment	3,075
% male/female	45/55
% from out of state	66
% live on campus	74
% spend weekend on campus	70
% transfers	12
% from public high school	54
% African-American	4
% Asian	3
% Caucasian	88
% Hispanic	2
% international	2
# of countries represented	10

WHAT'S HOT
dorms
student government
hard liquor
religion
beer

WHAT'S NOT
lack of diversity on campus
Greeks
students are cliquish
drugs
sex

ACADEMICS

Academic Rating	**85**
Profs Interesting Rating	89
Profs Accessible Rating	91
Calendar	semester
Student/teacher ratio	14:1
% profs PhD/tenured	89/76
Hours of study per day	3.23

MOST POPULAR MAJORS
business
biology
psychology

STUDENTS SPEAK OUT

Life

Located smack dab in the beautiful city of Baltimore, Loyola boasts a student body that loves to frequent their fair city's many bars. Explains one of Baltimore's diversity of opportunity, "Baltimore is great. They have a bar for every kind of student." Another tries valiantly to promote Baltimore's other fine features, "There is a lot to do...including museums, parks, clubs, bars, concerts, large malls," but it is a vain attempt. Alcohol, especially beer, reigns supreme with Loyola undergrads, especially on the weekends. Those who go against the grain (pun intended) report mixed feelings. "Even though Loyola is a bar school my friends and I don't drink [and] there is [still] a lot to do!" Warns one junior, though, "I am among the minority on this campus who doesn't drink." While "the school has implemented many alternatives" to off-campus carousing, and promotes a fairly strict drug and alcohol policy, you get the picture. Otherwise, Loyola dorms get high marks but "the food plan is horrendous." There are no sororities or frats at Loyola (perhaps another factor contributing to the huge bar scene), and student government is popular and active on campus.

Academics

"Most professors are great. None are TAs." That's a good summation of students' positive comments about their academic experience at Loyola. Fills in another, "All of my professors have been genuinely concerned about my current and future success. They push me to my full potential." Classes are small at Loyola, and the academic burden can be tough. There is a core curriculum that must be completed in the first two years. "The course load can be unbearable," says a senior studying political science. Adds a freshman, "The accelerated and high standards of teaching don't allow for catching up. You must be able to do the materials immediately." Along the same lines, "The honors program here is awesome!" The administration gets similar praise: "The administration is friendly and understanding." Indeed, registration procedures, lab facilities, computer facilities, and the bursar are all given high marks by students, leaving just a few harsh comments like this one: "When it comes to getting something done with finances or academics, no one knows anything and everyone sends you to everybody else." Students as a whole concur with this junior, "Loyola College is teaching me to be academically, socially, and spiritually advanced. I love it."

Student Body

"Everyone looks and dresses the same, but everyone is happy and nice." Yes, Loyola's student body is very white, and interaction between the white majority and minorities is lacking, but that doesn't seem to bother the students. Explains an Asian male, "Unfortunately, the school is lily white. But minority students don't have anything to worry about. They're very nice here." Wisecracks one of the college's J. Crew contingent, "Loyola has the highest concentration of plaid on the East Coast." Another comedian notes, "About three-fourths of the students here were cloned off the same...prototype, heavy-drinking frat boys without frats to live in so they trash the freshman dorm." Perhaps the only students that should worry about open discrimination are gays. Explains a sophomore studying psychology, "Generally we all get along. This campus is pretty homophobic though." Adds another, "Remember that no matter what the administration says—this is a Catholic school!" There is a real commitment to public service at Loyola, "Community service is an integral part of my life and most students' lives," and undergrads describe themselves as very sexually active. A Catholic school? Are these kids married?

ADMISSIONS

The admissions committee considers (in descending order of importance): HS record, test scores, class rank, essay, recommendations. *Also considered (in descending order of importance):* extracurriculars, alumni relationship, personality, special talents. An interview is recommended. Admissions process is need-blind. *High school units required/recommended:* 20 total units are recommended; 4 English recommended, 3 math recommended, 4 science recommended, 4 foreign language recommended, 3 social studies recommended, 2 history recommended. Maximum of 3 commercial, industrial, or technical courses may be counted. Minimum combined SAT I score of 1150, rank in top fifth of secondary school class, and 3.0 GPA recommended. TOEFL is required of all international students.

The Inside Word

Loyola is to be commended for notifying outstanding candidates of acceptance early in the applicant review cycle without demanding an early commitment in return. Traditional Early Decision plans are confusing, archaic, and unreasonable to students. A binding commitment is a huge price to pay to get a decision four months sooner. This is obviously one place that cares.

FINANCIAL AID

Students should submit: FAFSA (due February 1), CSS Profile, the school's own financial aid form (due February 1). The Princeton Review suggests that all financial aid forms be submitted as soon as possible after January 1. *The following grants/scholarships are offered:* Pell, SEOG, academic merit, athletic, the school's own scholarships, the school's own grants, state scholarships, state grants, private scholarships, private grants, ROTC. *Students borrow from the following loan programs:* Stafford, unsubsidized Stafford, Perkins, PLUS, private loans. Applicants will be notified of awards beginning April 15. College Work-Study Program is available. Institutional employment is available. Freshmen are discouraged from working.

FROM THE ADMISSIONS OFFICE

"To make a wise choice about your college plans, you will need to find out more. We extend to you these invitations. Question and answer periods with an admissions counselor are helpful to prospective students. An appointment should be made in advance. Admissions office hours are 9 a.m. to 5 p.m., Monday through Friday. College day programs and Saturday information programs are scheduled during the academic year. These programs include a film about Loyola, a general information session, a discussion of various majors, a campus tour, and lunch. Summer information programs can help high school juniors to get a head start on investigating colleges. These programs feature an introductory presentation about the college and a campus tour."

ADMISSIONS

Admissions Rating	77
% of applicants accepted	63
% of acceptees attending	23

FRESHMAN PROFILE

Average verbal SAT	600
Average math SAT	590
Average ACT	NR
Average TOEFL	560
Graduated top 20% of class	58
Graduated top 40% of class	84
Graduated top 60% of class	96
Average HS GPA or Avg.	2.9

DEADLINES

Early decision	NR
Regular admission	1/15
Regular notification	4/15
Non-fall registration	yes

APPLICANTS ALSO LOOK AT

AND OFTEN PREFER
Boston Coll.
Villanova

AND SOMETIMES PREFER
James Madison
U. Richmond
Fairfield
Lafayette
St. Joseph's U.

AND RARELY PREFER
U. Scranton
Fordham
Rutgers U.
Catholic
Penn State-U. Park

FINANCIAL FACTS

Financial Aid Rating	89
Tuition	$15,200
Room & board	$6,280
Estimated book expense	$600
% frosh receiving aid	65
% undergrads receiving aid	62
% aid is need-based	60
% frosh w/ grant (avg)	NR ($5,800)
% frosh w/ loan (avg)	NR ($3,000)
% UGs w/ job (avg)	15 ($1,200)
Off-campus job outlook	excellent

LOYOLA MARYMOUNT UNIVERSITY

LOYOLA BLVD. AT WEST 80TH ST., LOS ANGELES, CA 90045-2699   ADMISSIONS: 310-338-2750   FAX: 310-338-2732

CAMPUS LIFE

Quality of Life Rating 84
Type of school private
Affiliation Roman Catholic Church
(Society of Jesus/Marymount)
Environment metropolis

STUDENTS

FT undergrad enrollment	3,624
% male/female	43/57
% from out of state	21
% live on campus	49
% spend weekend on campus	50
% transfers	30
% from public high school	68
% in (# of) fraternities	13 (6)
% in (# of) sororities	11 (4)
% African-American	7
% Asian	15
% Caucasian	45
% Hispanic	20
% international	9
# of countries represented	73

WHAT'S HOT

student publications
college radio
religion
intramural sports
music associations

WHAT'S NOT

support groups
sex
dorms
students are unhappy
students are cliquish

ACADEMICS

Academic Rating	80
Profs Interesting Rating	89
Profs Accessible Rating	71
Calendar	semester
Student/teacher ratio	14:1
% profs PhD	85
Hours of study per day	3.64

MOST POPULAR MAJORS

business administration
communication arts
psychology

STUDENTS SPEAK OUT

Life

Students describe Loyola Marymount University as "a beautiful Catholic university in a nice part of Los Angeles." With just under 4,000 undergrads (and approximately another 1,000 graduate students), Loyola Marymount has "a smallness of the school [that] gives it a family-type atmosphere." Writes one student, "I can't walk from one side of campus to the other without seeing at least one person I know." Campus life is made even more intimate by the fact that only half the students live on campus. Students report that LMU is "a serious school, yet it is also fun on weekends." Says one, "If you want to drink, LMU's the place!" Greek life is popular, with almost one fifth the students joining. For those who choose not to go Greek, a wide assortment of vibrant clubs and organizations exist with which to fill one's happily sober, yet study-free hours, including: a newspaper and radio station, the school's popular Division I sports teams, an active intramural sports program, and, of course, the city of Los Angeles, which one student describes as "exciting, even though it smells a little bit funny." As an added bonus, the school is close to the beach.

Academics

According to one college counselor, Loyola Marymount University is "small and friendly," a true anomaly in a city that is neither. "It's not the most challenging academically," the same source continues, "but it's still an excellent choice for good students, especially those who underachieved in high school." Our survey results bore out this characterization of LMU. Students here enjoy a challenging but laid-back academic atmosphere, one that is helped by effective, caring professors with whom one-on-one contact is relatively easy. In response to our survey, students indicate a high degree of satisfaction with LMU, expressing their approval of class sizes, professors, and administrators. Many come here to learn about those art forms indigenous to California (and Los Angeles in particular), namely, film and music production. The College of Business Administration, however, attracts the most students. Studies in all popular liberal arts and social sciences, as well as in engineering, are also available. While requirements vary from major to major, most students are required to complete a core curriculum of humanities, sciences, math, and philosophy/theology courses in order to graduate. Exceptional students may enroll in the honors program, which affords them smaller, more demanding classes.

Student Body

LMU students we hear from get along so well that even those who declare that religious commitments prohibit them from certain kinds of partying refrain from censuring those who do partake. Joyful tolerance seems to be the watchword. LMU does a good job of recruiting minority students: nearly one-third of the student body is made up of minorities. Hispanics and Asians make up the largest groups; there are relatively few black students here. Students identified themselves as more religious than most student bodies, not at all unusual at a Catholic school.

ADMISSIONS

The admissions committee considers (in descending order of importance): HS record, test scores, essay, recommendations, class rank. *Also considered (in descending order of importance):* special talents, alumni relationship, extracurriculars, personality. Either the SAT or ACT is required; SAT is preferred. An interview is recommended. Admissions process is need-blind. *High school units required/recommended:* 16 total units are recommended; 4 English recommended, 3 math recommended, 2 science recommended, 3 foreign language recommended, 3 social studies recommended. *Special Requirements:* An audition is required for music program applicants. TOEFL is required of all international students. 4 units of mathematics required of computer science, engineering, and mathematics program applicants.

The Inside Word

Loyola Marymount's admissions committee is particular about candidate evaluation, but a large applicant pool has more to do with the university's moderate acceptance rate than does academic selectivity. Even so, underachievers will have difficulty getting in.

FINANCIAL AID

Students should submit: FAFSA, CSS Profile, state aid form (due March 2), a copy of parents' most recent income tax filing. The Princeton Review suggests that all financial aid forms be submitted as soon as possible after January 1. *The following grants/scholarships are offered:* Pell, SEOG, academic merit, athletic, the school's own scholarships, the school's own grants, state grants, private scholarships, private grants, ROTC. *Students borrow from the following loan programs:* Stafford, unsubsidized Stafford, Perkins, PLUS, the school's own loan fund, state loans, private loans. Applicants will be notified of awards beginning April 1. College Work-Study Program is available. Institutional employment is available.

FROM THE ADMISSIONS OFFICE

"The visionary statement which the Trustees adopted in 1976 commits Loyola Marymount University to the following goals: To strive toward all our goals within the context of a university that has an institutional commitment to Christianity and the Catholic tradition. To provide strong undergraduate humanistic education as an integral part of the academic program of each student. To offer sound professional programs on both the undergraduate and graduate level. To help the student advance significantly in personal, social, and professional growth through a program of services to students. To work toward the formation of a true spirit of community at all levels and in all areas of the University. To be at the service of the community beyond the campus, especially in the fostering of a more just society."

ADMISSIONS

Admissions Rating	70
% of applicants accepted	68
% of acceptees attending	27

FRESHMAN PROFILE

Average verbal SAT	550
Average math SAT	550
Average ACT	24
Average TOEFL	550
Graduated top 20% of class	58
Graduated top 40% of class	90
Graduated top 60% of class	NR
Average HS GPA or Avg.	3.2

DEADLINES

Early decision	NR
Regular admission	2/1
Regular notification	rolling
Non-fall registration	yes

APPLICANTS ALSO LOOK AT

AND OFTEN PREFER
UC-Davis
Stanford
UCLA

AND SOMETIMES PREFER
UC-Irvine
UC-San Diego
UC-Santa Barbara

AND RARELY PREFER
Santa Clara U.
UC-Riverside
Pepperdine

FINANCIAL FACTS

Financial Aid Rating	82
Tuition	$15,130
Room & board	$6,492
Estimated book expense	$572
% frosh receiving aid	80
% undergrads receiving aid	65
% aid is need-based	68
% frosh w/ grant (avg)	60
% frosh w/ loan (avg)	NR
% UGs w/ job (avg)	36 ($2,400)
Off-campus job outlook	excellent

LOYOLA UNIVERSITY NEW ORLEANS

6363 St. Charles Avenue, New Orleans, LA 70118   Admissions: 504-865-3240   Fax: 504-865-3383

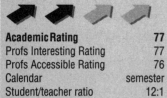
STUDENTS SPEAK OUT

Life

"Life in New Orleans is a ball," explains a Loyola University New Orleans accounting major. "There is all the art and music you want, fabulous architecture, an amazing zoo and aquarium, some of the best food I've ever tasted..." We don't have enough space to continue that student's list of fun, but you get the picture. Almost all Loyola students love New Orleans, a vibrant city world renowned for its glorification of good times. Many students are also impressed with on-campus activities. Writes one, "There are always activities going on at the residence halls as well as on campus. Students appreciate the fact that "student reps sit on most university committees and are involved in running everything, every aspect" of the school. Dorms get decent marks, as do off-campus frats and sororities, which are popular but don't dominate the social scene. Explains one undergrad of the social scene, "Since I am an honors student...I may not get to participate because of my academic obligations as often as I like, but when I do I have a blast!" Odds are that "blast" has something to do with drinking beer, rated "extremely" or "very" popular by more than 90 percent of the students surveyed, with liquor and pot not far behind. Indeed, if the following student's views of his classmates' habits reflect any general tendencies you may feel, Loyola may not be for you: "They drink too much and completely violate all that is proper and sacred."

Academics

"Loyola is a wonderfully liberal institution, much more so than typical private Catholic schools." A Jesuit institution, Loyola often forgives its freshmen of their previous academic sins. Explains this psychology major, "The great thing about Loyola is that it accepts students who may not have shown their true academic capabilities in high school and gives them a second chance." Coursework in religion and philosophy is mandatory, as is a sixteen-course Common Curriculum, so working in your major right off the bat is harder to do than it is at most schools. Professors are well-liked at Loyola: "Some are nutty but most of them really care and are friendly." Adds a business major, "The fact that most courses are taught by Ph.D.s makes the students appreciate the classes more." Beams another, "The Loyola classroom is as large and colorful as the city of New Orleans." Well, it's not as large, but it's the sentiment that counts. The school's strengths include business and communications, with the communications department housed in a $13 million complex, complete with TV and radio studios and production facilities. The administration gets high marks, with the university seen as smoothly run and well maintained.

Student Body

"They are overall a motley crew of heathenous, bastardous drunks," explains a philosophy major at Loyola University New Orleans. Well, that's one way of looking at it. Explains another, "Loyola students are extremely laid back. Most of us take our work seriously, but we don't take ourselves too seriously." Now that is a little more accurate. A diverse bunch, Loyola undergrads get along pretty well, with little discrimination or bad blood reported. Says this international student, "During my first few months at Loyola, I received a lot of support from my peers." This junior studying history adds, "Everyone for the most part gets along. There is a real sense of community." Interestingly, dating and sexual activity aren't as prevalent at Loyola as they are at most institutions we've surveyed, possibly due to Loyola's slightly older student body.

FINANCIAL AID: 504-865-3231   WEB SITE: HTTP://WWW.LOYNO.EDU/

ADMISSIONS

The admissions committee considers (in descending order of importance): HS record, test scores, class rank, recommendations, essay. *Also considered (in descending order of importance):* extracurriculars, special talents, personality, alumni relationship. Either the SAT or ACT is required. An interview is required of some applicants. Admissions process is need-blind. *High school units required/recommended:* 17 total units are required; 4 English required, 3 math required, 2 science required, 2 foreign language recommended, 2 social studies required. *Special Requirements:* A portfolio is required for art program applicants. An audition is required for music program applicants. An RN is required for nursing program applicants. TOEFL is required of all international students. *The admissions office says:* "Because of the diversity of high school curricula, cultural influences on test results, the various abilities required in collegiate programs, and the unique background of applicants, each applicant's admissions portfolio is reviewed individually."

The Inside Word

Students with a solid academic record can expect smooth sailing to admission at Loyola. The vast majority of the university's applicants get in, and a significant percentage of them are only average academically. The admissions process is truly personal, and many of the weaker applicants benefit from Loyola's willingness to consider more than just numbers.

FINANCIAL AID

Students should submit: FAFSA (due March 1). The Princeton Review suggests that all financial aid forms be submitted as soon as possible after January 1. *The following grants/scholarships are offered:* Pell, SEOG, academic merit, the school's own scholarships, the school's own grants, state grants, private scholarships, private grants, ROTC. *Students borrow from the following loan programs:* Stafford, unsubsidized Stafford, Perkins, PLUS. Applicants will be notified of awards beginning early in March. College Work-Study Program is available. Institutional employment is available.

FROM THE ADMISSIONS OFFICE

"Loyola University is a Jesuit university founded by the Society of Jesus and chartered on April 15, 1912, with ownership vested in the Loyola community of Jesuit fathers. The University was authorized to grant degrees by the General Assembly of Louisiana for the year 1912. Today, Loyola-New Orleans still operates under its founding purpose of offering a liberal arts education on the undergraduate level to all who seek knowledge and truth...Fronting on tree-lined St. Charles Avenue where streetcars are the mode of public transportation, Loyola's main campus faces Audubon Park directly across the avenue. The nineteen-acre campus is a collection of Tudor-Gothic buildings and modern architecture. Two blocks up St. Charles Avenue is the recently acquired four-acre Broadway Campus."

ADMISSIONS

Admissions Rating	71
% of applicants accepted	84
% of acceptees attending	38

FRESHMAN PROFILE

Average verbal SAT	590
Average math SAT	560
Average ACT	23
Average TOEFL	570
Graduated top 20% of class	46
Graduated top 40% of class	73
Graduated top 60% of class	88
Average HS GPA or Avg.	3.4

DEADLINES

Early decision	NR
Regular admission	rolling
Regular notification	rolling
Non-fall registration	yes

APPLICANTS ALSO LOOK AT

AND OFTEN PREFER
LSU-Baton Rouge
Tulane
U. New Orleans

AND SOMETIMES PREFER
Xavier U.
Texas Christian U.
U. Texas
U. Florida
Florida State U.

AND RARELY PREFER
NYU

FINANCIAL FACTS

Financial Aid Rating	93
Tuition	$12,450
Room & board	$5,760
Estimated book expense	$600
% frosh receiving aid	62
% undergrads receiving aid	70
% aid is need-based	65
% frosh w/ grant (avg)	73 ($6,832)
% frosh w/ loan (avg)	46 ($2,300)
% UGs w/ job (avg)	39
Off-campus job outlook	good

LOYOLA UNIVERSITY OF CHICAGO

820 N. MICHIGAN AVENUE, CHICAGO, IL 60611   ADMISSIONS: 800-262-2373   FAX: 312-915-7003

CAMPUS LIFE

Quality of Life Rating   **72**
Type of school   private
Affiliation   Roman Catholic Church
                        (Society of Jesus)
Environment   metropolis

STUDENTS

FT undergrad enrollment	5,451
% male/female	39/61
% from out of state	18
% live on campus	30
% spend weekend on campus	50
% transfers	29
% from public high school	62
% in (# of) fraternities	8 (6)
% in (# of) sororities	7 (9)
% African-American	5
% Asian	14
% Caucasian	66
% Hispanic	7
% international	1
# of countries represented	72

WHAT'S HOT
political activism
Chicago
ethnic diversity on campus
different students interact
religion

WHAT'S NOT
campus food
hard liquor
students are unhappy
inefficient administration
intercollegiate sports

ACADEMICS

Academic Rating   **73**
Profs Interesting Rating   72
Profs Accessible Rating   69
Calendar   semester
Student/teacher ratio   13:1
% profs PhD/tenured   93/95
Hours of study per day   2.88

MOST POPULAR MAJORS
psychology
business
biology

STUDENTS SPEAK OUT

Life

Loyola University has done much to change its image as a big commuter school. Nine residence halls accommodate 2,000 undergrads and an additional 2,000 find refuge each year in neighborhood apartments. But because lots of students go home on weekends and the overwhelming majority live off campus, the campus can still be a ghost town when Friday afternoon comes. One student complains, "The only neighborhood place that offers some amusement is Hamilton's (a bar reminiscent of high school hangouts like White Castle or the mall)." However, some residents who stick around say that there is "a great diversity of clubs and activities that enable the students to get involved." And of course, students are in Chicago, which is an amazingly cool city (except in winter, when it is an amazingly cold city). Frat parties are open to all, and the "Greek-independent" animosity common at many other schools is absent here. Parking, once "a nightmare," has improved since an on-campus parking garage was opened. Now, according to the administration, "parking could not be easier."

Academics

Chicago's Loyola University is actually five undergraduate institutions in one: the school maintains separate colleges for the arts and sciences, business administration, nursing, and education. At the College of Arts and Sciences, the most popular undergraduate division, the students face a group of core requirements so demanding that "it is rather difficult for many students to finish in four years." Students here pursue mandatory studies in theology and philosophy—as you might expect from a Jesuit institution—and also in history, science, mathematics, and writing. Requirements constitute nearly half the credits toward a B.A., and that doesn't even include courses required for one's major. When arts and sciences students do find time for electives, they often head for the popular School of Business Administration to take marketing and finance courses. According to college counselors, the psychology and pre-medical departments are the strongest divisions in Arts and Sciences; counselors also recommended the schools of Nursing and Business Administration. Loyola University has two undergraduate campuses, the Water Tower campus downtown and the Lake Shore campus, which is currently being expanded, on the north side of town. The school recently purchased a third campus in Wilmette. Residents live at Lake Shore.

Student Body

Minority students at Loyola complain that although they are well represented in the student body, interaction among ethnic groups just doesn't happen. Says one Latino student, "Although the university is ethnically diverse, the students do not hang together. It looks great on paper, but in reality it is not what it seems," and an African-American woman goes so far as to accuse administrators and fellow students of "racism and sexism." The commuter aspect still present at Loyola certainly doesn't create a bonding atmosphere. Those students who seek to break into new social circles reported that Loyola provided them with great experiences. A little over half the student body is Catholic.

ADMISSIONS

The admissions committee considers (in descending order of importance): HS record, test scores, class rank, recommendations. *Also considered (in descending order of importance):* extracurriculars, personality, special talents. Either the SAT or ACT is required. An interview is recommended. Admissions process is need-blind. *High school units required/recommended:* 15 total units are required; 4 English required, 2 math required, 4 math recommended, 1 science required, 2 science recommended, 4 foreign language recommended, 1 social studies required, 3 social studies recommended. Minimum 2.0 GPA required. *Special Requirements:* TOEFL is required of all international students. Biology and chemistry with labs required of nursing program applicants. *The admissions office says:* "We review student files on a rolling basis once they are complete with an application for admission, official transcripts, and ACT or SAT I scores."

The Inside Word

The admissions process is fairly formulaic, and the standards aren't too demanding for most candidates.

FINANCIAL AID

Students should submit: FAFSA, CSS Profile. The Princeton Review suggests that all financial aid forms be submitted as soon as possible after January 1. *The following grants/scholarships are offered:* SEOG, academic merit, athletic, the school's own scholarships, the school's own grants, state scholarships, state grants, private scholarships, private grants, federal nursing scholarship. *Students borrow from the following loan programs:* Stafford, unsubsidized Stafford, Perkins, PLUS, the school's own loan fund, state loans, federal nursing loans, health professions loans, private loans. College Work-Study Program is available. Institutional employment is available.

FROM THE ADMISSIONS OFFICE

"As a national research university, Loyola provides a superb academic program that is distinctive because of its personal approach. Nationally and internationally renowned scholars teach introductory freshman-level courses in classes that average twenty-one students. A special emphasis in our curriculum is placed on the examination of ethics and values as well as a commitment to instill intensive writing skills that will benefit the student throughout his/her life. Despite its large population, Loyola is committed to the individual student, and its programs and policies reflect the importance of community. Students from throughout the nation are attracted to Loyola for the opportunities offered by the University as well as the benefits of studying in Chicago, a world-class city."

ADMISSIONS

Admissions Rating	70
% of applicants accepted	86
% of acceptees attending	31

FRESHMAN PROFILE

Average verbal SAT	502
Average math SAT	556
Average ACT	24
Average TOEFL	500
Graduated top 20% of class	53
Graduated top 40% of class	80
Graduated top 60% of class	NR
Average HS GPA or Avg.	NR

DEADLINES

Early decision	NR
Regular admission	4/1
Regular notification	rolling
Non-fall registration	yes

APPLICANTS ALSO LOOK AT

AND OFTEN PREFER

De Paul
U. Illinois-Champaign
Illinois-Chicago
Northwestern
Marquette

AND SOMETIMES PREFER

Northern Illinois
Notre Dame
U. Chicago
Indiana U.-Bloomington

AND RARELY PREFER

Saint Louis U.

FINANCIAL FACTS

Financial Aid Rating	73
Tuition	$14,400
Room & board	$6,210
Estimated book expense	$770
% frosh receiving aid	78
% undergrads receiving aid	80
% aid is need-based	65
% frosh w/ grant (avg)	60 ($9,093)
% frosh w/ loan (avg)	62 ($2,925)
% UGs w/ job (avg)	25 ($1,200)
Off-campus job outlook	excellent

MACALESTER COLLEGE

1600 GRAND AVENUE, ST. PAUL, MN 55105   ADMISSIONS: 612-696-6357   FAX: 612-696-6689

STUDENTS SPEAK OUT

Life

Most Macalester College students point to the Twin Cities as their main source of free-time fun. The cities "become more important the more time you spend here." Despite the beer ban on campus, alcohol and drug use are very common. "Lots of pot-smoking and quasi-intellectual discussion," quips one student. Smaller gatherings are more common than full-school affairs, although the Spring Fest (an all-day concert party) and the Scottish Country Fair are popular. Daily interaction among students is infused with discussion of various issues, most recently, Comte, Sartre, artificial life technology, Gingrich, abortion, gay rights, and sexual harassment. Due to its size, Macalester is also "very social. By the time you get to your friends' friends, you know the entire school." Some popular activities are "volunteering, teaching ESL for example," playing the bagpipes, and getting involved with "a lot of political and activist issues." Also of note: (1) the weather (especially in winter) is unpleasant, and (2) food on campus is not good, but food is excellent off campus.

Academics

Located just twenty minutes from the Midwestern meccas of Minneapolis and St. Paul, Macalester enjoys a reputation as a diverse, challenging institution that stresses individuality. Students here love their professors ("they challenge you to go beyond your boundaries, to think in creative ways") and their courses, but "administrators are a mixed bag—some are great student advocates, some seem to have multiple personality disorder, and others are just evil." While there is concern by some that the administration is "trying to turn the place into a more boring, straitlaced place by cracking down on naked Frisbee games, etc.," the school is still "a good bit left of liberal" according to most. Attention from teachers is easy to come by—"I can just walk in and see anyone I need. By my sophomore year all the profs in my major knew me"—and professors are also well regarded for their teaching abilities. Students enjoy an unusual amount of freedom: core requirements are relatively few for a school of Mac's caliber, and independently designed majors and double majors are not uncommon. Students also voice their appreciation for the generally small class sizes (except at the intro level for some science courses).

Student Body

There are wide gaps in the ways Mac students view each other. Nearly everyone agrees that the student body is liberal and that the vast majority get along well, but some students mention various types of discord lurking in the shadows. Some students report that people get along with each other mostly because they stick to their own kind: "There's not much mingling between interest groups, but there's never conflict." Another student adds, "There's Macalester and then there's the football team." On the whole, however, most students feel that interaction on campus although "far from perfect," is "better than most of the world."

ADMISSIONS

The admissions committee considers (in descending order of importance): class rank, essay, HS record, recommendations, test scores. *Also considered (in descending order of importance):* extracurriculars, personality, alumni relationship, special talents. Either the SAT or ACT is required. An interview is recommended. Admissions process is need-blind. *High school units required/recommended:* 19 total units are recommended; 4 English recommended, 3 math recommended, 3 science recommended, 3 foreign language recommended, 3 social studies recommended, 3 history recommended. Honors, advanced placement, or International Baccalaureate courses recommended. *The admissions office says:* "[We make an] active effort to reach students personally, including interviews with admissions staff offered in fourteen to fifteen cities a year. Students report we're somewhat friendlier than other options."

The Inside Word

Macalester is just a breath away from moving into the highest echelon of American colleges; a gift of Reader's Digest stock several years ago has recently translated into over $500 million in endowment. As the college begins to reap the benefits of this generous gift, the applicant pool stands to grow in leaps and bounds. Macalester is already among the fifty or so most selective in the country. An interview can enhance your admissibility: even though they are offered across the country, we encourage you to visit the campus.

FINANCIAL AID

Students should submit: FAFSA (due March 1), CSS Profile (due March 1), the school's own financial aid form, a copy of parents' most recent income tax filing (due March 1). The Princeton Review suggests that all financial aid forms be submitted as soon as possible after January 1. *The following grants/scholarships are offered:* Pell, SEOG, academic merit, the school's own scholarships, the school's own grants, state grants, private scholarships, private grants, foreign aid. *Students borrow from the following loan programs:* Stafford, Perkins, PLUS, the school's own loan fund, state loans, private loans. Applicants will be notified of awards beginning March 15. College Work-Study Program is available. Institutional employment is available.

FROM THE ADMISSIONS OFFICE

"The Macalester admissions office works to bring to campus each year a group of students who will further our long-standing traditions of scholarship, international and multicultural awareness, and service to others. Our commitment to academic excellence requires that an evaluation of intellectual achievement and potential be central to the selection process. However, we try to make this evaluation as humanistic as possible, looking at recommendations, application essays, and personal interviews, as well as curriculum, class rank, and test scores. Because we aim as well to support a dynamic campus life, we also value leadership and participation in extracurricular and community activities, special talents in art, music, or athletics, and evidence of social and ethical concern. We try to evaluate applicants in the fullest possible context, and encourage students to schedule an interview or simply call with questions so that we can address their particular concerns."

ADMISSIONS

Admissions Rating	91
% of applicants accepted	54
% of acceptees attending	28

FRESHMAN PROFILE

Average verbal SAT	670
Average math SAT	640
Average ACT	29
Average TOEFL	550
Graduated top 20% of class	83
Graduated top 40% of class	99
Graduated top 60% of class	100
Average HS GPA or Avg.	NR

DEADLINES

Early decision	NR
Regular admission	1/15
Regular notification	3/29
Non-fall registration	no

APPLICANTS ALSO LOOK AT

AND OFTEN PREFER
Rice
Middlebury Coll.
Swarthmore

AND SOMETIMES PREFER
Carleton
Colorado Coll.

AND RARELY PREFER
Oberlin
U. Wisconsin-Madison
Earlham

FINANCIAL FACTS

Financial Aid Rating	91
Tuition	$16,585
Room & board	$4,772
Estimated book expense	$500
% frosh receiving aid	78
% undergrads receiving aid	79
% aid is need-based	97
% frosh w/ grant (avg)	77 ($10,793)
% frosh w/ loan (avg)	51 ($2,240)
% UGs w/ job (avg)	61
Off-campus job outlook	excellent

University of Maine

Orono, ME 04469   Admissions: 207-581-1561   Fax: 207-581-1517

CAMPUS LIFE

Quality of Life Rating 71
Type of school public
Affiliation none
Environment suburban

STUDENTS

FT undergrad enrollment	5,839
% male/female	53/47
% from out of state	20
% live on campus	52
% spend weekend on campus	50
% transfers	32
% from public high school	NR
% in (# of) fraternities	6 (12)
% in (# of) sororities	4 (7)
% African-American	1
% Asian	2
% Caucasian	95
% Hispanic	0
% international	4
# of countries represented	69

WHAT'S HOT
sex
old-fashioned dating
student publications
library
drugs

WHAT'S NOT
inefficient administration
student government
campus difficult to get around
students are unhappy
dorms

ACADEMICS

Academic Rating 70
Profs Interesting Rating 62
Profs Accessible Rating 64
Calendar semester
Student/teacher ratio 14:1
% profs PhD/tenured 72/83
Hours of study per day 2.95

MOST POPULAR MAJORS
business administration
elementary education
nursing

% GRADS WHO PURSUE...
Law 3, Med 2, MBA 5, MA 10

STUDENTS SPEAK OUT

Life

The social scenes at large state universities usually break down into several subdivisions. The largest is a party scene centered in dorms and frats; the others, off the mainstream, are mostly alcohol-free and focus on academics, the arts, and politics. The University of Maine is no exception to the rule. Students report that "most folks party and attempt to meet a mate for the night." Adds another, "UMaine is generally a fun campus, from hockey games to dances, concerts to plays, friends, and sorority and fraternity life to all other opportunities which wouldn't ever fit on this page. The student here is never at a loss for fun." Among other diversions: "Recent movies are shown on the big screen, we have spectacular sports teams, and the nearest mall is only about ten minutes away. People throw themselves into sports, clubs, and various other interests. I love the life at this school, mainly because there's never a lack of it." Primary among most students' devotions is the hockey team: "Hockey (men's) is very big on this campus. The team was the 1993 NCAA Champion." Of their hometown, students warn that "in Orono there are only two places students can go. People in town complain about the students. This is a college town—get a clue!"

Academics

Students at the University of Maine report that their school represents a good bargain for those in the engineering school. "It's a lot easier for engineers than for other students to get the classes they need," writes one student, while others in the school note that professors are excellent and that computer and experimental labs are accessible and up to date. Students in other schools complain more vigorously of the big-time red tape involved in any administrative process ("They always send you on a wild-goose chase when you need something. I get a year's exercise walking back and forth between the business office and financial aid when I need to correct my bill"); poor, uncaring professors ("I'm disappointed in being taught by TAs who don't even speak English fluently," notes one psychology major); and overall second-class treatment ("The University of Maine does not treat students well at all. Many of the facilities on campus, particularly financial aid, seem to have a negative view of students. We are not treated as the customers we are"). Orono is well known for its outdoors-oriented programs; its forest resources college is a magnet for out-of-state students.

Student Body

The vast majority of Orono students are white and from in-state. Still, our respondents report that students come from a wide variety of backgrounds and locations. Writes one, "The student body is made up of people of different ages, religions, etc. It's amazing to meet someone from Turkey living right in your dorm." Students also note that "This is a very diverse and liberal campus. Fellow students are involved and concerned."

ADMISSIONS

The admissions committee considers (in descending order of importance): HS record, class rank, test scores, recommendations, essay. *Also considered (in descending order of importance):* extracurriculars, geographical distribution, alumni relationship, personality, special talents. Either the SAT or ACT is required; SAT is preferred. An interview is recommended. Minimum combined SAT I score of 900, rank in top half of secondary school class, and minimum 2.5 GPA recommended. *Special Requirements:* An audition is required for music program applicants. TOEFL is required of all international students.

The Inside Word

The University of Maine is much smaller than most public flagship universities, and its admissions process reflects this; it is a much more personal approach than most others use. Candidates are reviewed carefully for fit with their choice of college and major, and the committee will contact students regarding a second choice if the first doesn't seem to be a good match. Prepare your application as if you are applying to a private university.

FINANCIAL AID

Students should submit: FAFSA, the school's own financial aid form (due March 1), state aid form. The Princeton Review suggests that all financial aid forms be submitted as soon as possible after January 1. *The following grants/scholarships are offered:* Pell, SEOG, academic merit, athletic, the school's own scholarships, the school's own grants, state scholarships, state grants, private scholarships, private grants, ROTC, foreign aid. *Students borrow from the following loan programs:* Stafford, unsubsidized Stafford, Perkins, PLUS, the school's own loan fund, private loans. Applicants will be notified of awards beginning April 1. College Work-Study Program is available. Institutional employment is available.

FROM THE ADMISSIONS OFFICE

"As an applicant to the University of Maine, we share with you a concern regarding appropriate 'institutional fit.' We want students who are comfortable with themselves and who are self-motivated. It is important to visit the campus to be certain that the academic, cultural and recreational offerings of the University are consistent with the student's needs. Meeting with faculty during the campus visit is particularly important to ensure that the student is comfortable with our academic expectations. The visit also provides an opportunity to talk with current students and to experience the high level of technical assistance available through our computer clusters and connectivity in our student residence halls. The University of Maine's strong commitment to educational excellence will be reinforced when the student visits our campus."

ADMISSIONS

Admissions Rating	69
% of applicants accepted	84
% of acceptees attending	38

FRESHMAN PROFILE

Average verbal SAT	550
Average math SAT	550
Average ACT	NR
Average TOEFL	NR
Graduated top 20% of class	43
Graduated top 40% of class	74
Graduated top 60% of class	93
Average HS GPA or Avg.	NR

DEADLINES

Early decision	12/1
Regular admission	2/1
Regular notification	rolling
Non-fall registration	yes

APPLICANTS ALSO LOOK AT

AND OFTEN PREFER
U. Vermont

AND SOMETIMES PREFER
U. New Hampshire
U. Mass.-Amherst
Colby

AND RARELY PREFER
U. Rhode Island
U. Conn
U. Maine-Farmington

FINANCIAL FACTS

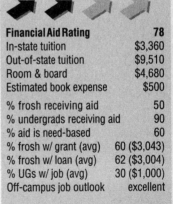

Financial Aid Rating	78
In-state tuition	$3,360
Out-of-state tuition	$9,510
Room & board	$4,680
Estimated book expense	$500
% frosh receiving aid	50
% undergrads receiving aid	90
% aid is need-based	60
% frosh w/ grant (avg)	60 ($3,043)
% frosh w/ loan (avg)	62 ($3,004)
% UGs w/ job (avg)	30 ($1,000)
Off-campus job outlook	excellent

MANHATTANVILLE COLLEGE

2900 PURCHASE STREET, PURCHASE, NY 10577   ADMISSIONS: 800-328-4553   FAX: 914-694-2386

STUDENTS SPEAK OUT

Life

Manhattanville College is located in the suburbs of New York City, about an hour away from Manhattan. The city is easily accessible by commuter train or by car. Closer to school is White Plains, a city of about 50,000 that is arguably one of the retail meccas of America; two huge malls within several blocks of each other anchor a shopping district that offers just about every type of store that one can imagine. The area is home to the headquarters of many large corporations, and internships are reportedly easy to come by. On campus, what was once a relative desert socially has gradually become an oasis: "When I was a freshman, this was a suitcase college, and we wanted to change that. We've worked hard, and I think we have changed it." There are lots of student groups and activities, many student-initiated, and "more people stay here on weekends." When students do leave the campus, many do so to participate in M'Ville's "Midnight Runs," which are trips to New York City in order to distribute clothing and food to the homeless.

Academics

Manhattanville students see themselves as self-starters and that quality, they feel, sets them apart from the pack. Explains one student, "What makes this a great learning environment is that students are encouraged to get involved and make a difference." The school's unusual curriculum demands that students take an active role in designing their education. Freshmen are assigned advisors and are required to devise a four-year program during their first semester. They must maintain a portfolio of work finished toward the completion of that curriculum; the portfolio is periodically evaluated by a faculty panel. Students continually revise their programs as their interests change and their perspectives broaden. A standard variety of liberal arts majors are available here, and students tend toward preprofessional pursuits. Science courses are said to be weak, mostly because the school is too small to adequately support them: "The biology department has only two full-time professors. Yet five percent of the students proceed from here to medical school. In previous editions of *Best Colleges*, the administration here received low grades, but an energetic, accessible new president seems to be working wonders. "You're going to see President Berman at the pub. You're going to see him at parties, dancing with his wife" says one student; "Sometimes I think to myself, 'How does he remember everyone's name?'"

Student Body

Manhattanville has a remarkably diverse student body for a small private college. Exclaims one student, "Manhattanville College has an important variety of cultures, religions, and people from all over the world." Many of the students are international, and American students come from all over the county. There is a relatively large black and Hispanic population. Race relations, reported here in the past as strained, have experienced a metamorphosis. Students now report little racial tension, and many social activities on campus focus on celebrating the wide range of cultural backgrounds found among the students here.

FINANCIAL AID: 914-694-2200

ADMISSIONS

The admissions committee considers (in descending order of importance): HS record, test scores, recommendations, class rank, essay. *Also considered (in descending order of importance):* personality, extracurriculars, alumni relationship, special talents. Either the SAT or ACT is required; SAT is preferred. An interview is recommended. Admissions process is need-blind. *High school units required/recommended:* 4 English required, 2 math required, 2 science required, 2 foreign language required, 2 social studies required, 2 history required. Minimum 3.0 GPA recommended. *Special Requirements:* A portfolio is required for art program applicants. An audition is required for music program applicants. TOEFL is required of all international students.

The Inside Word

Like many former women's colleges, Manhattanville has had a tough time building and keeping a male student body. This goes a long way toward explaining its gradual transformation into somewhat of a preprofessional bastion and the proliferation of men's athletic teams in just about every sport feasible for a college of its size and location. Athletes, both male and female, who show some talent often get a boost in the admissions process. So do candidates from elite prep schools, which are well represented in the student body.

FINANCIAL AID

Students should submit: FAFSA, a copy of parents' most recent income tax filing. The Princeton Review suggests that all financial aid forms be submitted as soon as possible after January 1. *The following grants/scholarships are offered:* Pell, SEOG, academic merit, the school's own scholarships, the school's own grants, state scholarships, private scholarships, private grants. *Students borrow from the following loan programs:* Stafford, unsubsidized Stafford, Perkins, PLUS. Applicants will be notified of awards beginning March 1. College Work-Study Program is available. Institutional employment is available.

FROM THE ADMISSIONS OFFICE

"In our community of learning and growing, Manhattanville College takes a genuine interest in each and every student. At the undergraduate level, the Portfolio System emphasizes student responsibility. Each student must submit a clear and precise plan for their education. They must accomplish the appropriate academic skills, and they are urged to carry these obtained skills to graduate study. This involvement through the Portfolio System, with a dedicated and sincere faculty advisor, helps the student actually measure their academic growth in an empirical manner. Our hope is to continue to attract students with this energy."

ADMISSIONS

Admissions Rating	72
% of applicants accepted	68
% of acceptees attending	34

FRESHMAN PROFILE

Average verbal SAT	540
Average math SAT	530
Average ACT	24
Average TOEFL	NR
Graduated top 20% of class	55
Graduated top 40% of class	83
Graduated top 60% of class	95
Average HS GPA or Avg.	3.1

DEADLINES

Early decision	NR
Regular admission	3/1
Regular notification	rolling
Non-fall registration	yes

APPLICANTS ALSO LOOK AT

AND OFTEN PREFER
Skidmore
NYU

AND SOMETIMES PREFER
SUNY Purchase
Fordham
Syracuse

AND RARELY PREFER
Mercy Coll.

FINANCIAL FACTS

Financial Aid Rating	91
Tuition	$15,500
Room & board	$7,330
Estimated book expense	$400
% frosh receiving aid	65
% undergrads receiving aid	65
% aid is need-based	70
% frosh w/ grant (avg)	91
% frosh w/ loan (avg)	65 ($2,600)
% UGs w/ job (avg)	44 ($1,050)
Off-campus job outlook	excellent

MARLBORO COLLEGE

MARLBORO, VT 05344   ADMISSIONS: 800-343-0049   FAX: 802-257-4154

CAMPUS LIFE

Quality of Life Rating 91
Type of school   private
Affiliation   none
Environment   rural

STUDENTS
FT undergrad enrollment   270
% male/female   42/58
% from out of state   83
% live on campus   75
% spend weekend on campus   75
% transfers   20
% from public high school   70
% African-American   1
% Asian   1
% Caucasian   91
% Hispanic   2
% international   3
# of countries represented   7

WHAT'S HOT
sex
student government
different students interact
theater
campus feels safe

WHAT'S NOT
lab facilities
Greeks
religion

ACADEMICS

Academic Rating   94
Profs Interesting Rating   97
Profs Accessible Rating   96
Calendar   semester
Student/teacher ratio   8:1
% profs PhD/tenured   70/60
Hours of study per day   3.61

STUDENTS SPEAK OUT

Life
Marlboro College students do not experience the "typical" college lifestyle: "The key to life here is to be able to be self-reliant. If you can't motivate yourself or learn to entertain yourself (there are times when the whole student body of 260 falls into a black hole so there is no one to hang out with and no town to walk to) then you will have a hard time surviving." Most students at this very small school agree they enjoy "a laid back and comfortable atmosphere conducive to learning," and they appreciate the outlying area: "Hiking the forested mountains and emerging onto the tiny, highly focused campus gives one a feeling of insular security which is unbeatable." Students meet twice monthly, using the New England town meeting model to "create and run activities and govern the student body." On-campus "theme parties, fencing tournaments, plays, lectures, concerts, and movies" help relieve student stress, as does the big Spring Cabaret ("almost everyone here is involved in theater"). For many, life is "an intense blur of all too significant coincidences culminating in full-moon bursts of creativity and catharsis." That's just how we were going to say it.

Academics
Cloistered away in the Vermont mountains, Marlboro College is ideal for free-thinking individualists. Most students choose Marlboro for its Plan of Concentration, a program that requires students to spend their junior and senior years following a self-devised curriculum, culminating in a senior research paper "analogous to a master's thesis." During those last two years, students work individually with professors. Students must also pass a writing proficiency exam, but otherwise, their course of study is left entirely to them. Explains one student, "Most students choose Marlboro because they know 'the plan' will prepare them for graduate school. Classes are informal, yet rigorous, and professors are easy to approach." But work can be terrifying: "Now that I'm a senior on plan, things are a little frightening. It's a lot more psychologically challenging to do your own self-designed work than just assignments." Students report a high level of satisfaction with their professors ("The professors are insane. There is no division between them and us except some respect from us for them"), administration ("You often sit with the college president at lunch"), and class availability ("As long as you can convince a professor that you need a certain study to learn what you want, they'll teach it to you").

Student Body
Marlboro students could be characterized as "a motley crew of manic gifted freaks," as one student summed it up. Notes another, "P.C./hep cats/hedonists dominate." And another reports, "There's not much diversity here, but students would welcome it." A Hispanic student agrees, writing, "because the students here are open minded and curious, a minority student is given a chance to educate others about his/her culture, mores and language." The only complaint seems to be unavoidable in a school so small: "the 'rumor mill.' You cannot sneeze without everyone knowing in ten minutes. There are no secrets here."

FINANCIAL AID: 802-257-4333

WEB SITE: HTTP://WWW.MARLBORO.EDU

ADMISSIONS

The admissions committee considers (in descending order of importance): HS record, essay, recommendations, class rank, test scores. *Also considered (in descending order of importance):* extracurriculars, personality, special talents. Either the SAT or ACT is required. An interview is required. Admissions process is need-blind. *High school units required/recommended:* 4 English required, 3 math recommended, 3 science recommended, 2 foreign language recommended, 2 social studies recommended, 2 history recommended. Minimum combined SAT I score of 1000 and minimum secondary school average of 85 recommended. TOEFL is required of all international students.

The Inside Word

Don't be misled by Marlboro's high acceptance rate; the college's applicant pool consists mainly of candidates who are sincerely interested in a nontraditional path to their BA. They also possess sincere intellectual curiosity, and students who don't should not bother applying. The admissions process here is driven by matchmaking and a search for those who truly want to learn. For the right kind of person, Marlboro can be a terrific college choice.

FINANCIAL AID

Students should submit: FAFSA (due March 1), the school's own financial aid form (due March 1), state aid form (due March 1), a copy of parents' most recent income tax filing (due March 1). The Princeton Review suggests that all financial aid forms be submitted as soon as possible after January 1. *The following grants/ scholarships are offered:* Pell, SEOG, the school's own grants, state scholarships, state grants, private grants, foreign aid. *Students borrow from the following loan programs:* Stafford, unsubsidized Stafford, Perkins, PLUS, the school's own loan fund, state loans, private loans. Applicants will be notified of awards beginning April 1. College Work-Study Program is available. Institutional employment is available.

FROM THE ADMISSIONS OFFICE

"Marlboro College is unlike any other college in the United States. It is distinguished by its curriculum, praised in higher education circles as unique; it is known for is self-governing philosophy, in which each student, faculty and staff has an equal vote on many issues affecting the community; and it is recognized for its fifty years' history of offering a rigorous, exciting, self-designed course if study taught in very small classes and individual tutorials. Marlboro's size also distinguishes it from most other schools. With 270 students and a student/faculty ratio of 8 to 1, it is one of the nation's smallest liberal arts colleges. Few other schools offer a program where students have such close interaction with faculty, and where community life is inseparable from academic life. The result, the self-designed, self-directed Plan of Concentration, allows students to develop their own unique academic work by defining a problem, setting clear limits on an area of inquiry, and analyzing, evaluating and reporting on the outcome of a significant project. A Marlboro education teaches you to think for yourself, to articulate your thoughts, express your ideas, believe in yourself, and do it all with the clarity, confidence and self-reliance necessary for later success, no matter what postgraduate path you take."

ADMISSIONS

Admissions Rating	83
% of applicants accepted	69
% of acceptees attending	38

FRESHMAN PROFILE

Average verbal SAT	670
Average math SAT	600
Average ACT	NR
Average TOEFL	NR
Graduated top 20% of class	NR
Graduated top 40% of class	NR
Graduated top 60% of class	NR
Average HS GPA or Avg.	NR

DEADLINES

Early decision	NR
Regular admission	3/1
Regular notification	rolling
Non-fall registration	yes

APPLICANTS ALSO LOOK AT

AND OFTEN PREFER
Sarah Lawrence
Bard
Hampshire

AND SOMETIMES PREFER
Bennington
Evergreen State
Antioch
Fairfield

AND RARELY PREFER
Goddard
U. Vermont

FINANCIAL FACTS

Financial Aid Rating	94
Tuition	$19,295
Room & board	$6,445
Estimated book expense	$400
% frosh receiving aid	83
% undergrads receiving aid	83
% aid is need-based	70
% frosh w/ grant (avg)	82 ($8,500)
% frosh w/ loan (avg)	83 ($2,625)
% UGs w/ job (avg)	70 ($1,430)
Off-campus job outlook	fair

MARQUETTE UNIVERSITY

P.O. Box 1881, Milwaukee, WI 53201-1881 · Admissions: 800-222-6544 · Fax: 414-288-3764

CAMPUS LIFE

Quality of Life Rating · **67**

Type of school	private
Affiliation	Roman Catholic Church
	(Society of Jesus)
Environment	metropolis

STUDENTS

FT undergrad enrollment	6,890
% male/female	47/53
% from out of state	60
% live on campus	41
% spend weekend on campus	NR
% transfers	15
% from public high school	55
% in (# of) fraternities	7 (10)
% in (# of) sororities	7 (8)
% African-American	5
% Asian	5
% Caucasian	83
% Hispanic	3
% international	2
# of countries represented	45

WHAT'S HOT
religion
old-fashioned dating
intercollegiate sports
political activism
registration is a breeze

WHAT'S NOT
students are unhappy
unattractive campus
support groups
campus difficult to get around
student government

ACACEMICS

Academic Rating	**70**
Profs Interesting Rating	61
Profs Accessible Rating	62
Calendar	semester
Student/teacher ratio	15:1
% profs PhD	95
Hours of study per day	2.81

MOST POPULAR MAJORS
mechanical engineering
accounting
electrical engineering

% GRADS WHO PURSUE...
Law 19, Med 9, MBA 9, MA 22

STUDENTS SPEAK OUT

Life

Marquette University is located in downtown Milwaukee, and location is definitely the number one quality-of-life issue at the school. Several area counselors warn that MU is in an unsafe neighborhood, and many respondents concur. Writes one, "The downtown scene has been problematic because of the nature of this area of the city and the police department's dislike for the students. The social problems of Milwaukee can be a great distraction." Not everyone agrees, however. One student notes that because the school is "located in downtown Milwaukee, there are a lot of things to do. It's unfortunate that most people just don't take the time to find out about them." Students report that drinking is popular. The Greek system barely exists—fewer than five percent of the students pledge—and social life centers on dorm parties, sporting events, and the city. Typical evening at Marquette? Writes one student, "My roommates and I spend our time studying, debating politics, discussing philosophy, and watching bad movies."

Academics

Area college counselors agree that Marquette is "a solid pre-professional college." Among the fields of study singled out for excellence, business, nursing, physical therapy, communications, and engineering (especially biomedical engineering) are the most frequently praised. A Jesuit school, Marquette does its best to create a supportive, caring environment for its students, and apparently it succeeds. Students we surveyed give their professors good grades for after-class accessibility and tell us that deans and other administrators are particularly helpful. As a large school, MU also provides great academic diversity and flexibility. Reports one student, "I was interested in developing an interdisciplinary degree in Medieval studies, and I was able to formulate such a program at MU. The academic depth here has been beneficial." While some students who apply to MU may expect a relaxed academic atmosphere—most schools with national reputations built primarily on sports are perceived as easy by those not attending them—that notion is trashed when they get here. "Marquette has a hard curriculum, and some of the students aren't up to it," explains one undergraduate who survived the distribution requirements, which for most students entail work in mathematics, science, liberal arts, and theology (different divisions of the school have different requirements). For the highly motivated/talented student, Marquette offers an honors program with smaller classes and more rigorous academics.

Student Body

Marquette has a reputation for diversity, but only sixteen percent of the students are minorities. "Diversity," writes one undergraduate, "is well publicized but superficial." Many of Marquette's students represent the first college-educated generation of their families, and many, accordingly, are career-oriented. Complains one undergrad, "On the whole, people here are too conservative and too blasé."

FINANCIAL AID: 414-288-7390

ADMISSIONS

The admissions committee considers (in descending order of importance): HS record, class rank, test scores, recommendations, essay. Either the SAT or ACT is required. An interview is recommended. *High school units required/recommended:* 16 total units are recommended; 4 English recommended, 3 math recommended, 2 science recommended, 2 foreign language recommended, 2 social studies recommended. Minimum composite ACT score of 21 (combined SAT I score of 800) and minimum 2.0 GPA required. *Special Requirements:* Additional math and/or science units required of business, engineering, and health profession program applicants.

The Inside Word

Class rank may be important to the admissions office as a required criterion, but not to worry—in practice, almost a tenth of Marquette's freshmen ranked in the bottom half of their graduating class. The university's low level of selectivity makes it a no-sweat proposition for most candidates.

FINANCIAL AID

Students should submit: FAFSA (due March 1). The Princeton Review suggests that all financial aid forms be submitted as soon as possible after January 1. *The following grants/scholarships are offered:* Pell, SEOG, academic merit, athletic, the school's own scholarships, the school's own grants, state scholarships, state grants, private scholarships, private grants, ROTC, foreign aid. *Students borrow from the following loan programs:* Stafford, unsubsidized Stafford, Perkins, PLUS, private loans. Applicants will be notified of awards beginning: rolling. College Work-Study Program is available. Institutional employment is available.

FROM THE ADMISSIONS OFFICE

"Since 1881, Marquette has been noted for its commitment to educational excellence in the 450 year-old Jesuit, Catholic tradition. Marquette embraces the philosophy that true education should be more than an acquisition of knowledge. Marquette seeks to develop your intellect as well as your moral and spiritual character. This all-encompassing education will challenge you to develop the goals and values that will shape the rest of your life. Each of Marquette's 7,500 undergraduates are admitted as freshman to one of six colleges: Arts and Sciences, Business Administration, Communication, Engineering, Health Sciences, or Nursing. Many co-enroll in the School of Education. The faculty within these colleges are prolific writers and researchers, but more important, they all teach and advise students. Marquette is nestled in the financial center of Milwaukee, the nation's eighteenth largest city, allowing you to take full advantage of the city's cultural, professional and governmental opportunities. Marquette's urban experience is unique: an 80 acre campus (with real grass and trees), an outdoor athletic complex, and an internationally diverse student body (85 percent of which live on campus) all make Marquette a close-knit community in which you can learn and live."

ADMISSIONS

Admissions Rating	71
% of applicants accepted	86
% of acceptees attending	34

FRESHMAN PROFILE

Average verbal SAT	570
Average math SAT	570
Average ACT	25
Average TOEFL	500
Graduated top 20% of class	61
Graduated top 40% of class	89
Graduated top 60% of class	99
Average HS GPA or Avg.	NR

DEADLINES

Early decision	NR
Regular admission	rolling
Regular notification	rolling
Non-fall registration	yes

APPLICANTS ALSO LOOK AT

AND OFTEN PREFER

U. Wisconsin-Madison
U. Wisconsin-Milwaukee
U. Illinois, Urbana-Champ.
Notre Dame
Miami U.

AND SOMETIMES PREFER

St. Louis
Purdue U.-West Lafayette
Case Western

AND RARELY PREFER

Vanderbilt
Villanova
U. Oklahoma

FINANCIAL FACTS

Financial Aid Rating	79
Tuition	$14,710
Room & board	$5,350
Estimated book expense	$600
% frosh receiving aid	92
% undergrads receiving aid	80
% aid is need-based	80
% frosh w/ grant (avg)	75 ($7,400)
% frosh w/ loan (avg)	73 ($4,625)
% UGs w/ job (avg)	35 ($1,200)
Off-campus job outlook	excellent

MARY WASHINGTON COLLEGE

1301 COLLEGE AVENUE, FREDERICKSBURG, VA 22401-5358   ADMISSIONS: 800-468-5614   FAX: 703-654-1857

CAMPUS LIFE

Quality of Life Rating   **83**
Type of school   public
Affiliation   none
Environment   town

STUDENTS

FT undergrad enrollment	3,024
% male/female	35/65
% from out of state	28
% live on campus	70
% spend weekend on campus	80
% transfers	20
% from public high school	84
% African-American	6
% Asian	3
% Caucasian	89
% Hispanic	2
% international	1
# of countries represented	20

WHAT'S HOT
campus is beautiful
student government
religion
honesty
student publications

WHAT'S NOT
computer facilities
health facilities
town-gown relations
drugs
Greeks

ACADEMICS

Academic Rating	**83**
Profs Interesting Rating	86
Profs Accessible Rating	90
Calendar	semester
Student/teacher ratio	17:1
% profs PhD/tenured	88/85
Hours of study per day	2.94

MOST POPULAR MAJORS
business administration
English
psychology

STUDENTS SPEAK OUT
Life
Mary Washington College boasts a beautiful campus, noteworthy "for its brick walkways and buildings with large white columns." Its classic southern appearance is matched in the surrounding town, colonial-era Fredericksburg, "a historic Civil War town...rich in older architecture." Town-gown relations are reportedly strained, however: one student writes that "We get along with each other but not with other Fredericksburg people." Still, students frequently venture off campus, especially when they want to drink. On campus, "There are many clubs...that keep people away from abusive substances." Otherwise, the social scene is somewhat stymied by the male/female ratio. But the school sponsors concerts and parties, and "students frequently find creative ways to have fun" like "Inter-Varsity Christian Fellowship" and Ultimate Frisbee. Social highlights include Junior Ring week ("juniors get humiliated [by their classmates] for a week and then get a ring at the ring dance").

Academics
As the cost of private college grows uncontrollably, small, liberal-arts-oriented public institutions like Mary Washington College have jumped a level in prominence. Such schools, which have always provided many of the amenities of the private schools—small classes, caring professors, a liberal arts emphasis—are now attracting a higher caliber of student, further enhancing their reputations. Students at MWC report an overall high level of satisfaction, particularly with their in-class experiences. Our respondents note that the teachers here are generally excellent ("the professors will go to any length to aid the students in their personal, academic, and career pursuits") and that the academic work, which includes a demanding core curriculum, is both rewarding and challenging ("I have found that there are no 'easy A' classes here at all. Just because you are in this school doesn't mean you are here to stay"). Many students express appreciation for the school's honor code (writes one, "[it is] a deeply cherished tradition here, and creates a community absent of lying, cheating, and stealing"). About the only sticking point with students is the administration, whom many are ticked off at for one or more of the following reasons: intersex dorm visitation is limited; tuition and enrollment are on the rise; and, the administration, characterized as pompous and overpaid, is predominantly male and white (while the student body is predominantly female and white).

Student Body
The MWC student body is "predominantly white," and, as one student reports, "Since there are a large number of Christians here and we are in the South, our school is quite conservative." Students not fitting that description indicate that they have some difficulty fitting into the mainstream, though most report that "everyone is extremely friendly." Another student explains how most deal with others: "There are many cliques here. You find your circle and float within it." Unfortunately, as the administration tries to diversify demographics, one student claims that "there are a lot of racial conflicts on campus."

FINANCIAL AID: 703-654-2001

WEB SITE: HTTP://WWW.MWC.EDU/

ADMISSIONS

The admissions committee considers (in descending order of importance): HS record, class rank, test scores, essay, recommendations. *Also considered (in descending order of importance):* extracurriculars, special talents, alumni relationship, personality. Admissions process is need-blind. *High school units required/recommended:* 19 total units are recommended; 4 English recommended, 3 math recommended, 3 science recommended, 3 foreign language recommended, 3 social studies recommended. Preference given to in-state applicants, but out-of-state applicants are encouraged to apply. TOEFL is required of all international students.

The Inside Word

It's hard to beat small, selective public colleges like Mary Washington for quality and cost, and more and more students are discovering this. The admissions process is very selective, and with the exception of preferential treatment for Virginia residents, functions in virtually the same manner as small private college admissions committees do. Students who are interested need to focus on putting their best into all aspects of the application.

FINANCIAL AID

Students should submit: FAFSA (due March 1). The Princeton Review suggests that all financial aid forms be submitted as soon as possible after January 1. *The following grants/scholarships are offered:* Pell, SEOG, academic merit, the school's own scholarships, state scholarships, private scholarships. *Students borrow from the following loan programs:* Stafford, unsubsidized Stafford, Perkins, PLUS. Applicants will be notified of awards beginning April 15. College Work-Study Program is available. Institutional employment is available.

FROM THE ADMISSIONS OFFICE

"Among institutions of higher learning in Virginia, Mary Washington College stands alone. The College is a unique blend of talented, inquisitive students and an exceptional faculty, brought together on a beautiful campus and served by superb facilities. The students come from all over the country and the world, and are instructed by a faculty that considers teaching its primary objective-research and publishing come second. The College is developing an innovative global awareness program that incorporates international perspectives into the academic curriculum. At the same time, the College offers its students exceptional opportunities for conducting and presenting undergraduate research. Through a program that provides more than $60,000 in research grant funds, undergraduates work individually with faculty members and can travel across the country to present their projects to a variety of conferences. The College recently completed a new campus art gallery and is currently renovating the fine arts complex."

ADMISSIONS

Admissions Rating	85
% of applicants accepted	52
% of acceptees attending	32

FRESHMAN PROFILE

Average verbal SAT	610
Average math SAT	580
Average ACT	NR
Average TOEFL	600
Graduated top 20% of class	69
Graduated top 40% of class	95
Graduated top 60% of class	98
Average HS GPA or Avg.	3.5

DEADLINES

Early decision	11/1
Regular admission	2/1
Regular notification	4/1
Non-fall registration	yes

APPLICANTS ALSO LOOK AT

AND OFTEN PREFER

William and Mary
Virginia

AND SOMETIMES PREFER

James Madison
U. Richmond

AND RARELY PREFER

George Mason
Longwood
Virginia Tech

FINANCIAL FACTS

Financial Aid Rating	80
In-state tuition	$2,086
Out-of-state tuition	$6,976
Room & board	$5,024
Estimated book expense	$650
% frosh receiving aid	55
% undergrads receiving aid	55
% aid is need-based	63
% frosh w/ grant (avg)	40 ($1,500)
% frosh w/ loan (avg)	50 ($2,500)
% UGs w/ job (avg)	20 ($1,250)
Off-campus job outlook	good

MARYLAND INSTITUTE, COLLEGE OF ART

1300 MOUNT ROYAL AVENUE, BALTIMORE, MD 21217   ADMISSIONS: 410-669-9200   FAX: 410-669-9206

CAMPUS LIFE

Quality of Life Rating **75**
Type of school   private
Affiliation   none
Environment   metropolis

STUDENTS
FT undergrad enrollment   788
% male/female   47/53
% from out of state   69
% live on campus   85
% spend weekend on campus   NR
% transfers   28
% from public high school   NR
% African-American   5
% Asian   7
% Caucasian   77
% Hispanic   5
% international   7
# of countries represented   36

WHAT'S HOT
different students interact
leftist politics
drugs
ethnic diversity on campus
cigarettes

WHAT'S NOT
student government
student publications

ACADEMICS

Academic Rating **85**
Profs Interesting Rating   84
Profs Accessible Rating   69
Calendar   semester
Student/teacher ratio   11:1
% profs PhD   81
Hours of study per day   4.05

MOST POPULAR MAJORS
general fine arts
painting
visual communications/graphic design

% GRADS WHO PURSUE...
MA 22

STUDENTS SPEAK OUT

Life
As one student explains, "The students here are very apathetic toward any community activities and toward starting student organization or clubs." Most students spend so much time in the studio and studying—about four hours a day, not including class time—that they simply don't have time to have fun ("We end up critiquing our work together a lot in our spare time"). A student organization does bring many fine, offbeat films to the school and students organize gallery showings. Drinking and drugs are not unheard of here, "since there is little to do on or around campus," as one student claims. Those who kick back seem to enjoy themselves: "For fun we go camping, throw a party, smoke weed, make a movie, go dancing." Many respondents extol the virtues of Baltimore. One brags that "Baltimore is deservedly famous for being full of weirdos. It has the nation's highest rate of mental illness [a dubious assertion—ed.]." Another points out that "being in Baltimore, between Philadelphia and Washington, gives us access to large art communities. This is important."

Academics
Students at MICA report that a cozy, homey atmosphere is the norm at this small school. "I feel that the teachers here are not 'teachers of art,' but rather are people who help us learn about ourselves, which is very important," writes one. Another exclaims, "The teachers possess fire for art. They aren't burnt out careless cement blocks." And one, apparently referring to the sometimes controversial nature of students' artwork here, reports that, "My experience here is that administration has been supportive of me and willing to take my side, even though I've raised the eyebrows of a few. I've especially had great support from my instructors and other faculty." Students tell us that the atmosphere here is intense—most spend practically every waking hour in the studio—but not cut-throat. "The pressure and the expected amount of work here pushes the students beyond their natural limits, but being surrounded by art and artists gives a vision of possibility." Most classes meet once a week for five to six hours a day, allowing students to work on one specific skill in concentrated bursts. Atypical of most arts schools, several students here note that the curriculum features "excellent foundation courses." And most agree with this praise: "I've never seen such an intelligent group of people remain so down to earth!"

Student Body
MICA students tend to be unconventional; wrote one, "They're all the people who stood out in H.S. They're made up of minds and talents which set them apart as freaks...Here these qualities are normal." And another offers, "We dig each other's different quirks." Students tend to be "extremely artistically expressive, socially liberal, scary looking but generally good-hearted individuals." Despite some complaints regarding clique formation "during the first week of classes" students note that at MICA, "you create strong bonds between your peers who experience this process and journey with you."

MARYLAND INSTITUTE, COLLEGE OF ART

FINANCIAL AID: 410-225-2285

WEB SITE: HTTP://WWW.MICA.EDU/

ADMISSIONS

The admissions committee considers (in descending order of importance): HS record, class rank, essay, test scores. *Also considered (in descending order of importance):* special talents, personality, extracurriculars. Either the SAT or ACT is required. An interview is recommended. Admissions process is need-blind. Portfolio of 12 to 20 pieces, including three drawings, required. Samples of drawing from observation (rather than from the imagination or copies of photographs) strongly recommended. Other pieces should represent best and most recent work. *Special Requirements:* A portfolio is required for art program applicants. TOEFL is required of all international students.

The Inside Word

Maryland Institute enjoys a very solid reputation among high school art teachers. This is one reason why the Institute is able to draw a sizable applicant pool of talented young artists year in and year out. Another reason is that it is truly a top quality choice. The admissions staff devotes a significant amount of their recruitment efforts towards helping students to understand how to put together a strong portfolio. Many talented students have little awareness of how to best showcase their skills, and Maryland Institute has done much to improve their knowledge. No doubt it has paid off in its student body.

FINANCIAL AID

Students should submit: FAFSA (due March 15), the school's own financial aid form (due March 15). The Princeton Review suggests that all financial aid forms be submitted as soon as possible after January 1. *The following grants/scholarships are offered:* Pell, SEOG, the school's own scholarships, the school's own grants, state scholarships, state grants, private scholarships, private grants. *Students borrow from the following loan programs:* Stafford, Perkins, PLUS. Applicants will be notified of awards beginning April 15. College Work-Study Program is available. Institutional employment is available.

FROM THE ADMISSIONS OFFICE

"Students who attend the Maryland Institute are generally certain about their decision to study art. They seek an academic and artistic community that is serious and supportive, but which allows them independence and self-direction. They are often interested in the connections that artists make between words, images, and ideas, and tend to integrate what they think and what they do into their lives in a way that most colleges do not. The Institute brings together some of the best students and faculty in the nation; individuals who are interested in the rich linkages that occur when the bright and the talented interact—student with student, student with faculty, and faculty with faculty. You will also find at the Institute philosophers and poets critiquing in the studio, photographers and painters writing books, and a physicist who paints! There is an unusual wholeness to living and learning at the Maryland Institute."

ADMISSIONS

Admissions Rating	81
% of applicants accepted	66
% of acceptees attending	38

FRESHMAN PROFILE

Average verbal SAT	NR
Average math SAT	NR
Average ACT	NR
Average TOEFL	525
Graduated top 20% of class	NR
Graduated top 40% of class	NR
Graduated top 60% of class	NR
Average HS GPA or Avg.	3.1

DEADLINES

Early decision	11/15
Regular admission	3/1
Regular notification	rolling
Non-fall registration	yes

APPLICANTS ALSO LOOK AT

AND OFTEN PREFER
RISD
Cooper Union

AND SOMETIMES PREFER
School of the Art Inst. of Chicago
Pratt Inst.
School of Visual Arts

FINANCIAL FACTS

Financial Aid Rating	82
Tuition	$15,950
Room & board	$5,490
Estimated book expense	$1,200
% frosh receiving aid	72
% undergrads receiving aid	70
% aid is need-based	65
% frosh w/ grant (avg)	65 ($4,178)
% frosh w/ loan (avg)	59 ($2,625)
% UGs w/ job (avg)	30 ($1,100)
Off-campus job outlook	good

UNIVERSITY OF MARYLAND-COLLEGE PARK

COLLEGE PARK, MD 20742   ADMISSIONS: 301-314-8385   FAX: 301-314-9560

CAMPUS LIFE

Quality of Life Rating	**69**
Type of school	public
Affiliation	none
Environment	city

STUDENTS

FT undergrad enrollment	20,344
% male/female	52/48
% from out of state	25
% live on campus	35
% spend weekend on campus	25
% transfers	42
% from public high school	87
% in (# of) fraternities	12 (26)
% in (# of) sororities	15 (19)
% African-American	14
% Asian	14
% Caucasian	63
% Hispanic	4
% international	5
# of countries represented	146

WHAT'S HOT
student publications
cigarettes
ethnic diversity on campus
health facilities
intercollegiate sports

WHAT'S NOT
students are unhappy
campus difficult to get around
theater
inefficient administration

ACADEMICS

Academic Rating	**70**
Profs Interesting Rating	62
Profs Accessible Rating	63
Calendar	semester
Student/teacher ratio	13:1
% profs PhD/tenured	92/88
Hours of study per day	2.87

MOST POPULAR MAJORS
government politics
electrical engineering
business

% GRADS WHO PURSUE...
Law 12, Med 7, MBA 2, MA 15

STUDENTS SPEAK OUT

Life

UMD students are active boosters of their varsity teams (called the Terrapins), and particularly love the football, lacrosse, and basketball teams. Especially basketball. "My freshman year, I had to camp out a couple of times for b-ball tickets." The university is a member of the Atlantic Coast Conference, competing against the likes of Duke, UNC, FSU, and other national athletic powers. While there once was a party atmosphere here, it has been tempered by Maryland's rising academic profile. The town of College Park is "not up to its potential," but with a student body of nearly 20,000, you're already in a small city while on campus. Frats and Sororities are "not as big as they were, but still very powerful and a big influence on campus life." For those who have cars and money to spend, D.C. is close by ("I live in D.C. on weekends," says one student) and Baltimore is not much farther away. Car owners complain to us that legal parking is scarce and that they are regularly ticketed.

Academics

Though Maryland is a fine institution all around, students in the university's honors program are hands down the most enthusiastic; for those who qualify, classes are smaller and easier to get into. "The honors program is what makes the difference for me." Says another, "professors in the honors program are wonderful...honors seminars give students a chance to interact with outstanding faculty in small-class, discussion-based environments." Students in regular classes are not as enthusiastic, but the university has given lots of attention to improving the academic experience for everyone. It appears to be working. According to one student, "for a big school, it feels a lot smaller." As at many of the large universities in *Best 310 Colleges*, some students complain of large lecture classes and science/engineering TAs whose command of English is unimpressive. But many students also point out that large size also translates into lots of choices. The school has excellent engineering, physics, and economics departments, theater majors are vocal boosters of their program, and business is "hugely popular." Maryland's core curriculum requires students to fulfill a wide range of distribution requirements and then, during senior year, take two seminars designed to help students integrate these disparate courses into their major fields of study. Finally, our respondents report that, while some of their classmates "coast through" their four years, many students here are serious about their studies and find their programs academically challenging. Some manage to find the perfect balance between the social and academic opportunities, as attested to by one student who tells us that "if beer weren't here I probably wouldn't be double-majoring now."

Student Body

One thing is certain about the students in College Park—the majority begin their experience on the same page. Literally two-thirds of the student body named Maryland as their first choice at the time they applied to college. By legislative mandate, three quarters of the university's students are residents of the state. Although the student body is ethnically diverse, different groups generally "don't mix as much as they could." But with this many classmates, almost any Maryland student will eventually find a group to fit into, although finding it may take a bit of time. Those who make the effort reap the benefits. Says one student, "most of my friends are from different backgrounds."

UNIVERSITY OF MARYLAND-COLLEGE PARK ▣(VHS)

FINANCIAL AID: 301-314-8313   E-MAIL: UMADMIT@UGA.UMD.EDU   WEB SITE: HTTP://INFORM.UMD.EDU/

ADMISSIONS

The admissions committee considers (in descending order of importance): HS record, test scores, class rank, recommendations, essay. *Also considered (in descending order of importance):* alumni relationship, extracurriculars, geographical distribution, personality, special talents. Either the SAT or ACT is required. Admissions process is need-blind. *High school units required/recommended:* 20 total units are recommended; 4 English recommended, 3 math recommended, 2 science recommended, 2 foreign language recommended, 3 social studies recommended. *Special Requirements:* A portfolio is required for art program applicants. An audition is required for music program applicants. TOEFL is required of all international students. Portfolio required of architecture and design program applicants. *The admissions office says:* "Honors or AP courses are strongly advised for students whose high schools offer them."

The Inside Word

Maryland's initial candidate review process emphasizes academic credentials and preparedness. Through this first review, roughly twenty percent of the applicant pool is either admitted or denied. The remaining eighty percent are then evaluated in depth by admissions officers and reviewed by an admissions committee of seven, who collectively decide upon each candidate. Don't take essays and the compilation of other personal material that is required of applicants lightly. It's uncommon for a large university to devote this kind of attention to candidate selection. Perhaps this explains why so many of the students here made Maryland their first choice.

FINANCIAL AID

Students should submit: FAFSA (due February 15). The Princeton Review suggests that all financial aid forms be submitted as soon as possible after January 1. *The following grants/scholarships are offered:* Pell, SEOG, academic merit, athletic, the school's own scholarships, the school's own grants, state scholarships, state grants, private scholarships, private grants. *Students borrow from the following loan programs:* Stafford, unsubsidized Stafford, Perkins, PLUS, the school's own loan fund. Applicants will be notified of awards beginning in early April. College Work-Study Program is available. Institutional employment is available.

FROM THE ADMISSIONS OFFICE

"Commitment to excellence, to diversity, to learning—these are the hallmarks of a Maryland education. As the state's flagship campus and one of the nation's leading public universities Maryland offers students and faculty the opportunity to come together to explore and create knowledge, to debate and discover our similarities and our differences, and to serve as a model of intellectual and cultural excellence for the state and the nation's capital. With leading programs in engineering, business, journalism, architecture and the sciences, the University offers an outstanding educational value."

ADMISSIONS

Admissions Rating	72
% of applicants accepted	69
% of acceptees attending	36

FRESHMAN PROFILE

Average verbal SAT	500
Average math SAT	590
Average ACT	NR
Average TOEFL	550
Graduated top 20% of class	53
Graduated top 40% of class	83
Graduated top 60% of class	96
Average HS GPA or Avg.	3.2

DEADLINES

Early decision	12/1
Regular admission	2/15
Regular notification	rolling
Non-fall registration	yes

APPLICANTS ALSO LOOK AT

AND OFTEN PREFER
UNC-Chapel Hill

AND SOMETIMES PREFER
Howard
Penn State-U. Park
Virginia Tech
NYU
U. Delaware

AND RARELY PREFER
George Washington
Hampton
Syracuse

FINANCIAL FACTS

Financial Aid Rating	70
In-state tuition	$3,494
Out-of-state tuition	$9,553
Room & board	$5,442
Estimated book expense	$566
% frosh receiving aid	57
% undergrads receiving aid	57
% aid is need-based	62
% frosh w/ grant (avg)	44 ($3,891)
% frosh w/ loan (avg)	38 ($4,837)
% UGs w/ job (avg)	22 ($1,818)
Off-campus job outlook	excellent

Massachusetts Institute of Technology

77 Massachusetts Avenue, Cambridge, MA 02139   Admissions: 617-253-4791   Fax: 617-258-8304

CAMPUS LIFE

Quality of Life Rating 79
Type of school private
Affiliation none
Environment metropolis

STUDENTS
FT undergrad enrollment 4,495
% male/female 62/38
% from out of state 92
% live on campus 94
% spend weekend on campus NR
% transfers 2
% from public high school 72
% in (# of) fraternities 50 (30)
% in (# of) sororities 30 (5)
% African-American 6
% Asian 29
% Caucasian 48
% Hispanic 9
% international 8
# of countries represented 104

WHAT'S HOT
ethnic diversity on campus
computer facilities
intramural sports
lab facilities
different students interact

WHAT'S NOT
unattractive campus
cigarettes
political activism
student government
sex

ACADEMICS

Academic Rating 94
Profs Interesting Rating 69
Profs Accessible Rating 63
Calendar 4-1-4
Student/teacher ratio 5:1
% profs tenured 99
Hours of study per day 4.25

MOST POPULAR MAJORS
electrical engineering/computer
mechanical engineering
computer science/engineering

% GRADS WHO PURSUE...
Law 1, Med 6, MBA 3, MA 45

STUDENTS SPEAK OUT

Life
For many MIT students, life begins and ends in the labs and libraries. "Cambridge may be great, but who has time to find out?" says one student. The word "hell" comes up a distressing number of times in students' descriptions of their surroundings; it's the kind of joke that must have a lot of truth behind it. One student tells us that the predominantly male population "requires girls to be bussed in from other colleges for parties. It's funny to see the 'meat trucks' come in with a new load every hour. The parties are composed mainly of dancing, beer drinking, and guys hitting on girls. It can be fun, but it leaves me searching for something more." "Meat trucks," eh? No wonder several students tell us that "sexism is pretty bad here." Why do students stay? One student lets us in on the MIT dark secret: "We'll all tell you we hate it, but it isn't so bad. I think we like it inside and just won't admit it."

Academics
There's an old MIT joke that goes, "MIT. Pick two: work, friends, sleep." By all indications, work is always one of the two choices. On average, MIT students put in four and a quarter hours of studying per day (only Cal Tech's students work harder). Not surprisingly, students here are under a lot of pressure to perform, and stress runs rampant. The school tries to relieve the pressure somewhat—freshmen take all courses pass/fail, and their fail grades are expunged from their records—but one sophomore expresses the prevalent attitude here: "I heard this is a great place to go to school and when I have graduated I'm sure I'll agree, but right now, it sucks." Those who can take the pressure benefit from "the best science education in the world, beyond doubt," one supplemented by "amazing resources" and world-famous professors. The Undergraduate Research Opportunities Program (UROP) allows undergrads to earn credit doing research, thereby giving them more autonomy than their peers at most other schools. Students who venture beyond the sciences will find excellent economics, humanities, and political science departments as well. The school offers so much that the opportunities can seem a little daunting: "Getting an education from MIT is like getting a drink from a firehose" is how one student puts it. The most common cause for complaint (besides the workload) is the quality of in-class instruction. Explains one student, "Classes are taught at a level to challenge Nobel prize-winners, so it's easy to get disillusioned and lost."

Student Body
Will all your classmates at MIT be nerds? More likely you'll find that there are "some pretty scary nerds here at MIT, but most people are pretty normal." MIT students are unhappy, particularly for a group of students at one of the nation's most prestigious institutions. For many, the pressure and intensity are overwhelming; says one, "It's too easy to turn into an emotionless machine, just doing problem sets. Only three months into my college career, I am losing my humanity." Minorities make up approximately forty percent of the student body: MIT is definitely an equal opportunity "hell." Still, when all is said and done, students keep coming here, and very few transfer out. Why subject yourself to this? Explains one student, "There are a large number of fantastically weird and frightfully smart people here—at last I have found people who understand me!"

FINANCIAL AID: 617-253-4971   E-MAIL: FROSH@MIT.EDU   WEB SITE: HTTP://WEB.MIT.EDU/

ADMISSIONS

The admissions committee considers (in descending order of importance): HS record, test scores, class rank, recommendations, essay. *Also considered (in descending order of importance):* extracurriculars, personality, special talents, alumni relationship. Either the SAT or ACT is required. An interview is required. Admissions process is need-blind. *High school units required/recommended:* 4 English recommended, 4 math recommended, 3 science recommended, 1 foreign language recommended, 2 history recommended. Rank in top tenth of secondary school class recommended. TOEFL is required of all international students.

The Inside Word

High academic achievement, lofty test scores, and the most rigorous high school course load possible are prerequisites for a successful candidacy. Among the most selective institutions in the country, MIT's admissions operation is easily one of the most down-to-earth and accessible. Over the years they have shown both a sense of humor in admissions literature and an awareness that applying to such a prestigious and demanding place creates a high level of anxiety in students. Their relaxed and helpful approach does much to temper such stress.

FINANCIAL AID

Students should submit: FAFSA (due March 1), the school's own financial aid form (due March 1), state aid form (due March 1), a copy of parents' most recent income tax filing (due March 1). The Princeton Review suggests that all financial aid forms be submitted as soon as possible after January 1. *The following grants/scholarships are offered:* Pell, SEOG, the school's own grants, state scholarships, state grants, private scholarships, private grants, ROTC, foreign aid. *Students borrow from the following loan programs:* Stafford, unsubsidized Stafford, Perkins, PLUS, the school's own loan fund. Applicants will be notified of awards beginning early April. College Work-Study Program is available. Institutional employment is available.

FROM THE ADMISSIONS OFFICE

"The students who come to the Massachusetts Institute of Technology are some of America's—and the world's—best and most creative. As graduates, they leave here to make real contributions—in science, technology, business, education, politics, architecture, and the arts. From any class, a handful will go on to do work that is historically significant. These young men and women are leaders, achievers, producers. Helping such students make the most of their talents and dreams would challenge any educational institution. MIT gives them its best advantages: a world-class faculty, unparalleled facilities, remarkable opportunities. In turn, these students help to make the Institute the vital place it is. They bring fresh viewpoints to faculty research: More than three-quarters participate in the Undergraduate Research Opportunities Program (UROP). They play on MIT's thirty-nine intercollegiate teams as well as in its fifteen musical ensembles. To their classes and to their out-of-class activities, they bring enthusiasm, energy, and individual style."

ADMISSIONS

Admissions Rating	99
% of applicants accepted	21
% of acceptees attending	54

FRESHMAN PROFILE

Average verbal SAT	700
Average math SAT	740
Average ACT	31
Average TOEFL	650
Graduated top 20% of class	99
Graduated top 40% of class	100
Graduated top 60% of class	NR
Average HS GPA or Avg.	NR

DEADLINES

Early decision	NR
Regular admission	1/1
Regular notification	4/1
Non-fall registration	no

APPLICANTS ALSO LOOK AT

AND SOMETIMES PREFER

Harvard/Radcliffe
Yale
Stanford
Cal Tech
Brown

AND RARELY PREFER

Princeton
Virginia
Cornell U.
Columbia
RPI

FINANCIAL FACTS

Financial Aid Rating	76
Tuition	$21,000
Room & board	$6,150
Estimated book expense	$800
% frosh receiving aid	62
% undergrads receiving aid	57
% aid is need-based	100
% frosh w/ grant (avg)	70 ($12,050)
% frosh w/ loan (avg)	63 ($5,202)
% UGs w/ job (avg)	55 ($1,650)
Off-campus job outlook	excellent

UNIVERSITY OF MASSACHUSETTS-AMHERST

WHITMORE BUILDING, AMHERST, MA 01003   ADMISSIONS: 413-545-3714   FAX: 413-545-4312

CAMPUS LIFE

Quality of Life Rating	**75**
Type of school	public
Affiliation	none
Environment	suburban

STUDENTS

FT undergrad enrollment	17,024
% male/female	52/48
% from out of state	27
% live on campus	61
% spend weekend on campus	80
% transfers	25
% from public high school	80
% in (# of) fraternities	8 (22)
% in (# of) sororities	6 (13)
% African-American	4
% Asian	6
% Caucasian	83
% Hispanic	4
% international	3
# of countries represented	77

WHAT'S HOT
political activism
student publications
ethnic diversity on campus
drugs
old-fashioned dating

WHAT'S NOT
inefficient administration
dorms
campus food
religion
unattractive campus

ACADEMICS

Academic Rating	**74**
Profs Interesting Rating	79
Profs Accessible Rating	66
Calendar	semester
Student/teacher ratio	17:1
% profs PhD/tenured	94/96
Hours of study per day	3.21

MOST POPULAR MAJORS
psychology
hotel/restaurant/travel admin.
English

STUDENTS SPEAK OUT

Life

Although references to the legendary style of partying abound in students' accounts of their present lives, the days of "Zoo Mass" are over. Still, the social scene thrives even if the "party school" reputation is dated. The social atmosphere is welcoming ("it's a place where anybody can fit in"); fraternities and sororities are available but students say there's no pressure to join. Amherst is considered "a great college town" that offers lots of opportunities for a good time. Many prefer to stay and make their own fun on campus, however, and the school's large scale affords students plenty of social and extracurricular opportunities. One blissful student describes his social life as "better than sex in summer rain." Students agree, however, "Opportunities don't come to you here; you've got to go out and get them yourself."

Academics

Students disagree about the quality of the education they receive at UMass. After a period of tuition hikes and the "loss of classes, professors, and library hours," things seem to be looking up recently after students raised their voices to the administration. A considerable number of students are satisfied with their experience here: "UMass does a damn good job living up to the strong reputation it has earned," writes one; the professors, who receive good grades for those at a public institution, are, according to one undergrad, "wonderful and very committed to teaching." In academics as well as social life, the school has effectively sobered up its image in the past decade. Respect for UMass as an academic institution has soared since then, as has the annual application rate. Recent budget cuts have hurt, and many students complain about their financial burdens. Membership in the Five College Consortium, however, lessens the impact of some of these cuts: students may use not only their own school's resources, but also those of four other highly regarded New England colleges (Amherst, Hampshire, Smith, and Mount Holyoke). The popularity of the consortium leads some to say that UMass-Amherst offers a private education "with a price a private school can't match." Preprofessional studies—business and management, communication, and engineering—are most popular here.

Student Body

Over seventy percent of the students here are Massachusetts natives; fourteen percent are minorities, which is a relatively small percentage, and black and Asian populations are pretty small. Students are generally very career- and goal-oriented, although, with over 18,000 classmates and potential friends at the four other consortium schools, most students can find others with common backgrounds without looking too hard.

ADMISSIONS

The admissions committee considers (in descending order of importance): HS record, class rank, test scores, recommendations, essay. *Also considered (in descending order of importance):* special talents, alumni relationship, extracurriculars, personality. Either the SAT or ACT is required; SAT is preferred. An interview is recommended. Admissions process is need-blind. *High school units required/recommended:* 16 total units are required; 4 English required, 3 math required, 3 science required, 2 foreign language required, 2 social studies required. *Special Requirements:* A portfolio is required for art program applicants. An audition is required for music program applicants. TOEFL is required of all international students. 4 units of math required of business, computer science, engineering, and math program applicants. 1/2 unit of trigonometry recommended of physical sciences and math program applicants. 1 unit of chemistry required of nursing program applicants. Chemistry and physics required of engineering program applicants.

The Inside Word

Gaining admission to UMass is not particularly difficult; most applicants with solid grades in high school are successful. A great choice for students who might have a tougher time getting in at other Five College Consortium members.

FINANCIAL AID

Students should submit: FAFSA (due February 15), state aid form (due May 1), a copy of parents' most recent income tax filing. The Princeton Review suggests that all financial aid forms be submitted as soon as possible after January 1. *The following grants/scholarships are offered:* Pell, SEOG, academic merit, athletic, the school's own scholarships, the school's own grants, state scholarships, state grants, private scholarships, ROTC. *Students borrow from the following loan programs:* Perkins, PLUS, state loans, private loans. College Work-Study Program is available. Institutional employment is available.

FROM THE ADMISSIONS OFFICE

"The University of Massachusetts Amherst is the largest public university in New England, offering its students an almost limitless variety of academic programs and activities. More than one hundred majors are offered, including a unique program called Bachelor's Degree with Individual Concentration (BDIC) in which students create their own program of study. The outstanding faculty of 1,100 includes novelist John Wideman, Pulitzer Prize winners Madeleine Blais and James Tate, Grammy nominee Max Roach, and five members of the prestigious National Academy of Sciences. Students can take courses through the honors program and sample classes at nearby Amherst, Hampshire, Mount Holyoke, and Smith Colleges at no extra charge. And the University's extensive library system is the largest at any public institution in the Northeast. "Extracurricular activities include more than two hundred and fifty clubs and organizations, fraternities and sororities, multicultural and religious centers, and NCAA Division I sports for men and women. Student-operated businesses, the largest college daily newspaper in the region, and an active student government provide hands-on experiences. More than ten thousand students a year participate in the intramural sports program. The picturesque New England town of Amherst offers shopping and dining and the ski slopes of western Massachusetts and southern Vermont are close by."

ADMISSIONS

Admissions Rating	68
% of applicants accepted	78
% of acceptees attending	29

FRESHMAN PROFILE

Average verbal SAT	610
Average math SAT	510
Average ACT	NR
Average TOEFL	550
Graduated top 20% of class	29
Graduated top 40% of class	61
Graduated top 60% of class	87
Average HS GPA or Avg.	NR

DEADLINES

Early decision	NR
Regular admission	2/1
Regular notification	rolling
Non-fall registration	yes

APPLICANTS ALSO LOOK AT
AND OFTEN PREFER

Dartmouth
Boston Coll.

AND SOMETIMES PREFER

U. Vermont
U. New Hampshire
U. Conn
Boston U.
Syracuse

AND RARELY PREFER

Northeastern
U. Rhode Island
SUNY Albany
U. Maine-Orono
Worcester Poly.

FINANCIAL FACTS

Financial Aid Rating	67
In-state tuition	$2,220
Out-of-state tuition	$8,566
Room & board	$4,022
Estimated book expense	$500
% frosh receiving aid	60
% undergrads receiving aid	55
% aid is need-based	NR
% frosh w/ grant (avg)	NR ($2,300)
% frosh w/ loan (avg)	55 ($2,600)
% UGs w/ job (avg)	50 ($1,600)
Off-campus job outlook	good

McGill University

847 Sherbrooke Street West, Montreal, Quebec, CN H3A 3N6   Admissions: 514-398-4455   Fax: 514-398-4193

CAMPUS LIFE

Quality of Life Rating	87
Type of school	public
Affiliation	none
Environment	metropolis

STUDENTS

FT undergrad enrollment	14,375
% male/female	45/55
% from out of state	NR
% live on campus	9
% spend weekend on campus	NR
% transfers	NR
% from public high school	NR
% in (# of) fraternities	(14)
% in (# of) sororities	1 (4)
% African-American	NR
% Asian	NR
% Caucasian	NR
% Hispanic	NR
% international	1
# of countries represented	120

WHAT'S HOT

Montreal, Quebec
off-campus food
different students interact
registration is a breeze
ethnic diversity on campus

WHAT'S NOT

computer facilities
religion
political activism
library
lab facilities

ACADEMICS

Academic Rating	83
Profs Interesting Rating	63
Profs Accessible Rating	63
Calendar	semester
Student/teacher ratio	NR
% profs PhD	85
Hours of study per day	3.01

STUDENTS SPEAK OUT

Life

"I'm having a ball. I love McGill," says one student. Jeez, so does everyone else! The outpouring of positive comments from McGill undergrads about their lives here is staggering. Here we go. "It is an unforgettable experience." "The beer is great, cold, and cheap." "The nightlife [in Montreal] is among the greatest in North America." "McGill is the best school in the world in the most amazing city." "Coffee in the cafeteria is fantastic." "It's an incredible experience, as an American, to study in Canada and be a part of Canadian culture." "Great smoked meat." "Montreal is a beautiful, historic, multicultural, safe city." "McGill provides an opportunity to study with people from all over the world. A friend I have is a princess when she is in Nairobi but is a student worrying about exams when she is in Montreal at McGill." "Montreal rocks!" Are there downsides, you ask? There are a few. "Not enough people get stoned." "Students are apathetic." "Undergrads, when bored, start inventing strange games." "Everybody smokes cigarettes! It's insane!" Do you get the picture here folks? Everyone loves Montreal, a city of over three million people. If you eat off campus, the food is incredible. The drug and alcohol policies are lenient. International students are treated well, about one-fifth of students speak French as a first language, and McGill is just a really neat place to go to school.

Academics

For all of the crowing from students about McGill being the best possible place to get a great education, the administration gets average to below-average marks. It's a shame, because McGill, one of Canada's most prestigious schools, has tons to offer academically. Students are distracted by the university's administrative problems: "Nobody cares about you at all, and they don't even do a good job faking it," says one dejected junior. "No matter what you need, you'll have to wait in line for it," says another. Professors fare better: "[Professors] are always willing to offer help if you need it." Still, even profs are by no means left unscathed. Says one, "Professors radiate self-importance. I have however learned good study skills, as well as independence." The difficulty-level of the coursework is high, with most students studying three to five hours or more a day. "Academic programs are challenging and course material interesting," explains a history major, while a junior studying biochemistry adds, "exams are really tough." The statement that seems to sum up the McGill academic experience is, unfortunately, this: "McGill is a triumph of bureaucracy over scholarship."

Student Body

"Never had any serious disagreements with my fellow students, except for the strange trend for those living away from home to slowly turn vegetarian. I hate feeling guilty for a good steak." So, if you're an inveterate carnivore, think twice about making the move to Canada. Otherwise, check out the student body at McGill, which is wonderfully diverse, yet unified. "It's amazing to see so many diverse individuals accepting and learning from each others' differences," lauds a sophomore. Another student explains, "Everyone does what they wish to. There are no barriers that stop my activities." Discrimination against minority groups does not seem to be much of a problem at McGill, perhaps due to its intense urban setting and that Canadian "je-ne-sais-quois." Politics lean left, yet few undergrads are active in political or social causes. Says one, "It is worth mentioning that the student body is quite apathetic." They do take sex seriously though, with the overwhelming majority describing themselves as sexually active.

McGill University

ADMISSIONS

The admissions committee considers (in descending order of importance): HS record, test scores, class rank, recommendations. *Also considered (in descending order of importance):* extracurriculars, special talents. Either the SAT or ACT is required; SAT is preferred. College-preparatory academic program recommended. Minimum SAT I scores of 550 in both verbal and math required of U.S. applicants. Three SAT II also required of U.S. applicants; specific tests required vary according to program. *Special Requirements:* Portfolio required of architecture program applicants; audition required of music program applicants; language tests required of English and/or French as a Second Language program applicants. *The admissions office says:* "Admissions requirements vary from school to school (there are six different schools, each specializing in a specific discipline, at McGill) and are very demanding. Students should have taken the most difficult courses in their chosen field; that is, engineers, nursing students, science students, etc., should have taken the maximum number of science and math courses available to them. American students with Advanced Placement grades of 3 or better will be granted some advanced standing."

The Inside Word

McGill is as tough as it comes in Canadian higher education; the university's entrance requirements are rigorous, and so are its academic standards. American citizens who aspire to attend McGill need to be especially well prepared; the university is heavily subsidized by the Canadian government, and few spaces in the entering class go to Americans looking to take advantage of favorable financial circumstances. The admissions process is thorough and demanding, and high SAT Is just don't have the same clout across the border. Students who are serious about McGill should put extra energy into French classes. While English is the language of instruction, French is the language of Montreal, and those who speak it fare much better than those who do not in everyday life.

FINANCIAL AID

Students should submit: FAFSA, the school's own financial aid form. The Princeton Review suggests that all financial aid forms be submitted as soon as possible after January 1. *The following grants/scholarships are offered:* academic merit, the school's own scholarships, foreign aid. *Students borrow from the following loan programs:* Stafford, unsubsidized Stafford, PLUS, the school's own loan fund. College Work-Study Program is available. Institutional employment is available. Freshmen are discouraged from working.

FROM THE ADMISSIONS OFFICE

McGill processes over 18,000 new applications for the September and January sessions.

ADMISSIONS

Admissions Rating	91
% of applicants accepted	46
% of acceptees attending	53

FRESHMAN PROFILE
Average verbal SAT	NR
Average math SAT	NR
Average ACT	NR
Average TOEFL	550
Graduated top 20% of class	NR
Graduated top 40% of class	NR
Graduated top 60% of class	NR
Average HS GPA or Avg.	NR

DEADLINES
Early decision	1/15
Regular admission	NR
Regular notification	4/15
Non-fall registration	yes

APPLICANTS ALSO LOOK AT
AND SOMETIMES PREFER
Duke
U. Michigan-Ann Arbor
U. Wisconsin-Madison
NYU
Boston U.
AND RARELY PREFER
Queens U. (Canada)

FINANCIAL FACTS

Financial Aid Rating	81
In-state tuition	$1,700
Out-of-state tuition	$7,460
Room & board	$4,461
Estimated book expense	$1,000
% frosh receiving aid	NR
% undergrads receiving aid	35
% aid is need-based	100
% frosh w/ grant (avg)	1 ($2,000)
% frosh w/ loan (avg)	NR
% UGs w/ job (avg)	NR
Off-campus job outlook	fair

MIAMI UNIVERSITY

Oxford, OH 45056
Admissions: 513-529-2531   Fax: 513-529-3841

STUDENTS SPEAK OUT

Life

Miami University is often referred to as "Mother Miami" by students frustrated by the numerous campus regulations. One explains, "The administration seems to forget that we are adults, and tightens the reins on our freedom daily," although "limited visitation" dorms (2 of 14) are now optional for first-years. A particularly onerous restriction is the campus-wide no car policy, which hinders some of the city-loving students ("Cincinnati and Dayton are an hour away by car"). Many students love the sheltered environment and isolation, however, contending that "once you are on campus, it is hard to leave due to its incredible beauty." Located in what one student sarcastically calls "the middle of a cornfield," the stately campus is described as "a haven for red bricklayers." Social life is dominated by the Greeks ("Although less than half of the students are in fraternities or sororities, the Greek system rules the school"). Off-campus socializing, popular among non-Greeks and those living off campus, centers on the "uptown" area, where most bars are found. The town of Oxford gets little praise from students; explains one student, "Oxford is an extremely rural town with limited night life. Either you go to a frat party, or you go drinking uptown and then come back for Bruno's Pizza or a Chuckburger." Intramural sports are extremely popular, as is intercollegiate men's basketball, and men's hockey games "are always sold out."

Academics

In its more than 180 years of existence, Miami University (located in Ohio, not Florida), has cultivated and maintained its reputation as a "public Ivy League" school. Selective by state university standards, Miami of Ohio offers nationally heralded programs at a low price tag. The School of Business Administration is known as the school's best; at the other end of the academic spectrum is the much-praised Western College, a liberal arts-intensive program stressing interdisciplinary study. Students in the business school and in many of the other major divisions complain that required classes can be difficult to get into and that classes can be large, but they also report an overall high level of satisfaction with the school. Students in the more intimate Western College are freer with their praise: writes one, "At Western, profs are accessible, discussions small, and there's lotsa community and student-faculty interaction." Professors in all programs receive good ratings from students, who praise them more for their "great accessibility" than their teaching. Of the administration, most students seem to agree that "Miami is run in a very businesslike manner. The result is a smoothly run yet less-personal atmosphere."

Student Body

The Miami University student body is almost all white and conservative ("College Republicans is the largest student organization on campus"). Students jokingly refer to Miami as "J. Crew U" and many report that "most students are cookie cutouts of each other: 'beautiful girls and macho men.' Not many dare to be different and if they do, the difference is obvious." The exceptions are students at Western, who have a decidedly "alternative" look.

ADMISSIONS

The admissions committee considers (in descending order of importance): HS record, class rank, test scores, recommendations, essay. *Also considered (in descending order of importance):* alumni relationship, extracurriculars, personality, special talents. Either the SAT or ACT is required. Admissions process is need-blind. *High school units required/recommended:* 15 total units are recommended; 4 English recommended, 3 math recommended, 3 science recommended, 2 foreign language recommended, 3 social studies recommended. *Special Requirements:* A portfolio is required for art program applicants. An audition is required for music program applicants. Interview required of architecture program applicants.

The Inside Word

Miami is one of the few selective public universities with an admissions process similar to those at highly selective private colleges. The university takes into account a variety of institutional needs as well as the qualifications of individual candidates when making admissions decisions. Don't be deceived by a high acceptance rate; the academic requirements for admission are quite high. Even so, students who are weak academically but add to Miami's "diversity" will get a leg up from the admissions committee.

FINANCIAL AID

Students should submit: FAFSA (due February 15). The Princeton Review suggests that all financial aid forms be submitted as soon as possible after January 1. *The following grants/scholarships are offered:* Pell, SEOG, academic merit, athletic, the school's own scholarships, the school's own grants, state scholarships, state grants, private scholarships, private grants, ROTC, foreign aid. *Students borrow from the following loan programs:* unsubsidized Stafford, Perkins, the school's own loan fund, supplemental loans, state loans, private loans. Applicants will be notified of awards beginning mid-March. College Work-Study Program is available. Institutional employment is available.

FROM THE ADMISSIONS OFFICE

"Miami's primary concern is its students. This concern is reflected in a broad array of efforts to develop the potential of each student. The University endeavors to individualize the educational experience. It provides personal and professional guidance; and it offers opportunities for its students to achieve understanding and appreciation not only of their own culture but of the cultures of others as well. Selected undergraduate, graduate, and professional programs of quality should be offered with the expectation of students achieving a high level of competence and understanding and developing a personal value system. Since the legislation creating Miami University stated that a leading mission of the University was to promote 'good education, virtue, religion, and morality,' the University has been striving to emphasize the supreme importance of dealing with problems relating to values."

ADMISSIONS

Admissions Rating	80
% of applicants accepted	74
% of acceptees attending	41

FRESHMAN PROFILE

Average verbal SAT	520
Average math SAT	610
Average ACT	26
Average TOEFL	530
Graduated top 20% of class	71
Graduated top 40% of class	94
Graduated top 60% of class	97
Average HS GPA or Avg.	NR

DEADLINES

Early decision	NR
Regular admission	1/31
Regular notification	3/15
Non-fall registration	yes

APPLICANTS ALSO LOOK AT

AND OFTEN PREFER

Northwestern U.
U. Michigan-Ann Arbor
Indiana U.-Bloomington

AND SOMETIMES PREFER

Ohio U.
Ohio State-Columbus
Dayton

AND RARELY PREFER

- Dickinson

FINANCIAL FACTS

Financial Aid Rating	75
In-state tuition	$5,098
Out-of-state tuition	$10,854
Room & board	$4,440
Estimated book expense	$550
% frosh receiving aid	54
% undergrads receiving aid	51
% aid is need-based	66
% frosh w/ grant (avg)	32 ($3,274)
% frosh w/ loan (avg)	42 ($4,422)
% UGs w/ job (avg)	23 ($1,400)
Off-campus job outlook	good

UNIVERSITY OF MIAMI

CORAL GABLES, FL 33124   ADMISSIONS: 305-284-4323   FAX: 305-284-2509

CAMPUS LIFE

Quality of Life Rating	**89**
Type of school	private
Affiliation	none
Environment	suburban

STUDENTS

FT undergrad enrollment	7,297
% male/female	51/49
% from out of state	49
% live on campus	43
% spend weekend on campus	NR
% transfers	29
% from public high school	NR
% in (# of) fraternities	15 (15)
% in (# of) sororities	13 (10)
% African-American	10
% Asian	5
% Caucasian	48
% Hispanic	25
% international	12
# of countries represented	108

WHAT'S HOT
ethnic diversity on campus
intercollegiate sports
intramural sports
different students interact
old-fashioned dating

WHAT'S NOT
political activism
theater
campus food

ACADEMICS

Academic Rating	**82**
Profs Interesting Rating	79
Profs Accessible Rating	85
Calendar	semester
Student/teacher ratio	7:1
% profs PhD/tenured	87/99
Hours of study per day	2.69

MOST POPULAR MAJORS
psychology
biology
finance

STUDENTS SPEAK OUT

Life

Students at the University of Miami note that "there is little on-campus entertainment, just bowling and pool." However, with the city of Miami and the beach close by, this lack of on-campus fun hardly matters. "Nearby fun spots abound—Coconut Grove, South Beach—and are close to campus. The city of Miami offers everything from trendy nightclubs to excellent beaches. Key West and the Everglades are only a couple of hours away." Also, students report, "The residential colleges provide some programs for students who live on campus. You don't have to live off campus to have fun!" Be forewarned that "the campus is located along US 1, which makes the location pretty inconvenient unless you have a car." Students boast that "this campus is so beautiful and the weather so nice that everything you do is made that much more enjoyable. It's motivating!" Primary in most students' minds are intercollegiate sports. "Sports are big, especially during football season. I can't imagine myself away from campus during Homecoming.

Academics

Like many larger universities, the University of Miami is best suited to self-starters who can handle the task of navigating lots of administrative red tape and the accompanying stress. Also, like similar schools, it is much more user-friendly to those in smaller departments. "The administration is a larger bureaucracy than Congress, but with less freedom," gripes one of the school's many accounting majors; "The administration is excellent. I have daily contact with them, and it is obvious that they care about the student body," counters an international studies major. As in all other aspects of the school, professors receive mixed grades. "Professors make the classroom interesting. They do their best to make the material fun." Writes one sophomore: "Professors seem to be more worried about research than about teaching." The overall impression one gets is that professors and administrators willingly make themselves available but rarely initiate contacts with students; they are, instead, receptive to those assertive enough to ask. All students agree that Honors students receive both "priority treatment" from administrators and the most lavish attention of their professors.

Student Body

UMiami students boast that an air of Southern cheerfulness pervades their campus. "This is an extremely social campus. People are easy to get along with," writes one student. Says another, "This is a close-knit student body. It's so diverse, but when it comes right down to it, we're all 'Canes!" Still, others complain that "campus life is fractured and cliquish. Lots of snobs." One warns, "A lot of people here are pretty wealthy and they like to flaunt it by driving Jags and carrying cellular phones or beepers to class. It's pretty obnoxious."

FINANCIAL AID: 305-284-5212

ADMISSIONS

The admissions committee considers (in descending order of importance): HS record, class rank, recommendations, test scores, essay. *Also considered (in descending order of importance):* alumni relationship, extracurriculars, geographical distribution, personality, special talents. Either the SAT or ACT is required. Admissions process is need-blind. *High school units required/recommended:* 4 English recommended, 3 math recommended, 3 science recommended, 2 foreign language recommended, 3 social studies recommended. *Special Requirements:* An audition is required for music program applicants. TOEFL is required of all international students. Three SAT II tests (English, chemistry, and math level II) required of applicants to dual-admission medical school program (enrolls Florida residents only).

The Inside Word

Miami gets far more national attention for the escapades of the 'Canes on and off the football field than it does for academic excellence. Anyone who takes a closer look will find national-caliber programs in several areas. While in general it is fairly easy for any good student to gain admission, candidates who apply for the Schools of Music and Marine Sciences will face lots of competition and rigorous screening from the admissions committee.

FINANCIAL AID

Students should submit: FAFSA, the school's own financial aid form, state aid form. The Princeton Review suggests that all financial aid forms be submitted as soon as possible after January 1. *The following grants/scholarships are offered:* Pell, SEOG, academic merit, athletic, the school's own scholarships, the school's own grants, state scholarships, state grants, private scholarships, private grants, federal nursing scholarship, ROTC. *Students borrow from the following loan programs:* Stafford, unsubsidized Stafford, Perkins, PLUS, the school's own loan fund, private loans. Applicants will be notified of awards beginning March 1. College Work-Study Program is available. Institutional employment is available.

FROM THE ADMISSIONS OFFICE

"A private university located in the beautiful, tropical suburb of Coral Gables, the University of Miami is moderate in size for a major research university (8,000 undergraduates), but comprehensive with one hundred and thirty majors. UM features the intimacy of a small school by virtue of its unique residential college system, where students live with a faculty master and associate masters. Three-fourths of all undergraduate classes have twenty-six or fewer students. Study abroad programs are available in twenty-two countries and fifty-two universities. The location of the University in suburban Coral Gables, just a Metrorail ride away from booming metropolitan Miami—a city of the twenty-first century—offers students a magnificent array of cultural and career opportunities."

ADMISSIONS

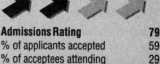

Admissions Rating	79
% of applicants accepted	59
% of acceptees attending	29

FRESHMAN PROFILE

Average verbal SAT	NR
Average math SAT	NR
Average ACT	25
Average TOEFL	550
Graduated top 20% of class	63
Graduated top 40% of class	85
Graduated top 60% of class	96
Average HS GPA or Avg.	NR

DEADLINES

Early decision	11/15
Regular admission	3/1
Regular notification	4/15
Non-fall registration	yes

APPLICANTS ALSO LOOK AT

AND OFTEN PREFER
Syracuse

AND SOMETIMES PREFER
Rollins
Florida International
Penn State-U. Park
Duke
Tulane

AND RARELY PREFER
Florida State

FINANCIAL FACTS

Financial Aid Rating	85
Tuition	$17,340
Room & board	$6,852
Estimated book expense	$630
% frosh receiving aid	78
% undergrads receiving aid	77
% aid is need-based	50
% frosh w/ grant (avg)	77 ($10,803)
% frosh w/ loan (avg)	59 ($5,539)
% UGs w/ job (avg)	40 ($2,000)
Off-campus job outlook	good

MICHIGAN STATE UNIVERSITY

EAST LANSING, MI 48824-0590   ADMISSIONS: 517-355-8332   FAX: 517-353-1647

CAMPUS LIFE

Quality of Life Rating   **77**
Type of school   public
Affiliation   none
Environment   city

STUDENTS
FT undergrad enrollment   27,011
% male/female   48/52
% from out of state   NR
% live on campus   46
% spend weekend on campus   60
% transfers   19
% from public high school   NR
% in (# of) fraternities   8 (35)
% in (# of) sororities   8 (19)
% African-American   8
% Asian   4
% Caucasian   82
% Hispanic   2
% international   2
# of countries represented   110

WHAT'S HOT
student publications
old-fashioned dating
intercollegiate sports
college radio
campus is beautiful

WHAT'S NOT
campus difficult to get around
inefficient administration
lab facilities
student government
theater

ACADEMICS

Academic Rating   **70**
Profs Interesting Rating   61
Profs Accessible Rating   62
Calendar   semester
Student/teacher ratio   16:1
% profs PhD/tenured   95/97
Hours of study per day   2.93

MOST POPULAR MAJORS
accounting
advertising
criminal justice

STUDENTS SPEAK OUT

Life

Michigan State University is located in East Lansing, a good college town. Almost half the students live in college housing, and Greek life is strong here. The annual spring concert and Greek Week are especially popular events. As in any very large school, there is a diversity of opinions as to what makes up MSU life. Some students enjoy it for its academic rigor. One premed comments that it's "an excellent pre-real world experience at MSU—a good test of your willingness to succeed." Others note the fanatical frenzy of the sports program, and student spirit for the Michigan State Spartans. Over forty-five percent of MSU students participate in intramural sports. One student summarizes the positive aspects of MSU life when she writes: "For fun? Who has time for fun? Just kidding—people here (including myself) go to the bars A LOT. Keg parties, intramural sports, Big Ten sports, etc. East Lansing is a great town with lots of things to do. Sometimes it's hard to study, because there is always a different drink special calling my name!"

Academics

MSU is a large school, which leads (necessarily) to some lack of personal attention—there are even six classes taught via television! One student writes us: "MSU is a huge school, so I expected large classes, but I was very disappointed by how many general education classes were overseen by TAs." TAs play a large role on campus because large lecture classes exist for most introductory subjects. Students at MSU have a wide range of majors to choose from—over 150, and if you don't find a major you like, you can design your own. The most popular majors are criminal justice, advertising, and accounting (reputedly excellent). MSU also has extensive international connections and offers the opportunity to study at seventy-six universities around the world. The students enjoy the contact (however limited) they have with the professors. One student comments that "Professors are great in upper-level classes." In spite of the size of the place they're trying to run, the administration gets reasonable marks; one sophomore writes that "The administration is helpful and hardworking."

Student Body

MSU has a mostly in-state Michigan population and eighty-two percent of the undergraduate student body is white. Some students feel that this leads to a homogeneous student body. One junior comments that MSU has "much racial tension." But others see it as a true melting pot because of the intensity of the desire for an education. Some students go as far as to say, "This place is very diverse—it seems most are accepting of others that are different. And if they aren't, they hide it pretty well."

FINANCIAL AID: 517-353-5940

WEB SITE: HTTP://WWW.MSU.EDU/

ADMISSIONS

The admissions committee considers (in descending order of importance): HS record, test scores, class rank, recommendations. *Also considered (in descending order of importance):* alumni relationship, extracurriculars, special talents. Either the SAT or ACT is required. *High school units required/recommended:* 4 English recommended, 3 math recommended, 2 science recommended, 2 foreign language recommended, 3 social studies recommended, 1 history recommended. Minimum composite ACT score of 21. *Special Requirements:* An audition is required for music program applicants.

The Inside Word

Gaining admission to MSU is a matter of following the formulas. Grades, tests, and rank—numbers, numbers, numbers. Solid extracurricular involvement and recommendations may help borderline candidates.

FINANCIAL AID

Students should submit: FAFSA (due rolling). The Princeton Review suggests that all financial aid forms be submitted as soon as possible after January 1. *The following grants/scholarships are offered:* Pell, SEOG, academic merit, athletic, the school's own scholarships, the school's own grants, state scholarships, state grants, private scholarships, private grants, ROTC. *Students borrow from the following loan programs:* Stafford, unsubsidized Stafford, Perkins, PLUS, the school's own loan fund, state loans, health professions loans, private loans. College Work-Study Program is available. Institutional employment is available.

FROM THE ADMISSIONS OFFICE

"Although Michigan State University is a graduate and research institution of international stature and acclaim, your undergraduate education is our highest priority. More than two thousand faculty members (ninety-five percent of whom hold the highest degree in their fields) are dedicated to providing academic instruction, guidance, and assistance to our undergraduate students. Our thirty-one thousand undergraduate students are a select group of academically motivated men and women. The diversity of ethnic, racial, religious, and socio-economic heritage makes the student body a microcosm of the state, national, and international community."

ADMISSIONS

Admissions Rating	67
% of applicants accepted	82
% of acceptees attending	40

FRESHMAN PROFILE

Average verbal SAT	550
Average math SAT	560
Average ACT	23
Average TOEFL	550
Graduated top 20% of class	42
Graduated top 40% of class	78
Graduated top 60% of class	95
Average HS GPA or Avg.	3.3

DEADLINES

Early decision	NR
Regular admission	7/30
Regular notification	rolling
Non-fall registration	yes

APPLICANTS ALSO LOOK AT

AND OFTEN PREFER

U. Michigan-Ann Arbor
Kalamazoo
Eastern Michigan
Central Michigan
Western Michigan

AND SOMETIMES PREFER

U. Illinois, Urbana-Champ.
Indiana U.-Bloomington
U. Wisconsin-Madison
Oakland

AND RARELY PREFER

Wayne State U.

FINANCIAL FACTS

Financial Aid Rating	78
In-state tuition	$3,983
Out-of-state tuition	$10,838
Room & board	$3,828
Estimated book expense	$608
% frosh receiving aid	61
% undergrads receiving aid	67
% aid is need-based	45
% frosh w/ grant (avg)	35 ($2,782)
% frosh w/ loan (avg)	50 ($4,949)
% UGs w/ job (avg)	22 ($2,420)
Off-campus job outlook	excellent

MICHIGAN TECHNOLOGICAL UNIVERSITY

1400 TOWNSEND DRIVE, HOUGHTON, MI 49931   ADMISSIONS: 906-487-2335   FAX: 906-487-3343

CAMPUS LIFE

Quality of Life Rating	**72**
Type of school	public
Affiliation	none
Environment	town

STUDENTS

FT undergrad enrollment	5,276
% male/female	75/25
% from out of state	23
% live on campus	36
% spend weekend on campus	80
% transfers	24
% from public high school	NR
% in (# of) fraternities	13 (16)
% in (# of) sororities	16 (8)
% African-American	2
% Asian	1
% Caucasian	89
% Hispanic	1
% international	4
# of countries represented	60

WHAT'S HOT
hard liquor
college radio
Greeks
student publications
intramural sports

WHAT'S NOT
dorms
theater
student government
sex
registration is a pain

ACADEMICS

Academic Rating	**76**
Profs Interesting Rating	68
Profs Accessible Rating	73
Calendar	quarter
Student/teacher ratio	16:1
% profs PhD	80
Hours of study per day	3.33

MOST POPULAR MAJORS
mechanical engineering
electrical engineering
civil engineering

STUDENTS SPEAK OUT

Life

"If you love small-town life and the great outdoors, you will love Tech," promises one satisfied Michigan Tech undergrad. Others concur. "Outdoor stuff is fun—like snowshoeing. Smelting in the Spring is always a blast." Smelting? And have you ever seen The Shining? Then pay attention to this quote: "A lot of people think the area is very pretty, but the long, cloudy winters get to some people." If you feel prone to Jack Nicholson-type outbursts, think hard about braving a Michigan winter in the small, isolated town of Houghton, which received fairly low marks from Tech students ("nothing to do"). Warns another, "Winter is pathetic, as well as six months long, so not much goes on except hockey and Winter Carnival. Alcohol warms up the body." Another adds, "Basically, here at Tech, if you don't drink, you don't have a social life. Frat parties and bars are usually the only places students can socialize." Greek life is indeed popular. Another student adds, "It is very white male, very conservative." He's right, men far outnumber women, and sometimes there are problems: "The common attitude [toward women] is 'We engineers, men only for engineers, uh, grunt, snort.'"

Academics

"I have yet to hear of a blow-off class at MTU." That's right, no Rocks for Jocks, no Underwater Basket Weaving. This is one of the top engineering schools in the country, and a bargain to boot. "To be successful here, you have to study a lot. If you expect to party much you'll probably be a C-D student," warns a mechanical engineering major. Luckily, students like their professors and classes, despite a few reservations (including the fact that a good percentage of introductory courses are also taught by TAs). Explains a senior studying chemical engineering, "Most of our professors care about the students and will spend hours outside of class explaining things we don't understand (or ever will)." The lectures are fairly large, as are most discussion groups and labs, so it's good that professors are accessible after class is over. The administration has some catching up to do. Registration procedures, health facilities, and the bursar all leave much to be desired. "When all is said and done...there is a lot more said than done," explains one MTU undergrad, while another rushes to the administration's defense. "I faced financial problems my first year," explains this sophomore, "and I received a tremendous amount of help from the administration."

Student Body

"The student body is small enough for a good education but large enough for everyone to be able to find people to get along with." This rosy view is held by many MTU students. Explains another, "Students are mostly geeks, but fun ones." This engineering major delves a bit deeper: "The majority of our student body consists of conservative, middle class white males. If you can get along with them, MTU is great." This student agrees, "I'm white, so I have to say that it's easier for me here than for non-whites, who tend to stay in their own cliques." Women of any color have it easier socially: "Female students date frequently." Indeed they report much better dating and sex lives than their male MTU counterparts. As far as diversity goes, well, listen to this sarcastic biology major: "Homosexuality is a word dared not spoken. Come on now, analytical and mathematical minds can't understand someone being different!" Counters another, however, "There are active minority, women's, and homosexual groups on campus."

MICHIGAN TECHNOLOGICAL UNIVERSITY

FINANCIAL AID: 906-487-2622   E-MAIL: CURT@MTU.EDU   WEB SITE: HTTP://WWW.MTU.EDU/

ADMISSIONS

The admissions committee considers (in descending order of importance): HS record, class rank, test scores, recommendations. *Also considered (in descending order of importance):* alumni relationship, extracurriculars, personality, special talents. ACT is preferred. An interview is recommended. Admissions process is need-blind. *High school units required/recommended:* 7 total units are required; 21 total units are recommended; 3 English required, 4 English recommended, 3 math required, 4 math recommended, 1 science required, 3 science recommended, 3 foreign language recommended, 3 social studies recommended, 1 history recommended. Recommended test scores and class rank vary with curriculum.

The Inside Word

Michigan Tech has a pretty good reputation and a highly self-selected applicant pool. In light of this, students who are interested should not be deceived by the high admit rate, and spend a little time on self-assessment of their ability to handle an engineering curriculum. There's nothing gained by getting yourself into a program that you can't get out of successfully.

FINANCIAL AID

Students should submit: FAFSA, state aid form. The Princeton Review suggests that all financial aid forms be submitted as soon as possible after January 1. *The following grants/scholarships are offered:* Pell, SEOG, academic merit, athletic, the school's own scholarships, the school's own grants, state scholarships, state grants, private scholarships, ROTC. *Students borrow from the following loan programs:* Stafford, unsubsidized Stafford, Perkins, PLUS, the school's own loan fund, state loans. Applicants will be notified of awards beginning March 30. College Work-Study Program is available. Institutional employment is available.

FROM THE ADMISSIONS OFFICE

"Michigan Tech is recognized as one of the nation's leading universities for undergraduate and graduate education in science and engineering. Its state-of-the-art campus is located near Lake Superior in Michigan's beautiful Upper Peninsula. The University owns and operates a downhill ski area and 18-hole golf course...MTU is one of Michigan's four nationally recognized research universities."

ADMISSIONS

Admissions Rating	76
% of applicants accepted	94
% of acceptees attending	44

FRESHMAN PROFILE

Average verbal SAT	650
Average math SAT	630
Average ACT	26
Average TOEFL	500
Graduated top 20% of class	64
Graduated top 40% of class	89
Graduated top 60% of class	97
Average HS GPA or Avg.	NR

DEADLINES

Early decision	NR
Regular admission	8/1
Regular notification	rolling
Non-fall registration	yes

APPLICANTS ALSO LOOK AT

AND SOMETIMES PREFER
Michigan State
U. Michigan-Ann Arbor
Wayne State U.

AND RARELY PREFER
GMI
Lawrence

FINANCIAL FACTS

Financial Aid Rating	81
In-state tuition	$3,717
Out-of-state tuition	$8,607
Room & board	$4,137
Estimated book expense	$900
% frosh receiving aid	71
% undergrads receiving aid	68
% aid is need-based	66
% frosh w/ grant (avg)	51 ($3,768)
% frosh w/ loan (avg)	50 ($3,529)
% UGs w/ job (avg)	34 ($1,200)
Off-campus job outlook	fair

UNIVERSITY OF MICHIGAN-ANN ARBOR

515 JEFFERSON, ANN ARBOR, MI 48104-2210   ADMISSIONS: 313-764-7433   FAX: 313-936-0740

CAMPUS LIFE

Quality of Life Rating **77**
Type of school   public
Affiliation   none
Environment   city

STUDENTS

FT undergrad enrollment	21,971
% male/female	52/48
% from out of state	33
% live on campus	32
% spend weekend on campus	NR
% transfers	4
% from public high school	80
% in (# of) fraternities	22 (39)
% in (# of) sororities	22 (23)
% African-American	8
% Asian	11
% Caucasian	72
% Hispanic	5
% international	3
# of countries represented	74

WHAT'S HOT
intercollegiate sports
computer facilities
library
Ann Arbor
hard liquor

WHAT'S NOT
student government
registration is a pain
students are unhappy
students are cliquish
theater

ACADEMICS

Academic Rating	**81**
Profs Interesting Rating	65
Profs Accessible Rating	66
Calendar	semester
Student/teacher ratio	11:1
% profs PhD/tenured	90/95
Hours of study per day	3.36

MOST POPULAR MAJORS
psychology
mechanical engineering
English

STUDENTS SPEAK OUT

Life
Social life at the University of Michigan has something for everyone: tons of extracurricular clubs, on-campus movies, concerts, and theatrical productions, an active Greek scene, and a successful and hugely popular intercollegiate athletic program (the men's basketball and football teams are widely followed, not only on campus, but by sports fans across the country). Students describe their social lives as "mostly laid-back"; writes a typical respondent, "Life at Michigan is generally fun. I go out to the movies with my roommates or my boyfriend. We hang out at the Union sometimes." Greek-sponsored parties are also a commonly exercised social option. Drinking and drugs are popular, although not inordinately so. Still, for some socially conservative Midwesterners, the amount of partying here is too much to take; complains one, "U of M is obscenely humanistic. If you're from a conservative background, get ready for a massive change. If you are a moralistic person, good luck maintaining those morals."

Academics
As one student puts it, "Quite simply, U of M is the quintessential state university. It has everything from the 'rah-rah' attitude at football games to ivy-covered buildings set in a beautiful campus." The school also has a number of outstanding academic departments scattered among its eleven undergraduate schools. The engineering school, for example, is among the nation's most highly regarded, as is the school of business; in the arts and sciences division, political science, history, and film and video studies earned student thumbs-up. The level of difficulty varies from program to program, but, overall, Michigan students work a little harder than the average public university student and consider their studies challenging. As at most large universities, students often have a hard time finding a full professor to help them with their work. Many courses, including a good number of upper-level classes, are taught by TAs of widely varying skills (complains one biology major, "TAs are often inadequate or do not have full command of the English language"). Sums up one student, "Michigan is a large school and it draws some of the best minds in the world to come to teach. If one doesn't mind the excessively bureaucratic processes here, then I would say that Michigan is a bargain for anyone."

Student Body
U of M has a decent minority population, which, combined with its huge enrollment, means that minority students are well represented. Students report that racial tensions exist; ""It's good to have a diverse student body, but there is still a lot of racial conflict," notes one Asian student. Explains another, "Different ethnicities do not interact at all because of prejudices or preconceptions of incompatibility."

UNIVERSITY OF MICHIGAN-ANN ARBOR

ADMISSIONS

The admissions committee considers (in descending order of importance): HS record, test scores, recommendations, class rank, essay. *Also considered (in descending order of importance):* special talents, alumni relationship, extracurriculars, geographical distribution. Either the SAT or ACT is required. Admissions process is need-blind. *High school units required/recommended:* 20 total units are recommended; 4 English recommended, 4 math recommended, 3 science recommended, 4 foreign language recommended, 3 social studies recommended, 1 history recommended. English units should include at least two rigorous writing courses. Some qualified in-state applicants admitted before receipt of test scores. In-state applicants from unaccredited schools may be asked to take additional exam before being considered. Higher GPA and test scores required of out-of-state applicants. *Special Requirements:* A portfolio is required for art program applicants. An audition is required for music program applicants. 3-4 units of math and 2 units of laboratory science including chemistry required of nursing program applicants. 4 units of math and at least 1 unit each of chemistry and physics required of engineering program applicants. 4 units of foreign language recommended of literature, science, and arts program applicants.

The Inside Word

Michigan's admissions process combines both formulaic and personal components in its evaluation of candidates. Making the cut is tough, and is getting even tougher for out-of-state applicants. The state legislature mandated a gradual but significant reduction in the percentage of nonresident enrollment a few years ago, and the university has loads of applicants from outside the state. If being a Wolverine is high on your list of choices, make sure you're well prepared. Last year, Michigan wait-listed 2,800 candidates.

FINANCIAL AID

Students should submit: FAFSA (due September 29), a copy of parents' most recent income tax filing (due September 29). The Princeton Review suggests that all financial aid forms be submitted as soon as possible after January 1. *The following grants/scholarships are offered:* Pell, SEOG, academic merit, athletic, the school's own scholarships, the school's own grants, state scholarships, state grants, private scholarships, private grants, federal nursing scholarship, ROTC. *Students borrow from the following loan programs:* Stafford, unsubsidized Stafford, Perkins, PLUS, the school's own loan fund, state loans, federal nursing loans, health professions loans, private loans. Applicants will be notified of awards beginning March 15. College Work-Study Program is available. Institutional employment is available.

FROM THE ADMISSIONS OFFICE

"The University of Michigan is continuing its dynamic mission into the twenty-first century—the commitment to diversity. To accomplish our goals, efforts are in place across the campus to meet the challenges of racism, community, and change, while preserving the important balance between tradition and preparation for the future. As the University's more than century-old tradition of excellence serves as its foundation, progress toward building a multicultural community is occurring at all levels of the institution. Students and scholars study and work closely together; the residence halls create a living community where lifelong friendships unfold."

ADMISSIONS

Admissions Rating	82
% of applicants accepted	68
% of acceptees attending	38

FRESHMAN PROFILE

Average verbal SAT	610
Average math SAT	630
Average ACT	28
Average TOEFL	NR
Graduated top 20% of class	88
Graduated top 40% of class	98
Graduated top 60% of class	100
Average HS GPA or Avg.	3.6

DEADLINES

Early decision	NR
Regular admission	2/1
Regular notification	rolling
Non-fall registration	yes

APPLICANTS ALSO LOOK AT

AND OFTEN PREFER

Brown
Pennsylvania
Dartmouth

AND SOMETIMES PREFER

Tufts
Brandeis
U. Chicago
Notre Dame

AND RARELY PREFER

Michigan State
Kenyon

FINANCIAL FACTS

Financial Aid Rating	78
In-state tuition	$5,550
Out-of-state tuition	$16,776
Room & board	$4,659
Estimated book expense	$500
% frosh receiving aid	40
% undergrads receiving aid	40
% aid is need-based	90
% frosh w/ grant (avg)	30 ($3,500)
% frosh w/ loan (avg)	42 ($2,000)
% UGs w/ job (avg)	40 ($2,520)
Off-campus job outlook	excellent

MIDDLEBURY COLLEGE

MIDDLEBURY, VT 05753-6002   ADMISSIONS: 802-388-3711   FAX: 802-388-9646

CAMPUS LIFE

Quality of Life Rating	**83**
Type of school	private
Affiliation	none
Environment	town

STUDENTS

FT undergrad enrollment	2,040
% male/female	51/49
% from out of state	96
% live on campus	98
% spend weekend on campus	95
% transfers	3
% from public high school	57
% African-American	3
% Asian	4
% Caucasian	80
% Hispanic	4
% international	10
# of countries represented	73

WHAT'S HOT
health facilities
theater
sex
hard liquor
beer

WHAT'S NOT
political activism
cigarettes
lack of diversity on campus
students are cliquish
off-campus food

ACADEMICS

Academic Rating	**92**
Profs Interesting Rating	84
Profs Accessible Rating	79
Calendar	4-1-4
Student/teacher ratio	11:1
% profs PhD/tenured	95/98
Hours of study per day	3.68

MOST POPULAR MAJORS
English
political science
economics

% GRADS WHO PURSUE...
Law 10, Med 7, MBA 25, MA 23

STUDENTS SPEAK OUT

Life

Middlebury College's mountain setting is "ideal for outdoor activities," particularly jogging, hiking, and skiing (the school has its own slope and lighted cross-country ski trail). "Last winter we even caught a glimpse of the Northern Lights," gushes one outdoorsman. But leisure options are otherwise limited; as one student puts it, "Don't come to Middlebury if you're seeking an active night life; you have to make your own fun." This situation suits some students perfectly; explains one undergrad, "Middlebury may be remote, but our isolation promotes creative social options and terrific friendships." Popular social events include social house and dorm parties, at which drinking is often the main attraction. Explains one student, "Social life is great for students who drink. But for everyone else, it gets pretty boring at times." Things may soon get boring for drinkers as well; several respondents tell us, "Socially, Middlebury is in a transition state. The college is trying to control much of the social life; this is evident in its attempts to abolish fraternities." Students also tell us, "Dating is nonexistent; the closest thing you'll find to a date is going down to Mr. Up's (local watering hole) in a group. Random hook-ups or serious relationships, however, are prevalent."

Academics

Some schools in New England (and in the West) attract a large number of skiing fanatics. Middlebury attracts students in that category who are also looking for a rigorous liberal arts education. Middlebury students work hard—about three and a half hours a day—and seem genuinely interested in academics for their own sake: foreign languages, English, history, theater, and other noncareer-related majors are pursued vigorously here. Premed departments are also popular and reportedly excellent. Professors are widely regarded as excellent, especially for their willingness to provide extra help; writes one student, "Never could I have imagined being able to find professors like these, who are so willing to help you late at night or on the weekends." Middlebury has a January semester, during which students concentrate on one course (usually in a less traditionally academic subject); students report that January is a "heavy ski period." Over half the undergrad population takes advantage of the school's Junior Year Abroad program.

Student Body

In response to our question about the diversity of the student body, one Middlebury student responds, "Diversity? Sure! I met a guy who isn't from Boston today. But his dad is a lawyer anyway, so it didn't count." The Middlebury student body is predominantly white, upper middle class and intelligent. This makes some people uneasy as many students "appear to have been molded in the same machine as everyone else," but others found these similarities reassuring. As one student puts it, "Middlebury is not a school for the depressed, brooding, coffee-drinking smoker; it is a school for the stoned Patagonia-wearing skier/hiker. We are a happy and rich sort." Students have "a sense of balance: They work hard and play hard, are moderately physically active, and are politically middle of the road. It's a pretty easy place to be whoever you are (even though most people are pretty much alike)."

ADMISSIONS

The admissions committee considers (in descending order of importance): HS record, recommendations, class rank, essay, test scores. *Also considered (in descending order of importance):* extracurriculars, personality, special talents, alumni relationship, geographical distribution. Admissions process is need-blind. *High school units required/recommended:* 19 total units are recommended; 4 English recommended, 4 math recommended, 3 science recommended, 4 foreign language recommended, 3 history recommended. One of the following options is required: SAT I and three SAT II (including writing and chemistry, mathematics, or physics); five SAT II (including writing); or ACT. Recommendations from guidance counselor and two teachers required. Mid-year grades from 12th year required. Additional units of music, art, or drama recommended. TOEFL is required of all international students.

The Inside Word

While Middlebury benefits tremendously from its age-old position as an Ivy League safety, it is nonetheless a very strong and demanding place in its own right. Middlebury has a broad national applicant pool and sees more ACT scores than most eastern colleges, so submitting ACT scores to Middlebury is a more comfortable option than at most eastern schools.

FINANCIAL AID

Students should submit: FAFSA (due December 15), CSS Profile, state aid form, a copy of parents' most recent income tax filing (due December 15). The Princeton Review suggests that all financial aid forms be submitted as soon as possible after January 1. *The following grants/scholarships are offered:* Pell, SEOG, the school's own scholarships, the school's own grants, state scholarships, state grants, private scholarships, private grants, foreign aid. *Students borrow from the following loan programs:* Stafford, unsubsidized Stafford, Perkins, PLUS, the school's own loan fund, private loans. Applicants will be notified of awards beginning April. College Work-Study Program is available. Institutional employment is available.

FROM THE ADMISSIONS OFFICE

"Nothing Middlebury College makes available to its students—a distinguished faculty, facilities for research, challenging programs, residential living—will be of any lasting value unless those who are chosen and come to learn are willing to give 'the gift outright' of their energies and talents. Accordingly, Middlebury seeks students willing to yield the full measure of their capacity in academics, athletics, the arts, leadership and service to others. The horizons of the Middlebury students are not bounded by the Adirondack Mountains to our west or by the Green Mountains to our east, but are limited only by the imagination and initiative of students who find themselves living at a school which has been described as 'an international university masquerading as a small liberal arts college in Vermont.' We seek those who wish not only to learn about themselves and their own traditions, but those who wish to expand their vision, and to see beyond the bounds of class, culture, reason or nation. It is this transcendence of one's self and one's own concerns which may come through the study of other people and other tongues or through the hard study that brings an understanding of physics or philosophy, mathematics or music."

ADMISSIONS

Admissions Rating	95
% of applicants accepted	27
% of acceptees attending	45

FRESHMAN PROFILE

Average verbal SAT	670
Average math SAT	660
Average ACT	29
Average TOEFL	NR
Graduated top 20% of class	85
Graduated top 40% of class	97
Graduated top 60% of class	99
Average HS GPA or Avg.	NR

DEADLINES

Early decision	12/15
Regular admission	1/1
Regular notification	4/1
Non-fall registration	yes

APPLICANTS ALSO LOOK AT

AND OFTEN PREFER

Dartmouth
Harvard/Radcliffe
Williams
Amherst
Princeton

AND SOMETIMES PREFER

Brown
Yale

AND RARELY PREFER

Bowdoin
Hamilton
Skidmore
St. Lawrence

FINANCIAL FACTS

Financial Aid Rating	80
Tuition	NR
Room & board	NR
Estimated book expense	$550
% frosh receiving aid	50
% undergrads receiving aid	45
% aid is need-based	100
% frosh w/ grant (avg)	37 ($16,000)
% frosh w/ loan (avg)	50 ($3,200)
% UGs w/ job (avg)	60 ($500)
Off-campus job outlook	good

MILLSAPS COLLEGE

JACKSON, MS 39210　　　　　　ADMISSIONS: 800-352-1050　　FAX: 601-354-2624

CAMPUS LIFE

Quality of Life Rating　　78
Type of school　　　　　private
Affiliation　　　Methodist Church
Environment　　　　　　　city

STUDENTS
FT undergrad enrollment　　1,175
% male/female　　　　　49/51
% from out of state　　　　40
% live on campus　　　　　73
% spend weekend on campus　70
% transfers　　　　　　　4
% from public high school　　57
% in (# of) fraternities　　62 (6)
% in (# of) sororities　　　60 (4)
% African-American　　　　5
% Asian　　　　　　　　2
% Caucasian　　　　　　91
% Hispanic　　　　　　　0
% international　　　　　　1
# of countries represented　　5

WHAT'S HOT
　lab facilities
　computer facilities
　Greeks
　hard liquor
　theater

WHAT'S NOT
　college radio
　student publications
　registration is a pain
　lack of diversity on campus
　intercollegiate sports

ACADEMICS

Academic Rating　　　83
Profs Interesting Rating　　93
Profs Accessible Rating　　85
Calendar　　　　　　semester
Student/teacher ratio　　14:1
% profs PhD/tenured　　83/90
Hours of study per day　　2.81

MOST POPULAR MAJORS
biology
English

% GRADS WHO PURSUE...
MA 18

STUDENTS SPEAK OUT

Life

Millsaps College students rave, "Jackson, Mississippi, offers a safe, friendly environment for us to learn and party in." There is a "real sense of community" among the small student body. One woman writes, "Everyone on this campus is super-friendly, and the small campus makes it easier to interact with other students." Participation in extracurricular activities is important; most students "utilize their chances to become involved in Greek societies, various clubs and honorary fraternities, college committees, and intercollegiate and intramural sports." Social life is ruled by the fraternities and sororities, which claim two-thirds of the students as members. Drinking is also integral; writes one student, "More than ninety percent of us use alcohol regularly. Marijuana is the drug of choice among most students." This reality runs counter to Millsaps's official policy, which prohibits drinking outside of dorm rooms, even for those of age. The general disregard for this stricture demonstrates the looseness of the college's religious ties. Students asserted that "although this is a church-affiliated would not notice if one did not know." Millsaps boasts some excellent intercollegiate sports teams, which receive only moderate support from students.

Academics

Millsaps, once unknown outside Mississippi, now boasts a solid reputation throughout the Deep South. Its greatest assets are its fine pre-professional programs and committed faculty. Although some students complain that "Millsaps College is caught up in the lawyer- and doctor-producing industry," most applaud their school's "rigorous academic environment," which extends to most areas of study. Standout departments are business, premedical sciences, political science, English, music, and history. Students who enroll in the interdisciplinary Heritage Program (a year-long Western Civilization survey) report that the curriculum is difficult and rewarding, and all students must complete "intense written and oral comprehensive exams before graduation"; still, the average student here studies only two and three-quarters hours a day, well below the national average. Professors receive good grades from students for teaching well and encouraging discussion. One student enthuses, "The professors are really cool—you often see them roaming down fraternity row with a beer in their hands on weekends." For many, this personalized, informal atmosphere is one of Millsaps's best features.

Student Body

The Millsaps student body is monochromatic; gripes one student, "The student body is almost completely made up of white, upper-middle-class Southerners." Still, Millsaps is an atypical Southern school in that "most of the student body is extremely liberal, surprising considering that so many come from small, conservative communities." Students agree that a spirit of hospitality pervades the campus. One student sums up, "If you are looking for a beautiful, friendly school and greater self-awareness, look at Millsaps College."

ADMISSIONS

The admissions committee considers (in descending order of importance): HS record, test scores, essay, recommendations, class rank. *Also considered (in descending order of importance):* personality, alumni relationship, extracurriculars. Either the SAT or ACT is required. An interview is recommended. Admissions process is need-blind. *High school units required/recommended:* 16 total units are required; 20 total units are recommended; 4 English required, 4 English recommended, 3 math recommended, 3 science recommended, 2 foreign language recommended. 16 secondary school units required, including at least 12 units (4 of English) in academic subjects. *The admissions office says:* "Millsaps's undergraduate catalog states: "Applicants must furnish evidence of: (1) good moral character; (2) sound physical and mental health; (3) adequate scholastic preparation; (4) intellectual maturity." Applicants are advised to apply for admission "well in advance of the date on which they wish to enter, particularly if housing accommodations on the campus are desired."

The Inside Word

Despite the college's seemingly deep-probing evaluation process, candidates with a solid track record in high school encounter little resistance in gaining admission. In reality, there is little room for extensive matchmaking by the admissions staff. The high percentage of acceptees who choose to enroll makes getting in less than definite for candidates with weak academic credentials.

FINANCIAL AID

Students should submit: FAFSA, the school's own financial aid form. The Princeton Review suggests that all financial aid forms be submitted as soon as possible after January 1. *The following grants/scholarships are offered:* Pell, SEOG, academic merit, the school's own scholarships, state scholarships, state grants, private scholarships, foreign aid. *Students borrow from the following loan programs:* Stafford, unsubsidized Stafford, Perkins, PLUS, the school's own loan fund, private loans. Applicants will be notified of awards beginning April 1. College Work-Study Program is available. Institutional employment is available.

FROM THE ADMISSIONS OFFICE

"Your academic experience at Millsaps begins with Introduction to Liberal Studies, a comprehensive freshman experience. You will be encouraged to develop critical thinking skills, analytical reasoning, and independence of thought as preparation for study in your major. The interdisciplinary Heritage Program offers a unique approach to the culture and development of society through lectures and small group discussions by a team of faculty who represent a cross-section of the humanities. Entering freshmen are primarily taught by full-time Ph.D. professors. The close relationship between faculty and students encourages classroom participation and enables students to explore their options as they choose a major field of study. Coursework in the major may begin as early as the freshman year."

ADMISSIONS

Admissions Rating	76
% of applicants accepted	86
% of acceptees attending	31

FRESHMAN PROFILE

Average verbal SAT	670
Average math SAT	600
Average ACT	26
Average TOEFL	500
Graduated top 20% of class	NR
Graduated top 40% of class	NR
Graduated top 60% of class	NR
Average HS GPA or Avg.	3.3

DEADLINES

Early decision	NR
Regular admission	3/1
Regular notification	4/1
Non-fall registration	yes

APPLICANTS ALSO LOOK AT

AND OFTEN PREFER

Duke
Emory

AND SOMETIMES PREFER

Vanderbilt
Tulane
Rhodes

AND RARELY PREFER

Hendrix

FINANCIAL FACTS

Financial Aid Rating	90
Tuition	$12,080
Room & board	$4,250
Estimated book expense	$500
% frosh receiving aid	90
% undergrads receiving aid	83
% aid is need-based	60
% frosh w/ grant (avg)	80 ($8,087)
% frosh w/ loan (avg)	75 ($4,000)
% UGs w/ job (avg)	40 ($1,000)
Off-campus job outlook	good

UNIVERSITY OF MINNESOTA

231 PILLSBURY DRIVE, SE, MINNEAPOLIS, MN 55455-0213   ADMISSIONS: 800-752-1000   FAX: 612-626-1693

Quality of Life Rating	**71**
Type of school	public
Affiliation	none
Environment	metropolis

STUDENTS

FT undergrad enrollment	16,457
% male/female	51/49
% from out of state	23
% live on campus	12
% spend weekend on campus	NR
% transfers	NR
% from public high school	NR
% in (# of) fraternities	6 (27)
% in (# of) sororities	5 (15)
% African-American	3
% Asian	7
% Caucasian	81
% Hispanic	2
% international	7
# of countries represented	85

WHAT'S HOT
ethnic diversity on campus
leftist politics
health facilities
Minneapolis
drugs

WHAT'S NOT
political activism
campus difficult to get around
inefficient administration
registration is a pain
support groups

ACADEMICS

Academic Rating	**66**
Profs Interesting Rating	63
Profs Accessible Rating	61
Calendar	quarter
Student/teacher ratio	15:1
% profs PhD/tenured	76/91
Hours of study per day	2.88

MOST POPULAR MAJORS
business administration
psychology
English

STUDENTS SPEAK OUT

Life

Only about 4,500 students at the University of Minnesota live on campus, but the campus is peppered with comfortable student unions where students can take refuge from the rough Minnesota winters. For those interested, there are close to 350 campus organizations in which to get involved. Off campus, students are never at a loss. The main campus is located in Minneapolis, home of the world's biggest mall and one of America's alternative rock capitals—the city was the breeding ground of such bands as The Replacements and Soul Asylum, not to mention His Paisliness, the Artist Formerly Known as Prince. Students often take advantage of the hopping Minneapolis nightclub scene. As one student puts it, "There's always something going on here." Yes, the progressive spirit is alive and well at this flagship campus in traditionally liberal Minnesota. Could it be true that even the Golden Gophers are planning to change their moniker to an unpronounceable symbol? We're impressed.

Academics

A looming velociraptor in the big-state-university Red Tape Era, the University of Minnesota has watched its bureaucracy slowly evolve into a warm-blooded creature that nurtures its young. With the advent of the Information Age, will the bureaucratic hassle of the twentieth century go the way of the dodo? At UM at least, the administration is trying to give its 16,000 undergrads streamlined services and personalized attention. Still, even an evolved University of Minnesota is not for everyone (although it's almost big enough to be); it's best for those not intimidated by the size of the place. "The U," as it is known to its students, "is a great place to get lost." About 37,000 students overall populate the two main campuses (St. Paul for students of forestry and agriculture, Minneapolis for just about everything else). Some classes are auditorium-sized. The upside of the U's enormity is that you can study just about anything you want. If you don't like any of the more than one hundred majors offered here, you can even design your own. Most students opt for career-track majors like business and management, journalism, psychology, and engineering. Says one student, "Every instructor is a specialist in his subfield, and the selection of upper division courses is excellent." Another accurately sums up the UMTC academic experience this way: "This is a professional school. You can work hard and have a good time both. If you want to excel here, get lots of advice and never stop asking questions."

Student Body

Diversity at the U far exceeds diversity in Minnesota in general, but that's not saying much. Students here are mostly white, mostly Minnesotan. Says one student, "Although the catalog claims diversity in the state university system, the majority of students at this campus are white, of Scandinavian-German descent." But in other ways there's plenty of variety to enjoy here—with 37,000 students, you can find everyone from Marxists to John Birchers.

ADMISSIONS

The admissions committee considers (in descending order of importance): class rank, HS record, test scores, recommendations, essay. Also considered (in descending order of importance): geographical distribution, extracurriculars, special talents. Either the SAT or ACT is required; ACT is preferred. High school units required/ recommended: 16 total units are required; 4 English required, 3 math required, 3 science required, 2 foreign language required, 2 social studies required. Special Requirements: A portfolio is required for art program applicants. An audition is required for music program applicants. TOEFL is required of all international students. The admissions office says: "Minority students, students with special talents, students active in extracurricular activities may receive special consideration if their admissions indices are not high enough for standard admission."

The Inside Word

Admissions strictly by formula at a place this large makes working up a sweat over getting in absolutely unnecessary for everyone but the most academically underprepared students.

FINANCIAL AID

Students should submit: FAFSA. The Princeton Review suggests that all financial aid forms be submitted as soon as possible after January 1. The following grants/ scholarships are offered: Pell, SEOG, academic merit, athletic, the school's own scholarships, the school's own grants, state scholarships, state grants, private scholarships, private grants, federal nursing scholarship, ROTC, foreign aid. Students borrow from the following loan programs: Stafford, unsubsidized Stafford, Perkins, PLUS, the school's own loan fund, state loans, federal nursing loans, health professions loans, private loans. College Work-Study Program is available. Institutional employment is available. Freshmen are discouraged from working.

FROM THE ADMISSIONS OFFICE

"The University of Minnesota is...empowering. Offering you boundless opportunities to realize your potential. Opportunities to make important decisions about your future, to take charge of your life. Education for adulthood. Diverse. Bringing together thousands of people from all over the world into a multicultural, international learning community. Education in an environment that will expand your world. Where you can find your own community, speak your own language, be among friends—whoever you are. Prestigious. Carrying on a tradition of high distinction and leadership in scholarship, research, academic excellence, and commitment to the personal and intellectual growth of students. Education that matters. A degree that you can be really proud of. Magnetic. Providing a high-powered, high-energy environment for dynamic sharing of ideas—with room for quiet reflection. Education that will stretch your imagination and take you to the boundaries of knowledge and beyond. Responsive. Meeting your needs with services and resources that provide both academic and personal guidance and support. Helping you feel connected, nourished. Education with a heart."

ADMISSIONS

Admissions Rating	77
% of applicants accepted	56
% of acceptees attending	55

FRESHMAN PROFILE

Average verbal SAT	570
Average math SAT	590
Average ACT	24
Average TOEFL	550
Graduated top 20% of class	49
Graduated top 40% of class	80
Graduated top 60% of class	92
Average HS GPA or Avg.	NR

DEADLINES

Early decision	12/15
Regular admission	6/1
Regular notification	rolling
Non-fall registration	yes

APPLICANTS ALSO LOOK AT

AND OFTEN PREFER
St. Olaf
Iowa State

AND SOMETIMES PREFER
U. Wisconsin-Madison
U. Iowa
U. Michigan-Ann Arbor
Michigan State

AND RARELY PREFER
Syracuse
Case Western

FINANCIAL FACTS

Financial Aid Rating	72
In-state tuition	$3,328
Out-of-state tuition	$9,814
Room & board	$3,876
Estimated book expense	$714
% frosh receiving aid	NR
% undergrads receiving aid	NR
% aid is need-based	NR
% frosh w/ grant (avg)	NR
% frosh w/ loan (avg)	NR
% UGs w/ job (avg)	NR
Off-campus job outlook	excellent

UNIVERSITY OF MISSOURI-COLUMBIA

COLUMBIA, MO 65211   ADMISSIONS: 573-882-2456   FAX: 573-882-7887

CAMPUS LIFE

Quality of Life Rating   **69**
Type of school   public
Affiliation   none
Environment   suburban

STUDENTS
FT undergrad enrollment   15,086
% male/female   48/52
% from out of state   13
% live on campus   47
% spend weekend on campus   NR
% transfers   25
% from public high school   NR
% in (# of) fraternities   24 (32)
% in (# of) sororities   24 (18)
% African-American   5
% Asian   2
% Caucasian   85
% Hispanic   1
% international   3
# of countries represented   117

WHAT'S HOT
old-fashioned dating
college radio
intercollegiate sports
political activism
intramural sports

WHAT'S NOT
students are unhappy
campus difficult to get around
support groups
theater
music associations

ACADEMICS

Academic Rating   **66**
Profs Interesting Rating   60
Profs Accessible Rating   60
Calendar   semester
Student/teacher ratio   14:1
% profs PhD   87
Hours of study per day   2.33

MOST POPULAR MAJORS
business administration
education
psychology

STUDENTS SPEAK OUT

Life

A land-grant university situated on 1,400 tree-filled acres, Mizzou is a sprawling campus done up in classic, big public school style. "Clubs and athletics are the heart of this school," explains a freshman studying biology. Indeed, at Mizzou, a reputed party school, basketball reigns supreme, with the Tigers consistently among the nation's best men's basketball teams. Intramural ports are also quite popular with students at Missouri. But what about life off-court? "Mizzou is a very Greek-oriented school," explains a psychology major. Fraternities and sororities are both very popular with Missouri undergrads, still, says one student, "if you aren't Greek there are still plenty of places to go and have fun." Columbia, a city of 75,000 people, is located between St. Louis and Kansas City. Many students do take advantage of the nightlife of each of their larger neighbors. Still, while Mizzou sports a high freshman retention rate, with over eighty percent returning for their sophomore year, few students we surveyed described themselves as "very happy" to be at Mizzou. Most say life is "fine," with little real enthusiasm.

Academics

"The professors are very helpful and always willing and ready to help outside of class," says one. Maybe that's because their salaries have been rising significantly in the 1990s and are finally closing in on the national average. See, Missouri is in the midst of a transformation. States President Charles A. Kiesler, "[We are] overhauling the way undergraduates are educated at a major research university." Explains one undergrad of this development, "Mizzou is seen as a party school...but for those of us who hit the books it is a serious educational setting." Adds another, "This school is tough academically, but I know that I'm getting a better education than most other students." Besides being tough academically, it is also tough to get into classes as a freshman, though registration improves considerably as you continue your studies. Lectures, labs, and discussions are all large, as they are at most major public institutions, so much of the responsibility for receiving personal attention rests with the student. Ellis Library and the school's computer facilities both received high marks from students, as did the performance of the administration a whole. Also, if you see a study-abroad program in your future, Mizzou has thirty programs to choose from in almost as many countries.

Student Body

Mizzou has a fairly diverse student population, especially for a public school. Mostly in-staters, "students interact well at this school." But, counters another, "the campus does tend to segregate racially at times." Indeed, discrimination on the basis of race, sex, and sexual preference are all perceived as problems by Missouri-Columbia undergrads. It must be said though that between 1993 and 1994, the number of black freshman tripled as a result of the school's efforts to attract a more diverse student body. Whatever their color, students date frequently at Mizzou, and these dates often lead to more than a good-night handshake.

ADMISSIONS

The admissions committee considers (in descending order of importance): class rank, test scores, HS record. Either the SAT or ACT is required; ACT is preferred. Admissions process is need-blind. *High school units required/recommended:* 16 total units are required; 4 English required, 3 math required, 2 science required, 2 foreign language recommended, 3 social studies required. Applicants must meet standards of scale based on SAT I/ACT scores and secondary school class rank. *Special Requirements:* TOEFL is required of all international students. Applicants to physical therapy program must be state residents.

The Inside Word

This flagship campus follows admission by formula, and a forgiving one at that. Solid "B" students will find a virtual open door to admission.

FINANCIAL AID

Students should submit: FAFSA. The Princeton Review suggests that all financial aid forms be submitted as soon as possible after January 1. *The following grants/ scholarships are offered:* Pell, SEOG, academic merit, athletic, the school's own scholarships, the school's own grants, state scholarships, state grants, private scholarships, private grants, federal nursing scholarship, ROTC. *Students borrow from the following loan programs:* unsubsidized Stafford, Perkins, the school's own loan fund, supplemental loans, state loans, federal nursing loans, health professions loans, private loans. Applicants will be notified of awards beginning April 1. College Work-Study Program is available. Institutional employment is available.

FROM THE ADMISSIONS OFFICE

"The University of Missouri-Columbia, MU, is the largest and oldest campus of the state's major public research institutions. A predominantly residential campus, MU serves select and diverse undergraduate and professional students from all parts of the state...MU aspires to achieve national and international prominence for its research and educational contributions. It will build on its research strengths in basic and applied biological and biomedical sciences; nuclear and related physical and engineering sciences; and selected social and behavioral sciences. It will strengthen its leadership roles in agriculture and journalism. Because of its large enrollment of undergraduates, MU will enhance the core disciplines required for all those seeking baccalaureate degrees, giving special attention to areas, such as languages and mathematical sciences, that provide the necessary foundation for truly educated citizens."

ADMISSIONS

Admissions Rating	75
% of applicants accepted	90
% of acceptees attending	51

FRESHMAN PROFILE

Average verbal SAT	600
Average math SAT	590
Average ACT	25
Average TOEFL	500
Graduated top 20% of class	54
Graduated top 40% of class	83
Graduated top 60% of class	96
Average HS GPA or Avg.	NR

DEADLINES

Early decision	NR
Regular admission	5/1
Regular notification	rolling
Non-fall registration	yes

APPLICANTS ALSO LOOK AT

AND OFTEN PREFER

Indiana U.-Bloomington
U. Illinois-Urbana-Champaign

AND SOMETIMES PREFER

Duke U.
Ohio State U.-Columbus
Southern Methodist U.
St. Louis U.
U. Arizona

FINANCIAL FACTS

Financial Aid Rating	73
In-state tuition	$3,388
Out-of-state tuition	$10,128
Room & board	$4,125
Estimated book expense	$700
% frosh receiving aid	58
% undergrads receiving aid	51
% aid is need-based	88
% frosh w/ grant (avg)	51 ($4,434)
% frosh w/ loan (avg)	39 ($3,645)
% UGs w/ job (avg)	24 ($1,213)
Off-campus job outlook	good

UNIVERSITY OF MISSOURI-ROLLA

1890 MINER CIRCLE, ROLLA, MO 65401 · ADMISSIONS: 314-341-4164 · FAX: 314-341-4082

CAMPUS LIFE

Quality of Life Rating 70
Type of school public
Affiliation none
Environment town

STUDENTS

FT undergrad enrollment	3,867
% male/female	76/24
% from out of state	26
% live on campus	50
% spend weekend on campus	NR
% transfers	26
% from public high school	88
% in (# of) fraternities	25 (21)
% in (# of) sororities	20 (5)
% African-American	3
% Asian	3
% Caucasian	85
% Hispanic	2
% international	5
# of countries represented	27

WHAT'S HOT
college radio
computer facilities
health facilities
Greeks
registration is a breeze

WHAT'S NOT
theater
dorms
music associations
sex
students are unhappy

ACADEMICS

Academic Rating 80
Profs Interesting Rating 68
Profs Accessible Rating 68
Calendar semester
Student/teacher ratio 14:1
% profs PhD/tenured 94/78
Hours of study per day 3.50

MOST POPULAR MAJORS
mechanical engineering
civil engineering
electrical engineering

STUDENTS SPEAK OUT

Life

"Who has time for life?" asks one chemistry major at the University of Missouri-Rolla. Not many students at Rolla, that's for sure. Lots of studying will necessarily take most free time away, but Rolla undergrads don't mind too much. Most are engineers and prepared for the large workload it takes to get a degree in their chosen field. "People [only] think about engineering," reports one student; "that's what they talk about at dinner at least." Apparently, this changes slightly on the weekends, when UMR students put away their slide rules and party. One respondent says his classmates "live for the weekends," especially St. Patrick's Day weekend, when there is "a BIG party at UMR" that has caused some tensions with the administration in the past. Not much goes on in town; located 100 miles southwest of St. Louis, Rolla has about 14,000 people. Accordingly, fun in Rolla is strictly "small-town"—movies, bowling, and a few bars. Students are fairly unsatisfied with UMR's dorms and food, which may be why a quarter of students go Greek. Another cause of dissatisfaction is the male/female ratio, skewed heavily in favor of the men (or against the men, depending on how you look at it). "More women are needed," succinctly states one undergrad.

Academics

Long hours of study and an emphasis on engineering of all kinds (electrical, mechanical, chemical, civil, nuclear, and aerospace are among the school's engineering departments) make Rolla tougher than most public universities. Although most students rate their profs accessible and helpful, some find them unavailable: "The professors are very knowledgeable of their disciplines, yet with the campus's focus on research, the professors devote most of their time to working on their own projects," complains one. TAs teach a few introductory and upper-level classes, but any problems this may cause seem to be offset by small lectures and discussions. On the whole, students are very satisfied with their education at UMR. Registration is painless, the library receives high marks, and the computer facilities at Rolla are exceptional.

Student Body

"You have to remember the type of school we go to," explains a freshman. "Most people were considered nerds back in high school." Says a student studying ceramic engineering, "I like my peers. They are a generally conservative bunch." Adds another, "[Students are] often intolerant of others' views and are, for the most part, extremely conservative." Rolla is predominantly an engineering school, which in this day and age means male, white, and, yes, conservative. "If you are not an engineer or an American, you are pretty much a second-rate citizen," explains one mechanical engineer. Discrimination on the basis of race, sex, and sexual orientation is in fact a concern on the UMR campus, where most students are from in state. Competitiveness is also a part of daily life for UMR undergrads.

FINANCIAL AID: 314-341-4282   E-MAIL: PARKJ@SHUTTLE.CC.UMR.EDU   WEB SITE: HTTP://WWW.UMR.EDU/

ADMISSIONS

The admissions committee considers (in descending order of importance): class rank, test scores, HS record, recommendations. *Also considered (in descending order of importance):* extracurriculars, alumni relationship, personality, special talents. Either the SAT or ACT is required; ACT is preferred. An interview is recommended. Admissions process is need-blind. *High school units required/recommended:* 19 total units are required; 4 English required, 3 math required, 4 math recommended, 2 science required, 3 science recommended, 2 foreign language recommended, 3 social studies required. TOEFL is required of all international students. *The admissions office says:* "(We) make every attempt to process applications and respond within two weeks."

The Inside Word

This public university admissions committee functions pretty much the same as most others; admission is based on numbers and course distribution requirements. The applicant pool is small, well-qualified, and self-selected; despite the extremely high admit rate, only strong students are likely to meet with success.

FINANCIAL AID

Students should submit: FAFSA, the school's own financial aid form (due November 1). The Princeton Review suggests that all financial aid forms be submitted as soon as possible after January 1. *The following grants/scholarships are offered:* Pell, SEOG, academic merit, athletic, the school's own scholarships, the school's own grants, state scholarships, state grants, private scholarships, private grants, ROTC. *Students borrow from the following loan programs:* Stafford, unsubsidized Stafford, Perkins, PLUS, the school's own loan fund, private loans. College Work-Study Program is available. Institutional employment is available. Freshmen are discouraged from working.

FROM THE ADMISSIONS OFFICE

"The University of Missouri-Rolla provides students with a vital, challenging, and stimulating environment. Rolla educates leaders in engineering and science. Students receive a comprehensive engineering and science education balanced by extraordinary offerings in liberal arts. The quality of student credentials and small size enhance the academic atmosphere."

ADMISSIONS

Admissions Rating	75
% of applicants accepted	97
% of acceptees attending	38

FRESHMAN PROFILE

Average verbal SAT	610
Average math SAT	650
Average ACT	28
Average TOEFL	570
Graduated top 20% of class	70
Graduated top 40% of class	91
Graduated top 60% of class	98
Average HS GPA or Avg.	NR

DEADLINES

Early decision	11/1
Regular admission	2/1
Regular notification	rolling
Non-fall registration	yes

APPLICANTS ALSO LOOK AT

AND OFTEN PREFER

U. Missouri-Columbia
U. Illinois, Urbana-Champ.
MIT
Northeast Missouri State
U. Wisconsin-Madison

AND SOMETIMES PREFER

U. Iowa
Georgia Tech.
Purdue U.-West Lafayette

FINANCIAL FACTS

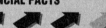

Financial Aid Rating	85
In-state tuition	$3,630
Out-of-state tuition	$10,851
Room & board	$3,422
Estimated book expense	$765
% frosh receiving aid	79
% undergrads receiving aid	78
% aid is need-based	44
% frosh w/ grant (avg)	74 ($2,750)
% frosh w/ loan (avg)	45 ($2,500)
% UGs w/ job (avg)	23 ($1,600)
Off-campus job outlook	fair

MONTANA TECH OF THE UNIV. OF MONTANA

1300 WEST PARK STREET, BUTTE, MT 59701-8997   ADMISSIONS: 800-445-8324   FAX: 406-496-4133

STUDENTS SPEAK OUT

Life

Montana Tech at the University of Montana students admit that "unfortunately, on-campus is a social bore. Off-campus isn't much better—only bars and very little culture. So one seeks comfort by enjoying great x-country skiing, snow boarding, rock climbing, mountaineering, back country skiing and the company of friends." Since most students live off campus in rented apartments or housing, and because they also meet non-students in co-op jobs, they develop social lives outside of school more readily than do most students. The school does provide a few opportunities for socializing. Homecoming is said to be one of the biggest days of the year and there are the occasional blow-out parties, such as St. Patrick's Day and M-Days (a weekend party during which students repaint a giant stone M). Otherwise, people hit the bars in Butte: "Everyone usually goes to a certain bar and dance club every week." Thanks to all of the above, the intense workload, and lopsided male/female ratio, "Life at Tech is a lot of studying, beer, and few women."

Academics

Montana Tech offers its students several perks not usually found at engineering and technical schools. In how many other such programs do students rave about small classes and accessible professors? Writes one student, "Teachers at Tech really care about their students and go to great lengths to make sure the students understand their courses." Another writes, "Most classes are small enough for one-on-one contact. Professors are great at helping on an individual basis." While students agree that teachers extend their time, they are less confident about their overall teaching abilities; as one undergrad explains, "although every professor is not on the upper echelon of education, there are some that make learning a joyride." Those who can find administrators mention that they are "open to discussion about classroom issues, provided criticism is constructive." The Montana Tech curriculum includes a number of distribution requirements (including English composition, social sciences, and the humanities), the opportunity for cooperative education (working at a major-related job, for credit, during the school year), and an emphasis on practical applications of engineering and mining. Mining and geology-related areas are strongest here, and the business and management program is growing in popularity.

Student Body

Nearly nine-tenths of the Montana Tech students are native Montanans. Forget the Unabomber; our surveys show Montana Tech students to be politically middle-of-the-road and pretty apathetic. They do not hold back on anti-gay and—a new one—anti-smoker sentiment. According to many, a little more diversity would be nice. One business major voices the need for more well-rounded students: "We need more people and less engineers!" Despite the intense workload, overly harsh competition is not a problem: "There's a willingness and openness about helping fellow students with various subjects." But nonetheless, the heavy work can isolate students, as one student illustrates with this answer to our call to describe his peers and their social life: "I don't care. I'm too busy."

MONTANA TECH OF THE UNIVERSITY OF MONTANA

FINANCIAL AID: 406-496-4212   E-MAIL: LNORMAN@MTUMSL.MTECH.EDU   WEB SITE: HTTP://WWW.MTECH.EDU

ADMISSIONS

The admissions committee considers (in descending order of importance): recommendations, test scores, HS record, class rank. *Also considered (in descending order of importance):* personality, alumni relationship, extracurriculars, special talents. Either the SAT or ACT is required; ACT is preferred. An interview is recommended. *High school units required/recommended:* 14 total units are required; 4 English required, 3 math required, 2 science required, 2 foreign language required, 3 social studies required. Minimum composite ACT score of 22 (combined SAT I score of 920), rank in top half of secondary school class, or minimum 2.5 GPA required. TOEFL is required of all international students. *The admissions office says:* "We admit students on a rolling basis. We also admit engineering students into their designated area of interest upon admission to Montana Tech; we do not make them wait until their sophomore or junior year."

The Inside Word

Underrecognized schools like Montana Tech can be a godsend for students who are strong academically but not likely to be offered admission to nationally renowned technical institutes. In fact, because of its small size and relatively remote location, Montana Tech is a good choice for anyone leaning toward a technical career. You'd be hard-pressed to find many other places which are as low-key and personal in this realm of academe.

FINANCIAL AID

Students should submit: FAFSA, a copy of parents' most recent income tax filing. The Princeton Review suggests that all financial aid forms be submitted as soon as possible after January 1. *The following grants/scholarships are offered:* Pell, SEOG, academic merit, athletic, the school's own scholarships, state scholarships, state grants, private scholarships. *Students borrow from the following loan programs:* Stafford, unsubsidized Stafford, Perkins, PLUS. Applicants will be notified of awards beginning June 1. College Work-Study Program is available. Institutional employment is available.

FROM THE ADMISSIONS OFFICE

"Located in Butte, Montana, and surrounded by the Rocky Mountains, Montana Tech is the only college in North America offering a full comprehensive array of degree programs in the areas of minerals, energy, safety, and environment. We are a dynamic college-always diversifying and moving ahead. Our academic programs clearly exemplify this attribute in that they offer both innovative and unique courses that continually change to meet the growing demands of business and industry. The personal approach at Montana Tech helps students achieve educational excellence. A student-to-faculty ratio of 16:1 makes students more than a number on our campus. Our quality is proven and guaranteed through our outstanding faculty; seventy percent of them have worked in industry before teaching, and a high percentage of our faculty have obtained doctorates..."

ADMISSIONS

Admissions Rating	70
% of applicants accepted	95
% of acceptees attending	68

FRESHMAN PROFILE

Average verbal SAT	560
Average math SAT	570
Average ACT	23
Average TOEFL	525
Graduated top 20% of class	43
Graduated top 40% of class	69
Graduated top 60% of class	88
Average HS GPA or Avg.	3.3

DEADLINES

Early decision	NR
Regular admission	3/1
Regular notification	rolling
Non-fall registration	yes

APPLICANTS ALSO LOOK AT

AND SOMETIMES PREFER

U. Montana
Montana St.-Billings
Colorado Mines
U. Washington
Eastern Montana

AND RARELY PREFER

Carroll (MT)

FINANCIAL FACTS

Financial Aid Rating	87
In-state tuition	$2,317
Out-of-state tuition	$6,745
Room & board	$3,456
Estimated book expense	$575
% frosh receiving aid	65
% undergrads receiving aid	80
% aid is need-based	100
% frosh w/ grant (avg)	62 ($1,636)
% frosh w/ loan (avg)	50 ($2,625)
% UGs w/ job (avg)	45 ($1,400)
Off-campus job outlook	good

MOREHOUSE COLLEGE

830 WESTVIEW DRIVE, SW, ATLANTA, GA 30314 · · · ADMISSIONS: 404-215-2632 · · · FAX: 404-681-2650

CAMPUS LIFE

Quality of Life Rating 80
Type of school private
Affiliation none
Environment metropolis

STUDENTS

FT undergrad enrollment	2,852
% male/female	100/0
% from out of state	80
% live on campus	55
% spend weekend on campus	55
% transfers	4
% from public high school	74
% in (# of) fraternities	3 (6)
% African-American	98
% Asian	0
% Caucasian	0
% Hispanic	0
% international	2
# of countries represented	15

WHAT'S HOT
old-fashioned dating
political activism
religion
leftist politics
Atlanta

WHAT'S NOT
students are cliquish
registration is a pain
hard liquor
town-gown relations
lack of diversity on campus

ACADEMICS

Academic Rating 81
Profs Interesting Rating 89
Profs Accessible Rating 66
Calendar semester
Student/teacher ratio 17:1
% profs PhD/tenured 75/74
Hours of study per day 3.54

MOST POPULAR MAJORS
engineering
business administration
biology/premedical

STUDENTS SPEAK OUT

Life

Students report that their historic campus has seen better days. The campus is undergoing renovations, but its current state leads one student to comment, "Morehouse is by no means a country club." Even though it is nominally a single-sex school, Morehouse classes are open to all students in the Atlanta University Center, and Morehouse students frequently take classes at the all-women's Spelman College. As a result, social life here is much more lively than at most single-sex institutions. Greek life is popular—too popular, some would claim (see *School Daze*, the film Spike Lee based on his experiences at Morehouse, for more information). Atlanta is popular with all its college students, and Morehouse is no exception.

Academics

Morehouse, an all-male, predominately black college in Atlanta, boasts a distinguished list of alumni: Martin Luther King, Jr., Julian Bond, Spike Lee, and Lerone Bennett are just some of the school's graduates. Ironically, this impressive list tends to overshadow Morehouse's current achievements. Most people know Morehouse only as "the school King attended." In fact, Morehouse continues to produce the nation's and the black community's potential leaders: half of all recent Morehouse graduates went on to pursue a graduate degree. Career-oriented study is the predominant focus of the student body: business and management, premedical sciences, engineering, and pre-law studies claim well over half the students. No student, however, can escape Morehouse without a well-rounded liberal arts, sciences, and ethnic studies background: the school's core curriculum, which takes two full years to complete, covers all these subjects. Because Morehouse is a member of the Atlanta University Center, a consortium of six predominantly black schools, students have a variety of course offerings to choose from. Students reported that their professors are excellent teachers but do not always make themselves readily available outside the classroom. Writes one student, "This school requires a dedication on the part of the student in order to work closely with the faculty." They also complain that administrative chores are unnecessarily difficult. Explains one undergrad, "A word my college should become more familiar with is organization!" While recognizing these problems, though, students report satisfaction with Morehouse. Concludes one student, "There is a true spirit of pride that flows through here. The school's positive effects can be seen in the attitudes of students and faculty. This school teaches you to know yourself."

Student Body

Morehouse draws students from all over the country. Outside the South, the Eastern Seaboard is the most prolific source of Morehouse undergrads. Students are politically progressive but also fairly religious, and therefore socially a little conservative. The typical Morehouse attitude is summed up by the student who writes, "Adversity builds character and the hotter the fire, the tougher the steel. If you come to Morehouse, you will either become a man or you will leave, plain and simple."

FINANCIAL AID: 404-215-2638

ADMISSIONS

The admissions committee considers (in descending order of importance): HS record, test scores, class rank, recommendations, essay. *Also considered (in descending order of importance):* extracurriculars, personality, alumni relationship, special talents. Either the SAT or ACT is required; SAT is preferred. An interview is required. *High school units required/recommended:* 16 total units are required; 4 English required, 3 math required, 2 science required, 2 foreign language recommended, 2 social studies required, 2 history recommended. Minimum combined SAT I score of 980 (composite ACT score of 21), rank in top half of secondary school class, and minimum 2.5 GPA required. TOEFL is required of all international students. *The admissions office says:* "Half of the college's current undergraduates (all four years) have graduated in the top 20 percent of their respective high school class."

The Inside Word

Morehouse is one of the most selective historically black colleges in the country. Applicants should prepare themselves for a rigorous candidate review process. Much more than a solid academic profile is necessary to gain admission; expect to devote significant energy toward demonstrating that you make a good match with the college.

FINANCIAL AID

Students should submit: FAFSA, state aid form, a copy of parents' most recent income tax filing (due April 1). The Princeton Review suggests that all financial aid forms be submitted as soon as possible after January 1. *The following grants/scholarships are offered:* Pell, SEOG, academic merit, athletic, the school's own scholarships, the school's own grants, state scholarships, state grants, private scholarships, private grants, ROTC, United Negro College Fund. *Students borrow from the following loan programs:* Stafford, Perkins, PLUS, private loans. Applicants will be notified of awards beginning April 15. College Work-Study Program is available. Institutional employment is available.

FROM THE ADMISSIONS OFFICE

"Morehouse College is the nation's only predominantly black, all-male, four-year liberal arts college. It is an independent institution located on a fifty-acre campus in Atlanta, Georgia. "The college was founded in 1867 as the Augusta Institute in Augusta, Georgia. The college was relocated to Atlanta in 1879 as the Atlanta Baptist College and was renamed Morehouse College in 1913." Morehouse is committed to educating and developing strong black leaders who will be dedicated to addressing the problems of society. The Morehouse education is designed to serve the three basic aspects of a well-rounded man: the personal, the social, and the professional."

ADMISSIONS

Admissions Rating	81
% of applicants accepted	45
% of acceptees attending	43

FRESHMAN PROFILE

Average verbal SAT	560
Average math SAT	600
Average ACT	NR
Average TOEFL	500
Graduated top 20% of class	28
Graduated top 40% of class	66
Graduated top 60% of class	91
Average HS GPA or Avg.	3.1

DEADLINES

Early decision	11/1
Regular admission	2/15
Regular notification	4/1
Non-fall registration	yes

APPLICANTS ALSO LOOK AT

AND OFTEN PREFER
Georgia Tech.

AND SOMETIMES PREFER
Fisk
Clark Atlanta
U. Maryland-Coll. Park
U. Georgia
Hampton

AND RARELY PREFER
Howard
Emory

FINANCIAL FACTS

Financial Aid Rating	74
Tuition	$7,430
Room & board	$5,490
Estimated book expense	$350
% frosh receiving aid	62
% undergrads receiving aid	71
% aid is need-based	65
% frosh w/ grant (avg)	40 ($3,000)
% frosh w/ loan (avg)	60 ($2,500)
% UGs w/ job (avg)	18 ($1,300)
Off-campus job outlook	fair

MOUNT HOLYOKE COLLEGE

COLLEGE STREET, SOUTH HADLEY, MA 01075-1488   ADMISSIONS: 413-538-2023   FAX: 413-538-2391

CAMPUS LIFE

Quality of Life Rating	**93**
Type of school	private
Affiliation	none
Environment	suburban

STUDENTS

FT undergrad enrollment	1,848
% male/female	0/100
% from out of state	80
% live on campus	99
% spend weekend on campus	NR
% transfers	NR
% from public high school	72
% African-American	4
% Asian	8
% Caucasian	71
% Hispanic	3
% international	13
# of countries represented	52

WHAT'S HOT
support groups
campus is beautiful
library
lab facilities
dorms

WHAT'S NOT
beer
Greeks
drugs
hard liquor
cigarettes

ACADEMICS

Academic Rating	**94**
Profs Interesting Rating	98
Profs Accessible Rating	96
Calendar	4-1-4
Student/teacher ratio	10:1
% profs PhD	96
Hours of study per day	3.96

MOST POPULAR MAJORS
English
politics
international relations

% GRADS WHO PURSUE...
Law 7, Med 7, MBA 2, MA 11

STUDENTS SPEAK OUT

Life
Most Mount Holyoke students love the sense of family they get here: one recalls, "From the first moment...the atmosphere was warm and homey. I felt like I was being baked by Betty Crocker." The all-female environment is a huge plus for many but takes a little getting used to. Reports one student, "Freshman year I couldn't wait to transfer—by senior year I didn't want to graduate." After making the adjustment to single-sex life, students find lots of intimacy and support. The college "gives you pure friendship minus the competition for most beautiful/skinniest/most attractive to guys." And of course, "If you want to see men you can just hop on the five-college bus and go to another college." Mount Holyoke is a member of the Five College Consortium, which also includes UMass-Amherst, Smith, Amherst, and Hampshire. Still, the Mount Holyoke way of life isn't for everyone. There "aren't many parties on campus, because of the no-keg rule." While many believe that "by working at your social life you get practice for the real world" and are proud that life does not revolve around parties, drinking, drugs, or boys, others wish the place were more lively. One mourns, "The weekends on campus consist of laundry and "Saturday Night Live." I suppose that is why there is a transfer club in my dorm (a collection of students determined to escape). I am one of them." Students strongly recommend bringing a car if you can.

Academics
Writes one Mount Holyoke College senior, "When I started applying to colleges, I never assumed I'd be at a women's school, but now I wouldn't trade my experience for the world." Such attitude readjustments are not unusual at Mount Holyoke, the nation's first all-women's college and still one of its most academically challenging and rewarding. Students here enjoy "great and very approachable" professors, a "nurturing and supportive atmosphere," and a gorgeous New England campus. Best of all, Mount Holyoke students agree that their school is a "uniquely challenging" place where "permanent self-confidence and unyielding motivation" are instilled from day one. Opportunities abound to study a variety of excellent liberal arts courses in very small classes. Life sciences departments, while small, are also effective enough to send five percent of MHC graduates on to medical school. In general, students here work extremely hard, take their course work very seriously and feel the tough workload rewards them by providing focus. "If you didn't know where you were going when you came, you sure do when you leave!" MHC women are also the nation's second happiest all-female student body (Sweet Briar is number one).

Student Body
Mount Holyoke claims a relatively diverse student body (about sixteen percent of the students are minorities), and interaction between everyone is frequent and casual. There are "not as many lesbians as people think. They're very vocal because they can 'get away with it'—that is, not be harassed." Most students here are very liberal and accepting of the gay community.

ADMISSIONS

The admissions committee considers (in descending order of importance): HS record, class rank, essay, test scores, recommendations. *Also considered (in descending order of importance):* alumni relationship, extracurriculars, geographical distribution, personality, special talents. Either the SAT or ACT is required. An interview is recommended. *High school units required/recommended:* 4 English recommended, 3 math recommended, 3 science recommended, 4 foreign language recommended, 2 history recommended. Additional courses in listed subject areas are recommended. TOEFL is required of all international students.

The Inside Word

Mount Holyoke has benefited well from the renaissance of interest in women's colleges; selectivity and academic quality is on the rise. Considering that the college was already fairly selective, candidates are well-advised to take the admissions process seriously. Matchmaking is a significant factor here; strong academic performance, well-written essays, and an understanding of and appreciation for "the Holyoke experience" will usually carry the day.

FINANCIAL AID

Students should submit: FAFSA (due February 1), the school's own financial aid form (due February 1), state aid form (due February 1), a copy of parents' most recent income tax filing (due February 1). The Princeton Review suggests that all financial aid forms be submitted as soon as possible after January 1. *The following grants/scholarships are offered:* Pell, SEOG, the school's own grants, state scholarships, state grants, private scholarships, private grants. *Students borrow from the following loan programs:* Stafford, Perkins, PLUS, the school's own loan fund, state loans. Applicants will be notified of awards beginning April 1. College Work-Study Program is available. Institutional employment is available.

FROM THE ADMISSIONS OFFICE

"Mount Holyoke's liberal tradition is strengthened by its special commitment to women. This is a time of great testing for women; opportunities for work and experience are vastly increased but real restraints, whether of attitude or of conflicting responsibilities, remain. In a sense every Mount Holyoke woman is a pioneer today, for each is charting new directions in circumstances radically altered from past expectations. As a community dedicated to the education of women, Mount Holyoke creates a sense of continuity and comradeship, which adds immeasurably to the confidence and resolve of its students."

ADMISSIONS

Admissions Rating	82
% of applicants accepted	65
% of acceptees attending	37

FRESHMAN PROFILE

Average verbal SAT	620
Average math SAT	600
Average ACT	NR
Average TOEFL	640
Graduated top 20% of class	84
Graduated top 40% of class	98
Graduated top 60% of class	100
Average HS GPA or Avg.	NR

DEADLINES

Early decision	NR
Regular admission	1/15
Regular notification	4/1
Non-fall registration	no

APPLICANTS ALSO LOOK AT

AND OFTEN PREFER

Dartmouth
Bryn Mawr
Trinity Coll. (CT)

AND SOMETIMES PREFER

Wellesley
Smith
Vassar
Connecticut Coll.
Randolph-Macon Woman's

AND RARELY PREFER

Skidmore
U. Mass.-Amherst

FINANCIAL FACTS

Financial Aid Rating	91
Tuition	$21,250
Room & board	$6,250
Estimated book expense	$750
% frosh receiving aid	73
% undergrads receiving aid	73
% aid is need-based	100
% frosh w/ grant (avg)	71 ($17,467)
% frosh w/ loan (avg)	73 ($2,400)
% UGs w/ job (avg)	60 ($900)
Off-campus job outlook	fair

MUHLENBERG COLLEGE

2400 CHEW STREET, ALLENTOWN, PA 18104-5586　　　ADMISSIONS: 610-821-3200　　FAX: 610-821-3234

CAMPUS LIFE

Quality of Life Rating	83
Type of school	private

AffiliationEvangelical Lutheran Church in America

| Environment | city |

STUDENTS

FT undergrad enrollment	1,674
% male/female	48/52
% from out of state	66
% live on campus	96
% spend weekend on campus	80
% transfers	4
% from public high school	71
% in (# of) fraternities	45 (5)
% in (# of) sororities	38 (4)
% African-American	2
% Asian	4
% Caucasian	91
% Hispanic	2
% international	1
# of countries represented	12

WHAT'S HOT
support groups
campus easy to get around
theater
cigarettes
Greeks

WHAT'S NOT
lack of diversity on campus
political activism
students are cliquish
student publications
Allentown

ACADEMICS

Academic Rating	83
Profs Interesting Rating	88
Profs Accessible Rating	91
Calendar	semester
Student/teacher ratio	14:1
% profs tenured	87
Hours of study per day	3.37

MOST POPULAR MAJORS
biology
psychology
English

% GRADS WHO PURSUE...
Law 6, Med 7, MBA 1, MA 16

STUDENTS SPEAK OUT

Life
Though only about one-third of Muhlenberg's students pledge fraternities and sororities, the Greeks are the mainstay of the social scene at Muhlenberg College. Writes one student, "All there is to do is go to Greek parties." In an effort to curtail student drinking, the administration has recently begun to pressure the fraternities and sororities into finding more creative ways to have a good time besides keg parties. But as a result, complains one student, "Fraternities have become more restricted. Let us have a good time while we're still young!" Despite these rough spots, students describe the atmosphere on campus as friendly—"We are all very close and it's like we are family," gushes one student. Another warns of the flip side of all that closeness, saying, "Everyone here knows who you are, what you do, and who with." As at many small schools, junior year abroad can be a welcome reprieve for restless students. The surrounding area of Allentown receives poor grades, with descriptions ranging from "boring" to "scungy." But Muhlenberg students are trying to change things for the better: over thirty percent of students involve themselves in community service activities, ranging from working with Muhlenberg's own Habitat for Humanity chapter to volunteering in local schools.

Academics
Muhlenberg College is currently experiencing a jump in applications, and one reason may be this impressive statistic: nearly ten percent of Muhlenberg students proceeds to medical school. The other pre-professional programs here are nearly as outstanding, especially business and management. Almost one-third of Muhlenberg's small student body pursues degrees in these highly touted majors. Not surprisingly, students here work hard, and several remark that "classes are difficult; there are no easy ones." Besides the rigorous major requirements, Muhlenberg students must also complete a battery of liberal arts-oriented distribution requirements designed to guarantee that the largely preprofessional students here get well-rounded education. Students are happy with their professors, and report that the school's size is to their benefit academically ("It is very small, and I like that, because all members of the faculty are extraordinarily accessible"). A final note on the Muhlenberg experience: one student reports that "Here at Muhlenberg, the student to squirrel ratio is about one-to-one."

Student Body
Although religious variety is plentiful, ethnic diversity is not one of Muhlenberg's strong suits, though the administration reports that the school is "making strides in terms of diversity." Several students describe themselves as "a homogeneous group." The typical Muhlenberg student is white, middle-class, and somewhat conservative. Muhlenberg is "just the type of place that you either love or don't." Many of the happiest students here seem to fit the Muhlenberg mold. "People here are afraid to look or act differently out of fear of not being accepted," reports one student.

FINANCIAL AID: 610-821-3175

ADMISSIONS

The admissions committee considers (in descending order of importance): HS record, class rank, test scores, essay, recommendations. *Also considered (in descending order of importance):* extracurriculars, personality, special talents, alumni relationship, geographical distribution. Either the SAT or ACT is required. An interview is recommended. *High school units required/recommended:* 18 total units are required; 4 English required, 3 math required, 4 math recommended, 2 science required, 2 foreign language required, 3 foreign language recommended, 2 social studies required, 2 history required. TOEFL is required of all international students.

The Inside Word

The college reports receiving a record number of both Early Decision applications and overall applications this year. Still, Muhlenberg loses a lot of accepted students to competitors, most of whom are very similar geographically and a bit stronger academically. This results in a more lenient admissions committee than would be the case otherwise.

FINANCIAL AID

Students should submit: FAFSA (due February 15), the school's own financial aid form (due February 15), state aid form (due February 15), a copy of parents' most recent income tax filing (due April 15). The Princeton Review suggests that all financial aid forms be submitted as soon as possible after January 1. *The following grants/scholarships are offered:* Pell, SEOG, academic merit, the school's own scholarships, the school's own grants, state scholarships, state grants, private scholarships, private grants, ROTC, foreign aid. *Students borrow from the following loan programs:* Stafford, unsubsidized Stafford, Perkins, PLUS, state loans, private loans. Applicants will be notified of awards beginning April 1. College Work-Study Program is available. Institutional employment is available.

FROM THE ADMISSIONS OFFICE

"Listening to our own students, we've learned that most picked Muhlenberg mainly because it has a long-standing reputation for being academically demanding on one hand, but personally supportive on the other. We expect a lot from our students, but we also expect a lot from ourselves in providing the challenge and support they need to stretch, grow and succeed. It's not unusual for professors to put their home phone numbers on the course syllabus and encourage students to call them at home with questions. Upperclassmen are helpful to underclassmen. 'We really know about collegiality here,' says an alumna who now works at Muhlenberg. 'It's that kind of place.' The supportive atmosphere and strong work ethic produce lots of successes. The premed and pre-law programs are very strong, as are programs in theatre arts, English, psychology, the sciences, business and accounting. 'When I was a student here,' recalls Dr. Walter Loy, now a professor of physics, 'we were encouraged to live life to its fullest, to do our best, to be honest, to deal openly with others, and to treat everyone as an individual. Those are important things, and they haven't changed at Muhlenberg.'"

ADMISSION__

Admissions R__		75
% of applican__ __epted		71
% of acceptee__ __nding		26

FRES___ __N PROFILE	
Average verba__	580
Average math__	580
Average ACT	25
Average TOE__	550
Graduated to__ __ of class	46
Graduated to__ __ of class	77
Graduated to__ __ of class	93
Average HS G__ __Avg.	3.3

___LINES	
Early decision__	NR
Regular admi__	2/15
Regular notif__ __h	4/1
Non-fall regis__ __n	yes

APPLICA__ __ALSO LOOK AT
AN__ __N PREFER
__more
__yette
__high
AND S__ __MES PREFER
Fra__ __& Marshall
__cknell
__ysburg
__inson
__anova
AND__ __LY PREFER
Pe__ __te-U. Park
__lehanna

FINANCIAL __TS

Financial Ai__ __ng	81
Tuition	$17,550
Room & bo__	$4,565
Estimated b__ __xpense	$500
% frosh rec__ __g aid	63
% undergra__ __ceiving aid	60
% aid is nee__ __ed	90
% frosh w/__ __(avg)	52 ($8,230)
% frosh w/__ __vg)	60 ($3,000)
% UGs w/ j__ __g)	18 ($1,000)
Off-campus__ __utlook	good

NEW COLLEGE OF THE UNIV. OF SOUTH FLORIDA

5700 NORTH TAMIAMI TRAIL, SARASOTA, FL 34243-2197   ADMISSIONS: 813-359-4269   FAX: 813-359-4298

CAMPUS LIFE

Quality of Life Rating	**80**
Type of school	public
Affiliation	none
Environment	suburban

STUDENTS

FT undergrad enrollment	586
% male/female	46/54
% from out of state	42
% live on campus	60
% spend weekend on campus	88
% transfers	27
% from public high school	84
% African-American	2
% Asian	8
% Caucasian	85
% Hispanic	5
% international	2
# of countries represented	7

WHAT'S HOT
sex
leftist politics
drugs
dorms
different students interact

WHAT'S NOT
campus food
computer facilities
lab facilities
intercollegiate sports
religion

ACADEMICS

Academic Rating	**92**
Profs Interesting Rating	96
Profs Accessible Rating	92
Calendar	4-1-4
Student/teacher ratio	11:1
% profs PhD/tenured	96/81
Hours of study per day	3.46

MOST POPULAR MAJORS
literature
biology
psychology

% GRADS WHO PURSUE...
Law 6, Med 8, MA 31

STUDENTS SPEAK OUT

Life

The social scene at New College is as self-directed as the intellectual one ("You learn to make your own fun and distractions. Creativity runs abundant from few resources"). There is little interaction with giant USF—New Collegians prefer their own intimate surroundings. Dorms are modern, comfortable, and safe, but demand exceeds supply. Many students opt to live off campus, where apartments are cheap and plentiful. Typical collegiate activities such as varsity sports and frat parties are nowhere to be found at NC; more common pastimes include casual, open get-togethers (with lots of music and pot). Students summarize their social calendars this way: "Go to Tampa, the beach. Emphasis on poetry readings, thrift shopping, concerts, hang out with friends on and off campus, skinny-dips in the hot tub, political and philosophical debates over everything, coffeehouses where everyone performs, and freeform dancing."

Academics

As one student writes, "New College is a world unto itself: an eclectic student body, a gifted faculty, an intimate and intense academic atmosphere...and all this at a bargain price in the beautiful Florida sunshine." The small, bright student body, combined with NC's excellent faculty and unique "contract" system ("instead of grades, each student receives a written evaluation in class, along with a pass/fail specification"), makes for a place well suited to self-motivated types. The academic system is "based on student initiative and flexibility; it requires self-reliance and individuality" in order to succeed. Distribution requirements, and structure in general, are minimal. Many find the lack of guidelines unsettling, so, the warning went, "Don't buy without a test drive" (i.e., visit the school before deciding). Professors are widely praised for their exceptional teaching skills and accessibility. Academic competition is rare, and as an added bonus, bureaucratic hassles are few (although "we don't really get along well with USF"). Students complain that "labs, both computer and natural science, are worse than they were at high school," and warn that the workload "is like being hit with a truck," but note that the rewards are great; explains one, "The experience is rigorous, because this is a grad-school prep program."

Student Body

New College students know that they are an oddball lot. Writes one, "We're a bunch of intellectual freaks who came here and learned to love themselves and each other." The diversity of the student body is best summed up by the student who writes, "I know a fourteen-year-old student and a thirty-two-year-old student, one who studied classical Indian music with a master in India, one who played and traveled with a rock band, one who wants to be an orthodox Jewish rabbi, and one who is now off training for the Olympic handball team." On the downside, one student warns, "It's difficult to get to know people closely, and most non-leftist viewpoints are repressed." It's true that students who aren't particularly gregarious might feel somewhat isolated, but self-confident conservatives have a history of success. One is now in Congress; another chairs the New Hampshire Republican Party.

FINANCIAL AID: 941-359-4255

ADMISSIONS

The admissions committee considers (in descending order of importance): HS record, essay, test scores, recommendations, class rank. *Also considered (in descending order of importance):* personality, extracurriculars, alumni relationship. Either the SAT or ACT is required. An interview is required of some applicants. Admissions process is need-blind. *High school units required/recommended:* 19 total units are required; 4 English required, 3 math required, 3 science required, 2 foreign language required, 3 social studies required. TOEFL is required of all international students. *The admissions office says:* "New College does not award grades. Students receive written evaluations at the end of each semester."

The Inside Word

Applications keep rolling in to New College like the evening tide on Sarasota Bay. Increases in the academic quality of entering students are virtually perpetual, as is recognition by the media. Perhaps the biggest drawback is a surprisingly high attrition rate for a college of this caliber—just as the admissions committee strives to choose wisely, so should prospective students. Don't apply simply because it's a great buy, make sure that it's what you're seeking. In order to be successful, candidates must demonstrate a high level of intellectual curiosity, self-awareness, and maturity. It also helps to be a strong writer, given that the application process requires candidates to submit three short essays, a long essay, and a graded paper from school. Did we forget to mention high grades and test scores? They'll help too, but if you're someone with lots of "potential" as opposed to "credentials," the admissions committee might still vote you in provided you've put together some very convincing evidence that you make a match and deserve a shot.

FINANCIAL AID

Students should submit: FAFSA. The Princeton Review suggests that all financial aid forms be submitted as soon as possible after January 1. *The following grants/scholarships are offered:* Pell, SEOG, academic merit, the school's own scholarships, the school's own grants, state scholarships, state grants, private scholarships, private grants. *Students borrow from the following loan programs:* Stafford, Perkins, PLUS, the school's own loan fund, state loans, private loans. Applicants will be notified of awards beginning April 15. College Work-Study Program is available. Institutional employment is available.

FROM THE ADMISSIONS OFFICE

"New College provides the opportunity to obtain a very high quality education at a low state tuition. Students work directly with senior faculty and are often exposed to levels of study not generally found outside of graduate institutions. The student who will do best at New College is one who is independent, broadminded, self-confident, and capable of rigorous academic work. The very nature of New College requires one to be dedicated to education and the pursuit of individual growth."

ADMISSIONS

Admissions Rating	91
% of applicants accepted	58
% of acceptees attending	50

FRESHMAN PROFILE

Average verbal SAT	680
Average math SAT	630
Average ACT	29
Average TOEFL	NR
Graduated top 20% of class	86
Graduated top 40% of class	97
Graduated top 60% of class	99
Average HS GPA or Avg.	3.8

DEADLINES

Early decision	NR
Regular admission	5/1
Regular notification	rolling
Non-fall registration	yes

APPLICANTS ALSO LOOK AT

AND OFTEN PREFER
Emory
Oberlin
Brown
U. Florida

AND SOMETIMES PREFER
Rice
UC-Santa Cruz

AND RARELY PREFER
Evergreen State
Eckerd
Florida State
Grinnell
Antioch

FINANCIAL FACTS

Financial Aid Rating	88
In-state tuition	$2,030
Out-of-state tuition	$7,949
Room & board	$3,848
Estimated book expense	$700
% frosh receiving aid	70
% undergrads receiving aid	84
% aid is need-based	60
% frosh w/ grant (avg)	60 ($5,035)
% frosh w/ loan (avg)	12 ($2,050)
% UGs w/ job (avg)	20 ($2,100)
Off-campus job outlook	excellent

UNIVERSITY OF NEW HAMPSHIRE

GRANT HOUSE, 4 GARRISON AVENUE, DURHAM, NH 03824

ADMISSIONS: 603-862-1360

CAMPUS LIFE

Quality of Life Rating 79
Type of school   public
Affiliation   none
Environment   town

STUDENTS

FT undergrad enrollment	10,001
% male/female	44/56
% from out of state	40
% live on campus	55
% spend weekend on campus	NR
% transfers	17
% from public high school	NR
% in (# of) fraternities	12 (11)
% in (# of) sororities	12 (6)
% African-American	0
% Asian	1
% Caucasian	91
% Hispanic	1
% international	NR
# of countries represented	32

WHAT'S HOT
drugs
sex
student publications
college radio
hard liquor

WHAT'S NOT
lack of diversity on campus
political activism
computer facilities
registration is a pain
students are cliquish

ACADEMICS

Academic Rating	73
Profs Interesting Rating	74
Profs Accessible Rating	69
Calendar	semester
Student/teacher ratio	17:1
% profs PhD/tenured	88/91
Hours of study per day	3.14

MOST POPULAR MAJORS
business administration
English
psychology

STUDENTS SPEAK OUT

Life

The University of New Hampshire still retains some vestiges of its party-school days. Writes one student, "Socially this school is great—my weekends start on Wednesdays too often!" Despite a new dry campus policy, students report a lot of drinking; pot smoking is still going strong with the considerable 'crunchy' Deadhead population. Students enjoy a wide variety of extracurricular activities: the radio station and school newspaper are popular, as are sports, both intramural and intercollegiate. The frat scene, while popular, is not monolithic, as it is at some schools located in small towns. Students give Durham below-average marks. Explains one student, "The towns surrounding Durham have much to offer students, and Boston is easily accessible. Durham and UNH itself, however, leave much to be desired in terms of the diversity of options available to students."

Academics

According to one undergraduate, "The University of New Hampshire has made the move toward academics and is trying to shun its 'party school' image." UNH has indeed worked to improve facilities and toughen academic requirements, so that now, according to one undergrad, "UNH is perfect for an undergraduate education. It clearly defines the students' purpose for being here: not to party, but to study and learn." A rigorous and varied core curriculum takes up a fourth of the credits necessary toward graduation (beware: students here have little room in their schedules for elective courses). Professors are extremely helpful compared to those at other public institutions: writes one molecular biology major, "Professors here are more than willing to sit down and explain the material if you have any questions. Some of my professors have become good friends of mine." Departments earning the most praise from students are English, business, premedical sciences, and the nursing program. Student complaints center mostly on administrative problems: the dean's office, the bursar, and the library all received below-average grades. Significant efforts to ease registration difficulties, such as phone-registration, have been made. Students also complain about the long semesters. Explains one, "UNH stands for the University of No Holidays. We go back earlier and get out later than any other area schools, which means that kids from other schools scavenge the summer jobs before you do."

Student Body

A whopping percentage of UNH students are white. Writes one student, "The biggest problem at UNH is the lack of ethnic diversity. It's really sad: when you see a black student, you wonder what sports team he's on." The student body is made up of both urbanites and earthy nature lovers, although there are more of the latter. As one student puts it, "If you wear Birkenstocks, L.L. Bean, and are at all 'crunchy,' you'll fit right in." Students identify themselves as politically left-of-center and as more politically concerned than most college students.

FINANCIAL AID: 603-862-3600 · WEB SITE: HTTP://SAMIZDAT.UNH.EDU:70/1/UNH

ADMISSIONS

The admissions committee considers (in descending order of importance): HS record, class rank, recommendations, test scores, essay. *Also considered (in descending order of importance):* personality, alumni relationship, extracurriculars, geographical distribution, special talents. Either the SAT or ACT is required; SAT is preferred. An interview is recommended. Admissions process is need-blind. *High school units required/recommended:* 18 total units are recommended; 4 English recommended, 4 math recommended, 4 science recommended, 3 foreign language recommended, 3 social studies recommended. Minimum rank in top three-tenths of secondary school class. *Special Requirements:* A portfolio is required for art program applicants. An audition is required for music program applicants. TOEFL is required of all international students.

The Inside Word

New Hampshire's emphasis on academic accomplishment in the admissions process makes it clear that the admissions committee is looking for students who have taken high school seriously. Standardized tests take as much of a backseat here as is possible at a large public university.

FINANCIAL AID

Students should submit: FAFSA. The Princeton Review suggests that all financial aid forms be submitted as soon as possible after January 1. *The following grants/ scholarships are offered:* Pell, SEOG, academic merit, athletic, the school's own scholarships, the school's own grants, state scholarships, state grants, private scholarships, private grants, ROTC, foreign aid. *Students borrow from the following loan programs:* Stafford, unsubsidized Stafford, Perkins, PLUS, the school's own loan fund, private loans. College Work-Study Program is available. Institutional employment is available.

FROM THE ADMISSIONS OFFICE

"The University of New Hampshire is a public University founded in 1866 offering over 100 majors to approximately 10,800 undergraduates. Durham is a small New England town rich in history set along Great Bay, an estuary fed by seven rivers. Nearby Portsmouth and Exeter present a variety of historic sites, restaurants, shops, and venues for the performing arts. Boston, Portland, the White Mountains, and the coastline and beaches of Maine, Massachusetts, and New Hampshire are all within easy reach. "UNH has a long tradition of offering a balance between liberal arts and professional studies. Students interested in going into law, medicine, dentistry, and other professional fields are encouraged to major in subjects of their choice for their bachelor's degree. The University's preprofessional advisory committee guide students toward meeting the entrance requirements of the professional schools."

ADMISSIONS

Admissions Rating	71
% of applicants accepted	77
% of acceptees attending	32

FRESHMAN PROFILE

Average verbal SAT	620
Average math SAT	560
Average ACT	NR
Average TOEFL	550
Graduated top 20% of class	43
Graduated top 40% of class	76
Graduated top 60% of class	88
Average HS GPA or Avg.	3.0

DEADLINES

Early decision	NR
Regular admission	2/1
Regular notification	4/15
Non-fall registration	yes

APPLICANTS ALSO LOOK AT

AND OFTEN PREFER

U. Colorado-Boulder
U. Vermont

AND SOMETIMES PREFER

U. Mass.-Amherst
Boston Coll.
U. Maine-Orono
St. Lawrence
Boston U.

AND RARELY PREFER

Providence
Bentley
Clark
Northeastern
U. Conn

FINANCIAL FACTS

Financial Aid Rating	80
In-state tuition	$3,760
Out-of-state tuition	$11,990
Room & board	$4,038
Estimated book expense	$550
% frosh receiving aid	78
% undergrads receiving aid	76
% aid is need-based	98
% frosh w/ grant (avg)	51 ($4,602)
% frosh w/ loan (avg)	68 ($3,418)
% UGs w/ job (avg)	34 ($1,814)
Off-campus job outlook	excellent

New Jersey Institute of Technology

University Heights, Newark, NJ 07102-1982   Admissions: 201-596-3300   Fax: 201-596-1528

CAMPUS LIFE

Quality of Life Rating **61**
Type of school   public
Affiliation   none
Environment   city

STUDENTS
FT undergrad enrollment   3,354
% male/female   82/18
% from out of state   9
% live on campus   25
% spend weekend on campus   50
% transfers   45
% from public high school   80
% in (# of) fraternities   15 (14)
% in (# of) sororities   8 (9)
% African-American   13
% Asian   17
% Caucasian   51
% Hispanic   13
% international   NR
# of countries represented   66

WHAT'S HOT
ethnic diversity on campus
different students interact
religion
registration is a breeze
Greeks

WHAT'S NOT
support groups
off-campus food
unattractive campus
students are unhappy
Newark

ACADEMICS

Academic Rating **70**
Profs Interesting Rating   64
Profs Accessible Rating   60
Calendar   semester
Student/teacher ratio   13:1
% profs PhD/tenured   90/98
Hours of study per day   2.95

MOST POPULAR MAJORS
engineering technology
electrical engineering
mechanical engineering

% GRADS WHO PURSUE...
Law 1, Med 2, MBA 2, MA 15

STUDENTS SPEAK OUT

Life
Students here uniformly agree that NJIT offers little in the way of social distractions. "This school has no social life except fraternities," is how one student describes the situation. The two main culprits are the very lopsided male/female ratio (more than 4:1) and the large commuter population, which causes the campus to thin out pretty quickly after classes. The city of Newark is among the dozen worst college towns, according to our survey, with safety students' chief concern; writes one commuter, "Professors who ask or even insist that students stay several hours beyond class time seem not to realize that Newark is not safe at night." Still, one student notes optimistically that "if you get involved—athletics, intramurals, Greek life, or newspapers—then life at NJIT can be fun. But no one is going to Shanghai you into a good time. If you don't get involved you won't enjoy your stay in lovely Newark, NJ."

Academics
To the in-state students who make up the majority of NJIT's student body, publicly funded NJIT provides "an excellent education for the money." NJIT is notable not only for its reasonable price but also for its quality programs in engineering (especially mechanical and electrical engineering), mathematics, science, and architecture. The school also offers a cooperative education program to its undergraduates, which allows them to make money and gain work experience while earning credit toward their degrees. Students report that class sizes were small for a public institution. They give their teachers poor marks, both for accessibility outside the classroom and for in-class instruction. TAs are a particular sore point. Other complaints concern class schedules ("courses are poorly scheduled, making it hard to make all the courses you need and want fit into one schedule"), the quality of labs ("The school's Physics labs are right out of the Flintstones"), and the administration ("takes no time to communicate with students"). Sums up one student: "NJIT may not offer the best social life, but it is preparing me for a promising future in the working world."

Student Body
NJIT has a large minority population: Asians, blacks, and Hispanics make up two-fifths of the student body. According to many, "There's a lot of self-imposed racial segregation." For many students, as well as for many teachers, English is a second language, leading one sarcastic student to note that "NJIT is great if you want the experience of studying in a foreign country without the expense of going to one." Very few students come here to find an intellectual environment. Most are interested in translating their hard work here immediately into a conventional, high-paying technical job.

FINANCIAL AID: 201-596-3480   E-MAIL: FENSTER@ADMIN.NJIT.EDU   WEB SITE: HTTP://WWW.NJIT.EDU/

ADMISSIONS

The admissions committee considers (in descending order of importance): HS record, class rank, test scores, essay, recommendations. *Also considered (in descending order of importance):* personality, alumni relationship, extracurriculars, special talents. Either the SAT or ACT is required; SAT is preferred. An interview is required of some applicants. Admissions process is need-blind. *High school units required/recommended:* 16 total units are required; 4 English required, 4 math required, 2 science required, 2 foreign language recommended, 1 social studies recommended, 1 history recommended. Minimum combined SAT I score of 1000 (original scoring) and rank in top quarter of secondary school class required. 1 unit of lab science required of management program applicants. 3 units of math required of management/science and science/technology/society programs. *Special Requirements:* TOEFL is required of all international students. Portfolio required of architecture program applicants. A.Appl.Sci. (or equivalent) required of engineering technology program applicants. Essay and interview required of Honors College applicants. *The admissions office says:* "Management applicants and Science Technology and Society applicants are required to take only 3 years of mathematics."

The Inside Word

NJIT is a great choice for students who aspire to technical careers but don't meet the requirements for better known and more selective universities. To top it off, it's a pretty good buy.

FINANCIAL AID

Students should submit: FAFSA. The Princeton Review suggests that all financial aid forms be submitted as soon as possible after January 1. *The following grants/scholarships are offered:* Pell, SEOG, academic merit, the school's own scholarships, the school's own grants, state scholarships, state grants, private scholarships, private grants, federal nursing scholarship, ROTC, foreign aid. *Students borrow from the following loan programs:* Stafford, unsubsidized Stafford, Perkins, PLUS, the school's own loan fund, supplemental loans, state loans, federal nursing loans, health professions loans, private loans. College Work-Study Program is available. Institutional employment is available. Freshmen are discouraged from working.

FROM THE ADMISSIONS OFFICE

"NJIT is a public research university providing instruction, research, and public service in engineering, computer science, management, architecture, engineering technology, applied sciences, and related fields. Approximately $25 million is spent annually for cutting-edge research. The campus is computing intensive and the university has been recognized as a national leader in integrating computer education into its curricula. All full-time freshmen are given a computer for their personal use while at NJIT. NJIT is composed of five units: Newark College of Engineering, School of Industrial Management, College of Science and Liberal Arts, Albert Dorman Honors College, and School of Architecture. The Admissions Office seeks to build a class of freshmen who will be comfortable and able to use the opportunities available at NJIT. The student should be one who wants a large technical university with a small-college atmosphere, high quality education at a modest cost, and close contact with faculty with a variety of academic, research, and business interests."

ADMISSIONS

Admissions Rating	73
% of applicants accepted	67
% of acceptees attending	44

FRESHMAN PROFILE

Average verbal SAT	560
Average math SAT	610
Average ACT	NR
Average TOEFL	520
Graduated top 20% of class	39
Graduated top 40% of class	64
Graduated top 60% of class	79
Average HS GPA or Avg.	72.0

DEADLINES

Early decision	NR
Regular admission	4/1
Regular notification	rolling
Non-fall registration	yes

APPLICANTS ALSO LOOK AT

AND OFTEN PREFER

Rutgers U.
Seton Hall
Stevens Tech.

AND SOMETIMES PREFER

Worcester Poly.
Montclair State
Trenton State
Virginia Tech

FINANCIAL FACTS

Financial Aid Rating	77
In-state tuition	$4,378
Out-of-state tuition	$8,722
Room & board	$5,376
Estimated book expense	$800
% frosh receiving aid	81
% undergrads receiving aid	69
% aid is need-based	82
% frosh w/ grant (avg)	69 ($5,134)
% frosh w/ loan (avg)	53 ($4,626)
% UGs w/ job (avg)	38 ($1,150)
Off-campus job outlook	good

New Mexico Inst. of Mining & Technology

Campus Station, Socorro, NM 87801   Admissions: 800-428-8324   Fax: 505-835-5989

CAMPUS LIFE

Quality of Life Rating	**67**
Type of school	public
Affiliation	none
Environment	town

STUDENTS

FT undergrad enrollment	1,013
% male/female	69/31
% from out of state	40
% live on campus	45
% spend weekend on campus	35
% transfers	22
% from public high school	83
% African-American	1
% Asian	3
% Caucasian	68
% Hispanic	17
% International	2
# of countries represented	33

WHAT'S HOT
different students interact
campus easy to get around
ethnic diversity on campus
library
computer facilities

WHAT'S NOT
campus food
health facilities
theater
student government
student publications

ACADEMICS

Academic Rating	**82**
Profs Interesting Rating	76
Profs Accessible Rating	79
Calendar	semester
Student/teacher ratio	13:1
% profs PhD/tenured	96/96
Hours of study per day	3.39

MOST POPULAR MAJORS
environmental engineering
physics

% GRADS WHO PURSUE...
Law 1, Med 1, MA 27

STUDENTS SPEAK OUT

Life

Do you like small cities that offer a bunch of outdoor activities and leave you plenty of time for your studies? Then Socorro might be just for you. Dubbed "Suckorro" by more than one student, this town has more hiking, camping, and rock-climbing opportunities than you can shake a crooked stick at. But that's about it. "There's not a lot of social life in the town itself, so the students have to keep themselves occupied," explains one. "Studying is a major part of college life," states another seemingly obviously, but at Tech, they're not kidding. "School is The Most Important Thing," drives home a freshman studying engineering. Still, one can have fun and work hard too, right? "Always easy to find a party," reassures one Techie, while another describes a good time as "going to Denny's and watching videos." Whatever you choose to do, if you're a guy, you may be doing it alone. With a disproportionately large number of men for every woman, dating is tough, which may be good in a way, because the school does not offer health services, reproductive or otherwise. Food also gets incredibly low marks. Begs one sad male, "The percentage of women is getting higher [but it] is still low. Please send help!" Women, are you listening?

Academics

"The sheer smallness of the school makes the red tape much more manageable than it might otherwise be," offers a senior physics major, diplomatically, about Tech's administration. Others took the low road. "[The registrar's office] consistently schedules multiple classes for the same room and grossly mismatches class sizes with classrooms. Perhaps they need a field trip around the campus," quips a biology major. A geology major waxes historical, "Lab facilities are from some necromancer of the 10th century." One reason students may be a bit cranky is the school's low graduation rate (only about forty percent of enrolled freshman graduate from Tech). Professors largely escape this considerable ire, however, being judged both qualified and accessible. "Most professors are extremely concerned with their students," offers one undergrad. Another agrees, "The professors are very good and nearly always available in their offices." Many classes are taught by TAs, but sometimes that's not necessarily a bad thing. Offers this student, "We've had many TAs teaching supplementary labs or tutoring sessions—these TAs have saved many grades. Sometimes TAs are better teachers than the profs." The classes at Tech are quite small, and remember, in Socorro, where minerals are many and distractions are few, "There is nothing to do but schoolwork."

Student Body

"A very diverse group of American misfits and foreigners. Very colorful!" An interesting self-description, eh? It wasn't an unusual one. Of his fellow students, this student comments, "We all seem to have had similar experiences in high school, i.e. we were all social lepers." Yes, "geek" and "nerd" pops up in many descriptions as well. Let's face it, this is a technical school, and nobody is ashamed of that! Praises one, "This is the most diverse, open-minded, and laid-back student body I have encountered." Cheers another, "They have a passion few liberal arts majors can match." While a few less-than-positive comments did pop up ("Students are politically uncaring and insensitive"), Techies by and large have few problems with each other, other than the fact that there are few women and many men. Discrimination is not an issue, and neither is a lack of diversity or interaction among students of different cultures. "Everyone is cool with each other," explains one freshman. Groovy.

ADMISSIONS

The admissions committee considers (in descending order of importance): HS record, test scores, class rank, recommendations. *Also considered (in descending order of importance):* alumni relationship, extracurriculars, geographical distribution, special talents. ACT is preferred. An interview is recommended. Admissions process is need-blind. *High school units required/recommended:* 15 total units are required; 24 total units are recommended; 4 English required, 3 math required, 4 math recommended, 2 science required, 4 science recommended, 2 foreign language recommended, 3 social studies required, 4 social studies recommended, 1 history recommended. Minimum composite ACT score of 21 and minimum 2.0 GPA required. TOEFL is required of all international students.

The Inside Word

A 2.0 GPA and a 21 ACT score is far from stringent. This is one of those situations that call for serious self-examination. Are you really ready to take on the demands of a fairly solid technical institute? If you aren't sure, you should probably pass, even if you're admissible.

FINANCIAL AID

Students should submit: FAFSA, the school's own financial aid form. The Princeton Review suggests that all financial aid forms be submitted as soon as possible after January 1. *The following grants/scholarships are offered:* Pell, SEOG, academic merit, the school's own scholarships, state scholarships, state grants, private scholarships. *Students borrow from the following loan programs:* Stafford, unsubsidized Stafford, Perkins, PLUS, the school's own loan fund. College Work-Study Program is available. Institutional employment is available.

FROM THE ADMISSIONS OFFICE

"Over a century old, Tech has internationally known programs in the areas of physics, geology, hydrology, and explosives research. At New Mexico Tech, we pride ourselves on the high quality of education we give to our students, in small classes where the professor will know you personally and take the time to help you. New Mexico Tech is also the parent body of several research organizations. These organizations and the many faculty research projects offer students the opportunity for hands-on research work. Many professors have research projects which students work on. Lanngmuir Laboratory for Atmospheric Research, for example, is one of the nation's foremost research organizations for areas such as the physics of clouds and thunderstorms and electrification of clouds. The lab often employs physics majors. The average Tech undergraduate graduating with a B.S. degree has the equivalent of seven months of full-time technical job experience. That's important when your looking for a job."

ADMISSIONS

Admissions Rating	77
% of applicants accepted	74
% of acceptees attending	42

FRESHMAN PROFILE

Average verbal SAT	590
Average math SAT	560
Average ACT	26
Average TOEFL	540
Graduated top 20% of class	60
Graduated top 40% of class	83
Graduated top 60% of class	95
Average HS GPA or Avg.	3.3

DEADLINES

Early decision	NR
Regular admission	8/1
Regular notification	rolling
Non-fall registration	yes

APPLICANTS ALSO LOOK AT

AND SOMETIMES PREFER

MIT
Cal Tech
Colorado Mines
U. New Mexico

AND RARELY PREFER

New Mexico State

FINANCIAL FACTS

Financial Aid Rating	90
In-state tuition	$1,366
Out-of-state tuition	$5,644
Room & board	$3,214
Estimated book expense	$600
% frosh receiving aid	88
% undergrads receiving aid	73
% aid is need-based	75
% frosh w/ grant (avg)	83 ($2,915)
% frosh w/ loan (avg)	35 ($3,347)
% UGs w/ job (avg)	70 ($1,750)
Off-campus job outlook	good

NEW YORK UNIVERSITY

22 WASHINGTON SQUARE NORTH, NEW YORK, NY 10011   ADMISSIONS: 212-998-4500   FAX: 212-995-4902

CAMPUS LIFE

Quality of Life Rating **72**
Type of school   private
Affiliation   none
Environment   metropolis

STUDENTS

FT undergrad enrollment	13,464
% male/female	42/58
% from out of state	40
% live on campus	40
% spend weekend on campus	95
% transfers	26
% from public high school	65
% in (# of) fraternities	7 (11)
% in (# of) sororities	5 (7)
% African-American	10
% Asian	21
% Caucasian	54
% Hispanic	9
% international	5
# of countries represented	120

WHAT'S HOT

ethnic diversity on campus
drugs
New York
political activism
old-fashioned dating

WHAT'S NOT

unattractive campus
students are unhappy
intramural sports
intercollegiate sports

ACADEMICS

Academic Rating **80**
Profs Interesting Rating   62
Profs Accessible Rating   65
Calendar   semester
Student/teacher ratio   13:1
% profs PhD/tenured   98/99
Hours of study per day   3.09

MOST POPULAR MAJORS
visual/performing arts
business
social science/history

% GRADS WHO PURSUE...
Law 25, Med 14, MBA 15, MA 13

STUDENTS SPEAK OUT

Life

Unlike most universities of its size, who have struggled to maintain their "status quo" through the fiscally demanding nineties, NYU has undergone significant growth and transformation. In the past NYU's lack of a campus, coupled with its large size, often caused students to feel detached from their school. Students characterized the administration as bureaucrats interested almost solely in collecting money. Registration was a process akin to Chinese water torture. To be sure, the NYU of today still shows room for improvement, but the positive changes are noteworthy. A huge increase in the amount of student housing and major efforts to create a campus feel around Washington Square have improved the sense of community about as much as one can reasonably expect. Students actually know the president, a departure from other recent NYU heads who seemed bent on avoiding them. And registration now occurs by computer and over the telephone, helping to ease long lines and bitter student emotions. The hefty price tag for attending NYU still makes for student frustration, but for most students Greenwich Village, the heart of the social universe of young New York, helps to make it all worth it. "NYU would be a great school if it were in the middle of Death Valley, but it isn't," explains one student from Florida. "It's in the middle of New York City, and that puts it past great, somewhere in the vicinity of orgasmic."

Academics

NYU's greatest strength is its diversity, both in academic programs and student body. Two divisions in particular stand out : the Stern Business School and the Tisch School of the Arts, both of which serve undergraduates and graduate students. Both are nationally recognized as leaders in their fields, the Tisch program mostly for its film program (alumni include Oliver Stone, Martin Scorsese, and many others). Art history is the best of the many solid liberal arts departments found in Washington Square College. As one student notes, "NYU is a perfect school if you're not really sure about your career goals. It embraces a wide spectrum of majors." Another puts it this way: "I am never bored and could never imagine being in a place less amazing and dynamic than here. NYU is like a miniature United Nations." On the downside, students find many professors cold and give them low marks for in-class and out-of-class performance.

Student Body

NYU's student body is one of the most diverse in the nation. Here are African-Americans, whites, Asians, and Hispanics, commuters and residents, hip urbanites and suburbanites, straights and gays, Jews, Christians, Muslims, Buddhists, and Hindus, all apparently united by one thing: their love/hate relationship with their school. Although NYU students gush about many aspects of the university—the diversity of programs it offers, the diversity of the student body, and Greenwich Village, most notably—they are also a generally unhappy lot. "Post-punk" definitely describes the prevalent attitude.

ADMISSIONS

The admissions committee considers (in descending order of importance): HS record, test scores, recommendations, essay. *Also considered (in descending order of importance):* extracurriculars, personality, special talents, alumni relationship. Either the SAT or ACT is required. Admissions process is need-blind. *High school units required/recommended:* 16 total units are required; 4 English required, 3 math required, 2 science required, 2 foreign language required, 3 social studies required. Specific requirements vary by program. Three SAT II exams required of applicants to B.A./M.D. program. *Special Requirements:* TOEFL is required of all international students. Submission of creative material or audition required of art, music, and performing arts program applicants and applicants to non-performance areas in the School of the Arts.

The Inside Word

NYU is more selective than most large private universities but, except for a few particularly choosy programs, no more personal in its evaluation of candidates. A solid GPA and test scores go farther toward getting in than anything else. Still, the university is very serious about projecting a highly selective image and it's dangerous to take your application too lightly. Since the completion of several major dormitories in the late 1980s, NYU has turned its attention to increasing the national profile of its student body. Applications have increased by more than half over the past four years.

FINANCIAL AID

Students should submit: FAFSA (due January 15). The Princeton Review suggests that all financial aid forms be submitted as soon as possible after January 1. *The following grants/scholarships are offered:* Pell, SEOG, academic merit, the school's own scholarships, the school's own grants, state scholarships, state grants, private scholarships, private grants. *Students borrow from the following loan programs:* Stafford, unsubsidized Stafford, Perkins, PLUS, state loans, federal nursing loans, private loans. Applicants will be notified of awards beginning April 1. College Work-Study Program is available. Institutional employment is available.

FROM THE ADMISSIONS OFFICE

"NYU is distinctive both in the quality of education we provide and in the exhilarating atmosphere in which our students study and learn. As an undergraduate in one of our seven small-to-medium-size colleges, you will enjoy a faculty/student ratio of only 13:1 and a dynamic, challenging learning environment that encourages lively interaction between students and professors. At the same time, you will have available to you all the resources of a distinguished university dedicated to research and scholarship at the highest levels, including a curriculum that offers over 2,500 courses and 160 programs of study and a faculty that include some of the most highly regarded scholars, scientists, and artists in the country. "New York University is a vital, vibrant community. There is an aura of energy and excitement here; a sense that possibilities and opportunities are limited only by the number of hours in a day. The educational experience at NYU is intense, but varied and richly satisfying. You will be actively engaged in your own education, both in the classroom and beyond."

ADMISSIONS

Admissions Rating	86
% of applicants accepted	46
% of acceptees attending	38

FRESHMAN PROFILE

Average verbal SAT	NR
Average math SAT	NR
Average ACT	NR
Average TOEFL	NR
Graduated top 20% of class	60
Graduated top 40% of class	NR
Graduated top 60% of class	NR
Average HS GPA or Avg.	3.3

DEADLINES

Early decision	11/15
Regular admission	1/15
Regular notification	4/1
Non-fall registration	yes

APPLICANTS ALSO LOOK AT

AND OFTEN PREFER

Columbia
Barnard
U. Pennsylvania
Cornell U.
Boston U.

AND SOMETIMES PREFER

UCLA
UC-Berkeley
U. Michigan
U. Chicago
Yale

AND RARELY PREFER

Hofstra
Rutgers U.

FINANCIAL FACTS

Financial Aid Rating	74
Tuition	$20,756
Room & board	$7,856
Estimated book expense	$450
% frosh receiving aid	86
% undergrads receiving aid	73
% aid is need-based	90
% frosh w/ grant (avg)	90 ($8,808)
% frosh w/ loan (avg)	NR
% UGs w/ job (avg)	29 ($3,000)
Off-campus job outlook	excellent

NORTH CAROLINA SCHOOL OF THE ARTS

P.O. Box 12189, Winston-Salem, NC 27117-2189   Admissions: 910-770-3291   Fax: 919-770-3375

CAMPUS LIFE

Quality of Life Rating   **78**
Type of school   public
Affiliation   none
Environment   city

STUDENTS
FT undergrad enrollment   419
% male/female   53/47
% from out of state   50
% live on campus   65
% spend weekend on campus   70
% transfers   18
% from public high school   95
% African-American   7
% Asian   1
% Caucasian   86
% Hispanic   2
% international   3
# of countries represented   9

WHAT'S HOT
different students interact
theater
cigarettes
music associations
sex

WHAT'S NOT
computer facilities
student publications
intramural sports
intercollegiate sports
student government

ACADEMICS

Academic Rating   **82**
Profs Interesting Rating   95
Profs Accessible Rating   83
Calendar   trimester
Student/teacher ratio   7:1
% profs PhD/tenured   15/40
Hours of study per day   2.97

MOST POPULAR MAJORS
theatre design/production
music
theatre

STUDENTS SPEAK OUT

Life

Students differ greatly in their views about social life at the North Carolina School of the Arts. Most agree that the school provides few traditional college social opportunities, as one students notes: "Not much to do on campus, but that keeps you studying." However, many students "try to have creative fun at all times...whether intoxicated or not. We climb all over campus, explore the city, listen to live music and generally go elsewhere to have fun over the weekends." Regardless, students concur that "students at NCSA work very hard in their fields and need time to unwind, which they also take very seriously." Many students report that stress is a pervasive state of being at NCSA, but, as one student notes, "Daily life is stressful, but only as stressful as you allow it to be." Special events during the year include: Beaux Arts ("an end of year weeklong festival of comedians, open mike performers, theater, musicians, etc.") and Intensive Arts ("two weeks before Christmas break, we begin a period in which academic work is suspended").

Academics

NCSA's goal is to serve students not in just one field of the arts but in virtually every field. Here musicians, dancers, and filmmakers attend classes alongside actors, graphic artists, and designers, creating in the process an exciting arts community in which students can fully explore different disciplines. Students approve of their instructors' performance ("The teachers here are the best"; "Most teachers are highly interactive with students, a luxury"). Students of music, drama, and arts are particularly positive; film students, while generally happy, note that "being a new school, there are a couple rough edges, but it's a good course." The School of the Arts maintains a General Studies division to provide students with more traditional academic work, which some students call "kind of a joke." But, as another notes, "More energy is spent on our art than academics—that's why we're here!" The administration here is also well regarded; as one student reports, "This school is very open to student input. Any suggestions by students are listened to." Overall, most agree, "I love my profs, and the programs. It's an excellent school for Arts."

Student Body

NCSA students report that student relations are very good. Explains one, "Students at NCSA are committed to each other in a strong bond of support. The arts require trust and teamwork." Students are accepting of alternative lifestyles; several report that there is a "large homosexual contingency. We have a homecoming 'Queen' and 'King.'" Despite "much inter-major rivalry and intra-major backstabbing...everyone gets along pretty well." Another tells us, "The worst thing about the attitude toward differences at this school is the realization that the rest of the world is not as open and accepting."

FINANCIAL AID: 919-770-3297

ADMISSIONS

The admissions committee considers (in descending order of importance): HS record, test scores, recommendations, class rank. *Also considered (in descending order of importance):* special talents, extracurriculars, personality, alumni relationship, geographical distribution. Either the SAT or ACT is required; SAT is preferred. An interview is required. *High school units required/recommended:* 20 total units are required; 4 English required, 3 math required, 3 science required, 2 foreign language recommended, 1 social studies required, 1 history required. *Special Requirements:* TOEFL is required of all international students. Portfolio required of design/production and filmmaking program applicants. *The admissions office says:* "Special consideration or exceptions may be granted for exceptionally talented applicants [who do not meet these requirements]."

The Inside Word

Getting into the North Carolina School of the Arts is about as difficult as one would expect from one of the best performing arts schools in the country. Keep in mind that staying in is even tougher. Anyone looking to attend a place such as NCSA needs to start preparing for auditions and related interviews well before the start of senior year. Once the school year begins, there are far too many other demands on your time, and it moves much too quickly. Speak with admissions officers and faculty in the spring of your junior year—it isn't nearly as hectic for them as it is immediately prior to and during auditions. You'll get much more contact and advice from them at other times.

FINANCIAL AID

Students should submit: FAFSA, the school's own financial aid form. The Princeton Review suggests that all financial aid forms be submitted as soon as possible after January 1. *The following grants/scholarships are offered:* Pell, the school's own scholarships, the school's own grants, state scholarships, state grants, private scholarships. *Students borrow from the following loan programs:* Stafford, Perkins, PLUS, state loans. Applicants will be notified of awards beginning April 15. College Work-Study Program is available. Institutional employment is available. Freshmen are discouraged from working.

FROM THE ADMISSIONS OFFICE

"There's no place like the North Carolina School of the Arts anywhere in the country—perhaps even the world. It's an exciting place where the best and the brightest young people emerge as polished professionals and exciting artists, ready to make their marks on the world, ready to enter productive and rewarding careers in the arts. The mission of the North Carolina School of the Arts is to train exceptionally talented students at the high school and college levels for professional careers in the arts: specifically, dance, design and production, drama, music, and the visual arts. NCSA also offers a range of general studies in the sciences and humanities."

ADMISSIONS

Admissions Rating	76
% of applicants accepted	NR
% of acceptees attending	NR

FRESHMAN PROFILE

Average verbal SAT	670
Average math SAT	580
Average ACT	NR
Average TOEFL	500
Graduated top 20% of class	9
Graduated top 40% of class	16
Graduated top 60% of class	22
Average HS GPA or Avg.	2.7

DEADLINES

Early decision	NR
Regular admission	NR
Regular notification	4/1
Non-fall registration	yes

APPLICANTS ALSO LOOK AT

AND SOMETIMES PREFER
Eastman

AND RARELY PREFER
UNC-Chapel Hill
North Carolina State

FINANCIAL FACTS

Financial Aid Rating	88
In-state tuition	$1,308
Out-of-state tuition	$9,159
Room & board	$3,706
Estimated book expense	$640
% frosh receiving aid	60
% undergrads receiving aid	79
% aid is need-based	75
% frosh w/ grant (avg)	60 ($875)
% frosh w/ loan (avg)	38 ($2,000)
% UGs w/ job (avg)	35 ($560)
Off-campus job outlook	good

NORTH CAROLINA STATE UNIVERSITY

P.O. Box 7103, Raleigh, NC 27695-7103   Admissions: 919-515-2434   Fax: 919-515-5039

STUDENTS SPEAK OUT

Life

Intercollegiate sports are an important feature of life at North Carolina State. Wolfpack basketball, football, and soccer each boast thousands of dedicated fans among the student body. Fraternities and sororities are also central to social life, but some who don't like them contend that they are too dominant on campus. "There is too much emphasis on Greek activities," says one student, "yeah, right, I wanna pay $600 a semester to buy a personality and some cheesy friends." But there are enough social activities that avoiding frat parties is not that difficult. One student assures us, "There is a wide variety of things to do—especially because we are located in a great city." Students praise Raleigh for its receptiveness to students. In fact, most NC State students end up living in Raleigh rather than on campus, because there is not nearly enough dorm space to go around. Drinking is big here, and the recent wave of crackdowns on underage drinking doesn't seem to have reached NC State...yet.

Academics

NC State, for years plagued by scandals involving the academic records of its athletes, has responded to the adversity by beefing up its commitment to academic quality and integrity. Especially in technical areas, NC State is thought of as "an excellent school." Particularly noteworthy departments are engineering, business management, design, architecture, and the top-notch textile school. All students must fulfill distribution requirements that include a number of liberal arts courses, but students say that most classes stress an analytical, science-oriented approach to their subjects. Although a few respondents report that the faculty are "very dedicated, helpful, and approachable," overall the faculty got low marks from students for both teaching ability and accessibility. Many classes do tend to be large and crowded, but few students complained. No one comes here expecting small classes. The overall atmosphere is easy going. Students we asked admit that doing "most or all the assigned reading for classes" is not overly important. NC State emphasizes a practical approach to education: an important part of its undergraduate curriculum is the cooperative education program, which allows students to work for credit outside the classroom. North Carolina State provides a quality education for the price, and its renewed focus on academics bodes well for the school's future.

Student Body

The large undergraduate population at NC State is "very diverse," despite the disproportionate number of native North Carolinians. Reasonable tuition prices combined with the many different scholarships make it possible for students of all socioeconomic backgrounds to attend. The political atmosphere is mostly "conservative-fundamentalist," but in a school this size, it is easy to find people of all stripes.

FINANCIAL AID: 919-515-2421   WEB SITE: HTTP://WWW.NCSU.EDU/

ADMISSIONS

The admissions committee considers (in descending order of importance): HS record, class rank, test scores, essay, recommendations. *Also considered (in descending order of importance):* geographical distribution, alumni relationship, extracurriculars, personality, special talents. Either the SAT or ACT is required. Admissions process is need-blind. *High school units required/recommended:* 20 total units are required; 4 English required, 3 math required, 4 math recommended, 3 science required, 2 foreign language required, 2 social studies required, 1 history required. *Special Requirements:* A portfolio is required for art program applicants. TOEFL is required of all international students. *The admissions office says:* "When students are accepted for admission at NC State University, they are admitted directly into the college of their choice. NCSU is divided into nine colleges: Agriculture and Life Sciences, Design, Education and Psychology, Engineering, Forest Resources, Humanities and Social Sciences, Management, Physical and Mathematical Sciences, and Textiles. Students who are interested in a particular college, but unsure about a major, may elect to apply for the undecided option in that college. For students who are truly undecided, NCSU's First-year College program allows students a year to explore their options before choosing a major."

The Inside Word

Prospective students should be certain to investigate additional requirements for the college they wish to enter; universities that admit students to specific programs often vary standards significantly. Nonresidents will find it dramatically easier to get in to NC State than to UNC.

FINANCIAL AID

Students should submit: FAFSA (due March 1), the school's own financial aid form (due March 1), state aid form (due March 1). The Princeton Review suggests that all financial aid forms be submitted as soon as possible after January 1. *The following grants/scholarships are offered:* Pell, SEOG, academic merit, athletic, the school's own scholarships, the school's own grants, state scholarships, state grants, private scholarships, private grants, ROTC. *Students borrow from the following loan programs:* Stafford, unsubsidized Stafford, Perkins, PLUS, the school's own loan fund, state loans, private loans. College Work-Study Program is available. Institutional employment is available. Freshmen are discouraged from working.

FROM THE ADMISSIONS OFFICE

"Our students select NC State for its strong programs, excellent reputation, location in the capital city of Raleigh, low cost, and friendly atmosphere. Our students like the excitement of a large campus and the many opportunities it offers, such as Cooperative Education, Study Abroad, extensive Scholars programming, and theme residence halls. An NC State education gives you real advantages in achieving your professional goals, whether they include a career or further study. Each year hundreds of NC State graduates are accepted in medical and law schools or other areas of advanced professional study."

ADMISSIONS

Admissions Rating	77
% of applicants accepted	72
% of acceptees attending	46

FRESHMAN PROFILE

Average verbal SAT	570
Average math SAT	580
Average ACT	NR
Average TOEFL	550
Graduated top 20% of class	59
Graduated top 40% of class	91
Graduated top 60% of class	98
Average HS GPA or Avg.	3.6

DEADLINES

Early decision	11/1
Regular admission	2/1
Regular notification	rolling
Non-fall registration	yes

APPLICANTS ALSO LOOK AT

AND OFTEN PREFER

U. Tennessee-Knoxville
UNC-Chapel Hill

AND SOMETIMES PREFER

Wake Forest
UNC-Charlotte
Catawba

AND RARELY PREFER

Clemson
U. South Carolina-Columbia
Auburn
Georgia Tech.
Virginia Tech.

FINANCIAL FACTS

Financial Aid Rating	75
In-state tuition	$1,732
Out-of-state tuition	$9,848
Room & board	$3,670
Estimated book expense	$600
% frosh receiving aid	47
% undergrads receiving aid	43
% aid is need-based	76
% frosh w/ grant (avg)	34 ($2,501)
% frosh w/ loan (avg)	30 ($3,011)
% UGs w/ job (avg)	NR
Off-campus job outlook	excellent

UNIVERSITY OF NORTH CAROLINA-ASHEVILLE

ONE UNIVERSITY HEIGHTS, ASHEVILLE, NC 28804-3299   ADMISSIONS: 704-251-6481   FAX: 704-251-6385

CAMPUS LIFE

Quality of Life Rating **84**

Type of school	public
Affiliation	none
Environment	city

STUDENTS

FT undergrad enrollment	2,190
% male/female	45/55
% from out of state	13
% live on campus	43
% spend weekend on campus	NR
% transfers	47
% from public high school	85
% in (# of) fraternities	8 (2)
% in (# of) sororities	6 (3)
% African-American	4
% Asian	2
% Caucasian	92
% Hispanic	1
% international	1
# of countries represented	18

WHAT'S HOT

health facilities
off-campus food
dorms
old-fashioned dating
town-gown relations

WHAT'S NOT

college radio
student publications
intercollegiate sports
campus food
music associations

ACADEMICS

Academic Rating **83**

Profs Interesting Rating	89
Profs Accessible Rating	88
Calendar	semester
Student/teacher ratio	14:1
% profs PhD/tenured	76/82
Hours of study per day	3.03

MOST POPULAR MAJORS

management
psychology
biology

STUDENTS SPEAK OUT

Life

Students report that life on the University of North Carolina at Asheville campus is sedate, its tone set by the fact that over half this small student body is made up of commuters. Writes one woman, "This is definitely not a party school. My only on-campus entertainment is hanging out with my boyfriend." Still, undergrads note that "UNCA offers many events throughout the week: bands, comedians, speakers, etc. Asheville is not a big city, but it has the basics: malls, restaurants, etc. We have ninety-nine cent-movies only five minutes from campus!" Asheville's campus is "small and quaint," and outdoor enthusiasts should take note that "we're in the mountains, and in the winter students like to ski and ice skate."

Academics

Asheville is one of a handful of small, state-run college-atmosphere universities that provide the liberal arts college experience at a state school price. "I really wanted to go to a small private college; UNCA has proven to be the next best thing," reports one student. "Teachers are down-to-earth, accomplished, and well equipped to share their knowledge." Writes another, "The school really seems to care about the student. Everyone's on a first-name basis here. Sometimes it seems that our academic success makes their day!" Students report that "we have very few large lectures. Most of our classes are relatively small," and find the small class sizes "helpful." Among the departments earning praise are environmental science, literature, and creative writing. Several students single out the Freshman Orientation program as particularly helpful. ("Orientation sessions and people answering my questions were more than I could ask for.") Overall students express high regard for professors and administrators; they are less thrilled with the core Humanities program. Writes one student, "this program is high profile, but I doubt many students chose UNCA because of it. We all refer to it as 'human-agonies.'" Warning: as UNCA becomes more prominent nationally, some of the personal charm that makes it special may disappear; according to one student, "Our professors are generally easy to get hold of and are willing to help students. However, the size of the school is doubling within the next ten years, and it seems this kind of intimacy will not remain possible."

Student Body

Asheville undergrads note that "overall the student body is a friendly group and most seem to get along despite the wide variety of values and beliefs," although several warn of "quite a few vocal religious fanatics." Asheville remains a well-kept secret nationally: over ninety percent of its students are North Carolina natives. Students rank themselves among the nation's most apolitical.

FINANCIAL AID: 704-251-6535   E-MAIL: PREED@UNCA.EDU   WEB SITE: HTTP://WWW.UNCA.EDU/

ADMISSIONS

The admissions committee considers (in descending order of importance): HS record, class rank, test scores, recommendations, essay. *Also considered (in descending order of importance):* alumni relationship, extracurriculars, geographical distribution, personality, special talents. Either the SAT or ACT is required. Admissions process is need-blind. *High school units required/recommended:* 15 total units are required; 4 English required, 3 math required, 4 math recommended, 3 science required, 2 foreign language required, 2 foreign language recommended, 2 social studies required, 1 history required. TOEFL is required of all international students. *The admissions office says:* "Preference given to those students who take additional college preparatory units, i.e., advanced or honors courses."

The Inside Word

UNC-Asheville is one of those relatively unknown gems in higher education. Recent publicity has fueled increases in applications and in turn boosted selectivity. The university is dynamic and eager to take advantage of this newfound recognition. No doubt admissions will become more and more competitive as the cycle repeats itself. For students who seek a public education in a smaller campus environment than places like Chapel Hill, this is a great choice.

FINANCIAL AID

Students should submit: FAFSA (due March 1), the school's own financial aid form (due March 1). The Princeton Review suggests that all financial aid forms be submitted as soon as possible after January 1. *The following grants/scholarships are offered:* Pell, SEOG, academic merit, athletic, the school's own scholarships, the school's own grants, state scholarships, state grants, private scholarships, private grants. *Students borrow from the following loan programs:* Stafford, Perkins, PLUS, the school's own loan fund, state loans, private loans. College Work-Study Program is available. Institutional employment is available. Freshmen are discouraged from working.

FROM THE ADMISSIONS OFFICE

"If you want to learn how to think, how to analyze and solve problems on your own, and how to become your own best teacher, a broad-based liberal arts education is the key. UNCA focuses on undergraduates, with a core curriculum covering humanities, language and culture, arts and ideas, and health and fitness. Students thrive in small classes, with a faculty dedicated first of all to teaching. The liberal arts emphasis develops discriminating thinkers, expert and creative communicators with a passion for learning. These are qualities you need for today's challenges and the changes of tomorrow."

ADMISSIONS

Admissions Rating	76
% of applicants accepted	59
% of acceptees attending	32

FRESHMAN PROFILE

Average verbal SAT	580
Average math SAT	560
Average ACT	24
Average TOEFL	590
Graduated top 20% of class	60
Graduated top 40% of class	92
Graduated top 60% of class	100
Average HS GPA or Avg.	3.4

DEADLINES

Early decision	10/15
Regular admission	4/15
Regular notification	rolling
Non-fall registration	yes

APPLICANTS ALSO LOOK AT

AND OFTEN PREFER
Warren Wilson

AND SOMETIMES PREFER
UNC-Chapel Hill
North Carolina State
Appalachian State

AND RARELY PREFER
UNC-Wilmington
UNC-Greensboro
Western Carolina
UNC-Charlotte

FINANCIAL FACTS

Financial Aid Rating	83
In-state tuition	$702
Out-of-state tuition	$6,742
Room & board	$3,556
Estimated book expense	$700
% frosh receiving aid	69
% undergrads receiving aid	40
% aid is need-based	53
% frosh w/ grant (avg)	57 ($2,480)
% frosh w/ loan (avg)	37 ($3,370)
% UGs w/ job (avg)	15 ($1,021)
Off-campus job outlook	good

UNIVERSITY OF NORTH CAROLINA-CHAPEL HILL

CHAPEL HILL, NC 27599-2200   ADMISSIONS: 919-966-3621   FAX: 919-962-5604

STUDENTS SPEAK OUT

Life

UNC-Chapel Hill is often called "the Southern Part of Heaven." This label fits the campus, widely admired for its great beauty and charm. Students also appreciate the town of Chapel Hill. One writes, "Chapel Hill is the quintessential college town. It has a small town atmosphere, but there's plenty to do. There are large cities close by, so there's something for everyone. The campus is beautiful, the people are friendly, the school is academically strong. What more could you want?" This vote of confidence is seconded by almost all the students. They love their school. The social scene is active and extends throughout campus and into town. Explains one student: "There's more going on here than you could ever hope to do. The religion of choice, of course, is basketball." Fraternities, sororities, and beer are very popular, as are the theater and intercollegiate and intramural sports. Besides Tar Heels men's basketball, the big sports draws are men's football, lacrosse, and baseball, and women's soccer, field hockey, and volleyball.

Academics

For many students, the University of North Carolina at Chapel Hill represents "the true college experience. From theater to tennis, baseball to basketball, academics to amusement, UNC provides students with the ability to discover that life is a test with more questions than answers." Sports and amusements notwithstanding, Chapel Hill's reputation as one of the nation's top state universities is based on its first-rate academic offerings; counselors cite the school's nationally known journalism and business programs, while students note that English, drama, and political science are also strong. On the downside is the school's big size. Because of it, classes are often fairly large (average for freshman/sophomore classes is 34; 26 for junior/senior) and led by teaching assistants. Students note that even some upper-level classes and labs are crowded. As a rule, opportunities here are sought out rather than simply handed to students. Professors are available, but only to students who take the initiative to ask for help. Of course, UNC's drawbacks are the same as those at most state universities, and UNC remains an excellent school. Its facilities are top-notch (the libraries receive especially high ratings), its faculty is extremely strong, and its students are bright and ambitious.

Student Body

The great majority of students are native to North Carolina. Out-of-state students face much stricter admissions standards but apply in droves anyway. The political climate on campus is moderate. Sadly, minority relations are strained. Notes one student, "Despite the enormous amount of diversity, blacks and whites are totally polarized." Another adds, "I like that there are many types of people. However, not everyone feels the same way. We are definitely more diverse and accepting than many other Southern universities, but we still have a way to go."

UNIVERSITY OF NORTH CAROLINA-CHAPEL HILL

FINANCIAL AID: 919-962-8396

WEB SITE: HTTP://WWW.UNC.EDU/

ADMISSIONS

The admissions committee considers (in descending order of importance): HS record, class rank, test scores, recommendations, essay. *Also considered (in descending order of importance):* alumni relationship, extracurriculars, special talents. Either the SAT or ACT is required; SAT is preferred. Admissions process is need-blind. *High school units required/recommended:* 16 total units are required; 4 English required, 3 math required, 3 science required, 2 foreign language required, 2 social studies required. Rigorous college-preparatory program recommended. *Special Requirements:* An audition is required for music program applicants. TOEFL is required of all international students.

The Inside Word

UNC's admissions process is formula driven and highly selective, which means high numbers go farther than anything else toward a successful candidacy. There are typically eight times as many out-of-state applicants as there are from in-state, an astonishing ratio when compared with the number of available spaces for nonresidents. For these students, it's one of the toughest admit offers to come by in the country.

FINANCIAL AID

Students should submit: FAFSA. The Princeton Review suggests that all financial aid forms be submitted as soon as possible after January 1. *The following grants/scholarships are offered:* Pell, SEOG, academic merit, athletic, the school's own scholarships, the school's own grants, state scholarships, state grants, private scholarships, private grants, ROTC. *Students borrow from the following loan programs:* Stafford, unsubsidized Stafford, Perkins, PLUS, the school's own loan fund, state loans, health professions loans, private loans. Applicants will be notified of awards beginning April 1. College Work-Study Program is available. Institutional employment is available.

FROM THE ADMISSIONS OFFICE

"What makes UNC-Chapel Hill different from other institutions? Atmosphere of academic rigor mingled with an unpretentious, friendly lifestyle; planetarium; commitment to vital teaching and cutting edge research; socioeconomic diversity; classic residential campus; a permeable honors program; study abroad; diversity permeates social life, classes, and curriculum and paces academic excellence; village-like atmosphere; the university is large enough to grant your individuality yet small enough for you to find your niche; academic quality of highest quality yet inexpensive cost; third among public universities in the production of Rhodes Scholars."

ADMISSIONS

Admissions Rating	87
% of applicants accepted	35
% of acceptees attending	58

FRESHMAN PROFILE

Average verbal SAT	600
Average math SAT	600
Average ACT	27
Average TOEFL	600
Graduated top 20% of class	92
Graduated top 40% of class	98
Graduated top 60% of class	NR
Average HS GPA or Avg.	NR

DEADLINES

Early decision	NR
Regular admission	1/15
Regular notification	rolling
Non-fall registration	no

APPLICANTS ALSO LOOK AT

AND OFTEN PREFER

Princeton
Duke

AND SOMETIMES PREFER

Harvard/Radcliffe
Brown
Virginia
Wake Forest
Davidson

AND RARELY PREFER

North Carolina State
U. Maryland-Coll. Park
Tulane
Rutgers U.

FINANCIAL FACTS

Financial Aid Rating	81
In-state tuition	$874
Out-of-state tuition	$8,400
Room & board	$4,350
Estimated book expense	$550
% frosh receiving aid	54
% undergrads receiving aid	44
% aid is need-based	80
% frosh w/ grant (avg)	51 ($2,000)
% frosh w/ loan (avg)	24 ($2,550)
% UGs w/ job (avg)	30 ($1,000)
Off-campus job outlook	good

UNIVERSITY OF NORTH DAKOTA

UNIVERSITY STATION, GRAND FORKS, ND 58202-8172   ADMISSIONS: 701-777-3821   FAX: 701-777-3650

CAMPUS LIFE

Quality of Life Rating   **78**
Type of school   public
Affiliation   none
Environment   suburban

STUDENTS

FT undergrad enrollment	8,123
% male/female	52/48
% from out of state	39
% live on campus	35
% spend weekend on campus	NR
% transfers	34
% from public high school	NR
% in (# of) fraternities	12 (17)
% in (# of) sororities	8 (7)
% African-American	1
% Asian	1
% Caucasian	91
% Hispanic	1
% international	5
# of countries represented	44

WHAT'S HOT
town-gown relations
old-fashioned dating
health facilities
intercollegiate sports
intramural sports

WHAT'S NOT
cigarettes
theater
music associations
drugs
student government

ACADEMICS

Academic Rating	**72**
Profs Interesting Rating	70
Profs Accessible Rating	68
Calendar	semester
Student/teacher ratio	17:1
% profs PhD/tenured	57/63
Hours of study per day	2.91

MOST POPULAR MAJORS
business administration
accounting
aerospace sciences

STUDENTS SPEAK OUT

Life

Most University of North Dakota students concede that life in Grand Forks can get "pretty boring." But many don't consider this a big negative; students brag of their classmates' "laid-back, easy-going lifestyles. There's no hurrying around," describe their peers as "polite, trusting, and giving," and note that simple entertainment, "We like to go out dancing and socializing on the weekends. Possibly to the movies," is readily available. Plus, explains one student, "The Twin Cities and Winnipeg are close by." Most undergrads come from "small or moderate cities or farming communities" that are "family-oriented, and promote religion and hard work." Not surprisingly, students frown on drugs and alternative lifestyles. The social scene centers on fraternities and sororities; although they attract only a small minority of students, they dominate the party scene as the only game in town. Other social and extracurricular options are certainly available, but most students go home on the weekends except when there is a major event, like a hockey game. Be forewarned that winters can get bitterly cold here. It is not unheard of for class to be canceled "on minus-sixty-degree days."

Academics

The University of North Dakota provides "a sound learning environment for students who really want to learn." It is large and well funded enough to offer state-of-the-art facilities in most areas, yet small enough to allow reasonably sized classes. Respondents report a surprising number (about thirty percent) of classes with fewer than twenty students. The strongest and most popular department at UND is aviation. The Center for Aerospace Science is highly respected nationwide, and attracts many of the out-of-state students to the school. Business and management departments are also popular and reputedly top-notch, as are most other career-oriented studies (physical and occupational therapy and education, for example). Although UND has a reputation for having a "relaxed" academic atmosphere, the students we spoke to take their academic responsibilities fairly seriously. Professors receive average marks for instruction and accessibility; writes one respondent, "There are as many professors who light a fire and keep you awake as there are to put you in a coma." Like most state universities, UND has its share of red tape. Complains one student, "The administration often make mistakes like messing up financial aid or bills."

Student Body

Wrote one student, "Most North Dakotans and Minnesotans (who make up the majority of the student body) are pretty easy-going and nice people." Still, as one student observed, UND is "smack dab in the middle of the Bible Belt, so left-wing or alternative lifestyles are not easily found or accepted." Students "are more conservative politically than the faculty." Minority students here are just that. UND's black, Asian, and Latino populations are minuscule.

FINANCIAL AID: 701-777-3121

WEB SITE: HTTP://WWW.UND.NODAK.EDU/

ADMISSIONS

The admissions committee considers (in descending order of importance): HS record, class rank, test scores, recommendations, essay. *Also considered (in descending order of importance):* extracurriculars, personality, special talents. Either the SAT or ACT is required; ACT is preferred. An interview is recommended. *High school units required/recommended:* 16 total units are required; 4 English required, 3 math required, 3 science required, 2 foreign language recommended, 3 social studies required, 2 history recommended. Minimum composite ACT score of 17 and completion of secondary school core curriculum required. TOEFL is required of all international students.

The Inside Word

North Dakota shapes up as a low-stress choice with little pressure on applicants. Its sound reputation serves as a reminder that a highly selective admissions profile isn't an indicator of the quality of a university. Who graduates is much more important than who gets admitted or denied.

FINANCIAL AID

Students should submit: FAFSA. The Princeton Review suggests that all financial aid forms be submitted as soon as possible after January 1. *The following grants/ scholarships are offered:* Pell, SEOG, academic merit, athletic, the school's own scholarships, state scholarships, state grants, private scholarships, federal nursing scholarship, ROTC, foreign aid. *Students borrow from the following loan programs:* Stafford, unsubsidized Stafford, Perkins, PLUS, the school's own loan fund, state loans, federal nursing loans, health professions loans, private loans. Applicants will be notified of awards beginning in late May. College Work-Study Program is available. Institutional employment is available.

FROM THE ADMISSIONS OFFICE

"More than 12,000 students come to the University of North Dakota each year, from every state in the nation and more than 40 countries. They're impressed by our academic excellence, 170 major fields of study, our dedication to the liberal arts mission, and alumni success record. Nearly all of the University's new students rank in the top half of their high school classes, with about 52 percent in the top quarter. As the largest institution of higher education in the Dakotas, Montana, Wyoming, and western Minnesota, UND is a comprehensive teaching and research university. Yet the University provides individual attention that may be missing at very large universities. UND graduates are highly regarded among prospective employers. Representatives from more than 200 regional and national companies recruit UND students every year."

ADMISSIONS

Admissions Rating	71
% of applicants accepted	80
% of acceptees attending	76

FRESHMAN PROFILE

Average verbal SAT	540
Average math SAT	550
Average ACT	23
Average TOEFL	525
Graduated top 20% of class	54
Graduated top 40% of class	87
Graduated top 60% of class	98
Average HS GPA or Avg.	NR

DEADLINES

Early decision	NR
Regular admission	7/1
Regular notification	rolling
Non-fall registration	yes

APPLICANTS ALSO LOOK AT

AND OFTEN PREFER

U. Nebraska-Lincoln
U. Colorado-Boulder
Notre Dame

AND SOMETIMES PREFER

Moorhead State
U. Minnesota
Bismarck State
Concordia Coll. (Moorehead-MN)
U. Wisconsin-Madison

AND RARELY PREFER

Marquette

FINANCIAL FACTS

Financial Aid Rating	72
In-state tuition	$2,428
Out-of-state tuition	$5,952
Room & board	$2,703
Estimated book expense	$600
% frosh receiving aid	47
% undergrads receiving aid	46
% aid is need-based	78
% frosh w/ grant (avg)	41 ($1,326)
% frosh w/ loan (avg)	55 ($1,611)
% UGs w/ job (avg)	10 ($1,350)
Off-campus job outlook	good

NORTHEASTERN UNIVERSITY

360 HUNTINGTON AVENUE, BOSTON, MA 02115

ADMISSIONS: 617-373-2200

CAMPUS LIFE

Quality of Life Rating	75
Type of school	private
Affiliation	none
Environment	metropolis

STUDENTS

FT undergrad enrollment	11,022
% male/female	56/44
% from out of state	35
% live on campus	65
% spend weekend on campus	NR
% transfers	16
% from public high school	NR
% in (# of) fraternities	9 (18)
% in (# of) sororities	5 (8)
% African-American	8
% Asian	7
% Caucasian	80
% Hispanic	4
% international	10
# of countries represented	107

WHAT'S HOT

computer facilities
Boston
ethnic diversity on campus
library
different students interact

WHAT'S NOT

music associations
theater
beer
unattractive campus
dorms

ACADEMICS

Academic Rating	72
Profs Interesting Rating	72
Profs Accessible Rating	68
Calendar	quarter
Student/teacher ratio	13:1
% profs PhD/tenured	84/63
Hours of study per day	3.42

MOST POPULAR MAJORS

business
engineering
criminal justice

% GRADS WHO PURSUE...

Law 1, Med 1, MBA 1, MA 6

STUDENTS SPEAK OUT

Life

Social life at Northeastern University is strongly influenced by the co-op plan (see Academics, below). With students spending one quarter on campus and the next at work, it can be difficult to form deep friendships with classmates. The campus, spread out and ugly, does little to help the situation, nor does the large commuter population. As a result, students find small groups of friends and stick with them: "Social interaction between groups doesn't happen," said one student. The lack of a cohesive social scene probably explains why Northeastern students gave themselves low grades in overall happiness despite their general satisfaction with their academic program. Still, the school is in downtown Boston, the college student's Mecca. Clubs, bars, record and bookstores, and Fenway Park are just a stone's throw away.

Academics

Ask Northeastern students why they chose their university and most mention the cooperative education program first. This five-year BA program requires students to spend two of their four quarters each year (after freshman year) at work for one of thousands of employers who participate in the program. Jobs are predominantly in the New England area, although the co-op does send students across the country and even overseas. Explains one student, "Because of co-op, I have had the experience of writing a résumé, negotiating for a higher salary, and working in my field. I think this school is underrated." Not surprisingly, studies at the university are predominantly geared toward the professions: over one third of the students are pre-business, and engineering, pharmacology, and physical therapy are also popular. Because the school is huge, it's easy to get lost in the crowd: "You need a lot of self-discipline because it's a big school and basically you're on your own," says one student. Yet for a school of its size, complaints about class size, administration, and inaccessible professors were rare. On the contrary, one student tells us, "The college of pharmacology is a small college in a large university, so I benefit from both," while another says that "business teachers at Northeastern have worked in the business world, owned businesses, etc., and they teach because they want to help students, not because they need the money."

Student Body

Students here are pretty serious about the programs they are pursuing. Many slacked off during high school and are attending Northeastern for the direction and discipline it imposes. Students here study hard and don't drink nearly as much as they are reputed to, but they aren't puritans. They're just a little more focused and conservative than the average college student. Says one, "If you want to drink, go to a less traditional school like Hampshire: if you want to get a job when you graduate, go to Northeastern." Northeastern is yet another school with a good ethnic mix where, sadly, most groups simply don't, or don't get the chance to, interact.

FINANCIAL AID: 617-373-3190   E-MAIL: ADMISSIONS@NEU.EDU   WEB SITE: HTTP://WWW.NEU.EDU/

ADMISSIONS

The admissions committee considers (in descending order of importance): HS record, class rank, test scores, recommendations, essay. *Also considered (in descending order of importance):* extracurriculars, alumni relationship, special talents, geographical distribution, personality. Either the SAT or ACT is required; SAT is preferred. An interview is recommended. Admissions process is need-blind. *High school units required/recommended:* 17 total units are recommended; 4 English recommended, 3 math recommended, 3 science recommended, 2 foreign language recommended, 3 social studies recommended, 2 history recommended. TOEFL is required of all international students. *The admissions office says:* "We make every effort to recruit qualified minority students. One senior staff member is dedicated to recruiting international students."

The Inside Word

Northeastern is one of the less selective of Boston's melange of colleges and universities, which makes it a popular safety for students who must go to school in Beantown. This translates into a large applicant pool and a lower acceptance rate than might otherwise be the case. The source of any true selectivity in NU's admissions process is a heavy reliance on the numbers: GPA, rank, and tests.

FINANCIAL AID

Students should submit: FAFSA (due March 1), CSS Profile (due March 1). The Princeton Review suggests that all financial aid forms be submitted as soon as possible after January 1. *The following grants/scholarships are offered:* Pell, SEOG, academic merit, athletic, the school's own scholarships, the school's own grants, state scholarships, state grants, private scholarships, private grants, ROTC. *Students borrow from the following loan programs:* Stafford, unsubsidized Stafford, Perkins, PLUS, state loans, federal nursing loans, health professions loans. Applicants will be notified of awards beginning April 1. College Work-Study Program is available. Institutional employment is available.

FROM THE ADMISSIONS OFFICE

Northeastern's vitality springs from our mission: serving students eager to pursue the American dream, doers with adventure in their souls, risk-takers with determination in their veins. As a major private urban university, we offer an extraordinary range of opportunities to students willing to seize them. As an institution committed to each student's personal growth since our founding in 1898, we provide the support essential for self-discovery. President Bill Clinton and many others have lauded Northeastern's role as a pioneer in cooperative education, which combines time in the classroom with time in the workplace. Indeed, in co-op we have no equal. But the benefits of the Northeastern experience extend well beyond co-op. Here, students learn from faculty whose first love is teaching and top priority is students. Here, in small classes, students discover the strands that link excellence in study with excellence in a career—and in life. Here, students experience education with a diverse and unpretentious mix of fellow adventurers from every state and around the world. Here, students use our campus as a base from which to make connections to people and organizations and neighborhoods—and, of course, to Boston, our greater campus, the world's most exciting college town. Northeastern is, as President Clinton said, "a symbol of the American dream."

ADMISSIONS

Admissions Rating	69
% of applicants accepted	73
% of acceptees attending	28

FRESHMAN PROFILE

Average verbal SAT	550
Average math SAT	550
Average ACT	23
Average TOEFL	550
Graduated top 20% of class	31
Graduated top 40% of class	59
Graduated top 60% of class	75
Average HS GPA or Avg.	NR

DEADLINES

Early decision	NR
Regular admission	3/1
Regular notification	rolling
Non-fall registration	yes

APPLICANTS ALSO LOOK AT

AND OFTEN PREFER
MIT
Drexel
Boston Coll.
Boston U.

AND SOMETIMES PREFER
U. Mass.-Amherst
Syracuse
U. Conn

FINANCIAL FACTS

Financial Aid Rating	77
Tuition	$15,045
Room & board	$8,025
Estimated book expense	$600
% frosh receiving aid	72
% undergrads receiving aid	70
% aid is need-based	88
% frosh w/ grant (avg)	68 ($7,616)
% frosh w/ loan (avg)	72 ($2,622)
% UGs w/ job (avg)	18
Off-campus job outlook	good

NORTHWESTERN UNIVERSITY

P.O. Box 3060, 1801 Hinman Avenue, Evanston, IL 60204-3060   Admissions: 708-491-7271

CAMPUS LIFE

Quality of Life Rating   **90**
Type of school   private
Affiliation   none
Environment   metropolis

STUDENTS
FT undergrad enrollment   7,570
% male/female   49/51
% from out of state   76
% live on campus   71
% spend weekend on campus   95
% transfers   6
% from public high school   75
% in (# of) fraternities   40 (21)
% in (# of) sororities   40 (11)
% African-American   6
% Asian   18
% Caucasian   68
% Hispanic   2
% international   1
# of countries represented   27

WHAT'S HOT
student publications
health facilities
theater
students are happy
Greeks

WHAT'S NOT
students are cliquish
sex
infrequent dating
town-gown relations
student government

ACADEMICS

Academic Rating   **90**
Profs Interesting Rating   74
Profs Accessible Rating   77
Calendar   quarter
Student/teacher ratio   11:1
% profs PhD   95
Hours of study per day   3.36

MOST POPULAR MAJORS
economics
political science
history

% GRADS WHO PURSUE...
Law 10, Med 10, MBA 23, MA 15

STUDENTS SPEAK OUT

Life

Northwestern University is in Evanston, only half an hour away from Chicago by public transportation. "Evanston's a bit dull," says one student of the school's suburban setting, "but the easy access to Chicago more than definitely makes up for it." Northwestern scores well in most quality-of-life categories, rating particularly high for its beautiful campus, comfortable dorms, and better-than-edible food. Extracurricular activities are popular here, which, along with the reasonable number of hours students study (three hours a day, about the national average), indicates that life at Northwestern doesn't begin and end in the classroom. Dating is not big here, however. In fact, students' response to the question, "How frequently do students date?" ranked eighteenth lowest in the nation. It's not that students have no social life; it's just that dating and sex seem to play a pretty small role in it. As one student says, "Most nights there are people going to bars and partying. But if you need to stay in and study, everyone understands and you won't be alone. There seems to be a really good balance between studying and fun." Students have few nice things to say about Chicago winters, which are severe.

Academics

Asked why they chose Northwestern, many of our respondents point to the many experiences available to the NU undergrad. Says one, "I came to NU because it seemed to have everything I wanted in a perfect package: great theater department with a wide variety of opportunities, strong Greek life, well-respected academic program, and Chicago, Chicago—what a wonderful town!" Academics at Northwestern are first-rate, with the school's programs in engineering, journalism, and theater receiving high praise; liberal arts departments are also uniformly strong, while the eleven percent of graduates who proceed to medical school attests to the success of NU's premed departments. Still, the school's reputation among college-bound students remains one notch below the Ivies. Students accepted here and at an Ivy League institution continue to choose the Ivy, although, given the overall satisfaction of NU students (see "Students," below), you might easily wonder why. One NU student did: "When I first came here I was a little disappointed because I'd wanted to go to Princeton. But now—wow! I'm a senior and I wouldn't have gone anyplace else had I known about Northwestern from the start."

Student Body

Students at Northwestern University score high in what is arguably the single most important category: overall happiness. Their answer to the question, "How happy are you here?" yields a 3.6, fifth highest among the schools we surveyed. The typical NU student is very bright, but in every other way is very much the average college student.

ADMISSIONS

The admissions committee considers (in descending order of importance): HS record, class rank, essay, test scores, recommendations. *Also considered (in descending order of importance):* extracurriculars, personality, special talents, alumni relationship. Either the SAT or ACT is required. An interview is recommended. Admissions process is need-blind. *High school units required/recommended:* 16 total units are recommended; 4 English recommended, 3 math recommended, 2 science recommended, 2 foreign language recommended, 3 social studies recommended. Electives may be chosen from all listed subjects. 3.5 to 4 units of math recommended of engineering program applicants. *Special Requirements:* An audition is required for music program applicants. TOEFL is required of all international students.

The Inside Word

Northwestern's applicant pool is easily among the best in the country annually. Candidates face both a rigorous evaluation by the admissions committee and serious competition from within the pool. The best approach (besides top grades and a strong personal background) is to take the committee up on their recommendations to interview and submit SAT II scores. The effort it takes to get in is well worth it.

FINANCIAL AID

Students should submit: FAFSA, CSS Profile, Divorced Parents form, a copy of parents' most recent income tax filing. The Princeton Review suggests that all financial aid forms be submitted as soon as possible after January 1. *The following grants/scholarships are offered:* Pell, SEOG, athletic, the school's own scholarships, the school's own grants, state scholarships, state grants, private scholarships, private grants, ROTC. *Students borrow from the following loan programs:* Stafford, unsubsidized Stafford, Perkins, PLUS, the school's own loan fund, state loans, health professions loans, private loans. Applicants will be notified of awards beginning April 15. College Work-Study Program is available. Institutional employment is available.

FROM THE ADMISSIONS OFFICE

"Consistent with its dedication to excellence, Northwestern provides both an educational and an extracurricular environment that enables its undergraduate students to become accomplished individuals and informed and responsible citizens. To the students in all its undergraduate schools, Northwestern offers liberal learning and professional education to help them gain the depth of knowledge that will empower them to become leaders in their professions and communities. Furthermore, Northwestern fosters in its students a broad understanding of the world in which we live as well as excellence in the competencies that transcend any particular field of study: writing and oral communication, analytical and creative thinking and expression, quantitative and qualitative methods of thinking."

ADMISSIONS

Admissions Rating	95
% of applicants accepted	40
% of acceptees attending	38

FRESHMAN PROFILE

Average verbal SAT	660
Average math SAT	650
Average ACT	29
Average TOEFL	600
Graduated top 20% of class	94
Graduated top 40% of class	99
Graduated top 60% of class	100
Average HS GPA or Avg.	NR

DEADLINES

Early decision	NR
Regular admission	1/1
Regular notification	4/15
Non-fall registration	yes

APPLICANTS ALSO LOOK AT

AND OFTEN PREFER
Yale
Harvard/Radcliffe

AND SOMETIMES PREFER
U. Chicago
Stanford
Princeton
Columbia

AND RARELY PREFER
DePaul
Marquette
Purdue U.—West Lafayette

FINANCIAL FACTS

Financial Aid Rating	80
Tuition	$17,184
Room & board	$5,520
Estimated book expense	$813
% frosh receiving aid	45
% undergrads receiving aid	60
% aid is need-based	97
% frosh w/ grant (avg)	45 ($11,300)
% frosh w/ loan (avg)	42 ($3,300)
% UGs w/ job (avg)	40 ($1,200)
Off-campus job outlook	excellent

University of Notre Dame

113 Main Building, Notre Dame, IN 46556   Admissions: 219-631-7505   Fax: 219-631-6947

STUDENTS SPEAK OUT

Life

The crux of extracurricular life at the University of Notre Dame is definitely sports. One student writes, "The football games generate incredible energy among the student body; it's truly a religious experience." Religion is also extremely important here. The Catholic tradition of the school is well preserved, and a large majority of the students are practicing Catholics. The emphasis on faith distinctly affects the social atmosphere. One student explains, for instance, that "every sexual issue here is also a spiritual one; sex is more or less out of the question." Long-term relationships are on many people's minds here, according to our surveys. One woman writes, "Students here pretend that marrying an ND guy isn't important, but many are searching for an 'MRS' degree along with an undergraduate one." To further complicate matters, men noticeably outnumber women. Most students live on campus, and submit to strict visitation rules. Many "live in the same dorm for all four years, and the dorm often plays the role of a fraternity/sorority." The Greek system is officially banned at ND. Drugs and smoking are "rarely seen at parties," but Domers know how to drink, describing themselves as "always the first to crack open a Bud." Some students insist that at Notre Dame, "beer is the fourth member of the Trinity."

Academics

Notre Dame is highly respected, not only in the sports arena but in nearly all academic fields as well. The strongest departments are considered to be in the pre-professional fields. Students tell us that the premed program, chemical engineering, architecture, and accounting are standouts. The College of Arts and Letters boasts fine programs as well. English, history, and philosophy are among its best. The core curriculum reflects Notre Dame's Catholic tenor: Among the usual math, science, and writing requirements are several courses in theology and philosophy. Students receive lots of academic guidance at Notre Dame, especially through the Freshman Year of Studies program, which prescribes the entire freshman curriculum. Many appreciate the extra structure, but some find it restrictive. One student complains, "The administration obviously has read Orwell's 1984." On the whole, the administration gets mixed-to-positive reviews. Some consider it "slow to respond to the students' needs. The red tape here would make the federal government gawk." Others praise it for running the school smoothly. Registration, for example, is a surprisingly painless process for a school of this size. The faculty are perceived as "taking interest in the students," and overall students rate their academic experiences as "incredible; words cannot describe the true sense of family here at the university."

Student Body

Such an academically strong school provides a socioeconomically diverse student body, but also one that's racially homogenous. As one junior notes, "we're white white white." One student sums up quite well: "If you seek true diversity, a Catholic school in Indiana may leave you disappointed. This is a bastion of conservatism, yet that also creates a stable, ethical environment. Notre Dame offers a comfortable atmosphere in which you may find the best friends of your life while getting an excellent education."

FINANCIAL AID: 219-631-6436   WEB SITE: HTTP://WWW.ND.EDU/

ADMISSIONS

The admissions committee considers (in descending order of importance): HS record, class rank, test scores, recommendations, essay. *Also considered (in descending order of importance):* extracurriculars, personality, special talents, alumni relationship. Either the SAT or ACT is required. Admissions process is need-blind. *High school units required/recommended:* 16 total units are required; 20 total units are recommended; 4 English required, 4 English recommended, 3 math required, 4 math recommended, 2 science required, 4 science recommended, 2 foreign language required, 4 foreign language recommended, 2 history required, 4 history recommended. *Special Requirements:* A portfolio is required for art program applicants. An audition is required for music program applicants. TOEFL is required of all international students.

The Inside Word

For most candidates, getting admitted to Notre Dame is pretty tough. Legacies, however, face some of the most favorable admissions conditions to be found at any highly selective university. Unofficially, athletic talents seem to have some influence on the committee as well: An enormous percentage of the total student body holds at least one varsity letter from high school, and many were team captains. Perhaps it's merely coincidence, but even so, candidates who tap well into the Notre Dame persona are likeliest to succeed.

FINANCIAL AID

Students should submit: FAFSA, CSS Profile, state aid form, Divorced Parents form, a copy of parents' most recent income tax filing. The Princeton Review suggests that all financial aid forms be submitted as soon as possible after January 1. *The following grants/scholarships are offered:* Pell, SEOG, athletic, the school's own scholarships, the school's own grants, state scholarships, state grants, private scholarships, private grants, ROTC. *Students borrow from the following loan programs:* Stafford, unsubsidized Stafford, Perkins, PLUS, state loans, private loans. College Work-Study Program is available. Institutional employment is available.

FROM THE ADMISSIONS OFFICE

"Notre Dame is a Catholic university, which means it offers unique opportunities for academic, ethical, spiritual, and social service development. The Freshman Year of Studies program provides special assistance to our students as they make the adjustment from high school to college. The first-year curriculum includes many core requirements, while allowing students to explore several areas of possible future study. Each residence hall is home to students from all classes; most will live in the same hall for all their years on campus. An average of 92 percent of entering students will graduate within five years."

ADMISSIONS

Admissions Rating	96
% of applicants accepted	39
% of acceptees attending	49

FRESHMAN PROFILE

Average verbal SAT	650
Average math SAT	660
Average ACT	29
Average TOEFL	600
Graduated top 20% of class	94
Graduated top 40% of class	98
Graduated top 60% of class	99
Average HS GPA or Avg.	NR

DEADLINES

Early decision	11/1
Regular admission	1/6
Regular notification	4/7
Non-fall registration	no

APPLICANTS ALSO LOOK AT

AND OFTEN PREFER
Princeton
Rice U.
US Naval Acad.
Stanford

AND SOMETIMES PREFER
Georgetown U.
Cornell U.
Duke
Northwestern

AND RARELY PREFER
U. Michigan-Ann Arbor
Holy Cross
U. Wisconsin-Madison
Boston Coll.

FINANCIAL FACTS

Financial Aid Rating	74
Tuition	$18,030
Room & board	$4,650
Estimated book expense	$600
% frosh receiving aid	75
% undergrads receiving aid	74
% aid is need-based	53
% frosh w/ grant (avg)	54 ($8,850)
% frosh w/ loan (avg)	66 ($4,000)
% UGs w/ job (avg)	38 ($1,500)
Off-campus job outlook	good

OBERLIN COLLEGE

101 NORTH PROFESSOR STREET, OBERLIN, OH 44074   ADMISSIONS: 216-775-8411   FAX: 216-775-6905

STUDENTS SPEAK OUT

Life

One Oberlin College student remarks, "Oberlin is a place where green hair is as common as Levi's in a country and western bar." The college's bohemian, slightly weird image is slowly changing, but this is certainly no place for the uptight prepster. The social scene is atypical as well: there are no fraternities or sororities, and Oberlin undergraduates prefer political debates, concerts, and plays to drinking or playing sports. Indeed, the enthusiastic responses we received to our questions about theater and music were virtually unparalleled at other colleges. The campus is described as beautiful and ugly, depending on where you are standing at the moment. The town of Oberlin is small and generally unremarkable and is "surrounded by farmland. We see corn, corn, and more corn," writes one student. However, Cleveland is not too far away, and students do enjoy tons of cultural offerings on campus. Overall, students claim to be quite happy here, and even some graduating seniors were not eager to leave their beloved community.

Academics

Oberlin students rate their college highly in nearly every academic category. An outstanding liberal arts school connected to a world-renowned conservatory of music, Oberlin has something to offer almost everyone. The atmosphere is "academically intense, yet noncompetitive"; classes are challenging and small; and the professors are "extremely accessible. You really get a sense that they are eager to meet you and help you with anything they can." The sciences are unusually strong and well supported for a small liberal arts school. Also popular among students are English, performing arts, history, and minority studies. All students must complete distribution requirements that include three courses geared toward promoting awareness of cultural diversity. Students study hard during the semester (almost four hours a day), but have a chance to lighten up during EXCO, which offers a variety of short, offbeat courses during January. A summary of the Oberlin experience is given by one student: "Oberlin consists of a group of highly motivated, bright, creative and alternatively oriented students. We are also immensely cynical and angst-ridden. Accordingly, we love the professors and hate the administration." Conservatory students are well integrated into academic life, with many of them opting for Oberlin's popular five-year combined BM/BA program. Over half the students take advantage of opportunities to spend at least one semester off campus, either in the U.S. or abroad: study in Asia is a particularly popular option here.

Student Body

Oberlin has been described as "the Mecca for the lesbian/gay/bisexual collegiate community. Oberlin pioneered race-, gender-, and faith-blind admissions in the U.S." Ethnic diversity, as well as acceptance of all racial and social groups, is very high: almost one fourth of the students here are minorities. The student body classifies itself as "largely liberal" with a commitment to progressive political issues unusual for a Midwestern school. Says one student: "If such a thing is possible, the majority of people here conform to nonconformity."

FINANCIAL AID: 216-775-8142

WEB SITE: HTTP://WWW.OBERLIN.EDU/

ADMISSIONS

The admissions committee considers (in descending order of importance): HS record, test scores, recommendations, essay, class rank. *Also considered (in descending order of importance):* extracurriculars, personality, special talents, alumni relationship, geographical distribution. Either the SAT or ACT is required. An interview is recommended. Admissions process is not need-blind. *High school units required/recommended:* 17 total units are recommended; 4 English recommended, 4 math recommended, 3 science recommended, 3 foreign language recommended, 3 social studies recommended. *Special Requirements:* An audition is required for music program applicants. TOEFL is required of all international students.

The Inside Word

The admissions process at Oberlin is especially demanding for candidates to the Conservatory of Music, which seeks only the best-prepared musicians for its excellent program. All applicants to the college face a thorough and rigorous review of their credentials by the admissions committee regardless of their choice of major. Take our advice—visit the campus to interview, and put extra effort into admissions essays.

FINANCIAL AID

Students should submit: FAFSA (due February 15), CSS Profile (due February 15), the school's own financial aid form (due February 15), a copy of parents' most recent income tax filing (due February 15). The Princeton Review suggests that all financial aid forms be submitted as soon as possible after January 1. *The following grants/scholarships are offered:* Pell, SEOG, academic merit, the school's own scholarships, the school's own grants, state scholarships, state grants, private scholarships, private grants. *Students borrow from the following loan programs:* Stafford, Perkins, PLUS, the school's own loan fund. Applicants will be notified of awards beginning April 1. College Work-Study Program is available. Institutional employment is available.

FROM THE ADMISSIONS OFFICE

"Oberlin College is an independent, coeducational liberal arts college. It comprises two divisions, the College of Arts and Sciences, with roughly 2,300 students enrolled, and the Conservatory of Music, with about 500 students. Students in both divisions share one campus; they also share residence and dining halls as part of one academic community. Many students take courses in both divisions. Oberlin awards the bachelor of arts and the bachelor of music degrees; a five-year program leads to both degrees. Selected master's degrees are offered in the Conservatory. Oberlin is located 35 miles southwest of Cleveland. Founded in 1833, Oberlin College is highly selective and dedicated to recruiting students from diverse backgrounds. Oberlin was the first coeducational college in the United States, as well as a historic leader in educating black students. Oberlin's 440-acre campus provides outstanding facilities, modern scientific laboratories, a large computing center, a library unexcelled by other college libraries for the depth and range of its resources, and the Allen Memorial Art Museum."

ADMISSIONS

Admissions Rating		85
% of applicants accepted		72
% of acceptees attending		25

FRESHMAN PROFILE

Average verbal SAT	730
Average math SAT	630
Average ACT	28
Average TOEFL	600
Graduated top 20% of class	76
Graduated top 40% of class	95
Graduated top 60% of class	100
Average HS GPA or Avg.	3.5

DEADLINES

Early decision	NR
Regular admission	1/15
Regular notification	4/1
Non-fall registration	yes

APPLICANTS ALSO LOOK AT

AND OFTEN PREFER

Yale
Swarthmore
Wesleyan U.
Stanford
Brown

AND SOMETIMES PREFER

Carleton
Haverford
Tufts
Grinnell
Williams

AND RARELY PREFER

Connecticut Coll.

FINANCIAL FACTS

Financial Aid Rating	72
Tuition	$20,600
Room & board	$5,820
Estimated book expense	$500
% frosh receiving aid	60
% undergrads receiving aid	60
% aid is need-based	97
% frosh w/ grant (avg)	56 ($12,618)
% frosh w/ loan (avg)	60 ($4,001)
% UGs w/ job (avg)	60 ($1,450)
Off-campus job outlook	good

OCCIDENTAL COLLEGE

1600 CAMPUS ROAD, LOS ANGELES, CA 90041   ADMISSIONS: 213-259-2700   FAX: 213-259-2907

STUDENTS SPEAK OUT

Life

Occidental College students agree that "Oxy is a very social place." "Greek parties and private parties abound," but "There's so much to do in L.A.—we don't just live and breathe the Oxy campus!" Indeed, students enjoy "Old Town Pasadena, concerts, theater, movies, theme parks, camping in Joshua Tree...shopping in Glendale, etc." Students spend a lot of time hanging out: "People here are intelligent and friendly. A popular pastime at Oxy is simply sitting around and talking about backgrounds, deep personal feelings, societal issues, etc." Community service activities are popular. Because the student body is small, Oxy "has the advantages or disadvantages of a family or a small town. If you breathe too loud, your friends will know, but so will your enemies." Oxy is located in an L.A. neighborhood called Eagle Rock, within driving distance of the fun parts of L.A. (Santa Monica, Venice Beach, Hollywood). As one respondent sums up, "Life here is good if you learn to temper your college life with frequent trips out into the 'real world,' i.e., off campus into L.A."

Academics

Like many small liberal arts schools, Occidental offers a number of talented, dedicated faculty with whom students work closely. Writes one student, "The interaction between students and faculty is fantastic! Most profs have their home phone numbers on their office doors. Some profs have the class over for dinner at the end of the term." Most students agree that the quality of instruction is "Excellent! Professors are committed to the intellectual development of the undergraduate student." Graduates' achievements are undeniably impressive: Nearly one-third of Oxy's graduates proceed to professional programs within a year, and as many again go on to academic graduate programs. Even more impressive is the fact that Oxy has not tailored its academic program to obtain these results: The school's program requires that students complete a core curriculum so demanding—it includes healthy doses of world culture, as well as math, science, humanities, and foreign language—that it takes a full two years to complete (although a brave few opt for the rigorous Core II, which allows students to finish all requirements during freshman year). Popular majors include the premedical sciences, economics, English, and political science. All are excellent.

Student Body

Oxy undergrads are notoriously politically correct, as one student notes: "My fellow students are highly intelligent and generally open-minded about new issues surrounding race, sexuality and gender." Students appreciate the school's commitment to diversity: "Occidental students learn more from each other than in the classroom." "I love the diversity. Our conversations never end." Some students point out, however, that "Despite knowing that you can only get through by being color blind, Oxy students 'hang' with only their own race/ethnicity. It's just like the damn real world."

ADMISSIONS

The admissions committee considers (in descending order of importance): HS record, class rank, essay, test scores, recommendations. *Also considered (in descending order of importance):* extracurriculars, special talents, personality, alumni relationship. Either the SAT or ACT is required. An interview is recommended. *High school units required/recommended:* 16 total units are recommended; 4 English recommended, 3 math recommended, 2 science recommended, 3 foreign language recommended, 2 history recommended. *Special Requirements:* TOEFL is required of all international students. 4 units of chemistry, math, and physics required of science and engineering program applicants. *The admissions office says:* "The Committee on Admissions looks for students with very strong academic and personal qualifications who demonstrate motivation, accomplishment, involvement, and commitment. The majority of students admitted to the college rank in the upper five to ten percent of their high school classes. Because the individual characteristics of each candidate are considered, no specific formula of grades and scores guarantees admission. Rigor of course work, grades, test scores [SAT I and ACT accepted; SAT I preferred], recommendations, and extracurricular activities are all taken into consideration when the freshman class is selected."

The Inside Word

Students who are considering Occidental, or any other college with a rigorous core curriculum, should take five full academic courses a year straight through to graduation from high school. Such work not only gives the admissions committee solid evidence of your ability to handle Oxy's core requirements, it will make completing them much less painful as well.

FINANCIAL AID

Students should submit: FAFSA, state aid form (due March 2), a copy of parents' most recent income tax filing. The Princeton Review suggests that all financial aid forms be submitted as soon as possible after January 1. *The following grants/scholarships are offered:* Pell, SEOG, academic merit, the school's own scholarships, the school's own grants, state scholarships, state grants, private scholarships, private grants, foreign aid. *Students borrow from the following loan programs:* Stafford, Perkins, PLUS, the school's own loan fund, state loans, private loans. Applicants will be notified of awards beginning April 1. College Work-Study Program is available. Institutional employment is available.

FROM THE ADMISSIONS OFFICE

"The college is committed to a philosophy of total education. Intellectual capability is a dominant component, but is conceived of as one dimension in a process that includes and stresses personal, ethical, social, and political growth toward maturation as well. The high percentage of students in residence at the college work toward the achievement of this objective. Successful Occidental students are self-motivated, independent-minded, and intellectually talented people. They base their judgments upon respect for evidence, ideas, and a deep concern for values, both private and public. They are alert to the possibilities of betterment in themselves, their college, and their society."

ADMISSIONS

Admissions Rating	82
% of applicants accepted	64
% of acceptees attending	23

FRESHMAN PROFILE

Average verbal SAT	590
Average math SAT	580
Average ACT	NR
Average TOEFL	600
Graduated top 20% of class	48
Graduated top 40% of class	70
Graduated top 60% of class	89
Average HS GPA or Avg.	NR

DEADLINES

Early decision	NR
Regular admission	2/1
Regular notification	4/1
Non-fall registration	no

APPLICANTS ALSO LOOK AT

AND OFTEN PREFER

Yale
Columbia
Pomona

AND SOMETIMES PREFER

UC—Berkeley
UCLA
UC—Davis
U. Southern Cal
Pitzer

FINANCIAL FACTS

Financial Aid Rating	84
Tuition	$17,666
Room & board	$5,440
Estimated book expense	$648
% frosh receiving aid	70
% undergrads receiving aid	66
% aid is need-based	85
% frosh w/ grant (avg)	89 ($12,412)
% frosh w/ loan (avg)	45 ($4,438)
% UGs w/ job (avg)	75 ($2,128)
Off-campus job outlook	good

OGLETHORPE UNIVERSITY

4484 PEACHTREE ROAD, NE, ATLANTA, GA 30319-2797   ADMISSIONS: 800-428-4484   FAX: 404-364-8500

STUDENTS SPEAK OUT

Life

Students at Oglethorpe give Atlanta an unqualified thumbs-up ("Atlanta is a big city and there are many things to do and other universities in the area to provide many different activities"), responding positively to its many clubs, restaurants, professional athletic teams, and "excellent weather." On campus, the Greek scene is popular: "The Greek life here is much more inclusive than at large schools." Otherwise, students report, campus life is slow: "Many people go home on weekends so sometimes it's hard to get a group together." Writes another, "Oglethorpe is so small that all parties seem to be the same one." Sums up one student, "One must become actively involved in the organizations at Oglethorpe to receive the full experience. If not, then the student gets lost as merely another student." Another major griping point is the food on campus. Notes a typical student, "Of all the things my friends and I do for fun off-campus, about 95 percent of them include eating: the food here is just that bad."

Academics

Out on the outskirts of Atlanta sits Oglethorpe University, an excellent school that inexplicably attracts only the peripheral attention of most South-bound students. The student body here receives a rigorous education, particularly in the preprofessional fields, and all Oglethorpe students must complete an unusually demanding and broad-based set of general education requirements, which constitute about forty percent of the credits required toward graduation. Despite the preprofessional inclinations of most undergrads, the core demands that students approach schoolwork with an attitude traditionally adopted by students at liberal arts—oriented colleges. Writes one student, "OU's classes and general atmosphere are extremely academic. Every part of life is open to a multipolitical, multicultural, objective debate in the quest for truth." Another reports approvingly, "The professors here treat students as colleagues. They are just as ready to learn from us as they are to teach us. This makes class a lot more exciting." OU has an excellent placement record with graduate programs, explaining why premedicine and business majors are so popular here. Students may cross-register at other Atlanta schools when desired courses are not offered at OU.

Student Body

Oglethorpe students are "politically right down the middle. They are very southern and, on social issues, conservative." Most agree that students have "A very ambitious focus. Students have very high professional aspirations." Although Oglethorpe pioneered the admission of black students to nonblack universities in the South, today the black population is low. OU works hard to make its education affordable to everyone it accepts—a large majority of students receive some form of financial aid—and students reported that, as a result, students of diverse social backgrounds are well represented.

FINANCIAL AID: 404-364-8356

ADMISSIONS

The admissions committee considers (in descending order of importance): HS record, test scores, recommendations, class rank, essay. *Also considered (in descending order of importance):* extracurriculars, personality, alumni relationship. Either the SAT or ACT is required. An interview is recommended. *High school units required/recommended:* 18 total units are required; 4 English required, 3 math required, 2 science required, 2 social studies required. Minimum combined SAT I score of 950 and minimum 2.8 GPA required.

The Inside Word

With rising national interest in the South, it won't be long before the academic strength found at Oglethorpe attracts wider attention and more applicants. At present, it's much easier to gain admission here than at many universities of similar quality. Go to Atlanta for a campus interview-you'll leave impressed.

FINANCIAL AID

Students should submit: FAFSA, the school's own financial aid form, state aid form, a copy of parents' most recent income tax filing. The Princeton Review suggests that all financial aid forms be submitted as soon as possible after January 1. *The following grants/scholarships are offered:* Pell, SEOG, academic merit, the school's own scholarships, the school's own grants, state scholarships, state grants, private scholarships, private grants, foreign aid. *Students borrow from the following loan programs:* Stafford, unsubsidized Stafford, Perkins, PLUS, the school's own loan fund, state loans, private loans. College Work-Study Program is available. Institutional employment is available.

FROM THE ADMISSIONS OFFICE

"Promising students and outstanding teachers come together at Oglethorpe University in an acclaimed program of liberal arts and sciences. Here you'll find an active intellectual community on a beautiful English Gothic campus just ten miles from the center of Atlanta, capital of the Southeast, site of the 1996 Summer Olympics and home to 2.8 million people. If you want challenging academics, the opportunity to work closely with your professors, and the stimulation of a great metropolitan area, consider Oglethorpe, a national liberal arts college in a world-class city."

ADMISSIONS

Admissions Rating	76
% of applicants accepted	83
% of acceptees attending	32

FRESHMAN PROFILE

Average verbal SAT	620
Average math SAT	600
Average ACT	28
Average TOEFL	500
Graduated top 20% of class	75
Graduated top 40% of class	90
Graduated top 60% of class	98
Average HS GPA or Avg.	3.7

DEADLINES

Early decision	NR
Regular admission	8/15
Regular notification	Rolling
Non-fall registration	yes

APPLICANTS ALSO LOOK AT

AND OFTEN PREFER
Emory
Florida State

AND SOMETIMES PREFER
U. Georgia
U. of the South
Furman
Georgia Tech.
Vanderbilt

AND RARELY PREFER
Mercer
Berry

FINANCIAL FACTS

Financial Aid Rating	96
Tuition	$13,950
Room & board	$4,650
Estimated book expense	$600

% frosh receiving aid	83
% undergrads receiving aid	85
% aid is need-based	44
% frosh w/ grant (avg)	82 ($8,781)
% frosh w/ loan (avg)	81 ($4,644)
% UGs w/ job (avg)	38 ($1,200)
Off-campus job outlook	good

OHIO NORTHERN UNIVERSITY

525 SOUTH MAIN STREET, ADA, OH 45810 | ADMISSIONS: 419-772-2260 | FAX: 419-772-2313

CAMPUS LIFE

Quality of Life Rating   **77**
Type of school   private
Affiliation   United Methodist Church
Environment   town

STUDENTS
FT undergrad enrollment   2,643
% male/female   51/49
% from out of state   21
% live on campus   70
% spend weekend on campus   33
% transfers   6
% from public high school   80
% in (# of) fraternities   25 (7)
% in (# of) sororities   25 (4)
% African-American   3
% Asian   1
% Caucasian   92
% Hispanic   1
% international   2
# of countries represented   20

WHAT'S HOT
religion
campus feels safe
Greeks
campus is beautiful
school runs like butter

WHAT'S NOT
off-campus food
drugs
Ada
dorms
sex

ACADEMICS

Academic Rating   **84**
Profs Interesting Rating   78
Profs Accessible Rating   90
Calendar   quarter
Student/teacher ratio   13:1
% profs PhD/tenured   78/79
Hours of study per day   3.63

MOST POPULAR MAJORS
pharmacy
mechanical engineering
electrical engineering

% GRADS WHO PURSUE...
Law 3, Med 1, MBA 1, MA 6

STUDENTS SPEAK OUT

Life
Ohio Northern boasts a "small, beautiful campus" in the small town of Ada, Ohio. Students admit that in town "there's little to do. We have a Hardee's and a gas station, that's about it." Another adds, "For fun, we go to Lima." An active social scene on campus partly makes up for the dull surrounding area, however. Explains one student: "There is a lot of life on campus, mainly because the town of Ada is so small. Student groups try to plan activities to make up for the small-town atmosphere." Among these events are an annual Fall Mud Volleyball tournament ("Tournaments are open to everyone on campus. It's something to look forward to when returning from summer break") and a spring festival called "Tunes on the Tundra," which features live music of all types. Fraternity parties are also well attended, and an unusual aspect of student life at ONU is that "the Greeks are involved with independents and other Greeks, which makes the campus more unified." Even more rare is the fact that "the administration is very supportive of the Greeks."

Academics
Engineering, health sciences, and pharmacology are three of the many strong fields that bring students to Ohio Northern University. ONU also has substantial and successful programs in business. A healthy serving of general education courses (most divisions of the school require about one-third of the courses toward graduation) prevents ONU from being just a professional training ground, however. Students mostly like the faculty and administration: respondents write that "our administration is excellent. If any student has a legitimate problem or request, it is taken care of as soon as possible" and "One thing that impressed me the most is the time that the professors take to sit down and help you. Even if they have a schedule conflict, they'll make time." One student tells us that, despite ONU's university status, "I have never seen a TA in any of my courses." Some complain, however, about their profs' teaching skills, noting that "Most profs are good, yet some are terrible, depends on luck." The school provides a safety net for those who fall behind: "Our tutoring system is sponsored by the university and is provided at no charge to students. This works well!" Overall, "the atmosphere is comfortable, the personal contacts with faculty and staff excellent."

Student Body
This is a white-bread campus. Sums up one ONU student: "The student body is mainly from white, middle-class, conservative families. There's a small-town atmosphere here." Most seem to get along well, but gays in particular may have a hard time. Reports one respondent: "Some students are very religious and it is for this reason, along with fear and ignorance, that some (e.g., gays) aren't accepted."

FINANCIAL AID: 419-772-2272

ADMISSIONS

The admissions committee considers (in descending order of importance): HS record, test scores, class rank, recommendations. *Also considered (in descending order of importance):* special talents, alumni relationship, extracurriculars, geographical distribution, personality. Either the SAT or ACT is required; ACT is preferred. An interview is recommended. Admissions process is need-blind. *High school units required/recommended:* 16 total units are required; 4 English required, 2 math required, 3 math recommended, 2 science required, 3 science recommended, 2 foreign language recommended, 2 social studies required, 2 history required. Minimum composite ACT score of 20, rank in top half of secondary school class, and minimum 2.5 GPA required. *Special Requirements:* 3 units of math and 3 units of science required of applicants to College of Pharmacy; 4 units of math and 2 units of science required of applicants to College of Engineering.

The Inside Word

Solid grades from high school are a pretty sure ticket for admission to Ohio Northern. A significant percentage of the university's admits enroll, which indicates a healthy level of self-selection in the applicant pool. Students who are above average academically are in good position to take advantage of a very large number of no-need scholarships.

FINANCIAL AID

Students should submit: FAFSA, the school's own financial aid form, state aid form. The Princeton Review suggests that all financial aid forms be submitted as soon as possible after January 1. *The following grants/scholarships are offered:* Pell, SEOG, academic merit, the school's own scholarships, the school's own grants, state scholarships, state grants, private scholarships, private grants, ROTC. *Students borrow from the following loan programs:* Stafford, unsubsidized Stafford, Perkins, PLUS, the school's own loan fund, health professions loans, private loans. College Work-Study Program is available. Institutional employment is available.

FROM THE ADMISSIONS OFFICE

"Ohio Northern's purpose is to help students develop into self-reliant, mature men and women capable of clear and logical thinking and sensitive to the higher values of truth, beauty, and goodness. ONU selects its student body from among those students possessing characteristics congruent with the institution's objectives. Generally, a student must be prepared to use the resources of the institution to achieve personal and educational goals."

ADMISSIONS

Admissions Rating	73
% of applicants accepted	88
% of acceptees attending	37

FRESHMAN PROFILE

Average verbal SAT	580
Average math SAT	570
Average ACT	24
Average TOEFL	500
Graduated top 20% of class	65
Graduated top 40% of class	88
Graduated top 60% of class	NR
Average HS GPA or Avg.	3.4

DEADLINES

Early decision	NR
Regular admission	8/1
Regular notification	rolling
Non-fall registration	yes

APPLICANTS ALSO LOOK AT
AND SOMETIMES PREFER

Miami U.
Ohio State-Columbus
U. Cincinnati
Bowling Green State
Toledo

FINANCIAL FACTS

Financial Aid Rating	85
Tuition	$17,970
Room & board	$4,500
Estimated book expense	$500
% frosh receiving aid	95
% undergrads receiving aid	94
% aid is need-based	82
% frosh w/ grant (avg)	91 ($7,100)
% frosh w/ loan (avg)	80 ($2,500)
% UGs w/ job (avg)	45 ($1,200)
Off-campus job outlook	good

OHIO STATE UNIVERSITY-COLUMBUS

3RD FLOOR LINCOLN TOWER, 1800 CANNON DRIVE, COLUMBUS, OH 43210-1200 ADMISSIONS: 614-292-3980 FAX: 614-292-9180

CAMPUS LIFE

Quality of Life Rating 76
Type of school public
Affiliation none
Environment metropolis

STUDENTS
FT undergrad enrollment 30,499
% male/female 53/47
% from out of state 6
% live on campus 20
% spend weekend on campus NR
% transfers 31
% from public high school NR
% in (# of) fraternities 10 (35)
% in (# of) sororities 11 (24)
% African-American 6
% Asian 4
% Caucasian 82
% Hispanic 1
% international 3
# of countries represented 78

WHAT'S HOT
drugs
cigarettes
hard liquor
beer
old-fashioned dating

WHAT'S NOT
campus difficult to get around
student government
support groups
inefficient administration
lab facilities

ACADEMICS

Academic Rating 70
Profs Interesting Rating 65
Profs Accessible Rating 66
Calendar quarter
Student/teacher ratio 13:1
% profs tenured 95
Hours of study per day 2.88

MOST POPULAR MAJORS
accounting
psychology
education

STUDENTS SPEAK OUT

Life
Getting involved in the Ohio State University community is the key to having a good time here, and students must take the initiative. Says one, "Because it's so large, you can't expect OSU to come to you—you have to get the most out of your education. Getting involved makes a big difference!" Once students become active in an organization, club, or social niche, the school's size is no problem. There's something here for everyone, particularly those who love intercollegiate sports (especially football). There's a very lively social scene, with plenty of drinking, drugs, and hooking up if you're interested, but there are also other things to do. Explains one student, "To attend this school is to have infinite control over your destiny. You can crouch in your room like Gregor Samsa transformed into a dung beetle, or you can plunge into the infinite sea of faces that each year flood OSU." Explains another, "This campus is so big, it's tough to categorize anything, except that OSU is justifiably famous for its lines (to pay fees, buy tickets, get classes, etc.)."

Academics
Most Ohio State students would agree with the classmate who told us that "OSU has anything and everything both academically and socially." With over 34,000 full-time undergraduates (and another 6,000 part-timers), OSU is like a small city. As one student explained, "OSU is great not only for academics but also for life. There is such a wide range of ethnic, political, religious, and social beliefs, all of which count and make OSU so diverse." Career-oriented programs—accounting, nursing, engineering, etc.--are uniformly strong. The journalism program also has a good reputation, while engineering and business are among the other popular majors. As an added perk, OSU is extremely affordable. One student complained that "tuition is going up and services, such as the bus system, library hours, and the number of courses offered, are diminishing," but even if fees were to double next year, OSU would still be a bargain. As you might expect at a school with 40,000 undergraduates, classes are frequently huge and professors can be hard to contact personally, but relatively few students complained about these issues. Quite a few undergraduates felt that graduate students taught too many undergrad courses, however.

Student Body
One student sums up her experiences at OSU this way: "I have been exposed to an incredible variety of people, an experience I could only have had at a large school. I have met people of many nationalities, religions, and economic backgrounds. Additionally, there is every social group here, from frat rats to progressives to punks to Deadheads to snobs." Another puts it more simply: "Because of OSU's size and diversity, you can always find another person like you." Students are generally politically conservative, and they report that both interaction between ethnic groups and acceptance of gays are low.

ADMISSIONS

The admissions committee considers (in descending order of importance): HS record, class rank, test scores, recommendations, essay. *Also considered (in descending order of importance):* special talents, extracurriculars, geographical distribution. Either the SAT or ACT is required. *High school units required/recommended:* 15 total units are required; 20 total units are recommended; 4 English required, 3 math required, 4 math recommended, 2 science required, 3 science recommended, 2 foreign language required, 3 foreign language recommended, 2 social studies required. *Special Requirements:* A portfolio is required for art program applicants. An audition is required for music program applicants. Audition required for applicants to dance program.

The Inside Word

Although admissions officers consider extracurriculars and other personal characteristics of candidates, there is a heavy emphasis on numbers—grades, rank, and test scores. Admissions standards are not as competitive as at many public flagship universities, which makes it worth a shot for average students. The university's great reputation makes it a good choice for anyone looking at large schools.

FINANCIAL AID

Students should submit: FAFSA, the school's own financial aid form. The Princeton Review suggests that all financial aid forms be submitted as soon as possible after January 1. *The following grants/scholarships are offered:* Pell, SEOG, academic merit, athletic, the school's own scholarships, the school's own grants, state scholarships, state grants, private scholarships, private grants, ROTC. *Students borrow from the following loan programs:* Stafford, Perkins, PLUS, the school's own loan fund, federal nursing loans, health professions loans, private loans. Applicants will be notified of awards beginning April 15. College Work-Study Program is available. Institutional employment is available.

FROM THE ADMISSIONS OFFICE

"The Ohio State University is Ohio's leading center for teaching, research, and public service. Our exceptional faculty, innovative programs, supportive services, and our extremely competitive tuition costs make Ohio State one of higher education's best values. Our central campus is in Columbus, Ohio—the state's capital and largest city. About 54,000 students from every county in Ohio, every state in the nation, and over 100 foreign nations are enrolled at Ohio State. Our faculty include Nobel Prize winners, Rhodes Scholars, members of the National Academy of Sciences, widely published writers, and noted artists and musicians. From classes and residence halls, to concerts and seminars, to clubs and sports and honoraries, to Frisbee games on the Oval, Ohio State offers lots of opportunities to develop talents and skills while meeting a variety of people. At Ohio State, you're sure to find a place to call your own."

ADMISSIONS

Admissions Rating	66
% of applicants accepted	91
% of acceptees attending	41

FRESHMAN PROFILE

Average verbal SAT	540
Average math SAT	550
Average ACT	23
Average TOEFL	NR
Graduated top 20% of class	40
Graduated top 40% of class	66
Graduated top 60% of class	86
Average HS GPA or Avg.	NR

DEADLINES

Early decision	NR
Regular admission	2/15
Regular notification	rolling
Non-fall registration	yes

APPLICANTS ALSO LOOK AT

AND OFTEN PREFER

Miami U.
Ohio U.
U. Illinois–Urbana-Champaign
Syracuse
U. Michigan-Ann Arbor

AND SOMETIMES PREFER

Pittsburgh
Bowling Green State
Kent State
U. Cincinnati

AND RARELY PREFER

Bellarmine

FINANCIAL FACTS

Financial Aid Rating	73
In-state tuition	$3,273
Out-of-state tuition	$9,819
Room & board	$2,844
Estimated book expense	NR
% frosh receiving aid	NR
% undergrads receiving aid	NR
% aid is need-based	NR
% frosh w/ grant (avg)	NR
% frosh w/ loan (avg)	NR
% UGs w/ job (avg)	NR
Off-campus job outlook	excellent

OHIO UNIVERSITY

ATHENS, OH 45701-2979   ADMISSIONS: 614-593-4100   FAX: 614-593-4229

CAMPUS LIFE

Quality of Life Rating	79
Type of school	public
Affiliation	none
Environment	town

STUDENTS

FT undergrad enrollment	15,339
% male/female	46/54
% from out of state	11
% live on campus	42
% spend weekend on campus	85
% transfers	14
% from public high school	86
% in (# of) fraternities	11 (17)
% in (# of) sororities	16 (11)
% African-American	4
% Asian	1
% Caucasian	91
% Hispanic	1
% international	2
# of countries represented	100

WHAT'S HOT
drugs
cigarettes
old-fashioned dating
intercollegiate sports
ethnic diversity on campus

WHAT'S NOT
campus difficult to get around
lab facilities
student government
support groups
inefficient administration

ACADEMICS

Academic Rating	70
Profs Interesting Rating	65
Profs Accessible Rating	65
Calendar	quarter
Student/teacher ratio	17:1
% profs PhD/tenured	93/73
Hours of study per day	2.81

MOST POPULAR MAJORS
communication
business management
education

% GRADS WHO PURSUE...
Law 3, Med 2, MBA 3, MA 10

STUDENTS SPEAK OUT

Life

Students describe life at Ohio University as "extremely nice." The generally relaxed academic atmosphere keeps stress at a minimum. Some admit to taking this laid-back attitude a bit too far. One student writes, "Beer and sex top the list of things to do. At the bottom there is studying." Partying opportunities are rarer now that the university is officially "dry," but many students join the fun- and alcohol-loving Greeks each year, and the numerous bars in Athens are usually crowded with students. Despite the official policy, the motto for many remains, "If you can't find a party on the weekend (Thursday through Monday), you are either blind, deaf, dumb or it's summer break." Ohio U's campus is "very attractive." Campus beauty was cited in our surveys as a major asset of the school. Intercollegiate basketball is big, and the intramural scene can get quite intense during the popular flag football and broomball competitions. The fact that Athens is far from any kind of urban center contributes to the feeling of isolation some get here, but the flip side for students is the freedom from unnecessary distractions. Students report a high level of happiness despite the lack of nearby skyscrapers, ski resorts, or beaches.

Academics

Ohio U's biggest academic strength is its ability to offer many of its students a private-style education for a reasonable, public-school price. The excellent honors tutorial program allows select students to work more closely with professors than is usually possible at a large university. Standout areas of study include communications and the "renowned journalism school." Also, education and business are both popular and high quality. Distribution requirements have become more rigorous in recent years with the introduction of the "tier" system. Freshmen must do Tier I (English, writing, and math), while upperclassmen must complete Tier II (assorted subjects including the natural sciences, social sciences, fine arts, Third World studies, and humanities), and Tier III (one interdisciplinary course for seniors). Although some classes are quite large, most are reasonable; in fact, students claim that many classes have fewer than twenty members, especially courses beyond required and introductory ones. Registration, however, is a hassle, with many students (especially underclassmen) running up against closed classes. The faculty and administration receive relatively high marks overall.

Student Body

Most students here are from in-state, and all in all, the OU crowd is fairly homogeneous. Approximately 600 African-Americans make up the only noticeable minority group here; other minority populations are much smaller, unless one counts foreign students as a minority. The preprofessional white contingent, on the other hand, is huge. Among these groups, however, interaction is relatively high, and the student body's size enables almost everyone at Ohio University to find a satisfying niche. Many students have such a good experience at OU, they return to the area to live after a few years. One student explains this phenomenon by describing the place as "spiritually healthy in a secular way."

FINANCIAL AID: 614-593-4141

ADMISSIONS

The admissions committee considers (in descending order of importance): HS record, class rank, test scores, recommendations. *Also considered (in descending order of importance):* special talents, alumni relationship, extracurriculars. Either the SAT or ACT is required; ACT is preferred. Admissions process is need-blind. *High school units required/ recommended:* 17 total units are recommended; 4 English recommended, 3 math recommended, 3 science recommended, 2 foreign language recommended, 3 social studies recommended. Rank in top third of secondary school class required. Minimum 2.5 GPA recommended. *Special Requirements:* A portfolio is required for art program applicants. An audition is required for music program applicants. An RN is required for nursing program applicants. TOEFL is required of all international students. *The admissions office says:* "Because of the varied backgrounds of the students, the climate of the campus is much more tolerant of people with differences than most competitive schools."

The Inside Word

There's little mystery in applying to Ohio U. The admissions process follows the formula approach very closely, and those whose numbers plug in well will get good news. Candidates who fall short academically should not expect to find much opportunity for redemption in a process that discounts essays and extracurriculars.

FINANCIAL AID

Students should submit: FAFSA, the school's own financial aid form, state aid form. The Princeton Review suggests that all financial aid forms be submitted as soon as possible after January 1. *The following grants/scholarships are offered:* Pell, SEOG, academic merit, athletic, the school's own scholarships, the school's own grants, state scholarships, state grants, private scholarships, private grants, federal nursing scholarship, ROTC. *Students borrow from the following loan programs:* Stafford, unsubsidized Stafford, Perkins, PLUS, the school's own loan fund, health professions loans. College Work-Study Program is available. Institutional employment is available.

FROM THE ADMISSIONS OFFICE

"Chartered in 1804, Ohio University symbolizes America's early commitment to higher education. Its historic campus provides a setting matched by only a handful of other universities in the country. Students choose Ohio University mainly because of its academic strength, but the beautiful setting and college-town atmosphere are also factors in their decision. Ohio University is the central focus of Athens, Ohio, located approximately seventy-five miles southeast of Columbus. We encourage prospective students to come for a visit and experience the beauty and academic excellence of Ohio University."

ADMISSIONS

Admissions Rating	72
% of applicants accepted	72
% of acceptees attending	40

FRESHMAN PROFILE

Average verbal SAT	630
Average math SAT	560
Average ACT	24
Average TOEFL	NR
Graduated top 20% of class	44
Graduated top 40% of class	81
Graduated top 60% of class	97
Average HS GPA or Avg.	3.2

DEADLINES

Early decision	NR
Regular admission	2/1
Regular notification	rolling
Non-fall registration	yes

APPLICANTS ALSO LOOK AT

AND OFTEN PREFER
Oberlin
Miami U.

AND SOMETIMES PREFER
Ohio State-Columbus
Michigan State
Penn State-U. Park
Wittenberg
U. Cincinnati

AND RARELY PREFER
Bowling Green State
Kent State
Purdue U.-West Lafayette
Indiana U.-Bloomington
Dayton

FINANCIAL FACTS

Financial Aid Rating	77
In-state tuition	$3,796
Out-of-state tuition	$8,035
Room & board	$4,260
Estimated book expense	$615
% frosh receiving aid	70
% undergrads receiving aid	60
% aid is need-based	62
% frosh w/ grant (avg)	39 ($2,085)
% frosh w/ loan (avg)	46 ($4,522)
% UGs w/ job (avg)	16 ($1,244)
Off-campus job outlook	poor

OHIO WESLEYAN UNIVERSITY

61 SOUTH SANDUSKY STREET, DELAWARE, OH 43015   ADMISSIONS: 800-862-8953   FAX: 614-368-3299

STUDENTS SPEAK OUT

Life

Most Ohio Wesleyan University students, even those with hard-core study habits, would probably agree that developing an active social life is crucial to enjoying yourself here. Several students voice opinions along these lines: "Life on OWU's campus revolves more closely around the social than the academic." Notes one, "There are plenty of opportunities to participate in campus organizations. The town does not have many night-time attractions except for three bars; however, Southern Ohio State provides some entertainment!" Students also report that they often go to Columbus for shopping, theater, and nightclub hopping. Students enjoy the school's Division III sports teams and intramural sports; writes one, "Athletics here are tremendous. Men's lacrosse and soccer are by far the most successful, but the other teams aren't slouches by any means. Intramural and club sports like ice hockey, flag football, soccer, and lacrosse are very popular." Beer-heavy fraternity parties represent students' number one social choice, leading one student to observe that "One has to look hard to be intellectually stimulated outside the classroom. This is still a party college."

Academics

OWU students are aware that their university is on the upswing. In the words of one student, the school's efforts over the past decade to create a more competitive academic atmosphere have made OWU "one of the best private liberal arts institutions in the Midwest." Midwestern independent college counselors agree. "Outstanding academics," writes one; another is enthusiastic about the "excellent teachers." OWU is a medium-sized university that offers a remarkably diverse array of studies. Strong programs include not only the most popular ones—business, English, political science—but also such "off the beaten path" majors as zoology, botany, and urban studies. Small classes and vibrant, accessible professors are the school's other big assets. "Most of the professors relate to the problems or questions that students have. Professors here bend over backwards for students," writes one of the many students who mentioned the teachers as the best thing about OWU. An honors program is available to top students who want a more challenging curriculum.

Student Body

According to many respondents, "OWU is made up of lots of white, middle-class, conservative students. The campus is both cliquish and segregated. The majority of the community comes from very isolated small towns, and when these individuals come to OWU, they have a hard time interacting with others different—racially, religiously, etc.—from themselves." Reports another, "There are definitely strong feelings against homosexuals/bisexuals/cross-dressers. There are some racial tensions which are being addressed." More than half the students are from Ohio with others from surrounding states; the number of students from the East and West Coasts is growing, however.

FINANCIAL AID: 614-368-3050   E-MAIL: OWUADMIT@CC.OWU.EDU   WEB SITE: HTTP://192.68.223.4:8000/

ADMISSIONS

The admissions committee considers (in descending order of importance): HS record, recommendations, class rank, test scores, essay. *Also considered (in descending order of importance):* alumni relationship, extracurriculars, personality, special talents, geographical distribution. Either the SAT or ACT is required. An interview is recommended. Admissions process is need-blind. *High school units required/recommended:* 16 total units are recommended; 4 English recommended, 3 math recommended, 3 science recommended, 3 foreign language recommended, 3 social studies recommended. *Special Requirements:* An audition is required for music program applicants. TOEFL is required of all international students. *The admissions office says:* "We use the SAT I/ACT less and we concentrate more on the students' personal contributions to their school and community. We also look at their personality and creativity. OWU is well known for enrolling students who are independent and individuals who seek a friendly and yet highly diverse environment. Applicants are asked to "weight" the components of their application: what they think best represents their capabilities, etc."

The Inside Word

The need to counter a low yield of admits who enroll keeps Ohio Wesleyan from higher academic expectations for its applicants. Students won't encounter super-selective academic standards for admission, but they will have to put some thought into the completion of their applications. The university's thorough admissions process definitely emphasizes the personal side of candidate evaluation.

FINANCIAL AID

Students should submit: FAFSA (due March 15), the school's own financial aid form (due March 15), a copy of parents' most recent income tax filing (due May 15). The Princeton Review suggests that all financial aid forms be submitted as soon as possible after January 1. *The following grants/scholarships are offered:* Pell, SEOG, academic merit, the school's own scholarships, the school's own grants, state grants, private scholarships, private grants, foreign aid. *Students borrow from the following loan programs:* Stafford, unsubsidized Stafford, Perkins, PLUS, the school's own loan fund, health professions loans, private loans. College Work-Study Program is available. Institutional employment is available.

FROM THE ADMISSIONS OFFICE

"Balance is the key word that describes Ohio Wesleyan. For example: 50 percent male, 50 percent female; 50 percent members of Greek life, 50 percent not; National Colloquium Program, Top Division III sports program; Small- town setting of 22,000, near sixteenth largest city in U.S. (Columbus, Ohio); Excellent faculty/student ratio, outstanding fine and performance arts programs."

ADMISSIONS

Admissions Rating	74
% of applicants accepted	84
% of acceptees attending	26

FRESHMAN PROFILE

Average verbal SAT	600
Average math SAT	590
Average ACT	26
Average TOEFL	550
Graduated top 20% of class	45
Graduated top 40% of class	69
Graduated top 60% of class	86
Average HS GPA or Avg.	3.4

DEADLINES

Early decision	NR
Regular admission	3/1
Regular notification	rolling
Non-fall registration	yes

APPLICANTS ALSO LOOK AT

AND OFTEN PREFER

Miami U.
Ohio State-Columbus
DePauw
Oberlin
U. Vermont

AND SOMETIMES PREFER

Wittenberg
Denison
Penn State-U. Park
Wooster
Dickinson

AND RARELY PREFER

Kenyon
Gettysburg
St. Lawrence
Skidmore

FINANCIAL FACTS

Financial Aid Rating	90
Tuition	$17,569
Room & board	$5,876
Estimated book expense	$550
% frosh receiving aid	82
% undergrads receiving aid	80
% aid is need-based	66
% frosh w/ grant (avg)	82 ($11,608)
% frosh w/ loan (avg)	61 ($3,825)
% UGs w/ job (avg)	43 ($1,200)
Off-campus job outlook	excellent

UNIVERSITY OF OKLAHOMA

NORMAN, OK 73019   ADMISSIONS: 405-325-2251   FAX: 405-325-7605

CAMPUS LIFE

Quality of Life Rating   **75**
Type of school   public
Affiliation   none
Environment   metropolis

STUDENTS
FT undergrad enrollment   13,118
% male/female   55/45
% from out of state   22
% live on campus   16
% spend weekend on campus   65
% transfers   37
% from public high school   NR
% in (# of) fraternities   18 (22)
% in (# of) sororities   18 (15)
% African-American   7
% Asian   5
% Caucasian   70
% Hispanic   3
% international   8
# of countries represented   100

WHAT'S HOT
political activism
intercollegiate sports
old-fashioned dating
ethnic diversity on campus
town-gown relations

WHAT'S NOT
health facilities
student government
campus difficult to get around
lab facilities
support groups

ACADEMICS

Academic Rating   **72**
Profs Interesting Rating   64
Profs Accessible Rating   62
Calendar   semester
Student/teacher ratio   NR
% profs PhD/tenured   83/85
Hours of study per day   2.97

MOST POPULAR MAJORS
psychology
accounting
management information systems

STUDENTS SPEAK OUT

Life

Most University of Oklahoma students live for football games and frat parties, but at a school this large, "a student can find a campus organization to meet any of his/her interests. Campus leadership, although dominated by the Greek system, is quite diverse." Most students agree that "life here depends on what group you hang out with. If you want to remain in high school you join a frat or a sorority. If not, it isn't hard to find a niche. We have everything from religious groups to a gay and lesbian society!" Most students enjoy the laid-back town location. Explains one city hater, "The school is beautifully set in Norman, OK. The only disadvantage is how close it is to Oklahoma City. The campus is phenomenally pretty, and I love the school spirit here, with the nationally recognized sports program."

Academics

"University of Oklahoma's reputation as a party school coaxed me from the East Coast," explains one Savannah, Georgia native. "Too bad for my GPA," he continues, "that my professors never heard of that reputation." Although it's still possible to get by at OU without doing much work—students report that studying and class attendance are well below the national average—it's also true that the school is providing more challenges for the motivated student. Full scholarships for National Merit Scholars and an honors program open to students who score above 1100 on the SATs have helped create a more ambitious intellectual atmosphere. Business and management programs are reputedly very good, as are engineering programs (studies in petroleum are especially strong, due to the proximity of the oil industry's center). Education majors are also popular. On the downside, OU is in many ways a typical large school. Professors vary widely in quality and are uniformly difficult to meet after class: "from my experience I would guess that the student/teacher ratio is 50:1," complains one accounting major. An engineering student adds, "Give us money so we can hire good teachers who don't have to do research." TAs teach a relatively large proportion of courses on all levels, and administrators are overtaxed in managing this small-town-sized school. The school's subdivision into sixteen smaller colleges seems to make management more difficult. A music education major explains that separate colleges (in this case, music and education) do not coordinate schedules, making it difficult for students taking courses at more than one school to schedule their semester.

Student Body

Around three-quarters of OU's student body are natives of Oklahoma. Minorities constitute more than 10 percent of the student body, an improvement from past years and a good indication that OU is actually working on diversifying the school. Students note that there is a visible gay presence on campus but also note that acceptance of the gay community is low.

FINANCIAL AID: 405-325-4521

ADMISSIONS

The admissions committee considers (in descending order of importance): HS record, class rank, test scores, recommendations, essay. *Also considered (in descending order of importance):* special talents, extracurriculars, personality. Either the SAT or ACT is required. Admissions process is need-blind. *High school units required/recommended:* 11 total units are required; 4 English required, 3 math required, 2 science required, 2 foreign language recommended, 2 social studies recommended, 2 history required. Minimum combined SAT I score of 1030 (composite ACT score of 22) or rank in top third of secondary school class and minimum 3.0 GPA required. *Special Requirements:* A portfolio is required for art program applicants. An audition is required for music program applicants. TOEFL is required of all international students.

The Inside Word

It's plain from the approach of Oklahoma's evaluation process that candidates needn't put much energy into preparing supporting materials for their applications. This is one place that is going to get you a decision pronto—your numbers will call the shots.

FINANCIAL AID

Students should submit: FAFSA. The Princeton Review suggests that all financial aid forms be submitted as soon as possible after January 1. *The following grants/scholarships are offered:* Pell, SEOG, academic merit, athletic, the school's own scholarships, the school's own grants, state scholarships, state grants, private scholarships, private grants, federal nursing scholarship. *Students borrow from the following loan programs:* Stafford, unsubsidized Stafford, Perkins, PLUS, the school's own loan fund, federal nursing loans, health professions loans, private loans. Applicants will be notified of awards beginning March 15. College Work-Study Program is available. Institutional employment is available.

FROM THE ADMISSIONS OFFICE

"Ask yourself some significant questions. What are your ambitions, goals and dreams? Do you desire opportunity and are you ready to accept challenge? What do you hope to gain from your educational experience? Are you looking for a university that will provide you with the tools, resources, and motivation to convert ambitions, opportunities, and challenges into meaningful achievement? To effectively answer these questions you must carefully seek out your options, look for direction, and make the right choice. The University of Oklahoma combines a unique mixture of academic excellence, varied social cultures, and a variety of campus activities to make your educational experience complete. At OU, comprehensive learning is our goal for your life. Not only do you receive a valuable classroom learning experience, but OU is also one of the finest research institutions in the United States. This allows OU students the opportunity to be a part of technology in progress. It's not just learning, it's discovery, invention and dynamic creativity, a hands-on experience that allows you to be on the cutting edge of knowledge. Make the right choice and consider the University of Oklahoma!"

ADMISSIONS

Admissions Rating	71
% of applicants accepted	88
% of acceptees attending	56

FRESHMAN PROFILE

Average verbal SAT	NR
Average math SAT	NR
Average ACT	24
Average TOEFL	550
Graduated top 20% of class	51
Graduated top 40% of class	79
Graduated top 60% of class	NR
Average HS GPA or Avg.	3.4

DEADLINES

Early decision	NR
Regular admission	7/15
Regular notification	rolling
Non-fall registration	yes

APPLICANTS ALSO LOOK AT

AND OFTEN PREFER
Washington U.
Rice

AND SOMETIMES PREFER
Baylor
U. Texas-Austin
U. Kansas

FINANCIAL FACTS

Financial Aid Rating	81
In-state tuition	$2,024
Out-of-state tuition	$5,714
Room & board	$3,708
Estimated book expense	$767
% frosh receiving aid	59
% undergrads receiving aid	62
% aid is need-based	75
% frosh w/ grant (avg)	50 ($3,378)
% frosh w/ loan (avg)	27 ($6,075)
% UGs w/ job (avg)	10 ($3,000)
Off-campus job outlook	good

UNIVERSITY OF OREGON

EUGENE, OR 97403-1217

ADMISSIONS: 800-232-3825   FAX: 503-346-3660

CAMPUS LIFE

Quality of Life Rating	**75**
Type of school	public
Affiliation	none
Environment	city

STUDENTS

FT undergrad enrollment	11,910
% male/female	48/52
% from out of state	39
% live on campus	25
% spend weekend on campus	80
% transfers	39
% from public high school	89
% in (# of) fraternities	7 (16)
% in (# of) sororities	7 (11)
% African-American	2
% Asian	7
% Caucasian	77
% Hispanic	3
% international	9
# of countries represented	90

WHAT'S HOT
drugs
health facilities
leftist politics
library
registration is a breeze

WHAT'S NOT
dorms
religion
students are unhappy
student government
students are cliquish

ACADEMICS

Academic Rating	**75**
Profs Interesting Rating	64
Profs Accessible Rating	66
Calendar	quarter
Student/teacher ratio	19:1
% profs PhD/tenured	80/97
Hours of study per day	2.97

MOST POPULAR MAJORS
psychology
sociology
English

% GRADS WHO PURSUE...
Law 3, Med 2, MBA 1, MA 6

STUDENTS SPEAK OUT

Life

The University of Oregon has a beautiful campus, complete with "grassy lawns, quiet walkways, and towering Douglas Fir trees." Classes are held in "ivy-covered brick buildings," and dorms are safe but uncomfortable (and hard to come by; most students live in apartments off campus). Students groove on Eugene; one writes, "The town is beautiful with much to offer in terms of active outlets (climbing, skiing, biking, snowboarding, rollerblading). We're only an hour from mountains, beaches, lakes, and other scenic tours. However, at night, there leaves a lot to be desired." On campus, social life revolves around "parties, movies, house dances," and mind-altering drugs. One student exclaims, "Friday and Saturday nights are frightening, as every block of this town has a drunken party and a lively drummer!" And as for the weather, it's no accident that the school's mascot is a duck: "It rains a lot here, except in the summer. There's unbelievable pollen here in the spring, but from July to September, there's no place on Earth I'd rather be."

Academics

A good-looking campus and a large "pseudo-hippie" population are the traits that most obviously distinguish UO from the typical state-sponsored university. Academically, UO's greatest strengths lie in the preprofessional majors, with psychology claiming the most students. Architecture, journalism, business, and the hard sciences are also excellent. Less popular programs have, in recent years, suffered from state and school budget problems. An honors program with special classes is available for top-notch students. Facilities are good; one psychology major reports, "My department includes a program that cuts the leading edge in the field of cognitive science and is well supported by neuroscience programs and laboratories." Students complain about class size, the number of introductory courses taught by TAs, and the overall quality of teaching. However, some students prefer TAs, because they are less intimidating than the professors, as one student notes: "When grad students teach, discussions are lively and people ask questions and even admit when they don't understand a concept. We fear the professor's stare." Says another, "Professors bite the heads off of live bats." And another, "I feel that some of the professors are unable to bring the material down to our level of comprehension."

Student Body

Says one student of her classmates, the "student body interacts pretty well—granola types, rural Oregon students, athletes. Life on campus opens up the eyes of even the most conservative to important political and social issues." However, some refuse to really look: "Many do not understand who I am and have many stereotypes about me being Asian American and a woman." Public protests are not unusual; writes one respondent, "We have students who protest and students who protest the protests, but there's always someone...protesting something or other. It's a conscientious campus."

FINANCIAL AID: 503-346-3211

WEB SITE: HTTP://WWW.UOREGON.EDU/

ADMISSIONS

The admissions committee considers (in descending order of importance): HS record, test scores. *Also considered (in descending order of importance):* geographical distribution. Either the SAT or ACT is required. An interview is recommended. *High school units required/recommended:* 14 total units are required; 4 English required, 3 math required, 2 science required, 2 foreign language recommended, 3 social studies required. Minimum 3.0 GPA required. *Special Requirements:* A portfolio is required for art program applicants. An audition is required for music program applicants. TOEFL is required of all international students. Portfolio required of architecture program applicants. *The admissions office says:* "A personal essay and two letters of recommendation are required if the applicant does not meet minimum admission requirements."

The Inside Word

Oregon's admissions process is essentially a formula; it's not likely that anything beyond your grades, rank, and tests will play much of a part in getting admitted.

FINANCIAL AID

Students should submit: FAFSA. The Princeton Review suggests that all financial aid forms be submitted as soon as possible after January 1. *The following grants/scholarships are offered:* Pell, SEOG, academic merit, athletic, the school's own scholarships, the school's own grants, state scholarships, state grants, ROTC. *Students borrow from the following loan programs:* Stafford, unsubsidized Stafford, Perkins, PLUS, the school's own loan fund, supplemental loans. Applicants will be notified of awards beginning April 15. College Work-Study Program is available. Institutional employment is available.

FROM THE ADMISSIONS OFFICE

"Five generations of outstanding leaders and citizens have studied at the University of Oregon since it opened in 1876. Today's students, like the 300,000 who came before them, have access to the most current knowledge in classes, laboratories, and seminars conducted by active researchers. In turn, by sharing their research through teaching, professors are better able to articulate their findings and to integrate their specialized studies with broader areas of knowledge. Their students learn that knowledge is a vital and changing commodity and that learning should be a lifelong activity."

ADMISSIONS

Admissions Rating	79
% of applicants accepted	90
% of acceptees attending	34

FRESHMAN PROFILE

Average verbal SAT	580
Average math SAT	560
Average ACT	NR
Average TOEFL	500
Graduated top 20% of class	NR
Graduated top 40% of class	NR
Graduated top 60% of class	NR
Average HS GPA or Avg.	3.3

DEADLINES

Early decision	NR
Regular admission	3/1
Regular notification	rolling
Non-fall registration	yes

APPLICANTS ALSO LOOK AT

AND OFTEN PREFER

UC-Berkeley
UC-Davis

AND SOMETIMES PREFER

U. Washington
U. Colorado-Boulder
U. Portland
U. Arizona
UC-Santa Cruz

AND RARELY PREFER

Willamette

FINANCIAL FACTS

Financial Aid Rating	75
In-state tuition	$3,510
Out-of-state tuition	$11,485
Room & board	$4,325
Estimated book expense	$600
% frosh receiving aid	45
% undergrads receiving aid	45
% aid is need-based	NR
% frosh w/ grant (avg)	25
% frosh w/ loan (avg)	45
% UGs w/ job (avg)	30 ($1,000)
Off-campus job outlook	good

UNIVERSITY OF THE PACIFIC

3601 PACIFIC AVENUE, STOCKTON, CA 95211 · ADMISSIONS: 209-946-2211 · FAX: 209-946-2413

STUDENTS SPEAK OUT

Life
Students at the University of the Pacific enjoy one of the nation's most stunning campuses, but the catch is it's located in one of the nation's most boring towns. "Stockton is dead socially," observes one student, "although bars are popular. Students frequently head to the Bay Area, Sacramento, or Tahoe for fun." On campus, "we have a movie theater, so often people head there on the weekends. The fraternities generally have open parties, so everyone is invited. People like to be active. U of P provides trips, coffeehouses, and other activities to please everyone." Adds another, "For fun we have a lot of school activities. Frats, sororities, sports, academic clubs, and general clubs are some of these." Parties, especially on weekends, are said to be frequent and wild. "Life during the week revolves around school, and on the weekends it seems to be based on partying and getting drunk," notes one student. Another complains, "I'm very sick of loud obnoxious partying idiots and they abound in this place. For fun I go to concerts or hang out with a couple of friends. Stockton is extremely boring."

Academics
Students at University of the Pacific most enjoy the personal attention they get from the professors and administrators. "I love it here because my profs all have time to help students, even if it's not during their regular office hours. Also, my classes are so small that the professors and students become friends," reports one student. Another writes "The administration is excellent. If you need something, the administration will get it for you right away. The professors in general are extremely helpful and understanding; they are there for you day and night." Health sciences are the school's strongest suit, although engineering and business-related majors are also popular and reportedly excellent. The school's well-regarded music programs are criticized by some as being too conservative and restrictive but overall also receive students' praises. Writes one student trying to sum up the University of the Pacific experience, "Overall, this is the perfect college for anyone who likes small-college atmosphere and big-time college sports, especially women's sports."

Student Body
University of the Pacific attracts a well-off crowd. Notes one student, "Students are generally friendly. Some have led very sheltered lives and it shows." Adds another, "Most people here are nice, white-bread Christian America. Some are very intelligent and mature. Most of them are also perpetually drunk." Students lean toward the conservative end of the political spectrum, although most simply don't care.

FINANCIAL AID: 209-946-2421

WEB SITE: HTTP://WWW.UOP.EDU/

ADMISSIONS

The admissions committee considers (in descending order of importance): HS record, test scores, essay, recommendations, class rank. *Also considered (in descending order of importance):* alumni relationship, extracurriculars, geographical distribution, personality, special talents. Either the SAT or ACT is required. An interview is recommended. *High school units required/recommended:* 16 total units are recommended; 4 English recommended, 3 math recommended, 2 science recommended, 2 foreign language recommended, 1 history recommended. *Special Requirements:* An audition is required for music program applicants. TOEFL is required of all international students. 4 units of math and 3 units of lab science recommended of science and technical program applicants.

The Inside Word

Pacific's small applicant pool and average yield of admits who enroll results in an admissions profile which is less competitive than the academic quality of the freshmen might predict. Test scores count less than a consistently solid academic performance in high school does toward getting admitted. The out-of-state population is small; candidates from far afield can expect this to benefit them to a minor degree.

FINANCIAL AID

Students should submit: FAFSA, the school's own financial aid form. The Princeton Review suggests that all financial aid forms be submitted as soon as possible after January 1. *The following grants/scholarships are offered:* Pell, SEOG, academic merit, athletic, the school's own scholarships, the school's own grants, state scholarships, state grants, private scholarships, private grants, ROTC, foreign aid. *Students borrow from the following loan programs:* Stafford, unsubsidized Stafford, Perkins, PLUS, the school's own loan fund, health professions loans, private loans. College Work-Study Program is available. Institutional employment is available.

FROM THE ADMISSIONS OFFICE

"We strive to make the admissions process as personal as the educational experience. Our primary concern is your academic preparation, because course selection and achievement are the best indicators of how you will do at our university."

ADMISSIONS

Admissions Rating	68
% of applicants accepted	83
% of acceptees attending	33

FRESHMAN PROFILE

Average verbal SAT	530
Average math SAT	560
Average ACT	NR
Average TOEFL	475
Graduated top 20% of class	59
Graduated top 40% of class	82
Graduated top 60% of class	92
Average HS GPA or Avg.	3.3

DEADLINES

Early decision	NR
Regular admission	3/1
Regular notification	rolling
Non-fall registration	yes

APPLICANTS ALSO LOOK AT

AND OFTEN PREFER
UC-Berkeley
UC-Davis
Cal State-Fresno

AND SOMETIMES PREFER
U. Southern Cal
Cal. Poly.-San Luis Obispo
UCLA
U. Redlands
U. Arizona

AND RARELY PREFER
Santa Clara

FINANCIAL FACTS

Financial Aid Rating	89
Tuition	$17,550
Room & board	$5,326
Estimated book expense	$710
% frosh receiving aid	56
% undergrads receiving aid	65
% aid is need-based	90
% frosh w/ grant (avg)	85 ($8,900)
% frosh w/ loan (avg)	56 ($3,000)
% UGs w/ job (avg)	23 ($1,200)
Off-campus job outlook	good

PARSONS SCHOOL OF DESIGN

66 FIFTH AVENUE, NEW YORK, NY 10011   ADMISSIONS: 212-229-8910   FAX: 212-229-8975

CAMPUS LIFE

Quality of Life Rating   **78**
Type of school   private
Affiliation   none
Environment   metropolis

STUDENTS

FT undergrad enrollment	1,713
% male/female	31/69
% from out of state	48
% live on campus	35
% spend weekend on campus	75
% transfers	50
% from public high school	NR
% African-American	3
% Asian	15
% Caucasian	35
% Hispanic	8
% international	8
# of countries represented	60

WHAT'S HOT
New York
different students interact
ethnic diversity on campus
leftist politics
town-gown relations

WHAT'S NOT
student publications
student government
political activism
theater
support groups

ACADEMICS

Academic Rating	**75**
Profs Interesting Rating	69
Profs Accessible Rating	60
Calendar	semester
Student/teacher ratio	15:1
Hours of study per day	3.93

MOST POPULAR MAJORS
fashion design
communication design
illustration

STUDENTS SPEAK OUT

Life

Parsons lacks most of the features of typical college life. Writes one student, "There really is no campus where students can meet. The social spots are the cafeteria and the library." And another tells us bluntly that "we don't do advanced high-school-type stuff like football 'n' beer. We go to school for a specific end, to learn, not to screw around." (With classmates this intense, it's no wonder one student writes that "we tend to make friends outside the school.") Not surprisingly, "there is no school spirit in Parsons." If students don't mind this lack of a traditional college setting, it's because (1) they're not traditional college students anyway, and (2) they are located in America's art and design capital, New York City. The city offers lots of galleries for art students, textile manufactures for fashion design students, advertising agencies for communications majors, and architecture of practically every style for architecture students. Writes one student, "New York is a great place to live if you have any money after art supplies. And, if you have any time." Another warns, however, that to survive at Parsons, you should expect to be "crazed. I run to stand still. During the semester there is not time to socialize and hardly time to sleep."

Academics

Parsons students are "very career-oriented. The serious students are the ones that stay." One student exemplifies the Parsons attitude: "Becoming a good and accurate artist is as difficult as becoming a good and accurate neurosurgeon, and the school you attend is vital to how serious and successful you become." Says another, "I highly recommend this school, but only if you have the drive (not just because you 'like' art in high school) and the funds." The prospective artists of Parsons spend almost four hours a day in the studios and libraries. Work is particularly intense during "foundation year," a first-year program during which students are given crash courses in all aspects of design. After foundation year, students focus on their majors, the best known of which is fashion design; other popular majors are illustration, photography, and communications design. Professors are "working professionals" who are "energetic, intelligent, and engaging in class." Or even "cooler than the other side of the pillow." Others consider them a little arrogant: "if you said you were an atheist, they'd think you don't believe in them." Because tuition is steep and the facilities old, students complain that they "expected more—equipment, materials, information—for the money." One offers this advice: "It's a good test for those who have it and those who don't."

Student Body

Over one-fourth of the students are minorities, and respondents describe the student body as "very diverse." One student explains, "It's NYC, capital of the world. There are many different types of people; you have to accept their differences." Students tend to be "hard working, independent, and creative." The school has a considerable gay community; writes one student, "Heterosexual students often complain how hard it is to find someone to go out with. I think it's easier for gay students because of the close-knit gay community."

ADMISSIONS

The admissions committee considers (in descending order of importance): essay, HS record, test scores, recommendations, class rank. *Also considered (in descending order of importance):* special talents, extracurriculars, personality. Either the SAT or ACT is required. An interview is recommended. Admissions process is need-blind. *High school units required/recommended:* 16 total units are required; 4 English recommended, 4 social studies recommended. Well-rounded secondary school program in academic subjects, with as much artwork as program will allow, and above-average grades recommended. Portfolio (minimum of 12 pieces) and home art test required. *Special Requirements:* A portfolio is required for art program applicants. TOEFL is required of all international students. *The admissions office says:* "All decisions are done by committee—the counselors who visit high schools and meet students on Portfolio Days are the same people who conduct the formal interviews and sit on the Admissions Committee."

The Inside Word

Sheer talent determines who gets in at Parsons. Applicants should spend a great deal of energy developing their portfolios and the ability to communicate a personal awareness of the creative process. Applying to fine arts colleges subjects students to intensive scrutiny on a very personal level; in addition to talent, solid self-esteem is a big asset to surviving such a judgmental process.

FINANCIAL AID

Students should submit: FAFSA (due April 1), CSS Profile (due April 1), the school's own financial aid form (due April 1), a copy of parents' most recent income tax filing (due April 1). The Princeton Review suggests that all financial aid forms be submitted as soon as possible after January 1. *The following grants/scholarships are offered:* Pell, SEOG, the school's own scholarships, the school's own grants, state scholarships, state grants, private scholarships, private grants, foreign aid. *Students borrow from the following loan programs:* Stafford, Perkins, PLUS, state loans, private loans. College Work-Study Program is available. Institutional employment is available.

FROM THE ADMISSIONS OFFICE

"In a world crowded with 'multipurpose' and 'comprehensive' colleges and universities, Parsons School of Design has a singular mission: to educate the leadership of tomorrow's art and design communities. Parsons students become polished craftsmen, expert technicians, skilled practitioners. Parsons graduates will lead the design and visual art professions during the early 21st century. The painters, photographers, sculptors, and craftsmen will enrich our cultural and intellectual environment. The designers will give form and shape and color to our everyday lives-to our homes and offices, our clothes and accessories, our books and magazines, movies and television, our logos, symbols and advertising, our furniture, appliances, and utensils."

ADMISSIONS

Admissions Rating	75
% of applicants accepted	51
% of acceptees attending	48

FRESHMAN PROFILE

Average verbal SAT	540
Average math SAT	520
Average ACT	NR
Average TOEFL	NR
Graduated top 20% of class	30
Graduated top 40% of class	56
Graduated top 60% of class	56
Average HS GPA or Avg.	NR

DEADLINES

Early decision	NR
Regular admission	7/1
Regular notification	rolling
Non-fall registration	yes

APPLICANTS ALSO LOOK AT

AND OFTEN PREFER

RISD
Cooper Union

AND SOMETIMES PREFER

NYU

FINANCIAL FACTS

Financial Aid Rating	72
Tuition	$17,100
Room & board	$8,028
Estimated book expense	$1,300
% frosh receiving aid	69
% undergrads receiving aid	71
% aid is need-based	100
% frosh w/ grant (avg)	69 ($6,500)
% frosh w/ loan (avg)	NR
% UGs w/ job (avg)	25 ($2,000)
Off-campus job outlook	good

PENNSYLVANIA STATE UNIV.-UNIVERSITY PARK

University Park, PA 16802   Admissions: 814-865-5471   Fax: 814-863-7590

CAMPUS LIFE

Quality of Life Rating   **76**
Type of school   public
Affiliation   none
Environment   suburban

STUDENTS

FT undergrad enrollment	30,638
% male/female	56/44
% from out of state	19
% live on campus	39
% spend weekend on campus	NR
% transfers	11
% from public high school	NR
% in (# of) fraternities	14 (55)
% in (# of) sororities	17 (25)
% African-American	3
% Asian	5
% Caucasian	88
% Hispanic	2
% international	1
# of countries represented	NR

WHAT'S HOT

student publications
beer
intercollegiate sports
hard liquor
old-fashioned dating

WHAT'S NOT

campus difficult to get around
theater
student government
music associations
computer facilities

ACADEMICS

Academic Rating	**76**
Profs Interesting Rating	66
Profs Accessible Rating	60
Calendar	semester
Student/teacher ratio	19:1
% profs PhD	90
Hours of study per day	3.03

MOST POPULAR MAJORS

elementary education
accounting
marketing

STUDENTS SPEAK OUT

Life

Because of its enormous student population, Penn State University offers social opportunities for just about everyone. Explains one student, "The social life here is extremely exciting. State has a million and one things to do, ranging from football games, women's field hockey, parties, Bible study groups, Unimart, the library, drinking, test reviews, the Nittany mall, and concerts." The Greeks are "huge, probably the largest in the country." Complained one student, "Greek life is overbearing, and those not involved in it see it as childish and annoying, which it is." For Greeks and GDIs alike, drinking is a major part of social life. Warns one student, "There have been a lot of problems with keg parties lately. Often the police are called in." One student reports that "the bars and liquor stores are all very strict about not selling to people under twenty-one, but there are many ways around them." With nationally ranked teams in football, wrestling, and women's basketball, it should come as no surprise that "PSU completely revolves around sports." Students give their hometown of University Park above-average marks; writes one, "The town is small but provides everything needed for the college student."

Academics

In nearly every way, Pennsylvania State University is the quintessential state-sponsored university. The school provides a reasonably priced education to a large number of students, offers studies in a mind-boggling range of areas, and maintains top departments in some fields, particularly those geared toward career training. Among many fine departments, those our respondents like most include administration of justice, engineering, business, agricultural economics and science, education, computer science ("there are a lot of computers on campus: learn to use them"), and meteorology. Overall, students agree that "you can get a great, well-rounded education here; the options are endless." Students also agree that tenacity is a must here, because the school's physical and administrative size make it very easy to get discouraged. One student writes optimistically, "Usually if you can't reach administration—it's pretty much like getting a busy signal, sooner or later, you'll get through." Again, as at most large state-sponsored schools, students can feel neglected by their professors, for whom undergraduates are but one of many responsibilities. Complains one student, "Sometimes you get the feeling that the professors would rather be doing strictly research, especially in science courses that you have to take!" Overall, however, students express satisfaction with the school, primarily because of Penn State's appealing blend of low pressure academics (for all except engineers and premeds) and varied social options.

Student Body

Most Penn State students are from the Quaker State. A proportionally small minority population still translates into more than 3,000 minority students. In general, "The level of apathy here toward political and social issues is very high." But there are definitely students committed to change: "Some sit back and do nothing, others dedicate long hours to improving 'Dear Old State'."

FINANCIAL AID: 814-865-6301

WEB SITE: HTTP://WWW.PSU.EDU

ADMISSIONS

The admissions committee considers (in descending order of importance): HS record, test scores. *Also considered (in descending order of importance):* alumni relationship, extracurriculars, geographical distribution. Either the SAT or ACT is required; SAT is preferred. Admissions process is need-blind. *High school units required/recommended:* 15 total units are required; 4 English required, 3 math required, 3 science required, 2 foreign language recommended. TOEFL is required of all international students.

The Inside Word

Penn State is deluged with applicants, which makes it especially important for candidates to have better than average grades and test scores. Little if anything else is taken into account in the university's formulas; at schools this large it's hard for the admissions process to be more individualized.

FINANCIAL AID

Students should submit: FAFSA, state aid form. The Princeton Review suggests that all financial aid forms be submitted as soon as possible after January 1. *The following grants/scholarships are offered:* Pell, SEOG, academic merit, athletic, the school's own scholarships, the school's own grants, state scholarships, state grants, private scholarships, private grants, ROTC. *Students borrow from the following loan programs:* Stafford, Perkins, PLUS, the school's own loan fund, state loans, private loans. College Work-Study Program is available. Institutional employment is available.

FROM THE ADMISSIONS OFFICE

"Unique among large public universities, Penn State combines the nearly 38,000—student setting of its University Park Campus with nineteen academically and administratively integrated undergraduate locations-small-college settings ranging in size from 600 to more than 3,500 students. Each year, over 60 percent of incoming freshman begin their studies at the residential and commuter campuses of the Commonwealth Education System or at Penn State-Erie, the Behrend College, while nearly 40 percent begin at the University Park Campus. The largest number of freshman begin at the seventeen Commonwealth Campuses. These locations focus on the needs of new students, offering the first two years of most Penn State baccalaureate degrees in settings that stress close interaction with faculty. Depending on the major selected, students complete their degree at either Penn State-Behrend, Penn State-Harrisburg (a junior, senior, and graduate student location), or at the University Park campus. Your application to Penn State qualifies you for review for any of our locations. Your three choices of location are reviewed in the order given. Entrance difficulty is based, in part, on the demand. Due to its popularity, the University Park Campus is the most competitive for admission. Each year Penn State receives approximately 33,000 freshmen applications, of which 22,000 list University Park Campus as their first choice; fall and summer sessions combined, 4,300 begin there."

ADMISSIONS

Admissions Rating	82
% of applicants accepted	51
% of acceptees attending	38

FRESHMAN PROFILE

Average verbal SAT	590
Average math SAT	600
Average ACT	NR
Average TOEFL	550
Graduated top 20% of class	75
Graduated top 40% of class	95
Graduated top 60% of class	99
Average HS GPA or Avg.	3.7

DEADLINES

Early decision	11/30
Regular admission	NR
Regular notification	rolling
Non-fall registration	yes

APPLICANTS ALSO LOOK AT

AND OFTEN PREFER

Carnegie Mellon
Georgia Tech.
Muhlenberg
Virginia
Lehigh

AND SOMETIMES PREFER

Bucknell
Miami U.

AND RARELY PREFER

U. Maryland-College Park

FINANCIAL FACTS

Financial Aid Rating	81
In-state tuition	$5,188
Out-of-state tuition	$11,240
Room & board	$4,300
Estimated book expense	$528
% frosh receiving aid	66
% undergrads receiving aid	80
% aid is need-based	NR
% frosh w/ grant (avg)	57 ($2,906)
% frosh w/ loan (avg)	43 ($4,284)
% UGs w/ job (avg)	29 ($1,258)
Off-campus job outlook	good

UNIVERSITY OF PENNSYLVANIA

PHILADELPHIA, PA 19104

ADMISSIONS: 215-898-7507   FAX: 215-898-5756

CAMPUS LIFE

Quality of Life Rating	86
Type of school	private
Affiliation	none
Environment	metropolis

STUDENTS

FT undergrad enrollment	9,454
% male/female	53/47
% from out of state	79
% live on campus	65
% spend weekend on campus	90
% transfers	11
% from public high school	62
% in (# of) fraternities	30 (29)
% in (# of) sororities	30 (14)
% African-American	7
% Asian	27
% Caucasian	60
% Hispanic	5
% international	8
# of countries represented	100

WHAT'S HOT

registration is a breeze
theater
computer facilities
drugs
student publications

WHAT'S NOT

town-gown relations
students are cliquish
sex
infrequent dating
campus difficult to get around

ACADEMICS

Academic Rating	94
Profs Interesting Rating	80
Profs Accessible Rating	73
Calendar	semester
Student/teacher ratio	10:1
% profs PhD/tenured	99/78
Hours of study per day	3.53

MOST POPULAR MAJORS

finance
history
psychology

% GRADS WHO PURSUE...

Law 8, Med 8, MBA 1, MA 4

STUDENTS SPEAK OUT

Life

University of Pennsylvania students are certain that they surpass their counterparts at other Ivies in at least one area: social life. "This is the social Ivy," writes one student; "It's the least nerdy of the Ivies," offers another. Although it may not exactly be "a four-year fiesta with an excellent education as the party favor," as one student claims, it does seem that while "the students here are serious about their studies, they also know how to relax on weekends and have fun. Penn offers true balance, not often found at colleges." Penn has an active frat scene, plenty of campus clubs and organizations, and a major city waiting beyond its gates. What lies immediately outside those gates, the neighborhood of West Philadelphia, is the hottest topic among our respondents. "I really don't feel too safe walking around at night," writes one. Explains another, "The upper-middle-class student body makes us a major target for crime." Others disagree. "The crime in West Philly gets a lot of bad press," writes one student, "but, if you're smart, you'll get along just fine." Most students agree that campus police do an adequate job patrolling the campus and that the dorms are "safe as fortresses." Safety concerns are greatest among the many upperclassmen who live off campus.

Academics

Penn is in the odd position of being considered a "second-tier Ivy League school": says one student, "Everyone knows we're just a safety for people who don't get into Harvard, Yale, or Princeton." In other words, Penn is probably the best school-with-an-inferiority-complex in the country. Wharton, its business school, is indisputably among the nation's best; and both the School of Nursing and the School of Engineering and Applied Sciences are top-rate (although "the engineering teachers are incomprehensible," according to one frustrated student). The College of Arts and Sciences, the school's most popular division, is easy only in comparison to the other three. Students are quick to remind us that "Penn is not one school but four, and each school is different." Students in all divisions agree, however, that the work is hard, their fellow students are "self-motivated and extremely preprofessional," and their professors are by and large disappointingly impersonal. Writes one, "Research is the primary concern of professors and administrators; as a result, graduate departments are strong, but the ability to teach undergrads is minimal." With over 9,000 undergraduates, Penn is smaller than only Cornell among the Ivies. Students say that because of Penn's size, "the opportunities for networking are amazing, but you need to actively persist; you will not be spoon-fed opportunities!"

Student Body

Penn attracts students of all types from around the world. The school has a 29 percent minority population, but one student explains that while "the number of different groups is many, the interactions between them are few." There is a noticeable Long Island contingent, notes several students, and some note a conformist tendency among the student body. Writes one, "Penn is one of those places where you are allowed to be yourself...provided that you're just like everyone else!"

FINANCIAL AID: 215-898-1988

ADMISSIONS

The admissions committee considers (in descending order of importance): HS record, class rank, test scores, recommendations, essay. *Also considered (in descending order of importance):* alumni relationship, extracurriculars, personality, geographical distribution, special talents. Either the SAT or ACT is required. An interview is recommended. Admissions process is need-blind. *High school units required/recommended:* 17 total units are recommended; 4 English recommended, 3 math recommended, 3 science recommended, 3 foreign language recommended, 2 social studies recommended, 2 history recommended. Rigorous, well-rounded academic preparation expected. SAT II (math level I or II) required of business and engineering program applicants. TOEFL is required of all international students.

The Inside Word

Penn is coming off of a couple of great years in admissions. Although it's the least selective of the Ivies, it is by no means easy to gain admission. The competition in the applicant pool is formidable, and the University typically stays mum about the inner workings of the admissions process. It's hard to put your best foot forward when it is unclear how your efforts will be measured. Applicants can safely assume that they need to be one of the stronger students in their graduating class in order to be successful.

FINANCIAL AID

Students should submit: FAFSA, the school's own financial aid form, a copy of parents' most recent income tax filing. The Princeton Review suggests that all financial aid forms be submitted as soon as possible after January 1. *The following grants/scholarships are offered:* Pell, SEOG, the school's own scholarships, the school's own grants, state scholarships, state grants, private scholarships, private grants, ROTC, foreign aid. *Students borrow from the following loan programs:* Stafford, unsubsidized Stafford, Perkins, PLUS, the school's own loan fund, state loans, federal nursing loans, private loans. Applicants will be notified of awards beginning April 3. College Work-Study Program is available. Institutional employment is available.

FROM THE ADMISSIONS OFFICE

"The University of Pennsylvania combines both tradition and change. From modest beginnings in 1740 as a college for the 'complete education' of youth, the university has become one of the foremost multidisciplinary institutions in the nation, a major repository of humanistic and scientific research. Its undergraduate and graduate schools comprise more than 20,000 students and 1,700 faculty, pursuing scores of disciplines in more than 2,500 courses, including 1,500 at the undergraduate level alone."

ADMISSIONS

Admissions Rating	96
% of applicants accepted	29
% of acceptees attending	47

FRESHMAN PROFILE

Average verbal SAT	670
Average math SAT	670
Average ACT	29
Average TOEFL	610
Graduated top 20% of class	95
Graduated top 40% of class	100
Graduated top 60% of class	100
Average HS GPA or Avg.	NR

DEADLINES

Early decision	NR
Regular admission	1/1
Regular notification	early April
Non-fall registration	no

APPLICANTS ALSO LOOK AT

AND OFTEN PREFER

Yale
Harvard/Radcliffe
Stanford
Princeton
MIT

AND SOMETIMES PREFER

Cornell U.
Duke
Brown
Columbia

AND RARELY PREFER

Johns Hopkins
Georgetown
Northwestern
UC-Berkeley

FINANCIAL FACTS

Financial Aid Rating	72
Tuition	$17,974
Room & board	$7,500
Estimated book expense	$520
% frosh receiving aid	46
% undergrads receiving aid	44
% aid is need-based	100
% frosh w/ grant (avg)	43 ($13,679)
% frosh w/ loan (avg)	46 ($3,832)
% UGs w/ job (avg)	47
Off-campus job outlook	good

PEPPERDINE UNIVERSITY

MALIBU, CA 90263-4392

ADMISSIONS: 310-456-4392   FAX: 310-456-4861

CAMPUS LIFE

Quality of Life Rating — **85**

Type of school	private
Affiliation	Church of Christ
Environment	suburban

STUDENTS

FT undergrad enrollment	2,661
% male/female	42/58
% from out of state	39
% live on campus	75
% spend weekend on campus	50
% transfers	17
% from public high school	NR
% in (# of) fraternities	15 (5)
% in (# of) sororities	17 (6)
% African-American	4
% Asian	9
% Caucasian	70
% Hispanic	9
% international	10
# of countries represented	60

WHAT'S HOT
religion
campus is beautiful
Malibu
intercollegiate sports
campus feels safe

WHAT'S NOT
beer
infrequent dating
library
cigarettes
hard liquor

ACADEMICS

Academic Rating — **82**

Profs Interesting Rating	83
Profs Accessible Rating	83
Calendar	semester
Student/teacher ratio	13:1
% profs PhD/tenured	99/99
Hours of study per day	2.71

MOST POPULAR MAJORS
business administration
telecommunications
sports medicine

% GRADS WHO PURSUE...
Law 9, Med 5

STUDENTS SPEAK OUT

Life
Pepperdine University's campus and location are among the nation's best. One student calls the area "a beautiful resort," and few would disagree. "Peace and serenity" characterize life on campus. Social life is subdued: the school's religious affiliation results in tough regulations; drinking is prohibited and hanging out in your dorm room with members of the opposite sex is restricted. These rules lead one student to comment, "For a university dedicated to higher learning, it would be nice to get out of the Middle Ages." And, although Pepperdine accepts students of all faiths, those who are not members of the Church of Christ may find that "religiously this school is not open-minded. It's affiliated with the Church of Christ and therefore doesn't allow any other religious clubs on campus. Students of different faiths have to leave campus if they want to worship; it's a bit unfair." The small student body also works against an active social scene. Students report that "rumors spread here like VD. Classmates are very judgmental." Sums up one student: "The frat/sorority scene happens—sports, too—but that's about it."

Academics
Two things immediately set Pepperdine apart. One is its beach-front location in idyllic Malibu; the other is its affiliation with the Church of Christ. Those attracted by the school's setting should be aware that the school's stated purpose is "to pursue the very highest academic standards within a context that celebrates and extends the spiritual and ethical ideals of the Christian faith." Pepperdine takes its mission seriously: A weekly assembly is mandatory, the core curriculum contains three religion surveys, and all courses emphasize "Christian values." Students who can fit in at such a school are rewarded with excellent academic programs, particularly in preprofessional areas such as communications, business, and computer science. Classes "are small enough that you can really get to know your professors and classmates," professors and administrators "are very personable and approachable," and school life features "a strong sense of community, which helps encourage the learning environment." Recommends another student, "The year-in-Europe program is a must. It is the most incredible opportunity of a Pepperdine education." Sums up one respondent: "Interesting and definitely not boring, what with riots, floods, earthquakes and all."

Student Body
The student body is clearly divided between devout members of the Church of Christ and those less religious; writes one of the former, "I think most students forget that this is a Christian school. Unfortunately, nothing is done about sexual promiscuity. It is 'in' to be either gay or promiscuous and to hate Christians. Drug and alcohol use are rampant." Pepperdine students are also notoriously "elitist and materialistic." Minority enrollment here is high; Asians, Pacific Islanders, and Hispanics are well represented.

PEPPERDINE UNIVERSITY

FINANCIAL AID: 310-456-4301   WEB SITE: HTTP://WWW.PEPPERDINE.EDU/

ADMISSIONS

The admissions committee considers (in descending order of importance): HS record, test-scores, recommendations, essay, class rank. *Also considered (in descending order of importance):* personality, special talents, alumni relationship, extracurriculars. Either the SAT or ACT is required. An interview is recommended. *High school units required/recommended:* 4 English recommended, 3 math recommended, 2 science recommended, 2 foreign language recommended, 2 social studies recommended. Minimum combined SAT I score of 1100 (composite ACT score of 24) and minimum 3.4 GPA recommended. TOEFL is required of all international students. *The admissions office says:* "Academic improvement, triumph over circumstance, and a student's character go a long way in Pepperdine's admissions process. These subjective factors allow us to find the best and brightest students among those who have not excelled in the areas of cumulative GPA or standardized tests. Relation to alumni or membership in the Church of Christ 'may have a positive effect' for marginal candidates."

The Inside Word

A stunning physical location enables the admissions office to produce beautiful catalogs and viewbooks, which, when combined with the university's reputation for academic quality, help to attract a large applicant pool. In addition to solid grades and test scores, successful applicants typically have well-rounded extracurricular backgrounds. Involvement in school, church, and community is an overused cliché in the world of college admissions, but at Pepperdine it's definitely one of the ingredients in successful applications.

FINANCIAL AID

Students should submit: FAFSA (due February 15), the school's own financial aid form (due February 15), a copy of parents' most recent income tax filing (due February 15). The Princeton Review suggests that all financial aid forms be submitted as soon as possible after January 1. *The following grants/scholarships are offered:* Pell, SEOG, academic merit, athletic, the school's own scholarships, the school's own grants, state scholarships, state grants, private scholarships, private grants, ROTC, foreign aid. *Students borrow from the following loan programs:* Stafford, unsubsidized Stafford, Perkins, PLUS, the school's own loan fund, state loans, private loans. Applicants will be notified of awards beginning April 15. College Work-Study Program is available. Institutional employment is available.

FROM THE ADMISSIONS OFFICE

"As a selective university, Pepperdine seeks students who show promise of academic achievement at the collegiate level. However, we also seek students who are committed to serving the university community, as well as others with whom they come into contact. We look for community service activities, volunteer efforts, and strong leadership qualities, as well as a demonstrated commitment to academic studies and an interest in the liberal arts."

ADMISSIONS

Admissions Rating	**80**
% of applicants accepted	64
% of acceptees attending	29

FRESHMAN PROFILE

Average verbal SAT	580
Average math SAT	570
Average ACT	24
Average TOEFL	550
Graduated top 20% of class	73
Graduated top 40% of class	96
Graduated top 60% of class	NR
Average HS GPA or Avg.	3.5

DEADLINES

Early decision	11/15
Regular admission	2/1
Regular notification	4/1
Non-fall registration	yes

APPLICANTS ALSO LOOK AT

AND OFTEN PREFER

UC-Berkeley
Stanford
UC-Irvine
U. Southern Cal
Loyola Marymount

AND SOMETIMES PREFER

UC-Santa Cruz
UC-San Diego
UC-Santa Barbara
U. Colorado-Boulder
Claremont McKenna

AND RARELY PREFER

Notre Dame
Vanderbilt
Boston Coll.
BYU

FINANCIAL FACTS

Financial Aid Rating	**85**
Tuition	$20,140
Room & board	$6,860
Estimated book expense	$500
% frosh receiving aid	70
% undergrads receiving aid	76
% aid is need-based	NR
% frosh w/ grant (avg)	NR ($11,320)
% frosh w/ loan (avg)	70 ($3,625)
% UGs w/ job (avg)	58 ($1,500)
Off-campus job outlook	excellent

UNIVERSITY OF PITTSBURGH

4200 FIFTH AVENUE, PITTSBURGH, PA 15260

ADMISSIONS: 412-624-7488   FAX: 412-648-8815

CAMPUS LIFE

Quality of Life Rating	72
Type of school	public
Affiliation	none
Environment	metropolis

STUDENTS

FT undergrad enrollment	12,933
% male/female	48/52
% from out of state	12
% live on campus	39
% spend weekend on campus	NR
% transfers	28
% from public high school	NR
% in (# of) fraternities	11 (21)
% in (# of) sororities	8 (15)
% African-American	9
% Asian	3
% Caucasian	85
% Hispanic	1
% international	1
# of countries represented	60

WHAT'S HOT
cigarettes
drugs
hard liquor
intercollegiate sports
old-fashioned dating

WHAT'S NOT
campus difficult to get around
unattractive campus
political activism
inefficient administration
registration is a pain

ACACEMICS

Academic Rating	77
Profs Interesting Rating	63
Profs Accessible Rating	64
Calendar	semester
Student/teacher ratio	15:1
% profs PhD/tenured	90/87
Hours of study per day	3.04

MOST POPULAR MAJORS
engineering
psychology
business

% GRADS WHO PURSUE...
Law 2, Med 3, MBA 6, MA 6

STUDENTS SPEAK OUT

Life

University of Pittsburgh students love their sports teams and are particularly crazy about football and basketball. The Greek system is alive and well here, but because the university is located in a major city, the Greeks don't dominate the social scene as they do at many small-town institutions. Explains one, "Social life at Pitt is very diverse because of its urban environment. Anything that you want to do is within walking distance." For fun, Pitt students go to sporting events, attend cultural and theatrical events in Pittsburgh, participate in one of the university's 250 student clubs and organizations, and, oh yes, they drink. "Most people do the bar scene. So that just about tops everything." Many students live off campus, because of Pittsburgh's many options.

Academics

Pitt is a large, research-oriented public university with especially strong programs in health sciences and engineering. Comments one student, "Pitt has wonderful opportunities for any student interested in the health professions. The University of Pittsburgh Medical Center consists of four hospitals that all welcome students as volunteers." Pitt has other assets: affordability, location, and a broad range of well-maintained programs, particularly in preprofessional fields. However, as is often the case at research centers, many of the students here see their professors as average teachers at best. Complains one English major, "You need a teaching certificate to teach high school, WHY NOT COLLEGE?" Some students say they are annoyed by the lack of understandable English among teaching assistants. However, top students seeking individual attention can enter an honors program (the University Honors College) in which classes are smaller and more focused. Students report that dealing with administrative stuff is particularly unpleasant. Writes one sophomore, "Getting to voice complaints to the administration is as painless as a colonoscopy." The introductory STEP program receives rave reviews. One freshman comments that "I love school! I've met many nice people and teachers. I recommend it for anyone."

Student Body

The Pitt student body is largely from western Pennsylvania and mainly white and middle class. One student comments that "Most students get along with each other, with the exception of the football team." A small but not negligible percentage (9 percent) of the students are African-American, though interaction between whites and blacks is limited, according to some students. Other students say there is a feeling of unity among the student body, and describe their experience as "friendly and warm." Students are moderate to conservative politically, but mostly they don't care much: one student dubs the school "Apathy State U." Many students work their ways through Pitt, and it is not uncommon for students to take up to six years to get their degrees.

FINANCIAL AID: 412-624-PITT   WEB SITE: HTTP://WWW.PITT.EDU/

ADMISSIONS

The admissions committee considers (in descending order of importance): HS record, class rank, test scores, recommendations, essay. *Also considered (in descending order of importance):* alumni relationship, extracurriculars, geographical distribution, personality, special talents. Either the SAT or ACT is required. An interview is recommended. Admissions process is need-blind. *High school units required/recommended:* 15 total units are required; 4 English required, 3 math required, 3 science required, 3 foreign language recommended, 1 social studies required. *Special Requirements:* An audition is required for music program applicants. TOEFL is required of all international students. *The admissions office says:* "In addition to basic curriculum, different schools have specific curricular requirements: Engineering—chemistry, physics, math through trigonometry; Nursing-2 lab sciences, one chemistry; Pharmacy—chemistry, biology, math through trig; School of Health and Rehabilitation Sciences—biology, chemistry; College of Business Administration—4 units of math (through trig)."

The Inside Word

Applicants to Pitt, as at most large public universities, are admitted primarily on the strength of basic qualifiers like grades and test scores. If you are serious about Pitt, rolling admissions allows you to get a decision earlier than most colleges notify their applicants.

FINANCIAL AID

Students should submit: FAFSA, the school's own financial aid form, state aid form, a copy of parents' most recent income tax filing. The Princeton Review suggests that all financial aid forms be submitted as soon as possible after January 1. *The following grants/scholarships are offered:* Pell, SEOG, academic merit, athletic, the school's own scholarships, the school's own grants, state grants, private scholarships, private grants, ROTC. *Students borrow from the following loan programs:* Stafford, unsubsidized Stafford, Perkins, PLUS, the school's own loan fund, state loans, federal nursing loans, health professions loans, private loans. College Work-Study Program is available. Institutional employment is available.

FROM THE ADMISSIONS OFFICE

"The University of Pittsburgh is ranked one of the top fifty-six research institutions in the United States by the Association of American Universities. Over 400 degree granting programs are available from among ten undergraduate and fourteen graduate school and four regional campuses, allowing students a wide latitude of choices, both academically and in setting, style, size, and pace of campus life. Schools of Engineering, Nursing and Pharmacy offer strong professional programs; the College of Arts and Sciences' highest ranked departments, nationally, include philosophy, history, chemistry, microbiology, physics, psychology, and Spanish. The University Center for International Studies is ranked one of the exemplary international programs in the country by the Council on Learning; and a Semester at Sea Program takes students to different ports of call around the world on an ocean liner."

ADMISSIONS

Admissions Rating	79
% of applicants accepted	66
% of acceptees attending	39

FRESHMAN PROFILE

Average verbal SAT	570
Average math SAT	560
Average ACT	NR
Average TOEFL	500
Graduated top 20% of class	47
Graduated top 40% of class	83
Graduated top 60% of class	98
Average HS GPA or Avg.	NR

DEADLINES

Early decision	NR
Regular admission	rolling
Regular notification	rolling
Non-fall registration	yes

APPLICANTS ALSO LOOK AT

AND OFTEN PREFER

Penn State U.
Duquesne U.
Temple U.
Indiana U. (PA)
Slippery Rock U.

AND SOMETIMES PREFER

U. Delaware
Carnegie Mellon
Dickinson
Drexel

AND RARELY PREFER

Villanova

FINANCIAL FACTS

Financial Aid Rating	74
In-state tuition	$5,184
Out-of-state tuition	$11,270
Room & board	$4,834
Estimated book expense	$400
% frosh receiving aid	70
% undergrads receiving aid	60
% aid is need-based	90
% frosh w/ grant (avg)	74 ($2,933)
% frosh w/ loan (avg)	59 ($3,419)
% UGs w/ job (avg)	26 ($1,701)
Off-campus job outlook	good

PITZER COLLEGE

1050 NORTH MILLS AVENUE, CLAREMONT, CA 91711   ADMISSIONS: 909-621-8129   FAX: 909-621-8521

CAMPUS LIFE

Quality of Life Rating   83
Type of school   private
Affiliation   none
Environment   suburban

STUDENTS
FT undergrad enrollment   729
% male/female   48/52
% from out of state   46
% live on campus   92
% spend weekend on campus   70
% transfers   6
% from public high school   45
% African-American   7
% Asian   17
% Caucasian   59
% Hispanic   16
% international   8
# of countries represented   28

WHAT'S HOT
leftist politics
drugs
lab facilities
library
registration is a breeze

WHAT'S NOT
religion
intramural sports
unattractive campus
intercollegiate sports
campus food

ACADEMICS

Academic Rating   86
Profs Interesting Rating   95
Profs Accessible Rating   94
Calendar   semester
Student/teacher ratio   10:1
% profs PhD   99
Hours of study per day   3.05

MOST POPULAR MAJORS
anthropology
political studies
sociology

% GRADS WHO PURSUE...
Law 16, Med 6, MA 49

STUDENTS SPEAK OUT

Life

Pitzer College students are aptly known as "modern-day hippies." "People think about politics, how to make life better, and what to do in the future. For fun we go to parties or movies or go to the clubs or beaches in L.A." But be warned, "L.A. might as well be 20 million miles away if you don't have a car. This leads to an abundance of partying and drug use." If you don't like the drug/party scene there's still plenty to do, "like exploring the underground storm tunnels, playing Ghosts in the Graveyard at midnight, or dancing at an impromptu student ball," and "there are a lot of art shows and performances," plus "jazz at the Grove House [and] good discussions at the women's center," as well as gripe sessions: "We talk about what's wrong with Pitzer but not how to change it." Pitzer's big annual event is a spring fair called Kohoutek, after the disappointing comet; the festival "is pretty groovy—bands, liquor, crafts, ethnic foods, fun stuff."

Academics

Note: The Claremont Colleges are five small undergraduate schools (Claremont McKenna, Harvey Mudd, Pitzer, Pomona, and Scripps) and one graduate school sharing a central location and facilities. Each school serves a distinct purpose and maintains its own faculty and campus. Cross-registration among colleges is encouraged. Pitzer College, founded in 1963 as a women's school, is now a coed college whose curriculum "emphasizes the social and behavioral sciences, particularly psychology, sociology, anthropology, and political science." Pitzer is by far the most liberal of the Claremont Colleges, and its students and professors are marked by their openness to progressive ideas and educational approaches: "Pitzer is a place of experimentation. In fact, one is encouraged to take the road less traveled." Besides the above-mentioned majors, history, economics, English, and the arts are popular, and "a growing interest in independent studies exists." Students give their professors excellent grades, explaining, "When your professor is your friend, it makes a school a place of learning." To other Claremont students, Pitzer is "the easy school." And some students here happily concur: "Students at Pitzer are not exactly gunning for Ivy League law schools. But the relaxed atmosphere can be...well, relaxing."

Student Body

Pitzer students explain that "most of them are very different (i.e., into alternative lifestyles)," and "a lot of them have drug and alcohol problems," but some feel that a bit of hypocrisy pervades, since one must be sufficiently "alternative" to fit in: "I think it would be hard to be openly conservative here, for example." The school's approach and curriculum naturally serve as a magnet for students inclined towards p.c. attitudes—explains one, "The students are very diverse but most hold in common the social responsibility ideals of Pitzer, and the commitment to 'make the world a better place.'"

FINANCIAL AID: 909-621-8208

ADMISSIONS

The admissions committee considers (in descending order of importance): HS record, test scores, recommendations, essay, class rank. *Also considered (in descending order of importance):* extracurriculars, geographical distribution, personality, alumni relationship, special talents. Either the SAT or ACT is required. An interview is recommended. *High school units required/recommended:* 16 total units are required; 4 English required, 2 math required, 2 science required, 2 foreign language required, 3 social studies required. Full program of challenging work is more important than specific number of units. Minimum SAT I scores of 500 in both verbal and math, rank in top quarter of secondary school class, and minimum 3.0 GPA recommended. TOEFL is required of all international students. *The admissions office says:* "We are less [standardized] test oriented than most selective colleges. [We look] for students that are socially and politically aware and concerned. We attract more liberal-oriented students, both socially and politically. We also tend to get very creative and unconventional students as well as students that are very traditional but choose to attend a more liberal school."

The Inside Word

This is a place where applicants can feel confident in letting their thoughts flow freely on admissions essays. Not only does the committee read them (a circumstance more rare in college admissions than one is led to believe), but they've set up the process to emphasize them! Thus, what you have to say for yourself will go much farther than numbers in determining your suitability for Pitzer. Paying greater attention to essays also helps Pitzer create a dynamic and engaging freshman class each year.

FINANCIAL AID

Students should submit: FAFSA (due February 1), CSS Profile (due February 1), state aid form. The Princeton Review suggests that all financial aid forms be submitted as soon as possible after January 1. *The following grants/scholarships are offered:* Pell, the school's own scholarships, the school's own grants, state scholarships, state grants, private scholarships, private grants. *Students borrow from the following loan programs:* Stafford, Perkins, PLUS, the school's own loan fund, private loans. Applicants will be notified of awards beginning April 1. College Work-Study Program is available. Institutional employment is available.

FROM THE ADMISSIONS OFFICE

"Pitzer is about opportunities. It's about possibilities. The students who come here are looking for something different from the usual 'take two courses from column A, two courses from column B, and two courses from column C.' That kind of arbitrary selection doesn't make a satisfying education at Pitzer. So we look for students who want to have an impact on their own education, who want the chief responsibility-with help from their faculty advisers-in designing their own futures."

ADMISSIONS

Admissions Rating	82
% of applicants accepted	53
% of acceptees attending	30

FRESHMAN PROFILE

Average verbal SAT	630
Average math SAT	590
Average ACT	26
Average TOEFL	550
Graduated top 20% of class	61
Graduated top 40% of class	84
Graduated top 60% of class	96
Average HS GPA or Avg.	3.4

DEADLINES

Early decision	12/1
Regular admission	2/1
Regular notification	4/1
Non-fall registration	yes

APPLICANTS ALSO LOOK AT

AND OFTEN PREFER

UC-Berkeley
Stanford
Pomona
Oberlin
Reed

AND SOMETIMES PREFER

Occidental
UCLA
Colorado Coll.
Scripps
UC-Santa Cruz

AND RARELY PREFER

UC-Davis
UC-San Diego
Middlebury Coll.
Grinnell

FINANCIAL FACTS

Financial Aid Rating	93
Tuition	$21,086
Room & board	$6,454
Estimated book expense	$650
% frosh receiving aid	50
% undergrads receiving aid	48
% aid is need-based	100
% frosh w/ grant (avg)	38 ($15,550)
% frosh w/ loan (avg)	50 ($3,330)
% UGs w/ job (avg)	65 ($2,000)
Off-campus job outlook	good

POMONA COLLEGE

333 NORTH COLLEGE WAY, CLAREMONT, CA 91711-6312 · ADMISSIONS: 909-621-8134 · FAX: 909 621-8403

STUDENTS SPEAK OUT

Life

Many students tell us that Pomona College's biggest social problem is that students depend too heavily on the campus for their social lives. One student notes, "The main problem with Pomona is that hardly anyone ever goes out, but it's been getting better." Another offers this advice: "You need to bring a car if you plan on having any fun" because there is plenty to do in the nearby metropolis, but "the L.A. public transportation system is remarkably inefficient." However, many find campus life cozy and fun: "I've never had so much fun in a hallway before! We eat, sleep, talk, watch movies—play sports in our halls," which are very friendly thanks to the Sponsor groups, "15 - 20 freshmen and 2 sophomores who live next to each other" and participate in planned activities. More than one person says "Sponsor groups are one of the best things about Pomona." Many tend to overcommit themselves with extracurricular activities like sports, theatre, orchestra, choir, and volunteer work. For the most part, "It's almost your typical 'work hard, play hard' place—but a lot of people don't seem to go out much."

Academics

Note: the Claremont Colleges are five small undergraduate schools (Claremont McKenna, Harvey Mudd, Pitzer, Pomona, and Scripps) and one graduate school sharing a central location and facilities. Each school serves a distinct purpose and maintains its own faculty and campus. Cross-registration among colleges is encouraged. Pomona College, the most prestigious school in the Claremont cluster, offers a "traditional liberal arts program." Area college counselors report that the school is "academically superior across the board," and students enrolled in most departments express satisfaction with their academic programs and say the sciences are particularly demanding. Students must fulfill general education requirements that can take all of freshman and sophomore years to complete. Then, students concentrate in one field, finishing up with a comprehensive exam or senior project that must be completed successfully to graduate. Most students relish the challenges they find here: "Club Med setting aside, students can find as much academic challenge as they wish." Student/teacher interaction is great: "Pomona encourages freethinking, and provides an excellent atmosphere in which to do so. My professors are extremely friendly and open to anything from an intellectual discussion to a casual chat." Most important, "students work together."

Student Body

Writes one Pomona student, "If there is a Pomona stereotype, it is that we are the snobby nerds of the five colleges." Another adds, "Most of them are smart and pretty friendly. Too many nerdfaces, though, and smug intellectuals. But overall good." One student offers his (and others') definition: "Pomona College: the most politically correct college with the least ability to understand the reasons behind it." And although the campus is mostly left-leaning, "the students really are incredibly inactive politically. We have L.A. just an hour away but there is no political or activist movement on campus."

FINANCIAL AID: 909-621-8205   E-MAIL: POMONA-ADM@POMADM.POMONA.EDU   WEB SITE: HTTP://WWW.POMONA.EDU.

ADMISSIONS

The admissions committee considers (in descending order of importance): HS record, test scores, essay, recommendations, class rank. *Also considered (in descending order of importance):* extracurriculars, personality, alumni relationship, geographical distribution, special talents. Either the SAT or ACT is required. An interview is recommended. Admissions process is need-blind. *High school units required/recommended:* 4 English recommended, 3 math recommended, 2 science recommended, 3 foreign language recommended, 2 social studies recommended. College-preparatory program strongly recommended. TOEFL is required of all international students.

The Inside Word

Even though it is tough to get admitted to Pomona, students will find the admissions staff to be accessible and engaging. An applicant pool full of such well-qualified students as those who typically apply, in combination with the college's small size, necessitates that candidates undergo as personal an admissions evaluation as possible. This is how solid matches are made, and how Pomona does a commendable job of keeping an edge on the competition.

FINANCIAL AID

Students should submit: state aid form (due March 1), Divorced Parents form (due February 11), a copy of parents' most recent income tax filing. The Princeton Review suggests that all financial aid forms be submitted as soon as possible after January 1. *The following grants/scholarships are offered:* Pell, SEOG, the school's own scholarships, the school's own grants, state scholarships, state grants, private scholarships, private grants, foreign aid. *Students borrow from the following loan programs:* Stafford, Perkins, PLUS, the school's own loan fund, private loans. Applicants will be notified of awards beginning in mid-April. College Work-Study Program is available. Institutional employment is available.

FROM THE ADMISSIONS OFFICE

"Perhaps the most important thing to know about Pomona College is that we are what we say we are. There is enormous integrity between the statements of mission and philosophy governing the College and the reality that students, faculty, and administrators experience. The balance in the curriculum is unusual. Sciences, social sciences, humanities, and the arts receive equal attention, support, and emphasis. Most importantly, the commitment to undergraduate education is absolute. Teaching awards remain the highest honor the trustees can bestow upon faculty. The typical method of instruction is the seminar and the average class size of fourteen offers students the opportunity to become full partners in the learning process. Our location in the Los Angeles basin and in Claremont, with five other colleges, provides a remarkable community."

ADMISSIONS

Admissions Rating	96
% of applicants accepted	32
% of acceptees attending	36

FRESHMAN PROFILE

Average verbal SAT	700
Average math SAT	700
Average ACT	31
Average TOEFL	600
Graduated top 20% of class	95
Graduated top 40% of class	100
Graduated top 60% of class	NR
Average HS GPA or Avg.	NR

DEADLINES

Early decision	11/15
Regular admission	1/1
Regular notification	4/10
Non-fall registration	no

APPLICANTS ALSO LOOK AT

AND OFTEN PREFER

Harvard/Radcliffe
UC-Berkeley
Stanford
Yale
Princeton

AND SOMETIMES PREFER

UCLA
Dartmouth
Williams
Wesleyan U.
Claremont McKenna

AND RARELY PREFER

UC-Davis
Pitzer

FINANCIAL FACTS

Financial Aid Rating	94
Tuition	$19,530
Room & board	$7,860
Estimated book expense	$850
% frosh receiving aid	50
% undergrads receiving aid	55
% aid is need-based	100
% frosh w/ grant (avg)	51 ($14,800)
% frosh w/ loan (avg)	50 ($3,700)
% UGs w/ job (avg)	65 ($1,800)
Off-campus job outlook	good

PRINCETON UNIVERSITY

PRINCETON, NJ 08544

ADMISSIONS: 609-258-3060   FAX: 609-258-6743

CAMPUS LIFE

Quality of Life Rating	**84**
Type of school	private
Affiliation	none
Environment	town

STUDENTS

FT undergrad enrollment	4,609
% male/female	54/46
% from out of state	87
% live on campus	96
% spend weekend on campus	NR
% transfers	NR
% from public high school	59
% African-American	7
% Asian	11
% Caucasian	70
% Hispanic	6
% international	5
# of countries represented	69

WHAT'S HOT
library
school runs like butter
campus feels safe
lab facilities
beer

WHAT'S NOT
infrequent dating
cigarettes
drugs
off-campus food
sex

ACADEMICS

Academic Rating	**98**
Profs Interesting Rating	87
Profs Accessible Rating	81
Calendar	semester
Student/teacher ratio	5:1
% profs PhD/tenured	83/84
Hours of study per day	3.34

MOST POPULAR MAJORS
history
economics
politics

% GRADS WHO PURSUE...
Law 5, Med 9, MA 11

STUDENTS SPEAK OUT

Life

Princeton University is located in Princeton, New Jersey, and, as one student explains, "The town and the university are like a divorced couple no longer on speaking terms. They ignore each other and the students suffer. The town offers no student-oriented cafés or amusements within a student's budget. Off-campus housing is exorbitant." Accordingly, social life centers on the beautiful Gothic campus. Underclassmen live in groups of dorms called "colleges," each of which provides meals and sponsors a roster of extracurricular activities. Fraternities exist but are not officially sanctioned and have limited memberships. However, "eating clubs" (which are a lot like fraternities: they provide meals, host parties, and place students in a "subcommunity") are crucial. During sophomore year, most students join one of the thirteen eating clubs, eight of which choose members by lottery; the other five hand-pick members (in a process called "bicker"). Students explain that there is a "big gulf between residential college underclassmen and upperclassmen in eating clubs." Parties here tend to be "orgies of beer"; explained one student, "If you're not into the drinking scene, your social life could be a bit mundane." Students also actively support their sports teams. Finally: "The most bizarre phenomenon on campus is the popularity of the a cappella singing groups. We have eight of them, seven more than campuses ten times our size."

Academics

In the words of one college counselor, "Princeton University offers the best undergraduate education in the country." Other prestigious institutions feature famous medical, law, and/or business schools, but Princeton has none of these: Here, the focus is on the college student. Academic departments are all excellent: particularly noteworthy are engineering ("It has a friendly 'we're in this together' atmosphere—no 'cutthroat, kill-the-curve-breaker' competition like at MIT," writes one engineer), political science, history, religion, and English. Students enjoy a great deal of personal attention thanks to "precepts," once-a-week-small - group discussion meetings with each class's professor or TA. Core distribution requirements guarantee that all students are schooled in the classic academic disciplines (math, natural and social sciences, humanities). A series of independent projects, culminating in a yearlong senior thesis, give upperclassmen an unusual amount of autonomy in structuring their workloads. The amount of work here is "difficult but not overbearing"; in fact, Princeton students study no more than the average student profiled in this book.

Student Body

Almost a quarter of Princeton's students are minorities. Writes one Hispanic student, "If you are a minority, you must come here." Several students express surprise that their classmates were not nerds ("The guy next door blasting Guns N' Roses is probably brilliant; cool people can be found here"), but others complain that their classmates were "anti-intellectual: it's not considered cool to talk about your work or seem passionately committed to it." Says another student: "It's a place to grow, but only a place for soul-searching if you step outside the mainstream."

FINANCIAL AID: 609-258-3330

ADMISSIONS

The admissions committee considers (in descending order of importance): class rank, essay, HS record, recommendations, test scores. *Also considered (in descending order of importance):* extracurriculars, personality, special talents, alumni relationship. Either the SAT or ACT is required; SAT is preferred. An interview is recommended. *High school units required/recommended:* 20 total units are recommended; 4 English recommended, 4 math recommended, 2 science recommended, 4 foreign language recommended, 2 history recommended. Additional units should be chosen from social studies, science, foreign language, art, and music. *Special Requirements:* TOEFL is required of all international students. SAT II (math level I or II, physics or chemistry, and one of applicant's choice) required of engineering program applicants.

The Inside Word

Princeton is much more open about the admissions process than the rest of their Ivy compatriots. The admissions staff evaluates candidates' credentials using a 1 to 5 rating scale, common among highly selective colleges. In the initial screening of applicants, admissions staff members assigned to particular regions of the country eliminate weaker students before the admissions committee makes its evaluation. Princeton's recommendation to interview and submit three SAT II Subject Test scores should be considered a requirement, given the ultracompetitive nature of the applicant pool.

FINANCIAL AID

Students should submit: FAFSA (due April 15), CSS Profile (due February 1), the school's own financial aid form (due February 1), Divorced Parents form (due February 1), a copy of parents' most recent income tax filing (due June 1). The Princeton Review suggests that all financial aid forms be submitted as soon as possible after January 1. *The following grants/scholarships are offered:* Pell, SEOG, the school's own scholarships, the school's own grants, state scholarships, state grants, private scholarships, private grants, ROTC, foreign aid. *Students borrow from the following loan programs:* Stafford, unsubsidized Stafford, Perkins, PLUS, the school's own loan fund. Applicants will be notified of awards beginning early April. College Work-Study Program is available. Institutional employment is available.

FROM THE ADMISSIONS OFFICE

"Methods of instruction [at Princeton] vary widely, but common to all areas...is a strong emphasis on individual responsibility and the free interchange of ideas. This is displayed most notably in the wide use of preceptorials and seminars, in the provision of independent study for all upperclass students and qualified underclass students, and in the availability of a series of special programs to meet a range of individual interests. The undergraduate college encourages the student to be an independent seeker of information...and to assume responsibility for gaining both knowledge and judgment that will strengthen later contributions to society."

ADMISSIONS

Admissions Rating	99
% of applicants accepted	14
% of acceptees attending	59

FRESHMAN PROFILE

Average verbal SAT	690
Average math SAT	680
Average ACT	NR
Average TOEFL	NR
Graduated top 20% of class	96
Graduated top 40% of class	100
Graduated top 60% of class	100
Average HS GPA or Avg.	NR

DEADLINES

Early decision	NR
Regular admission	1/2
Regular notification	early April
Non-fall registration	no

APPLICANTS ALSO LOOK AT

AND SOMETIMES PREFER

Harvard/Radcliffe
Yale
UC-Berkeley
Columbia

AND RARELY PREFER

Johns Hopkins
Wesleyan U.
U. Chicago
Pennsylvania
Northwestern U.

FINANCIAL FACTS

Financial Aid Rating	80
Tuition	$20,960
Room & board	$5,910
Estimated book expense	$675
% frosh receiving aid	48
% undergrads receiving aid	44
% aid is need-based	100
% frosh w/ grant (avg)	46 ($13,900)
% frosh w/ loan (avg)	44 ($3,000)
% UGs w/ job (avg)	70 ($1,200)
Off-campus job outlook	good

PROVIDENCE COLLEGE

RIVER AVENUE AND EATON STREET, PROVIDENCE, RI 02918   ADMISSIONS: 401-865-2535   FAX: 401-865-2826

CAMPUS LIFE

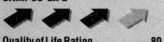

Quality of Life Rating   **80**
Type of school	private
Affiliation	Roman Catholic Church
	(Dominican Fathers)
Environment	suburban

STUDENTS
FT undergrad enrollment	3,471
% male/female	44/56
% from out of state	85
% live on campus	74
% spend weekend on campus	88
% transfers	10
% from public high school	62
% African-American	4
% Asian	2
% Caucasian	91
% Hispanic	2
% international	NR
# of countries represented	14

WHAT'S HOT
religion
intramural sports
intercollegiate sports
hard liquor
beer

WHAT'S NOT
students are cliquish
lack of diversity on campus
town-gown relations
music associations
Greeks

ACADEMICS

Academic Rating   **77**
Profs Interesting Rating	71
Profs Accessible Rating	76
Calendar	semester
Student/teacher ratio	13:1
% profs PhD/tenured	82/72
Hours of study per day	2.69

MOST POPULAR MAJORS
business
English
history

% GRADS WHO PURSUE...
Law 6, Med 2, MBA 2, MA 12

STUDENTS SPEAK OUT

Life

Providence College students keep a full schedule of parties and extracurriculars. As one students puts it: "At PC I am able to study, interact with others, and play sports." Another agrees, "If you are looking for a school that offers a great social environment, excellent sports facilities, and a workload that is definitely manageable, PC is the school for you." Run by the Dominican Order of Preachers, PC is attended mainly by Catholics. The college has both single-sex and coed dorms, with visitation rules for single-sex dorms. Not surprisingly, many upperclassmen move off campus. Neither the presence of Dominicans nor the lack of Greeks hamper the party scene. Students report that their classmates are "a bunch of heavy drinkers." One nondrinker says: "Most people go to bars or parties on weekends. They think about sensual pleasure." PC's Division I sports teams are very popular. The city of Providence itself, however, received low marks (excluding the bars): "The neighborhood is awful. It's dirty and dangerous."

Academics

While the influence of Catholicism on PC campus life is undeniable, most students' interests lie in more mundane matters: namely, their careers. Many of PC's students are business and management majors. Marketing, education, and accounting are among the other popular profession-oriented paths. The social sciences (particularly history and political science) and English are also popular. All students must complete a two-year interdisciplinary Western Civilization survey as well as an array of distribution requirements. With fewer than 4,000 undergraduates, PC is "rather small, so it sometimes seems like high school, but the closeness of the students and the faculty more than make up for it. You couldn't be 'just a number' if you tried." Academically, most students describe the school as "low pressure." Explains one: "The most important thing that I've learned so far is that if you pick the right prof, you don't have to learn. Grade inflation goes hand in hand with this college. Amen." Students generally approve of the faculty. Several students offer appraisals similar to this student's: "They teach very well, they are always there for you." Many student complaints concern the administration, whom some describe as "too conservative, too Catholic, and [in] need [of] a huge shot of adrenaline."

Student Body

The big majority of PC students fit the description "white, middle class, and Catholic. There is virtually no diversity." Writes one student, "We're a friendly group but too homogeneous. The administration is so concerned with its 'Catholic image' that it overlooks the need for student diversity." Many indicate that they get along with their classmates, but one explains just how: "The majority of students on this campus travel in packs and seldom venture outside of them. It is their loss." Another warns, "School is very cliquey. Any problems with your friends...and you're screwed for 4 years."

FINANCIAL AID: 401-865-2286

ADMISSIONS

The admissions committee considers (in descending order of importance): HS record, test scores, class rank, essay, recommendations. *Also considered (in descending order of importance):* extracurriculars, personality, special talents, alumni relationship, geographical distribution. Either the SAT or ACT is required. An interview is recommended. Admissions process is need-blind. *High school units required/recommended:* 18 total units are required; 4 English required, 2 math required, 3 math recommended, 2 science required, 3 science recommended, 3 foreign language required, 4 foreign language recommended, 2 social studies required, 1 history required. Minimum SAT I scores of 510 verbal and 550 math (composite ACT score of 25), rank in top third of secondary school class, and minimum 3.0 GPA recommended. *Special Requirements:* TOEFL is required of all international students. 4 units each of math and science recommended of biology, chemistry, and pre-engineering program applicants.

The Inside Word

Providence's reputation for quality is solidly in place among above-average graduates of northeastern parochial schools, who account for 22 percent of the applicant pool. The strength of these candidates and the high percentage of admits who enroll allows the college to be choosy about who gets in. Successful candidates usually project a well-rounded, conservative image.

FINANCIAL AID

Students should submit: FAFSA (due February 1), CSS Profile (due February 1), a copy of parents' most recent income tax filing (due May 15). The Princeton Review suggests that all financial aid forms be submitted as soon as possible after January 1. *The following grants/scholarships are offered:* Pell, SEOG, academic merit, athletic, the school's own scholarships, the school's own grants, state scholarships, private scholarships, private grants, ROTC. *Students borrow from the following loan programs:* Perkins, PLUS, supplemental loans. Applicants will be notified of awards beginning April 1. College Work-Study Program is available. Institutional employment is available.

FROM THE ADMISSIONS OFFICE

"Infused with the history, tradition, and learning of a 700-year-old Catholic teaching order, the Dominican Friars, Providence College offers a value-affirming environment where students are enriched through spiritual, social, physical and cultural growth as well as through intellectual development. Providence College offers over thirty-six programs of study leading to baccalaureate degrees in business, education, the sciences, arts, and humanities. Our faculty is noted for a strong commitment to teaching. A close student/faculty relationship allows for in-depth classwork, independent research projects and detailed career exploration. While noted for the physical facilities and academic opportunities associated with larger universities, Providence also fosters personal growth through a small, spirited, family-like atmosphere that encourages involvement in student activities and athletics."

ADMISSIONS

Admissions Rating	74
% of applicants accepted	75
% of acceptees attending	33

FRESHMAN PROFILE

Average verbal SAT	490
Average math SAT	550
Average ACT	25
Average TOEFL	550
Graduated top 20% of class	52
Graduated top 40% of class	85
Graduated top 60% of class	97
Average HS GPA or Avg.	NR

DEADLINES

Early decision	11/15
Regular admission	1/15
Regular notification	4/1
Non-fall registration	yes

APPLICANTS ALSO LOOK AT

AND OFTEN PREFER

Boston Coll.
Holy Cross
Fairfield
Villanova
Stonehill

AND SOMETIMES PREFER

Villanova
U. Vermont
U. New Hampshire
U. Conn
U. Mass.-Amherst

AND RARELY PREFER

U. Rhode Island
Bentley
Boston U.
Fordham

FINANCIAL FACTS

Financial Aid Rating	78
Tuition	$15,800
Room & board	$6,670
Estimated book expense	$650
% frosh receiving aid	80
% undergrads receiving aid	71
% aid is need-based	90
% frosh w/ grant (avg)	80 ($8,000)
% frosh w/ loan (avg)	62 ($3,600)
% UGs w/ job (avg)	35 ($1,600)
Off-campus job outlook	good

UNIVERSITY OF PUGET SOUND

1500 NORTH WARNER STREET, TACOMA, WA 98416   ADMISSIONS: 206-756-3211   FAX: 206-756-3500

CAMPUS LIFE

Quality of Life Rating   86
Type of school   private
Affiliation   none
Environment   city

STUDENTS
FT undergrad enrollment	2,611
% male/female	42/58
% from out of state	69
% live on campus	65
% spend weekend on campus	70
% transfers	19
% from public high school	82
% in (# of) fraternities	30 (6)
% in (# of) sororities	25 (6)
% African-American	2
% Asian	10
% Caucasian	75
% Hispanic	3
% international	1
# of countries represented	16

WHAT'S HOT
school runs like butter
music associations
health facilities
campus food
college radio

WHAT'S NOT
lack of diversity on campus
political activism
sex
Tacoma
library

ACADEMICS

Academic Rating	**89**
Profs Interesting Rating	92
Profs Accessible Rating	93
Calendar	semester
Student/teacher ratio	12:1
% profs PhD/tenured	85/80
Hours of study per day	3.56

MOST POPULAR MAJORS
English
business
psychology

% GRADS WHO PURSUE...
Law 4, Med 2, MBA 5, MA 20

STUDENTS SPEAK OUT

Life
"Come to UPS," extols one junior. "Ollie North did!" There are, however, many, many additional reasons to consider the University of Puget Sound as a place to spend your next four years. Situated near the Sound and Mt. Rainier Park, UPS boasts a large number of outdoor activities. There's also plenty to do on and around campus. "There are always lots of fun activities, along with different bands that perform and guest speakers," one student reports. Parties, sports, movies, crew ("You gotta row"), restaurants, bars, coffee houses, and Mariners games are only some of the available options. "There's a lot of things to do if you want to get involved. There are all kinds of groups," says another. And Seattle, with its many distractions, is a mere half-hour drive away. UPS students work hard—over half of the students we surveyed admitted to spending at least four hours a day on their studies—but still manage to fit fun into their busy schedules. One student notes that "people are always trying to make time to study, fit in all their activities, and, of course, sleep," while another finds that "classes, homework, and jobs keep people here very busy. But people are still very social."

Academics
UPS received many accolades from its students on the small size of its classes: "Small class size and great professors equal a great opportunity for learning," said one. Another reported that "having numerous classes with less than ten people in them has been wonderful." Professors were also lauded. Students repeatedly referred to their competence and challenging teaching methods as their strong points. "My classes are hard, but valuable and interesting," observed one respondent. "The instructors foster a creative, stimulating atmosphere where students can express any idea that comes to mind." "It's difficult," said another, "but the professors like to probe your brain; they make you think, and it's worth it." The professors were especially praised for their accessibility and approachability. As one student reports, "I had one math professor who volunteered to show up for a study session with my study group. He did this on a day when he taught no classes on campus. All of my professors have flexible office hours and try to accommodate their students' schedules." Others note that "the professors are friendly, try to be funny, and are available to meet with students. It's easy to talk to a professor outside of class." "They're friends, not overbearing know-it-alls," claims one freshman. The administration received average to above-average marks ("Our school is like an old `63 Mercedes: it looks cool and it usually runs smooth, but it costs a lot to keep up"), and while there were a few complaints ranging from campus food ("The food needs to be healthier and cheaper") to departmental resources (one disgruntled theater major complains: "Theatre at UPS hath made me mad!"), most UPS students agree that they would prefer to be here than anywhere else.

Student Body
UPS students find their classmates to be an easygoing, sociable, and supportive bunch. "Everyone at UPS is really friendly. It's easy to make friends and to have fun," and "Most of the other students here are great; upperclassmen are very supportive of freshmen," were common remarks. A lot of students do seem disappointed, however, with the homogenous makeup of the student body. Comments included "The people are friendly. The population is not diverse though, mostly white middle-class" and "We're white. Very, very white." Little discrimination was reported, however, and UPS students seem to generally agree that their fellow students are "excellent, understanding, and chill."

FINANCIAL AID: 206-756-3214　　　　　　E-MAIL: ADMISSION@UPS.EDU　　　WEB SITE: HTTP://WWW.UPS.EDU/

ADMISSIONS

The admissions committee considers (in descending order of importance): HS record, test scores, recommendations, essay, class rank. *Also considered (in descending order of importance):* special talents, alumni relationship, personality, extracurriculars, geographical distribution. Either the SAT or ACT is required; SAT is preferred. An interview is recommended. Admissions process is need-blind. *High school units required/recommended:* 16 total units are recommended; 4 English recommended, 3 math recommended, 3 science recommended, 2 foreign language recommended, 3 social studies recommended. *Special Requirements:* An audition is required for music program applicants. TOEFL is required of all international students. *The admissions office says:* "[Our admissions committee] reviews each application carefully. At least three people will read each application before a decision is made. The entire committee [11 members] will review the files over which there is some question of admissibility. Members of the admissions staff will meet with any candidate at any time during the admissions process."

The Inside Word

The University of Puget Sound is on the right track with its willingness to supply students with detailed information about how the selection process works. If universities in general were more forthcoming about candidate evaluation, college admission wouldn't be the angst-ridden exercise which it is for so many students. All students are aware that their academic background is the primary consideration of every admissions committee. How they are considered as individuals remains mysterious. At Puget Sound, it is clear that people mean more to the University than its freshman profile, and that candidates can count on a considerate and caring attitude before, during, and after the review process.

FINANCIAL AID

Students should submit: FAFSA (due February 1), CSS Profile (due February 1). The Princeton Review suggests that all financial aid forms be submitted as soon as possible after January 1. *The following grants/scholarships are offered:* Pell, SEOG, academic merit, the school's own scholarships, the school's own grants, state scholarships, state grants, private scholarships, private grants, ROTC. *Students borrow from the following loan programs:* Stafford, unsubsidized Stafford, Perkins, PLUS, the school's own loan fund, private loans. Applicants will be notified of awards beginning March 15. College Work-Study Program is available. Institutional employment is available.

FROM THE ADMISSIONS OFFICE

"For over 100 years, students from many locations and backgrounds have chosen to join our community. It is a community committed to excellence—excellence in the classroom and excellence in student organizations and activities. Puget students are serious about rowing and writing, management and music, skiing and sciences, leadership and languages. At Puget Sound you'll be challenged—and helped—to perform at the peak of your ability."

ADMISSIONS

Admissions Rating	80
% of applicants accepted	78
% of acceptees attending	21

FRESHMAN PROFILE

Average verbal SAT	670
Average math SAT	600
Average ACT	26
Average TOEFL	550
Graduated top 20% of class	76
Graduated top 40% of class	97
Graduated top 60% of class	NR
Average HS GPA or Avg.	3.6

DEADLINES

Early decision	NR
Regular admission	2/1
Regular notification	4/1
Non-fall registration	yes

APPLICANTS ALSO LOOK AT

AND OFTEN PREFER

Stanford
Northwestern U.
Pomona Coll.

AND SOMETIMES PREFER

U. Washington
Whitman
Lewis & Clark
Willamette
Colorado Coll.

AND RARELY PREFER

U. Oregon
Gonzaga

FINANCIAL FACTS

Financial Aid Rating	90
Tuition	$18,030
Room & board	$4,800
Estimated book expense	$660
% frosh receiving aid	80
% undergrads receiving aid	80
% aid is need-based	65
% frosh w/ grant (avg)	80 ($7,090)
% frosh w/ loan (avg)	60 ($4,600)
% UGs w/ job (avg)	40 ($2,100)
Off-campus job outlook	excellent

PURDUE UNIVERSITY-WEST LAFAYETTE

WEST LAFAYETTE, IN 47907   ADMISSIONS: 317-494-1776   FAX: 317-494-0544

CAMPUS LIFE

Quality of Life Rating **80**
Type of school   public
Affiliation   none
Environment   suburban

STUDENTS
FT undergrad enrollment   25,858
% male/female   58/42
% from out of state   26
% live on campus   38
% spend weekend on campus   50
% transfers   15
% from public high school   NR
% in (# of) fraternities   20 (46)
% in (# of) sororities   18 (24)
% African-American   4
% Asian   4
% Caucasian   88
% Hispanic   2
% international   2
# of countries represented   77

WHAT'S HOT
hard liquor
old-fashioned dating
intercollegiate sports
beer
Greeks

WHAT'S NOT
library
campus difficult to get around
dorms
theater
students are cliquish

ACADEMICS

Academic Rating **70**
Profs Interesting Rating   68
Profs Accessible Rating   68
Calendar   semester
Student/teacher ratio   17:1
% profs PhD   84
Hours of study per day   3.10

MOST POPULAR MAJORS
electrical engineering
mechanical engineering
elementary education

STUDENTS SPEAK OUT

Life

Purdue students give the campus's surrounding area low -to- average marks. Activities do exist on campus for those students who make the effort to find them: "You basically make your own fun." An overwhelmingly large number of our respondents cite drinking as a popular activity. "In terms of entertainment, there ain't much," says one. "Most people go to pubs to drink and hang out." Another observes that "the emphasis surrounding Purdue's campus seems to be on alcohol and party-like behavior. Everyone tends to live for the weekends, if only to get away from the humdrumness of classes." But Purdue students still take their studies very seriously: "More students are concerned with their grades here than at other schools. I study a lot." Purdue's large Greek system used to dominate the social scene here, but more than one respondent notes that "Greek life isn't as popular as it used to be. It's a very conservative campus, but that's starting to change."

Academics

Purdue University is one of the great buys of higher education, especially for in-staters, who make up the vast majority of students. With career-minded undergrads and great programs in business and engineering (one in five pursues an engineering degree), Purdue is run efficiently and effectively. The administration receives above-average marks from students for its accessibility and responsiveness: "The administration at Purdue makes itself extremely accessible. The student body and the school administration offer constructive feedback on a regular basis," reports one respondent. Some groan about long lines ("It's a long wait at the bursar's office,") and old systems ("The school needs to automate most processes including registering for classes"), but most feel that the school is smoothly run overall, especially given its size. Classes tend to be rigorous ("The academic program is challenging for all majors. I like the environment here because the pressure keeps me on my feet"), and some students complain of overwork ("I love taking classes where the professors think that the class is the only one I'm enrolled in," as one student sarcastically put it). Professors receive good marks for competence ("Professors are well-known and respected in their fields" and are "really good at getting their points across"), but students feel they need improvement in enthusiasm and accessibility. Facilities receive average marks ("Library needs improvement in its computers"; "Labs are now open later"). But more than one student claimed that Purdue is "completely underrated. It's a great academic experience. Purdue is the `sleeper' education of the U.S.!"

Student Body

The happiest students in our survey were the ones who were most accepting of Purdue's conservative leanings. "I feel the students of Purdue U are very friendly and typically lean toward the conservative side." One Prairie Village, KS native proclaimed; "Very easy-going student body. Most relaxed, clean-cut, crime-free major university in the nation!" Other respondents, while happy with their fellow students, were dissatisfied with the lack of diversity and acceptance they felt was apparent on their campus. "I get along with my fellow students, yet I think, for being such a large campus, that it is very narrow-minded, culturally biased, and dull. There are too many small-town students and too many engineers." Notes another, "Students are friendly in general, but the campus is very segregated. Members of different ethnic groups often socialize with only each other."

ADMISSIONS

The admissions committee considers (in descending order of importance): HS record, class rank, test scores, recommendations, essay. *Also considered (in descending order of importance):* alumni relationship. Either the SAT or ACT is required. An interview is recommended. Admissions process is need-blind. *High school units required/recommended:* 4 English required, 2 math required, 1 science required. 1-2 units of history and social studies recommended. Out-of-state applicants must meet higher standards than in-state applicants. *Special Requirements:* TOEFL is required of all international students. Minimum SAT I scores of 400 verbal and 500 math (composite ACT scores of 21 English and 23 math) required of engineering program applicants. Interview required of veterinary technology program applicants. SAT II (English, chemistry, and math) recommended of science and engineering program applicants; required of all home-schooled applicants.

The Inside Word

The fact that Purdue holds class rank as one of its most important consideration in the admission of candidates is troublesome. There are far too many inconsistencies in ranking policies and class size among the 25,000-plus high schools in the U.S. to place so much weight on an essentially incomparable number. The university's high admit rate thankfully renders the issue relatively moot.

FINANCIAL AID

Students should submit: FAFSA, the school's own financial aid form. The Princeton Review suggests that all financial aid forms be submitted as soon as possible after January 1. *The following grants/scholarships are offered:* Pell, SEOG, academic merit, athletic, the school's own scholarships, the school's own grants, state scholarships, state grants, private scholarships, private grants, ROTC. *Students borrow from the following loan programs:* Stafford, unsubsidized Stafford, Perkins, PLUS, the school's own loan fund, state loans, health professions loans. Applicants will be notified of awards beginning April 15. College Work-Study Program is available. Institutional employment is available.

FROM THE ADMISSIONS OFFICE

"Although it is one of America's largest universities, Purdue does not 'feel' big to its students. The main campus in West Lafayette was built around a master plan that keeps walking time between classes to a maximum of 12 minutes. Purdue is a comprehensive university with an international reputation in a wide range of academic fields. A strong work ethic prevails at Purdue. As a member of the Big Ten, Purdue has a strong and diverse athletic program. Hundreds of student organizations, including a large and active Greek system, offer opportunities for students with every kind of special interest."

ADMISSIONS

Admissions Rating	68
% of applicants accepted	90
% of acceptees attending	41

FRESHMAN PROFILE

Average verbal SAT	530
Average math SAT	560
Average ACT	24
Average TOEFL	550
Graduated top 20% of class	46
Graduated top 40% of class	74
Graduated top 60% of class	89
Average HS GPA or Avg.	NR

DEADLINES

Early decision	NR
Regular admission	NR
Regular notification	rolling
Non-fall registration	yes

APPLICANTS ALSO LOOK AT

AND OFTEN PREFER

Indiana U.—Bloomington
Valparaiso
U. Illinois
Rose—Hulman

AND SOMETIMES PREFER

Penn State—U. Park
U. Wisconsin-Madison

AND RARELY PREFER

Hanover

FINANCIAL FACTS

Financial Aid Rating	82
In-state tuition	$3,056
Out-of-state tuition	$10,128
Room & board	$4,310
Estimated book expense	$600
% frosh receiving aid	96
% undergrads receiving aid	53
% aid is need-based	91
% frosh w/ grant (avg)	59 ($3,086)
% frosh w/ loan (avg)	40 ($4,723)
% UGs w/ job (avg)	15 ($2,000)
Off-campus job outlook	good

RANDOLPH-MACON COLLEGE

P.O. Box 5005, Ashland, VA 23005-5505 Admissions: 800-888-1762   Fax: 804-752-7231

CAMPUS LIFE

Quality of Life Rating   **84**
Type of school   private
Affiliation   United Methodist Church
Environment   city

STUDENTS
FT undergrad enrollment	1,067
% male/female	52/48
% from out of state	42
% live on campus	90
% spend weekend on campus	70
% transfers	8
% from public high school	65
% in (# of) fraternities	49 (8)
% in (# of) sororities	45 (4)
% African-American	4
% Asian	2
% Caucasian	92
% Hispanic	1
% international	1
# of countries represented	12

WHAT'S HOT
Greeks
beer
hard liquor
cigarettes
sex

WHAT'S NOT
music associations
college radio
health facilities
student publications
theater

ACADEMICS

Academic Rating	**80**
Profs Interesting Rating	87
Profs Accessible Rating	93
Calendar	4-1-4
Student/teacher ratio	11:1
% profs tenured	82
Hours of study per day	2.84

MOST POPULAR MAJORS
economics/business
psychology
English

% GRADS WHO PURSUE...
Law 3, Med 3, MBA 5, MA 16

STUDENTS SPEAK OUT

Life

Many Randolph-Macon College students are happy about the "incredibly personable" attitude of their peers, as well as the school's "tight community" atmosphere. Although the social scene often involves traveling off the Ashland, Virginia campus ("Ashland is NOT the center of the universe!"), no one seems to mind—distractions are within easy reach. As one student reports, "You can't beat the location of Randolph-Macon: it's fifteen minutes from Richmond, ninety minutes from Virginia Beach, sixty minutes from the Blue Ridge Mountains, and ninety minutes from Washington, D.C. Everything is extremely accessible." On campus, athletics draw strong support, and the Greeks are popular; they are the center of the party scene, although not everyone loves them ("the frats are always breaking rules"). R-MC students say they do not appreciate being "forced to go off campus to drink," and there is talk of starting a campus pub for those twenty-one and over. On the whole, however, students find life at Randolph-Macon quite enjoyable. As one student writes, "Everyone makes the most, academically and energetically, of their time."

Academics

R-MC has a variety of solid academic offerings. Students describe the school as "academically competitive with a very strong liberal arts program." Popular majors include psychology, English, economics and business, and biology. Distribution requirements are rigorous and include courses in English, math, natural and social sciences, fine arts, and foreign languages. Small class size is a plus and contributes to the "family" atmosphere on campus. Students appreciate the fact that "teachers are always willing to help," and write that "students are often invited to dine with their professors." Randolph-Macon's 4-1-4 calendar includes a January term, which students use for nontraditional academic courses, field study, or travel. During the rest of the year, interested students may apply for internships in Washington, D.C., or terms of study at any of the other schools in the Seven College Consortium of Virginia (Washington and Lee, Hampden-Sydney, Sweet Briar, Mary Baldwin, Hollins, or Randolph-Macon Woman's College). Student complaints that "the administration needs to listen more and be open to the feelings of the students" seem to have been heard, and the student population as a whole is satisfied with the way the school is run. R-MC offers a challenging, intimate academic setting, with an "excellent" faculty that wins high praise from students.

Student Body

Randolph-Macon is mostly Caucasian, with very small African-American and Asian contingents. There are plenty of "upper-class, nice-dressing southerners," and student interest in political issues is minimal, though diversity and tolerance are reportedly big issues now. Reports one student, "People here didn't care during the Gulf war, but are currently banding together to protest keg restrictions."

FINANCIAL AID: 804-752-7259

WEB SITE: HTTP://WWW.RMC.EDU/

ADMISSIONS

The admissions committee considers (in descending order of importance): HS record, class rank, test scores, recommendations, essay. *Also considered (in descending order of importance):* alumni relationship, extracurriculars, geographical distribution, personality, special talents. Either the SAT or ACT is required; SAT is preferred. An interview is recommended. Admissions process is need-blind. *High school units required/recommended:* 16 total units are required; 22 total units are recommended; 4 English required, 3 math required, 2 science required, 4 science recommended, 2 foreign language required, 4 foreign language recommended, 1 social studies required, 2 history required. TOEFL is required of all international students.

The Inside Word

Candidates who are above-average students and testers are very likely to receive scholarships at Randolph-Macon. The college has a low yield of admits who enroll, and every strong student who signs on gives the freshman academic profile a boost. It's a great choice for average students—if the competition among Virginia colleges weren't so strong, admission to Randolph-Macon would be much tougher.

FINANCIAL AID

Students should submit: FAFSA, the school's own financial aid form, state aid form (due July 31), a copy of parents' most recent income tax filing. The Princeton Review suggests that all financial aid forms be submitted as soon as possible after January 1. *The following grants/scholarships are offered:* Pell, SEOG, academic merit, the school's own scholarships, the school's own grants, state scholarships, state grants, private scholarships, private grants, ROTC. *Students borrow from the following loan programs:* Stafford, unsubsidized Stafford, Perkins, PLUS, the school's own loan fund, state loans, private loans. Applicants will be notified of awards beginning April 1. College Work-Study Program is available. Institutional employment is available.

FROM THE ADMISSIONS OFFICE

"Randolph-Macon is an independent, coeducational college with the broadest liberal arts core curriculum in Virginia. The academic program is designed to allow students considerable freedom in planning their own program, while showing them that they will acquire not only the breadth of knowledge traditionally emphasized in a liberal education but also a sound foundation in a particular field. Students receive solid support from advisors, faculty, and peers. The Counseling and Career Center provides personal and career counseling as well as workshops and seminars. The combination of people, programs, and services prepares students for any future, including success in securing a job or in gaining acceptance to graduate or professional school. The college offers a wide variety of social and recreational opportunities. A full-time Student Activities Director works in conjunction with over sixty-five campus organizations to ensure that almost every day there are activities and events in which students can participate; 40 percent of the students participate in one or more community service activities; 70 percent play intramural sports; 45 percent join a fraternity or sorority; and everyone has a voice in student government. Construction of a new $9 million sports and recreation center began in the spring of 1996.

ADMISSIONS

Admissions Rating	72
% of applicants accepted	77
% of acceptees attending	24

FRESHMAN PROFILE

Average verbal SAT	550
Average math SAT	534
Average ACT	NR
Average TOEFL	610
Graduated top 20% of class	36
Graduated top 40% of class	68
Graduated top 60% of class	90
Average HS GPA or Avg.	3.1

DEADLINES

Early decision	12/1
Regular admission	3/1
Regular notification	Rolling
Non-fall registration	yes

APPLICANTS ALSO LOOK AT

AND OFTEN PREFER

U. Virginia

AND SOMETIMES PREFER

James Madison
Virginia Tech
Washington and Lee
Hampden—Sydney

AND RARELY PREFER

Mary Washington
Roanoke
Sweet Briar
U. Richmond

FINANCIAL FACTS

Financial Aid Rating	86
Tuition	$15,255
Room & board	$3,995
Estimated book expense	$400
% frosh receiving aid	84
% undergrads receiving aid	79
% aid is need-based	78
% frosh w/ grant (avg)	82 ($5,500)
% frosh w/ loan (avg)	57 ($4,987)
% UGs w/ job (avg)	30 ($900)
Off-campus job outlook	excellent

RANDOLPH-MACON WOMAN'S COLLEGE

LYNCHBURG, VA 24503   ADMISSIONS: 800-745-7692   FAX: 804-947-8996

CAMPUS LIFE

Quality of Life Rating	**93**
Type of school	private
Affiliation	United Methodist Church
Environment	city

STUDENTS

FT undergrad enrollment	674
% male/female	0/100
% from out of state	63
% live on campus	85
% spend weekend on campus	NR
% transfers	12
% from public high school	73
% African-American	5
% Asian	2
% Caucasian	84
% Hispanic	2
% international	7
# of countries represented	22

WHAT'S HOT
campus easy to get around
campus food
school runs like butter
registration is a breeze
support groups

WHAT'S NOT
drugs
student publications
college radio
intramural sports
beer

ACADEMICS

Academic Rating	**92**
Profs Interesting Rating	99
Profs Accessible Rating	98
Calendar	semester
Student/teacher ratio	9:1
% profs PhD/tenured	75/71
Hours of study per day	3.60

MOST POPULAR MAJORS
English
politics
psychology

% GRADS WHO PURSUE...
Law 3, Med 2, MBA 2, MA 26

STUDENTS SPEAK OUT

Life
Randolph-Macon Woman's College has one of the nation's most beautiful campuses. "Beautiful setting, great architecture," is how one student describes it. Writes another, "We get spoiled by huge rooms, great food, security, and cable TV." A classic Southern college, R-MWC is full of tradition. "There are a lot of traditions which spill over into social life. Many are based on the sister classes (odd- and even-graduation year classes are paired up as 'sisters')—Ring Night, Pumpkin Parade, Skeller Sings, Odd or Even Day, etc." Says another, "The best part about R-MWC is the traditions, like Sister classes, secret societies, Mary's Garden, and Engagement Tower." Students note that campus life provides "lots of clubs, lots of leadership opportunities." But despite all the mysterious goings-on, "At R-MWC, the weekends are usually spent off-campus." Explains one student, "For fun, many students party at a local men's or coed college (Hampden-Sydney, VMI, Washington and Lee), or go to a local bar." Overall, "Students study very hard during the week and party very hard on the weekends, at nearby colleges." Students warn that Lynchburg is pretty boring. "It's a small Bible town, and there is not much to do besides the movies and the terrible mall. There are a few good bars. The school, however, offers various entertainment, such as dances, movies, and panel discussions."

Academics
Writes one typical Randolph-Macon Woman's College student, "The week of orientation, the Dean found out that I was concerned about a math class, and called me for reassurance. I knew then that I had come to the right school." The small class sizes here are a big hit. "My average class size this semester is six people, and I'm a sophomore," reports one student. Says another, "R-MWC is a place to call home. Professors and administrators are family; living in dorms is like having 800 sisters." Faculty and staff "are always friendly, very accessible, and generally very cooperative. Often, they are more than just people who work here, they are our friends." One student points out that "the most wonderful thing about my school is the amount of student-faculty interaction. It's not unusual for large discussion groups, of which the professor is a member, to form immediately after class and for the conversation to continue well into mealtimes." Natural sciences are singled out among the many excellent departments here. An effective Honor Code means that "Everyone is committed to maintaining an atmosphere where cheating will not occur." Sums up one student: "There is a definite commitment to the ideals of a liberal arts education and single-sex education."

Student Body
One student describes the R-MWC student body this way: "An interesting combination from all over the U.S. There are Southern belles and the grunge-influenced and everything between. Everyone seems able to find her own niche." Another observes that, "Most of the students are rich and act that way. The school is very conservative, but I'm a liberal and I feel very at home here. We respect each others' differences."

FINANCIAL AID: 804-947-8128

WEB SITE: HTTP://WWW.RMWC.EDU/

ADMISSIONS

The admissions committee considers (in descending order of importance): HS record, recommendations, class rank, test scores, essay. *Also considered (in descending order of importance):* extracurriculars, personality, alumni relationship, geographical distribution, special talents. Either the SAT or ACT is required. An interview is recommended. Admissions process is need-blind. *High school units required/recommended:* 16 total units are recommended; 4 English recommended, 3 math recommended, 2 science recommended, 3 foreign language recommended, 2 history recommended. TOEFL is required of all international students. *The admissions office says:* "This curriculum is required of any student seeking honors scholarship consideration."

The Inside Word

The admissions process at Randolph-Macon Woman's College works pretty much as it does at most small liberal arts colleges, with one worthwhile exception: each candidate is assigned to an admissions staff member who functions as an advocate for the student throughout the process. It's nice to have somewhat regular contact with someone in the admissions office over the course of the cycle. This saves restating problems, questions, and circumstances every time you call or write. It also helps the college make a strong positive impression on applicants.

FINANCIAL AID

Students should submit: FAFSA (due March 15), the school's own financial aid form (due March 15), state aid form (due March 15), a copy of parents' most recent income tax filing. The Princeton Review suggests that all financial aid forms be submitted as soon as possible after January 1. *The following grants/scholarships are offered:* Pell, SEOG, academic merit, the school's own scholarships, the school's own grants, state scholarships, state grants, private scholarships, private grants, foreign aid. *Students borrow from the following loan programs:* Stafford, Perkins, PLUS. College Work-Study Program is available. Institutional employment is available.

FROM THE ADMISSIONS OFFICE

"At Randolph-Macon Woman's College, we want to know what you think. Our students follow a multitude of career paths—lawyer, psychologist, banker, oceanographer, teacher, artist, physician. But a Randolph-Macon education consists of much more than coursework and skill-building. As a student, you start with your own thoughtful response to the world. Then, in small groups, with other energetically thoughtful women—and under the guidance of a committed professor—you engage in the real activity of education: Exploring. Analyzing. Talking. Writing. Imagining. Sharing. Realizing. Enjoying.

ADMISSIONS

Admissions Rating	72
% of applicants accepted	89
% of acceptees attending	34

FRESHMAN PROFILE

Average verbal SAT	600
Average math SAT	550
Average ACT	25
Average TOEFL	500
Graduated top 20% of class	69
Graduated top 40% of class	89
Graduated top 60% of class	99
Average HS GPA or Avg.	NR

DEADLINES

Early decision	11/15
Regular admission	3/1
Regular notification	rolling
Non-fall registration	yes

APPLICANTS ALSO LOOK AT

AND OFTEN PREFER

Duke
U. Richmond
Virginia
Smith
Mount Holyoke

AND SOMETIMES PREFER

Sweet Briar
Hollins
William and Mary

AND RARELY PREFER

Washington and Lee
U. South Carolina—Columbia
Virginia Tech
Rhodes

FINANCIAL FACTS

Financial Aid Rating	93
Tuition	$15,420
Room & board	$6,520
Estimated book expense	$400
% frosh receiving aid	64
% undergrads receiving aid	62
% aid is need-based	73
% frosh w/ grant (avg)	88 ($7,763)
% frosh w/ loan (avg)	77 ($2,534)
% UGs w/ job (avg)	66 ($1,550)
Off-campus job outlook	fair

University of Redlands

1200 East Colton Avenue, P.O. Box 3080, Redlands, CA 92373-0999   Admissions: 800-455-5064   Fax: 909-335-4089

CAMPUS LIFE

Quality of Life Rating   **86**
Type of school   private
Affiliation   American Baptist Church
Environment   suburban

STUDENTS

FT undergrad enrollment	1,369
% male/female	48/52
% from out of state	37
% live on campus	93
% spend weekend on campus	70
% transfers	25
% from public high school	87
% in (# of) fraternities	15 (6)
% in (# of) sororities	20 (4)
% African-American	4
% Asian	9
% Caucasian	67
% Hispanic	11
% international	8
# of countries represented	35

WHAT'S HOT
health facilities
music associations
campus food
support groups
computer facilities

WHAT'S NOT
library
student publications
lab facilities
college radio
Redlands

ACADEMICS

Academic Rating	**87**
Profs Interesting Rating	94
Profs Accessible Rating	93
Calendar	4-1-4
Student/teacher ratio	13:1
% profs PhD/tenured	76/88
Hours of study per day	3.47

MOST POPULAR MAJORS
government
education

% GRADS WHO PURSUE...
Law 13, Med 2, MBA 5, MA 51

STUDENTS SPEAK OUT

Life

The city of Redlands—a small town with a population of about 64,000—gets only fair marks from our students ("For fun we sit around and make fun of the city of Redlands") but does receive kudos for its proximity to other attractions: "The beach is ninety minutes away, excellent skiing is sixty minutes away, and the cultural Mecca that is Los Angeles is just over the hill. Too bad you need a car for EVERYTHING." But students do admit that there are more than enough things to do on campus. "Redlands life is kind of dull...but clubs on campus make an effort to make it better. Activities are planned for every weekend, and they include a lot of interesting and unusual things." These things include the usual fraternity- and sorority-sponsored parties, free movies, and campus-wide arts and entertainment festivals. Respondents report a great sense of community on this small and friendly campus: "The University of Redlands is a tight community, and a very academically oriented one. We work hard, but we also know how to have fun. There's something for everyone here." Dating, alcohol, and smoking are all very popular.

Academics

One outstanding feature of the University of Redlands is the Johnston Center, an integrative studies program that allows students to choose a concentration, rather than a major with a set core curriculum. Instead of grades, students receive detailed evaluations from their professors. U of R undergrads had nothing but praise for the center. Says one student: "The Johnston Center for Integrative Studies, an experimental program within the U of R, allowed me to fully customize my major. Without the Johnston Center, many students would not even be here. It's the number one resource for getting a truly excellent education here." Another student puts it this way: "Sometimes you find a place just like heaven. This isn't it, but it is a good, solid university. The alternative education available at the Johnston Center is beyond compare." The administration receives average marks overall. While praised for its warmth ("The administration is generally helpful and friendly. Some of them know me by name") it is also criticized for trying to add red tape to an already efficient system ("The administration attempts to make U of R more bureaucratic than it needs to be"). The professors at U of R are universally lauded. One senior physics major remarks: "The professors in my field are outstanding. Their knowledge of the subject is amazing." Others comment on their professors' accessibility and genuine caring for their students. "The professors I've had are great," says one. "They're really interested in who you are and what you do. Conversations outside class are common." Another observes: "I have had some truly outstanding professors here who challenge each of us to create, to analyze, and to think in sophisticated terms. I feel this is an excellent school because of the extremely strong student-faculty involvement." The facilities receive average marks all around, but some feel that the library needs some improvement: "Computers, nice! Class size, nice! Library, sucks out loud!"

Student Body

Almost all of the students surveyed express satisfaction with their peers. "People here are really friendly. I must say `hi' to a dozen people on my way to class each day" says one. However, the student body receives only average marks for diversity: "School needs to be a little more diverse. People here are very nice, but there seems to be a gap between people who are different." Tolerance levels appear to be high, though, and no tensions along racial or sexual lines are reported.

FINANCIAL AID: 909-335-4047

ADMISSIONS

The admissions committee considers (in descending order of importance): HS record, test scores, recommendations, essay, class rank. *Also considered (in descending order of importance):* extracurriculars, alumni relationship, personality, special talents. Either the SAT or ACT is required. An interview is recommended. Admissions process is need-blind. *High school units required/recommended:* 4 English recommended, 3 math recommended, 2 science recommended, 2 foreign language recommended, 1 social studies recommended, 2 history recommended. Minimum combined SAT I score of 950 and minimum 2.85 GPA recommended. *Special Requirements:* An audition is required for music program applicants. TOEFL is required of all international students. Interview required of applicants to Johnston Center for Individualized Learning.

The Inside Word

The University of Redlands is a solid admit for any student with an above average high school record. Candidates who are interested in pursuing self-designed programs through the University's Johnston Center will find the admissions process to be distinctly more personal than it generally is; the center is interested in intellectually curious, self-motivated students and puts a lot of energy into identifying and recruiting them.

FINANCIAL AID

Students should submit: FAFSA, the school's own financial aid form. The Princeton Review suggests that all financial aid forms be submitted as soon as possible after January 1. *The following grants/scholarships are offered:* Pell, SEOG, academic merit, the school's own scholarships, the school's own grants, state grants, private scholarships, private grants, foreign aid. *Students borrow from the following loan programs:* Stafford, unsubsidized Stafford, Perkins, PLUS, the school's own loan fund, private loans. College Work-Study Program is available. Institutional employment is available.

FROM THE ADMISSIONS OFFICE

"We've created an unusually blended curriculum of the liberal arts and pre-professional study because we think education is about learning how to think and learning how to do. For example, our environmental studies students have synthesized their study of computer science, sociology, biology, and economics to develop an actual resource management plan for the local mountain communities. Our creative writing program encourages internships with publishing or television production companies so that when our graduates send off their first novel, they can pay the rent as magazine writers. We educate managers, poets, environmental scientists, teachers, musicians, and speech therapists to be reflective about culture and society, so that they can better understand and improve the world they'll enter upon graduation."

ADMISSIONS

Admissions Rating	70
% of applicants accepted	79
% of acceptees attending	28

FRESHMAN PROFILE

Average verbal SAT	570
Average math SAT	560
Average ACT	23
Average TOEFL	550
Graduated top 20% of class	NR
Graduated top 40% of class	NR
Graduated top 60% of class	NR
Average HS GPA or Avg.	3.5

DEADLINES

Early decision	12/15
Regular admission	3/1
Regular notification	rolling
Non-fall registration	yes

APPLICANTS ALSO LOOK AT
AND OFTEN PREFER
Occidental
Pomona

AND SOMETIMES PREFER
Pitzer
UC—Irvine
UC—Santa Barbara
U. of the Pacific
U. San Diego

AND RARELY PREFER
Whittier
Pepperdine
U. Southern Cal

FINANCIAL FACTS

Financial Aid Rating	86
Tuition	$17,110
Room & board	$6,515
Estimated book expense	$600
% frosh receiving aid	75
% undergrads receiving aid	75
% aid is need-based	84
% frosh w/ grant (avg)	75 ($8,890)
% frosh w/ loan (avg)	69 ($2,625)
% UGs w/ job (avg)	50 ($1,200)
Off-campus job outlook	good

REED COLLEGE

3203 S.E. WOODSTOCK BOULEVARD, PORTLAND, OR 97202   ADMISSIONS: 800-547-4750   FAX: 503-777-7775

STUDENTS SPEAK OUT

Life

Explains one Reed College student, "When Reedies party, which is generally infrequently, they do so with the same intensity they devote to their studies." Drugs "are kinda big here but everyone's cool about it," and alcohol is also popular. Several students note that drugs no longer occupy the center of Reed social life, as they did in the 1960s and 1970s. Student activism and community service are hot, as are creative outlets (newspaper, literary and political journals, radio station, etc.). Students also note a number of recreational options in the area: the city of Portland, Mt. Hood, several nearby national parks, and the Pacific Ocean all offer relief from the school's high stress level.

Academics

In many ways, Reed epitomizes the ideal of a progressive undergraduate institution. Its students are hardworking, intelligent, and open to unconventional ideas; its philosophy de-emphasizes the traditional (grades, while recorded, are neither reported nor discussed; restrictions on student behavior are minimal); and its professors and academic programs constantly challenge the students' preconceptions and capacities for work. As several Reed students note, "This school is not for everyone." Because of its nontraditional aspects, Reed scares off some potential applicants, and many who do attend leave before graduation. About half of Reed freshmen make it through all four years. But students are excited about the school's assets: writes one, "The classes are tiny and the profs are fantastic. Reed treats you like an adult. Students and faculty are accepting of just about everything. If you want to work really hard, hang out with brilliant, strange, intelligent, and interesting people, Reed is the place." They are equally forthcoming about its less appealing side. As one student writes, "The ethos here is, if you're not haggard, sleep-deprived, and lonely, you're not living up to your academic potential." The academic program includes an introductory humanities course, an array of general education requirements, and a senior thesis. Academic departments are all reportedly excellent. History, English, and the sciences drew frequent praise. Reed is best for "self-motivated, intelligent students; it's a place of many sticks and few carrots." For those who survive, there is one huge carrot: Reed's excellent reputation among graduate schools (over two-thirds of Reed graduates continue on to graduate work).

Student Body

Reed's student body is the most left-leaning politically of all those included in our survey. Alternative lifestyles—drug usage, homosexuality—are openly accepted here. Frequent gripes against the student body are its lack of political and ethnic diversity ("This school is so white!" writes one Asian student), and its propensity toward cynicism and an obsession with work that borders on the antisocial. As one student puts it, "Reed students do things like study or write rather than bathe, eat, sleep, or other things that 'normal' humans do. If students' nerves could generate electricity, we might be able to light all of Southern California during finals week." Another student mentions that "an informal study conducted by a bunch of psych majors a few years back found that 80 percent of Reedies report having been picked last for kickball in elementary school."

ADMISSIONS

The admissions committee considers (in descending order of importance): HS record, essay, test scores, class rank, recommendations. *Also considered (in descending order of importance):* alumni relationship, personality. Either the SAT or ACT is required. An interview is recommended. *High school units required/recommended:* 16 total units are recommended; 4 English recommended, 3 math recommended, 2 science recommended, 2 foreign language recommended, 1 social studies recommended, 1 history recommended. TOEFL is required of all international students. *The admissions office says:* "The Committee on Admission takes into account many integrated factors, but academic accomplishments and talents are given the greatest weight in the selection process. Strong verbal and qualitative skills and demonstrated writing ability are important considerations. The Committee on Admission may give special consideration to applicants who represent a particular culture, region, or background that will contribute to the diversity of the college. Qualities of character—in particular, motivation, attitude toward learning, and social consciousness—also are important considerations."

The Inside Word

Reed's applicant pool draws heavily from the same students who are attracted to such bastions of nontraditional higher education as Hampshire, New College, and Evergreen. Despite the progressive nature of the educational attitudes and student body at Reed, the college zealously avoids such labeling in admissions literature, preferring to portray itself in a much more traditional fashion. While a social conscience is definitely an asset, applicants should devote particular attention to discussing their intellectual curiosity and academic interests in essays and/or interviews—Reed seems to like it best when their different side is downplayed.

FINANCIAL AID

Students should submit: FAFSA (due March 1), CSS Profile (due March 1), the school's own financial aid form (due march 1), a copy of parents' most recent income tax filing. The Princeton Review suggests that all financial aid forms be submitted as soon as possible after January 1. *The following grants/scholarships are offered:* Pell, SEOG, the school's own grants, ROTC. *Students borrow from the following loan programs:* Stafford, unsubsidized Stafford, Perkins, PLUS, the school's own loan fund. Applicants will be notified of awards beginning April 1. College Work-Study Program is available. Institutional employment is available.

FROM THE ADMISSIONS OFFICE

"Dedication to the highest standards of academic scholarship is central to a Reed education. A well-structured curriculum and small classes with motivated students and dedicated faculty provide the environment in which a student's quest for learning can be given broad rein. Students most likely to derive maximum benefit from a Reed education are individuals who possess a high degree of self-discipline and a genuine enthusiasm for academic work."

ADMISSIONS

Admissions Rating	85
% of applicants accepted	71
% of acceptees attending	23

FRESHMAN PROFILE

Average verbal SAT	740
Average math SAT	650
Average ACT	29
Average TOEFL	600
Graduated top 20% of class	NR
Graduated top 40% of class	NR
Graduated top 60% of class	NR
Average HS GPA or Avg.	3.7

DEADLINES

Early decision	12/1
Regular admission	2/1
Regular notification	4/1
Non-fall registration	yes

APPLICANTS ALSO LOOK AT

AND OFTEN PREFER

UC—Berkeley
Oberlin

AND SOMETIMES PREFER

New Coll. (FL)
Colorado Coll.
Grinnell

AND RARELY PREFER

Hampshire
UC—Santa Cruz
Evergreen State

FINANCIAL FACTS

Financial Aid Rating	74
Tuition	$20,610
Room & board	$5,750
Estimated book expense	NR
% frosh receiving aid	46
% undergrads receiving aid	45
% aid is need-based	100
% frosh w/ grant (avg)	46 ($14,200)
% frosh w/ loan (avg)	30 ($2,500)
% UGs w/ job (avg)	65 ($700)
Off-campus job outlook	good

RENSSELAER POLYTECHNIC INSTITUTE

TROY, NY 12180

ADMISSIONS: 800-448-6562

CAMPUS LIFE

Quality of Life Rating	**65**
Type of school	private
Affiliation	none
Environment	suburban

STUDENTS

FT undergrad enrollment	4,346
% male/female	77/23
% from out of state	56
% live on campus	54
% spend weekend on campus	65
% transfers	14
% from public high school	79
% in (# of) fraternities	40 (30)
% in (# of) sororities	40 (6)
% African-American	4
% Asian	13
% Caucasian	71
% Hispanic	4
% international	6
# of countries represented	74

WHAT'S HOT
computer facilities
Greeks
ethnic diversity on campus
student publications
intramural sports

WHAT'S NOT
Troy
students are unhappy
off-campus food
political activism
sex

ACADEMICS

Academic Rating	**80**
Profs Interesting Rating	62
Profs Accessible Rating	67
Calendar	semester
Student/teacher ratio	12:1
% profs PhD	99
Hours of study per day	3.55

MOST POPULAR MAJORS
mechanical engineering
electrical engineering
computer science

STUDENTS SPEAK OUT

Life

Students at the Rensselaer Polytechnic Institute give their hometown of Troy low marks. Writes one woman, "If you like rain, freezing temperatures, and secluded and remote old industrial towns, this is the school for you." She also complains that her male classmates are chauvinists. Perhaps their difficulties interacting with women come from the fact that they rarely see one: the male/female ratio is approximately 4:1. Writes one student, "The social scene is pretty bad due to the male/female ratio, but that happens at nearly all big engineering colleges. Don't worry, though, you'll be out in only four years." The Greeks play "a major part on campus and a major role in many people's social lives." Sports are also popular, both for spectators and participants. One student sums up, "You can get a great education in engineering here and they try hard to get you a job, but if you're looking for fun, excitement, or friends who won't kill you for your homework, go somewhere else or join a fraternity."

Academics

Students looking for four carefree years don't usually look to engineering schools first, and for good reason; as the students of Rensselaer Polytechnic Institute demonstrate, pursuing an engineering degree entails single-minded devotion to the task. "I would definitely describe this as a high-pressure school," writes one student in what may be an understatement. Stress is a way of life for RPI students. Sentiments such as "college is boot camp: deal with it!" were common among students' responses. Electrical engineering is the most popular major, but mechanical and aeronautic engineering are also strong, as is computer science. Business and management courses are also surprisingly strong. Writes one management major, "Although the School of Management is regarded as 'where the hockey players go,' it has a very good program and is small, which allows for more student/faculty interaction." This student/faculty mix, however, sometimes leads to inter—departmental scuffles for research positions and teaching assistantships. Notes one student, "RPI is a scrappy institution where political skills and personal savvy are just as important as academic skills." As is common at engineering schools, overall satisfaction levels here are low. One student, however, reports that things do get easier after the first year: "RPI makes the transition from high school to college life during freshman year very difficult. During first year the professors were unreachable, many of my labs were taught by foreign TAs so there was a language barrier, and most of my classes were taught as if we were reviewing material rather than learning it for the first time. Oddly, it gets better as you move on. This school supports you least just when you need it most." Perhaps in response to this kind of frustration, RPI has been experimenting with redesigned course structures that emphasize close student-faculty interaction.

Student Body

As previously mentioned, the student body is overwhelmingly male. Because RPI is a technical school, students are also similar in terms of their interests; nearly all share more than a mild fascination with computers and science. Still, students rank their student body "very diverse," probably because of the relatively large minority population.

FINANCIAL AID: 518-276-6813   E-MAIL: ADMISSIONS@RPI.EDU   WEB SITE: HTTP://WWW.RPI.EDU/

ADMISSIONS

The admissions committee considers (in descending order of importance): HS record, test scores, recommendations, class rank, essay. *Also considered (in descending order of importance):* alumni relationship, extracurriculars, geographical distribution, personality, special talents. Either the SAT or ACT is required. An interview is recommended. Admissions process is need-blind. *High school units required/recommended:* 13 total units are required; 4 English required, 4 math required, 2 science required, 3 social studies required. Essay required of all applicants. The following courses are strongly recommended (in order of importance): calculus, AP chemistry, and AP physics. *Special Requirements:* TOEFL is required of all international students. Portfolio required of architecture program applicants. *The admissions office says:* "Here at Rensselaer, we personally read every application on an individual basis. Our primary concern is a student's ability to handle Rensselaer's demanding curriculum!"

The Inside Word

Although scores and numbers may not be the only consideration of the admissions committee at RPI, it is important to remember that you have to have high ones in order to stay in the running for admission. Here in Troy and at many other highly selective colleges and universities, the first review weeds out those who are academically weak and without any special considerations. Underrepresented minorities and women are high on the list of desirables in the applicant pool here, and go through the admissions process without any hitches if reasonably well qualified.

FINANCIAL AID

Students should submit: FAFSA, the school's own financial aid form. The Princeton Review suggests that all financial aid forms be submitted as soon as possible after January 1. *The following grants/scholarships are offered:* Pell, SEOG, academic merit, athletic, the school's own scholarships, the school's own grants, state scholarships, state grants, private scholarships, private grants, ROTC, foreign aid. *Students borrow from the following loan programs:* unsubsidized Stafford, Perkins, PLUS, the school's own loan fund, supplemental loans, state loans, private loans. Applicants will be notified of awards beginning early in April. College Work-Study Program is available. Institutional employment is available.

FROM THE ADMISSIONS OFFICE

"Rensselaer emphasizes the study of technology and science, preparing students for today's high-tech world. The university is devoted to the discovery and dissemination of knowledge and its application to the service of humanity. Rensselaer has been in the forefront of scientific and professional education since its founding in 1824, and today its reputation for educational excellence draws students from every state and more than sixty foreign countries. Rensselaer offers a wide variety of recreational and social activities. Students enjoy thirty fraternities and five sororities, an award-winning newspaper, a progressively programmed radio station (WRPI), and over 120 drama, music, sports and special interest clubs."

ADMISSIONS

Admissions Rating	79
% of applicants accepted	85
% of acceptees attending	25

FRESHMAN PROFILE

Average verbal SAT	620
Average math SAT	600
Average ACT	30
Average TOEFL	550
Graduated top 20% of class	80
Graduated top 40% of class	96
Graduated top 60% of class	100
Average HS GPA or Avg.	NR

DEADLINES

Early decision	12/1
Regular admission	1/1
Regular notification	3/15
Non-fall registration	yes

APPLICANTS ALSO LOOK AT

AND OFTEN PREFER

Yale
MIT
Cornell U.

AND SOMETIMES PREFER

Carnegie Mellon
Boston U.
Lehigh
Worcester Poly.
U. Rochester

AND RARELY PREFER

SUNY Binghamton
Clarkson
SUNY Buffalo
Syracuse
RIT

FINANCIAL FACTS

Financial Aid Rating	77
Tuition	$17,995
Room & board	$6,155
Estimated book expense	$825
% frosh receiving aid	85
% undergrads receiving aid	85
% aid is need-based	80
% frosh w/ grant (avg)	85 ($12,138)
% frosh w/ loan (avg)	58 ($4,400)
% UGs w/ job (avg)	22 ($1,400)
Off-campus job outlook	good

RHODE ISLAND SCHOOL OF DESIGN

2 COLLEGE STREET, PROVIDENCE, RI 02903   ADMISSIONS: 401-454-6300   FAX: 401-454-6309

CAMPUS LIFE

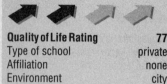

Quality of Life Rating	**77**
Type of school	private
Affiliation	none
Environment	city

STUDENTS

FT undergrad enrollment	1,848
% male/female	44/56
% from out of state	92
% live on campus	33
% spend weekend on campus	90
% transfers	28
% from public high school	56
% African-American	2
% Asian	8
% Caucasian	63
% Hispanic	3
% international	21
# of countries represented	50

WHAT'S HOT
cigarettes
drugs
leftist politics
honesty
different students interact

WHAT'S NOT
music associations
student government
student publications
support groups
college radio

ACADEMICS

Academic Rating	**83**
Profs Interesting Rating	86
Profs Accessible Rating	69
Calendar	4-1-4
Student/teacher ratio	12:1
% profs PhD/tenured	78/71
Hours of study per day	4.32

MOST POPULAR MAJORS
illustration
architecture
graphic design

STUDENTS SPEAK OUT

Life

RISD students report that "there are so few school functions or activities that people really aren't involved schoolwide. There is very little 'school spirit.'" Students generally get obsessive about their work, to the extent that many of them don't spend much time having fun. One student explains, "Work dominates everyone's center of concerns and many trivial issues, such as parties, slide to secondary places." To most students, this is not a negative: the same student continues, "I love the mentality that accompanies individuals who dedicate their lives to creative areas and that's why I'm here. The environment is alternative to the mainstream and offers unlimited options to explore new fields, philosophies, and artistic languages. I just wish more people had the opportunity to experience it." When they do take time off from work, RISD students smoke a ton of pot (ninth most per capita of all student bodies profiled in this book). They give the city of Providence below average marks.

Academics

The Rhode Island School of Design is one of the nation's finest and most demanding art schools. Students here work hard (they spend over four hours a day in their studios) with a determination that few but those who are certain of their life's goals can muster. Writes one student, "RISD is pretty intense—long studio hours; lots of people survive on coffee—but I wouldn't choose any other way of life." Says another, "Do NOT go to RISD if you are indecisive about your future. Knowing that you want to go into an art field is recommended, and it also saves time, money, and headaches over transferring to another school." The payoff for all the hard work is the chance to study with skilled, often excellent teachers (who, however, are only moderately accessible to their students after classes), the use of top—notch facilities, and the opportunity to participate in a community of similarly dedicated, similarly offbeat artists. Students are uniformly happy with courses in commercial arts, architecture, and fine arts.

Student Body

RISD's student body, in the words of one student, is made up of "lots of loony people all doing their own thang." Explains another, "The student body here is more accepting of eccentric personalities and strong opinions than most." There is a visible gay population that encounters little prejudice from the straight students. Students come from all over the country, and 10 percent are foreign nationals. Some are unhappy with the state of minority representation on campus. Explains one who is active in student government, "Unfortunately, this is an expensive school with very little endowment, so financial aid is limited. As a result, there are not many African- American, Native- American, or Hispanic students here." The most frequent negative rap on RISD students: they're arrogant. Says one, "Although it may not seem like it, RISD is a very religious school. Everyone thinks they're God."

ADMISSIONS

The admissions committee considers (in descending order of importance): HS record, essay, class rank, test scores, recommendations. *Also considered (in descending order of importance):* special talents, alumni relationship, extracurriculars, geographical distribution, personality. Either the SAT or ACT is required; SAT is preferred. Admissions process is need-blind. College-preparatory program with courses in studio art and art history strongly recommended. *Special Requirements:* A portfolio is required for art program applicants. TOEFL is required of all international students. Portfolio optional for architectural program applicants. *The admissions office says:* "RISD 'urges' applicants to pursue a college preparatory program in high school, including studio art and art history classes whenever possible; architecture applicants should also have completed two years of algebra, one semester of trigonometry, and one year of science (physics preferred)."

The Inside Word

Artistic talent as shown through your portfolio means far more than anything else for most applicants to RISD; an eye goes a lot further than an A toward gaining admission. Even so, a flip attitude about academics can be detrimental to all but the most talented artists. Prospective architecture majors must show academic strength in addition to artistic sensibilities. Art schools take a considerable amount of time to make and release decisions; it is best to submit materials as early as possible even though it may be a long time before notification of the committee's decision.

FINANCIAL AID

Students should submit: FAFSA (due February 15). The Princeton Review suggests that all financial aid forms be submitted as soon as possible after January 1. *The following grants/scholarships are offered:* Pell, SEOG, the school's own scholarships, the school's own grants, state scholarships, state grants, private scholarships, private grants. *Students borrow from the following loan programs:* Stafford, Perkins, PLUS. Applicants will be notified of awards beginning April 1. College Work-Study Program is available. Institutional employment is available. Freshmen are discouraged from working.

FROM THE ADMISSIONS OFFICE

"Education at RISD is a blend of long and rich tradition, intellectual stimulation, creativity, and a commitment to the visual arts. Our outstanding faculty form the cornerstone of a RISD education. With impressive educational backgrounds, scholarship, and professional artistic achievements, RISD faculty members bring great expertise and sensitivity to their teaching. This superb faculty...yield an atmosphere charged with energy. Here, at once, is the freedom to create and the challenge to produce. This experience—and this place—have attracted international recognition, as may be seen from RISD's student body."

ADMISSIONS

Admissions Rating	78
% of applicants accepted	59
% of acceptees attending	45

FRESHMAN PROFILE

Average verbal SAT	580
Average math SAT	570
Average ACT	NR
Average TOEFL	550
Graduated top 20% of class	47
Graduated top 40% of class	76
Graduated top 60% of class	90
Average HS GPA or Avg.	85.0

DEADLINES

Early decision	NR
Regular admission	2/15
Regular notification	4/1
Non-fall registration	yes

APPLICANTS ALSO LOOK AT

AND OFTEN PREFER
Cooper Union
Parsons

AND SOMETIMES PREFER
Carnegie Mellon
Maryland Inst., Coll. of Art
Syracuse
School of the Art Inst. of Chicago

AND RARELY PREFER
Mass. Coll. of Art

FINANCIAL FACTS

Financial Aid Rating	63
Tuition	$17,600
Room & board	$6,618
Estimated book expense	$300
% frosh receiving aid	49
% undergrads receiving aid	59
% aid is need-based	NR
% frosh w/ grant (avg)	20 ($8,921)
% frosh w/ loan (avg)	40 ($2,625)
% UGs w/ job (avg)	57 ($1,100)
Off-campus job outlook	good

UNIVERSITY OF RHODE ISLAND

KINGSTON, RI 02881   ADMISSIONS: 401-792-9800   FAX: 401-792-7198

CAMPUS LIFE

Quality of Life Rating   **77**
Type of school   public
Affiliation   none
Environment   town

STUDENTS
FT undergrad enrollment   8,333
% male/female   45/55
% from out of state   42
% live on campus   48
% spend weekend on campus   50
% transfers   23
% from public high school   87
% in (# of) fraternities   17 (17)
% in (# of) sororities   14 (8)
% African-American   3
% Asian   3
% Caucasian   78
% Hispanic   3
% international   NR
# of countries represented   72

WHAT'S HOT
student publications
student government
Greeks
old-fashioned dating
college radio

WHAT'S NOT
lab facilities
dorms
beer
music associations
hard liquor

ACADEMICS

Academic Rating   **70**
Profs Interesting Rating   68
Profs Accessible Rating   69
Calendar   semester
Student/teacher ratio   15:1
% profs PhD   87
Hours of study per day   3.20

MOST POPULAR MAJORS
pharmacy
psychology
human development/family studies

STUDENTS SPEAK OUT

Life
Students at the University of Rhode Island wish to put their school's reputation as the top party school to rest. So does the administration—so much so that they banned alcohol from campus at the start of the 1995-96 academic year. "We don't believe we are a big party school. Short and simple," says one. In fact, many students pride themselves and their classmates on the equal emphasis they place on their studies and their leisure: "Life at URI is well balanced. The academics are challenging, but there are also a lot of things to do to relax." URI's surrounding area receives high marks for its beauty and accessibility. As one student says: "Being on the coast, the rocks and the beaches are a must. Rhode Island is a small state, so everything is relatively close. The area nightlife always presents something to do." There are also things to do on campus for those students willing to go out and find them: "There are many different organizations on campus that cater to many different interests. I've been happy here. It's all a matter of how involved you get and what you make of it." Campus-wide activities include the Coffee House, Midnight Madness, Homecoming, and Oozeball (mud volleyball).

Academics
Most of the students at the University of Rhode Island are on a professional track. Education and business are popular majors, followed by engineering ("In the chemical engineering program, all of the professors are willing to help you, even if you're not one of their students"), nursing ("Nursing is a great major here. Instructors are intelligent and resources are excellent"), and pharmacological studies ("As a pharmacy major, I have been lucky enough to have an outstanding and supportive faculty guiding me through my curriculum") says one student. Overall, URI's professors receive respectable marks. While a few respondents find them dull and uninterested in their students, most call them very caring and capable. One student even goes so far as to say that his "professors here are considerate...and some teach with unstoppable dynamism and even wild abandon!" The administration at URI receives lukewarm marks, mostly for its inaccessibility "Welcome to the University of Rhode Island Telephone Registration System" are the words you will hate to hear after your sophomore year" and its perceived indifference. "Some members of the administration could be more helpful towards and respectful of undergrads." Like most large institutions, URI is a school best suited to the self-starter: "If you do not make the effort to meet with professors, you will have virtually no connections or friendships with them," offers one junior. "My academic experience was hard at first, until I began talking to my professors." Many options are open for those students willing to make the effort: "No doors have been closed to me at URI," says one. "I've done independent studies, volunteer work for credit, even studied in London!"

Student Body
Most students at URI are struck by the fact that despite the size of the school, their fellow classmates are extremely open and friendly to friends and strangers alike. "The majority will flash a smile or say `hi', even if they don't know you. It's nice to have a stranger smile and ask what's up." There is some racial tension reported; however, most students feel that the student body is willing to work its issues out: "The student body is socially diverse, but not ethnically diverse. URI tends to be very homophobic, but this is starting to change. The ability for groups to mingle and form coalitions is encouraged."

FINANCIAL AID: 401-874-2314   E-MAIL: MUSKRAT@URIACC.URI.EDU   WEB SITE: HTTP://WWW.URI.EDU/

ADMISSIONS

The admissions committee considers (in descending order of importance): HS record, test scores, class rank, recommendations, essay. *Also considered (in descending order of importance):* alumni relationship, geographical distribution, special talents, extracurriculars, personality. Either the SAT or ACT is required. An interview is recommended. Admissions process is need-blind. *High school units required/recommended:* 18 total units are required; 4 English required, 3 math required, 4 math recommended, 2 science required, 3 science recommended, 2 foreign language required, 3 foreign language recommended, 2 social studies required, 3 social studies recommended, 2 history recommended. Minimum combined SAT I score of 1100 and rank in top third of secondary school class. *Special Requirements:* An audition is required for music program applicants. 4 units of math and 1 unit each of chemistry and physics required of engineering program applicants. *The admissions office says:* "We have no restriction on the number of out-of-state students, as most public universities do. We recommend interviews and look forward to meeting with as many candidates as possible."

The Inside Word

Any candidate with solid grades is likely to find the university's admissions committee to be welcoming. The yield of admits who enroll is low and the state's population small. Out-of-state students are attractive to URI because they are sorely needed to fill out the student body. Students who graduate in the top 10 percent of their class are good scholarship bets.

FINANCIAL AID

Students should submit: FAFSA (due March 1), the school's own financial aid form (due March 1). The Princeton Review suggests that all financial aid forms be submitted as soon as possible after January 1. *The following grants/scholarships are offered:* Pell, SEOG, academic merit, athletic, the school's own scholarships, the school's own grants, state scholarships, state grants, private scholarships, private grants, federal nursing scholarship, ROTC, foreign aid. *Students borrow from the following loan programs:* Perkins, PLUS, the school's own loan fund, supplemental loans, state loans, federal nursing loans, health professions loans, private loans. Applicants will be notified of awards beginning rolling. College Work-Study Program is available. Institutional employment is available.

FROM THE ADMISSIONS OFFICE

"Like the permanent granite cornerstones that grace its stately buildings, the University of Rhode Island was founded in the lasting tradition of the land-grant colleges and later became one of the original crop of national sea-grant colleges. Observing its centennial in 1992, the state's largest university prepares its students to meet the challenges of the twenty-first century."

ADMISSIONS

Admissions Rating	68
% of applicants accepted	78
% of acceptees attending	29

FRESHMAN PROFILE

Average verbal SAT	540
Average math SAT	540
Average ACT	23
Average TOEFL	550
Graduated top 20% of class	38
Graduated top 40% of class	67
Graduated top 60% of class	94
Average HS GPA or Avg.	3.0

DEADLINES

Early decision	12/15
Regular admission	3/1
Regular notification	rolling
Non-fall registration	yes

APPLICANTS ALSO LOOK AT

AND OFTEN PREFER

U. Mass.—Amherst
U. Conn

AND SOMETIMES PREFER

Boston U.
U. Delaware
U. Vermont
U. New Hampshire

AND RARELY PREFER

Providence
U. Maine—Orono

FINANCIAL FACTS

Financial Aid Rating	77
In-state tuition	$3,154
Out-of-state tuition	$10,846
Room & board	$5,564
Estimated book expense	$600
% frosh receiving aid	72
% undergrads receiving aid	65
% aid is need-based	87
% frosh w/ grant (avg)	NR ($2,000)
% frosh w/ loan (avg)	72 ($3,400)
% UGs w/ job (avg)	46 ($1,300)
Off-campus job outlook	good

RHODES COLLEGE

2000 NORTH PARKWAY, MEMPHIS, TN 38112-1690   ADMISSIONS: 901-726-3700   FAX: 901-726-3718

STUDENTS SPEAK OUT

Life

Most Rhodes College students agree that the strong sense of community (a word we saw over and over in our surveys) is integral to life at Rhodes. People here are filled with "southern hospitality; there is a warm smile on every face you encounter." The campus is "incredibly gorgeous" by all accounts, and students consider the surrounding city of Memphis "a perfect blend between a small-town community and a big metropolis." Greeks dominate the social scene, claiming over half the students as members, but are not the only options. "There are plenty of opportunities to get involved elsewhere." Student life has been dramatically affected by what students perceive as an "overly restrictive" alcohol policy; many contended the new restrictions "have seriously damaged the social scene at Rhodes. Parties are 'closed' and taken off campus, although there is a 'care cab' service, some students fear alcohol policy violations and risk accidents instead of fines." In the end, though, students seem happy with their academic/social mix: "The best thing about school life is that such a high percentage of people hang out on campus. This leads to lots of intellectual discussions and 'creative' activities."

Academics

Like Tulane University in Louisiana, Rhodes College offers its students the best of many worlds: a highly touted academic program, a beautiful campus, and accessibility to a major metropolis. Rhodes students enjoy one benefit their counterparts in New Orleans don't: tremendous intimacy. With over 1,400 undergraduates, Rhodes is only one fourth Tulane's size (and, unlike Tulane, has no graduate students). Its academic offerings, both in preprofessional and liberal arts fields, are considered "superior." Probably Rhodes's finest asset is its excellent, highly committed faculty. As one satisfied student reports, "Professors are always available and very challenging. Teaching is their main objective, and personal relationships easily develop between profs and students." Another concurs: "Professors keep their doors open while they are in their offices, and encourage students to stop by and discuss reading material, debate current events, or just chat." The administration also wins praise for being "open to students' ideas. If you have the initiative, anything can be done." Most respondents agreed that "the school's administration always hears what students need, if not always what they want." The honor code is widely respected: tests are not proctored, yet "cheating incidents are rare," according to students, and those that occur are handled by a student-run honor council. For most students, Rhodes's big attraction is its reputation with graduate schools: the school claims its students' acceptance rate in such programs is over 90 percent.

Student Body

One Rhodes undergrad sums up: "Rhodes is pretty conservative, but the student body is intelligent and open to new ideas." There isn't a lot of ethnic diversity here—the minority population is small, but students asserted that "race relations are good," such as they are. Students come from forty-two states and eighteen foreign countries, but the predominant feel in the student body is definitely southern and definitely wealthy.

FINANCIAL AID: 901-726-3810   E-MAIL: ADMINFO@RHODES.EDU   WEB SITE: HTTP://WWW.RHODES.EDU/

ADMISSIONS

The admissions committee considers (in descending order of importance): HS record, class rank, test scores, recommendations, essay. *Also considered (in descending order of importance):* personality, alumni relationship, extracurriculars, geographical distribution, special talents. Either the SAT or ACT is required. An interview is recommended. Admissions process is need-blind. *High school units required/recommended:* 16 total units are required; 4 English required, 3 math required, 2 science required, 2 foreign language required, 2 social studies required. Minor program deviations may be accepted from applicants of superior ability. TOEFL is required of all international students. *The admissions office says:* "Our admissions counseling staff travels and reads by territory with individual attention given to each and every application."

The Inside Word

Rhodes is one of the best kept secrets in higher education, familiar mainly to those in the Southeast but beginning to develop more national recognition. Its student body is very impressive academically. Only the college's upper-echelon competition—the best universities in the South—prevents the admissions committee from being even more selective. Even so, candidates should be prepared for a thorough review of their academic qualifications and the match they make with Rhodes.

FINANCIAL AID

Students should submit: FAFSA (due March 1), the school's own financial aid form (due March 1), state aid form (due March 1). The Princeton Review suggests that all financial aid forms be submitted as soon as possible after January 1. *The following grants/scholarships are offered:* Pell, SEOG, academic merit, the school's own scholarships, the school's own grants, state scholarships, state grants, private scholarships, private grants, ROTC, foreign aid. *Students borrow from the following loan programs:* Stafford, unsubsidized Stafford, Perkins, PLUS, the school's own loan fund, state loans, private loans. Applicants will be notified of awards beginning April 1. College Work-Study Program is available. Institutional employment is available.

FROM THE ADMISSIONS OFFICE

"It's not just one characteristic that makes Rhodes different from other colleges, it's a special blend of features that sets us apart. We are a selective liberal arts college, yet without a cutthroat atmosphere; we are a small community, yet located in a major city; we are in a metropolitan area, yet offer one of the most beautiful and serene campuses in the nation. Our students are serious about learning and yet know how to have fun...in an atmosphere of trust and respect brought about by adherence to the honor code. And they know that learning at Rhodes doesn't mean sitting in a lecture hall and memorizing the professor's lecture. It means interaction, discussion, and a process of teacher and student discovering knowledge together. Rhodes is a place that welcomes new people and new ideas. It's a place of energy and light, not of apathy and complacency. Everyone who is a part of the Rhodes community is striving to be the best at what she/he does."

ADMISSIONS

Admissions Rating	81
% of applicants accepted	70
% of acceptees attending	24

FRESHMAN PROFILE

Average verbal SAT	650
Average math SAT	610
Average ACT	28
Average TOEFL	550
Graduated top 20% of class	74
Graduated top 40% of class	96
Graduated top 60% of class	98
Average HS GPA or Avg.	3.5

DEADLINES

Early decision	11/15
Regular admission	2/1
Regular notification	4/1
Non-fall registration	yes

APPLICANTS ALSO LOOK AT

AND OFTEN PREFER

Duke
Davidson
U. of the South

AND SOMETIMES PREFER

Wake Forest
U. Tennessee—Knoxville
Emory
Wesleyan Coll.
Vanderbilt

AND RARELY PREFER

Centre
Randolph-Macon Woman's

FINANCIAL FACTS

Financial Aid Rating	93
Tuition	$15,762
Room & board	$4,912
Estimated book expense	$600
% frosh receiving aid	76
% undergrads receiving aid	74
% aid is need-based	60
% frosh w/ grant (avg)	71 ($8,590)
% frosh w/ loan (avg)	58 ($3,172)
% UGs w/ job (avg)	30 ($1,068)
Off-campus job outlook	good

RICE UNIVERSITY

OFFICE OF ADMISSIONS, P.O. BOX 1892, HOUSTON, TX 77251   ADMISSIONS: 800-5276957   FAX: 713-523-4117

CAMPUS LIFE

Quality of Life Rating **85**
Type of school   private
Affiliation   none
Environment   metropolis

STUDENTS

FT undergrad enrollment	2,674
% male/female	59/41
% from out of state	53
% live on campus	70
% spend weekend on campus	70
% transfers	5
% from public high school	90
% African-American	5
% Asian	13
% Caucasian	69
% Hispanic	8
% international	NR
# of countries represented	9

WHAT'S HOT
intramural sports
registration is a breeze
school runs like butter
beer
computer facilities

WHAT'S NOT
Greeks
infrequent dating
cigarettes
drugs
campus food

ACADEMICS

Academic Rating	**95**
Profs Interesting Rating	76
Profs Accessible Rating	83
Calendar	semester
Student/teacher ratio	9:1
% profs PhD/tenured	95/100
Hours of study per day	3.52

MOST POPULAR MAJORS
political science
English
engineering

% GRADS WHO PURSUE...
Law 10, Med 8, MBA 3, MA 26

STUDENTS SPEAK OUT

Life

What is it about Rice that makes students want to strip and run naked in the streets? A strange club called Baker 13 promotes such behavior, but there must be something else going on to account for the number of students who cite public nudity as a popular pastime. Whatever the case may be, Rice undergrads have plenty of fully-clothed fun as well. "There is always something to do on campus," explains one. Another concurs, "I feel I have plenty of options for activities outside of class, like clubs, parties, dances, etc." Another trumpets Houston's attractions, "If you want to do something/anything, you can find it in Houston." Rice has no Greek system, but beer is still a big part of life, and definitely the drug of choice (few smoke pot, and stronger drugs are almost nonexistent on the Rice campus). Dorms are comfortable, though the food is barely edible. A sophomore studying sports medicine sums up the Rice lifestyle, "Study, study, party, party, party, cram, pull an all-nighter, party." He forgot to mention running around naked, though.

Academics

Known as the "Ivy of the South," Rice has a varied and challenging academic program without some of the intense competition that often accompanies such stature. The professors "make it clear that a university is a place to learn from one another [rather than being] a place to compete with one another," says one satisfied Owl. "Work is taken very, very seriously," adds another. Most students study 4 to 5 hours a day. Getting the classes you want is easy for freshman and seniors alike. Lectures are small and few classes are taught by TAs. The science and engineering departments are still stronger than Rice's liberal arts offerings, but the gap is quickly closing. Says one student, "Rice offers both strong science and humanities courses for a good, well-rounded education." Profs are respected and accessible, "You can take a test in the morning and then eat lunch with the professor afterwards," explains a junior studying biology. An honor code, lenient alcohol policy, and coed housing all reflect the administration's reliance on the personal responsibility of each student, and Rice undergrads appreciate that trust. Says one, "the best thing about Rice is being able to find yourself socially without compromising yourself intellectually."

Student Body

"Everyone is really nice, which especially helps during orientation. Cliques are very rare, so it is very likely that you will get to know just about everyone else in your class." Comments like this typify Rice undergrads' love affair with each other: "Diverse and accepting as a whole...people rarely exclude someone like they do in high school," explains a sophomore studying music. Adds a math major, "The students here are intelligent, articulate, and approachable." With such a caring, diverse student body, we have to wonder why dating is such an anathema on the Rice campus. Explains one student, "For fun we don't date and laugh at people who do." Hmm. The fact that men outnumber women may have something to do with it; in any case, the lack of dating is never cited as a problem. Regardless, discrimination is not much of a factor on the Rice campus, and people of different skin colors even interact to a decent extent.

FINANCIAL AID: 713-527-4958

ADMISSIONS

The admissions committee considers (in descending order of importance): HS record, test scores, recommendations, essay, class rank. *Also considered (in descending order of importance):* extracurriculars, personality, special talents, alumni relationship, geographical distribution. An interview is recommended. *High school units required/recommended:* 16 total units are required; 4 English required, 3 math required, 2 science required, 2 foreign language required, 2 social studies required. *Special Requirements:* TOEFL is required of all international students. Chemistry, physics, trigonometry, and further advanced mathematics required of engineering and science program applicants. Audition and theory test required of music program applicants. Portfolio strongly recommended of architecture program applicants. *The admissions office says:* "Admissions committee decisions are based not only on high school grades and test scores but also on such qualities as leadership, participation in extracurricular activities, and personal creativity. Admissions are extremely competitive; the school attempt[s] to seek out and identify those students who have demonstrated exceptional ability and the potential for personal and intellectual growth." Applicants are required to take the SAT I and three SAT II Subject Tests (different programs require different scores; contact the school for details).

The Inside Word

Rice has gotten loads of positive publicity over the past few years. As a result, what was already an extremely selective university is even more so. Candidates with less than the most impressive applications are not likely to last long in the admissions process.

FINANCIAL AID

Students should submit: FAFSA, the school's own financial aid form, a copy of parents' most recent income tax filing. The Princeton Review suggests that all financial aid forms be submitted as soon as possible after January 1. *The following grants/scholarships are offered:* Pell, SEOG, academic merit, athletic, the school's own scholarships, the school's own grants, state scholarships, state grants, private scholarships, private grants, ROTC. *Students borrow from the following loan programs:* Stafford, unsubsidized Stafford, Perkins, PLUS, the school's own loan fund, state loans, private loans. Applicants will be notified of awards beginning April 15. College Work-Study Program is available. Institutional employment is available.

FROM THE ADMISSIONS OFFICE

"Dedicated to 'the advancement of letters, science, and art,' Rice is private, independent, nonsectarian, and coeducational. It includes among its academic divisions both undergraduate and graduate studies in the humanities, social sciences, natural sciences, engineering, architecture, administrative sciences, and music. Highly talented students with diverse interests are attracted to Rice by the opportunities for creative learning. They find rewarding student/faculty relationships, options for individually tailored programs of study, opportunities for research, cooperative activities with other institutions in the nation's fourth largest city, and the unique experience of residential colleges."

ADMISSIONS

Admissions Rating	99
% of applicants accepted	19
% of acceptees attending	42

FRESHMAN PROFILE

Average verbal SAT	710
Average math SAT	700
Average ACT	NR
Average TOEFL	NR
Graduated top 20% of class	96
Graduated top 40% of class	99
Graduated top 60% of class	NR
Average HS GPA or Avg.	NR

DEADLINES

Early decision	NR
Regular admission	1/2
Regular notification	4/1
Non-fall registration	no

APPLICANTS ALSO LOOK AT

AND OFTEN PREFER

Harvard/Radcliffe
Stanford
Virginia
Princeton

AND SOMETIMES PREFER

Columbia
Duke

AND RARELY PREFER

Emory
U. Texas—Austin

FINANCIAL FACTS

Financial Aid Rating	90
Tuition	$11,650
Room & board	$5,900
Estimated book expense	$525
% frosh receiving aid	86
% undergrads receiving aid	84
% aid is need-based	45
% frosh w/ grant (avg)	92 ($7,376)
% frosh w/ loan (avg)	39 ($2,822)
% UGs w/ job (avg)	60 ($1,500)
Off-campus job outlook	excellent

UNIVERSITY OF RICHMOND

RICHMOND, VA 23173

ADMISSIONS: 804-289-8640   FAX: 804-287-6003

CAMPUS LIFE

Quality of Life Rating   **93**
Type of school   private
Affiliation   Baptist General
                               Association of Virginia
Environment   city

STUDENTS
FT undergrad enrollment   2,872
% male/female   51/49
% from out of state   82
% live on campus   94
% spend weekend on campus   90
% transfers   4
% from public high school   73
% in (# of) fraternities   51 (11)
% in (# of) sororities   61 (8)
% African-American   5
% Asian   3
% Caucasian   90
% Hispanic   2
% international   3
# of countries represented   42

WHAT'S HOT
campus food
off-campus food
intramural sports
student government
Greeks

WHAT'S NOT
lack of diversity on campus
students are cliquish
infrequent dating
sex
drugs

ACADEMICS

Academic Rating   **90**
Profs Interesting Rating   90
Profs Accessible Rating   95
Calendar   semester
Student/teacher ratio   11:1
% profs PhD/tenured   96/95
Hours of study per day   2.98

MOST POPULAR MAJORS
business
biology
political science

% GRADS WHO PURSUE...
Law 7, Med 5, MBA 2, MA 14

STUDENTS SPEAK OUT

Life
Richmond has a "country club" campus, and although it's plain that the university has many attractive features, the physical beauty is a magnet. "You would never know from being on campus that you were in a city, yet fifteen minutes down the road is downtown Richmond." Smack in the middle is a large man-made lake that separates the men's college from the women's. Says one student, "The lake in the middle of campus does a whole lot more than provide scenery." Indeed: The lake bears imposing physical testimony to what many think is Richmond's greatest shortcoming: the "co-ordinate system" (the school's name for its separation of undergraduates into single-sex colleges). Although men and women attend classes together, "relationships between men and women are limited. This is obvious in classrooms and the dining hall, where the majority of men and women sit at separate tables." The Greeks play a major role in the school's social life. For a woman to attend a frat party, she must make sure her name has been included on a guest list drawn up in advance. "It's a big hassle," writes one woman. For non-Greeks, "there are options if you have a car and money to burn." These options include the mountains, the beach, downtown Richmond, and Washington, D.C. There are on-campus options as well. Writes one student, "There's something to do every night on campus. The university provides a lot of activities for free: movies, concerts, food, etc." In all, satisfaction runs quite high; one student exclaims, "This is the perfect school!"

Academics
The undergraduate division of the University of Richmond is divided into three co-educational schools: the School of Arts and Sciences, the School of Business, and the School of Leadership Studies. In addition, students are members of a residential college: Richmond College (for men) and Westhampton College (for women). Business and biology are the most popular majors, although political science, English, international studies, and psychology are among the other popular departments. Academics are challenging, and many students praise the faculty and administration in their survey responses. "Professors treat us like peers and friends. They're always available. This attitude seems to be instilled by the university—even in visiting professors." Most agree that the motivated student will find plenty to keep him busy. Other assets: professors are very helpful ("most teachers give out their home phone numbers, and all my professors know my name"); classes are small and are never taught by TAs.

Student Body
Students readily admit that the UR student body is homogeneous. Says one, "I like my fellow students; they are all like me." But another describes her fellow students as "diverse in attitudes, opinions. Intelligent, active, extremely involved in community service." "Those who don't fit the mold," writes another, "may find it hard to fit in." Despite these divergent views, "everyone seems to get along fine—we are very happy here!" Students are politically conservative and report that there is a healthy interest in religion on campus. They also spend a far-above-average amount of time volunteering for a variety of charitable and educational organizations. The experience here seems to be contagious; in the words of a survey respondent, "One of the things that is seldom mentioned, but plays a huge role in each student's happiness, is that...complete strangers will smile and say 'hello' before you get a chance to do the same."

FINANCIAL AID: 804-289-8438

ADMISSIONS

The admissions committee considers (in descending order of importance): HS record, class rank, test scores, recommendations, essay. *Also considered (in descending order of importance):* special talents, extracurriculars, alumni relationship, geographical distribution. Either the SAT or ACT is required. Admissions process is need-blind. *High school units required/recommended:* 16 total units are required; 4 English required, 3 math required, 4 math recommended, 1 science required, 4 science recommended, 2 foreign language required, 4 foreign language recommended, 1 history required, 4 history recommended. *Special Requirements:* An audition is required for music program applicants. TOEFL is required of all international students. Audition and theory placement tests required of music scholarship applicants. Audition required of theatre scholarship applicants. *The admissions office says:* "Fifty percent of the decision is based on the applicant's high school record, 30 percent on two required SAT II Subject Tests (Writing, Math I or IIC), and 20 percent on the SAT I. Essays, recommendations, and activities are tie-breakers. These figures are guidelines; no formula is used."

The Inside Word

There may not be an admissions formula, but Richmond is very precise about just how much each of the major admissions criteria counts toward a decision. Two SAT II Subject Tests are an important application requirement; we'd advise candidates to prepare thoroughly, since they outweigh the SAT I. When used with a measure of flexibility and a willingness to consider other factors, as Richmond does, there is nothing inherently wrong with such an approach. There does appear to be an effort to look at the candidate's record carefully and thoroughly. Make no mistake: course of study, high-school performance, and test scores are the most important parts of your application, but Richmond also makes sure that all files are read at least three times before a final decision has been rendered.

FINANCIAL AID

Students should submit: FAFSA (due February 25), the school's own financial aid form (due February 25), state aid form (due July 31). The Princeton Review suggests that all financial aid forms be submitted as soon as possible after January 1. *The following grants/scholarships are offered:* Pell, SEOG, academic merit, athletic, the school's own scholarships, the school's own grants, state scholarships, state grants, private scholarships, private grants, ROTC, foreign aid. *Students borrow from the following loan programs:* Stafford, unsubsidized Stafford, Perkins, PLUS, private loans. Applicants will be notified of awards beginning April 1. College Work-Study Program is available. Institutional employment is available.

FROM THE ADMISSIONS OFFICE

"The University of Richmond combines the characteristics of a small college with the range and diversity of a major university. Small class size and close interaction with professors give each student a personal angle in the learning process. At the same time, the university offers a wide range of academic opportunities through internships, study abroad, and undergraduate research, in over forty-four majors in the Arts and Sciences, Business, and Leadership Studies. The university's unique coordinate colleges provide a single-gender residential system within the framework of a fully coeducational academic program."

ADMISSIONS

Admissions Rating	90
% of applicants accepted	53
% of acceptees attending	29

FRESHMAN PROFILE

Average verbal SAT	630
Average math SAT	640
Average ACT	28
Average TOEFL	550
Graduated top 20% of class	77
Graduated top 40% of class	98
Graduated top 60% of class	100
Average HS GPA or Avg.	3.0

DEADLINES

Early decision	1/15
Regular admission	2/1
Regular notification	4/1
Non-fall registration	no

APPLICANTS ALSO LOOK AT

AND OFTEN PREFER

William and Mary
Virginia
UNC—Chapel Hill
Duke

AND SOMETIMES PREFER

Wake Forest
James Madison
Tulane
Vanderbilt
Washington and Lee

AND RARELY PREFER

Lafayette
Lehigh

FINANCIAL FACTS

Financial Aid Rating	80
Tuition	$16,570
Room & board	$3,595
Estimated book expense	$600
% frosh receiving aid	60
% undergrads receiving aid	60
% aid is need-based	38
% frosh w/ grant (avg)	55 ($8,500)
% frosh w/ loan (avg)	34 ($5,600)
% UGs w/ job (avg)	25 ($850)
Off-campus job outlook	good

RIPON COLLEGE

P.O. Box 248, 300 Seward Street, Ripon, WI 54971   Admissions: 800-947-4766   Fax: 414-748-7243

CAMPUS LIFE

Quality of Life Rating   **74**
Type of school   private
Affiliation   none
Environment   town

STUDENTS
FT undergrad enrollment   731
% male/female   43/57
% from out of state   45
% live on campus   91
% spend weekend on campus   93
% transfers   9
% from public high school   60
% in (# of) fraternities   45 (5)
% in (# of) sororities   33 (3)
% African-American   1
% Asian   2
% Caucasian   91
% Hispanic   2
% international   3
# of countries represented   17

WHAT'S HOT
hard liquor
college radio
intramural sports
beer
registration is a breeze

WHAT'S NOT
political activism
student publications
computer facilities
lack of diversity on campus
health facilities

ACADEMICS

Academic Rating   **84**
Profs Interesting Rating   87
Profs Accessible Rating   90
Calendar   semester
Student/teacher ratio   10:1
% profs PhD   91
Hours of study per day   3.22

MOST POPULAR MAJORS
history
economics
politics/government

% GRADS WHO PURSUE...
Law 5, Med 14, MBA 2, MA 22

STUDENTS SPEAK OUT
Life
"Life" at Ripon means many different things to many different people. One student explains this diversity by writing, "Depending on which clique or Greek organization you're in, comments made range from the new J. Crew catalog to how many hits of acid you've taken in the past week." Students have fun at Ripon, and much of it is a reaction to the hard work they undertake as students. "Life is generally a get-by situation," writes one overworked junior. Another student notes that "[Ripon] is a very athletically active school. If one is not participating in a sport they are spectating." Of course, Wisconsin winters curtail some of that fun. As a sophomore comments, "Life here is somewhat confined as campus is rather small; we have somewhat of a rural location and social activity is limited on the weekends, but we all manage to have our fun, especially when it snows." Frat life rules at Ripon. Forty-five percent of the men are involved in it and 35 percent of the women. One junior frat guy writes "The fraternities on campus is the life on campus. Socially, that's it." Springfest Weekend is especially noted as the fun time on campus to visit.

Academics
Ripon students get personal attention and individual care from their professors. One student notes that "I can only marvel at the excellent facilities on campus, the academic excellence of the professors and the friendliness of all the students." What else would you expect from the university that graduated Harrison Ford and Spencer Tracy? Ripon is a small school which offers majors in twenty-nine different subjects. The most popular majors are economics and biology. Study abroad is available in twenty-two different locations. The biggest attraction, however, remains the personal relationship between faculty and students. One junior writes that Ripon has "excellent professors, easily accessible and willing to help in any way." Students work hard at Ripon, and sometimes it takes its toll. One junior comments that "There's too much work to do. You have to attend all lectures and get stacks of homework, which is no fun." Ripon also offers an Educational Development Program free of charge to physically impaired and learning disabled students, which includes tutoring in subject areas, skill development workshops, and personal advisement. Some students found this program less than successful: one student complains that "The Educational Development program does not help at ALL." Also the administration, gets less- than-perfect marks.

Student Body
Ripon attracts a fairly homogeneous student body. Although Ripon students come from a variety of geographical regions, the standard profile seems to be white and upper-middle class. Ninety-one percent of the student body is white. One student notices this and comments "The students at this college have a very difficult time accepting those who do not portray a traditional upper-middle- class image." Another writes: "Ripon College is very accepting of white heterosexuals. If you aren't in that category, you will have a rough time adjusting." The student body is fairly conservative, politically and socially.

ADMISSIONS

The admissions committee considers (in descending order of importance): HS record, class rank, test scores, recommendations, essay. *Also considered (in descending order of importance):* extracurriculars, geographical distribution, personality, alumni relationship, special talents. Either the SAT or ACT is required. An interview is required of some applicants. Admissions process is need-blind. *High school units required/recommended:* 17 total units are required; 4 English required, 2 math required, 4 math recommended, 2 science required, 4 science recommended, 2 foreign language recommended, 2 social studies required, 4 social studies recommended, 2 history recommended. Rank in top quarter of secondary school class recommended. TOEFL is required of all international students.

The Inside Word

Candidates for admission to Ripon should prepare their applications with the knowledge that they will be subjected to a very thorough and demanding review. Even though the college faces formidable competition from other top midwestern liberal arts colleges and highly selective universities, the admissions staff succeeds at enrolling a very impressive freshman class each year. That doesn't happen without careful matchmaking and a lot of personal attention.

FINANCIAL AID

Students should submit: FAFSA (due April 1), a copy of parents' most recent income tax filing. The Princeton Review suggests that all financial aid forms be submitted as soon as possible after January 1. *The following grants/scholarships are offered:* Pell, SEOG, academic merit, the school's own scholarships, the school's own grants, state scholarships, state grants, private scholarships, private grants, ROTC, foreign aid. *Students borrow from the following loan programs:* Stafford, unsubsidized Stafford, Perkins, PLUS. College Work-Study Program is available. Institutional employment is available.

FROM THE ADMISSIONS OFFICE

"Since its founding in 1851, Ripon College has adhered to the philosophy that the liberal arts offer the richest foundation for intellectual, cultural, social, and spiritual growth. Academic strength is a 140-year tradition at Ripon. We attract excellent professors who are dedicated to their disciplines; they in turn attract bright, committed students from forty states and nineteen countries. Ripon has a national reputation for academic excellence as well a friendly, relaxed atmosphere, small class size, and the availability of outstanding facilities. Ripon is also a community. Not only do you see your professors in the classroom, but you can relate to them in a variety of other social situations. "Ripon offers a rigorous curriculum in twenty-nine major areas, including unique preprofessional programs. There is also ample opportunity for co-curricular involvement."

ADMISSIONS

Admissions Rating	73
% of applicants accepted	83
% of acceptees attending	39

FRESHMAN PROFILE

Average verbal SAT	620
Average math SAT	590
Average ACT	24
Average TOEFL	NR
Graduated top 20% of class	58
Graduated top 40% of class	85
Graduated top 60% of class	96
Average HS GPA or Avg.	3.2

DEADLINES

Early decision	12/1
Regular admission	3/15
Regular notification	rolling
Non-fall registration	yes

APPLICANTS ALSO LOOK AT

AND SOMETIMES PREFER

Lawrence
U. Wisconsin-Madison
Beloit

AND RARELY PREFER

U. Wisconsin-Stevens Point
U. Wisconsin-Whitewater

FINANCIAL FACTS

Financial Aid Rating	97
Tuition	$16,780
Room & board	$4,400
Estimated book expense	$350
% frosh receiving aid	85
% undergrads receiving aid	80
% aid is need-based	85
% frosh w/ grant (avg)	95 ($10,477)
% frosh w/ loan (avg)	66 ($3,568)
% UGs w/ job (avg)	45 ($1,080)
Off-campus job outlook	good

ROCHESTER INSTITUTE OF TECHNOLOGY

ONE LOMB MEMORIAL DRIVE, ROCHESTER, NY 14623   ADMISSIONS: 716-475-6631   FAX: 716-475-7424

CAMPUS LIFE

Quality of Life Rating	76
Type of school	private
Affiliation	none
Environment	suburban

STUDENTS

FT undergrad enrollment	7,899
% male/female	68/32
% from out of state	35
% live on campus	70
% spend weekend on campus	90
% transfers	38
% from public high school	85
% in (# of) fraternities	10 (15)
% in (# of) sororities	10 (9)
% African-American	5
% Asian	5
% Caucasian	81
% Hispanic	3
% international	4
# of countries represented	84

WHAT'S HOT
computer facilities
health facilities
lab facilities
campus food
library

WHAT'S NOT
theater
political activism
unattractive campus
music associations
student government

ACADEMICS

Academic Rating	74
Profs Interesting Rating	70
Profs Accessible Rating	70
Calendar	quarter
Student/teacher ratio	12:1
% profs PhD/tenured	70/76
Hours of study per day	2.92

MOST POPULAR MAJORS
business administration
engineering technology
engineering

STUDENTS SPEAK OUT

Life

As one undergrad puts it, "Come to RIT for the education, not for the social life." Several factors conspire to make social life less than ideal at the school. The male/ female ratio is a concern for some folks; there's location (even though the school is located in a small city, students are "very much detached from the mainstream local and downtown social scenes"); and there's the weather. "The weather here is not for wimps!" exclaims one student; says another, referring to frequently windy conditions, "Art students beware! Your portfolio will magically transform into a kite as you walk across campus." Campus decor can be summed up in one word: brick. "This school looks like one extensive sidewalk to the Wizard of Oz," writes one student; another offered this insight: "Too many bricks and not enough chicks." Students give the food above average marks.

Academics

Looking for a demanding arts and technology school, one that has valuable relation-ships with major industries, state-of-the-art facilities, and an intense (but not cut-throat) student body? If you can stand cold weather, Rochester Institute of Technology just might be the place. Computer science, electrical engineering, photography, and business and management are among the most popular majors here; the biology and chemistry departments also received students' praise. The photography department is nationally respected and boasts outstanding facilities. Facilities for the hearing im-paired are also reportedly among the best in the country. Located in the hometown of Xerox, Kodak, and Bausch & Lomb, RIT provides its career-minded students with plenty of opportunities for internships. The pressure to succeed is great here: writes one student, "Classes are difficult and require a lot of work. But if you are determined and have the will, you can succeed. The school is very prestigious and graduates are in demand." The pressure is intensified by a quarterly academic schedule, which causes courses to fly by. "It's impossible to get ahead of your work," writes one stu-dent, "the trick is not to fall too far behind." Professors receive below average grades from students. A civil engineer reports that "the professors have great knowledge about the subjects but have trouble conveying their ideas to students."

Student Body

Although almost one fourth of the RIT student body is made up of minorities, each of the minority populations is, in itself, relatively small. Almost two-thirds of the stu-dents are from New York State, and most of the rest are from neighboring states. They are a serious, studious, apolitical lot. Among the student bodies profiled in this book, they are among the bottom ten percent in terms of their overall happiness.

FINANCIAL AID: 716-475-2186   E-MAIL: ADMISSIONS@RIT.EDU   WEB SITE: HTTP://WWW.RIT.EDU/

ADMISSIONS

The admissions committee considers (in descending order of importance): HS record, test scores, class rank, essay, recommendations. *Also considered (in descending order of importance):* alumni relationship, extracurriculars, geographical distribution, personality, special talents. Either the SAT or ACT is required. An interview is required of some applicants. Admissions process is need-blind. *High school units required/recommended:* 16 total units are recommended; 4 English recommended, 3 math recommended, 3 science recommended, 4 social studies recommended. *Special Requirements:* A portfolio is required for art program applicants. Early application and supplementary information required of applicants to physician assistant program.

The Inside Word

RIT is not as competitive as the top tier of technical schools, but its location and contacts with major research corporations make it a top choice for many students. The acceptance rate is deceptively high when considered in conjunction with the student academic profile and the high yield of admitted students who enroll. There is a strong element of self-selection at work in the applicant pool; the successful candidate is one who is solid academically and ready to hit the ground running.

FINANCIAL AID

Students should submit: FAFSA (due March 15), state aid form (due March 15), a copy of parents' most recent income tax filing (due March 15). The Princeton Review suggests that all financial aid forms be submitted as soon as possible after January 1. *The following grants/scholarships are offered:* Pell, SEOG, academic merit, the school's own scholarships, the school's own grants, state scholarships, state grants, private scholarships, private grants, ROTC, foreign aid. *Students borrow from the following loan programs:* Stafford, unsubsidized Stafford, Perkins, PLUS, supplemental loans, state loans, private loans. College Work-Study Program is available. Institutional employment is available.

FROM THE ADMISSIONS OFFICE

"A nationally respected leader in professional and career-oriented education, RIT has been described as one of America's most imitated institutions and has been recognized as one of the nation's leading universities. RIT has also been rated the number one comprehensive university in the East for its scientific and technology programs. RIT's strength lies in its dedication to providing superior career preparation for today's students. This has attracted excellent faculty to RIT and has led to the development of academic programs that combine small classes and an emphasis on undergraduate teaching, modern classroom facilities, and work experience gained through the university's cooperative education program. Few universities provide RIT's variety of career-oriented services. Our eight colleges offer outstanding programs in business, engineering, art and design, science and mathematics, liberal arts, photography, hotel management, computer science, and other areas."

ADMISSIONS

Admissions Rating	75
% of applicants accepted	76
% of acceptees attending	38

FRESHMAN PROFILE

Average verbal SAT	570
Average math SAT	590
Average ACT	25
Average TOEFL	525
Graduated top 20% of class	50
Graduated top 40% of class	79
Graduated top 60% of class	91
Average HS GPA or Avg.	3.7

DEADLINES

Early decision	NR
Regular admission	8/1
Regular notification	Rolling
Non-fall registration	yes

APPLICANTS ALSO LOOK AT

AND OFTEN PREFER
Cornell U.
RPI

AND SOMETIMES PREFER
SUNY Binghamton
SUNY Buffalo
Clarkson U.
Carnegie Mellon
U. Rochester

AND RARELY PREFER
SUNY Albany
Drexel
Syracuse
Boston U.
Northeastern

FINANCIAL FACTS

Financial Aid Rating	82
Tuition	$14,670
Room & board	$5,898
Estimated book expense	$625
% frosh receiving aid	85
% undergrads receiving aid	70
% aid is need-based	90
% frosh w/ grant (avg)	85 ($8,500)
% frosh w/ loan (avg)	80 ($3,700)
% UGs w/ job (avg)	45 ($1,800)
Off-campus job outlook	excellent

UNIVERSITY OF ROCHESTER

WILSON BOULEVARD, ROCHESTER, NY 14627

ADMISSIONS: 716-275-3221   FAX: 716-275-0359

CAMPUS LIFE

Quality of Life Rating 81
Type of school   private
Affiliation   none
Environment   city

STUDENTS
FT undergrad enrollment	5,020
% male/female	52/48
% from out of state	50
% live on campus	82
% spend weekend on campus	90
% transfers	15
% from public high school	NR
% in (# of) fraternities	18 (14)
% in (# of) sororities	13 (9)
% African-American	8
% Asian	10
% Caucasian	70
% Hispanic	4
% international	8
# of countries represented	40

WHAT'S HOT
library
music associations
computer facilities
dorms
beer

WHAT'S NOT
political activism
intercollegiate sports
students are cliquish
town-gown relations
cigarettes

ACADEMICS

Academic Rating 80
Profs Interesting Rating	77
Profs Accessible Rating	68
Calendar	semester
Student/teacher ratio	12:1
% profs PhD	99
Hours of study per day	3.20

MOST POPULAR MAJORS
psychology
political science
biology

% GRADS WHO PURSUE...
Law 5, Med 6, MBA 11, MA 50

STUDENTS SPEAK OUT

Life
Cold weather is a given in Rochester: "Siberia for eight months of the year" is a popular description among students we surveyed. It is actually possible to avoid a great deal of winter misery because of the convenient sets of indoor tunnels beneath the campus. Nevertheless, the consensus seems to be that of one student who notes "I just wish we could take the whole school and place it in California or somewhere where there is no snow." Despite the academic pressures at the U of R (or perhaps because of them), weekends are full of partying opportunities. Fraternities and sororities figure prominently in the social scene, and Greek activities dominate. One student observes, "Many people claim to be anti-Greek, but they tend to show up at frat parties anyway." There are varying degrees of social contentment here: some students have "too many parties to choose from," some contend that "freshman males lead lives of quiet desperation," and some prefer to socialize electronically in the generally comfy and spacious dorms.

Academics
The University of Rochester has traditionally been known best for its math and science departments. However, the "home of the Bausch & Lomb scholars, Wilson scholars, and Xerox" has enough diversity in its academic offerings to "dispel the myth that the U of R is solely an engineering/premed breeding ground." Although numerous students consider the workload "heavy and tough - they don't mess around!" most also believe their rigorous courses are "extremely rewarding." Rochester has several unique opportunities to offer its students: one is the world-renowned Eastman School of Music (the administration encourages qualified students to take courses there). Distinct to the U of R is a program called "Take Five," an attractive option for students who find themselves unable to fit enough courses of interest into a four-year schedule. One student writes, "As a chemical engineer, I have very little time to take courses outside my major. The U of R has given me the opportunity to stay here for an additional year—tuition—free—to pursue my interest in Japanese history and culture." While some students claim that certain professors "are more interested in their research than they are in undergrads," in general students here are positive and enthusiastic about their academic life; some consider the U of R "better than the Ivies but without the reputation—it's the jewel of upper New York State."

Student Body
The typical student at the University of Rochester is relatively conservative ("we need more liberals on campus!"), although the majority of students we asked are politically apathetic. A small private school despite its public-sounding name, the U of R has trouble living up to the diversity described in its brochures. "The minority population is sorely lacking both in presence and diversity, especially in the black and Hispanic sectors. After the quotas are met, the administration doesn't seem to put any real effort into finding interesting minority students—in fact, any minority students at all."

FINANCIAL AID: 716-275-3226

ADMISSIONS

The admissions committee considers (in descending order of importance): HS record, recommendations, class rank, test scores, essay. *Also considered (in descending order of importance):* extracurriculars, personality, alumni relationship, geographical distribution, special talents. Either the SAT or ACT is required. An interview is recommended. Admissions process is need-blind. *High school units required/recommended:* 15 total units are recommended; 4 English recommended, 3 math recommended, 2 science recommended, 2 foreign language recommended, 4 social studies recommended. *Special Requirements:* Physics required of physics and physics/astronomy program applicants; recommended of engineering program applicants. Chemistry strongly recommended of biology, chemical engineering, chemistry, and nursing program applicants. Audition required of B.Mus. program applicants; recommended of B.A. music program applicants. *The admissions office says:* "We consider very strongly the demand of course selection. Honors, Regents or Advanced Placement are expected of students in secondary schools offering these programs. [The admission staff prides] itself on the personalization of the [selection] process."

The Inside Word

The University of Rochester is definitely a good school, but the competition takes away three-quarters of the university's admits. Many students use Rochester as a safety; this hinders the university's ability to move up among top national institutions in selectivity. It also makes U of R a very solid choice for above-average students who aren't Ivy material.

FINANCIAL AID

Students should submit: FAFSA (due February 1), CSS Profile, state aid form. The Princeton Review suggests that all financial aid forms be submitted as soon as possible after January 1. *The following grants/scholarships are offered:* Pell, SEOG, academic merit, the school's own scholarships, the school's own grants, state scholarships, state grants, private scholarships, private grants, ROTC, foreign aid. *Students borrow from the following loan programs:* Stafford, unsubsidized Stafford, Perkins, PLUS, the school's own loan fund, federal nursing loans, private loans. Applicants will be notified of awards beginning March 15. College Work-Study Program is available. Institutional employment is available.

FROM THE ADMISSIONS OFFICE

"A campus visit can be one of the most important (and most enjoyable) components of a college search. Visiting Rochester can provide you with the opportunity to experience for yourself the traditions and innovations of our University. Whether you visit a class, tour the campus, or meet with a professor or coach, you'll learn a great deal about the power of a Rochester education—with advantages that begin during your undergraduate years and continue after graduation. No other school combines the wealth of academic programs on the personal scale that the University of Rochester offers. Our students achieve academic excellence in a university setting that encourages frequent, informal contact with distinguished faculty."

ADMISSIONS

Admissions Rating	84
% of applicants accepted	61
% of acceptees attending	22

FRESHMAN PROFILE

Average verbal SAT	620
Average math SAT	630
Average ACT	28
Average TOEFL	NR
Graduated top 20% of class	78
Graduated top 40% of class	94
Graduated top 60% of class	NR
Average HS GPA or Avg.	NR

DEADLINES

Early decision	NR
Regular admission	NR
Regular notification	4/15
Non-fall registration	yes

APPLICANTS ALSO LOOK AT

AND OFTEN PREFER

Cornell U.
Washington U.
SUNY Binghamton
SUNY Buffalo

AND SOMETIMES PREFER

Boston U.
SUNY Albany
U. Vermont
Syracuse
NYU

AND RARELY PREFER

Franklin & Marshall

FINANCIAL FACTS

Financial Aid Rating	81
Tuition	$19,630
Room & board	$6,930
Estimated book expense	$500
% frosh receiving aid	91
% undergrads receiving aid	89
% aid is need-based	89
% frosh w/ grant (avg)	89 ($15,540)
% frosh w/ loan (avg)	75 ($3,600)
% UGs w/ job (avg)	60 ($2,800)
Off-campus job outlook	good

ROLLINS COLLEGE

1000 HOLT AVENUE, WINTER PARK, FL 32789 ADMISSIONS: 407-646-2161 FAX: 407-646-2600

STUDENTS SPEAK OUT

Life

Rollins is located in Winter Park, which "provides a small-town feeling, while Orlando adds big city life. The combination of these two communities makes life at Rollins enjoyable and different from day to day." Another student remarks that "Orlando, with its clubs and Disney provides plenty of entertainment. On campus, we hang out, rent movies, shoot pool, drink, have parties, and do lots of homework." Because of these offerings and because of the excellent weather, students rate Rollins' location very high. Some students note that the school does sponsor activities, but even they concede that "on-campus events are not widely attended," and that "fun is off campus." Such survey sentiments are not rare, despite the fact that the majority of Rollins students stay on campus on weekends. One student who writes that "if you don't have ID, you have no life other than the frats and sororities." Says another, "You have to find your own fun here, and mostly that means leaving campus."

Academics

Rollins College students just glow about their academic experiences. "Academically it has been just about everything I've ever wanted and more. The facilities are beautiful and well maintained and offer tremendous opportunities," gushes one senior. Writes another, "Our administration and faculty are friendly in the truest sense of the word. They always take time to talk with you about things within and without the school. They care about the Rollins community and are obviously proud members of it." Students admire their professors, who "involve all students in discussion. They seem very willing to help us in any way possible. The small classes make it very easy to get one-on-one attention." They also report that "The profs here teach so that you will gain knowledge. What's going to be on the exam is always secondary to that goal." Administrators also receive excellent grades; explains one student, "The administration is very helpful and extremely friendly. That friendliness is partly why I chose this school." As one student sums up: "Rollins is as I always dreamed college would be. My professors even make dinner for our night sessions."

Student Body

Students note a definite division by class among their peers. Writes one, "Money creates social stratifications that make it undesirable for some of the poorer students to feel welcome within many social cliques." Students are further polarized by an "active, exclusionary Greek system." Rollins' minority community is small. Latinos are the best represented minority here.

ADMISSIONS

The admissions committee considers (in descending order of importance): HS record, class rank, test scores, essay, recommendations. *Also considered (in descending order of importance):* extracurriculars, personality, special talents, alumni relationship, geographical distribution. Either the SAT or ACT is required. An interview is recommended. Admissions process is need-blind. *High school units required/recommended:* 4 English required, 3 math required, 2 science required, 2 foreign language required, 3 social studies required. TOEFL is required of all international students.

The Inside Word

It's fairly important to put together a well-rounded candidacy when applying to Rollins. Academic standards are moderate, but the admissions committee puts a great deal of emphasis on the whole package when evaluating candidates. Despite this thorough personal approach, solid numbers will still be enough on their own to get you admitted, provided you don't take the process too lightly.

FINANCIAL AID

Students should submit: FAFSA (due March 1), the school's own financial aid form (due March 1), state aid form. The Princeton Review suggests that all financial aid forms be submitted as soon as possible after January 1. *The following grants/scholarships are offered:* Pell, SEOG, academic merit, athletic, the school's own scholarships, the school's own grants, state scholarships, state grants, private scholarships, private grants. *Students borrow from the following loan programs:* Perkins, the school's own loan fund, supplemental loans, private loans. College Work-Study Program is available. Institutional employment is available.

FROM THE ADMISSIONS OFFICE

"As you begin the college selection process, you should remember that you're in control of your destiny. While the grades you've earned and the scores you've achieved are very important in the college's review of your credentials, places like Rollins pay serious attention to your personal side—your interests, talents, strengths, values, and potential to contribute to college life. Don't sell yourself short in the process. Be proud of what you've accomplished and who you are, and be ready to describe yourself honestly. If you can get an interview at a college, take it. You'll find that we encourage you to talk about yourself and what you do well. If you have a portfolio of your artwork or a scrapbook of your athletic accomplishments, bring it with you. If you play the violin, maybe your interviewer would like to hear you play. Your essay is equally important in describing yourself. Write it in your own voice, and read it aloud when you're finished. It shouldn't sound like an essay, but like a conversation. And most of all, it should be about you! Many colleges appreciate your personal side and look for ways to know you better. Take advantage of that in the college selection process."

ADMISSIONS

Admissions Rating	78
% of applicants accepted	70
% of acceptees attending	33

FRESHMAN PROFILE

Average verbal SAT	600
Average math SAT	570
Average ACT	25
Average TOEFL	550
Graduated top 20% of class	54
Graduated top 40% of class	77
Graduated top 60% of class	92
Average HS GPA or Avg.	3.0

DEADLINES

Early decision	NR
Regular admission	2/15
Regular notification	4/1
Non-fall registration	yes

APPLICANTS ALSO LOOK AT

AND OFTEN PREFER

U. Richmond

AND SOMETIMES PREFER

Emory
Tulane
U. Central Florida
U. Miami

AND RARELY PREFER

Roanoke
U. Florida
Florida State
Stetson
Eckerd

FINANCIAL FACTS

Financial Aid Rating	82
Tuition	$18,545
Room & board	$5,885
Estimated book expense	$600
% frosh receiving aid	63
% undergrads receiving aid	62
% aid is need-based	65
% frosh w/ grant (avg)	47 ($10,000)
% frosh w/ loan (avg)	31 ($3,400)
% UGs w/ job (avg)	12 ($1,500)
Off-campus job outlook	good

ROSE-HULMAN INSTITUTE OF TECHNOLOGY

5500 WABASH AVENUE, TERRE HAUTE, IN 47803   ADMISSIONS: 812-877-1511   FAX: 812-877-9925

CAMPUS LIFE

Quality of Life Rating	**75**
Type of school	private
Affiliation	none
Environment	suburban

STUDENTS

FT undergrad enrollment	1,548
% male/female	94/6
% from out of state	40
% live on campus	65
% spend weekend on campus	NR
% transfers	2
% from public high school	73
% in (# of) fraternities	44 (8)
% African-American	2
% Asian	2
% Caucasian	95
% Hispanic	1
% international	NR
# of countries represented	NR

WHAT'S HOT
computer facilities
lab facilities
school runs like butter
intramural sports
campus easy to get around

WHAT'S NOT
drugs
Terre Haute
sex
music associations
theater

ACADEMICS

Academic Rating	**93**
Profs Interesting Rating	91
Profs Accessible Rating	92
Calendar	other
Student/teacher ratio	13:1
% profs PhD	94
Hours of study per day	3.90

MOST POPULAR MAJORS
electrical engineering
mechanical engineering
chemical engineering

% GRADS WHO PURSUE...
Law 1, Med 2, MBA 5

STUDENTS SPEAK OUT

Life
Rose-Hulman Institute, which had been all-male since 1874, is a coeducational school as of 1995. Students here traditionally study almost nonstop, but perhaps the long-awaited addition of women to the campus will improve the moribund social scene a bit. The town in which it's located, Terre Haute, is often referred to by students as "Terrible Hole." There are two other colleges close by, a women's school (St. Mary's of the Woods) and a large state school (Indiana State University), but, as one student reports, "The other two schools have very little to do with us. And, there's nothing to do in town." Most students claim not to mind the dull social atmosphere, explaining that they would have no time to enjoy themselves even if things were better. When students do leave the computer labs and libraries, they step out onto a campus that is "very nice, a lot like home. I can go out in the woods or go swimming or fishing in the pond."

Academics
Students and professors at Rose-Hulman have a truly strange relationship. Everybody knows that engineers are supposed to complain that their professors are incomprehensible and/or completely unconcerned with their undergraduate students. At Rose-Hulman, however, students have nothing but nice things to say about their instructors. "Although this college is very intense," writes one; "the amount of time given to students by the lecturers is first-class. Professors are always willing to help." Says another, "The faculty and staff are friendly and really care about their work," and one student even reports that "most faculty accept phone calls at home." Several students complain that professors are quick to try new, unproven methods of teaching this difficult material ("which makes us feel like guinea pigs in a lab," writes one student), but overall it's hard to imagine a happier group of engineers. The "extraordinarily polite" and "dedicated" administration is well-loved; one student reports that they "definitely have their fingers on the pulse of the student body." As for the workload, one student puts it this way: "Sleep is for wimps." RH students put in over four hours a day outside the classroom, and many are practically glued to their computers. The education they receive is universally loved: "It's like getting a drink of water from a fire hose," analogizes one student. All engineering majors are reputedly of uniform quality. The school offers a unique program in applied optics.

Student Body
Nearly one hundred women were among the 460 new students who began RH last fall, ending a 121-year all-male tradition at the undergraduate level. Most students looked forward to the change ("it should improve both social conditions and student work ethics"), although a few expressed fears that "nobody's going to get any work done." Students are very conservative, and the few gays who attend school here keep their preferences low-key, although there is a gay student association. Even though the students are hardworking engineers, one insists, "We are not a bunch of zit-popping, paste-eating, mouth-breathing, pencil-neck geeks who sit around discussing this week's episode of Star Trek."

ROSE-HULMAN INSTITUTE OF TECHNOLOGY

FINANCIAL AID: 812-877-1511   E-MAIL: ADMIS.OFC@ROSE-HULMAN.EDU   WEB SITE: HTTP://WWW.ROSE-HULMAN.EDU/

ADMISSIONS

The admissions committee considers (in descending order of importance): HS record, class rank, test scores, recommendations, essay. *Also considered (in descending order of importance):* personality, extracurriculars, special talents. Either the SAT or ACT is required. An interview is recommended. *High school units required/recommended:* 16 total units are required; 4 English required, 4 math required, 2 science required, 2 social studies required. Minimum combined SAT I score of 1000 and rank in top quarter of secondary school class required; minimum combined SAT I score of 1200 and rank in top fifth of secondary school class recommended. TOEFL is required of all international students.

The Inside Word

After over one hundred years as an all-male institution, Rose-Hulman opened its doors to women last fall, leaving Wabash, Hampden-Sydney, and Morehouse as the only remaining all-male colleges in the US. Going coed should alleviate some of the Institute's enrollment pressures and result in even more creativity from the admissions office, long known for its uncommon literature and unique recruitment approaches. Academic standards are high, but for adventurous, ambitious, and technologically minded women, Rose-Hulman will be a relatively easy admit for the foreseeable future.

FINANCIAL AID

Students should submit: FAFSA, the school's own financial aid form, state aid form, a copy of parents' most recent income tax filing. The Princeton Review suggests that all financial aid forms be submitted as soon as possible after January 1. *The following grants/scholarships are offered:* Pell, SEOG, academic merit, the school's own scholarships, the school's own grants, state scholarships, state grants, private scholarships, private grants, ROTC. *Students borrow from the following loan programs:* Stafford, Perkins, PLUS, private loans. College Work-Study Program is available. Institutional employment is available.

FROM THE ADMISSIONS OFFICE

"Rose-Hulman is generally considered one of the premier undergraduate colleges of engineering and science. We are naturally known as an institution that puts teaching above research and graduate programs. At Rose-Hulman, professors (not graduate students) teach the courses and conduct their own labs. Department chairmen teach freshmen. To enhance the teaching at Rose-Hulman, computers have become a prominent addition to not only our labs but also many of our classrooms. Additionally, all students are now required to purchase laptop computers."

ADMISSIONS

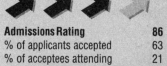

Admissions Rating	86
% of applicants accepted	63
% of acceptees attending	21

FRESHMAN PROFILE

Average verbal SAT	640
Average math SAT	690
Average ACT	30
Average TOEFL	NR
Graduated top 20% of class	93
Graduated top 40% of class	100
Graduated top 60% of class	100
Average HS GPA or Avg.	3.5

DEADLINES

Early decision	12/1
Regular admission	4/1
Regular notification	rolling
Non-fall registration	no

APPLICANTS ALSO LOOK AT

AND OFTEN PREFER

MIT
Caltech
Notre Dame

AND SOMETIMES PREFER

U. Illinois, Urbana-Champ.
Washington U.
Georgia Tech.
Carnegie Mellon
Lehigh

AND RARELY PREFER

Purdue U. - West Lafayette
U. Missouri - Columbia

FINANCIAL FACTS

Financial Aid Rating	83
Tuition	$15,600
Room & board	$4,700
Estimated book expense	$700
% frosh receiving aid	90
% undergrads receiving aid	91
% aid is need-based	80
% frosh w/ grant (avg)	80 ($4,000)
% frosh w/ loan (avg)	80 ($4,100)
% UGs w/ job (avg)	40 ($1,000)
Off-campus job outlook	good

RUTGERS UNIVERSITY-RUTGERS COLLEGE

New Brunswick, NJ 08903   Admissions: 908-445-3770   Fax: 908-932-8060

CAMPUS LIFE

Quality of Life Rating   72
Type of school	public
Affiliation	none
Environment	suburban

STUDENTS
FT undergrad enrollment	9,221
% male/female	49/51
% from out of state	12
% live on campus	76
% spend weekend on campus	NR
% transfers	24
% from public high school	NR
% in (# of) fraternities	11 (31)
% in (# of) sororities	7 (15)
% African-American	7
% Asian	18
% Caucasian	58
% Hispanic	11
% international	2
# of countries represented	51

WHAT'S HOT
ethnic diversity on campus
student publications
sex
drugs
library

WHAT'S NOT
campus difficult to get around
inefficient administration
unattractive campus
health facilities
support groups

ACADEMICS

Academic Rating   77
Profs Interesting Rating	62
Profs Accessible Rating	64
Calendar	semester
Student/teacher ratio	18:1
% profs tenured	98
Hours of study per day	2.94

MOST POPULAR MAJORS
psychology
English
political science

STUDENTS SPEAK OUT

Life

Life in New Brunswick, home of Rutgers College, is what you make it. Says one student, "New Brunswick offers alot to do if you keep open ears and an open mind." And if you get bored, "Going to New York City or Philadelphia is easy, students just hop a train." At RU, individual initiative is the key. "For someone to get the best out of the campus, they must join many of its clubs and activities," says a sophomore studying biology. Indeed, there are numerous opportunities for just about anyone, from die-hard young Republicans to flaming liberals. Offers one satisfied student, "I'm involved in numerous women's organizations, and Rutgers has provided me with the opportunity to cultivate my feminism." Adds another about RU's social scene, "If you want to use drugs and alcohol, they're easily accessible. If you don't, it's easy to avoid them." Dorms receive moderate marks (about half the students live on campus) but no one is raving about the food they serve.

Academics

Rutgers College is a medium-sized liberal arts college in the middle of Rutgers University, New Jersey's state university. For some students, this unique relationship gives them "the best of both worlds"—the opportunities and resources of a big, affordable state school along with the personal attention of a smaller college. Says one, "The range of courses is enormous. You can take anything from "White Collar Crime" to "Sexuality in Religion." The professors are "the best around," as another puts it. For other students, however, RU is "a circus." "You must do everything twice before it gets done," says an economics major. Lectures and discussions can be enormous, and getting into classes as a freshman is not easy, although it improves dramatically for upperclassmen. Over and over students note the need to be assertive when dealing with RU. "To succeed at Rutgers you must have ambition. You can get the best of everything here, only if you make it happen."

Student Body

"We have everything from commie pinko leftists to skater Green Day pseudo-punks to loser preppie Republicans," says one first-year Rutgers College student. Adds another, "The best part about Rutgers is that there are so many diverse social groups." The variety we found in students' responses to our survey bears this out. While some whine that students are too liberal, just as many moan that their classmates are too conservative and Greek-obsessed (which can hardly be true; only a small percentage of Rutgers undergrads go Greek). Maybe the only way in which many students are alike here is the state they call home: New Jersey. Still, even with a large in-state contingent, this is a huge place, so there are plenty of undergrads from around the country and the world. Explains one, "A good percentage [of the student body] are freaks because Rutgers, being a state university, has to have diversity." What a lovely sentiment. Another states more eloquently, "Few campuses, I imagine, offer the same diversity of lifestyles."

FINANCIAL AID: 908-932-8811   WEB SITE: HTTP://WWW.RUTGERS.EDU/INDEX.HTML

ADMISSIONS

The admissions committee considers (in descending order of importance): HS record, class rank, test scores, recommendations. *Also considered (in descending order of importance):* special talents, extracurriculars, geographical distribution. Either the SAT or ACT is required. Admissions process is need-blind. *High school units required/recommended:* 16 total units are required; 4 English required, 3 math required, 4 math recommended, 2 science required, 2 foreign language required. TOEFL is required of all international students.

The Inside Word

New Jersey residents are finally acknowledging that the flagship of their state university system is among the finest public universities in the nation. As a result, getting in keeps getting tougher every year as more and more New Jersey residents elect to stay home for college.

FINANCIAL AID

Students should submit: FAFSA, a copy of parents' most recent income tax filing. The Princeton Review suggests that all financial aid forms be submitted as soon as possible after January 1. *The following grants/scholarships are offered:* Pell, SEOG, academic merit, athletic, the school's own scholarships, the school's own grants, state scholarships, state grants, ROTC. *Students borrow from the following loan programs:* Stafford, Perkins, PLUS, the school's own loan fund, state loans. College Work-Study Program is available. Institutional employment is available.

FROM THE ADMISSIONS OFFICE

"What does it take to be accepted for admission to Rutgers University? There's no single answer to that question. Our primary emphasis is on your past academic performance as indicated by your high school grades (particularly in required academic subjects), your class rank, the strength of your academic program, your standardized test scores on the SAT or ACT, any special talents you may have, and your participation in school and community activities. We seek students with a broad diversity of talents, interests, and backgrounds. Above all else, we're looking for students who will get the most out of a Rutgers education—students with the intellect, initiative, and motivation to make full use of the opportunities we have to offer."

ADMISSIONS

Admissions Rating	83
% of applicants accepted	53
% of acceptees attending	24

FRESHMAN PROFILE

Average verbal SAT	660
Average math SAT	610
Average ACT	NR
Average TOEFL	550
Graduated top 20% of class	63
Graduated top 40% of class	84
Graduated top 60% of class	88
Average HS GPA or Avg.	NR

DEADLINES

Early decision	12/15
Regular admission	NR
Regular notification	2/28
Non-fall registration	no

APPLICANTS ALSO LOOK AT

AND OFTEN PREFER
Pennsylvania
Cornell U.
Virginia

AND SOMETIMES PREFER
Penn State
Boston Coll.
New Jersey Tech
Montclair State

AND RARELY PREFER
Trenton State
Seton Hall
George Washington

FINANCIAL FACTS

Financial Aid Rating	75
In-state tuition	$3,786
Out-of-state tuition	$7,707
Room & board	$4,936
Estimated book expense	$800
% frosh receiving aid	62
% undergrads receiving aid	72
% aid is need-based	84
% frosh w/ grant (avg)	73 ($4,399)
% frosh w/ loan (avg)	41 ($3,450)
% UGs w/ job (avg)	30 ($1,550)
Off-campus job outlook	good

SAMFORD UNIVERSITY

800 LAKESHORE DRIVE, BIRMINGHAM, AL 35229   ADMISSIONS: 800-888-7218   FAX: 205-870-2754

CAMPUS LIFE

Quality of Life Rating   **88**
Type of school	private
Affiliation	Southern Baptist Church
Environment	metropolis

STUDENTS
FT undergrad enrollment	2,729
% male/female	40/60
% from out of state	55
% live on campus	58
% spend weekend on campus	40
% transfers	30
% from public high school	75
% in (# of) fraternities	30 (5)
% in (# of) sororities	33 (8)
% African-American	5
% Asian	1
% Caucasian	92
% Hispanic	1
% international	1
# of countries represented	24

WHAT'S HOT
religion
town-gown relations
campus is beautiful
Greeks
off-campus food

WHAT'S NOT
sex
beer
hard liquor
drugs
students are cliquish

ACADEMICS

Academic Rating   **81**
Profs Interesting Rating	82
Profs Accessible Rating	80
Calendar	4-1-4
Student/teacher ratio	14:1
% profs tenured	83
Hours of study per day	2.82

MOST POPULAR MAJORS
elementary education
pharmacy
management

% GRADS WHO PURSUE...
Law 10, MBA 1, MA 16

STUDENTS SPEAK OUT

Life

Samford University students must live within the often restrictive boundaries set by the administration of this Southern Baptist school. Class attendance is frequently mandatory and homework assignments are numerous. The campus, and all frat parties, are completely dry. "Our school is simply encouraging driving under the influence," charges one student, because the rules force students to go off campus if they want to drink. Dorms are single-sex with extremely limited visitation privileges. Many students chose Samford because these policies reflect their beliefs—but others remark that the school needs to "let open some of the strict rules." Students also report that they "do not date very much unless you are in the Greek system." The Baptist Student Union, which is associated with almost every student organization, plays an integral role in student life. Big annual events include: Spring Fling, Welcome Back Week, and Step Sing, "a song and dance variety show and competition. It is a tradition that dates back many years and is sold out every night, every year."

Academics

Because of its strict Southern Baptist affiliation, Samford University is not for everyone. For those who fit into this conservative religious community, however, the rewards can be great. Samford combines affordability with a small-school atmosphere and the academic diversity of a university; the school maintains separate divisions for arts and sciences, business, education, music, nursing, and pharmacy. All students must complete general education requirements in the humanities, social sciences, lab sciences, and Bible. Students report that professors are good teachers and very accessible. One notes, "the teachers want to talk with you out of class and are ready to assist students with internships and other problems." Furthermore, they note that faculty members are less dogmatic than either the administration or the students. Praises one, "I commend Samford for trying to hire professors that are varied in their views." Students agree that the administration does a good job directing the school. Writes one, "The university strives to promote spiritual values, yet truly encourages academic and social unity." Despite those who wish for more lax social guidelines, many agree that "Samford is not your average university. It exceeds others socially, academically, and spiritually."

Student Body

"Not all students are, of course, but many seem closed and even at times defensive of their own beliefs, as if they are fragile," explains one student. Another notes most "come from white, middle-class families. Christianity is important, if not the focal point of the lives of most. The diversity comes mainly from students whose parents are missionaries." An African-American undergrad reports "some students act snobbish towards me because of my color." And another student adds "There are also problems with Greek/independent relations." As at other strongly religious schools, students either fit in here or they don't. Those who fit in love the place; those who don't are generally miserable.

FINANCIAL AID: 800-888-7245

WEB SITE: HTTP://SERVER1.SAMFORD.EDU/HOMEPAGE.HTML

ADMISSIONS

The admissions committee considers (in descending order of importance): HS record, test scores, class rank, recommendations, essay. *Also considered (in descending order of importance):* extracurriculars, personality, alumni relationship, special talents. Either the SAT or ACT is required; SAT is preferred. An interview is recommended. Admissions process is need-blind. *High school units required/recommended:* 18 total units are required; 4 English required, 4 English recommended, 3 math recommended, 3 science recommended, 2 foreign language recommended, 3 social studies recommended. Minimum combined SAT I score of 900 and minimum 3.0 GPA required. *Special Requirements:* An audition is required for music program applicants. TOEFL is required of all international students. *The admissions office says:* "Samford uses the application credentials as the scholarship application as well (scores, grades, résumés). [Our students typically have a] Christian background, strong leadership skills, [and a] well-developed sense of social consciousness. Alumni relations receive some special consideration."

The Inside Word

Samford's use of admission credentials in scholarship considerations is something that is quite common at colleges across the country. Students should always complete their applications as if such is the case. Even for universities where you are clearly admissible academically, giving some additional attention to essays and visiting for an interview can make the difference between being a scholarship winner and taking on an additional summer job.

FINANCIAL AID

Students should submit: FAFSA (due March 1), the school's own financial aid form (due March 1). The Princeton Review suggests that all financial aid forms be submitted as soon as possible after January 1. *The following grants/scholarships are offered:* Pell, SEOG, academic merit, athletic, the school's own scholarships, state scholarships, state grants, private scholarships, ROTC. *Students borrow from the following loan programs:* Stafford, unsubsidized Stafford, Perkins, PLUS, health professions loans, private loans. Applicants will be notified of awards beginning March 1. College Work-Study Program is available. Institutional employment is available.

FROM THE ADMISSIONS OFFICE

"Students who are drawn to Samford are well-rounded individuals who not only expect to be challenged, but are excited by the prospect. It is the critical and creative way you think, it is the articulate way you write and speak, it is the joy of learning that stays with you throughout your life, and it is the clarity of decision-making guided by Christian principles."

ADMISSIONS

Admissions Rating	71
% of applicants accepted	84
% of acceptees attending	42

FRESHMAN PROFILE

Average verbal SAT	NR
Average math SAT	NR
Average ACT	24
Average TOEFL	550
Graduated top 20% of class	52
Graduated top 40% of class	79
Graduated top 60% of class	85
Average HS GPA or Avg.	3.4

DEADLINES

Early decision	12/15
Regular admission	6/1
Regular notification	rolling
Non-fall registration	yes

APPLICANTS ALSO LOOK AT

AND OFTEN PREFER

Vanderbilt
Furman

AND SOMETIMES PREFER

Baylor
U. Alabama - Birmingham
Florida State
U. Georgia
Auburn

FINANCIAL FACTS

Financial Aid Rating	90
Tuition	$9,070
Room & board	$4,106
Estimated book expense	$500
% frosh receiving aid	80
% undergrads receiving aid	80
% aid is need-based	NR
% frosh w/ grant (avg)	70 ($1,500)
% frosh w/ loan (avg)	45 ($3,400)
% UGs w/ job (avg)	25 ($1,020)
Off-campus job outlook	excellent

SAN FRANCISCO ART INSTITUTE

800 CHESTNUT STREET, SAN FRANCISCO, CA 94133 · ADMISSIONS: 800-345-7234 · FAX: 415-749-4590

CAMPUS LIFE

Quality of Life Rating — **82**

Type of school	private
Affiliation	none
Environment	metropolis

STUDENTS

FT undergrad enrollment	463
% male/female	53/47
% from out of state	40
% live on campus	NR
% spend weekend on campus	NR
% transfers	80
% from public high school	NR
% African-American	2
% Asian	6
% Caucasian	73
% Hispanic	7
% international	12
# of countries represented	20

WHAT'S HOT

leftist politics
San Francisco
campus food
drugs
cigarettes

WHAT'S NOT

health facilities
religion

ACADEMICS

Academic Rating — **82**

Profs Interesting Rating	77
Profs Accessible Rating	66
Calendar	semester
Student/teacher ratio	9:1
% profs tenured	62
Hours of study per day	3.46

MOST POPULAR MAJORS

painting/drawing
photography
film

% GRADS WHO PURSUE...

MA 100

STUDENTS SPEAK OUT

Life

Students at the San Francisco Art Institute work. A lot. Comments like "Good place to work at 3 AM and really get work done!" are so common it's scary. Surprisingly, few of the undergrads we talked to cite the city of San Francisco as a consistent source of outside entertainment. Observations such as "Tuition is getting pretty outrageous and financial aid simply cannot adequately cover the costs incurred from an education," and "Not much social interaction. We're too busy and too poor," might be partial explanations. While activities involving the student government are quite popular, fraternities, sports, and student-run radio are not. Students also go to parties or local bars and clubs, and many involve themselves in the local art world outside of campus.

Academics

"Work, work, work" is a comment typical of SFAI students. "You need to be very focused to get anything out of this school" is another. Most undergrads suggest that the disciplined and self-motivated student will get the most out of the Institute. Course loads can be tough, and over a third of the school's population admitted to studying over five hours a day outside of class. One happy student notes: "The school is absolutely wonderful; everything I need is within spitting distance." Students give the facilities at SFAI moderate marks ("Studio space is a main problem in this school"), with the lack of health-care resources a main concern. On the plus side, the faculty receives a high rating overall. Students cite their accessibility ("Most of my teachers were very available outside of class. One of them even helped me move with her van") and competence ("Our professors have a real knowledge of what it takes and what it means to be an artist functioning in the world"; "It was valuable to hang out with teachers outside of class") as their strong points. In general, the students seem to see the Institute as a haven within which to work and learn as artists, as expressed by this candid undergrad: "They don't prepare us for the hostile, cold, and materialistic world. We're f@%&ing spoiled!"

Student Body

In general, SFAI students seem to get along with their classmates, regarding them as talented, friendly people. Nonetheless, they are not above criticizing the sometimes self-centered dispositions of their peers: "Art-school attitude" is how one student describes the behavior of her fellow SFAI students. Another sees two (three?) sides to this phenomenon: "A little pretentious, but generally a good sense of humor. Lots of nudity." Okay, fine. Although the angst-ridden, multiple-body-pierced "art-school type" is not unknown at SFAI, they don't necessarily last here: "They usually either drop out or grow out of it when they realize they don't have to work so hard to look like an artist." Racially, the students describe themselves as rather homogeneous. One student describes them as "peas in a pod," while another notes: "This school is not ethnically diverse. Sometimes people of color get pigeonholed or stereotyped."

ADMISSIONS

The admissions committee considers (in descending order of importance): HS record, test scores, essay, recommendations, class rank. *Also considered (in descending order of importance):* personality, special talents. Either the SAT or ACT is required. An interview is recommended. Admissions process is need-blind. Minimum verbal SAT I score of 420 (English ACT score of 20) recommended. *Special Requirements:* A portfolio is required for art program applicants. TOEFL is required of all international students.

The Inside Word

Students who are considering the San Francisco Art Institute need to be particularly strong individuals. Those who show self-awareness, self-discipline, and motivation in addition to serious artistic talent and potential are likely to be successful in gaining admission. Such personal characteristics are an absolute must in order to be successful at the Institute. Only well-focused students are ready for such a demanding program.

FINANCIAL AID

Students should submit: FAFSA. The Princeton Review suggests that all financial aid forms be submitted as soon as possible after January 1. *The following grants/scholarships are offered:* Pell, SEOG, academic merit, the school's own scholarships, the school's own grants, state scholarships, state grants. *Students borrow from the following loan programs:* Stafford, unsubsidized Stafford, PLUS. Applicants will be notified of awards beginning April 1. College Work-Study Program is available. Institutional employment is available.

FROM THE ADMISSIONS OFFICE

"The lure of the San Francisco Art Institute is more than its glorious history and more than the magical stimulus of the historic Spanish colonial complex on Chestnut Street. The lure of the Art Institute is also in its teaching philosophy. Our abiding principle is an emphasis on the development of the personal values of the individual artist."

ADMISSIONS

Admissions Rating	81
% of applicants accepted	75
% of acceptees attending	50

FRESHMAN PROFILE

Average verbal SAT	NR
Average math SAT	NR
Average ACT	NR
Average TOEFL	500
Graduated top 20% of class	NR
Graduated top 40% of class	NR
Graduated top 60% of class	NR
Average HS GPA or Avg.	NR

DEADLINES

Early decision	3/1
Regular admission	8/1
Regular notification	rolling
Non-fall registration	yes

APPLICANTS ALSO LOOK AT
AND SOMETIMES PREFER

School of the Art Inst. of Chicago
CalArts
Sch. of the Museum of Fine Arts

FINANCIAL FACTS

Financial Aid Rating	86
Tuition	$16,416
Room & board	NR
Estimated book expense	$1,400
% frosh receiving aid	60
% undergrads receiving aid	80
% aid is need-based	85
% frosh w/ grant (avg)	NR ($5,912)
% frosh w/ loan (avg)	60 ($6,625)
% UGs w/ job (avg)	36 ($1,000)
Off-campus job outlook	good

SAN FRANCISCO CONSERVATORY OF MUSIC

1201 ORTEGA STREET, SAN FRANCISCO, CA 94122   ADMISSIONS: 415-759-3431   FAX: 415-759-3499

CAMPUS LIFE

Quality of Life Rating	**84**
Type of school	private
Affiliation	none
Environment	metropolis

STUDENTS

FT undergrad enrollment	139
% male/female	38/62
% from out of state	41
% live on campus	NR
% spend weekend on campus	NR
% transfers	40
% from public high school	60
% African-American	3
% Asian	17
% Caucasian	50
% Hispanic	7
% international	23
# of countries represented	21

WHAT'S HOT
music associations
different students interact
town-gown relations
San Francisco
theater

WHAT'S NOT
intramural sports
student government
intercollegiate sports
student publications
support groups

ACADEMICS

Academic Rating	**93**
Profs Interesting Rating	84
Profs Accessible Rating	79
Calendar	semester
Student/teacher ratio	7:1
% profs PhD/tenured	15/36
Hours of study per day	4.41

MOST POPULAR MAJORS
piano
classical guitar
voice

% GRADS WHO PURSUE...
Law 5, MA 40

STUDENTS SPEAK OUT

Life

San Francisco Conservatory of Music is located in one of America's greatest cities, a city that seems to offer almost as much of an education as the school itself does. As one student puts it, "I go to the opera and symphony for fun. I love my life and producing art. I love San Francisco's open and accepting attitude." Indeed, San Francisco offers a limitless array of things to do, and music of all kinds thrives here. Students spend most of their time practicing, but there are "Lots of parties over weekends, lots of concerts," says a student. The Conservatory consists of one building, meaning there are no dormitories or on-campus dining facilities, which some students dislike. The school is located in a safe neighborhood, but one student describes it as "a depressing, boring place in a great city." Most students claim that they are happy here, and report that there is little discrimination against homosexuals or minorities.

Academics

The San Francisco Conservatory of Music is extremely small, which allows students a lot of individual attention from their teachers. Says one student, "Most professors are excellent and they try to make themselves very accessible." Most students feel that "the teachers seem to have a genuine concern for the musical development of their students." One student raves, "My teachers are amazing, witty, and intelligent." However, most agree that "Choosing the right studio instructor is paramount," and "Some classes are ridiculous." This is a very typical sentiment to have at a school of this size. Students claim that the competition between them is slight, no doubt in part because of a more laid-back attitude from the teachers. One student complains, "Most professors are outstanding, but far too lenient towards students." Despite this, most students surveyed spend five or more hours a day practicing. Another student has this to say: "This is not a school for the unmotivated person. You have to be completely self-motivated. If you are, it's the best school because you learn to be your own best teacher. It's not the situation, but what you make of it." Most are happy enough with the administration, probably yet another benefit of the school's small size.

Student Body

Despite its diminutive size, the San Francisco Conservatory of Music is well represented by international students and minorities. Students point out that what binds them together is the love of music: "We really just are in school together. There doesn't seem to be competition. Everyone's in for themselves and they have a very mature and professional attitude." Another student adds "I love the student body here. Unlike other conservatories, the students here are doing music for the love of it." Some students, however, wish that their classmates were broader in mind. As one student complains, "The students here may be gifted musically, but are lacking in an overall political and philosophical scope." Another says, "I expected to find lots of open-minded, artistic people. But training to be a musician is much like training to be a plumber."

FINANCIAL AID: 415-759-3422

ADMISSIONS

The admissions committee considers (in descending order of importance): HS record, recommendations, test scores, class rank. *Also considered (in descending order of importance):* special talents, extracurriculars, personality. Either the SAT or ACT is required; SAT is preferred. Admissions process is need-blind. *High school units required/recommended:* 3 English recommended, 3 foreign language recommended. Minimum 2.0 GPA required; minimum 3.0 GPA recommended. Audition required of all applicants. TOEFL is required of all international students. *The admissions office says:* "The most important criteria for admission is an applicant's musical proficiency. Our students are totally committed to their musical development."

The Inside Word

Students considering the San Francisco Conservatory of Music and similar conservatory programs need to begin preparing for the admissions process as early as possible, preferably before the end of junior year of high school. Expectations are high, and cover a wide range of criteria. Beyond a very demanding audition, candidates must demonstrate a sound grasp of the fundamental concepts of music theory and exposure to as much classical repertoire as possible. Applying to music school is far more demanding of students than filing typical college admission applications, and far more stressful as well. Most successful candidates are as well-prepared mentally as they are musically.

FINANCIAL AID

Students should submit: FAFSA (due March 1), the school's own financial aid form (due March 1). The Princeton Review suggests that all financial aid forms be submitted as soon as possible after January 1. *The following grants/scholarships are offered:* Pell, SEOG, the school's own scholarships, state grants, private scholarships, foreign aid. *Students borrow from the following loan programs:* Stafford, unsubsidized Stafford, Perkins, PLUS. College Work-Study Program is available. Institutional employment is available.

FROM THE ADMISSIONS OFFICE

"Students at the Conservatory have many opportunities to perform both at the Conservatory and throughout the Bay Area while studying here. The San Francisco Bay Area offers students many performing opportunities. Prospective students have found that classroom and rehearsal visits, in addition to concert attendance, provide an important glimpse at the musical life and demands of the Conservatory."

ADMISSIONS

Admissions Rating	92
% of applicants accepted	59
% of acceptees attending	46

FRESHMAN PROFILE

Average verbal SAT	540
Average math SAT	530
Average ACT	23
Average TOEFL	520
Graduated top 20% of class	NR
Graduated top 40% of class	NR
Graduated top 60% of class	NR
Average HS GPA or Avg.	NR

DEADLINES

Early decisi	NR
Regular admission	3/1
Regular notification	rolling
Non-fall registration	yes

APPLICANTS ALSO LOOK AT

AND SOMETIMES PREFER

New England Conservatory
Eastman
Juilliard

FINANCIAL FACTS

Financial Aid Rating	92
Tuition	$14,800
Room & board	NR
Estimated book expense	$620
% frosh receiving aid	82
% undergrads receiving aid	69
% aid is need-based	95
% frosh w/ grant (avg)	NR ($7,400)
% frosh w/ loan (avg)	65 ($3,600)
% UGs w/ job (avg)	25 ($900)
Off-campus job outlook	excellent

SANTA CLARA UNIVERSITY

Santa Clara, CA 95053   Admissions: 408-554-4700   Fax: 408-554-5255

CAMPUS LIFE

Quality of Life Rating	**89**
Type of school	private
Affiliation	Roman Catholic Church
	(Society of Jesus)
Environment	metropolis

STUDENTS

FT undergrad enrollment	3,977
% male/female	47/53
% from out of state	33
% live on campus	43
% spend weekend on campus	NR
% transfers	15
% from public high school	58
% in (# of) fraternities	12 (4)
% in (# of) sororities	14 (3)
% African-American	3
% Asian	21
% Caucasian	56
% Hispanic	14
% international	2
# of countries represented	29

WHAT'S HOT
intramural sports
students are happy
support groups
religion
school runs like butter

WHAT'S NOT
cigarettes
infrequent dating
sex
drugs
library

ACADEMICS

Academic Rating	**86**
Profs Interesting Rating	92
Profs Accessible Rating	91
Calendar	quarter
Student/teacher ratio	15:1
% profs PhD/tenured	92/92
Hours of study per day	3.58

MOST POPULAR MAJORS
finance
political science
English

% GRADS WHO PURSUE...
Law 9, Med 7, MBA 22, MA 26

STUDENTS SPEAK OUT

Life

Santa Clara University's campus is beautiful, and for some students, social life begins and ends there. Explains one student: "At SCU most people go to fraternity parties on weekends or to the local bars. Soccer and basketball games are the most popular sporting events. There are not a lot of people who go off campus on weekends." Other campus-area attractions include "coffeehouses, comedy clubs, dancing, parties." As at many Catholic schools, students fill spare time with participation in community service programs. Options expand dramatically for those with cars-writes one student, "If you have a car, the possibilities are endless. You can go to the city (San Francisco), Santa Cruz, Monterey, Napa Valley, hiking, etc. However, parking is a big pain in the ass." Mass transit (Cal Train) to San Francisco runs right to the campus, although strangely, few students report using it. Most students agree that the "city of Santa Clara is pretty boring," and that "in the area of alternative social activities, Santa Clara has a long way to go."

Academics

Santa Clara is a small school with big ambitions. Originally exclusively Catholic, this increasingly diverse institution continues to funnel its considerable resources into improving itself. The school has definitely improved its facilities, faculty, and reputation in recent years. Classes (especially in SCU's strong engineering program) are small, taught by professors (rarely by TAs), and generally "challenging and excellent." Sums up one student: "SCU provides the appropriate environment: small classes, good, available teachers (better than TAs of famous teachers)." Classes "are very difficult." Warns one student: "Work hard and you'll get a B; but don't work too hard because it is impossible to get an A." There are isolated complaints that SCU has drifted too far away from its original mission ("to educate, not to train"). One student writes that "the school claims to be a Jesuit university, but the Jesuit philosophy does not coincide with the curriculum, especially in the schools of Business and Engineering" (SCU's most popular divisions). Others point out, however, that the school requires a comprehensive liberal arts core curriculum for all students. Overall, the level of satisfaction here is high. Writes one typical junior, "The classroom and learning environment here at SCU are amazing! Levels of discussion are mind-numbing, and access to professors is excellent."

Student Body

The once "mostly Catholic, elite white population" of SCU is changing rapidly. It is now over one-third minority. The administration continues to emphasize its ethnic recruiting program. Students are studious, socially and politically conservative, and friendly: several respondents comment that "the people at SCU are very relaxed and it is very easy for people to meet one another."

FINANCIAL AID: 408-554-4505

ADMISSIONS

The admissions committee considers (in descending order of importance): HS record, test scores, recommendations, class rank, essay. *Also considered (in descending order of importance):* extracurriculars, alumni relationship, geographical distribution, personality, special talents. Either the SAT or ACT is required; SAT is preferred. An interview is recommended. Admissions process is need-blind. *High school units required/recommended:* 16 total units are recommended; 4 English recommended, 3 math recommended, 1 science recommended, 3 foreign language recommended, 1 history recommended. Electives should be chosen from advanced courses in foreign language, math, lab science, or history. *Special Requirements:* An audition is required for music program applicants. TOEFL is required of all international students.

The Inside Word

Santa Clara deserves recognition as a rising star that still manages to be highly personal and accessible. It's always better when an admissions staff regards you as a person, not an enrollment target. Unfortunately, such is not always the case. It would be hard to find a place that is more receptive to minority students. There is a very significant minority presence here because Santa Clara works hard and earnestly to make everyone feel at home. The university's popularity is increasing across the board, which proves that nice guys sometimes finish first.

FINANCIAL AID

Students should submit: FAFSA (due January 15), CSS Profile (due January 15). The Princeton Review suggests that all financial aid forms be submitted as soon as possible after January 1. *The following grants/scholarships are offered:* Pell, SEOG, academic merit, athletic, the school's own scholarships, the school's own grants, state scholarships, state grants, private scholarships, private grants, ROTC. *Students borrow from the following loan programs:* Perkins, PLUS, supplemental loans, private loans. College Work-Study Program is available. Institutional employment is available. Freshmen are discouraged from working.

FROM THE ADMISSIONS OFFICE

"Santa Clara University, located one hour south of San Francisco, offers its undergraduates an opportunity to be educated within a challenging, dynamic and caring community. The university blends a sense of tradition and history (as the oldest college in California) with a vision that values innovation and a deep commitment to social justice. Santa Clara's faculty members are talented scholars who are demanding, supportive, and accessible. The students are serious about academics, ethnically diverse and enjoy a full range of athletic, social, community service, religious, and cultural activities—both on campus and through the many options presented by our Northern California location. The undergraduate program includes three divisions: the College of Arts and Sciences, the School of Business and the School of Engineering."

ADMISSIONS

Admissions Rating	**75**
% of applicants accepted	76
% of acceptees attending	32

FRESHMAN PROFILE

Average verbal SAT	580
Average math SAT	590
Average ACT	NR
Average TOEFL	550
Graduated top 20% of class	56
Graduated top 40% of class	75
Graduated top 60% of class	80
Average HS GPA or Avg.	3.5

DEADLINES

Early decision	NR
Regular admission	1/15
Regular notification	rolling
Non-fall registration	yes

APPLICANTS ALSO LOOK AT

AND OFTEN PREFER

UC - Berkeley
UC - Davis
Stanford
Notre Dame
UCLA

AND SOMETIMES PREFER

Pomona
UC - Irvine
UC - Santa Barbara
UC - San Diego
Loyola Marymount U.

AND RARELY PREFER

U. Oregon
UC - Santa Cruz
U. San Francisco
San Jose State

FINANCIAL FACTS

Financial Aid Rating	**85**
Tuition	$15,450
Room & board	$6,780
Estimated book expense	$612
% frosh receiving aid	72
% undergrads receiving aid	68
% aid is need-based	85
% frosh w/ grant (avg)	86 ($10,505)
% frosh w/ loan (avg)	65 ($4,422)
% UGs w/ job (avg)	30 ($1,800)
Off-campus job outlook	good

SARAH LAWRENCE COLLEGE

One Meadway, Bronxville, NY 10708

Admissions: 800-888-2858   Fax: 914-395-2668

CAMPUS LIFE

Quality of Life Rating 78
Type of school   private
Affiliation   none
Environment   metropolis

STUDENTS
FT undergrad enrollment   948
% male/female   26/74
% from out of state   76
% live on campus   90
% spend weekend on campus   85
% transfers   17
% from public high school   60
% African-American   6
% Asian   5
% Caucasian   81
% Hispanic   6
% international   5
# of countries represented   24

WHAT'S HOT
theater
cigarettes
drugs
leftist politics
honesty

WHAT'S NOT
Greeks
town-gown relations
college radio
religion
intramural sports

ACADEMICS

Academic Rating 93
Profs Interesting Rating   98
Profs Accessible Rating   96
Calendar   semester
Student/teacher ratio   6:1
% profs PhD/tenured   94/95
Hours of study per day   3.51

MOST POPULAR MAJORS
writing
creative/performing arts
psychology

% GRADS WHO PURSUE...
Law 10, Med 8, MBA 6, MA 46

STUDENTS SPEAK OUT

Life

Sarah Lawrence College students overwhelmingly prefer Bronxville's proximity to New York City over Bronxville itself. One student writes that "[New York City] is a must for sanity," while another writes "At other schools there are more things to do on campus. New York City makes it all worthwhile." The majority of students live on campus and give high marks to the dormitories and food. Over two-thirds of the students are women, which leads to complaints about dating possibilities, although there is such a high acceptance of homosexuality that the statistics might not be as depressing as they seem. Students use the word "diversity" a lot when describing their classmates, although over two-thirds of the students are white. "It's a great place to be an individual," one student says. Others describe life at Sarah Lawrence as "accepting" and "totally cool." Some express dismay over the lack of social activity on campus. "My social life is taking a break at the vending machine," writes one student.

Academics

Sarah Lawrence students praise the faculty above all else, and find the professors to be "accessible, caring, and intelligent." They are only slightly less impressed with the administration. "The administration is friendly, if flaky, and only very vaguely and inconsistently fascistic or blatantly deceitful," writes one student. Students meet often with advisors (referred to as "dons"), and enjoy a lot of individual attention from their teachers, who are described as "like butter," and "as intelligent and strange as the students." There is a great deal of interaction between teachers and students, and students are very enthusiastic about this aspect of Sarah Lawrence. Although letter grades are kept on file for graduate schools, no official grades are given. Students instead receive lengthy written responses to their work. Liberal arts majors such as writing, drama, English, art, and art history are the most popular, but the sciences offer very strong programs as well. "This is the best school for academics."

Student Body

As one Sarah Lawrence student writes, "If you're a lesbian, you have friends who are lesbians; if you're a Christian, you have friends who are Christians; if you don't like the people here, you have friends who don't like the people here." Undergrads are pretty far to the left politically, and repeatedly emphasize how accepting the student body is of all types of people. However, some think that students need to lighten up. "There's a disturbingly widespread tendency of students to take everything, including themselves, far too seriously—everything becomes fraught with dire implications." Another student feels that "students here are too set on being different," undermining the very spirit of acceptance they are trying to create. But overall, students here are a happy bunch who revel in their own and each other's individuality.

FINANCIAL AID: 914-395-2570

ADMISSIONS

The admissions committee considers (in descending order of importance): HS record, essay, recommendations, class rank, test scores. *Also considered (in descending order of importance):* extracurriculars, personality, special talents, alumni relationship, geographical distribution. Either the SAT or ACT is required. An interview is recommended. *High school units required/recommended:* 17 total units are recommended; 4 English recommended, 3 math recommended, 2 science recommended, 2 foreign language recommended, 3 social studies recommended, 3 history recommended. TOEFL is required of all international students. *The admissions office says:* "The education at Sarah Lawrence demands that a student possess a facility and a desire to work with the written word. The structure of the education requires a student to be self-motivated, comfortable working closely with adults, and interested in an interdisciplinary approach to knowledge. The arts are an integrated part of the curriculum at SLC; many students successfully balance concentrations in both academics and the creative or performing arts."

The Inside Word

The public generally views Sarah Lawrence as an artsy "alternative" college. The college itself avoids this image, preferring instead to evoke an impression that aligns them with more traditional and prestigious northeastern colleges such as the Ivies, Little Ivies, and Seven Sisters. The admissions process tends to be more benevolent toward guys, who are in short supply at Sarah Lawrence even though the college has been coed for many years.

FINANCIAL AID

Students should submit: FAFSA (due February 1), CSS Profile (due February 1), the school's own financial aid form (due February 1), state aid form (due February 1), Divorced Parents form (due February 1), a copy of parents' most recent income tax filing (due February 1). The Princeton Review suggests that all financial aid forms be submitted as soon as possible after January 1. *The following grants/scholarships are offered:* Pell, SEOG, the school's own grants, state grants, private scholarships, private grants. *Students borrow from the following loan programs:* Stafford, Perkins, PLUS. Applicants will be notified of awards beginning April 1. College Work-Study Program is available. Institutional employment is available.

FROM THE ADMISSIONS OFFICE

"Students who come to Sarah Lawrence are curious about the world, and they have an ardent desire to satisfy that curiosity. Most are bored with the conventions of high school. They are seeking a place where large, difficult questions are valued more than smooth answers—where their work will be driven by their need to know and their passion for reading, writing, and creating. Sarah Lawrence offers such students two innovative academic structures: the seminar/conference system and the arts components. Courses in the humanities, social sciences, natural sciences and mathematics are taught in the seminar/conference style. The seminars enroll an average of eleven students and consist of lecture, discussion, readings and assigned papers. For each seminar, students also have private tutorials, called conferences, where they conceive of individualized projects and shape them under the careful direction of professors in biweekly meetings. Arts components let students combine history and theory with practice. Painters, printmakers, photographers, sculptors and filmmakers, composers, musicians, choreographers, dancers, actors, and directors work 'round the clock' in readily available studios, editing facilities and darkrooms, guided by accomplished professionals. The secure, wooded campus 30 minutes from New York City and the diversity of people and ideas at Sarah Lawrence make it an extraordinary educational environment."

ADMISSIONS

Admissions Rating	85
% of applicants accepted	59
% of acceptees attending	32

FRESHMAN PROFILE

Average verbal SAT	720
Average math SAT	590
Average ACT	26
Average TOEFL	550
Graduated top 20% of class	57
Graduated top 40% of class	89
Graduated top 60% of class	98
Average HS GPA or Avg.	3.3

DEADLINES

Early decision	NR
Regular admission	2/1
Regular notification	4/1
Non-fall registration	yes

APPLICANTS ALSO LOOK AT
AND OFTEN PREFER
NYU
Smith
Vassar
AND SOMETIMES PREFER
Barnard
Bard
Oberlin
Skidmore
AND RARELY PREFER
Hampshire
Brown
Bryn Mawr

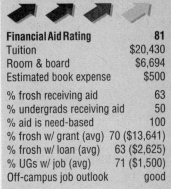

FINANCIAL FACTS

Financial Aid Rating	81
Tuition	$20,430
Room & board	$6,694
Estimated book expense	$500
% frosh receiving aid	63
% undergrads receiving aid	50
% aid is need-based	100
% frosh w/ grant (avg)	70 ($13,641)
% frosh w/ loan (avg)	63 ($2,625)
% UGs w/ job (avg)	71 ($1,500)
Off-campus job outlook	good

SCRIPPS COLLEGE

1030 COLUMBIA AVENUE, CLAREMONT, CA 91711 ADMISSIONS: 800-770-1333 FAX: 909-621-8323

STUDENTS SPEAK OUT

Life

Students at Scripps College, the women's school in the Claremont-McKenna cluster, are generally unexcited about their social lives. Some blame the lackluster scene on "the enormous emphasis on academics and doing well. I don't feel there is an equal balance between social life and school work." Others point to the town of Claremont ("not a college town. It's run by rich white men who don't want college kids having any fun"). Students tell us that, as a result, intercollegiate activities, such as the women's rugby team, are very popular, and many students exploit the nearby Southern California cities for their rich internship material. Others point out that the Scripps campus is truly beautiful, "You can't beat studying for finals while basking by the pool in the warm California sun." and that housing accommodations are generous: "You can have a single by the time you're a sophomore." And some even defend the town. Writes one, "The small-town atmosphere inspires and is an excellent outlet for free time spent just aimlessly walking."

Academics

Note: The Claremont Colleges are five small undergraduate schools (Claremont McKenna, Harvey Mudd, Pitzer, Pomona, and Scripps) and one graduate school sharing a central location and facilities with 5,300 total students and 2,500 total courses. Each school serves a distinct purpose and maintains its own faculty and campus. Scripps College is "well known for its core curriculum in the humanities, as well as for its emphasis on interdisciplinary study." Thanks to its proximity to the Claremont sibling schools, Scripps is a great choice "for women who want a women's school but also want the advantages of coed," according to one area counselor. One student reports that this association "gives you the opportunity to experience a small school but still have the benefits of a large college." English, economics, political science, international relations, biology, and studio arts are popular majors here. A strong contingent explores women's studies and ethnic studies in this particularly encouraging enclave. One student notes, "Scripps is an interesting place to explore being a feminist. It provides a strong foundation to develop as a modern woman." Students approve of and admire their professors, since they "talk with the students, not at them. There is a strong sense of mutual respect." Scripps offers welcome escape routes for the weary; half spend at least a semester at another school, in the US or abroad: "Scripps is a small college and gets boring pretty quickly. If you get tired of [it], go to Europe for a year."

Student Body

Scripps students do not consider their student body to be quite as diverse as they'd like, despite a good minority representation. In fact, many students note that "the issue of diversity could not be hotter." Several students relish the benefits of the single-sex environment, which fosters serious scholarship and congenial competition, and write that "the all-female support group on campus creates a home away from home."

ADMISSIONS

The admissions committee considers (in descending order of importance): HS record, test scores, class rank, recommendations, essay. *Also considered (in descending order of importance):* personality, alumni relationship, extracurriculars, geographical distribution, special talents. Either the SAT or ACT is required. An interview is recommended. Admissions process is need-blind. *High school units required/recommended:* 20 total units are recommended; 4 English recommended, 4 math recommended, 3 science recommended, 3 foreign language recommended, 3 social studies recommended, 3 history recommended. Rank in top tenth of secondary school class and minimum 3.4 GPA recommended. *Special Requirements:* TOEFL is required of all international students. Portfolio, audition, or tape recommended of art, dance, and music program applicants. *The admissions office says:* "Applicants must submit a graded paper from a junior or senior year academic class."

The Inside Word

With a graded paper required in addition to application essays, it is safe to say that Scripps is going to take a long, hard look at the writing ability of its candidates. Colleges that require such papers usually use them to temper the unnatural aura that sometimes envelops the application essay-writing process; a school paper will usually reflect a student's work under more normal circumstances. Candidates should also submit SAT II test scores; anything that is strongly recommended by a college admissions committee should never be regarded as optional.

FINANCIAL AID

Students should submit: FAFSA (due February 1), CSS Profile (due February 1). The Princeton Review suggests that all financial aid forms be submitted as soon as possible after January 1. *The following grants/scholarships are offered:* Pell, SEOG, academic merit, the school's own scholarships, the school's own grants, state grants, private scholarships, private grants, ROTC, foreign aid. *Students borrow from the following loan programs:* Stafford, unsubsidized Stafford, Perkins, PLUS, the school's own loan fund. Applicants will be notified of awards beginning April 1. College Work-Study Program is available. Institutional employment is available.

FROM THE ADMISSIONS OFFICE

"At Scripps we believe that learning involves much more than amassing information. The truly educated person is one who can think analytically, communicate effectively, and make confident, responsible choices. Scripps classes are small (the average class size is 15) so that they foster an atmosphere where students feel comfortable participating, testing old assumptions and exploring new ideas. Our curriculum is based on the traditional components of a liberal arts education: a set of general requirements in a wide variety of disciplines including foreign language, natural science, and writing; a multicultural requirement; a major that asks you to study one particular field in depth; and a variety of electives that allows considerable flexibility. What distinguishes Scripps from other liberal arts colleges is an emphasis on interdisciplinary courses."

ADMISSIONS

Admissions Rating	77
% of applicants accepted	80
% of acceptees attending	29

FRESHMAN PROFILE

Average verbal SAT	670
Average math SAT	600
Average ACT	25
Average TOEFL	550
Graduated top 20% of class	68
Graduated top 40% of class	87
Graduated top 60% of class	96
Average HS GPA or Avg.	3.6

DEADLINES

Early decision	1/1
Regular admission	2/1
Regular notification	4/1
Non-fall registration	yes

APPLICANTS ALSO LOOK AT

AND OFTEN PREFER

UCLA
Pomona
Smith
Wellesley
UC - Berkeley

AND SOMETIMES PREFER

Smith
UC - Santa Barbara
Occidental
UC - San Diego
Claremont McKenna

FINANCIAL FACTS

Financial Aid Rating	91
Tuition	$18,068
Room & board	$7,500
Estimated book expense	$700
% frosh receiving aid	50
% undergrads receiving aid	50
% aid is need-based	95
% frosh w/ grant (avg)	58 ($13,617)
% frosh w/ loan (avg)	52 ($3,500)
% UGs w/ job (avg)	46 ($1,600)
Off-campus job outlook	good

Seton Hall University

400 South Orange Avenue, South Orange, NJ 07079-2689 ADMISSIONS: 201-761-9332 FAX: 201-761-9452

CAMPUS LIFE

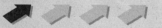

Quality of Life Rating **71**

Type of school	private
Affiliation	Roman Catholic Church (Archdiocese of Newark)
Environment	metropolis

STUDENTS

FT undergrad enrollment	4,160
% male/female	47/53
% from out of state	13
% live on campus	47
% spend weekend on campus	50
% transfers	30
% from public high school	NR
% in (# of) fraternities	25 (12)
% in (# of) sororities	25 (9)
% African-American	12
% Asian	5
% Caucasian	58
% Hispanic	8
% international	1
# of countries represented	43

WHAT'S HOT

sex
health facilities
cigarettes
college radio
intercollegiate sports

WHAT'S NOT

political activism
students are unhappy
lab facilities
off-campus food
support groups

ACADEMICS

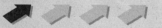

Academic Rating **68**

Profs Interesting Rating	63
Profs Accessible Rating	65
Calendar	semester
Student/teacher ratio	17:1
% profs PhD/tenured	87/60
Hours of study per day	2.47

MOST POPULAR MAJORS

communication
criminal justice
accounting

% GRADS WHO PURSUE...

Law 26, Med 10, MBA 10, MA 23

STUDENTS SPEAK OUT

Life

Seton Hall University students enjoy "a small, closely knit community where everyone knows each other." Unfortunately, social life at Seton Hall is curtailed by the fact that fewer than half the students live on campus (the school has a large commuter population). To make matters worse, "too many people go home over the weekend," and hometown South Orange, while close to New York City, is itself no hotbed of excitement. Explains one student, "Since the surrounding city doesn't offer much socially, I feel like I am trapped. On weekends, there is absolutely nothing to do. I came to college to get away from home, yet I find myself going back home almost every weekend." Says another, "The weekend life at this campus is so lame. Thursday, though, is a major drinking night. There are about five or six quality bars and clubs within walking distance, and they're very easy to get into without proof of age." Campus activities are plentiful "but very few take advantage of them," and "fraternities and sororities are very active on campus: over one quarter of all students belong to a Greek organization." Of course, there's Seton Hall basketball, still popular even though the team has failed to match its "mouse that roared" feat of 1989, when it beat out schools five times its size to earn a berth in the NCAA finals. A final note to commuters: "Be sure to get a club and a car alarm. Also, the speed bumps at the front gate are too high!"

Academics

"It may have taken a Big East championship to get us noticed," explains one current Seton Hall University student, "but we're NOT just basketball." These days Seton Hall is trying to make the same big splash in the academic world that it made in the sports world. The school still primarily serves those looking for career-specific education. Nursing, communications, education, and business-related majors are the most popular choices here. However, curriculum requirements incorporate a heavy dose of liberal arts courses into every undergraduate's studies. Like many Catholic universities, SHU is cheap by private school standards, but services for students are top-notch. Says one student, "People working at SHU are very cooperative, helpful, and are very easy to associate with." A business student notes the accessibility of SHU professors, writing, "Although recently becoming a more popular school, SHU has maintained a very good student/teacher ratio. This provides the opportunities for teachers to meet and know the students as people, not as a number." Students do complain about administrative hassles and red tape. A brand new library, however, has received nothing but raves.

Student Body

Seton Hall has a minority population made up predominantly of African-Americans and Hispanics. Although a few respondents write that "racial tensions are high," most tell us that relations between groups are about normal. Students are very conservative politically. New Jersey natives make up over three-quarters of the student body.

ADMISSIONS

The admissions committee considers (in descending order of importance): HS record, class rank, test scores, essay, recommendations. *Also considered (in descending order of importance):* alumni relationship, extracurriculars, geographical distribution, personality, special talents. Either the SAT or ACT is required. An interview is recommended. Admissions process is need-blind. *High school units required/recommended:* 16 total units are required; 4 English required, 3 math required, 1 science required, 2 foreign language required, 2 social studies required. Minimum combined SAT I score of 900, rank in top two-fifths of secondary school class, and minimum 2.5 GPA recommended. *Special Requirements:* TOEFL is required of all international students. 2 units of lab science required of nursing program applicants. *The admissions office says:* "The personal attention given each application is what makes the admissions process at Seton Hall different. Every prospective student's file is read by two counselors, a committee review is held weekly, and folders are not assigned numeric averages."

The Inside Word

Getting into Seton Hall shouldn't be too stressful for most average students who have taken a full college-prep curriculum in high school. In the New York metropolitan area there are a lot of schools with similar characteristics, and collectively they take away the large proportion of Seton Hall's admits. Above average students who are serious about the university should be able to parlay their interest into some scholarship dollars, although the largest awards go to basketball players.

FINANCIAL AID

Students should submit: FAFSA. The Princeton Review suggests that all financial aid forms be submitted as soon as possible after January 1. *The following grants/scholarships are offered:* Pell, SEOG, academic merit, athletic, the school's own scholarships, the school's own grants, state scholarships, state grants, private scholarships, private grants, federal nursing scholarship, ROTC. *Students borrow from the following loan programs:* Stafford, unsubsidized Stafford, Perkins, PLUS, the school's own loan fund, state loans, federal nursing loans, private loans. College Work-Study Program is available. Institutional employment is available.

FROM THE ADMISSIONS OFFICE

"As a leading Catholic institution of higher learning, Seton Hall is committed to offering a superior academic environment fostering personal growth and career development. With a focus on the twenty-first century, the University has implemented a five-year information technology plan and completed a new $20 million library. Our computerized information retrieval system and CD-ROM technology have been expanded considerably to meet the needs of our students. A state-of-the-art classroom facility is also scheduled for completion in 1997."

ADMISSIONS

Admissions Rating	67
% of applicants accepted	75
% of acceptees attending	26

FRESHMAN PROFILE

Average verbal SAT	533
Average math SAT	529
Average ACT	21
Average TOEFL	550
Graduated top 20% of class	26
Graduated top 40% of class	52
Graduated top 60% of class	73
Average HS GPA or Avg.	3.0

DEADLINES

Early decision	NR
Regular admission	3/1
Regular notification	rolling after 1/1
Non-fall registration	yes

APPLICANTS ALSO LOOK AT

AND OFTEN PREFER
Rutgers U.
NYU
Villanova

AND SOMETIMES PREFER
Montclair State
Trenton State
Providence
U. Conn

AND RARELY PREFER
St. Bonaventure
Fairfield
Hofstra

FINANCIAL FACTS

Financial Aid Rating	73
Tuition	$12,300
Room & board	$6,958
Estimated book expense	$700
% frosh receiving aid	74
% undergrads receiving aid	74
% aid is need-based	70
% frosh w/ grant (avg)	62 ($4,345)
% frosh w/ loan (avg)	60 ($2,950)
% UGs w/ job (avg)	25 ($1,000)
Off-campus job outlook	excellent

SIENA COLLEGE

Loudonville, NY 12211-1462　　　　　　Admissions: 518-783-2423　　　Fax: 518-783-4293

CAMPUS LIFE

Quality of Life Rating	76
Type of school	private
Affiliation	Roman Catholic Church
	(Franciscan Friars)
Environment	city

STUDENTS

FT undergrad enrollment	2,529
% male/female	46/54
% from out of state	18
% live on campus	74
% spend weekend on campus	80
% transfers	5
% from public high school	70
% African-American	2
% Asian	2
% Caucasian	93
% Hispanic	2
% international	NR
# of countries represented	3

WHAT'S HOT
beer
hard liquor
intramural sports
sex
town-gown relations

WHAT'S NOT
health facilities
music associations
library
political activism
lack of diversity on campus

ACADEMICS

Academic Rating	77
Profs Interesting Rating	72
Profs Accessible Rating	81
Calendar	semester
Student/teacher ratio	16:1
% profs PhD/tenured	76/81
Hours of study per day	3.08

MOST POPULAR MAJORS
accounting
marketing/management
biology

% GRADS WHO PURSUE...
Law 3, Med 5, MBA 2, MA 9

STUDENTS SPEAK OUT

Life

Students at Siena College report that partying represents the number one on-campus diversion. Writes one student, "For fun, how about partying every night of the week? Not that I do, but that's all most people do here!" Adds another, "On weekends, most students think about partying and drinking. Thursday night is generally the big night out, and if you can close Dap's, the local bar, you're awesome!" Siena has no fraternities, and as a result most parties take place in the dorms and neighborhood bars. Many students complain that Siena's size ("In a small school, gossip travels fast") and the fact that students are very similar drives most off campus for entertainment. "For fun, we go over to other colleges and attend their parties," writes one student. Another explains, "I go to other schools such as SUNY and RPI, where there are many different types of people."

Academics

Siena College's best departments are in a variety of fields, often leading to advanced degrees: accounting, biology, marketing management, and psychology. Siena's appeal also lies in its affiliation to the Roman Catholic church; over three-quarters of the students are Catholic, and many describe it as a primary factor in their choice of Siena. One student writes that "Siena College, with its Franciscan tradition and small classes, gives me the opportunity and guidance to achieve the goals I set for myself." Students report that classes are small and that professors are dedicated. "Our professors are very committed to the academic excellence of the school and see that opportunities are given to all students interested in a particular major," observes one student. Noted another, "The professors are very easy to negotiate with. If you have problems, you can work it out with them and both sides will be happy." Students warn that "[Siena is a] small school, with good student-teacher relations, but a limited number of majors and courses," although course offerings in the most popular departments are reportedly satisfactory. Students have mixed feelings about administrators. One tells us that the "administration has gone from years and years of putting the student first to the present system of putting dollars first."

Student Body

Students at Siena are, according to most, "conservative and close-minded." The mostly Catholic population holds strongly to traditional values, especially those concerning sexual orientation; warns one student, "You have to be careful. If you are perceived as being gay, you will be persecuted by the fascists that pervade this school." Most students come from middle- to upper-middle-class backgrounds and act accordingly. Reports one student: "There are three types of students at Siena: Gap, J. Crew, and L. L. Bean."

FINANCIAL AID: 518-783-2427

ADMISSIONS

The admissions committee considers (in descending order of importance): HS record, class rank, recommendations, test scores, essay. *Also considered (in descending order of importance):* personality, alumni relationship, extracurriculars, special talents. Either the SAT or ACT is required. An interview is recommended. Admissions process is need-blind. *High school units required/recommended:* 19 total units are required; 23 total units are recommended; 4 English required, 3 math required, 4 math recommended, 3 science required, 4 science recommended, 2 foreign language required, 3 foreign language recommended, 4 social studies required, 3 history required, 4 history recommended. Additional units of math and science recommended. TOEFL is required of all international students.

The Inside Word

Students who have consistently solid grades should have no trouble getting admitted. There is hot competition for students between colleges in New York State; Siena has to admit the large majority of its applicants in order to meet freshman class enrollment targets.

FINANCIAL AID

Students should submit: FAFSA, the school's own financial aid form, state aid form, a copy of parents' most recent income tax filing. The Princeton Review suggests that all financial aid forms be submitted as soon as possible after January 1. *The following grants/scholarships are offered:* Pell, SEOG, academic merit, athletic, the school's own scholarships, the school's own grants, state scholarships, state grants, private scholarships, private grants, ROTC. *Students borrow from the following loan programs:* Stafford, unsubsidized Stafford, Perkins, PLUS, private loans. Applicants will be notified of awards beginning April 1. College Work-Study Program is available. Institutional employment is available.

FROM THE ADMISSIONS OFFICE

"Siena is a coeducational, independent liberal arts college with a Franciscan tradition. It is a community where the intellectual, personal, and social growth of all students is paramount. Siena's faculty calls forth the best Siena students have to give—and the students do the same for them. Students are competitive, but not at each other's expense. Siena's curriculum includes 73 majors in three divisions—liberal arts, science and business. In addition, there are over a dozen preprofessional and special academic programs. With a student-faculty ratio of 16:1, class size ranges between 15 and 35 students. Siena's 152-acre campus is located in Loudonville, a suburban community within two miles of the New York State seat of government in Albany. With fifteen colleges in the area, there is a wide variety of activities on weekends. Regional theater, performances by major concert artists, and professional sports events compete with the activities on the campus. Within 50 miles are the Adirondacks, the Berkshires, and the Catskills, providing outdoor recreation throughout the year. Because the capital region's easy, friendly lifestyle is so appealing, many Siena graduates try to find their first jobs in upstate New York."

ADMISSIONS

Admissions Rating		70
% of applicants accepted		81
% of acceptees attending		30

FRESHMAN PROFILE

Average verbal SAT	550
Average math SAT	560
Average ACT	23
Average TOEFL	500
Graduated top 20% of class	39
Graduated top 40% of class	88
Graduated top 60% of class	99
Average HS GPA or Avg.	NR

DEADLINES

Early decision	NR
Regular admission	3/1
Regular notification	3/15
Non-fall registration	yes

APPLICANTS ALSO LOOK AT

AND OFTEN PREFER

Villanova
Providence

AND SOMETIMES PREFER

Fairfield
Marist
SUNY Albany
Scranton
Loyola Coll. (MD)

AND RARELY PREFER

Oswego State
Fredonia State
LeMoyne
Syracuse
U. Conn

FINANCIAL FACTS

Financial Aid Rating	82
Tuition	$11,340
Room & board	$5,270
Estimated book expense	$600
% frosh receiving aid	82
% undergrads receiving aid	86
% aid is need-based	81
% frosh w/ grant (avg)	79 ($7,937)
% frosh w/ loan (avg)	NR ($2,921)
% UGs w/ job (avg)	10 ($1,200)
Off-campus job outlook	good

SIMMONS COLLEGE

300 THE FENWAY, BOSTON, MA 02115

ADMISSIONS: 800-345-8468   FAX: 617-521-3199

CAMPUS LIFE

Quality of Life Rating	**81**
Type of school	private
Affiliation	none
Environment	metropolis

STUDENTS

FT undergrad enrollment	1,111
% male/female	0/100
% from out of state	38
% live on campus	70
% spend weekend on campus	75
% transfers	13
% from public high school	82
% African-American	7
% Asian	7
% Caucasian	61
% Hispanic	3
% international	3
# of countries represented	26

WHAT'S HOT
Boston
off-campus food
leftist politics
lab facilities
honesty

WHAT'S NOT
political activism
theater
music associations
intramural sports
beer

ACADEMICS

Academic Rating	**82**
Profs Interesting Rating	87
Profs Accessible Rating	83
Calendar	semester
Student/teacher ratio	10:1
% profs PhD	78
Hours of study per day	3.36

MOST POPULAR MAJORS
nursing
communications
physical therapy

% GRADS WHO PURSUE...
Law 1, Med 1, MBA 10, MA 14

STUDENTS SPEAK OUT

Life

A common complaint at single-sex colleges is that there's not enough chance to meet and hang out with the opposite sex. However, at Simmons College, not a single student mentions the lack of men as a problem for their social life. "Because we are in Boston, most partying is done off campus," comments one student, and its location is a major attraction for many students who want the single-sex education experience without the isolation of a more rural school. Many believe that "Boston is the number one college town, no doubt about it." This urban setting, however, doesn't subtract from the feeling that Simmons is a small, caring school where some faculty members "invite you home for dinner with their family."

Academics

Simmons is a women's college with excellent preprofessional and career-oriented programs (especially in the fields of nursing, physical therapy, and business and management). Nearly as impressive is its location in central Boston. A hidden asset, however, seems to be its all-female student body. Most Simmons students feel that "Simmons college is a woman's institution that is committed to showing women how to achieve their goals in a supportive, growing environment." Students enjoy the nurturing environment, but don't let that fool you; Simmons students work hard. In terms of hours spent studying per day outside of class, they are among the top 15 percent of student bodies profiled in this book. The Simmons curriculum is demanding, requiring all students to complete forty hours of liberal arts and science classes, another twenty to forty hours of courses in their major fields, and between eight and sixteen hours of independent study. A low student/teacher ratio led to positive comments: "Our professors have a very personal one-on-one relationship with us." Simmons is difficult but respected: "Simmons sure ain't no crystal staircase, but it will get you to where you want to go." As far as the administration goes, one student reported: "How about [having] Sunday brunch at the President's house, and having the Vice President return your call in the evening?...we are recognized as individuals, and not as numbers."

Student Body

The minority population is split fairly evenly among Asians, Afican-Americans, and Hispanics. The tone of the student body is set by the wealthy, white, New England women who make up the majority. Many students complain that this majority can be close-minded when it comes to anyone or anything different from itself. One minority student describes the majority of students as "a lot of narrow-minded suburban girls who couldn't get into Smith or Wellesley." Students of all backgrounds, however, are exposed to a community of strong, intellectually independent academics. "Simmons is the definition of feminism," writes one student. Another adds that "the respect here is wonderful. Women here will stand up for one another and develop strong friendships."

FINANCIAL AID: 617-521-2036

WEB SITE: HTTP://WWW.SIMMONS.EDU

ADMISSIONS

The admissions committee considers (in descending order of importance): HS record, class rank, test scores, recommendations, essay. Also considered (in descending order of importance): alumni relationship, extracurriculars. Either the SAT or ACT is required. An interview is recommended. Admissions process is need-blind. High school units required/recommended: 15 total units are recommended; 4 English recommended, 3 math recommended, 3 science recommended, 2 foreign language recommended, 3 social studies recommended. TOEFL is required of all international students. The admissions office says: "To retain [Simmons's] diversity means its policies must be flexible, focusing on each applicant's qualities of scholarship and character."

The Inside Word

Most of the best women's colleges in the country are in the Northeast, including those Seven Sister schools (roughly the female equivalent of the formerly all-male Ivies) that remain women's colleges. The competition for students is intense, and although Simmons is a strong attraction for many women, there are at least a half-dozen competitors who draw the better students away. For the majority of applicants there is little need for anxiety while awaiting a decision. Its solid academics, Boston location, and bountiful scholarship program make Simmons well worth considering for any student opting for a women's college.

FINANCIAL AID

Students should submit: FAFSA (due February 1), the school's own financial aid form (due February 1), a copy of parents' most recent income tax filing (due February 1). The Princeton Review suggests that all financial aid forms be submitted as soon as possible after January 1. The following grants/scholarships are offered: Pell, SEOG, academic merit, the school's own scholarships, the school's own grants, state scholarships, private scholarships, private grants. Students borrow from the following loan programs: Stafford, unsubsidized Stafford, Perkins, PLUS, the school's own loan fund, state loans. Applicants will be notified of awards beginning April 1. College Work-Study Program is available. Institutional employment is available.

FROM THE ADMISSIONS OFFICE

"The Simmons idea is not novel today; indeed, its time has come. Since the early 1900s there have been dramatic changes in society's attitudes toward women and in women's perception of themselves and what they contribute in every field of activity. Simmons College has not only kept pace with these changes, it also has helped to shape them in its classrooms and by the example of its graduates in the careers they have undertaken and the leadership they have provided."

ADMISSIONS

Admissions Rating	73
% of applicants accepted	67
% of acceptees attending	31

FRESHMAN PROFILE

Average verbal SAT	560
Average math SAT	520
Average ACT	24
Average TOEFL	550
Graduated top 20% of class	47
Graduated top 40% of class	86
Graduated top 60% of class	96
Average HS GPA or Avg.	NR

DEADLINES

Early decision	1/1
Regular admission	2/1
Regular notification	4/15
Non-fall registration	yes

APPLICANTS ALSO LOOK AT

AND OFTEN PREFER

Boston Coll.
Boston U.
Mount Holyoke
Wellesley
Bryn Mawr

AND SOMETIMES PREFER

Wheaton (MA)
Northeastern
Smith

AND RARELY PREFER

U. Mass. - Amherst
U. New Hampshire

FINANCIAL FACTS

Financial Aid Rating	83
Tuition	$16,960
Room & board	$7,228
Estimated book expense	$500
% frosh receiving aid	76
% undergrads receiving aid	74
% aid is need-based	65
% frosh w/ grant (avg)	NR ($12,000)
% frosh w/ loan (avg)	76 ($3,825)
% UGs w/ job (avg)	65 ($1,086)
Off-campus job outlook	good

SIMON'S ROCK COLLEGE OF BARD

84 ALFORD ROAD, GREAT BARRINGTON, MA 01230

ADMISSIONS: 800-235-7186   FAX: 413-528-7334

CAMPUS LIFE

Quality of Life Rating   **80**
Type of school   private
Affiliation   none
Environment   town

STUDENTS

FT undergrad enrollment	304
% male/female	38/62
% from out of state	87
% live on campus	95
% spend weekend on campus	90
% transfers	1
% from public high school	77
% African-American	7
% Asian	8
% Caucasian	65
% Hispanic	2
% international	2
# of countries represented	5

WHAT'S HOT
cigarettes
theater
different students interact
leftist politics
sex

WHAT'S NOT
beer
student publications
Greeks
computer facilities
lab facilities

ACADEMICS

Academic Rating	**92**
Profs Interesting Rating	97
Profs Accessible Rating	95
Calendar	4-1-4
Student/teacher ratio	8:1
% profs PhD/tenured	90/90
Hours of study per day	3.64

MOST POPULAR MAJORS
arts and aesthetics
literary studies
social sciences

% GRADS WHO PURSUE...
Med 1, MA 33

STUDENTS SPEAK OUT

Life

One literature major writes, "Simon's Rock is the only place where every human being misunderstood socially, politically, emotionally, sexually, and intellectually comes together for a once-in-a-lifetime challenge." It is true that most students are here because they were unsatisfied intellectually, some perhaps socially, in high school; this shared history creates "a special bond among students." The social life is varied; some love the fact that "there's no single social norm," while others find it "insane," lamenting the lack of "normal extracurricular activities." The campus is "very liberal, very sexually active, and there is an unmistakable drug presence (mostly pot and acid)." One student explains, "Since classes are very challenging, the weekends are for decompression." The size and intimacy of "the Rock" help early entrants "to make the transition from high school to college, from living at home to living on your own." But most do not stay for four years. As one student tells us, "After a while it just gets too small and it becomes time to move on. Usually two years are enough."

Academics

Simon's Rock provides a welcome academic haven for about three hundred unique students. What sets them apart is their age (usually between fifteen and eighteen), and the fact that most of them have fled high school in search of greater academic challenges. Indeed, this innovative college prides itself on rescuing extremely gifted young people who are bored or unhappy in high school. Simon's Rock is "for people who feel that our educational system has them in a choke hold. It is a welcome release and a wonderful opportunity," writes one student. The academics are considered "astounding" and professors are "vital and exciting." Classes are small and very difficult; half of the course load consists of requirements, but independent studies and creative arts are very common. An advantage of the College's small size is "as much student/teacher contact as you need." One student says, "In an atmosphere that provides almost unequaled support for learning (intellectual or otherwise), one is limited only by the difficult transition between adolescence and freedom that we go through. Never has there been a greater concentration of unique and intelligent life."

Student Body

Simon's Rock is "not for the fainthearted and/or conservative," according to students. Political opinions, mostly quite liberal ones, are expressed strongly and often; one student wryly calls his peers "a bunch of rich kids pretending to be working-class revolutionaries." They actually are a bunch of young, lively, extremely bright students who have forsaken limited high school experiences in exchange for a great educational head start. Lauds one happy student, "I can't thank my fellow students enough for not being typical."

FINANCIAL AID: 413-528-7297

WEB SITE: HTTP://WWW.SIMONS-ROCK.EDU/

ADMISSIONS

The admissions committee considers (in descending order of importance): essay, HS record, recommendations, test scores. *Also considered (in descending order of importance):* personality, extracurriculars, special talents, alumni relationship. Either the SAT or ACT is required; SAT is preferred. An interview is required. Admissions process is need-blind. TOEFL is required of all international students. *The admissions office says:* "Most other competitive schools don't permit bright, highly motivated sixteen-year-olds to apply. We do object to the 'dumbing down' style of instruction offered in even the 'best' secondary schools and usually feel that the last year of high school, while fun for some, rarely provides a powerful intellectual experience."

The Inside Word

There is no other college like Simon's Rock in the country, and no other similar admissions process. Applying to college doesn't get any more personal, and thus any more demanding, than it does here. If you're not ready to tap your potential as a thinker in college beginning with completion of the application, avoid Simon's Rock. Simply hating high school isn't going to get you in. Self-awareness, intellectual curiosity, and a desire for more formidable academic challenges than those typically found in high school will.

FINANCIAL AID

Students should submit: FAFSA, CSS Profile, the school's own financial aid form, state aid form, a copy of parents' most recent income tax filing. The Princeton Review suggests that all financial aid forms be submitted as soon as possible after January 1. *The following grants/scholarships are offered:* Pell, SEOG, academic merit, the school's own scholarships, the school's own grants, state scholarships, state grants, private scholarships, private grants. *Students borrow from the following loan programs:* Stafford, Perkins, PLUS, state loans. College Work-Study Program is available. Institutional employment is available.

FROM THE ADMISSIONS OFFICE

"Simon's Rock is, as far as we know, the only four-year college in the U.S. wholly devoted to early admission. Our students typically enroll after completing the tenth or eleventh grade, and pursue a full-time course of study in the liberal arts and sciences. The college offers a two-year AA degree and a four-year BA degree. Who goes to college two years early? Very serious students, for the most part. Our freshman have often had excellent high school records, but found themselves wanting more challenge than even AP or honors classes could offer. Simon's Rock also believes that sixteen-year-olds deserve to be taken seriously, which is an idea many students find attractive."

ADMISSIONS

Admissions Rating	87
% of applicants accepted	60
% of acceptees attending	54

FRESHMAN PROFILE

Average verbal SAT	670
Average math SAT	600
Average ACT	27
Average TOEFL	500
Graduated top 20% of class	NR
Graduated top 40% of class	NR
Graduated top 60% of class	NR
Average HS GPA or Avg.	3.2

DEADLINES

Early decision	NR
Regular admission	7/1
Regular notification	rolling
Non-fall registration	yes

APPLICANTS ALSO LOOK AT

AND SOMETIMES PREFER

See note below left: "From The Admissions Office"

FINANCIAL FACTS

Financial Aid Rating	85
Tuition	$17,690
Room & board	$5,860
Estimated book expense	$400
% frosh receiving aid	89
% undergrads receiving aid	85
% aid is need-based	65
% frosh w/ grant (avg)	90 ($9,500)
% frosh w/ loan (avg)	80 ($2,625)
% UGs w/ job (avg)	50 ($1,000)
Off-campus job outlook	fair

SKIDMORE COLLEGE

SARATOGA SPRINGS, NY 12866   ADMISSIONS: 800-867-6007   FAX: 518-584-3023

CAMPUS LIFE

Quality of Life Rating   **93**
Type of school   private
Affiliation   none
Environment   suburban

STUDENTS

FT undergrad enrollment	2,150
% male/female	40/60
% from out of state	70
% live on campus	80
% spend weekend on campus	85
% transfers	1
% from public high school	61
% African-American	2
% Asian	4
% Caucasian	84
% Hispanic	5
% international	2
# of countries represented	29

WHAT'S HOT

off-campus food
theater
cigarettes
dorms
college radio

WHAT'S NOT

Greeks
library
religion
health facilities
intramural sports

ACADEMICS

Academic Rating	**85**
Profs Interesting Rating	91
Profs Accessible Rating	95
Calendar	semester
Student/teacher ratio	11:1
% profs PhD/tenured	80/67
Hours of study per day	3.06

MOST POPULAR MAJORS

business
English
government

% GRADS WHO PURSUE...

Law 5, Med 2, MBA 1, MA 17

STUDENTS SPEAK OUT

Life

Skidmore College students love Saratoga Springs, "a beautiful town with a great history." The town "has excellent work/internship opportunities, great social opportunities, and of course the famous racetrack." Students head into town to hit the bars: a student tells us that "for nondrinkers or those without ID, alternative social activities are sometimes tough to find." The area offers outdoorsmen/women opportunities for white-water rafting, skiing, and hiking. Campus clubs and organizations are plentiful, and the college radio station is very popular in the area. Dating is made a little difficult by the disproportionate number of women here—the male/female ratio is about 2:3. Skidmore's dorms are among the highest-rated of the schools in Best 310. Reports one student, "About half the sophomore class has single rooms. Juniors are pretty much guaranteed a single with a window!"

Academics

Major renovations to the campus and administration efforts to attract a more competitive student body led several independent counselors to report that Skidmore College "has come a long way and continues to improve." Long a popular choice with Eastern prepsters, Skidmore strengths are in the "liberal arts, fine arts, and performing arts," according to another area counselor. A core curriculum, called Liberal Studies, exposes students to a solid grounding in the "greatest hits" of Western arts and sciences. Says one student, "The Liberal Studies sequence at Skidmore is a valuable supplement to a solid liberal arts education. Liberal Studies I: The Human Experience epitomizes Skidmore's vision of the student body as open-minded and appreciative of today's diverse, complex, and often ambiguous global community." Multiculturalism and political correctness are hot issues here, more so with professors and administrators than with students. Students praise their professors and administrators ("President Porter is very accessible; there was even a raffle to change places with the president for a day, where a student would perform his duties and he would attend classes," reports one student).

Student Body

Skidmore's student body has traditionally included a large share of rich preppies. The administration has made efforts recently to attract a more diverse student body, with mixed results. Reports one senior, "Skidmore is a lot less materialistic than it was three years ago when I got here. In fact, the school now has a Deadhead feel. Diversity is still lacking, but awareness is more prevalent than it used to be." Most students find their classmates superficially open and friendly, but cliquish and difficult to get to know well. While students identify themselves as politically left-of-center, many write to tell us that their classmates are basically apathetic: says one, "The professors are more liberal than the student body, and that division widens yearly."

ADMISSIONS

The admissions committee considers (in descending order of importance): HS record, recommendations, test scores, class rank, essay. *Also considered (in descending order of importance):* extracurriculars, personality, geographical distribution, special talents, alumni relationship. Either the SAT or ACT is required. An interview is recommended. *High school units required/recommended:* 16 total units are required; 4 English required, 3 math required, 3 science required, 3 foreign language required, 1 social studies required, 2 history required. TOEFL is required of all international students. *The admissions office says:* "We seek students who demonstrate intellectual curiosity, open-mindedness, an energetic commitment to learning, and a concern for others. The admissions committee's primary emphasis is on the strength of the candidate's academic record, personal qualities, accomplishments, interests, and capacity for growth. Although a personal interview is not required, it is strongly recommended."

The Inside Word

Although Skidmore overlaps applicants with some of the best colleges and universities in the Northeast, it's mainly as a safety. Still, this makes for a strong applicant pool, and those students who do enroll give the college a better-than-average freshman academic profile. The entire admissions operation at Skidmore is impressive and efficient, proof that number two does indeed try harder.

FINANCIAL AID

Students should submit: FAFSA (due February 1), CSS Profile (due February 1). The Princeton Review suggests that all financial aid forms be submitted as soon as possible after January 1. *The following grants/scholarships are offered:* Pell, SEOG, the school's own grants, state scholarships, state grants, private scholarships, private grants, ROTC. *Students borrow from the following loan programs:* Stafford, Perkins, PLUS, the school's own loan fund. Applicants will be notified of awards beginning April 1. College Work-Study Program is available. Institutional employment is available.

FROM THE ADMISSIONS OFFICE

"Skidmore's Liberal Studies Curriculum is a highly interdisciplinary core curriculum that enriches a student's first two years of study. Students take one course in each of four liberal studies areas, beginning with Liberal Studies I: The Human Experience. This is a cornerstone course which is team-taught to all freshmen by twenty-eight professors from virtually every department in the college. It involves lectures, performances, films, and regular small group discussions. Students then take one liberal studies course in each of the three succeeding semesters in the following areas: Cultural Traditions and Social Change, Artistic Forms and Critical Concepts, and Science, Society, and Human Values. The purpose of this constellation of courses is to show the important academic interrelationships across disciplines, across cultures, and across time. The result is that our students learn to look for connections among the disciplines rather than see them in isolation. With this interdisciplinary foundation under their belts by the end of the sophomore year, students are better prepared to then select a major (or combination of majors) that matches their interests."

ADMISSIONS

Admissions Rating	76
% of applicants accepted	65
% of acceptees attending	20

FRESHMAN PROFILE

Average verbal SAT	610
Average math SAT	600
Average ACT	28
Average TOEFL	NR
Graduated top 20% of class	47
Graduated top 40% of class	78
Graduated top 60% of class	95
Average HS GPA or Avg.	NR

DEADLINES

Early decision	NR
Regular admission	2/1
Regular notification	4/1
Non-fall registration	yes

APPLICANTS ALSO LOOK AT

AND OFTEN PREFER

Trinity (CT)
Middlebury Coll.
Vassar

AND SOMETIMES PREFER

American
Syracuse
Boston U.

AND RARELY PREFER

Clark

FINANCIAL FACTS

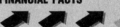

Financial Aid Rating	84
Tuition	$20,671
Room & board	$6,110
Estimated book expense	$550
% frosh receiving aid	40
% undergrads receiving aid	49
% aid is need-based	NR
% frosh w/ grant (avg)	30 ($13,013)
% frosh w/ loan (avg)	35 ($2,600)
% UGs w/ job (avg)	47 ($900)
Off-campus job outlook	good

SMITH COLLEGE

NORTHAMPTON, MA 01063   ADMISSIONS: 413-585-2500   FAX: 413-585-2075

CAMPUS LIFE

Quality of Life Rating   **92**
Type of school   private
Affiliation   none
Environment   city

STUDENTS

FT undergrad enrollment	2,592
% male/female	0/100
% from out of state	82
% live on campus	90
% spend weekend on campus	80
% transfers	19
% from public high school	67
% African-American	3
% Asian	11
% Caucasian	73
% Hispanic	4
% international	8
# of countries represented	63

WHAT'S HOT
campus feels safe
dorms
library
off-campus food
support groups

WHAT'S NOT
beer
hard liquor
Greeks
intramural sports
sex

ACADEMICS

Academic Rating	**94**
Profs Interesting Rating	97
Profs Accessible Rating	96
Calendar	semester
Student/teacher ratio	10:1
% profs PhD/tenured	96/73
Hours of study per day	4.10

MOST POPULAR MAJORS
government
psychology
art

% GRADS WHO PURSUE...
Law 15, Med 4, MA 42

STUDENTS SPEAK OUT

Life

Undergrads at all-women Smith are quite happy with their choice of college. "Smith is the perfect combination for me. During the week it's like a sleepover party with all my best friends. You can concentrate and relax. On weekends you can catch the bus to Amherst or U Mass and party with the boys." Another adds, "Every student makes her own social life at Smith. Between the five colleges, the lesbian community on campus, and the men in the area, everyone can find some way to have fun." The majority of the students live on campus, and rate their dorms (which are actually large houses) very well. According to one student, "They are homes, not just a bunch of beds." Students also seem to like the food ("We get Thursday night candlelit dinners and Friday teas"), which is rare at most colleges. "Smithies" feel safe, and report that "The campus is absolutely beautiful and easy to get around." Smith students report that overall, they are quite happy. As one student puts it, "I feel like I'm taking a four-year break from the real world, but ultimately one that will prepare me to do whatever I want to do out there." Another is certain, "I will leave this school with confidence and power."

Academics

Smith students describe their professors as "dynamic," "caring," and "an honor to study with." All courses are taught by professors, and students surveyed have almost no complaints at all about their teachers. "The teachers engage you in real, intelligent conversation and they respect you, if not always your opinions," says one student, while another raves "My professors are wonderful. They are extremely accessible and always willing to exchange ideas about an off-topic issue." The students also herald the administration, which is extremely rare for most student bodies. "The administration is pretty smooth and well-organized," reported one student, while others went so far as to describe the administration as "like a family," and "stellar." There is no core curriculum at Smith, instead students design their own course of study within their majors, a feature that they love: "I came here for the academic structure that allowed and encouraged independent work. I have thrived through taking initiatives, and am impressed with fellow students who've attacked their work the same way." Another admitted "I'm finally doing the work I've always wanted to do." Students work hard (one student attributed this to the fact that they are "very competitive"), studying an average of over three hours a day. Liberal arts majors are popular, as are the natural sciences.

Student Body

Students tend to lean to the left politically and "care a lot about issues," which led some Smithies to describe classmates as "too intense," while others complain, "There is an incredible push to be politically correct." "This school is very liberal and very vocal," says another, "liberal issues are often the only ones taken seriously. In general, though, we get along and are supportive of each other." Indeed, Smithies repeatedly described their peers as accepting of one another, and intelligent as well. "Everyone here is very open and friendly. It's a very supportive atmosphere." Although some complained about the heavy politics at Smith ("The feminists here are slightly too radical"), students at Smith are overwhelmingly happy about the friends they make. As one student describes, "Relationships here are based on respect. I find that I can disagree with someone and still be very good friends with them."

ADMISSIONS

The admissions committee considers (in descending order of importance): HS record, class rank, test scores, essay, recommendations. *Also considered (in descending order of importance):* extracurriculars, special talents, alumni relationship, geographical distribution, personality. Either the SAT or ACT is required. An interview is recommended. Admissions process is not need-blind. *High school units required/recommended:* 16 total units are recommended; 4 English recommended, 3 math recommended, 2 science recommended, 3 foreign language recommended, 2 social studies recommended, 2 history recommended. TOEFL is required of all international students.

The Inside Word

Don't be fooled by high acceptance rates at Smith and other top women's colleges. The applicant pools are small and highly self-selected. Ultimately it is every bit as tough to get admitted. Only women who have taken the toughest courses available to them in high school will be competitive.

FINANCIAL AID

Students should submit: FAFSA (due February 1), CSS Profile (due February 1), the school's own financial aid form (due February 1), state aid form, Divorced Parents form (due February 1), a copy of parents' most recent income tax filing (due February 1). The Princeton Review suggests that all financial aid forms be submitted as soon as possible after January 1. *The following grants/scholarships are offered:* Pell, SEOG, the school's own scholarships, the school's own grants, state scholarships, state grants, private scholarships, private grants, foreign aid. *Students borrow from the following loan programs:* Stafford, unsubsidized Stafford, Perkins, PLUS, state loans, private loans. College Work-Study Program is available. Institutional employment is available.

FROM THE ADMISSIONS OFFICE

"Smith students choose from 1,000 courses in more than fifty areas of study. There are no specific course requirements outside the major; students meet individually with faculty advisers to plan a balanced curriculum. Smith programs offer unique opportunities, including the chance to study abroad, or at another college in the United States, and to learn firsthand about the federal government. The Ada Cornstock Scholars Program encourages women beyond the traditional age to return to college and complete their undergraduate studies. Smith is located in the scenic Connecticut River valley of western Massachusetts near a number of other outstanding educational institutions. Through the Five College Consortium, Smith, Amherst, Hampshire, and Mount Holyoke colleges and the University of Massachusetts enrich their academic, social, and cultural offerings by means of joint faculty appointments, joint courses, student and faculty exchanges, shared facilities, and other cooperative arrangements."

ADMISSIONS

Admissions Rating	92
% of applicants accepted	49
% of acceptees attending	39

FRESHMAN PROFILE

Average verbal SAT	NR
Average math SAT	NR
Average ACT	NR
Average TOEFL	NR
Graduated top 20% of class	84
Graduated top 40% of class	97
Graduated top 60% of class	100
Average HS GPA or Avg.	NR

DEADLINES

Early decision	NR
Regular admission	1/15
Regular notification	4/1
Non-fall registration	no

APPLICANTS ALSO LOOK AT

AND OFTEN PREFER

Wellesley
Brown
Cornell U.
Williams

AND SOMETIMES PREFER

Bryn Mawr
Wesleyan U.
Barnard
Amherst
Vassar

AND RARELY PREFER

Boston U.
Mt. Holyoke
Oberlin

FINANCIAL FACTS

Financial Aid Rating	80
Tuition	$20,380
Room & board	$6,920
Estimated book expense	$550
% frosh receiving aid	57
% undergrads receiving aid	52
% aid is need-based	100
% frosh w/ grant (avg)	56 ($13,799)
% frosh w/ loan (avg)	51 ($2,473)
% UGs w/ job (avg)	47 ($1,472)
Off-campus job outlook	fair

UNIVERSITY OF SOUTH CAROLINA-COLUMBIA

COLUMBIA, SC 29208   ADMISSIONS: 803-777-7700   FAX: 803-777-0101

CAMPUS LIFE

Quality of Life Rating	77
Type of school	public
Affiliation	none
Environment	city

STUDENTS

FT undergrad enrollment	12,403
% male/female	46/54
% from out of state	16
% live on campus	38
% spend weekend on campus	NR
% transfers	29
% from public high school	80
% in (# of) fraternities	9 (20)
% in (# of) sororities	9 (14)
% African-American	17
% Asian	3
% Caucasian	75
% Hispanic	1
% international	2
# of countries represented	116

WHAT'S HOT

old-fashioned dating
ethnic diversity on campus
sex
health facilities
intercollegiate sports

WHAT'S NOT

campus difficult to get around
dorms
support groups
unattractive campus
lab facilities

ACADEMICS

Academic Rating	68
Profs Interesting Rating	67
Profs Accessible Rating	65
Calendar	semester
Student/teacher ratio	16:1
% profs PhD	84
Hours of study per day	2.82

MOST POPULAR MAJORS

biology
psychology
nursing

STUDENTS SPEAK OUT

Life

Columbia, South Carolina is home to the state's flagship university, great barbecue, and the best rock and roll band in America. We speak, of course, of Hootie and the Blowfish. One thing USC is not known for, however, is sports. The Gamecocks "may suck on the football field, but we sure know how to tailgate!" USC tailgate parties, which reputedly feature every manner of intoxicant, are notorious throughout the South. Of course, Saturday mornings in the fall don't account for the entirety of social life here. For those students who go Greek, there are frequent frat parties; for the rest there's hanging out in dorms, off-campus residences, and the city of Columbia, to which students give average marks. Fewer than half the students live on campus and some of them pack up and go home every weekend, but with 12,000-plus undergrads, there's always plenty of people around.

Academics

International studies (particularly international business), a challenging honors program for qualified students, and an attractive tuition draw the serious student to USC's Columbia campus. The weather also helps: "The academic experience is great, especially when the SC weather allows you to get outside with your books." Another nobly defends the school: "Everyone thinks this is a party school, and it is, but you can still get some semblance of a college education here." Majors other than international studies receiving the undergrads' praise are business, criminal justice, political science, English, and history. One student reports that the school is taking "big strides toward improving all liberal arts." As at many inexpensive public institutions, TAs teach more than their fair share of courses, classes can be very large ("It's a hard being in such big classes at first, but by your sophomore year it kind of grows on you"), and there are "plenty of bureaucrats!" Many like the TAs: "They give good advice about tests and are more concerned about you than your professors." Another sums up, "You sometimes feel like a number, but that is to be expected at a flagship state university. Overall you get about what you put in—but no one is going to guide you by the hand."

Student Body

Around seventy-five percent of the student body is from South Carolina. The USC student body is also nearly twenty percent African-American, which makes it one of the nation's largest black student populations. But race relations could be better: "Both whites and blacks are racist." As another puts it, "We all hate each other equally." The Mason-Dixon line still holds emotional sway here: "I feel that this campus is segregated, especially Yankee-Rebel," one student reveals. Students recognize the existence of a considerable gay population, but they, too, are shunned by the majority. Most students are politically conservative, and a significant portion consider themselves religious.

FINANCIAL AID: 803-777-8134   WEB SITE: HTTP://WWW.CSD.SCAROLINA.EDU/

ADMISSIONS

The admissions committee considers (in descending order of importance): HS record, test scores, class rank, recommendations. *Also considered (in descending order of importance):* special talents. Either the SAT or ACT is required. Admissions process is need-blind. *High school units required/recommended:* 16 units are required; 4 English required, 3 math required, 2 science required, 2 foreign language required, 2 social studies required. Minimum 2.0 GPA or 15 academic secondary school units required. TOEFL is required of all international students.

The Inside Word

The admissions process at USC is formulaic, and not particularly demanding. A solid performance in high school should do the trick.

FINANCIAL AID

Students should submit: FAFSA, the school's own financial aid form. The Princeton Review suggests that all financial aid forms be submitted as soon as possible after January 1. *The following grants/scholarships are offered:* Pell, SEOG, academic merit, athletic, the school's own scholarships, private scholarships, private grants, federal nursing scholarship, ROTC. *Students borrow from the following loan programs:* Stafford, Perkins, PLUS, federal nursing loans, health professions loans, private loans. Applicants will be notified of awards beginning May 1. College Work-Study Program is available. Institutional employment is available.

FROM THE ADMISSIONS OFFICE

"The University of South Carolina offers over 80 undergraduate majors and areas of concentration. It has a graduate school, school of law, and professional-degree programs. Fully accredited by the Southern Association of Colleges and Schools, USC awards baccalaureate, master's, and doctoral degrees, and is known for its programs: accounting (US top ten), marketing and advertising (top eight), and marine science (number four) are examples. USC's Honors College is one of the nation's best. The New York Times calls it a 'thriving undergraduate honors college that operates at Ivy League standards.' Many students decide to attend USC after visiting its campus— one of America's most beautiful—in Columbia, South Carolina. This Sunbelt city offers great entertainment, cultural, and recreational activities, all within walking distance of campus. And South Carolina's world-famous beaches and the Blue Ridge Mountains are less than a three-hour drive away. Growing numbers of students are discovering that the University of South Carolina is the right choice for them."

ADMISSIONS

Admissions Rating	70
% of applicants accepted	76
% of acceptees attending	40

FRESHMAN PROFILE

Average verbal SAT	550
Average math SAT	550
Average ACT	22
Average TOEFL	550
Graduated top 20% of class	61
Graduated top 40% of class	92
Graduated top 60% of class	99
Average HS GPA or Avg.	2.9

DEADLINES

Early decision	NR
Regular admission	rolling
Regular notification	rolling
Non-fall registration	yes

APPLICANTS ALSO LOOK AT

AND OFTEN PREFER

UNC-Chapel Hill
William and Mary
SMU
Duke

AND SOMETIMES PREFER

Furman
Clemson
U. Georgia
Coll. of Charleston
Randolph-Macon Woman's

AND RARELY PREFER

Francis Marion
Winthrop
Florida State

FINANCIAL FACTS

Financial Aid Rating	77
In-state tuition	$3,278
Out-of-state tuition	$8,282
Room & board	$3,650
Estimated book expense	$545
% frosh receiving aid	50
% undergrads receiving aid	60
% aid is need-based	90
% frosh w/ grant (avg)	40 ($2,500)
% frosh w/ loan (avg)	50 ($2,625)
% UGs w/ job (avg)	7 ($1,300)
Off-campus job outlook	excellent

UNIVERSITY OF THE SOUTH

735 UNIVERSITY AVENUE, SEWANEE, TN 37383-1000   ADMISSIONS: 800-522-2234   FAX: 615-598-1667

CAMPUS LIFE

Quality of Life Rating	87
Type of school	private
Affiliation	Episcopal Church
Environment	rural

STUDENTS

FT undergrad enrollment	1,216
% male/female	50/50
% from out of state	82
% live on campus	93
% spend weekend on campus	85
% transfers	5
% from public high school	52
% in (# of) fraternities	68 (18)
% in (# of) sororities	55 (7)
% African-American	2
% Asian	0
% Caucasian	95
% Hispanic	0
% international	2
# of countries represented	17

WHAT'S HOT
beer
hard liquor
campus is beautiful
campus feels safe
students are happy

WHAT'S NOT
off-campus food
lack of diversity on campus
students are cliquish
campus food
student government

ACADEMICS

Academic Rating	91
Profs Interesting Rating	97
Profs Accessible Rating	96
Calendar	semester
Student/teacher ratio	11:1
% profs PhD/tenured	100/93
Hours of study per day	3.39

MOST POPULAR MAJORS
English
history
fine arts

% GRADS WHO PURSUE...
Law 15, Med 14, MBA 5, MA 20

STUDENTS SPEAK OUT

Life

Located in the Tennessee mountains, there are vast opportunities to enjoy the outdoors at the University of the South. "There are an unlimited number of outdoor activities. One can go mountain biking and caving on the same day and never leave the campus." Sports are very popular and so is drinking, although policies are strict enough that kegs have been banned from campus. In spite of this, University of the South is known as a party school. This doesn't mean that it's not academically challenging—students spend the vast majority of their time studying. As one student explains, "Sewanee has two strengths: academics and partying," and another, "People at Sewanee work hard Sunday through Thursday, but they make up for it by playing very, very hard on the weekends." A large number of students belong to fraternities or sororities, which is where a lot of the drinking apparently occurs: "Life is ruled by the Greek system. All parties are Greek related, but are open to anyone and most fraternities accept others. Overall, there is plenty to do and always a place to have fun." The majority of students live on campus, and students report that they feel very safe here. These students are some of the happiest in the nation. Explains one undergrad, "Sewanee provides a fine blend of academic excellence, social variation, and campus beauty."

Academics

University of the South is a small school, and students enjoy a lot of personal attention from their professors. According to one, "The intimate relationship between students and faculty is unbeatable. Students get all the attention they desire. How could you devise a study session any better than reviewing material over dessert and coffee at a professor's home?" Another student raves, "Sewanee claims primary concern with the quality of the teaching and doesn't disappoint. The students and their education really do come first." For the most part, students believe that the administration is smoothly run, although one student referred to the administration as "a bunch of Nerf-world dancing monkeys." Even so, most students agree with this one: "The administration made a few mistakes, but they're real open to hear suggestions. They can be very fair, just, and compassionate." The school abides by a strict honor code, which students are very happy with. As one student explains, "The honor code is an integral part of the Sewanee experience: the students' commitment to abstain from lying, cheating, and stealing fosters an overwhelming trust that inspires students to feel safe leaving doors unlocked and backpacks unattended." Humanities majors are very popular, but the school offers strong curricula in the sciences as well. As one student warns, "Despite Sewanee's reputation as a party school, most students are generally concerned about academics; if not, they're not around for very long."

Student Body

The average Sewanee undergrad is white, fairly conservative politically, and slightly more religious than most. One student describes his classmates as "waspy and not very diverse," while another says "The student body is completely homogenous and boring. I feel like I'm in high school for the second time," and still another asks, "Why would minority students go to a place called The University of the South? Our school screams `white.'" Perhaps because of the like-mindedness of the students, they seem to like each other a lot. One student attests that "Sewanee's students must be among the friendliest anywhere; it's rare to walk past a stranger and not receive a "hi," or at least a smile."

FINANCIAL AID: 615-598-1312   E-MAIL: SWILLIAM@SEWANEE.EDU   WEB SITE: HTTP://WWW.SEWANEE.EDU/

ADMISSIONS

The admissions committee considers (in descending order of importance): HS record, test scores, class rank, recommendations, essay. *Also considered (in descending order of importance):* extracurriculars, personality, alumni relationship, geographical distribution, special talents. Either the SAT or ACT is required. An interview is recommended. *High school units required/recommended:* 18 total units are required; 4 English required, 3 math required, 2 science required, 2 foreign language required, 2 social studies required, 2 history required. TOEFL is required of all international students. *The admissions office says:* "We expect students to challenge themselves with advanced classes [in high school], when they are offered."

The Inside Word

The admissions office at Sewanee is very personable and accessible to students. Its staff includes some of the most well-respected admissions professionals in the South, and it shows in the way they work with students. Despite a fairly high acceptance rate, candidates who take the admissions process here lightly may find themselves disappointed. Applicant evaluation is too personal for a lackadaisical approach to succeed.

FINANCIAL AID

Students should submit: FAFSA, the school's own financial aid form, a copy of parents' most recent income tax filing. The Princeton Review suggests that all financial aid forms be submitted as soon as possible after January 1. *The following grants/scholarships are offered:* Pell, SEOG, academic merit, the school's own scholarships, the school's own grants, state scholarships, state grants, private scholarships, private grants, foreign aid. *Students borrow from the following loan programs:* Stafford, unsubsidized Stafford, Perkins, PLUS, the school's own loan fund, state loans, private loans. Applicants will be notified of awards beginning April 1. College Work-Study Program is available. Institutional employment is available.

FROM THE ADMISSIONS OFFICE

"The University of the South, popularly known as Sewanee, is consistently ranked among the top tier of national liberal arts universities. Sewanee is committed to an academic curriculum that focuses on the liberal arts as the most enlightening and valuable form of undergraduate education. Founded by leaders of the Episcopal church in 1857, Sewanee continues to be owned by twenty-eight Episcopal dioceses in twelve states. The university is located on a 10,000-acre campus atop Tennessee's Cumberland Plateau between Chattanooga and Nashville. The university has an impressive record of academic achievement—twenty-two Rhodes Scholars and eighteen NCAA Postgraduate Scholarship recipients have graduated from Sewanee."

ADMISSIONS

Admissions Rating	83
% of applicants accepted	64
% of acceptees attending	31

FRESHMAN PROFILE

Average verbal SAT	640
Average math SAT	620
Average ACT	27
Average TOEFL	NR
Graduated top 20% of class	74
Graduated top 40% of class	94
Graduated top 60% of class	100
Average HS GPA or Avg.	3.4

DEADLINES

Early decision	11/15
Regular admission	2/1
Regular notification	4/1
Non-fall registration	yes

APPLICANTS ALSO LOOK AT

AND OFTEN PREFER

UNC - Chapel Hill
Washington and Lee
Virginia

AND SOMETIMES PREFER

Davidson
Vanderbilt
Wake Forest

AND RARELY PREFER

Rhodes
U. Georgia
U. Tennessee - Knoxville

FINANCIAL FACTS

Financial Aid Rating	89
Tuition	$16,790
Room & board	$4,460
Estimated book expense	$500
% frosh receiving aid	54
% undergrads receiving aid	59
% aid is need-based	87
% frosh w/ grant (avg)	55 ($9,035)
% frosh w/ loan (avg)	34 ($4,005)
% UGs w/ job (avg)	NR
Off-campus job outlook	fair

UNIVERSITY OF SOUTHERN CALIFORNIA

UNIVERSITY PARK, LOS ANGELES, CA 90089   ADMISSIONS: 213-740-1111

STUDENTS SPEAK OUT

Life

The University of Southern California is located just south of downtown Los Angeles. While the neighborhood may not be all that safe, students report that the campus is. Many feel that a car is a necessity here; for entertainment, most drive the short distance to L.A. nightspots or the beach. This does not mean that there is nothing to do if you don't have a car, however: "L.A. gives us plenty of distractions from campus life, but there is still plenty to do on campus. There must have been 2,000 things to do on campus last year." However, some students commented that on-campus activities would be more fun if more students got involved. The Greek system is popular; about a tenth of the USC student body joins. One student claims, "fraternities rule the weekends." USC students are some of the most school-spirited in the nation. Over three-quarters of the school attends the USC Trojan football games. "Athletics are a strong unifying force on campus," says one student, "campus pride and the Trojan family are very real things here."

Academics

"Our professors are experts in their fields but still accessible," one student comments. "USC has the advantages of a small private school, but also the size and strength of a large research university." More than one student tells us that "you get what you pay for," and the price of a USC education is not low. One student beams, "we have great professors who are active in real world jobs as well as at the school," and another concurs, "It's cool to see your professor's name attached to a good New York Times book review." Students enjoy the attention they get from the faculty: "The professors still remember my name years after I've taken their courses." However, one dissenter notes, "USC is good because classes are small, unlike state schools. But the professors need to spend less time doing research and more time committed to teaching. Especially at a school like USC, which is so expensive." USC offers a plethora of majors. As one might expect from a school located in Los Angeles, the film, television, drama, and journalism majors are very popular. Engineering, business, and the social sciences are also highly pursued here. For the motivated student USC offers the Thematic Option, an honors program with small classes of fewer than thirty students and a varied curriculum. More than half the students rated the library and computer facilities on campus well. Most students spend between three and five hours a day studying.

Student Body

When asked to describe their classmates, USC students use one word over and over again: diversity. "At USC I come across all walks of life and I enjoy the experience," says one. Another undergrad points out "Diversity is part of what makes USC so rich." Despite these warm sentiments, most students report that there is little interaction between the various ethnic groups. But, students maintain, "Everybody gets along well, regardless of ethnicity or social class." The minority population at USC consists mostly of Asian and Hispanic students, but African Americans are also well represented on campus. Overall, the majority of USC students are happy and extremely enthusiastic about their school. As one student writes, "USC is great! Coming to this school was the best decision I ever made. There are so many different and interesting people here!"

FINANCIAL AID: 213-740-1111

ADMISSIONS

The admissions committee considers (in descending order of importance): HS record, test scores, class rank, recommendations, essay. *Also considered (in descending order of importance):* alumni relationship, extracurriculars, personality, special talents. Either the SAT or ACT is required. An interview is recommended. Admissions process is need-blind. *High school units required/recommended:* 16 total units are required; 4 English required, 3 math required, 2 science required, 2 foreign language required, 2 social studies required. *Special Requirements:* A portfolio is required for art program applicants. An audition is required for music program applicants. Supplemental application required of cinema/television program applicants. *The admissions office says:* "The various schools and departments at USC have their own individual requirements for admission, and some have separate deadlines as well. Contact the school for details. Recommended high school curriculum: college prep."

The Inside Word

The high national visibility of its athletic teams and glamorous image enables USC to maintain a large applicant pool. Admissions standards for specific programs will do more to trip up individual candidates than the general process itself—solid students with above-average academic records should encounter smooth sailing.

FINANCIAL AID

Students should submit: FAFSA (due March 1), state aid form (due March 1), a copy of parents' most recent income tax filing (due May 1). The Princeton Review suggests that all financial aid forms be submitted as soon as possible after January 1. *The following grants/scholarships are offered:* Pell, SEOG, academic merit, athletic, the school's own scholarships, the school's own grants, state scholarships, state grants, private scholarships, private grants, ROTC. *Students borrow from the following loan programs:* Stafford, Perkins, PLUS, the school's own loan fund, health professions loans, private loans. Applicants will be notified of awards beginning rolling. College Work-Study Program is available. Institutional employment is available.

FROM THE ADMISSIONS OFFICE

USC administers one of the largest financial aid programs in the world. More than 20 percent of USC students receive scholarships based on merit. The scholarship application deadline is December 15.

ADMISSIONS

Admissions Rating	77
% of applicants accepted	72
% of acceptees attending	29

FRESHMAN PROFILE

Average verbal SAT	510
Average math SAT	600
Average ACT	25
Average TOEFL	NR
Graduated top 20% of class	65
Graduated top 40% of class	96
Graduated top 60% of class	99
Average HS GPA or Avg.	3.5

DEADLINES

Early decision	NR
Regular admission	1/31
Regular notification	4/1
Non-fall registration	yes

APPLICANTS ALSO LOOK AT

AND OFTEN PREFER

UCLA
Georgetown U.

AND SOMETIMES PREFER

Loyola Marymount
U. Washington
U. Texas - Austin
U. of the Pacific
UC - Riverside

AND RARELY PREFER

U. Arizona

FINANCIAL FACTS

Financial Aid Rating	79
Tuition	$18,246
Room & board	$6,482
Estimated book expense	$600
% frosh receiving aid	64
% undergrads receiving aid	56
% aid is need-based	62
% frosh w/ grant (avg)	NR
% frosh w/ loan (avg)	54
% UGs w/ job (avg)	11 ($2,700)
Off-campus job outlook	good

SOUTHERN METHODIST UNIVERSITY

6422 BOAZ STREET, P.O. BOX 296, DALLAS, TX 75275-0296   ADMISSIONS: 214-768-2058   FAX: 214-768-4138

STUDENTS SPEAK OUT

Life

Though SMU students make some use of metropolitan Dallas' nightclubs, cultural spots, and "bars, bars, bars," most point out that there is little reason to leave campus for entertainment. "There are more activities, guest speakers, and seminars available (on campus) than I can attend," one respondent tells us. "This school is extremely Greek-oriented," another adds, "That is where campus life is." "As a freshman, every upperclassman is extremely nice and congenial towards you due mostly to deferred rush," a student reports. She added that rush is a major part of life at SMU "whether you're a freshman or an upperclassman, because the Greeks are the ones hosting the weekend entertainment." As at most frat-dominated universities (and most colleges in general) drinking is extremely popular, but peer pressure is not a problem; as one student puts it, "there is a lot of heavy drinking here and heavy partying. However, people are not looked down upon for not drinking or partaking in any vices."

Academics

"My professors are excellent," more than one Southern Methodist University student writes. A large percentage of SMU students opt for business and management and other pre-professional degrees, but there are excellent liberal arts and fine arts programs as well. One respondent to our survey tells us, "I love this school because it caters to every student's needs." While many students have the typical big-school experience with the administration ("The red tape is awful"), more than half of our freshman respondents find it relatively easy to get into the classes they want. "Persistence pays off and there are some smart, terrific administrators who will help you out," one student tells us. Another says, "Professors are always available...Academically, every course is challenging, but there is always someone to help around." About the level of academic challenge at SMU there has been some skepticism for a number of years. Indeed, more than half of the students we surveyed claim to spend fewer than three hours a day studying outside of class. Unlike the students in last year's survey, however, those in this year's group don't seem to mind. None of them, at least, complain about it. "I love SMU!" one exclaimed. "Small, interacting student body, beautiful campus, and fun town." Another's suggestion is even more succinct, if equally ungrammatical: "The only thing I would change is more parking."

Student Body

"Despite various backgrounds, we usually treat each other with mutual respect," one SMU student writes about the social atmosphere on campus. The emphasis placed on the word *usually* is apropos of a concern shared by many SMU students: that a large number of their classmates are upper-class snobs. "SMU is composed of a homogeneous student body," one comments. "If you are like a typical SMU student, things will be great. If you are not it could be a rough four to five years." Another respondent put it more bluntly: "The students here live in a bubble. They are sheltered and often opinionated and not accepting of people who are different." While these sentiments are echoed by other students, just as many praise their classmates' friendliness and remark on how well everyone gets along.

FINANCIAL AID: 214-SMU-3417

WEB SITE: HTTP://WWW.COX.SMU.EDU/

ADMISSIONS

The admissions committee considers (in descending order of importance): HS record, class rank, recommendations, test scores, essay. *Also considered (in descending order of importance):* extracurriculars, special talents, alumni relationship, personality. Either the SAT or ACT is required. Admissions process is need-blind. *High school units required/recommended:* 15 total units are required; 4 English required, 3 math required, 3 science required, 2 foreign language required, 3 social studies required. *Special Requirements:* An audition is required for music program applicants. TOEFL is required of all international students. Portfolio recommended of art scholarship applicants. *The admissions office says:* "No one item is given precedence over another. The entire application package is considered for acceptance at Southern Methodist University. Though an interview is optional, it is always recommended."

The Inside Word

SMU's School of the Arts is one of the best in the country, and applicants face a very competitive admissions process. The university in general is not quite as selective, but the expectations are high enough so that average students with academic inconsistencies or weak test scores can expect to encounter a rocky road to admission.

FINANCIAL AID

Students should submit: FAFSA, the school's own financial aid form. The Princeton Review suggests that all financial aid forms be submitted as soon as possible after January 1. *The following grants/scholarships are offered:* Pell, SEOG, academic merit, athletic, the school's own scholarships, the school's own grants, state grants, private scholarships, private grants, ROTC, foreign aid. *Students borrow from the following loan programs:* Stafford, unsubsidized Stafford, Perkins, PLUS, the school's own loan fund, state loans, private loans. Applicants will be notified of awards beginning March 15. College Work-Study Program is available. Institutional employment is available.

FROM THE ADMISSIONS OFFICE

"Southern Methodist University is a private, coeducational university five miles north of the heart of Dallas, situated on a park-like campus with tree-lined streets. Founded in 1911 by what today is the United Methodist Church, the university welcomes students of every religion, race, ethnic origin, and economic background and furthermore meets the demonstrated financial need of qualified students. SMU's programs are characterized by small classes and a low student/faculty ratio of 14:1. Undergraduates are taught by faculty members, not graduate assistants. The opportunities available to undergraduates in four schools—Dedman College, the School of Humanities and Sciences; the Meadows School of the Arts; the Edwin L. Cox School of Business; and the School of Engineering and Applied Science—are enhanced by the resources, facilities, and faculty of the university's graduate and professional programs (in communication, the arts, engineering, the humanities and sciences, business, theology, and law)."

ADMISSIONS

Admissions Rating	75
% of applicants accepted	90
% of acceptees attending	35

FRESHMAN PROFILE

Average verbal SAT	NR
Average math SAT	NR
Average ACT	26
Average TOEFL	550
Graduated top 20% of class	53
Graduated top 40% of class	82
Graduated top 60% of class	97
Average HS GPA or Avg.	3.2

DEADLINES

Early decision	1/15
Regular admission	4/1
Regular notification	rolling
Non-fall registration	yes

APPLICANTS ALSO LOOK AT

AND OFTEN PREFER

Northwestern U.
Georgetown U.

AND SOMETIMES PREFER

Tulane
Emory
U. Texas - Austin
Rhodes
Vanderbilt

AND RARELY PREFER

TCU
Pepperdine
Baylor
U. Southern Cal

FINANCIAL FACTS

Financial Aid Rating	90
Tuition	$13,510
Room & board	$5,078
Estimated book expense	$576
% frosh receiving aid	80
% undergrads receiving aid	72
% aid is need-based	65
% frosh w/ grant (avg)	77 ($6,788)
% frosh w/ loan (avg)	43 ($5,412)
% UGs w/ job (avg)	19 ($2,000)
Off-campus job outlook	good

SOUTHWESTERN UNIVERSITY

UNIVERSITY AT MAPLE, GEORGETOWN, TX 78626 · · · · · ADMISSIONS: 800-252-3166 · · · FAX: 512-863-5788

CAMPUS LIFE

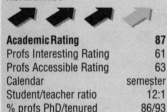

Quality of Life Rating	81
Type of school	private
Affiliation	United Methodist Church
Environment	town

STUDENTS

FT undergrad enrollment	1,213
% male/female	44/56
% from out of state	13
% live on campus	75
% spend weekend on campus	65
% transfers	11
% from public high school	87
% in (# of) fraternities	36 (4)
% in (# of) sororities	38 (4)
% African-American	3
% Asian	5
% Caucasian	79
% Hispanic	11
% international	2
# of countries represented	14

WHAT'S HOT
old-fashioned dating
sex
student government
leftist politics
college radio

WHAT'S NOT
cigarettes
registration is a pain
dorms
inefficient administration
lab facilities

ACADEMICS

Academic Rating	87
Profs Interesting Rating	61
Profs Accessible Rating	63
Calendar	semester
Student/teacher ratio	12:1
% profs PhD/tenured	86/93
Hours of study per day	2.92

MOST POPULAR MAJORS
psychology
biology
accounting

% GRADS WHO PURSUE...
Law 5, Med 7, MBA 5, MA 12

STUDENTS SPEAK OUT

Life

Southwestern University is located in Georgetown, a sleepy town that both attracts and repels students. "There is a mix of people who either really like Georgetown's small-town life or people who try to go to Austin every chance they get." Either way, you need a car, because after fraternity parties, the most popular activity with the first set is "rolling": "driving down the Georgetown country roads very slowly and drinking lots." Thankfully, the driver remains sober. For the second group, "the 20 minute trip to Austin makes it very bearable," thanks to bars with great bands and good clubs for dancing. On campus, students enjoy one another intellectually, since "nobody shies away from intellectual and political discussions." And if the school's surrounding area doesn't have much in the way of excitement, it does offer students a rewarding engagement with the community and each other: as one student relates his activities, "since service is big, first it's over to Taylor, a town of mud, to build a house. Then it's back to Georgetown, for a playground construction. Then back to some campus gathering to drink the favorite local beer, Shiner Bock."

Academics

Southwestern is a small, private liberal arts school where professors make teaching their top priority. A core curriculum requires all students to acquire a solid liberal arts background. Students praise the school's "excellent studies abroad programs" (nearly a third spend time overseas) and the Brown Symposium, a two-day series of seminars during spring semester for which classes are suspended; scholars from around the world deliver lectures and lead discussions. But SU students save their greatest praise for their teachers, whom they rank among the highest in the nation. One student remarks, "The school is constructed so that the professors challenge your views but respect them. They open doors of thought." And another adds, "Most of the professors here are extremely cool, many are downright brilliant...I'm just overshadowed by genius." And they not only love to teach, they love their students: "My professors are always begging me to come visit them. I think they get offended if I have to cut my visits Then it's back to Georgetown, for a playground construction. Then back to some campus gathering to drink the favorite local beer, Shiner Bock."

Student Body

SU Students are politically middle-of-the-road, which makes them liberal by Texas standards. Some students mention that the student body is nice but could be more interesting: "The campus is very friendly and most students are easy to talk to and get along with but [the school] lacks diversity." Minority students suffer from this lack, as one Latina woman tells us, "Being a minority has made it worse living on this campus...The only thing you can accomplish at Southwestern is to get a great education, but I feel college life is supposed to be so much more." According to one student, "major improvements have been made the past four years regarding the treatment of gays, lesbians, and bisexuals on campus, but much education still needs to be done." A considerable minority feel their classmates are "cliquish," and gossip is a big annoyance.

ADMISSIONS

The admissions committee considers (in descending order of importance): HS record, class rank, test scores, essay, recommendations. *Also considered (in descending order of importance):* alumni relationship, extracurriculars, geographical distribution, personality, special talents. Either the SAT or ACT is required; SAT is preferred. An interview is required of some applicants. Admissions process is need-blind. *High school units required/recommended:* 17 total units are recommended; 4 English recommended, 4 math recommended, 3 science recommended, 2 foreign language recommended, 2 social studies recommended, 1 history recommended. *Special Requirements:* A portfolio is required for art program applicants. An audition is required for music program applicants. TOEFL is required of all international students. Audition required of music and theatre program applicants. *The admissions office says:* "[Our admissions process includes] a participatory and democratic review process. All decisions involve agreement from at least two readers."

The Inside Word

Southwestern is one of the best "sleepers" in the nation. Admissions standards are high, but they would be even more so if more people knew of this place. Academic excellence abounds, the administration is earnest and helpful, and the school is beginning to attract national recognition. If you could thrive in a small-town, close-knit environment, Southwestern definitely deserves a look.

FINANCIAL AID

Students should submit: FAFSA (due March 15), the school's own financial aid form (due March 1). The Princeton Review suggests that all financial aid forms be submitted as soon as possible after January 1. *The following grants/scholarships are offered:* Pell, SEOG, academic merit, the school's own scholarships, the school's own grants, state grants, private scholarships, private grants, foreign aid. *Students borrow from the following loan programs:* Stafford, unsubsidized Stafford, Perkins, PLUS, the school's own loan fund, state loans, private loans. College Work-Study Program is available. Institutional employment is available.

FROM THE ADMISSIONS OFFICE

"The college selection process can often be very difficult and confusing. What I hope we all remember is the importance of helping students make good choices that will be in line with meeting their needs. There is often a big difference between what a person wants and needs. Students must concentrate on meeting their needs and not simply satisfying their wants. Colleges are very different, just as people are. Our responsibility is to help students have a complete and accurate view of Southwestern. The student's responsibility is to present himself or herself honestly. Together we can approach our selections with the ultimate goal of having students successfully complete their educations at our institution, becoming satisfied alumni, and knowing that their college years had a positive and lasting impact on their lives."

ADMISSIONS

Admissions Rating	78
% of applicants accepted	76
% of acceptees attending	35

FRESHMAN PROFILE

Average verbal SAT	670
Average math SAT	600
Average ACT	26
Average TOEFL	550
Graduated top 20% of class	NR
Graduated top 40% of class	NR
Graduated top 60% of class	NR
Average HS GPA or Avg.	3.4

DEADLINES

Early decision	1/1
Regular admission	2/15
Regular notification	4/1
Non-fall registration	yes

APPLICANTS ALSO LOOK AT

AND OFTEN PREFER

Rice
Trinity U.

AND SOMETIMES PREFER

SMU
TCU
Rhodes
Tulane
Vanderbilt

AND RARELY PREFER

Texas A&M
Austin
U. Texas - Austin
Baylor

FINANCIAL FACTS

Financial Aid Rating	91
Tuition	$13,400
Room & board	$4,868
Estimated book expense	$600

% frosh receiving aid	78
% undergrads receiving aid	73
% aid is need-based	74
% frosh w/ grant (avg)	78 ($8,091)
% frosh w/ loan (avg)	51 ($3,136)
% UGs w/ job (avg)	41 ($1,200)
Off-campus job outlook	good

SPELMAN COLLEGE

350 SPELMAN LANE, SW, ATLANTA, GA 30314 ADMISSIONS: 404-681-3643 FAX: 404-223-1449

STUDENTS SPEAK OUT

Life

"Atlanta is great!" writes one student, summing up the attitudes of students at Spelman College (as, indeed, at every area college). Another Spelman student reports that "Atlanta is a big city and there is always something to do. In the Atlanta University Center, there are so many students that many different activities are provided for our entertainment and fun." One drawback, also common to urban campuses, is that "our public safety sucks. Any weirdo can get on our campus far too easily." The single-sex orientation of Spelman makes life "interesting. At an all-girls' school, it's rare to see a guy in class or outside. Many people enjoy going over to Morehouse, an all-male school just across the street." Greek life plays a major part in the social scene (even though only 15 percent of the students actually pledge a sorority); Greek parties at Spelman and Morehouse are generally big events. Also popular are extracurricular clubs, particularly community service and leadership organizations. Students complain that athletic facilities are poor, which might explain students' lack of interest in intercollegiate and intramural sports. Concludes one woman: "I would recommend Spelman College to any young lady who wants to get the full experience of college life."

Academics

Spelman College is one of only two remaining all-female historically black colleges in the country. It is also one of the nation's pre-eminent historically black institutions. Women who choose Spelman do so for the opportunity to be surrounded by others like themselves: black, bright, and highly motivated. Explains one, "Spelman College is a great school for up-and-coming African-American females. The school gives us the opportunity to relate our life experiences to the outside world. Here, we learn to express ourselves and to stand up for what we believe in." Preprofessional majors—computer science, premed, pre-law, and pre-business—are most popular with Spelman women, but all students receive a well-rounded education in communication skills, science, math, social science, fine arts, and literature because of a rigorous core curriculum. Of their professors, students note that "The vast majority of the professors are wonderful teachers. I love the fact that I have many brilliant black professors. It does wonders for your self-esteem when your professors look just like you." To expand their academic options even more, Spelman students can, and do, take courses at all-male Morehouse College across the street.

Student Body

The typical Spelman student is dedicated to career pursuits. She is also religious (church services are a regular part of most students' lives), socially conservative (drug use and homosexuality are generally frowned upon), and politically liberal but not activist. Explains one senior: "It has been my experience that Spelman students are not very politically minded, i.e., not concerned with the ramifications of their actions and beliefs outside the microcosm of Spelman."

FINANCIAL AID: 404-681-3643

ADMISSIONS

The admissions committee considers (in descending order of importance): HS record, test scores, essay, recommendations, class rank. *Also considered (in descending order of importance):* extracurriculars, alumni relationship, geographical distribution, special talents. Either the SAT or ACT is required. Admissions process is need-blind. *High school units required/recommended:* 15 total units are required; 4 English required, 2 math required, 3 math recommended, 2 science required, 3 science recommended, 2 foreign language required, 3 foreign language recommended, 2 social studies required. TOEFL is required of all international students. *The admissions office says:* "Alumnae relations receive special consideration."

The Inside Word

No historically black college in the country has a more competitive admissions process than Spelman. Successful candidates have done well academically in high school while taking an ambitious course schedule. Applicant evaluation here is very personal; it is quite important to show depth of character and social consciousness.

FINANCIAL AID

Students should submit: FAFSA (due April 1), the school's own financial aid form (due April 1). The Princeton Review suggests that all financial aid forms be submitted as soon as possible after January 1. *The following grants/scholarships are offered:* Pell, SEOG, academic merit, the school's own grants, state grants, private scholarships, private grants, ROTC, foreign aid. *Students borrow from the following loan programs:* Stafford, Perkins, PLUS. Applicants will be notified of awards beginning April 2. College Work-Study Program is available. Institutional employment is available.

FROM THE ADMISSIONS OFFICE

"As an outstanding historically black college for women, Spelman strives for academic excellence in liberal education. This predominantly residential private college provides students with an academic climate conducive to the full development of their intellectual and leadership potential. The college is a member of the Atlanta University Center consortium, and Spelman students enjoy the benefits of a small college while having access to the resources of the other five participating institutions. The purpose extends beyond intellectual development and professional career preparation of students. It seeks to develop the total person. The college provides an academic and social environment that strengthens those qualities that enable women to be self-confident as well as culturally and spiritually enriched. This environment attempts to instill in students both an appreciation for the multicultural communities of the world and a sense of responsibility for bringing about positive change in those communities."

ADMISSIONS

Admissions Rating	81
% of applicants accepted	38
% of acceptees attending	33

FRESHMAN PROFILE

Average verbal SAT	NR
Average math SAT	NR
Average ACT	23
Average TOEFL	NR
Graduated top 20% of class	NR
Graduated top 40% of class	NR
Graduated top 60% of class	NR
Average HS GPA or Avg.	3.4

DEADLINES

Early decision	NR
Regular admission	2/1
Regular notification	3/15
Non-fall registration	yes

APPLICANTS ALSO LOOK AT

AND OFTEN PREFER
Georgia Tech.

AND SOMETIMES PREFER
Howard
Hampton
Clark Atlanta
Tuskegee
Florida A & M

AND RARELY PREFER
U. Maryland
Emory
U. Georgia

FINANCIAL FACTS

Financial Aid Rating	68
Tuition	$7,550
Room & board	$5,890
Estimated book expense	$500
% frosh receiving aid	NR
% undergrads receiving aid	76
% aid is need-based	100
% frosh w/ grant (avg)	NR
% frosh w/ loan (avg)	NR
% UGs w/ job (avg)	25 ($1,500)
Off-campus job outlook	fair

ST. BONAVENTURE UNIVERSITY

P.O. Box D, St. Bonaventure, NY 14778-2284   Admissions: 716-375-2400   Fax: 716-375-2005

CAMPUS LIFE

Quality of Life Rating 77
Type of school	private
Affiliation	Roman Catholic Church
	(Franciscan Friars)
Environment	town

STUDENTS
FT undergrad enrollment	1,795
% male/female	49/51
% from out of state	23
% live on campus	78
% spend weekend on campus	75
% transfers	16
% from public high school	71
% in (# of) fraternities	1 (1)
% in (# of) sororities	1 (1)
% African-American	2
% Asian	1
% Caucasian	87
% Hispanic	1
% international	1
# of countries represented	16

WHAT'S HOT
college radio
cigarettes
hard liquor
beer
sex

WHAT'S NOT
campus food
lab facilities
town-gown relations
music associations
theater

ACADEMICS

Academic Rating 75
Profs Interesting Rating	79
Profs Accessible Rating	77
Calendar	semester
Student/teacher ratio	17:1
% profs PhD/tenured	93/93
Hours of study per day	2.73

MOST POPULAR MAJORS
elementary education
accounting
journalism/mass communication

STUDENTS SPEAK OUT

Life

St. Bonaventure University's reputation is that of a party school. Agrees one student, "At Bona, the weekends start on Tuesday and end on Sunday. Sunday and Monday are study days—mostly!" Another observes, "I believe we are making great strides in finding nonparty activities for students. Programming is going very well this year—every week, they have different comedians come to campus who are really good." The Regina A. Quick Center for the Arts opened during the Spring '95 semester, and should provide even more options. Students keep active in on-campus clubs and student government; sports are also popular on campus. The school allows no fraternities or sororities: parties occur in off-campus apartments or, in smaller groups in the dorms. Dormitories are single-sex, and "intervisitation" rules are strictly enforced. The rules prohibit opposite-sex visitors after 1:00 a.m. during the week, 2:00 a.m. during the weekend. "It's ridiculous," writes one student. "What are two people going to do after 1:00 or 2:00 that cannot be done earlier?" Students give the town of St. Bonaventure low grades but agree that the campus is "a beautiful place, quite tranquil." Boasts one student: "In the winter we go sledding at the local golf course on trays 'stole' (sic) from Hickey Dining Hall."

Academics

St. Bonaventure is a Franciscan school catering to the career-minded student: business and management, communication, and education majors claim well over half the enrollees. That doesn't mean that instruction begins and ends with these fields, however: Required courses in theology, liberal arts, math, science, and philosophy account for half the credits needed to graduate. Other notable features of a St. Bonaventure education include its numerous opportunities for internships and the school's Mentor Program, through which students meet one-on-one with professionals in their chosen fields for guidance. Students report that their classes are small, leading one to write that "The focus of Bona is the student. The professors are highly involved with my progress and are more than willing to aid me when I run into difficulties. They relate to us well, in and outside of the classroom." Adds another, "I enjoy the classes that have friars for instructors. So far in my experience, they are the most understanding and concerned with my progress." One student offers this glowing recommendation: "Bonaventure is in a class by itself as far as the combination of academics, athletics, and social life is concerned."

Student Body

Minorities represent a tiny fraction of the student body here. Writes one African-American student, "If you are a black student, Bonaventure may give you extreme culture shock...If you're looking to be empowered by a militant black professor, go to Howard." Students are predominantly white, Catholic, and conservative. Several non-Catholics report that liberal opinions meet with antagonism, and one undergrad reports, "If you do not drink, are a minority, or don't play sports, don't bother to apply."

FINANCIAL AID: 716-375-2528

ADMISSIONS

The admissions committee considers (in descending order of importance): HS record, test scores, recommendations, class rank, essay. *Also considered (in descending order of importance):* alumni relationship, extracurriculars, personality, special talents. Either the SAT or ACT is required. An interview is recommended. Admissions process is need-blind. *High school units required/recommended:* 16 total units are required; 4 English required, 3 math required, 3 science required, 2 foreign language required, 4 social studies required. Minimum combined SAT I score of 1050, rank in top two-fifths of secondary school class, and minimum 3.0 GPA recommended. TOEFL is required of all international students. *The admissions office says:* "[We] highly encourage students to submit a personal essay—it is an excellent opportunity to point out individual uniqueness or experiences, and situations that have affected academic performance."

The Inside Word

St. Bonaventure is a safety for many students applying to more selective Catholic universities, but it does a good job of enrolling a sizable percentage of its admits. Most solid students needn't worry about admission; even so, candidates who rank St. Bonnie as a top choice should still submit essays and interview.

FINANCIAL AID

Students should submit: FAFSA, the school's own financial aid form. The Princeton Review suggests that all financial aid forms be submitted as soon as possible after January 1. *The following grants/scholarships are offered:* Pell, SEOG, academic merit, athletic, the school's own scholarships, the school's own grants, state scholarships, state grants, private scholarships, private grants, ROTC, foreign aid. *Students borrow from the following loan programs:* Stafford, unsubsidized Stafford, Perkins, PLUS, the school's own loan fund, private loans. Applicants will be notified of awards beginning April 1. College Work-Study Program is available. Institutional employment is available.

FROM THE ADMISSIONS OFFICE

"The St. Bonaventure University family has been imparting the Franciscan tradition to men and women of a rich diversity of backgrounds for more than 130 years. This tradition encourages all who become a part of it to face the world confidently, respect the earthly environment and work for productive change in the world. The charm of our campus and the inspirational beauty of the surrounding hills provide a special place where growth in learning and living is abundantly realized. Academics at St. Bonaventure are challenging. Small classes and personalized attention encourage individual growth and development for students. St. Bonaventure's nationally known Schools of Arts and Sciences, Business Administration, Journalism/Mass Communication and Education offer majors in thirty-one disciplines. The School of Graduate Studies also offers several programs leading to the Masters degree."

ADMISSIONS

Admissions Rating			69
% of applicants accepted			89
% of acceptees attending			38

FRESHMAN PROFILE

Average verbal SAT	560
Average math SAT	560
Average ACT	24
Average TOEFL	550
Graduated top 20% of class	44
Graduated top 40% of class	79
Graduated top 60% of class	88
Average HS GPA or Avg.	88.0

DEADLINES

Early decision	NR
Regular admission	4/15
Regular notification	rolling
Non-fall registration	yes

APPLICANTS ALSO LOOK AT

AND OFTEN PREFER
Villanova
Geneseo State
Providence

AND SOMETIMES PREFER
LeMoyne
Siena
Ithaca
SUNY Buffalo
Niagara

AND RARELY PREFER
Syracuse

FINANCIAL FACTS

Financial Aid Rating	86
Tuition	$11,084
Room & board	$5,005
Estimated book expense	$500
% frosh receiving aid	93
% undergrads receiving aid	92
% aid is need-based	85
% frosh w/ grant (avg)	93 ($7,217)
% frosh w/ loan (avg)	85 ($3,036)
% UGs w/ job (avg)	39 ($800)
Off-campus job outlook	fair

ST. JOHN'S COLLEGE (MD)

P.O. BOX 2800, ANNAPOLIS, MD 21404   ADMISSIONS: 800-727-9238   FAX: 410-263-4828

CAMPUS LIFE

Quality of Life Rating	**85**
Type of school	private
Affiliation	none
Environment	suburban

STUDENTS

FT undergrad enrollment	418
% male/female	52/48
% from out of state	86
% live on campus	75
% spend weekend on campus	95
% transfers	19
% from public high school	65
% African-American	2
% Asian	3
% Caucasian	88
% Hispanic	4
% international	4
# of countries represented	6

WHAT'S HOT

campus easy to get around
registration is a breeze
honesty
cigarettes
different students interact

WHAT'S NOT

campus food
college radio
computer facilities
Greeks
lab facilities

ACADEMICS

Academic Rating	**93**
Profs Interesting Rating	98
Profs Accessible Rating	98
Calendar	semester
Student/teacher ratio	8:1
% profs PhD	57
Hours of study per day	3.57

% GRADS WHO PURSUE...

Law 7, Med 6, MBA 3, MA 42

STUDENTS SPEAK OUT

Life

As one student puts it, "St. John's is one long conversation." A small student body creates an environment of closeness between students and faculty. Annapolis, a naval town, doesn't seem to offer much ("claustrophobic"), but that doesn't appear to matter to Johnnies, who are some of the happiest students in the country. More than one student maintains that they would be happy nowhere else (maybe some should check out SJC's sister school in Santa Fe). Intramural sports are popular, as are the bimonthly waltz parties, held on campus. SJC students do drink, although one student notes that "a tea party is as common as a beer party." More than half of the students surveyed smoke cigarettes, and most of them rated the food on campus (over three-fourths of the students live on campus) poorly. Many claim that classes and studying spill over into every aspect of their lives ("we continue class outside of class"), but no one seemed to be complaining about that. "I think we constantly evaluate our situation here," one student writes, "sometimes it's hard to understand why I persist with the course of study offered here because it can be frustrating. However, time and time again I come to the conclusion that I would be happy in no other place." Another simply states, "St. John's stands out as a place where students can go to think."

Academics

There are no electives offered at St. John's. Instead, students are required to study a strict curriculum of ancient Greek, French, classical mathematics, science, music, literature, and philosophy. Students cannot transfer in, but instead must complete the four-year program from beginning to end. No grades are given. Teachers (referred to as "tutors") meet with students once every semester to discuss their work. One student sums it up this way: "St. John's is a close academic community. The level of dedication to the St. John's program comes through in relationships with teachers, administration, and peers." Tutors are able to teach any of the courses offered at St. John's. Says one student, "This gives them a wide breadth of knowledge that enables them to tie together diverse subject matters." The vast majority of the students strongly agree that teachers are accessible ("Your tutor is your friend"), and rate the administration very highly. Class attendance is mandatory, and the focus of class is discussion, which leads one student to comment "Since you rely so much on your classmates' participation for learning, there is a possibility of having bad classes. But when it works, there's nothing like it." Overall, SJC has disappointed few in its academic approach. "This school has an incredible academic environment. Where else do people sit around at parties and passionately discuss Plato, Aristotle, and other philosophy?"

Student Body

Most students are white, with a slightly larger percentage of men than women making up the student body. Typically, students here lean to the left politically. Students describe themselves as "very sheltered," psycho-liberal," and "disaffected, nervous, chain-smoking, bitter individuals," as well as "sometimes individual to a fault." However, undergrads generally report that they are very happy. There is a definite sense of community among Johnnies, who consider themselves to be somewhat different as a whole from other college students across the country. "Only the slightly eccentric really fit in," writes one student, while another comments, "we are a small, intellectual community with respect for one another's ideas."

FINANCIAL AID: 410-263-2371

WEB SITE: HTTP://WWW.SJCA.EDU

ADMISSIONS

The admissions committee considers (in descending order of importance): essay, HS record, recommendations, class rank, test scores. *Also considered (in descending order of importance):* personality, extracurriculars, alumni relationship, special talents. An interview is recommended. Admissions process is need-blind. *High school units required/recommended:* 4 English recommended, 3 math recommended, 2 science recommended, 2 foreign language recommended, 2 social studies recommended, 2 history recommended. 2 units of algebra, 1 unit of geometry, and 2 units of a single foreign language recommended. Additional math, science, and foreign language units recommended. TOEFL is required of all international students. *The admissions office says:* "The very things that attract students to other competitive colleges—prestige, name brands, competition for grades, intense career ambition, the 'we-have-it-all' and 'are the best' mentalities—arouse suspicion in our students and tend to repel them from other competitive schools. Furthermore, after examining other competitive colleges, they are confident that St. John's offers the best liberal arts education."

The Inside Word

St. John's has one of the most personal admissions processes in the country. The applicant pool is highly self-selected and extremely bright, so don't be fooled by the high acceptance rate—every student who is offered admission deserves to be here. Candidates who don't give serious thought to the kind of match they make with the college and devote serious energy to their essays are not likely to be successful.

FINANCIAL AID

Students should submit: FAFSA (due March 1), CSS Profile (due March 1), Divorced Parents form (due March 1). The Princeton Review suggests that all financial aid forms be submitted as soon as possible after January 1. *The following grants/scholarships are offered:* Pell, SEOG, the school's own grants, state scholarships, state grants, foreign aid. *Students borrow from the following loan programs:* Stafford, Perkins, PLUS, the school's own loan fund. College Work-Study Program is available. Institutional employment is available.

FROM THE ADMISSIONS OFFICE

"The purpose of the admission process is to determine whether an applicant has the necessary preparation and ability to complete the St. John's program satisfactorily. The essays are designed to enable applicants to give a full account of themselves. They can tell the Committee much more than statistical records reveal. Previous academic records show whether an applicant has the habits of study necessary at St. John's. Letters of reference, particularly those of teachers, are carefully read for indications that the applicant has the maturity, self-discipline, ability, energy and initiative to succeed in the St. John's program. St. John's attaches little importance to 'objective' test scores, and no applicant is accepted or rejected because of such scores."

ADMISSIONS

Admissions Rating	80
% of applicants accepted	86
% of acceptees attending	38

FRESHMAN PROFILE

Average verbal SAT	690
Average math SAT	600
Average ACT	NR
Average TOEFL	NR
Graduated top 20% of class	54
Graduated top 40% of class	74
Graduated top 60% of class	91
Average HS GPA or Avg.	NR

DEADLINES

Early decision	NR
Regular admission	rolling
Regular notification	rolling
Non-fall registration	yes

APPLICANTS ALSO LOOK AT

AND OFTEN PREFER

Oberlin
Harvard/Radcliffe
Princeton

AND SOMETIMES PREFER

Brown
U. Chicago
Reed

AND RARELY PREFER

Kenyon
Grinnell
Bard

FINANCIAL FACTS

Financial Aid Rating	93
Tuition	$19,840
Room & board	$5,950
Estimated book expense	$275
% frosh receiving aid	60
% undergrads receiving aid	65
% aid is need-based	100
% frosh w/ grant (avg)	55 ($13,305)
% frosh w/ loan (avg)	62 ($2,625)
% UGs w/ job (avg)	35 ($1,700)
Off-campus job outlook	excellent

ST. JOHN'S COLLEGE (NEW MEXICO)

1160 CAMINO CRUZ BLANCA, SANTA FE, NM 87501   ADMISSIONS: 800-331-5232   FAX: 505-984-6003

STUDENTS SPEAK OUT

Life

St. John's has created, and fosters, a very intimate community of scholars. "Great books; no gym," is how one student puts it. Nature has provided a wonderful setting. Almost all students surveyed rate both the city of Sante Fe and the campus, with its Spanish colonial (adobe-style) buildings set among the Sangre de Cristo foothills, as beautiful. The people seem to be pretty nice, too. There is little discrimination of any kind on campus; the few minority students at SJC are the third-happiest group of minority students at any college surveyed for this book. "St. John's is a veritable haven. Lacking the difficult social and political barriers prevalent at other schools, SJC induces sentiments of inclusion and ease." When it comes to basic partying, students here aren't particularly unique—beer, liquor, cigarettes and pot are the lubricants of choice—but how many colleges throw a serious midnight bash to collectively celebrate the seniors turning in "final essays," their thesis papers?

Academics

Budding intellectuals looking to dive into the "great books" but who prefer the panorama of the southwest to the historic streets of Annapolis need look no further than St. John's younger sibling in Santa Fe. In academic terms, it's virtually the same program here in New Mexico as that in Maryland. The curriculum is composed entirely of required courses in areas ranging from ancient Greek and classical mathematics to science, music, literature, and philosophy. All classes are small and discussion-oriented, following the Socratic method. Many students we surveyed made it clear that St. John's methods bring out the best in them. Class attendance is mandatory, and St. John's students put in an average of nearly four hours per day preparing themselves. One senior wrote us that "The most excellent thing about St. John's...is that students get smarter, more serious and more committed to learning as they move through the four-year program. The most intense, intellectual seniors might have been the wildest, flakiest freshmen. If you stick with the program, you will inevitably work hard and learn." Nearly everyone seems to thrive on the demands; our surveys place these students not only among the hardest working, but also among the happiest collegians around. Cautioned one student, "If you think you want to come, the only way to decide is to visit. This is a wonderful place for some, but very different, and very challenging."

Student Body

From an intellectual standpoint, SJC is a magnet for distinct individuals; the college clearly seeks independent thinkers. Demographically, it's a different story. As is the case with most atypical colleges, SJC's student body is very homogeneous. The students here are largely white and liberal to left-leaning politically. But again, our research makes it pretty clear that just about anyone is welcome—"we are a...highly intellectual community that doesn't need to divide itself into racial, religious, or economic cliques."

FINANCIAL AID: 505-984-6058   E-MAIL: ADMISSIONS@SHADOW.SJCSF.EDU   WEB SITE: HTTP://WWW.SJCSF.EDU

ADMISSIONS

The admissions committee considers (in descending order of importance): essay, HS record, recommendations, class rank, test scores. *Also considered (in descending order of importance):* personality, special talents, alumni relationship, extracurriculars. An interview is recommended. Admissions process is need-blind. *High school units required/recommended:* 4 English recommended, 4 math recommended, 3 science recommended, 2 foreign language recommended, 2 social studies recommended, 2 history recommended. College-preparatory courses required. TOEFL is required of all international students. *The admissions office says:* "The Admissions Committee—five tutors and the Director of Admissions—regards the application as being a question from the applicant: 'Do you think I am ready to profit from the program of studies at St. John's?' In the essays, applicants are asked to discuss their previous education, reasons for choosing St. John's, and their experience with books. Optional topics are also suggested. These can tell the Committee much more than statistical records reveal."

The Inside Word

Self-selection drives this admissions process—over one-half of the entire applicant pool each year indicates that St. John's is their first choice, and half of those admitted send in tuition deposits. Even so, no one in admissions takes things for granted, and neither should any student considering an application. The admissions process is highly personal on both sides of the coin. Only the intellectually curious and highly motivated need apply.

FINANCIAL AID

Students should submit: FAFSA (due February 15), CSS Profile (due February 15), the school's own financial aid form (due February 15), state aid form, a copy of parents' most recent income tax filing. The Princeton Review suggests that all financial aid forms be submitted as soon as possible after January 1. *The following grants/scholarships are offered:* Pell, SEOG, the school's own grants, state scholarships, state grants, private scholarships, foreign aid. *Students borrow from the following loan programs:* Stafford, Perkins, PLUS. College Work-Study Program is available. Institutional employment is available.

FROM THE ADMISSIONS OFFICE

"St. John's appeals to students who value good books, love to read and are passionate about discourse and debate. There are no lectures, and virtually no tests or electives. Instead, classes of twenty students occur around conference tables where professors are as likely to be asked to defend their points of view as are students. Great books provide the direction, context, and stimulus for conversation. The entire student body adheres to the same, all-required arts and science curriculum. Someone once said 'A classic is a house we still live in,' and at St. John's, students and professors alike approach each reading on the list as if the ideas it holds were being expressed for the first time—questioning the logic behind a geometrical proof, challenging the premise of a scientific development, or dissecting the progression of modern political theory as it unfolds."

ADMISSIONS

Admissions Rating	80
% of applicants accepted	82
% of acceptees attending	50

FRESHMAN PROFILE

Average verbal SAT	670
Average math SAT	620
Average ACT	30
Average TOEFL	NR
Graduated top 20% of class	55
Graduated top 40% of class	79
Graduated top 60% of class	95
Average HS GPA or Avg.	NR

DEADLINES

Early decision	NR
Regular admission	3/1
Regular notification	rolling
Non-fall registration	yes

APPLICANTS ALSO LOOK AT
AND SOMETIMES PREFER

Colorado Coll.
Reed
Oberlin
UC - Santa Cruz
U. Chicago

FINANCIAL FACTS

Financial Aid Rating	92
Tuition	$17,980
Room & board	$5,995
Estimated book expense	$275
% frosh receiving aid	85
% undergrads receiving aid	85
% aid is need-based	100
% frosh w/ grant (avg)	72 ($11,325)
% frosh w/ loan (avg)	72 ($2,625)
% UGs w/ job (avg)	60 ($1,750)
Off-campus job outlook	excellent

CAMPUS LIFE

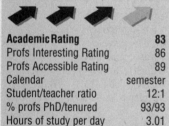

Quality of Life Rating	**87**
Type of school	private
Affiliation	none
Environment	town

STUDENTS

FT undergrad enrollment	1,976
% male/female	50/50
% from out of state	48
% live on campus	96
% spend weekend on campus	95
% transfers	5
% from public high school	65
% in (# of) fraternities	23 (7)
% in (# of) sororities	30 (4)
% African-American	2
% Asian	2
% Caucasian	90
% Hispanic	2
% international	1
# of countries represented	20

WHAT'S HOT

Greeks
students are happy
drugs
campus easy to get around
campus food

WHAT'S NOT

students are cliquish
lack of diversity on campus
Canton
religion
infrequent dating

ACADEMICS

Academic Rating	**83**
Profs Interesting Rating	86
Profs Accessible Rating	89
Calendar	semester
Student/teacher ratio	12:1
% profs PhD/tenured	93/93
Hours of study per day	3.01

MOST POPULAR MAJORS

English
government
economics

% GRADS WHO PURSUE...

Law 2, Med 5, MBA 1, MA 12

STUDENTS SPEAK OUT

Life

The social scene at St. Lawrence University is "very intense. There is always something going on at night. As such, the social climate of SLU produces two types of students. There are those who, except for attending classes, just hang out all day, every day. They usually do very, very poorly. Then there are those who devote three hours an afternoon or morning to their studies. Both go out every night, but the latter end up with a solid education after four years." Drinking is very popular, "Especially," writes one student, "on weekends and Wednesdays ('flip night' at two favorite local bars—you call 'heads' or 'tails' and if the bartender's coin matches your call, the beer is free!)." The Greeks play a major role here. There are plenty of opportunities for outdoor activities, although a tolerance for bitter cold is a prerequisite for enjoying them. A car is recommended since "the population of Canton frequently matches our winter temperature. Students travel to Burlington, Syracuse, Ottawa, and Montreal." Intercollegiate sports, especially SLU's Division I hockey team, are very popular. "Whether or not you like hockey before you get here, you will by the time you leave," writes one student.

Academics

SLU offers a traditional liberal arts education in the seclusion of frigid upstate New York. By reputation it's a laid-back party school, but many students here are eager to refute that stereotype. One writes that "the school's undeserved party reputation overshadows the facilities and faculty, which are first-rate. You will get incredible attention and opportunities if you wish to excel. Too many people sell SLU short." Whether or not the school has earned its reputation, students do put in their hours of work here—"More than they're willing to let on," says several respondents. English, economics, history, political science, and government are all popular majors here, and, according to one bio major, "This school has a phenomenal science department, especially biology and chemistry, for a small liberal arts school. The faculty prepare us well to continue our education, especially in medical or dental school." SLU sponsors a wide variety of semester abroad programs, which many of our respondents recommended enthusiastically. Profs receive high marks, as does class size.

Student Body

Most SLU students will agree that their student body is very alike and that their classmates are laid-back and friendly. Whether all SLU students are wealthy prepsters, as they are reputed to be, is another question. Says one student: "SLU students truly wear L. L. Bean and Patagonia ensembles, summer on Nantucket or the Vineyard, and desire jobs on Wall Street or in a law office." A minority, but a vocal minority, disagrees. One student writes that "the stereotype of St. Lawrence as a playground for the children of the rich and famous no longer applies." There is a fair-sized "crunchy granola" contingent, and Deadheads abound. Students are politically conservative and not terribly tolerant of alternative lifestyles.

FINANCIAL AID: 315-379-5265

WEB SITE: HTTP://WWW.STLAWU.EDU

ADMISSIONS

The admissions committee considers (in descending order of importance): HS record, class rank, recommendations, essay, test scores. *Also considered (in descending order of importance):* personality, extracurriculars, special talents, alumni relationship. Either the SAT or ACT is required. An interview is recommended. Admissions process is not need-blind. *High school units required/recommended:* 16 total units are required; 4 English recommended, 3 math recommended, 3 science recommended, 3 foreign language recommended, 3 social studies recommended. *The admissions office says:* "We are assured by prospective students that the high level of personal attention they receive distinguishes St. Lawrence's [admissions] process. On average, an inquirer receives information about St. Lawrence every two weeks. Prospective students feel nurtured."

The Inside Word

St. Lawrence has a rough time convincing students to commit to spending four years in relative isolation. Serious competition from many fine Northeastern colleges also causes admissions standards to be less selective than the University would like. This makes St. Lawrence an especially good choice for academically sound but average students who are seeking an excellent small college experience and/or an outdoorsy setting.

FINANCIAL AID

Students should submit: FAFSA (due February 15), the school's own financial aid form (due February 15), a copy of parents' most recent income tax filing (due May 31). The Princeton Review suggests that all financial aid forms be submitted as soon as possible after January 1. *The following grants/scholarships are offered:* Pell, SEOG, academic merit, the school's own scholarships, the school's own grants, state scholarships, state grants, private scholarships, private grants, foreign aid. *Students borrow from the following loan programs:* Stafford, Perkins, PLUS, the school's own loan fund. Applicants will be notified of awards beginning March 15. College Work-Study Program is available. Institutional employment is available.

FROM THE ADMISSIONS OFFICE

"St. Lawrence is an independent, nondenominational liberal arts and sciences university, and the oldest coeducational institution in New York State. The campus is composed of thirty buildings, two of which are on the National Historic Register, in a country setting at the edge of the village of Canton, NY. St. Lawrence's 1,000 acres include a golf course, cross-country ski trails, and jogging trails at the outer edges of campus. Canton is a town of 7,000 people who welcome St. Lawrence students into their gift and clothing shops, grocery stores, restaurants, and movie theater. The university is ninety minutes from the capital of Canada, one-half hour from Adirondack Park and the Thousand Islands, and two hours from Montreal, Canada."

ADMISSIONS

Admissions Rating	79
% of applicants accepted	60
% of acceptees attending	33

FRESHMAN PROFILE

Average verbal SAT	650
Average math SAT	580
Average ACT	NR
Average TOEFL	600
Graduated top 20% of class	54
Graduated top 40% of class	77
Graduated top 60% of class	93
Average HS GPA or Avg.	NR

DEADLINES

Early decision	NR
Regular admission	2/15
Regular notification	rolling after 3/15
Non-fall registration	yes

APPLICANTS ALSO LOOK AT

AND OFTEN PREFER

Middlebury Coll.
Colby
Colgate
U. Vermont

AND SOMETIMES PREFER

Hamilton
Syracuse
Bates
Skidmore
U. New Hampshire

AND RARELY PREFER

Union (NY)
Denison

FINANCIAL FACTS

Financial Aid Rating	82
Tuition	$19,640
Room & board	$5,885
Estimated book expense	$650
% frosh receiving aid	76
% undergrads receiving aid	72
% aid is need-based	99
% frosh w/ grant (avg)	74 ($11,879)
% frosh w/ loan (avg)	66 ($3,154)
% UGs w/ job (avg)	56 ($1,330)
Off-campus job outlook	poor

ST. LOUIS UNIVERSITY

221 NORTH GRAND BOULEVARD, ST. LOUIS, MO 63103

ADMISSIONS: 314-977-2500   FAX: 314-977-3874

CAMPUS LIFE

Quality of Life Rating | **70**
Type of school | private
Affiliation | Roman Catholic Church
 | (Society of Jesus)
Environment | metropolis

STUDENTS

FT undergrad enrollment	4,671
% male/female	48/52
% from out of state	65
% live on campus	33
% spend weekend on campus	50
% transfers	11
% from public high school	NR
% in (# of) fraternities	17 (9)
% in (# of) sororities	12 (5)
% African-American	8
% Asian	4
% Caucasian	66
% Hispanic	2
% international	8
# of countries represented	83

WHAT'S HOT
religion
political activism
ethnic diversity on campus
registration is a breeze
St. Louis

WHAT'S NOT
hard liquor
unattractive campus
dorms
students are cliquish
students are unhappy

ACADEMICS

Academic Rating	78
Profs Interesting Rating	67
Profs Accessible Rating	72
Calendar	semester
Student/teacher ratio	10:1
% profs PhD/tenured	95/95
Hours of study per day	3.17

MOST POPULAR MAJORS
nursing
finance
psychology

% GRADS WHO PURSUE...
Law 6, Med 6, MBA 15, MA 3

STUDENTS SPEAK OUT

Life

St. Louis University is primarily a commuter school. About half of its students live on campus, and many of them are from the St. Louis area. Accordingly, "the parking lots are empty on weekends," and the social scene quiets down after Thursday night. Students agree that "to make the most of SLU, you have to get involved in student activities." Participation in community service programs is particularly common: Other activities, though popular, reportedly suffer from a lack of funding. SLU's Jesuit tradition carries on today in the form of nightly student mass and perennial commitment to the Catholic faith for about two thirds of the student population. The campus itself, right in the middle of St. Louis, is not beautiful, but it is constantly improving, as is the surrounding urban area ("although it could be better," warns one student). The first-rate sports complex garners compliments from students, and SLU boasts an athletic shining star in the form of the highly ranked Billikens soccer team. A new theater complex has also recently been added to the campus.

Academics

St. Louis University's slogan is "Excellence is Affordable," and SLU indeed provides a private school education at a reasonable price. Preprofessional programs are most popular here, especially premedicine. Education, international business, and communication all also receive good grades from students. Course offerings are touted by students as "challenging," and professors receive high ratings for teaching and accessibility. One student writes, "The teachers are always willing to help; they want you to learn and do well. They seem to take students' doing well as a personal achievement." Another agrees: "The student/teacher ratio is excellent, and the professors are wonderful." All students must complete a core curriculum meant to guarantee a broad-based education. Science, math, humanities, and ethics all figure into the core. The core emphasizes classical literature and philosophy, leading several students to joke that "SLU provides the best twelfth-century education money can buy." All in all, though, we find student attitudes toward academics at SLU to be quite positive.

Student Body

More than half of SLU's students hail from Missouri, and by their own account, the undergraduate population is not terribly diverse. Students describe themselves as "very conservative and midwestern" as a group. However, the atmosphere here is relatively accepting of everyone, and, although students identify themselves as politically apathetic, they are extremely involved in community service. A lot of students fall into the "nontraditional" category: they are older students returning for degrees while continuing their careers. Among the "traditional" population, there is a strong trend toward preprofessionalism ("Sometimes I feel like I'm at a trade school for doctors and lawyers," writes one student).

ADMISSIONS

The admissions committee considers (in descending order of importance): HS record, test scores, class rank, recommendations, essay. *Also considered (in descending order of importance):* alumni relationship, extracurriculars, personality, special talents. Either the SAT or ACT is required; ACT is preferred. An interview is recommended. Admissions process is need-blind. *High school units required/recommended:* 16 total units are recommended; 4 English recommended, 3 math recommended, 2 science recommended, 2 foreign language recommended, 2 social studies recommended. *Special Requirements:* A portfolio is required for art program applicants. An audition is required for music program applicants. Personal statement required of physical and occupational therapy program applicants.

The Inside Word

Students who are ranked in the top half of their graduating class will have a fairly straight path to admission at St. Louis. Those who are not can find success through minority status, a top parochial school diploma, or major talent in soccer.

FINANCIAL AID

Students should submit: FAFSA. The Princeton Review suggests that all financial aid forms be submitted as soon as possible after January 1. *The following grants/scholarships are offered:* Pell, SEOG, academic merit, athletic, the school's own scholarships, the school's own grants, state scholarships, state grants, private scholarships, private grants, ROTC, foreign aid. *Students borrow from the following loan programs:* Stafford, unsubsidized Stafford, Perkins, PLUS, the school's own loan fund, state loans, federal nursing loans, health professions loans, private loans. College Work-Study Program is available. Institutional employment is available.

FROM THE ADMISSIONS OFFICE

"For more than 175 years, St. Louis University has earned a reputation for excellence in education. In its history, St. Louis has accomplished a list of firsts that make it a true center of higher learning: first university west of Mississippi; first Catholic college in the United States to have faculty in schools of philosophy, theology, medicine, law and business; first federally certified air college (Park College); and first freestanding European campus (Madrid, Spain) operated by an American university. St. Louis' academic reputation is the foundation for its success today. As a Jesuit institution, our goal is to graduate men and women of competence and conscience-individuals who are not only capable of making wise decisions, but who also understand why they made them. Today, we enroll more than 11,000 students dedicated to our long tradition to excel academically, to serve others, and to be leaders in society."

ADMISSIONS

Admissions Rating	71
% of applicants accepted	85
% of acceptees attending	33

FRESHMAN PROFILE

Average verbal SAT	NR
Average math SAT	NR
Average ACT	25
Average TOEFL	500
Graduated top 20% of class	47
Graduated top 40% of class	66
Graduated top 60% of class	77
Average HS GPA or Avg.	NR

DEADLINES

Early decision	12/1
Regular admission	8/1
Regular notification	rolling
Non-fall registration	yes

APPLICANTS ALSO LOOK AT

AND OFTEN PREFER
Washington U.

AND SOMETIMES PREFER
Northeast Missouri State
Marquette
U. Illinois, Urbana-Champ.
U. Wisconsin-Madison
U. Missouri-Columbia

AND RARELY PREFER
Creighton
Indiana U.-Bloomington
Kansas State

FINANCIAL FACTS

Financial Aid Rating	87
Tuition	$13,900
Room & board	$5,110
Estimated book expense	$800
% frosh receiving aid	93
% undergrads receiving aid	84
% aid is need-based	66
% frosh w/ grant (avg)	85 ($7,850)
% frosh w/ loan (avg)	64 ($3,535)
% UGs w/ job (avg)	25 ($1,157)
Off-campus job outlook	excellent

ST. MARY'S COLLEGE (CA)

1928 SAINT MARY'S ROAD, MORAGA, CA 94575   ADMISSIONS: 510-631-4224   FAX: 510-376-7193

STUDENTS SPEAK OUT

Life

Student comments at St. Mary's College of California overwhelmingly focus on the beauty of the campus. Sums up one student, "This is more like a spa or a country club. If you want to maintain the high school feel while simultaneously wowing Mom and Dad by debating in proper fashion, this is the college for you." Also noteworthy is the school's location, "set apart and beautiful but also close to Berkeley and San Francisco." The area is conducive to sports, outdoor activities, and just lounging around. Writes one student, "I row crew, race mountain bikes, surf, skate, and snow board. This area has a lot to offer." Concludes another, "If you love sports, St. Mary's is a great school to attend." Otherwise, students agree that the "campus can get a little boring on the weekends. Most of the best activities take place off campus, such as in San Francisco."

Academics

Described by students as "an excellent place to get a personalized education," St. Mary's provides a solid liberal arts education even to the business-oriented students who make up the majority. Popular majors include business and management, premedical sciences, communication, and psychology. All students must complete a core curriculum centered on the Great Books Seminar Program. Students liked this program for its provocative, discussion-oriented approach to the classics: "It really makes you think and discuss." Adds another student, "The seminar style of teaching is used not only in the Great Books program, but also in the more traditional type of classes. It's awesome!" Students agree that "The teachers are wonderful, they all know me by name. They even call when I'm sick at home. They're always available to meet to discuss the class, personal information, or our grades." Other perks include a January semester, during which students are encouraged to pursue experimental studies, internships, and travel; and the possibility of overseas study with affiliated Catholic institutions in Rome, France, and England. In general, courses here are difficult. However, students feel that the immediate challenge leads to greater rewards, so they study quite hard. The emphasis is on individual achievement rather than head-to-head competition.

Student Body

St. Mary's students, most of whom are Roman Catholic and heading toward business careers, are predictably conservative. Reportedly, "Students are fairly laid-back and able to get along with others, liberal minded and accepting of everyone not part of the norm." Attitudes toward alternative lifestyles are more tolerant than at most Catholic schools but still less accepting than the norm. The school has a large minority population, and the different ethnicities represented on campus feel they are well accepted. But, perhaps because of their similar backgrounds and goals, students rate the diversity of their student body as low.

ADMISSIONS

The admissions committee considers (in descending order of importance): HS record, test scores, recommendations, class rank, essay. *Also considered (in descending order of importance):* personality, special talents, alumni relationship, extracurriculars, geographical distribution. Either the SAT or ACT is required. An interview is recommended. Admissions process is need-blind. *High school units required/recommended:* 16 total units are recommended; 4 English recommended, 3 math recommended, 2 science recommended, 2 foreign language recommended, 2 social studies recommended, 1 history recommended. *Special Requirements:* TOEFL is required of all international students. Algebra I and II, plane geometry, trigonometry, physics, and chemistry recommended of applicants to School of Science.

The Inside Word

The typical St. Mary's admit is a better-than-average student who has attending a Catholic college very high on his or her list of preferences. The applicant pool is full of such candidates. Candidates should give serious attention to the application process, as they are guaranteed close scrutiny despite the college's high admit rate.

FINANCIAL AID

Students should submit: FAFSA (due March 2). The Princeton Review suggests that all financial aid forms be submitted as soon as possible after January 1. *The following grants/scholarships are offered:* Pell, SEOG, academic merit, athletic, the school's own scholarships, the school's own grants, state grants, foreign aid. *Students borrow from the following loan programs:* Stafford, unsubsidized Stafford, Perkins, PLUS, private loans. Applicants will be notified of awards beginning April 15. College Work-Study Program is available. Institutional employment is available.

FROM THE ADMISSIONS OFFICE

"Today St. Mary's College continues to offer a value-oriented education by providing a classical liberal arts background second to none. The emphasis here is on teaching an individual how to think independently and responsibly, how to analyze information in all situations, and how to make choices based on logical thinking and rational examination. Such a program develops students' ability to ask the right questions and to formulate meaningful answers, not only within their professional careers but also for the rest of their lives. St. Mary's College is committed to preparing young men and women for the challenge of an ever-changing world, while remaining faithful to an enduring academic and spiritual heritage. We believe the purpose of a college experience is to prepare men and women for an unlimited number of opportunities. We believe this is best accomplished by educating the whole person, both intellectually and ethically. And we believe this is reaffirmed in our community of Brothers, in our faculty, and in our personal concern for each student."

ADMISSIONS

Admissions Rating	73
% of applicants accepted	86
% of acceptees attending	23

FRESHMAN PROFILE

Average verbal SAT	640
Average math SAT	570
Average ACT	23
Average TOEFL	525
Graduated top 20% of class	71
Graduated top 40% of class	98
Graduated top 60% of class	100
Average HS GPA or Avg.	3.4

DEADLINES

Early decision	11/30
Regular admission	2/1
Regular notification	rolling
Non-fall registration	yes

APPLICANTS ALSO LOOK AT

AND OFTEN PREFER

Notre Dame
UC-Berkeley

AND SOMETIMES PREFER

UC-Davis
Villanova
Loyola Marymount

AND RARELY PREFER

Santa Clara U.
Gonzaga U.
UC-Santa Barbara
U. of the Pacific

FINANCIAL FACTS

Financial Aid Rating	88
Tuition	$14,132
Room & board	$6,608
Estimated book expense	$600
% frosh receiving aid	74
% undergrads receiving aid	61
% aid is need-based	78
% frosh w/ grant (avg)	79 ($8,667)
% frosh w/ loan (avg)	66 ($2,832)
% UGs w/ job (avg)	25 ($1,200)
Off-campus job outlook	excellent

ST. MARY'S COLLEGE OF MARYLAND

St. Mary's City, MD 20686

Admissions: 800-492-7181   Fax: 301-862-0999

CAMPUS LIFE

Quality of Life Rating 78
Type of school public
Affiliation none
Environment rural

STUDENTS

FT undergrad enrollment	1,401
% male/female	44/56
% from out of state	16
% live on campus	76
% spend weekend on campus	60
% transfers	14
% from public high school	82
% African-American	10
% Asian	4
% Caucasian	84
% Hispanic	2
% international	3
# of countries represented	28

WHAT'S HOT
campus is beautiful
lab facilities
hard liquor
campus easy to get around
campus feels safe

WHAT'S NOT
campus food
off-campus food
computer facilities
St. Mary's City
Greeks

ACADEMICS

Academic Rating	87
Profs Interesting Rating	85
Profs Accessible Rating	88
Calendar	semester
Student/teacher ratio	13:1
% profs tenured	97
Hours of study per day	3.07

MOST POPULAR MAJORS
psychology
biology
economics

% GRADS WHO PURSUE...
Law 5, Med 1, MBA 2, MA 29

STUDENTS SPEAK OUT

Life

Writes one St. Mary's student, "You can't go wrong telling people where we are: We're St. Mary's College at St. Mary's City on the St. Mary's River in St. Mary's County!" The college has a "gorgeous campus" and the river provides a "great waterfront," but the city of St. Mary's...well, as one student puts it, "The nearest town is only eight miles away! It's historic St. Mary's City, a popular attraction consisting of two shacks and a dirt path. Come visit and you will find out why we say, 'St. Mary's isn't the edge of the world, but you can see it from here!'" One student notes, "Historic ruins are great for tripping in," but most agreed that "St. Mary's is like a paradise in the middle of a barren desert. The campus is beautiful and fun, but, beyond the campus gates, there is nothing." School-sponsored activities are relatively sparse, and partly as a result, students report that drinking is a very popular pastime. One student complains, "As a student who does not drink, it is pretty hard to find things to d

Academics

Although its name might lead you to think otherwise, St. Mary's is a public school, not a Catholic school. Nor is it a typical public school: in fact, in size, approach to academics, and level of commitment on the part of the faculty, St. Mary's is much more comparable to a small private liberal arts college. Located on a riverfront, St. Mary's maintains an excellent department in marine biology; economics, psychology, English, and history are other departments that were popular with our respondents. Students report that access to faculty is good, classes are small and personal, and, "although it is a serious academic school, it is not a tense school." Best of all, St. Mary's is affordable, although some students worry that may not remain the case indefinitely. Writes one undergrad, "With recent popularity, as indicated by issues of popular news magazines, St. Mary's has become very image-conscious, which, combined with tuition increases to decrease institutional dependence on state funds, will probably turn

Student Body

The student body here is made up mostly of Maryland natives, although a recent surge in publicity about the school's quality and cost is drawing more out-of-state students. About 100 black students make up most of the minority population; those we spoke with report a high level of satisfaction with the school. Several students note that the student body is "generally very close and friendly because it's like one big fraternity."

FINANCIAL AID: 301-862-0300

ADMISSIONS

The admissions committee considers (in descending order of importance): HS record, essay, recommendations, class rank, test scores. *Also considered (in descending order of importance):* special talents, alumni relationship, extracurriculars, geographical distribution, personality. Either the SAT or ACT is required; SAT is preferred. An interview is recommended. Admissions process is need-blind. *High school units required/recommended:* 22 total units are required; 4 English required, 3 math required, 3 science required, 2 foreign language recommended, 3 social studies required. Minimum 2.5 GPA required. Minimum combined SAT I score of 1050 and rank in top half of secondary school class recommended. TOEFL is required of all international students. *The admissions office says:* "Very personalized admissions process. Each counselor is responsible for a specific geographic region, particularly with regard to the State of Maryland. This gives the staff an opportunity to meet a given student in a variety of settings. The staff really gives consideration to each student's individual merits."

The Inside Word

There are few better choices than St. Mary's for better than average students who are not likely to get admitted to one of the top 50 or so colleges in the country. It is likely that if funding for public colleges is able to stabilize, or even grow, that this place will soon be joining the ranks of the best. Now is the time to take advantage, before the academic expectations of the admissions committee start to soar.

FINANCIAL AID

Students should submit: FAFSA. The Princeton Review suggests that all financial aid forms be submitted as soon as possible after January 1. *The following grants/scholarships are offered:* Pell, SEOG, academic merit, the school's own scholarships, the school's own grants, state scholarships, private scholarships, private grants. *Students borrow from the following loan programs:* Stafford, Perkins, PLUS, the school's own loan fund, state loans. Applicants will be notified of awards beginning April 1. College Work-Study Program is available. Institutional employment is available.

FROM THE ADMISSIONS OFFICE

"St. Mary's College of Maryland...occupies a distinctive niche and represents a real value in American higher education. It is a public college, dedicated to the ideal of affordable, accessible education but committed to quality teaching and excellent programs for undergraduate students. The result is that St. Mary's offers the small college experience of the same high caliber usually found at prestigious private colleges, but at public college prices. Recently designated by the state of Maryland as 'A Public Honors College,' one of only two public colleges in the nation to hold that distinction, St. Mary's has become increasingly attractive to high school students. Admission is very selective, with eight to ten applicants for each spot in the freshman class."

ADMISSIONS

Admissions Rating	85
% of applicants accepted	54
% of acceptees attending	41

FRESHMAN PROFILE

Average verbal SAT	710
Average math SAT	630
Average ACT	NR
Average TOEFL	NR
Graduated top 20% of class	36
Graduated top 40% of class	47
Graduated top 60% of class	52
Average HS GPA or Avg.	3.5

DEADLINES

Early decision	12/1
Regular admission	1/15
Regular notification	4/1
Non-fall registration	yes

APPLICANTS ALSO LOOK AT

AND OFTEN PREFER

Johns Hopkins
U. Delaware
Lehigh
Bucknell

AND SOMETIMES PREFER

Dickinson
James Madison
Loyola Coll. (MD)
U. Maryland-Coll. Park

FINANCIAL FACTS

Financial Aid Rating	81
In-state tuition	$5,000
Out-of-state tuition	$8,550
Room & board	$5,220
Estimated book expense	$750
% frosh receiving aid	75
% undergrads receiving aid	63
% aid is need-based	42
% frosh w/ grant (avg)	49 ($3,200)
% frosh w/ loan (avg)	55 ($2,298)
% UGs w/ job (avg)	27 ($1,875)
Off-campus job outlook	good

ST. OLAF COLLEGE

1520 SAINT OLAF AVENUE, NORTHFIELD, MN 55057-1098   ADMISSIONS: 800-800-3025   FAX: 507-646-3832

CAMPUS LIFE

Quality of Life Rating 88
Type of school private
Affiliation Evangelical Lutheran Church in America
Environment town

STUDENTS
FT undergrad enrollment	2,854
% male/female	41/59
% from out of state	43
% live on campus	91
% spend weekend on campus	85
% transfers	2
% from public high school	NR
% African-American	1
% Asian	4
% Caucasian	90
% Hispanic	1
% international	2
# of countries represented	20

WHAT'S HOT
music associations
town-gown relations
support groups
religion
library

WHAT'S NOT
sex
lack of diversity on campus
infrequent dating
drugs
cigarettes

ACADEMICS

Academic Rating	91
Profs Interesting Rating	96
Profs Accessible Rating	96
Calendar	4-1-4
Student/teacher ratio	11:1
% profs PhD/tenured	79/79
Hours of study per day	3.82

MOST POPULAR MAJORS
economics
English
biology

STUDENTS SPEAK OUT

Life

St. Olaf College offers a beautiful campus coupled with strict policies on everything from having a car (it's difficult to get permission) to drinking (it's a dry campus, although students at St. Olaf drink about as much as students in the rest of the country). Drug use, however, is scarce. Says one student, "Parties are usually a couple friends in a dorm room. No big ragers. But people do a surprising amount of drinking." Another student says "Movies, dances, lectures, and other on-campus events are good, but Northfield doesn't offer a lot in entertainment." Despite what Northfield may be lacking ("Northfield isn't someplace to stay on a Friday or Saturday night"), buses run regularly to the Twin Cities, which allows students to leave town easily enough. Dating isn't prevalent, and a few students wonder why condoms are not available on campus, though women can get the pill. "Sexuality at times comes across as real taboo, due in part to it being a college of the church," writes a student. St. Olaf is affiliated with the Lutheran Church, and has no Greek system. Sports are very popular, almost as popular as studying. "The social life is definitely lacking but if a student is creative and looks hard enough, they won't be bored. Besides, there's always homework. I'm not sure if that's good or not, but it's a popular weekend activity nonetheless." The vast majority of students live on campus (making the cost of living low), and seem to have a strong sense of community. "Although this student body is fairly homogenous, there is great freedom for differences, and each student is accepted whether they are part of the whole or not."

Academics

Students here like their teachers more than any other one thing at their school. "The professors are the best! I've been to their houses for dinner and discussion. They constantly keep in contact by e-mail," says one. Classes are small, and teachers seem to be very interested in the students themselves ("All of my professors know my name, and that's important to me."). Students compliment the administration as well, which is rare at most colleges. According to one student, "Part of the reason I came to St. Olaf is I knew I would be a person and not a number on the computer—I received a handwritten message on my acceptance letter." St. Olaf has a very good liberal arts program ("This is a great school for the high achieving high school student who has an appreciation for the arts and music. The classes are stimulating for the most part and many are challenging."), with strong curricula in economics and the sciences as well. The core classes are numerous, including two required religion courses. A "paracollege" is another option, which allows students to create their own major and curricula. One student sums up the St. Olaf academic program this way: "This school is extremely dedicated to the success of the student—if you want to do well, the resources are there."

Student Body

The average St. Olaf student is fairly religious, white, and politically middle-of-the road. Many complain about a lack of diversity, but seem to get along with each other quite well: "I think the students here have a lot in common, interests, socioeconomic status, etc. I get along with them because they are so much like me." Finally, a student has this to say about his classmates' priorities: "The average `ole' thinks about school, sex, and beer, in that order."

FINANCIAL AID: 507-646-3015

ADMISSIONS

The admissions committee considers (in descending order of importance): HS record, recommendations, test scores, essay, class rank. *Also considered (in descending order of importance):* alumni relationship, extracurriculars, geographical distribution, personality, special talents. Either the SAT or ACT is required. An interview is recommended. Admissions process is need-blind. *High school units required/recommended:* 15 total units are recommended; 4 English recommended, 3 math recommended, 2 science recommended, 2 foreign language recommended, 3 social-studies recommended. Minimum 3.0 GPA in academic courses recommended. *Special Requirements:* An audition is required for music program applicants. TOEFL is required of all international students. Audition required of B.Mus. program applicants.

The Inside Word

St. Olaf truly deserves a more national reputation; the place is a bastion of excellence and has always crossed applications with the best schools in the Midwest. Despite its lack of widespread recognition, it is a great choice. Candidates benefit from the relative anonymity of the college through an admissions process, which, while demanding, isn't as tough as other colleges of St. Olaf's caliber.

FINANCIAL AID

Students should submit: FAFSA, the school's own financial aid form. The Princeton Review suggests that all financial aid forms be submitted as soon as possible after January 1. *The following grants/scholarships are offered:* Pell, SEOG, academic merit, the school's own scholarships, the school's own grants, state scholarships, state grants, federal nursing scholarship. *Students borrow from the following loan programs:* Stafford, Perkins, PLUS, the school's own loan fund, state loans, federal nursing loans. College Work-Study Program is available. Institutional employment is available.

FROM THE ADMISSIONS OFFICE

"St. Olaf College provides an education in the liberal arts that is rooted in the Christian gospel and offered with a global perspective. 50 to 60 percent of each graduating class will have studied overseas during the four years at St. Olaf. The Paracollege and Great Conversation programs offer alternatives to the traditional curriculum."

ADMISSIONS

Admissions Rating	79
% of applicants accepted	74
% of acceptees attending	43

FRESHMAN PROFILE

Average verbal SAT	620
Average math SAT	620
Average ACT	26
Average TOEFL	550
Graduated top 20% of class	69
Graduated top 40% of class	91
Graduated top 60% of class	98
Average HS GPA or Avg.	3.5

DEADLINES

Early decision	NR
Regular admission	2/1
Regular notification	rolling
Non-fall registration	yes

APPLICANTS ALSO LOOK AT

AND OFTEN PREFER

Gustavus Adolphus
Northwestern U.

AND SOMETIMES PREFER

Carleton

AND RARELY PREFER

U. Minnesota-Twin Cities
Luther

FINANCIAL FACTS

Financial Aid Rating	94
Tuition	$15,000
Room & board	$3,760
Estimated book expense	$350
% frosh receiving aid	76
% undergrads receiving aid	81
% aid is need-based	95
% frosh w/ grant (avg)	76 ($8,599)
% frosh w/ loan (avg)	63 ($2,782)
% UGs w/ job (avg)	65 ($200)
Off-campus job outlook	fair

STANFORD UNIVERSITY

STANFORD, CA 94305   ADMISSIONS: 415-723-2091   FAX: 415-725-2846

CAMPUS LIFE

Quality of Life Rating   **90**

Type of school	private
Affiliation	none
Environment	suburban

STUDENTS

FT undergrad enrollment	6,577
% male/female	50/50
% from out of state	54
% live on campus	92
% spend weekend on campus	95
% transfers	7
% from public high school	70
% in (# of) fraternities	10 (18)
% in (# of) sororities	10 (8)
% African-American	8
% Asian	24
% Caucasian	50
% Hispanic	12
% international	4
# of countries represented	57

WHAT'S HOT

registration is a breeze
computer facilities
library
leftist politics
student publications

WHAT'S NOT

infrequent dating
cigarettes
sex
student government
theater

ACADEMICS

Academic Rating   **94**

Profs Interesting Rating	76
Profs Accessible Rating	70
Calendar	quarter
Student/teacher ratio	10:1
% profs PhD	100
Hours of study per day	3.21

MOST POPULAR MAJORS

economics
English
engineering

STUDENTS SPEAK OUT

Life

"It was cool when we could go to Dead shows, but oh well!" With the responses we get about life at Stanford, one has to wonder, did the fun die with Jerry? One thing you have to get used to at Stanford is not having a steady, because dating on campus is almost nonexistent. Says one frustrated student, "My only complaints are that there's not much formal dating and it's hard to get off campus on the weekends without a car." Indeed, a car is pretty necessary if San Francisco is your destination on the weekend. "People sometimes go to San Francisco to experience a real atmosphere," explains one student, "to get away from the suburban snobbiness." If you do stay on campus (as most actually do), "the drug/alcohol policy is wonderfully lenient." Says another, "Dorm life is central to a lot of people." Luckily, Stanford dorms get high marks. So does the Greek system, a very popular way to socialize. Food on campus is okay, off campus is better, but it's expensive. Stanford's campus itself is huge ("You definitely need a bike") and drop-dead gorgeous, drawing nothing but raves. Sports are big too; most undergrads are involved at some level. Maybe that's enough—maybe love can wait.

Academics

"Profs are good but the administration bites." That's the general mood surrounding Stanford's academics ("Some of the brightest minds in the world are here") and administration ("Lots of bureaucracy and red tape"). With large lecture classes "you've got to be brave or a brown-noser to get to know your freshman-year profs." But, adds a junior studying political science, "The upper-division profs are more accessible and interested in getting to know you." Keeping up with schoolwork takes up three to five hours each day for most students at Stanford, which is understandable—this is one of the very best schools in the country, an Ivy-caliber university with a California atmosphere. The engineering, physical sciences, and liberal arts programs are all nationally renowned. Lab facilities and the bursar got high marks, while student health services were a cause of concern. "Cowell Student Health Center is entirely made up of incompetent doctors," writes one. First-year classes are easy to get into, especially with computerized registration, and the library at Stanford is great, though some students complain that books they're looking for are usually checked out ("Buy more copies!" pleads one). One student sums up undergrads' general happiness with Stanford's academic standards with "You get what you pay (a lot) for."

Student Body

Comments like "Students all get along really well" and "The people here are smart and cool" pop up here and there, but Stanford undergrads for the most part seem a little bummed these days. "If you are a social butterfly into shallow (yet significant) relationships, Stanford's social climate will fit you perfectly." Ouch. While students consider their school ethnically diverse (and it is), they also own up to the fact that people tend to stick in their cliques, and that there is "a degree of racial tension" on campus. Says one, "I am comfortable with other students. I feel as if we are all on the same level, but most ethnic groups tend to stick together." Says another of his comrades, "They're okay. Too bad I only see them in the library." But don't think Stanford undergrads are a bunch of carrel-bound complainers! They have plenty of sex and imbibe many legal and illegal intoxicants to keep their mood somewhat in line with the gorgeous setting in which they spend their days.

FINANCIAL AID: 415-723-3058 · WEB SITE: HTTP://WWW.STANFORD.EDU

ADMISSIONS

Applicants must submit: letters of recommendation, high school grades and curriculum, SAT I/ACT scores, essays, extracurricular activities. Also considered: SAT II Subject Test scores. Recommended high school curriculum: standard college prep.

The Inside Word

Not only is Stanford a pinnacle of academic excellence, but among the nation's ultra-selective universities it is one of the most compassionate toward students, both those who attend and those who aspire to attend. It isn't easy for an admissions staff to be warm and caring when your reputation is based in part on how many candidates you say "no" to. In our opinion, Stanford is the best of the best in this regard. Students who haven't devoted themselves to excellence in the same fashion that Stanford itself has are not likely to meet with success in gaining admission.

FINANCIAL AID

Students should submit: FAFSA (due February 1), CSS Profile, the school's own financial aid form (due February 1), a copy of parents' most recent income tax filing. The Princeton Review suggests that all financial aid forms be submitted as soon as possible after January 1. *The following grants/scholarships are offered:* Pell, SEOG, athletic, the school's own scholarships, the school's own grants, state scholarships, state grants, private scholarships, private grants, ROTC, foreign aid. *Students borrow from the following loan programs:* Stafford, Perkins, PLUS, the school's own loan fund. Applicants will be notified of awards beginning early April. College Work-Study Program is available. Institutional employment is available.

FROM THE ADMISSIONS OFFICE

Stanford University is an independent, coeducational, nondenominational, residential institution with goals of practicality, humanism and excellence. It provides students an abundant and challenging environment and much personal and academic freedom. Located in a residential area, 40 minutes from San Francisco and the Pacific and four hours from the Sierra, Stanford's 8,800 acres consist of a central cluster of academic and residence buildings surrounded by rolling foothills and open space. The setting promotes an informal atmosphere and encourages use of the extensive academic, athletic, and fine arts facilities which include an 85,000-seat football stadium, golf course, riding stables, and intimate theater, and one of the largest Rodin sculpture collections in the U.S. Academic facilities and features include a faculty of over 1,300, more than sixty majors, many interdepartmental and innovative programs, advanced scientific equipment, a network of twenty-five libraries, plus the opportunity for all students to study at one of the seven Overseas Studies Centers.

ADMISSIONS

Admissions Rating	99
% of applicants accepted	20
% of acceptees attending	54

FRESHMAN PROFILE

Average verbal SAT	650
Average math SAT	720
Average ACT	31
Average TOEFL	NR
Graduated top 20% of class	96
Graduated top 40% of class	NR
Graduated top 60% of class	NR
Average HS GPA or Avg.	NR

DEADLINES

Early decision	12/1
Regular admission	12/15
Regular notification	4/1
Non-fall registration	no

APPLICANTS ALSO LOOK AT

AND OFTEN PREFER
Harvard/Radcliffe

AND SOMETIMES PREFER
Duke
MIT
Caltech
Yale
Princeton

AND RARELY PREFER
UC-Berkeley
UCLA
Gonzaga
Virginia
Northwestern U.

FINANCIAL FACTS

Financial Aid Rating	76
Tuition	$20,490
Room & board	$7,340
Estimated book expense	$900
% frosh receiving aid	47
% undergrads receiving aid	61
% aid is need-based	100
% frosh w/ grant (avg)	39 ($15,583)
% frosh w/ loan (avg)	43 ($3,700)
% UGs w/ job (avg)	44 ($1,500)
Off-campus job outlook	good

STATE UNIVERSITY OF NEW YORK AT ALBANY

1400 WASHINGTON AVENUE, ALBANY, NY 12222

ADMISSIONS: 518-442-5435

CAMPUS LIFE

Quality of Life Rating   **65**
Type of school   public
Affiliation   none
Environment   city

STUDENTS

FT undergrad enrollment	9,742
% male/female	52/48
% from out of state	3
% live on campus	54
% spend weekend on campus	NR
% transfers	34
% from public high school	NR
% in (# of) fraternities	22 (29)
% in (# of) sororities	12 (18)
% African-American	9
% Asian	8
% Caucasian	70
% Hispanic	7
% international	NR
# of countries represented	22

WHAT'S HOT
drugs
cigarettes
hard liquor
sex
ethnic diversity on campus

WHAT'S NOT
campus food
unattractive campus
political activism
students are unhappy
dorms

ACADEMICS

Academic Rating	**72**
Profs Interesting Rating	61
Profs Accessible Rating	63
Calendar	semester
Student/teacher ratio	18:1
% profs tenured	96
Hours of study per day	2.52

MOST POPULAR MAJORS
psychology
English
political science

STUDENTS SPEAK OUT

Life

SUNY-Albany students give the Empire State's capital city mixed reviews. According to one student, "The city of Albany is fun and energetic. There are a million things to do." Others complain, as does this freshman student, "It's a nice area, but boring! And cold!" A large number of our respondents find most of their diversions center around the school's thriving Greek scene, but admit that this is not their only option. "There are a lot of Greeks, "reports one, "but there are also many opportunities to meet people who are similar to you, through groups, clubs, and activities." "People are concerned with parties and bars and dating (for the most part)," claims another. "But there are some cultural and intellectual groups, events, places, etc. Thank goodness." Dorm life also provides a social scene ("My hall is very unified, and they are my second family"). Other students take advantage of activities in the surrounding area, and even make the trek to NYC, a three-hour drive away. Says one student (or was this a well-placed corporate plant?), "We go to Denny's, go bar hopping, go to the movies, rent from Blockbuster Video, go to McDonald's or the mall, or drive into NYC with a group of friends to see a sporting event."

Academics

SUNY-Albany continues to attract students with its strong preprofessional programs—most notably in its business and psychology departments. As with many of the large schools we survey, students find that the number of academic opportunities available to them is directly related to the amount of energy spent in searching them out. "This is a university with tremendous opportunities; however, the students must seek out these opportunities or they will be overlooked." Overall, the faculty receives moderate grades, but a large number of glowing reports caught our attention. "Teachers are insightful and accessible," writes one student. "My algebra professor would teach class even if no students would show up." "Professors here are good teachers and are willing to help students with their problems," says another. "In a school so big, you'd think that professors and TAs wouldn't take an interest in students. To the contrary, they do. They are always at office hours and are always available when needed." And still another reports, "I came from a small school and was a little overwhelmed at first. But the professors here really believed in me and that made all the difference." Facilities receive low-to-medium marks for, among other things, library hours ("There is no place to study after 11 P.M."), particular department resources ("The music department is about 200 years behind the times"), and the food ("The food sucks! Tell the administrators!").

Student Body

While many students agree that SUNY-Albany has "a very diverse student body and, considering that, there are few difficulties," many others admit that, despite this, "people are still scared to mingle interracially." Some conflicts are reported ("Serious incidents do occur; however, they are few and far between"), and other respondents find that "students tend to stick with their own kind (fraternities, sororities, cliques"). But overall, most of our respondents cite "a sense of community that is obvious to everyone," and that "most people here are really friendly."

STATE UNIVERSITY OF NEW YORK AT ALBANY

FINANCIAL AID: 518-442-5757   E-MAIL: UGADMIT@SAFNET.ALBANY.EDU   WEB SITE: HTTP://WWW.ALBANY.EDU/HOME.HTML

ADMISSIONS

The admissions committee considers (in descending order of importance): HS record, test scores, class rank, recommendations. *Also considered (in descending order of importance):* extracurriculars, personality, special talents. Either the SAT or ACT is required; SAT is preferred. Admissions process is need-blind. *High school units required/recommended:* 18 total units are required; 4 English required, 2 math required, 2 science required, 3 foreign language recommended, 3 social studies required. Minimum combined SAT I score of 1100, rank in top quarter of secondary school class, and minimum 86 grade average recommended. *Special Requirements:* A portfolio is required for art program applicants. An audition is required for music program applicants. TOEFL is required of all international students.

The Inside Word

New York State's budget woes continue to have a costly effect on the SUNY system. Adverse publicity continues, and its result is readily evidenced by the University at Albany's low yield of enrollees. It's now significantly easier to get admitted to Albany than it is to several of the SUNY Colleges, and there doesn't seem to be an end in sight. Perhaps the selection of SUNY Albany as the new training camp site for the New York Giants will bring both revenue and facilities that will help a turnaround. Without increased private funding, Albany will remain the easiest path into a University Center.

FINANCIAL AID

Students should submit: FAFSA. The Princeton Review suggests that all financial aid forms be submitted as soon as possible after January 1. *The following grants/scholarships are offered:* Pell, SEOG, academic merit, athletic, the school's own scholarships, state scholarships, state grants, private scholarships, private grants, ROTC. *Students borrow from the following loan programs:* Stafford, unsubsidized Stafford, Perkins, PLUS, the school's own loan fund. College Work-Study Program is available. Institutional employment is available.

FROM THE ADMISSIONS OFFICE

"As one of the small number of schools in New York State accredited by the American Assembly of Collegiate Schools of Business, The School of Business of the University at Albany: State University of New York, provides one of the finest preprofessional undergraduate educations in accounting and business administration in the Northeast. Because of demand, a secondary admission to the School of Business is required at the end of the sophomore year. Of the group that applies each year, fifty to sixty percent are admitted as majors in accounting or business administration. Each year, large numbers of seniors are actively recruited by the Big Six accounting firms, as well as by many other medium and smaller size firms."

ADMISSIONS

Admissions Rating	73
% of applicants accepted	62
% of acceptees attending	20

FRESHMAN PROFILE

Average verbal SAT	580
Average math SAT	590
Average ACT	NR
Average TOEFL	550
Graduated top 20% of class	43
Graduated top 40% of class	85
Graduated top 60% of class	98
Average HS GPA or Avg.	87.0

DEADLINES

Early decision	11/15
Regular admission	2/15
Regular notification	rolling
Non-fall registration	yes

APPLICANTS ALSO LOOK AT

AND OFTEN PREFER

Cornell U.
Binghamton U.

AND SOMETIMES PREFER

U. Rochester
Fordham
Syracuse
Siena
U. Mass.-Amherst

AND RARELY PREFER

Hofstra

FINANCIAL FACTS

Financial Aid Rating	66
In-state tuition	$3,400
Out-of-state tuition	$8,300
Room & board	$4,836
Estimated book expense	$700
% frosh receiving aid	81
% undergrads receiving aid	75
% aid is need-based	84
% frosh w/ grant (avg)	56 ($2,700)
% frosh w/ loan (avg)	71 ($3,425)
% UGs w/ job (avg)	12 ($851)
Off-campus job outlook	good

BINGHAMTON UNIVERSITY

P.O. BOX 6000, BINGHAMTON, NY 13902-6000   ADMISSIONS: 607-777-2171   FAX: 607-777-4000

CAMPUS LIFE

Quality of Life Rating — **76**

Type of school	public
Affiliation	none
Environment	suburban

STUDENTS

FT undergrad enrollment	8,813
% male/female	46/54
% from out of state	7
% live on campus	53
% spend weekend on campus	75
% transfers	33
% from public high school	83
% in (# of) fraternities	15 (21)
% in (# of) sororities	15 (14)
% African-American	6
% Asian	18
% Caucasian	68
% Hispanic	7
% international	5
# of countries represented	87

WHAT'S HOT
drugs
college radio
leftist politics
political activism
health facilities

WHAT'S NOT
students are cliquish
students are unhappy
town-gown relations
Binghamton
off-campus food

ACADEMICS

Academic Rating — **82**

Profs Interesting Rating	64
Profs Accessible Rating	64
Calendar	semester
Student/teacher ratio	19:1
% profs PhD/tenured	95/75
Hours of study per day	3.15

MOST POPULAR MAJORS
management
English
psychology

% GRADS WHO PURSUE...
Law 11, Med 8, MBA 2, MA 24

STUDENTS SPEAK OUT

Life
"I like the atmosphere. People are very ambitious here" was an opinion voiced many times over by Binghamton University students. Most of our respondents say that their classmates are serious about their work, if not about the university itself: "Most are apathetic about the school, but very serious about their career goals." The upstate New York town of Binghamton received less-than-stellar reviews. "The town is barren and relies on the university for everything" grumbles one sophomore. "If we had a football team, this town could come alive." Most concur that "there is little fun to be had in Bingo-Land." On-campus fun for most students revolves around the fraternity scene and dormitories, although people do get involved in other activities. "The student clubs on campus are terrific," claims one, "namely because the students get to run them completely." Campus facilities offer other venues in which students can let their hair down: "I like the way people socialize here. We have a pub on campus where the atmosphere is very lighthearted and relaxed."

Academics
Binghamton University, often known as "the ivy of the SUNYs," offers a top-notch education at a state-school price. Preprofessional programs, most notably in psychology, accounting, and nursing, are particularly strong. But Binghamton also has state-school-sized classes, to the dismay of some students: "Getting the classes one needs is very difficult, sometimes even for an upperclassman in the major!" gripes a senior. Most agree, however, that large class size does not compromise quality ("I am still learning a lot, besides the huge classes"), and claim that the problem does improve with upper-level classes ("As a junior and a senior, my classes were much smaller and more beneficial to my needs"). The school's administration receives average marks, with higher marks for efficiency ("Very few bottlenecks"), and lower marks for its efforts to communicate with students ("Some of the administrative types seem more interested in building fiefdoms instead of ensuring a quality education"). Professors receive good marks overall; while a few students wish their profs "could be a bit more involved with their students," most feel their teachers made special efforts to get to know and be available to them—not a small feat considering the large class sizes. "Professors are very accessible and willing to get to know the students if an effort is shown by the student" reports one respondent. "While many professors are really busy with their work, there are some who will be more than willing to offer their time to you" says another. Facilities receive average marks. Offers one student: "I live in a campus-owned apartment—very nice, very expensive." Another notes, "I like my classes and I've never had a problem with the administration; however, the infirmary is a different story."

Student Body
A very large percentage of Binghamton's student body comes from New York state. "There are all nationalities of Long Islanders," says one student, "but not enough out-of-staters." Otherwise, the population is considered to be quite diverse by our respondents: "The student body is diverse not only in race, religion, and culture, but in personality as well," says another. "It is very refreshing. I find myself getting along with a lot of different people." Students report social divisions along racial lines, but little open conflict.

FINANCIAL AID: 607-777-2428

ADMISSIONS

The admissions committee considers (in descending order of importance): HS record, class rank, essay, recommendations, test scores. *Also considered (in descending order of importance):* extracurriculars, personality, special talents, alumni relationship, geographical distribution. Either the SAT or ACT is required. Admissions process is need-blind. *High school units required/recommended:* 21 total units are recommended; 4 English required, 3 math required, 4 math recommended, 4 science recommended, 3 foreign language recommended, 2 social studies recommended, 2 history recommended. *Special Requirements:* TOEFL is required of all international students. 3 units of one foreign language or 2 units of two languages required of Harpur College applicants. 1 unit of chemistry recommended of nursing program applicants.

The Inside Word

While Binghamton has a developing national reputation, its admissions operation focuses virtually entirely on New York residents—unlike at other top public universities, there appears to be little interest in out-of-state students. The university's admissions process is highly selective, but fairly simple. Candidates go through a process that first considers academic qualifications, primarily through numbers, and then takes a relatively brief look at other components of the application. Binghamton hasn't been hurt by New York's budget problems as much as the rest of the SUNY system has, and may escape relatively free from harm.

FINANCIAL AID

Students should submit: FAFSA (due March 1). The Princeton Review suggests that all financial aid forms be submitted as soon as possible after January 1. *The following grants/scholarships are offered:* Pell, SEOG, academic merit, the school's own scholarships, the school's own grants, state scholarships, state grants, private scholarships, private grants, federal nursing scholarship, ROTC. *Students borrow from the following loan programs:* Perkins, PLUS, supplemental loans, federal nursing loans. College Work-Study Program is available. Institutional employment is available.

FROM THE ADMISSIONS OFFICE

"Binghamton University prides itself on excellent teaching and solid research from a faculty remarkably accessible to students. Students have the opportunity to engage in research with faculty and, together, they have designed projects and co-authored papers. Teaching and mentoring by faculty builds students' confidence and competence, encouraging them to become independent learners. Binghamton University welcomes serious students interested in working toward a productive future in our dynamic academic community."

ADMISSIONS

Admissions Rating	89
% of applicants accepted	40
% of acceptees attending	28

FRESHMAN PROFILE

Average verbal SAT	670
Average math SAT	620
Average ACT	NR
Average TOEFL	580
Graduated top 20% of class	89
Graduated top 40% of class	99
Graduated top 60% of class	100
Average HS GPA or Avg.	92.1

DEADLINES

Early decision	11/1
Regular admission	2/15
Regular notification	4/15
Non-fall registration	yes

APPLICANTS ALSO LOOK AT

AND OFTEN PREFER
Cornell U.
NYU
U. Pennsylvania

AND SOMETIMES PREFER
SUNY Geneseo
Clarkson U.
SUNY Buffalo

AND RARELY PREFER
Queens (CUNY)
Fordham

FINANCIAL FACTS

Financial Aid Rating	64
In-state tuition	$3,650
Out-of-state tuition	$8,300
Room & board	$4,654
Estimated book expense	$800
% frosh receiving aid	92
% undergrads receiving aid	49
% aid is need-based	95
% frosh w/ grant (avg)	31 ($3,801)
% frosh w/ loan (avg)	20 ($1,284)
% UGs w/ job (avg)	10 ($1,000)
Off-campus job outlook	excellent

STATE UNIVERSITY OF NEW YORK AT BUFFALO

BUFFALO, NY 14260   ADMISSIONS: 716-645-2000   FAX: 716-645-2895

STUDENTS SPEAK OUT

Life

One student reports that SUNY-Buffalo (referred to as UB—University of Buffalo—by its students), like many large universities, "offers something for everyone. The number and variety of athletic, academic, and social organizations to choose from are great. People might think that by coming to such a large school they sacrifice their identity and become 'just a number.' But if a person is willing to make some effort and interact with the staff here, he doesn't necessarily lose his identity. I'll probably pursue my master's degree here, too." Students like the city of Buffalo a lot. Unfortunately, as a student who lives off campus tells us, "The campus is completely isolated from the city. I can't imagine how dorm life is bearable." In fact, undergrads give all aspects of dorm life low grades; the food received similarly poor marks. The campus is impersonal and a little difficult to get around: "We need a transportation system between the campus and dormitories," complains one student. Students enjoy an active dating scene despite a lopsided male/female ratio. Beware: winters are long and cold.

Academics

SUNY-Buffalo is by far the largest school in the SUNY system. The Amherst campus, where undergraduates study, covers a vast expanse of territory, so the school's size can at first be overwhelming. But as one student explains, "Some students are intimidated by a large school, but you get lost only if you let yourself." Engineering, business, and premed are the school's main drawing cards, although the liberal arts and several other career-oriented programs (physical and occupational therapy, architecture) are reportedly very good. Introductory classes are huge, and labs and recitations are frequently taught by graduate students, but a physical therapy major writes, "Once you advance in your major, classes are smaller (twenty to forty students) and most are taught by professors." Students give the library excellent marks but feel that, on the whole, the school is poorly administered. For one thing, it's not always easy to get into mandatory classes. Says one student of the amount of effort she put into registration, "If I actually got into my classes, life would become very boring." All in all, though, the school is no better or worse run than other comparably sized universities.

Student Body

Practically all UB students are from New York State. Locals make up the majority of the student body, but the school is good enough to draw from all over the state, and many students are from New York City and Long Island. One quarter of the students are minorities. Most students identify themselves as politically apathetic. Explains one, "With all the diversity this school offers (ethnic, communal, language, cultural, racial, economic), it is a great place to be. What it needs, however, is more socio-political consciousness and comfort from subzero temperatures."

FINANCIAL AID: 716-829-3724   E-MAIL: UBADMISSIONS@ACSU.BUFFALO.EDU   WEB SITE: HTTP://WWW.BUFFALO.EDU

ADMISSIONS

The admissions committee considers (in descending order of importance): class rank, HS record, test scores. Either the SAT or ACT is required. Admissions process is need-blind. *High school units required/recommended:* 4 English recommended, 3 math recommended, 3 science recommended, 3 foreign language recommended, 4 social studies recommended. Minimum composite SAT I score of 1050, rank in top fifth of secondary school class, and grade average of 85 recommended. *Special Requirements:* A portfolio is required for art program applicants. An audition is required for music program applicants. TOEFL is required of all international students. *The admissions office says:* "Competition for available places is keen. Mean combined SAT I scores for accepted students are typically above 1100 and mean high school averages are above 90. A limited number of freshmen may be offered admission to the University based upon evidence of special talents [such as] exceptional creative talent in art, media study, music, theater, writing, special academic achievement, demonstrated leadership, outstanding athletic ability, and community service."

The Inside Word

Buffalo was formerly a private university, and was absorbed into the SUNY system. Its admissions process reflects this private heritage to the extent possible (applications are centrally processed for the entire system in Albany). It's one of the few SUNY schools with a freshman academic profile higher than its published admissions standards. Although Binghamton is academically the most selective of the SUNY University Centers, Buffalo is in many ways closer to what other states refer to as the flagship of the state system.

FINANCIAL AID

Students should submit: FAFSA (due May 1), state aid form (due May 1). The Princeton Review suggests that all financial aid forms be submitted as soon as possible after January 1. *The following grants/scholarships are offered:* Pell, SEOG, academic merit, athletic, the school's own scholarships, the school's own grants, state scholarships, state grants, private scholarships, private grants, federal nursing scholarship. *Students borrow from the following loan programs:* Stafford, unsubsidized Stafford, Perkins, PLUS, the school's own loan fund, supplemental loans, federal nursing loans, health professions loans, private loans. Applicants will be notified of awards beginning in February. College Work-Study Program is available. Institutional employment is available.

FROM THE ADMISSIONS OFFICE

"Steeped in tradition, modern in focus, large in concept, and personal in form, the State University of New York at Buffalo (UB) is a university in the richest sense. Important in graduate and professional education, it displays also remarkable breadth, diversity, and quality in undergraduate programs in the humanities, natural sciences, social sciences, and fine arts. In short, New York State's major public university provides unparalleled opportunities for learning, for career preparation, for developing a rewarding way of life. On the cutting edge of technology, UB offers its students electronic mail and a campus-wide electronic information service which provides a direct gateway to the internet's World Wide Web. Prospective transfer students receive a transfer credit evaluation report, and UB students can take advantage of touch-tone registration and an automated degree audit system to monitor their progress toward a degree. We encourage students and their families to visit the University at Buffalo and to feel the many textures of the campus—its personalities, paths and facilities. Campus tours and presentations are offered year-round. To schedule a campus visit, call (716) 645-6900."

ADMISSIONS

Admissions Rating	**75**
% of applicants accepted	69
% of acceptees attending	25

FRESHMAN PROFILE

Average verbal SAT	630
Average math SAT	600
Average ACT	25
Average TOEFL	550
Graduated top 20% of class	57
Graduated top 40% of class	91
Graduated top 60% of class	100
Average HS GPA or Avg.	89.0

DEADLINES

Early decision	11/1
Regular admission	NR
Regular notification	rolling
Non-fall registration	yes

APPLICANTS ALSO LOOK AT

AND OFTEN PREFER

SUNY Albany
SUNY Binghamton
Cornell U.
NYU

AND SOMETIMES PREFER

Syracuse
Alfred
U. Rochester
SUNY Stony Brook
Boston U.

AND RARELY PREFER

U. Mass.-Amherst
Penn State-U. Park
U. Conn.

FINANCIAL FACTS

Financial Aid Rating	**76**
In-state tuition	$3,400
Out-of-state tuition	$8,300
Room & board	$5,300
Estimated book expense	$800
% frosh receiving aid	65
% undergrads receiving aid	59
% aid is need-based	90
% frosh w/ grant (avg)	50 ($1,642)
% frosh w/ loan (avg)	53 ($5,283)
% UGs w/ job (avg)	NR
Off-campus job outlook	good

STATE UNIV. OF NEW YORK AT STONY BROOK

STONY BROOK, NY 11794   ADMISSIONS: 516-632-6868   FAX: 516-632-9027

CAMPUS LIFE

Quality of Life Rating   **64**
Type of school   public
Affiliation   none
Environment   town

STUDENTS
FT undergrad enrollment   10,082
% male/female   49/51
% from out of state   2
% live on campus   55
% spend weekend on campus   60
% transfers   13
% from public high school   85
% in (# of) fraternities   (15)
% in (# of) sororities   (11)
% African-American   10
% Asian   17
% Caucasian   49
% Hispanic   7
% international   3
# of countries represented   57

WHAT'S HOT
ethnic diversity on campus
cigarettes
drugs
leftist politics
sex

WHAT'S NOT
campus difficult to get around
students are unhappy
inefficient administration
dorms
support groups

ACADEMICS

Academic Rating   **67**
Profs Interesting Rating   60
Profs Accessible Rating   62
Calendar   other
Student/teacher ratio   17:1
% profs PhD/tenured   95/74
Hours of study per day   2.83

MOST POPULAR MAJORS
psychology
biological sciences
social sciences

% GRADS WHO PURSUE...
Law 6, Med 9, MA 21

STUDENTS SPEAK OUT

Life
SUNY-Stony Brook is considered a commuter school, but with a sizable undergraduate population living on campus, there is a significant campus community. Living conditions here leave something to be desired: A striking number of students rate the dorms, campus, and food "uncomfortable," "ugly," and "awful," respectively. The social scene here is lively; students find plenty of ways to party. Our survey shows drug use to be common, but drinking, while popular, is not any more so than on other campuses we surveyed. Offsetting the school's nondescript modern campus is the historic town of Stony Brook; the surrounding area is beautiful. Students report that "the bars in Stony Brook are located within a one-mile radius of campus and are jammed with students." Long Island's South Shore is only a half-hour's drive (or bus ride) away and provides excellent distraction in the early fall and late spring. And New York City is about an hour away via the Long Island Railroad.

Academics
Stony Brook is a big university with a staff devoted primarily to research. Accordingly, students get the opportunity to study with some brilliant scholars, particularly in the hard sciences, engineering, and the psychology department. The downside is that some professors are more dedicated to their research than to their undergraduates and, not surprisingly, professors here receive low grades for in-class and out-of-class performance. Be prepared to fend for yourself: Students tell us that a good education is available here, but you'll have to find it on your own. "Large" and "impersonal" are words commonly used to describe the administration, which students give uniformly poor grades. State budget cuts have hurt the school, and several students complain of overcrowded or canceled courses. Still, the school is academically strong and students are very competitive. Perhaps too competitive: Respondents tell us that there is "excessive cheating during final exams." Most students agree that they're getting a good deal: Says one, "Stony Brook is a large public university and functions well within those parameters," while another describes his school as "a very good deal for the money, very academically oriented, and very thorough."

Student Body
Many SUNY-Stony Brook students are from the area. The science and engineering programs attract some students from outside the area and even a few hundred foreign nationals. One student mentions the school's very big minority population, and says, "Stony Brook is cultural diversity." However, because of the school's size and the large commuter population, there is little sense of community among the students, and interaction among different groups is minimal, but not impossible. Some students report that this large size results in relationships that are "totally plastic."

STATE UNIVERSITY OF NEW YORK AT STONY BROOK

FINANCIAL AID: 516-632-6840

WEB SITE: HTTP://WWW.SUNYSB.EDU

ADMISSIONS

The admissions committee considers (in descending order of importance): HS record, class rank, recommendations, test scores. *Also considered (in descending order of importance):* extracurriculars, special talents, alumni relationship, geographical distribution, personality. Either the SAT or ACT is required. An interview is recommended. Admissions process is need-blind. *High school units required/recommended:* 4 English recommended, 3 math recommended, 3 science recommended, 3 foreign language recommended, 3 social studies recommended. Minimum combined SAT I score of 1100, rank in top third of secondary school class, and grade average of 85 required. *Special Requirements:* TOEFL is required of all international students. Chemistry, physics, and 4 units of math recommended of engineering, mathematics, and sciences program applicants. Applicants planning to major in computer science must successfully complete one semester at Stony Brook. Additional requirements for upper-division nursing and engineering program applicants.

The Inside Word

After Albany, Stony Brook has suffered more from New York State's fiscal woes than the other University Centers. It's a long road back to its former image of academic strength, given several years of lost momentum. The university is moving its athletic programs to NCAA Division I in the hope of generating greater positive visibility and increases in applications for admission. Until such time as Stony Brook emerges from budget insecurity, admission will remain relatively easy for solid students.

FINANCIAL AID

Students should submit: FAFSA (due March 1). The Princeton Review suggests that all financial aid forms be submitted as soon as possible after January 1. *The following grants/scholarships are offered:* Pell, SEOG, academic merit, athletic, the school's own scholarships, state scholarships, state grants, private scholarships, private grants. *Students borrow from the following loan programs:* Stafford, Perkins, PLUS, state loans, federal nursing loans, health professions loans. College Work-Study Program is available. Institutional employment is available.

FROM THE ADMISSIONS OFFICE

"As New York State's only public university to be classified by the Carnegie Foundation as one of the nation's seventy leading research institutions, Stony Brook has exceptional strength in the sciences, mathematics, humanities, fine arts, social sciences, engineering, and health professions. Stony Brook's undergraduate degree programs are augmented by a number of special academic opportunities. Among them are: living/learning centers that integrate academic pursuits with residential life; the Honors College for outstanding students which offers a four-year sequence of interdisciplinary seminars taught by some of Stony Brook's most respected faculty; and federated learning communities, a nationally acclaimed "experiment" in interdisciplinary education that brings a small group of students together with a faculty "Master Learner" in six courses centered on a common theme."

ADMISSIONS

Admissions Rating	75
% of applicants accepted	54
% of acceptees attending	24

FRESHMAN PROFILE

Average verbal SAT	540
Average math SAT	560
Average ACT	NR
Average TOEFL	550
Graduated top 20% of class	68
Graduated top 40% of class	97
Graduated top 60% of class	NR
Average HS GPA or Avg.	3.4

DEADLINES

Early decision	NR
Regular admission	7/10
Regular notification	rolling
Non-fall registration	yes

APPLICANTS ALSO LOOK AT

AND OFTEN PREFER

Yale
Columbia
Pennsylvania
Brown
Cornell U.

AND SOMETIMES PREFER

Wesleyan U.
Williams
NYU
Cooper Union
Binghamton U.

AND RARELY PREFER

St. John's U. (NY)
Vassar

FINANCIAL FACTS

Financial Aid Rating	69
In-state tuition	$3,400
Out-of-state tuition	$8,300
Room & board	$5,166
Estimated book expense	$750
% frosh receiving aid	53
% undergrads receiving aid	85
% aid is need-based	43
% frosh w/ grant (avg)	NR
% frosh w/ loan (avg)	NR
% UGs w/ job (avg)	16 ($1,200)
Off-campus job outlook	good

STEPHENS COLLEGE

1200 EAST BROADWAY, COLUMBIA, MO 65215   ADMISSIONS: 800-876-7207   FAX: 573-876-7248

CAMPUS LIFE

Quality of Life Rating **68**
Type of school   private
Affiliation   none
Environment   suburban

STUDENTS

FT undergrad enrollment	607
% male/female	3/97
% from out of state	68
% live on campus	95
% spend weekend on campus	90
% transfers	9
% from public high school	NR
% in (# of) sororities	20 (4)
% African-American	8
% Asian	2
% Caucasian	88
% Hispanic	2
% international	NR
# of countries represented	NR

WHAT'S HOT
old-fashioned dating
registration is a breeze
sex
different students interact
religion

WHAT'S NOT
lab facilities
support groups
student government
campus difficult to get around

ACADEMICS

Academic Rating	**68**
Profs Interesting Rating	66
Profs Accessible Rating	67
Calendar	semester
Student/teacher ratio	11:1
% profs tenured	85
Hours of study per day	2.46

MOST POPULAR MAJORS
theatre arts
business administration
mass communication

STUDENTS SPEAK OUT

Life

Social activities at Stephens College, which enrolls almost no men, are polite and well mannered. That's why most Stephens students follow this junior's example: When they want to party, "I go to Mizzou." Students report that the life off campus is much more fun than the life on. One student comments that "Columbia [MO] is not exactly the cultural hub of the world. Most of my time is spent talking with friends. The nightlife is severely limited." The 30:1 female-to-male ratio can't help either. Many have relationships with students at other schools. For those who aren't interested in relationships, drinking or doing the club scene in St. Louis, there still are other options. One sophomore sings the praises of on-campus life when she mentions the following: "Quiet coffeehouses are the best! The penthouse in our library is a wonderful getaway."

Academics

Stephens College students love the feeling Stephens gives them. One junior writes, "One thing I love about this school is class size, teacher availability and the overall atmosphere because it is so small and everyone is friends with each other." Stephens enrolls just over 600 students; about 97 percent of them are women. Men are admitted to select programs at the school. This beautiful campus includes an eleven-acre lake, a riding arena and stables. Not surprisingly, equestrian science is one of the more popular majors, along with business (highly recommended by students), fashion, and communications. Students are mixed on the professors, but downright negative about the administration. One student notes, "If you have something good to say about our school, your comments are welcomed. If you have a complaint, the administration suddenly becomes deaf, blind, and dumb." Stephens College offers a BFA degree with two additional summers of study, and also offers cross degrees with Missouri and Washington University. Study abroad is encouraged, as Stephens has affiliations with many international programs. Located close to St. Louis, Stephens provides a blend of experience. As one student puts it, "At Stephens, it is the best of both worlds...small classes-community spirit, but in a partying college town right down the street from Mizzou."

Student Body

As the 30:1 ratio implies, Stephens is primarily a women's college. The student body is active and aware of gender issues, and this awareness leads to students being very active in other areas of political and social life. Stephens is mainly white, but minorities are not invisible on campus. Some note an economic distinction between the wealthy and the not-so-wealthy, but students give Stephens high marks for their friendships. One sophomore comments: "There are very distinct social types here that do not generally interact, but when it comes to relationships within these groups, we are blind to race and sexual preference. We see each other as women, friends and human beings." This awareness, however, should not be confused with liberal beliefs; "My fellow students can be extremely conservative. It's hard to be surrounded by an abundance of white, sheltered conservatives." Gay and lesbian groups are visible, but support for them is "nonexistent."

FINANCIAL AID: 573-876-7106

ADMISSIONS

The admissions committee considers (in descending order of importance): HS record, essay, class rank, recommendations, test scores. *Also considered (in descending order of importance):* extracurriculars, personality, alumni relationship, special talents. Either the SAT or ACT is required. An interview is required of some applicants. Admissions process is need-blind. *High school units required/recommended:* 12 total units are recommended; 4 English recommended, 2 math recommended, 2 science recommended, 2 foreign language recommended, 2 social studies recommended. Minimum combined SAT I score of 750 (composite ACT score of 19) and minimum 2.25 GPA required. TOEFL is required of all international students. *The admissions office says:* "Women at Stephens College never hear the words, 'You can't do that because you're a woman.' Their self-confidence, self-esteem, and self-concept grow in an accelerated manner."

The Inside Word

Each candidate's application is read by three members of the admissions committee, and essays carry much more significance than test scores. You'll get a lot of personal attention from the admissions staff here; with the kind of competition Stephens faces for students, they have to work pretty hard here to bring in the freshman class. Their success is a testament to the quality of the college.

FINANCIAL AID

Students should submit: FAFSA. The Princeton Review suggests that all financial aid forms be submitted as soon as possible after January 1. *The following grants/ scholarships are offered:* Pell, SEOG, academic merit, the school's own scholarships, the school's own grants, state scholarships, state grants, private scholarships, private grants. *Students borrow from the following loan programs:* Stafford, unsubsidized Stafford, Perkins, PLUS, the school's own loan fund. Applicants will be notified of awards beginning in March. College Work-Study Program is available. Institutional employment is available.

FROM THE ADMISSIONS OFFICE

"Stephens College encourages applications from women who are interested in developing their self-confidence and 'voice.' As a women's college, Stephens works with women who are independent, inquisitive, intelligent and creative— be sure your application demonstrates this when you apply."

ADMISSIONS

Admissions Rating	67
% of applicants accepted	85
% of acceptees attending	50

FRESHMAN PROFILE

Average verbal SAT	520
Average math SAT	490
Average ACT	21
Average TOEFL	550
Graduated top 20% of class	25
Graduated top 40% of class	51
Graduated top 60% of class	81
Average HS GPA or Avg.	3.0

DEADLINES

Early decision	12/1
Regular admission	rolling
Regular notification	rolling
Non-fall registration	yes

APPLICANTS ALSO LOOK AT
AND SOMETIMES PREFER

U. Missouri-Columbia
William Woods

AND RARELY PREFER

Butler

FINANCIAL FACTS

Financial Aid Rating	85
Tuition	$14,830
Room & board	$5,540
Estimated book expense	$500
% frosh receiving aid	70
% undergrads receiving aid	70
% aid is need-based	75
% frosh w/ grant (avg)	90 ($7,500)
% frosh w/ loan (avg)	75 ($2,200)
% UGs w/ job (avg)	40 ($1,500)
Off-campus job outlook	good

STEVENS INSTITUTE OF TECHNOLOGY

CASTLE POINT ON HUDSON, HOBOKEN, NJ 07030   ADMISSIONS: 800-458-5323   FAX: 201-216-8348

CAMPUS LIFE

Quality of Life Rating	72
Type of school	private
Affiliation	none
Environment	metropolis

STUDENTS

FT undergrad enrollment	1,289
% male/female	79/21
% from out of state	25
% live on campus	80
% spend weekend on campus	80
% transfers	1
% from public high school	NR
% in (# of) fraternities	40 (10)
% in (# of) sororities	40 (3)
% African-American	7
% Asian	25
% Caucasian	57
% Hispanic	11
% international	NR
# of countries represented	13

WHAT'S HOT
different students interact
ethnic diversity on campus
off-campus food
Hoboken
Greeks

WHAT'S NOT
students are unhappy
drugs
sex
library
campus food

ACADEMICS

Academic Rating	80
Profs Interesting Rating	66
Profs Accessible Rating	68
Calendar	semester
Student/teacher ratio	9:1
% profs PhD/tenured	90/90
Hours of study per day	3.23

MOST POPULAR MAJORS
engineering
computer science

% GRADS WHO PURSUE...
Law 1, Med 2, MBA 6, MA 1

STUDENTS SPEAK OUT

Life
Explains one student: "The bottom line is this: if you come here for the education, you made the right choice. If you come here for social life, athletics, or extracurricular activities, I have a bridge I'd like to sell you." Students complain that the workload and the extremely unfavorable male/female ratio (4:1— "Stevens needs a LOT more females," writes one man) kill any chances students here might have for a normal social life. For those who can make leisure time, New York City is a short commuter train ride away. Hoboken has some nice restaurants and clubs, but students go to New York when they really want to blow off steam. The campus is pleasant, "aesthetically pleasing as well as conveniently situated alongside the Hudson, and, we have the best view of New York."

Academics
How often do you hear a technological institute described as "caring"? Not one, but two area college counselors use that word to describe the Stevens Institute of Technology. That's because the school has initiated programs intended to relieve the stress common to students at all engineering schools. Extensive tutoring is available to students who fall below the class average, and smaller review sessions are part of all large lecture courses. All courses taken by freshmen and sophomores are mandatory, taking the pressure out of schedule-making. Finally, students who feel the workload is too great to complete in four years may continue to take courses toward their degrees for a fifth year, at no additional cost. The quality of academics at Stevens is, according to another area counselor, "solid, nearly as good as that at Rensselaer." Students agree that "you are not allowed to sleep or have fun, but the education is the best!" Electrical, computer, mechanical, and civil engineering are both excellent and popular with the students; physics and management are among the other popular majors. Students give their professors bad grades as teachers, mainly because "most don't speak English too well," but the overwhelming majority feel that they are getting a good education nonetheless. Many students feel that the administration could stand improvement, however, complaining that it is large and obtrusive ("there's an entire floor of the administration building for every hundred students"), yet also ineffective (the registrar, bursar, and library system all receive extremely low grades). All these complaints, however, pale beside Stevens's ability to serve the student body's chief goals, summed up by the student who writes, "This school is hard, but when I graduate I will be set."

Student Body
Two-thirds of Stevens's student body is white. Asians make up a sizable part of the minority population, and Hispanics are also well represented. One student writes that "the vast diversity among the students provides for interesting interactions." Students are extremely goal-oriented and single-minded in pursuit of their degrees.

ADMISSIONS

The admissions committee considers (in descending order of importance): HS record, recommendations, class rank, test scores, essay. *Also considered (in descending order of importance):* extracurriculars, personality, special talents, alumni relationship. Either the SAT or ACT is required; SAT is preferred. An interview is required. Admissions process is need-blind. *High school units required/recommended:* 4 English required, 4 math required, 3 science required, 2 foreign language recommended, 4 social studies recommended, 2 history recommended. Minimum SAT I score of 500 on verbal and 600 on math, and rank in top fifth of secondary school class required. TOEFL is required of all international students. *The admissions office says:* "Rolling admissions and our personalized service [distinguish our admissions process]."

The Inside Word

Stevens is indeed impressive, and legitimately near the top of the "second tier" of technical schools. Above-average students who would run into difficulty trying to gain admission to the MITs and Caltechs of the world will find a much more receptive admissions process here. Given its solid reputation and metropolitan New York location, it's an excellent choice for techies who want to establish their careers in the area.

FINANCIAL AID

Students should submit: FAFSA, the school's own financial aid form (due March 1), a copy of parents' most recent income tax filing. The Princeton Review suggests that all financial aid forms be submitted as soon as possible after January 1. *The following grants/scholarships are offered:* Pell, SEOG, academic merit, the school's own scholarships, the school's own grants, state scholarships, state grants, private scholarships, private grants, ROTC. *Students borrow from the following loan programs:* unsubsidized Stafford, Perkins, PLUS, supplemental loans, state loans, private loans. College Work-Study Program is available. Institutional employment is available.

FROM THE ADMISSIONS OFFICE

"The quality and achievement of Stevens graduates in many quarters is one of the great hallmarks of the Institute's academic excellence. One striking indication of this is the number of Stevens undergraduate alumni who succeed in becoming top industry executives, ranking Stevens in the top 3 percent of all U.S. colleges. Our graduates have an extremely high pass rate, 80 percent on the rigorous New Jersey Engineer-In-Training exam (EIT), the highest in the state, and 92 percent of all undergraduate alumni from the class of 1993 are either employed or in graduate school. Stevens boasts a student/faculty ratio of 9:1, which affords each student with the individual attention so vital to a thorough education."

ADMISSIONS

Admissions Rating	80
% of applicants accepted	70
% of acceptees attending	33

FRESHMAN PROFILE

Average verbal SAT	600
Average math SAT	660
Average ACT	NR
Average TOEFL	550
Graduated top 20% of class	70
Graduated top 40% of class	90
Graduated top 60% of class	96
Average HS GPA or Avg.	NR

DEADLINES

Early decision	NR
Regular admission	3/1
Regular notification	rolling
Non-fall registration	no

APPLICANTS ALSO LOOK AT

AND OFTEN PREFER

RPI
Cooper Union

AND SOMETIMES PREFER

Carnegie Mellon
Rutgers U.
New Jersey Tech

FINANCIAL FACTS

Financial Aid Rating	76
Tuition	$18,200
Room & board	$6,400
Estimated book expense	$300
% frosh receiving aid	75
% undergrads receiving aid	85
% aid is need-based	80
% frosh w/ grant (avg)	88
% frosh w/ loan (avg)	67 ($4,000)
% UGs w/ job (avg)	55 ($1,000)
Off-campus job outlook	excellent

SUSQUEHANNA UNIVERSITY

SELINSGROVE, PA 17870   ADMISSIONS: 717-373-4260   FAX: 717-372-2745

CAMPUS LIFE

Quality of Life Rating 86
Type of school   private
Affiliation   Evangelical Lutheran
                     Church in America (Upper
                         Susquehanna Synod)
Environment   town

STUDENTS
FT undergrad enrollment   1,457
% male/female   48/52
% from out of state   42
% live on campus   80
% spend weekend on campus   87
% transfers   7
% from public high school   85
% in (# of) fraternities   30 (4)
% in (# of) sororities   30 (4)
% African-American   2
% Asian   2
% Caucasian   95
% Hispanic   1
% international   1
# of countries represented   12

WHAT'S HOT
hard liquor
sex
Greeks
beer
music associations

WHAT'S NOT
political activism
lack of diversity on campus
student publications
computer facilities
library

ACADEMICS

Academic Rating 81
Profs Interesting Rating   84
Profs Accessible Rating   89
Calendar   semester
Student/teacher ratio   14:1
% profs PhD/tenured   87/90
Hours of study per day   3.14

MOST POPULAR MAJORS
business administration
communication/theatre arts
biology

% GRADS WHO PURSUE...
Law 3, Med 2, MBA 2, MA 10

STUDENTS SPEAK OUT
Life
Susquehanna University is a small school in a "quaint" rural town. The campus is gorgeous, and there is a positive relationship between the locals and the students, many of whom volunteer within the community. "The town is very pretty but it takes a little getting used to. I had to get used to shopping with Amish people," writes one student. There is heavy Greek participation at SU, although students maintain that people who do not want to go Greek will still fit in. However, one student counters, "Greek life tends to control social activities so people feel they have to join." Another writes, "If a fraternity isn't having a party, there's not much to do." Drinking and parties seem to be the most popular social activities. As one student explains, "The town is boring. There are no decent nearby places to go, so drinking is popular on weekends." Almost all undergrads live on campus, and the cost of living is extremely low, one of the reasons most students report they are happy. Many believe that Susquehanna University has too many cliques ("a high school with ash trays"), but for the most part, students seem to get along: "SU has got to be the friendliest campus around. If you walk by five people on the sidewalk, five people will say hello." Another sums up Susquehanna University this way: "I am having the typical college experience—exactly what I expected and exactly what I was looking for."

Academics
Susquehanna students are nearly unanimous in praising their professors for their accessibility and teaching ability. "The professors love to teach," remarks one student, while another raves "The professors are `real people,' not just lecturers. They are there to talk to, even on an individual and personal basis." Compliments are also given to Susquehanna's tutoring program. SU emphasizes job planning as well as undergraduate success, requiring students to take courses that relate to their future careers. "The curriculum is very flexible, accommodating to one's desires," says one student, while another warns, "The academic experience overall is very challenging. This is not a school for slackers." English, math, and communications are popular majors, as well as humanities, social sciences and the natural sciences. The administration does not fare well with SU undergrads: "The academic program is fantastic. I only wish I could say the same about the administration." "There is an underlying feeling of conspiracy in the administration," says another student. Still, some students are quite happy with the administration: "The administration is very helpful in helping students achieve desired goals."

Student Body
Students here are conservative politically, typically white, and from a slightly higher-than-average social class. "This campus needs some loud voices and some different people," complains one student, "there are a lot of cliques on campus. If you don't have a circle of friends, you're lost. However, it's easy to find a group and fit in." With such a low minority enrollment it is perhaps unsurprising that so many students complain about the lack of diversity here. "Students at Susquehanna tend to be superficial," writes one student, while another remarks, "The students are generally very close-minded and snotty." It seems that relations are nonetheless harmonious between the students of Susquehanna University. Writes one, "I feel we are an extended family." Undergrads do feel confident that "Most students have a place they belong."

ADMISSIONS

The admissions committee considers (in descending order of importance): HS record, class rank, test scores, recommendations, essay. *Also considered (in descending order of importance):* extracurriculars, personality, special talents, alumni relationship, geographical distribution. Either the SAT or ACT is required; SAT is preferred. An interview is recommended. Admissions process is need-blind. *High school units required/recommended:* 18 total units are required; 21 total units are recommended; 4 English required, 3 math required, 4 math recommended, 3 science required, 4 science recommended, 2 foreign language required, 3 foreign language recommended, 2 social studies recommended, 1 history required. Applicants ranked in top fifth of secondary school class may substitute two writing samples. Rank in top fifth of secondary school class and strong college preparatory program recommended. *Special Requirements:* A portfolio is required for art program applicants. An audition is required for music program applicants. TOEFL is required of all international students.

The Inside Word

Susquehanna is about as low profile as universities come in the age of MTV. Getting in is made easier by the serious competition the university faces from numerous like institutions in the region, some with significantly better reputations.

FINANCIAL AID

Students should submit: FAFSA (due May 1), state aid form (due May 1), a copy of parents' most recent income tax filing (due May 1). The Princeton Review suggests that all financial aid forms be submitted as soon as possible after January 1. *The following grants/scholarships are offered:* Pell, SEOG, academic merit, the school's own scholarships, the school's own grants, state scholarships, state grants, private scholarships, private grants, ROTC, foreign aid. *Students borrow from the following loan programs:* Stafford, unsubsidized Stafford, Perkins, PLUS, the school's own loan fund, private loans. College Work-Study Program is available. Institutional employment is available.

FROM THE ADMISSIONS OFFICE

"Students tell us they are getting both a first-rate education and practical experience to help them be competitive upon graduation. Faculty, especially in psychology, marketing, and the sciences, regularly encourage students in their research. Students also do internships at such sites as the White House, Continental Insurance, Estee Lauder, State Street Global Advisors, and Cable News Network. About 90 percent of our graduates go on for advanced degrees or get jobs in their chosen field within six months of graduation. Keeping up with the latest in information technology is easy for our students now that all residence hall rooms have connections to the computer network. Even though the university has four micro-computing laboratories, including one open twenty-four hours a day, many students find it convenient to use their own PCs to 'surf the 'net' from their rooms...Small classes, the opportunity to work closely with professors, and the sense of campus community all contribute to the educational experience here...More than 100 student organizations provide lots of opportunity for leadership and involvement in campus life."

ADMISSIONS

Admissions Rating	75
% of applicants accepted	74
% of acceptees attending	27

FRESHMAN PROFILE

Average verbal SAT	580
Average math SAT	570
Average ACT	NR
Average TOEFL	550
Graduated top 20% of class	54
Graduated top 40% of class	81
Graduated top 60% of class	94
Average HS GPA or Avg.	NR

DEADLINES

Early decision	12/15
Regular admission	3/15
Regular notification	rolling
Non-fall registration	yes

APPLICANTS ALSO LOOK AT

AND OFTEN PREFER
Ithaca

AND SOMETIMES PREFER
Franklin & Marshall
Bucknell
Dickinson
Gettysburg

AND RARELY PREFER
Penn State-U. Park

FINANCIAL FACTS

Financial Aid Rating	94
Tuition	$16,800
Room & board	$4,900
Estimated book expense	$600
% frosh receiving aid	85
% undergrads receiving aid	80
% aid is need-based	80
% frosh w/ grant (avg)	85 ($10,000)
% frosh w/ loan (avg)	75 ($3,000)
% UGs w/ job (avg)	70 ($1,500)
Off-campus job outlook	good

SWARTHMORE COLLEGE

500 COLLEGE AVENUE, SWARTHMORE, PA 19081   ADMISSIONS: 215-328-8300   FAX: 215-328-8673

CAMPUS LIFE

Quality of Life Rating 88
Type of school private
Affiliation none
Environment metropolis

STUDENTS
FT undergrad enrollment	1,353
% male/female	48/52
% from out of state	88
% live on campus	91
% spend weekend on campus	95
% transfers	3
% from public high school	65
% in (# of) fraternities	5 (2)
% African-American	6
% Asian	11
% Caucasian	73
% Hispanic	5
% international	5
# of countries represented	42

WHAT'S HOT
support groups
health facilities
campus is beautiful
music associations
computer facilities

WHAT'S NOT
cigarettes
off-campus food
infrequent dating
hard liquor
drugs

ACADEMICS

Academic Rating 97
Profs Interesting Rating 95
Profs Accessible Rating 96
Calendar semester
Student/teacher ratio 9:1
% profs PhD 95
Hours of study per day 4.24

MOST POPULAR MAJORS
English literature
biology
political science

% GRADS WHO PURSUE...
Law 8, Med 4, MA 62

STUDENTS SPEAK OUT

Life
Most members of the generally happy Swarthmore College family concede that they "could use more frolicking." The intense academic emphasis prompts many to make even Friday night "a study night." Some students entirely "refuse to date, because it may distract them from their work." Not all are this Spartan, however. One student comments, "If Swarthmore isn't a party school on the weekends, I'd hate to see what a party school is." Students rate the beauty and comfort of their surroundings very highly, and most love living on campus. Casual dating is not a popular option; people tend to go for "serious long-term relationships." The small size of the school (about 1,300) makes for an intimate, homey community, although some consider it a little too small. Everyone definitely "knows everyone else's business." Nearby Philadelphia is accessible via a train from the campus, for times when students need to escape to urban anonymity.

Academics
As a popular T-shirt at Swarthmore reads, "Anywhere else it would have been an A...really!" Swarthmore is one of the most academically intense schools in the country. "Compared to Swarthmore, an operating room is relaxed," is how one student puts it. Our survey results confirm that reputation. "Swatties" rate among the top 5 percent in the nation in terms of workload and commitment to their studies. Most report spending many hours daily on course work, and one characteristically explains, "Even if you do your work it's a struggle to do well." The liberal arts and premedical sciences are the most popular fields here; nearly half the students go on to graduate school. Students have little but praise for their professors. Writes one student, "The best thing about Swat is having the privilege to study with amazing profs who not only know their fields, but WANT to be teaching them to undergrads." Classes are uniformly small enough to include lots of individual attention. "The professors are accessible," notes one student oddly, "like a fast rodent coming out of a garbage can, they are there to help us." Students rave about the high level of intellectual curiosity on campus— "every tree is labeled" for the edification of the interested—and report an exceptionally low incidence of cheating. About their only complaint concerns the stress level, which most agree is unhealthy.

Student Body
The student body here is "diverse and very opinionated." A left-leaning community overall, Swarthmore has an unusually visible and well-accepted gay minority. According to one student, most people are "generally well informed and sensitized to political events. This stimulates compelling discussion and debate at the dinner table and in the dorm room. I have learned as much from my friends as from my professors." Minority students make up over 20 percent of the student body, with blacks and Asians accounting for the largest minority populations.

FINANCIAL AID: 610-328-8353

ADMISSIONS

The admissions committee considers (in descending order of importance): HS record, recommendations, essay, test scores. *Also considered (in descending order of importance):* alumni relationship, extracurriculars, personality, special talents, geographical distribution. Either the SAT or ACT is required. An interview is recommended. Admissions process is need-blind. Strong preparation in English and 4 units of foreign language recommended. Other units should be chosen from natural science and math, history and social studies, and literature, art, and music.

The Inside Word

Swarthmore is as good as they come; among liberal arts colleges there is no better. Candidates face an admissions process that is appropriately demanding and thorough. Even the best qualified of students need to complete their applications with a meticulous approach-during candidate evaluation, serious competition is just another file away. Those who are fortunate enough to be offered admission usually have shown the committee that they have a high level of intellectual curiosity, self-confidence, and motivation.

FINANCIAL AID

Students should submit: FAFSA (due early February), CSS Profile, the school's own financial aid form (due early February), Divorced Parents form (due early February), a copy of parents' most recent income tax filing (due early February). The Princeton Review suggests that all financial aid forms be submitted as soon as possible after January 1. *The following grants/scholarships are offered:* Pell, SEOG, academic merit, the school's own scholarships, the school's own grants, state scholarships, state grants, foreign aid. *Students borrow from the following loan programs:* Stafford, unsubsidized Stafford, Perkins, PLUS, the school's own loan fund, state loans. Applicants will be notified of awards beginning April 15. College Work-Study Program is available. Institutional employment is available.

FROM THE ADMISSIONS OFFICE

"The purpose of Swarthmore College is to make its students more valuable human beings and more useful members of society. While it shares this purpose with other educational institutions, each school, college, and university seeks to realize that purpose in its own way. Each must select those tasks it can do best. By such selection it contributes to the diversity and richness of educational opportunity which is part of the American heritage. Swarthmore seeks to help its students realize their fullest intellectual and personal potential combined with a deep sense of ethical and social concern."

ADMISSIONS

Admissions Rating	94
% of applicants accepted	35
% of acceptees attending	29

FRESHMAN PROFILE

Average verbal SAT	710
Average math SAT	680
Average ACT	NR
Average TOEFL	600
Graduated top 20% of class	NR
Graduated top 40% of class	NR
Graduated top 60% of class	NR
Average HS GPA or Avg.	NR

DEADLINES

Early decision	NR
Regular admission	1/1
Regular notification	4/15
Non-fall registration	no

APPLICANTS ALSO LOOK AT

AND OFTEN PREFER

Harvard/Radcliffe
Princeton
Yale

AND SOMETIMES PREFER

Amherst
Wesleyan U.
Columbia
Brown
Williams

AND RARELY PREFER

Vassar
Haverford
U. Chicago
Dickinson
Pennsylvania

FINANCIAL FACTS

Financial Aid Rating	82
Tuition	$19,992
Room & board	$6,880
Estimated book expense	$500
% frosh receiving aid	NR
% undergrads receiving aid	NR
% aid is need-based	97
% frosh w/ grant (avg)	48 ($15,685)
% frosh w/ loan (avg)	60 ($2,500)
% UGs w/ job (avg)	77 ($1,200)
Off-campus job outlook	fair

SWEET BRIAR COLLEGE

SWEET BRIAR, VA 24595

ADMISSIONS: 804-381-6142   FAX: 804-381-6173

CAMPUS LIFE

Quality of Life Rating	93
Type of school	private
Affiliation	none
Environment	rural

STUDENTS

FT undergrad enrollment	671
% male/female	3/97
% from out of state	71
% live on campus	91
% spend weekend on campus	65
% transfers	6
% from public high school	78
% African-American	5
% Asian	3
% Caucasian	84
% Hispanic	2
% international	4
# of countries represented	17

WHAT'S HOT
campus feels safe
campus food
campus is beautiful
student government
students are happy

WHAT'S NOT
health facilities
drugs
Sweet Briar, VA
off-campus food
student publications

ACADEMICS

Academic Rating	89
Profs Interesting Rating	98
Profs Accessible Rating	97
Calendar	4-1-4
Student/teacher ratio	8:1
% profs PhD/tenured	94/82
Hours of study per day	3.54

MOST POPULAR MAJORS
psychology
biology
government

% GRADS WHO PURSUE...
Law 2, Med 1, MBA 2, MA 15

STUDENTS SPEAK OUT

Life
Sweet Briar College has a gorgeous, large wooded campus—"3,300 acres of green forest and rolling hills." Also first-rate are the dorms, library, and cafeteria: says one student, "The dining hall has first-class five-star chefs." As one woman puts it, "At times we are pampered to the extent that my family calls this place a country club." Sports, outdoor activities, and extracurricular clubs are all popular at SBC. So, too, are the two annual formals (one each semester). But most of the social life of this all-women school takes place off campus, at neighboring schools like Hampden-Sydney and Washington and Lee. Explains one student, "We have entertainment—a band or a comedian—on campus every weekend, but to meet men, we have to road trip to other schools. Lately, some events have been bringing some men to our campus, which is nice." The town of Amherst is small "with not much to do. The closest movie theater is twenty minutes away by car."

Academics
Sweet Briar College students resent the false perception that their school is "a finishing school and a stepping-stone toward marriage," explains one. "The women who are here are serious about their studies and their future careers." Our survey results back up this assertion: the women of Sweet Briar take their academics seriously, attending all classes (a must: the school is so small that any absences are obvious) and then studying an additional three-and-a-half hours a day. A traditional liberal arts college, Sweet Briar requires all students to complete a wide range of distribution requirements. Many students pursue double majors. English, government, economics, psychology, and international affairs are among the popular departments. Most Sweet Briar women are very happy with the school they chose. Writes one, "At Sweet Briar, a student's opportunities are endless, ranging from one-on-one attention she receives from professors, to the small classes (average size: eight to twelve), to going abroad to study for a semester or year, to doing an internship in your field of study." Students praise their teachers (who "take both a professional and a personal interest in the students," and who "concentrate on teaching, not on publishing their own work, during the semester"), administrators ("the administration is receptive to students' opinions—we have a College Council every two months at which students, faculty, and administrators communicate"), classmates, and surroundings. And, they appreciate the benefits of attending a small school. Sums up one, "Because the school is so small women are able to develop their strengths, improve on their weaknesses, and really focus on themselves."

Student Body
Sweet Briar students are a fairly homogenous group. Most are white, conservative, Southern, and from well-off families. The students report that their classmates are generally warm, friendly, and outgoing, but that alternative lifestyles and progressive politics are not entirely welcome on their campus. Change may be in the offing; students report that the school has recently stepped up efforts to attract minority students.

ADMISSIONS

The admissions committee considers (in descending order of importance): HS record, essay, recommendations, class rank, test scores. *Also considered (in descending order of importance):* personality, extracurriculars, alumni relationship, special talents. Either the SAT or ACT is required. An interview is recommended. Admissions process is need-blind. *High school units required/recommended:* 16 total units are required; 4 English required, 3 math required, 2 science required, 2 foreign language required, 3 social studies required, 1 history required. *Special Requirements:* An audition is required for music program applicants. TOEFL is required of all international students. *The admissions office says:* "Faculty are highly involved in our admissions process. We encourage prospective students to work closely with their Sweet Briar admissions counselor, particularly if there are extenuating circumstances in regard to the academic record."

The Inside Word

An extremely small applicant pool tempers selectivity greatly, but also allows the admissions committee to take a longer look at most candidates than is typical in college admission. Despite the small applicant pool, candidates are usually well-qualified academically. A lackadaisical application can spell denial.

FINANCIAL AID

Students should submit: FAFSA, a copy of parents' most recent income tax filing. The Princeton Review suggests that all financial aid forms be submitted as soon as possible after January 1. *The following grants/scholarships are offered:* Pell, SEOG, academic merit, the school's own scholarships, the school's own grants, state scholarships, state grants, private scholarships, private grants. *Students borrow from the following loan programs:* Stafford, Perkins, PLUS, the school's own loan fund, state loans. Applicants will be notified of awards beginning February 15. College Work-Study Program is available. Institutional employment is available.

FROM THE ADMISSIONS OFFICE

"The young woman who applies to Sweet Briar is mature and farsighted enough to know what she wants from her college experience. She realizes that the college she chooses must be right for her own personal growth and intellectual development. Sweet Briar attracts the ambitious student who enjoys being immersed not only in a first-rate academic program, but in a variety of meaningful activities outside the classroom. Our students take charge and revel in their accomplishments. This attitude follows graduates, enabling them to compete confidently in the corporate world and in graduate school."

ADMISSIONS

Admissions Rating	72
% of applicants accepted	85
% of acceptees attending	41

FRESHMAN PROFILE

Average verbal SAT	520
Average math SAT	540
Average ACT	24
Average TOEFL	580
Graduated top 20% of class	38
Graduated top 40% of class	69
Graduated top 60% of class	NR
Average HS GPA or Avg.	3.2

DEADLINES

Early decision	11/15
Regular admission	2/15
Regular notification	4/1
Non-fall registration	yes

APPLICANTS ALSO LOOK AT

AND OFTEN PREFER
Smith
Mount Holyoke
Randolph-Macon Woman's

AND SOMETIMES PREFER
Hollins
Vanderbilt
U. Richmond

AND RARELY PREFER
Mount Vernon

FINANCIAL FACTS

Financial Aid Rating	94
Tuition	$14,990
Room & board	$6,510
Estimated book expense	$500
% frosh receiving aid	65
% undergrads receiving aid	87
% aid is need-based	78
% frosh w/ grant (avg)	66 ($11,176)
% frosh w/ loan (avg)	64 ($3,577)
% UGs w/ job (avg)	65 ($1,000)
Off-campus job outlook	poor

SYRACUSE UNIVERSITY

201 ADMINISTRATION BUILDING, SYRACUSE, NY 13244

ADMISSIONS: 315-443-3611

CAMPUS LIFE

Quality of Life Rating	74
Type of school	private
Affiliation	none
Environment	city

STUDENTS

FT undergrad enrollment	10,102
% male/female	47/53
% from out of state	58
% live on campus	78
% spend weekend on campus	80
% transfers	14
% from public high school	80
% in (# of) fraternities	16 (23)
% in (# of) sororities	25 (19)
% African-American	9
% Asian	5
% Caucasian	78
% Hispanic	6
% international	3
# of countries represented	66

WHAT'S HOT
student publications
hard liquor
intercollegiate sports
college radio
sex

WHAT'S NOT
students are cliquish
campus difficult to get around
registration is a pain
political activism
town-gown relations

ACADEMICS

Academic Rating	75
Profs Interesting Rating	66
Profs Accessible Rating	70
Calendar	semester
Student/teacher ratio	11:1
% profs tenured	87
Hours of study per day	2.97

MOST POPULAR MAJORS
psychology
broadcast journalism
architecture

% GRADS WHO PURSUE...
Law 5, Med 2, MBA 7

STUDENTS SPEAK OUT

Life

Students at Syracuse University give the city of Syracuse low grades, and rank their relations with their neighbors particularly poorly. Reports one, "There is a very poor relationship between the community and the university. It's very upsetting as a student to live in a community that, for the most part, resents your entire existence." The city's freezing winter climate means that "Hanging out with friends is what we do for fun. Most people just stay in and drink because its too cold to go outside. We might go to a club off-campus once a month." Sports are the main rallying point for students—"The only time there is unity among a majority of students is during a Dome football or basketball game," says one student. The lacrosse team is among the best in the country and is also extremely popular with students. Fraternities and sororities play a major role in the social scene here. Sums up one student: "There are four choices during the weekend: bars; Greek houses; house parties; and, doing nothing."

Academics

Syracuse is a large private university best known for its excellent communications department, which continues to offer one of the nation's top programs for journalists and telecasters. The engineering, pre-business, public affairs, and natural sciences departments are also strong, however, and very popular with undergraduates. Size is one of the chief benefits of SU, whose undergraduate programs are so extensive that they are subdivided into eleven "academic units." Says one student, "I came here because I wanted a wide variety of academic and social opportunities in a nonurban setting." Overall, "Here at SU, lazy and unmotivated students have a chance to take an easy route, but bright and motivated students can pursue a challenging and enjoyable route as well. The university provides many opportunities to those who want to make the most of their investment." It takes networking skills and personal initiative to navigate the bureaucracy here, but even students with these traits aren't guaranteed smooth sailing. Class size and administrators receive low marks, especially for a private school.

Student Body

Syracuse attracts a relatively well-diversified student body, but students overwhelmingly feel that "There is disunity and constant conflict between blacks and whites, frats and sororities. This school is more segregated than integrated." Notes one student, "Yes we have diversity, but what's the point if the different groups don't interact at all?!?" Although students here complain about almost every aspect of school life, they also give themselves a solid B, just below the national average, when grading their own happiness.

ADMISSIONS

The admissions committee considers (in descending order of importance): HS record, class rank, test scores, recommendations, essay. *Also considered (in descending order of importance):* personality, alumni relationship, extracurriculars, special talents. Either the SAT or ACT is required; SAT is preferred. An interview is recommended. Admissions process is need-blind. *High school units required/recommended:* 20 total units are required; 4 English required, 3 math required, 3 science required, 2 foreign language required, 3 social studies required. *Special Requirements:* A portfolio is required for art program applicants. An audition is required for music program applicants. TOEFL is required of all international students. Portfolio required of architecture program applicants.

The Inside Word

Thanks to nationally competitive athletic teams and the Newhouse School of Communications, Syracuse draws a large applicant pool. At the same time, it needs a large freshman class every year, so the university is only moderately selective. Most above-average students should be very strong candidates; many weaker students are also able to benefit from Syracuse's individualized admissions process.

FINANCIAL AID

Students should submit: FAFSA (due February 15). The Princeton Review suggests that all financial aid forms be submitted as soon as possible after January 1. *The following grants/scholarships are offered:* Pell, SEOG, academic merit, athletic, the school's own scholarships, the school's own grants, state scholarships, state grants, private scholarships, private grants, ROTC. *Students borrow from the following loan programs:* Stafford, unsubsidized Stafford, Perkins, PLUS, state loans, federal nursing loans, private loans. Applicants will be notified of awards beginning April 1. College Work-Study Program is available. Institutional employment is available.

FROM THE ADMISSIONS OFFICE

"Syracuse University offers students a world of opportunities. Opportunities to explore over 200 majors; to be an active participant in shaping the course of their education; to participate in extracurricular clubs and organizations (there are nearly 300). There are events that provide the chance to hear the experiences of distinguished alumni such as NBC sportscaster Bob Costas or CEO and president of Estee Lauder, Robin Burns. Other academic opportunities include participation in the Honors Program, undergraduate research, and programs abroad. The Syracuse University community is alive with the excitement of scholarship and discovery. Our faculty continue to find new and innovative ways to combine research and teaching, involving undergraduates at all levels. Syracuse University is a student-centered research university, and is committed to giving students the very best educational experience available."

ADMISSIONS

Admissions Rating	81
% of applicants accepted	66
% of acceptees attending	36

FRESHMAN PROFILE

Average verbal SAT	600
Average math SAT	600
Average ACT	NR
Average TOEFL	550
Graduated top 20% of class	60
Graduated top 40% of class	88
Graduated top 60% of class	98
Average HS GPA or Avg.	NR

DEADLINES

Early decision	NR
Regular admission	2/1
Regular notification	3/15
Non-fall registration	yes

APPLICANTS ALSO LOOK AT

AND OFTEN PREFER

Cornell U.
Union (NY)
Lehigh
Boston U.
NYU

AND SOMETIMES PREFER

Penn State-U. Park
Ithaca
Lafayette
Bucknell
Geneseo State

AND RARELY PREFER

Hobart & William Smith
Siena
Northeastern

FINANCIAL FACTS

Financial Aid Rating	73
Tuition	$15,910
Room & board	$6,520
Estimated book expense	$660
% frosh receiving aid	75
% undergrads receiving aid	75
% aid is need-based	85
% frosh w/ grant (avg)	70 ($8,600)
% frosh w/ loan (avg)	63 ($3,500)
% UGs w/ job (avg)	40 ($1,900)
Off-campus job outlook	good

TEMPLE UNIVERSITY

BROAD STREET AND MONTGOMERY AVENUE, PHILADELPHIA, PA 19122-1803 ADMISSIONS: 215-204-7200 FAX: 215-204-5694

CAMPUS LIFE

Quality of Life Rating	66
Type of school	public
Affiliation	none
Environment	metropolis

STUDENTS

FT undergrad enrollment	15,457
% male/female	48/52
% from out of state	20
% live on campus	10
% spend weekend on campus	NR
% transfers	48
% from public high school	63
% in (# of) fraternities	7 (13)
% in (# of) sororities	3 (7)
% African-American	19
% Asian	12
% Caucasian	64
% Hispanic	3
% international	3
# of countries represented	77

WHAT'S HOT
ethnic diversity on campus
old-fashioned dating
sex
cigarettes
different students interact

WHAT'S NOT
town-gown relations
unattractive campus
students are unhappy
inefficient administration
dorms

ACADEMICS

Academic Rating	66
Profs Interesting Rating	60
Profs Accessible Rating	60
Calendar	semester
Student/teacher ratio	12:1
% profs PhD	86
Hours of study per day	2.89

MOST POPULAR MAJORS
business administration
radio/television/film
accounting

STUDENTS SPEAK OUT

Life
One Temple University student reports, "There is a wide variety of activities available because we are in the city and your fellow students won't let you get bored. You stay active whether you want to or not." Philadelphia offers students a wide variety of museums, stores, night spots, and sporting events. Life in the city is not without its drawbacks, however. Students complain that Temple's neighborhood is unsafe: "This school is surrounded by a ghetto. At all times beggars accost you for money. Walking off campus, especially at night, would be ill-advised," writes one student. Also, because Temple is mostly attended by commuters, "we have very little campus consciousness or social life. Still, the city provides plenty of entertainment, so I cannot complain." What on-campus social life there is centers on parties, the student activity center (with a first-run movie theater), and the school's athletic teams, which are very popular (particularly the men's basketball team).

Academics
Like DePaul University in Chicago, Temple has traditionally provided an excellent preprofessional education to a largely working-class student body. Most Temple students cite cost as their chief reason for choosing the school; as one student explains, Temple undergrads receive "a down-and-dirty, no-frills inexpensive institution that gives you what you need." Temple is large enough to offer something for everybody. Communications is the hottest field—Temple's School of Communications and Theatre is nationally renowned. Business and education majors are also popular. Unfortunately, like many schools dependent on the government for funding, Temple currently seems to be weathering a pretty rough period. Students complain that "too much red tape" surrounds administration and financial aid, that advisers "are often unavailable or unwilling to help," and that professors are overworked and/or inaccessible—all of which indicate that Temple is terribly underfunded. Professors also take it on the chin for poor teaching skills and for p.c. orthodoxy ("If you don't espouse a liberal viewpoint you may as well not participate! The attitude is 'left is best and right is wrong.'"). Students describe the administration as being "exceptionally sensitive to minority needs," and appreciate the fact that "Temple gives anybody a chance to succeed no matter what his background. If I had to do it all over I'd go to Temple not once but twice."

Student Body
Many students here have major responsibilities other than school, such as families and jobs. Most are commuters; the typical student is rarely on campus except to attend classes and study. Outside of historically black colleges, very few schools have as proportionally large an African-American population as Temple does. Students agree that Temple's "richly diverse student body" is one of its best assets.

ADMISSIONS

The admissions committee considers (in descending order of importance): HS record, class rank, test scores, essay, recommendations. *Also considered (in descending order of importance):* special talents, alumni relationship, extracurriculars. Either the SAT or ACT is required. An interview is recommended. *High school units required/recommended:* 16 total units are required; 4 English required, 2 math required, 3 math recommended, 1 science required, 2 science recommended, 2 foreign language required, 3 foreign language recommended, 1 social studies required. At least 12 of the required units should have been completed in last three years. *Special Requirements:* A portfolio is required for art program applicants. An audition is required for music program applicants. Audition required of dance program applicants.

The Inside Word

Applicants to Temple are overwhelmingly local, and very eager to attend the university. Admissions standards are lenient in general, but candidates for the College of Music in particular face a rigorous review.

FINANCIAL AID

Students should submit: the school's own financial aid form, state aid form. The Princeton Review suggests that all financial aid forms be submitted as soon as possible after January 1. *The following grants/scholarships are offered:* Pell, SEOG, academic merit, athletic, the school's own scholarships, the school's own grants, state scholarships, state grants, ROTC. *Students borrow from the following loan programs:* Stafford, unsubsidized Stafford, Perkins, PLUS, federal nursing loans, health professions loans. Applicants will be notified of awards beginning in February. College Work-Study Program is available. Institutional employment is available.

FROM THE ADMISSIONS OFFICE

"Dr. Russell H. Conwell started Temple in 1884 with just seven students. Now, over 100 years later, the University, with approximately 30,000 students, is one of the nation's senior comprehensive research institutions with specialized programs all over the world. Using their undergraduate education and training, Temple alumni/ae have helped shape the fields of government, business, industry, the performing and communication arts, science, research, law, medicine and technology. At Temple, students have all the excitement of a large city at their fingertips. They also have a choice of campuses. They can experience the vitality of the city with courses on the Main Campus, Center City and Health Sciences Center, or they can select a slower-paced suburban environment at the beautiful Ambler Campus or Tyler School of Art. Temple University is choice and challenge, offering unlimited possibilities to each undergraduate to shape his or her future."

ADMISSIONS

Admissions Rating	71
% of applicants accepted	64
% of acceptees attending	44

FRESHMAN PROFILE

Average verbal SAT	530
Average math SAT	530
Average ACT	NR
Average TOEFL	500
Graduated top 20% of class	34
Graduated top 40% of class	63
Graduated top 60% of class	85
Average HS GPA or Avg.	NR

DEADLINES

Early decision	NR
Regular admission	6/15
Regular notification	rolling
Non-fall registration	yes

APPLICANTS ALSO LOOK AT

AND OFTEN PREFER

Pittsburgh
Penn State-U. Park

AND SOMETIMES PREFER

Villanova
Rutgers U.
LaSalle
Drexel
Lehigh

AND RARELY PREFER

Gettysburg
St. Joseph's U.
NYU

FINANCIAL FACTS

Financial Aid Rating	72
In-state tuition	$5,314
Out-of-state tuition	$10,096
Room & board	$5,062
Estimated book expense	$500
% frosh receiving aid	68
% undergrads receiving aid	80
% aid is need-based	NR
% frosh w/ grant (avg)	NR
% frosh w/ loan (avg)	NR
% UGs w/ job (avg)	NR ($1,500)
Off-campus job outlook	good

UNIVERSITY OF TENNESSEE-KNOXVILLE

320 STUDENT SERVICES BUILDING, KNOXVILLE, TN 37996-0230   ADMISSIONS: 423-974-2184   FAX: 423-974-6341

CAMPUS LIFE

Quality of Life Rating	**75**
Type of school	public
Affiliation	none
Environment	city

STUDENTS

FT undergrad enrollment	18,608
% male/female	51/49
% from out of state	18
% live on campus	28
% spend weekend on campus	45
% transfers	36
% from public high school	NR
% in (# of) fraternities	16 (26)
% in (# of) sororities	16 (19)
% African-American	5
% Asian	3
% Caucasian	91
% Hispanic	1
% international	1
# of countries represented	64

WHAT'S HOT
old-fashioned dating
political activism
intercollegiate sports
college radio
library

WHAT'S NOT
campus difficult to get around
support groups
student government
inefficient administration
students are unhappy

ACADEMICS

Academic Rating	**71**
Profs Interesting Rating	70
Profs Accessible Rating	67
Calendar	semester
Student/teacher ratio	17:1
% profs PhD/tenured	80/72
Hours of study per day	2.63

MOST POPULAR MAJORS
pre-professional
psychology
electrical engineering

STUDENTS SPEAK OUT

Life

If you don't know who the Volunteers are, you probably don't belong at the University of Tennessee-Knoxville. As one student puts it, "This is a huge sports school." Some students complain that too much attention is paid to sports, particularly football and basketball, but the fact is that these laments will almost certainly go unheeded: the alumni are aggressive Big Orange supporters. Frats and sororities claim about 10 percent of the population and form a social universe of their own. No alcohol is served on campus, but there are plenty of alcohol-free activities. And there's always the Knoxville bar scene—"You only need to be eighteen to get in a bar and a baby could probably buy a beer"—is how one student explains it—and an active dating scene ("If you can't find girls here, you're not looking," enthuses one man). This is definitely not a suitcase college and the campus is jumping on weekends. Because of its size, UTK's campus can be a little difficult to get around.

Academics

If you are a Tennessean looking for the most demanding academic program in your state, UTK is not where you come looking first (not with Vanderbilt, Sewanee, Fisk, and Rhodes around). As one student explains, "A student here will not be immediately inundated with intellectual fervor—not by a long shot! However, there are enough innovative, intelligent, and inspiring instructors on the faculty that a student who wishes to make the most of his or her college experience can certainly do so." The key here is that UTK's size provides a lot of academic opportunities, as long as you know where to look. "Hard sciences are strong, and so is engineering," says one student. The school has nationally respected academic programs in education, law, and business, and programs in textiles and advertising have been rated outstanding by professional organizations. Some students feel that humanities take a back seat here: "Programs that generate money are better supported by the administration; therefore, humanities programs such as art history and music are not funded as well as those in engineering, sciences, business, etc." Although a sense of "businesslike impersonality" at times can prevail, professors are remarkably accessible after class compared with those at other public universities.

Student Body

Almost all UTK students are from Tennessee. Cost, convenience, and a love of big-time sports are what bring them here. They are a politically conservative bunch, very much the typical southern college students. They're not so concerned with appearing tolerant of difference as their northern counterparts, and they certainly do not care about being p.c. Typical of men's attitudes toward women here is the student who tells us "Southern girls (ooh-la-la) are the best." A gay student tells us that his straight classmates' attitude toward him was either to ignore him or to treat him with outright hostility, an assertion borne out by his classmates' answers to questions relating to tolerance of gays on campus. In short, if you're a jock, or comfortable around jocks, you'll fit right in here; otherwise, you'll have to look around to find your niche.

ADMISSIONS

The admissions committee considers (in descending order of importance): HS record, test scores, essay, recommendations. *Also considered (in descending order of importance):* alumni relationship, extracurriculars, geographical distribution, special talents. Either the SAT or ACT is required. An interview is recommended. Admissions process is need-blind. *High school units required/recommended:* 14 total units are required; 4 English required, 3 math required, 2 science required, 2 foreign language required, 1 social studies required, 1 history required. Minimum composite ACT score of 18 and minimum 2.0 GPA (2.25 GPA for out-of-state) required. *Special Requirements:* An audition is required for music program applicants. TOEFL is required of all international students. Additional units in math required of architecture and engineering program applicants.

The Inside Word

Don't expect any attention to be given to your essays or extracurriculars at Tennessee unless you are not "automatically admissible." The university takes in a jumbo freshman class and has to use a fairly straightforward approach to getting these kids admitted. Standards are the same for out-of-state applicants as for in-state, but the school's mix of in-state/out-of state students is firm, since it is set by policy of the Board of Trustees.

FINANCIAL AID

Students should submit: FAFSA, state aid form. The Princeton Review suggests that all financial aid forms be submitted as soon as possible after January 1. *The following grants/scholarships are offered:* Pell, SEOG, academic merit, athletic, the school's own scholarships, state scholarships, state grants, private scholarships, ROTC, foreign aid. *Students borrow from the following loan programs:* Stafford, Perkins, PLUS, the school's own loan fund, state loans, private loans. Applicants will be notified of awards beginning April 1. College Work-Study Program is available. Institutional employment is available.

FROM THE ADMISSIONS OFFICE

"The University of Tennessee-Knoxville is the place where you belong if you're interested in outstanding resources and unlimited opportunities to foster your personal and academic growth. Ten colleges offer more than 100 majors to students from all fifty states and ninety-five foreign countries. More than 300 clubs and organizations on campus offer opportunities for fun, challenge, and service. UTK is a place where students take pride in belonging to a 200-year-old tradition and celebrate the excitement of 'the Volunteer spirit.' We invite you to explore the many advantages UTK has to offer."

ADMISSIONS

Admissions Rating	71
% of applicants accepted	74
% of acceptees attending	56

FRESHMAN PROFILE

Average verbal SAT	550
Average math SAT	550
Average ACT	23
Average TOEFL	NR
Graduated top 20% of class	43
Graduated top 40% of class	71
Graduated top 60% of class	90
Average HS GPA or Avg.	3.2

DEADLINES

Early decision	NR
Regular admission	7/1
Regular notification	rolling
Non-fall registration	yes

APPLICANTS ALSO LOOK AT

AND OFTEN PREFER
Middle Tennessee State
Auburn
Emory

AND SOMETIMES PREFER
U. Florida
Vanderbilt
U. Georgia

AND RARELY PREFER
U. Kentucky
East Tennessee State
Clemson
U. of the South

FINANCIAL FACTS

Financial Aid Rating	80
In-state tuition	$2,164
Out-of-state tuition	$6,294
Room & board	$3,252
Estimated book expense	$750
% frosh receiving aid	52
% undergrads receiving aid	88
% aid is need-based	NR
% frosh w/ grant (avg)	29 ($2,270)
% frosh w/ loan (avg)	12 ($2,635)
% UGs w/ job (avg)	NR ($2,000)
Off-campus job outlook	good

TEXAS A&M UNIVERSITY-COLLEGE STATION

COLLEGE STATION, TX 77843-0100   ADMISSIONS: 409-845-3741   FAX: 409-845-0727

CAMPUS LIFE

Quality of Life Rating   **85**
Type of school   public
Affiliation   none
Environment   suburban

STUDENTS
FT undergrad enrollment   34,371
% male/female   54/46
% from out of state   8
% live on campus   28
% spend weekend on campus   60
% transfers   22
% from public high school   NR
% in (# of) fraternities   9 (29)
% in (# of) sororities   12 (15)
% African-American   3
% Asian   4
% Caucasian   80
% Hispanic   11
% international   2
# of countries represented   111

WHAT'S HOT
old-fashioned dating
town-gown relations
intercollegiate sports
intramural sports
religion

WHAT'S NOT
health facilities
campus difficult to get around
theater
drugs
cigarettes

ACADEMICS

Academic Rating   **77**
Profs Interesting Rating   64
Profs Accessible Rating   67
Calendar   semester
Student/teacher ratio   20:1
% profs PhD/tenured   76/88
Hours of study per day   2.84

MOST POPULAR MAJORS
biomedical science
psychology
mechanical engineering

% GRADS WHO PURSUE...
Law 2, Med 3, MBA 2, MA 7

STUDENTS SPEAK OUT

Life

Texas A&M is, as one student explains, "one of the most spirited and traditional schools in the nation. The bonding here is incredible—there are no ex-Aggies, only former Aggies. Aggies hire Aggies, drink and play together, work together, and stay together." Traditions are big, particularly those originating with the school's Corps of Cadets, the military training program that accounts for 6 percent of the student body. Cadets lead the Silver Taps ceremony (which honors students who died the previous month), midnight yell practice (a meeting of students to practice football yells before games), and Bonfire, the annual late-night party before the A&M/UT-Austin football game; and cadets make up the extremely popular marching band, the Fightin' Texas Aggie Band. Other traditions here include the Big Event ("it is a huge project where Aggies do any services that are needed for the community") and Twelfth Man (A&M fans stand through football games, attempting to distract and intimidate opponents, essentially serving as the team's "twelfth man"). For those in the spirit, "Nothing is perfect, but A&M is close."

Academics

Although it has been long regarded as strong in the fields of agricultural sciences, engineering, and business and management, Texas A&M was until recently considered lightweight in terms of classic academics. To remedy this perception, in 1989 the school instituted a thorough core curriculum consisting of one-third of the credits toward graduation and covering the humanities, the natural and social sciences, and computer literacy. While students still report a much lighter than average workload (under three hours of study per day), A&M is definitely headed in a more serious direction. Not that A&M needed improvement, at least according to its students, most of whom are fanatical boosters. Aggies report a high overall level of satisfaction with their school and particularly appreciate the way the administration manages this gigantic campus. "A&M has 40,000-plus students and is still growing. For a school this size, the transition and details and paperwork are fairly smooth. Plus, our administration encourages student feedback and wants to continue to make this university the best for us." "Every time I have a question, all I have to do is pick up the phone." Class size, professors, and especially TAs receive lower marks, although many students note that things get much better once intro-level courses are completed.

Student Body

Aggies are among the nation's most conservative students, and proud of it. Muticulturalism has become a major point of conversation on campus in recent years, with many white students opposed. Says one black student, "I have learned to accept [that] Texas A&M will always be a conservative school. I see Confederate flags in every other room in my dorm, the multicultural services dept. is in Texas A&M's basement. Oh! Well!" And another adds, "I am not racist or homophobic, but there are too many who are."

Texas A&M University-College Station

FINANCIAL AID: 409-845-3236   E-MAIL: R-BOWEN@TAMU.EDU   WEB SITE: HTTP://WWW.TAMU.EDU/

ADMISSIONS

The admissions committee considers (in descending order of importance): HS record, class rank, test scores. *Also considered (in descending order of importance):* extracurriculars, alumni relationship, geographical distribution, personality, special talents. Either the SAT or ACT is required. *High school units required/recommended:* 18 total units are required; 19 total units are recommended; 4 English required, 3 math required, 4 math recommended, 2 science required, 4 science recommended, 2 foreign language required, 3 foreign language recommended, 3 social studies required, 4 social studies recommended. TOEFL is required of all international students.

The Inside Word

Texas A&M has a very impressive record of enrolling strong students. A super high percentage of these admits enroll which, when combined with the university's impressive graduation rate, is probably the best testament to A&M's reputation. Don't be deceived by the fairly high admit rate—for it to be significantly lower, there would have to be a huge increase in the size of the already enormous applicant pool.

FINANCIAL AID

Students should submit: FAFSA, the school's own financial aid form, state aid form. The Princeton Review suggests that all financial aid forms be submitted as soon as possible after January 1. *The following grants/scholarships are offered:* Pell, SEOG, academic merit, athletic, the school's own scholarships, the school's own grants, state scholarships, state grants, private scholarships, ROTC, foreign aid. *Students borrow from the following loan programs:* Stafford, Perkins, PLUS, the school's own loan fund, state loans, health professions loans. Applicants will be notified of awards beginning April 15. College Work-Study Program is available. Institutional employment is available.

FROM THE ADMISSIONS OFFICE

"Established in 1876 as the first public college in the state, Texas A&M University today has become a world leader in teaching, research and public service. Located in College Station in the heart of Texas, it is centrally situated among three of the country's 10 largest cities—Dallas, Houston and San Antonio. Texas A&M is the only university to be ranked nationally among the top 10 in these four areas: enrollment (Fall 1994 enrollment is 43,256), enrollment of top students (4th in number of new National Merit Scholars for Fall 1994), value of research, and endowment (6th in endowment)."

ADMISSIONS

Admissions Rating	80
% of applicants accepted	69
% of acceptees attending	56

FRESHMAN PROFILE

Average verbal SAT	640
Average math SAT	600
Average ACT	25
Average TOEFL	NR
Graduated top 20% of class	77
Graduated top 40% of class	85
Graduated top 60% of class	NR
Average HS GPA or Avg.	NR

DEADLINES

Early decision	NR
Regular admission	3/1
Regular notification	rolling
Non-fall registration	yes

APPLICANTS ALSO LOOK AT

AND OFTEN PREFER
Rice

AND SOMETIMES PREFER
U. Texas-Austin
Texas Tech
LSU-Baton Rouge
Baylor

AND RARELY PREFER
SMU
Stephen F. Austin
Southwest Texas

FINANCIAL FACTS

Financial Aid Rating	88
In-state tuition	$900
Out-of-state tuition	$7,380
Room & board	$3,414
Estimated book expense	$626
% frosh receiving aid	50
% undergrads receiving aid	63
% aid is need-based	35
% frosh w/ grant (avg)	41 ($2,829)
% frosh w/ loan (avg)	21 ($3,446)
% UGs w/ job (avg)	23 ($1,665)
Off-campus job outlook	good

TEXAS CHRISTIAN UNIVERSITY

2800 SOUTH UNIVERSITY DRIVE, FORT WORTH, TX 76129   ADMISSIONS: 800-828-3764   FAX: 817-921-7268

CAMPUS LIFE

Quality of Life Rating	**90**
Type of school	private
Affiliation	Christian Church (Disciples of Christ)
Environment	metropolis

STUDENTS

FT undergrad enrollment	5,245
% male/female	42/58
% from out of state	30
% live on campus	52
% spend weekend on campus	90
% transfers	26
% from public high school	88
% in (# of) fraternities	28 (12)
% in (# of) sororities	34 (14)
% African-American	4
% Asian	2
% Caucasian	79
% Hispanic	6
% international	4
# of countries represented	67

WHAT'S HOT
off-campus food
support groups
town-gown relations
library
Greeks

WHAT'S NOT
students are cliquish
hard liquor
drugs
sex
cigarettes

ACADEMICS

Academic Rating	**81**
Profs Interesting Rating	90
Profs Accessible Rating	87
Calendar	semester
Student/teacher ratio	15:1
% profs PhD/tenured	93/67
Hours of study per day	3.18

MOST POPULAR MAJORS
marketing
nursing
psychology

STUDENTS SPEAK OUT

Life

Texas Christian University students are, overall, a happy group. They don't work too hard, love their surroundings (Fort Worth and nearby Dallas), and find each other extraordinarily attractive. "This school has had the best-looking women in Texas four years running!" enthuses one senior man. The lopsided male/female ratio can be problematic, as one woman points out: "If you're a girl looking for lots of dates, just remember that the 'girl to guy' ratio is 3:2 and getting asked out is a feat in itself!" Conservative politically and socially (hey, TCU women! Why not do some asking out yourselves?), students rate marriage very high among their goals. Greek life is very important here—second only to football in the hearts of most students.

Academics

TCU students are enthusiastic about their professors, whom they find personable and approachable. Comments such as "the majority of the teachers at TCU work very closely with the students" and "the teaching staff here is incredible and there are few 'weed out' classes; I have yet to take a class that was not exhilarating in some way" are common on our surveys. Pre-business is big here: nearly one in ten graduates enters an MBA program within a year of graduation. So, too, are most other career-track majors: education, communications, the health sciences, and computer science are all strong and popular departments. Despite the preprofessional leanings of the student body, the traditional arts and sciences are hardly neglected at TCU: All students here must complete, by the end of sophomore year, a broad range of distribution requirements in the humanities, sciences, fine arts, and religion. A frequent complaint among those we surveyed is that the administration is secretive and unresponsive to student input: These complaints are particularly surprising in light of the apolitical nature of TCU students. If you have trouble dealing with powerful and occasionally arbitrary authorities, you might want to think twice before applying here.

Student Body

"If diversity at college is what you're looking for, don't look here!" reports one TCU student, and this sentiment is echoed by many of her classmates. Not everyone matches the description "white, affluent, and conservative," but many do. Add "attractive" and "fraternity/sorority member" to the description and you won't eliminate many students. The lack of diversity and the domination of social life by the Greeks are about the only complaints students seem to have about their classmates, however. As one student puts it, "I expect I'll never find another body of individuals so kind or friendly again." For those few students who don't fit into the mainstream here, however, things can be a bit more difficult. As one Hispanic student tells us, "Racism here is not usually blatant, but is subtle and therefore harder to combat. I don't see a great deal of school-based support, and students who aren't members of a minority tend to be apathetic. I've pretty much been left to my own devices, but I'm doing fine anyway." TCU actively seeks to recruit under-represented students.

ADMISSIONS

The admissions committee considers (in descending order of importance): HS record, class rank, test scores, essay, recommendations. *Also considered (in descending order of importance):* extracurriculars, personality, alumni relationship, special talents. Either the SAT or ACT is required; SAT is preferred. An interview is recommended. Admissions process is need-blind. *High school units required/recommended:* 17 total units are required; 4 English required, 3 math required, 3 science required, 2 foreign language required, 3 social studies required. *Special Requirements:* An audition is required for music program applicants. TOEFL is required of all international students. *The admissions office says:* "Students who wish to be considered for academic scholarship awards and students who would like to be evaluated on their transcript through junior year only should apply by January 15. Recommended high school curriculum: English, 4 yrs.; math, social studies, 3 yrs. each; foreign language, science, 2 yrs. each; biology, 1 yr."

The Inside Word

The most important element of the admissions process at TCU for most candidates is deciding whether they want to be here. Most applicants are admitted, and the academic standards aren't too high.

FINANCIAL AID

Students should submit: FAFSA, a copy of parents' most recent income tax filing. The Princeton Review suggests that all financial aid forms be submitted as soon as possible after January 1. *The following grants/scholarships are offered:* Pell, SEOG, academic merit, athletic, the school's own scholarships, the school's own grants, state scholarships, state grants, private scholarships, private grants, federal nursing scholarship, ROTC, foreign aid. *Students borrow from the following loan programs:* Stafford, unsubsidized Stafford, Perkins, PLUS, the school's own loan fund, state loans, federal nursing loans, private loans. Applicants will be notified of awards beginning April 1. College Work-Study Program is available. Institutional employment is available.

FROM THE ADMISSIONS OFFICE

"Our objective is to provide undergraduate and graduate instruction informed by research; to offer such undergraduate and graduate studies as will enable students to enter fruitful careers; to promote a mental, spiritual, and physical well-being of our students; to encourage continuous self-education; and to maintain a vital and inviting setting for learning and living in which the resources of the University are available while the atmosphere of a residential college is preserved...We are convinced that there must be a general compatibility among the values and daily practices of the University and its several units. We hope to perpetuate diversity in our programs and people, for we believe that no single vision will suffice for direction in a complex enterprise."

ADMISSIONS

Admissions Rating	75
% of applicants accepted	73
% of acceptees attending	43

FRESHMAN PROFILE

Average verbal SAT	NR
Average math SAT	NR
Average ACT	25
Average TOEFL	550
Graduated top 20% of class	51
Graduated top 40% of class	81
Graduated top 60% of class	95
Average HS GPA or Avg.	3.5

DEADLINES

Early decision	NR
Regular admission	2/15
Regular notification	4/1
Non-fall registration	yes

APPLICANTS ALSO LOOK AT

AND SOMETIMES PREFER
SMU
Trinity U.
Baylor
Rice

AND RARELY PREFER
Southwestern
U. Texas-Austin
Texas A&M

FINANCIAL FACTS

Financial Aid Rating	83
Tuition	$9,420
Room & board	$3,500
Estimated book expense	$650
% frosh receiving aid	63
% undergrads receiving aid	55
% aid is need-based	30
% frosh w/ grant (avg)	60 ($5,067)
% frosh w/ loan (avg)	34 ($4,592)
% UGs w/ job (avg)	8 ($1,396)
Off-campus job outlook	good

UNIVERSITY OF TEXAS-AUSTIN

UNDERGRADUATE ADMISSIONS, AUSTIN, TX 78712-1157   ADMISSIONS: 512-471-7601   FAX: 512-471-8102

CAMPUS LIFE

Quality of Life Rating	86
Type of school	public
Affiliation	none
Environment	metropolis

STUDENTS

FT undergrad enrollment	30,100
% male/female	50/50
% from out of state	5
% live on campus	13
% spend weekend on campus	NR
% transfers	6
% from public high school	NR
% in (# of) fraternities	11 (34)
% in (# of) sororities	13 (20)
% African-American	4
% Asian	12
% Caucasian	65
% Hispanic	14
% international	3
# of countries represented	116

WHAT'S HOT

intercollegiate sports
Austin
library
intramural sports
student publications

WHAT'S NOT

campus difficult to get around
dorms
unattractive campus
theater

ACADEMICS

Academic Rating	77
Profs Interesting Rating	67
Profs Accessible Rating	67
Calendar	semester
Student/teacher ratio	19:1
% profs tenured	92
Hours of study per day	3.01

STUDENTS SPEAK OUT

Life

Students love Austin, arguably the hippest small city in the country. "All Austin needs is a beach," says one student. It does have almost everything else, including museums, theaters, bookstores, and one of America's most vibrant bar/live music scenes. Students blend right into the Austin community: relations between students and locals rank very high. For those who stay on campus, there are hundreds of clubs and organizations to get involved with. Fraternities and sororities are very popular, but the school is large enough and offers enough in the way of activities that a student could have a full social life without ever attending a frat event. Longhorn football is huge, and other intercollegiate sporting events are also very popular.

Academics

UT-Austin is more than affordable; it is, in the words of one undergraduate, "damn cheap!" Tuition is so low that some out-of-state students pay less than they would to go to public institutions in their own home states. But UT-Austin has more than just price going for it. It also boasts excellent, varied academic programs. The school's huge endowment allows it to recruit scholars aggressively, and it has attracted top professors in many fields. Business-related majors claim a large number of students here; engineering and communications are also popular, and the film school is "up and coming." The only drawback is that UT-Austin is huge. No, it's damn huge! Around 30,000 undergraduates (and another 12,000 graduate students) crowd the 300-acre campus. Accordingly, students usually have to assert themselves to get to know their professors (although top students qualify for an honors program with smaller classes). Also as you might expect, administering such a large institution is difficult, and the red tape can be a little daunting; as one student says, "It is a huge bureaucracy, but this is inevitable considering the size of the student body." Most students know what they're getting into before they arrive, and feel that UT-Austin is a "great school with great diversity, even though it has all the bureaucracy associated with large schools."

Student Body

It's a cliche, but at a school of 30,000, you're going to find someone who fits just about any description. One student details the mix: "People range from sorority and fraternity goers to strong environmentalists to avid Cliff (our campus Christian speaker) watchers." The vast majority of students, nine out of ten, are Texans. Although Texas is a conservative state, UT-Austin seems to attract more than its fair share of "alternative" types. Liberal political ideas score surprisingly high, and people are concerned about "discrimination against women and minorities."

ADMISSIONS

The admissions committee considers (in descending order of importance): class rank, test scores, HS record, essay, recommendations. *Also considered (in descending order of importance):* special talents, extracurriculars, personality. Either the SAT or ACT is required. Admissions process is not need-blind. *High school units required/recommended:* 15 total units are required; 4 English required, 3 math required, 4 math recommended, 2 science required, 3 science recommended, 2 foreign language required, 3 social studies required. In-state applicants who rank in top tenth of secondary school class may be admitted with minimum combined SAT I score of 1010 (composite ACT score of 22); those in next 15% must have minimum combined SAT I score of 1140 (composite ACT score of 25); those in second quarter must have minimum combined SAT I score of 1230 (composite ACT score of 28). Minimum combined SAT I score of 1270 (composite ACT score of 29) and rank in top quarter of secondary school class required of out-of-state applicants. *Special Requirements:* An audition is required for music program applicants. TOEFL is required of all international students.

The Inside Word

Texas has a huge endowment. Much of it comes from University-owned oil wells (the profits from which are shared with Texas A&M). Top faculty and super facilities draw a mega-sized applicant pool. So does football. UT wants top athletes in each entering class, to be sure. But it also expects students who are well qualified academically, and it gets loads of them. Both the University and Austin are thriving intellectual communities; Austin has the highest per capita book sales of any city in the United States. Many students continue to grad school without ever leaving, which is understandable. It's hard to spend any time there without developing an attachment.

FINANCIAL AID

Students should submit: FAFSA. The Princeton Review suggests that all financial aid forms be submitted as soon as possible after January 1. *The following grants/scholarships are offered:* Pell, SEOG, academic merit, athletic, the school's own scholarships, the school's own grants, state scholarships, state grants, private scholarships, ROTC. *Students borrow from the following loan programs:* Stafford, Perkins, PLUS, state loans, federal nursing loans, health professions loans, private loans. College Work-Study Program is available. Institutional employment is available.

FROM THE ADMISSIONS OFFICE

"UT-Austin is a large, research-oriented university located in the capital of Texas, at the edge of the beautiful hill country of Texas. Over 48,500 students representing 50 states and 126 countries live and learn in a competitive academic environment. A strong intercollegiate athletic program for both men and women is supplemented by an intramural athletic program that is available to all students as well as faculty and staff. An Undergraduate Advising Center for undeclared majors, a Career Choice Information Center, and College Placement Centers provide advising, career counseling and placement. Other student services include an Honors Center, Counseling and Student Health Centers, and a Study Abroad Office. The University serves as a cultural center to the community at large as well as to the students, faculty, and staff. A Performing Arts Center is host to Broadway plays, the Austin Civic Opera, the Austin Symphony and visiting musical and dance groups."

ADMISSIONS

Admissions Rating	83
% of applicants accepted	65
% of acceptees attending	59

FRESHMAN PROFILE

Average verbal SAT	670
Average math SAT	620
Average ACT	25
Average TOEFL	550
Graduated top 20% of class	NR
Graduated top 40% of class	NR
Graduated top 60% of class	NR
Average HS GPA or Avg.	NR

DEADLINES

Early decision	NR
Regular admission	3/1
Regular notification	rolling
Non-fall registration	yes

APPLICANTS ALSO LOOK AT

AND OFTEN PREFER

Rice
Baylor

AND SOMETIMES PREFER

Texas A&M
Texas Tech
U. Houston

AND RARELY PREFER

Clemson
Southwest Texas State

FINANCIAL FACTS

Financial Aid Rating	81
In-state tuition	$840
Out-of-state tuition	$5,130
Room & board	$4,420
Estimated book expense	$650
% frosh receiving aid	60
% undergrads receiving aid	53
% aid is need-based	44
% frosh w/ grant (avg)	50 ($2,450)
% frosh w/ loan (avg)	33 ($3,250)
% UGs w/ job (avg)	19 ($2,100)
Off-campus job outlook	good

University of Toronto

315 Bloor Street West, Toronto, Ontario, CN M5S 1A3

Admissions: 416-978-2190

CAMPUS LIFE

Quality of Life Rating	71
Type of school	public
Affiliation	none
Environment	metropolis

STUDENTS

FT undergrad enrollment	28,965
% male/female	48/52
% from out of state	6
% live on campus	15
% spend weekend on campus	NR
% transfers	NR
% from public high school	NR
% African-American	NR
% Asian	NR
% Caucasian	NR
% Hispanic	NR
% international	NR
# of countries represented	NR

WHAT'S HOT

ethnic diversity on campus
Toronto, Ontario
health facilities
library
different students interact

WHAT'S NOT

political activism
campus difficult to get around
students are unhappy
support groups
music associations

ACADEMICS

Academic Rating	75
Profs Interesting Rating	60
Profs Accessible Rating	60
Calendar	other
Student/teacher ratio	NR
Hours of study per day	2.98

STUDENTS SPEAK OUT

Life

"Life here is: go to campus, go to class, go home," writes one University of Toronto junior, pointing out the lack of school spirit and social life. But there are activities and events on campus for students to attend. One student informs us that "There are many clubs on campus to get involved with. I'm in the outdoor club, the camera club, and the wine-tasting club." Some people note the lack of ethnic-group interactions, but overall, it is not mentioned as a large problem. If the campus does not satisfy, most people find solace in Toronto, a major-league city with tons of entertainment. "Toronto is an amazing city, diverse and full of culture, with excellent food. This makes the university experience worthwhile." Still, life revolves around the academic challenge that U of T poses, so "People here tend to be very focused on their academics and their futures. However, there are many who find a balance with their academic and social lives."

Academics

Students in different majors have different experiences at the University of Toronto, and that's to be expected with its huge undergraduate enrollment. "The hugeness of some classes is overwhelming and scary, especially to first-years," comments one student, and others agree—size matters. U of T is not for the weak-kneed—like most public, large universities, it is very impersonal and businesslike. But the university divides into majors, and some majors provide the students with greater personal attention than others. One junior physical therapy major writes, "Overall, my academic experience thus far has been excellent. Because I am in a small department, I am receiving a great deal of personal attention." Science majors are popular at the U of T. Pure and applied sciences and engineering are regarded among the best in Canada. The other side of this large university is the competitive nature of the student body. One sophomore notes that "It's extremely competitive. Good grades are difficult to come by, and a 200 percent effort is needed in order to do well." School spirit is small, partially due to a large commuter population. One commuter complains, "Academically the school is quite good, but for students that live off-campus, there really is no attempt by the university to include them, and considering that the makeup is over 50 percent commuter, that shouldn't occur." The administration receives low marks as well, for its delays, hesitancy to advise, and overly burdensome rules.

Student Body

As with most large, public institutions, it is hard to generalize about the student body. One thing is for sure—94 percent of them are from the provinces of Canada. One student mentions that "This university is so big it's hard...to meet lots of people unless you belong to a social organization like a frat." The student body studies the sciences more than the arts, works many hours outside of class, and packs the libraries on weekends (or at least they say they do). With such an emphasis on sciences and premedical/pregraduate study programs, the students can be a bit competitive with each other. "A cutthroat student body," is how one junior describes his fellow classmates.

FINANCIAL AID: 416-978-7950   E-MAIL: ASK@ADM.UTORONTO.CA   WEB SITE: HTTP://WWW.UTORONTO.CA

ADMISSIONS

The admissions committee considers (in descending order of importance): HS record, test scores. High secondary school GPA and good scores on SAT I and three SAT II required of applicants to the Faculty of Arts and Science, Erindale College, Faculty of Music, Faculty of Nursing, Scarborough College, School of Architecture and Landscape Architecture, and School of Physical and Health Education. ACT and/or CEEB Advanced Placement Tests will also be considered. 30 semester hours (45 quarter hours) from accredited institutions for applicants to the Faculty of Applied Science and Engineering. Applicants with excellent secondary school records and two CEEB Advanced Placement exams may be considered. *The admissions office says:* "Province residents are given special consideration for the Pharmacy program. Canadian citizens are given special consideration for the Dentistry, Physical and Occupational Therapy, and Rehabilitation Medicine programs."

The Inside Word

The University of Toronto is one of Canada's best, and its admissions process is appropriately selective. American candidates: give yourself extra time to research and prepare for filing an application; you're a foreign student here, and some additional paperwork is required in order to attend.

FROM THE ADMISSIONS OFFICE

"The University of Toronto is committed to being an internationally significant research university with undergraduate, graduate, and professional programs of study."

ADMISSIONS

Admissions Rating	77
% of applicants accepted	NR
% of acceptees attending	NR

FRESHMAN PROFILE

Average verbal SAT	NR
Average math SAT	NR
Average ACT	NR
Average TOEFL	NR
Graduated top 20% of class	NR
Graduated top 40% of class	NR
Graduated top 60% of class	NR
Average HS GPA or Avg.	NR

DEADLINES

Early decision	NR
Regular admission	6/1
Regular notification	NR
Non-fall registration	no

FINANCIAL FACTS

Financial Aid Rating	86
In-state tuition	NR
Out-of-state tuition	NR
Room & board	$5,500
Estimated book expense	$800
% frosh receiving aid	NR
% undergrads receiving aid	NR
% aid is need-based	NR
% frosh w/ grant (avg)	NR
% frosh w/ loan (avg)	NR
% UGs w/ job (avg)	NR

TRENTON STATE COLLEGE

HILLWOOD LAKES, CN 4700, TRENTON, NJ 08650-4700 ADMISSIONS: 800-345-7354 FAX: 609-771-2836

CAMPUS LIFE

Quality of Life Rating	79
Type of school	public
Affiliation	none
Environment	suburban

STUDENTS

FT undergrad enrollment	5,298
% male/female	40/60
% from out of state	7
% live on campus	59
% spend weekend on campus	NR
% transfers	23
% from public high school	68
% in (# of) fraternities	19 (14)
% in (# of) sororities	19 (16)
% African-American	7
% Asian	5
% Caucasian	77
% Hispanic	5
% international	NR
# of countries represented	20

WHAT'S HOT
old-fashioned dating
sex
ethnic diversity on campus
campus food
dorms

WHAT'S NOT
political activism
lab facilities
library
students are cliquish
off-campus food

ACADEMICS

Academic Rating	82
Profs Interesting Rating	77
Profs Accessible Rating	70
Calendar	semester
Student/teacher ratio	14:1
% profs PhD/tenured	85/73
Hours of study per day	2.68

MOST POPULAR MAJORS
elementary education
business
biology

% GRADS WHO PURSUE...
Law 3, Med 2, MBA 8, MA 17

STUDENTS SPEAK OUT

Life

While Trenton State College students enjoy the school's campus, they give the surrounding area low grades. Writes one student, "There's nothing within walking distance. There are few clubs and bars and no coffeehouses." Social life revolves almost entirely around drinking, leading one student to warn that "Social life is awful. Until you turn twenty-one there is no way to do anything off campus and there is nothing on campus to do. If you don't drink or 'hook up' you're out of luck on Saturday night." There is a fairly popular Greek system, but all the frat houses are located off campus, "which is stupid because it promotes drinking and driving." One student notes that "The school tries to provide lots of activities, including an on-campus bar with great bands and a social atmosphere." The campus itself is "scenic" and the dorms are "comfortable, once you get used to group showers," one student claims. Another sums up: "If you're looking for a good, challenging education, then TSC is for you. But if you want an all-around college experience, I'd suggest other schools."

Academics

Which is the real TSC: the one highly touted by U.S. News & World Report and Money magazine, or the one that drew gripes from students in our survey with such surprising frequency? The truth is somewhere in the middle. TSC has earned a good reputation, but it's perhaps not as good a school as the rep would have it, which explains why so many students are disappointed. TSC's strengths are its affordability, competitive student body, and uniformly strong academic departments. The school's honors program also allows strong students a great degree of autonomy in designing their studies. All students complete a wide assortment of math, science, and liberal arts courses, regardless of major. Despite the school's assets, however, most students we surveyed express reservations about TSC. The administration is the favorite target of most; students feel that the school shows more concern for presenting "a good front" and attracting future students than for providing for currently enrolled students. Students complain that "advisement and guidance overall are substandard" and that "administrative offices are understaffed." Furthermore, students give below-average grades to the faculty, purported to be one of TSC's great strengths.

Student Body

TSC students hail mostly from the Garden State. Students are cliquish, "one-dimensional suburban types, but very courteous and friendly"; warns one student, "Greeks stick together, minorities stick together, clubs stick together, even people with the same majors or who live on the same floor stick together." Students are "generally conservative and a little close-minded," but because TSC is one of the most competitive public institutions in the country, students are very bright. Sums up one student: "Overall, folks are very friendly and easy to get along with. They are, however, extremely competitive in the classroom."

ADMISSIONS

The admissions committee considers (in descending order of importance): HS record, class rank, test scores, essay, recommendations. *Also considered (in descending order of importance):* extracurriculars, special talents. Either the SAT or ACT is required; SAT is preferred. Admissions process is need-blind. *High school units required/recommended:* 16 total units are required; 4 English required, 3 math required, 2 science required, 2 foreign language recommended, 2 social studies required, 2 history recommended. Minimum combined SAT I score of 800 and rank in top half of secondary school class required. *Special Requirements:* A portfolio is required for art program applicants. An audition is required for music program applicants. TOEFL is required of all international students. Interview and portfolio required of some communication studies program applicants.

The Inside Word

Trenton State's newfound visibility has given a boost to the applicant pool, but selectivity remains at about the level it has been for the past few years. Since the pool is now somewhat better than before, this still translates into a stronger entering class.

FINANCIAL AID

Students should submit: FAFSA, the school's own financial aid form. The Princeton Review suggests that all financial aid forms be submitted as soon as possible after January 1. *The following grants/scholarships are offered:* Pell, SEOG, academic merit, the school's own scholarships, state scholarships, state grants, private scholarships, ROTC. *Students borrow from the following loan programs:* Stafford, unsubsidized Stafford, Perkins, PLUS, state loans, federal nursing loans. Applicants will be notified of awards beginning April 1. College Work-Study Program is available. Institutional employment is available.

FROM THE ADMISSIONS OFFICE

"Twin lakes form the border of the Trenton State College campus, which is set on 250 acres of wooded and landscaped grounds in suburban Ewing Township, NJ...TSC offers more than 40 baccalaureate degree programs in the arts and science. The campus is residential, with more than half of the 5,300 full-time students housed on campus. Classes are small and are all taught by faculty members: there are no graduate teaching assistants. The College is strongly committed to retaining and graduating the students it enrolls. This commitment is reflected in the high return rate of entering students, which has consistently been over 90 percent for the past five years.

ADMISSIONS

Admissions Rating	87
% of applicants accepted	45
% of acceptees attending	41

FRESHMAN PROFILE

Average verbal SAT	660
Average math SAT	600
Average ACT	NR
Average TOEFL	NR
Graduated top 20% of class	82
Graduated top 40% of class	94
Graduated top 60% of class	98
Average HS GPA or Avg.	NR

DEADLINES

Early decision	11/15
Regular admission	3/1
Regular notification	4/1
Non-fall registration	yes

APPLICANTS ALSO LOOK AT

AND OFTEN PREFER
Rutgers U.

AND SOMETIMES PREFER
Penn State-U. Park
U. Delaware
Villanova
Lafayette
Seton Hall

AND RARELY PREFER
Drexel
U. Mass.-Amherst
Boston Coll.
Providence

FINANCIAL FACTS

Financial Aid Rating	75
In-state tuition	$4,410
Out-of-state tuition	$6,940
Room & board	$5,824
Estimated book expense	$700
% frosh receiving aid	53
% undergrads receiving aid	51
% aid is need-based	58
% frosh w/ grant (avg)	60 ($2,600)
% frosh w/ loan (avg)	54 ($3,250)
% UGs w/ job (avg)	23 ($900)
Off-campus job outlook	good

TRINITY COLLEGE (CT)

SUMMIT STREET, HARTFORD, CT 06016 · ADMISSIONS: 203-297-2180 · FAX: 203-297-2257

CAMPUS LIFE

Quality of Life Rating | **78**
Type of school | private
Affiliation | none
Environment | city

STUDENTS

FT undergrad enrollment | 1,787
% male/female | 51/49
% from out of state | 73
% live on campus | 92
% spend weekend on campus | 80
% transfers | 5
% from public high school | 50
% in (# of) fraternities | 33 (10)
% in (# of) sororities | 11 (2)
% African-American | 6
% Asian | 5
% Caucasian | 82
% Hispanic | 4
% international | 2
# of countries represented | 23

WHAT'S HOT
drugs
hard liquor
campus food
intercollegiate sports
cigarettes

WHAT'S NOT
town-gown relations
students are cliquish
Hartford
sex
lack of diversity on campus

ACADEMICS

Academic Rating | **86**
Profs Interesting Rating | 76
Profs Accessible Rating | 75
Calendar | semester
Student/teacher ratio | 10:1
% profs PhD/tenured | 97/98
Hours of study per day | 2.92

MOST POPULAR MAJORS
economics
English
political science

STUDENTS SPEAK OUT

Life

Clubs, sports and community service are very popular at Trinity College. The Division III intercollegiate sports, particularly basketball and hockey, are extremely popular. The social life is hopping seven nights a week. One student notes that "Trinity is a school for students who like to get their work done and then booze all night." In response to all the partying, the administration a few years ago limited weeknight parties to groups of 100 or fewer. Fraternities are very active on campus and are responsible for many of the social events. One student comments that "Greek life dominates. The school doesn't have many alternatives." There is, however, little peer pressure to rush, only to participate. One student writes, "This is not a suitcase school—there is usually stuff to do every weekend. We try not to be bored. Fraternity parties are most popular, but there's always good food, bars, comedy and bands on- and off-campus."

Academics

Traditionally known as Connecticut's safety school for Ivy League aspirants, Trinity is becoming the first choice of more and more top students. Its small class size, competitive academic structure and its excellent professors garners praise from students. One transfer student comments, "I transferred to Trinity two years ago from St. John's College in Annapolis, MD. I have also taken classes at Dartmouth and the University of Iowa. The education I have received at Trinity is better than any of these schools. The professors could not be much better and they go out of their way to help students." Standout departments include most liberal arts offerings (with reportedly "excellent" history and philosophy departments), economics, psychology, and the interdisciplinary, by-invitation-only Guilded Studies program. The amount of academic pressure depends largely on the individual and the individual's major. One student notes that the "philosophy department is very demanding." But another student writes, "If you want to excel, there's plenty of room, and if you want to slide there's plenty of beer—it's up to you." Requirements are demanding. Students must complete distribution requirements (five courses) and an interdisciplinary minor (six courses) as well as a major. Trinity offers a vast array of internships; more than half of the students take advantage of the opportunity to work at local insurance companies or in state government. Study abroad is also encouraged—Trinity has a campus in Rome and is part of a consortium in Spain.

Student Body

Despite efforts by the administration to increase diversity on campus, Trinity remains in essence a white, preppie enclave. One student refers to the student body as "Boarding School II-the sequel." The political climate is basically conservative, but not actively so. The contentedness that pervades the campus translates into apathy toward outside issues. There is no visible gay community at Trinity, nor is there evidence of alternative lifestyle consciousness in general. This does not stop the student body from studying and relaxing in "cliques." Students at Trinity College are primarily interested in getting a high-quality education while having fun, and most agree that Trinity provides them with anything they're looking for.

TRINITY COLLEGE (CT)

ADMISSIONS

The admissions committee considers (in descending order of importance): HS record, recommendations, class rank, test scores, essay. *Also considered (in descending order of importance):* extracurriculars, personality, special talents, alumni relationship, geographical distribution. Either the SAT or ACT is required. An interview is recommended. *High school units required/recommended:* 13 total units are required; 4 English required, 3 math required, 2 science required, 2 foreign language required, 2 history required. TOEFL is required of all international students. *The admissions office says:* "Trinity College's bulletin notes that students don't always realize the significance of personal qualities in the admissions process: Colleges are interested in more than prospective students' achievements or skills. We are keenly interested in attracting and admitting candidates who not only give ample proof of academic prowess but also show evidence of such personal qualities as honesty, fairness, compassion, altruism, leadership, and initiative in their high school years."

The Inside Word

Trinity's Ivy safety status enables it to enroll a fairly impressive student body, but the majority of its best applicants go elsewhere. The price tag is high, and the college's competitors include a large portion of the best schools in the country. Minority candidates with sound academic backgrounds will encounter a most accommodating admissions committee.

FINANCIAL AID

Students should submit: FAFSA (due February 1), CSS Profile, the school's own financial aid form, a copy of parents' most recent income tax filing. The Princeton Review suggests that all financial aid forms be submitted as soon as possible after January 1. *The following grants/scholarships are offered:* Pell, SEOG, the school's own scholarships, the school's own grants, state scholarships, state grants, private scholarships, private grants, ROTC, foreign aid. *Students borrow from the following loan programs:* Stafford, Perkins, PLUS, the school's own loan fund, state loans. Applicants will be notified of awards beginning April 1. College Work-Study Program is available. Institutional employment is available.

FROM THE ADMISSIONS OFFICE

"Trinity's location in a major metropolitan area offers its students opportunities not as readily available at other selective New England liberal arts colleges in more rural settings. Well over one-half of Trinity's students take advantage of internships in business, the arts, government, law, education, medicine, etc., in the Hartford area. Additionally, several hundred students are engaged in volunteer activities in the broader community through the Community Outreach program. However, Trinity's beautiful campus means that students need not give up a classical collegiate atmosphere in order to take advantage of the opportunities made possible by the college's city setting."

ADMISSIONS

Admissions Rating	87
% of applicants accepted	57
% of acceptees attending	29

FRESHMAN PROFILE
Average verbal SAT	690
Average math SAT	610
Average ACT	27
Average TOEFL	550
Graduated top 20% of class	72
Graduated top 40% of class	94
Graduated top 60% of class	100
Average HS GPA or Avg.	NR

DEADLINES
Early decision	NR
Regular admission	1/15
Regular notification	early April
Non-fall registration	no

APPLICANTS ALSO LOOK AT
AND OFTEN PREFER
Amherst
Yale
Harvard/Radcliffe
Pennsylvania
Tufts
AND SOMETIMES PREFER
Middlebury Coll.
Wesleyan U.
Boston Coll.
Georgetown U.
Colgate
AND RARELY PREFER
Connecticut Coll.
Fairfield

FINANCIAL FACTS

Financial Aid Rating	84
Tuition	$19,690
Room & board	$6,130
Estimated book expense	$500
% frosh receiving aid	51
% undergrads receiving aid	47
% aid is need-based	100
% frosh w/ grant (avg)	47 ($14,440)
% frosh w/ loan (avg)	45 ($3,625)
% UGs w/ job (avg)	50 ($1,500)
Off-campus job outlook	good

TRINITY UNIVERSITY

715 STADIUM DRIVE, SAN ANTONIO, TX 78212-7200 ADMISSIONS: 800-874-6489 FAX: 210-736-7696

STUDENTS SPEAK OUT

Life
Located just outside history-rich San Antonio, home of the Alamo, Trinity is a small liberal arts institution where students seem to have big-time fun. "San Antonio has a variety of intercultural activities—poetry readings, open mics...and there are some local bands worth hearing." There's also country-western dancing, a favorite pastime of many undergrads. Students at Trinity are also sports crazy. Never mind the NBA Spurs, "Intramurals are, one word, HUGE." And if San Antonio runs out of allure, there are "the group retreats over the weekend to isolated towns near the Mexican border that are something worth experiencing." For homebodies, dorms receive glowing reviews, as does the campus food. Dinner and a movie is another popular way to spend a few extra hours, but usually it's done in groups because dating on the Trinity campus is almost nonexistent, and sexual activity, as reported by the students, is on the low side. The Greek system at Trinity is also popular, but not dominant, and, as at most small schools, many parties are open to the entire student body. Indeed, most students are more than happy with their daily lives at Trinity.

Academics
"Everything's bigger in Texas and so are the IQ's of our professors," boasts a sophomore studying communications. Such praise is almost universal among Trinity undergrads, probably a result of the university's aggressive recruitment of top profs (made possible by its big-time endowment). Says one, "The administration did a tremendous job of building up the academic reputation of Trinity." Beams another, "All my professors are willing to offer one-on-one assistance to all those students who are willing to learn, even if their office hours have lapsed." TAs don't teach upper-level classes, another reason students are quite satisfied with the level of instruction. Lectures and discussion sections are small, with average enrollments of about twenty students. Trinity undergrads are required to complete a fairly rigorous set of general education courses that take up close to 25 percent of their total credits. This can lead to a somewhat inflexible schedule for students who remain undecided about their major for too long. Labs, the library, Trinity's computer system, and financial aid packages all receive high marks from a satisfied student body.

Student Body
"If you go to Trinity be prepared for a strange crowd. We have people who play guitars in the elevators and stairwells, people who wear lab coats, fireman's hats, and bathrobes to class, and people who jump on cafeteria tables to give speeches." Wait, aren't those scenes from Animal House? No matter, Trinity students do like to have a good time. Explains one, "There are no cliques...Greeks and independents interact openly." Another adds, "Well, lots are from Texas and know how to hunt and such, but we all get along." Lots may be from Texas, but about four in ten aren't. Trinity is working hard to buck the homogeneity label attached to many small, private institutions, but it still has a ways to go. Apart from fairly large Asian and Hispanic populations, Trinity is basically white, which is a special problem at such a small school where small percentages equal very small populations. Says one dissatisfied student, "The lack of ethnic diversity is disappointing." Still, interaction among students is given fairly high marks, and the friendliness of the student body is trumpeted by Trinity undergrads over and over again.

FINANCIAL AID: 210-736-8315

ADMISSIONS

The admissions committee considers (in descending order of importance): HS record, class rank, test scores, essay, recommendations. *Also considered (in descending order of importance):* extracurriculars, personality, special talents, alumni relationship, geographical distribution. Either the SAT or ACT is required; SAT is preferred. An interview is recommended. *High school units required/recommended:* 16 total units are required; 4 English required, 3 math required, 2 science required, 2 foreign language required, 2 social studies required. TOEFL is required of all international students.

The Inside Word

There is no disputing that Trinity has bought academic excellence in its student body. For this reason alone, above-average students who need significant financial assistance in order to attend college should definitely consider applying. While Trinity's actions may be less than noble, there is no question that it's an extremely capable student body, and that there are significant benefits to be derived from attending.

FINANCIAL AID

Students should submit: FAFSA (due February 1), the school's own financial aid form (due February 1), a copy of parents' most recent income tax filing (due February 1). The Princeton Review suggests that all financial aid forms be submitted as soon as possible after January 1. *The following grants/scholarships are offered:* Pell, SEOG, academic merit, the school's own scholarships, the school's own grants, state grants, private scholarships, private grants, ROTC. *Students borrow from the following loan programs:* Stafford, Perkins, PLUS, the school's own loan fund, private loans. Applicants will be notified of awards beginning April 1. College Work-Study Program is available. Institutional employment is available. Freshmen are discouraged from working.

FROM THE ADMISSIONS OFFICE

"Three qualities separate Trinity University from other selective, academically challenging institutions around the country. First, Trinity is unusual in the quality and quantity of resources devoted almost exclusively to its undergraduate students. Those resources give rise to a second distinctive aspect of Trinity—its emphasis on undergraduate research. Our students prefer being involved over observing. With superior laboratory facilities and strong, dedicated faculty, our undergraduates fill many of the roles formerly reserved for graduate students. With no graduate assistants, our professors often go to their undergraduates for help with their research. Finally, Trinity stands apart for the attitude of its students. In an atmosphere of academic camaraderie and fellowship, our students work together to stretch their minds and broaden their horizons. For quality of resources, for dedication to undergraduate research, and for the disposition of its student body, Trinity University holds a unique position in American higher education."

ADMISSIONS

Admissions Rating	83
% of applicants accepted	79
% of acceptees attending	32

FRESHMAN PROFILE

Average verbal SAT	640
Average math SAT	640
Average ACT	28
Average TOEFL	500
Graduated top 20% of class	81
Graduated top 40% of class	96
Graduated top 60% of class	99
Average HS GPA or Avg.	3.8

DEADLINES

Early decision	11/15
Regular admission	2/1
Regular notification	4/1
Non-fall registration	yes

APPLICANTS ALSO LOOK AT

AND OFTEN PREFER

Rice
Duke
U. Texas-Austin

AND SOMETIMES PREFER

TCU
Tulane
Vanderbilt
SMU
Texas A&M

AND RARELY PREFER

Rhodes

FINANCIAL FACTS

Financial Aid Rating	83
Tuition	$13,500
Room & board	$5,545
Estimated book expense	$500
% frosh receiving aid	78
% undergrads receiving aid	78
% aid is need-based	48
% frosh w/ grant (avg)	70
% frosh w/ loan (avg)	NR
% UGs w/ job (avg)	25 ($1,500)
Off-campus job outlook	good

TRUMAN STATE UNIVERSITY

KIRKSVILLE, MO 63501   ADMISSIONS: 816-785-4000   FAX: 816-785-4181

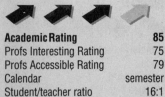

CAMPUS LIFE

Quality of Life Rating   **81**
Type of school   public
Affiliation   none
Environment   town

STUDENTS
FT undergrad enrollment   5,787
% male/female   44/56
% from out of state   29
% live on campus   46
% spend weekend on campus   75
% transfers   8
% from public high school   80
% in (# of) fraternities   28 (17)
% in (# of) sororities   21 (9)
% African-American   3
% Asian   2
% Caucasian   90
% Hispanic   2
% international   3
# of countries represented   50

WHAT'S HOT
library
religion
beer
campus easy to get around
hard liquor

WHAT'S NOT
political activism
registration is a pain
computer facilities
town-gown relations
Kirksville

ACADEMICS

Academic Rating   **85**
Profs Interesting Rating   75
Profs Accessible Rating   79
Calendar   semester
Student/teacher ratio   16:1
% profs PhD/tenured   76/79
Hours of study per day   3.27

MOST POPULAR MAJORS
business administration
biology
psychology

% GRADS WHO PURSUE...
Law 1, Med 4, MBA 5, MA 28

STUDENTS SPEAK OUT

Life
Kirksville, Truman State University's hometown, gets a bad rap from many of its temporary inhabitants, who cite "extreme culture shock" and a "dearth of activities to relieve the stress of academic work." Nevertheless, some students stick up for their town. Writes one enthusiast, "Kirksville is a much better city than most people give it credit for; one must search out its beauty (the Blue Moon Cafe is excellent)." Students here are more involved in religion than at many colleges, and religious clubs are quite popular. The dating scene is very active, and people who have found a comfortable social niche claim to be happy here. The campus itself is described in not-so-flattering terms—as a matter of fact, the word most often used to describe it rhymes with "nerd."

Academics
Formerly known as Northeast Missouri State University, Truman has grown from a regional teacher's college into a nationally-recognized university with quality programs in business, communications, and (of course) education. The curriculum here features one of the nation's most comprehensive liberal arts core requirements and stresses the development of communication skills (writing, speaking, etc.) for all students. The school also uses a battery of standardized tests to assess students' progress continually. Many students appreciate what the school provides: "a quality liberal arts and sciences education at an affordable price." They also assert that "the faculty and administration are very involved in individual students' progress and are always willing to help." Many feel proud that Truman "is in the middle of a renaissance." While they admit that "the development of a liberal arts and sciences culture has caused some growing pains," they also assert that "those who are interested have a wonderful opportunity to shape a new university community." Still, many students here are definitely less than satisfied. Our surveys were filled with complaints about everything from registration ("closed classes are a real problem"), to courses ("the theme in evaluation for grading purposes is still 'memorize and regurgitate'"), to the overall mission of the university ("if you want job training come here—if you want an education, DON'T!").

Student Body
Truman State University is not the place to come seeking a paradise of ethnic diversity and harmony. Although a few students think different groups interact with each other very easily, most believe just the opposite. Writes one African-American student, "Our school is completely Eurocentric: a whitewashed faculty with a whitewashed student body." Complains another student, "Minority students and organizations do not receive the support of the school community." Most students would agree that "the campus needs to start integrating itself academically. If minorities are good enough to come here and play sports, [Truman] should incorporate studies and have guest speakers that deal with different ethnic backgrounds." Truman's small minority population is made up mostly of African Americans.

FINANCIAL AID: 816-785-4130   E-MAIL: AD03%NEMOMUS@ACADEMIC.NEMOSTATE.EDU   WEB SITE: HTTP://WWW.TRUMAN.EDU

ADMISSIONS

The admissions committee considers (in descending order of importance): HS record, test scores, class rank, essay, recommendations. *Also considered (in descending order of importance):* extracurriculars, personality, special talents, alumni relationship, geographical distribution. An interview is recommended. Admissions process is need-blind. *The admissions office says:* "The admissions committee is seeking applicants with varied talents and interests...Successful applicants tend to demonstrate significant co-curricular involvement and strong leadership potential."

The Inside Word

Truman is next in line among public universities joining the ranks of the highly selective. It's tough to get admitted here, and it's only going to get tougher as increased name recognition prompts annual increases in application totals. Serious students with conservative attitudes make the best match with this rising star.

FINANCIAL AID

Students should submit: FAFSA (due April 1). The Princeton Review suggests that all financial aid forms be submitted as soon as possible after January 1. *The following grants/scholarships are offered:* Pell, SEOG, academic merit, athletic, the school's own scholarships, state scholarships, state grants, private scholarships, private grants, ROTC. *Students borrow from the following loan programs:* Stafford, unsubsidized Stafford, Perkins, PLUS, the school's own loan fund, state loans, federal nursing loans, private loans. College Work-Study Program is available. Institutional employment is available.

FROM THE ADMISSIONS OFFICE

"The 5,900 undergraduate students that attend Truman State...have already discovered...an institution that is committed to providing the undergraduate student with an exemplary liberal arts and sciences education."

ADMISSIONS

Admissions Rating	76
% of applicants accepted	74
% of acceptees attending	32

FRESHMAN PROFILE

Average verbal SAT	NR
Average math SAT	NR
Average ACT	26
Average TOEFL	500
Graduated top 20% of class	63
Graduated top 40% of class	92
Graduated top 60% of class	98
Average HS GPA or Avg.	3.5

DEADLINES

Early decision	11/15
Regular admission	3/1
Regular notification	rolling
Non-fall registration	yes

APPLICANTS ALSO LOOK AT

AND OFTEN PREFER
Washington U.

AND SOMETIMES PREFER
U. Missouri-Columbia
Lawrence
U. Illinois, Urbana-Champ.
St. Louis

AND RARELY PREFER
U. Iowa
Illinois State
Illinois Wesleyan
Purdue U.-West Lafayette

FINANCIAL FACTS

Financial Aid Rating	85
In-state tuition	$3,008
Out-of-state tuition	$5,416
Room & board	$3,808
Estimated book expense	$600
% frosh receiving aid	92
% undergrads receiving aid	85
% aid is need-based	45
% frosh w/ grant (avg)	80 ($2,137)
% frosh w/ loan (avg)	35 ($2,836)
% UGs w/ job (avg)	37 ($816)
Off-campus job outlook	good

TUFTS UNIVERSITY

MEDFORD, MA 02155

ADMISSIONS: 617-627-3170   FAX: 617-627-3860

CAMPUS LIFE

Quality of Life Rating	**84**
Type of school	private
Affiliation	none
Environment	metropolis

STUDENTS

FT undergrad enrollment	4,550
% male/female	47/53
% from out of state	73
% live on campus	80
% spend weekend on campus	NR
% transfers	5
% from public high school	61
% in (# of) fraternities	14 (10)
% in (# of) sororities	4 (3)
% African-American	4
% Asian	13
% Caucasian	71
% Hispanic	4
% international	7
# of countries represented	61

WHAT'S HOT
student publications
political activism
student government
campus food
music associations

WHAT'S NOT
library
cigarettes
sex
drugs
support groups

ACADEMICS

Academic Rating	**87**
Profs Interesting Rating	71
Profs Accessible Rating	75
Calendar	semester
Student/teacher ratio	13:1
% profs PhD/tenured	96/100
Hours of study per day	2.99

MOST POPULAR MAJORS
English
international relations
biology

% GRADS WHO PURSUE...
Law 24, Med 11, MBA 20, MA 35

STUDENTS SPEAK OUT

Life

Tufts University offers students an attractive, hilly, suburban campus less than a half-hour's commute from Boston. Many students call the location "perfect." Says one enthusiast, "Tufts has just about everything a college student would want, from hills to flatlands, parties to quiet nights, a city and a suburb, as well as all kinds of people. There's nowhere else I'd rather be at this time in my life." Another student warns that "people who don't like walking up and down hills may not be particularly happy here at Tufts." School spirit is low—"Nobody goes to the games or pep rallies"—and on-campus activities that don't serve alcohol are poorly attended. Dating seems to be rare. As one student explains: "The dating scene stinks—everyone already has someone at home, someone here, or is just looking for sex." But the food is great.

Academics

Tufts has a reputation as the "Ivy League dumping ground"—the "safety" choice of Easterners applying to the Ivies. As one student explains, "Many here apply to an Ivy as their reach, but have Tufts as their first real choice. The result is really smart hard workers who weren't quite genius-geeky enough for their first-choice schools." Once here, students settle into a demanding academic environment notable for several things. First are the professors, whom students find accessible and friendly. Second are "the nation's best orientation program, especially the Exploration Program from the Experimental College," which has students and professors co-teach introductory courses in fields of common interest and expertise. There's also a popular junior year abroad. Students rave about the size of the student body, large enough to support a wide range of academic fields but small enough to feel like a community: "Walking around you always see people you know, but you also see people you don't." What was once the "big negative" in our survey is now one of TU's biggest, in the truest sense of the word, attributes—a brand new, $20 million library.

Student Body

Our respondents have a lot of mostly negative things to say about the diversity of the student body here. The comment, "For all the hype about diversity, I have not found Tufts to be a particularly diverse university," was typical. Students feel that administrators are more interested in the perception of diversity than in diversity itself, and characterize their classmates as friendly but cliquish. There is a sizable leftist population here, and gay students are active, but there is also a large group of students who resent their p.c. classmates. One goes so far as to say that "there is an atmosphere of barely checked violence at Tufts." Still, students rank themselves "very happy" overall, so these complaints are not major, regardless of how strenuously students voice them. Students don't work terribly hard yet express overall satisfaction with their education: They are bright but not driven in the way many of their Ivy League peers are.

TUFTS UNIVERSITY

Financial Aid: 617-627-3528   E-mail: uadmiss inquiry@infonet.tufts.edu   Web Site: http://www.tufts.edu

ADMISSIONS

The admissions committee considers (in descending order of importance): class rank, HS record, recommendations, test scores, essay. *Also considered (in descending order of importance):* extracurriculars, personality, special talents, alumni relationship, geographical distribution. Either the SAT or ACT is required. An interview is recommended. *High school units required/recommended:* 16 total units are recommended; 4 English recommended, 3 math recommended, 2 science recommended, 3 foreign language recommended, 1 history recommended. *Special Requirements:* TOEFL is required of all international students. 4 units of math and 2 units of lab science recommended of engineering, math, and sciences program applicants. SAT II (chemistry or physics and math level I or II) required of engineering program applicants who submit SAT I scores.

The Inside Word

Tufts has little visibility outside the Northeast, and little personality either. Still it manages to attract and keep an excellent student body, mostly from right inside its own backyard. In order to be successful, candidates must have significant academic accomplishments and submit a thoroughly well-prepared application—the review is rigorous and the standards are high.

FINANCIAL AID

Students should submit: FAFSA (due February 15), CSS Profile (due February 1), a copy of parents' most recent income tax filing (due February 15). The Princeton Review suggests that all financial aid forms be submitted as soon as possible after January 1. *The following grants/scholarships are offered:* Pell, SEOG, academic merit, the school's own scholarships, the school's own grants, state scholarships, state grants, private scholarships, ROTC. *Students borrow from the following loan programs:* Stafford, unsubsidized Stafford, Perkins, PLUS, the school's own loan fund, state loans. Applicants will be notified of awards beginning April 1. College Work-Study Program is available. Institutional employment is available.

FROM THE ADMISSIONS OFFICE

"Tufts University, on the boundary between Medford and Somerville, sits on a hill overlooking Boston, five miles northwest of the city. The campus is a tranquil New England setting within easy access by subway and bus to the cultural, social, and entertainment resources of Boston and Cambridge. "Since its founding in 1852 by members of the Universalist church, Tufts has grown from a small liberal arts college into a nonsectarian university of over 7,000 students. By 1900 the college had added a medical school, a dental school, and graduate studies. The University now also includes the Fletcher School of Law and Diplomacy, the Graduate School of Arts and Sciences, the School of Veterinary Medicine, the School of Nutrition, the Sackler School of Graduate Biomedical Sciences, and the Gordon Institute of Engineering Management."

ADMISSIONS

Admissions Rating	93
% of applicants accepted	45
% of acceptees attending	33

FRESHMAN PROFILE

Average verbal SAT	650
Average math SAT	650
Average ACT	28
Average TOEFL	NR
Graduated top 20% of class	87
Graduated top 40% of class	97
Graduated top 60% of class	99
Average HS GPA or Avg.	NR

DEADLINES

Early decision	NR
Regular admission	1/1
Regular notification	4/1
Non-fall registration	no

APPLICANTS ALSO LOOK AT

AND OFTEN PREFER

Harvard/Radcliffe
Duke
Brown
Dartmouth
Pennsylvania

AND SOMETIMES PREFER

Northwestern U.
U. Mass.-Amherst

AND RARELY PREFER

Boston Coll.
Brandeis

FINANCIAL FACTS

Financial Aid Rating	77
Tuition	$20,557
Room & board	$5,968
Estimated book expense	$600
% frosh receiving aid	38
% undergrads receiving aid	40
% aid is need-based	100
% frosh w/ grant (avg)	32 ($12,950)
% frosh w/ loan (avg)	36 ($3,060)
% UGs w/ job (avg)	48 ($1,500)
Off-campus job outlook	excellent

TULANE UNIVERSITY

6823 ST. CHARLES AVENUE, NEW ORLEANS, LA 70118   ADMISSIONS: 504-865-5731   FAX: 504-862-8715

CAMPUS LIFE

Quality of Life Rating	**87**
Type of school	private
Affiliation	none
Environment	metropolis

STUDENTS

FT undergrad enrollment	4,830
% male/female	50/50
% from out of state	86
% live on campus	48
% spend weekend on campus	98
% transfers	3
% from public high school	55
% in (# of) fraternities	32 (16)
% in (# of) sororities	35 (8)
% African-American	10
% Asian	5
% Caucasian	78
% Hispanic	5
% international	4
# of countries represented	90

WHAT'S HOT
hard liquor
off-campus food
registration is a breeze
sex
beer

WHAT'S NOT
music associations
dorms
library
lab facilities
theater

ACADEMICS

Academic Rating	**83**
Profs Interesting Rating	70
Profs Accessible Rating	75
Calendar	semester
Student/teacher ratio	11:1
% profs PhD/tenured	98/98
Hours of study per day	3.04

MOST POPULAR MAJORS
engineering
business
psychology

% GRADS WHO PURSUE...
Law 13, Med 14, MBA 12, MA 35

STUDENTS SPEAK OUT

Life

Tulane University is "a miniature New Orleans in the middle of New Orleans, a true party-like atmosphere," which leads one college counselor to describe Tulane as "outstanding in spite of, or because of, its location." Overall, students love New Orleans. New Orleans has a very active night life that centers on its homegrown Zydeco and Cajun cultures, and spending a night out on the town is a very popular diversion for students. The conveniently located campus is also really pretty: One happy camper comments, "I think one of the best parts of Tulane is the beauty of the campus. I love walking around and seeing the growth of flowers." The Greek system is surprisingly popular considering the school's urban location, but social pressure seems to be low. One student wants to make "A comment about drugs and alcohol—I have been at Tulane for five years and I have never been pressured by my peers concerning the use of these things. Also, sororities/fraternities are not important. Plenty of people in and out of Greek systems go out together."

Academics

In the past few years Tulane has made some major changes in an effort to up-grade further its already excellent facilities and programs. Completed are a new home for the law school, a new student recreation center, a new baseball stadium, a new track and tennis stadium, and a new a 600-space parking garage; two new dorms, a complete renovation of existing dorms, a visual arts complex, a science building, and a home for the Latin American Studies program are in the works. Business, international studies, architecture, engineering, and English are reported to be the top programs here. All liberal arts students (everyone except engineers, architects, and business students) must complete a demanding core curriculum. Ethnic studies students offer negative comments about Tulane; "This institution REALLY does not cater to ETHNIC (nonwhite) students!!!" However, another student describes Tulane as "a comfortable-sized school in a good-sized city with personable teachers and plenty of help programs for students." Numerous counseling and tutoring options help prevent students from becoming just numbers on an attendance sheet.

Student Body

Tulane attracts a decent minority population, over half of which is made up of African Americans. Students call the student body diverse, but report that cliquishness prevails. Sometimes, this tendency leads to a segregated atmosphere. One student notes that "I'm concerned about how conservative and classist my fellow students are. Some are bluntly racist." The school draws students from nearly every state and ninety foreign countries, but the majority of students are southerners. This southern, well-groomed student can be off-putting to others. One student writes: "At first, I was put off by the general 'preppiness' of the student body but I've discovered many people who don't fit into the yuppie Eddie Bauer model. So my outlook has brightened considerably."

FINANCIAL AID: 504-865-5723   E-MAIL: UNDERGRAD.ADMISSION@TULANE.EDU   WEB SITE: HTTP://WWW.TULANE.EDU

ADMISSIONS

The admissions committee considers (in descending order of importance): HS record, class rank, test scores, recommendations, essay. *Also considered (in descending order of importance):* extracurriculars, alumni relationship, personality, special talents. Either the SAT or ACT is required. *High school units required/recommended:* 15 total units are recommended; 4 English recommended, 3 math recommended, 3 science recommended, 3 foreign language recommended, 2 social studies recommended. Strong college-preparatory program recommended; English units should include extensive reading and writing; math units should include algebra, geometry, trigonometry, and calculus or other advanced courses; 3 or 4 years of a single foreign language recommended; social studies should emphasize history. Even if academic requirements are met in first three years of secondary school, final year should include a minimum of 4 units of college-preparatory subjects. *Special Requirements:* TOEFL is required of all international students. Portfolio recommended of architecture program applicants.

The Inside Word

Tulane's applicant pool is highly national in origin, and very sound academically. The university's competitors include many of the best universities in the country, which tempers its selectivity significantly due to the loss of admitted students. Nonetheless, Tulane is an excellent choice for just about anyone looking for a quality institution that is on the move. Prestige and the value of a Tulane degree stand to increase as the South continues to grow in population and political influence.

FINANCIAL AID

Students should submit: FAFSA. The Princeton Review suggests that all financial aid forms be submitted as soon as possible after January 1. *The following grants/ scholarships are offered:* Pell, SEOG, academic merit, athletic, the school's own scholarships, state grants, ROTC, foreign aid. *Students borrow from the following loan programs:* Stafford, Perkins, PLUS, private loans. College Work-Study Program is available. Institutional employment is available.

FROM THE ADMISSIONS OFFICE

"With 5,000 full-time undergraduate students in five divisions, Tulane University offers the personal attention and teaching excellence traditionally associated with liberal arts colleges together with the facilities and interdisciplinary resources found only at major research universities—with both complemented by the exciting, historic setting of New Orleans, America's most interesting city. Senior faculty regularly teach introductory and lower-level courses, and 74 percent of the classes have twenty-five or fewer students. The close student-teacher relationship pays off. Tulane graduates are among the country's most likely to be selected for several prestigious fellowships that support graduate study abroad. Founded in 1834 and reorganized as Tulane University in 1884, Tulane is one of the major private research universities in the South. The Tulane campus offers a traditional collegiate setting in an attractive residential neighborhood."

ADMISSIONS

Admissions Rating	80
% of applicants accepted	73
% of acceptees attending	20

FRESHMAN PROFILE

Average verbal SAT	630
Average math SAT	620
Average ACT	29
Average TOEFL	600
Graduated top 20% of class	79
Graduated top 40% of class	89
Graduated top 60% of class	98
Average HS GPA or Avg.	NR

DEADLINES

Early decision	11/1
Regular admission	1/15
Regular notification	4/1
Non-fall registration	yes

APPLICANTS ALSO LOOK AT
AND OFTEN PREFER
Duke
Vanderbilt
Emory

AND SOMETIMES PREFER
U. Texas-Austin
Northwestern U.
Florida State
Washington U.

AND RARELY PREFER
Skidmore
SMU
U. Richmond
Rollins

FINANCIAL FACTS

Financial Aid Rating	94
Tuition	$19,700
Room & board	$6,312
Estimated book expense	$350
% frosh receiving aid	79
% undergrads receiving aid	74
% aid is need-based	80
% frosh w/ grant (avg)	58 ($14,858)
% frosh w/ loan (avg)	55 ($3,349)
% UGs w/ job (avg)	25 ($1,300)
Off-campus job outlook	fair

TUSKEGEE UNIVERSITY

TUSKEGEE, AL 36088   ADMISSIONS: 800-622-6531   FAX: 334-727-5276

CAMPUS LIFE

Quality of Life Rating	64
Type of school	private
Affiliation	none
Environment	town

STUDENTS

FT undergrad enrollment	2,990
% male/female	47/53
% from out of state	75
% live on campus	55
% spend weekend on campus	55
% transfers	NR
% from public high school	83
% in (# of) fraternities	6 (4)
% in (# of) sororities	5 (4)
% African-American	95
% Asian	0
% Caucasian	1
% Hispanic	2
% international	4
# of countries represented	36

WHAT'S HOT
old-fashioned dating
leftist politics
religion
sex
political activism

WHAT'S NOT
library
registration is a pain
inefficient administration
dorms
Tuskegee, AL

ACADEMICS

Academic Rating	72
Profs Interesting Rating	62
Profs Accessible Rating	66
Calendar	semester
Student/teacher ratio	13:1
% profs PhD	68
Hours of study per day	3.40

MOST POPULAR MAJORS
electrical engineering
biology
business administration

% GRADS WHO PURSUE...
Law 1, Med 2, MBA 3, MA 7

STUDENTS SPEAK OUT

Life

"We play video games, play cards, and watch TV. We talk about our future," writes a junior majoring in aerospace engineering of life at historic Tuskegee University. Indeed, students here say they enjoy each other's company and form close friendships. Tuskegee, Alabama is a sleepy town, and students feel that a car makes a big difference here: "If you don't have a car then you are out of luck." For those who do have cars, Auburn University and Atlanta are popular weekend destinations, as are events that bring Tuskegee students together with students from other historically black colleges, such as Freaknic in Atlanta and Black College Week in Daytona Beach. On campus, Greek life is very popular; fraternity and sorority parties are well attended and Greek Week draws a lot of attention. Students also look forward to Homecoming ("the best time of the year—the campus is overrun by many visitors, alumni, and thrill seekers") and an annual spring festival.

Academics

Founded by agricultural scientist Booker T. Washington over a century ago as Tuskegee Institute, Tuskegee University continues to prepare its mostly black student population for careers in the sciences, engineering, and the professions. The engineering program gets especially high marks, enrolling nearly a quarter of the student body. Education students enjoy the chance to student-teach at the kindergarten and Montessori classes right on campus. In all majors, incredibly small classes afford personal attention, and profs even make time after class to help individual students. A senior studying chemistry says of her profs, "They are good with one-on-one help." Another writes, "Many professors are excellent and class size is wonderful." Professors teach almost all classes, and class discussion is considered important here. Tuskegee students are studious: schoolwork takes up over 3 hours of the average student's day. Some students feel that the administration and the facilities could stand improvement, but even so, most praise their school: "The Tuskegee experience is like no other. We have our problems as all institutions of higher learning do, but the 'family' atmosphere here more than makes up for it." Indeed, students here value their choice to attend a traditionally black college and feel that Tuskegee is preparing them for the rest of their lives: "As far as establishing a sound African-American foundation for students, it's the best there is."

Student Body

"Our student body isn't the most racially diverse," states a senior studying biology, "but it is extremely socially diverse (geographically, financially, religiously), and the different groups interact well, providing a stimulating environment." Indeed, with African Americans making up over 90 percent of Tuskegee undergrads, it's the varied backgrounds of its mostly black students that lends diversity to the school. Whatever their backgrounds, students here get along well. "People are very friendly because [much] of the student body is southern," says one student, and another voices the popular consensus that "Everyone's pretty much a family here." Still, "there is some discrimination due to social class," and homophobia is a concern on campus, though not a pervasive problem.

FINANCIAL AID: 205-727-8210

ADMISSIONS

The admissions committee considers (in descending order of importance): test scores, HS record, class rank, recommendations, essay. *Also considered (in descending order of importance):* personality, extracurriculars, special talents. Either the SAT or ACT is required; SAT is preferred. *High school units required/recommended:* 16 total units are required; 4 English required, 3 math required, 2 science required, 3 social studies required. Minimum combined SAT I score of 800 and minimum 2.0 GPA required; combined SAT I score of 900 and 2.5 GPA recommended. *Special Requirements:* TOEFL is required of all international students. National League of Nursing exam required of nursing program applicants.

The Inside Word

Tuskegee University has a solid reputation, and draws a large pool of above-average candidates. Academic accomplishments in high school are first and foremost ingredients of a successful application for admission, but there is no doubt that the committee takes a close look at all aspects of candidate files. Don't downplay the importance of strong essays, recommendations, and a well-rounded extracurricular background.

FINANCIAL AID

Students should submit: FAFSA (due March 31), the school's own financial aid form (due March 31). The Princeton Review suggests that all financial aid forms be submitted as soon as possible after January 1. *The following grants/scholarships are offered:* Pell, SEOG, academic merit, athletic, the school's own scholarships, the school's own grants, state scholarships, state grants, private scholarships, private grants, federal nursing scholarship, ROTC, United Negro College Fund. *Students borrow from the following loan programs:* Stafford, unsubsidized Stafford, Perkins, PLUS, state loans, federal nursing loans, health professions loans. Applicants will be notified of awards beginning April 1. College Work-Study Program is available.

FROM THE ADMISSIONS OFFICE

"With distinctive strengths in the sciences, engineering and other professions, the University's basic mission is to provide educational programs of exceptional quality which promote the development of liberally prepared and professionally-oriented people. The University is rooted in a history of successfully educating black Americans to understand themselves against the background of their total heritage and the promise of their individual and collective future. A primary mission has been to prepare them to play effective professional and leadership roles in society and to become productive citizens in the national and world community. Tuskegee University continues to be dedicated to these broad aims."

ADMISSIONS

Admissions Rating	71
% of applicants accepted	70
% of acceptees attending	36

FRESHMAN PROFILE

Average verbal SAT	430
Average math SAT	480
Average ACT	NR
Average TOEFL	NR
Graduated top 20% of class	NR
Graduated top 40% of class	NR
Graduated top 60% of class	NR
Average HS GPA or Avg.	NR

DEADLINES

Early decision	NR
Regular admission	4/15
Regular notification	rolling
Non-fall registration	yes

APPLICANTS ALSO LOOK AT

AND SOMETIMES PREFER

Florida A & M
Spelman
Howard
Hampton
Alabama A&M

AND RARELY PREFER

U. Alabama
Auburn
Alabama State

FINANCIAL FACTS

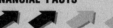

Financial Aid Rating	76
Tuition	$7,424
Room & board	$3,750
Estimated book expense	$600
% frosh receiving aid	90
% undergrads receiving aid	85
% aid is need-based	65
% frosh w/ grant (avg)	25 ($3,000)
% frosh w/ loan (avg)	NR
% UGs w/ job (avg)	65 ($1,540)
Off-campus job outlook	good

U.S. MILITARY ACADEMY

WEST POINT, NY 10996   ADMISSIONS: 914 938-4011   FAX: 914 938-3828

CAMPUS LIFE

Quality of Life Rating	**75**
Type of school	public
Affiliation	none
Environment	town

STUDENTS

FT undergrad enrollment	3,973
% male/female	88/12
% from out of state	92
% live on campus	100
% spend weekend on campus	95
% transfers	13
% from public high school	86
% African-American	7
% Asian	5
% Caucasian	83
% Hispanic	4
% international	1
# of countries represented	19

WHAT'S HOT
different students interact
school runs like butter
health facilities
honesty
intramural sports

WHAT'S NOT
Highland Falls
drugs
sex
beer
hard liquor

ACADEMICS

Academic Rating	**94**
Profs Interesting Rating	96
Profs Accessible Rating	98
Calendar	semester
Student/teacher ratio	NR
% profs PhD	34
Hours of study per day	3.49

MOST POPULAR MAJORS
engineering
social sciences
mathematical and physical sciences

% GRADS WHO PURSUE...
Law 5, Med 5, MA 80

STUDENTS SPEAK OUT

Life

The United States Military Academy is the training ground for the women and men who will one day be given the keys to our national security. In the hallowed halls of West Point, future generations of Eisenhowers and Schwarzkopfs learn how to "selflessly serve God and country" and train in hand-to-hand combat and modern warfare. Cadets are blessed with serious perks. "We have the opportunity to try most anything that interests us (i.e., rock climbing, parachuting)," explains a senior. They also get to use live ammunition. Overall, the cadets of West Point say they relish the challenges of officer training even though there is precious little freedom or down time. Life here is "strict, but in a good way." West Point "teaches you how to entertain yourself without the use of alcohol or drugs. Students here strive for a loftier goal than just passing their classes; they strive to serve their country." It's no day at the beach. Cadets must lead a very disciplined life (first-years—or "plebes"—have it especially rough), and the academic and physical demands can be exhausting. "Life at West Point is very regimented. We don't have much leeway in what we do. We cannot leave the campus except on weekends and holidays." Army chow and cramped, uncomfortable dorms don't help. The town outside the gates, Highland Falls, is small, so even when cadets do leave campus, there is very little to do. Luckily, New York City is only an hour away.

Academics

The academic atmosphere at West Point is rigorous. Cadets hit the books for nearly four hours each day. "Minimal effort here is comparable to a lot of effort at any other school," asserts a senior. Cadets heap praise on their "top notch, but tough" professors who are "always available" for extra help. "They are very competent and concerned that we succeed," explains one cadet. Professors are demanding, though, and they have broad latitude to punish students who break the rules. "Tardiness, rudeness, or falling asleep in class is not allowed." One candid senior relates, "there are two levels of instruction here: what you should do (academics) and what you wish you had done (disciplinary repercussions)." As you might expect, "the administration runs this university like clockwork." Registration is a breeze, and the facilities boast the most state-of-the-art technology in the world. "Plebes" begin Cadet Basic Training the summer before classes start. The following summer, cadets participate in artillery, air defense, and military field exercises, then it's off to Kentucky for armor training. During the summer before junior year, cadets study mountain warfare in Vermont and winter warfare in Alaska, take airborne training in Georgia, and practice survival techniques in the Colorado wilderness. Upon graduation, cadets are commissioned as Second Lieutenants in the U.S. Army and must serve a minimum of five years of active duty.

Student Body

West Point is the first stop on the road to glory for over 1,100 aspiring military leaders each year. Cadets describe themselves as people who hate to lose and are "smart, hard-working, driven, dedicated, and career-minded." Oh, and "funny." Politically, most cadets lean toward the right politically—not shocking since "it is a military school" after all. "Minority discrimination does not occur because it is simply not allowed here," declares a senior. There is "a very strong sense of camaraderie" among the cadets of West Point. "The spirit of cooperation is high" reports one cadet. "The saying is 'cooperate and graduate'", says another. West Point cadets form bonds that will last the rest of their lives. "I love my classmates," sums up a senior. "I would die for them in battle."

FINANCIAL AID: 914-938-3516

WEB SITE: HTTP://WWW.USMA.EDU/

ADMISSIONS

The admissions committee considers (in descending order of importance): test scores, class rank, HS record, recommendations, essay. *Also considered (in descending order of importance):* extracurriculars, personality, special talents. Either the SAT or ACT is required. *High school units required/recommended:* 19 total units are recommended; 4 English recommended, 4 math recommended, 2 science recommended, 2 foreign language recommended, 3 social studies recommended, 1 history recommended. Applicants must obtain a nomination from an approved source (Congress, the President, Vice President, or Department of the Army). All entrants must be at least 17 years of age and not yet 22 on July 1 of year of entry. All applicants must be unmarried U.S. citizens (foreign nationals with approval) in good health with no parental obligations or responsibilities and must demonstrate leadership ability. Applicant should seek nomination and submit Service Academies Precandidate Questionnaire in spring of 11th year. Applicants are advised to seek nominations from as many sources as possible and to contact the Admissions Office between July 1 and January 15 of 12th year. TOEFL is required of all international students.

The Inside Word

Students considering a candidacy at West Point need to hit the ground running in the second half of their junior year. Don't delay initiating the application and nomination processes; together they constitute a long, hard road that includes not one, but several highly competitive elements. Successful candidates must demonstrate strength both academically and physically, be solid citizens and contributors to society, and show true fortitude and potential for leadership. Admissions processes at other top schools can seem like a cakewalk compared to this, but those who get a nomination and pass muster through the physical part of the process have made it through the hardest part.

FROM THE ADMISSIONS OFFICE

As a young man or woman considering your options for obtaining a quality college education, you may wonder what unique aspects the United States Military Academy has to offer. West Point offers one of the most highly respected, quality education programs in the nation. A West Point cadetship includes a fully funded four-year college education. Tuition, room, board, medical and dental care are provided by the U.S. Army. As members of the Armed Forces, cadets also receive an annual salary of more than $6,500. This pay covers the cost of uniforms, books, a personal computer, and living incidentals. By law, graduates of West Point are appointed on active duty as commissioned officers and serve in the U.S. Army for a minimum of five years.

Each year the United States Military Academy admits 1,150 to 1,200 young men and women. These new members of the cadet corps come from all corners of the United States and represent nearly every race, religion and culture in the country. Nurtured by the West Point environment, this diversity of background helps cadets gain a cultural as well as a rich educational experience.

ADMISSIONS

Admissions Rating	99
% of applicants accepted	13
% of acceptees attending	72

FRESHMAN PROFILE

Average verbal SAT	630
Average math SAT	650
Average ACT	28
Average TOEFL	NR
Graduated top 20% of class	79
Graduated top 40% of class	96
Graduated top 60% of class	99
Average HS GPA or Avg.	NR

DEADLINES

Early decision	12/1
Regular admission	3/21
Regular notification	NR
Non-fall registration	no

APPLICANTS ALSO LOOK AT

AND OFTEN PREFER

U. Rochester

AND SOMETIMES PREFER

US Naval Acad.
U. Notre Dame
Villanova U.
Tulane U.
U. Oklahoma

AND RARELY PREFER

U. Florida
Carnegie Mellon U.

FINANCIAL FACTS

Financial Aid Rating	99
In-state tuition	$0
Out-of-state tuition	$0
Room & board	$0
Estimated book expense	$700
% frosh receiving aid	NR
% undergrads receiving aid	NR
% aid is need-based	NR
% frosh w/ grant (avg)	NR
% frosh w/ loan (avg)	NR
% UGs w/ job (avg)	NR

U.S. NAVAL ACADEMY

LEAHY HALL, ANNAPOLIS, MD 21402-5018   ADMISSIONS: 410 293-1000

STUDENTS SPEAK OUT

Life

The U. S. Naval Academy prepares its students (known as midshipmen) for life on the high seas with a rigorous academic and military training program. As a result, the future leaders who attend the academy are extremely busy: "We have about 30 hours' worth of activities in a 24-hour day." No doubt about it, life is very demanding here, but things get better after the first year. Opinion is unanimous that "Plebe year (first year) is the hardest." Soon after entering the gate on Induction Day (the first week in July), students don uniforms and commence a "frantic and exhausting" period of summer military training to get ready for the academic year and learn to "think under pressure." Relations with upperclassmen are "tough," and "most freshmen and sophomores go to their sponsor family's home during free time." Students stress that theirs is not the typical college experience: "it's hard to consider this place a school," as one puts it. Midshipmen are encouraged to participate in several intercollegiate and intramural athletics, and to get involved in clubs, bands, and choirs. The historic town of Annapolis gets high marks for its attractiveness and good food, making up somewhat for the dormitories that are currently under renovation. But the bottom line is that students at Annapolis know what they're here for—"service to our country"—and find their training to be the best entertainment: "For fun, we shoot guns, drive ships, jump out of airplanes, and navigate submarines. We practice our future jobs."

Academics

The U.S. Naval Academy offers a great education at a great price—it's free. Midshipmen have one of the "toughest academic programs around," yet the "outstanding" professors are "always willing and ready to help in every way possible." Classes are small and are all taught by faculty members. "Tough but rewarding" is how one midshipman sums up his experience here. "If you've never been challenged by academics, get ready for a surprise." Midshipmen must handle a demanding courseload along with naval officer training, and academically they find that "it's a challenge to do well on top of all the military responsibilities." Facilities are absolutely state-of-the-art, and the administration, as might be expected, runs a tight, efficient ship. The innovative core curriculum balances technical and non-technical subjects and has received national acclaim: As one midshipman remarks, "This is the only place I know where history majors are required to take electrical engineering, calculus, and physics courses." All students, regardless of major, are awarded a bachelor of science degree upon graduation.

Student Body

Midshipmen form strong bonds with one another. "We're very close because we depend on each other. No one can make it through this school alone." The overall impression is that "students get along extremely well"; one midshipman reports that the Academy feels like "the biggest fraternity in the world." The Academy boasts that nearly 20% of its Midshipmen are members of minority groups. And once an all-male bastion, the Naval Academy currently claims well over 500 women within its ranks. Recently, the position of Brigade Commander—the biggest kahuna of all midshipmen—was held by a woman.

U.S. NAVAL ACADEMY

ADMISSIONS

The admissions committee considers (in descending order of importance): class rank, HS record, test scores, recommendations, essay. *Also considered (in descending order of importance):* extracurriculars, geographical distribution, personality, alumni relationship, special talents. Either the SAT or ACT is required; SAT is preferred. An interview is required. *High school units required/recommended:* 15 total units are recommended; 4 English recommended, 4 math recommended, 4 science recommended, 2 foreign language recommended, 1 history recommended. Applicants must be at least age 17 and not yet age 22 on July 1 of year of admission, and be unmarried U.S. citizens (except for limited quota of foreign students), with no parental obligations or responsibilities. Highly competitive admissions process. Minimum SAT I scores of 600 in both verbal and math (ACT scores of 22 English and 26 math), and rank in top fifth of secondary school class recommended. *Special Requirements:* TOEFL is required of all international students. Strict medical qualifications required of Navy and Marine Corps applicants for commissioning standards upon graduation.

The Inside Word

It doesn't take a genius to recognize that getting admitted to Annapolis requires true strength of character; simply completing the arduous admissions process is an accomplishment worthy of remembrance. Those who have successful candidacies are strong, motivated students, and leaders in both school and community. Perseverance is an important character trait for anyone considering the life of a midshipman—the application process is only the beginning of a truly challenging and demanding experience.

FROM THE ADMISSIONS OFFICE

"The Naval Academy offers you a unique opportunity to associate with a broad cross-section of the country's finest young men and women. You will have the opportunity to pursue a four-year program that develops you mentally, morally, and physically as no civilian college can. As you might expect, this program is demanding, but the opportunities are limitless and more than worth the effort. To receive an appointment to the academy, you need four years of high school preparation to develop the strong academic, athletic, and extracurricular background required to compete successfully for admission. You should begin preparing in your freshman year and apply for admission at the end of your junior year. Selection for appointment to the Academy comes as a result of a complete evaluation of your admissions package and completion of the nomination process."

ADMISSIONS

Admissions Rating	99
% of applicants accepted	14
% of acceptees attending	79

FRESHMAN PROFILE

Average verbal SAT	630
Average math SAT	650
Average ACT	27
Average TOEFL	NR
Graduated top 20% of class	78
Graduated top 40% of class	95
Graduated top 60% of class	99
Average HS GPA or Avg.	3.7

DEADLINES

Early decision	NR
Regular admission	3/1
Regular notification	NR
Non-fall registration	no

APPLICANTS ALSO LOOK AT

AND OFTEN PREFER

Harvard/Radcliffe
Duke
Stanford
U. Virginia
US Air Force Acad.

AND SOMETIMES PREFER

US Military Acad.
Georgia Tech.
Massachusetts Tech.
Penn State
U. Michigan

AND RARELY PREFER

Purdue U.
Boston U.

FINANCIAL FACTS

Financial Aid Rating	99
Tuition	$0
Room & board	$0
Estimated book expense	$0
% frosh receiving aid	NR
% undergrads receiving aid	NR
% aid is need-based	NR
% frosh w/ grant (avg)	NR
% frosh w/ loan (avg)	NR
% UGs w/ job (avg)	NR

UNION COLLEGE (NY)

SCHENECTADY, NY 12308

ADMISSIONS: 518-388-6112   FAX: 518-388-6986

STUDENTS SPEAK OUT

Life

Social life at Union College pretty much fits the stereotype for a small school in an unexciting town. Social opportunities are limited, with fraternities providing the setting for most of the socializing. Says one student, "If you don't like fraternity parties, don't come here." The development of a healthy dating scene is hindered by the lopsided male/female ratio, as men outnumber women. Drinking is a very popular way to spend free time, as are occasional road trips to Saratoga Springs. Schenectady is not popular with students, who rank it the seventh-worst college town in the nation. The campus is "absolutely breathtaking," and the dorms are comfortable, although the lack of kitchen facilities drives many students to off-campus housing. Students sharing common interests take houses together. Explains one student, "The best feature is the houses...I have learned firsthand what they have to offer: friendship, support, and a very strong environment. Our motto is: 'We do more after midnight than most people do all day.'"

Academics

One Union student reports that "this school offers just about everything a large school does, without all of the people." Indeed, two of Union's great assets are its comfortable size and diverse programs: the school's 2,000 undergrads pursue a wide variety of career-oriented and liberal arts studies. Engineering is popular and excellent, as are the premedical majors. Political science, history, economics, and English are among the favorite liberal arts departments. The school recently instituted a core curriculum that requires all students to acquire a comprehensive education in Western culture, as well as a grounding in math and the sciences. Classes are small and, best of all, the professors are extremely accessible. "When professors offer their home phone numbers so you can get help over the weekend, you know you're getting your money's worth," reports one student. Several students remark on the Term Abroad program, which half of Union's students take advantage of. Says one, "I spent my junior fall semester in Bath, England. It was a fabulous experience. I can't imagine another school offering a better program." Students give the library low marks, but repairs and expansion are underway, according to administrators. A new theater has also been added to the campus. The school's trimester schedule means that the school year does not end until June.

Student Body

As one Union student puts it, "The student body is overly homogenous but students are very friendly and down-to-earth." There is a small minority population, but, "for the most part, students of different cultures stick closely together. We say we want to teach each other about our different cultures but it is mostly talk...how sad." Some students seem overwhelmed by the fraternity scene. Comments one frustrated sophomore, "They lose their individuality as a result of the Greek system." The school's pricey tuition guarantees that a lot of undergrads are from affluent families.

ADMISSIONS

The admissions committee considers (in descending order of importance): HS record, class rank, recommendations, essay, test scores. *Also considered (in descending order of importance):* extracurriculars, personality, special talents, alumni relationship, geographical distribution. An interview is recommended. Admissions process is need-blind. *High school units required/recommended:* 16 total units are required; 4 English required. 2-1/2 units of math and 2 units of foreign language required of liberal arts program applicants. Intermediate algebra, plane geometry, trigonometry, chemistry, and physics required of engineering program applicants. 3-1/2 units of math required of seven-year B.S./M.D. program applicants. TOEFL is required of all international students. *The admissions office says:* "The goal of the admissions process is to bring together [students] who will have general educational impact on each other, in and out of class. A strong academic track record is certainly necessary. We have designed our application process to allow students to highlight their candidacies as 'whole people.'"

The Inside Word

In this age of MTV-type admissions videos and ultraglossy promotional literature, Union is decidedly more low-key than most colleges. The College is a bastion of tradition and conservatism, and sticks to what it knows best when it comes to recruitment and admission. Students who are thinking about Union need to be prepared with as challenging a high school curriculum as possible and solid grades across the board. The ACT is the easier and less costly of the standardized testing options, but as with most highly selective Northeastern colleges offering such a choice, it is wise to proceed with caution—few of these admissions committees are as experienced in interpreting ACT scores as they are in evaluating SAT Is or SAT IIs.

FINANCIAL AID

Students should submit: FAFSA, CSS Profile, the school's own financial aid form (due May 1), state aid form. The Princeton Review suggests that all financial aid forms be submitted as soon as possible after January 1. *The following grants/scholarships are offered:* Pell, SEOG, the school's own scholarships, the school's own grants, state scholarships, state grants, private scholarships, private grants. *Students borrow from the following loan programs:* Stafford, Perkins, PLUS, the school's own loan fund, private loans. Applicants will be notified of awards beginning March 30. College Work-Study Program is available. Institutional employment is available.

FROM THE ADMISSIONS OFFICE

"Union College is an independent, primarily undergraduate, residential college for men and women of high academic promise and strong personal motivation. Throughout its history Union has been distinguished by its commitment to the idea that both experience and reflection are necessary to a proper education. In the past, that commitment was evidenced when Union became the first liberal arts college to offer engineering. Today, that commitment is reflected in our nationally recognized General Education Curriculum, which combines elements of choice within a structure of requirements and incentives; our extensive Terms Abroad program, which attracts 50 percent of our students; and our vigorous encouragement of undergraduate research."

ADMISSIONS

Admissions Rating	**76**
% of applicants accepted	52
% of acceptees attending	28

FRESHMAN PROFILE

Average verbal SAT	600
Average math SAT	640
Average ACT	27
Average TOEFL	NR
Graduated top 20% of class	75
Graduated top 40% of class	97
Graduated top 60% of class	100
Average HS GPA or Avg.	NR

DEADLINES

Early decision	NR
Regular admission	2/1
Regular notification	4/1
Non-fall registration	no

APPLICANTS ALSO LOOK AT

AND OFTEN PREFER

Brown
Hamilton

AND SOMETIMES PREFER

Tufts
SUNY Buffalo
Cornell U.
St. Lawrence
Franklin & Marshall

AND RARELY PREFER

Connecticut Coll.
Lehigh

FINANCIAL FACTS

Financial Aid Rating	**83**
Tuition	$19,782
Room & board	$6,234
Estimated book expense	$450
% frosh receiving aid	60
% undergrads receiving aid	57
% aid is need-based	99
% frosh w/ grant (avg)	55 ($13,000)
% frosh w/ loan (avg)	56 ($3,400)
% UGs w/ job (avg)	41 ($952)
Off-campus job outlook	good

URSINUS COLLEGE

Box 1000 Main Street, Collegeville, PA 19426   Admissions: 610-489-4111   Fax: 610-489-0627

STUDENTS SPEAK OUT

Life

Ursinus is a very small liberal arts college in Collegeville, a very small town located just outside of Philadelphia, a very big city. Says one undergrad, "Life is fun, we go to parties, movies, shopping, and occasionally study!" One place you'd better like being is your dorm room, because unless you live with your parents, you must live in a dorm for your entire Ursinus career. Luckily, Ursinus has 29 different halls and houses that hold between 5 and 250 students. There's even a "quiet hall" if you need that extra silence to finish your homework. Food at the dorms, unfortunately, is pretty bad. Greek life is big at Ursinus, and even if you're not Greek, many parties are open to the entire student body. And if there's a party, there's most likely beer and liquor flowing freely (although the administration has been trying to crack down on alcohol on campus). Pot is also popular in Collegeville. Many other activities center around Wismer Hall, the meeting place on the beautiful 150-acre Ursinus campus.

Academics

Six years ago Ursinus instituted a liberal studies curriculum to ensure that all undergrads receive a quality general education along with their chosen major. Encompassing English, math, science, and foreign languages, the liberal studies curriculum may be one of the reasons that three out of four eventually go to grad or professional school. One problem the required curriculum causes, however, is that "it is impossible to get all the classes you want. There is very little flexibility in scheduling." The administration is very involved in each student's education, something many students appreciate. "The administration forms personal relationships with students, they get involved in a positive way." Profs are also given high marks. "Professors are very accessible both on and off campus," explains one sophomore. One reason for this accessibility is the small class sizes, with large lectures rarely hitting 100 students, and most enrolling 50 or fewer. Lab and computer facilities are both given high marks, while Myrin Library fares a little worse. Ursinus also offers study abroad programs in Mexico, Japan, France, and Spain.

Student Body

There is a word for the Ursinus student body that many students use themselves. It is "homogenous." At such a small school that is so predominantly white, minority students are few in number. Still, racial discrimination is not seen as a big problem on campus. Says one minority student, "I haven't experienced racial tension or discrimination." However, another adds "Because Ursinus is such a small school, everyone seems to label each other from the beginning. Many cliques form, making it feel like high school all over again." Another chimes in, "Very cliquey—most everyone is broken up into respective groups: Greeks, athletes, bio majors, etc." Interaction among different groups is indeed low. Even with these problems, however, most describe the student body as friendly and easy to get along with, and few allow it to get in the way of dating, which is big on campus, and sexual activity, which is even more popular.

FINANCIAL AID: CALL ADMISSIONS   E-MAIL: ADMISSIONS@URSINUS.EDU   WEB SITE: HTTP://WWW.URSINUS.EDU

ADMISSIONS

The admissions committee considers (in descending order of importance): HS record, test scores, class rank, recommendations, essay. *Also considered (in descending order of importance):* extracurriculars, special talents, alumni relationship, geographical distribution, personality. Either the SAT or ACT is required; SAT is preferred. An interview is recommended. Admissions process is need-blind. *High school units required/recommended:* 14 total units are required; 20 total units are recommended; 4 English required, 3 math required, 1 science required, 2 foreign language required, 1 social studies required. TOEFL is required of all international students. *The admissions office says:* "Personality, motivation, and activities are considered. Rank in the top fifth of high school graduating class is preferred."

The Inside Word

Unless you are academically inconsistent or other colleges are also asking for them, there is little reason to take SAT II Subject Tests for admission to Ursinus. Four-fifths of those who apply get in, and grades and rank count for more than anything else.

FINANCIAL AID

Students should submit: FAFSA, state aid form (due February 15). The Princeton Review suggests that all financial aid forms be submitted as soon as possible after January 1. *The following grants/scholarships are offered:* Pell, SEOG, academic merit, the school's own scholarships, the school's own grants, state grants, foreign aid. *Students borrow from the following loan programs:* Stafford, Perkins, PLUS, state loans, private loans. Applicants will be notified of awards beginning April 1. College Work-Study Program is available. Institutional employment is available.

FROM THE ADMISSIONS OFFICE

"Located one-half hour from center-city Philadelphia, the college boasts a beautiful 140-acre campus which includes the Residential Village (renovated Victorian-style homes which decorate the Main Street and house our students), and the nationally recognized Berman Museum of Art. Ursinus is a member of the Centennial Conference, competing both in academics and in intercollegiate athletics with institutions such as Dickinson, Franklin and Marshall, Gettysburg, and Muhlenberg. The academic environment is enhanced with such fine programs as a chapter of Phi Beta Kappa, an Early Assurance Program to Medical School with the Medical College of Pennsylvania, and myriad student exchanges both at home and abroad. A heavy emphasis is placed upon student research— an emphasis which can only be carried out with the one-on-one attention Ursinus students receive from their professors."

ADMISSIONS

Admissions Rating	74
% of applicants accepted	77
% of acceptees attending	28

FRESHMAN PROFILE

Average verbal SAT	590
Average math SAT	580
Average ACT	NR
Average TOEFL	550
Graduated top 20% of class	68
Graduated top 40% of class	90
Graduated top 60% of class	97
Average HS GPA or Avg.	88.0

DEADLINES

Early decision	NR
Regular admission	2/15
Regular notification	4/1
Non-fall registration	yes

APPLICANTS ALSO LOOK AT

AND OFTEN PREFER

Swarthmore
Princeton
Brown

AND SOMETIMES PREFER

Villanova
Penn State-U. Park
Rutgers U.
St. Joseph's U.
Muhlenberg

FINANCIAL FACTS

Financial Aid Rating	91
Tuition	$15,650
Room & board	$5,160
Estimated book expense	NR
% frosh receiving aid	82
% undergrads receiving aid	80
% aid is need-based	90
% frosh w/ grant (avg)	71 ($8,421)
% frosh w/ loan (avg)	65 ($3,430)
% UGs w/ job (avg)	50 ($1,000)
Off-campus job outlook	good

VALPARAISO UNIVERSITY

ADMISSIONS OFFICE, KRETZMANN HALL, VALPARAISO, IN 46383-6493   ADMISSIONS: 800-348-2611   FAX: 219-464-5381

CAMPUS LIFE

Quality of Life Rating	74
Type of school	private
Affiliation	Lutheran Church
Environment	suburban

STUDENTS

FT undergrad enrollment	2,755
% male/female	44/56
% from out of state	61
% live on campus	62
% spend weekend on campus	85
% transfers	16
% from public high school	80
% in (# of) fraternities	32 (10)
% in (# of) sororities	23 (8)
% African-American	4
% Asian	2
% Caucasian	87
% Hispanic	2
% international	4
# of countries represented	39

WHAT'S HOT
religion
Greeks
old-fashioned dating
music associations
honesty

WHAT'S NOT
library
health facilities
political activism
students are cliquish
unattractive campus

ACADEMICS

Academic Rating	81
Profs Interesting Rating	81
Profs Accessible Rating	83
Calendar	semester
Student/teacher ratio	12:1
% profs PhD/tenured	81/81
Hours of study per day	3.14

MOST POPULAR MAJORS
nursing
business administration
education

% GRADS WHO PURSUE...
Law 1, Med 1, MBA 1, MA 20

STUDENTS SPEAK OUT

Life

The Greek system dominates life outside the classroom at Valparaiso University. Over 40 percent of the students pledge a fraternity or sorority. Indeed, for better or for worse, most students tend to agree that "socially, Greek life is all there is." Strict drug, alcohol, and intervisitation policies and "lame" campus-sponsored activities don't help matters much. According to one student, "There is nothing to do if you are under 21 unless you go to frat parties." Another confesses, "We go to the frats to have beer." Students who don't enjoy the fraternity scene still keep themselves entertained, though. "Life at Valpo is what you make it. If you want to get involved, you can!" Religious organizations and student government provide two of the most popular extracurricular alternatives. Geographically, the Valparaiso campus receives high marks for safety and ease of navigation. The surrounding town of Valparaiso offers bars, shopping, and "many tasty restaurants." However, as many students are quick to point out, that's about all it offers. Life in rural Indiana can get "boring on the weekends." Several students also complain about the weather, but none of them seem to be doing anything about it. Luckily, the bright lights of Chicago are only about an hour away by car.

Academics

Valparaiso's greatest strength lies in its ability to offer a broad variety of majors across four different colleges (Arts & Sciences, Nursing, Business, and Engineering) while still managing to provide its students with the flexibility, small classes, and personal attention found at small liberal arts colleges. And while Valparaiso definitely caters to career-oriented students, it provides a well-rounded undergraduate education. Nearly all students must complete core freshman courses and a senior seminar, and fulfill an array of liberal arts requirements before graduating. This best-of-both-worlds approach is a hit with students. As far as they are concerned, Valparaiso is a "first rate" and "very prestigious" university that offers a "fabulous academic experience" and "the best education money can buy." What else is the cause of all this student satisfaction? Well, it certainly isn't the library, which students rate dreadfully low. Instead, and without a doubt, the outstanding and dedicated faculty share the blame. "Our professors are extremely helpful; they are here for the students first and the research second," declares one junior. "The faculty here are downright cool and great motivators," explains a senior. And student after student maintains that profs are "always willing to give extra assistance." Unfortunately, however, this fond embrace of authority does not extend so completely to the administration. Although a few students insist that they do "a magnificent job of accommodating students," the administration is generally perceived as "out of touch" and reactionary.

Student Body

Valparaiso is comprised of a "huge majority of Anglo students," most of whom know each other. In general, "a strong sense of community" permeates campus life. The majority of Valpo students are "turtleneck-wearing conservatives." The university is affiliated with the Lutheran church, and religion maintains a noticeable (though by no means predominant) presence on campus. Dating and sexual activity are popular pastimes with the student population. Still, many complain about being inhibited by the overall social atmosphere. As one student so aptly sums up, "Students are too reserved. They need to loosen up. Toga! Toga! Toga!"

FINANCIAL AID: 219-464-5015

ADMISSIONS

The admissions committee considers (in descending order of importance): HS record, class rank, test scores, recommendations, essay. *Also considered (in descending order of importance):* extracurriculars, personality, alumni relationship, geographical distribution, special talents. Either the SAT or ACT is required. An interview is recommended. Admissions process is need-blind. *High school units required/recommended:* 4 English recommended, 3 math recommended, 2 science recommended, 2 foreign language recommended, 2 social studies recommended, 1 history recommended. *Special Requirements:* An audition is required for music program applicants. TOEFL is required of all international students.

The Inside Word

Valparaiso admits the vast majority of those who apply, but candidates should not be overconfident. Places like this fill a special niche in higher education, and spend a good deal of time assessing the match a candidate makes with the University, even if the expected better-than-average high school record is present. Essays and extracurriculars can help you get admitted if your transcript is weak.

FINANCIAL AID

Students should submit: FAFSA (due March 1), state aid form. The Princeton Review suggests that all financial aid forms be submitted as soon as possible after January 1. *The following grants/scholarships are offered:* Pell, SEOG, academic merit, athletic, the school's own scholarships, the school's own grants, state grants, private scholarships, private grants, foreign aid. *Students borrow from the following loan programs:* Perkins, PLUS, the school's own loan fund, supplemental loans, private loans. Applicants will be notified of awards beginning March 15. College Work-Study Program is available. Institutional employment is available.

FROM THE ADMISSIONS OFFICE

"As a Lutheran-affiliated university, Valparaiso has a sincere sense of values and purpose. The University is dedicated to academic excellence within the framework of our Christian commitment. This is demonstrated by the concern of our faculty and administration for the total well-being of our students."

ADMISSIONS

Admissions Rating	75
% of applicants accepted	86
% of acceptees attending	34

FRESHMAN PROFILE

Average verbal SAT	570
Average math SAT	570
Average ACT	25
Average TOEFL	NR
Graduated top 20% of class	56
Graduated top 40% of class	82
Graduated top 60% of class	94
Average HS GPA or Avg.	NR

DEADLINES

Early decision	NR
Regular admission	NR
Regular notification	rolling
Non-fall registration	yes

APPLICANTS ALSO LOOK AT

AND OFTEN PREFER

Indiana U.-Bloomington
Purdue U.-West Lafayette
U. Illinois-Urbana-Champ.

AND SOMETIMES PREFER

Marquette
Illinois State
Augustana (IL)
Western Illinois
U. Indianapolis

FINANCIAL FACTS

Financial Aid Rating	78
Tuition	$13,510
Room & board	$3,450
Estimated book expense	$500
% frosh receiving aid	79
% undergrads receiving aid	79
% aid is need-based	60
% frosh w/ grant (avg)	70 ($5,100)
% frosh w/ loan (avg)	70 ($3,625)
% UGs w/ job (avg)	35 ($900)
Off-campus job outlook	fair

VANDERBILT UNIVERSITY

2305 WEST END AVENUE, NASHVILLE, TN 37203-1700 ADMISSIONS: 615-322-2561 FAX: 615-343-5555

CAMPUS LIFE

Quality of Life Rating	87
Type of school	private
Affiliation	none
Environment	metropolis

STUDENTS

FT undergrad enrollment	5,792
% male/female	54/46
% from out of state	87
% live on campus	86
% spend weekend on campus	NR
% transfers	2
% from public high school	59
% in (# of) fraternities	38 (17)
% in (# of) sororities	50 (12)
% African-American	4
% Asian	7
% Caucasian	80
% Hispanic	3
% international	2
# of countries represented	47

WHAT'S HOT
health facilities
registration is a breeze
off-campus food
Greeks
hard liquor

WHAT'S NOT
students are cliquish
lack of diversity on campus
theater
music associations
college radio

ACADEMICS

Academic Rating	89
Profs Interesting Rating	79
Profs Accessible Rating	83
Calendar	semester
Student/teacher ratio	8:1
% profs PhD/tenured	97/43
Hours of study per day	3.62

MOST POPULAR MAJORS
human/org. development
English
psychology

% GRADS WHO PURSUE...
Law 11, Med 10, MBA 11, MA 26

STUDENTS SPEAK OUT

Life

As one student puts it, "Vanderbilt University can be the ideal situation for college or your worst nightmare. When you arrive as a freshman, you pretty much deduce within weeks if you love it or hate it." To love it, you have to love (or be able to ignore) a very active Greek scene that defines many students' social lives. One student explains that "this campus is segregated into a Greek and non-Greek faction, and there is unfortunately little social activity outside the Greek system for students under twenty-one." The Greeks have been so dominant a force that Vandy's administration works with the Greeks to help control the problems associated with hazing and alcohol. Reports one student, "The party scene and the Greek scene have been actively toned down by the administration, and a happy result of this is that more of us are exploring Nashville (the 'hip' Nashville, not the 'country' Nashville)." Drinking is a popular pastime. Writes one, "While this school is tough academically, it's also very social. Parties start on Tuesdays, except during test weeks." Reports from campus, however, cite a "significant" growing minority of students who do not drink. Students praise the Student Recreation Center ("it's incredible—the majority of students work out all the time!"), and the campus. The most often cited negative: the Nashville weather. Advises one undergrad, "Bring your umbrella."

Academics

Students at Vanderbilt claim the best of both worlds: top-notch academics (nearly half the school's graduates proceed to graduate school) and a friendly, laid-back Southern atmosphere. "There is a sense of academic excellence here," writes one undergraduate, "but without cutthroat competition." It's the kind of place where students can admit to studying over three hours a day, then turn around and report that "academic pressure is virtually nonexistent, unless one places it on one's self." A smooth-running administration nurtures this atmosphere, as do approachable, caring professors. "Dedicated" is a word several respondents use to describe the faculty. Writes one student, "Professors are so accessible, many of them welcome students to their homes." Students favor preprofessional studies, but a broad-ranging core curriculum covers writing, humanities, mathematics, and natural and social sciences. Prebusiness majors, such as economics, are both popular and strong, as are the premedical sciences, engineering, English, and psychology.

Student Body

One Vandy student describes her classmates as "a microcosm of the country club set, a cult of Southern gentility and graciousness cut off from the 'real world.'" The generalization is fairly accurate, but is becoming less so every year because of efforts to recruit a more diverse student body. Several students report that the school is becoming "much less conservative and less homogenous." Still, Vandy has one of the nation's most politically and socially conservative student bodies, and more than a few students say they want it to remain that way.

FINANCIAL AID: 615-322-3591   E-MAIL: ADMISSIONS@VANDERBILT.EDU   WEB SITE: HTTP://WWW.VANDERBILT.EDU

ADMISSIONS

The admissions committee considers (in descending order of importance): HS record, test scores, recommendations, class rank, essay. *Also considered (in descending order of importance):* personality, special talents, alumni relationship, extracurriculars. Either the SAT or ACT is required; SAT is preferred. Admissions process is need-blind. *High school units required/recommended:* 15 total units are required; 20 total units are recommended; 4 English required, 4 English recommended, 3 math required, 4 math recommended, 2 science required, 3 science recommended, 2 foreign language required, 4 foreign language recommended, 3 social studies recommended. Additional unit requirements vary by school. *Special Requirements:* An audition is required for music program applicants. TOEFL is required of all international students. *The admissions office says:* "For students who apply to the Blair School of Music, an audition is the primary factor in the application. Required high school curriculum: Four years of English, two years of a foreign language, and three years of mathematics. It is recommended that engineering applicants complete an additional year of math and two years of science."

The Inside Word

Vanderbilt's strong academic reputation has positioned the university among the most selective in the South. Despite an admissions process that is largely formulaic, the applicant pool is competitive enough so that students should not downplay the importance of submitting strong essays and recommendations—they make the difference for some candidates.

FINANCIAL AID

Students should submit: FAFSA, CSS Profile, the school's own financial aid form (due February 15), state aid form, a copy of parents' most recent income tax filing. The Princeton Review suggests that all financial aid forms be submitted as soon as possible after January 1. *The following grants/scholarships are offered:* Pell, SEOG, academic merit, athletic, the school's own scholarships, the school's own grants, state scholarships, state grants, private scholarships, private grants, ROTC. *Students borrow from the following loan programs:* Stafford, unsubsidized Stafford, Perkins, PLUS, the school's own loan fund, state loans, private loans. College Work-Study Program is available. Institutional employment is available.

FROM THE ADMISSIONS OFFICE

"Exceptional accomplishment and high promise in some field of intellectual endeavor are essential. The student's total academic and nonacademic record is reviewed in conjunction with recommendations and personal essays. For students at Blair School of Music, the audition is a prime consideration."

ADMISSIONS

Admissions Rating	86
% of applicants accepted	58
% of acceptees attending	30

FRESHMAN PROFILE

Average verbal SAT	700
Average math SAT	650
Average ACT	28
Average TOEFL	570
Graduated top 20% of class	52
Graduated top 40% of class	60
Graduated top 60% of class	61
Average HS GPA or Avg.	3.5

DEADLINES

Early decision	11/1
Regular admission	1/15
Regular notification	4/1
Non-fall registration	yes

APPLICANTS ALSO LOOK AT

AND OFTEN PREFER

U. Virginia
Princeton
Notre Dame
Cornell U.
Georgetown

AND SOMETIMES PREFER

Duke
Emory
Wake Forest
Northwestern
Dartmouth

AND RARELY PREFER

Tulane
Washington U.
Boston Coll.
SMU

FINANCIAL FACTS

Financial Aid Rating	82
Tuition	$19,920
Room & board	$7,088
Estimated book expense	$690
% frosh receiving aid	55
% undergrads receiving aid	53
% aid is need-based	62
% frosh w/ grant (avg)	51 ($13,200)
% frosh w/ loan (avg)	39 ($4,431)
% UGs w/ job (avg)	35 ($1,068)
Off-campus job outlook	good

VASSAR COLLEGE

RAYMOND AVENUE, POUGHKEEPSIE, NY 12601   ADMISSIONS: 914-437-7300   FAX: 914-437-7187

CAMPUS LIFE

Quality of Life Rating	72
Type of school	private
Affiliation	none
Environment	suburban

STUDENTS

FT undergrad enrollment	2,253
% male/female	38/62
% from out of state	68
% live on campus	98
% spend weekend on campus	90
% transfers	4
% from public high school	60
% African-American	6
% Asian	9
% Caucasian	77
% Hispanic	5
% international	NR
# of countries represented	29

WHAT'S HOT
theater
drugs
cigarettes
campus is beautiful
support groups

WHAT'S NOT
town-gown relations
Poughkeepsie
infrequent dating
Greeks
religion

ACADEMICS

Academic Rating	90
Profs Interesting Rating	87
Profs Accessible Rating	90
Calendar	semester
Student/teacher ratio	11:1
% profs PhD/tenured	90/95
Hours of study per day	3.14

MOST POPULAR MAJORS
English
political science
art

% GRADS WHO PURSUE...
Law 9, Med 5, MBA 3, MA 13

STUDENTS SPEAK OUT

Life

Vassar College is close to New York City, in both geography and spirit. The college is quite cosmopolitan, and there is some tension between Vassar and the neighboring industrial town of Poughkeepsie. One student reports that "the people at Vassar are trying to move the city-sophisticate attitude from New York City into a very economically depressed community. Maybe that's why there isn't much communication between the city and the college." The campus itself is "incredible," and students enjoy the social life available there. The mood is "generally cheery" and students like the fact that people "support everything you do, from experimenting with drugs to not drinking at a keg party." The male/female ratio is still nearly 1:2 even after years of coeducation (Vassar was once an all-women's school), but the neurotic dating scene on campus still draws criticism. One student asserts that dating at Vassar is "typified by those who seem married and those who sleep around, leaving little room for the more casual, yet less promiscuous approach." Several respondents point out that there are many social options and activities on campus, including "a wide range of clubs, lectures, and movies when one needs to get closer to or farther away from the people here." And, of course, there's always New York City.

Academics

According to one counselor, Vassar is a school that "the students adore." Its academics are first-rate and geared toward the preferences of students: enthuses one, "The lack of a core curriculum enables me to major in sociology with a molecular biology correlate, and still go premed." Many students design their own majors and are given free rein to explore and grow academically ("The top-flight teaching staff has given me a passion for study I never knew was there," writes one student). Professors are extremely accessible; most, in fact, live on campus. Says one student, "I like the fact that two professors live in each dorm. They are often seen at ACDC (All-Campus Dining Center), where sharing meals with students is commonplace." Courses are generally small, and liberal arts departments are still the best here, especially English and art history. The visual and performing arts are also popular, particularly drama. The library wins raves for its aesthetic appeal and conduciveness to study.

Student Body

"If the college would pay as much attention to diversity of students as they do to the landscape, we would be very multicultural," writes one Vassar student. The truth is, it does and they are. Vassar has good minority representation, and students are proud of their "microcosm of America." There are strong, visible gay and alternative communities (some even believe "it is becoming 'in' to be bisexual at Vassar"), and "issues like homosexuality and race relations are full-blown." Says one student, "Vassar offers a little bit of everything: Democrats, hippies, gays, feminists, conservatives, fascists, communists, activists, and people with no opinion are all rampant here."

ADMISSIONS

The admissions committee considers (in descending order of importance): HS record, essay, recommendations, class rank, test scores. *Also considered (in descending order of importance):* extracurriculars, special talents, personality, alumni relationship, geographical distribution. Either the SAT or ACT is required; SAT is preferred. An interview is recommended. Admissions process is need-blind. *High school units required/recommended:* 4 English recommended, 3 math recommended, 2 science recommended, 3 foreign language recommended, 3 social studies recommended, 1 history recommended. *Special Requirements:* TOEFL is required of all international students. Audiotape recommended of music program applicants. Portfolio recommended of art program applicants. *The admissions office says:* "There are no rigid requirements as to secondary school programs, and patterns vary, but Vassar expects candidates to have elected the most demanding courses available. Ordinarily, the candidate should have had four years of English, including both literature and continuous practice in writing; at least three years of mathematics; at least two years of laboratory science; three years of social science with a minimum of one year of history; and three years of one ancient or modern foreign language or two years of one language and two of a second. Additional work should be elected in fully credited academic subjects in the humanities, the natural and social sciences, and the arts. Students should take some portion of their work in enriched or honors courses or in the CEEB Advanced Placement Program where they are available. Special attention is given to the academic content of the program candidates select in the senior year."

The Inside Word

Vassar is relatively frank about its standards; you won't get much more direct advice from colleges about how to get admitted. The admissions process here follows very closely the practices of most prestigious Northeastern schools. Your personal side—essays, extracurriculars, interview, etc.—is not going to do a lot for you if you don't demonstrate significant academic accomplishments. Multiple applicants from the same high school will be compared against each other as well as the entire applicant pool, and candidates from prep schools have an advantage over public school grads. Males and minorities are actively courted by the admissions staff, and the College is sincere in its commitment.

FINANCIAL AID

Students should submit: FAFSA (due January 1), the school's own financial aid form (due January 1), a copy of parents' most recent income tax filing (due January 1). The Princeton Review suggests that all financial aid forms be submitted as soon as possible after January 1. *The following grants/scholarships are offered:* Pell, SEOG, the school's own scholarships, state scholarships, state grants, private scholarships, private grants, foreign aid. *Students borrow from the following loan programs:* Stafford, Perkins, PLUS, the school's own loan fund. Applicants will be notified of awards beginning in early April. College Work-Study Program is available. Institutional employment is available.

FROM THE ADMISSIONS OFFICE

"Vassar presents a rich variety of social and cultural activities, clubs, sports, living arrangements, and regional attractions. Vassar is a vital, residential college community recognized for its respect for the rights and individuality of others."

ADMISSIONS

Admissions Rating	91
% of applicants accepted	48
% of acceptees attending	33

FRESHMAN PROFILE

Average verbal SAT	680
Average math SAT	650
Average ACT	29
Average TOEFL	600
Graduated top 20% of class	80
Graduated top 40% of class	99
Graduated top 60% of class	NR
Average HS GPA or Avg.	NR

DEADLINES

Early decision	NR
Regular admission	1/1
Regular notification	early April
Non-fall registration	no

APPLICANTS ALSO LOOK AT

AND OFTEN PREFER

Wesleyan U.
Brown

AND SOMETIMES PREFER

Barnard
Northwestern U.
Middlebury Coll.

AND RARELY PREFER

Skidmore
Union (NY)

FINANCIAL FACTS

Financial Aid Rating	82
Tuition	$19,940
Room & board	$6,150
Estimated book expense	$650
% frosh receiving aid	63
% undergrads receiving aid	62
% aid is need-based	100
% frosh w/ grant (avg)	51 ($15,201)
% frosh w/ loan (avg)	62 ($2,765)
% UGs w/ job (avg)	60 ($950)
Off-campus job outlook	fair

UNIVERSITY OF VERMONT

194 SOUTH PROSPECT STREET, BURLINGTON, VT 05405-3596   ADMISSIONS: 802-656-3370   FAX: 802-656-8432

STUDENTS SPEAK OUT

Life

Burlington, Vermont, home of the University of Vermont, has been described as the ideal college town. Students here are in love with this clean and picturesque city, and rank it among the top fifteen percent of college sites. No wonder so many students flock here from neighboring Massachusetts and Connecticut; Burlington is "a small city with big-city opportunities (concerts, malls, people) and small-town hospitality, safety, and fun." Nearby are all the benefits of rural Vermont: skiing, mountain biking, hiking, climbing, and other outdoor pastimes are very accessible and popular among students. Explains one student, "If you can't find students in the library on a Saturday or Sunday, then they're probably on the slopes." UVM's campus is beautiful as well, and most are happy living there; dorms are within easy walking distance of both classes and downtown. Sports are, predictably, a big draw. Greek life, while popular, is not a dominant force on campus. As successful as it is academically, UVM is also a big party school. Drinking is a very popular pastime, and a large "pseudo-hippie" contingent guarantees the availability of pot and countless Grateful Dead bootlegs. However, balance is the key: "If you want to party, ski, and have fun, go to UVM. But if you want to stay, you've got to work HARD!!!"

Academics

UVM toes the precarious line between good academics and good parties—and for the most part manages to succeed at both. Students here study more than the average, and attend classes more regularly than is usual at large state schools. Students give their professors relatively high grades for in-class teaching skills and out-of-class accessibility (again, no small feat at a large university). UVM is particularly strong in health- and environment-related areas. "The Environmental Studies program is fantastic!" reports one major. Business and management majors are also popular, as are psychology and political science. As at most state universities, many courses are overcrowded, and registration is annoying at best ("Classes are always full, especially English," writes one undergrad); students find the school poorly run and the administration "a source of dismay." One student contends, "Intro classes have the consistency of Cheez Whiz—they go down easy, they taste horrible, and they are not good for you." However, UVM's overall academic reputation is quite good, and deservedly so. Its strong record has attracted many non-Vermont residents ("flatlanders"), despite a hefty out-of-state fee.

Student Body

Diversity is not one of UVM's assets: all but a handful of students are white. Politically, students are conservative and basically uninvolved. Although there is a fairly visible gay presence on campus, tolerance of gay students is low. One student further complains that UVM "is still extremely sexist. It needs more women faculty in all departments and more attention paid to women's issues and sexual crimes on campus." Most students encounter no big problems, however, and describe their classmates as "laid-back and extremely friendly."

ADMISSIONS

The admissions committee considers (in descending order of importance): HS record, class rank, test scores, recommendations, essay. *Also considered (in descending order of importance):* alumni relationship, extracurriculars, geographical distribution, special talents. Either the SAT or ACT is required; SAT is preferred. An interview is recommended. *High school units required/recommended:* 16 total units are required; 4 English required, 3 math required, 2 science required, 2 foreign language required, 3 social studies required. Additional electives strongly recommended; nonacademic electives may be counted. Qualified in-state applicants accepted first; out-of-state applicants then accepted on competitive basis. *Special Requirements:* TOEFL is required of all international students. Trigonometry required of business, engineering, mathematics, physical therapy, and science program applicants; biology, chemistry, and physics required of physical therapy program applicants; chemistry and physics required of engineering program applicants; biology and chemistry required of professional nursing program applicants. Audition required of music performance program applicants.

The Inside Word

UVM is one of the most popular public universities in the country, and its admissions standards are significantly more competitive for out-of-state students. Nonresidents shouldn't get too anxiety-ridden about getting in; more than half of the student body comes from elsewhere. Candidates with above-average academic profiles should be in good shape.

FINANCIAL AID

Students should submit: FAFSA, the school's own financial aid form, a copy of parents' most recent income tax filing. The Princeton Review suggests that all financial aid forms be submitted as soon as possible after January 1. *The following grants/scholarships are offered:* Pell, SEOG, academic merit, athletic, the school's own scholarships, the school's own grants, state grants, private scholarships, private grants, ROTC. *Students borrow from the following loan programs:* Stafford, unsubsidized Stafford, PLUS, the school's own loan fund, state loans, federal nursing loans, health professions loans, private loans. Applicants will be notified of awards beginning March 15. College Work-Study Program is available. Institutional employment is available.

FROM THE ADMISSIONS OFFICE

"The University of Vermont was founded in the classic tradition: with a primary emphasis on liberal arts and undergraduate education. UVM has since expanded to include eight colleges and schools: Arts & Sciences, Agriculture & Life Sciences, Allied Health, Business, Education & Social Services, Engineering & Math, Natural Resources, Nursing, as well as a highly respected medical school and a graduate college. Each of our professional programs combines a broad educational background with specialized training for its students. As a medium sized public university with 8,000 undergraduates and 1,500 graduates and medical students, UVM offers students the best of a large, comprehensive university environment, with a small college atmosphere. If you are up to the challenge of our academics, if you are concerned about the environment, if you enjoy being physically active, and if you are interested in being involved in our community, take a close look at the University of Vermont. We can offer you a lot."

ADMISSIONS

Admissions Rating	71
% of applicants accepted	81
% of acceptees attending	29

FRESHMAN PROFILE

Average verbal SAT	560
Average math SAT	560
Average ACT	NR
Average TOEFL	550
Graduated top 20% of class	36
Graduated top 40% of class	78
Graduated top 60% of class	96
Average HS GPA or Avg.	NR

DEADLINES

Early decision	NR
Regular admission	2/1
Regular notification	3/15
Non-fall registration	yes

APPLICANTS ALSO LOOK AT

AND OFTEN PREFER

Dartmouth
U. Colorado-Boulder
Cornell U.
Middlebury Coll.
Brown

AND SOMETIMES PREFER

SUNY Binghamton
Boston Coll.
Boston U.
Tufts
Colby

AND RARELY PREFER

Bates
U. Rochester
Skidmore

FINANCIAL FACTS

Financial Aid Rating	69
In-state tuition	$6,210
Out-of-state tuition	$15,512
Room & board	$5,198
Estimated book expense	$500
% frosh receiving aid	53
% undergrads receiving aid	58
% aid is need-based	98
% frosh w/ grant (avg)	40 ($4,027)
% frosh w/ loan (avg)	54 ($4,867)
% UGs w/ job (avg)	27 ($1,680)
Off-campus job outlook	good

VILLANOVA UNIVERSITY

800 LANCASTER AVENUE, VILLANOVA, PA 19085   ADMISSIONS: 610-519-4500   FAX: 610-519-7599

STUDENTS SPEAK OUT

Life

The quality of life at Villanova University leaves a lot to be desired. The school is located in an affluent suburb of Philadelphia, and many students complain that "local residents despise Villanova students. The local police have nothing else to keep them busy so they search out off-campus parties with a vengeance." To make things worse, on-campus housing is in short supply, and off-campus residences welcoming students are scarce. It's a problem partly created by the Roman Catholic-affiliated school's strict dorm policies: dorms are single sex, and much-resented visitation rules are enthusiastically enforced (note: the school has one coed dormitory). These rules along with drinking regulations force all partying to off-campus residences. VU students party hard, so it's no wonder local landlords don't actively seek them as tenants. The social scene centers on drinking and can get pretty monotonous. Writes one student, "Social life is lacking for anyone who doesn't dig the cliquish sorority/fraternity scene. For a person like me, getting to Philadelphia is virtually my only hope of salvation from this pit of boredom." On the positive side, "Access to Philadelphia is excellent (two trains on campus) and relatively quick (30 minutes)." Also, VU students have a tremendous amount of school spirit, nurtured by the school's fanatically supported athletic teams.

Academics

The students at Villanova report that their school "places a definite emphasis on spiritual and personal growth." Although non-Catholics also attend VU, the influence of the Augustinian fathers who govern the school is felt everywhere, from the well-attended daily Masses to the strict dorm policies. VU's business subdivision, the College of Commerce and Finance, is the school's best, although, as one student reports, "The nursing program is one of the best in the state," and the engineering school is also good. Students warn that "There is no communication between colleges and departments." Among other negatives: "The school's administration sometimes act like they're going to convict some students of heresy when they try to make any small changes." On the positive side, "Professors are extremely helpful in class and whenever I need anything explained in or outside the classroom." Concludes one student, "Because Villanova is a liberal arts college, I feel that I've received a broad education, which should provide a sturdy base for whatever I choose to do in the future."

Student Body

Villanova students rank themselves among the least diverse student bodies profiled in this book. Says one, "There is a definite need for more diversity. This student body is like one big bowl of vanilla ice cream, with a couple of chocolate chips." Students are conservative politically, but mostly they just don't care. VU students also rank among the nation's least interested in politics. The atmosphere here, explains one student, is "very uptight; also, everyone has a tendency to be rather clone-like J. Crew wannabes."

ADMISSIONS

The admissions committee considers (in descending order of importance): HS record, class rank, test scores, recommendations, essay. *Also considered (in descending order of importance):* alumni relationship, extracurriculars, geographical distribution, personality, special talents. Either the SAT or ACT is required; SAT is preferred. An interview is required of some applicants. Admissions process is need-blind. *High school units required/recommended:* 16 total units are required; 4 English required, 3 math required, 4 math recommended, 2 science required, 3 science recommended, 2 foreign language required, 1 social studies required, 2 history required. *Special Requirements:* Interview required of pre-dental, pre-optometry, allied health, and accelerated medical school program applicants.

The Inside Word

Villanova has a very solid and growing reputation among Catholic universities nationally, yet is significantly less competitive for admissions than the top tier of schools like Georgetown, Notre Dame, and Boston College. If Villanova is your first choice, be careful. As is the case at many universities, Early Action applicants face dramatically higher academic standards than those for the regular pool. The University is a very sound option, whether high on your list of choices or as a safety school.

FINANCIAL AID

Students should submit: FAFSA, the school's own financial aid form, a copy of parents' most recent income tax filing. The Princeton Review suggests that all financial aid forms be submitted as soon as possible after January 1. *The following grants/scholarships are offered:* Pell, SEOG, academic merit, athletic, the school's own scholarships, the school's own grants, state scholarships, state grants, private scholarships, private grants, ROTC. *Students borrow from the following loan programs:* Stafford, Perkins, PLUS, state loans, federal nursing loans, private loans. Applicants will be notified of awards beginning April 1. College Work-Study Program is available. Institutional employment is available.

FROM THE ADMISSIONS OFFICE

"It is sometimes difficult to find a college or university that is absolutely right for you. Maybe you're looking for a school that offers a wide choice of academic programs and has a reputation for solid academic quality. You probably want a friendly, small-campus atmosphere with faculty that give personal attention to every student, preferably with the cultural attractions of a big campus and close to a major city. A high-quality student body is also important...You will want to make recreation and fun an important part of your college experience, too. Finding all this at one campus can be tough; but it's all here at Villanova...Our goal at Villanova is to help each student realize his and her full potential for development, with the added hope that each one also grows in staunch independence of mind and in generous commitment to the service of God, society, and our fellow humans."

ADMISSIONS

Admissions Rating	79
% of applicants accepted	74
% of acceptees attending	28

FRESHMAN PROFILE

Average verbal SAT	600
Average math SAT	600
Average ACT	NR
Average TOEFL	550
Graduated top 20% of class	57
Graduated top 40% of class	89
Graduated top 60% of class	99
Average HS GPA or Avg.	NR

DEADLINES

Early decision	12/1
Regular admission	1/15
Regular notification	4/1
Non-fall registration	no

APPLICANTS ALSO LOOK AT

AND OFTEN PREFER
Georgetown U.

AND SOMETIMES PREFER
Boston Coll.
Fordham
Holy Cross
St. Joseph's U.
Dickinson

AND RARELY PREFER
Seton Hall
U. Rhode Island
Trenton State
Gettysburg

FINANCIAL FACTS

Financial Aid Rating	74
Tuition	$17,500
Room & board	$6,300
Estimated book expense	$500
% frosh receiving aid	68
% undergrads receiving aid	67
% aid is need-based	70
% frosh w/ grant (avg)	56 ($13,170)
% frosh w/ loan (avg)	52 ($4,744)
% UGs w/ job (avg)	18 ($1,500)
Off-campus job outlook	excellent

VIRGINIA TECH

BLACKSBURG, VA 24061-0202   ADMISSIONS: 540-231-6267   FAX: 540-231-7826

STUDENTS SPEAK OUT

Life

Virginia Tech is situated on a huge, beautiful campus. One student reports that she has "fallen in love with Tech's campus. It's set near Jefferson National Park and the Appalachian Mountains. Our hokey stone buildings give an appearance of an Ivy League college, but we also have the quiet country atmosphere." Says another, "The campus seems very big at first, but the longer you are here and the more people you meet, the smaller it gets." City slickers may feel out of place here, but for the outdoorsy types, "There are tons of things to do nearby: the New River (tubing, rafting, kayaking), the Cascades, Mountain Lake (Dirty Dancing was filmed there), good campsites, hiking trails, snow skiing, the list is endless." Students tell us they get along well with the people of Blacksburg and give the town slightly better than average grades. Fraternities and sororities are popular, and there's a fair amount of drinking. Intramural and intercollegiate sports are also enjoyed by many. A small number of students are enrolled in the Corps of Cadets, a military outfit.

Academics

Virginia Tech is not just a technical school. In fact, according to one undergrad, "When it comes to variety of majors, classes, people, activities, almost anything, Tech is the best school in the state. You name it, Tech has it!" Other students are less cocky, deferring to the University of Virginia by calling their school "Virginia's other great university." With over 18,000 undergraduates, Tech has the resources to offer undergraduates programs in just about any field of study. Technical and preprofessional programs are the most popular: almost one quarter of the students pursue engineering degrees. Students here work hard (says one, "My advice is to hit the books hard from the beginning"), but they must not mind that much, because they rank high in overall happiness. Virginia Tech does have its share of problems. Professors receive subpar grades for both in-class performance and accessibility. One student explains: "Virginia Tech is a research-oriented school. That fact unfortunately shows up in the quality of the teaching. There is a lot of knowledge here, and resources are available, but they are not complemented with communication between professors and students." Upperclassmen remark that professors are more attentive to their needs than they were when they were sophomores and freshmen. Students give the library very high marks, and give the administration average grades, which is good: administrators at large schools almost invariably receive poor grades.

Student Body

Three quarters of Virginia Tech's students come from Virginia, and most of the rest come from nearby states. Most students are white, but there are also decent-sized Asian and African-American populations. Students are conservative and very dedicated to their studies. Says one about his classmates, "People here are generally very nice and very down-to-earth."

ADMISSIONS

The admissions committee considers (in descending order of importance): HS record, class rank, test scores, recommendations, essay. *Also considered (in descending order of importance):* geographical distribution, alumni relationship, extracurriculars, personality, special talents. Either the SAT or ACT is required; SAT is preferred. Admissions process is need-blind. *High school units required/recommended:* 18 total units are required; 4 English required, 3 math required, 2 science required, 1 social studies required, 1 history required. Lab science units must be in biology, chemistry, or physics. 4 units of mathematics and 3 units of lab science required for engineering and science-related program applicants. Minimum 2.0 GPA required; higher GPA recommended. *Special Requirements:* A portfolio is required for art program applicants. An audition is required for music program applicants. TOEFL is required of all international students. Portfolio required of B.A. or B.F.A. studio art applicants. *The admissions office says:* "Admission to Virginia Tech is selective. We look for a strong B to B+ average in college preparatory courses, including English, advanced math, and lab sciences. Students who have challenged themselves in high school are much more likely to receive an offer of admission and to succeed at Virginia Tech."

The Inside Word

When compared to applying to UVA or William and Mary, getting into Virginia Tech is a cakewalk. Tech has a great reputation, which from a careerist point of view makes it well worth considering.

FINANCIAL AID

Students should submit: FAFSA (due February 1), the school's own financial aid form (due February 1), state aid form (due February 1), a copy of parents' most recent income tax filing (due February 1). The Princeton Review suggests that all financial aid forms be submitted as soon as possible after January 1. *The following grants/scholarships are offered:* Pell, SEOG, academic merit, athletic, the school's own scholarships, the school's own grants, state scholarships, state grants, private scholarships, private grants, ROTC. *Students borrow from the following loan programs:* Stafford, unsubsidized Stafford, Perkins, PLUS, the school's own loan fund, health professions loans, private loans. Applicants will be notified of awards beginning April 15. College Work-Study Program is available. Institutional employment is available.

FROM THE ADMISSIONS OFFICE

"At Virginia Tech, more than 19,000 undergraduate students choose from over 75 majors in seven colleges: Agriculture & Life Sciences, Architecture & Urban Studies, Arts & Sciences (the largest), Business, Engineering, Forestry and Wildlife Resources, Education, and Human Resources. More than 400 student organizations—including academic, social, and religious clubs; student government and media; and special-interest groups—thrive on campus. At Virginia's largest university, students have unlimited opportunities. But they also benefit from a low student/teacher ratio (17:1) and a variety of academic programs such as Honors and CO-OP. Virginia Tech offers the best of both worlds in an ideal environment—southwest Virginia's Blue Ridge Mountains."

ADMISSIONS

Admissions Rating	75
% of applicants accepted	79
% of acceptees attending	32

FRESHMAN PROFILE

Average verbal SAT	580
Average math SAT	690
Average ACT	NR
Average TOEFL	600
Graduated top 20% of class	60
Graduated top 40% of class	92
Graduated top 60% of class	98
Average HS GPA or Avg.	3.0

DEADLINES

Early decision	11/1
Regular admission	2/1
Regular notification	4/15
Non-fall registration	yes

APPLICANTS ALSO LOOK AT

AND OFTEN PREFER

Georgia Tech.
Virginia

AND SOMETIMES PREFER

James Madison
George Mason
William and Mary
Hampton

AND RARELY PREFER

Radford
Penn State-U. Park
U. Tennessee-Knoxville
Randolph-Macon Woman's

FINANCIAL FACTS

Financial Aid Rating	73
In-state tuition	$3,500
Out-of-state tuition	$10,152
Room & board	$3,250
Estimated book expense	$800
% frosh receiving aid	64
% undergrads receiving aid	45
% aid is need-based	65
% frosh w/ grant (avg)	72 ($2,500)
% frosh w/ loan (avg)	95 ($2,625)
% UGs w/ job (avg)	17 ($1,500)
Off-campus job outlook	good

UNIVERSITY OF VIRGINIA

P.O. Box 9017, Charlottesville, VA 22906   Admissions: 804-982-3200   Fax: 804-924-0938

CAMPUS LIFE

Quality of Life Rating 77
Type of school   public
Affiliation   none
Environment   suburban

STUDENTS

FT undergrad enrollment	11,861
% male/female	47/53
% from out of state	34
% live on campus	48
% spend weekend on campus	NR
% transfers	17
% from public high school	77
% in (# of) fraternities	30 (39)
% in (# of) sororities	30 (22)
% African-American	11
% Asian	10
% Caucasian	75
% Hispanic	2
% international	NR
# of countries represented	39

WHAT'S HOT

student publications
beer
Greeks
hard liquor
intercollegiate sports

WHAT'S NOT

town-gown relations
students are cliquish
campus food
political activism
students are unhappy

ACADEMICS

Academic Rating	87
Profs Interesting Rating	68
Profs Accessible Rating	71
Calendar	semester
Student/teacher ratio	11:1
% profs tenured	90
Hours of study per day	3.23

MOST POPULAR MAJORS

commerce
English
psychology

STUDENTS SPEAK OUT

Life

Movies set at idealized universities might very well model their settings after University of Virginia. The grounds are beautiful, the dorms are livable, and the students are well dressed, clean scrubbed, and good looking. In fact, UVA is so meticulous about its campus that one student complains: "They'll slash our budget and reduce the number of courses available to an ever-growing number of students, but you'd better believe all the leaves will be raked up." An honor and judicial system "that works" deals with the problem of cheating: Students caught can either withdraw from school or go before a jury of their peers. School spirit is very big here: Students refer to themselves as Cavaliers (after the sports teams) or "hoos" (short for "wahoos") and dress up to go to sporting events, which are extremely popular. UVA has long had a reputation as a party school, and its students continue to maintain that tradition. Fraternities and sororities play a major role in social life, as does drinking.

Academics

Founded by Thomas Jefferson, UVA is a state-affiliated university with a reputation most private schools would envy. U.S. News & World Report ranked it among the nation's twenty-five best: among state schools, only UC-Berkeley ranked higher. Most state universities accept over two thirds of their applicants; UVA rejects over two thirds. UVA offers a tremendously diverse array of programs, and many of those programs are among the best in the country. English, religious studies, engineering, history, and government are the best known, but academics are uniformly excellent. What's more, students receive more personal attention from their professors than do others at large universities. One environmental science major reports, "I just transferred from a small, private liberal arts college, and the amount of attention I've received from professors here exceeds what I got there tenfold. I can't imagine the professors anywhere being more dedicated to the success of their students." While most state-funded schools are, at best, adequately run, at this one students actually like their deans and administrators, and the library is also excellent. About the only real complaint we hear concerning academics is that lecture classes tend to be large.

Student Body

There is a 21 percent minority population here, but the students are the first to admit that the student body is segregated. Preppie attire is de rigueur, and a social, if not political, conservatism is pervasive. Still, students of every demographic group are measurably happier here than their average counterparts elsewhere. Explains one, "Although the student body itself isn't very well integrated, something about being a student here does tie us all together. I know it sounds corny to non-Cavaliers, but something pervasive and contagious is alive and well in Hoo-ville. I won't call it Mr. Jefferson's spirit, but it is something that settles into your heart first year and never leaves. At worst, it'll make you wear orange pants (one of the school's colors). At best, it'll hum in the back of your thoughts for the rest of your life."

ADMISSIONS

The admissions committee considers (in descending order of importance): HS record, class rank, test scores, essay, recommendations. *Also considered (in descending order of importance):* geographical distribution, alumni relationship, extracurriculars, personality, special talents. Either the SAT or ACT is required; SAT is preferred. Admissions process is need-blind. *High school units required/recommended:* 16 total units are required; 4 English required, 4 math required, 2 science required, 2 foreign language required, 1 social studies required. More competitive requirements for out-of-state applicants. *Special Requirements:* TOEFL is required of all international students. Chemistry and physics required of engineering program applicants.

The Inside Word

Even many Virginia residents regard trying to get into UVA as a feeble attempt. The competition doesn't get much more severe, and only the most capable and impressive candidates stand to be offered admission. The volume of out-of-state applications borders on enormous when considered in conjunction with available spots in the entering class. Those who do give it a shot won't encounter the world's most personal and compassionate admissions process.

FINANCIAL AID

Students should submit: FAFSA, the school's own financial aid form, a copy of parents' most recent income tax filing. The Princeton Review suggests that all financial aid forms be submitted as soon as possible after January 1. *The following grants/scholarships are offered:* Pell, SEOG, academic merit, athletic, the school's own scholarships, the school's own grants, state scholarships, state grants, private scholarships, private grants, ROTC. *Students borrow from the following loan programs:* unsubsidized Stafford, Perkins, PLUS, supplemental loans, federal nursing loans. Applicants will be notified of awards beginning April 1. College Work-Study Program is available. Institutional employment is available.

FROM THE ADMISSIONS OFFICE

"Admission to competitive schools requires strong academic credentials. Students who stretch themselves and take rigorous courses (honors level and Advanced Placement courses, when offered) are significantly more competitive than those who do not. Experienced admission officers know that most students are capable of presenting superb academic credentials, and the reality is that a very high percentage of those applying do so. Other considerations, then, come into play in important ways for academically strong candidates, as they must be seen as 'selective' as well as academically competitive."

ADMISSIONS

Admissions Rating	91
% of applicants accepted	37
% of acceptees attending	50

FRESHMAN PROFILE

Average verbal SAT	650
Average math SAT	650
Average ACT	NR
Average TOEFL	600
Graduated top 20% of class	56
Graduated top 40% of class	60
Graduated top 60% of class	60
Average HS GPA or Avg.	NR

DEADLINES

Early decision	12/1
Regular admission	1/2
Regular notification	4/1
Non-fall registration	no

APPLICANTS ALSO LOOK AT

AND OFTEN PREFER

Duke
Georgetown U.

AND SOMETIMES PREFER

William and Mary
UNC-Chapel Hill
Virginia Tech

AND RARELY PREFER

George Washington
Bucknell
Boston U.

FINANCIAL FACTS

Financial Aid Rating	78
In-state tuition	$3,832
Out-of-state tuition	$13,140
Room & board	$3,846
Estimated book expense	$600
% frosh receiving aid	48
% undergrads receiving aid	38
% aid is need-based	95
% frosh w/ grant (avg)	40 ($5,950)
% frosh w/ loan (avg)	32 ($4,600)
% UGs w/ job (avg)	18 ($1,400)
Off-campus job outlook	fair

WABASH COLLEGE

P.O. Box 352, Crawfordsville, IN 47933-0352 ADMISSIONS: 800-345-5385 FAX: 317-364-4424

STUDENTS SPEAK OUT

Life

There's a lot of lofty talk about values among students at Wabash College, an "extremely difficult and prestigious" all-male enclave in rural Indiana. The school's emphasis on "a tradition of commitment" allows "the student to feel like an important part of the college and its history." Students promise to abide by the Gentleman's Rule: "A Wabash man will conduct himself at all times, both on and off campus, as a gentleman and a responsible citizen." When they aren't hitting the books or aspiring to such high water marks, students do pursue leisurely endeavors. Wabash is a "big drinking school" with a huge Greek presence (almost 3 in 4 undergrads belong to fraternities). "We study hard during the week but party hard during the weekend," a Wabash man explains. Though somewhat limited, social opportunities outside of Greek life are available. "From chapel-singing to just fishing with some friends before class, life at Wabash is well worth living." Varsity and intramural athletics enjoy understandable popularity. Still, students gripe that the town of Crawfordsville is ho-hum at best, and relations with "townies" are strained. These qualms notwithstanding, Wabash is outstanding "if you can live without women for a little while." Admits one sophomore, "some of us drink a lot and perform self-gratifying acts because of the lack of women." That may be more information than we wanted to know.

Academics

Wabash offers a profoundly rewarding academic experience that "challenges students to a high degree of competition and self-improvement." But it's not for the faint-hearted. To put it mildly, "Wabash is a bit more focused and rigorous than most liberal arts institutions." The course load is "very hectic. If you want an easy ride, look elsewhere. As Wabash says: 'It won't be easy; it will be worth it.'" Students must complete a required core of liberal arts courses, fulfill a major concentration, and pass comprehensive written and oral examinations in order to graduate. Classes are very small and students heap praise on their professors, whose attentiveness and caring offset the intense academic demands. "The professors here will fight for you," maintains one student. Another asserts, "Professors here are very helpful in every aspect. You'll look around and find guys standing around talking with them, or just hanging out with them." Students also give rave reviews to the library, the computer facilities, the class registration process, and even the administration, which runs the school "like a well-oiled machine." And although the majority of Wabash men spend four or more hours studying outside of class each day, they are convinced that it is worth it. "Wabash is a unique experience for young men where tradition, academics, arts, science, and sports combine to change the entering freshman into a mature young man ready to succeed in the world."

Student Body

Wabash students "smell bad, drink too much, fight a lot, and are probably ten times smarter and better prepared for post-graduate life" than students at other schools. Most Wabash men are conservative "good ol' boys" who interact splendidly, provided they aren't "too busy studying or drinking." A student explains, "There will be a preppy football player living in the same house as a coffee-sipping poet, and they get along. The college does unique things to people." Save for a notable prevalence of gay discrimination, genuine animosity is mostly confined to rival fraternities and is "usually dealt with amicably." Wabash men also stick together; a network of tightly-knit alums provides grads with "good connections in the business, professional, and graduate school worlds."

FINANCIAL AID: 317-361-6370

WEB SITE: HTTP://RUBY.WABASH.EDU

ADMISSIONS

The admissions committee considers (in descending order of importance): HS record, class rank, test scores, recommendations, essay. *Also considered (in descending order of importance):* personality, alumni relationship, extracurriculars, geographical distribution, special talents. Either the SAT or ACT is required; SAT is preferred. An interview is recommended. Admissions process is not need-blind. *High school units required/recommended:* 15 total units are recommended; 4 English recommended, 3 math recommended, 2 science recommended, 2 foreign language recommended, 2 social studies recommended, 2 history recommended. Additional math units recommended. Minimum SAT I scores of 500 in both math and verbal, rank in top third of secondary school class, and minimum 2.7 GPA recommended. *The admissions office says:* "[T]he selection committee primarily focuses on the four-year academic record. Positive consideration is given to applicants who have sought academic challenge through high school by enrolling in the most advanced level classes."

The Inside Word

Wabash is one of the few remaining all-male colleges in the country, and like the rest it has a small applicant pool. The vast majority of candidates are offered admission; the pool is highly self-selected and the academic standards for admission, while selective, are not particularly demanding. However, though not tough to gain admission to, Wabash is tough to graduate from—don't consider it if you aren't prepared to work.

FINANCIAL AID

Students should submit: FAFSA, CSS Profile, the school's own financial aid form, a copy of parents' most recent income tax filing. The Princeton Review suggests that all financial aid forms be submitted as soon as possible after January 1. *The following grants/scholarships are offered:* Pell, academic merit, the school's own scholarships, the school's own grants, state scholarships, state grants, private scholarships, private grants, foreign aid. *Students borrow from the following loan programs:* Stafford, unsubsidized Stafford, PLUS, the school's own loan fund. Institutional employment is available. Freshmen are discouraged from working.

FROM THE ADMISSIONS OFFICE

"Wabash College is different-and distinctive-from other liberal arts colleges. Different in that Wabash is an outstanding college for men only. Distinctive in the quality and character of the faculty, in the demanding nature of the academic program, in the farsightedness and maturity of the men who enroll, and in the richness of the traditions that have evolved throughout its 160-year history. Wabash is, preeminently, a teaching institution, and fundamental to the learning experience is the way faculty and students talk to each other: with mutual respect for the expression of informed opinion. For example, students who collaborate with faculty on research projects are considered their peers in the research-an esteem not usually extended to undergraduates. The college takes pride in the sense of community that such a learning environment fosters. But perhaps the single most striking aspect of student life at Wabash is personal freedom. The college has only one rule: 'The student is expected to conduct himself at all times, both on and off the campus, as a gentleman and a responsible citizen.' Wabash College treats students as adults, and such treatment attracts responsible freshmen and fosters their independence and maturity.'"

ADMISSIONS

Admissions Rating	79
% of applicants accepted	78
% of acceptees attending	39

FRESHMAN PROFILE

Average verbal SAT	600
Average math SAT	620
Average ACT	NR
Average TOEFL	550
Graduated top 20% of class	68
Graduated top 40% of class	93
Graduated top 60% of class	99
Average HS GPA or Avg.	3.5

DEADLINES

Early decision	NR
Regular admission	3/1
Regular notification	4/1
Non-fall registration	yes

APPLICANTS ALSO LOOK AT

AND OFTEN PREFER

Indiana U.-Bloomington
Notre Dame

AND SOMETIMES PREFER

DePaul
Valparaiso

AND RARELY PREFER

Purdue U.-West Lafayette

FINANCIAL FACTS

Financial Aid Rating	94
Tuition	$13,700
Room & board	$4,405
Estimated book expense	$500
% frosh receiving aid	95
% undergrads receiving aid	95
% aid is need-based	74
% frosh w/ grant (avg)	81 ($10,951)
% frosh w/ loan (avg)	54 ($2,164)
% UGs w/ job (avg)	32 ($600)
Off-campus job outlook	good

WAKE FOREST UNIVERSITY

Box 7305 Reynolda Station, Winston-Salem, NC 27109   ADMISSIONS: 910-759-5201   FAX: 910-759-6074

CAMPUS LIFE

Quality of Life Rating   **86**
Type of school   private
Affiliation   none
Environment   city

STUDENTS
FT undergrad enrollment   3,607
% male/female   49/51
% from out of state   67
% live on campus   83
% spend weekend on campus   60
% transfers   NR
% from public high school   77
% in (# of) fraternities   42 (15)
% in (# of) sororities   51 (10)
% African-American   7
% Asian   1
% Caucasian   90
% Hispanic   0
% international   1
# of countries represented   25

WHAT'S HOT
library
intercollegiate sports
Greeks
intramural sports
religion

WHAT'S NOT
infrequent dating
students are cliquish
registration is a pain
lack of diversity on campus
sex

ACADEMICS

Academic Rating   **90**
Profs Interesting Rating   86
Profs Accessible Rating   87
Calendar   semester
Student/teacher ratio   13:1
% profs PhD/tenured   87/90
Hours of study per day   3.18

MOST POPULAR MAJORS
biology
business
history

% GRADS WHO PURSUE...
Law 6, Med 6, MBA 2, MA 16

STUDENTS SPEAK OUT

Life
Most Wake Forest University students "are active about campus, whether in Greek life, musical groups, theater, sports, religious groups, or university programs (radio, newspaper, etc.)." These activities are essential to students' social lives. One student writes, "If you find your niche here, then you're set: parties, friends, road trips, etc. If you somehow miss out, then there is very little to do except watch everybody else go by. The sure-fire bet is to take a semester at the Wake Forest House in London or Venice. It's almost like 'insta-family' with bonds that last all through college." Students agree that fraternities and sororities are the "most important factor in the school's social and political spheres." Drinking is popular, drugs are not. Students report, "Beer is like mother's milk to Wake students. We all work so hard during the week that by the time the weekend rolls around many of us stay inebriated for two days straight." Students are conservative about sex; says one, "This place would be a monastery if it weren't for beer and frat parties!" The campus is beautiful (several students write that "Wake Forest is like a country club"), the dorms are comfortable, and the food is not that bad. The city of Winston-Salem, writes one student, "is accessible by car, but the campus is self-supporting and self-contained."

Academics
Students at Wake Forest are impressed with their school's growing national reputation, but also wary of the changes this newfound prestige might bring. Says one, "In seeking to gain the national recognition it deserves, Wake must be vigilant not to lose its small-school, friendly character." Another reports that "This can be a frustrating time to be at Wake, yet also exciting, since students are involved in the shaping of its future." Students here work hard, and are rewarded with excellent, accessible professors and facilities that are "fantastic." One freshman says: "I'm a freshman taking introductory classes with the most widely sought after and professionally esteemed professors on campus. It's as if they wanted students with fresh minds, as if the departments were competing to win over potential majors. Great!" Students also give administrators high marks. A solid, broad-based core curriculum requires all students to pursue a well-rounded academic program. Students live by an honor code; one tells us it is "very strictly adhered to; I am unaware of any infractions in my semesters here," and all students report that incidents of cheating are very rare.

Student Body
Wake Forest draws a large proportion of out-of-state students, but the overall feel of the student body remains Southern and wealthy. A 9 percent minority population is made up mostly of African Americans. Students are politically conservative but largely apathetic, and they are fairly religious. They rank in the top 15 percent of the nation's happiest students.

FINANCIAL AID: 910-759-5176

WEB SITE: HTTP://WWW.WFU.EDU/WWW-DATA/START.HTML

ADMISSIONS

The admissions committee considers (in descending order of importance): HS record, class rank, test scores, recommendations, essay. *Also considered (in descending order of importance):* extracurriculars, personality, special talents, alumni relationship, geographical distribution. Admissions process is need-blind. *High school units required/recommended:* 16 total units are required; 4 English required, 3 math required, 1 science required, 2 foreign language required, 2 social studies required, 2 history required. TOEFL is required of all international students. *The admissions office says:* "The 'typical' Wake Forest student is characterized by a commitment to personal honor and integrity, a serious and industrious pursuit of academic excellence, and a tradition of service to others within and outside the campus community."

The Inside Word

An applicant to Wake Forest undergoes very close scrutiny from the admissions committee; many very solid candidates wind up on the wait list. Fortunately, the admissions staff is as friendly and accessible as the University's students rate the whole place. Successful candidates typically show impressive extracurricular accomplishments as well as academic excellence, and are good matches with the University's personality.

FINANCIAL AID

Students should submit: FAFSA, the school's own financial aid form, a copy of parents' most recent income tax filing. The Princeton Review suggests that all financial aid forms be submitted as soon as possible after January 1. *The following grants/scholarships are offered:* Pell, SEOG, academic merit, athletic, the school's own scholarships, the school's own grants, state scholarships, state grants, private scholarships, private grants, ROTC. *Students borrow from the following loan programs:* Stafford, unsubsidized Stafford, Perkins, PLUS, the school's own loan fund, state loans, private loans. Applicants will be notified of awards beginning April 15. College Work-Study Program is available. Institutional employment is available.

FROM THE ADMISSIONS OFFICE

"Recognized as one of the country's finest private liberal arts universities, Wake Forest offers undergraduates the intimacy of a smaller college and the complete resources, facilities and faculty of a larger institution. Recently, Wake Forest has intensified its commitment to small classes, individualized instruction and faculty-student interaction. First year students will benefit from a new plan bringing first-year seminars and additional faculty, classes and scholarships to the University. Students will be issued powerful IBM Think Pads providing every student with access to the extensive resources available on campus and through the Internet and World-Wide Web."

ADMISSIONS

Admissions Rating	91
% of applicants accepted	46
% of acceptees attending	36

FRESHMAN PROFILE	
Average verbal SAT	650
Average math SAT	620
Average ACT	NR
Average TOEFL	550
Graduated top 20% of class	73
Graduated top 40% of class	79
Graduated top 60% of class	80
Average HS GPA or Avg.	NR

DEADLINES	
Early decision	NR
Regular admission	1/15
Regular notification	4/1
Non-fall registration	yes

APPLICANTS ALSO LOOK AT

AND OFTEN PREFER

Duke
UNC-Chapel Hill

AND SOMETIMES PREFER

Washington and Lee
Vanderbilt
William and Mary
Davidson

AND RARELY PREFER

Furman
U. Richmond
North Carolina State

FINANCIAL FACTS

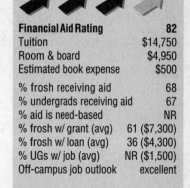

Financial Aid Rating	82
Tuition	$14,750
Room & board	$4,950
Estimated book expense	$500
% frosh receiving aid	68
% undergrads receiving aid	67
% aid is need-based	NR
% frosh w/ grant (avg)	61 ($7,300)
% frosh w/ loan (avg)	36 ($4,300)
% UGs w/ job (avg)	NR ($1,500)
Off-campus job outlook	excellent

WARREN WILSON COLLEGE

P.O. Box 9000, Asheville, NC 28815   Admissions: 704-298-3325   Fax: 704-299-4841

STUDENTS SPEAK OUT

Life

Warren Wilson College life involves everything that surrounds the school. One junior notes, "My social life consists of late-night discussions with friends, watching movies, going hiking and camping (when weather permits), and taking part in theater productions here...WWC is a very 'outdoorsy' school with regular mountain biking, kayaking, canoeing, rock climbing, and camping trips scheduled." Other activities at the college include a large community service program. Each student does twenty hours a year of community service. Intense student discussions rank high among things to do: "We have lots of discussions about important things: environmental problems, politics, gun control, abortion." Political and environmental groups also have strong student support. Swannanoa residents and students don't seem to mix much. One student explains that "the townspeople don't have a very positive image of us, probably because we deviate from the 'norm,' whatever that is."

Academics

With such a small student population, Warren Wilson seems like it would be confining. However, the students respond that the size of Warren Wilson is one of its major assets. One junior writes that "professors are great and down to earth. You get to call them by their first names and they are very personable and friendly. That is why I chose WWC." Comments another student, "Warren Wilson is a very comfortable place to study possibly uncomfortable things. Work hard, explore religion, make friends, get involved with politics. It is the place for anyone who has a desire to work and make the world a better place." This environment makes WWC students offer high grades on faculty accessibility. As one sophomore puts it, "Over 90 percent of the staff live on campus and they are always willing to help you anytime." Academics can be rigorous at WWC, with education, environmental sciences, and business the most popular majors. But "Academics are as difficult as the student wants them to be," notes one junior.

Student Body

Students at WWC are diverse and liberal—make no mistake about it. One senior describes the college to be "As close to a liberal utopia as a college can get." One student notes that "WWC attracts students who are interested in working for change in their community and the world they live in." Another adds, "Most people could be called weird. It's a diverse group all right. But everyone is very friendly and accepting of all kinds of personalities." WWC is described as "a very gay-friendly environment." The school's highly involved community and liberal environment tends to attract the type of person who interacts well with others and is socially and environmentally aware. One student sums it up by saying "Most people here tend to be environmentalists or hippies. Because our school is so tiny, everybody knows one another. This creates a warm feeling of intimacy. Fellow students always smile at each other."

FINANCIAL AID: 704-298-3325 WEB SITE: HTTP://WWW.WARREN-WILSON.EDU

ADMISSIONS

The admissions committee considers (in descending order of importance): HS record, class rank, test scores, recommendations, essay. *Also considered (in descending order of importance):* personality, alumni relationship, extracurriculars, geographical distribution, special talents. An interview is recommended. Admissions process is need-blind.

The Inside Word

Warren Wilson is a college for thinkers with a deep sense of social commitment. The admissions process clearly reflects the committee's desire for solid academic achievement in successful candidates, but they also take a close and careful look at the person being considered. It isn't supercompetitive to get in here, but only candidates who make good matches with the College are offered admission.

FINANCIAL AID

Students should submit: FAFSA (due March 15), the school's own financial aid form (due March 15), state aid form, a copy of parents' most recent income tax filing. The Princeton Review suggests that all financial aid forms be submitted as soon as possible after January 1. *The following grants/scholarships are offered:* Pell, SEOG, academic merit, the school's own scholarships, the school's own grants, state grants, private scholarships, private grants, foreign aid. *Students borrow from the following loan programs:* Stafford, unsubsidized Stafford, Perkins, PLUS, the school's own loan fund. College Work-Study Program is available. Institutional employment is available.

FROM THE ADMISSIONS OFFICE

"This book is a 'Guide to the Best 310 Colleges,' but Warren Wilson College may not be the best college for many students. There are 3,500 colleges in the U.S., and there is a best place for everyone. The 'best college' is one that has the right size, location, programs, and above all, the right feel for you, even if it is not listed here. Warren Wilson College may be the best choice if you think and act independently, actively participate in your education, and want a college that provides a sense of community. Your hands will get dirty here, your mind will be stretched, and you'll not be anonymous. If you are looking for the traditional college experience with football and frats, and a campus-on-a-quad, this probably is not the right place. However, if you want to be a part of an academic community that works and serves together, this might be exactly what you are looking for."

ADMISSIONS

Admissions Rating	77
% of applicants accepted	70
% of acceptees attending	39

FRESHMAN PROFILE

Average verbal SAT	600
Average math SAT	560
Average ACT	24
Average TOEFL	500
Graduated top 20% of class	46
Graduated top 40% of class	72
Graduated top 60% of class	85
Average HS GPA or Avg.	3.3

DEADLINES

Early decision	11/15
Regular admission	3/15
Regular notification	2/1
Non-fall registration	yes

APPLICANTS ALSO LOOK AT

AND SOMETIMES PREFER

UNC-Asheville
UNC-Chapel Hill
Guilford
Earlham
North Carolina State

AND RARELY PREFER

Appalachian State
Antioch

FINANCIAL FACTS

Financial Aid Rating	95
Tuition	$11,450
Room & board	$3,125
Estimated book expense	$600
% frosh receiving aid	100
% undergrads receiving aid	89
% aid is need-based	82
% frosh w/ grant (avg)	52 ($5,200)
% frosh w/ loan (avg)	54 ($2,753)
% UGs w/ job (avg)	100 ($2,040)
Off-campus job outlook	good

WASHINGTON AND LEE UNIVERSITY

LEXINGTON, VA 24450 ADMISSIONS: 703-463-8710 FAX: 703-463-8945

CAMPUS LIFE

Quality of Life Rating   **91**
Type of school   private
Affiliation   none
Environment   town

STUDENTS

FT undergrad enrollment	1,618
% male/female	59/41
% from out of state	88
% live on campus	61
% spend weekend on campus	98
% transfers	1
% from public high school	67
% in (# of) fraternities	80 (15)
% in (# of) sororities	65 (4)
% African-American	3
% Asian	1
% Caucasian	93
% Hispanic	1
% international	1
# of countries represented	20

WHAT'S HOT

campus is beautiful
Greeks
hard liquor
students are happy
beer

WHAT'S NOT

lack of diversity on campus
students are cliquish
infrequent dating
off-campus food
theater

ACADEMICS

Academic Rating	**97**
Profs Interesting Rating	98
Profs Accessible Rating	97
Calendar	other
Student/teacher ratio	11:1
% profs PhD/tenured	94/94
Hours of study per day	3.35

MOST POPULAR MAJORS

history
economics
biology

% GRADS WHO PURSUE...

Law 7, Med 5, MBA 1, MA 10

STUDENTS SPEAK OUT

Life

Washington and Lee University is a big Greek school. One student explains: "80 percent of our students pledge to frats and sororities. With sixteen frats and 4 sororities, we work hard and play hard here." Greeks dominate the social agenda. Writes one student, "The student body (which, at W&L, means the Greeks) runs the school's activities." Frat parties are frequent, and beer and alcohol, not surprisingly, are practically staples. "If you want to sleep before 2 a.m.," reports one undergrad, "forget it—there are so many drunk people coming in from parties that you could call an AA convention in the hallway." When students stumble home late at night, they do so across a beautiful campus, which one student describes this way: "When you think about the classic example of college on a postcard, the image you call up would be W&L. Ivy on the walls, lush green setting, and excellent academics." The housing situation is reportedly excellent; says one student, "Everyone, including freshmen, can get single rooms. Upperclassmen can (and often do) live off campus, or in on campus apartments with kitchens." With its grassy surroundings, comfortable housing, good food, and upwardly mobile Southern student body, it's no wonder many people liken W&L to a country club.

Academics

Washington and Lee University offers a classic "small liberal arts school" experience for a moderate private school price. Students at this traditional Southern school—Robert E. Lee was once college president—enjoy small classes with personable, accessible professors, and a "strong sense of community among the students, faculty, and administration. When students graduate, they feel like they're leaving part of their family behind." An honor code contributes to that sense of community: students here schedule their own unproctored exams and leave their dorm rooms unlocked, confident that nothing will get stolen. Students also love the unusual academic schedule, which features two full-length terms (fall and winter) and a mandatory six-week term in the spring, during which students participate in seminars and internships or travel abroad. Professors often use the spring term to develop new course ideas and teaching methods. 10 percent of all graduates go on to law school within a year. History, economics, and English are among the most popular majors.

Student Body

Washington and Lee has few minority students, most of whom are African American. Students report a pervasive conformity among the majority of students. "People here don't like change," warned one; another elaborated, "Make sure you know who you are before you get here. Confidence in who you are will make or break you at W&L. Being an individual is hard but worth it; the price of conformity is too high." The stereotypical W&L student is "Southern gentility who drives a BMW and refers to his or her father as Daddy," an image repeated by enough students that it must have some truth to it. Others report that admissions that traditionally keep a male-majority on campus leave the women on campus with a "secondary role." Still, those who fit in and enjoy this lifestyle are very satisfied with W&L.

FINANCIAL AID: 540-463-8715

WEB SITE: HTTP://LIBERTY.UC.WLU.EDU

ADMISSIONS

The admissions committee considers (in descending order of importance): HS record, class rank, recommendations, test scores, essay. *Also considered (in descending order of importance):* personality, alumni relationship, extracurriculars, geographical distribution, special talents. Either the SAT or ACT is required. An interview is recommended. Admissions process is need-blind. *High school units required/recommended:* 16 total units are required; 4 English required, 3 math required, 1 science required, 2 foreign language required, 1 social studies required, 1 history required. Other subjects may be considered. TOEFL is required of all international students. *The admissions office says:* "Individuals are welcome to submit materials that speak of their special talents."

The Inside Word

If you're looking for a bastion of Southern tradition, Washington and Lee is one of the foremost. Its admissions process is appropriately traditional, and highly selective. Under these circumstances, it is always best to take a cautious and conservative approach to preparing your candidacy. Smart applicants have taken the toughest courses available to them in high school—the minimum requirements aren't likely to help you gain admission. Neither will a glib approach to the personal side of the application; avoid controversial issues in essays and choose your recommenders wisely.

FINANCIAL AID

Students should submit: FAFSA, CSS Profile, state aid form, a copy of parents' most recent income tax filing. The Princeton Review suggests that all financial aid forms be submitted as soon as possible after January 1. *The following grants/scholarships are offered:* Pell, SEOG, academic merit, the school's own scholarships, the school's own grants, state scholarships, state grants, private scholarships, private grants, foreign aid. *Students borrow from the following loan programs:* Stafford, unsubsidized Stafford, Perkins, PLUS, the school's own loan fund, private loans. Applicants will be notified of awards beginning April 1. College Work-Study Program is available. Institutional employment is available.

FROM THE ADMISSIONS OFFICE

"W&L, the nation's sixth oldest college, is a small, private, liberal arts school located in the heart of the beautiful Shenandoah Valley. As one might expect, W&L possesses an inordinate amount of history. Quality teaching both in and out of the classroom, and the development of students into well-rounded leaders, summarize the school's primary goals. An average W&L class contains fifteen students, and courses are taught by the school's full-time faculty members; no graduate students or teacher assistants are on the faculty. W&L possesses a uniquely broad and deep curriculum, as well as a time-honored, student-run Honor Code that allows students a wide range of freedoms. W&L is a highly competitive school, where students will receive a first-rate, personalized education, develop leadership skills, enjoy life outside of the classroom, and reap the innumerable postgraduation benefits of a W&L education."

ADMISSIONS

Admissions Rating	96
% of applicants accepted	31
% of acceptees attending	41

FRESHMAN PROFILE

Average verbal SAT	680
Average math SAT	650
Average ACT	29
Average TOEFL	NR
Graduated top 20% of class	91
Graduated top 40% of class	99
Graduated top 60% of class	100
Average HS GPA or Avg.	NR

DEADLINES

Early decision	12/1
Regular admission	1/15
Regular notification	4/1
Non-fall registration	no

APPLICANTS ALSO LOOK AT

AND OFTEN PREFER

Virginia
UNC-Chapel Hill

AND SOMETIMES PREFER

Davidson
William and Mary
Vanderbilt
Wake Forest

AND RARELY PREFER

Rhodes
SMU
Franklin & Marshall
James Madison
Tulane

FINANCIAL FACTS

Financial Aid Rating	83
Tuition	$14,500
Room & board	$4,620
Estimated book expense	$715
% frosh receiving aid	54
% undergrads receiving aid	52
% aid is need-based	75
% frosh w/ grant (avg)	41 ($10,540)
% frosh w/ loan (avg)	38 ($2,963)
% UGs w/ job (avg)	15 ($1,150)
Off-campus job outlook	fair

WASHINGTON UNIVERSITY

ONE BROOKINGS DRIVE, BOX 1089, ST. LOUIS, MO 63130   ADMISSIONS: 800-638-0700   FAX: 314-935-4290

CAMPUS LIFE

Quality of Life Rating	80
Type of school	private
Affiliation	none
Environment	metropolis

STUDENTS

FT undergrad enrollment	4,993
% male/female	53/47
% from out of state	78
% live on campus	60
% spend weekend on campus	95
% transfers	11
% from public high school	65
% in (# of) fraternities	25 (11)
% in (# of) sororities	25 (6)
% African-American	5
% Asian	14
% Caucasian	69
% Hispanic	2
% international	6
# of countries represented	83

WHAT'S HOT
support groups
registration is a breeze
leftist politics
lab facilities
off-campus food

WHAT'S NOT
intercollegiate sports
music associations
sex
infrequent dating
campus food

ACADEMICS

Academic Rating	90
Profs Interesting Rating	72
Profs Accessible Rating	77
Calendar	semester
Student/teacher ratio	6:1
% profs PhD/tenured	99/53
Hours of study per day	3.28

MOST POPULAR MAJORS
psychology
biology
economics

% GRADS WHO PURSUE...
Law 13, Med 12, MBA 37, MA 11

STUDENTS SPEAK OUT

Life
Washington University students tell us that their campus is quite beautiful and that "life is grand," often in all capital letters. The campus is just outside the borders of St. Louis in a setting more suburban than one might expect. As one student puts it, "Don't look to St. Louis to fulfill your wildest dreams of the big city." Despite over 200 organizations and clubs on campus, including a spectacular women's volleyball team, on-campus social life elicits some critical comments. Says one student, "Get off campus or you will go insane." Another adds, "Students focus on school work and studying and less on social fun." Other students express exuberant satisfaction with the entertainment possibilities (school-sponsored or otherwise): "It's simple. If you want to learn something, go to any other school in the world. If you want to have a blast while you learn, attend Wash U." Not surprisingly, considering the last comment, drinking and drugs are more popular here than at the average school in this book. As for romantic life, "students don't date here—they scam on each other and don't go out until they've been seeing each other for months." Hey, whatever it takes—WU students rank high in overall happiness, so their complaints may be best taken with a large grain of salt.

Academics
Wash U is a paradox, a school best known for being underrated. Many comments from students begin, "Although WU isn't that well known..." and then go on to explain something great about the school. WU has a lot of success in sending students to graduate programs, particularly medical school (over 10 percent of all graduates go directly to med school). Students think highly of most of their professors, although quite a few complain that the school emphasizes research and publishing in its tenure process, with the result being the occasional brilliant-but-entirely-incomprehensible professor. And, as one student tells us, "It's not as difficult as its reputation would lead you to believe," an assertion borne out by student response to the question, "How many hours a day do you study?" Their answer, 3.3 hours, is just slightly above the average of the colleges profiled in this book. The preprofessional programs are excellent, as are the economics and science departments.

Student Body
WU may not entirely be "the rich kids' college everyone thinks it is...many students receive financial aid," but some students do note that "Yes, we get along. Too many are rich. This isn't the real world." The school received its reputation because its tuition fees are very high, and because it draws a lot of well-to-do students. Students come to WU from all over the country (and many other countries as well), but many gravitate to familiar types once they get here: Says one student, "I thought I was being unique by going to school in St. Louis and being a New Yorker, but I don't have one friend who is not from the East Coast." Although the students believe they have a well-diversified student body, they give themselves low marks for interaction. Still, every demographic group ranks quite high for overall happiness—maybe because, as one students tells us, "My fellow students are very non-judgmental, good-hearted people."

Crystal Overstreet
314-935-4826

FINANCIAL AID: 314-935-5900

WEB SITE: HTTP://WWW.WUSTL.EDU

ADMISSIONS

The admissions committee considers (in descending order of importance): HS record, class rank, recommendations, test scores, essay. *Also considered (in descending order of importance):* alumni relationship, extracurriculars, personality, special talents, geographical distribution. Either the SAT or ACT is required. An interview is recommended. Admissions process is not need-blind. *High school units required/recommended:* 18 total units are recommended; 4 English recommended, 3 math recommended, 3 science recommended, 2 foreign language recommended, 1 social studies recommended, 2 history recommended. Rigorous secondary school academic program recommended. *Special Requirements:* Portfolio recommended of School of Art program applicants.

The Inside Word

The fact that Washington U. doesn't have much play as a nationally respected car window decal is about all that prevents it from being among the most selective universities. In every other respect—that is, in any way which really matters—this place is hard to beat, and easily ranks as one of the best. No other university with as impressive a record of excellence across the board has a more accommodating admissions process. Not that it's easy to get in here, but lack of instant name recognition does affect Washington's admission rate. Students with above-average academic records who are not quite Ivy material are the big winners. Marginal candidates with high financial need may find difficulty; the admissions process at Washington U. is not need-blind, and may take into account candidates' ability to pay if they are not strong applicants.

FINANCIAL AID

Students should submit: FAFSA (due February 15), CSS Profile (due February 15), state aid form, Divorced Parents form (due February 15). The Princeton Review suggests that all financial aid forms be submitted as soon as possible after January 1. *The following grants/scholarships are offered:* Pell, SEOG, academic merit, the school's own scholarships, the school's own grants, state scholarships, state grants, private scholarships, private grants, ROTC, foreign aid. *Students borrow from the following loan programs:* Stafford, Perkins, PLUS, the school's own loan fund, private loans. Applicants will be notified of awards beginning April 1. College Work-Study Program is available. Institutional employment is available.

FROM THE ADMISSIONS OFFICE

"A research university with world-renowned scholars and professional schools, Washington University is also a college with exceptionally high teaching standards in the liberal arts and in professional schools of architecture, art, business, engineering and applied science. "At Washington, you are limited by nothing except your imagination and your willingness to take initiatives. Whichever college or school you choose, you can take courses in any other, and you can transfer between them. We encourage interdisciplinary work. "Our students come from all over the country and the world, and from all manner of social, economic, ethnic, and racial backgrounds. Campus events are inclusive, not exclusive-more than 200 clubs and activities including community service and multicultural groups, and fraternities and sororities are open to anyone at any level of skill and interest."

ADMISSIONS

Admissions Rating	90
% of applicants accepted	56
% of acceptees attending	23

FRESHMAN PROFILE

Average verbal SAT	630
Average math SAT	650
Average ACT	29
Average TOEFL	600
Graduated top 20% of class	87
Graduated top 40% of class	98
Graduated top 60% of class	100
Average HS GPA or Avg.	NR

DEADLINES

Early decision	NR
Regular admission	1/1
Regular notification	4/1
Non-fall registration	no

APPLICANTS ALSO LOOK AT

AND OFTEN PREFER

Northwestern U.
Cornell U.
Tufts

AND SOMETIMES PREFER

U. Michigan-Ann Arbor
Pennsylvania
Emory
Vanderbilt
St. Louis

AND RARELY PREFER

American
U. Illinois, Urbana-Champ.
Brandeis
U. Wisconsin-Madison
Lafayette

FINANCIAL FACTS

Financial Aid Rating	83
Tuition	$20,000
Room & board	$6,284
Estimated book expense	$780
% frosh receiving aid	52
% undergrads receiving aid	51
% aid is need-based	88
% frosh w/ grant (avg)	51 ($13,740)
% frosh w/ loan (avg)	42 ($3,710)
% UGs w/ job (avg)	50 ($1,500)
Off-campus job outlook	excellent

UNIVERSITY OF WASHINGTON

1400 N.E. CAMPUS PARKWAY, SEATTLE, WA 98195 ADMISSIONS: 206-543-9686 FAX: 206-543-2100

CAMPUS LIFE

Quality of Life Rating 85
Type of school public
Affiliation none
Environment metropolis

STUDENTS

FT undergrad enrollment	20,448
% male/female	50/50
% from out of state	10
% live on campus	15
% spend weekend on campus	NR
% transfers	40
% from public high school	NR
% in (# of) fraternities	16 (30)
% in (# of) sororities	16 (18)
% African-American	3
% Asian	20
% Caucasian	63
% Hispanic	4
% international	2
# of countries represented	56

WHAT'S HOT
library
health facilities
Seattle
intercollegiate sports
off-campus food

WHAT'S NOT
political activism
music associations
student government
theater
dorms

ACADEMICS

Academic Rating	74
Profs Interesting Rating	68
Profs Accessible Rating	66
Calendar	quarter
Student/teacher ratio	11:1
% profs PhD	99
Hours of study per day	2.92

MOST POPULAR MAJORS
business administration
psychology
English

STUDENTS SPEAK OUT

Life

Both the University of Washington and the city of Seattle get high ratings from students. This is not your typical urban campus. The view of Mt. Rainier is stunning on clear days, as are campus views of the Olympic and Cascade mountain ranges and Lake Washington. The university is chock full of outdoorsy types, and there are plenty of outlets for those looking to get in touch with Mother Nature. How many colleges offer an artificial "climbing rock" on their grounds to accommodate mountaineers-in-training? Fraternities and sororities, student government, the newspaper, athletic teams, and the marching band are some of the more popular groups on campus. Some students are decidedly less active; more than one mention that "the chairs in Suzzalo library are the best place to sleep on campus." The center of off-campus social activity is "the Ave," the university district's main thoroughfare and home to many restaurants, coffeehouses, and shops geared to students.

Academics

UW has come a long way since its beginnings in 1861 as the Territorial University of Washington, when a sole professor taught across the complete curriculum. The university now boasts seventeen colleges staffed by over 3,000 instructional faculty; thirteen of the colleges offer programs for undergraduates. While the academic options at schools like Washington are broad, attending a large university does have its drawbacks. Despite the fact that about 20,000 of the university's 34,000 students are full-time undergraduates, they hardly seem to be the focus of attention on campus. One student comments that "Professors really seem to care—about their research!" Another describes his experiences dealing with the housing and financial aid offices as "about as rewarding as being beaten to death with a rotten sturgeon." To be fair, the university puts a lot of energy into efforts designed to make students feel a part of a smaller, more close-knit community. Freshman seminars are weekly one-credit courses taught by UW faculty and limited to ten students. Freshman Interest Groups (FIGs) are optional interest groups of twenty to twenty-four students who share the same class schedule and go to a bi-weekly student-led discussion group. Much larger classes are generally the rule, but once students begin to focus on a major they sometimes find more of a "small college" feel within their academic departments.

Student Body

UW's Pacific Rim location helps the minority enrollment significantly—Asians are well represented in the student body. Other minorities are decidedly less well represented, but generally feel welcome. Most students we surveyed report little discrimination on campus overall, but it's also apparent that the university community tends to segment itself into smaller microcosms. Many of these smaller groups, be they classes, clubs, cliques or clans, tend to focus their energy inwardly, which may explain why many respondents mention a lack of school spirit.

FINANCIAL AID: 206-543-6101

ADMISSIONS

The admissions committee considers (in descending order of importance): HS record, test scores, class rank. *Also considered (in descending order of importance):* alumni relationship, extracurriculars, special talents. Either the SAT or ACT is required. Admissions process is need-blind. *High school units required/recommended:* 15 total units are required; 4 English required, 3 math required, 2 science required, 2 foreign language required, 3 social studies required. 1 unit of electives including 1/2 unit of academic elective and 1/2 unit of arts required. Minimum 2.0 GPA required. *Special Requirements:* An audition is required for music program applicants. Audition required of dance, music, and drama program applicants.

The Inside Word

Admission at UW follows a fairly strict formula that factors the student's combined SAT I or composite ACT scores with GPA to arrive at an admission index (AI). The minimum "AI" changes annually depending on the strength of the applicant pool, and is significantly higher for out-of-state students. Those who come close to qualifying for admission based on their AI but still fall short may be considered by the Freshman Review Committee, which evaluates grade trends, course selection, rigor of the candidate's high school, and special talents. In any case, solid numbers will do more to get you in than anything else.

FINANCIAL AID

Students should submit: FAFSA. The Princeton Review suggests that all financial aid forms be submitted as soon as possible after January 1. *The following grants/ scholarships are offered:* Pell, SEOG, academic merit, athletic, the school's own scholarships, the school's own grants, state scholarships, state grants, private scholarships, federal nursing scholarship, ROTC. *Students borrow from the following loan programs:* Stafford, unsubsidized Stafford, Perkins, PLUS, the school's own loan fund, supplemental loans, federal nursing loans, health professions loans, private loans. College Work-Study Program is available. Institutional employment is available.

FROM THE ADMISSIONS OFFICE

"Undergraduates benefit in special ways by learning from professors who are at the forefront of generating new knowledge."

ADMISSIONS

Admissions Rating	76
% of applicants accepted	65
% of acceptees attending	46

FRESHMAN PROFILE	
Average verbal SAT	560
Average math SAT	580
Average ACT	25
Average TOEFL	540
Graduated top 20% of class	40
Graduated top 40% of class	97
Graduated top 60% of class	NR
Average HS GPA or Avg.	3.6

DEADLINES	
Early decision	2/1
Regular admission	NR
Regular notification	March
Non-fall registration	yes

APPLICANTS ALSO LOOK AT

AND OFTEN PREFER
Washington State
Western Washington
U. Oregon

AND SOMETIMES PREFER
U. Puget Sound
UC-Berkeley
UCLA
Stanford

AND RARELY PREFER
U. Colorado-Boulder
Central Washington
U. Southern Cal

FINANCIAL FACTS

Financial Aid Rating	80
In-state tuition	$2,875
Out-of-state tuition	$8,599
Room & board	$5,118
Estimated book expense	$735

% frosh receiving aid	41
% undergrads receiving aid	43
% aid is need-based	76
% frosh w/ grant (avg)	16 ($3,962)
% frosh w/ loan (avg)	28 ($5,401)
% UGs w/ job (avg)	NR
Off-campus job outlook	good

WELLESLEY COLLEGE

WELLESLEY, MA 02181

ADMISSIONS: 617-283-1000   FAX: 617-283-3639

CAMPUS LIFE

Quality of Life Rating	**86**
Type of school	private
Affiliation	none
Environment	suburban

STUDENTS

FT undergrad enrollment	2,158
% male/female	0/100
% from out of state	86
% live on campus	98
% spend weekend on campus	NR
% transfers	3
% from public high school	64
% African-American	8
% Asian	23
% Caucasian	62
% Hispanic	6
% international	6
# of countries represented	66

WHAT'S HOT

support groups
lab facilities
campus is beautiful
ethnic diversity on campus
student government

WHAT'S NOT

beer
drugs
hard liquor
intramural sports
cigarettes

ACADEMICS

Academic Rating	**95**
Profs Interesting Rating	94
Profs Accessible Rating	96
Calendar	semester
Student/teacher ratio	10:1
% profs tenured	97
Hours of study per day	3.73

MOST POPULAR MAJORS

economics
political science
English

% GRADS WHO PURSUE...

Law 24, Med 22, MBA 6, MA 38

STUDENTS SPEAK OUT

Life

Wellesley College offers students a trade off: "I may not enjoy the social life at Wellesley, but the academics are well worth the sacrifice," writes one. "You have to make an effort to have a social life" is another comment we hear frequently. Finding a social scene means taking a thirty-minute ride to Cambridge for parties at Harvard and MIT. There are those who find this situation ideal; says one, "I have a great social life, find the academics challenging, and I can balance the two—academics during the week, social life on weekends." The neighboring town is "not much more than a country club gift shop" (although some students mention that the "town thinks we are psycho Amazons"), but Boston makes up for it. So, too, does the campus, which students rank among the nation's most beautiful. Sprawling, bucolic, and full of Oxford-style Gothic architecture, it was just edged out by Rhodes and College of the Atlantic in our survey. Life at Wellesley takes a little getting used to—"many first-years consider transferring, but by winter break they love it here!"

Academics

Because of its unique situation as a competitive, all-women's school, Wellesley inspires great enthusiasm in its students. "Wellesley is a small liberal arts women's college dedicated to developing able, confident, and ambitious women to lead in the forefront of all fields," writes one senior. Although we also hear from detractors, most of our respondents are very happy with their choice: as one points out, Wellesley's student body is "self-selecting," so most know what they're getting into before they get here, and few leave disappointed. Academics are "quite difficult but invariably interesting"—even those who hate the social scene conceded this—professors are "excellent and caring," and classes are small. Junior year in Aix-en-Provence is highly recommended, both as a mind-broadening experience and as an escape from the sometimes stifling Wellesley community. Art history, English, and political science are among the most popular majors here, and counselors report that the science departments are strong. Students are torn over the issues of multiculturalism and "political correctness," both of which have taken root here. As students at a women's school they are especially sensitive to race and gender issues: They just don't agree on the best way to address them.

Student Body

Wellesley attracts a good cross-section of bright women, including a sizable number of foreign nationals. Students here are, on average, considerably left-of-center politically, but there's enough of everybody for students to find their peers. There is a visible lesbian population, but, as one student puts it, the "perception that this school is only for staunch feminists and homosexuals is totally false." Conservatives, radicals, lesbians, and fringe-type rebels all complain that there's too much of everyone else and not enough of them, indicating that Wellesley may have gotten the mix just about right. And remember: "Wellesley is not a girls' school without men but rather a women's college without boys."

FINANCIAL AID: 617-283-2360

ADMISSIONS

The admissions committee considers (in descending order of importance): HS record, class rank, recommendations, test scores, essay. *Also considered (in descending order of importance):* extracurriculars, personality, special talents, alumni relationship, geographical distribution. An interview is recommended. *High school units required/recommended:* 17 total units are recommended; 4 English recommended, 3 math recommended, 3 science recommended, 4 foreign language recommended, 3 social studies recommended. TOEFL is required of all international students.

The Inside Word

While the majority of women's colleges have gone coed or even closed over the past two decades, Wellesley has continued with vigor. As a surviving member of the Seven Sisters, the nation's most prestigious women's colleges, Wellesley enjoys even more popularity with students who choose the single-sex option. Admissions standards are rigorous, but among institutions of such high reputation Wellesley's admissions staff is friendlier and more open than the majority. Their willingness to conduct preliminary evaluations for candidates is especially commendable, and in some form or another should be the rule rather than an exception at highly selective colleges.

FINANCIAL AID

Students should submit: FAFSA (due February 1), the school's own financial aid form (due February 1), a copy of parents' most recent income tax filing (due February 1). The Princeton Review suggests that all financial aid forms be submitted as soon as possible after January 1. *The following grants/scholarships are offered:* Pell, SEOG, the school's own grants, state scholarships, state grants, private scholarships, private grants, ROTC, foreign aid. *Students borrow from the following loan programs:* Stafford, Perkins, PLUS, the school's own loan fund, state loans, private loans. Applicants will be notified of awards beginning April 1. College Work-Study Program is available. Institutional employment is available.

FROM THE ADMISSIONS OFFICE

"A student's years at Wellesley are the beginning—not the end—of an education. A Wellesley College degree signifies not that the graduate has memorized certain blocks of material, but that she has acquired the curiosity, the desire, and the ability to seek and assimilate new information. Four years at Wellesley can provide the foundation for the widest possible range of ambitions, and the necessary self-confidence to fulfill them. At Wellesley, a student has every educational opportunity. Above all, it is Wellesley's purpose to teach students to apply knowledge wisely, and to use the advantages of talent and education to seek new ways to serve the wider community."

ADMISSIONS

Admissions Rating	94
% of applicants accepted	43
% of acceptees attending	46

FRESHMAN PROFILE

Average verbal SAT	670
Average math SAT	640
Average ACT	NR
Average TOEFL	600
Graduated top 20% of class	94
Graduated top 40% of class	100
Graduated top 60% of class	NR
Average HS GPA or Avg.	NR

DEADLINES

Early decision	NR
Regular admission	1/15
Regular notification	4/1
Non-fall registration	no

APPLICANTS ALSO LOOK AT

AND OFTEN PREFER

Brown
Swarthmore

AND SOMETIMES PREFER

Boston Coll.
Vassar
Barnard
Smith
Cornell U.

AND RARELY PREFER

Johns Hopkins
Mount Holyoke

FINANCIAL FACTS

Financial Aid Rating	82
Tuition	$19,240
Room & board	$6,155
Estimated book expense	$500
% frosh receiving aid	54
% undergrads receiving aid	55
% aid is need-based	100
% frosh w/ grant (avg)	54 ($13,600)
% frosh w/ loan (avg)	47 ($2,525)
% UGs w/ job (avg)	55 ($1,600)
Off-campus job outlook	good

WESLEYAN COLLEGE

4760 FORSYTH ROAD, MACON, GA 31297

ADMISSIONS: 912-477-1110   FAX: 912-757-4030

CAMPUS LIFE

Quality of Life Rating **84**
Type of school   private
Affiliation   United Methodist Church
Environment   city

STUDENTS
FT undergrad enrollment   396
% male/female   0/100
% from out of state   38
% live on campus   78
% spend weekend on campus   60
% transfers   7
% from public high school   87
% African-American   17
% Asian   4
% Caucasian   74
% Hispanic   3
% international   NR
# of countries represented   5

WHAT'S HOT
student government
campus easy to get around
town-gown relations
registration is a breeze
music associations

WHAT'S NOT
drugs
library
beer
health facilities
college radio

ACADEMICS

Academic Rating **83**
Profs Interesting Rating   94
Profs Accessible Rating   96
Calendar   semester
Student/teacher ratio   10:1
% profs PhD/tenured   82/91
Hours of study per day   3.20

MOST POPULAR MAJORS
business administration
psychology
English

% GRADS WHO PURSUE...
Law 15, Med 15, MBA 10, MA 40

STUDENTS SPEAK OUT
Life
Campus life at Wesleyan College revolves around academics; off-campus life revolves around academics, too. As one student at this all-women's college puts it, "This school is geared only toward academics, so if you are looking for a social life, this is not the place to come." Wesleyan has a freshman curfew and a dry campus, which leads some to leave campus for fun, although Macon receives only average marks. One junior mentions that "Macon is not the most culturally enriched city. I go to Atlanta whenever I can; most people leave campus on weekends." Atlanta isn't too far away—but you do need a car. On campus, people tend to stick together and stress-release with casual events. One student describes the average night as "We spend a lot of time in each others' rooms. We talk, watch movies, go out and play cards or board games." Some students mention community service as important among the student body. "I teach a 35-year-old man how to read. It is the most rewarding volunteer work I have ever done." A number of students also mention intramural sports as both fun and important to social life.

Academics
The friendly atmosphere of Wesleyan inspires personal relationships between students and faculty. The small single-sex student body creates a sense of personal attention. "Each of my professors is a friend. Wesleyan has provided me with immeasurable opportunities, such as my semester abroad in Bulgaria and summer programs in France and Spain," offers one English major. Study abroad is popular among Wesleyan students. Communication, business administration, and psychology are all well-respected majors among the Wesleyan students. And it seems like the small size suits the students themselves: "Wesleyan's size is perfect. Professors, deans and administrators are easily accessible, and lifetime friendships are made." Some students mention that professors have invited them back to their homes for dinner. There is a strong sense of academic family at Wesleyan. The administration doesn't receive completely high marks, though. One student writes, "The administration does not always come through with the product as advertised. For example, you cannot design your own major here, public proclamations to the contrary. Also, getting financial aid is like pulling teeth." All in all, students respect the faculty and the education they receive and like the personal attention. One sophomore explains that "Profs treat students as equals and try in every way to cater to the students' needs."

Student Body
The student body, 500-600 women, comes from a range of backgrounds, and Wesleyan's diverse students get along well. Because most students live on campus, sometimes Wesleyan seems smaller than it is. One student comments that "You can't help but get to know everyone here, it's so small. If you sneeze in one dorm, everyone across campus hears it." Students are politically divided, but none mention that the environment becomes unpleasant or tension-filled because of it. Comments one student, "Some [students] are prejudiced, some are cool...we're all different!"

FINANCIAL AID: 800-447-6610 E-MAIL: BACKERMAN@POST.WESLEYAN.PEACHNET.EDU WEB SITE: HTTP://WWW.POST.WESLEYAN.PEACHNET.EDU

ADMISSIONS

The admissions committee considers (in descending order of importance): HS record, test scores, recommendations, class rank, essay. *Also considered (in descending order of importance):* extracurriculars, personality, special talents, alumni relationship. Either the SAT or ACT is required. An interview is recommended. Admissions process is need-blind. *High school units required/recommended:* 16 total units are required; 4 English required, 3 math required, 2 science required, 3 social studies required. *Special Requirements:* A portfolio is required for art program applicants. An audition is required for music program applicants. Audition required of theatre program applicants.

The Inside Word

The College has gotten lots of national publicity of late, but its applicant pool is still primarily Southeastern in origin. Candidates from outside the usual sphere of influence of any college draw the attention of admissions officers, and it's no exception here. Recommendations are important at Wesleyan; we'd advise that such letters make at least some reference to your interest in and suitability for a women's college; your own essay won't carry nearly as much weight.

FINANCIAL AID

Students should submit: FAFSA, the school's own financial aid form, a copy of parents' most recent income tax filing. The Princeton Review suggests that all financial aid forms be submitted as soon as possible after January 1. *The following grants/scholarships are offered:* Pell, SEOG, academic merit, the school's own scholarships, the school's own grants, state scholarships, state grants, private scholarships, private grants, foreign aid. *Students borrow from the following loan programs:* unsubsidized Stafford, Perkins, PLUS, the school's own loan fund, supplemental loans, state loans, private loans. Applicants will be notified of awards beginning February 1. College Work-Study Program is available. Institutional employment is available.

FROM THE ADMISSIONS OFFICE

"Wesleyan College has put women first since 1836. As the world's first college for women, Wesleyan has led the way in curriculum development designed for women. Committed faculty who consider students as colleagues and collaborate with them on research, papers, internships, or designing interdisciplinary majors. Faculty/Student ratio of 1 to 10; average class size of 15; Computer Focus Program provides each entering student with a Macintosh computer to use during college and to keep upon graduation."

ADMISSIONS

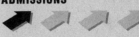

Admissions Rating	66
% of applicants accepted	91
% of acceptees attending	47

FRESHMAN PROFILE

Average verbal SAT	590
Average math SAT	520
Average ACT	23
Average TOEFL	550
Graduated top 20% of class	32
Graduated top 40% of class	NR
Graduated top 60% of class	NR
Average HS GPA or Avg.	3.4

DEADLINES

Early decision	11/1
Regular admission	rolling
Regular notification	rolling
Non-fall registration	yes

APPLICANTS ALSO LOOK AT
AND SOMETIMES PREFER

U. Georgia
Emory
Agnes Scott
Mercer

AND RARELY PREFER

Berry
Rhodes
U. Florida
Florida State

FINANCIAL FACTS

Financial Aid Rating	95
Tuition	$12,500
Room & board	$4,800
Estimated book expense	$515
% frosh receiving aid	97
% undergrads receiving aid	89
% aid is need-based	88
% frosh w/ grant (avg)	90 ($6,900)
% frosh w/ loan (avg)	92 ($3,948)
% UGs w/ job (avg)	50 ($1,200)
Off-campus job outlook	good

WESLEYAN UNIVERSITY

MIDDLETOWN, CT 06457

ADMISSIONS: 860-685-3000   FAX: 860-685-3001

STUDENTS SPEAK OUT

Life

Students at Wesleyan University "get very involved in extracurricular activities like political groups, radio station, news journals (especially alternative ones), theater groups, and music groups. They also study a lot, sometimes even on Saturday night." Notes one student, "Activities are easy to get involved in and have short ladders to success. We have wild concerts, sleazy but subdued frat parties, coffeehouses, small house parties, even unofficial dorm parties." Social situations "run from super-raging to ultra-mellow. You're likely to go to a wild frat party and hang out in a dorm discussing politics and philosophy, all in the same night." Among student complaints are the lack of school spirit ("Even football games against our arch rivals, Williams and Amherst, are poorly attended") and the quality of their hometown, Middletown. "If New York is the city that never sleeps, Middletown is the city that never wakes up. Everything closes at 9 p.m. If you want to do anything, it's got to be on campus or in Boston. The closest city is New Haven, which is New England's answer to Beirut."

Academics

Wesleyan University is in many ways a model liberal arts institution. Despite its university standing, Wesleyan is a small school, with fewer than 2,700 undergraduates and only about 150 graduate students. Over half its students major in liberal arts, and although relatively few students proceed from here directly to graduate programs, they still attack their studies with vigor (over three-and-a-half hours of study a day). Professors here are excellent, "wonderful and really accessible." They teach all courses, despite the presence of graduate students to serve as TAs. Students are allowed a lot of flexibility in determining their curricula; independent studies in fields of the students' choosing are not uncommon. Students report that the liberal arts and natural and social science departments are uniformly strong, but note that the performing and fine arts (except for film) are not as well supported by the school. Students also complain about the inordinate number of bureaucratic chores; writes one, "Bureaucracy is the name of the game. This is a small school where you'll still feel like a number. Registration is a nightmare, including a six-hour line for financial 'holds.'"

Student Body

What type of student attends Wesleyan U? Some appropriate adjectives: "Progressive, innovative, creative, alternative, intellectual, politically active, artistic." Politically, "Wesleyan students are monolithically liberal—frustrating for me as a radical, frightening for those unlucky few Republicans." Adds another, "Students are intelligent but self-involved. There are many creative people here. The student body is a little less self-righteous than it was three years ago, which is good." With a large minority population, WU earns its reputation as the "diversity university."

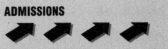

FINANCIAL AID: 203-685-2800

WEB SITE: HTTP://WESLEYAN.EDU/HOME/HOME.HTML

ADMISSIONS

The admissions committee considers (in descending order of importance): HS record, class rank, test scores, recommendations, essay. *Also considered (in descending order of importance):* personality, alumni relationship, extracurriculars, geographical distribution, special talents. Either the SAT or ACT is required. An interview is recommended. Admissions process is need-blind. *High school units required/recommended:* 16 total units are recommended; 4 English recommended, 3 math recommended, 3 science recommended, 3 foreign language recommended, 3 social studies recommended. TOEFL is required of all international students.

The Inside Word

Wesleyan stacks up well against its very formidable competitors academically, yet due to these same competitors the University admits at a fairly high rate for an institution of its high caliber. Candidate evaluation is nonetheless rigorous. If you aren't one of the best students in your graduating class, it isn't likely that you will be very competitive in Wesleyan's applicant pool. Strong communicators can help open the doors by submitting persuasive essays and interviews that clearly demonstrate an effective match with the University.

FINANCIAL AID

Students should submit: FAFSA (due January 15), CSS Profile, the school's own financial aid form (due January 15), state aid form, a copy of parents' most recent income tax filing (due January 15). The Princeton Review suggests that all financial aid forms be submitted as soon as possible after January 1. *The following grants/scholarships are offered:* Pell, SEOG, the school's own scholarships, the school's own grants, state scholarships, state grants, private scholarships, private grants. *Students borrow from the following loan programs:* Stafford, PLUS, the school's own loan fund, state loans, private loans. Applicants will be notified of awards beginning April 15. College Work-Study Program is available. Institutional employment is available.

FROM THE ADMISSIONS OFFICE

"Wesleyan offers only one undergraduate degree, the bachelor of arts. Students may choose from about 950 courses each year and may be counted upon to devise, with the faculty, some 1,500 individual tutorials and lessons. True to its name, the University also offers master's degrees in eleven fields of study and doctoral degrees in six. Outstanding facilities permit Wesleyan's faculty and students to teach, learn, and live in a very attractive environment. Sophisticated laboratories and an observatory housing Connecticut's largest reflecting telescope serve introductory courses and advanced research alike. More than half of the student body participates in intramural athletics; men and women form twenty-nine teams in intercollegiate competition."

ADMISSIONS

Admissions Rating	94
% of applicants accepted	31
% of acceptees attending	38

FRESHMAN PROFILE

Average verbal SAT	670
Average math SAT	650
Average ACT	29
Average TOEFL	NR
Graduated top 20% of class	85
Graduated top 40% of class	97
Graduated top 60% of class	NR
Average HS GPA or Avg.	NR

DEADLINES

Early decision	NR
Regular admission	1/1
Regular notification	4/15
Non-fall registration	no

APPLICANTS ALSO LOOK AT
AND OFTEN PREFER

Harvard/Radcliffe
Columbia
Brown
Stanford
Duke

AND SOMETIMES PREFER

Amherst
Princeton
Williams
Bowdoin
Swarthmore

AND RARELY PREFER

Oberlin
Brandeis
Vassar
Middlebury Coll.

FINANCIAL FACTS

Financial Aid Rating	75
Tuition	$21,910
Room & board	$6,030
Estimated book expense	$800
% frosh receiving aid	49
% undergrads receiving aid	49
% aid is need-based	100
% frosh w/ grant (avg)	44 ($13,993)
% frosh w/ loan (avg)	49 ($5,000)
% UGs w/ job (avg)	50 ($1,500)
Off-campus job outlook	good

WEST VIRGINIA UNIVERSITY

P.O. Box 6009, Morgantown, WV 26506-6009   Admissions: 800-344-9881   Fax: 304-293-3080

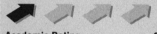
STUDENTS SPEAK OUT

Life

Most West Virginia University students would agree with one who writes, "The social life here is great!" WVU students seem to find ample time to socialize. Despite a lopsided male/female ratio, students express satisfaction with the romantic scene. Fraternities and sororities provide the setting for most parties and sponsor several major campus-wide festivals (complains one student, "Fraternities and sororities basically control all student activities"). Still, the nucleus of the WVU social universe is intercollegiate sports. Students are ardent supporters of Mountaineer football and basketball. Students give Morgantown average grades, but noted that relations with local residents could be better. Explains one student, "It's the only town in the U.S. where the students are blamed for every wrongdoing that goes on in town."

Academics

"West Virginia University is known for its party atmosphere, so many overlook the true value of the education available here," explains one student. "The school has its weaker courses, it's true, but overall the education provided here is strong." Another concurs: "I've noticed that those who come to learn do indeed succeed, and those who come to party are gone within a year." Our survey shows that WVU students attend nearly all classes and put in close to three hours of studying a day afterward, so the days of "all party, no study" truly are in WVU's past. Business and management, engineering, and health sciences are the most popular fields, and all students must meet challenging distribution requirements: four courses each in the humanities, natural sciences/mathematics, and social sciences are necessary for graduation. As at most large universities, classes are often huge, professors are often inaccessible, and the bureaucracy can reach nightmarish proportions. Still, those who stick around for all four years feel that, in the end, a WVU education is worth the trouble (particularly considering its bargain-basement price). Says one senior, "Course registration, core curriculum classes, and financial aid can be so frustrating and intense that you feel like you're dealing with the federal government. However, once you are far into your major, the school can begin to shine. Classes delve more deeply into the subjects and the professors give you more attention. I can't say enough good about my program (journalism)." An honors program provides approximately 600 undergrads with smaller classes and more rigorous academics.

Student Body

A little more than half of WVU's students come from in-state. Many others are from neighboring states, but the school does draw students from all across the country and over fifty foreign countries to boot. Over 90 percent of the students are white.

FINANCIAL AID: 304-293-5242

WEB SITE: HTTP://WWW.WVU.EDU

ADMISSIONS

The admissions committee considers (in descending order of importance): HS record, test scores, recommendations, class rank. *Also considered (in descending order of importance):* alumni relationship, extracurriculars, geographical distribution, personality, special talents. Either the SAT or ACT is required. *High school units required/recommended:* 18 total units are required; 4 English required, 3 math required, 2 science required, 2 foreign language recommended, 2 social studies required, 1 history required. Recommended electives may include fine arts, computer science, and typing. Listed units are general minimum requirements; some programs have higher requirements. Minimum combined SAT I score of 770 (composite ACT score of 19) and minimum 2.0 GPA required of in-state applicants. Combined SAT I score of 820 (composite ACT score of 20) and minimum 2.25 GPA required of out-of-state applicants. *Special Requirements:* A portfolio is required for art program applicants. An audition is required for music program applicants. TOEFL is required of all international students. 3.5 units of mathematics required of computer science, engineering, and mineral and energy resources program applicants. *The admissions office says:* "Students are urged to focus on laboratory sciences."

The Inside Word

West Virginia's admissions office made an excellent point about rolling admission in their response to us, which applies to candidates for admission at any university that uses such an approach. As the admissions committee gets closer to its enrollment targets, the admissions process becomes progressively more selective. At West Virginia the early bird usually gets a worm, and there is often another one for a late bird. Still, don't hold off on rolling admission applications just because others have more pressing deadlines. Forget that there's a rolling plan, and complete your application as if it has to be in at the same time as all the rest.

FINANCIAL AID

Students should submit: FAFSA (due March 1), the school's own financial aid form (due March 1). The Princeton Review suggests that all financial aid forms be submitted as soon as possible after January 1. *The following grants/scholarships are offered:* Pell, SEOG, academic merit, athletic, the school's own scholarships, the school's own grants, state scholarships, state grants, private scholarships, private grants, federal nursing scholarship, ROTC. *Students borrow from the following loan programs:* Stafford, unsubsidized Stafford, Perkins, PLUS, the school's own loan fund, federal nursing loans, health professions loans, private loans. College Work-Study Program is available. Institutional employment is available.

FROM THE ADMISSIONS OFFICE

"West Virginia University combines the breadth of academic opportunities offered by a major research institution with the atmosphere of a small school; the undergraduate student/faculty ratio is 17:1. Enrollment in one of the University's fifteen colleges and schools offers students the warmth and friendliness of a small academic community. WVU encourages diversity and promotes social justice in all of its activities."

ADMISSIONS

Admissions Rating	66
% of applicants accepted	83
% of acceptees attending	37

FRESHMAN PROFILE

Average verbal SAT	520
Average math SAT	520
Average ACT	22
Average TOEFL	550
Graduated top 20% of class	NR
Graduated top 40% of class	NR
Graduated top 60% of class	NR
Average HS GPA or Avg.	3.1

DEADLINES

Early decision	NR
Regular admission	3/1
Regular notification	rolling
Non-fall registration	yes

APPLICANTS ALSO LOOK AT

AND OFTEN PREFER

Miami U.
Marquette
Washington U.
James Madison

AND SOMETIMES PREFER

U. Pittsburgh
Virginia Tech
U. Maryland-Coll. Park

AND RARELY PREFER

Ohio State-Columbus
Penn State-U. Park

FINANCIAL FACTS

Financial Aid Rating	69
In-state tuition	$2,192
Out-of-state tuition	$6,784
Room & board	$4,434
Estimated book expense	$560
% frosh receiving aid	56
% undergrads receiving aid	54
% aid is need-based	77
% frosh w/ grant (avg)	49 ($1,113)
% frosh w/ loan (avg)	41 ($1,971)
% UGs w/ job (avg)	18 ($1,400)
Off-campus job outlook	excellent

WESTMINSTER COLLEGE (PA)

SOUTH MARKET STREET, NEW WILMINGTON, PA 16172   ADMISSIONS: 412-946-7100   FAX: 412-946-7171

CAMPUS LIFE

Quality of Life Rating	**79**
Type of school	private
Affiliation	Presbyterian Church USA
Environment	rural

STUDENTS

FT undergrad enrollment	1,473
% male/female	41/59
% from out of state	25
% live on campus	90
% spend weekend on campus	NR
% transfers	4
% from public high school	70
% in (# of) fraternities	60 (5)
% in (# of) sororities	45 (5)
% African-American	1
% Asian	1
% Caucasian	97
% Hispanic	0
% international	NR
# of countries represented	1

WHAT'S HOT
Greeks
religion
intercollegiate sports
hard liquor
student government

WHAT'S NOT
off-campus food
campus food
lack of diversity on campus
students are cliquish
computer facilities

ACADEMICS

Academic Rating	**80**
Profs Interesting Rating	83
Profs Accessible Rating	83
Calendar	4-1-4
Student/teacher ratio	16:1
% profs PhD/tenured	87/87
Hours of study per day	3.35

MOST POPULAR MAJORS
business administration
elementary education
history

% GRADS WHO PURSUE...
Law 3, Med 3, MBA 2

STUDENTS SPEAK OUT

Life

Westminster College is located in the secluded Amish town of New Wilmington, apparently a well-coifed and religious place that boasts "seven hair salons and six churches." On campus, one student reports, "There really is not anything exciting to do unless you go to a fraternity. I go to Taco Bell." Many others do choose the former route, because "If the students did not have fraternities or sororities, we would be bored out of our minds." And some still seem to be. More than one person tells us that "Westminster is doing an incredibly better job at recruiting students who do not know how to have fun." Another informs, "Aside from hanging out at frats, those who have cars...pack up and go home." For those with a little more imagination, there are outlets besides frats on campus, including a national service group, music clubs, an active student government, a radio station, and Bible study groups. WC has a considerable population of religious Christians, many of whom take exception to the rowdy fraternity parties, but some of whom manage to blend their religious and worldly interests. One student tells us that his peers are concerned with "God, beer, sex, and weed—honestly."

Academics

Two features set Westminster apart from other small private schools. One is its relatively low tuition: Although not cheap by public school standards, WC charges four to five thousand dollars a year less than similar schools (and, the vast majority of students receive financial aid). The other is the school's admissions demographic: Students who might not get into schools with similar profiles, such as Gettysburg or Dickinson, are much more likely to be accepted by WC. Once here, undergraduates enjoy a homey atmosphere, involved professors ("I have been in study groups late at night when we have run into questions concerning our book or our lesson. I am not at all uncomfortable in calling professors at home and asking them these questions"), and small, "relaxed" classes. The administration, however, can be less friendly, "outside of the president," whom everyone likes and refers to as "Oscar." A core curriculum requires most students to take several courses in the sciences, humanities, mathematics, computer science, and religion. An Honors Program is available for advanced students. Preprofessional tracks—business and education—are most popular with students. The school holds a mandatory January term, which may be used for internships, academic travel, or independent study.

Student Body

The Westminster student body is overwhelmingly white and "middle to lower-middle-class, and predominantly Republican." According to most students, everyone is so friendly that "When walking to classes, you have to allow 'Hi time' because everyone will stop and ask you how you are." However, "The students group themselves by Greek organizations and segregate themselves as such. Those not included are viewed as outsiders." The truth of that comment is evidenced by this dissenter: "Most times, I feel out of place because I do not drink, smoke, do drugs, or have sex." Another problem that stems from the enclosed lifestyle is gossip, which "runs deep enough here to drown most vertebrates."

WESTMINSTER COLLEGE (PA)

ADMISSIONS

The admissions committee considers (in descending order of importance): HS record, class rank, test scores, recommendations, essay. *Also considered (in descending order of importance):* extracurriculars, personality, alumni relationship, geographical distribution, special talents. Either the SAT or ACT is required. An interview is recommended. Admissions process is need-blind. *High school units required/recommended:* 18 total units are required; 4 English required, 3 math required, 2 science required, 2 foreign language required, 3 social studies required, 1 history required. *The admissions office says:* "Applicants must have a minimum 2.5 GPA in high school."

The Inside Word

The vast majority of those who apply to Westminster gain admission, but the applicant pool is strong enough to enable the College to weed out those who don't measure up to the solid entering class academic profile. Candidates who are shooting for academic scholarships should play the admissions game all the way, and put a solid effort into the completion of their applications.

FINANCIAL AID

Students should submit: FAFSA, the school's own financial aid form (due May 1), a copy of parents' most recent income tax filing. The Princeton Review suggests that all financial aid forms be submitted as soon as possible after January 1. *The following grants/scholarships are offered:* Pell, SEOG, academic merit, athletic, the school's own scholarships, the school's own grants, state scholarships, state grants, private scholarships, private grants, foreign aid. *Students borrow from the following loan programs:* Stafford, Perkins, PLUS. Applicants will be notified of awards beginning: rolling. College Work-Study Program is available. Institutional employment is available. Freshmen are discouraged from working.

FROM THE ADMISSIONS OFFICE

"Since its founding, Westminster has been dedicated to a solid foundation in today's most crucial social, cultural, and ethical issues. Related to the Presbyterian Church (U.S.A.), Westminster is home to people of many faiths. The diversity of our students and faculty, tradition of campus, and small-town setting all contribute to an enlightening educational experience."

ADMISSIONS

Admissions Rating	69
% of applicants accepted	86
% of acceptees attending	47

FRESHMAN PROFILE

Average verbal SAT	550
Average math SAT	540
Average ACT	24
Average TOEFL	550
Graduated top 20% of class	57
Graduated top 40% of class	82
Graduated top 60% of class	95
Average HS GPA or Avg.	3.2

DEADLINES

Early decision	NR
Regular admission	4/15
Regular notification	rolling
Non-fall registration	yes

APPLICANTS ALSO LOOK AT

AND OFTEN PREFER
Miami U.

AND SOMETIMES PREFER
Penn State-U. Park
Allegheny

AND RARELY PREFER
Duquesne
Indiana U.-Bloomington
Washington & Jefferson
Kent State
Slippery Rock

FINANCIAL FACTS

Financial Aid Rating	**90**
Tuition	$12,810
Room & board	$3,980
Estimated book expense	$250
% frosh receiving aid	90
% undergrads receiving aid	91
% aid is need-based	75
% frosh w/ grant (avg)	82 ($7,000)
% frosh w/ loan (avg)	75 ($3,100)
% UGs w/ job (avg)	25 ($1,300)
Off-campus job outlook	poor

WHEATON COLLEGE (MA)

NORTON, MA 02766

ADMISSIONS: 800-394-6003   FAX: 508-285-8270

CAMPUS LIFE

Quality of Life Rating   **77**
Type of school   private
Affiliation   none
Environment   town

STUDENTS
FT undergrad enrollment   1,299
% male/female   31/69
% from out of state   58
% live on campus   98
% spend weekend on campus   75
% transfers   3
% from public high school   62
% African-American   2
% Asian   3
% Caucasian   85
% Hispanic   3
% international   4
# of countries represented   26

WHAT'S HOT
cigarettes
support groups
theater
registration is a breeze
student government

WHAT'S NOT
off-campus food
Norton
Greeks
town-gown relations
religion

ACADEMICS

Academic Rating   **86**
Profs Interesting Rating   93
Profs Accessible Rating   92
Calendar   semester
Student/teacher ratio   13:1
% profs PhD   96
Hours of study per day   3.47

MOST POPULAR MAJORS
psychology
English literature
history

% GRADS WHO PURSUE...
Law 12, Med 4, MBA 8, MA 23

STUDENTS SPEAK OUT

Life

Wheaton College is located in Norton, a town that is "boring, but located between Boston and Providence, so it's okay." Students warn, however, that "access to a car is a must to reach entertainment." On campus, "students are encouraged to get involved in extracurricular activities, and do!" There is no Greek system here, but that does not curtail drinking. Reported one student, "Like many rural campuses, Wheaton has a strong alcohol presence, but it is kept under control." One student warned that "weekends are pretty dead here. Parties are usually just a bunch of people standing and drinking. The main point is to get drunk, not to enjoy yourself. It's boring." Students reported that things have been "changing rapidly" at Wheaton College since the school went coeducational in 1988. The most important quality of life issue on campus remains the lopsided male/female ratio—women currently outnumber men by more than 2:1. One man wrote that this "is a big plus for many guys on campus, who, shall we say, try to take advantage of the situation." Many women feel that the school, in its effort to boost its male population, has denigrated its admissions standards, "the men here are all slovenly lackadaisical goof-offs," wrote one fed-up woman. One other important quality of life issue is the small student body: "Be careful what you say here," wrote one student, "because it will get around."

Academics

Wheaton offers a rigorous liberal arts education provided by "very knowledgeable and extraordinarily accessible" professors. Our respondents lauded their professors in unqualified terms: wrote one, "Close relationships with instructors and students [are] of vital importance to Wheaton students. Wheaton offers that personal touch that every young adult needs and wants." Said another, "Most of my profs have great senses of humor. They help make Wheaton what it is: a fun, enthusiastic, competitive college." Students also praised the administration ("although sometimes they're a little uptight and self righteous," offered one student), and particularly appreciated the active career services office. "The Filene Center for Work and Learning has been very helpful in providing info regarding internships and jobs," wrote one student. "It also helps students write résumés and cover letters." Wheaton demands a lot of its students, who must complete a broad range of general education requirements and who study, on average, about three and a quarter hours a day.

Student Body

Wheaton's student body is not a terribly diverse one. One student described the campus climate as "many WASPs, many Saabs, and a lot of money." A good number feel that students here would be better served if the student body were more diverse, in terms of both class and ethnicity. One student summed up the mood on campus this way: "There is simply no unity, and besides classes it feels like a prep school." A number of women did note, however, that Wheaton remains a "strong women's college-Wheaton still holds over a lot of ideas from the pre-1987 move to coeducation."

FINANCIAL AID: 508-285-8232   E-MAIL: ADMISSION@WHEATONMA.EDU   WEB SITE: HTTP://WWW.WHEATONMA.EDU

ADMISSIONS

The admissions committee considers (in descending order of importance): HS record, class rank, essay, recommendations, test scores. *Also considered (in descending order of importance):* extracurriculars, personality, special talents, alumni relationship, geographical distribution. An interview is recommended. Admissions process is need-blind. *High school units required/recommended:* 18 total units are required; 4 English required, 3 math required, 3 science required, 3 foreign language required, 3 social studies required. No standardized tests required for admission but may be taken for placement purposes. TOEFL is required of all international students.

The Inside Word

Wheaton is to be applauded for periodically reexamining its admissions process; some colleges use virtually the same application process eternally, never acknowledging the fluid nature of societal attitudes and institutional circumstances. Approaches that emphasize individuals, or even their accomplishments, over their numbers are unfortunately rare in the world of college admission, where GPA and SAT I reign supreme. Wheaton has an easier time than some colleges in taking this step because it isn't particularly selective. Getting in is even easier for men, and will be for the foreseeable future.

FINANCIAL AID

Students should submit: FAFSA, the school's own financial aid form, a copy of parents' most recent income tax filing. The Princeton Review suggests that all financial aid forms be submitted as soon as possible after January 1. *The following grants/scholarships are offered:* Pell, SEOG, the school's own grants, state scholarships, state grants, private scholarships. *Students borrow from the following loan programs:* Stafford, Perkins, PLUS, the school's own loan fund, state loans, private loans. Applicants will be notified of awards beginning March 24. College Work-Study Program is available. Institutional employment is available.

FROM THE ADMISSIONS OFFICE

"What makes for a 'best college'? Is it merely the hard-to-define notions of prestige or image? We don't think so. We think what makes college 'best' and best for you is a school that will make you a first-rate thinker and writer, a pragmatic professional in your work, and an ethical practitioner in your life. "To get you to all these places, Wheaton takes advantage of its great combinations: a beautiful, secluded New England campus combined with access to Boston and Providence; a high quality, classic liberal arts and sciences curriculum combined with award-winning internship, job, and community service programs; and a campus that respects your individuality in the context of the larger community. "What's the 'best' outcome of a Wheaton education? A start on life that combines meaningful work, significant relationships, and a commitment to your local and global community. Far more than for what they've studied or for what they've gone on to do for a living, we're most proud of Wheaton graduates for who they become."

ADMISSIONS

Admissions Rating	71
% of applicants accepted	76
% of acceptees attending	30

FRESHMAN PROFILE

Average verbal SAT	600
Average math SAT	560
Average ACT	24
Average TOEFL	550
Graduated top 20% of class	40
Graduated top 40% of class	70
Graduated top 60% of class	88
Average HS GPA or Avg.	3.1

DEADLINES

Early decision	NR
Regular admission	2/1
Regular notification	4/1
Non-fall registration	yes

APPLICANTS ALSO LOOK AT

AND OFTEN PREFER

Connecticut Coll.
Boston Coll.

AND SOMETIMES PREFER

Skidmore
Clark
U. Rhode Island
Bates

AND RARELY PREFER

Providence
U. Mass.-Amherst

FINANCIAL FACTS

Financial Aid Rating	83
Tuition	$19,020
Room & board	$6,050
Estimated book expense	$700
% frosh receiving aid	70
% undergrads receiving aid	64
% aid is need-based	100
% frosh w/ grant (avg)	62 ($13,700)
% frosh w/ loan (avg)	68 ($2,400)
% UGs w/ job (avg)	80 ($550)
Off-campus job outlook	good

WHITMAN COLLEGE

WALLA WALLA, WA 99362

ADMISSIONS: 509-527-5176   FAX: 509-527-5859

CAMPUS LIFE

Quality of Life Rating — **87**

Type of school	private
Affiliation	none
Environment	city

STUDENTS

FT undergrad enrollment	1,300
% male/female	48/52
% from out of state	52
% live on campus	77
% spend weekend on campus	95
% transfers	10
% from public high school	85
% in (# of) fraternities	38 (4)
% in (# of) sororities	39 (6)
% African-American	1
% Asian	7
% Caucasian	85
% Hispanic	3
% international	2
# of countries represented	23

WHAT'S HOT
college radio
school runs like butter
intramural sports
theater
health facilities

WHAT'S NOT
off-campus food
town-gown relations
lack of diversity on campus
student government
cigarettes

ACADEMICS

Academic Rating	**92**
Profs Interesting Rating	95
Profs Accessible Rating	96
Calendar	semester
Student/teacher ratio	11:1
% profs PhD/tenured	91/92
Hours of study per day	3.66

MOST POPULAR MAJORS
history
politics
English

% GRADS WHO PURSUE...
Law 11, Med 5, MBA 14, MA 47

STUDENTS SPEAK OUT

Life

Citing its small campus, remote location, and air that is "clean and beautiful," students at Whitman College describe their school's atmosphere as "peaceful." Very few schools offer the housing option of "living in the mountains on a river off campus." At Whitman it's possible to "ride around in the hills on motorcycles" after classes! Students describe their school as "a very positive place" where "you can learn so much more than just academics." As one student exclaims, "I can't rave enough about this school." Whitman students share the surrounding community of Walla Walla with two other colleges and about 30,000 residents, and relations among these factions are generally strained. As a result, most social activity at Whitman takes place on campus. One in five students pledges a fraternity or sorority each year. Ultimate Frisbee, lacrosse, and something called "beer pong" are big. "Movie rentals are another bonding experience." A social activity unique to Whitman, called "cruising the wheatfields," is also very popular. "Friends either drive to the wheatfields to watch the awesome sunsets or go at night to see the stars. There is always the possibility that an irate farmer will come running at you with a shotgun, which adds a little excitement," explains one student. Finally, and this fact cannot be taken lightly, "the washers and dryers are free."

Academics

Whitman is "one of the best-kept secrets west of the Mississippi." This highly competitive but largely undiscovered gem of the inland Northwest has almost everything going for it: a beautiful setting, a rigorous, "difficult" curriculum; a dedicated and "exceptionally willing" faculty; an attentive and "helpful" administration; and a phenomenal success rate among its graduates (three-quarters of whom continue on to professional or graduate school within a year of graduation). Students proclaim that their school is the "land of accessibility," a place where "professors will answer your questions even if you catch them in the local grocery store." As one student explains: "The president of the college dropped by my fraternity house for lunch one day. You can't get more accessible than that." These professors are awfully demanding in return, and students must work very hard academically. On average, students spend a relatively high three hours studying each day. Also, "the grading is very tough." A smattering of students criticize Whitman for failing to standardize "grading and subject material in courses with the same title." Overall, Whitties report a high level of satisfaction with all aspects of their academic experience, which includes a Western Civilization-oriented freshman core curriculum and a wide array of distribution requirements. Seniors must also pass comprehensive written and oral exams to get their diplomas.

Student Body

"I love the close-knit, family atmosphere here," declares a well-adjusted freshman. "You feel like hugging every one of your classmates." According to another student, "the typical Whittie comes from a white, well-to-do family, has a deep concern for the environment, and is studious, down-to-earth, outdoorsy, and very friendly." However, warns a sophomore, "some students are a little pretentious." Minority students are in short supply. But despite the homogeneous exterior of the student population, "the Whitman student motto is 'do your own thing.' You can do whatever you want and probably even find at least ten people who are into the same thing." There is some animosity between Greeks and independents. And, laments one student, "There's not enough weirdos."

FINANCIAL AID: 509-527-5178

ADMISSIONS

The admissions committee considers (in descending order of importance): HS record, class rank, essay, test scores, recommendations. *Also considered (in descending order of importance):* extracurriculars, alumni relationship, geographical distribution, personality, special talents. Either the SAT or ACT is required; SAT is preferred. An interview is recommended. Admissions process is need-blind. *High school units required/recommended:* 18 total units are recommended; 4 English recommended, 4 math recommended, 3 science recommended, 2 foreign language recommended. TOEFL is required of all international students. *The admissions office says:* "It is difficult to compare the inner workings of your operation with others you are not privy to. Having said that, several things distinguish us. Our admissions committee is faculty-driven and they meet with us to evaluate over 50 percent of our candidates. Also, our process is highly personalized, and an individual's human qualities (motivation, drive, initiative, concern for others) are given consideration. [Our students are] probably much more concerned about the environment and environmental issues [than average students]. It's a very 'green' student body."

The Inside Word

Whitman's admissions committee is to be applauded; any admissions process that emphasizes essays and extracurriculars over the SAT I has truly gotten it right. The college cares much more about who you are and what you have to offer if you enroll than it does about what your numbers will do for the freshman academic profile. Whitman is a mega-sleeper Educators all over the country know it as an excellent institution, and the College's alums support it at one of the highest rates of giving at any college in the nation. Student looking for a top-quality liberal arts college owe it to themselves to take a look.

FINANCIAL AID

Students should submit: FAFSA (due February 15), the school's own financial aid form. The Princeton Review suggests that all financial aid forms be submitted as soon as possible after January 1. *The following grants/scholarships are offered:* Pell, SEOG, academic merit, the school's own scholarships, the school's own grants, state scholarships, state grants, private scholarships, private grants, foreign aid. *Students borrow from the following loan programs:* Stafford, unsubsidized Stafford, Perkins, PLUS, the school's own loan fund, private loans. College Work-Study Program is available. Institutional employment is available.

FROM THE ADMISSIONS OFFICE

"Whitman is a place which encourages you to explore past the boundaries of disciplines because learning and living don't always fall neatly into tidy little compartments. Many students choose Whitman specifically because they're interested in a particular career such as business or engineering but want the well-rounded preparation that only a liberal arts education provides."

ADMISSIONS

Admissions Rating	86
% of applicants accepted	52
% of acceptees attending	35

FRESHMAN PROFILE

Average verbal SAT	630
Average math SAT	620
Average ACT	27
Average TOEFL	560
Graduated top 20% of class	76
Graduated top 40% of class	95
Graduated top 60% of class	100
Average HS GPA or Avg.	3.7

DEADLINES

Early decision	NR
Regular admission	2/1
Regular notification	4/1
Non-fall registration	yes

APPLICANTS ALSO LOOK AT

AND OFTEN PREFER
Stanford

AND SOMETIMES PREFER
U. Puget Sound
Colorado Coll.
Lewis & Clark
U. Oregon

AND RARELY PREFER
Western Washington
Willamette
U. Washington

FINANCIAL FACTS

Financial Aid Rating	91
Tuition	$18,650
Room & board	$5,420
Estimated book expense	$750
% frosh receiving aid	85
% undergrads receiving aid	82
% aid is need-based	63
% frosh w/ grant (avg)	80 ($8,150)
% frosh w/ loan (avg)	51 ($3,550)
% UGs w/ job (avg)	48 ($806)
Off-campus job outlook	good

WHITTIER COLLEGE

13406 East Philadelphia Street, Whittier, CA 90608 · Admissions: 310-907-4238 · Fax: 310-698-4067

CAMPUS LIFE

Quality of Life Rating	79
Type of school	private
Affiliation	none
Environment	city

STUDENTS

FT undergrad enrollment	1,301
% male/female	45/55
% from out of state	25
% live on campus	62
% spend weekend on campus	85
% transfers	21
% from public high school	68
% in (# of) fraternities	17 (4)
% in (# of) sororities	24 (5)
% African-American	5
% Asian	10
% Caucasian	53
% Hispanic	29
% international	3
# of countries represented	15

WHAT'S HOT

different students interact
town-gown relations
old-fashioned dating
dorms
ethnic diversity on campus

WHAT'S NOT

library
college radio
computer facilities
campus food
unattractive campus

ACADEMICS

Academic Rating	83
Profs Interesting Rating	92
Profs Accessible Rating	95
Calendar	4-1-4
Student/teacher ratio	14:1
% profs PhD/tenured	89/63
Hours of study per day	3.15

MOST POPULAR MAJORS

business administration
political science
English

% GRADS WHO PURSUE...

Law 2, Med 2, MBA 2, MA 5

STUDENTS SPEAK OUT

Life

Life at Whittier College "has its ups and downs." On the one hand, "it's really easy to meet people" and students rave about belonging to a widely diverse "little community." Also, the location is great: "Whittier is close to LA, so there are many things to do." Beautiful beaches and majestic mountains are nearby, and "Disneyland and Universal Studios are only 20 minutes away." The school provides "a wide variety of political, social, and musical events" in which student involvement is very high, and a new social center has been eagerly anticipated. On the other hand, "the weekends are dead if you don't get off campus." In recent years, the administration has vigilantly cracked down on drug use and underage drinking, which has led some students to accuse the administration of putting "a stranglehold on student activities." In fact, some students complain that "campus safety is used for the wrong reasons." The zeal of the administration notwithstanding, life at Whittier still features a thriving social scene, though most drinking occurs off campus, "which is stupid because then we all have to drive." A new food service, chosen by a committee that included students, may put an end to complaints about campus food. Student societies, the Whittier equivalent of fraternities and sororities, are popular.

Academics

Only Whittier College can claim former President Richard Nixon as an alumnus. Nixon, a Quaker, was drawn by the school's Quaker affiliation. Although Whittier has all but severed its religious ties, it remains true to its Quaker roots, emphasizing innovation and community in its curriculum. Students must choose between two courses of study. The first, called the Liberal Education track, focuses on the development of creative and analytical skills. Students who choose the second track, called the Whittier Scholars Program, work with advisors to design their own majors and programs of study. Either way, students here are given a lot of academic independence and are blessed with "endless academic options." Both tracks feature team-taught courses, discussion-intensive seminars on weighty issues ("the nature of civilization," for example) that "really get people to think," and a unique interdisciplinary approach. But be warned: "We write a lot at this school." Overall, students approve heartily of the "very positive academic experience" offered at Whittier. Profs are "personable and approachable" and "eager to help." As one student sums up, "Since I've been at Whittier, I've felt wittier!" Ha, ha! Student opinion of the administration is, again, a very different story. Many students complain that "the administration cares only about the Whittier image" instead of its students. "The Admissions Office is commonly referred to as the Propaganda Department" explains one student. Another gripes that "priorities are pretty mixed up; we need a new library but the president needs to spend $150,000 on a new office."

Student Body

Despite sparse vestiges of elitism and a few cliques of "Melrose and 90210 wannabes," students at Whittier report that they are largely a "friendly," "laid back," and "very cohesive group." (Except for a few students who are "loud, obnoxious and stupid," but that stands to reason.) There is a great deal of diversity here, and "very little discrimination" against anyone. Students seem very proud about how well the student population gets along. What's the secret? Whittier students assert that they maintain as much respect and tolerance for their fellow students as they can muster. "We are all individuals and respect one another, which is part of the Quaker heritage."

FINANCIAL AID: 310-907-4285   E-MAIL: JASH@WHITTIER.EDU   WEB SITE: HTTP://WWW.WHITTIER.EDU/

ADMISSIONS

The admissions committee considers (in descending order of importance): HS record, recommendations, test scores, class rank, essay. *Also considered (in descending order of importance):* personality, alumni relationship, extracurriculars, special talents. Either the SAT or ACT is required. An interview is recommended. Admissions process is need-blind. *High school units required/recommended:* 17 total units are recommended; 4 English recommended, 3 math recommended, 3 science recommended, 2 foreign language recommended, 2 social studies recommended, 3 history recommended. TOEFL is required of all international students. *The admissions office says:* "What really happens? Picture yourself making a point in a heated class discussion, researching a paper that you and your professor will present together, preparing a senior project that seems to tie in almost everything you've learned. Then imagine yourself feeling more intellectually alive than you've ever felt before. That's what happens to you at Whittier. Want to learn more? Call us, write us, or better yet, visit us and see if we are all we claim to be!"

The Inside Word

The admissions committee at Whittier subjects each candidate to very close scrutiny. Their academic expectations aren't too high, but their interest in making good solid matches between candidates and the college is paramount. If Whittier is high on your list, make sure you put forth a serious effort to demonstrate what you want out of the college and what you'll bring to the table in return.

FINANCIAL AID

Students should submit: FAFSA, CSS Profile, a copy of parents' most recent income tax filing. The Princeton Review suggests that all financial aid forms be submitted as soon as possible after January 1. *The following grants/scholarships are offered:* Pell, SEOG, academic merit, the school's own scholarships, the school's own grants, state scholarships, state grants, private scholarships, private grants, ROTC, foreign aid. *Students borrow from the following loan programs:* Stafford, unsubsidized Stafford, Perkins, PLUS, the school's own loan fund, private loans. Applicants will be notified of awards beginning April 1. College Work-Study Program is available. Institutional employment is available.

FROM THE ADMISSIONS OFFICE

"Faculty and students at Whittier share a love of learning and delight in the life of the mind. They join in understanding the value of the intellectual quest, the use of reason, and a respect for values. They seek knowledge of their own culture and the informed appreciation of other traditions, and they explore the interrelatedness of knowledge and the connections among disciplines. An extraordinary community emerges from teachers and students representing a variety of academic pursuits, individuals who have come together at Whittier in the belief that study within the liberal arts forms the best foundation for rewarding endeavor throughout a lifetime."

ADMISSIONS

Admissions Rating	69
% of applicants accepted	66
% of acceptees attending	27

FRESHMAN PROFILE

Average verbal SAT	530
Average math SAT	520
Average ACT	22
Average TOEFL	580
Graduated top 20% of class	45
Graduated top 40% of class	71
Graduated top 60% of class	89
Average HS GPA or Avg.	3.0

DEADLINES

Early decision	12/1
Regular admission	2/1
Regular notification	rolling
Non-fall registration	no

APPLICANTS ALSO LOOK AT

AND OFTEN PREFER
Pomona

AND SOMETIMES PREFER
Claremont McKenna
UCLA

AND RARELY PREFER
U. Redlands
UC—San Diego

FINANCIAL FACTS

Financial Aid Rating	95
Tuition	$17,800
Room & board	$6,047
Estimated book expense	$500
% frosh receiving aid	83
% undergrads receiving aid	81
% aid is need-based	88
% frosh w/ grant (avg)	83 ($10,812)
% frosh w/ loan (avg)	83 ($4,651)
% UGs w/ job (avg)	61 ($1,250)
Off-campus job outlook	good

WILLAMETTE UNIVERSITY

SALEM, OR 97301   ADMISSIONS: 503-370-6303   FAX: 503-375-5363

CAMPUS LIFE

Quality of Life Rating   **80**
Type of school   private
Affiliation   United Methodist Church
Environment   city

STUDENTS
FT undergrad enrollment   1,713
% male/female   44/56
% from out of state   48
% live on campus   70
% spend weekend on campus   90
% transfers   16
% from public high school   83
% in (# of) fraternities   31 (6)
% in (# of) sororities   23 (3)
% African-American   1
% Asian   5
% Caucasian   80
% Hispanic   3
% international   2
# of countries represented   23

WHAT'S HOT
computer facilities
library
town-gown relations
school runs like butter
campus food

WHAT'S NOT
student publications
college radio
lack of diversity on campus
cigarettes
health facilities

ACADEMICS

Academic Rating   **85**
Profs Interesting Rating   88
Profs Accessible Rating   92
Calendar   semester
Student/teacher ratio   13:1
% profs PhD/tenured   90/95
Hours of study per day   3.19

MOST POPULAR MAJORS
politics
English
business economics

% GRADS WHO PURSUE...
Law 3, Med 3, MBA 4, MA 10

STUDENTS SPEAK OUT
Life
Willamette University is in the heart of the lush Pacific Northwest, and, not surprisingly, the campus is easy on the eyes: says one student, "I love WU, especially the stream with the ducks!" "Size and atmosphere," says another, "is what makes the school a wonderful place to spend your college years." Because the academic mood here is pretty intense, most socializing and partying is confined to the weekends. A third of the students go Greek, and while frats and sororities play a sizable role in the school's social life, animosity between Greeks and independents is minimal, "especially after second semester rush." One complaint students have is that the school "has no substantial structure for student interaction. There is no student union and the only café is très chic." When students start craving city life, they trek up to Portland, about an hour's drive.

Academics
According to one student at Willamette, his school is "overall, the best small liberal arts school in the Northwest." Students here say they enjoy small classes and excellent professors, and they're among the nation's happier student bodies despite the fact that they study hard. Says one environmental science major, "The students are very smart and the competition is stiff." The premed program is top-notch, as are most of the natural science departments. Students interested in political science benefit from the school's location, right across the street from the state capitol; an internship program in Washington, D.C., run in conjunction with American University, is also available to poli-sci majors. Music and preprofessional programs are also said to be strong. Distribution requirements guarantee that WU undergrads are exposed to some math, literature, social sciences, natural sciences, and fine arts, whether they want to be or not. All students must also complete a senior project, which can be a major scientific research project, a senior thesis, or a professional internship.

Student Body
As one Willamette student puts it, "The student body is fairly monochromatic and moderate politically, but gradually this is improving. I've seen a lot of progress on this campus, and there is momentum growing in the liberal direction." Says another, "WU is making a concerted effort to recruit a more diverse student body." They are a bright group of people, half of whom will go directly on to graduate school after graduation. Although one West Coast student finds his classmates "rich and stuck up," they're down to earth by East Coast standards: says one transfer from Williams College in Massachusetts, "Students here are a lot less pretentious and snooty than they were at Williams."

FINANCIAL AID: 503-370-6273

WEB SITE: HTTP://WWW.WILLAMETTE.EDU/

ADMISSIONS

The admissions committee considers (in descending order of importance): HS record, class rank, essay, test scores, recommendations. *Also considered (in descending order of importance):* extracurriculars, special talents, geographical distribution, personality, alumni relationship. Either the SAT or ACT is required. An interview is recommended. *High school units required/recommended:* 16 total units are required; 4 English required, 3 math required, 3 science required, 2 foreign language required, 3 social studies required. TOEFL is required of all international students.

The Inside Word

Willamette's admissions process is relatively standard for small liberal arts colleges. Extracurriculars, recommendations, and essays help the admissions committee do some matchmaking, but ultimately it's a candidate's grades that determine admissibility.

FINANCIAL AID

Students should submit: FAFSA. The Princeton Review suggests that all financial aid forms be submitted as soon as possible after January 1. *The following grants/scholarships are offered:* Pell, SEOG, academic merit, the school's own scholarships, the school's own grants, state scholarships, state grants, private scholarships, private grants, foreign aid. *Students borrow from the following loan programs:* Stafford, unsubsidized Stafford, Perkins, PLUS, state loans, private loans. Applicants will be notified of awards beginning April 1. College Work-Study Program is available. Institutional employment is available.

FROM THE ADMISSIONS OFFICE

"Two of the primary reasons students choose Willamette are the challenge of the academic experience and the opportunity for significant involvement in co-curricular activities. They see Willamette as a place where they can engage in a rigorous liberal arts and sciences education, and enjoy exceptional, varied, and exciting opportunities outside the classroom. Students are also attracted to Willamette because of its unique location; in particular, they are attracted by the internships and political activity at the adjacent Oregon State Capitol Building, cultural exchange with Willamette's adjacent sister school, the U.S. campus of Tokyo International University, and the fact that Portland, the Oregon Coast, and the Cascade Mountains are within an hour of campus. Some of the words that best describe Willamette: academic, challenging, personal, friendly, well-located, beautiful, balanced, historic."

ADMISSIONS

Admissions Rating	81
% of applicants accepted	70
% of acceptees attending	30

FRESHMAN PROFILE

Average verbal SAT	670
Average math SAT	600
Average ACT	26
Average TOEFL	600
Graduated top 20% of class	71
Graduated top 40% of class	95
Graduated top 60% of class	99
Average HS GPA or Avg.	3.6

DEADLINES

Early decision	NR
Regular admission	2/1
Regular notification	4/1
Non-fall registration	yes

APPLICANTS ALSO LOOK AT

AND OFTEN PREFER

Colorado Coll.
Santa Clara
Claremont McKenna
Stanford

AND SOMETIMES PREFER

Lewis & Clark
U. Oregon
Oregon State
Whitman
U. Puget Sound

AND RARELY PREFER

Portland State

FINANCIAL FACTS

Financial Aid Rating	88
Tuition	$18,300
Room & board	$5,070
Estimated book expense	$400
% frosh receiving aid	85
% undergrads receiving aid	84
% aid is need-based	80
% frosh w/ grant (avg)	81 ($8,300)
% frosh w/ loan (avg)	54 ($4,500)
% UGs w/ job (avg)	70 ($1,200)
Off-campus job outlook	good

THE COLLEGE OF WILLIAM AND MARY

WILLIAMSBURG, VA 23187

ADMISSIONS: 757-221-4223   FAX: 757-221-1242

CAMPUS LIFE

Quality of Life Rating	86
Type of school	public
Affiliation	none
Environment	town

STUDENTS

FT undergrad enrollment	5,326
% male/female	42/58
% from out of state	35
% live on campus	75
% spend weekend on campus	95
% transfers	12
% from public high school	82
% in (# of) fraternities	44 (16)
% in (# of) sororities	42 (12)
% African-American	6
% Asian	7
% Caucasian	82
% Hispanic	2
% international	1
# of countries represented	36

WHAT'S HOT
religion
Greeks
campus is beautiful
intramural sports
music associations

WHAT'S NOT
drugs
sex
cigarettes
library
infrequent dating

ACADEMICS

Academic Rating	90
Profs Interesting Rating	90
Profs Accessible Rating	89
Calendar	semester
Student/teacher ratio	13:1
% profs tenured	93
Hours of study per day	2.98

MOST POPULAR MAJORS
business administration
English
biology

% GRADS WHO PURSUE...
Law 15, Med 14, MBA 5, MA 28

STUDENTS SPEAK OUT

Life

The College of William and Mary is within spitting distance of a major tourist attraction, Colonial Williamsburg. One student comments, "Williamsburg itself is very touristy and artificial in lots of ways (students equal or outnumber locals, with whom there is no contact). On the flip side, there are many interesting historic things around and the town is damn picturesque, tourists notwithstanding." The town does provide some job opportunities for students, but most students hang out on or immediately around campus, socializing either at frat parties or at local delicatessens. Greek life is very important; says one student, "The main thing to do on weekends is go to fraternity parties and sorority formals—for which it is a huge effort to get a date." But students claim that other social outlets exist, and note that extracurricular clubs and organizations are popular. The campus itself is gorgeous; writes one student, "W&M is a beautiful place to spend your college years. Unfortunately, sometimes it seems that the school pays more attention to the landscaping than it does to the students."

Academics

William and Mary is among the most competitive public schools in the nation. New general education requirements emphasize competence in seven arts and sciences areas. Professors are generally good teachers and are very accessible for those at a public institution. One student tells us, "Professors here are readily available—I got to know my Russian professor well enough that he spent an afternoon with our family over Christmas break. Most profs don't go quite that far, but it is not uncommon to have lunch with a professor." Another significant feature is the honor code, which the school claims is the oldest in the nation: it allows students to take exams in an unproctored setting. William and Mary has recently felt the pressure of Virginia's fiscal crisis. Writes one student, "The school is in the midst of serious budget problems, which are exacerbated by the fact that the administration concentrates on expansion and graduate work rather than maintaining its reputation as an excellent undergraduate liberal arts school." Course selection is among the victims of the budget ax; so far other assets remain intact, but many students voiced concerns that, without more state support, big changes may be in the offing for the school.

Student Body

The William and Mary student body is predominantly white; about 350 blacks constitute the largest minority population. In general, students are socially conservative. Says one, "Those who choose not to dress and act like the majority have to form their own groups outside the mainstream." Most students believe there is a sizable gay community on campus, but one gay student writes: "It is rumored that this is a gay campus, but let me tell you, I'm gay and it's been hard to find too many others." Politically, one student explains that "This school is liberal if you're from Virginia, conservative if you're from anywhere else." Students are the fourth most religious among those at a nonaffiliated university.

ADMISSIONS

The admissions committee considers (in descending order of importance): HS record, class rank, test scores, essay, recommendations. *Also considered (in descending order of importance):* extracurriculars, geographical distribution, personality, special talents, alumni relationship. Either the SAT or ACT is required. An interview is required of some applicants. *High school units required/recommended:* 20 total units are recommended; 4 English recommended, 4 math recommended, 3 science recommended, 4 foreign language recommended, 4 social studies recommended. TOEFL is required of all international students. *The admissions office says:* "[We have] two differently selective pools: in-state students—very competitive; out-of-state students—highly competitive. Special consideration is given to alumni children, athletes, and underrepresented ethnic minority students."

The Inside Word

The volume of applications at William and Mary is extremely high, thus admission is ultracompetitive. Only very strong students from out of state should apply. The large applicant pool necessitates a rapid-fire candidate evaluation process; each admissions officer reads roughly 100 application folders per day during the peak review season. But this is one admissions committee that moves fast without sacrificing a thorough review. There probably isn't a tougher public college admissions committee in the country.

FINANCIAL AID

Students should submit: FAFSA, the school's own financial aid form (due February 15). The Princeton Review suggests that all financial aid forms be submitted as soon as possible after January 1. *The following grants/scholarships are offered:* Pell, SEOG, academic merit, athletic, the school's own scholarships, the school's own grants, state scholarships, state grants, private scholarships, private grants, ROTC. *Students borrow from the following loan programs:* Stafford, Perkins, PLUS. Applicants will be notified of awards beginning April 1. College Work-Study Program is available. Institutional employment is available.

FROM THE ADMISSIONS OFFICE

"The College of William and Mary is a multifaceted university dedicated to intellectual inquiry, discovery, and dissemination of knowledge. For almost three hundred years, the college's commitment to 'the good arts and sciences' has attracted students of talent and achievement from Virginia and beyond. As we embark on our fourth century in 1993, we continue to honor and build upon our traditional strengths, which are at the center of a liberal education, while responding with energy to the emerging needs of the future. We are excited about the breadth of our curriculum, the richness of our offerings, and the opportunities we provide for students to gain a global perspective. The distinction of its scholar-teachers, the timeless and historic beauty of its campus, the celebration of learning and working together that invigorates its students make William and Mary a community unlike any other, a place of learning that serves as a beacon as well as an anchor."

ADMISSIONS

Admissions Rating	93
% of applicants accepted	39
% of acceptees attending	41

FRESHMAN PROFILE

Average verbal SAT	720
Average math SAT	640
Average ACT	29
Average TOEFL	630
Graduated top 20% of class	90
Graduated top 40% of class	96
Graduated top 60% of class	NR
Average HS GPA or Avg.	NR

DEADLINES

Early decision	11/1
Regular admission	1/15
Regular notification	4/1
Non-fall registration	yes

APPLICANTS ALSO LOOK AT

AND OFTEN PREFER

Virginia
Georgetown U.
Williams
Duke
Dartmouth

AND SOMETIMES PREFER

Wake Forest
Randolph-Macon Woman's
Washington and Lee
Johns Hopkins
Rice

AND RARELY PREFER

James Madison
U. Richmond

FINANCIAL FACTS

Financial Aid Rating	74
In-state tuition	$4,906
Out-of-state tuition	$14,916
Room & board	$4,490
Estimated book expense	$600
% frosh receiving aid	60
% undergrads receiving aid	53
% aid is need-based	91
% frosh w/ grant (avg)	NR ($3,300)
% frosh w/ loan (avg)	45 ($2,400)
% UGs w/ job (avg)	30 ($800)
Off-campus job outlook	good

WILLIAMS COLLEGE

WILLIAMSTOWN, MA 01267

ADMISSIONS: 413-597-2211   FAX: 413-458-2158

CAMPUS LIFE

Quality of Life Rating	**89**
Type of school	private
Affiliation	none
Environment	town

STUDENTS

FT undergrad enrollment	1,960
% male/female	51/49
% from out of state	88
% live on campus	96
% spend weekend on campus	90
% transfers	4
% from public high school	57
% African-American	6
% Asian	11
% Caucasian	73
% Hispanic	7
% international	3
# of countries represented	52

WHAT'S HOT
health facilities
school runs like butter
intercollegiate sports
dorms
intramural sports

WHAT'S NOT
infrequent dating
cigarettes
Greeks
drugs
religion

ACADEMICS

Academic Rating	**98**
Profs Interesting Rating	96
Profs Accessible Rating	96
Calendar	4-1-4
Student/teacher ratio	11:1
% profs tenured	95
Hours of study per day	3.61

MOST POPULAR MAJORS
English
history
economics

% GRADS WHO PURSUE...
Law 3, Med 6, MBA 1, MA 12

STUDENTS SPEAK OUT

Life

The gorgeous campus of Williams College is located in Williamstown, Massachussetts, an "uneventful" hamlet hemmed in by "purple mountains" and "good skiing." For many students, "the quality of life is just incredible." As one blissful freshman professes, "there hasn't been a single day when I haven't stopped and looked around and said, 'What am I doing here? It's so beautiful!'" Sometimes, though, "there's not enough to do" in Williamstown, a place which "has failed in its role as a college town," according to a junior. The campus and the surrounding area are great for athletics, and students take maximum advantage of the excellent facilities. "Sports are very big "at Williams, as is the consumption of beer, which makes for a "high proportion of keg-seeking athletes" and, later in the evening, "a whole lot of drunk jocks." On campus, living conditions are outstanding: "Our dormitory arrangements—suites with a common room—are very comfortable and particularly conducive to forming close groups of friends," explains one student. There is no Greek scene, but frat-style parties are nevertheless abundant. A broad range of extracurricular activities, including the campus newspaper, radio station, and theater and musical groups, are popular. Although students are extremely social, they "don't date much" which must be a bummer because "everyone looks like a J. Crew model."

Academics

Does Williams offer "the best undergraduate education in America"? Its students think so and—a strange penchant to bash Harvard notwithstanding—the evidence is compelling. Blessed with "a dedicated faculty" of "brilliant, accessible, and devoted professionals," Williams is a traditional liberal arts college of the highest caliber. "If you can handle being taught by world-class professors who know your name and start conversations when they see you outside of class," explains one student, "you might like it here." The academic atmosphere at Williams is "extremely challenging" and "the level of instruction and discourse is outstanding." To top it all off, "the alumni are well-connected and quite helpful to current students." Even the administration receives very high marks overall, despite more than a few complaints. The computer center "needs more attention" and the financial aid office can be unpleasant. Williams students must complete a variety of distribution requirements and attend winter session, a month-long term during which students pursue individualized and less traditional areas of academic interest. English, economics, history, and political science are among the most popular majors. The premedical sciences, while attracting fewer students, are also reputedly excellent.

Student Body

The consummate Williams student is "a white, jeans-, Patagonia-, and baseball cap-wearing, upper-middle class athlete" but there is a "great deal of tolerance for all kinds of people and interests." The proportion of minority students is considerable. A "hard-working but not cut-throat" attitude prevails at Williams and "everybody gets along remarkably well." Students are "motivated and focused" and "boy! can they hold creative conversations," though they worry that they will seem to be nerds: "Most are closet workhorses but would have you think they spend all their time partying," says a junior. Politically, "the majority of students is moderate to somewhat left-of-center." Not permanently, though. "People are so open-minded that they can change their minds about something really basic within the course of one conversation, but maybe that's due to less-strongly-held convictions."

FINANCIAL AID: 413-597-4181

WEB SITE: HTTP://WWW.WILLIAMS.EDU/

ADMISSIONS

The admissions committee considers (in descending order of importance): HS record, class rank, test scores, recommendations, essay. *Also considered (in descending order of importance):* extracurriculars, special talents, alumni relationship, geographical distribution, personality. Either the SAT or ACT is required. Admissions process is need-blind. *High school units required/recommended:* 4 English recommended, 4 math recommended, 2 science recommended, 3 foreign language recommended, 2 social studies recommended. TOEFL is required of all international students.

The Inside Word

As is typical of highly selective colleges, at Williams high grades and test scores work more as qualifiers than to determine admissibility. Beyond a strong record of achievement, evidence of intellectual curiosity, noteworthy non-academic talents, and a noncollege family background are some aspects of a candidate's application which might make for an offer of admission. But there are no guarantees—the evaluation process here is rigorous. The admissions committee (the entire admissions staff) discusses each candidate in comparison to the entire applicant pool. The pool is divided alphabetically for individual reading; after weak candidates are eliminated, those who remain undergo additional evaluations by different members of the staff. Admission decisions must be confirmed by the agreement of a plurality of the committee. Such close scrutiny demands a well-prepared candidate and application.

FINANCIAL AID

Students should submit: FAFSA (due February 1), CSS Profile (due February 1), the school's own financial aid form (due February 1), state aid form (due February 1), Divorced Parents form (due February 1), a copy of parents' most recent income tax filing (due February 1). The Princeton Review suggests that all financial aid forms be submitted as soon as possible after January 1. *The following grants/scholarships are offered:* Pell, SEOG, academic merit, the school's own scholarships, the school's own grants, state scholarships, state grants, private scholarships, private grants, foreign aid. *Students borrow from the following loan programs:* Stafford, unsubsidized Stafford, Perkins, PLUS, the school's own loan fund, supplemental loans, state loans, private loans. Applicants will be notified of awards beginning April 10. College Work-Study Program is available. Institutional employment is available.

FROM THE ADMISSIONS OFFICE

"Special Course offerings at Williams include Oxford-style tutorials, where students research and defend ideas, engaging in weekly debate with a peer and a faculty tutor. Annually thirty Williams students devote a full year to the tutorial method of study at Oxford; a quarter of Williams students pursue their education overseas. Four weeks of Winter Study each January provide time for individualized projects, research and novel fields of study. Students compete in 28 Division III athletic teams, perform in 25 musical groups, stage 10 theatrical productions, and volunteer in 30 service organizations. The college receives several million dollars annually for undergraduate science research and equipment. The town offers two distinguished art museums, and 2,200 forest acres-complete with a treetop canopy walkway-for environmental research and recreation."

ADMISSIONS

Admissions Rating	99
% of applicants accepted	26
% of acceptees attending	40

FRESHMAN PROFILE

Average verbal SAT	660
Average math SAT	700
Average ACT	30
Average TOEFL	600
Graduated top 20% of class	91
Graduated top 40% of class	99
Graduated top 60% of class	100
Average HS GPA or Avg.	NR

DEADLINES

Early decision	NR
Regular admission	1/1
Regular notification	4/9
Non-fall registration	no

APPLICANTS ALSO LOOK AT

AND OFTEN PREFER
Harvard/Radcliffe
Princeton
Yale
Amherst
Brown

AND SOMETIMES PREFER
Stanford
Dartmouth
Bowdoin
Cornell U.
Wesleyan U.

AND RARELY PREFER
Hamilton
Middlebury Coll.
U. Vermont
U. Chicago

FINANCIAL FACTS

Financial Aid Rating	81
Tuition	$21,759
Room & board	$6,140
Estimated book expense	$600
% frosh receiving aid	50
% undergrads receiving aid	50
% aid is need-based	100
% frosh w/ grant (avg)	NR ($15,500)
% frosh w/ loan (avg)	NR ($2,000)
% UGs w/ job (avg)	50 ($1,000)
Off-campus job outlook	fair

UNIVERSITY OF WISCONSIN-MADISON

750 UNIVERSITY AVENUE, MADISON, WI 53706   ADMISSIONS: 608-262-3961   FAX: 608-262-0123

CAMPUS LIFE

Quality of Life Rating	**85**
Type of school	public
Affiliation	none
Environment	city

STUDENTS

FT undergrad enrollment	26,207
% male/female	49/51
% from out of state	36
% live on campus	40
% spend weekend on campus	90
% transfers	5
% from public high school	67
% in (# of) fraternities	14 (34)
% in (# of) sororities	14 (17)
% African-American	3
% Asian	4
% Caucasian	86
% Hispanic	3
% international	5
# of countries represented	78

WHAT'S HOT
hard liquor
beer
drugs
student publications
library

WHAT'S NOT
student government
religion
theater
campus difficult to get around
students are cliquish

ACADEMICS

Academic Rating	**80**
Profs Interesting Rating	66
Profs Accessible Rating	67
Calendar	semester
Student/teacher ratio	12:1
% profs PhD/tenured	88/97
Hours of study per day	2.67

MOST POPULAR MAJORS
political science
mechanical engineering
history

STUDENTS SPEAK OUT

Life

Wisconsin-Madison is a world-class American university located in a world-class college town. With over 800 campus organizations, 14,000 works of art, and even a nuclear reactor to call their own, the nearly 30,000 undergraduate students at Wisconsin-Madison would be hard-pressed not to find something to do. Big 10 sports, especially "Badger hockey and football," are perennial student favorites, as are "hanging out at the Union" and watching the school's marching band, called the Fifth Quarter. For a small midwestern city, Madison is an oasis of culture and progressivism. The downtown area offers a stunning array of "shopping, ethnic restaurants" and even street performers, the "unbelievably cold winters" permitting. There are also a lot of bars, and Wisconsin-Madison students can consume about as much beer and liquor as any student body in the country. Some students find the "terrible alcohol/drug abuse and the ease with which it occurs in the community" lamentable. Other drugs, especially marijuana, are prevalent. "Most students have smoked a bowl in their stay here," observes a senior.

Academics

Make no mistake about it, the University of Wisconsin-Madison is a humongous institution, which is both a blessing and a curse for its students. Although you just aren't going to find a finer collection of academic facilities on the planet (let alone at these tuition rates), you cannot avoid massive amounts of administrative red tape. It comes with the territory. Not surprisingly, students fawn over the library (with its five million bound volumes and 50,000 periodical subscriptions) and the state-of-the-art research facilities. Because of the huge lectures for introductory classes and a generally inaccessible faculty, independent and self-reliant students will probably enjoy the most success at Wisconsin-Madison. Most undergrads complain that obtaining assistance from professors, teaching assistants, and administrators is a formidable task. "It's hard to find exactly who you need to talk to," explains one. All undergraduate students must complete a broad and difficult assortment of distribution requirements throughout the liberal arts and sciences. "It's harder than I thought," says one undergrad. The engineering and business schools are national powerhouses, and career-track majors—journalism, education and the premedical sciences—and the social sciences are also highly regarded. Still, for such an academically—acclaimed school, students rate the quality of teaching pretty low.

Student Body

"A lot of international students" attend the University of Wisconsin-Madison, and visible populations of all manner of ethnic and minority groups dot the campus landscape. On the surface, anyway, Wisconsin-Madison "is a liberal community" where "everyone seems to get along and fit in." And, indeed, the school upholds a rich tradition of liberalism; the first social security legislation was drafted here (young neoconservatives beware!). Underneath the multicultural veneer, however, there is some friction among ethnic and political groups. Female students and black students in particular complain that discrimination is alive and well. Further strife occurs between independents and the Greek community, which, despite its commanding role in social life, makes up only about 10 percent of the student population.

FINANCIAL AID: 608-262-3060

WEB SITE: HTTP://WWW.WISCINFO.WISC.EDU

ADMISSIONS

The admissions committee considers (in descending order of importance): class rank, HS record, test scores, recommendations, essay. *Also considered (in descending order of importance):* alumni relationship, special talents, extracurriculars, geographical distribution, personality. Either the SAT or ACT is required. Admissions process is need-blind. *High school units required/recommended:* 17 total units are required; 22 total units are recommended; 4 English required, 3 math required, 4 math recommended, 3 science required, 4 science recommended, 2 foreign language required, 4 foreign language recommended, 3 social studies required, 4 social studies recommended. *Special Requirements:* An audition is required for music program applicants. Portfolio recommended of art program applicants.

The Inside Word

Wisconsin has high expectations of its candidates, and virtually all of them relate to numbers. Though not at the top tier of selectivity, this is admissions by formula at its most refined state. Nonresidents will encounter a very selective process.

FINANCIAL AID

Students should submit: FAFSA, the school's own financial aid form, a copy of parents' most recent income tax filing. The Princeton Review suggests that all financial aid forms be submitted as soon as possible after January 1. *The following grants/scholarships are offered:* Pell, SEOG, academic merit, athletic, the school's own scholarships, the school's own grants, state scholarships, state grants, private scholarships, private grants, ROTC. *Students borrow from the following loan programs:* Stafford, Perkins, PLUS, the school's own loan fund, state loans, federal nursing loans, health professions loans, private loans. College Work-Study Program is available. Institutional employment is available.

FROM THE ADMISSIONS OFFICE

"Admission decisions of quality and fairness take time. We don't promise to be the fastest out of the box, but we do guarantee a complete, fair and thorough decision. We want applicants to provide us with as much information about themselves as they think is necessary for a group of people who don't know them to reach a favorable decision."

ADMISSIONS

Admissions Rating	**84**
% of applicants accepted	71
% of acceptees attending	44

FRESHMAN PROFILE

Average verbal SAT	670
Average math SAT	630
Average ACT	27
Average TOEFL	550
Graduated top 20% of class	80
Graduated top 40% of class	99
Graduated top 60% of class	NR
Average HS GPA or Avg.	3.5

DEADLINES

Early decision	NR
Regular admission	2/1
Regular notification	rolling
Non-fall registration	yes

APPLICANTS ALSO LOOK AT

AND OFTEN PREFER
Northwestern U.
Miami U.
UC-Berkeley
U. Texas-Austin

AND SOMETIMES PREFER
U. Michigan-Ann Arbor
U. Minnesota-Twin Cities
Marquette
Indiana U.-Bloomington

AND RARELY PREFER
U. Missouri-Rolla

FINANCIAL FACTS

Financial Aid Rating	**74**
In-state tuition	$2,730
Out-of-state tuition	$9,050
Room & board	$4,520
Estimated book expense	$565
% frosh receiving aid	46
% undergrads receiving aid	41
% aid is need-based	90
% frosh w/ grant (avg)	36 ($2,900)
% frosh w/ loan (avg)	26 ($2,841)
% UGs w/ job (avg)	50 ($1,500)
Off-campus job outlook	excellent

WITTENBERG UNIVERSITY

P.O. Box 720, Springfield, OH 45501   Admissions: 800-677-7558   Fax: 513-327-6340

STUDENTS SPEAK OUT

Life

Wittenberg University is a very good small liberal arts school in a sub-par college town, which can make Wittenberg "pretty boring outside of academic life." However, students insist that they manage to have a good time in spite of the fact that the surrounding town of Springfield, Ohio "is a dump." Wittenberg students enjoy a "great sense of community" and they agree that "the people make it worth staying." For fun, students "play sports, watch movies, or roadtrip to nearby Columbus, Dayton, and Cincinnati." They also go "hiking, mountain climbing" and even "frolic in the moonlight" for excitement. "Getting involved in clubs and organizations helps me keep my sanity," explains one student. Greek life also provides social outlets for students who pledge. While some students boldly claim that "there is always something to do," the majority contend that "there is not enough to do here except party." Indeed, drinking, sexual activity, and drug use are perennially popular pastimes. As one student sums up, "The Witt social scene is simple: go to a party, get drunk, and randomly hook up." Another declares that "Wittenberg has a reputation for having some great parties. The people around here like to have a good time and will make up any excuse to celebrate."

Academics

Strong liberal arts credentials and the quality of Wittenberg's academic experience more than make up for the town of Springfield. "What they sell in the brochure is what you get and more!" exclaims one satisfied sophomore. Wittenberg is a "great place to learn and grow as a person," chimes in another student. "I know I am getting a good education," asserts yet another. Wittenberg prides itself on its small classes and an intense academic atmosphere ("harder than hell"). A unique trimester system keeps academic life interesting. The professors here "are very good teachers who really care" and "are eager to help." Moreover, "profs always give out their phone numbers." Still, several students would "get rid of a few tenures" in a heartbeat if given the opportunity. The administration, which "can be more of a pain in the ass than a help," receives mixed reviews. Explains one student: "The administration makes decisions that affect our lives without really consulting the students. However, most of the administration is friendly and willing to help out with problems." Students gripe that there is "too much bickering" among departments and that some facilities are "outdated" or in short supply ("not enough computers"). All in all, though, most students give the administration above-average marks in all areas. The financial aid office receives especially high praise.

Student Body

The amount of diversity that anyone could possibly achieve in rural Ohio is limited. Thus, the fact that the Wittenberg student population is "not very diverse" isn't too much of a shocker. Most Wittenberg students are white and run the gamut from middle class to downright wealthy. "You can tell a majority of the students come from a very sheltered, comfortable background." Not surprisingly, "everyone gets along pretty well," although the "rich kids tend to stick with themselves." Even those who do come from different backgrounds seem to live harmoniously. Maybe that's because "Witt students have character." Wittenberg students belong to a "unique community" with a "happy, friendly atmosphere." Again and again, students assert that it is impossible "to walk through campus without getting a friendly greeting from someone." Of course, "with the school being so small, people are always in each other's business" which can become "very annoying." And for all the social harmony, the gender gap here may be a problem: one woman reports that "Witt guys must take a course in how to treat women badly before they can get accepted."

FINANCIAL AID: 513-327-7321

ADMISSIONS

The admissions committee considers (in descending order of importance): HS record, class rank, test scores, recommendations, essay. *Also considered (in descending order of importance):* personality, alumni relationship, extracurriculars, special talents, geographical distribution. Either the SAT or ACT is required. An interview is required of some applicants. Admissions process is need-blind. *High school units required/recommended:* 16 total units are required; 4 English required, 3 math required, 3 science required, 3 foreign language required, 3 social studies required. *Special Requirements:* A portfolio is required for art program applicants. An audition is required for music program applicants. TOEFL is required of all international students. *The admissions office says:* "The admissions committee evaluates each applicant on individual merit and accomplishment as well as potential for growth. Acceptance to Wittenberg is not based solely on GPA, class rank, or testing data. We want individuals who will contribute to all aspects of the community."

The Inside Word

Applications showed a significant increase at Wittenberg this year. The pool is still small, but students who haven't achieved at an above-average level in high school meet with little success in the admissions process. Candidate evaluation is thorough and personal; applicants should devote serious attention to all aspects of their candidacy.

FINANCIAL AID

Students should submit: FAFSA, state aid form, a copy of parents' most recent income tax filing. The Princeton Review suggests that all financial aid forms be submitted as soon as possible after January 1. *The following grants/scholarships are offered:* Pell, SEOG, academic merit, the school's own scholarships, the school's own grants, state scholarships, state grants, private scholarships, private grants, ROTC, foreign aid. *Students borrow from the following loan programs:* Stafford, unsubsidized Stafford, Perkins, PLUS, the school's own loan fund, private loans. College Work-Study Program is available. Institutional employment is available.

FROM THE ADMISSIONS OFFICE

"At Wittenberg, we believe that helping you to achieve symmetry demands a special environment, a setting where you can refine your definition of self yet gain exposure to the varied kinds of knowledge, people, views, activities, options, and ideas that add richness to our lives. Wittenberg is neither a huge university where students are usually mass produced, nor a very small college with few options which can provide for the intellectual and personal growth required to achieve balance. Campus life is as diverse as the interests of our students. Wittenberg attracts students from all over the United States and from many other countries. Historically, the university has been committed to geographical, educational, cultural, and religious diversity. With their diverse backgrounds and interests, Wittenberg students have helped initiate many of the more than 100 student organizations that are active on campus. The students will be the first to tell you there's never a lack of things to do on or near the campus any day of the week, if you're willing to get involved."

ADMISSIONS

Admissions Rating	74
% of applicants accepted	85
% of acceptees attending	33

FRESHMAN PROFILE

Average verbal SAT	600
Average math SAT	590
Average ACT	25
Average TOEFL	550
Graduated top 20% of class	60
Graduated top 40% of class	79
Graduated top 60% of class	85
Average HS GPA or Avg.	3.5

DEADLINES

Early decision	1/15
Regular admission	3/15
Regular notification	rolling
Non-fall registration	yes

APPLICANTS ALSO LOOK AT

AND OFTEN PREFER

Miami U.
Denison

AND SOMETIMES PREFER

Ohio State-Columbus
Ohio Wesleyan
Wooster
DePauw

FINANCIAL FACTS

Financial Aid Rating	87
Tuition	$16,854
Room & board	$4,536
Estimated book expense	$1,200
% frosh receiving aid	68
% undergrads receiving aid	65
% aid is need-based	90
% frosh w/ grant (avg)	68 ($9,500)
% frosh w/ loan (avg)	90 ($2,400)
% UGs w/ job (avg)	55 ($1,275)
Off-campus job outlook	good

WOFFORD COLLEGE

429 NORTH CHURCH STREET, SPARTANBURG, SC 29303-3663   ADMISSIONS: 864-597-4130   FAX: 864-597-4219

CAMPUS LIFE

Quality of Life Rating   **88**
Type of school   private
Affiliation   United Methodist Church
Environment   suburban

STUDENTS

FT undergrad enrollment	1,062
% male/female	55/45
% from out of state	33
% live on campus	82
% spend weekend on campus	NR
% transfers	7
% from public high school	79
% in (# of) fraternities	52 (8)
% in (# of) sororities	58 (3)
% African-American	6
% Asian	2
% Caucasian	90
% Hispanic	0
% international	NR
# of countries represented	4

WHAT'S HOT
Greeks
students are happy
town-gown relations
student government
school runs like butter

WHAT'S NOT
college radio
lab facilities
student publications
drugs
lack of diversity on campus

ACADEMICS

Academic Rating   **88**
Profs Interesting Rating   94
Profs Accessible Rating   92
Calendar   4-1-4
Student/teacher ratio   15:1
% profs tenured   91
Hours of study per day   3.22

MOST POPULAR MAJORS
biology
English language/literature
psychology

% GRADS WHO PURSUE...
Law 6, Med 9, MBA 3, MA 14

STUDENTS SPEAK OUT

Life

Students at Wofford College are proud of the school's traditional approach to academics and college life. Writes one student, "Wofford has a style all its own. We say there's a right way, a wrong way, and a Wofford way, which is to always do things in a classic and traditional manner." According to our respondents, the Greeks are firmly planted at the top of Wofford's social hierarchy. One student reported that "Most of the fun activities at Wofford are centered on the fraternities and sororities. Every weekend there is something happening at the row." Not surprisingly, some students, particularly independents, complain that the frat-centered social scene is monotonous. "At frat parties," explains one student, "we just stand around and ask everyone else what they're drinking. Independents go elsewhere for fun and the frats haven't really figured out that they aren't any fun." Relations between the Greeks and independents are strained, although the greatest animus exists between those pledged to different houses. Sports are quite popular, and while "the athlete is a student first here," tiny Wofford has put together a solid enough program to gain entry into Division II athletics. Also noteworthy is the fact that "Wofford is a service-oriented place. Everyone participates in some form of community service."

Academics

Wofford caters to a pre-professional crowd—one in five graduates goes on to business, medical, or law school—and most students choose majors such as business, economics, and biology to facilitate their goals. The liberal arts definitely take a backseat here, although the English department is reportedly strong. The school's insular environment could be a turnoff: one student warns, "There are certainly things about Wofford that could be unappealing to some people. It is very small, very Southern, and not very diverse." The availability of the professors receives high marks. Small classes and a caring administration are among the school's other assets. Students are hardworking and goal-oriented but not intellectual. Writes one student, "Wofford has something to offer those aspiring young intellectuals who are grasping for more than a second run at high school, but most students are just going for that second run."

Student Body

Most of Wofford's small minority population is African-American. The rest of the students tend to fit what one student called "the Wofford mold," defining such students as "conservative, upper-middle-class Caucasians who love fraternities." One minority student warns that, "Life here is not the best for minority students. There are not many activities that minorities feel comfortable attending. There is not much social life for minorities unless they make it." The majority of students are happy here, however, and explain, "Wofford is like a family. Even though you may not know each student by name, a bond still exists."

ADMISSIONS

The admissions committee considers (in descending order of importance): HS record, class rank, test scores, essay, recommendations. *Also considered (in descending order of importance):* extracurriculars, personality, alumni relationship, geographical distribution, special talents. Either the SAT or ACT is required. An interview is recommended. Admissions process is need-blind. *High school units required/recommended:* 16 total units are recommended; 4 English recommended, 4 math recommended, 3 science recommended, 2 foreign language recommended, 2 social studies recommended. Minimum combined SAT I score of 1000 recommended. TOEFL is required of all international students.

The Inside Word

Wofford is under-recognized among excellent college options in the South. Matchmaking plays a large part in the decisions of the admissions committee, which means that it takes much more than just above-average grades and solid test scores to get admitted. The admissions staff is friendly, and eager to help students put their best foot forward in the process. Wofford is a particularly good choice for those who, while strong academically, are not likely candidates for admission to Duke and other top Southern schools.

FINANCIAL AID

Students should submit: FAFSA (due March 15), CSS Profile (due March 15), the school's own financial aid form (due March 15). The Princeton Review suggests that all financial aid forms be submitted as soon as possible after January 1. *The following grants/scholarships are offered:* Pell, SEOG, academic merit, athletic, the school's own scholarships, the school's own grants, state scholarships, state grants, private scholarships, private grants, ROTC. *Students borrow from the following loan programs:* Stafford, unsubsidized Stafford, Perkins, PLUS, private loans. Applicants will be notified of awards beginning in March. College Work-Study Program is available. Institutional employment is available.

FROM THE ADMISSIONS OFFICE

"In 1856, Samuel Dibble received the first diploma from Wofford. He went on to serve in the U.S. House of Representatives, becoming the first in a long line of leaders who studied at the college. The list includes five Rhodes Scholars, two U.S. Senators, the founder of the National Beta Club, and the leaders of Duke and Vanderbilt as they became great universities. Of about 11,000 living Wofford alumni, 1,160 are presidents or owners of corporations or organizations; 402 are college faculty or staff members; 1,042 practice in medicine, dentistry, or other health care professions; and 560 are attorneys or judges. "In 1987, the Board of Trustees approved a master plan, "To Improve Quality," that set some ambitious new goals. Increasing financial support indicates that challenge is being accepted and met. The F. W. Olin Foundation gave the college almost $6 million to build and equip a new high-technology academic building, and Wofford recently received a $12.2 million bequest for the endowment from Mrs. Charles Daniel. Always regarded as one of the South's most respected liberal arts colleges, Wofford today is rapidly earning a national reputation as a college on the move."

ADMISSIONS

Admissions Rating	77
% of applicants accepted	87
% of acceptees attending	29

FRESHMAN PROFILE

Average verbal SAT	600
Average math SAT	590
Average ACT	26
Average TOEFL	550
Graduated top 20% of class	70
Graduated top 40% of class	93
Graduated top 60% of class	100
Average HS GPA or Avg.	NR

DEADLINES

Early decision	12/1
Regular admission	2/1
Regular notification	3/15
Non-fall registration	yes

APPLICANTS ALSO LOOK AT

AND OFTEN PREFER
Wake Forest

AND SOMETIMES PREFER
U. South Carolina - Columbia
Furman

AND RARELY PREFER
Clemson

FINANCIAL FACTS

Financial Aid Rating	97
Tuition	$13,490
Room & board	$4,185
Estimated book expense	$625
% frosh receiving aid	85
% undergrads receiving aid	76
% aid is need-based	51
% frosh w/ grant (avg)	75 ($7,597)
% frosh w/ loan (avg)	50 ($5,256)
% UGs w/ job (avg)	40 ($1,200)
Off-campus job outlook	excellent

COLLEGE OF WOOSTER

WOOSTER, OH 44691   ADMISSIONS: 800-877-9905   FAX: 330-263-2594

CAMPUS LIFE

Quality of Life Rating 85
Type of school   private
Affiliation   Presbyterian Church
Environment   town

STUDENTS

FT undergrad enrollment	1,644
% male/female	49/51
% from out of state	56
% live on campus	93
% spend weekend on campus	98
% transfers	4
% from public high school	79
% in (# of) fraternities	20 (8)
% in (# of) sororities	15 (8)
% African-American	5
% Asian	1
% Caucasian	82
% Hispanic	1
% international	9
# of countries represented	32

WHAT'S HOT
music associations
dorms
college radio
computer facilities
students are happy

WHAT'S NOT
town-gown relations
political activism
off-campus food
sex
hard liquor

ACADEMICS

Academic Rating	86
Profs Interesting Rating	91
Profs Accessible Rating	91
Calendar	semester
Student/teacher ratio	12:1
% profs PhD/tenured	90/94
Hours of study per day	3.43

MOST POPULAR MAJORS
English
history
psychology

% GRADS WHO PURSUE...
Law 8, Med 8, MBA 5, MA 47

STUDENTS SPEAK OUT

Life
The College of Wooster boasts a satisfied student body. "I'm happy" is the norm for Wooster undergrads across the board. "The campus is very beautiful" says one COW undergrad, "so that makes a big difference." While few students seem daunted by the limitations of a small campus in a small town, the range of options at Wooster is small. "I do everything from going to parties to traveling to Cleveland to watching a movie," explains one student. Adds another, "there is not a lot to do in the city." Most are happy hanging out with their group of friends, a situation that lends itself to a somewhat "cliquey" atmosphere. While one student described life at Wooster as "peachy as pie," others bemoan the predominance of frats and sororities in Wooster's social scene. Unlike many small schools, dating is big here. There are four bars in the town of Wooster and few town-related activities, so students have to make the fun happen themselves, which they do through the Greek system, clubs, or athletics. All in all, while there is some disenchantment with Wooster—"Living at Wooster is like sucking blood from a slug"—for the most part, "Wooster rocks!"

Academics
Academics are very important to Wooster undergrads, most of whom study 3-5 hours a day. One reason is that COW undergrads love their profs. "Most every member of the administration, faculty, and staff lives in Wooster, so it is very common to see them around town, at the stores, out mowing their lawns, walking their dogs, going on a jog. It's great!" Says another, "I like the small classroom atmosphere and having my professors know who I am." Small classes is right—non-lecture classes usually have fewer than 15 students. Another student states reverently, "It is with the respect [for Wooster professors] that I become motivated to work harder and succeed." Praise for profs falls just short of universal, with the most damning response being, "Some professors are just fabulous, and some I wonder why they are teaching." The administration doesn't fare quite as well as the profs, receiving barely passing marks. "The administration treats the students like dollars," says one disgruntled student. Another states, "Administratively, it is surprisingly difficult to get things done around here, considering how small Wooster is." Getting into the classes they want is not always easy for freshmen. International students had nothing but raves for the faculty and administration. "They make international students feel right at home." Those receiving financial aid were, on the whole, satisfied with their aid packages. The library and health services are also top-notch according to COW students.

Student Body
"It isn't a 1968 hippie commune, but I think we generally accept and get along with one another." That statement sums up the majority opinion of COW's student body. Adds another, "While it is possible to interact only with students like yourself, most students enjoy...interacting with those that are different." Not everyone agrees, however. Concerns with homophobia, black/white relations, and general snobbery are all raised. Sexual and minority discrimination are also concerns on campus, but not prevailing problems. Says one student, mysteriously, "If we don't get along, we go swim in Jell-O until problems are resolved." Hmm. Says another, "There are many people here from outside Ohio, so that gives Wooster a special flavor." The flavor of Fruit Medley Jell-O, perhaps?

FINANCIAL AID: 330-263-2317   E-MAIL: ADMISSION@ACS.WOOSTER.EDU   WEB SITE: HTTP://WWW.WOOSTER.EDU/

ADMISSIONS

The admissions committee considers (in descending order of importance): HS record, test scores, recommendations, class rank, essay. *Also considered (in descending order of importance):* personality, special talents, extracurriculars, geographical distribution, alumni relationship. Either the SAT or ACT is required. An interview is recommended. *High school units required/recommended:* 16 total units are required; 4 English required, 3 math required, 3 science required, 2 foreign language required, 3 social studies required.

The Inside Word

Wooster has a solid academic reputation, and holds its own against formidable competition for students with many national-caliber liberal arts colleges. Applicants should not take the admissions process lightly, because candidate evaluations are very thorough and personal.

FINANCIAL AID

Students should submit: FAFSA, a copy of parents' most recent income tax filing. The Princeton Review suggests that all financial aid forms be submitted as soon as possible after January 1. *The following grants/scholarships are offered:* Pell, SEOG, academic merit, the school's own scholarships, the school's own grants, state grants, private scholarships, private grants, foreign aid. *Students borrow from the following loan programs:* Stafford, Perkins, PLUS, private loans. Applicants will be notified of awards beginning March 1. College Work-Study Program is available. Institutional employment is available. Freshmen are discouraged from working.

FROM THE ADMISSIONS OFFICE

The College of Wooster has always been an innovator. In his inaugural address in 1870, Wooster's first president, Willis Lord, said the College "should be not only a place of all studies; it should be a place of studies for all." We were one of America's first co-educational colleges, the first to award a Ph.D. to a woman, and an early advocate of undergraduate research. African-American and international students have been an integral part of our campus community since the 1890's.

For almost 50 years, a senior Independent Study tutorial has been the centerpiece of Wooster's curriculum. Wooster is one of the very few colleges in the nation that asks every senior to design and complete an original project. The Independent Study program sets Wooster apart and consistently draws praise for fostering creativity, resourcefulness, and self-reliance. It is a prime example of the way Wooster students control their own educational experience, blending theory and knowledge with the skills that all successful people need in today's world.

ADMISSIONS

Admissions Rating	72
% of applicants accepted	32
% of acceptees attending	27

FRESHMAN PROFILE

Average verbal SAT	600
Average math SAT	530
Average ACT	25
Average TOEFL	620
Graduated top 20% of class	57
Graduated top 40% of class	83
Graduated top 60% of class	95
Average HS GPA or Avg.	3.0

DEADLINES

Early decision	12/1
Regular admission	2/15
Regular notification	4/1
Non-fall registration	yes

APPLICANTS ALSO LOOK AT

AND OFTEN PREFER
Middlebury
DePauw U.
St. Olaf
Lawrence U.
Wittenberg U.

AND SOMETIMES PREFER
Ohio U.
Smith
Grinnell
Ohio Wesleyan U.
Kenyon

AND RARELY PREFER
Denison U.
Case Western Reserve U.
Dickinson
Penn State U.

FINANCIAL FACTS

Financial Aid Rating	90
Tuition	$17,600
Room & board	$4,680
Estimated book expense	$560

% frosh receiving aid	85
% undergrads receiving aid	83
% aid is need-based	88
% frosh w/ grant (avg)	78 ($10,000)
% frosh w/ loan (avg)	51 ($2,900)
% UGs w/ job (avg)	50 ($900)
Off-campus job outlook	excellent

WORCESTER POLYTECHNIC INSTITUTE

100 INSTITUTE ROAD, WORCESTER, MA 01609   ADMISSIONS: 508-831-5286   FAX: 508-831-5875

STUDENTS SPEAK OUT

Life

There is a disproportionate male/female ratio at Worcester Polytechnic Institute, and, as you might imagine, this is a problem for a lot of students. Several WPI women express pleasure with the imbalance, but the situation isn't really healthy for anyone: very few things in this world are as unpleasant as a rutting engineer. As for the party scene, one student typically recounts, "The life of the school is the Greek system. With so many local students, if it were not for fraternities and sororities, everyone would go home on weekends." Says another, "Weekends are dead if you're not on a fraternity party list." The school has no student center, a real sticking point for some: "Staring at walls is a popular pastime. We NEED a student center!" As for the city of Worcester, "It sucks!" is the consensus (not just here, but at all three of the colleges in this book that are located there.). "Fortunately," says one student, "there is no reason to go into town, except the Centrum (an arena that sometimes features the Bruins, Celtics, and national rock tours)." The campus is "very homey and comfortable, an excellent offset to the technically based curriculum."

Academics

With the East Coast's most famous technical school only 40 miles away, it's understandable that WPI is sometimes overlooked. However, for students looking for an excellent engineering and science education that will also require them to broaden their horizons (with a minimum of five humanities courses) and allow them to pursue independent research (through the Major Qualifying Project program), WPI may just be the place. In certain respects, WPI students have it all over their counterparts at MIT. WPI students find their professors better in class and out; like their financial aid packages much more and spend less because they live in Worcester; and don't study nearly as hard while still pursuing rigorous engineering and science programs. Some students praise the quarter system, which allows students to concentrate on fewer courses at a time. But WPI offerings in subjects not related to engineering are generally weak, and although the school belongs to the Worcester Consortium (a group of ten area schools that allows students at any one to take courses at the others), WPI's quarterly schedule can make participation in the consortium difficult.

Student Body

Unlike MIT, WPI does not have an ethnically or geographically diverse student body. 85 percent of the students are white, and 42 percent are from Massachusetts. They are intense and studious, but they are not nerds (at least not by their own account!). As one student explains, "I think that students from other schools assume that every student at WPI is a total dork, but they'd be surprised how many different kinds of people there really are here."

WORCESTER POLYTECHNIC INSTITUTE

FINANCIAL AID: 508-831-5469

WEB SITE: HTTP://WWW.WPI.EDU

ADMISSIONS

The admissions committee considers (in descending order of importance): HS record, recommendations, test scores, class rank, essay. *Also considered (in descending order of importance):* personality, special talents, alumni relationship, extracurriculars, geographical distribution. Either the SAT or ACT is required. An interview is recommended. Admissions process is need-blind. *High school units required/recommended:* 10 total units are recommended; 4 English recommended, 4 math recommended, 2 science recommended. TOEFL is required of all international students.

The Inside Word

Worcester's applicant pool is small, but very well qualified. Its high acceptance rate makes it a good safety choice for those aiming at more difficult tech schools, and for those who are solid but aren't MIT material. As is the case at most technical institutes, women will meet with a very receptive admissions committee.

FINANCIAL AID

Students should submit: FAFSA (due April 1), CSS Profile (due April 1), Divorced Parents form (due April 1), a copy of parents' most recent income tax filing (due May 1). The Princeton Review suggests that all financial aid forms be submitted as soon as possible after January 1. *The following grants/scholarships are offered:* Pell, SEOG, academic merit, the school's own scholarships, the school's own grants, state scholarships, state grants, private scholarships, private grants, ROTC, foreign aid. *Students borrow from the following loan programs:* Stafford, unsubsidized Stafford, Perkins, PLUS, the school's own loan fund, state loans, private loans. Applicants will be notified of awards beginning April 1. College Work-Study Program is available. Institutional employment is available.

FROM THE ADMISSIONS OFFICE

"Projects and research are a distinctive element of the WPI plan. WPI believes that in these times simply passing courses and accumulating theoretical knowledge is not enough to truly educate tomorrow's leaders. Tomorrow's professionals ought to be involved in project work that prepares them today for future challenges. Projects at WPI come as close to professional experience as a college program can possibly achieve. In fact, WPI works with more than 200 companies, government agencies, and private organizations each year. These groups provide project opportunities where students get a chance to work in real, professional settings. Students gain experience in planning, coordinating team efforts, meeting deadlines, writing proposals and reports, making oral presentations, doing cost analyses, and making decisions."

ADMISSIONS

Admissions Rating	81
% of applicants accepted	82
% of acceptees attending	30

FRESHMAN PROFILE

Average verbal SAT	620
Average math SAT	660
Average ACT	29
Average TOEFL	600
Graduated top 20% of class	75
Graduated top 40% of class	96
Graduated top 60% of class	100
Average HS GPA or Avg.	NR

DEADLINES

Early decision	12/1
Regular admission	2/15
Regular notification	4/1
Non-fall registration	yes

APPLICANTS ALSO LOOK AT

AND OFTEN PREFER

MIT
RPI
Caltech
Cornell U.

AND SOMETIMES PREFER

Rose-Hulman
U. Mass.-Amherst
Clarkson
Case Western Reserve
Carnegie-Mellon

AND RARELY PREFER

U. Rhode Island
U. New Hampshire
U. Conn
Clarkson U.
Drexel

FINANCIAL FACTS

Financial Aid Rating	83
Tuition	$18,060
Room & board	$5,940
Estimated book expense	$590
% frosh receiving aid	78
% undergrads receiving aid	70
% aid is need-based	98
% frosh w/ grant (avg)	77 ($8,600)
% frosh w/ loan (avg)	50 ($3,500)
% UGs w/ job (avg)	32 ($1,000)
Off-campus job outlook	good

YALE UNIVERSITY

208234 YALE STATION, NEW HAVEN, CT 06520-8234   ADMISSIONS: 203-432-9300   FAX: 203-432-9392

STUDENTS SPEAK OUT

Life

It would be foolish to pass up a chance to attend Yale University for just about any reason. But if you're unsure whether you could be happy living and studying for four years in a cold, economically depressed, dangerous city, you owe it to yourself to visit New Haven before deciding that Yale is the school for you. Yale students have survived there for centuries, but they're not thrilled about it. Yalies give New Haven extremely low marks. One has this to say about his new hometown: "Yale's worst problem is New Haven. It is dangerous and unreceptive to students. Life on and immediately around campus is great, but otherwise it's a real problem." Says another, "New Haven is pretty gross—very dangerous. It's a great eye opener to the 'real world,' though." Yale's social scene centers on its residential colleges (groups of students live together for their entire four-year stay): "Our residential college system really improves social life!" There's lots of hanging out, but some students complain that dates are in short supply. Writes one student, "The dating scene here is as much fun as a root canal." Popular student organizations include theater and music groups, the campus newspaper, and numerous political organizations.

Academics

Yale "is truly one of America's great schools," writes one college counselor. It's an assertion that's hard to debate. As a major national research center, Yale attracts many of the world's great scholars. But unlike other research institutes, Yale also devotes a lot of attention to undergraduates. Reports one student, "There is a genuine focus on undergraduates here, the professors seem genuinely to enjoy teaching, and you really do learn a lot in classes." Students do complain, however, that too many classes at all levels are taught by TAs and that they occasionally encounter professors who are poor teachers. Strife on campus over TAs' demands for higher wages and union representation has also been a cause for concern, with the recent "grade strike" by TAs a cause of heated debate, high anxiety, and student anger at the administration. Indeed, the administration is uniformly cited as the worst aspect of the Yale undergrad experience. As one student puts it, "The administration does its absolute best to squelch student input." Academic departments are "uniformly excellent" here: among the school's many fine departments, standouts include drama, English, history, and the premed program. Yale has no core curriculum, instead requiring students to complete a broad range of general education requirements. Students tell us they like the "shopping period" registration system: they don't formally register for classes until two weeks into the semester, so the likelihood of getting stuck with a lousy class is minimized.

Student Body

Yale is famous enough to attract, and wealthy enough to finance, students from all backgrounds, and the result is a lively, diverse academic atmosphere. Be prepared to enter a fast-paced, very competitive community here: As one student puts it, "'Intense' is definitely the word for Yalies—we get very involved whatever we do here, be it classes, drama, sports or what have you." Yale students' reputation for being eccentric still holds. One respondent puts it this way: "Everyone here has quirks. Yalies are fascinating people, very self absorbed, but terrific when they decide to think about others."

FINANCIAL AID: 203-432-0360   WEB SITE: HTTP://WWW.CS.YALE.EDU/HTML/YALE/FRONTDOOR.HTML

ADMISSIONS

The admissions committee considers (in descending order of importance): HS record, test scores, class rank, recommendations, essay. *Also considered (in descending order of importance):* extracurriculars, personality, alumni relationship, special talents, geographical distribution. Either the SAT or ACT is required. Applicants urged to take honors and advanced placement courses. TOEFL is required of all international students.

The Inside Word

Yale is ultraselective, and the admissions committee considers virtually all of its decisions to be final—there's nothing to be gained in appealing a denial here. The University has a regional review process that serves as a preliminary screening of all candidates. Only the best-qualified, well-matched candidates actually come before the admissions committee.

FINANCIAL AID

Students should submit: FAFSA (due February 1), the school's own financial aid form (due February 1), state aid form, a copy of parents' most recent income tax filing. The Princeton Review suggests that all financial aid forms be submitted as soon as possible after January 1. *The following grants/scholarships are offered:* Pell, SEOG, the school's own grants, state scholarships, state grants, private scholarships, private grants, ROTC, foreign aid. *Students borrow from the following loan programs:* Stafford, unsubsidized Stafford, Perkins, PLUS, the school's own loan fund, state loans, private loans. Applicants will be notified of awards beginning around April 1. College Work-Study Program is available. Institutional employment is available.

FROM THE ADMISSIONS OFFICE

"The most important questions the Admissions Committee must resolve are 'Who is likely to make the most of Yale's resources?' and 'Who will contribute significantly to the Yale community?' These questions suggest an approach to evaluating applicants that is more complex than whether Yale would rather admit well-rounded people or those with specialized talents. In selecting a class of 1,300 from approximately 11,000 applicants, the Admissions Committee looks for academic ability and achievement combined with such personal characteristics as motivation, curiosity, energy, and leadership ability. The nature of these qualities is such that there is no simple profile of grades, scores, interests, and activities that will assure admission. Diversity within the student population is important, and the Admissions Committee selects a class of able and contributing individuals from a variety of backgrounds and with a broad range of interests and skills."

ADMISSIONS

Admissions Rating	99
% of applicants accepted	20
% of acceptees attending	54

FRESHMAN PROFILE

Average verbal SAT	720
Average math SAT	690
Average ACT	NR
Average TOEFL	600
Graduated top 20% of class	NR
Graduated top 40% of class	NR
Graduated top 60% of class	NR
Average HS GPA or Avg.	NR

DEADLINES

Early decision	NR
Regular admission	12/31
Regular notification	4/15
Non-fall registration	no

APPLICANTS ALSO LOOK AT

AND SOMETIMES PREFER

Harvard/Radcliffe
Princeton
Stanford
MIT
Swarthmore

AND RARELY PREFER

Brown
Amherst
Williams
Wesleyan U.
Pennsylvania

FINANCIAL FACTS

Financial Aid Rating	72
Tuition	$21,000
Room & board	$6,630
Estimated book expense	$630
% frosh receiving aid	52
% undergrads receiving aid	53
% aid is need-based	NR
% frosh w/ grant (avg)	58 ($12,624)
% frosh w/ loan (avg)	55 ($2,625)
% UGs w/ job (avg)	NR ($2,205)
Off-campus job outlook	good

PART 3

"MY ROOMMATE'S FEET REALLY STINK."

The questionnaire we distributed to college students closed with a free-form "essay question." We told students that we didn't care *what* they wrote: if it was "witty, informative, or accurate," we'd try to get it into this book. We used all the informative and accurate essays to write the student view boxes; below are excerpts from the wittiest, pithiest, and most outrageous essays.

LITERARY ALLUSIONS...

"To study at this school is to have infinite control over your destiny: you can crouch in your room like Gregor Samsa transformed into a dung beetle, or you can plunge into the infinite sea of faces that each year flood OSU like a tidal wave."

— A.W., Ohio State University

"'Prosperity unbruised cannot endure a single blow, but a man who has been at constant feud with misfortunes develops a skin calloused by time...and even if he falls he can carry the fight upon one knee.' —Seneca on Providence."

— Matthew D., U. of Connecticut

Two jokes about St. John's College students:
1. Q: How many Johnnies does it take to change a light bulb?
   A: Let's define "change" before we go any further.
2. Q: What did the Chorus say to Creon after Oedipus poked out his eyes?
   A: Now that's a face only a mother could love.

— April W., St. John's College

"Very definitely a love/hate relationship here. This is the level of hell that Dante missed."

—Amy P., Caltech

"It is a shame that my family pays $12,000 annually for me to eat a different casserole every day."

— S.W., Southwestern University

"The food here is really bad; it's either bland or sickening. You're lucky if they don't screw up the bread."

— Scott P., Bentley College

"When students first arrive, they call the Observatory Hill Dining Facility 'O-Hill.' They soon learn to call it 'O-Hell,' because the food here is beyond revolting."

— Greg F., U. of Virginia

"If I had known that I'd be rooming with roaches and poisoned by the cafeteria staff I would have gone to Wayne State. I really can't complain, though, because I have met my husband here, like my mom did twenty years before."

— M.L.P., Fisk University

"The food here has particularly fancy names, and it seems as though they spend more time thinking of these names than they spend on making decent food."

— Andrew Z., Wheaton College

"If you're looking for gray skies, a gray campus, and gray food, then Albany is the place to be!"

— Michele G., SUNY Albany

"The food isn't that bad, if you don't mind varying shades of brown. On a good day the food on your tray will remind you of the brown paint sampler at your local Sherwin-Williams dealer."

— Rob P., College of the Holy Cross

"You should mention Lil', the lady who has worked in the dining hall for fifty years and who everyone loves. She plays the spoons all the time and runs around."

— Aaron R., Tufts University

"You should mention Lil', who works in the dining hall. She's loony and she knows everyone."

— Mitchell D., Tufts University

"People ask me, 'Mike Z., why did you come to NYU?' I tell them, 'I didn't come to NYU, I came to New York City.'"

— Mike Z., NYU

"Change the name of UC—Irvine to UC—Newport Beach and we would have more girls."

— Pat M., UC–Irvine

"As this school is located in a tiny Texas town, a favorite activity is called 'rolling.' Rolling entails piling into a car with many drinks and driving the back country roads. Very slowly."

— Anonymous, Southwestern University

"Worcester—the fart of the commonwealth."

— David R., Clark University

"Connecticut is a cute state. It's a great place to go to school, but I wouldn't want to live here."

— Claire S., NJ native, Fairfield University

"Binghamton is always gray. The two days a week we have sun, it's beautiful, but otherwise, sunglasses are not a must unless you're an artsy-fartsy pseudo chic literature and rhetoric/ philosophy major."

— Deborah C., SUNY–Binghamton

"Socially, the surrounding area is so dead that the Denny's closes at night."

— Thomas R., UC–Riverside

"The local liquor stores and towing companies make a lot of money."

— Katherine R., U. of Rhode Island

"Last week's major crime was that my left headlight was out, for which the busy Hanover police pulled me over three times."

— Jon K., Dartmouth College

"Davis is boring; you need a lot of drugs."

— Anonymous, UC–Davis

"It is definitely important to have a car, as the population of Canton frequently matches our winter temperature. 'Canton gray,' our perennial sky color, is one Crayola missed."

— Daniel R., St. Lawrence University

"I'm from L.A. and in my opinion Boston sucks. If you're into the frat/ Spuds McKenzie crowd, Boston's the place to be. If you ain't, it's a lame social scene."

— Josh M., Emerson College

"Bloomington, Illinois, was recently voted the sixth most normal location in the U.S. Unfortunately, this translates into one of the most boring places. I liken it to New Haven on an overdose of valium."

— Matthew G., Illinois Wesleyan University

"Contrary to popular belief, cow tipping is definitely passé here."

— Anonymous, U. of Connecticut, Storrs

"Life in New Orleans—'And the people sat down to eat and to drink, and rose up to play.'—Exodus 32:6."

— Theresa W., Tulane University

"Fredericksburg is boring if one is not amused by the simple pleasures of existence such as breathing, sleep, and other things."

— Rich W., Mary Washington College

"I love escaping from Claremont. I wish I had a car! Claremont seems to be stuck in a white, bureaucratic, conservative nightmare. I feel cut off from the rest of the world, like I've fallen into Wonderland—the rules of the outside world don't apply here. However, I do feel like I've gotten and am getting a good education."

— Anonymous, Scripps College

SECURITY...

"Campus security is made up of a bunch of midget high school dropouts with Napoleonic complexes who can spot a beer can from a mile away."

— Anonymous, UC–San Diego

"Public safety here is a joke. The public safety officers are like the Keystone Kops on Thorazine."

— Anonymous, Bryn Mawr College

"I would not recommend walking alone at night because security is not well staffed, and also not armed. What if someone has a gun, what are those rent-a-cops going to do? Say, 'I'll hit you with this club if you don't drop the gun?' Come on!"

— Anonymous, St. Joseph's University

"Our alcohol policy sucks. All of our campus police now think they're T. J. Hooker."

— Anonymous, Dartmouth College

"Sure, our campus is diverse if you call diverse a campus full of white kids looking to make thirty to fifty grand after graduation."

— Joseph M. C., Davidson College

"If you're thinking of applying to MIT, go ahead. Because, believe it or not, most people here are at least as stupid as you are."

— Patrick L., MIT

"Yes, we shave our legs and underarms."

— Dawn P., Wellesley College

"Most of the students are unwashed and wear too much Patchouli."

— Anonymous, Maryland Institute, College of Art

"People who go to school here are all pretty good-looking, especially the women. It should be renamed UKB, the University of Ken and Barbie."

— Tony H., Arizona State University

"Wesleyan is not only the 'diversity university' but also the 'controversy university,' the 'fight adversity university,' and the 'if we keep trying we might have some unity' university. We satisfy all types."

— John P., Wesleyan University

"The student body is much more diverse than its stereotype. Only about one-third of the students are illiterate guitar-toting drug dealers."

— Ben J., Berklee College of Music

"Everyone walks too fast around here. You try to say 'hi' to someone, you've got to time it just right 'cause they aren't going to stop to talk to you. Plus, everyone wears the same clothes!"

— Terry B., Wittenberg University

"Girls over 5'8", watch out—for some reason, guys here have munchkin blood in them or something."

— Robyn A., Tufts University

"Life in some dorms can be very distressing. It's amazing how strange some people are."

—Anonymous, Penn State U.

"A school can be defined by its graffiti and its level of cleverness. Three quarters of our school graffiti is pro- or anti- a specific fraternity, with the other one quarter devoted to homophobic or misogynist theories."

— Matthew E., College of William and Mary

"This is a great university if you're not studying sciences involving animal research, politics, teacher education (certification), or anything that offends any long-haired leftist who's a vegetarian."

— Brock M., U. of Oregon

"This school is filled with wealthy, well-dressed egomaniacs who are about as socially conscious as Marie Antoinette."

— Anonymous, Hofstra University

"There's a lot of discrimination against drummers here, but rightly so!"

—Anonymous, Berklee College of Music

"When you first come here, you think everybody's really strange. Over time, though, you realize everybody is, and so are you. No big deal."

— Josh B., St. John's College

"University of Chicago's reputation is not entirely deserved. It's not true the place is completely full of nerds. It's only partially completely full of nerds."

— David G., U. of Chicago

"Everyone seems to know someone who invented something like Velcro or whose father is a CEO of a corporation."

— William K., Denison University

"I have this really big booger in my nose that I can't quite handle. What do I do? Pick it in public and look like a typical Brown freak, or just deal with it?"

—"Optional," Brown University

"Don't let anyone try to tell you that this is a diverse but close-knit atmosphere. The people here are about as diverse as a box of nails."

— Cari L., College of the Holy Cross

"UNH is about as diverse as the NHL."

— Curtis E., U. of New Hampshire

"We are cheeseballs, but rather enlightened, thus we condescendingly tolerate almost everyone."

—Cache M., Lawrence U.

"Denison has attempted to lose the 'rich kid party school' image and expand the diversity of the student body, but now it is becoming the 'I wish this were still a rich kid party school.' There is an awful lot available here, but students seem unmotivated and lazy."

— Anonymous, Denison University

"Most of my peers are narrow-minded morons who seem to live in the fifties. Because of this constant annoyance, the rest of us have a camaraderie that allows us to see how the other half lives."

—Gary A., LSU

"They say that Harvard students are arrogant, but where else can you find world-class professors and guest lecturers, world-class students, and world-class attitudes?"

— Edward S., Harvard University

"Everyone here is too smart for their [sic] own good. As one upper-level executive in the Houston area put it, 'The students at Rice know how to make it rain, but they don't know to come in out of it.'"

— John B., Rice U.

"My roommate's feet really stink."

— Anonymous, Claremont McKenna

"Although it may not seem like it, RISD is a very religious school. Everyone thinks they're God."

— Neil M., Rhode Island School of Design

"Sometimes people complain about the lack of student involvement. I think someone should really do something about the apathy at St. Lawrence."

— Bill P., St. Lawrence University

"Bates is so diverse! Yesterday I met somebody from Connecticut!"

— Ellen H., Bates College

"If it weren't for me, this university would suck. People were sitting around with their thumbs up their butts until I came here. Now everyone is happier and has more fun. In fact, I bet this survey sucked until I gave you my almighty wisdom."

— Patrick W., U. of Illinois–Urbana

"Rose-Hulman is one of the few places where it's safer to leave a $20 bill on your desk than it is to forget to log out of the computer network."

—Zac C., Rose-Hulman Institute of Technology

"The only thing the administration does well is tasks involving what Kenneth Boulding would call 'suboptimization.' Give them something that really doesn't need doing and it will be accomplished efficiently."

— *Dana T., U. of Minnesota–Twin Cities*

"Our business office may be the smoothest running machine since the Pinto!"

— *Robert C., University of Dallas*

"Despite the best efforts of the administration to provide TSC students with an inefficient, cold-hearted, red-tape infested, snafu-riddled Soviet-style administrative bureaucracy, Trenton State College is a pretty decent place to go for a fairly reasonable amount of money."

— *Anonymous, Trenton State College*

"The admissions office tries to make you apply based on, 'Well, we're very old and...and...well, we look nice. We'll do whatever it takes to make you happy! Really! I mean it. See my honest smile?' If you visit the school, ditch the tour and the gimmicks and talk to the professors."

— *Anonymous, Southwestern University*

"Going to a school as small as Emerson means that instead of saying 'screw you, Mr. 90803,' the administration will say, 'screw you, Joe.'"

— *"Joe Bloggs," Emerson College*

"The dean of students here makes Cruella de Ville look like Cinderella."

— *Anonymous, Goucher College*

"Our president is very accessible. He gave me some of his neckties to cut up."

— *Martha B., Maryland Institute, College of Art*

"Illinois Wesleyan University is unique in that our president also greatly resembles Phil Hartman, the Saturday Night Live cast member."

— *Kyle C. H., Illinois Wesleyan University*

"Columbia is like a fruit truck. It picks up varied and exotic fruits and deposits them rotten at their destination."

— *Paul L., Columbia University*

"The U. of Minnesota is a huge black hole of knowledge. It sucks things into it from far and wide, compressing to the essence. Unfortunately, it is very hard to get anything out of a black hole. What I have managed to eke out has been both rewarding and depressing."

— *James McDonald, U. of Minnesota*

"BU reminds me of a warm summer day: sweaty, sticky, and smelly."

— *Douglas G. H., Boston University*

"Boulder is the world in a nutshell, served with alfalfa sprouts."

— Glenn H., U. of Colorado, Boulder

"Going to Northwestern is like having a beautiful girlfriend who treats you like crap."

— Jonathan J. G., Northwestern University

"Unless you are totally committed to science, do not come. Caltech has as much breadth as a Russian grocery store."

— Daniel S., Caltech

"Being at Marlboro is like having a recurring bizarre dream. You're not quite sure what it all means, but it happens a lot. If it stopped you'd probably wonder why, but then you'd just eat breakfast."

— Mark L., Marlboro College

"Life at school is an oxymoron."

—Dave G., UC–Davis

"Y'know, sometimes you don't smoke a cigarette, the cigarette smokes ya."

— Anonymous, St. John's College

"Vassar is like a sexual disease: once you've accepted it it's great, but when you realize you've got another three years to put up with it you go see a medical adviser immediately."

— Henry R., Vassar College

"Vassar is like a big walrus butt: lots of hair but also very moist."

— Calder M., Vassar College

"Attending UC Riverside is like having your wisdom teeth pulled—not very enjoyable, but necessary."

— David E. Y., UC–Riverside

"I feel that this school is a maze with snakes and bulls. If you live with a raised fist or a raised phallus it is easy. If you are earthly, bound to do nothing, come."

— Anonymous, U. of Oregon

"Getting an education from MIT is like getting a drink from a firehose."

— Juan G., MIT

"If Bates was a bakery, many goods would be fresh and rats would be under the counter."

— Anne W., Bates College

"Pomona College is a swirling, sucking eddy of despair, filled with small moments of false hope, in an ever-blackening universe."

— Anonymous, Pomona College

"My life here is as the torrential rains of Dhamer upon the Yaktong Valley. I bleat like a llama shedding out of season."

— Ronald M., James Madison University

"This school is like a tight anus: there's tremendous pressure to come out straight and conformed."

— Stephen J., Washington and Lee University

"Intro classes have the consistency of Cheez Whiz: they go down easy, they taste horrible, and they are not good for you."

— Pat T., U. of Vermont

SEX, DRUGS, ROCK & ROLL...

"This school is no good for people who like art, music, and Sonic Youth. 'Society is a hole.' There's a quote by Sonic Youth."

— Meghan S., Lake Forest College

"I hate the Grateful Dead! Blech! Why can't my generation listen to their own damn music! AAAARRRGH."

— Anonymous, College of William and Mary

"I am the Lizard King, I can do anything."

— Michael M., U. of Connecticut

"Beam, Bud, beer, babes—the four essential B's."

— "Jim Beam," Wittenberg University

"William and Mary: where you can drink beer and have sex in the same place your forefathers did."

— Adam L., College of William and Mary

"Yeah, there aren't any guys, but who doesn't like doing homework on a Saturday night?"

— Nicole C., Wellesley College

"UCSB is the only place where U Can Study Buzzed and still ace an exam the next day."

— Tracy B., UC–Santa Barbara

"It may take an 'ee' to spell 'geek,' but it also takes an 'ee' to spell 'beer.'"

— H. B., U. of Missouri–Rolla

"When I visited schools, I went to Brown and Northwestern on the same trip. I went to NU on a Wednesday and Thursday night. I partied like a champ. At Brown on Friday I was invited to two parties (I should be psyched) but they were both for NUDE people. AUGH YUCK!"

— Silvy N., Northwestern University

"A Denison student might be quoted as saying, 'Life is a waste of time, and time is a waste of life; so get wasted all the time, and have the time of your life.'"

— Katherine H., Denison University

"We have a Spring party called Mockstock. Fraternities and sororities join together and hire several bands to play throughout a day. Like Woodstock!"

—Anonymous, Hanover College

"This campus is an extremely great place to spend four college years, but it is still plagued, as all other campuses are, including Christian colleges, with sin. Therefore this campus needs to come under submission to Jesus Christ."

— Laura D., James Madison University

NEANDERTHALS

"If U R looking to settle down with an unattractive big woman, Hofstra is the place."

— Anonymous, Hofstra University

"One thing about Sewanee women is that beauty is only a light switch away. So basically we need some better-looking girls."

— Will B., University of the South, Sewanee

"Girls at BYU are like parking spaces: the good ones are taken, the close ones are handicapped or reserved, and the rest are too far out!"

— Todd P., Brigham Young University

"In Rolla, we have tons of women, but not many of them!"

— Todd O., U. of Missouri–Rolla

"The faculty is great, academics are challenging, but the women are liberated and become difficult to live with. To sum it all up, Hendrix is so cool."

— Mike S., Hendrix College

"All the girls are nasty. But I drink and sometimes fool around with them anyway."

— Dan F., Swarthmore College

"UCSD rages—NOT! If you like the ocean and the library and have a fear of parties and girls without facial hair, you've hit the jackpot!!!"

— Spencer M., UC–San Diego

"There's a saying I've heard around: nine out of ten girls in California look good, the tenth goes to UCSD."

— Michael K., UC–San Diego

"U of C is OK if all you want to do is work, but if you are looking for a good social scene or a hot stinkin' babe, go to California, young man!"

—Benjamin D., University of Chicago

"Stay away from 'big haired' babes!"

— Skip S., Clemson University

"Beer, football, and boobies are what Clemson is all about!"

— Paul S., Clemson University

"The men here often complain that there are too few women here; if they took a look in the mirror, maybe they'd realize why girls don't come here!"

— Tara L., Stevens Institute of Technology

SCHOOL VS. THE "REAL WORLD"...

"College is the best time of your life. Never again will you be surrounded by people the same age as you, free from grown-ups and the threat of working in the real world. Your parents give you money when you ask for it and all you have to do is learn!"

— Jennifer F., Syracuse University

"Real life experience in such concepts—alienation, depression, suppression, isolationism, edge of racial tension, apathy, etc.—before the 'Real World.'"

— Anonymous, NYU

"When we lose a football game to a college with lower academic standards, we console ourselves by saying that one day they will work for us and then we'll get even!"

— Michael J., University of the South, Sewanee

"This place sucks. Hell is probably better than Hanover College. At least there are things to do in hell. At Hanover all people do is drink and study."

— Anonymous, Hanover College

SCHOOLS VS. "CATS"...

"Irvine is a charming place to live, work, and shop. It's better than Cats, and it makes me laugh when the ink goes up the wrong pipe."

— Peter T., UC–Irvine

"This is the best college in the country. I loved it. It was better than Cats. I laughed, I cried, I'd go again and again."

— Bob D., Dartmouth College

"I love it! It's much better than Cats! I'll go here again and again!"

— Nicolas A., Carnegie Mellon University

"I laughed, I cried, but it was NOT better than Cats!"

— R. W., Carnegie Mellon University

"I laugh, I cry, it's better than Cats. I'll do it again and again!"

— Jeff V., Wofford College

"I love it! It's much better than Cats! I want to live here again and again!"

— Shannon C., Eastman School of Music

IN CASE YOU WERE WONDERING...

"You forgot to ask the most pertinent question, which is: 'Have you ever seen Elvis teach your 100 level courses?'"

— Adam L., Alfred University

"I was smart once. I used to sleep. Then I majored in chemical engineering."

— C. C. Smith, Clemson University

"This school has nothing to enjoy but Oregon green bud. A lot of beer subsists by itself and acid grows like mushrooms on turds. The turds being Eugene."

—Anonymous, U. of Oregon

"About dating, it simply hasn't happened, although there is this one girl—Liz—that's in one of my classes. She's smart, nice, friendly, and pretty, too. But she has a boyfriend—she says she's 'involved'—so I don't know anybody else that I want to date even though there's another girl that likes me."

—"Joe B," Lawrence U

"Classes are hard to get. Usually you have to cheat and just add the class, telling them you are a graduating senior. I've done that for the last three years and it works!"

—Anonymous, UC–Davis

"Moon men landed in the middle quad last week while my peers and I sipped ice milk and listened to passing jets (this happens quite frequently). However, nine people saw my mother on a Tuesday wearing nothing but clothes and a plain tarpaulin, moistened with lemming poop."

— *Glenn S., Rhode Island School of Design*

"My school is a melting pot of genius. Whether it is apparent or not, still, as far as all of us being adopted by outer space brothers and made kings and queens of our vast universe, I'd say we'd have the greatest chance of contact with the master outer space race."

— *Steve G., Rhode Island School of Design*

"At the spring and fall equinox, students sacrifice stray dogs to Gartog, god of foot disease."

— *Wally F., Rhode Island School of Design*

"Those who oppose the Dark Lord will be crushed, but those who are its friend will receive rewards beyond the dreams of avarice."

— *Anonymous, Sarah Lawrence College*

"There is a real problem with moles on this campus; no one is willing to talk about them."

— *Alexander D., Bates College*

"Bates College is a phallocentric, logocentric, Greco-Roman, linear-rational, ethnocentric, homophobic, patriarchal institution. How's that for a list of catchwords?"

— *Stephen H., Bates College*

"I think if our generation's parents knew how consumptive, ill-informed, and drug-addicted their children were, they'd suffer a collective nervous breakdown."

— *Anonymous, U. of Denver*

"Our school is the school of the future and always will be."

— *Chuck C., Rhodes College*

"A crust of bread is better than nothing. Nothing is better than true love. Therefore, by the transitive property, a crust of bread is better than true love."

—Jason G., Gettysburg College

"Bentley College has fulfilled all and more of my expectations than I ever imagined."

— Dawn T., Bentley College

"Everyone seems to be really into political correctness, but in the wake of the recent Supreme Court decision, I don't see that lasting very long."

—John R., Birmingham Southern College

"Sarah Lawrence is a haven of unity and acceptance. Every morning at sunrise the entire campus gathers around the flagpole, holds hands, and sings 'We Are The World.' If you're really lucky you get to be Dionne Warwick or Willie Nelson. If you show up late you have to be Bob Dylan. But everyone gets free doughnuts and it's the happiest time of the day for most students. One morning I went hung over and threw up in the middle of the circle. I was so ashamed but then I looked around at the diverse group of smiling faces from all over the country and the world and suddenly I felt better. I went home and threw up some more, thankful to live in the world of love that is Sarah Lawrence."

— Matt F., Sarah Lawrence College

PART 4

INDEXES

INDEX OF COLLEGE COUNSELORS

The authors relied heavily on the following independent counselors for their assistance:

■ Arizona

Adrienne Feuer
The College Workshop
2525 E. Camelback Road, Suite 730
Phoenix, AZ 85016

■ California

Barbara Barnett
9336 Hidden Valley Drive
Villa Park, CA 92667
(714) 998-5533

College and Career Consultants
250 E. 17 Street, Suite N
Costa Mesa, CA 92627
(714) 646-0156

Mark Corkery
NIEP
2402 Michelson Dr. #230
Irvine, CA 92715
(714) 833-7862

Arlene Corsello
P.O. Box 5629
Napa, CA 94581
(707) 255-8276

Elizabeth Hayward
4425 Jamboree Road
Newport Beach, CA 92660
(714) 955-0581

Anne Kogen, Director
American College Placement Service
15928 Ventura Blvd., Suite 227
Encino, CA 91436
(818) 784-6206

Jane McClure
Jackson, McClure and Mallory
200 Lombard Street
San Francisco, CA 94111
(415) 421-4177; 421-4183 Fax
  Also:
Jackson, McClure, Mallory
164 West Napa
Sonoma, CA 95476
(707) 935-7277

■ Colorado

Dr. Steven R. Antonoff
Antonoff Associates, Inc.
425 S. Cherry Street, Suite 215
Denver, CO 80222
(303) 394-2929

Estelle R. Meskin
Educational Consultant
282 Monroe Street
Denver, CO 80206
(303) 781-4145

■ Connecticut

Margery Andrews
Director, College Guidance Service
1471 Ridge Road
North Haven, CT 06473
(203) 281-3746

William M. Morse, MA, PhD
260 Riverside Avenue
Westport, CT 06880
(203) 222-1066

Cornelia Nicholson
Independent Educational Consultant
123 North Street
Watertown, CT 06795
(203) 274-1238

Howard Greene Associates
60 Post Road W.
Westport, CT 06880
(203) 226-4257

Phyllis Steinbrecher
225 Main Street
Westport, CT 06880
(203) 227-3190

Florida

Melvin F. Droszcz
10100 W. Sample Road
Coral Springs, FL 33065
(305) 731-1848, (305) 344-7888

Susan Braunstein & Associates
900 E. Ocean Blvd., Suite B-110
Stuart, FL 34994
(407) 283-2211

Jan Leach Janus
College and Career Placement Services
525 North Park Ave., Suite 218
Winter Park, FL 32789
(407) 628-1090

Georgia

Dr. Carol E. DeLucca
235 Lachaize Circle
Atlanta, GA 30327
(404) 303-0314; 303-1813 Fax

Illinois

Dennis Beemer, MEd
1071 Creekside Drive
Wheaton, IL 60187
(708) 665-1353

Susan Jeanette Bigg
1410K West Wrightwood Ave.
Chicago IL 60614
(312) 404-1699

Nancy Gore Marcus
560 Green Bay Road
Winnetka, IL 60093
(708) 446-7557

Robert J. Simmons
College Counseling Network
3026 North Dryden Place
Arlington Heights, IL 60004
(708) 398-7214

Jeanette B. Spires
111 Fallstone Court
Lake Forest, IL 60045
(708) 234-7211

Indiana

Cynthia Kleit, MS
Educational Consultant
9016 Buckthorne Court
Indianapolis, IN 46260
(317) 872-0829

Louisiana

Adele R. Williamson
Nancy W. Cadwaller
Collegiate Advisory Placement Service
P.O. Box 66371
Baton Rouge, LA 70896
(504) 928-1818; 383-8323 Fax

Maryland

Zola Dincin Schneider
The College Advisory Service
5812 Warwick Place
Chevy Chase, MD 20815
(301) 654-5889

Massachusetts

College Admissions Consultants
94 Station Street
Hingham, MA 02043
(617) 749-2970

Leslie Goldberg
Educational Consultant
15 Sentinel Road
Hingham, MA 02043
(617) 749-2074

Timothy Lee
Sudbury Educational Center
323 Boston Post Road
Sudbury, MA 01776
(508) 443-0055

Bonny Musinsky
Musinsky and Associates
49 Kendal Common Road
Weston, MA 02193
(617) 899-5759

Missouri

Patricia Adkins Rochette
1001-B West 101 Terrace
Kansas City, MO 64114
(816) 942-0727

Nevada

Andrew T. C. Stifler
Educational Consulting Services
2393 Potosi Street
Las Vegas, NV 89102
(702) 253-6464, (702) 877-3589

New Jersey

David Mason
1398 Axel Avenue
North Brunswick, NJ 08902
(908) 247-1543

Ronna Morrison
11 Maple Avenue
Demarest, NJ 07627
(201) 768-8250

Stacy Needle
221 Castlewall Avenue
Elderon, NJ 07740
(908) 229-8400

David Peterson
20 Mount Horeb Road
Warren, NJ 07059
(908) 356-3899

New Mexico

Rusty Haynes
4165 Montgomery NE
Albuquerque, NM 87109
(505) 884-1798

New York

Kalman Chaney
Financial Aid & Financial Planning
968 Lexington Avenue
New York, NY 10021
(212) 861-8806

Edward T. Custard
Carpe Diem ETC
259 Sugar Loaf Mountain Road
Chester, NY 10918-9565
(914) 469-9182

Geraldine C. Fryer
1066 Boston Post Road
Rye, NY 10580
(914) 967-7952
 Also:
4725 MacArthur Blvd.
Washington, DC 20007
(202) 333-3230

Carol Gill
369 Ashford Avenue
Dobbs Ferry, NY 10522
(914) 693-8200

Pearl Glassman
Pearl Glassman Counseling, Inc.
30 White Birch Road
Pound Ridge, NY 10576
(914) 764-5153

Pearl Glassman Counseling
RRI, BX 350
Pound Ridge, NY 10576
(914) 764-5153

Gladys Kleiman
164 Guyon Avenue
Staten Island, NY 10306
(718) 351-7232
 Also:
C.A.P.S.
10 Village Plaza
South Orange, NJ 07079

Jane E. Kolber
Educational Consultant
142 East 71st Street
New York, NY 10021
(212) 734-1704

Frank C. Leana, PhD
Howard Greene & Associates
176A East 75th Street.
New York, NY 10021
(212) 737-8866

New York (continued)

M and M College Advisors
3 Birch Grove Drive
Armonk, NY 10504
(914) 273-9618

Allan W. McLeod
51 East 73rd Street
New York, NY 10021
(212) 535-5824

Joan Tager
34 Emerson Avenue
Staten Island, NY 10301
(718) 727-1914
 Also:
10 Village Plaza
South Orange, NJ 07079
(201) 467-1773

Judy Wacht
15 Tulip Lane
New Rochelle, NY 10804
(914) 633-3636

North Carolina

Judith Goetzl, MA
College Bound Consultants
3325 Chapel Hill Boulevard
Suite #184
Durham, NC 27707
(919) 493-7788

Anne Jones
Olive Jordan
Marnie Ruskin
College Connections
P.O. Box 29342
Greensboro, NC 27429
(910) 282-1202

Eric B. Moore
1208 Providence Road
Charlotte, NC 28207
(704) 334-1482

Marnie Ruskin
College Connections
5 Parkmont Court
Greensboro, NC 27408

Ann Crandall Sloan
Independent Educational Consultant
501 Spring Valley Drive
Raleigh, NC 27609
(919) 782-2634

Oregon

Gail Durham
Catlin Gabel School
8825 SW Barnes Road
Portland, OR 97225
(503) 297-1894

Cynthia Doran
3105 NW Cumberland Road
Portland, OR 97210
(503) 228-2281

Nancy Knocke
College Search
2830 SW Vista Drive
Portland, OR 97225
(503) 292-8666

Lloyd Thacker
2188 SW Park Place, Suite 303
Portland, OR 97205
(503) 228-0357

Pennsylvania

Edith W. Barnes
Academic Directions
1476 Morstein Road
Westchester, PA 19580
(215) 647-2862

Elizabeth Lohmann
EPL Inc.
224 S. Wayne Avenue
Wayne, PA 19087
(215) 687-3385

Lynne H. Martin
105 Bala Avenue
Bala Cynwyd, PA 19004
(215) 399-6787

Suzanne F. Scott, EdM
1538 Woodland Road
Rydal, PA 19046
(215) 884-0656

Barbara B. Snyderman, PhD
401 Shady Avenue, Suite C107
Pittsburgh, PA 15206
(412) 361-8887

■ Texas

Bill Fleming
The Educational Group
5952 Royal, Suite #203
Dallas, TX 75230
(214) 987-2433; 369-4979 Fax

■ Utah

Jill G. Kennedy
College Selection Consultants
1385 Yale Avenue
Salt Lake City, UT 84105
(801) 583-6170

■ Vermont

James Ten Broeck, Ben Mason
Mason & Associates
100 Dorset Street
South Burlington, VT 05403
(802) 658-9622

■ Washington

Linda Jacobs, MEd
Linda Jacobs and Associates
College Placement Services
2400 E. Louisa
Seattle, WA 98112
(206) 323-8902

Pauline B. Reiter, PhD
College Placement Consultants
40 Lake Bellevue #100
Bellevue, WA 98005
(206) 453-1730

INDEX OF LEARNING DISABLED PROGRAMS

Following is a list by college of telephone numbers—including a few basic services—for programs designed for students with learning disabilities. The nature of these programs varies from school to school. If you would like specific information, contact the schools directly at the numbers below.

> KEY: *staff*—total of full- and part-time LD staff
> *time*—extra time is allowed for LD to finish degree
> *$*—extra fees, above tuition, are required of LD
> *tutor*—individual or group tutoring is available to LD
> *SOS*—support services available to LD
> *intvw*—interview is required for LD

Agnes Scott College 404-371-6284
tutor, SOS

Alabama, University of 205-348-8326
intvw, tutor

Alfred University 607-871-2792
time, tutor, SOS

American University, The 202-885-3360
2 staff, time, SOS, intvw

Amherst College 413-542-2529
SOS

Arizona, University of 602-621-1242
11 staff, time, $, tutor, SOS

Arizona State University 602-965-1234
2 staff, tutor, SOS

Atlantic, College of the 800-528-0025
time

Auburn University 205-844-5943
1 staff, time, SOS

Austin College 903-813-3000

Babson College 617-239-4322
tutor, SOS

Bard College 914-758-7472

Barnard College 212-854-4634
1 staff, time, tutor, SOS

Bates College 207-786-6222
SOS

Baylor University 817-755-1811
SOS

Bellarmine College 502-452-8131
tutor, SOS

Beloit College 608-363-2620
2 staff, tutor, SOS

Bennington College 800-833-6845
intvw

Bentley College 617-891-2274
SOS

Berklee College of Music 617-266-1400
SOS

Birmingham-Southern College 205-226-4686
SOS, intvw

Boston College 617-552-3100
1 staff, time, SOS

Boston University 617-353-6880
1 staff, $, tutor, SOS

Boston Conservatory, The	617-536-6340	Carleton College	507-663-4190
		tutor, SOS	
Bowdoin College	207-725-3224		
time, tutor, SOS		**Carnegie Mellon University**	412-268-6878
		1 staff, tutor, SOS	
Brandeis University	617-736-3500		
tutor, SOS		**Case Western Reserve U.**	216-368-5230
		4 staff, tutor, SOS	
Brigham Young University	801-378-2723		
1 staff, tutor, SOS		**Catawba College**	800-CATAWBA
Brown University	401-863-2315	**Catholic Univ. of America**	202-319-5618
4 staff, time, tutor, SOS		*time, tutor, SOS*	
Bryn Mawr College	215-526-5152	**Centenary College of LA**	318-869-5131
Bucknell University	717-524-1101	**School of the Art Institute**	
tutor, SOS		**of Chicago**	312-899-5231
		tutor, SOS	
UC–Berkeley	510-642-0518		
SOS		**Chicago, University of**	312-702-8650
UC–Davis	916-752-3184	**CUNY–Hunter College**	212-772-4490
2 staff, time, tutor, SOS		*4 staff, time, tutor, SOS*	
UC-Irvine	714-856-7494	**CUNY–Queens College**	718-997-5600
SOS		*time, SOS*	
UC–Los Angeles	310-825-1501	**Claremont McKenna**	909-621-8088
1 staff, time, tutor, SOS		*SOS*	
UC–Riverside	909-787-4538	**Harvey Mudd College**	909-621-8011
1 staff, time, tutor, SOS			
		Pitzer College	909-621-8129
UC–San Diego	619-534-4382		
SOS		**Pomona College**	909-621-8134
UC–Santa Barbara	805-893-8897	**Scripps College**	909-621-8149
1 staff, time, tutor, SOS		*time, SOS*	
UC–Santa Cruz	408-459-2089	**Clark University**	508-793-7468
1 staff, time, $, tutor, SOS		*1 staff, SOS, intvw*	
California Inst. of the Arts	805-255-2185	**Clarkson University**	315-268-7643
tutor, SOS		*time, tutor*	
California Inst. of Tech.	818-564-8136	**Clemson University**	803-656-0511
SOS		*time, tutor, SOS*	
California State Poly	909-869-3268	**Colby College**	207-872-3106
1 staff, time, tutor, SOS, intvw		*tutor, SOS*	
Calvin College	616-957-6113	**Colgate University**	315-824-7401
2 staff, time, tutor, SOS		*time*	

Colorado College	719-389-6689	**Dickinson College**	717-245-1740
SOS		*time, tutor, SOS*	
Colorado–Boulder, Univ. of	303-556-3406	**Drew University**	201-408-3514
2 staff, tutor, SOS		*time, tutor, SOS*	
Colorado School of Mines	303-273-3297	**Drexel University**	215-895-2400
2 staff, time, tutor, SOS			
		Duke University	919-684-5917
Columbia University	212-854-2521	*tutor, SOS*	
Connecticut, University of	203-486-0178	**Duquesne University**	412-434-6636
2 staff, time, tutor, SOS		*time, SOS*	
Connecticut College	203-439-2173	**Earlham College**	317-983-1311
1 staff, tutor, SOS		*tutor, SOS*	
Cooper Union	212-353-4116	**Eastman School of Music**	716-274-1060
time, SOS		*staff*	
Cornell University	607-255-3976	**Eckerd College**	813-864-8331
1 staff, tutor, SOS		*time, SOS, intvw*	
Creighton University	402-280-2749	**Emerson College**	617-578-8600
3 staff, time, SOS		*2 staff, time, tutor, SOS*	
Dallas, University of	214-721-5266	**Emory University**	404-727-3300
		tutor, SOS	
Dartmouth College	603-646-2014	**Eugene Lang College**	212-229-5665
SOS		*tutor*	
Davidson College	704-892-2225	**Evergreen State College**	206-866-6000
1 staff, time, tutor, SOS		*1 staff, time, tutor, SOS*	
Dayton, University of	513-229-3634	**Fairfield University**	203-254-4100
1 staff, time, tutor, SOS			
Deep Springs College	619-872-2000	**Fisk University**	615-329-8666
staff		**Florida, University of**	904-392-1261
Delaware, University of	302-831-8123	*1 staff, time, tutor, SOS*	
time, SOS		**Florida A&M**	904-599-3180
Denison University	614-587-6666	*tutor, SOS*	
tutor, SOS		**Florida State University**	904-644-1741
Denver, University of	303-871-2372	*2 staff, time, tutor, SOS*	
4 staff, $, tutor, SOS		**Fordham University**	718-817-4000
DePaul University	312-362-6897	*tutor, SOS*	
time, $, tutor, SOS		**Franklin & Marshall**	717-291-4083
DePauw University	800-447-2495	**Furman University**	803-294-2034

George Mason University	703-993-2474	**Hendrix College**	504-388-4423
1 staff, time, tutor, SOS		*1 staff, time, tutor, SOS*	
George Washington Univ.	202-994-6710	**Hiram College**	800-362-5280
SOS			
Georgetown University	202-687-3600	**Hobart & William Smith**	315-781-3351
SOS, intvw		*SOS*	
Georgia Tech	404-894-2564	**Hofstra University**	516-463-5840
1 staff, time, tutor, SOS		*3 staff, $, tutor, SOS, intvw*	
Gettysburg College	717-337-6100	**Hollins College**	703-362-6226
		tutor, SOS	
Goddard College	800-468-4888	**Holy Cross, College of the**	508-793-2443
Golden Gate University	415-442-7200	**Howard University**	202-806-2920
		tutor, SOS	
Gonzaga University	509-328-4220	**Idaho, University of**	208-885-6746
tutor, SOS		*tutor, SOS*	
Goucher College	410-337-6529	**Illinois Inst. of Tech.**	312-808-7100
1 staff, time, tutor, SOS		*SOS*	
Grinnell College	515-269-3702	**Illinois–Urbana, Univ. of**	217-333-8705
1 staff, time, tutor, SOS		*1 staff, time, $, tutor, SOS*	
Grove City College	412-458-2100	**Illinois Wesleyan Univ.**	800-332-2498
SOS			
Guilford Coll.	910-316-2200	**Indiana Univ.,**	812-855-7578
time, tutor, SOS		**–Bloomington**	
		tutor, SOS	
Gustavus Adolphus College	507-933-7676	**Iowa, University of**	319-335-1462
time, SOS		*2 staff, time, tutor, SOS*	
Hamilton College	315-859-4421	**Iowa State University**	515-294-1020
		1 staff, time, tutor, SOS	
Hampden-Sydney College	804-223-6106	**James Madison University**	703-568-6705
1 staff, SOS		*time, SOS*	
Hampshire College	413-582-5471	**Johns Hopkins University**	410-516-8171
SOS		*time, SOS*	
Hampton University	800-624-3328	**Juilliard School**	212-799-5000
SOS		*time, tutor, SOS*	
Hanover College	812-866-7021	**Kalamazoo College**	616-383-8492
		time, tutor, SOS	
Harvard-Radcliffe Colleges	617-495-1551	**Kansas, University of**	913-864-4064
SOS, intvw		*1 staff, tutor, SOS*	
Haverford College	610-896-1350		
$, SOS			

Kentucky, University of *SOS*	606-257-9000	**Maryland Inst., Coll. of Art** *3 staff, tutor, SOS*	410-728-6703
Kenyon College *tutor, SOS*	614-427-5145	**Mass.–Amherst, U. of** *3 staff, time, tutor, SOS*	413-545-4602
Knox College *1 staff, tutor, SOS*	309-343-0112	**M.I.T.** *intvw*	617-253-4861
Lafayette College *time, tutor, SOS*	215-250-5100	**McGill University**	514-398-3910
Lake Forest College	708-735-5000	**Miami University** *1 staff, time, tutor, SOS*	513-529-6841
Lawrence University	414-832-6500	**Miami, University of**	305-284-4323
Lehigh University *time, tutor, SOS*	215-758-4152	**Michigan–Ann Arbor,** **University of** *4 staff, time, tutor, SOS*	313-763-3000
Lewis & Clark College *1 staff, tutor, SOS*	503-768-7175	**Michigan State University** *2 staff, tutor, SOS*	517-355-8332
Louisiana State Univ.	504-388-1175	**Michigan Tech. University** *SOS*	906-487-2335
Loyola College	800-221-9107	**Middlebury College** *tutor, SOS*	802-388-3711
Loyola Marymount Univ. *time, tutor, SOS*	310-338-8453	**Millsaps College**	601-974-1050
Loyola University, Chicago *SOS*	312-508-2740	**Minnesota–Duluth, U. of,** *2 staff, time, tutor, SOS*	218-726-8727
Loyola University	504-865-3240	**Missouri-Columbia,** **University of** *tutor*	314-882-2493
Macalester College *3 staff, tutor, SOS*	612-696-6724	**Missouri–Rolla, Univ. of** *time, tutor, SOS*	314-341-4292
Maine, University of *1 staff, time, tutor, SOS*	207-581-2319	**Montana College** *time, tutor, SOS, intvw*	406-496-4198
Manhattanville College *2 staff, $, tutor, SOS, intvw*	914-694-2200	**Morehouse College** *SOS*	800-992-0642
Marlboro College *time, SOS, intvw*	802-257-4333	**Mount Holyoke College**	413-538-2855
Marquette University *tutor, SOS*	414-288-1645	**Muhlenberg College** *1 staff, time, tutor, SOS*	215-821-3433
Mary Washington College	703-899-4662	**New College**	813-359-4269
Maryland, Univ. of *SOS*	301-314-7651		

New Hampshire, Univ. of *2 staff, tutor, SOS*	603-862-2607	**Oklahoma, University of** *1 staff, time, tutor, SOS*	405-325-1459
New Jersey Inst. of Tech. *SOS*	201-596-3516	**Oregon, University of** *tutor, SOS*	503-346-3201
New Mexico Inst. *4 staff, time, tutor, SOS*	505-835-5208	**Pacific, University of the**	503-359-2201
New York University *2 staff, time, $, tutor, SOS, intvw*	212-998-4975	**Parsons School of Design**	212-229-8910
UNC–Chapel Hill *SOS*	919-966-3621	**Pennsylvania State Univ.** *tutor, SOS*	814-863-1807
North Carolina Schl. Arts	919-770-3290	**Pennsylvania, Univ. of** *time, tutor, SOS*	215-898-1886
UNC–Asheville *SOS*	704-251-6517	**Pepperdine University** *1 staff, time, tutor, SOS*	310-456-4208
North Carolina State *1 staff, tutor, SOS*	919-515-7653	**Pittsburgh, University of** *SOS*	412-648-7890
North Dakota, Univ. of *time, tutor, SOS*	701-777-3425	**Princeton University**	609-258-3060
Northeastern University *1 staff, time, $, tutor, SOS, intvw*	617-373-2675	**Providence College** *time, tutor, SOS*	401-865-2494
Northwestern University *tutor, SOS*	708-491-7458	**Puget Sound, University of** *3 staff, time, tutor, SOS*	206-756-1355
Notre Dame, University of *time, tutor, SOS*	219-631-7505	**Purdue University** *3 staff, tutor, SOS*	317-494-1144
Oberlin College *time, tutor, SOS*	216-775-8467	**Randolph-Macon College** *tutor, SOS*	804-752-7343
Occidental College *tutor*	213-259-2700	**Randolph-Macon Woman's** *time, tutor, SOS*	804-947-8126
Oglethorpe University *tutor, SOS, intvw*	404-364-8307	**Redlands, University of** *SOS*	909-335-4074
Ohio University *1 staff, time, tutor, SOS*	614-593-2620	**Reed College** *tutor, SOS*	503-771-1112
Ohio Northern University *time, tutor*	419-772-2260	**Rensselaer Poly. Inst.** *1 staff, time, tutor, SOS*	518-276-2746
Ohio State University *10 staff, tutor, SOS*	614-292-3307	**Rhode Island, Univ. of** *1 staff, time, SOS*	401-792-7100
Ohio Wesleyan University *time, SOS*	614-368-3276	**Rhode Island Schl. Design** *time, SOS*	401-454-6639

Rhodes College	901-726-3849
tutor, SOS	
Rice University	713-527-4036
Richmond, University of	804-289-8640
Ripon College	414-748-8107
2 staff, tutor, SOS, intvw	
Rochester, University of	716-275-9049
1 staff, time, tutor, SOS	
Rochester Institute of Tech.	716-475-2215
18 staff, time, $, tutor, SOS	
Rollins College	407-646-2222
2 staff, tutor, SOS	
Rose-Hulman Inst. of Tech.	812-877-1511
Rutgers University	908-932-7107
time, tutor, SOS	
St. Bonaventure University	716-375-2066
1 staff, time, tutor, SOS	
St. John's College	800-331-5232
St. Lawrence University	315-379-5104
1 staff, time, tutor, SOS	
Saint Louis University	314-658-2930
1 staff, tutor, SOS, intvw	
Saint Mary's College, CA	510-631-4224
tutor	
St. Mary's College of MD	301-862-0339
tutor, SOS	
Saint Olaf College	507-646-3288
1 staff, tutor, SOS	
Samford University	205-870-2736
time, $, tutor, SOS	
San Francisco Art Institute	415-749-4500
SOS	
San Francisco Cons. Music	415-759-3431
Santa Clara University	408-554-4700

Sarah Lawrence College	914-395-2249
Seton Hall University	201-761-9167
SOS	
Siena College	518-783-2423
SOS	
Simmons College	617-521-2120
time, tutor, SOS	
Simon's Rock Coll. of Bard	800-235-7186
Skidmore College	518-584-5000
time, $, SOS	
Smith College	413-585-2071
time, tutor, SOS	
South, University of the	615-598-1248
time, SOS	
South Carolina, Univ. of	803-777-6142
SOS, intvw	
Southern California, U. of	213-740-0776
1 staff, time, SOS	
Southern Methodist Univ.	214-768-4019
3 staff, tutor, SOS	
Southwestern University	512-863-1200
Spelman College	404-681-3643
Stanford University	415-723-2091
Stephens College	314-876-7207
intvw	
Stevens Institute of Tech.	201-216-5194
SUNY–Albany	518-442-5435
SOS	
SUNY–Binghamton	607-777-2171
tutor, SOS	
SUNY–Buffalo	716-645-2608
3 staff, time, tutor, SOS	
SUNY–Stony Brook	516-632-6868
Susquehanna University	717-372-4238
1 staff, time, tutor, SOS, intvw	

Swarthmore College	215-328-8300	**Vanderbilt University** *1 staff, time, tutor, SOS*	615-322-4705
Sweet Briar College *SOS*	804-381-6142	**Vassar College** *4 staff, time, tutor, SOS*	814-437-5578
Syracuse University *time, tutor, SOS*	315-443-4498	**Vermont, University of** *time, tutor, SOS*	802-656-7753
Temple University *1 staff, SOS*	215-204-1280	**Villanova University** *time, SOS*	610-519-4079
Tennessee–Knoxville, U. of *tutor, SOS*	615-974-6087	**Virginia, University of** *5 staff, time, tutor, SOS*	804-924-3139
Texas–Austin, Univ. of *tutor, SOS*	512-471-1201	**Virginia Polytechnic** *1 staff, tutor, SOS*	703-231-3787
Texas A&M University *time, tutor, SOS*	409-845-1637	**Wabash College** *SOS*	317-364-4251
Texas Christian University	817-921-7490	**Wake Forest University** *1 staff, time, tutor, SOS*	919-759-5929
Toronto, University of	416-978-2190	**Warren Wilson College**	704-298-3325
Trenton State College *tutor, SOS*	609-771-2571	**Washington University** *time, tutor, SOS*	314-935-5040
Trinity College (CT) *3 staff, time, tutor, SOS*	203-297-2154	**Washington and Lee**	703-463-8710
Trinity University *SOS*	210-736-7207	**Wellesley College** *SOS*	617-283-2270
Truman State University	816-785-4114	**Wesleyan University**	203-347-9411
Tufts University *SOS*	617-628-5000	**Wesleyan College**	800-447-6610
Tulane University *4 staff, tutor, SOS*	504-865-5113	**West Virginia University** *SOS*	304-293-6700
Tuskegee University	205-727-8500	**Westminster College** *SOS*	412-946-7100
U.S. Military Academy	914-938-4011	**Wheaton College** *time, tutor, SOS*	508-285-8215
U.S. Naval Academy	410-293-1000		
Union College	518-388-6112	**Whitman College** *2 staff, tutor, SOS*	509-527-5213
Ursinus College *SOS*	215-489-4111	**Whittier College**	310-907-4233
Valparaiso University	219-464-5011		

Willamette University   503-370-6447
1 staff, tutor, SOS

William and Mary   804-221-2510
1 staff, time, SOS

Williams College   413-597-2211
SOS

Wisconsin–Madison, U. of   608-263-2741
time, SOS

Wittenberg University   303-492-8671
1 staff, time, $, SOS

Wofford College   803-597-4130

College of Wooster   216-263-2595
tutor

Worcester Polytechnic Inst.   508-831-5381
time, tutor, SOS

Yale University   203-432-1900

INDEX OF SCHOOLS

Tom Meltzer is a graduate of Columbia University. He has taught and written test-preparation materials for *The Princeton Review* since 1986. He is also a professional musician and songwriter, and performs regularly with his band, Five Chinese Brothers. Tom grew up in Baltimore and now lives in Brooklyn, New York. He is an avid Orioles booster.

Zachary Knower is a graduate of Princeton University. He has done everything there is to do for *The Princeton Review* since 1989 while simultaneously pursuing a burgeoning acting career. He, too, was raised in Baltimore, now lives in New York, and is a die-hard Orioles fan. Zachary recently made his television debut, appearing as a jewelry store owner on FOX-TV's *America's Most Wanted*.

John Katzman graduated from Princeton University. After working briefly on Wall Street, he founded *The Princeton Review*. Beginning his career in test preparation with nineteen high school students in his parents' apartment, Katzman now oversees courses that prepare tens of thousands of high school and college students annually for tests including the SAT, GRE, GMAT, LSAT, MCAT, and TOEFL. John now hates baseball.

Edward T. Custard is a graduate of Manhattanville College and has done grad work at New York University. He has lectured on college admissions throughout the United States and Europe. His educational consulting firm, Carpe Diem ETC, is based in Chester, NY. He has held positions as Director of Admissions at New College of the University of South Florida and the State University of New York at Purchase, and was an admissions counselor for the Tisch School of the Arts at New York University. In the course of a personal crusade against the mundane, he has also been a bridge worker on high steel above the Hudson River and played drums in a band with Hulk Hogan in Florida. During baseball season Ed watches New York Giants videotapes, but he aspires to one day be part owner of the Carolina Mudcats.

Each year, thousands of students from countries throughout the world prepare for the TOEFL and for U.S. college and graduate school admissions exams. Whether you plan to prepare for your exams in your home country or the United States, The Princeton Review is committed to your success.

INTERNATIONAL LOCATIONS: If you are using our books outside of the United States and have questions or comments, or want to know if our courses are being offered in your area, be sure to contact The Princeton Review office nearest you:

- ◆ CANADA (Montreal)   514-499-0870
- ◆ HONG KONG   852-517-3016
- ◆ JAPAN (Tokyo)   8133-463-1343
- ◆ KOREA (Seoul)   822-508-0081
- ◆ MEXICO (Mexico City)   525-564-9468
- ◆ PAKISTAN (Lahore)   92-42-571-2315
- ◆ SAUDI ARABIA   413-584-6849 (a U.S. based number)
- ◆ SPAIN (Madrid)   341-323-4212
- ◆ TAIWAN (Taipei)   886-27511293

U.S. STUDY ABROAD: *Review USA* offers international students many advantages and opportunities. In addition to helping you gain acceptance to the U.S. college or university of your choice, *Review USA* will help you acquire the knowledge and orientation you need to succeed once you get there.

Review USA is unique. It includes supplements to your test-preparation courses and a special series of *AmeriCulture* workshops to prepare you for the academic rigors and student life in the United States. Our workshops are designed to familiarize you with the different U.S. expressions, real-life vocabulary, and cultural challenges you will encounter as a study-abroad student. While studying with us, you'll make new friends and have the opportunity to personally visit college and university campuses to determine which school is right for you.

Whether you are planning to take the TOEFL, SAT, GRE, GMAT, LSAT, MCAT, or USMLE exam, The Princeton Review's test preparation courses, expert instructors, and dedicated International Student Advisors can help you achieve your goals.

For additional information about *Review USA*, admissions requirements, class schedules, F-1 visas, I-20 documentation, and course locations, write to:

The Princeton Review • Review USA

2315 Broadway, New York, NY 10024

Fax: 212/874-0775